Annotated Teacher's Edition

Prentice Hall
LITERATURE
Timeless Voices, Timeless Themes

GOLD

ISBN 0-13-434862-1

2 3 4 5 6 7 8 9 10   02 01 00 99 98

PRENTICE HALL
Simon & Schuster Education Group
A VIACOM COMPANY

Prentice Hall
LITERATURE
Timeless Voices, Timeless Themes

What's special about *Prentice Hall Literature: Timeless Voices, Timeless Themes?*

This exciting new program sets a new standard in quality language arts instructional materials. No other literature program provides a more complete blend of classic and contemporary literature; such an extensive array of motivating, real-world connections; such consistent and comprehensive instruction in communication skills; or a more flexible array of teaching materials.

The program also includes a library of longer works and technology in the form of literature videodiscs, audiocassettes of selections, and CD-ROM software. Use the materials you want in the medium that is most convenient for you to address your students' needs.

◇ **A unique, flexible organization**
Prentice Hall Literature: Timeless Voices, Timeless Themes is the first literature program that lets you choose a thematic approach, a genre-based organization, or a combination of the two.

◇ **Strong real-world connections make literature relevant to students**
Prentice Hall Literature: Timeless Voices, Timeless Themes provides features that make all literature, including the classics, relevant to today's students.

◇ **A new level of skills instruction**
Prentice Hall Literature: Timeless Voices, Timeless Themes is the only program to provide instruction in all of the following skills with *every selection:*

Reading Strategies	Literary Elements and Forms
Writing	Vocabulary
Grammar	Critical Thinking
Visual Literacy	Speaking and Listening

◇ **Teaching support that you can customize to your needs**
A wide array of print and technology resources make it easy for you to customize instruction to meet the needs of all students.

A unique, flexible organization *fits any teaching approach.*

The Gold and Platinum levels of *Prentice Hall Literature: Timeless Voices, Timeless Themes* let you choose a thematic approach, a genre-based approach, or a combination of the two. Each book is organized into five thematic units, followed by five genre-based units. If you prefer a strictly thematic or a purely genre-based approach, however, you can use one of the alternative tables of contents:
- complete contents by theme
- complete contents by genre

The Platinum level also offers a contents of literature from around the world.

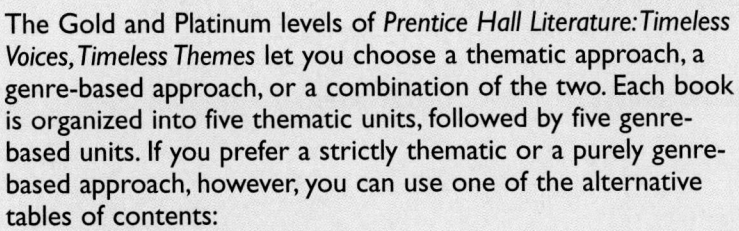

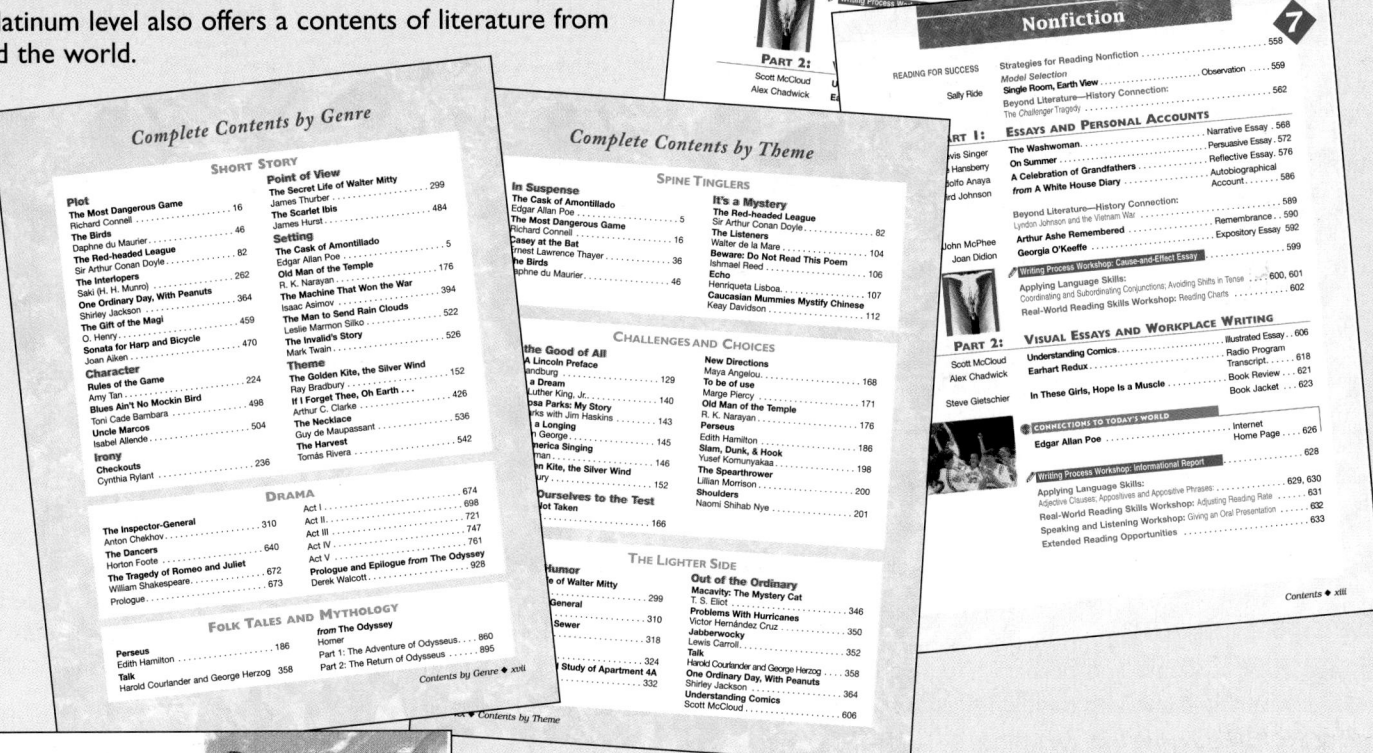

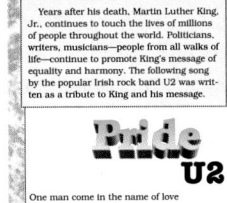

. . . I say to you today, my friends, that in spite of the difficulties and frustrations of the moment I still have a dream. It is a dream deeply rooted in the American dream.

I have a dream that one day this nation will rise up and live out the true meaning of its creed: "We hold these truths to be self-evident; that all men are created equal."

I have a dream that one day on the red hills of Georgia the sons of former slaves and the sons of former slaveowners will be able to sit down together at the table of brotherhood.

I have a dream that one day even the state of Mississippi, a desert state sweltering with the heat of injustice and oppression, will be transformed into an oasis of freedom and justice.

I have a dream that my four little children will one day live in a nation where they will not be judged by the color of their skin but by the content of their character.

I have a dream today.

I have a dream that one day the state of Alabama, whose governor's lips are presently dripping with the words of interposition and nullification, will be transformed into a situation where little black boys and black girls will be able to join hands with little white boys and white girls and walk together as sisters and brothers.

I have a dream today.

I have a dream that one day every valley shall be exalted, every hill and mountain shall be made low, the rough places will be made plains.

1. Interposition (in' tər pə zish' ən) **and nullification** (nul' ə fi kā' shən): Disputed doctrine that a state can reject federal laws considered to be violations of its rights.

◆ **Build Vocabulary**
creed (krēd) *n.*: Statement of belief
oppression (ə presh' ən) *n.*: Keeping others down by the unjust use of power
oasis (ō ā' sis) *n.*: Fertile place in the desert
exalted (eg zôlt' ed) *v.*: Lifted up

◀ **Critical Viewing** What does this photograph tell you about the importance of Dr. King's message to those who heard his speech? [Draw Conclusions]

CONNECTIONS TO TODAY'S WORLD

Years after his death, Martin Luther King, Jr., continues to touch the lives of millions of people throughout the world. Politicians, writers, musicians—people from all walks of life—continue to promote King's message of equality and harmony. The following song by the popular Irish rock band U2 was written as a tribute to King and his message.

Pride
U2

One man come in the name of love
One man come and go
One man come, he to justify
One man to overthrow

Chorus:

In the name of love
What more in the name of love
In the name of love
What more in the name of love

One man caught on a barbed wire fence
One man he resist
One man washed on an empty beach
One man betrayed with a kiss

(Chorus)

Early morning, April four
Shot rings out in the Memphis sky
Free at last
They took your life
They could not take your pride

(Chorus)

1. What emotion does this song evoke? Explain.
2. What message does the song convey? Support your answer.
3. How does the song's message relate to King's message in "I Have a Dream"?

I Have a Dream ◆ 141

Strong real-world connections

Each unit includes a Connections to Today's World feature that links classic literature to high-interest contemporary writings, including songs, sports articles, cartoons, and Internet Web sites. The program also provides Beyond Literature features that lead students into an exploration of careers, communities, and other subject areas.

Comprehensive skills instruction with every selection

Prentice Hall Literature: Timeless Voices, Timeless Themes is the only literature program to provide instruction in all language arts skills with *every selection*. The following instructional options are provided before, during, and after each selection. Choose the ones that best fit your curricular goals.

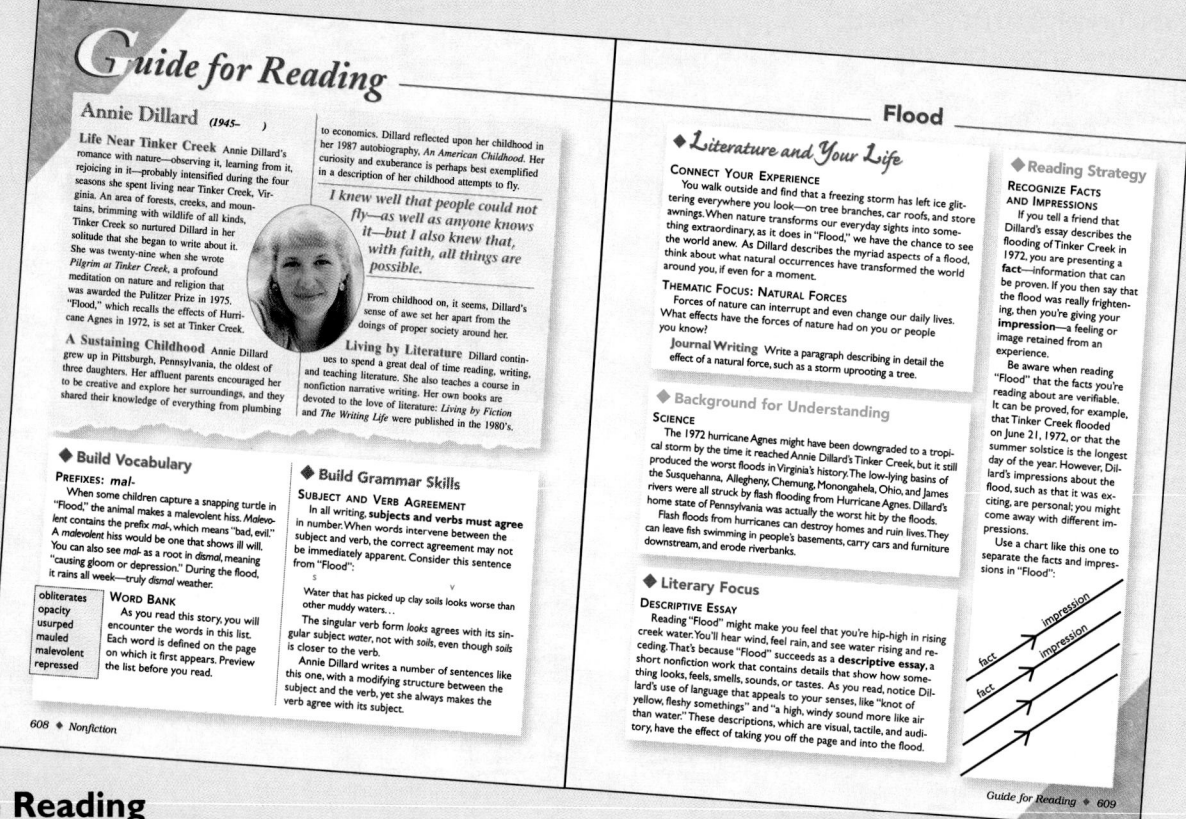

Before Reading

Engage your students and prepare them to read each selection through the unparalleled prereading support offered in the **Guide for Reading**.

◆ **An extensive author biography** brings the author to life for students.

◆ **Build Vocabulary** previews new words and teaches a vocabulary building strategy.

◆ **Build Grammar Skills** provides instruction in a grammar skill modeled in the selection.

◆ **Literature and Your Life** captures students' interest by linking the literature to their own experiences.

◆ **Background for Understanding** provides context related to history, science, culture, and more.

◆ **Reading Strategy** helps students read more critically and with a higher level of comprehension.

◆ **Literary Focus** teaches a literary form or element.

During Reading

To help students through the selection, *Prentice Hall Literature: Timeless Voices, Timeless Themes* offers the following support:

◆ **Reading Strategy** prompts support comprehension and guide students in using the strategy introduced before the selection.

> ◆ Reading Strategy
> Is this a fact or an impression? How do you know?

◆ **Literary Focus** prompts help students see how the literary element is illustrated in specific passages.

> ◆ Literary Focus
> In what specific ways is this passage typical of a descriptive essay?

◆ **Literature and Your Life** prompts help students connect details in the selection to their lives.

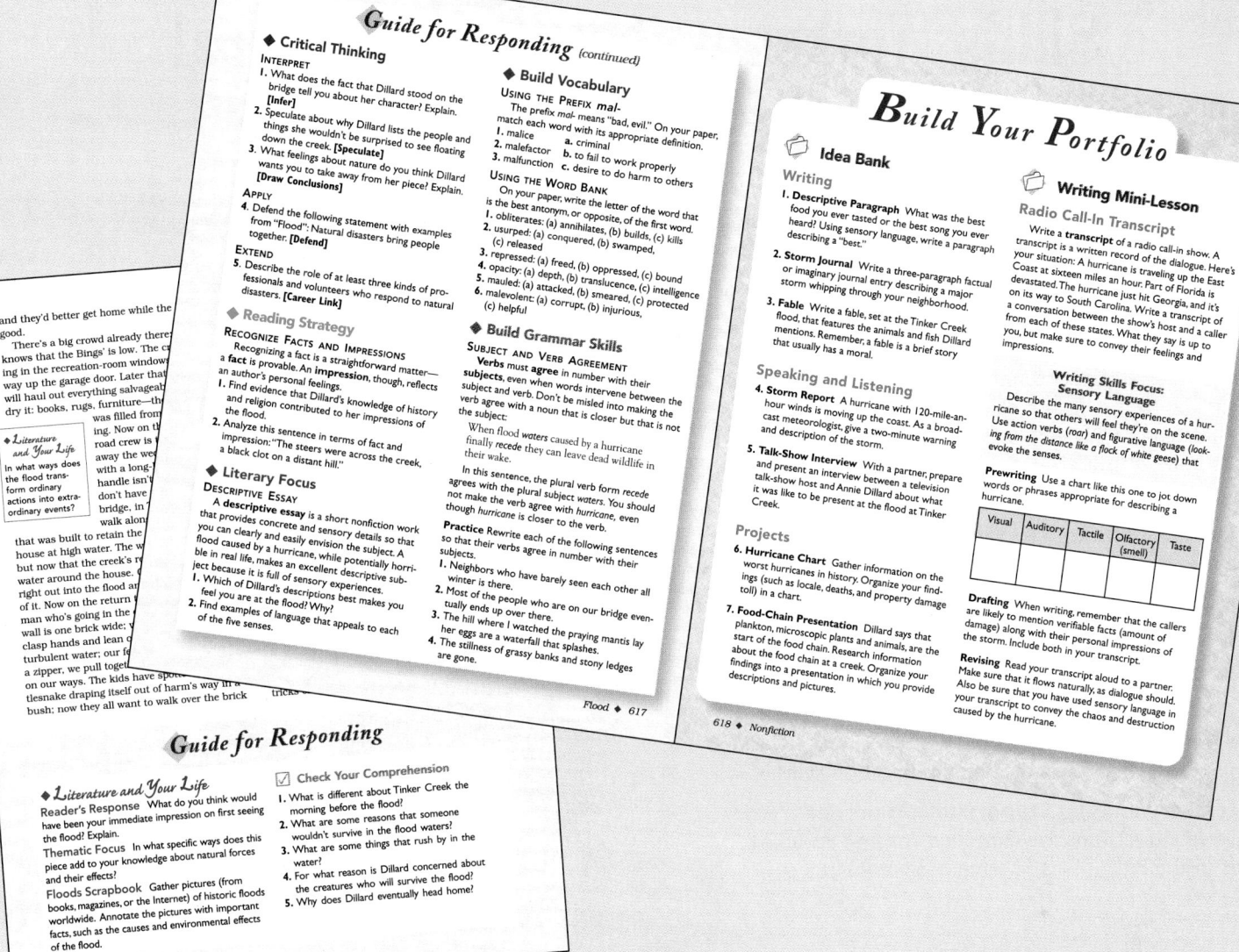

After Reading

Assess students' understanding and **extend** their learning through the **Guide for Responding** after each selection. Additional instruction and practice are provided for <u>all of the skills</u> introduced before the literature.

◆ **Literature and Your Life** promotes reader response and thematic connections.

☑ **Check Your Comprehension** questions assess students' literal understanding of the selection.

◆ **Critical Thinking** questions assess students' ability to use higher-level thinking skills to construct meaning.

◆ **Reading Strategy** assesses students' mastery of the reading strategy.

◆ **Literary Focus** reinforces students' understanding of the literary element.

◆ **Build Vocabulary** checks students' mastery of both the vocabulary strategy and the words used in the selection, often in an SAT-style format.

◆ **Build Grammar Skills** provides reteaching and assessment with practice activities and a writing application.

Build Your Portfolio provides a wealth of activities for students to demonstrate their understanding.

📁 **Idea Bank** provides:

- Three writing activities keyed to varying performance levels
- Two speaking and listening activities
- Two projects, often linked to cross-curricular topics

📁 **Writing Mini-Lesson** provides step-by-step writing process instruction and focuses students on developing a specific writing skill.

Skills Workshops provide additional in-depth skills instruction.

Writing Process Workshops provide detailed step-by-step writing process instruction in all modes of writing.

- Provides 20 opportunities for extended writing projects
- Linked to the end-of-selection Writing Mini-Lesson through the Writing Skills Focus sections; enables students to build on skills they've already learned

Two **Applying Language Skills** mini-lessons accompany each Writing Process Workshop to provide additional grammar instruction right at point-of-use.

Real-World Reading Skills Workshops help students build reading skills essential to success in careers and in daily life.

- 20 lessons in each book

Speaking and Listening Workshops provide instruction and practice in real-life communication skills.

Extended Reading Opportunities provide a wide range of suggestions for extended reading, including titles in the *Prentice Hall Literature Library*.

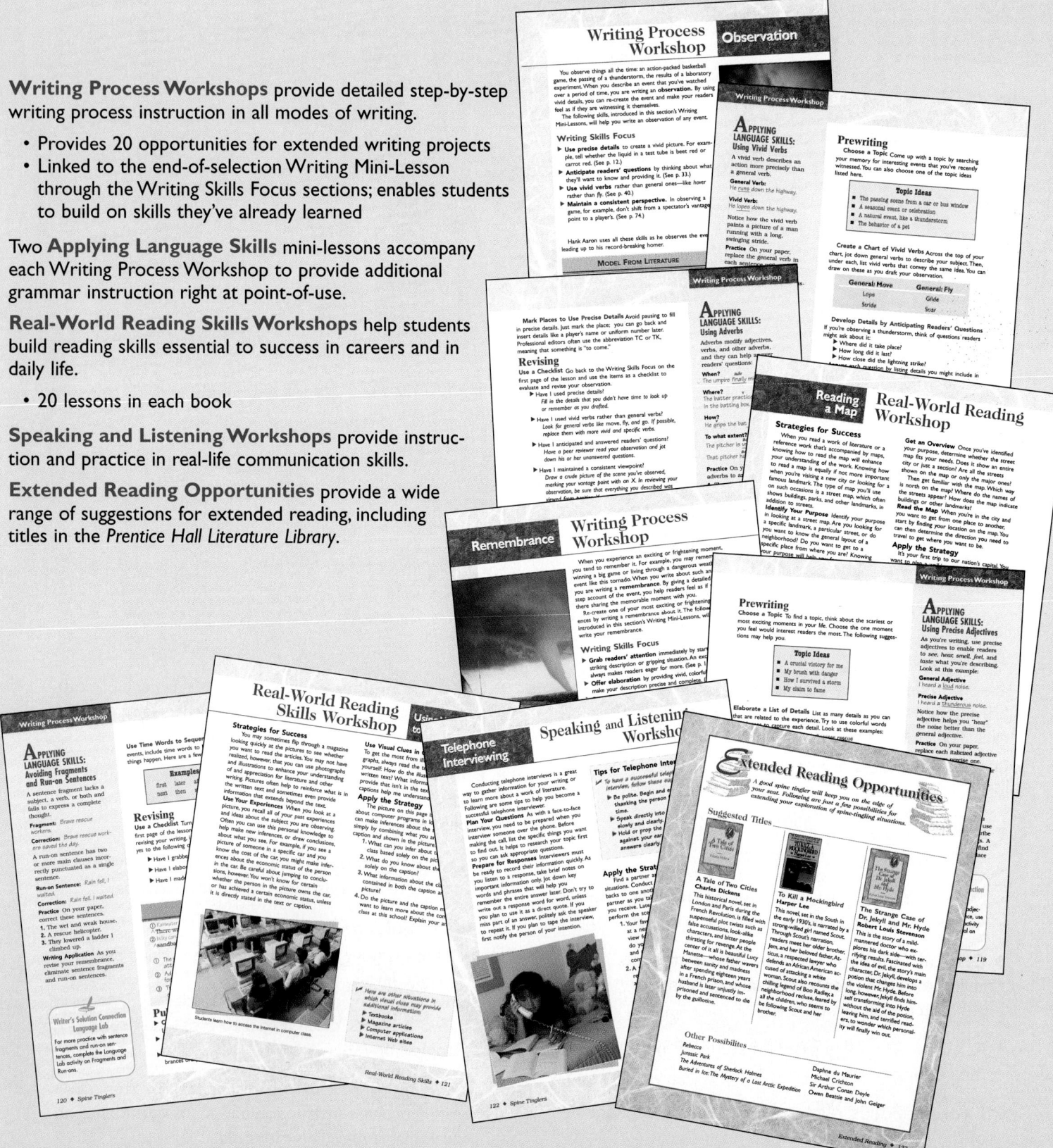

The Annotated Teacher's Edition provides flexible teaching pathways and customized strategies to meet your curricular goals and your students' individual needs.

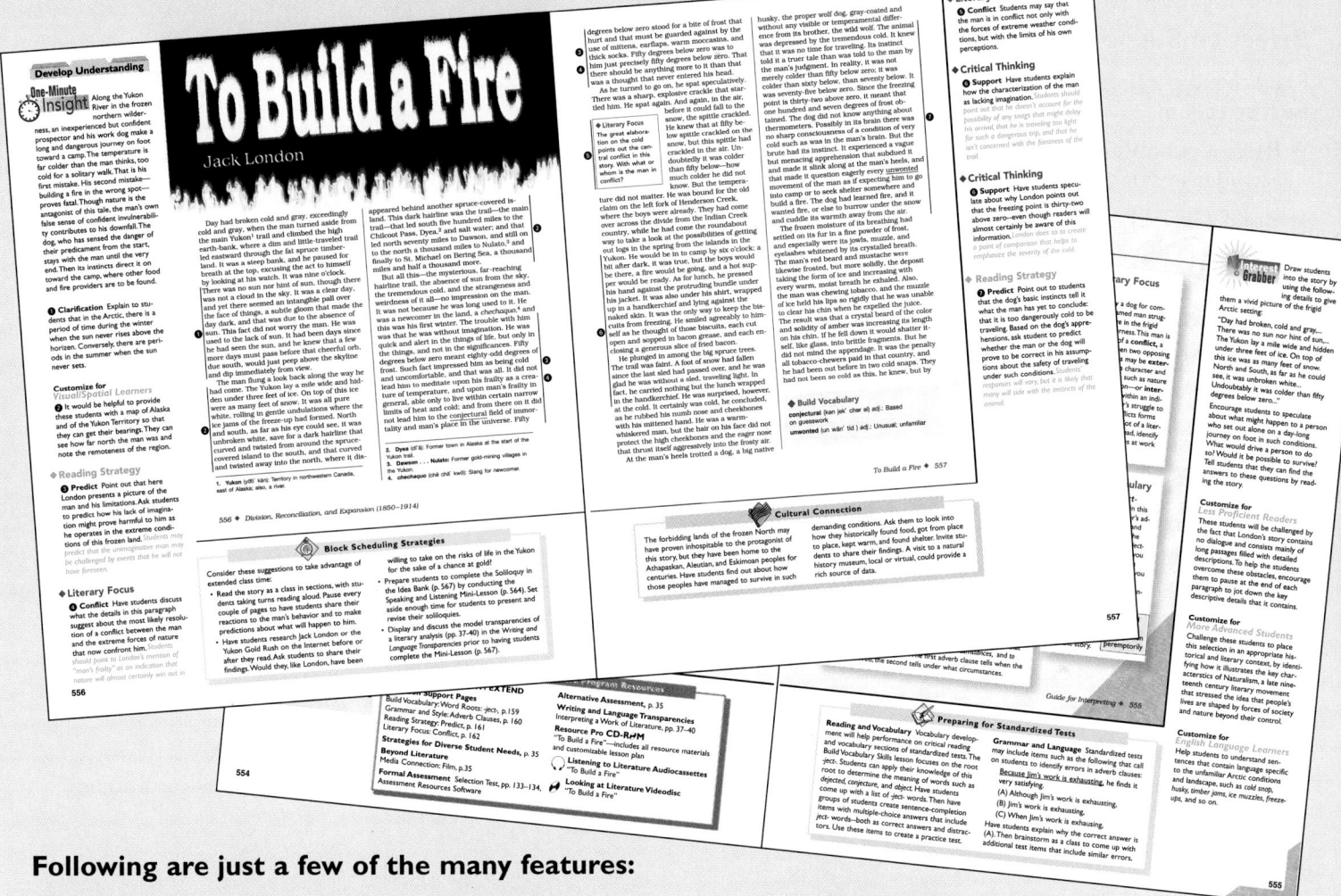

Following are just a few of the many features:

Customize notes provide tips and strategies for addressing the needs of various student populations: Less Proficient Readers, More Advanced Students, English Language Learners, Visual/Spatial Learners, and so on.

Interest Grabber notes at the beginning of every selection provide a quick activity or teaching strategy for piquing students' interest.

One-Minute Insight provides a summary and an explanation of the selection's underlying meaning.

Preparing for Standardized Tests shows you how to connect skills instruction to a standardized test format.

Beyond the Selection notes with every selection provide **Internet Links** to appropriate Web sites.

Other notes include:

Humanities Notes

Cross-Curricular Connections

Cultural Connections

Beyond the Classroom (Career and Community Connections)

Literary Focus

Reading Strategy

Build Grammar Skills

Build Vocabulary

Enrichment

Check Your Comprehension

Comprehension Check

A wealth of options for reteaching, extension, and assessment

Teacher Resources

Selection Support: Skills Development

Practice pages reinforce the skills taught with each selection:

◆ **Build Vocabulary** includes practice activities in standardized test formats.

◆ **Build Grammar Skills** includes practice activities and a writing application.

◆ **Reading Strategy** often provides graphic organizers to aid students as they read the selection.

◆ **Literary Focus** reinforces literary concepts.

Beyond Literature
◆ Cross Curricular, Career, and Community Connections

Daily Language Practice
Brief daily activities, ready for easy class presentation

Art Transparencies
20 full-color transparencies

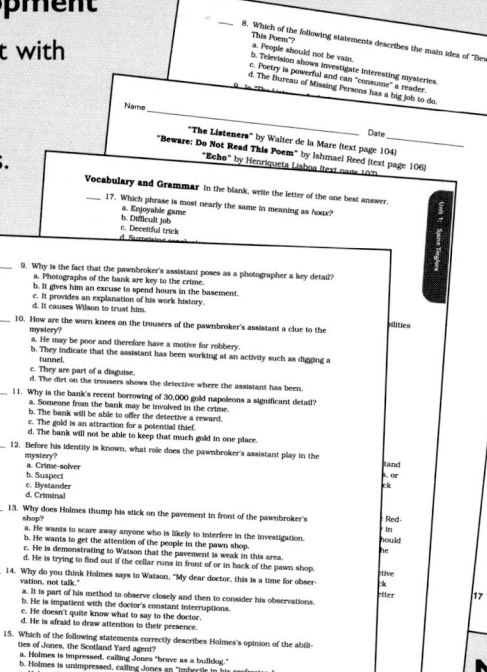

Formal Assessment

◆ **Selection Tests** assess all skills objectives and include essay questions geared to varying performance levels.

◆ **Unit Tests** assess mastery of unit skills objectives in a standardized-test format.

◆ **Assessment Resources Software** allows you to easily customize tests to performance levels or curricular goals.

Alternative Assessment

Alternative assessment activities, rubrics, portfolio forms, peer and parental assessment support, and much more

Strategies for Diverse Student Needs

Selection summaries in English and Spanish and guided support for every selection

Professional Development
Professional articles on a wide range of topics

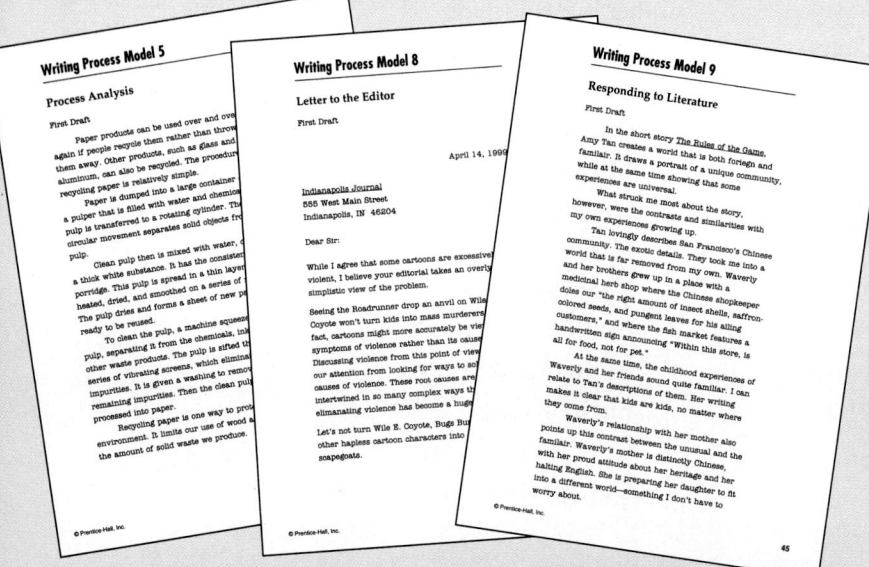

Writing and Language Transparencies

◆ Provides over 100 transparencies for writing and grammar instruction

◆ Complete writing models for various types of writing—ranging from reports to persuasive essays—including rough drafts, revised drafts, and proofread drafts

◆ Graphic organizers for support of both writing and reading

◆ Daily Language Practice overheads that make it easy to provide five-minute activities to improve language skills

Extend your students' appreciation of fine literature.

Prentice Hall Literature Library

- ◆ 24 titles to choose from
- ◆ Special hardcovers with a beautiful design for attractiveness and durability
- ◆ Uncut editions so students enjoy complete works
- ◆ Classic novels by honored writers
- ◆ Great drama, including additional Shakespeare offerings
- ◆ Literature collections featuring writings from specific regions, cultures, or genre

Study Guides for each title provide expert teaching support with summaries, teaching strategies, and more.

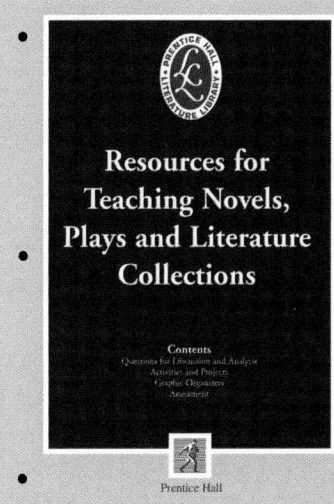

Resources for Teaching Novels, Plays, and Literature Collections provides a wealth of teaching materials and assessment aids for use with any of the titles in our library. Includes transparencies, graphic organizers, and tests.

A wide range of quality technology enhances and extends literature instruction.

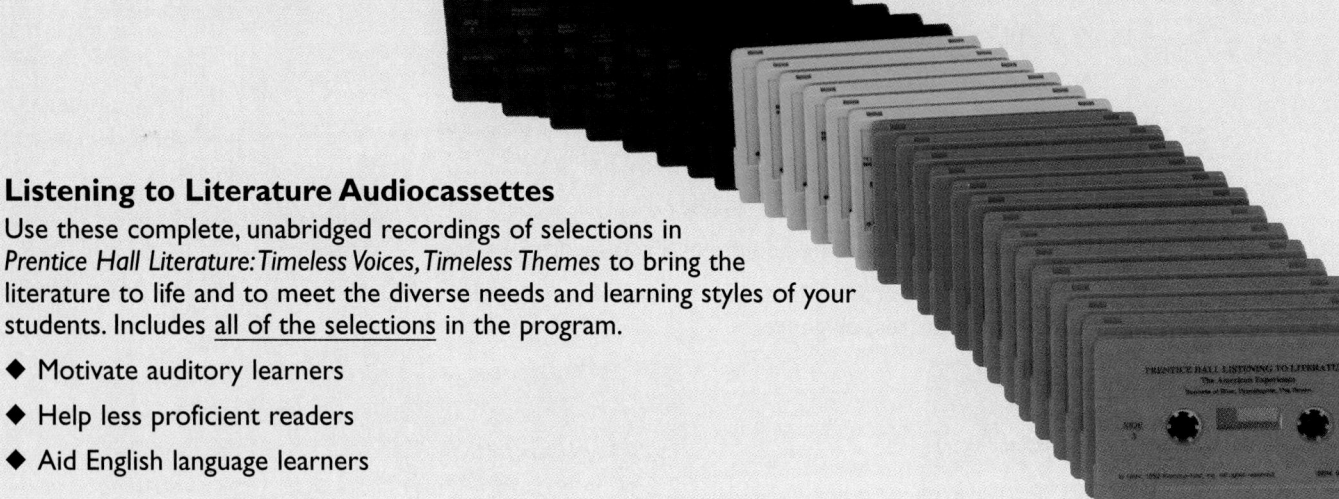

Listening to Literature Audiocassettes

Use these complete, unabridged recordings of selections in *Prentice Hall Literature: Timeless Voices, Timeless Themes* to bring the literature to life and to meet the diverse needs and learning styles of your students. Includes <u>all of the selections</u> in the program.

◆ Motivate auditory learners

◆ Help less proficient readers

◆ Aid English language learners

Looking at Literature Videodiscs and Videotapes

Full-motion video segments provide a wide range of support for the literature—from student response to historical context to connections to today's world.

◆ Motivate students

◆ Build background

◆ Establish relevance

◆ Encourage class discussion of the literature

Resource Pro and Literature Database CD-ROM

Imagine a complete Teaching Resources, a customizable Lesson Planner, and a wide range of additional literature selections that fits in your hand! With this CD-ROM, you can customize lesson plans at the touch of a button. You can also review, edit, and print an entire year's worth of blackline masters and other teaching support materials. In addition, more than 100 supplemental literature selections are provided for every grade level.

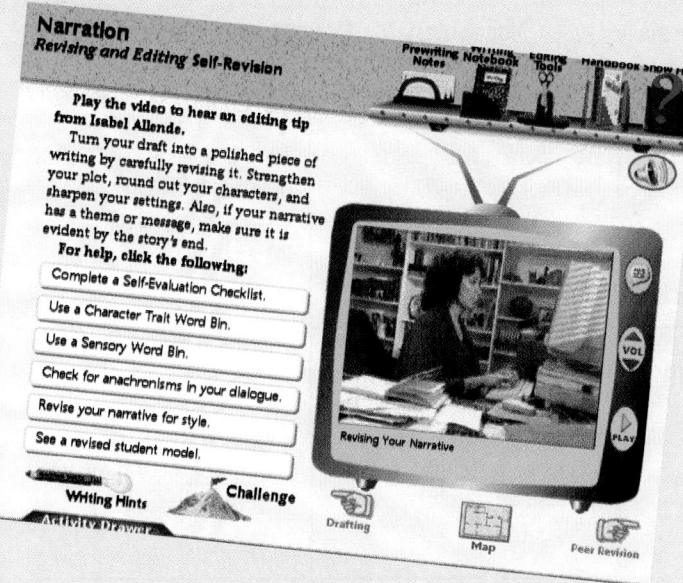

Writer's Solution

Writer's Solution, Prentice Hall's award-winning interactive writing instruction program, has been fully integrated into *Prentice Hall Literature: Timeless Voices, Timeless Themes*. Components include:

◆ Writing Lab CD-ROM provides interactive tutorials on the major modes of writing, including Response to Literature.

◆ Language Lab CD-ROM provides self-directed instruction and practice in grammar, usage, and mechanics.

◆ Writers at Work videodisc and videotape bring real writers into the classroom.

◆ Writer's Toolkit networked software provides tools and activities for all stages of writing.

Formal Assessment CD-ROM

All selection tests and unit tests are available on software so you can customize assessment for your students. The software is also available on floppy disk for Windows and Macintosh. The software enables you to:

◆ Customize tests to ability levels

◆ Customize tests by skills objectives

◆ Administer tests on-line in the computer lab

Literature CD-ROM Library

Multimedia presentations; hyperlinks to glossaries, indexes, and encyclopedias; and complete, on-line testing are just some of the outstanding features on these interactive CD-ROMs. Titles include the following:

◆ How to Read and Understand Poetry

◆ How to Read and Understand Drama

◆ The Time, Life, and Works of Shakespeare

◆ The History of American Literature, Part 1

◆ The History of American Literature, Part 2

◆ Greek Myths and Legends

Internet Home Page

Visit the Prentice Hall Web site at **phschool.com** for features that support *Prentice Hall Literature: Timeless Voices, Timeless Themes:*

◆ Visit literary sites through our updated Links.

◆ Share ideas through our Faculty Forum electronic bulletin board.

◆ Take part in special events such as electronic dialogues with notable authors.

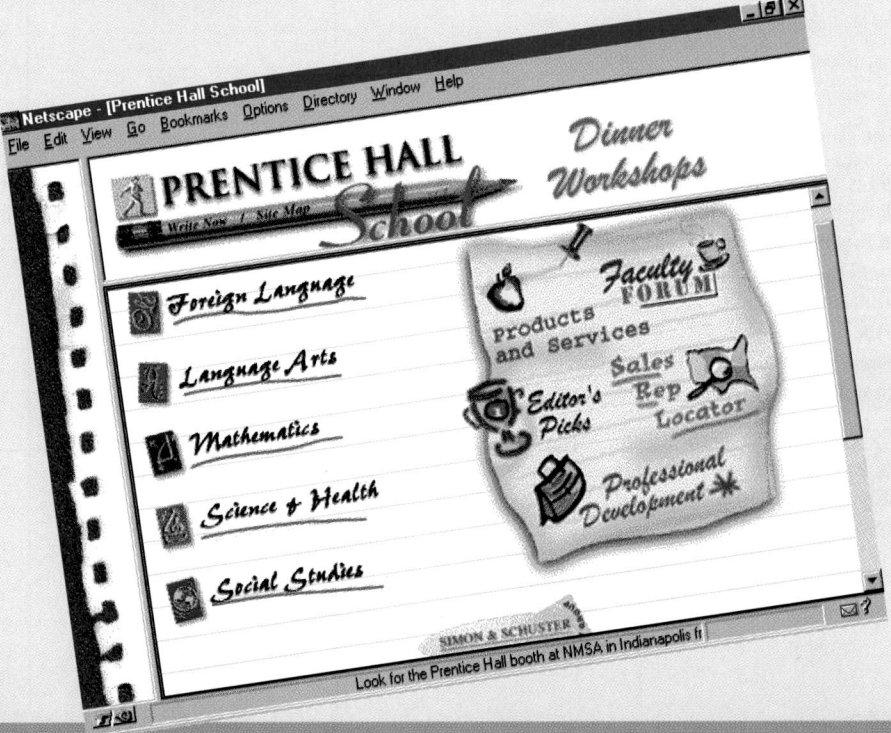

Program Planner   Unit 1 Spine Tinglers

Selection	Reading	Literary Elements/Forms	Vocabulary	Grammar
"The Cask of Amontillado," Edgar Allan Poe, SE p. 5. Reading Level: Challenging	• Reading for Success: Literal Comprehension Strategies, SE pp. 4, 11; TR Selection Support, pp. 3–4 • Model Selection, SE pp. 5–10 • Form a Mental Picture, TR Str. for Diverse St. Needs, p. 1	• Mood, SE pp. 3, 11; TR Selection Support, p. 5	• Prefixes: *pre-,* SE pp. 2, 11; TR Selection Support, p. 1 Word Bank: precluded, retribution, p. 5; accosted, afflicted, explicit, p. 6: recoiling, termination, subsided, p. 9	• Pronoun Case, SE pp. 2, 11; TR Selection Support, p. 2 • WS Language Lab CD-ROM, Nouns and Pronouns • WS Gram. Pr. Book, pp. 7–10
"The Most Dangerous Game," Richard Connell, SE p. 16 Reading Level: Average	• Context Clues, SE pp. 15, 32; TR Selection Support, p. 8 • Identify Chain of Events, TR Str. for Diverse St. Needs, p. 2	• Suspense, SE pp. 15, 32; TR Selection Support, p. 9	• Related Words: Forms of *scruples,* SE pp. 14, 32; TR Selection Support, p. 6 Word Bank: palpable, p. 17; indolently, p. 18; bizarre, p. 21; naive, scruples, p. 24; blandly, grotesque, p. 25; futile, p. 27	• Past and Past Perfect Tenses, SE pp. 14, 32; TR Selection Support, p. 7 • WS Gram. Pr. Book, p. 73 • WS Language Lab CD-ROM, Verb Tense Lesson
"Casey at the Bat," Ernest Lawrence Thayer, SE p. 36 Reading Level: Average	• Summarizing, SE pp. 35, 39; TR Selection Support, p. 12 • Translate Baseball Phrases, TR Str. for Diverse St. Needs, p. 3	• Climax and Anticlimax, SE pp. 35, 39; TR Selection Support, p. 13	• Related Words: Forms of *tumult,* SE pp. 34, 39; TR Selection Support, p. 10 Word Bank: pallor, wreathed, writhing, p. 37; tumult, p. 38	• Participles, SE pp. 34, 39; TR Selection Support, p. 11 • WS Gram. Pr. Book, p. 44
"The Birds," Daphne du Maurier, SE p. 46 Reading Level: Average	• Predict, SE pp. 45, 73; TR Selection Support, p. 16 • Use a Timeline, TR Str. for Diverse St. Needs, p. 4	• Foreshadowing, SE pp. 45, 73; TR Selection Support, p. 17	• Suffixes: *-ful,* SE pp. 44, 73; TR Selection Support, p. 14 Word Bank: placid, p. 47; garish, p. 50; recounted, p. 55; sullen, p. 57; furtively, imperative, p. 60; reconnaissance, p. 63; fretful, p. 67	• Compound Sentences, SE pp. 44, 73; TR Selection Support, p. 15 • WS Gram. Pr. Book, p. 57
"The Red-headed League," Sir Arthur Conan Doyle, SE p. 82 Reading Level: Challenging	• Key Details, SE pp. 81, 100; TR Selection Support, p. 20 • Break Down Sentences, TR Str. for Diverse St. Needs, p. 5	• The Mystery, SE pp. 81, 100; TR Selection Support, p. 21	• Word Roots: *-spec-,* SE pp. 80, 100; TR Selection Support, p. 18 Word Bank: singular, p. 84; avail, p. 88; hoax, p. 89; introspective, p. 92; vex, conundrums, astuteness, formidable, p. 93	• Coordinate Adjectives, SE pp. 80, 100; TR Selection Support, p. 19 • WS Gram. Pr. Book, pp. 15–17 • WS Language Lab CD-ROM, Comma Lesson
"The Listeners," Walter de la Mare; **"Beware: Do Not Read Beyond This Poem,"** Ishmael Reed; **"Echo,"** Henriqueta Lisboa, SE pp. 104, 106, 107 Reading Levels: Average, Average, Easy	• Use Your Senses, SE pp. 103, 108; TR Selection Support, p. 24 • Restate Poetry as Prose, TR Str. for Diverse St. Needs, p. 6	• Imagery, SE pp. 103, 108; TR Selection Support, p. 25	• Poetic License and Vocabulary, SE pp. 102, 108; TR Selection Support, p. 22 Word Bank: perplexed, thronging, p. 104; legendary, p. 106; strafing, p. 107	• Parallelism, SE pp. 102, 108; TR Selection Support, p. 23
"Caucasian Mummies Mystify Chinese," Keay Davidson, SE p. 110 Reading Level: Average	• Main Idea, SE pp. 111, 116; TR Selection Support, p. 28 • Analyze Nonfiction Sources, TR Str. for Diverse St. Needs, p. 7	• News Article, SE pp. 11, 116; TR Selection Support, p. 29	• Suffixes: *-ist,* SE pp. 110, 116; TR Selection Support, p. 26 Word Bank: dogmas, parched, archaeologist, imperialist, p. 113; subjugation, reconcile, p. 115	• Active and Passive Voice, SE pp. 110, 116; TR Selection Support, p. 27 • WS Language Lab CD-ROM, Verb Tense Lesson

KEY: SE: Student Edition;   ATE: Annotated Teacher's Edition;   TR: Teaching Resources;   LL: Listening to Literature;   WS: Writer's Solution

Writing	Speaking and Listening	Projects	Assessment	Technology
• Monologue, Opening Argument, Letter to Edgar Allan Poe, SE p. 12 • Mini-Lesson: Description of a Set [Precise Details], SE p. 12 • Diary Entries, Reflection, Sequel, TR Alt. Assess., p. 1	• Casting Discussion, Resolving Interpersonal Conflicts, SE p. 12 • Mini-Lesson: Resolving Interpersonal Conflicts, ATE p. 8 • Nonverbal Communication, TR Alt. Assess., p. 1	• Pantomime, Storyboard, SE p. 12 • Model and Demonstration, Mardi Gras, TR Alt. Assess., p. 1	• Selection Test, TR Formal Assessment, pp. 1–3; Assess. Res. Software • Description Rubric [for Wr. Mini-Lesson], TR Alt. Assess., p. 90 • TR Alt. Assess., p. 1	• "The Cask of Amontillado," LL Audiocassettes • WS Writing Lab CD-ROM Description Tutorial; Wr. at Work Videodisc, Ch. 1
• Review, Persuasive Essay, Movie Script, SE p. 33 • Mini-Lesson: Survival Manual [Anticipate Readers' Questions], SE p. 33 • Film Critique, Attorney's Brief, TR Alt. Assess., p. 2	• Interview, Trial, SE p. 33 • Mini-Lessons: Interview, Trial, ATE pp. 29, 30 • Story Dialogue, Report on Hunting, TR Alt. Assess., p. 2	• Video Game Design, Technical Diagrams, SE p. 33 • Costume Design, Movie Score, Visual Geography, TR Alt. Assess., p. 2	• Selection Test, TR Formal Assessment, pp. 4–6; Assess. Res. Software • How-to/Process Explanation Rubric [for Wr. Mini-Lesson], TR Alt. Assess., p. 93 • TR Alt. Assess., p. 2	• "The Most Dangerous Game," LL Audiocassettes • WS Writing Lab CD-ROM Exposition Tutorial
• Sports Headlines, Sports How-to, Résumé, SE p. 40 • Mini-Lesson: Sportscast [Vivid Verbs], SE p. 40 • Poem Reworking, Alternative Endings, TR Alt. Assess., p. 3	• Sports Interview, Pep Talk, SE p. 40 • Mini-Lesson: Sports Interview, ATE p. 41 • Dialogue, Summary, TR Alt. Assess., p. 3	• Statistics Chart, Sports in Other Countries, SE p. 40 • World Records, Movie Score, TR Alt. Assess., p. 3	• Selection Test, TR Formal Assessment, pp. 7–9; Assess. Res. Software • Description Rubric [for Wr. Mini-Lesson], TR Alt. Assess., p. 90 • TR Alt. Assess., p. 3	• "Casey at the Bat," LL Audiocassettes • Looking at Lit., Ch. 1 • WS Writing Lab CD-ROM Description Tutorial
• The Final Outcome, Public Service Announcement, Book vs. Movie, SE p. 74 • Mini-Lesson: Bird's-Eye View of a Place [A Consistent Viewpoint], SE p. 74 • Short Story, Story Addition, TR Alt. Assess., p. 4	• Panel Discussion, Scene, SE p. 74 • Mini-Lesson: Panel Discussion, ATE p. 64 • Emergency Plans Oral Report, News Report, Persuasive Dialogue, Oral Report, TR Alt. Assess., p. 4	• Multimedia Presentation, A Picture of Flight, SE p. 74	• Selection Test, TR Formal Assessment, pp. 10–12; Assess. Res. Software • Description Rubric [for Wr. Mini-Lesson], TR Alt. Assess., p. 90 • TR Alt. Assess., p. 4	• "The Birds," LL Audiocassettes • WS Writing Lab CD-ROM Description Tutorial
• Observation Journal, Dramatic Scene, Cause-and-Effect Essay, SE p. 101 • Mini-Lesson: Detec-tive Story [Elaboration], SE p. 101 • Character Comparison, School Mystery, Character Description, TR Alt. Assess., p. 5	• Summary, Grilling the Suspect, SE p. 101 • Mini-Lesson: Summary, Grilling the Suspect, ATE pp. 97, 98 • Trial Preparation, Author Interview, TR Alt. Assess., p. 5	• The Science of Detection, Planning the Heist, SE p. 101 • City Guide, Theatrical Production, TR Alt. Assess., p. 5	• Selection Test, TR Formal Assessment, pp. 13–15; Assess. Res. Software • Narration Rubric [for Wr. Mini-Lesson], TR Alt. Assess., p. 89 • TR Alt. Assess., p. 5	• "The Red-headed League," LL Audiocassettes • Looking at Lit., Ch. 2 • WS Writing Lab CD-ROM Narration Tutorial; Wr. at Work Videodisc, Ch. 2
• Comic Strip, TV Review, Dramatic Scene, SE p. 109 • Mini-Lesson: Movie Summary [Sequence of Events], SE p. 109 • Paragraph, Poetic License, Compare-and-Contrast Essay, Narrative Poem, TR Alt. Assess., p. 6	• Oral Interpretation, Storytelling, SE p. 109 • Mini-Lesson: Oral Interpretation, ATE p. 106 • Background Music Description, TR Alt. Assess., p. 6	• Multimedia Presentation, Art Exhibit, SE p. 109 • Painting, TR Alt. Assess., p. 6	• Selection Test, TR Formal Assessment, pp. 16–18; Assess. Res. Software • Summary Rubric [for Wr. Mini-Lesson], TR Alt. Assess., p. 91 • TR Alt. Assess., p. 6	• "The Listeners," "Beware: Do Not Read Beyond This Poem," "Echo," LL Audiocassettes • WS Writing Lab CD-ROM Exposition Tutorial; Wr. at Work Videodisc, Ch. 1
• Book Jacket, Short Story, Travel Brochure, SE p. 117 • Mini-Lesson: News Feature [Grabbing the Reader's Attention], SE p. 117 • Present-Day Puzzle Report, Burial Practices Report, Follow-Up Questions, TR Alt. Assess., p. 7	• Group Discussion, Oral Presentation, SE p. 117 • Mini-Lesson: Resolving Interpersonal Conflicts, ATE p. 10 • Dialogue, Oral Presentation, TR Alt. Assess., p. 7	• Photo Essay, Costume Drawing, SE p. 117 • Archaeological Tools Presentation, Model, TR Alt. Assess., p. 7	• Selection Test, TR Formal Assessment, pp. 19–21; Assess. Res. Software • Description Rubric [for Wr. Mini-Lesson], TR Alt. Assess., p. 52 • TR Alt. Assess., p. 7	• "The Cask of Amontillado," LL Audiocassettes • WS Writing Lab CD-ROM Description Tutorial; Wr. at Work Videodisc, Ch. 1

Program Planner   Unit 2 Challenges and Choices

Selection	Reading	Literary Elements/Forms	Vocabulary	Grammar
from **"A Lincoln Preface,"** **Carl Sandburg,** SE p. 129 Reading Level: Challenging	• Reading for Success: Interactive Reading Strategies, SE pp. 128, 135; TR Selection Support, pp. 32–33 • Model Selection, SE pp. 129–134 • Summarize, TR Str. for Diverse St. Needs, p. 8	• Anecdote, SE pp. 127, 135; TR Selection Support, p. 34	• Suffixes: -ic, SE pp. 126, 135; TR Selection Support, p. 30 Word Bank: despotic, chattel, p. 129; cipher, slouching, censure, p. 131; gaunt, p. 133; droll, p. 134	• Independent and Subordinate Clauses, SE pp. 126, 135; TR Selection Support, p. 31 • WS Language Lab CD-ROM, Combining Sentences Lesson • WS Gram. Pr. Book, pp. 53–59
"I Have a Dream," Martin **Luther King, Jr.;** from *Rosa Parks: My Story;* **"There Is a Longing . . . ,"** Chief Dan **George; "I Hear America Singing," Walt Whitman,** SE pp. 140, 143, 145, 146 Reading Levels: Average, Easy, Average, Average	• Respond, SE pp. 139, 148; TR Selection Support, p. 37 • Identify Key Ideas, TR Str. for Diverse St. Needs, p. 9	• Author's Purpose, SE pp. 139, 148; TR Selection Support, p. 38	• Word Roots: -cred-, SE pp. 138, 148; TR Selection Support, p. 35 Word Bank: creed, oppression, oasis, exalted, p. 141; prodigious, hamlet, p. 142; complied, manhandled, p. 144; determination, endurance, p. 145	• Use of *shall* and *will,* SE pp. 138, 148; TR Selection Support, p. 36
"The Golden Kite, the Silver Wind," Ray Bradbury, SE p. 152 Reading Level: Average	• Predict Consequences of Actions, SE pp. 151, 157; TR Selection Support, p. 41 • Recognize Cause and Effect, TR Str. for Diverse St. Needs, p. 10	• Fable, SE pp. 151, 157; TR Selection Support, p. 42	• Word Roots: -clam-, SE pp. 150, 157; TR Selection Support, p. 39 Word Bank: portents, vile, ravenous, p. 153; acclaimed, pandemonium, spurn, p. 154	• Action Verbs and Linking Verbs, SE pp. 150, 157; TR Selection Support, p. 40 • WS Language Lab CD-ROM, Eight Parts of Speech Lesson • WS Gram. Pr. Book, pp. 11–14
"The Road Not Taken," Robert Frost; "New Directions," Maya Angelou; "To Be of Use," Marge Piercy, SE pp. 166, 168, 171 Reading Levels: Easy, Average, Average	• Generate Questions, SE pp. 164, 172; TR Selection Support, p. 45 • Paraphrase, TR Str. for Diverse St. Needs, p. 11	• Figurative Language, SE pp. 165, 172; TR Selection Support, p. 46	• Suffixes: -ly, SE pp. 164, 172; TR Selection Support, p. 43 Word Bank: diverged, p. 167; amicably, meticulously, p. 168; specters, ominous, unpalatable, p. 170; dallying, submerged, harness, p. 171	• Commas in Series, SE pp. 164, 172; TR Selection Support, p. 44 • WS Language Lab CD-ROM, Commas Lesson • WS Gram. Pr. Book, pp. 100–101
"Old Man of the Temple," **R. K. Narayan,** SE p. 176 Reading Level: Average	• Distinguish Fantasy From Reality, SE pp. 175, 182; TR Selection Support, p. 49 • Prepare a Readers Theater, TR Str. for Diverse St. Needs, p. 12	• Fantasy, SE pp. 175, 182; TR Selection Support, p. 50	• Suffixes: -ity, SE pp. 174, 182; TR Selection Support, p. 47 Word Bank: sobriety, p. 177; awry, p. 178; literally, longevity, imperative, venture, p. 180	• Compound Predicates, SE pp. 174, 82; TR Selection Support, p. 48 • WS Gram. Pr. Book, pp. 26–29
"Perseus," Edith Hamilton, SE p. 186 Reading Level: Challenging	• Predict, SE pp. 185, 194; TR Selection Support, p. 53 • Identify Characters, TR Str. for Diverse St. Needs, p. 13	• Hero in a Myth, SE pp. 185, 194; TR Selection Support, p. 54	• Word Roots: -mort-, SE pp. 184, 194; TR Selection Support, p. 51 Word Bank: kindred, p. 186; mortified, despair, p. 189; wavering, revelry, p. 191; deity, reconciled, p. 193	• Possessive Nouns, SE pp. 184, 194; TR Selection Support, p. 52 • WS Language Lab CD-ROM, The Eight Parts of Speech • WS Gram. Pr. Book, p. 112
"Slam, Dunk, & Hook," Yusef Komunyakaa; "The Spearthrower," Lillian Morrison; "Shoulders," Naomi Nye, SE pp. 198, 200, 201 Reading Levels: Average, Easy, Easy	• Form Mental Images, SE pp. 197, 202; TR Selection Support, p. 57 • Explain Poetic Phrases, TR Str. for Diverse St. Needs, p. 14	• Theme in Poetry, SE pp. 197, 202; TR Selection Support, p. 58	• Specialized Vocabulary: Jargon, SE pp. 196, 202; TR Selection Support, p. 55 Word Bank: metaphysical, jibed, feint, p. 199; surge, p. 200	• Prepositional Phrases, SE pp. 196, 202; TR Selection Support, p. 56 • WS Gram. Pr. Book, p. 41

KEY: SE: Student Edition;   ATE: Annotated Teacher's Edition;   TR: Teaching Resources;   LL: Listening to Literature;   WS: Writer's Solution

Writing	Speaking and Listening	Projects	Assessment	Technology
• Gettysburg Address, Newspaper Article, Character Profile, SE p. 136 • Mini-Lesson: Anecdote [Show, Don't Tell], SE p. 136 • Char. Analysis, Job Description, Historical Role Play, Analysis, TR Alt. Assess., p. 8	• Dramatic Scene, Panel Discussion, SE p. 136 • Mini-Lesson: Panel Discussion, ATE p. 132 • Praise Song, TR Alt. Assess., p. 8	• Timeline, Conflict Resolution, SE p. 136 • Sketch, TR Alternative Assess., p. 8	• Selection Test, TR Formal Assessment, pp. 26-28; Assess. Res. Software • Narrative Rubric [for Wr. Mini-Lesson], TR Alt. Assess., p. 89 • TR Alt. Assess., p. 8	• from "A Lincoln Preface," LL Audiocassettes • LL Writing Lab CD-ROM Narration Tutorial; Wr. at Work Videodisc, Ch. 2
• The American Dream, The Song of America, Argument for the Defense, SE p. 149 • Mini-Lesson: Proposal for a School Speaker [Benefits of Proposed Ideas], SE p. 149 • News Account, Occupation List, Compare-and-Contrast, Poem, TR Alt. Assess., p. 9	• Interview, Radio News Report, SE p. 149 • Mini-Lesson: Interview, ATE p. 148 • Public Speaking Essay, TR Alt. Assess., p. 9	• America in Poetry, Multimedia Presentation, SE p. 149 • Mind Map, TR Alt. Assess., p. 9	• Selection Test, TR Formal Assessment, pp. 29–31; Assess. Res. Software • Persuasion Rubric [for Wr. Mini-Lesson], TR Alt. Assess., p. 98 • TR Alt. Assess., p. 9	• "I Have a Dream," from *Rosa Parks: My Story*, "There Is a Longing . . . ," "I Hear America Singing," LL Audiocassettes • Looking at Lit., Ch. 3 • LL Writing Lab CD-ROM Persuasion Tutorial; Wr. at Work Videodisc, Ch. 4
• Good Advice, Fable, Persuasive Letter, SE p. 158 • Mini-Lesson: Public Service Ad Campaign [Use Appropriate Style for the Medium], SE p. 158 • Children's Story, Campaign Speech, TR Alt. Assess., p. 10	• Dramatization, Improvisation, SE p. 158 • Mini-Lesson: Dramatization, ATE p. 154 • Oral Presentation, TR Alt. Assess., p. 10	• Science Report, Map, SE p. 158 • Timeline, Stage Design, Creative Movement, TR Alt. Assess., p. 10	• Selection Test, TR Formal Assessment, pp. 32–34; Assess. Res. Software • Persuasion Rubric [for Wr. Mini-Lesson], TR Alt. Assess., p. 98 • TR Alt. Assess., p. 10	• "The Golden Kite, the Silver Wind," LL Audiocassettes • WS Writing Lab CD-ROM Persuasion Tutorial
• Recipe, Dialogue, Job Description, SE p. 173 • Mini-Lesson: Evaluation of Figurative Language [Effective Figurative Lang.], SE p. 173 • Observation and Description, Analyzing Character, Prediction, TR Alt. Assess., p. 11	• Job Interview, Group Discussion, SE p. 173 • Mini-Lesson: Job Interview, ATE p. 170 • Humorous Poem, TR Alt. Assess., p. 11	• Docudrama, Nutrition Report, SE p. 173 • Interview, Advertisement, TR Alt. Assess., p. 11	• Selection Test, TR Formal Assessment, pp. 35–37; Assess. Res. Software • Evaluation/Review Rubric [for Wr. Mini-Lesson], TR Alt. Assess., p. 97 • TR Alt. Assess., p. 11	• "The Road Not Taken, "New Directions," "To Be of Use," LL Audiocassettes • LL Writing Lab CD-ROM Response to Literature Tutorial; Wr. at Work Videodisc, Ch. 7
• Police Report, Obituary, Real Estate, SE p. 183 • Mini-Lesson: Travel Brochure [Tone], SE p. 183 • What-if, Compare-and-Contrast, Ghost Story, Observation, Explanatory Essay, TR Alt. Assess., p. 12	• Dramatic Reading, Dramatic Monologue, SE p. 183 • Mini-Lesson: Dramatic Monologue, ATE p. 178	• Cultural Map of India, Report on Hinduism, SE p. 183 • Temple Illustration, TR Alt. Assess., p. 12	• Selection Test, TR Formal Assessment, pp. 38–40; Assess. Res. Software • Description Rubric [for Wr. Mini-Lesson] TR Alt. Assess., p. 52 • TR Alt. Assess., p. 12	• "Old Man of the Temple," LL Audiocassettes • LL Writing Lab CD-ROM Description Tutorial
• Review, Feature Article, Modern-day Myth, SE p. 195 • Mini-Lesson: Speech Introduction [Appealing to Your Audience], SE p. 195 • Intrapersonal Reflection, Retold Myth, Critical Analysis, TR Alt. Assess., p. 13	• Comic Skit, Trial, SE p. 195 • Mini-Lesson: Trial, ATE p. 190 • Retold Myth, TR Alt. Assess., p. 13	• Mask, Map, SE p. 195 • Motive and Conflict Chart, Modern and Ancient Maps report, Lyre Report, TR Alt. Assess., p. 13	• Selection Test, TR Formal Assessment, pp. 41–43; Assess. Res. Software • Description Rubric [for Wr. Mini-Lesson], TR Alt. Assess., p. 90 • TR Alt. Assess., p. 13	• "Perseus," LL Audiocassettes • Literature CD-ROMs, Greek Myths and Legends • LL Writing Lab CD-ROM Description Tutorial
• Poem, Description, Story, SE p. 203 • Mini-Lesson: Sports Editorial [Anticipation of Questions], SE p. 203	• Oral Interpretation, Sportscast, SE p. 203 • Mini-Lesson: Sportscast, ATE p. 200 • Interview, Soundtrack, Debate, TR Alt. Assess., p. 14	• Painting/Drawing, Multimedia Presentation, SE p. 203 • Textbook Illustration, Three-Dimensional Art, Journal Entry, TR Alt. Assess., p. 14	• Selection Test, TR Formal Assessment, pp. 44–46; Assess. Res. Software • Persuasion Rubric [for Wr. Mini-Lesson], TR Alt. Assess., p. 98 • TR Alt. Assess., p. 14	• "Slam, Dunk, & Hook," "The Spearthrower," "Shoulders," LL Audiocassettes • Looking at Lit., Ch. 4 • LL Writing Lab CD-ROM Persuasion Tutorial

Program Planner   Unit 3 Moments of Discovery

Selection	Reading	Literary Elements/Forms	Vocabulary	Grammar
"Children in the Woods," **Barry Lopez,** SE p. 215 Reading Level: Challenging	• Reading for Success: Strategies for Constructing Meaning, SE pp. 214, 219; TR Selection Support, pp. 61–62 • Model Selection, SE pp. 215–218 • Outline an Argument, TR Str. for Diverse St. Needs, p. 15	• Central Idea and Support, SE pp. 213, 219; TR Selection Support, p. 63	• Prefixes: extra-, SE pp. 212, 219; TR Selection Support, p. 59 Word Bank: charged, p. 215; acutely, elucidate, extrapolation, p. 216; detritus, effervesce, insidious, ineffable, p. 217	• Forms of Adjectives, SE pp. 212, 219; TR Selection Support, p. 60 • WS Language Lab CD-ROM, The Eight Parts of Speech Lesson • WS Gram. Pr. Book, pp. 88–89
"Rules of the Game," **Amy Tan,** SE p. 224 Reading Level: Average	• Contrast Characters, SE pp. 223, 232; TR Selection Support, p. 66 • Respond to Characters' Actions, TR Str. for Diverse St. Needs, p. 16	• Generational Conflict, SE pp. 223, 232; TR Selection Support, p. 67	• Word Origins: Words From French, SE pp. 222, 232; TR Selection Support, p. 64 Word Bank: pungent, p. 225; benevolently, retort, prodigy, malodorous, p. 229; concessions, p. 230	• Complex Sentences, SE pp. 222, 232 ; TR Selection Support, p. 65 • WS Language Lab CD-ROM, Sentence Style Lesson • WS Gram. Pr. Book, p. 57
"Checkouts," Cynthia Rylant; "Fifteen," William Stafford, SE pp. 236, 241 Reading Levels: Average, Easy	• Relate to Personal Experience, SE pp. 235, 242; TR Selection Support, p. 70 • Analyze Characters' Behavior, TR Str. for Diverse St. Needs, p. 17	• Irony, SE pp. 235, 242; TR Selection Support, p. 71	• Suffixes: -ment, SE pp. 234, 242; TR Sel. Support, p. 68 Word Bank: intuition, p. 236; reverie, p. 238; shards, harried, brazen, dishevelment, p. 239; perverse, articulate, lingered, p. 240; demure, p. 241	• Pronouns and Antecedents, SE pp. 234, 242; TR Selection Support, p. 69 • WS Gram. Pr. Book, pp. 85–87
"Sympathy," Paul Laurence Dunbar; "Caged Bird," Maya Angelou; "We never . . ." **Emily Dickinson;** from ***In My Place,* Charlayne Hunter-Gault,** SE pp. 246, 247, 248, 250 Reading Levels: Average, Average, Average, Challenging	• Draw Conclusions, SE pp. 245, 253; TR Selection Support, p. 74 • Compare and Contrast Images, TR Str. for Diverse St. Needs, p. 18	• Symbol, SE pp. 245, 253; TR Selection Support, p. 75	• Levels of Diction, SE pp. 244, 253; TR Selection Support, p. 72 Word Bank: keener, p. 246; warp, p. 249; epithets, effigies, disperse, p. 250; imbued, perpetuated, p. 252	• Commonly Confused Words: Accept and Except, SE pp. 244, 253; TR Selection Support, p. 73
"The Interlopers," Saki (H. H. Munro), SE p. 262 Reading Level: Challenging	• Identify Causes and Effects, SE pp. 261, 268; TR Selection Support, p. 78 • Follow Dialogue, TR Str. for Diverse St. Needs, p. 19	• Conflict, SE pp. 261, 268; TR Selection Support, p. 79	• Word Roots: -obl-, SE pp. 260, 268; TR Selection Support, p. 76 Word Bank: precipitous, marauders, p. 262; medley, condolence, languor, p. 264; succor, p. 267	• Commonly Confused Words: Between and Among, SE pp. 260, 268; TR Selection Support, p. 77 • WS Gram. Pr. Book, p. 93
"The Rug Merchant," James A. Michener, SE p. 272 Reading Level: Average	• Make Inferences About Characters, SE pp. 271, 278; TR Selection Support, p. 82 • Question Author's Purpose, TR Str. for Diverse St. Needs, p. 20	• Characterization in Essays, SE pp. 271; TR Selection Support, p. 83	• Word Roots: -vis-, SE pp. 270, 278; TR Selection Support, p. 80 Word Bank: improvised, laden, p. 272; encompassed, p. 274; impose, ingeniously, p. 277	• Correct Use of Like and As/As If, SE pp. 270, 278; TR Selection Support, p. 81 • WS Gram. Pr. Book, p. 92
"Combing," Gladys Cardiff; "Women," Alice Walker; "maggie and milly . . ." E. E. Cummings; "Astonishment," Wisława Szymborska, SE pp. 282, 283, 284, 285 Reading Levels: Easy, Average, Average, Average	• Interpret Meaning, SE pp. 281, 286; TR Selection Support, p. 86 • Connect, TR Str. for Diverse St. Needs, p. 21	• Moment of Insight, SE pp. 281, 286; TR Selection Support, p. 87	• Words With Multiple Meanings, SE pp. 280, 286; SE p. 286; TR Selection Support, p. 84 Word Bank: intent, plaiting, p. 282; stout, p. 283; languid, p. 284	• Reflexive and Intensive Pronouns, SE pp. 280, 286; TR Selection Support, p. 85 • WS Gram. Pr. Book, p. 8

KEY: SE: Student Edition;   ATE: Annotated Teacher's Edition;   TR: Teaching Resources;   LL: Listening to Literature;   WS: Writer's Solution

Writing	Speaking and Listening	Projects	Assessment	Technology
• Poem, Dialogue, Persuasive Essay, SE p. 220 • Mini-Lesson: Field Guide [Specific Examples], SE p. 220 • Learning Environments, Persuasive Speech, TR Alt. Assess., p. 15	• Teaching Children, Dramatization, SE p. 220 • Mini-Lesson: Teaching Children Oral Interpretation, ATE p. 217 • Job Profile, TR Alt. Assess., p.15	• Relationship Map, Rain Forest Presentation, SE p. 220 • Teamwork, Nature Recording, Nature Study, TR Alt. Assess., p. 15	• Selection Test, TR Formal Assessment, pp. 51–53; Assess. Res. Software • Description Rubric [for Wr. Mini-Lesson], TR Alt. Assess., p. 90 • TR Alt. Assess., p.15	• "Children in the Woods," LL Audiocassettes • WS Writing Lab CD-ROM Description Tutorial; Wr. at Work Videodisc, Ch. 1
• Magazine Article, Letter, Extension, SE p. 233 • Mini-Lesson: Proposal [Clear Organization], SE p. 233 • Sequel, Short Story, Journal Entry, TR Alt. Assess., p. 16	• Radio Commentary, Dialogue, SE p. 233 • Mini-Lesson: Dialogue, ATE p. 230 • Soundtrack Explanation, TR Alt. Assess., p. 16	• Chess Set, Game, SE p. 233 • Technical Illustration, List, TR Alt. Assess., p. 16	• Selection Test, TR Formal Assessment, pp. 54–56; Assess. Res. Software • How-to/Process Explanation Rubric [for Wr. Mini-Lesson], TR Alt. Assess., p. 93 • TR Alt. Assess., p. 16	• "Rules of the Game," LL Audiocassettes • WS Writing Lab CD-ROM Persuasion Tutorial
• Classified Advertisement, Job Evaluation, Love Poem, SE p. 243 • Mini-Lesson: Scene From a Teen Soap Opera [Audience], SE p. 243 • Human Nature, TR Alt. Assess., p. 17	• Television News Report, Oral Story, SE p. 243 • Mini-Lesson: Oral Story, ATE p. 238 • Debate, Career Profile, Role Play, TR Alt. Assess., p. 17	• Audio Montage, Historic Homes, SE p. 243 • Illustration, Pamphlet, TR Alt. Assess., p. 17	• Selection Test, TR Formal Assessment, pp. 57–59; Assess. Res. Software • Drama Rubric [for Wr. Mini-Lesson], TR Alt. Assess., p. 102 • TR Alt. Assess., p. 17	• "Checkouts," "Fifteen," LL Audiocassettes • WS Writing Lab CD-ROM Creative Writing Tutorial
• Editorial, Letter, Dialogue, SE p. 254 • Mini-Lesson: Song [Purpose], SE p. 254 • Letter, TR Alt. Assess., p.18	• Choral Reading, Dramatic Monologue, SE p. 254 • Mini-Lesson: Dramatic Monologue, ATE p. 251 • Debate, TR Alt. Assess., p. 18	• Multimedia Presentation, Music, SE p. 254 • Civil Rights Timeline, Illustration, Measurement Report, Body Language Chart, TR Alt. Assess., p. 18	• Selection Test, TR Formal Assessment, pp. 60–62; Assess. Res. Software • Poetry Rubric [for Wr. Mini-Lesson], TR Alt. Assess., p. 101 • TR Alt. Assess., p. 18	• "Sympathy," "Caged Bird," "We never know how high we are," from In My Place, LL Audiocassettes • Looking at Lit., Ch. 5 • WS Writing Lab CD-ROM Creative Writing Tutorial
• Last Letter, Happy Ending, Peaceful Speech, SE p. 269 • Mini-Lesson: News Story [Elaboration for Understanding], SE p. 269 • Final Journal Entries, Creating Suspense, TR Alt. Assess., p. 19	• Persuasive Argument, Performance, SE p. 269 • Mini-Lesson: Persuasive Argument, ATE p. 266 • Celebration, Conflict Report, Improvisation, TR Alt. Assess., p. 19	• Real Estate Advertisement, Presentation on Wolves, SE p. 269 • Conflict Report, TR Alt. Assess., p. 19	• Selection Test, TR Formal Assessment, pp. 63–65; Assess. Res. Software • Description Rubric [for Wr. Mini-Lesson], TR Alt. Assess., p. 90 • TR Alt. Assess., p. 19	• "The Interlopers," LL Audiocassettes • WS Writing Lab CD-ROM Exposition Tutorial; Wr. at Work Videodisc, Ch. 3
• Sales Catalog, Dramatic Scene, Short Story, SE p. 279 • Mini-Lesson: Letter of Complaint [Clear Explanation of the Problem], SE p. 109 • Reflection, Description, Tale, Compare-and-Contrast, TR Alt. Assess., p. 20	• Conversation, Dramatic Monologue, SE p. 279 • Mini-Lesson: Dramatic Monologue, ATE p. 276 • Portrait of a Culture, TR Alt. Assess., p. 20	• Design a Rug, Report on Afghanistan, SE p. 279 • Tourist Guide, TR Alt. Assess., p. 20	• Selection Test, TR Formal Assessment, pp. 66–68; Assess. Res. Software • Cause-Effect Rubric [for Wr. Mini-Lesson], TR Alt. Assess., p. 95 • TR Alt. Assess., p. 20	• "The Rug Merchant," LL Audiocassettes • WS Writing Lab CD-ROM Practical and Technical Writing Tutorial
• Postcard, Poem, Dialogue, SE p. 287 • Mini-Lesson: Journal Entry [Elaboration to Add Emotional Depth], SE p. 287 • News Report, Sequel, TR Alt. Assess., p. 21	• Oral Interpretation, Television Interview, SE p. 287 • Mini-Lesson: Oral Interpretation, ATE p. 284 • Oral History, TR Alt. Assess., p. 21	• Multimedia Presentation, Photo Essay, SE p. 287 • A Genealogy of Women, Drawing, Report: Quilting, TR Alt. Assess., p. 21	• Selection Test, TR Formal Assessment, pp. 69–71; Assess. Res. Software • Expression Rubric [for Wr. Mini-Lesson], TR Alt. Assess., p. 87 • TR Alt. Assess., p. 21	• "Combing," "Women," "maggie and milly and molly and may," "Astonishment," LL Audiocassettes • WS Writing Lab CD-ROM Description Tutorial; Wr. at Work Videodisc, Ch. 1

Program Planner   Unit 4 The Lighter Side

Selection	Reading	Literary Elements/Forms	Vocabulary	Grammar
"The Secret Life of Walter Mitty," James Thurber, SE p. 299 Reading Level: Average	• Interactive Reading Strategies, SE pp. 298, 305; TR Selection Support, pp. 90–91 • Model Selection, SE pp. 299–304 • Distinguish Between Fantasy and Reality, TR Str. for Diverse St. Needs, p. 22	• Point of View, SE pp. 297, 305; TR Selection Support, p. 92	• Word Roots: *-scrut-*, SE pp. 296, 305; TR Selection Support, p. 88 Word Bank: rakishly, hurtling, p. 299; distraught, haggard, insolent, p. 301; insinuatingly, cur, cannonading, p. 302; derisive, inscrutable, p. 304	• Pronoun and Antecedent Agreement, SE pp. 296, 305; TR Selection Support, p. 89 • WS Language Lab CD-ROM, Pronouns Lesson • WS Gram. Pr. Book, pp. 78–81
"The Inspector-General," Anton Chekhov, SE p. 310 Reading Level: Average	• Read Between the Lines, SE pp. 309, 314; TR Selection Support, 95 • Prepare a Readers Theater, TR Str. for Diverse St. Needs, p. 23	• Irony, SE pp. 309, 314; TR Selection Support, p. 96	• Word Roots: *-nym-*, SE pp. 308, 314; TR Selection Support, p. 93 Word Bank: incognito, anonymous, trundle, p. 310; valet, p. 312; buffet, p. 313	• Double Negatives, SE pp. 308, 314; TR Selection Support, p. 94 • WS Language Lab CD-ROM, Problems With Modifiers Lesson • WS Gram. Pr. Book, p. 92
"Go Deep to the Sewer," Bill Cosby; **"Fly Away,"** Ralph Helfer, SE pp. 318, 324 Reading Levels: Average, Average	• Recognize Situational Humor, SE pp. 317, 328; TR Selection Support, p. 99 • Translate Jargon, TR Str. for Diverse St. Needs, p. 24	• Humorous Remembrance, SE pp. 317, 328; TR Selection Support, p. 100	• Sports Jargon, SE pp. 316, 328; TR Selection Support, p. 97 Word Bank: lateral, p. 319; yearned, decoy, p. 321; interpretation, p. 323; skeptical, p. 325	• Adjective Clauses, SE pp. 316, 328; TR Selection Support, p. 98 • WS Language Lab CD-ROM, Varying Sentence Structure Lesson • WS Gram. Pr. Book, pp. 53–54
"An Entomological Study of Apartment 4A," Patricia Volk, SE p. 332 Reading Level: Challenging	• Set a Purpose for Reading, SE pp. 331, 337; TR Selection Support, p. 103 • Recognize Puns and Word Play, TR Str. for Diverse St. Needs, p. 25	• Feature Article, SE pp. 331, 337; TR Selection Support, p. 104	• Prefixes: *micro-*, SE pp. 330, 337; TR Selection Support, p. 101 Word Bank: microcosms, metaphors, p. 332; poignant, malevolence, p. 334; immortalized, p. 336	• Participial Phrases, SE pp. 330, 337; TR Selection Support, p. 102 • WS Language Lab CD-ROM, Misplaced Modifiers Lesson • WS Gram. Pr. Book, pp. 44–45
"Macavity: The Mystery Cat," T. S. Eliot; **"Problems With Hurricanes,"** Victor Hernandez Cruz; **"Jabberwocky,"** Lewis Carroll, SE pp. 346, 350, 352 Reading Levels: Average, Easy, Average	• Contrast the Serious and the Ridiculous, SE pp. 345, 354; TR Selection Support, p. 107 • Identify Incongruity, TR Str. for Diverse St. Needs, p. 26	• Humorous Diction, SE pp. 345, 354; TR Selection Support, p. 108	• Word Origins: Portmanteau Words, SE pp. 344, 354; TR Selection Support, p. 105 Word Bank: bafflement, levitation, feline, depravity, larder, p. 347; suavity, p. 349; projectiles, p. 351; chortled, p. 353	• Parts of Speech Determined by Function, SE pp. 344, 354; TR Selection Support, p. 106 • WS Language Lab CD-ROM, The Eight Parts of Speech Lesson • WS Gram. Pr. Book, p. 25
"Talk," Harold Courlander, SE p. 358 Reading Level: Easy	• Recognize Illogical Situations, SE pp. 357, 360; TR Selection Support, p. 111 • Read Aloud, TR Str. for Diverse St. Needs, p. 27	• Humorous Folk Tale, SE pp. 357, 360; TR Selection Support, p. 112	• Prefixes: *re-*, SE pp. 356, 360; TR Selection Support, p. 109 Word Bank: ford, refrain, scowling, p. 359	• Adverb Clauses, SE pp. 356, 360; TR Selection Support, p. 110 • WS Language Lab CD-ROM, Varying Sentence Structure Lesson • WS Gram. Pr. Book, p. 55
"One Ordinary Day, With Peanuts," Shirley Jackson, SE p. 364 Reading Level: Challenging	• Question Characters' Actions, SE pp. 363, 372; TR Selection Support, p. 115 • Use a Chain-of-Events Organizer, TR Str. for Diverse St. Needs, p. 28	• Surprise Ending, SE pp. 363, 372; TR Selection Support, p. 116	• Related Words: Forms of *Omen,* SE pp. 362, 372; TR Selection Support, p. 113 Word Bank: irradiated, p. 364; loitered, endeavoring, p. 365; ominously, p. 366; buffeted, insatiable, p. 369; omen, impertinent, p. 371	• Capitalization of Proper Nouns, SE pp. 362, 372; TR Selection Support, p. 114 • WS Language Lab CD-ROM, Types of Nouns Lesson • WS Gram. Pr. Book, pp. 5–6, 94–95

KEY: SE: Student Edition;   ATE: Annotated Teacher's Edition;   TR: Teaching Resources;   LL: Listening to Literature;   WS: Writer's Solution

Writing	Speaking and Listening	Projects	Assessment	Technology
• Daydream, Recommendation, Diary Entry, SE p. 306 • Mini-Lesson: Character Profile [Main Impression], SE p. 306 • Counseling, Lyrics, Article, Interpersonal Communication, TR Alt. Assess., p. 22	• Performance, Panel Discussion, SE p. 306 • Mini-Lesson: Performance, ATE p. 302 • Drama, TR Alt. Assess., p. 22	• Daydream Illustrations, Report on Dreaming, SE p. 306 • Painting, Plot Representation, TR Alt. Assess., p. 22	• Selection Test, TR Formal Assessment, pp. 76–78; Assess. Res. Software • Description Rubric [for Wr. Mini-Lesson], TR Alt. Assess., p. 90 • TR Alt. Assess., p. 22	• "The Secret Life of Walter Mitty," LL Audiocassettes • WS Writing Lab CD-ROM Description Tutorial; Wr. at Work Videodisc, Ch. 1
• Advice Column, Letter to the Czar, Dialogue, SE p. 315 • Mini-Lesson: Ad for Inspector-General [Background], SE p. 315 • Personal Irony, Neighborhood Improvement, Recommendations, TR Alt. Assess., p. 23	• Speech to Town Officials, Performance, SE p. 315 • Mini-Lesson: Speech to Town Officials, ATE p. 312 • Double Negative Dialogue, Skit, TR Alt. Assess., p. 23	• Report on Russian Life, Multimedia Report, SE p. 315 • Interview, Pie Chart, TR Alt. Assess., p. 23	• Selection Test, TR Formal Assessment, pp. 79–81; Assess. Res. Software • Persuasion Rubric [for Wr. Mini-Lesson], TR Alt. Assess., p. 98 • TR Alt. Assess., p. 23	• "The Inspector-General," LL Audiocassettes • WS Writing Lab CD-ROM Persuasion Tutorial; Wr. at Work Videodisc, Ch. 4
• Sports Report, Résumé, Dramatic Scene, SE p. 329 • Mini-Lesson: Personal Narrative [Introduction], SE p. 329 • Essay, Process Explanation, TR Alt. Assess., p. 24	• Stand-up Comic Monologue, Interview, SE p. 329 • Mini-Lesson: Stand-up Comic Monologue, ATE p. 322 • Genetics Report, TR Alt. Assess., p. 24	• Research Report, Multimedia Biography, SE p. 329 • FX Report, Pantomime, Sketch/Drawing, Game, TR Alt. Assess., p. 24	• Selection Test, TR Formal Assessment, pp. 82–84; Assess. Res. Software • Narrative Based on Personal Experience Rubric [for Wr. Mini-Lesson], TR Alt. Assess., p. 89 • TR Alt. Assess., p. 24	• "Go Deep to the Sewer," "Fly Away," LL Audiocassettes • WS Writing Lab CD-ROM Narration Tutorial; Wr. at Work Videodisc, Ch. 2
• Animal Organizer, Bug Story, Campaign, SE p. 338 • Mini-Lesson: Letter [Level of Formality], SE p. 338 • Point of View, Two Perspectives, Personal Essay, Feature Article, TR Alt. Assess., p. 25	• Oral Report, Dialogue, SE p. 338 • Mini-Lesson: Dialogue, ATE p. 334 • Jingle, TR Alt. Assess., p. 25	• Insect Survey, Pet Arthropod, SE p. 338 • Pesticide Report, Children's Zoology Fair, TR Alt. Assess., p. 25	• Selection Test, TR Formal Assessment, pp. 85–87; Assess. Res. Software • Business Letter/Memo Rubric [for Wr. Mini-Lesson], TR Alt. Assess., p. 106 • TR Alt. Assess., p. 25	• "An Entomological Study of Apartment 4A," LL Audiocassettes • WS Writing Lab CD-ROM Practical and Technical Writing Tutorial
• Wanted Poster, News Report, Rewrite, SE p. 355 • Mini-Lesson: Poem [Precise Details], SE p. 355 • Descriptions, Journal Entry, Comparison and Contrast, Poem, TR Alt. Assess., p. 26	• Choral Reading, Oral Report, SE p. 355 • Mini-Lesson: Oral Report, ATE p. 350 • Portmanteau Words, TR Alt. Assess., p. 26	• Glossary, Farm Report, SE p. 355 • Children's Play, Mural, TR Alt. Assess., p. 26	• Selection Test, TR Formal Assessment, pp. 88–90; Assess. Res. Software • Poetry Rubric [for Wr. Mini-Lesson], TR Alt. Assess., p. 101 • TR Alt. Assess., p. 26	• "Macavity: The Mystery Cat," "Problems With Hurricanes," "Jabberwocky," LL Audiocassettes • Looking at Lit., Ch. 6 • WS Writing Lab CD-ROM Creative Writing Tutorial
• Sequel, News Report, Humorous Folk Tale, SE p. 361 • Mini-Lesson: Book-Jacket Blurb [Clear and Consistent Purpose], SE p. 361 • Reflection, Summary, Character Analysis, Bibliography, Limerick, Cultural Study, TR Alt. Assess., p. 27	• Dramatic Reading, Interview, SE p. 361 • Mini-Lesson: Dramatic Reading, ATE p. 358	• Storyboard, Multimedia Report, SE p. 361 • Logic Rating System, TR Alt. Assess., p. 27	• Selection Test, TR Formal Assessment, pp. 91–93; Assess. Res. Software • Persuasion Rubric [for Wr. Mini-Lesson], TR Alt. Assess., p. 98 • TR Alt. Assess., p. 27	• "Talk," LL Audiocassettes • WS Writing Lab CD-ROM Persuasion Tutorial; Wr. at Work Videodisc, Ch. 4
• Classified Ad, Diary Entry, Job Description, SE p. 373 • Mini-Lesson: Summary [Following Criteria], SE p. 373 • Know Thyself, Chapter Two, Humorous Essay, TR Alt. Assess., p. 28	• Dramatic Scene, Retold Story, SE p. 373 • Mini-Lesson: Dramatic Scene, Retold Story, ATE pp. 366, 370 • Incident Report, TR Alt. Assess., p. 28	• Map, Economic Report, SE p. 373 • Relaxation Techniques, Script, Mural, TR Alt. Assess., p. 28	• Selection Test, TR Formal Assessment, pp. 94–96; Assess. Res. Software • Summary Rubric [for Wr. Mini-Lesson], TR Alt. Assess., p. 91 • TR Alt. Assess., p. 28	• "One Ordinary Day, With Peanuts," LL Audiocassettes • WS Writing Lab CD-ROM Exposition Tutorial; Wr. at Work Videodisc, Ch. 3

Program Planner   Unit 5 Visions of the Future

Selection	Reading	Literary Elements/Forms	Vocabulary	Grammar
from *The Road Ahead,* **Bill Gates,** SE p. 385 Reading Level: Challenging	• Reading for Success: Strategies for Reading Critically, SE pp. 384, 389; TR Selection Support, pp. 119–120 • Model Selection, SE pp. 385–388 • Outline Main Idea and Supporting Details, TR Str. for Diverse St. Needs, p. 29	• Expository Writing, SE pp. 383, 389; TR Selection Support, p. 121	• Word Roots: *-simul-,* SE pp. 382, 389; TR Selection Support, p. 117 Word Bank: simultaneously, p. 385; capacious, precursors, p. 387; parlance, infrared, p. 388	• Pronoun Agreement With Indefinite Pronoun Antecedents, SE pp. 382, 389; TR Selection Support, p. 118 • WS Language Lab CD-ROM, Pronouns and Antecedents Lesson • WS Gram. Pr. Book, p. 85
"The Machine That Won the War," Isaac Asimov, SE p. 394 Reading Level: Average	• Identify Relevant Details, SE pp. 393, 400; TR Selection Support, p. 124 • Paraphrase Conversations, TR Str. for Diverse St. Needs, p. 30	• Science Fiction, SE pp. 393, 400; TR Selection Support, p. 125	• Prefixes: *circum-,* SE pp. 392, 400; TR Selection Support, p. 122 Word Bank: erratic, grisly, imperturbable, oracle, p. 395; surcease, subsidiary, p. 396; circumvent, p. 398	• Contractions, SE pp. 392, 400; TR Selection Support, p. 123 • WS Gram. Pr. Book, p. 112
"Fire and Ice," Robert Frost; "All Watched Over by Machines of Loving Grace," Richard Brautigan; "There Will Come Soft Rains," Sara Teasdale; "The Horses," Edwin Muir, SE pp. 412, 413, 414, 415 Reading Levels: Easy, Average, Easy, Challenging	• Recognize a Poet's Purpose, SE pp. 411, 417; TR Selection Support, p. 128 • Interpret Poetic Images, TR Str. for Diverse St. Needs, p. 31	• Alliteration, SE pp. 411, 417; TR Selection Support, p. 129	• Suffixes: *-ous,* SE pp. 410, 417; TR Selection Support, p. 126 Word Bank: perish, suffice, p. 412; tremulous, p. 414; covenant, confounds, p. 415; steeds, archaic, p. 416	• Commonly Confused Words: *lie* and *lay,* SE pp. 410, 417; TR Selection Support, p. 127 • WS Gram. Pr. Book, pp. 11–14
"If I Forget Thee, Oh Earth," Arthur C. Clarke; from *Silent Spring,* **Rachel Carson; "To the Residents of A.D. 2029," Bryan Woolley,** SE pp. 426, 430, 434 Reading Levels: Average, Average, Average	• Distinguish Between Fact and Opinion, SE pp. 425, 438; TR Selection Support, p. 132 • Identify Predictions, TR Str. for Diverse St. Needs, p. 32	• Exhortation, SE pp. 425, 438; TR Selection Support, p. 133	• Word Roots: *-ann-,* SE pp. 424, 438; TR Selection Support, p. 130 Word Bank: purged, p. 426; pyre, perennial, p. 428; blight, p. 432; moribund, p. 433; postulated, beleaguered, schism, p. 437	• Correlative Conjunctions, SE pp. 424, 438; TR Selection Support, p. 131 • WS Language Lab CD-ROM, Varying Sentence Structure Lesson, • WS Gram. Pr. Book, p. 23
"Gifts," Shu Ting; "Glory and Hope," Nelson Mandela, SE pp. 442, 443 Reading Levels: Average, Challenging	• Evaluate the Writer's Message, SE pp. 441, 446; TR Selection Support, p. 136 • Break Down Long Sentences, TR Str. for Diverse St. Needs, p. 33	• Tone, SE pp. 441, 446; TR Selection Support, p. 137	• Suffixes: *-logy,* SE pp. 440, 446; TR Selection Support, p. 134 Word Bank: pinions, hieroglyphics, p. 442; confer, p. 443; pernicious, ideology, chasms, covenant, inalienable, p. 445	• Subject and Verb Agreement, SE pp. 440, 446; TR Selection Support, p. 135 • WS Language Lab CD-ROM, Subject-Verb Agreement Lesson • WS Gram. Pr. Book, pp. 82–84

T20   **KEY:**   SE: Student Edition;   ATE: Annotated Teacher's Edition;   TR: Teaching Resources;   LL: Listening to Literature;   WS: Writer's Solution

Writing	Speaking and Listening	Projects	Assessment	Technology
• Interview Questions, Description of the Future, Business Proposal, SE p. 390 • Mini-Lesson: Letter for a Time Capsule [Clear Beginning, Middle, and End], SE p. 390 • Advice Column, Job Description, Newspaper Editorial, Rebuttal, TR Alt. Assess., p. 29	• Role Play, Oral Report, SE p. 390 • Mini-Lesson: Oral Report, ATE p. 387 • Software Instruction, Debate, TR Alt. Assess., p. 29	• Multimedia Presentation, Advertising Campaign, SE p. 390 • Work Plan, TR Alt. Assess., p. 29	• Selection Test, TR Formal Assessment, pp. 101–103; Assess. Res. Software • Expression Rubric [for Wr. Mini-Lesson], TR Alt. Assess., p. 87 • TR Alt. Assess., p. 29	• from The Road Ahead, LL Audiocassettes • WS Writing Lab CD-ROM Exposition Tutorial
• Diary Entry, Newspaper Story, Title Memo, SE p. 401 • Mini-Lesson: Directions for Operating a Simple Machine [Clear Explanation of Procedures], SE p. 401 • Creative Writing, Definition, TR Alt. Assess., p. 30	• Discussion of a Concept, Performance, SE p. 401 • Mini-Lesson: Discussion of a Concept, ATE p. 398 • Astronomy Report, Demonstration: Probability Theory, TR Alt. Assess., p. 30	• Poster, History of Computers, SE p. 401 • Sci-Fi Family Tree, Soundtrack, Sketch, TR Alt. Assess., p. 30	• Selection Test, TR Formal Assessment, pp. 104–106; Assess. Res. Software • How-to/Process Explanation Rubric [for Wr. Mini-Lesson], TR Alt. Assess., p. 93 • TR Alt. Assess., p. 30	• "The Machine That Won the War," LL Audiocassettes • WS Writing Lab CD-ROM Exposition Tutorial
• Diary Entry, Poem, Short Story, SE p. 418 • Mini-Lesson: Poem to a Future Generation [Brevity and Clarity], SE p. 418 • Images of Fire and Ice, Descriptive Scene, Personal Essay, TR Alt. Assess., p. 31	• Panel Discussion, Oral Interpretation, SE p. 418 • Mini-Lesson: Panel Discussion, ATE p. 414 • Alliterative Poem, Science-Fiction Scene, TR Alt. Assess., p. 31	• Bumper Stickers, Job Expo, SE p. 418 • Cybernetic Town, Technology Poll, TR Alt. Assess., p. 31	• Selection Test, TR Formal Assessment, pp. 107–109; Assess. Res. Software • Poetry Rubric [for Wr. Mini-Lesson], TR Alt. Assess., p. 101 • TR Alt. Assess., p. 31	• "Fire and Ice," "All Watched Over by Machines of Loving Grace," "There Will Come Soft Rains," "The Horses," LL Audiocassettes • WS Writing Lab CD-ROM Creative Writing Tutorial; Wr. at Work Videodisc, Ch. 6
• Bumper Sticker Slogan, Memo, Poem, SE p. 439 • Mini-Lesson: Environmental Report [Elaboration to Prove a Point], SE p. 439 • Journal Entry, Planning Document, Dear Bryan, TR Alt. Assess., p. 32	• Speech, Storytelling, SE p. 439 • Mini-Lesson: Storytelling, Speech, ATE pp. 428, 436 • Interpretive Reading, TR Alt. Assess., p. 32	• Poster, Time Capsule, SE p. 439 • Map the Colony, Beauty and Art, Pamphlet, TR Alt. Assess., p. 32	• Selection Test, TR Formal Assessment, pp. 110–112; Assess. Res. Software • Research Report/Paper Rubric [for Wr. Mini-Lesson], TR Alt. Assess., p. 99 • TR Alt. Assess., p. 32	• "If I Forget Thee, Oh Earth," from Silent Spring, "To the Residents of A.D. 2029," LL Audiocassettes • Looking at Lit., Ch. 7 • WS Writing Lab CD-ROM Research Writing Tutorial
• Letter to Nelson Mandela, SE p. 447 • Mini-Lesson: Speech for a Historic Figure [Transitions to Show Importance], SE p. 447 • Letter, Report, Letter to the Editor, TR Alt. Assess., p. 33	• Oral Interpretation, Panel Discussion, SE p. 447 • Mini-Lesson: Panel Discussion, ATE p. 444 • Oral Interpretation, Dialogue, Cause-and-Effect Report, TR Alt. Assess., p. 33	• Multimedia Presentation, Poster, SE p. 447 • Artistic Interpretation, TR Alt. Assess., p. 33	• Selection Test, TR Formal Assessment, pp. 113–115; Assess. Res. Software • Persuasion Rubric [for Wr. Mini-Lesson], TR Alt. Assess., p. 98 • TR Alt. Assess., p. 33	• "Gifts," "Glory and Hope," LL Audiocassettes • WS Writing Lab CD-ROM Persuasion Tutorial; Wr. at Work Videodisc, Ch. 4

Program Planner   Unit 6 Short Stories

Selection	Reading	Literary Elements/Forms	Vocabulary	Grammar
"The Gift of the Magi," **O. Henry,** SE p. 459 Reading Level: Average	• Reading for Success: Literal Comprehension Strategies, SE pp. 458, 465; TR Selection Support, p. 140–141 • Model Selection, SE pp. 459–464 • Simplify Word Order, TR Str. for Diverse St. Needs, p. 34	• Plot, SE pp. 457, 464; TR Selection Support, p. 142	• Prefixes: *de-*, SE pp. 456, 464; TR Selection Support, p. 138 Word Bank: instigates, p. 459; depreciate, p. 460; cascade, p. 460; chaste, p. 462; meretricious, p. 462; ravages; p. 462; discreet p. 463	• Sentence Fragments, SE pp. 456, 464; TR Selection Support, p. 139 • WS Language Lab CD-ROM, Sentence Style Lesson, • WS Gram. Pr. Book, pp. 62–63
"Sonata for Harp and Bicycle," Joan Aiken, SE p. 470 Reading Level: Average	• Predict, SE pp. 469, 480; TR Selection Support, p. 145 • Explain Comparisons, TR Str. for Diverse St. Needs, p. 35	• Rising Action and Climax, SE pp. 469, 480; TR Selection Support, p. 146	• Word Origins: Words From Myths, SE pp. 468, 480; TR Selection Support, p. 143 Word Bank: encroaching, p. 471; tantalizingly, p. 472; furtive, p. 475; menacing, p. 475; reciprocate, p. 476; ardent, p. 478; gossamer, p. 478; preposterous, p. 478; engendered, p. 478; improbably, p. 478	• Commas Before Interrogative Elements, SE pp. 468, 480; TR Selection Support, p. 144 • WS Language Lab CD-ROM, Commas Lesson, • WS Gram. Pr. Book, pp. 100–103
"The Scarlet Ibis," **James Hurst,** SE p. 484 Reading Level: Average	• Identify With a Character, SE pp. 483, 494; TR Selection Support, p. 149 • Classify Descriptive Details, TR Str. for Diverse St. Needs, p. 36	• Point of View, SE pp. 483, 494; TR Selection Support, p. 150	• Irregular Plurals: *-x* to *-ces*, SE pp. 482, 494; TR Selection Support, p. 147 Word Bank: imminent, p. 489; iridescent, p. 489; vortex, p. 489; infallibility, p. 489; entrails, p. 491; precariously, p. 491; evanesced, p. 493	• Infinitives and Infinitive Phrases, SE pp. 482, 494; Selection Support, p. 148 • WS Gram. Pr. Book, pp. 48–49
"Blues Ain't No Mockin Bird," Toni Cade Bambara; **"Uncle Marcos,"** Isabel Allende, SE pp. 498, 504 Reading Levels: Average, Challenging	• Make Inferences About Characters, SE pp. 497, 513; TR Selection Support, p. 153 • Understand Dialect, TR Str. for Diverse St. Needs, p. 37	• Direct and Indirect Characterization, SE pp. 497, 513; TR Selection Support, p. 154	• Prefixes: *dis-*, SE pp. 496, 513; TR Selection Support, p. 151 Word Bank: lassoed, p. 499; formality, p. 501; pallid, p. 504; vanquished, p. 504; fetid, p. 506; impassive, p. 506; disconsolately, p. 508; unrequited, p. 510	• Possessive Nouns, SE pp. 496, 513; TR Selection Support, p. 152
"The Man to Send Rain Clouds," Leslie Marmon Silko; **"The Invalid's Story,"** Mark Twain, SE pp. 522, 526 Reading Level: Easy, Average	• Your Senses, SE pp. 520, 532; TR Selection Support, p. 157 • Identify Cause and Effect, TR Str. for Diverse St. Needs, p. 38	• Setting, SE pp. 521, 532; TR Selection Support, p. 158	• Suffixes: *-ous,* SE pp. 520, 532; TR Selection Support, p. 155 Word Bank: cloister, p. 524; pagans, p. 524; perverse, p. 524; prodigious, p. 526; deleterious, p. 526; ominous, p. 528; judicious, p. 528; placidly, p. 528; desultory, p. 528	• Punctuating Dialogue, SE pp. 520, 532; TR Selection Support, p. 156 • WS Writing Lab CD-ROM Creative Writing Tutorial
"The Necklace," Guy de Maupassant; **"The Harvest,"** Thomás Rivera, SE pp. 536, 542	• Theme, SE pp. 458, 465; TR Selection Support, p. 161 • Sequence Events, TR Str. for Diverse St. Needs, p. 39	• Draw Conclusions, SE pp. 457, 464; TR Selection Support, p. 162	• Prefixes: *de-,* SE pp. 534, 546; TR Selection Support, p. 159 Word Bank: déclassé, p. 537; rueful, p. 537; resplendent, p. 539; disheveled, p. 540; profoundly, p. 540; harrowed, p. 543; astutely p. 544	• Participial Phrases, SE pp. 534, 546; TR Selection Support, p. 160 • WS Gram. Pr. Book, pp. 44–45

KEY: SE: Student Edition;   ATE: Annotated Teacher's Edition;   TR: Teaching Resources;   LL: Listening to Literature;   WS: Writer's Solution

Writing	Speaking and Listening	Projects	Assessment	Technology
• Letter of Appreciation, Sequel, Surprise Ending, SE p. 466 • Mini-Lesson: Thank-You Letter [Elaboration to Make Writing Personal], SE p. 466 • Story Award, Diary Entries, The Magi, Analysis, TR Alt. Assess., p. 34	• Play, Monologue, SE p. 466 • Mini-Lesson: Monologue, ATE p. 463	• Pantomime, Storyboard, SE p. 466 • Cultural Collage, Gift Budget, Diorama, TR Alt. Assess., p. 34	• Selection Test, TR Formal Assessment, pp. 120–122; Assess. Res. Software • Expression Rubric [for Wr. Mini-Lesson], TR Alt. Assess., p. 87 • TR Alt. Assess., p. 34	• "The Gift of the Magi," LL Audiocassettes • WS Writing Lab CD-ROM Practical and Technical Writing Tutorial
• Memo, Continuation, Evaluation, SE p. 481 • Mini-Lesson: Newspaper Report [Dramatic Effects], SE p. 481 • Security Memo, Script, Damage Report, Technology Report, TR Alt. Assess., p 35	• Talk-Show Interview, Debate, SE p. 481 • Mini-Lesson: Planning a Debate, ATE p. 476 • Interview, Strange Music, TR Alt. Ass., p. 35	• Mystery Timeline, Illustration, SE p. 481 • Model, TR Alt. Assess., p. 35	• Selection Test, TR Formal Assessment, pp. 123–125; Assess. Res. Software • Fictional Narrative Rubric, Narrative Based on Personal Experience Rubric [for Wr. Mini-Lesson], TR Alt. Assess., pp. 88, 89 • TR Alt. Assess., p. 35	• "Sonata for Harp and Bicycle," LL Audiocassettes • WS Writing Lab CD-ROM Exposition Tutorial; Wr. at Work Videodisc, Ch. 3
• Journal Entry, About a Symbol, Analysis of a Theme, SE p. 495 • Mini-Lesson: Character Sketch [Elaborate by Providing Details], SE p. 495 • Relationship Journal Entry, Physical Therapy Report, Sequel, TR Alt. Assess., p. 36	• Eulogy, Skit, SE p. 495 • Mini-Lesson: Eulogy, Skit, ATE pp. 488, 492	• Travel Brochure, Map, SE p. 495 • Foreshadowing Chart, Botanical Guide, Meteorological Report, Watercolor, TR Alt. Assess., p. 36	• Selection Test, TR Formal Assessment, pp. 126–128; Assess. Res. Software • Description Rubric [for Wr. Mini-Lesson], TR Alt. Assess., p. 90 • TR Alt. Assess., p. 36	"The Scarlet Ibis," LL Audio-cassettes • WS Writing Lab CD-ROM Description Tutorial
• Letter, Character Sketch, Persuasive Essay, SE p. 514 • Mini-Lesson: Magazine Feature [Main Impression], SE p. 514 • Newspaper Tribute, Letter to Granny, Revision, Journal Entry, Character Development, TR Alt. Assess., p. 37	• Debate, Monologue, SE p. 514 • Mini-Lesson: Monologue, ATE p. 500 • Dramatization, TR Alt. Assess., p. 37	• Illustrated Report, Illustration, SE p. 514 • Encyclopedia Map and Entry, TR Alt. Assess., p. 37	• Selection Test, TR Formal Assessment, pp. 129–131; Assess. Res. Software • Description Rubric [for Wr. Mini-Lesson], TR Alt. Assess., p. 90 • TR Alt. Assess., p. 37	• "Blues Ain't No Mockin Bird," "Uncle Marcos," LL Audiocassettes • Looking at Lit., Ch. 8 • WS Writing Lab CD-ROM Description Tutorial; Wr. at Work Videodisc, Ch. 1
• Suggestion Letter, Essay, Research, SE p. 533 • Mini-Lesson: Eulogy [Tone], SE p. 533 • Paragraph, Ceremony, Description, Elegy, Essay About Symbols, TR Alt. Assess., p 38	• Dramatic Reading, Persuasive Speech, p. 533 • Mini-Lesson: Persuasive Speech, Dramatic Reading, ATE pp. 524, 526 • Exaggeration Story, Mark Twain Reading, TR Alt. Assess., p. 38	• Map, Diagram, SE p. 533 • Mural, TR Alt. Assess., p. 38 • Illustration, Music, SE p. 547 • Harvest Fair, TR Alt. Assess., p. 39	• Selection Test, TR Formal Assessment, pp. 132–134; Assess. Res. Software • Expression Rubric [for Wr. Mini-Lesson], TR Alt. Assess., p. 87 • TR Alt. Assess., p. 38	• "The Man to Send Rain Clouds," "The Invalid's Story," LL Audiocassettes • WS Writing Lab CD-ROM Narration Tutorial
• Character Sketch, Different Point of View, Essay About Irony, SE p. 547 • Mini-Lesson: Scene for a Television Drama [Climax and Resolution], SE p. 547 • Journal Entry, Envy and Gossip Story, Sequel, Character Sketch, TR Alt. Assess., p. 39	• Improvisation, Debate, SE p. 547 • Mini-Lesson: Improvisation, ATE p. 537 • Round Table Discussion, Reading, TR Alt. Assess., p. 39	• Illustration, Music, SE p. 547 • Harvest Fair, TR Alt. Assess., p. 39	• Selection Test, TR Formal Assessment, pp. 135–137; Assess. Res. Software • Drama Rubric [for Wr. Mini-Lesson], TR Alt. Assess., p. 102 • TR Alt. Assess., p. 39	• "The Necklace," "The Harvest," LL Audiocassettes, • WS Writing Lab CD-ROM Creative Writing Tutorial

Program Planner   Unit 8 Drama

Selection	Reading	Literary Elements/Forms	Vocabulary	Grammar
"The Dancers," Horton Foote, SE p. 640 Reading Level: Average	• Envision the Action, SE pp. 639, 659; TR Selection Support, p. 186 • Prepare a Readers' Theater, TR Str. for Diverse St. Needs, p. 45	• Staging, SE pp. 639, 659; TR Selection Support, p. 187	• Homographs, SE pp. 638, 659; TR Selection Support, p. 184 Word Bank: genteel, p. 645; mortified, p. 646; defiance, p. 646; console, p. 652	• Linking Verbs and Predicate Adjectives, SE pp. 638, 659; TR Selection Support, p. 185 • WS Language Lab CD-ROM, Eight Parts of Speech Lesson • WS Gram. Pr. Book, pp. 12–13
The Tragedy of Romeo and Juliet, **William Shakespeare, Act I,** SE p. 672 Reading Level: Challenging	• Use Text Aids, SE pp. 670, 696; TR Selection Support, p. 190 • Summarize Plot, TR Str. for Diverse St. Needs, p. 46	• Character, SE pp. 671, 696; TR Selection Support, p. 191	• Prefixes: *trans-,* SE pp. 671, 696; TR Selection Support, p. 188 Word Bank: pernicious, p. 677; augmenting, p. 677; grievance, p. 678; transgression, p. 678; heretics, p. 683	• Punctuating Words of Direct Address SE pp. 671, 696; TR Selection Support, p. 189 • WS Language Lab CD-ROM, Commas Lesson • WS Gram. Pr. Book, p. 101
The Tragedy of Romeo and Juliet, **William Shakespeare, Act II,** SE p. 698 Reading Level: Challenging	• Reading Blank Verse, SE pp. 697, 719; TR Selection Support, p. 194 • Analyze Characters, TR Str. for Diverse St. Needs, p. 47	• Blank Verse, SE pp. 697, 719; TR Selection Support, p. 195	• Prefixes: *inter-,* SE pp. 697, 719; TR Selection Support, p. 192 Word Bank: cunning, p. 702; procure, p. 704; vile, p. 705; predominant, p. 706; intercession, p. 706; sallow, p. 707; waverer, p. 707; lamentable, p. 708; unwieldy, p. 714	• Logical Comparisons, SE pp. 697, 719; TR Selection Support, p. 193 • WS Language Lab CD-ROM, Double and Illogical Comparisons Lesson • WS Gram. Pr. Book, p. 91
The Tragedy of Romeo and Juliet, **William Shakespeare, Act III,** SE p. 721 Reading Level: Challenging	• Paraphrase, SE pp. 720, 745; TR Selection Support, p. 198 • Recognize Dramatic Irony, TR Str. for Diverse St. Needs, p. 48	• Soliloquy, Aside, and Monologue, SE pp. 720, 745; TR Selection Support, p. 199	• Words From Myths, SE pp. 720, 745; TR Selection Support, p. 196 Word Bank: gallant, p. 724; fray, p. 725; martial, p. 726; exile, p. 726; eloquence, p. 727; fickle, p. 738	• Commonly Confused Words: *Who* and *Whom,* SE pp. 720, 745; TR Selection Support, p. 197 • WS Language Lab CD-ROM, Using Pronouns Correctly Lesson • WS Gram. Pr. Book, pp. 78–81
The Tragedy of Romeo and Juliet, **William Shakespeare, Act IV,** SE p. 747 Reading Level: Challenging	• Predict, SE pp. 746, 759; TR Selection Support, p. 202 • Use a Story Map Organizer, TR Str. for Diverse St. Needs, p. 49	• Dramatic Irony, SE pp. 746, 759; TR Selection Support, p. 203	• Suffixes: *-ward,* SE pp. 746, 759; TR Selection Support, p. 200 Word Bank: pensive, p. 748; vial, p. 749; enjoined, p. 750; wayward, p. 750; dismal, p. 752; loathsome, p.753; pilgrimage, p. 756	• Parallel Structure, SE pp. 746, 759; TR Selection Support, p. 201 • WS Language Lab CD-ROM, Varying Sentence Structure and Combining Sentences Lesson
The Tragedy of Romeo and Juliet, **William Shakespeare, Act V,** SE p. 761 Reading Level: Challenging	• Identify Causes and Effects, SE pp. 760, 776; TR Selection Support, p. 206 • Recognize Metaphors, TR Str. for Diverse St. Needs, p. 50	• Tragedy, SE pp. 760, 776; TR Selection Support, p. 207	• Prefixes: *ambi-,* SE pp. 760, 776; TR Selection Support, p. 204 Word Bank: remnants, p. 762; penury, p. 762; haughty, p. 766; sepulcher, p. 769; ambiguities, p. 771; scourge, p. 774	• Subject and Verb Agreement in Inverted Sentences, SE pp. 760, 776; TR Selection Support, p. 205 • WS Language Lab CD-ROM, Special Problems in Agreement Lesson • WS Gram. Pr. Book, p. 82

KEY: SE: Student Edition;   ATE: Annotated Teacher's Edition;   TR: Teaching Resources;   LL: Listening to Literature;   WS: Writer's Solution

Writing	Speaking and Listening	Projects	Assessment	Technology
• Diary Entry, Casting Notes, News Report, SE p. 660 • Mini-Lesson: Script [Realistic Dialogue], SE p. 660 • Diary Entry, Letter for Advice, Venn Diagram and Paragraph, TR Alt. Assess., p. 45	• Musical Accompaniment, Counseling, SE p. 660 • Mini-Lesson: Role-Playing a Counseling Session, ATE p. 652 • Performance, 1950's Dance Music, TR Alt. Assess., p. 45	• Demonstrate a Dance, Design Costumes, SE p. 660 • Stage Design, Gulf Coast Map, TR Alt. Assess., p. 45	• Selection Test, TR Formal Assessment, pp. 161-163; Assess. Res. Software • Drama Rubric [for Wr. Mini-Lesson], TR Alt. Assess., p. 102 • TR Alt. Assess., p. 45	• "The Dancers," LL Audiocassettes • WS Writing Lab CD-ROM Creative Writing Tutorial; Wr. at Work Videodisc, Ch. 6
• Advice Column, Character Analysis, SE p. 696 • Summary, Movie Review, Stage Directions, Musical Review, TR Alt. Assess., p. 46	• Reading, SE p. 696 • Mini-Lesson: Reading, ATE p. 693 • Peace-Keeping Speech, TR Alt. Assess., p. 46	• Costume Design, Biographical Timeline, TR Alt. Assess., p. 46	• Selection Test, TR Formal Assessment, pp. 164–166; Assess. Res. Software • Persuasion Rubric [for Wr. Mini-Lesson], TR Alt. Assess., p. 98 • TR Alt. Assess., p. 46	• The Tragedy of Romeo and Juliet, Act I, LL Audiocassettes • Looking at Lit., Ch. 10 • Lit. CD-ROMs, The Life, Times, and Works of Shakespeare
• Poem in Iambic Pentameter, SE p. 719 • Summary, Movie Review, Stage Directions, Musical Review, TR Alt. Assess., p. 46	• Set Design, SE p. 719 • Mini-Lesson: Persuasion, ATE p. 717 • Peace-Keeping Speech, TR Alt. Assess., p. 46	• Costume Design, Biographical Timeline, TR Alt. Assess., p. 46	• Selection Test, TR Formal Assessment, pp. 167–169; Assess. Res. Software • Persuasion Rubric [for Wr. Mini-Lesson], TR Alt. Assess., p. 719 • TR Alt. Assess., p. 46	• The Tragedy of Romeo and Juliet, Act II, LL Audiocassettes • Lit. CD-ROMs, The Life, Times, and Works of Shakespeare
• Editorial, Soliloquy, SE p. 745 • Scene Organizer, Miniature Plot Summaries, Medical Report, Text Aids, TR Alt. Assess., p. 47	• Debate, SE p. 745 • Mini-Lesson: Debate, ATE p. 743 • Panel Discussion, TR Alt. Assess., p. 47	• Poster Design, Timeline, TR Alt. Assess., p. 47	• Selection Test, TR Formal Assessment, pp. 170–172; Assess. Res. Software • TR Alt. Assess., p. 47	• The Tragedy of Romeo and Juliet, Act III, LL Audiocassettes • Lit. CD-ROMs, The Life, Times, and Works of Shakespeare
• Love Letter, Your Own Ending, SE p. 759 • Scene Organizer, Miniature Plot Summaries, Medical Report, Text Aids, TR Alt. Assess., p. 47	• Renaissance Music Presentation, SE p. 759 • Mini-Lesson: Renaissance Music Presentation, ATE p. 757 • Panel Discussion, TR Alt. Assess., p. 47	• Poster Design, Timeline, TR Alt. Assess., p. 47	• Selection Test, TR Formal Assessment, pp. 173–175; Assess. Res. Software • TR Alt. Assess., p. 47	• The Tragedy of Romeo and Juliet, Act IV, LL Audiocassettes • Lit. CD-ROMs, The Life, Times, and Works of Shakespeare
• Executive Summary, Alternate Ending, Response to Literary Criticism, SE p. 777 • Mini-Lesson: Persuasive Letter [Precise Details], SE p. 777 • Letter From Juliet, Study of Motion, Guide to Preventing Civil Strife, TR Alt. Assess., p. 48	• Modern Scene, Rap Song, SE p. 777 • Mini-Lesson: Modern Scene, Rap Song, ATE p. 770, 773 • Mock Trial, Drama, TR Alt. Assess., p. 48	• Set Design, Shakespeare Display, p. 777 • Magazine Cover, Survey, TR Alt. Assess., p. 48	• Selection Test, TR Formal Assessment, pp. 176–178; Assess. Res. Software • Persuasion Rubric [for Wr. Mini-Lesson], TR Alt. Assess., p. 777 • TR Alt. Assess., p. 48	• The Tragedy of Romeo and Juliet, Act V, LL Audiocassettes • WS Writing Lab CD-ROM Persuasion Tutorial; Wr. at Work Videodisc, Ch. 4 • Lit. CD-ROMs, The Life, Times, and Works of Shakespeare

Program Planner Unit 9 Poetry

Selection	Reading	Literary Elements/Forms	Vocabulary	Grammar
"I Wandered Lonely as a Cloud," William Wordsworth, SE p. 789 Reading Level: Average	• Reading for Success: Strategies for Reading Poetry, SE pp. 4, 10; TR Selection Support, p. 210-211 • Model Selection, SE pp. 789–790 • Infer Feelings From Statements, TR Str. for Diverse St. Needs, p. 51	• Rhyme Scheme, SE pp. 787, 791; TR Selection Support, p. 212	• Specialized Vocabulary: Poetic Contractions, SE pp. 786, 791; TR Selection Support, p. 208 Word Bank: host, p. 789; glee, p. 789; pensive, p. 790; bliss, p. 790	• Inverted Word Order, SE pp. 787, 791; TR Selection Support, p. 209 • WS Language Lab CD-ROM, Varying Sentence Structure Lesson • WS Gram. Pr. Book, p. 31
"The Eagle," Alfred, Lord Tennyson; "'Hope' is the thing with feathers—," Emily Dickinson; "Dream Deferred," "Dreams," Langston Hughes, SE pp. 796, 797, 798, 799 Reading Levels: Easy, Average, Average, Easy	• Paraphrase, SE pp. 795, 800; TR Selection Support, p. 215 • Recognize Unusual Comparisons, TR Str. for Diverse St. Needs, p. 52	• Figurative Language, SE pp. 795, 800; TR Selection Support, p. 216	• Color Words, SE pp. 794, 800; TR Selection Support, p. 213 Word Bank: azure, p. 797; sore, p. 797; abash, p. 797; deferred, p. 798; fester, p. 798; barren, p. 799	• Coordinating Conjunctions, SE pp. 794, 800; TR Selection Support, p. 214 • WS Language Lab CD-ROM, Eight Parts of Speech Lesson • WS Gram. Pr. Book, pp. 23–24
"Blackberry Eating," Galway Kinnell; "Memory," Margaret Walker; "Women's Work," Julia Alvarez; "Eulogy for a Hermit Crab," Pattiann Rogers; "Meciendo," Gabriela Mistral, SE pp. 804, 805, 806, 807 Reading Levels: Easy, Easy, Average, Average, Average	• Envision the Imagery, SE pp. 803, 810; TR Selection Support, p. 219 • Identify Speaker's Attitude, TR Str. for Diverse St. Needs, p. 53	• Imagery, SE pp. 803, 810; TR Selection Support, p. 220	• Word Roots: -primo-, SE pp. 802, 810; TR Selection Support, p. 217 Word Bank: unbidden, p. 804; sinister, p. 805; primed, p. 806; divine, p. 807; meticulously, p. 809	• Parallel Structure, SE pp. 802, 810; TR Selection Support, p. 218 • WS Language Lab CD-ROM, Unity and Coherence in Paragraphs Lesson • WS Gram. Pr. Book, p. 129
"Uphill," Christina Rossetti; "Summer," Walter Dean Michaels; Ecclesiasties 3: 1–8, The King James Bible; "The Bells," Edgar Allan Poe, SE pp. 814, 815, 817, 818 Reading Levels: Average, Easy, Average, Challenging	• Listen, SE pp. 813, 823; TR Selection Support, p. 223 • Identify Sensory Words, TR Str. for Diverse St. Needs, p. 54	• Lyric Poetry and Sound Devices, SE pp. 813, 823; TR Selection Support, p. 224	• Prefixes: mono-, SE pp. 812, 823; TR Selection Support, p. 221 Word Bank: wayfarers, p. 814; voluminously, p. 819; palpitating, p. 819; monotone, p. 820; paean, p. 822	• End Punctuation, SE pp. 812, 823; TR Selection Support, p. 222 • WS Language Lab CD-ROM, Fragments and Run-On Sentences Lesson • WS Gram. Pr. Book, p. 99
"The Raven," Edgar Allan Poe; "The Seven Ages of Man," William Shakespeare, SE pp. 832, 836 Reading Levels: Challenging, Challenging	• Make Inferences About the Speaker, SE pp. 831, 838; TR Selection Support, p. 227 • Summarize Poetic Narrative, TR Str. for Diverse St. Needs, p. 55	• Narrative and Dramatic Poetry, SE pp. 831, 838; TR Selection Support, p. 228	• Word Roots: -sol-, SE pp. 830, 838; TR Selection Support, p. 225 Word Bank: quaint, p. 832; beguiling, p. 834; respite, p. 834; desolate, p. 834; pallid, p. 834; woeful, p. 836; treble, p. 836	• Participial Phrases, SE pp. 830, 838; TR Selection Support, p. 226 • WS Language Lab CD-ROM, Misplaced Modifiers Lesson • WS Gram. Pr. Book, pp. 44–45
"On the Grasshopper and the Cricket," John Keats; Sonnet 30, William Shakespeare; Three Haiku; Hokku Poems, SE pp. 842, 843, 844, 845 Reading Levels: Average, Average, Easy, Easy	• Read in Sentences, SE pp. 841, 846; TR Selection Support, p. 231 • Restate Poetic Language, TR Str. for Diverse St. Needs, p. 56	• Sonnets and Haiku, SE pp. 841, 846; TR Selection Support, p. 232	• Suffixes: -ness, SE pp. 840, 846; TR Selection Support, p. 229 Word Bank: ceasing, p. 842; wrought, p. 842; drowsiness, p. 842; woes, p. 843	Concrete and Abstract Nouns, SE pp. 840, 846; TR Selection Support, p. 230 • WS Language Lab CD-ROM, Types of Nouns Lesson

KEY: SE: Student Edition; ATE: Annotated Teacher's Edition; TR: Teaching Resources; LL: Listening to Literature; WS: Writer's Solution

Writing	Speaking and Listening	Projects	Assessment	Technology
• Personal Response, Poem With Similes, Support for a Definition, SE p. 792 • Mini-Lesson: Word Picture of a Natural Scene [Unnecessary Details], SE p. 792 • Description, Your "Inward" Eye, Conversation Poem or Story, Nature Essay, TR Alt. Assess., p. 49	• Speech, Memorized Presentation, SE p. 792 • Group Poem, Musical Reading, TR Alt. Assess., p. 49	• Anthology, Illustration, SE p. 792 • Nature Walk, TR Alt. Assess., p. 49	• Selection Test, TR Formal Assessment, pp. 183–185; Assess. Res. Software • Description Rubric [for Wr. Mini-Lesson], TR Alt. Assess., p. 90 • TR Alt. Assess., p. 49	• "I Wandered Lonely as a Cloud," LL Audiocassettes • WS Writing Lab CD-ROM Description Tutorial; Wr. at Work Videodisc, Ch. 1
• Advertisement, Guidebook Description, Analysis, SE p. 801 • Wr. Mini-Lesson: Comparison Poem [Using Figurative Language], SE p. 801 • Environmental Research, Letter, Comparison-Contrast Essay, Analysis, Physical Description, Advice Column, TR Alt. Assess., p. 50	• Inspirational Speech, Oral Presentation, SE p. 801 • Mini-Lesson: Inspirational Speech, ATE p. 795	• Illustration, Biographical Report, SE p. 801 • Pro-Con Chart, TR Alt. Assess., p. 50	• Selection Test, TR Formal Assessment, pp. 186–188; Assess. Res. Software • Poetry Rubric [for Wr. Mini-Lesson], TR Alt. Assess., p. 101 • TR Alt. Assess., p. 50	• "The Eagle," " 'Hope' is the thing with feathers—," "Dream Deferred," "Dreams," LL Audiocassettes • WS Writing Lab CD-ROM Creative Writing Tutorial; Wr. at Work Videodisc, Ch. 6
• Menu, Diary Entry, Evaluation, SE p. 811 • Mini-Lesson: Remember When . . . [Main Impression], SE p. 811 • Eulogy, Defense Strategies, TR Alt. Assess., p. 51	• Dramatic Reading, Monologue, p. 811 • Mini-Lesson: Opinion, ATE p. 805 • Word List, TR Alt. Assess., p. 51	• Concrete Image, Research Poem, SE p. 811 • Art Collection, Graph, Cityscape, Children's Story, TR Alt. Assess., p. 51	• Selection Test, TR Formal Assessment, pp. 189–191; Assess. Res. Software • Description Rubric [for Wr. Mini-Lesson], TR Alt. Assess., p. 90 • TR Alt. Assess., p. 51	• "Blackberry Eating," "Memory," "Women's Work," "Eulogy for a Hermit Crab," "Meciendo," LL Audiocassettes • WS Writing Lab CD-ROM Description Tutorial; Wr. at Work Videodisc, Ch. 1
• Written Recommendation, Lyric Poem, Compare-and-Contrast Essay, SE p. 824 • Mini-Lesson: Rap Song [Repetition], SE p. 824 • Summary, Speaker Profile, Structural Analysis, TR Alt. Assess., p. 52	• Dramatic Reading, Listening Activity, SE p. 824 • Mini-Lesson: Dramatic Reading, ATE p. 816 • Clapping, Discussion, TR Alt. Assess., p. 52	• Illustration, Multimedia Presentation, SE p. 824 • Season Chart, Opposites Chart, TR Alt. Assess., p. 52	• Selection Test, TR Formal Assessment, pp. 192–194; Assess. Res. Software • Poetry Rubric [for Wr. Mini-Lesson], TR Alt. Assess., p. 101 • TR Alt. Assess., p. 52	• "Uphill," "Summer," Ecclesiastes 3: 1–8, "The Bells," LL Audiocassettes • WS Writing Lab CD-ROM Creative Writing Tutorial; Wr. at Work Videodisc, Ch. 6
• Poem Summary, Story, Essay About the Stages of Life, SE p. 839 • Mini-Lesson: Scene for a Movie [Setting a Mood], SE p. 839 • Letter of Condolence, Raven Report, TR Alt. Assess., p. 53	• Choral Reading, Debate, SE p. 839 • Mini-Lesson: Choral Reading, Debate, ATE p. 832, 836 • Mime, TR Alt. Assess., p. 53	• Photo Exhibit, Fact Sheet, SE p. 839 • Photo Album, Portrait of the Artist, Stage Set, Life Expectancy Graph, TR Alt. Assess., p. 53	• Selection Test, TR Formal Assessment, pp. 195–197; Assess. Res. Software • Description Rubric [for Wr. Mini-Lesson], TR Alt. Assess., p. 90 • TR Alt. Assess., p. 53	• "The Raven," "The Seven Ages of Man," LL Audiocassettes • Looking at Lit., Ch. 11 • WS Writing Lab CD-ROM Description Tutorial; Wr. at Work Videodisc, Ch. 1
• Journal Entry, Introduction, Literary Analysis, SE p. 847 • Mini-Lesson: Haiku Series [Keeping to a Format], SE p. 847 • Response, Rhyme Analysis, Venn Diagram, Letter, TR Alt. Assess., p. 54	• Poetry Reading, Dialogue, SE p. 847 • Mini-Lesson: Dialogue, ATE p. 841	• Illustrated Book, Internet Research, SE p. 847 • Senses Chart, Science Exhibit, Watercolor, TR Alt. Assess., p. 54	• Selection Test, TR Formal Assessment, pp. 198–200; Assess. Res. Software • Poetry Rubric [for Wr. Mini-Lesson], TR Alt. Assess., p. 101 • TR Alt. Assess., p. 54	• "On the Grasshopper and the Cricket," Sonnet 30, Three Haiku; Hokku Poems, LL Audiocassettes • WS Writing Lab CD-ROM Creative Writing Tutorial; Wr. at Work Videodisc, Ch. 6

Program Planner   Unit 10 The Epic

Selection	Reading	Literary Elements/Forms	Vocabulary	Grammar
from the *Odyssey,* Homer: **Part 1: The Adventure of Odysseus,** SE p. 860 Reading Level: Challenging	• Read in Sentences, SE pp. 859, 893; TR Selection Support, p. 235 • Selection, SE pp. 5–9 • Identify Story Elements, TR Str. for Diverse St. Needs, p. 57	• The Epic Hero, SE pp. 859, 893; TR Selection Support, p. 236	• Word Origins: Words From Myths, SE pp. 858, 893; TR Selection Support, p. 233 Word Bank: plundered, p. 860; squall, p. 864; dispatched, p. 868; mammoth, p. 872; titanic, p. 876; assuage, p. 878; bereft, p. 881; ardor, p. 884; insidious, p. 888	• Pronoun Case, SE pp. 858, 893; TR Selection Support, p. 234 • WS Language Lab CD-ROM, Commas Lesson • WS Gram. Pr. Book, p. 101
from the *Odyssey,* Homer: **Part 2: The Return of Odysseus,** SE p. 895 Reading Level: Challenging	• Summarize, SE pp. 894, 917; TR Selection Support, p. 239 • Selection, SE pp. 895–916 • Use Parenthetical Expressions, TR Str. for Diverse St. Needs, p. 58	• Epic Simile, SE pp. 894, 917; TR Selection Support, p. 240	• Word Roots: *-equi-,* SE pp. 894, 917; TR Selection Support, p. 237 Word Bank: dissemble, p. 896; lithe, p. 896; incredulity, p. 896; bemusing, p. 901; glowering, p. 902; equity, p. 905; maudlin, p. 905; contempt, p. 910	• Participial Phrases, SE pp. 894, 917; TR Selection Support, p. 238 • WS Language Lab CD-ROM, Misplaced Modifiers Lesson • WS Gram. Pr. Book, p. 44
"An Ancient Gesture," Edna St. Vincent Millay; **"Siren Song,"** Margaret Atwood; **Prologue and Epilogue from the** *Odyssey,* Derek Walcott; **"Ithaca,"** Constance Cavafy, SE pp. 926, 927, 928, 930 Reading Levels: Easy, Average, Average, Average	• Compare and Contrast, SE pp. 925, 932; TR Selection Support, p. 243 • Selections, SE pp. 926–931 • Recognize Allusions, TR Str. for Diverse St. Needs, p. 59	• Contemporary Interpretations, SE pp. 925, 932; TR Selection Support, p. 244	• Suffixes: *-esque,* SE pp. 924, 932; TR Selection Support, p. 241 Word Bank: beached, p. 927; picturesque, p. 927; tempests, p. 928; amber, p. 931; ebony, p. 931; defrauded, p. 931	• Adverb Clauses, SE pp. 924, 932; TR Selection Support, p. 242 • WS Gram. Pr. Book, p. 55

KEY: SE: Student Edition;   ATE: Annotated Teacher's Edition;   TR: Teaching Resources;   LL: Listening to Literature;   WS: Writer's Solution

Writing	Speaking and Listening	Projects	Assessment	Technology
• Letter, Comparison-and-Contrast Essay, SE p. 893 • Job Description, Math Analysis, Film Treatment, TR Alt. Assess., p. 55	• Play-by-Play Broadcast, p. 893 • Mini-Lesson: Play-by-Play Broadcast, ATE p. 890 • Siren Songs, TR Alt. Assess., p. 55	• Sailing Terminology, Comic Book, Cause-and-Effect Chart, TR Alt. Assess., p. 55	• Selection Test, TR Formal Assessment, pp. 205–207; Assess. Res. Software • Fictional Narrative Rubric [for Wr. Mini-Lesson], TR Alt. Assess., p. 88 • TR Alt. Assess., p. 55	• from the *Odyssey*, Part 1: The Adventure of Odysseus, LL Audiocassettes • Looking at Lit., Ch. 12
• Epic Simile, Modern Heroic Poem, Literary Essay, SE p. 918 • Mini-Lesson: Letter Home [Sequence of Events], SE p. 918 • Biographical Sketch, Thoughts on Waiting, Analysis of Greek Art, TR Alt. Assess., p. 56	• Debate, Oral Report, SE p. 918 • Mini-Lesson: Oral Report, Debate, ATE p. 899, 914 • Storytelling, Mediation, TR Alt. Assess., p. 56	• Odyssey Map, Board Game, SE p. 918 • Technical Illustrations, Timeline, TR Alt. Assess., p. 56	• Selection Test, TR Formal Assessment, pp. 208–210; Assess. Res. Software • Fictional Narrative Rubric [for Wr. Mini-Lesson], TR Alt. Assess., p. 88 • TR Alt. Assess., p. 56	• from the *Odyssey*, Part 2: The Return of Odysseus, LL Audiocassettes • WS Writing Lab CD-ROM Narration Tutorial; Wr. at Work Videodisc, Ch. 2
• Metaphor, Comparison-and-Contrast Essay, Adaptation, SE p. 933 • Mini-Lesson: Now-and-Then Report [Accuracy], SE p. 933 • Journey of Life Journal Entry, Letter to Penelope, Siren Song, Point of View Rewrite, TR Alt. Assess., p. 57	• Monologue, Choral Reading, SE p. 933 • Mini-Lesson: Choral Reading, ATE p. 930 • Greek Myth Oral Report, Walcott's the *Odyssey* Performance, TR Alt. Assess., p. 57	• Illustration, Collection, SE p. 933 • Group Epic, TR Alt. Assess., p. 57	• Selection Test, TR Formal Assessment, pp. 211–213; Assess. Res. Software • Research Report/Paper Rubric [for Wr. Mini-Lesson], TR Alt. Assess., p. 99 • TR Alt. Assess., p. 57	• "An Ancient Gesture," "Siren Song," Prologue and Epilogue from the *Odyssey*, "Ithaca," LL Audiocassettes • WS Writing Lab CD-ROM Research Writing Tutorial; Wr. at Work Videodisc, Ch. 5

Skills Workshops

Unit	Writing Process Workshops	Applying Language Skills	Real-World Reading Skills Workshops	Speaking and Listening Workshops
Spine Tinglers	Observation, p. 75 Remembrance, p. 118	Vivid Verbs; Using Adjectives, pp. 76, 77 Precise Adjectives; Fragments, Run-ons, pp. 119, 120	Reading a Map, p. 78 Using Visuals, p. 121	Telephone Interviewing, p. 122
Challenges and Choices	Persuasive Speech, p. 159 Persuasive Essay, p. 204	Active/Passive Voice; Parallel Structure, pp. 160, 161 Double Comparisons; Faulty Logic, pp. 205, 206	Evaluating Advertising, p. 162 Challenge the Text, p. 207	Resisting Persuasion, p. 208
Moments of Discovery	Comparison/Contrast Essay, p. 255 Problem/Solution Essay, p. 288	Comparisons; Compound Sentences, pp. 256, 257 Coordinating/Subordinating; Adverb Clauses, pp. 289, 290	Reading Consumer Reports, p. 258 Reading for Specific Information, p. 291	Conducting Business, p. 291
The Lighter Side	Letter to an Author, p. 339 Critical Evaluation, p. 374	Run-ons; Misplaced Modifiers, pp. 340, 341 Quotations; Degrees of Comparison, pp. 375, 376	Reading Novels, p. 342 Judging an Author's Purpose, p. 377	Body Language, p. 378
Visions of the Future	Process Explanation, p. 419 Test Essay, p. 448	Transitions; Concise Language, pp. 420, 421 Commonly Confused Words; Sentence Variety, pp. 449, 450	Following Directions, p. 422 Key Words, p. 451	Following Oral Directions, p. 452
Short Stories	Personal Narrative, p. 515 Short Story, p. 548	Active/Passive Voice; Pronouns, pp. 516, 517 Punctuating Dialogue; Subject-Verb Agreement, pp. 549, 550	Recognizing Main Ideas, p. 518 Recognizing Bias, p. 551	Oral Storytelling, p. 552
Nonfiction	Cause/Effect Essay, p. 599 Informational Report, p. 628	Coordinating/Subordinating Conjunctions; Shifts in Tense, pp. 600, 601 Adjective Clauses; Appositives, pp. 629, 630	Reading Charts, p. 602 Adjusting Reading Rate, p. 631	Giving an Oral Presentation, p. 632
Drama	Dramatic Scene, p. 661 Editorial, p. 778	Fragments; Brackets/Parentheses, pp. 662, 663 Compound-Complex Sentences, pp. 779, 780	Analyze a Position, p. 664 Break Down Difficult Texts, p. 781	Giving a Persuasive Speech, p. 782
Poetry	Song Lyrics, p. 825 Poem, p. 848	Figurative Language; Punctuating Song Lyrics, pp. 826, 827 Concrete Nouns; Parallel Structure, pp. 849, 850	Interpreting Song Lyrics, p. 828 Using Headlines, p. 851	Choral Reading, p. 852
The Epic	Biographical Report, p. 919 Research Paper, p. 936	Who/Whom; Problems With Agreement, pp. 937, 938 Citing Sources; Quotation Marks, pp. 937, 938	Evaluating Sources, p. 922 Sort Information on the Internet, p. 939	Critically Viewing News Reports, p. 939

Prentice Hall

LITERATURE
Timeless Voices, Timeless Themes

Copper

Bronze

Silver

Gold

Platinum

The American Experience

The British Tradition

World Masterpieces

PROGRAM ADVISORS

The program advisors provided ongoing input throughout the development of Prentice Hall Literature: Timeless Voices, Timeless Themes. Their valuable insights ensure that the perspectives of the teachers throughout the country are represented within this literature series.

Diane Cappillo
Language Arts Department Chair
Barbara Goleman Senior High School
Miami, Florida
Facilitator at the University of Miami/Dade County Public Schools Summer Writing Institute. Past president of the Dade County Council of Teachers of English.

Anita Clay
English Instructor
Gateway Institute of Technology
St. Louis, Missouri
Former supervisory positions:
Middle School Team Leader Chairman, High School English Department; Coordinator Effective and Efficient School; Coordinator, Writing Across the Curriculum Project.

Nancy M. Fahner
Language Arts Instructor
Charlotte High School
Charlotte, Michigan
Recipient of Charlotte Teacher of the Year Award 1992. Currently working on School-to-Work Curriculum Development.

Terri Fields
Language Arts and Communication Arts Teacher,
Author
Sunnyslope High School
Phoenix, Arizona
Recipient of both Arizona Teacher of the Year and U. S. WEST Outstanding Arizona Teacher

awards. Member of the Northern Arizona University Center for Excellence in Education Advisory Council. First place award for educational writing from National Federation of PressWomen.

Argelia Arizpe Guadarrama
Secondary Curriculum Coordinator
Phar-San Juan-Alamo Independent School District
San Juan, Texas
Recognized by Texas Education Agency for work on Texas Assessment of Academic Skills. Recipient of National Recognition of Positive Avenues for Student Success Program.

V. Pauline Hodges, Ph.D.
Teacher and Educational Consultant
Forgan High School
Forgan, Oklahoma
Formerly Language Arts Coordinator
Jefferson County, Colorado
Denver Professor in English Education/Reading, Colorado State University. President-elect of the National Rural Education Association. Recipient of Oklahoma Foundation for Excellence Award for Secondary Teaching 1993 and Outstanding Educator Award from the Colorado Language Arts Society.

Jennifer Huntress
Secondary Language Arts Coordinator
Putnam City Schools
Oklahoma City, Oklahoma
National trainer for writing evaluation, curriculum integration, and alternative assessment strategies. Instructor of language arts methods classes at Oklahoma City University.

Angelique McMath Jordan
English Teacher
Dunwoody High School
Dunwoody, Georgia
*Teacher of the Year at Dunwoody
High School, 1991.*

Nancy L. Monroe
English and Speed Reading Teacher
Bolton High School
Alexandria, Louisiana
*Past president of the Rapides Council of
Teachers of English and the Louisiana Council
of Teachers. National Advanced Placement
Consultant.*

Rosemary A. Naab
English Chairperson
Ryan High School
Archdiocese of Philadelphia
Philadephia, Pennsylvania
*English Curriculum Committee.
Awarded Curriculum Quill Award by the
Archdiocese of Philadelphia for the
development of effective strategies
for the teaching of writing and the
integration of technology and writing.*

Ann Okamura
English Teacher
Luguna Creek High School
Elk Grove, California
*Participant of the College Board
Pacesetters Program. Formerly K–12
District Resource Specialist in Writing,
Foreign Languages, Lay Readers,
District Writing, Competency Assessment,
and the Elk Grove Writing Project. A
fellow in the San Joaquin Valley Writing
Project and California Literature Project.*

Jonathan L. Schatz
English Teacher/Team Leader
Tappan Zee High School
Orangeburg, New York
*Creator of a literacy program to assist students
with reading in all content areas.*

John Scott
English Teacher
Hampton High School
Hampton, Virginia
*Recipient of the Folger Shakespeare Library
Renaissance Forum Award. Master Teacher
in Shakespeare who produces workshops for
professional development at the local, state,
and national level. Selected to participate in four
National Endowment for the Humanities teacher
programs.*

Ken Spurlock
Assistant Principal
Boon County High School
Florence, Kentucky
*Former English Teacher at Holmes High School
and district writing supervisor. Past president of
Kentucky Council of Teachers of English.*

ISBN 0-13-434056-6
1 2 3 4 5 6 7 8 9 10 02 01 00 99 98

 PRENTICE HALL
Simon & Schuster Education Group
A Viacom Company

STAFF CREDITS FOR PRENTICE HALL LITERATURE

(in alphabetical order)

Advertising and Promotion: Judy Goldstein, Carol Leslie, Rip Odell, Rob Richman, Ann Shea

Business Office: Emily Heins

Design: Laura Jane Bird, Sarah Carroll, Annemarie Franklin, Monduane Harris, Jim O'Shea, AnnMarie Roselli, Gerry Shrenck

Director of Language Arts: Douglas McCollum

Editorial: Ellen Bowler, Pam Cardiff, Megan Chill, Barbara W. Coe, Donna C. DiCuffa, Elisa Mui Eiger, Amy E. Fleming, Philip Fried, Rebecca Z. Graziano, James S. Jeglikowski, Jacqueline M. Regan

Electronic Publishing: Gregory Myers, Cleasta Wilburn

Manufacturing: Katherine Clarke, Rhett Conklin

Marketing: Glenn E. Bell, Jean Faillace, Belinda Loh

Market Research: Eileen Friend, Joan McCulley

Media Resources: Martha Conway, Libby Forsyth, Melanie Jones, Vickie Menanteaux, Maureen Raymond, Melissa Shustyk, Keirsten Wallace

National Language Arts Consultants: Linda Alexander, Kelly Ford, Karen Massey, Gail Witt

Permissions: Doris Robinson

PrePress Production: Kathryn Dix, William J. Hanna

Production: Christina Burghard, Holly Gordon, Elizabeth Torjussen

Technology: Rick Hickox

Art/Photograph Credits begin on p. 995.

ACKNOWLEDGMENTS

Grateful acknowledgment is made to the following for permission to reprint copyrighted material:

Margaret Walker Alexander
"Memory" from *For My People* by Margaret Walker, copyright 1942 Yale University Press. Reprinted by permission of Margaret Walker Alexander.

Rudolfo A. Anaya
"A Celebration of Grandfathers," copyright by Rudolfo Anaya, from *New Mexico Magazine,* March 1983. Reprinted by permission of the author.

(Acknowledgments continue on p. 991)

Looking at Universal Themes

Spine Tinglers

Unit 4

Looking at Universal Themes

The Lighter Side

Contents ◆ xi

Unit 8

Drama

Poetry

Unit 9

Contents ◆ xv

Unit 10

The Epic

Complete Contents by Genre

Complete Contents by Genre (continued)

NONFICTION

POETRY

Complete Contents by Genre (continued)

Planning Instruction and Assessment

Unit Objectives

1. To read selections in different genre that develop the theme of Spine Tinglers
2. To apply a variety of reading strategies, particularly literal comprehension strategies, appropriate for reading these selections
3. To recognize literary elements used in these selections
4. To increase vocabulary
5. To learn elements of grammar and usage
6. To write in a variety of modes and about situations based on the selections
7. To develop speaking and listening skills, by doing proposed activities

Meeting the Objectives

With each selection, you will find instructional material and portfolio opportunities through which students can meet these objectives. Further, you will find additional practice pages for reading strategies, literary elements, vocabulary, and grammar in the **Selection Support** booklet in the Teaching Resources box.

Setting Goals Work with your students at the beginning of the unit to set goals for unit outcomes. Plan what skills and concepts you wish students to acquire. You may individualize according to students' performance levels or learning modalities.

Portfolios You may have students keep portfolios of their work or of their work in progress. The activities and prompts on the Build Your Portfolio page of each selection provide opportunities for students to apply the concepts presented with the selection.

The Storm, 1893, Edvard Munch, ©1997 The Museum of Modern Art, New York

 Humanities: Art

The Storm, 1893, by Edvard Munch.
Edvard Munch (1863–1944) was a painter and graphic artist who studied in Paris as well as in his native Norway. Munch's complex psychological style is considered one of the earliest manifestations of Expressionism, a movement in art marked by the use of symbols and images distorted to give expression to emotion and inner experience. Munch's identity as an artist came from his obsession with depression, fear, and death; his exploration of these dark themes infused his art with a harrowing power.

Like so many of Munch's works, *The Storm* focuses more on the emotional effect of an event than on the event itself. The postures of all the people with their hands raised suggests they are paralyzed by a terror that seems larger and deeper than that caused by a storm. The woman in white is separated from the group by her position and also by her clothing, her pale dress emphasizing her stark isolation from the others and from the darkness of the natural forces gathering around her.

Have students answer these questions:

1. What emotions do you think the people in the painting are feeling, and why?
   Answers may include terror and helplessness; people fear the coming storm.
2. Imagine that this painting is illustrating a spine-tingling story. Why might the woman in white be separated from the others?
   Students may suggest the following: They are forcing her to go get help; she is driven mad by their terror and is running away.

Spine Tinglers

Turn the page to enter a world of suspense and mystery. Here, extraordinary events are commonplace, and desperate acts or unexplained phenomena can change the course of a life forever. Experience these stories, poems, and essays—if you dare! Your heart will race, your fists will clench, and your spine will tingle.

◆ 1

Assessing Student Progress

The following tools are available to measure the degree to which students meet the unit objectives:

Informal Assessment

The questions on the Guide for Responding sections are a first level of response to the concepts and skills presented with the selection. Students' responses are a brief informal measure of their grasp of the material. Their responses on this level can indicate where further instruction and practice are needed. You may then follow up with the practice pages in the *Selection Support* booklet.

You will find literature and reading guides in the *Alternative Assessment* booklet, which you may give students on an individual basis for informal assessment of their performance.

Formal Assessment

In the *Formal Assessment* booklet, you will find selection tests and a unit test.

Selection Tests The selection tests measure comprehension and skills acquisition for each selection or group of selections.

Unit Test The unit test, which calls on students to read a passage of literature they have not previously seen, applies the unit skills on a broader level. The Critical Reading section measures Unit Objectives 1, 2, and 3. The Vocabulary and Grammar section measures Objectives 4 and 5. The Essay section measures Objectives 1 and 6. Both the Critical Reading and Vocabulary and Grammar sections use formats similar to those found on many standardized tests, including the SAT.

Alternative Assessment

Portfolios As you review individual pieces or the collected work in students' portfolios, you will find assessment sheets available in the portfolio section of the *Alternative Assessment* booklet.

Scoring Rubrics You will find scoring rubrics for writing modes in the *Alternative Assessment* booklet. You can apply these to Writing Mini-Lessons and to Writing Process Workshop lessons.

Speaking and Listening The *Alternative Assessment* booklet contains assessment sheets for speaking and listening activities.

Learning Modalities The *Alternative Assessment* contains activities that appeal to different learning styles. You may use these to as an alternative measurement of students' growth.

OBJECTIVES

1. To read, comprehend, and interpret a short story
2. To relate a story to personal experience
3. To apply literal comprehension reading strategies
4. To identify mood
5. To build vocabulary in context and learn the prefix *pre-*
6. To develop skill in using correct pronoun case
7. To write a description of a set using precise details
8. To respond to the story through writing, speaking and listening, and projects

SKILLS INSTRUCTION

Vocabulary:
Prefixes: *pre-*

Grammar:
Pronoun Case

Reading for Success: Literal Comprehension Strategies

Literary Focus:
Mood

Writing: Precise Details

Speaking and Listening:
Resolving Interpersonal Conflicts (teacher edition)

Critical Viewing:
Explain; Analyze; Compare and Contrast

PORTFOLIO OPPORTUNITIES

Writing: Monologue; Opening Argument; Letter to Edgar Allan Poe

Writing Mini-Lesson: Describing a Set

Speaking and Listening: Casting Discussion; Resolving Interpersonal Conflicts

Projects: Pantomime; Story Board

More About the Author
Edgar Allan Poe not only wrote great short stories, he helped define what a short story should be. He asserted that a short story should be constructed to achieve "a certain unique or single effect." Every character, detail, and incident in a story should contribute to this effect. He believed that if a writer's "very initial sentence tend not to the out-bringing of this effect, then he has failed in his first step."

Guide for Reading

Edgar Allan Poe (1809–1849)

One of the first great American storytellers, Edgar Allan Poe blazed the trail for writers like Stephen King.

To this day, writers of spine tinglers point to Poe as the master of horror.

Poe's dark imagination may have its roots in his troubled childhood. Both of his parents died before he was three, and he was raised by John Allan, a wealthy Virginia merchant.

A Bitter Break While attending the University of Virginia, Poe amassed gambling debts, which his stepfather refused to pay. Forced to leave school, Poe later attended the United States Military Academy at West Point. Within a year, however, he was expelled for academic violations, causing an irreparable break with his stepfather.

The Downward Spiral Poe found brief happiness when he married Virginia Clemm. Tragically, however, Clemm succumbed to tuberculosis in 1847. Poe, heartbroken over the death of his wife, became increasingly antisocial. In 1849, he was discovered in a delirious condition on a Baltimore street. Three days later he was dead at the age of forty.

The Story Behind the Story This story has its roots in Poe's experiences in the First Artillery at Fort Independence. Soldiers told a story about a bullying officer who killed a younger officer named Robert Massie in 1817. Massie's friends avenged his death by leading the killer into the dungeons. There, they chained him to the floor and sealed him inside to die a horrible death. The story was confirmed in 1905 during renovations to the fort. Behind a wall, workmen found a skeleton, chained to the floor, with tatters of a military uniform hanging from the bones.

◆ Build Vocabulary

PREFIXES: *pre-*
The word *precluded* in this story begins with the prefix *pre-*, which means "before." The prefix *pre-* can help you unlock the meanings of words in which it appears. You can determine, for example, that *precluded* refers to something happening before something else. It actually means "made something impossible in advance."

| precluded |
| retribution |
| accosted |
| afflicted |
| explicit |
| recoiling |
| termination |
| subsided |

WORD BANK
As you read this story, you will encounter the words on this list. Each word is defined on the page where it first appears. Preview the list before you read.

◆ Build Grammar Skills

PRONOUN CASE
Pronouns help writers avoid repeating names. The use of pronouns is especially important in this story because there are only two characters.

Pronoun case refers to the different forms a pronoun takes to indicate its function in a sentence.

Subjective case pronouns—*I, we, you, she, it, they*—are used when the pronoun performs the action or renames the subject. In this example, *I* renames *it*.

It is *I*.

The objective case—*me, us, you, him, he, it, they*—is used when the pronoun receives the action of the verb or is the object of a preposition.

subject   obj. of prep.
In this respect *I* did not differ from *him* materially.

Prentice Hall Literature Program Resources

REINFORCE / RETEACH / EXTEND

Selection Support Pages
Build Vocabulary: Prefixes: *pre-*, p. 1
Build Grammar Skills: Pronoun Case, p. 2
Reading for Success: Literal Comprehension Strategies, pp. 3–4
Literary Focus: Mood, p. 5

Strategies for Diverse Student Needs, p. 1

Beyond Literature
Humanities Connection: Coats of Arms, p. 1

Formal Assessment Selection Test, pp. 1–3,

Assessment Resources Software

Alternative Assessment, p. 1

Writing and Language Transparencies
Descriptive and Observational Writing, pp. 17–20

Resource Pro CD-ROM
"The Cask of Amontillado"—includes all resource material and customizable lesson plan

Listening to Literature Audiocassettes
"The Cask of Amontillado"

The Cask of Amontillado

◆ *Literature and Your Life*

CONNECT YOUR EXPERIENCE

Often, it doesn't take much to spark a desire for revenge. It can start with a simple insult, an unresolved dispute, even an unhappy loser in a hard-fought game. You encounter these situations in books, movies, television programs, and in real life. Sometimes, as in this story, a quest for revenge can get out of hand.

Journal Writing Think about why some people become obsessed with revenge and jot down all the reasons that come to mind. Then note some of the negative consequences of such an obsession. If possible, cite examples.

THEMATIC FOCUS: SPINE TINGLERS

In this spine-tingling tale, suspense builds about how far one character will go in his quest for revenge against another character. As you read, you may find yourself wondering: How far will a character go to satisfy such a desire?

◆ Background for Understanding

CULTURE

The mask you see on this page might remind you of Halloween, but it's related to a different cultural custom. Masks and costumes are an important part of Carnival—a mad, wild celebration that precedes Lent, a period of fasting and penance before Easter. Because the masks and costumes of Carnival hide a person's real identity, many people feel free to enter into the Carnival spirit and loosen their usual rules of behavior. This week-long celebration of costumes, food, and dancing serves as the setting for "The Cask of Amontillado," providing cover for a gruesome act of revenge.

HISTORY

Much of the action in this story takes place in underground burial chambers known as catacombs. These long passages and side tunnels with hollowed-out cavities along the walls stretch out like hidden cities of the dead. Until recent centuries, many wealthy European families had their own catacombs beneath the family manor. In these stone vaults beneath their homes, families held funerals for their dead, surrounded by the bones of ancient ancestors. The most extensive known catacombs are the early Christian catacombs outside Rome.

◆ Literary Focus

MOOD

As the two characters in this tale descend into the depths of the catacombs, you can't help feeling that something sinister is about to happen. Poe creates this eerie, suspenseful **mood**, or feeling that the reader experiences, with carefully chosen words and details, such as *drops of moisture trickle among the bones* and *torches glow dimly in the foulness of the air*. Notice the many other descriptive details that contribute to the mood in Poe's classic tale of horror.

Jot down the details and the effect that they create in a graphic organizer like this one.

Detail		Effect
____	→	____
____	→	____
____	→	____

Guide for Reading ◆ 3

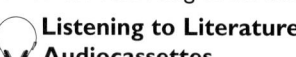
✎ Preparing for Standardized Tests

Reading and Vocabulary Vocabulary development will enable students to improve performance on the verbal portions of tests—both reading comprehension and vocabulary items. The Build Vocabulary lesson focuses on learning word meanings through the use of the prefix *pre-*. Students can apply this skill when working with verbal reasoning items on standardized tests. For additional practice, use the Build Vocabulary page in *Selection Support*, p. 1.

Grammar and Language Portions of some standardized tests require students to understand the distinction between subjective case and objective case pronouns. Students may be asked to select the correct pronoun case to complete a sentence, as in the following:

Felix and (I, me) play trumpet in the band. *I*
That is (she, her) in the red uniform. *she*

The Build Grammar Skills lesson for this selection focuses on this topic. For additional practice, use the Build Grammar Skills page on Pronoun Case, p. 2, in *Selection Support.*

❶ Ask students whether Montresor really wants to turn back. *No.* Then ask if students have ever convinced someone to do something by leading him or her to do the opposite. *Students may answer that they have prodded someone into doing something by telling the person that he or she couldn't do it.*

◆ Literary Focus

❷ **Mood** How do students' impressions of the setting change as the characters wind their way through the arches and descend deeper and deeper into the catacombs? *Students should note that the mood becomes increasingly sinister and ominous.*

◆ Literary Focus

❸ **Mood** By providing measurements of the recess, the narrator lets on that he has carefully planned something chilling.

Customize for
Less Proficient Readers
To help these students visualize the interior crypt, help them identify benchmarks—a phone booth, a refrigerator, or a stall shower—that match the size of the crypt.

Customize for
More Advanced Students
Help these students to appreciate the care with which Montresor has plotted his revenge. For instance, the numbering of the tiers of bricks shows how precisely he planned ahead. Challenge students to look back to identify other examples of Montresor's careful planning. Students can point to the methods Montresor used to get Fortunato to his house, to empty the house of witnesses, and to provide the necessary tools and materials on site.

"*Nemo me impune lacessit.*"[9]

"Good!" he said.

The wine sparkled in his eyes and the bells jingled. My own fancy grew warm with the Medoc. We had passed through long walls of piled skeletons, with casks and puncheons[10] intermingling, into the inmost recesses of the catacombs. I paused again, and this time I made bold to seize Fortunato by an arm above the elbow.

❶ "The niter!" I said; "see, it increases. It hangs like moss upon the vaults. We are below the river's bed. The drops of moisture trickle among the bones. Come, we will go back ere it is too late. Your cough—"

"It is nothing," he said; "let us go on. But first, another draft of the Medoc."

I broke and reached him a flagon of De Grâve. He emptied it at a breath. His eyes flashed with a fierce light. He laughed and threw the bottle upwards with a gesticulation I did not understand.

I looked at him in surprise. He repeated the movement—a grotesque one.

"You do not comprehend?" he said.

"Not I," I replied.

"Then you are not of the brotherhood."

"How?"

"You are not of the masons."[11]

"Yes, yes," I said; "yes, yes."

"You? Impossible! A mason?"

"A mason," I replied.

"A sign," he said, "a sign."

"It is this," I answered, producing from beneath the folds of my *roquelaure* a trowel.

"You jest," he exclaimed, recoiling a few paces. "But let us proceed to the Amontillado."

"Be it so," I said, replacing the tool beneath the cloak and again offering him my arm. He leaned upon it heavily. We continued our route in search of the Amontillado. We passed through a range of low arches, descended, passed on, and descending again, arrived at a deep crypt, in which the foulness of

> **Summarize:** They are going deeper into these burial vaults, where there are hollowed-out sections in the walls.

---

9. *Nemo me impune lacessit:* Latin for "No one attacks me with impunity."
10. **puncheons** (pun´ chənz) *n.*: Large barrels.
11. **masons:** The Freemasons, an international secret society.

---

the air caused our flambeaux rather to glow than flame.

❷ At the most remote end of the crypt there appeared another less spacious. Its walls had been lined with human remains, piled to the vault overhead, in the fashion of the great catacombs of Paris. Three sides of this interior crypt were still ornamented in this manner. From the fourth side the bones had been thrown down, and lay promiscuously upon the earth, forming at one point a mound of some size. Within the wall thus exposed by the displacing of the bones, we perceived a still interior crypt or recess, in depth about four feet, in width three, in height six or seven. It seemed to ❸ have been constructed for no especial use within itself, but formed merely the interval between two of the colossal supports of the roof of the catacombs, and was backed by one of their circumscribing walls of solid granite.

It was in vain that Fortunato, uplifting his dull torch, endeavored to pry into the depth of the recess. Its termination the feeble light did not enable us to see.

"Proceed," I said: "herein is the Amontillado. As for Luchesi—"

"He is an ignoramus," interrupted my friend, as he stepped unsteadily forward, while I followed immediately at his heels. In an instant he had reached the extremity of the niche, and finding his progress arrested by the rock, stood stupidly bewildered. A moment more and I had fettered him to the granite. In its surface were two iron staples, distant from each other about two feet, horizontally. From one of these depended a short chain, from the other a padlock. Throwing the links about his waist, it was but the work of a few seconds to secure it. He was too much astounded to resist. Withdrawing the key I stepped back from the recess.

"Pass your hand," I said, "over the wall; you cannot help feeling the niter. Indeed, it is *very* damp. Once more let me *implore* you to return. No? Then I must positively leave you. But I must first render you all the little

> **Break down** these sentences and **paraphrase** them: Fortunato tried unsuccessfully to feel the depth of the recess, but the light was too feeble to enable us to see the end.

> **Read ahead** to clarify what *fettered* means and what has happened here: Fortunato is chained to the wall.

Speaking and Listening Mini-Lesson

Resolving Interpersonal Conflicts
This mini-lesson supports the Speaking and Listening activity in the Idea Bank on page 11.

Introduce the Concept Have students discuss situations in which unresolved conflicts between individuals or groups have resulted in unfortunate consequences. You might point out that Montresor's action is an extreme case of unresolved conflict.

Develop Background Before students begin their role-playing, have them explore and discuss ways to approach and resolve conflicts.

Lead students to consider these points:

• Individuals involved in conflict must be willing to take responsibility for their actions or lack of actions.

• Responsible individuals must be willing to put aside their own concerns and to take steps to change the situation positively.

Apply the Information With this background, students should be able to develop constructive resolutions to the situations they stated. Remind them to follow the rules stated in their book as they role-play.

Assess the Outcome Have students evaluate their own and other groups' resolutions of conflicts. As a final discussion, they might consider if any of their solutions might have helped prevent the outcome of the conflict between Montresor and Fortunato.

The Court Jester, 1875 (detail), William Merritt Chase, Pennsylvania Academy of the Fine Arts, Philadelphia

▲ **Critical Viewing** How does this costume compare with your image of the costume worn by Fortunato? [Compare and Contrast]

❹

attentions in my power."

"The Amontillado!" ejaculated my friend, not yet recovered from his astonishment.

"True," I replied; "the Amontillado."

As I said these words I busied myself among the pile of bones of which I have before spoken. Throwing them aside, I soon uncovered a quantity of building stone and mortar. With these materials and with the aid of my trowel, I began vigorously to wall up the entrance of the niche.

I had scarcely laid the first tier of the masonry when I discovered that the intoxication of Fortunato had in a great measure worn off. The earliest indication I had of this was a low moaning cry from the depth of the recess. It was *not* the cry of a drunken man. There was then a long and obstinate silence. I laid the second tier, and the third, and the fourth; and then I heard the furious vibrations of the chain. The noise lasted for several minutes, during which, that I might hearken to it with the more satisfaction, I ceased my labors and sat down upon the bones. When at last the clanking <u>subsided</u>, I resumed the trowel, and finished without interruption the fifth, the sixth, and the seventh tier. The wall was now nearly upon a level with my breast. I again paused, and holding the flambeaux over the masonwork, threw a few feeble rays upon the figure within.

A succession of loud and shrill screams, bursting suddenly from the throat of the chained form, seemed to thrust me violently back. For a brief moment I hesitated, I trembled. Unsheathing my rapier, I began to grope with it about the recess; but the thought of an instant reassured me. I placed my hand upon the solid fabric of the catacombs, and felt satisfied. I reapproached the wall; I replied to the yells of him who clamored. I reechoed, I aided, I surpassed them in volume and in strength. I did this, and the clamorer grew still.

❺

❻

◆ **Build Vocabulary**

recoiling (ri koil´ iŋ) v.: Staggering back

termination (tʉr mə nā´ shən) n.: End

subsided (səb sīd´ id) v.: Settled down; became less active or intense

The Cask of Amontillado ◆ 9

 Humanities: Art

Keying Up—The Court Jester (detail), 1875, by William Merritt Chase.

This piece of art illustrates a jester's costume, similar to that worn by Fortunato in this story.

William Merritt Chase, an American artist, studied in New York with artist Joseph O. Eaton. He also took classes at the National Academy of Design. *Keying Up— The Court Jester* was Chase's first highly acclaimed work. It won the Medal of Honor at the Centennial Exhibition in Philadelphia, although many critics objected to the "overpowering" color used. Nevertheless, the painting established Chase's career as artist and teacher.

Use these questions for discussion:
1. What effect would this kind of clothing have on the story? *A costumed figure such as this would probably be unsuspecting of someone's evil intents.*

2. What elements of the setting in this painting convey an appropriate mood for the story? *The dark background and polished wood panels suggest a location like the Montresor family home with catacombs beneath.*

❶ Summarize Have students summarize the activity described here.

Montresor has completed eleven tiers of masonry, sealing Fortunato into the crypt.

Reinforce and Extend

Customize for
Less Proficient Readers
Your less proficient readers will benefit greatly from rereading all or part of the story. In reviewing the story, students should focus on specific elements, such as Poe's use of foreshadowing and irony.

Answers
◆ *Literature and Your Life*

Reader's Response Students might point to the chaining scene (p. 8), which shows how thorough was the planning for the entrapment. Students could use the following words to describe Montresor: *cold-blooded, heartless, calculating, obsessed,* and *evil.*

Thematic Focus Answers may include the idea that people often feel that revenge, however unethical or cruel, is one way they can get a measure of justice or satisfaction.

☑ Check Your Comprehension

1. Montresor believes that Fortunato has repeatedly insulted him.
2. Montresor appeals to Fortunato's pride as a wine connoisseur.
3. Montresor makes certain that his house will be empty by telling his servants he will be out all night; he has supplied chains and wall-building materials to entrap his victim.
4. He is sealed up in the crypt.

The **signal words** "It was now midnight . . ." indicate that the narrator's tale is coming to a conclusion."

❶

Break down and **paraphrase** this sentence to start with the subject: A low laugh that raised the hairs on my head now came out of this space.

It was now midnight, and my task was drawing to a close. I had completed the eighth, the ninth, and the tenth tier. I had finished a portion of the last and the eleventh; there remained but a single stone to be fitted and plastered in. I struggled with its weight; I placed it partially in its destined position. But now there came from out the niche a low laugh that erected the hairs upon my head. It was succeeded by a sad voice, which I had difficulty in recognizing as that of the noble Fortunato. The voice said—

"Ha! ha! ha!—he! he! he!—a very good joke, indeed—an excellent jest. We will have many a rich laugh about it at the palazzo—he! he! he!—over our wine—he! he! he!"

"The Amontillado!" I said.

"He! he! he!—he! he! he!—yes, the Amontillado. But is it not getting late? Will not they be awaiting us at the palazzo, the Lady Fortunato

and the rest? Let us be gone."

"Yes," I said, "let us be gone."

"For the love of God, Montresor!"

"Yes," I said, "for the love of God!"

But to these words I hearkened in vain for a reply. I grew impatient. I called aloud—

"Fortunato!"

No answer. I called again—

"Fortunato!"

No answer still. I thrust a torch through the remaining aperture and let it fall within. There came forth in return only a jingling of the bells. My heart grew sick; it was the dampness of the catacombs that made it so. I hastened to make an end of my labor. I forced the last stone into its position; I plastered it up. Against the new masonry I reerected the old rampart of bones. For the half of a century no mortal has disturbed them. *In pace requiescat!*[12]

Paraphrase this last paragraph: Not getting any response from Fortunato, Montresor puts the last stone in place. For fifty years, no one has disturbed that bricked-up section.

12. *In pace requiescat:* Latin for "May he rest in peace!"

Guide for Responding

◆ *Literature and Your Life*

Reader's Response At what point in the story did you find Montresor most disturbing? Explain.

Thematic Focus Poe's tale is a spine-tingling exploration of one man's obsession with revenge. Why do you think revenge is a popular subject for suspenseful movies, novels, and stories?

Journal Writing Explore how this story influenced your answer to the question: What happens when a desire for revenge gets out of hand?

☑ Check Your Comprehension

1. Why does Montresor hate Fortunato?
2. How does Montresor persuade Fortunato to follow him to the catacombs?
3. What specific steps does Montresor take to ensure that his plan works?
4. What happens to Fortunato at the end of the story?

Beyond the Selection

FURTHER READING

Other Works by Edgar Allan Poe
"Murders in the Rue Morgue"
"The Tell-Tale Heart"
"The Black Cat"

Other Works With the Theme of Revenge
"Arturo's Flight," Judith Ortiz Cofer
"Dragon's Bait," Vivian Vande Velde
The Righteous Revenge of Artemis Bonner, Walter Dean Myers

INTERNET

The Internet provides excellent opportunities for students to learn more about Poe. We suggest the following sites. Please be aware, however, that sites may have changed from the time we published this information. For essays about Poe and his life, go to **http://www.iptweb. com/www/lib/authors/poe.html**

For a bibliography of Poe's works, go to **http://www. cat.pdx.edu/~caseyh/horror/author/poe.html**

We *strongly recommend* that you preview the sites before you send students to them.

Guide for Responding (continued)

◆ Critical Thinking

INTERPRET

1. In what ways are Montresor and Fortunato alike? How are they different? **[Compare and Contrast]**
2. What character traits make Fortunato such an easy prey for Montresor? **[Analyze]**
3. Which of Montresor's words and actions could have revealed his plan to Fortunato? **[Infer]**
4. Why does Montresor feel justified in carrying out his plan against Fortunato? **[Infer]**
5. Why does Montresor keep urging Fortunato to turn back? **[Infer]**

EVALUATE

6. Montresor acts as judge and executioner in this story. Explain whether you think individuals are ever justified in taking justice into their own hands. **[Evaluate]**

APPLY

7. If you were on the jury of Montresor's murder trial, would you agree to a plea of innocent by reason of insanity? Explain. **[Make a Decision]**

◆ Reading for Success

LITERAL COMPREHENSION STRATEGIES

Review the reading strategies and the notes showing how to comprehend a writer's words and meanings. Then apply them to answer the following:

1. Using context clues, identify the meaning of *gesticulation* on p. 8.
2. Summarize what has happened in the paragraph beginning, "Pass your hand . . ." on p. 8.
3. Paraphrase the paragraph on p. 9 that begins, "A succession of loud and shrill screams . . ."

◆ Literary Focus

MOOD

The eerie, sinister **mood,** or atmosphere, adds to the suspense of Poe's story. Poe creates this mood with descriptive details the way movie makers use visual effects.

1. Find three or four specific images that contribute to the story's eerie mood.
2. Using a scene from the story, explain how you would create a movie scene with an eerie mood.

◆ Build Vocabulary

USING THE PREFIX *pre-*

The prefix *pre-* means "before" or "in advance." Define each of these words. Incorporate the definition of *pre-* into each answer.

1. preview   2. precondition   3. precaution

USING THE WORD BANK

In your notebook, write the letter of the word that is the best antonym, or opposite, of the first word.

1. precluded: (a) prevented, (b) aided, (c) started
2. retribution: (a) reward, (b) disaster, (c) assignment
3. accosted: (a) sought, (b) retreated, (c) discovered
4. subsided: (a) increased, (b) created, (c) challenged
5. afflicted: (a) weary, (b) skeptical, (c) blessed
6. explicit: (a) unnecessary, (b) vague, (c) impatient
7. recoiling: (a) unfastening, (b) releasing, (c) advancing
8. termination: (a) height, (b) beginning, (c) extension

◆ Build Grammar Skills

PRONOUN CASE

When you use pronouns, be careful to choose the correct form, especially when using pairs of pronouns or when pairing a pronoun with a proper noun.

Practice In your notebook, write each of these sentences. Choose *I, he, we, me, him,* or *us* to complete each one.

1. Fortunato and ____?____ ran into each other at Carnival.
2. No one followed____?____to my home.
3. It was time to settle the score between ____?____ and____?____.
4. ____?____ and____?____ reached the end of the catacombs.
5. ____?____ two entered the catacombs together, but only one would return.

> The **subjective case** is used when a pronoun is the subject or renames the subject. The **objective case** is used when the pronoun receives the action of the verb or when it is the object of a preposition.

The Cask of Amontillado ◆ 11

◆ Build Vocabulary

Using the Prefix *pre-*

Answers should be similar to these:
1. To see in advance
2. A requirement that must be met before something else can occur
3. Care taken in advance

Using the Word Bank

1. b   2. a   3. b   4. a
5. c   6. b   7. c   8. b

◆ Build Grammar Skills

1. I;   2. me;   3. him, me;
4. He, I;   5. We

✎ Writer's Solution

For additional instruction and practice, use the lesson in the **Language Lab CD-ROM** on Pronoun Case. You may also use the practice pages on the Cases of Pronouns in the *Writer's Solution Grammar Practice Book,* pp. 78–80.

Answers
◆ Critical Thinking

1. Both characters are concerned with reputation: Montresor wants revenge for Fortunato's supposed insults against his honor; Fortunato wants to be admired for his knowledge of wines. However, Montresor is bitter, clever, and devious, while Fortunato is trusting and vain.
2. Fortunato is egocentric, vain, trusting, and foolish.
3. Students' answers should come from the conversation between the two men as they descend into the catacombs, and may include examples such as: "You are a man to be missed"; "Nemo me impune lacessit"; and "Then I must positively leave you."
4. Montresor feels that Fortunato's insults give him the right to avenge himself. His obsession with real or imagined insults twists his mind to the point where he believes that Fortunato deserves the horrible death he has planned for him.
5. Montresor knows that Fortunato is vain, so by feigning concern and offering him the chance to leave, Montresor ensures that Fortunato will stay.
6. Students may feel that there are times when there is no other recourse to redress a wrong.
7. Students may say that Montresor was too aware of his actions, that his plan was too premeditated to warrant an insanity plea.

◆ Reading for Success

1. The phrase "threw the bottle upward" indicates that *gesticulation* means a physical movement.
2. Montresor has chained Fortunato to the wall of the crypt.
3. Fortunato's screams unnerve Montresor; he nearly strikes out to stab his screaming victim, but instead screams back at him until his victim falls silent.

◆ Literary Focus

1. Answers may include: Montresor's black cape and mask suggest an executioner's outfit; the long, winding staircase to the deep catacombs adds to a feeling of isolation.
2. Responses should include specific visual elements that will convey the mood.

11

Idea Bank
Customizing for *Performance Levels*

Following are suggestions for matching the Idea Bank topics with your students' ability levels:

Less Advanced Students: 1, 4, 7
Average Students: 2, 4, 6
More Advanced Students: 3, 5

Customizing for *Learning Modalities*

Following are suggestions for matching Idea Bank topics with your students' learning modalities:

Visual/Spatial: 6, 7
Auditory: 4, 5
Kinesthetic: 6, 7

Writing Mini-Lesson

Refer students to the Writing Handbook, page 962, for instruction on the writing process, and page 964 for further information on Description.

Writer's Solution

Writers at Work Videodisc
Have students view the videodisc segment (Ch. 1) featuring science fiction writer Anne McCaffrey to see how she uses her imagination to come up with vivid details for her descriptions. Have students discuss how McCaffrey builds on her observations of the real world to create descriptions of places that exist only in the imagination.

Play frames 335 to 10785

Writing Lab CD-ROM
Have students complete the Tutorial on Description. Follow these steps:
1. Use the sensory word bins for gathering precise details.
2. Have students draft on computer.
3. Use the Vague Adjectives Checker to aid revision.

Sourcebook
Have students use Chapter 1, Description (pp. 1–29) for additional support. The chapter includes in-depth instruction on gathering sensory details (pp. 17–18).

Build Your Portfolio

Idea Bank

Writing

1. **Monologue** Write a brief monologue—a speech delivered by a single character—in which Montresor explains the "injury" he has suffered at Fortunato's hands. **[Performing Arts Link]**

2. **Opening Argument** Create the prosecution's opening argument for the murder trial of Montresor. **[Social Studies Link]**

3. **Letter to Edgar Allan Poe** Respond to the story by writing a letter to Poe. Explain whether you found the characters believable and the ending satisfying.

Speaking and Listening

4. **Casting Discussion** With a small group, discuss actors who would be good choices to play each of the characters in "The Cask of Amontillado." Through discussion, agree on one actor that the group would recommend for each role. Present your recommendation and reasons to the class. **[Performing Arts Link]**

5. **Resolving Interpersonal Conflicts** Montresor's evil plot of revenge arises from a conflict between him and Fortunato. With a small group, brainstorm for situations that could cause conflicts among you and your friends. Then take turns role-playing constructive resolutions.

Projects

6. **Pantomime** With a partner, convey the plot of the story through facial expressions and broad gestures, but not words. **[Performing Arts Link]**

7. **Storyboard** Create a storyboard that outlines the main events in the plot for a movie version of "The Cask of Amontillado." **[Art Link]**

Writing Mini-Lesson

Description of a Set

Imagine that "The Cask of Amontillado" is being made into a movie. Choose one of the settings in the story and write a description of a set design that incorporates Poe's descriptive details and your imagination.

Writing Skills Focus: Precise Details
Use **precise details** to create a vivid picture of your set. For example, if a tree is tall, tell *how tall*. If the setting is damp, use words like *clammy* or *humid* to indicate whether the dampness is cool or warm.

Poe uses precise details to create an image of a specific crypt of a certain size. With these precise details, you can imagine how Fortunato looks standing in the crypt because you know how big it is compared with a person.

Model from the Story
Within the wall thus exposed . . . we perceived a still interior crypt or recess, in depth about four feet, in width three, in height six or seven.

Prewriting Set designers usually make a sketch of the set. Drawing to scale—using one size to represent another (1/4 inch to represent a foot)—helps keep the dimensions of the set in proportion. Make a sketch or model to work out details of sizes, colors, and placement.

Drafting Begin your description with a few striking images that will capture the mood you want the set to convey. Refer to your sketch as you draft.

Revising Try making a second sketch of your set based on the details provided in your draft. This will help you discover places where you may need to add precise details to complete the picture.

✓ ASSESSMENT OPTIONS

Formal Assessment, Selection Test, pp. 1–3, and Assessment Resources Software. The selection test is designed so that it can be easily customized to the performance levels of your students.
Alternative Assessment, p. 1, includes options for less advanced students, more advanced students, visual and spatial learners, and auditory learners.

PORTFOLIO ASSESSMENT
Use the following rubrics in the *Alternative Assessment* booklet to assess student writing:
Monologue: Narrative Rubric, p. 88
Opening Argument: Persuasion Rubric, p. 98
Letter to Edgar Allan Poe: Expression, p. 87
Writing Mini-Lesson: Description Rubric, p. 90

PART 1 *In Suspense*

New Moon, New York, 1945, George Ault
Museum of Modern Art, New York

In Suspense ◆ 13

One-Minute Planning Guide

The selections in this section capture a wide range of suspenseful situations. In "The Most Dangerous Game," suspense builds as a hunter seeks the ultimate challenge by stalking human prey. While the situation in "Casey at the Bat" is much less threatening, it is no less tense, as a famous slugger steps to the plate with the game of the line. The poem is paired with a suspenesul article about a real-life slugger—all-time home run champion, Hank Aaron. Part 1 ends with a story made famous by filmmaker Alfred Hitchcock; Daphne du Maurier's "The Birds." The tension in du Maurier's story is built around a conflict between humanity and the natural world—a type of conflict that often occurs in real-life in today's world.

Customize for
Varying Student Needs
When assigning the selections in this part, keep in mind these factors:

"The Most Dangerous Game"
• A long short story (15 pp.)
• Less proficient readers may need to read in sections
• High-interest plot will appeal to virtually all students

"Casey at the Bat"
• Accessible narrative poem
• Setting may seem dated to students

from *I Had a Hammer*
• High-interest nonfiction account about a real-life sports success story perfect for pairing with "Casey at the Bat"
• Very brief, with simple vocabulary

"The Birds"
• Very long short story (26 pp.)
• Less proficient readers may need to read in sections
• High-interest plot and connection to film will interest students

 Humanities: Art

New Moon, New York, 1945, by George Ault.

Born in New York, George Ault (1891–1948) spent much of his childhood and adolescence in England. His work is characterized as Cubist Realism, a style that combines representation of objective reality with Cubism's geometric imagery.

The oil painting *New Moon, New York* suggests a deserted city street with its tall geometric forms and shadows, as a sliver of a new moon hangs in the sky. The suspenseful, foreboding mood is heightened by the pair of lights hovering in the bottom half of the painting. They could be streetlights, but they have no apparent base. They seem to come from a gravityless, bodiless world where anything can happen.

Have students link the art to the theme of Part I ("In Suspense") by answering the following questions:

1. What is the most exciting explanation you can give for the pair of lights in the lower half of the painting? *Answers may include ghosts, aliens, or a split car or train.*

2. If you saw a scene that looked like this in a suspenseful movie, what would you expect to happen next? *Students' responses should indicate something frightening or violent, like the appearance of a stalker or a ghost.*

Guide for Reading

OBJECTIVES

1. To read, comprehend, and interpret a story
2. To relate a story to personal experience
3. To use context clues to facilitate comprehension
4. To recognize suspense
5. To build vocabulary in context and learn forms of *scruples*
6. To recognize and use the past and past perfect tenses of verbs
7. To use the skill of anticipating readers' questions in writing a survival manual
8. To respond to the story through writing, speaking and listening, and projects

SKILLS INSTRUCTION

Vocabulary:
Related Words:
Forms of *Scruples*

Grammar:
Past and Past
Perfect Tenses

Reading Strategy:
Context Clues

Literary Focus:
Suspense

Writing:
Anticipate Readers'
Questions

Speaking and Listening:
Interview
(teacher edition)

Critical Viewing:
Analyze; Predict;
Speculate

PORTFOLIO OPPORTUNITIES

Writing: Review; Persuasive Essay; Movie Script

Writing Mini-Lesson: Survival Manual

Speaking and Listening: Interview; Trial

Projects: Video Game Design; Technical Diagrams

More About the Author

Richard Connell never achieved critical acclaim to match his popular success as a writer. *The New York Times* criticized him for courting popularity by using "tricks," rather than devoting his talents "to a ... more critical study of the contemporary scene." Have students discuss this criticism. Ask: Is it enough for a piece of fiction to simply be entertaining? Or is it essential for a writer to address important issues in his or her work?

Richard Connell *(1893–1949)*

Some authors have a wide variety of jobs before they settle on being a writer. Others seem destined from the start to be writers. Richard Connell belongs to the second category.

Connell began his writing career as a sports reporter —at the age of ten!

Wartime Experiences By the time he was sixteen, Connell had graduated from reporting on sports to editing his father's newspaper in Poughkeepsie, New York. He continued his involvement in journalism at Harvard University, where he was an editor for the *Daily Crimson*. After enlisting in the army during World War I, Connell served as editor for his division's newspaper. The wartime events that Connell reported are echoed in the experiences of Rainsford in "The Most Dangerous Game," who fought in the trenches of France during World War I.

Hollywood Hotshot After the war, Connell changed his focus from journalism to fiction and movie screenplays. In 1924, he published his unforgettable short story "The Most Dangerous Game."

A year later, he settled in Beverly Hills, California. Many of his popular stories were soon made into movies. The film version of "The Most Dangerous Game" was released in 1932 and has been the inspiration for a number of other adventure movies. Connell's success as a screenwriter continued throughout the remainder of his life, and he received two Academy Award nominations for his work.

◆ Build Vocabulary

RELATED WORDS: FORMS OF *SCRUPLES*

You can increase your word power by learning other forms of a word. For example, in this story you learn the noun *scruples*, referring to the uncomfortable feelings one has about something one thinks is wrong. By adding the suffix *-ous*, meaning "having" or "full of," you form the adjective *scrupulous*, which means "having scruples."

palpable
indolently
bizarre
naive
scruples
blandly
grotesque
futile

WORD BANK

As you read "The Most Dangerous Game," you will encounter the words in this list. Each word is defined on the page where it first appears. Preview the list before you read the story. What other words can you form from the words in the list?

◆ Build Grammar Skills

PAST AND PAST PERFECT TENSES

The **tense** of a verb indicates the time of the action. "The Most Dangerous Game" is told in the past tense. Sometimes it's important to indicate when two events in the past occurred in relation to each other. The **past perfect tense** shows that an action took place before another action in the past.

In this passage from the story, Richard Connell uses the past perfect tense.

past   past perfect
... he *stopped* before he *had swum* fifty feet.

To form the past perfect tense, use *had* with the past participle of the verb.

14 ◆ Spine Tinglers

Prentice Hall Literature Program Resources

REINFORCE / RETEACH / EXTEND

Selection Support Pages
Build Vocabulary: Related Words:
Forms of *Scruples*, p. 6
Build Grammar Skills: Past and Past
Perfect Tenses, p. 7
Reading Strategy: Context Clues, p. 8
Literary Focus: Suspense, p. 9

Strategies for Diverse Student Needs, p. 2

Beyond Literature
Workplace Skills: Dealing With Competition

Formal Assessment Selection Test, pp. 4–6,
Assessment Resources Software

Alternative Assessment, p. 2

Writing and Language Transparencies
Process Analysis, pp. 29–32

Resource Pro CD-ROM
"The Most Dangerous Game"—includes all
resource material and customizable lesson plan

 Listening to Literature Audiocassettes
"The Most Dangerous Game"

The Most Dangerous Game

◆ *Literature and Your Life*

CONNECT YOUR EXPERIENCE

Some competitions, like a one-on-one basketball game, can be relaxed and friendly. Others can be fierce. If one side takes the competition more seriously than the other, the situation can become unpleasant—or even dangerous. Sometimes, as in this story, a competition gets so intense, it becomes a life-or-death situation.

Journal Writing Describe the most memorable competitive situation you have ever experienced or seen. How did it make you feel?

THEMATIC FOCUS: IN SUSPENSE

Competition can sometimes be so intense that it frightens you. This suspenseful adventure story is sure to send shivers down your spine as you wonder whether the hero has what it takes to win a life-threating competition.

◆ Background for Understanding

CULTURE

Both of the main characters in this story are big-game hunters, people who enjoy hunting large wild animals, such as bears, for sport. For hunting enthusiasts, big-game hunting is the ultimate test of their skill, pitting them against large, often dangerous, animals in unfamiliar, exotic surroundings. In recent times, this sport has become the subject of controversy as populations of big-game animals have dwindled.

◆ Literary Focus

SUSPENSE

When you read a spine-tingling story, you just *have* to find out what happens next. This feeling of curiosity, uncertainty, even anxiety about the outcome of events is called **suspense**. Writers can create suspense by placing characters in tense, risky, or unpredictable situations. Often, writers provide hints about events to come while withholding enough information to keep readers guessing. As you read "The Most Dangerous Game," pay attention to the unsettling events and details that create suspense and look for clues to the story's outcome.

◆ Reading Strategy

CONTEXT CLUES

An author's choice of words can increase your enjoyment of a story by making people, places, and situations more vivid and lifelike. Occasionally, however, an author might select a word that is unfamiliar. Don't reach for the dictionary the minute you see an unfamiliar word. Often, you can determine its meaning from its **context**; that is, the words, phrases, and sentences that surround it. Try to use context clues to determine the meaning of the word *appraising* in this passage from "The Most Dangerous Game."

> . . . he found the general studying him, *appraising* him narrowly.

The key clue to the meaning of *appraising* is the word *studying*. From this context clue, you can guess that the word *appraising* is close in meaning to the word *studying*. You might then ask yourself why the general is studying the other man closely, and you could conclude that the general is trying to figure the man out, or is evaluating him. Thus the word *appraising* means "evaluating."

Guide for Reading ◆ 15

One-Minute Insight In addition to keeping readers on the edges of their seats, "The Most Dangerous Game" asks an important question about human nature: Are human beings really "civilized"? The author contrasts Zaroff, whose style of living reflects highly cultured tastes, but who hunts other humans for sport, with Rainsford, who is horrified at the idea of taking a human life. However, when Rainsford is forced into the role of "a beast at bay," he kills Zaroff in the end. The role reversal from hunter to hunted has brought out the savage, primitive side of Rainsford's nature. The author may be saying that, although we humans consider ourselves civilized, in the jungle of life, the "beast" within us is not as far below the surface as we may think.

Listening to Literature Audiocassettes Since this is a long story, you may want to break up students' reading by having them listen to sections of the story on audiocassette. You might, for example, have students listen to the portion of the story covering Rainsford's first day on the island, then have students read the rest of the story on their own. Doing so may hook students' interest and make them want to read ahead on their own.

Customize for
Visual/Spatial Learners
Encourage visual learners to use the artwork on this opening page to help picture the story's setting and envision the action that will take place.

16 ◆ Spine Tinglers

Block Scheduling Strategies

Consider these suggestions to take advantage of extended class time:

• Have students complete the journal activity in Literature and Your Life (p. 15) and discuss their entries in small groups.

• Students may work in groups with the Word Bank in Build Vocabulary (p. 14) using dictionaries to see if they can find other word forms of each word. You may also have them use the Build Vocabulary page in *Selection Support,* p. 6.

• Students might stage a debate on "Hunting: Pro or Con." Have them read Background for Understanding (p. 15) and do additional research on hunting to prepare for the debate.

• Have students listen to all or part of the selection on audiocassette. Have them discuss how the reader's portrayal of the characters compares to the way they imagine the characters would talk.

The Most Dangerous Game

Richard Connell

"Off there to the right—somewhere—is a large island," said Whitney. "It's rather a mystery—"

"What island is it?" Rainsford asked.

"The old charts call it 'Ship-Trap Island,'" Whitney replied. "A suggestive name, isn't it? Sailors have a curious dread of the place. I don't know why. Some superstition—"

"Can't see it," remarked Rainsford, trying to peer through the dank tropical night that was palpable as it pressed its thick warm blackness in upon the yacht.

"You've good eyes," said Whitney, with a laugh, "and I've seen you pick off a moose moving in the brown fall bush at four hundred yards, but even you can't see four miles or so through a moonless Caribbean[1] night."

"Not four yards," admitted Rainsford. "Ugh! It's like moist black velvet."

◄ **Critical Viewing** How does this painting create a feeling of suspense? **[Analyze]**

"It will be light in Rio," promised Whitney. "We should make it in a few days. I hope the jaguar guns have come from Purdey's. We should have some good hunting up the Amazon.[2] Great sport, hunting."

"The best sport in the world," agreed Rainsford.

"For the hunter," amended Whitney. "Not for the jaguar."

"Don't talk rot, Whitney," said Rainsford. "You're a big-game hunter, not a philosopher. Who cares how a jaguar feels?"

"Perhaps the jaguar does," observed Whitney.

---

1. **Caribbean** (karʹ ə bēʹ ən): The Caribbean Sea, a part of the Atlantic Ocean, bounded by South America, Central America, and the West Indies.
2. **Amazon** (amʹ ə zänʹ): Large river in South America.

◆ **Build Vocabulary**

palpable (palʹ pə bəl) *adj.*: Able to be touched or felt

Peering Through the Jungle, Larry Noble, Sal Barracca & Associates

The Most Dangerous Game ◆ 17

Humanities: Art

17

◆ Literature and Your Life

❶ Ask students: Have you ever encountered a place about which there were superstitions—a house that was said to be haunted, for example? Whether or not you are superstitious, how did you feel about going near that place? *Some students might believe in superstitions. Those who do not might report feeling nervous about going near such places, just because of the stories they have heard.*

◆ Literary Focus

❷ Suspense Students may say that, often, in fiction, when characters boast that they are not afraid of something, that thing will turn out to "get them." Therefore, there is a good chance that something evil connected with the island is about to happen to Rainsford.

◆ Reading Strategy

❸ Context Clues Call students' attention to the word *brier*. Ask students: Which word in this sentence provides a clue to the meaning of *brier*? What do they think the word means? Give students a moment to look back or read ahead until they come to another word that confirms their guess. *Students should cite the word "puffed" as a clue that "brier" means a kind of pipe. The previous sentence, "I'm going to smoke another pipe on the after deck," and the later words, ". . . his pipe, striking a rope, was knocked from his mouth," both confirm this guess.*

◆ Build Grammar Skills

❹ Past and Past Perfect Tenses Have students identify the uses of the past perfect tense in this passage. Then have them explain why the past perfect was called for in each instance. *"had swum": Rainsford stops swimming when he sees how futile his effort would be; "had come to him": Rainsford became cool-headed before he stopped swimming; "he had been in a tight place": Rainsford had been in dangerous situations before this one.*

"Bah! They've no understanding."

"Even so, I rather think they understand one thing—fear. The fear of pain and the fear of death."

"Nonsense," laughed Rainsford. "This hot weather is making you soft, Whitney. Be a realist. The world is made up of two classes—the hunters and the huntees. Luckily, you and I are the hunters. Do you think we've passed that island yet?"

"I can't tell in the dark. I hope so."

"Why?" asked Rainsford.

"The place has a reputation—a bad one."

"Cannibals?" suggested Rainsford.

"Hardly. Even cannibals wouldn't live in such a God-forsaken place. But it's gotten into sailor lore, somehow. Didn't you notice that the crew's nerves seemed a bit jumpy today?"

"They were a bit strange, now you mention it. Even Captain Nielsen—"

"Yes, even that tough-minded old Swede, who'd go up to the devil himself and ask him for a light. Those fishy blue eyes held a look I never saw there before. All I could get out of him was: 'This place has an evil name among sea-faring men, sir.' Then he said to me, very gravely: 'Don't you feel anything?'—as if the air about us was actually poisonous. Now, you mustn't laugh when I tell you this —I did feel something like a sudden chill.

"There was no breeze. The sea was as flat as a plate-glass window. We were drawing near the island then. What I felt was a—a mental chill; a sort of sudden dread."

"Pure imagination," said Rainsford. "One superstitious sailor can taint the whole ship's company with his fear."

❶ ◆ Literary Focus
Do you think that Rainsford is "tempting fate" with his outlook on life? Predict what is going to happen to him.

"Maybe. But sometimes I think sailors have an extra sense that tells them when they are in danger. Sometimes I think evil is a tangible thing—with wave lengths, just as sound and light have. An evil place can, so to speak, broadcast vibrations of evil. Anyhow, I'm glad we're getting out of this zone. Well, I think I'll turn in now, Rainsford."

18 ◆ *Spine Tinglers*

"I'm not sleepy," said Rainsford. "I'm going to smoke another pipe on the after deck."

"Good night, then, Rainsford. See you at breakfast."

"Right. Good night, Whitney."

There was no sound in the night as Rainsford sat there, but the muffled throb of the engine that drove the yacht swiftly through the darkness, and the swish and ripple of the wash of the propeller.

Rainsford, reclining in a steamer chair, **❸** indolently puffed on his favorite brier. The sensuous drowsiness of the night was on him. "It's so dark," he thought, "that I could sleep without closing my eyes; the night would be my eyelids—"

An abrupt sound startled him. Off to the right he heard it, and his ears, expert in such matters, could not be mistaken. Again he heard the sound, and again. Somewhere, off in the blackness, someone had fired a gun three times.

Rainsford sprang up and moved quickly to the rail, mystified. He strained his eyes in the direction from which the reports had come, but it was like trying to see through a blanket. He leaped upon the rail and balanced himself there, to get greater elevation; his pipe, striking a rope, was knocked from his mouth. He lunged for it; a short, hoarse cry came from his lips as he realized he had reached too far and had lost his balance. The cry was pinched off short as the blood-warm waters of the Caribbean Sea closed over his head.

He struggled up to the surface and tried to cry out, but the wash from the speeding yacht slapped him in the face and the salt water in his open mouth made him gag and strangle. Desperately he struck out with strong strokes after the receding lights of the yacht, but he stopped before he had swum fifty feet. A certain cool-headedness had come to him; it was not the first time he had been in a tight place. There was a chance that his cries could be heard by someone aboard the yacht, but that chance was

❹

◆ Build Vocabulary

indolently (in´ də lənt lē) *adv.*: Lazily; idly

Cross-Curricular Connection: Social Studies

The Caribbean, Rio, the Amazon, Malacca, Burma, Sudan—all these exotic names evoke thoughts of faraway, fabulous places.

• The Caribbean Sea is the part of the Atlantic Ocean bounded by South America, Central America, and the West Indies.

• Rio, short for Rio de Janeiro, is on the southern Atlantic coast of Brazil. The Amazon, the world's second longest river, originates high in the Andes Mountains of Peru, from where it flows westward across northern Brazil and into the Atlantic Ocean.

• Malacca is in Malaya, on the southwest coast of the Malay Peninsula, northwest of Singapore.

• Burma is bordered by Thailand on the south, China on the east, India on the north, and the Bay of Bengal on the west.

• Sudan is in northeastern Africa.

Have students look up these places in an Atlas or encyclopedia to gather information about the location, climate, and landscape in each place. Then have them discuss how naming these exotic places contributes to a mood of suspense and mystery.

slender, and grew more slender as the yacht raced on. He wrestled himself out of his clothes, and shouted with all his power. The lights of the yacht became faint and ever-vanishing fireflies; then they were blotted out entirely by the night.

Rainsford remembered the shots. They had come from the right, and doggedly he swam in that direction, swimming with slow, deliberate strokes, conserving his strength. For a seemingly endless time he fought the sea. He began to count his strokes; he could do possibly a hundred more and then—

5 Rainsford heard a sound. It came out of the darkness, a high screaming sound, the sound of an animal in an extremity of anguish and terror.

He did not recognize the animal that made the sound; he did not try to; with fresh vitality he swam toward the sound. He heard it again; then it was cut short by another noise, crisp, staccato.

"Pistol shot," muttered Rainsford, swimming on.

Ten minutes of determined effort brought another sound to his ears—the most welcome he had ever heard—the muttering and growling of the sea breaking on a rocky shore. He was almost on the rocks before he saw them; on a night less calm he would have been shattered against them. With his remaining strength he dragged himself from the swirling waters. Jagged crags appeared to jut into the opaqueness, he forced himself upward, hand over hand. Gasping, his hands raw, he reached a flat place at the top. Dense jungle came down to the very edge of the cliffs. What **6** perils that tangle of trees and underbrush might hold for him did not concern Rainsford just then. All he knew was that he was safe from his enemy, the sea, and that utter weariness was on him. He flung himself down at the jungle edge

Hat, Knife, and Gun in Woods, David Mann, Sal Barracca & Associates

▲ **Critical Viewing** Based on this painting, predict what is going to happen in the story. **[Predict]** **7**

and tumbled headlong into the deepest sleep of his life. **6**

When he opened his eyes he knew from the position of the sun that it was late in the afternoon. Sleep had given him new vigor; a sharp hunger was picking at him. He looked about him, almost cheerfully.

"Where there are pistol shots, there are men. Where there are men, there is food," he thought. But what kind of men, he wondered, in so forbidding a place? An unbroken front of snarled and ragged jungle fringed the shore.

He saw no sign of a trail through the closely knit web of weeds and trees; it was easier to go

The Most Dangerous Game ◆ 19

◆ **Build Vocabulary**

5 **Related Words** Point out that, while the word *extremity* may be unfamiliar, it is a form of another word most students know. Ask students: What other word does *extremity* remind you of? How can the related word help you define this one? *"Extremity" is a form of "extreme." The word "extreme" can be substituted for the words "in an extremity of": "... the sound of an animal in extreme anguish and terror."*

◆ **Literary Focus**

6 **Suspense** Although in this passage Rainsford feels safe enough to go to sleep, the author never lets the suspense drop. Ask students: Which words in this passage create suspense? *The words, "What perils that tangle of trees and underbrush might hold for him ..." hint that there will be dangers ahead.* Ask students to predict what those dangers might be. *Students will not be able to predict specific dangers, but should be able to predict that someone or something is about to threaten Rainsford's safety.*

▶**Critical Viewing**◀

7 **Predict** Students may observe that the abandoned hat and weapons indicate that someone will die.

Customize for
Less Proficient Readers
Less proficient readers may find it helpful to jot down key details of the setting. Noting the key features of this rugged landscape will help them to better understand the challenges that Rainsford faces later in the story, when he is forced to elude Zaroff.

 Humanities: Art

Hat, Knife, and Gun in Woods, 1940, by David Mann.

David Mann creates illustrations for books and magazines. *Hat, Knife, and Gun in Woods* was originally a book-cover illustration.

Use these questions for discussion:
1. Why do you think the artist chose not to include human beings in the painting? *The absence of human figures creates mystery. The viewer wonders: "Where and who is the owner of the objects?" "Is the blood on the knife that of a human or an animal?"*

2. How do light and darkness create drama and suspense in both the painting and the story? *The dark, murky colors in the background of the painting make the viewer wonder who or what might be lurking there; Connell heightens suspense in the story by having the hunting scenes take place at night. Lighter, brighter colors highlight the central objects in the painting; Connell uses brightness to highlight the scene in which Rainsford first enters Zaroff's house: "... Rainsford stood blinking in the river of glaring gold light that poured out."*

① Synthesize Information Have students identify the two meanings of the word "game." *The word "game" in the title refers to both the "game" of hunting and the "game," or animal, that is hunted.*

◆ **Literary Focus**

② Suspense Ask students: How is the author increasing the suspense in this passage? *By putting off answering Rainsford's questions about the nature of Zaroff's game, the author makes the reader increasingly impatient to find out the answer.*

◆ **Reading Strategy**

③ Context Clues Draw students' attention to the word *ardent* in this passage. Ask them to locate words and phrases that they can use as clues to determine the meaning of the word. *Clues include the examples Zaroff gives to show how his father encouraged his interest in hunting when Zaroff was a small child. Students should conclude that anyone who would compliment a child on shooting prize turkey or allow a ten-year-old to hunt bear would be an ardent, or enthusiastic, hunter himself.*

finding the general a most thoughtful and affable host, a true cosmopolite.[8] But there was one small trait of the general's that made Rainsford uncomfortable. Whenever he looked up from his plate he found the general studying him, appraising him narrowly.

"Perhaps," said General Zaroff, "you were surprised that I recognized your name. You see, I read all books on hunting published in English, French, and Russian. I have but one passion in my life, Mr. Rainsford, and it is the hunt."

"You have some wonderful heads here," said Rainsford as he ate a particularly well cooked filet mignon. "That Cape buffalo is the largest I ever saw."

"Oh, that fellow. Yes, he was a monster."

"Did he charge you?"

"Hurled me against a tree," said the general. "Fractured my skull. But I got the brute."

"I've always thought," said Rainsford, "that the Cape buffalo is the most dangerous of all big game."

For a moment the general did not reply; he was smiling his curious red-lipped smile. Then he said slowly: "No. You are wrong, sir. The Cape buffalo is not the most dangerous big game." He sipped his wine. "Here in my preserve on this island," he said in the same slow tone, "I hunt more dangerous game."

Rainsford expressed his surprise. "Is there big game on this island?"

The general nodded. "The biggest."

"Really?"

"Oh, it isn't here naturally, of course. I have to stock the island."

"What have you imported, general?" Rainsford asked. "Tigers?"

The general smiled. "No," he said. "Hunting tigers ceased to interest me some years ago. I exhausted their possibilities, you see. No thrill left in tigers, no real danger. I live for danger, Mr. Rainsford."

The general took from his pocket a gold cigarette case and offered his guest a long black

---

8. **cosmopolite** (käz mäp´ ə lit´) *n.:* Person at home in all parts of the world.

cigarette with a silver tip; it was perfumed and gave off a smell like incense.

"We will have some capital hunting, you and I," said the general. "I shall be most glad to have your society."

"I have hunted every kind of game in every land. It would be impossible for me to tell you how many animals I have killed."

"But what game—" began Rainsford.

"I'll tell you," said the general. "You will be amused, I know. I think I may say, in all modesty, that I have done a rare thing. I have invented a new sensation. May I pour you another glass of port, Mr. Rainsford?"

"Thank you, general."

The general filled both glasses, and said: "God makes some men poets. Some He makes kings, some beggars. Me He made a hunter. My hand was made for the trigger, my father said. He was a very rich man with a quarter of a million acres in the Crimea,[9] and he was an ardent sportsman. When I was only five years old he gave me a little gun, specially made in Moscow for me, to shoot sparrows with. When I shot some of his prize turkeys with it, he did not punish me; he complimented me on my marksmanship. I killed my first bear in the Caucasus[10] when I was ten. My whole life has been one prolonged hunt. I went into the army—it was expected of noblemen's sons—and for a time commanded a division of Cossack cavalry, but my real interest was always the hunt. I have hunted every kind of game in every land. It would be impossible for me to tell you how many animals I have killed."

---

9. **Crimea** (krī mē´ ə): Region in southwestern Russia on the Black Sea.

10. **Caucasus** (kô´ kə səs): Mountain range in southern Russia.

Cultural Connection

Connell's story focuses on hunting—an activity that is part of the heritage of all cultures. While farming has been practiced for about 1 percent of human history, hunting was humankind's occupation for more than half a million years. Anthropologists think hunting may have encouraged many traits common to human beings in modern societies, including cooperation, organization, and aggression. There are few hunting and gathering societies left in the world. The only people who still exist solely by hunting are the Mbuti Pygmies of the Central African rain forest and the disappearing Bushmen of the Kalahari in Southern Africa. Societies that combine hunting with other means of sustenance include the Eskimos, the Pacific Northwest Indians, some Plains Indians, the Siriono Indians of Bolivia, and the Aborigines of Australia. These hunting societies are quite egalitarian: Cooperation is paramount for successful hunting, and individualism and authoritarianism are discouraged. Identification with the environment is very strong, as reflected in such religious ceremonies as the Mbuti songs to the forest god, Eskimo poetry celebrating the sea goddess, and the giraffe dance of the Kalahari Bushmen.

Ask students to read further about one of the above groups or about the history of hunting in various cultures.

The general puffed at his cigarette. "After the debacle[11] in Russia I left the country, for it was imprudent for an officer of the Czar to stay there. Many noble Russians lost everything. I, luckily, had invested heavily in American securities, so I shall never have to open a tea room in Monte Carlo or drive a taxi in Paris. Naturally, I continued to hunt—grizzlies in your Rockies, crocodiles in the Ganges, rhinoceroses in East Africa. It was in Africa that the Cape buffalo hit me and laid me up for six months. As soon as I recovered I started for the Amazon to hunt jaguars, for I had heard they were unusually cunning. They weren't." The Cossack sighed. "They were no match at all for a hunter with his wits about him, and a high-powered rifle. I was bitterly disappointed. I was lying in my tent with a splitting headache one night when a terrible thought pushed its way into my mind. Hunting was beginning to bore me! And hunting, remember, had been my life. I have heard that in America business men often go to pieces when they give up the business that has been their life."

"Yes, that's so," said Rainsford.

The general smiled. "I had no wish to go to pieces," he said. "I must do something. Now, mine is an analytical mind, Mr. Rainsford. Doubtless that is why I enjoy the problems of the chase."

"No doubt, General Zaroff."

"So," continued the general, "I asked myself why the hunt no longer fascinated me. You are much younger than I am, Mr. Rainsford, and have not hunted as much, but you perhaps can guess the answer."

"What was it?"

"Simply this: hunting had ceased to be what you call 'a sporting proposition.' It had become too easy. I always got my quarry. Always. There is no greater bore than perfection."

The general lit a fresh cigarette.

"No animal had a chance with me any more. That is no boast; it is a mathematical certainty. The animal had nothing but his legs and his

11. **debacle** (di bäk´ əl) *n.*: Bad defeat—Zaroff is referring to the Russian Revolution of 1917, a defeat for upper-class Russians like himself.

instinct. Instinct is no match for reason. When I thought of this it was a tragic moment for me, I can tell you."

Rainsford leaned across the table, absorbed in what his host was saying.

"It came to me as an inspiration what I must do," the general went on.

"And that was?"

The general smiled the quiet smile of one who has faced an obstacle and surmounted it with success. "I had to invent a new animal to hunt," he said.

"A new animal? You're joking."

"Not at all," said the general. "I never joke about hunting. I needed a new animal. I found one. So I bought this island, built this house, and here I do my hunting. The island is perfect for my purpose—there are jungles with a maze of trails in them, hills, swamps—"

"But the animal, General Zaroff?"

"Oh," said the general, "it supplies me with the most exciting hunting in the world. No other hunting compares with it for an instant. Every day I hunt, and I never grow bored now, for I have a quarry with which I can match my wits."

Rainsford's bewilderment showed in his face.

"I wanted the ideal animal to hunt," explained the general. "So I said: 'What are the attributes of an ideal quarry?' And the answer was, of course: 'It must have courage, cunning, and, above all, it must be able to reason.'"

"But no animal can reason," objected Rainsford.

"My dear fellow," said the general, "there is one that can."

"But you can't mean—" gasped Rainsford.

"And why not?"

"I can't believe you are serious, General Zaroff. This is a grisly joke."

"Why should I not be serious? I am speaking of hunting."

"Hunting? General Zaroff, what you speak of is murder."

The general laughed with entire good nature. He regarded Rainsford quizzically. "I refuse to believe that so modern and civilized a young

◆ **Literary Focus**
Predict what Zaroff is going to identify as the "most dangerous game."

The Most Dangerous Game ◆ 23

◆ **Build Grammar Skills**

4 Past and Past Perfect Tenses
Ask students to identify two uses of the past perfect tense in this passage and to explain why the past perfect is appropriate in each case. *"had invested":The general had invested his money in America before the Russian Revolution and, therefore, avoided losing his wealth, as did many other members of the Russian nobility;"had heard":The general had heard that jaguars were cunning before he ever hunted them.*

◆ *Literature and Your Life*

5 Ask students: Have you ever had the experience of getting so good at something that it bored you because it was no longer a challenge? Have students describe such experiences and discuss different ways of responding to them. *Responses may include: playing a video game and getting a perfect score every time or playing a sport against an opponent the students can always beat. Different ways of responding may be to find a more difficult game to play or a more highly skilled opponent.*

◆ **Literary Focus**

6 Suspense Students should cite the passage "It must have courage, cunning, and, above all, it must be able to reason." The last quality—the ability to reason—should lead students, as it leads Rainsford, to predict that Zaroff will identify man as the "most dangerous game."

Customize for
More Advanced Students
Point out that the plot reaches a climax when Rainsford discovers the identity of Zaroff's new "animal," yet the story is only approximately half over. Suggest that these students begin a diagram of the story showing where the plot builds, reaches a climax, levels off, and then builds again.

Listening to Literature Audiocassettes Play the audiocassette recording of this conversation to highlight its drama and suspense. Discuss with the class how Rainsford's shock is reflected as he realizes the identity of Zaroff's "new animal."

23

① **Clarification** Explain that *mid-Victorian* refers to the period in British history that lasted from 1840 to 1900, during the reign of Queen Victoria. One of the characteristics of the period was excessive prudishness. Also point out that the Puritans, who were among the early settlers of the original thirteen colonies, demanded a strict observance of religious laws. Zaroff obviously approves of neither.

▶**Critical Viewing**◀

② **Speculate** Students may observe that the density of the jungle foliage would make the hunter as much at risk from the prey as the prey is from the hunter.

◆ **Critical Thinking**

③ **Compare and Contrast** Ask students to compare and contrast the two men's use of the word *civilized.* Ask them to conjecture about which word each man would suggest as an opposite of *civilized.* *To Zaroff, to be civilized is to enjoy the finer luxuries in life, including elegant food, wine, and such amenities as electricity. The opposite might be "primitive," or "crude." To Rainsford, civilized may mean "enlightened," "law-abiding," or "human." Opposites might be "ruthless," "savage," "barbarous."*

Customize for
More Advanced Students

Ask more advanced students to compare Zaroff's words in this passage ("Life is for the strong, to be lived by the strong. . . .") with those of Rainsford to Whitney at the beginning of the story (p. 18): "The world is made up of two classes—the hunters and the huntees. Luckily, you and I are the hunters." Ask students if they view Rainsford's words in a different light now. *The two men express similar ideas. After reading Zaroff's speech, one wonders if Rainsford would reconsider his earlier words.* Explain that a literary term for this technique is *irony.*

---

man as you seem to be harbors romantic ideas about the value of human life. Surely your experiences in the war—"

"Did not make me condone cold-blooded murder," finished Rainsford stiffly.

Laughter shook the general. "How extraordinarily droll you are!" he said. "One does not expect nowadays to find a young man of the educated class, even in America, with such a naive, and, if I may say so, mid-Victorian point of view.[12] It's like finding a snuff-box in a limousine. Ah, well, doubtless you had Puritan ancestors. So many Americans appear to have had. I'll wager you'll forget your notions when you go hunting with me. You've a genuine new thrill in store for you, Mr. Rainsford."

"Thank you, I'm a hunter, not a murderer."

"Dear me," said the general, quite unruffled, "again that unpleasant word. But I think I can show you that your scruples are quite ill founded."

"Yes?"

"Life is for the strong, to be lived by the strong, and, if need be, taken by the strong. The weak of the world were put here to give the strong pleasure. I am strong. Why should I not use my gift? If I wish to hunt, why should I not? I hunt the scum of the earth—sailors from tramp ships—lascars,[13] blacks, Chinese, whites, mongrels—a thoroughbred horse or hound is worth more than a score of them."

"But they are men," said Rainsford hotly.

"Precisely," said the general. "That is why I use them. It gives me pleasure. They can reason, after a fashion. So they are dangerous."

"But where do you get them?"

The general's left eyelid fluttered down in a wink. "This island is called Ship-Trap," he

---

12. **mid-Victorian point of view:** A point of view emphasizing proper behavior and associated with the time of Queen Victoria of England (1819–1901).
13. **lascars** (las´ kərz) *n.*: Oriental sailors, especially natives of India.

◆ **Build Vocabulary**

naive (nä ēv´) *adj.*: Unsophisticated
scruples (scrōō´ pəlz) *n.*: Misgivings about something one feels is wrong

24 ◆ *Spine Tinglers*

▲ **Critical Viewing** What might it be like to hunt in an environment such as the one pictured here? **[Speculate]**

answered. "Sometimes an angry god of the high seas sends them to me. Sometimes, when Providence is not so kind, I help Providence a bit. Come to the window with me."

Rainsford went to the window and looked out toward the sea.

"Watch! Out there!" exclaimed the general, pointing into the night. Rainsford's eyes saw only blackness, and then, as the general pressed a button, far out to sea Rainsford saw the flash of lights.

The general chuckled. "They indicate a channel," he said, "where there's none: giant rocks with razor edges crouch like a sea monster with wide-open jaws. They can crush a ship as easily as I crush this nut." He dropped a walnut on the hardwood floor and brought his heel grinding down on it. "Oh, yes," he said, casually, as if in answer to a question, "I have electricity. We try to be civilized here."

"Civilized? And you shoot down men?"

A trace of anger was in the general's black

❹

eyes, but it was there for but a second, and he said, in his most pleasant manner: "Dear me, what a righteous young man you are! I assure you I do not do the thing you suggest. That would be barbarous. I treat these visitors with every consideration. They get plenty of good food and exercise. They get into splendid physical condition. You shall see for yourself tomorrow."

"What do you mean?"

"We'll visit my training school," smiled the general. "It's in the cellar. I have about a dozen pupils down there now. They're from the Spanish bark *San Lucar* that had the bad luck to go on the rocks out there. A very inferior lot, I regret to say. Poor specimens and more accustomed to the deck than to the jungle."

He raised his hand, and Ivan, who served as waiter, brought thick Turkish coffee. Rainsford, with an effort, held his tongue in check.

"It's a game, you see," pursued the general blandly. "I suggest to one of them that we go hunting. I give him a supply of food and an excellent hunting knife. I give him three hours'

❺

> # He need not play the game if he doesn't wish to. If he does not wish to hunt, I turn him over to Ivan.

start. I am to follow, armed only with a pistol of the smallest caliber and range. If my quarry eludes me for three whole days, he wins the game. If I find him"—the general smiled—"he loses."

"Suppose he refuses to be hunted?"

"Oh," said the general, "I give him his option, of course. He need not play the game if he doesn't wish to. If he does not wish to hunt, I turn him over to Ivan. Ivan once had the honor of serving as official knouter[14] to the Great

White Czar, and he has his own ideas of sport. Invariably, Mr. Rainsford, invariably they choose the hunt."

"And if they win?"

The smile on the general's face widened. "To date I have not lost," he said.

Then he added, hastily: "I don't wish you to think me a braggart, Mr. Rainsford. Many of them afford only the most elementary sort of problem. Occasionally I strike a tartar.[15] One almost did win. I eventually had to use the dogs."

❻

"The dogs?"

"This way, please. I'll show you."

The general steered Rainsford to a window. The lights from the windows sent a flickering illumination that made grotesque patterns on the courtyard below, and Rainsford could see moving about there a dozen or so huge black shapes; as they turned toward him, their eyes glittered greenly.

"A rather good lot, I think," observed the general. "They are let out at seven every night. If anyone should try to get into my house—or out of it—something extremely regrettable would occur to him." He hummed a snatch of song from the Folies Bergère.[16]

"And now," said the general, "I want to show you my new collection of heads. Will you come with me to the library?"

❼

"I hope," said Rainsford, "that you will excuse me tonight, General Zaroff. I'm really not feeling at all well."

"Ah, indeed?" the general inquired solicitously. "Well, I suppose that's only natural, after your long swim. You need a good, restful night's sleep. Tomorrow you'll feel like a new man, I'll wager. Then we'll hunt, eh? I've one rather promising prospect—"

---

14. **knouter** (nout´ ər) *n.*: Someone who beats criminals with a leather whip, or knout.
15. **tartar** (tär´ tər) *n.*: Stubborn, violent person.
16. **Folies Bergère** (fô lē ber zhär´): Musical theater in Paris.

◆ **Build Vocabulary**

blandly (bland´ lē) *adv.*: In a mild and soothing manner
grotesque (grō tesk´) *adj.*: Having a strange, bizarre design

The Most Dangerous Game ◆ 25

◆ **Literary Focus**

❹ **Suspense** Students should respond to this question as follows: *The momentary "trace of anger" in the general's eyes lets readers know that Rainsford is making the general angry by questioning whether he is really "civilized." Later in the story, Zaroff might want to get back at Rainsford for the insult.* Some students may predict that Zaroff will force Rainsford to be hunted himself.

◆ **Critical Thinking**

❺ **Synthesize Information** Ask students: In which ways is what Zaroff does like a game? Who are the players? What are the rules? Is the game fair? Why, or why not? *Responses can include: What Zaroff does is like a game because there are players (Zaroff and the person being hunted), and there are rules (the hunted person gets certain supplies and a three-hour start, Zaroff is armed only with a small pistol, the winner is decided after three days). The game is unfair because Zaroff makes up the rules, and he knows the area better. Students who read ahead will probably find the use of dogs unfair, as well.*

◆ **Build Vocabulary**

❻ **Related Words** Draw students' attention to the word *braggart* in this passage. Ask them to find in the word a smaller word of which *braggart* is a form. Then have them deduce the meaning of *braggart* if the word is unfamiliar to them. *"Brag" is a smaller word that can be found in "braggart." A braggart is a person who is always bragging.*

Comprehension Check ☑

❼ What kind of heads are likely to be in Zaroff's "new collection" in the library? The preceding conversation about the new "game" Zaroff has invented should lead students to guess that the heads are human.

◆ Literary Focus

❶ Suspense Ask students: Which details build suspense in this passage? Invite them to explain why each detail contributes to the suspense of the story. *"stealthy steps in the corridor outside his room": The steps Rainsford thinks he hears may be those of Ivan. This would indicate that Rainsford is being watched or guarded. "it would not open": The fact that Rainsford is locked in his room suggests that Zaroff has an evil plan up his sleeve. One doesn't ordinarily lock in one's guests.*

❷ Clarification Explain that *crêpes suzette* are thin dessert pancakes heated in butter and orange-flavored liqueur and served flaming. *Chablis* is a white wine. These details are further examples of the general's "civilized" way of life, contrasted with his most uncivilized description of last night's hunting.

◆ Literary Focus

❸ Suspense The change in Zaroff's facial expression, from angry (studying Rainsford with "dead black eyes") to suddenly brightening, should lead students to respond: *Zaroff has just gotten the idea to hunt Rainsford.*

Comprehension Check ☑

❹ What will happen to Rainsford if he chooses not to participate in the hunt? *He will be tortured by Ivan and probably killed.*

Customize for
More Advanced Students

Have students read once more the passage at the beginning of the story in which Rainsford speaks of two classes: the "hunters" and the "huntees." In which class did Rainsford include himself? In which class will he be now? Explain briefly that in most short stories, the main character undergoes some sort of change or growth. Ask students: Do you think Rainsford might rethink his comment to Whitney, "Who cares how a jaguar feels?" *Earlier, Rainsford considered himself among the hunters; now he is about to become a huntee. Students might imagine that Rainsford would now feel more sympathetic to the jaguar.*

Rainsford was hurrying from the room.

"Sorry you can't go with me tonight," called the general. "I expect rather fair sport—a big, strong black. He looks resourceful—Well good night, Mr. Rainsford; I hope you have a good night's rest."

The bed was good, and the pajamas of the softest silk, and he was tired in every fiber of his being, but nevertheless Rainsford could not quiet his brain with the opiate of sleep. He lay, eyes wide open. Once he thought he heard stealthy steps in the corridor outside his room. He sought to throw open the door; it would not open. He went to the window and looked out. **❶** His room was high up in one of the towers. The lights of the château were out now, and it was dark and silent, but there was a fragment of sallow moon, and by its wan light he could see, dimly, the courtyard; there, weaving in and out in the pattern of shadow, were black, noiseless forms; the hounds heard him at the window and looked up, expectantly, with their green eyes. Rainsford went back to the bed and lay down. By many methods he tried to put himself to sleep. He had achieved a doze when, just as morning began to come, he heard, far off in the jungle, the faint report of a pistol.

General Zaroff did not appear until luncheon. He was dressed faultlessly in the tweeds of a country squire. He was solicitous about the state of Rainsford's health.

"As for me," sighed the general, "I do not feel so well. I am worried, Mr. Rainsford. Last night I detected traces of my old complaint."

To Rainsford's questioning glance the general said: "Ennui. Boredom."

Then, taking a second helping of crêpes suzette, the general explained: "The hunting was not good last night. The fellow lost his head. He made a straight trail that offered no problems at all. That's the trouble with these sailors; they **❷** have dull brains to begin with, and they do not know how to get about in the woods. They do excessively stupid and obvious things. It's most annoying. Will you have another glass of Chablis, Mr. Rainsford?"

"General," said Rainsford firmly, "I wish to leave this island at once."

He nodded toward the corner to where the giant stood, scowling, his thick arms crossed on his hogshead of chest.

The general raised his thickets of eyebrows; he seemed hurt. "But, my dear fellow," the general protested, "you've only just come. You've had no hunting—"

"I wish to go today," said Rainsford. He saw the dead black eyes of the general on him, studying him. General Zaroff's face suddenly brightened.

◆ Literary Focus
What idea has just come to Zaroff's mind? **❸**

He filled Rainsford's glass with venerable Chablis from a dusty bottle.

"Tonight," said the general, "we will hunt—you and I."

Rainsford shook his head. "No, general," he said. "I will not hunt."

The general shrugged his shoulders and delicately ate a hothouse grape. "As you wish, my friend," he said. "The choice rests entirely with you. But may I not venture to suggest that you will find my idea of sport more diverting than Ivan's?" **❹**

He nodded toward the corner to where the giant stood, scowling, his thick arms crossed on his hogshead of chest.

"You don't mean—" cried Rainsford.

"My dear fellow," said the general, "have I not told you I always mean what I say about hunting? This is really an inspiration. I drink to a foeman worthy of my steel—at last."

The general raised his glass, but Rainsford sat staring at him.

"You'll find this game worth playing," the general said enthusiastically. "Your brain against mine. Your woodcraft against mine. Your strength and stamina against mine. Outdoor chess! And the stake is not without value, eh?"

"And if I win—" began Rainsford huskily.

"I'll cheerfully acknowledge myself defeated if I do not find you by midnight of the third day," said General Zaroff. "My sloop will place you on the mainland near a town."

The general read what Rainsford was thinking.

"Oh, you can trust me," said the Cossack. "I will give you my word as a gentleman and a sportsman. Of course you, in turn, must agree to say nothing of your visit here."

"I'll agree to nothing of the kind," said Rainsford.

"Oh," said the general, "in that case— But why discuss that now? Three days hence we can discuss it over a bottle of Veuve Cliquot, unless—"

The general sipped his wine.

Then a businesslike air animated him. "Ivan," he said to Rainsford, "will supply you with hunting clothes, food, a knife. I suggest you wear moccasins; they leave a poorer trail. I suggest too that you avoid the big swamp in the southeast corner of the island. We call it Death Swamp. There's quicksand there. One foolish fellow tried it. The deplorable part of it was that Lazarus followed him. You can imagine my feelings, Mr. Rainsford. I loved Lazarus; he was the finest hound in my pack. Well, I must beg you to excuse me now. I always take a siesta after lunch. You'll hardly have time for a nap, I fear. You'll want to start, no doubt. I shall not follow till dusk. Hunting at night is so much more exciting than by day, don't you think? Au revoir,[17] Mr. Rainsford, au revoir."

General Zaroff, with a deep, courtly bow, strolled from the room.

From another door came Ivan. Under one arm he carried khaki hunting clothes, a haversack of food, a leather sheath containing a long-bladed hunting knife; his right hand rested on a cocked revolver thrust in the crimson sash about his waist. . . .

Rainsford had fought his way through the bush for two hours. "I must keep my nerve. I must keep my nerve," he said through tight teeth.

He had not been entirely clear-headed when the château gates snapped shut behind him. His whole idea at first was to put distance between himself and General Zaroff, and, to this end, he had plunged along, spurred on by the sharp rowels of something very like panic. Now he had got a grip on himself, had stopped, and was taking stock of himself and the situation.

He saw that straight flight was futile; inevitably it would bring him face to face with the sea. He was in a picture with a frame of water, and his operations, clearly, must take place within that frame.

"I'll give him a trail to follow," muttered Rainsford, and he struck off from the rude paths he had been following into the trackless wilderness. He executed a series of intricate loops; he doubled on his trail again and again, recalling all the lore of the fox hunt, and all the dodges of the fox. Night found him leg-weary, with his hands and face lashed by the branches, on a thickly wooded ridge. He knew it would be insane to blunder on through the dark, even if he had the strength. His need for rest was imperative and he thought: "I have played the fox, now I must play the cat of the fable." A big tree with a thick trunk and outspread branches was nearby, and, taking care to leave not the slightest mark, he climbed up into the crotch, and stretching out on one of the broad limbs, after a fashion, rested. Rest brought him new confidence and almost a feeling of security. Even so zealous a hunter as General Zaroff could not trace him there, he told himself; only the devil himself could follow that complicated trail through the jungle after dark. But, perhaps, the general was a devil—

An apprehensive night crawled slowly by like a wounded snake, and sleep did not visit Rainsford, although the silence of a dead world was on the jungle. Toward morning when a dingy gray was varnishing the sky, the cry of some startled bird focused Rainsford's attention in

---

17. **au revoir** (ō´ rə vwär´): French for "until we meet again."

◆ **Build Vocabulary**

futile (fyōōt´ əl) *adj.*: Useless; hopeless

The Most Dangerous Game ◆ 27

❺ **Clarification** Explain that *Veuve Cliquot* is an expensive French champagne—yet further evidence of the general's taste for "civilization."

◆ **Reading Strategy**

❻ **Context Clues** Call students' attention to the word *rowel* in this passage. Ask them if they can find clues to its meaning. *A rowel is the small wheel on the end of a riding spur. Students might use the words "spurred" and "sharp" to conclude that a rowel is something sharp, knifelike, or needlelike. They are not likely to figure out the exact definition of this little-used word. Either give the definition or have students look it up.*

❼ **Clarification** Explain to students that Rainsford is referring to a fable by the seventeenth-century poet Jean de la Fontaine, famous for his fables. In La Fontaine's fables, as in Aesop's, human behavior is portrayed by animal characters; but La Fontaine suggests more forcefully than Aesop that life is a jungle. In the fable to which Rainsford is referring, a fox and a cat are arguing about who is more clever. The fox says he has a hundred ways of eluding a pack of hounds; the cat claims only one. When they are actually pursued by hounds, the fox runs into a hundred holes, but is finally caught and killed. The cat, who immediately climbs a tree, is safe. The fable ends with the lines "Too many resources can be the ruin of a plan;/We waste our time in choosing, in trying all we can./Let's use one, but one that will suffice." Ask students: How does Rainsford compare his plight to that of the fox and the cat? *Responses should include: Rainsford has already tried all the "dodges of the fox." Now he plans to hide in a tree, like the cat.*

◆ **Reading Strategy**

❽ **Context Clues** Point out the word *zealous* to students. Ask them if they can use what they know about Zaroff's character to figure out the meaning of the word, if it is unfamiliar to them. Invite a volunteer to reason aloud. *Students know that Zaroff's main interest in life is hunting. If he is a zealous hunter, "zealous" must mean "enthusiastic" or "devoted"—or "ardent," a word students learned earlier in the story.*

Customize for
More Advanced Students

Draw students' attention to the sentence "Rainsford knew now how an animal at bay feels." Ask students: How has Rainsford changed since the beginning of the story? *At the beginning of the story, Rainsford remarked, "Who cares how a jaguar feels?" Now he not only cares, but knows from firsthand experience. Students might think that Rainsford's experience will make him more sensitive . . . or that it will make him more savage—more like a jaguar.*

▶Critical Viewing◀

❶ Speculate The dangers include drowning and being smashed against the rocks. On the other hand, the water offers Rainsford freedom from his pursuers.

◆ Critical Thinking

❷ Evaluate Character Ask students: How does Rainsford feel about having killed Ivan? *He seems to have no feelings about Ivan's death at all.* Ask students: Does Rainsford's lack of concern for Ivan's life show a change in his character? *Earlier in the story, Rainsford viewed human life as sacred; now that he is an "animal at bay," he cares only about saving his own life.*

◆ Literary Focus

❸ Suspense Responses can include: *The darkness of the scene contributes to the suspense because readers know that Zaroff cannot see who might be in the room with him; readers don't know if Rainsford is alive or dead, but the words "so thought the general . . ." hint that Rainsford might be alive—and in the general's room; the sentence "Then he switched on the light" signals the reader that the lamplight will reveal something surprising.*

▲ Critical Viewing Imagine Rainsford at the edge of the cliff. What will result from his leaping into the crashing waves? **[Speculate]** ❶

there, thinking. An idea that held a wild chance came to him, and, tightening his belt, he headed away from the swamp.

The baying of the hounds drew nearer, then still nearer, nearer, ever nearer. On a ridge Rainsford climbed a tree. Down a watercourse, not a quarter of a mile away, he could see the bush moving. Straining his eyes, he saw the lean figure of General Zaroff; just ahead of him Rainsford made out another figure whose wide shoulders surged through the tall jungle weeds; it was the giant Ivan, and he seemed pulled forward by some unseen force; Rainsford knew that Ivan must be holding the pack in leash.

They would be on him any minute now. His mind worked frantically. He thought of a native trick he had learned in Uganda. He slid down the tree. He caught hold of a springy young sapling and to it he fastened his hunting knife, with the blade pointing down the trail; with a bit of wild grapevine he tied back the sapling. Then he ran for his life. The hounds raised their voices as they hit the fresh scent. Rainsford knew now how an animal at bay feels.

30 ◆ Spine Tinglers

He had to stop to get his breath. The baying of the hounds stopped abruptly, and Rainsford's heart stopped too. They must have reached the knife.

He shinnied excitedly up a tree and looked back. His pursuers had stopped. But the hope that was in Rainsford's brain when he climbed died, for he saw in the shallow valley that General Zaroff was still on his feet. But Ivan was not. The knife, driven by the recoil of the springing tree, had not wholly failed. ❷

"Nerve, nerve, nerve!" he panted, as he dashed along. A blue gap showed between the trees dead ahead. Ever nearer drew the hounds. Rainsford forced himself on toward that gap. He reached it. It was the shore of the sea. Across a cove he could see the gloomy gray stone of the château. Twenty feet below him the sea rumbled and hissed. Rainsford hesitated. He heard the hounds. Then he leaped far out into the sea. . . .

Speaking and Listening Mini-Lesson

Trial

This mini-lesson supports the Speaking and Listening Activity in the Idea Bank on page 33.

Introduce the Concept Before students begin their trial, provide research materials to help them become acquainted with trial-and-jury proceedings. Suggest that students look up *trial, jury, murder, homicide,* and *manslaughter.* They should come up with definitions for the following: justifiable homicide, voluntary manslaughter, and murder. Remind students that a jury must decide if a person is guilty, not if he or she was morally right.

Develop Background Review Rainsford's acts at the end of the story. Lead students to infer what Rainsford did from when he leaps into the sea to when he appears in Zaroff's bedroom.

Apply the Information With this background, students should be able to plan and carry out their trial of Rainsford.

Assess the Outcome Have different groups—the jury, the defense, the prosecution team, witnesses—evaluate their own and other groups' performances for clarity of presentation and effective use of specific evidence.

When the general and his pack reached the place by the sea, the Cossack stopped. For some minutes he stood regarding the blue-green expanse of water. He shrugged his shoulders. Then he sat down, took a drink of brandy from a silver flask, lit a perfumed cigarette, and hummed a bit from *Madame Butterfly*.[19]

General Zaroff had an exceedingly good dinner in his great paneled dining hall that evening. With it he had a bottle of Pol Roger and half a bottle of Chambertin. Two slight annoyances kept him from perfect enjoyment. One was the thought that it would be difficult to replace Ivan; the other was that his quarry had escaped him; of course the American hadn't played the game—so thought the general as he tasted his after-dinner liqueur. In his library he read, to soothe himself, from the works of Marcus Aurelius.[20] At ten he went up to his bedroom. He was deliciously tired, he said to himself,

◆ **Literary Focus**
This paragraph describes a peaceful scene. However, it contributes to suspense. Explain why.

❸

as he locked himself in. There was a little moonlight, so, before turning on his light, he went to the window and looked down at the courtyard. He could see the great hounds, and he called: "Better luck another time," to them. Then he switched on the light.

A man, who had been hiding in the curtain of the bed, was standing there.

"Rainsford!" screamed the general. "How in God's name did you get here?"

"Swam," said Rainsford. "I found it quicker than walking through the jungle."

The general sucked in his breath and smiled. "I congratulate you," he said. "You have won the game."

Rainsford did not smile. "I am still a beast at bay," he said, in a low, hoarse voice. "Get ready, General Zaroff."

The general made one of his deepest bows. "I see," he said. "Splendid! One of us is to furnish a repast for the hounds. The other will sleep in this very excellent bed. On guard, Rainsford. . . ."

He had never slept in a better bed, Rainsford decided.

---

19. ***Madame Butterfly:*** An opera by Giacomo Puccini.
20. **Marcus Aurelius** (   ): Roman emperor and philosopher (A.D. 121–180).

❹

Guide for Responding

◆ *Literature and Your Life*

Reader's Response What do you admire about Rainsford? What don't you admire? Why?
Thematic Focus Sometimes, as in this story, competition is too intense. What are some of the potential consequences (aside from the ones in this story) of a competition that gets too fierce?
Group Discussion Discuss with a group what you can learn from this story about competition.

☑ Check Your Comprehension

1. How does Rainsford come to Ship-Trap Island?
2. What, according to Zaroff, is the most dangerous game? Why?
3. Explain how Zaroff's treatment of Rainsford changes during the course of the story.
4. Describe three of the tricks Rainsford uses to elude Zaroff. What is the outcome of each trick?
5. Why does Zaroff think that Rainsford "hasn't played the game"?

The Most Dangerous Game ◆ 31

Beyond the Selection

FURTHER READING

Other Works With the Theme of Suspense
"The Monkey's Paw," W. W. Jacobs
"August Heat," W. F. Harvey
"Contents of the Dead Man's Pocket," Jack Finney

INTERNET

You and your students may find additional information about "The Most Dangerous Game" on the Internet. We suggest the following site. Please be aware, however, that sites may have changed from the time we published this information.

For a review of a film about the story, go to **http://www.the cinemalaser.com/dangerous.htm**

You may also find related information on the Caribbean on the Internet. We *strongly recommend* that you preview the site before you send students to it.

◆ **Critical Thinking**
❹ **Synthesize Information** Ask students if they are surprised that Rainsford survived. Then ask: Which skills and qualities enabled Rainsford to survive the hunt in the jungle?
Responses should include the following: He is a strong swimmer, a quick thinker, a skilled and experienced woodsman; he is clever and resourceful; he is in excellent physical condition; he never panics or loses his nerve.

Reinforce and Extend

Answers
◆ *Literature and Your Life*

Reader's Response Students may admire Rainsford's resourcefulness and courage, as well as his physical stamina. They may be uneasy that he resorted to killing, even if it was in self-defense.

Thematic Focus Students can cite examples from films and literature, as well as from personal experience, where competition leads to broken friendships or even emotional breakdowns.

☑ **Check Your Comprehension**

1. He falls overboard from a yacht that is sailing near the island and swims to shore.
2. People are the most dangerous game because they have courage, cunning, and the ability to reason.
3. At first, Zaroff treats Rainsford as an equal, a potential hunting companion. When Rainsford will not participate in hunting people, Zaroff regards Rainsford with disbelief and scorn. Then Zaroff designates Rainsford as his next quarry. During the hunt, Zaroff first treats Rainsford with mocking condescension. Rainsford's traps make the general more wary, and he unsportingly brings in the assistance of hunting dogs and his servant Ivan.
4. Rainsford creates a convoluted trail and hides in a tree, but Zaroff tracks him down. Rainsford builds a Malay mancatcher that slightly wounds Zaroff. Rainsford's Burmese tiger pit kills one of Zaroff's hunting dogs. The Ugandan knife-and-sapling trap kills Zaroff's servant Ivan.
5. Zaroff thinks that Rainsford leapt into the sea to escape, rather than continuing to elude or kill Zaroff on the island.

OBJECTIVES

1. To read, comprehend, and interpret a poem
2. To relate a poem to personal experience
3. To summarize
4. To identify climax and anticlimax in a poem
5. To build vocabulary in context and learn related forms of *tumult*
6. To identify participles
7. To write a sportscast using vivid verbs
8. To respond to the poem through writing, speaking and listening, and projects

SKILLS INSTRUCTION

Vocabulary:
Related Words:
Forms of *Tumult*

Grammar:
Participles

Reading Strategy:
Summarizing

Literary Focus:
Climax and
Anticlimax

Writing:
Vivid Verbs

Speaking and Listening:
Sports Interview
(teacher edition)

Critical Viewing:
Compare and
Contrast

PORTFOLIO OPPORTUNITIES

Writing: Sports Headlines; Sports How-To; Résumé

Writing Mini-Lesson: Sportscast

Speaking and Listening: Sports Interview (teacher's edition)

Projects: Statistics Chart; Sports in Other Countries

More About the Author
Ernest Lawrence Thayer had to defend his right of ownership for "Casey at the Bat" when other poets tried to take credit for it. Some even tried to claim royalties! The operetta *The Mighty Casey*, based on the poem, had music by noted American composer William Schuman (b. 1910), who is known for using complex jazz rhythms in his work; the libretto was by Jeremy Gury. Comedian De Wolf Hopper claimed to have recited the ballad on the stage more than 15,000 times.

Guide for Reading

Ernest Lawrence Thayer (1863–1940)

It's not surprising that "Casey at the Bat" reads like a sports story in verse. The poet, Ernest Lawrence Thayer, spent many years working as a newspaper reporter. Thayer began his reporting career as editor-in-chief of Harvard University's humor magazine, *The Lampoon*. He later worked at newspapers in both New York and California. "Casey at the Bat" was published in the *San Francisco Examiner* on June 3, 1888, under Thayer's pen name, Phin. The comedian De Wolf Hopper popularized the poem by reciting it as part of his act, and in 1953 the poem inspired an operetta called *The Mighty Casey*.

◆ Build Vocabulary

RELATED WORDS: FORMS OF *TUMULT*
Learning other forms of a word can help you expand your vocabulary. For example, you may already know that the adjective *tumultuous* means "wild and noisy." If so, when you come across the noun *tumult* in "Casey at the Bat," you'll be able to figure out that it means "a noisy commotion."

pallor
wreathed
writhing
tumult

WORD BANK
As you read "Casey at the Bat," you'll encounter the words on this list. Each word is defined on the page where it first appears. Preview the list before you read.

◆ Build Grammar Skills

PARTICIPLES
In his poem "Casey at the Bat," Ernest Lawrence Thayer captures the action of a baseball game by using **participles**—forms of verbs that act as adjectives. Participles fall into two groups: present participles and past participles. **Present participles** end in *-ing*. **Past participles** usually end in *-ed* but may also have irregular endings, such as *-t* or *-en*. Look at these examples from the poem:

present participle
Then when the *writhing* pitcher ground the ball into his hip,

past participle
Then from the *gladdened* multitude went up a joyous yell–

34 ◆ *Spine Tinglers*

Prentice Hall Literature Program Resources

REINFORCE / RETEACH / EXTEND

Selection Support Pages
Build Vocabulary: Forms of *Tumult*, p. 10
Build Grammar Skills: Participles, p. 11
Reading Strategy: Summarizing, p. 12
Literary Focus: Climax and Anticlimax, p. 13

Strategies for Diverse Student Needs, p. 3

Beyond Literature
Cross-Curricular Connection: Math, p. 3

Formal Assessment Selection Test, pp. 7–9, Assessment Resources Software

Alternative Assessment, p. 3

Writing and Language Transparencies
Process Analysis, pp. 29–32

Resource Pro CD-ROM
"Casey at the Bat"—includes all resource material and customizable lesson plan

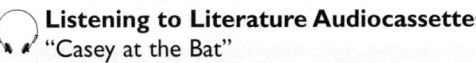 **Listening to Literature Audiocassettes**
"Casey at the Bat"

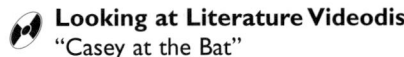 **Looking at Literature Videodisc**
"Casey at the Bat"

Casey at the Bat

◆ *Literature and Your Life*

CONNECT YOUR EXPERIENCE

Sporting events can really keep you on the edge of your seat! An athlete can break a world record or a losing team can charge to victory at the last minute. As you read this poem about a suspenseful baseball game, you may be reminded of nail-biting moments you've experienced while either watching or playing a sport.

Journal Writing Write a brief description of a suspenseful sporting event that you've either played in or witnessed.

THEMATIC FOCUS: IN SUSPENSE

The game of baseball can be filled with spine-tingling moments. No matter how skilled a player may be, or how important a game is, you never know just what will happen once the players take the field. Notice how this poem proves that point.

◆ Background for Understanding

SPORTS

Baseball is one of only a few sports in which there is no time clock. Unless a game is shortened by rain, it won't end until nine innings (or six or seven innings in some leagues) have been played and one team has come out on top. As a result, a team that's behind always has a chance to come back—even if they're behind by ten runs at the end of eight innings—as long as they keep getting base hits and avoid making the final out. "Casey at the Bat" captures the hopes of a team that's behind by two runs heading into the ninth inning. Notice how suspense builds as the game comes down to a final pitch.

◆ Literary Focus

CLIMAX AND ANTICLIMAX

The biggest moment of a story, or any type of narrative, is its **climax**. It is the turning point at which readers learn how the conflict, or central struggle in the story, will turn out. An **anticlimax** is similar to a climax because it also is the key event in the story. However, an anticlimax is always a letdown. It's the point at which you learn that the story will not turn out the way you'd expected.

◆ Reading Strategy

SUMMARIZING

If you want to describe a story or a poem to someone who has never read it, you'd probably do so by summarizing. When you **summarize**, you state briefly in your own words the main points and key details of the piece. This example shows one way to summarize the first stanza of the poem "Casey at the Bat":

Thayer's Version

It looked extremely rocky for the Mudville nine that day;

The score stood two to four, with but an inning left to play.

So, when Cooney died at second, and Burrows did the same, A pallor wreathed the features of the patrons of the game.

Summary

It is the last inning of a baseball game in which the Mudville team is losing by two runs. There are two outs against Mudville, and their fans are worried.

Preparing for Standardized Tests

Reading and Vocabulary The Build Vocabulary lesson, focusing on the related word forms *tumult/tumultuous,* can be expanded to show the development of other adjectives from nouns, both in similar patterns, such as *uproar/uproarious.* Students can apply this skill not only to vocabulary and reading comprehension, but also to verbal analogy items, in which one word on each side of the analogy is a noun, and the other, the adjective form of the noun, as in the following example:

tumult : tumultuous :: uproar : (a) roaring (b) deafening (c) uproarious c

For further practice, use the Build Vocabulary page in *Selection Support,* p. 10.

Grammar and Language The Build Grammar Skills lesson on Participles can help students improve their scores on the grammar portions of standardized tests. For additional practice with participles, use the Build Grammar Skills page on Participles, p. 11, in *Selection Support.*

"Casey at the Bat" is a narrative poem that uses vivid words and dramatic details to create suspense leading to an anticlimax. Until the last stanza, the whole poem develops the idea that Casey is a "mighty" hitter. The anticlimax is a comical letdown. Yet the ending is satisfying because Casey is the kind of arrogant hero readers enjoy seeing deflated.

Listening to Literature Audiocassettes Have students listen to the audiocassette from beginning to end as they read "Casey at the Bat." The highly dramatic nature of the poem, with its building tension, its stadium setting, and its mixture of drama and comedy, make this a classic read-aloud.

Customize for
Less Proficient Readers
Have students summarize lines 9–10, or ask a more advanced volunteer to work with them. *Flynn and Blake, two weak hitters, would have to hit safely for Casey to get a turn at bat.*

Customize for
Musical/Rhythmic Learners
Invite students to find words that help them "hear" the roar of the crowd. *Joyous yell; rumbled; rattled; struck; rebounded*

❶ **Clarification** Point out that Cooney and Burrows did not really "die" at second base. The word *die* is used as slang, meaning the runners were "put out."

◆ **Critical Thinking**
❷ **Evaluate** Ask students: Do you think Casey will come to bat? Does this line help build suspense? Why or why not? *Some students may feel it is a foregone conclusion that Casey will get to bat; others may be uncertain about the outcome.*

◆ **Reading Strategy**
❸ **Summarizing** Ask students to summarize lines 17–24. *Casey seems confident and at ease as he steps proudly to the plate; he gives a friendly response to the crowd.*

Casey at the Bat

Ernest Lawrence Thayer

It looked extremely rocky for the Mudville nine that day;
The score stood two to four, with but an inning left to play.
❶ So, when Cooney died at second, and Burrows did the same,
A <u>pallor</u> <u>wreathed</u> the features of the patrons of the game.

5   A straggling few got up to go, leaving there the rest,
With that hope which springs eternal within the human breast.
For they thought: "If only Casey would get a whack at that,"
They'd put even money now, with Casey at the bat.

But Flynn preceded Casey, and likewise so did Blake,
10 And the former was a pudd'n, and the latter was a fake.
So on that stricken multitude a deathlike silence sat;
❷ For there seemed but little chance of Casey's getting to the bat.

But Flynn let drive a "single," to the wonderment of all.
And the much-despised Blakey "tore the cover off the ball."
15 And when the dust had lifted, and they saw what had occurred,
There was Blakey safe at second, and Flynn a-huggin' third.

Then from the gladdened multitude went up a joyous yell—
❸ It rumbled in the mountaintops, it rattled in the dell;[1]
It struck upon the hillside and rebounded on the flat;
20 For Casey, mighty Casey, was advancing to the bat.

---

1. **dell** (del) *n.*: Small, secluded valley.

36 ◆ Spine Tinglers

Block Scheduling Strategies

Consider these suggestions to take advantage of extended class time:

- Invite students to read their Literature and Your Life (p. 35) journal entries aloud. You might encourage students to turn their entries into sportscasts in order to link Literature and Your Life with the Writing Mini-Lesson (p. 40).
- Encourage students to critique one another's Idea Bank sports how-to's (p. 40) in small groups.

- After Speaking and Listening pep talks have been given (p. 40), invite discussion of students' responses to the talks.
- Have students use the Internet to find more examples of the following: young-adult baseball literature, including biographies; narrative poems for reading aloud.
- In order to create sportscasts based on real events, students might do library or Internet research in order to select and learn the details of great moments in sports history.

There was ease in Casey's manner as he stepped into his place,
There was pride in Casey's bearing and a smile on Casey's face;
And when responding to the cheers he lightly doffed[2] his hat,
No stranger in the crowd could doubt 'twas Casey at the bat.

25 Ten thousand eyes were on him as he rubbed his hands with dirt,
Five thousand tongues applauded when he wiped them on his shirt;
Then when the <u>writhing</u> pitcher ground the ball into his hip,
Defiance glanced in Casey's eye, a sneer curled Casey's lip.

And now the leather-covered sphere came hurtling through the air,
30 And Casey stood a-watching it in haughty grandeur there.
Close by the sturdy batsman the ball unheeded sped;
"That ain't my style," said Casey. "Strike one," the umpire said.

2. **doffed** (däft) v.: Lifted.

◆ **Build Vocabulary**
pallor (pal´ ər) n.: Paleness
wreathed (rēthd) v.: Curled around
writhing (rīth´ iŋ) v.: Twisting; turning

Baseball Players Practicing, 1875, Thomas Eakins Museum of Art, Rhode Island School of Design

▲ **Critical Viewing** Compare and contrast the stance and uniform of the batter in the painting with that of players today. [Compare and Contrast] ❼

Casey at the Bat ◆ 37

◆ **Critical Thinking**
❹ **Compare and Contrast**
Compare and contrast Casey's attitude toward the pitcher with his attitude toward the crowd. *He is hostile to the pitcher, friendly to the crowd. Both attitudes indicate his cockiness.*

◆ **Build Grammar Skills**
❺ **Participles** What is the participle in line 29 and what kind of participle is it? *Leather-covered; past participle.*

◆ **Critical Thinking**
❻ **Draw a Conclusion** What does Casey's line "That ain't my style" and his refusal to swing tell you about the kind of player he is? *He is an arrogant showman, a "hot dog."*

▶**Critical Viewing**◀
❼ **Compare and Contrast** The stance is straighter and stiffer than today's stances, reflecting an era before modern advances in batting instruction. The uniform is similar, but lacks modern additions such as batting helmets and gloves; and the leather shoes appear old-fashioned by today's standards.

Customize for
Visual/Spatial Learners
Lines 29–30 use sensory details to create a clear visual picture of the ball and the batter. You might ask students to close their eyes and picture the scene, as if they were watching the event on television.

Customize for
Musical/Rhythmic Learners
The strong rhythms and rhymes of "Casey at the Bat" have captivated listeners for more than a century. Encourage students to join in a recitation and to suggest sound effects such as the crack of the bat and the roar of the crowd.

 Humanities: Art

Baseball Players Practicing, 1875, by Thomas Eakins.

The painting shows a batter in antiquated costume, apparently waiting for the pitch, while a gloveless player crouches behind him in the catcher's position.

Thomas Eakins (1844–1916) is considered perhaps the greatest American realist painter of the nineteenth century. He is known for his scenes of sports, such as the boxing painting *Between Rounds* and the rowing painting *Max Schmitt in a Single Scull.*

Among his other masterpieces are two dark-hued interiors of medical clinics: *The Gross Clinic* and *The Agnew Clinic.* Critics and audiences appreciate Eakins' achievement of intense feeling combined with realistic details.

Use these questions for discussion:
1. How does this painting help you visualize Casey and his surroundings? *The players in the painting have uniforms and equipment typical of Casey's era.*

2. Compare and contrast your image of Casey with the batter in the picture. *They are probably similarly outfitted, but the batter in the picture is realistic, rather than a larger-than-life hero.*

3. Compare and contrast the surroundings in the painting with those in the poem. *The grandstands and grass are similar, but the ambiance of the painting is tranquil, that of the poem tumultuous.*

◆ Critical Thinking

❶ Infer What does it show you about Casey when he "stilled the rising tumult" to protect the umpire? *He appears noble—but this reveals his arrogance or even condescension.*

◆ Critical Thinking

❷ Evaluate Ask students whether they feel suspense at line 44, and why or why not. *Point out that the line builds suspense by making us anticipate the pitch that is to come.*

◆ Build Grammar Skills

❸ Participles What is the participle in line 49, and what kind of participle is it? *Favored; past participle.*

◆ Literary Focus

❹ Climax and Anticlimax Is the ending of "Casey at the Bat" a climax or an anticlimax? Explain. *It is an anticlimax because it is a letdown after a buildup of suspense.*

Reinforce and Extend

Answers

◆ Literature and Your Life

Reader's Response Students should include reasons for their response. Details may include suspense about whether or not Casey will get to bat, the crowd's outrage at the umpire for the first strike, the anticipated shattering of the air by the force of Casey's swing.

Thematic Focus Students may recall a big letdown when their team did not win. A glum silence could have resulted, but probably not the stunned disappointment of the Mudville crowd.

☑ Check Your Comprehension

1. The crowd thinks Casey can win the game for his team. They cheer when it's his turn to bat.
2. (a) At first Casey is confident, proud, and defiant. (b) By the time the last pitch is thrown, his smile has turned to a sneer, and he appears angry.
3. Suggested responses: When Casey advances to the plate; Casey's first strike; Casey's second strike; Casey's swing at the last pitch.
4. Casey strikes out.

(Answers continue on page 39.)

From the benches, black with people, there went up a muffled roar,
Like the beating of the storm waves on the stern and distant shore.
35   "Kill him! kill the umpire!" shouted someone on the stand;
And it's likely they'd have killed him had not Casey raised his hand.

❶ With a smile of Christian charity great Casey's visage[3] shone;
He stilled the rising <u>tumult</u>, he made the game go on;
He signaled to the pitcher, and once more the spheroid flew;
40   But Casey still ignored it, and the umpire said, "Strike two."

"Fraud!" cried the maddened thousands, and the echo answered "Fraud!"
But one scornful look from Casey and the audience was awed;
❷ They saw his face grow stern and cold, they saw his muscles strain,
And they knew that Casey wouldn't let the ball go by again.

45   The sneer is gone from Casey's lips, his teeth are clenched in hate.
He pounds with cruel vengeance his bat upon the plate:
And now the pitcher holds the ball, and now he lets it go,
And now the air is shattered by the force of Casey's blow.

❸ Oh, somewhere in this favored land the sun is shining bright,
50   The band is playing somewhere, and somewhere hearts are light:
❹ And somewhere men are laughing, and somewhere children shout,
But there is no joy in Mudville: Mighty Casey has struck out.

---

3. **visage** (vĭz´ ĭj) *n.*: Face.

◆ Build Vocabulary
tumult (tōō´ məlt) *n.*: Noisy commotion

Guide for Responding

◆ Literature and Your Life

Reader's Response Did you expect the poem to end the way it did? Why or why not? What details made reading this poem a suspenseful experience?

Thematic Focus Think of a suspenseful sporting event in which your team lost and recall the reaction of the crowd. How did this situation compare with the situation described in "Casey at the Bat"?

☑ Check Your Comprehension

1. Explain how the crowd feels about Casey.
2. (a) What is Casey's attitude when he first comes to the plate? (b) How does his attitude change?
3. List three suspenseful points in the poem.
4. What is the outcome of Casey's turn at bat?

38 ◆ Spine Tinglers

◆ Critical Thinking

INTERPRET
1. Describe the type of baseball player Casey is, citing examples from the poem. **[Analyze]**
2. How might Casey's attitude have affected his game? **[Draw Conclusions]**
3. Based on what you know about Casey, what do you think was his reaction after he struck out? **[Speculate]**

EVALUATE
4. Explain whether or not the poet is successful in building suspense in the poem. **[Analyze]**

Beyond the Selection

FURTHER READING

Other Works About Spine-Tingling Moments in Baseball
The Annotated Casey at the Bat: A Collection of Ballads About the Mighty Casey, Martin Gardner
One for the Road: The Inside Story of Hank Aaron's Chase for the Home-Run Record, George Plimpton
Baseball's Best: The Hall of Fame Gallery, Martin Appel and Burt Goldblatt
Baseball's Greatest Quotations, Paul Dickson

INTERNET
You and your students may find more information about "Casey at the Bat" on the Internet. We suggest the following site. Please be aware, however, that sites may have changed since this information was published. Go to **http://www.clark.net/pub/cosmic/catbl.html**

We *strongly recommend* that you preview the site before sending students there.

Guide for Responding *(continued)*

◆ Reading Strategy

SUMMARIZING

Any time you describe the plot of a movie, television show, or novel to a friend, you're putting your **summarizing** skills to use. Summarize stanzas 4, 5, 8, 10, 12, and 13 (a summary of stanza 1 appears on page 35) of "Casey at the Bat." Include only the main ideas and the key details that support those ideas. Your summary should include enough information so that you could use it as the basis for a sports report about the game.

◆ Literary Focus

CLIMAX AND ANTICLIMAX

When you get to the point in a story or a narrative poem at which you learn how the conflict will be resolved, you've finally reached the **climax**. If the outcome is a downward turn of events, and one you had not expected, it is called an **anticlimax**.
1. Why is the climax the "high point" of a story?
2. Is the turning point of "Casey at the Bat" a climax or an anticlimax? Explain.

◆ Build Vocabulary

RELATED WORDS: FORMS OF *TUMULT*

On your paper, complete the following sentences with the appropriate form of the word *tumult*:
1. His supporters gave the senator a _____?_____ greeting following his reelection.
2. An explosion at the factory caused quite a _____?_____ downtown.

USING THE WORD BANK

For each numbered item, write a sentence that uses one word from the Word Bank.
1. Write the first sentence of a news article describing a noisy demonstration in the city.
2. Describe how a snake is moving along a tree branch in a rain forest.
3. Explain why you think your friend may not be feeling well today.
4. Tell about an old house that has ivy growing around its pillars.

◆ Build Grammar Skills

PARTICIPLES

Thayer vividly captures the actions of the players and the emotions of the audience through the use of carefully chosen **participles**—forms of verbs that act as adjectives. He uses both **present participles,** which end in *-ing,* and **past participles,** which usually end in -ed.

Practice Write these passages in your notebook. Identify the participle in each passage. Indicate whether it is a present or a past participle.
1. A straggling few got up to go, leaving there the rest,
2. So on that stricken multitude a deathlike sentence sat;
3. From the benches, black with people, there went up a muffled roar, Like the beating of the waves on the stern and distant shore.
4. He stilled the rising tumult, he made the game go on;
5. "Fraud!" cried the maddened thousands, and the echo answered "Fraud!"

Beyond Literature

Math Connection

Statistics in Sports Although you might not think of it, math plays an important role in baseball and in other sports. Statistics are kept on just about everything—from a baseball player's batting average during night games to the number of seconds a basketball player hangs in the air when performing a slam dunk. Not only do statistics help fans track how well their favorite players are performing, but they also help coaches and managers make key on-field decisions. For example, a baseball manager might check a player's batting average against a specific pitcher when deciding whether to pinch-hit for him or her. What types of statistics might have prompted the Mudville manager to pinch-hit for the Mighty Casey?

Casey at the Bat/I Had a Hammer ◆ 39

◆ Critical Thinking

1. Casey is most likely a strong hitter because the crowd expects him to win the game. In the poem he is referred to as "Mighty Casey."
2. If he hadn't been overconfident, he might have swung at the first two pitches and gotten on base.
3. Casey was probably angry. He might have blamed the pitcher or the umpire for his defeat.
4. The poet is successful. The narrative is a "play-by-play" description of the game, so each moment seems important. The contrast between Casey's confidence and the crowd's anxiety heightens the suspense.

Writer's Solution

Idea Bank

Customizing for
Performance Levels

Following are suggestions for matching the Idea Bank topics with your students' performance levels:
    Less Advanced Students: 1, 5, 7
    Average Students: 2, 4
    More Advanced Students: 3, 6

Customizing for
Learning Modalities

Following are suggestions for matching Idea Bank topics with your students' learning modalities:
    Visual/Spatial: 1, 7
    Auditory: 4, 5
    Logical/Mathematic: 3, 6

Writing Mini-Lesson

Refer students to the Writing Handbook, page 962, for instruction on the writing process, and page 964 for further information on Description.

Writer's Solution

Writing Lab CD-ROM

Have students complete the tutorial on Description. Follow these steps:

1. Have students view the video segment from a sports broadcast (in the Audience section) to provide a model for their sportscasts.
2. To ensure that your students' sportscasts are appropriate for their audiences, have them complete the Audience Profile in the section on Audience and Purpose.
3. Have students draft on computer.
4. Use the Vague Adjectives Checker to aid revision.

You will need approximately 90 minutes of class time to complete the preceding steps.

Sourcebook

Have students use Chapter 1, Description (pp. 1–29) for additional support. This chapter includes in-depth instruction on gathering sensory details (p. 17) and using vivid verbs (p. 25).

Build Your Portfolio

Idea Bank

Writing

1. **Sports Headlines** Brainstorm for a list of suspenseful sports moments. Then write a list of attention-grabbing sports headlines based on your list. **[Career Link]**

2. **Sports How-to** Write a step-by-step explanation of how to perform a sports-related activity. For example, you might tell how to throw a curve ball or how to execute a tennis serve. **[Physical Education Link]**

3. **Résumé** Research a baseball player. Then list his career highlights as if you were compiling information for a résumé—a summary of a person's job experience and education. **[Career Link]**

Speaking and Listening

4. **Sports Interview** Work with a partner to present a sports interview to the class. Have one person portray the interviewer and the other person portray a sports figure you admire. **[Career Link]**

5. **Pep Talk** What might the coach of the Mudville team say to boost the morale of his players? Compose a "pep talk" and present it to the class. **[Physical Education Link]**

Projects

6. **Statistics Chart** Create a chart comparing two different sets of baseball statistics. For example, you might compare the statistics of two different players or statistics from two different time periods. **[Math Link]**

7. **Sports in Other Countries** Research a sport that is very popular in another country and create a presentation based on your findings. **[Social Studies Link]**

Writing Mini-Lesson

Sportscast

"The running back *blasted* through the defensive line." "She *spiked* the ball over the net." "The champs *annihilated* the challengers." The language of a good sportscast is vivid and lively. It captures the thrills and sometimes the disappointments of a sports event. Write a sportscast that really hooks your audience. You can base it on any sport you choose. The tip given here will help you.

Writing Skills Focus: Vivid Verbs

One of the keys to a good sportscast is the use of vivid verbs. **Vivid verbs** are action words with punch. They give life to your writing by making your descriptions precise and interesting. Notice how Ernest Lawrence Thayer uses vivid verbs to set the scene in "Casey at the Bat."

Model From the Poem

But Flynn *let drive* a "single," to the wonderment of all.

Prewriting Choose a topic by recalling a sports event you recently witnessed or in which you participated. As an alternative, you can make up an event. Then create a list of vivid verbs that apply to the sport you've chosen. For example, list ways a pitcher might throw a baseball or ways a batter might hit.

Drafting As you draft your sportscast, choose precise, descriptive verbs that are appropriate to your sport. For example, a figure skater probably would not careen across the ice, but a hockey player might.

Revising Remember, your sportscast should make your audience feel as if they attended the event it describes. Look for places where you can liven up your descriptions by adding vivid verbs.

✓ ASSESSMENT OPTIONS

Formal Assessment, Selection Test, pp. 7–9, and Assessment Resources Software. The selection test is designed so that it can be easily customized to the performance levels of your students.
Alternative Assessment, p. 3, includes options for less advanced students, more advanced students, musical/rhythmic learners, and verbal/linguistic learners.

PORTFOLIO ASSESSMENT
Use the following rubrics in the *Alternative Assessment* booklet to assess student writing:
Sports Headlines: Description Rubric, p. 90
Sports How-to: How-to/Process Explanation Rubric, p. 93
Résumé: Résumé and Cover Letter Rubric, p. 107
Writing Mini-Lesson: Description Rubric, p. 90

The mighty Casey is probably the most famous fictional slugger—a player who could build nervous excitement among the fans because of his ability to change the outcome of a game with a single swing of the bat. One of the greatest real-life sluggers of all time is Hank Aaron. Aaron, who played in the major leagues from 1954 to 1976, holds more batting records than any other player. His crowning achievement came when he hit his 715th home run, breaking the record held by the legendary Babe Ruth. In the following section from his autobiography, Aaron describes this achievement.

from I Had a Hammer

Hank Aaron

My father threw out the first ball, and then we took the field against the Dodgers. Their pitcher was Al Downing, a veteran lefthander whom I respected. Downing always had an idea of what he was doing when he was on the mound, and he usually pitched me outside with sliders and screwballs.[1] I crowded the plate against him to hit the outside pitch, but at the same time, I knew he would be trying to outthink me, which meant that I had to be patient and pick my spot. It didn't come in the second inning, when Downing walked me before I could take the bat off my shoulder. I scored when Dusty Baker doubled and Bill Buckner mishandled the ball in left field. Nobody seemed to care too much, but my run broke Willie Mays's National League record for runs scored—Willie had retired at the end of the 1973 season—and put me third all-time behind Ty Cobb and Ruth. I had always put great store in runs scored ever since Jackie Robinson pointed out that the purpose of coming up to the plate was to make it around the bases. The way I saw it, a run scored was just as important as one batted in. Apparently, though, Jackie and I were in the minority on that score.

I came up again in the fourth, with two outs and Darrell Evans on first base. The Dodgers were ahead 3–1, and I knew that Downing was not going to walk me and put the tying run on base. He was going to challenge me with everything he had—which was what it was going to take for me to hit my 715th home run. I knew all along that I wouldn't break the record against a rookie pitcher, because a rookie would be scared to come at me. It had to

---

1. pitched me . . . screwballs: Threw two types of pitches that cause the ball to move in an unnatural way. They are intended to confuse a batter and make the ball more difficult to hit.

Connections to Today's World
Though "Casey at the Bat" dates from an earlier time, students can easily relate the poem to contemporary times. Baseball heroes and record breakers abound. An outstanding record breaker is Hank Aaron, who, in 1974, broke the home run record of Babe Ruth. Ask students to cite more recent record breakers in baseball.

More About the Author
Henry "Hank" Aaron was born in 1934 in Mobile, Alabama. He was one of seven brothers and sisters; one brother, the late Tommy Aaron, played on the Braves for seven years. Hank Aaron played football in high school, and began playing semiprofessional baseball for an all-black team in Mobile when he was sixteen. His professional career was spent with the Milwaukee Braves (later the Atlanta Braves), and, for his last two years, with the Milwaukee Brewers. His professional records include most runs batted in, most extra-base hits, and most total bases; he is in the top ten in several other categories, including most games played, most times at bat, most runs scored, most doubles, and most putouts. He appeared in twenty-four All-Star games and was Most Valuable Player for the 1957 season. He led the National League in home runs four times, in RBIs four times, and in batting average twice. An excellent fielder, he won the Gold Glove award in 1958. He was elected to the Hall of Fame in 1982, receiving more votes than any player ever except Willie Mays. Since retiring, he has been director of player development for the Atlanta Braves.

Speaking and Listening Mini-Lesson

Sports Interview
This mini-lesson supports the Speaking and Listening activity in the Idea Bank on page 40.

Introduce the Concept Tell students that most of an interview happens before the participants go on camera. Competent interviewers must prepare carefully before going face-to-face with their subjects; preparation includes researching the background and carefully planning questions.

Develop Background Before students perform their interviews, ask questions such as the following, regarding the practical aspects of the preparation stage:

• On what basis would you decide to choose to interview one sports figure rather than another?

• How would you go about doing research on an athlete's life and career?

Apply the Information Invite pairs to select a sports figure to interview, and then to do the required research. Students may draw up interview questions as a pair, or the interviewer alone may do this. Remind students to think about the personalities of the people they will role-play.

Assess the Outcome Have pairs perform their interviews for the class. You might allow students in the audience to ask follow-up questions of the sports figure and even of the interviewer. Invite the audience to help evaluate the interview.

Customize for
More Advanced Students

Point out that Aaron emphasizes the mental aspect of baseball, which is especially important in the duel between pitcher and batter. Encourage students to share their knowledge of how pitchers and batters try to outfox each other. Students can compare Aaron's "duel" with Downing with Casey's relationship with the pitcher.

Customize for
Logical/Mathematical Learners

Help students see that a situation at any point in a game presents a strategic puzzle in which batter, pitcher, runners, and fielders all must ask themselves (with the help of signals from coaches) what they should try to do and to which possible events they should be ready to enact. Aaron reveals his thinking on coming up to the plate in the fourth inning.

42 ◆ *Spine Tinglers*

⬧ **Beyond the Classroom**

Career Connection

Sports Students in the United States today are exposed to numerous sports heroes as role models, and often dream of entering professional sports themselves. Both the fictional Casey and the real Henry Aaron carved extremely successful careers.

Realistically, few people have the outstanding skills and talent required to be a highly paid professional athlete. However, for those interested in sports, there are many

career possibilities in related fields. Have students explore the following career possibilities: sports writing and photography, sports medicine, fitness and training, sports equipment businesses, and so on.

Community Connection

Sports (and Other) Heroes Many communities have residents or former residents who are locally prominent. There might be a local athlete who went on to become a pro-

fessional, or a former athlete who lives in your town, or someone in a different field entirely who has contributed either to your community or to the world at large. Challenge students to discover the identities of such local heroes by consulting local newspapers, newscasts, and official records. Ask students to tell the class what they have found about the heroes in their midst. Students might even persuade a hero to talk to your class.

42

be a pitcher with some confidence and nerve—a solid veteran like Downing.

Downing's first pitch was a change of pace that went into the dirt. The umpire, Satch Davidson, threw it out, and the first-base umpire, Frank Pulli, tossed Downing another one of the specially marked infrared balls. Downing rubbed it up and then threw his slider low and down the middle, which was not where he wanted it but which was fine with me. I hit it squarely, although not well enough that I knew it was gone. The ball shot out on a line over the shortstop, Bill Russell, who bent his knees as if he were going to jump up and catch it. That was one of the differences between Ruth and me: he made outfielders look up at the sky, and I made shortstops bend their knees.

I used to say that I never saw one of my home runs land, but when I see photographs or films of myself hitting home runs, I'm always looking out toward left field. I never realized I was doing it, though, and I still don't think I was watching to see the ball go over the fence. I think it was just a matter of following the ball with my eyes. From the time the pitcher gripped it, I was focused on the ball, and I didn't look away until it was time to run the bases. Anyway, I saw this one go out. And before it did, I saw Buckner run to the fence like he was going to catch it. During the pregame warm-ups, Buckner had practiced leaping against the fence, as if he planned to take the home run away from me, and I believe he was thinking about doing that as he ran back to the wall and turned. But the ball kept going. It surprised him, and it surprised me. I'm still not sure I hit that ball hard enough for it to go out. I don't know—maybe I did but I was so keyed up that I couldn't feel it. Anyway, something carried the ball into the bullpen, and about the time I got to first base I realized that I was the all-time home run king of baseball. Steve Garvey, the Dodgers' first baseman, shook my hand as I passed first, and Davey Lopes, the second baseman, stuck out his hand at second. I'm not sure if I ever shook with Lopes, though, because about that time a couple of college kids appeared out of nowhere and started running alongside me and pounding me on the back. I guess I was aware of them, because the clips show that I sort of nudged them away with my elbow, but I honestly don't remember them being there. I was in my own little world at the time. It was like I was running in a bubble and I could see all these people jumping up and down and waving their arms in slow motion. I remember that every base seemed crowded, like there were all these people I had to get through to make it to home plate. I just couldn't wait to get there. I was told I had a big smile on my face as I came around third. I purposely never smiled as I ran the bases after a home run, but I suppose I couldn't help it that time.

1. What would be your reaction to hitting a record-breaking home run? Compare your feelings with those Aaron describes.
2. How does Aaron feel about baseball? Support your answer.
3. Compare and contrast Aaron's personality with that of the mighty Casey.

 ◀ **Critical Viewing** Judging from the look on his face, how does Hank Aaron feel at this moment? [Infer]

from I Had a Hammer ◆ 43

OBJECTIVES

1. To read, comprehend, interpret, and respond to a story
2. To relate the story to personal experience
3. To predict events
4. To identify foreshadowing
5. To build vocabulary in context and learn the suffix -ful
6. To develop skill in using compound sentences
7. To write a bird's eye view of a place, maintaining a consistent point of view
8. To respond to the story through writing, speaking and listening, and projects

SKILLS INSTRUCTION

Vocabulary:
Suffixes: -ful
Grammar:
Compound Sentences
Literary Focus:
Foreshadowing
Reading Strategy:
Predict
Writing: Maintaining a Consistent Viewpoint

Speaking and Listening:
Panel Discussion (teacher edition)
Critical Viewing:
Predict; Compare and Contrast; Infer; Describe

PORTFOLIO OPPORTUNITIES

Writing: The Final Outcome; Public Service Announcement; Book vs. Movie
Writing Mini-Lesson: Writing a Bird's Eye View of a Place
Speaking and Listening: Panel Discussion; Create a Scene
Projects: Multimedia Presentation; A Picture of Flight

More About the Author
The daughter of a famous actor, Daphne du Maurier gave up a chance at an acting career herself, determined to succeed as a writer. Her first novel, *The Loving Spirit*, written when du Maurier was 24, so impressed Major Frederick Browning, a 35-year-old major in the Grenadier Guards, that he managed to meet her and immediately asked for—and won—her hand in marriage. Du Maurier's fiction was so popular that in 1969 she was given the title of Dame Commander, Order of the British Empire. Of her writing, du Maurier said that she was "not so much interested in people as in types—types who represent great forces of good and evil."

Guide for Reading

Daphne du Maurier
(1907–1989)

You may already be familiar with Daphne du Maurier's work—without ever having opened one of her books.

Du Maurier's stories have inspired some of the most gripping movies ever made.

Among these is Alfred Hitchcock's film *The Birds*, based on the story of the same name.

A Family of Artists Du Maurier was born in London into a family of actors, artists, and writers. Her father was an actor and theater manager who specialized in playing criminals on the stage, and her grandfather was a novelist and artist who illustrated his own writings.

A Successful Career *The Loving Spirit* (1931) was du Maurier's first novel, which she wrote while secluded in a house in Cornwall on the southwest coast of England. The novel became a bestseller, propelling her into a life-long career as a writer. She followed with a series of romantic novels that were tinged with mystery and suspense: *Jamaica Inn* (1936), *Rebecca* (1938), and *Frenchman's Creek* (1941). Du Maurier also wrote numerous short stories and, in 1977, completed an autobiography, *Myself When Young*.

A Box Office Attraction Du Maurier's stories attracted the attention of film director Alfred Hitchcock, who specialized in suspenseful movies. In addition to *The Birds*, Hitchcock made two other films based on du Maurier's tales, including *Rebecca*, which won the Academy Award for Best Picture in 1940.

◆ Build Vocabulary

SUFFIXES: -ful
In "The Birds," the children are described as *fretful*. The word *fretful* contains the suffix *-ful*. The suffix *-ful* can mean "having the quality of," as in *forgetful*; "having the quantity that would fill," as in *handful*; or "full of," as in *fretful*. Therefore, the word *fretful* literally means "full of fret or worry." Thus, a person who is fretful, full of fret or worry, is irritable or discontented.

WORD BANK
Before you read, preview this list of words from the story.

placid
garish
recounted
sullen
furtively
imperative
reconnaissance
fretful

◆ Build Grammar Skills

COMPOUND SENTENCES
As Daphne du Maurier develops this story, she makes frequent use of compound sentences as a way to express a lot of detailed information. A **compound sentence** consists of two or more equally important, or coordinate, independent clauses joined by a coordinating conjunction—*and*, *but*, or *or*—or by a semicolon.

                 indep. clause
On December the third, the wind changed overnight,
   indep. clause
and it was winter.

As you read "The Birds," notice the compound sentences and consider the effect they have on the telling of the story.

Prentice Hall Literature Program Resources

REINFORCE / RETEACH / EXTEND

Selection Support Pages
Build Vocabulary: Suffixes: -ful, p. 14
Build Grammar Skills: Compound Sentences, p. 15
Reading Strategy: Predict, p. 16
Literary Focus: Foreshadowing, p. 17

Strategies for Diverse Student Needs, p. 4

Beyond Literature
Cross-Curricular Connection: Science, p. 4

Formal Assessment Selection Test, pp. 10–12, Assessment Resources Software

Alternative Assessment, p. 4

Writing and Language Transparencies
Descriptive and Observational Writing, pp. 17–20

Resource Pro CD-ROM
"The Birds"—includes all resource material and customizable lesson plan

Listening to Literature Audiocassettes
"The Birds"

The Birds

◆ Literature and Your Life

CONNECT YOUR EXPERIENCE

You step outside and the sky is dark and threatening, with clouds closing in on you. Low rumbles of thunder are becoming louder by the second. You look at the threatening scene and an eerie feeling runs through you. Nature appears to be brooding, about to strike.

Writers have often been fascinated by nature's dark side. Sometimes—as du Maurier does in "The Birds"—they use fiction to ask questions about nature's moods.

THEMATIC FOCUS: IN SUSPENSE

One question that du Maurier explores in this suspenseful tale is, What happens when nature, whose moods are familiar to us, shows a darker side than has ever been seen before?

◆ Background for Understanding

SCIENCE

Use these silhouettes to help you picture the birds that appear in du Maurier's story. Try to imagine what it would be like to have thousands of these birds descend upon your town.

starling

crow

meadowlark

robin

Journal Writing Jot down three species of birds you commonly observe. Draw a silhouette of each bird and briefly describe it.

◆ Literary Focus

FORESHADOWING

As its name suggests, **foreshadowing** is the shadow of things to come—an author's use of clues to hint at future events. In "The Birds," for instance, du Maurier hints at danger to come when she writes, "The birds had been more restless than ever this fall of the year." Notice other examples of foreshadowing, details that seem disturbing or unusual.

◆ Reading Strategy

PREDICT

You can use foreshadowing to **predict** the outcome of a story before you actually read what happens. For example, by noticing small but troubling events, you can foresee much bigger troubles to come.

In reading "The Birds," base your predictions of future events on telltale details that some or all of the characters ignore. Jot down anything that seems disturbing, unusual, or out of place. Then apply an imaginary magnifying glass to these details. Ask yourself what would happen if this small trouble were multiplied many times. Use a graphic organizer like this one to help you record your details.

Unusual Detail	What Will Happen If It Intensifies

Guide for Reading ◆ 45

Guide for Reading ◆ 45

Preparing for Standardized Tests

Vocabulary Students can use their knowledge of the suffix *-ful* to improve performance on standardized tests. When taking a test, students may come across words containing this suffix. The words may not at first be familiar. However, if they remove the suffix *-ful* from these words, they may be left with a word with which they're familiar. For example, they may be familiar with the word *fret* but not with the word *fretful*.

Writing Students can use their knowledge of compound sentences to improve their performance on writing sections of standardized tests. Explain that by using compound sentences that contain more than one idea, along with other sentences that contain a single idea, they will be able to establish better sentence variety in their writing. Doing so will help their writing flow better. In addition, they can emphasize a key point by following a series of compound sentences with a short, simple sentence that sums up the main point in the previous sentences.

Interest Grabber Playing a brief segment from Alfred Hitchcock's film adaptation of "The Birds" is a great way to hook your students' interest. You may want to play, for example, the scene in which the character Melanie cautiously nudges a door open and steps into a room. Suddenly, large birds swoop at her from all directions, and she frantically fights to fend off their attack. Ask students: What do you think causes the birds to attack? What would it be like to live in fear of attacks by flocks of birds? How do the characters in the story try to combat the birds? Tell students that they can find answers to all of these questions by reading the story.

Engage students' interest by having them discuss what could be the possible effects of the situation described in this report. With their interest thus engaged, have them read the story.

Customize for
Less Proficient Readers
Help these students follow this rather long story by having them stop at several points within the story to summarize what has already happened and predict what might happen next.

Customize for
More Advanced Students
Advanced students can meet in small groups to discuss their opinions about the underlying meaning of the story. Suggest they address questions such as, "What might the birds symbolize in the story?" "Did the author have a message to convey, or is this just a good suspense story?"

Customize for
English Language Learners
Students for whom English is a second language might find certain British terms and expressions confusing. Point out definitions of words such as *shingles* and *pips* in the footnotes, and explain words such as *flat* (apartment) when they appear in the text.

Customize for
Musical/Rhythmic Learners
Have these students note the descriptions of sounds from nature: bird calls, wind, and water. Ask them to explain how the sounds contribute to the story.

In addition to entertaining readers through a gripping series of events involving attacks on humans by flocks of birds, this story conveys an important message about the unpredictability of nature and people's inability to control nature's forces. This message is conveyed through such details as Mr. Trigg's and Jim's uncaring attitudes toward the dangers the birds represent and Nat's reference to a time when people didn't depend on modern conveniences. Have students discuss why it is impossible for people to predict outcomes in conflicts with the forces of nature.

Customize for
Visual/Spatial Learners
The photographs and illustrations on pages 46, 52, 59, and 62 can serve as an invaluable reading aid for these students. Have them preview the photographs before they begin reading and use the visuals to make predictions about the story's setting and plot. Then, as they read, encourage them to help them picture what's happening in the story.

Listening to Literature Audiocassettes Because this is a long story, you may want to have students listen to a portion of it on audiocassette. For example, you might want to have students listen to the beginning of the story to hook their interest and get them into the action. Students can then read the remainder of the story.

▶**Critical Viewing◀**

❶ **Predict** Since the story is called "The Birds," and because the painting shows birds with prominent beaks and claws flying close overhead, students might predict that the story will be about dangerous birds.

THE BIRDS

Daphne du Maurier

Attack of the Birds, 1994, Lev Tabenkin, Maya Polsky

▲ **Critical Viewing** Based on this painting, what do you think might happen in this story? [Predict] ❶

46 ◆ *Spine Tinglers*

Block Scheduling Strategies

Consider these suggestions to take advantage of extended class time:

• Have students read the story in class in three or four segments. Pause after each segment for a class discussion. Have students share their reactions to the events they've just read about and make predictions as a class about what will happen next.

• After students have finished reading the selection, have them view an extended portion

(possibly 30 minutes) of Hitchcock's film adaptation of the story. Have students compare and contrast the film and the story.

• Have students complete the Writing Mini-Lesson using the Description tutorial on the *Writer's Solution Writing Lab* CD-ROM (see the teaching suggestions on p. 74).

2 n December the third the wind changed overnight and it was winter. Until then the autumn had been mellow, soft. The leaves had lingered on the trees, golden-red, and the hedgerows were still green. The earth was rich where the plow had turned it.

Nat Hocken, because of a wartime disability, had a pension and did not work full-time at the farm. He worked three days a week, and they gave him the lighter jobs: hedging, thatching, repairs to the farm buildings.

Although he was married, with children, his was a solitary disposition; he liked best to work alone. It pleased him when he was given a bank to build up, or a gate to mend at the far end of the peninsula, where the sea surrounded the farmland on either side. Then, at midday, he would pause and eat the pasty[1] that his wife had baked for him, and, sitting on the cliff's edge, watch the birds. Autumn was best for this, better than spring. In spring the birds flew inland, purposeful, intent; they knew where they were bound; the rhythm and ritual of their life brooked no delay. In autumn those that had not migrated overseas but remained to pass the winter were caught up in the same driving urge, but because migration was denied them followed a pattern of their own. **3** Great flocks of them came to the peninsula, restless, uneasy, spending themselves in motion; now wheeling, circling in the sky, now settling to feed on the rich new-turned soil, but even when they fed it was as though they did so without hunger, without desire. Restlessness drove them to the skies again.

Black and white, jackdaw and gull, mingled in strange partnership, seeking some sort of liberation, never satisfied, never still. Flocks of starlings, rustling like silk, flew to fresh pasture, driven by the same necessity of movement, and the smaller birds, the finches and the larks, scattered from tree to hedge as if compelled.

Nat watched them, and he watched the sea birds too. Down in the bay they waited for the tide. They had more patience. Oyster catchers, redshank, sanderling, and curlew watched by the water's edge; as the slow sea sucked at the shore and then withdrew, leaving the strip of seaweed bare and the shingle churned, the sea birds raced and ran upon the beaches. Then that same impulse to flight seized upon them too. Crying, whistling, calling, they skimmed the placid sea and left the shore. Make haste, make speed, hurry and begone; yet where, and to what purpose? The restless urge of autumn, unsatisfying, sad, had put a spell upon them and they must flock, and wheel, and cry; they must spill themselves of motion before winter came.

"Perhaps," thought Nat, munching his pasty by the cliff's edge, "a message comes to the birds in autumn, like a warning. Winter is coming. Many of them perish. And **4** like the people who, apprehensive of death before their time, drive themselves to work or folly, the birds do likewise."

The birds had been more restless than ever this fall of the year, the agitation more marked because the days were still. As the tractor traced its path up and down the western hills, the figure of the farmer silhouetted on the driving seat, the whole machine and the man upon it would be lost momentarily in the great cloud of wheeling, crying birds. There were many more than usual; Nat was sure of this.

> ◆ **Literary Focus**
> What might the birds' restlessness and large numbers foreshadow? **5**

◆ **Build Vocabulary**

placid (plas´ id) *adj.*: Tranquil; calm

---

1. **pasty** (pas´ tē) *n.*: A meat pie.

The Birds ◆ 47

◆ **Critical Thinking**

2 **Infer** Have students discuss what the opening paragraph reveals about the story's setting. *The opening paragraph reveals that it is winter and that the story takes place in a rural setting that has farms.*

◆ **Literary Focus**

3 **Foreshadowing** Ask students: How does this description of the birds' activities foreshadow what might happen later in the story? *The birds are "restless, uneasy" and feed "without desire," foreshadowing their unusual behavior later in the story.*

◆ **Critical Thinking**

4 **Analyze Character** Ask students what Nat's thoughts reveal about his relationship with nature. *He is sensitive to nature and attuned to the birds and their response to the cycle of the seasons.*

◆ **Literary Focus**

5 **Foreshadowing** Students should respond as follows: *The birds' restlessness and large numbers might foreshadow unusual or destructive behavior.*

◆ **Humanities: Art**

Attack of the Birds, 1994, by Lev Tabenik.

Lev Tabenik is a Moscow artist, the son of an artist. He graduated from the Moscow Polygraphic Institute. Much of his art was created when Russia was still part of the Soviet Union. His paintings often include images of animals seen in unusual ways—exaggerated in size or threatening in aspect.

In this painting, a Russian peasant woman is attacked by birds. She is surrendering to the birds, her arms held up to them.

Use these questions for discussion:
1. Does viewing this painting make you want to read the story? Why or why not? *Students may respond that the painting does make them want to read the story, because it captures a terrifying situation that they'd like to learn more about.*
2. After seeing this painting, would you like to see other works by the artist? Why or why not? *Students may respond that they would like to see other works by the artist because of the action-packed, suspenseful nature of his work.*

◆ **Critical Thinking**

❶ **Analyze** Ask students why Nat doesn't want his wife to know how he feels about the bird attack. *He is afraid that if she sees his real feelings, she may panic.*

Comprehension Check ☑

❷ How does Nat explain the birds' desperate behavior? *He believes it is the hard weather that has driven them to act that way, and that they may be birds from another area.*

◆ **Build Grammar Skills**

❸ Have students identify the two main clauses in each of these compound sentences. Ask them why they think the author wrote two compound sentences in a row. *She wanted to increase the suspense in the story by adding on ominous details about the weather in quick succession.*

◆ **Literary Focus**

❹ **Foreshadowing** Students may say that the change in the weather is unnatural, foreshadowing even more unnatural behavior from the birds.

◆ **Critical Thinking**

❺ **Analyze** Ask students what effect Nat wants his response to have on his family. *He wants to calm and soothe them.*

---

passage to his own. His wife sat up in bed, one child asleep beside her, the smaller in her arms, his face bandaged. The curtains were tightly drawn across the window, the candles lit. Her face looked garish in the yellow light. She shook her head for silence.

"He's sleeping now," she whispered, "but only just. Something must have cut him, there was blood at the corner of his eyes. Jill said it was the birds. She said she woke up, and the birds were in the room."

❶ His wife looked up at Nat, searching his face for confirmation. She looked terrified, bewildered, and he did not want her to know that he was also shaken, dazed almost, by the events of the past few hours.

"There are birds in there," he said, "dead birds, nearly fifty of them. Robins, wrens, all the little birds from hereabouts. It's as though a madness seized them, with the east wind." He sat down on the bed beside his wife and held her hand. "It's the weather," he said, "it must be that, it's the hard weather. They aren't the birds, maybe, ❷ from here around. They've been driven down from upcountry."

"But, Nat," whispered his wife, "it's only this night that the weather turned. There's been no snow to drive them. And they can't be hungry yet. There's food for them out there in the fields."

"It's the weather," repeated Nat. "I tell you, it's the weather."

His face, too, was drawn and tired, like hers. They stared at one another for a while without speaking.

"I'll go downstairs and make a cup of tea," he said.

The sight of the kitchen reassured him. The cups and saucers, neatly stacked upon the dresser, the table and chairs, his wife's roll of knitting on her basket chair, the children's toys in a corner cupboard.

◆ **Build Vocabulary**
garish (gar´ ish) *adj.*: Too bright or gaudy

He knelt down, raked out the old embers, and relit the fire. The glowing sticks brought normality, the steaming kettle and the brown teapot comfort and security. He drank his tea, carried a cup up to his wife. Then he washed in the scullery,[2] and, putting on his boots, opened the back door.

The sky was hard and leaden, and the brown hills that had gleamed in the sun the day before looked dark and bare. The east wind, like a razor, stripped the trees, and the leaves, crackling and dry, shivered and scattered with the wind's blast. Nat stubbed the earth with his boot. It was frozen hard. He had never known a change so swift and sudden. Black winter had descended in a single night.

> ❸
> ◆ **Literary Focus**
> What might this description of the sudden change in the weather fore-shadow?
> ❹

The children were awake now. Jill was chattering upstairs and young Johnny crying once again. Nat heard his wife's voice, soothing, comforting. Presently they came down. He had breakfast ready for them, and the routine of the day began.

"Did you drive away the birds?" asked Jill, restored to calm because of the kitchen fire, because of day, because of breakfast.

"Yes, they've all gone now," said Nat. "It was the east wind brought them in. They were frightened and lost, they wanted shelter." ❺

"They tried to peck us," said Jill. "They went for Johnny's eyes."

"Fright made them do that," said Nat. "They didn't know where they were in the dark bedroom."

"I hope they won't come again," said Jill. "Perhaps if we put bread for them outside the window they will eat that and fly away."

She finished her breakfast and then went for her coat and hood, her schoolbooks and her satchel. Nat said nothing, but his wife

2. scullery (skul´ er ē) *n.*: A room next to the kitchen where pots and pans are washed and stored.

looked at him across the table. A silent message passed between them.

"I'll walk with her to the bus," he said. "I don't go to the farm today."

And while the child was washing in the scullery he said to his wife, "Keep all the windows closed, and the doors too. Just to be on the safe side. I'll go to the farm. Find out if they heard anything in the night." Then he walked with his small daughter up the lane. She seemed to have forgotten her experience of the night before. She danced ahead of him, chasing the leaves, her face whipped with the cold and rosy under the pixie hood.

"Is it going to snow, Dad?" she said. "It's cold enough."

He glanced up at the bleak sky, felt the wind tear at his shoulders.

6 "No," he said, "it's not going to snow. This is a black winter, not a white one."

All the while he searched the hedgerows for the birds, glanced over the top of them to the fields beyond, looked to the small wood above the farm where the rooks and jackdaws gathered. He saw none.

The other children waited by the bus stop, muffled, hooded like Jill, the faces white and pinched with cold.

Jill ran to them, waving. "My dad says it won't snow," she called, "it's going to be a black winter."

She said nothing of the birds. She began to push and struggle with another little girl. The bus came ambling up the hill. Nat saw her on to it, then turned and walked back towards the farm. It was not his day for work, but he wanted to satisfy himself that all was well. Jim, the cowman, was clattering in the yard.

"Boss around?" asked Nat.

"Gone to market," said Jim. "It's Tuesday, isn't it?"

He clumped off round the corner of a shed. He had no time for Nat. Nat was said to be superior. Read books, and the like.

Nat had forgotten it was Tuesday. This showed how the events of the preceding night had shaken him. He went to the back door of the farmhouse and heard Mrs. Trigg singing in the kitchen, the wireless[3] making a background to her song.

"Are you there, missus?" called out Nat.

She came to the door, beaming, broad, a good-tempered woman.

"Hullo, Mr. Hocken," she said. "Can you tell me where this cold is coming from? Is it Russia? I've never seen such a change. And it's going on, the wireless says. Something to do with the Arctic Circle."

"We didn't turn on the wireless this morning," said Nat. "Fact is, we had trouble in the night."

"Kiddies poorly?"

"No . . ." He hardly knew how to explain it. Now, in daylight, the battle of the birds would sound absurd.

He tried to tell Mrs. Trigg what had happened, but he could see from her eyes that she thought his story was the result of a nightmare.

"Sure they were real birds," she said, smiling, "with proper feathers and all? Not the funny-shaped kind that the men see after closing hours on a Saturday night?"

"Mrs. Trigg," he said, "there are fifty dead birds, robins, wrens, and such, lying low on the floor of the children's bedroom. They went for me; they tried to go for young **7** Johnny's eyes."

Mrs. Trigg stared at him doubtfully.

"Well there, now," she answered, "I suppose the weather brought them. Once in the bedroom, they wouldn't know where they were to. Foreign birds maybe, from that Arctic Circle."

"No," said Nat, "they were the birds you see about here every day."

"Funny thing," said Mrs. Trigg, "no explaining it, really. You ought to write up

---

3. **wireless** (wīr′ lis) *n*.: Radio.

The Birds ◆ 51

◆ **Reading Strategy**

6 Predict Ask students to infer what Nat means by "black winter" and to predict what might happen in a "black winter," as opposed to a "white winter." *A "black winter" is probably one without snow; it implies darkness and danger, while a "white winter" sounds lighter and more normal. In a black winter, fearsome and dangerous things might happen.*

◆ *Literature and Your Life*

7 Ask students: Have you ever witnessed a dangerous or unusual event, but worried that people would not believe you when you reported it? If so, how do you imagine Mrs. Trigg's reaction makes Nat feel? Why does he keep trying to convince her? *Nat must feel frustrated by having his terrifying experience treated so lightly, but he feels obligated to warn her of the impending danger.*

❶ Predict Have students predict how Nat will react to Jim's response to Nat's description of the birds' aggressive behavior. *Students may predict that Nat will be frustrated that others are unaware of the behavior of the birds and are skeptical about whether what he is describing actually happened.*

❷ Clarification Explain that during World War II, an air raid was an attack by enemy planes dropping bombs. It was usually signaled with loud sirens. During an air raid, people were told to turn off their lights so that buildings would not be visible as targets for bomber planes.

►**Critical Viewing**◄

❸ Compare and Contrast The painting shows a stark landscape that is empty of life except for two birds. The mood seems lonely and a little unsettling. The mood in the story so far could also be described as unsettling because of the disturbing bird behavior.

and ask the *Guardian*. They'd have some answer for it. Well, I must be getting on."

She nodded, smiled, and went back into the kitchen.

Nat, dissatisfied, turned to the farm gate. Had it not been for those corpses on the bedroom floor, which he must now collect and bury somewhere, he would have considered the tale exaggeration too.

Jim was standing by the gate.

"Had any trouble with the birds?" asked Nat.

"Birds? What birds?"

"We got them up our place last night. Scores of them, came in the children's bedroom. Quite savage they were."

"Oh?" It took time for anything to penetrate Jim's head. "Never heard of birds acting savage," he said at length. "They get tame, like, sometimes. I've seen them come to the windows for crumbs."

"These birds last night weren't tame."

❶

"No? Cold, maybe. Hungry. You put out some crumbs."

Jim was no more interested than Mrs. Trigg had been. It was, Nat thought, like air raids in the war. No one down this end of the country knew what the Plymouth folk had seen and suffered. You had to endure something yourself before it touched you. He walked back along the lane and crossed the stile to his cottage. He found his wife in the kitchen with young Johnny.

❷

"See anyone?" she asked.

"Mrs. Trigg and Jim," he answered. "I don't think they believed me. Anyway, nothing wrong up there."

"You might take the birds away," she said. "I daren't go into the room to make the beds until you do. I'm scared."

▼ **Critical Viewing** Compare and contrast the mood of the painting with the mood of the story so far. [Compare and Contrast]

❸

Landscape From a Dream, 1936-38, Paul Nash, Tate Gallery, London

 Humanities: Art

Landscape From a Dream, 1936–1938, by Paul Nash.

This eerie, dreamlike landscape populated only by a bird, its reflection, and another distant bird in the sky seems to illustrate both the mood and subject matter of du Maurier's story.

Paul Nash (1889–1946) was an English painter who lived through both World War I and World War II. He enlisted in the army

in 1914, and was appointed an official war artist in 1917 and again in 1940. Nash's paintings from the middle 1930's are mostly landscapes in deep perspective in which unlikely objects are brought together in a dreamlike atmosphere.

Use these questions for discussion:
1. How does the mirror reflection convey an ominous mood? *The perplexing blending of reflection and reality is bewildering*

and disturbing to the viewer, and suggests that things are confused and not as they should be.

2. How does the painting reflect the content and theme of "The Birds"? *Content: It shows a harsh, barren landscape in which birds are the only living creatures. Theme: It depicts nature as threatening and confusing, rather than safe and predictable.*

"Nothing to scare you now," said Nat. "They're dead, aren't they?"

He went up with a sack and dropped the stiff bodies into it, one by one. Yes, there were fifty of them, all told. Just the ordinary, common birds of the hedgerow, nothing as large even as a thrush. It must have been fright that made them act the way they did. Blue tits, wrens—it was incredible to think of the power of their small beaks jabbing at his face and hands the night before. He took the sack out into the garden and was faced now with a fresh problem. The ground was too hard to dig. It was frozen solid, yet no snow had fallen, nothing had happened in the past hours but the coming of the east wind. It was unnatural, queer. The weather prophets must be right. The change was something connected with the Arctic Circle.

The wind seemed to cut him to the bone as he stood there uncertainly, holding the sack. He could see the white-capped seas breaking down under in the bay. He decided to take the birds to the shore and bury them.

When he reached the beach below the headland he could scarcely stand, the force of the east wind was so strong. It hurt to draw breath, and his bare hands were blue. Never had he known such cold, not in all the bad winters he could remember. It was low tide. He crunched his way over the shingle[4] to the softer sand and then, his back to the wind, ground a pit in the sand with his heel. He meant to drop the birds into it, but as he opened up the sack the force of the wind carried them, lifted them, as though in flight again, and they were blown away from him along the beach, tossed like feathers, spread and scattered, the bodies of the fifty frozen birds. There was something ugly in the sight. He did not

4. **shingle** *n.*: Area of beach covered with water-worn gravel.

like it. The dead birds were swept away from him by the wind.

"The tide will take them when it turns," he said to himself.

He looked out to sea and watched the crested breakers, combing green. They rose stiffly, curled, and broke again, and because it was ebb tide the roar was distant, more remote, lacking the sound and thunder of the flood.

Then he saw them. The gulls. Out there, riding the seas.

What he had thought at first to be the whitecaps of the waves were gulls. Hundreds, thousands, tens of thousands . . . They rose and fell in the trough of the seas, heads to the wind, like a mighty fleet at anchor, waiting on the tide. To eastward, and to the west, the gulls were there. They stretched as far as his eye could reach, in close formation, line upon line. Had the sea been still they would have covered the bay like a white cloud, head to head, body packed to body. Only the east wind, whipping the sea to breakers, hid them from the shore.

> ◆ **Literary Focus**
> What might this deceptively calm scene foreshadow?

Nat turned and, leaving the beach, climbed the steep path home. Someone should know of this. Someone should be told. Something was happening, because of the east wind and the weather, that he did not understand. He wondered if he should go to the call box by the bus stop and ring up the police. Yet what could they do? What could anyone do? Tens of thousands of gulls riding the sea there in the bay because of storm, because of hunger. The police would think him mad, or drunk, or take the statement from him with great calm. "Thank you. Yes, the matter has already been reported. The hard weather is driving the birds inland in great numbers." Nat looked about him. Still no sign of any other bird. Perhaps the cold had sent them all

The Birds ◆ 53

53

Customize for
Less Proficient Readers

Check students' understanding of the story by having them explain why the information in the pull-out quotation is an essential detail in the story. *Students should note that the passage is important because it highlights the fact that the danger posed by the birds is widespread and very real.*

◆ Critical Thinking

❶ Make a Judgment How do students think listeners would respond to the radio announcement? Why? *They would probably be calmed by it and believe it, since it gives an explanation that sounds scientific.*

❷ Clarification Point out to students that Nat knows gulls eat fish, so he cannot accept the radio announcer's statement that they are hungry because of the cold weather. Nat's knowledge would lead him to believe that the gulls are motivated by something more sinister than hunger.

◆ Literary Focus

❸ Foreshadowing Ask students to tell what Nat's thoughts about the gulls might foreshadow. *Nat knows that gulls are larger and stronger than robins and sparrows; they could break through windows. His thoughts might foreshadow this possibility.*

❹ Clarification Explain that blackout boards were boards that were placed over windows during bombing raids in World War II. They ensured that no light would show from indoors and give the Germans a target at which to aim.

---

from upcountry? As he drew near to the cottage his wife came to meet him at the door. She called to him, excited. "Nat," she said, "it's on the wireless. They've just read out a special news bulletin. I've written it down."

"What's on the wireless?" he said.

"About the birds," she said. "It's not only here, it's everywhere. In London, all over the country. Something has happened to the birds."

Together they went into the kitchen. He read the piece of paper lying on the table.

❶ "Statement from the Home Office at 11 A.M. today. Reports from all over the country are coming in hourly about the vast quantity of birds flocking above towns, villages, and outlying districts, causing obstruction and damage and even attacking individuals. It is thought that the Arctic airstream, at present covering the British Isles, is causing birds to migrate south in immense numbers, and that intense hunger may drive these birds to attack human beings. Householders are warned to see to their windows, doors, and chimneys, and to take reasonable precautions for the safety of their children. A further statement will be issued later."

A kind of excitement seized Nat; he looked at his wife in triumph.

"There you are," he said. "Let's hope they'll hear that at the farm. Mrs. Trigg will know it wasn't any story. It's true. All over the country. I've been telling myself all morning there's something wrong. And just now, down on the beach, I looked out to sea and there are gulls, thousands of them, tens of thousands—you couldn't put a pin between their heads—and they're all out there, riding on the sea, waiting."

"What are they waiting for, Nat?" she asked.

> **Householders are warned to see to their windows, doors, and chimneys, and to take reasonable precautions for the safety of their children.**

He stared at her, then looked down again at the piece of paper.

"I don't know," he said slowly. "It says here the birds are hungry." ❷

He went over to the drawer where he kept his hammer and tools.

"What are you going to do, Nat?"

"See to the windows and the chimneys too, like they tell you."

"You think they would break in, with the windows shut? Those sparrows and robins and such? Why, how could they?"

He did not answer. He was not thinking of the robins and the sparrows. He was thinking of the gulls . . . ❸

He went upstairs and worked there the rest of the morning, boarding the windows of the bedrooms, filling up the chimney bases. Good job it was his free day and he was not working at the farm. It reminded him of the old days, at the beginning of the war. He was not married then, and he had made all the black-out boards for his mother's house in Plymouth. ❹ Made the shelter too. Not that it had been of any use when the moment came. He wondered if they would take these precautions up at the farm. He doubted it. Too easygoing, Harry Trigg and his missus. Maybe they'd laugh at the whole thing. Go off to a dance or a whist drive.[5]

"Dinner's ready." She called him, from the kitchen.

"All right. Coming down."

He was pleased with his handiwork. The frames fitted nicely over the little panes and at the bases of the chimneys.

When dinner was over and his wife was washing up, Nat switched on the one

---

5. **whist drive** *n.*: A card game organized for a group.

Cross-Curricular Connection: Social Studies

During World War II, the German air force, the Luftwaffe, began attacking British Royal Air Force (RAF) bases in England. After raids in August and September of 1940, the Germans believed they had destroyed the RAF. They then began to bomb civilian targets in what was called the *Blitz*, which means "lightning" in German. The Blitz continued until May of 1941, with attacks almost every night.

Ask students what Nat's references to the war and the bombing raids add to the story. *These references encourage readers to draw a parallel between the events of the story and the terrors and horrors of war. Students might say that the events of the story are even worse than war, because in war, people are fighting a human against whom they know how to defend themselves. The attack of the birds is completely unnatural and unprecedented.*

o'clock news. The same announcement was repeated, the one which she had taken down during the morning, but the news bulletin enlarged upon it. "The flocks of birds have caused dislocation in all areas," read the announcer, "and in London the sky was so dense at ten o'clock this morning that it seemed as if the city was covered by a vast black cloud.

"The birds settled on rooftops, on window ledges, and on chimneys. The species included blackbird, thrush, the common house sparrow, and, as might be expected in the metropolis, a vast quantity of pigeons and starlings, and that frequenter of the London river, the black-headed gull. The sight has been so unusual that traffic came to a standstill in many thoroughfares, work was abandoned in shops and offices, and the streets and pavements were crowded with people standing about to watch the birds."

Various incidents were recounted, the suspected reason of cold and hunger stated again, and warnings to householders repeated. The announcer's voice was smooth and suave. Nat had the impression that this man, in particular, treated the whole business as he would an elaborate joke. There would be others like him, hundreds of them, who did not know what it was to struggle in darkness with a flock of birds. There would be parties tonight in London, like the ones they gave on election nights. People standing about, shouting and laughing . . . "Come and watch the birds!"

Nat switched off the wireless. He got up and started work on the kitchen windows. His wife watched him, young Johnny at her heels.

"What, boards for down here too?" she said. "Why, I'll have to light up before three o'clock. I see no call for boards down here."

◆ **Build Vocabulary**
recounted (ri kount′ ed) *v.*: Told in detail; narrated

"Better be sure than sorry," answered Nat. "I'm not going to take any chances."

"What they ought to do," she said, "is to call the Army out and shoot the birds. That would soon scare them off."

"Let them try," said Nat. "How'd they set about it?"

"They have the Army to the docks," she answered, "when the dockers strike. The soldiers go down and unload the ships."

"Yes," said Nat, "and the population of London is eight million or more. Think of all the buildings, all the flats and houses. Do you think they've enough soldiers to go around shooting birds from every roof?"

"I don't know. But something should be done. They ought to do something."

Nat thought to himself that "they" were no doubt considering the problem at that very moment, but whatever "they" decided to do in London and the big cities would not help the people here, three hundred miles away. Each householder must look after his own.

"How are we off for food?" he said.

"Now, Nat, whatever next?"

"Never mind. What have you got in the larder?"[6]

"It's shopping day tomorrow, you know that. I don't keep uncooked food hanging about, it goes off. Butcher doesn't call till the day after. But I can bring back something when I go in tomorrow."

Nat did not want to scare her. He thought it possible that she might not go to town tomorrow. He looked in the larder for himself, and in the cupboard where she kept her tins. They would do for a couple of days. Bread was low.

"What about the baker?"

"He comes tomorrow too."

He saw she had flour. If the baker did not call she had enough to bake one loaf.

"We'd be better off in the old days," he said, "when the women baked twice a week,

---

6. **larder** (lärd′ ər) *n.*: Place where food is kept; pantry.

The Birds ◆ 55

◆ *Literature and Your Life*

❺ Have students think of situations either in their real-life experiences or in movies or television programs they've seen in which people gathered to witness some unusual (and possibly dangerous) event. Why are people drawn to unusual events? *Students may recall seeing movies in which people gathered to witness upheavals in nature, such as a tornado or the eruption of a volcano, and they may explain that people are drawn to such events because they are curious and find the events exciting.*

◆ **Reading Strategy**

❻ **Predict** Nat predicts parties in London because of the birds. Ask students for their predictions of what would really happen in London that night. *Answers may include mass fright, panic, and destruction caused by the birds' attacks.*

❼ **Clarification** Explain that in British English, a *flat* is an apartment.

◆ **Critical Thinking**

❽ **Analyze** Ask students why they think Nat is asking his wife these questions. What is he really trying to find out? Why doesn't he come right out and say what he means? *He wants to learn how long they can last if the birds attack, but he doesn't want to terrify his wife.*

◆ Literary Focus

❶ Foreshadowing Students may respond that the circling gulls foreshadow a new movement and attack, in which humans are surrounded and the gulls "try their strength" against them.

◆ Build Grammar Skills

❷ Have students identify the two independent clauses in this sentence (there's actually a subordinate clause also). Ask them to explain why the author chose to use a semicolon rather than a comma to join them. Then ask why the coordinating conjunction *but* is used rather than *and*. *The semicolon signals a more pronounced pause than a comma, increasing the dramatic effect of the second clause. The conjunction "but" rather than "and" is appropriate here because the birds were not looking for smaller species to prey on; rather, they are on a mission to attack human beings.*

Comprehension Check ☑

❸ What does Nat believe the different groups of birds are going to do? *He believes that the birds of prey have been ordered to attack the people who live in towns and cities, while the less aggressive gulls have been assigned the people who live in rural areas.*

and had pilchards[7] salted, and there was food for a family to last a siege, if need be."

"I've tried the children with tinned fish, they don't like it," she said.

Nat went on hammering the boards across the kitchen windows. Candles. They were low in candles too. That must be another thing she meant to buy tomorrow. Well, it could not be helped. They must go early to bed tonight. That was, if . . .

He got up and went out of the back door and stood in the garden, looking down toward the sea. There had been no sun all day, and now, at barely three o'clock, a kind of darkness had already come, the sky <u>sullen</u>, heavy, colorless like salt. He could hear the vicious sea drumming on the rocks. He walked down the path, halfway to the beach. And then he stopped. He could see the tide had turned. The rock that had shown in midmorning was now covered, but it was not the sea that held his eyes. The gulls had risen. They were circling, hundreds of them, thousands of them, lifting their wings against the wind. It was the gulls that made the darkening of the sky. And they were silent. They made not a sound. They just went on soaring and circling, rising, falling, trying their strength against the wind.

> ◆ **Literary Focus**
> ❶ What might the circling gulls foreshadow?

Nat turned. He ran up the path, back to the cottage.

"I'm going for Jill," he said. "I'll wait for her at the bus stop."

"What's the matter?" asked his wife. "You've gone quite white."

"Keep Johnny inside," he said. "Keep the door shut. Light up now, and draw the curtains."

"It's only just gone three," she said.

"Never mind. Do what I tell you."

He looked inside the tool shed outside the back door. Nothing there of much use.

---

7. **pilchards** (pil´ cherdz) *n.*: Small fish similar to sardines.

56 ◆ *Spine Tinglers*

A spade was too heavy, and a fork no good. He took the hoe. It was the only possible tool, and light enough to carry.

He started walking up the lane to the bus stop, and now and again glanced back over his shoulder.

The gulls had risen higher now, their circles were broader, wider, they were spreading out in huge formation across the sky.

He hurried on; although he knew the bus would not come to the top of the hill before four o'clock he had to hurry. He passed no one on the way. He was glad of this. No time to stop and chatter.

At the top of the hill he waited. He was much too soon. There was half an hour still to go. The east wind came whipping across the fields from the higher ground. He stamped his feet and blew upon his hands. In the distance he could see the clay hills, white and clean, against the heavy pallor of the sky. Something black rose from behind them, like a smudge at first, then widening, becoming deeper, and the smudge became a cloud, and the cloud divided again into five other clouds, spreading north, east, south, and west, and they were not clouds at all; they were birds. He watched them travel across the sky, and as one section passed overhead, within two or three hundred feet of him, he knew, from their speed, they were bound inland, upcountry; they had no business with the people here on the peninsula. They were rooks, crows, jackdaws, magpies, jays, all birds that usually preyed upon the smaller species; but this afternoon they were bound on some other mission. ❷

"They've been given the towns," thought Nat; "they know what they have to do. We don't matter so much here. The gulls will serve for us. The others go to the towns." ❸

He went to the call box, stepped inside, and lifted the receiver. The exchange would do. They would pass the message on.

"I'm speaking from Highway," he said, "by the bus stop. I want to report large for-

---

Beyond the Classroom

Career Connection

Ornithology In this story, Nat can identify many birds and knows their habits. Ornithologists are scientists who make a career of studying birds and their behavior. Have interested students find out what background an ornithologist must have.

Discuss with students how Nat acquired his knowledge of birds—through formal education or from experience? How does his knowledge help him in his attempt to defend his home and his family?

mations of birds traveling upcountry. The gulls are also forming in the bay."

"All right," answered the voice, laconic, weary.

"You'll be sure and pass this message on to the proper quarter?"

"Yes . . . yes . . ." Impatient now, fed-up. The buzzing note resumed.

"She's another," thought Nat, "she doesn't care. Maybe she's had to answer calls all day. She hopes to go to the pictures tonight. She'll squeeze some fellow's hand and point up at the sky and say 'Look at all them birds!' She doesn't care."

The bus came lumbering up the hill. Jill climbed out, and three or four other children. The bus went on towards the town.

❹ "What's the hoe for, Dad?"

They crowded around him, laughing, pointing.

"I just brought it along," he said. "Come on now, let's get home. It's cold, no hanging about. Here, you. I'll watch you across the fields, see how fast you can run."

He was speaking to Jill's companions, who came from different families, living in the council houses.[8] A short cut would take them to the cottages.

"We want to play a bit in the lane," said one of them.

"No, you don't. You go off home or I'll tell your Mammy."

They whispered to one another, round-eyed, then scuttled off across the fields. Jill stared at her father, her mouth sullen.

"We always play in the lane," she said.

"Not tonight, you don't," he said. "Come on now, no dawdling."

He could see the gulls now, circling the fields, coming in toward the land. Still silent. Still no sound.

---

8. **council houses** *n*.: Housing units built by the government.

◆ Build Vocabulary

sullen (sul´ ən) *adj*.: Gloomy; dismal

"Look, Dad, look over there, look at all the gulls."

"Yes. Hurry, now."

"Where are they flying to? Where are they going?"

"Upcountry, I dare say. Where it's warmer."

He seized her hand and dragged her after him along the lane.

"Don't go so fast. I can't keep up."

The gulls were copying the rooks and crows. They were spreading out in formation across the sky. They headed, in bands of thousands, to the four compass points.

"Dad, what is it? What are the gulls doing?"

They were not intent upon their flight, as the crows, as the jackdaws had been. They still circled overhead. Nor did they fly so high. It was as though they waited upon some signal. As though some decision had **❺** yet to be given. The order was not clear.

"Do you want me to carry you, Jill? Here, come pick-a-back."

This way he might put on speed; but he was wrong. Jill was heavy. She kept slipping. And was crying too. His sense of urgency, of fear, had communicated itself to the child.

> **◆ Reading Strategy**
> Predict why Nat is hurrying his daughter along frantically. **❻**

"I wish the gulls would go away. I don't like them. They're coming closer to the lane."

He put her down again. He started running, swinging Jill after him. As they went past the farm turning he saw the farmer backing his car out of the garage. Nat called to him.

"Can you give us a lift?" he said.

"What's that?"

Mr. Trigg turned in the driving seat and stared at them. Then a smile came to his cheerful, rubicund face.

"It looks as though we're in for some fun," he said. "Have you seen the gulls? Jim

The Birds ◆ 57

◆ **Critical Thinking**

❹ Analyze Encourage students to explain why Nat avoids answering Jill's question. *He doesn't want to frighten her or her companions.*

◆ **Reading Strategy**

❺ Predict Ask students to predict what the "order" will be. *Predictions should indicate that the "order" will be to attack and kill the humans.*

◆ **Reading Strategy**

❻ Predict Students should predict that Nat is hurrying because he believes the gulls will attack soon.

① **Analyze Character** Ask students to describe Mr. Trigg's attitude toward the birds. Why wouldn't Nat want to join him? *Mr. Trigg thinks that getting rid of the birds will be easy and fun. Nat knows that shooting at them won't help.*

◆ **Critical Thinking**

② **Interpret** Ask students to explain how Nat's knowledge of birds and their habits increases his awareness of the danger his family faces. *He knows that the black-backed gulls are smart and vicious, and since they are leading the attack, he knows the danger is extreme.*

③ **Clarification** Explain that the story was written during the Cold War, the period after World War II and the building of the Berlin Wall. During this time, the Soviet Union, which included Russia, was seen as a threat to Western Europe. Discuss how the idea that the Russians had poisoned the birds could result from fears that grew up during this period.

◆ **Reading Strategy**

④ **Predict** Possible prediction: The farmer will be attacked by the birds and killed; his attitude is too careless.

① and I are going to take a crack at them. Everyone's gone bird-crazy, talking of nothing else. I hear you were troubled in the night. Want a gun?"

Nat shook his head.

The small car was packed. There was just room for Jill, if she crouched on top of petrol tins on the back seat.

"I don't want a gun," said Nat, "but I'd be obliged if you'd run Jill home. She's scared of the birds."

He spoke briefly. He did not want to talk in front of Jill.

"O.K.," said the farmer, "I'll take her home. Why don't you stop behind and join the shooting match? We'll make the feathers fly."

Jill climbed in, and turning the car, the driver sped up the lane. Nat followed after. Trigg must be crazy. What use was a gun against a sky of birds?

Now Nat was not responsible for Jill, he had time to look about him. The birds were circling still above the fields. Mostly herring gull, but the black-backed gull amongst them. Usually they kept apart. Now they were united. Some bond had brought them together. It was the black-backed gull that **②** attacked the smaller birds, and even new-born lambs, so he'd heard. He'd never seen it done. He remembered this now, though, looking above him in the sky. They were coming in towards the farm. They were circling lower in the sky, and the black-backed gulls were to the front, the black-backed gulls were leading. The farm, then, was their target. They were making for the farm.

Nat increased his pace toward his own cottage. He saw the farmer's car turn and come back along the lane. It drew up beside him with a jerk.

"The kid has run inside," said the farmer. "Your wife was watching for her. Well, what do you make of it? They're saying in town **③** the Russians have done it. The Russians have poisoned the birds."

"How could they do that?" asked Nat.

"Don't ask me. You know how stories get around. Will you join my shooting match?"

"No, I'll get along home. The wife will be worried else."

"My missus says if you could eat gull there'd be some sense in it," said Trigg. "We'd have roast gull, baked gull, and pickle 'em into the bargain. You wait until I let off a few barrels into the brutes. That'll scare 'em."

"Have you boarded your windows?" asked Nat.

"No. Lot of nonsense. They like to scare you on the wireless. I've had more to do today than to go round boarding up my windows."

"I'd board them now, if I were you."

"Garn. You're windy. Like to come to our place to sleep?"

"No, thanks all the same."

"All right. See you in the morning. Give you a gull breakfast."

The farmer grinned and turned his car to the farm entrance.

Nat hurried on. Past the little wood, past the old barn, and then across the stile to the remaining field.

As he jumped the stile he heard the whir of wings. A black-backed gull dived down at him from the sky, missed, swerved in flight, and rose to dive again. In a moment it was joined by others, six, seven, a dozen, black-backed and herring mixed. Nat dropped his hoe. The hoe was useless. Covering his head with his arms, he ran toward the cottage. They kept coming at him from the air, silent save for the beating wings. The terrible, fluttering wings. He could feel the blood on his hands, his wrists, his neck. Each stab of a swooping beak tore his flesh. If only he could keep them from his eyes. Nothing else mattered. He must keep them from his eyes. They had not learned yet how to cling to a shoulder, how to rip cloth- **⑤**

⑤ ing, how to dive in mass upon the head, upon the body. But with each dive, with each attack, they became bolder. And they had no thought for themselves. When they dived low and missed, they crashed, bruised and broken, on the ground. As Nat ran he stumbled, kicking their spent bodies in front of him.

⑥ He found the door; he hammered upon it with his bleeding hands. Because of the boarded windows no light shone. Everything was dark.

"Let me in," he shouted, "it's Nat. Let me in."

He shouted loud to make himself heard above the whir of the gulls' wings.

Then he saw the gannet, poised for the dive, above him in the sky. The gulls circled, retired, soared, one after another, against the wind. Only the gannet re-mained. One single gannet above him in the

⑦ sky. The wings folded suddenly to its body. It dropped like a stone. Nat screamed, and

the door opened. He stumbled across the threshold, and his wife threw her weight against the door.

They heard the thud of the gannet as it fell.

His wife dressed his wounds. They were not deep. The backs of his hands had suf-fered most, and his wrists. Had he not worn a cap they would have reached his head. As to the gannet . . . the gannet could have split his skull.

The children were crying, of course. They had seen the blood on their father's hands.

"It's all right now," he told them. "I'm not hurt. Just a few scratches. You play with Johnny, Jill. Mammy will wash these cuts."

He half shut the door to the scullery so that they could not see. His wife was ashen. She began running water from the sink.

▼ **Critical Viewing** What do the scraggly tree and the scores of birds in the photograph convey about the setting of this story? [Infer] **⑧**

The Birds ◆ 59

◆**Reading Strategy**

⑤ Predict Ask students to predict what the word "yet" implies about the birds. *The birds will soon learn to cling, rip, and dive in mass.*

◆**Build Grammar Skills**

⑥ Have students identify the main clauses in this compound sentence. Then ask them why they think the author used a semicolon rather than a conjunction to connect the clauses. *The semicolon provides a pause in the sentence; in the story, the pause between finding the door and hammer-ing on it must have seemed endless to Nat. A conjunction here would interrupt that "endless" pause.*

⑦ Clarification Explain to students that gannets, like gulls, are seabirds. They are larger than gulls, and their bills are long, tapered, and sharply pointed. They plunge headfirst at high speeds into the sea to catch fish. Gannets can dive from heights of 60 to 100 feet.

▶**Critical Viewing**◀

⑧ Infer The elements in this photo-graph indicate a bleak, unfriendly set-ting, overrun with birds, like the set-ting in the story.

Customize for
Musical/Rhythmic Learners
Challenge these students to note how the author uses sound in this section of the story to heighten sus-pense. Have them list words that name sounds the birds make and note how the sounds become pro-gressively more menacing. *Sliding, scraping, shuffling, thud, tapping, splinter, scraping, jostling*

Customize for
Visual/Spatial Learners
Encourage these students to carefully study the details in the photograph on this page and to use the photo-graph to help them envision the action of the story.

◆ *Literature and Your Life*

❶ Have students compare the details in this passage to those in action or horror movies they've seen. *Students may note that they've seen horror movies in which a community or a country is caught off-guard at the time when a disastrous event is about to occur.*

◆ **Reading Strategy**

❷ Predict Have students predict whether the birds will prove Nat wrong by finding a way to get inside. *Based on horror movies they've seen or horror stories they've read, students may predict that Nat has overlooked something and that the birds will find a way in.*

"I saw them overhead," she whispered. "They began collecting just as Jill ran in with Mr. Trigg. I shut the door fast, and it jammed. That's why I couldn't open it at once when you came."

"Thank God they waited for me," he said. "Jill would have fallen at once. One bird alone would have done it."

Furtively, so as not to alarm the children, they whispered together as she bandaged his hands and the back of his neck.

"They're flying inland," he said, "thousands of them. Rooks, crows, all the bigger birds. I saw them from the bus stop. They're making for the towns."

"But what can they do, Nat?"

"They'll attack. Go for everyone out in the streets. Then they'll try the windows, the chimneys."

❶ "Why don't the authorities do something? Why don't they get the Army, get machine guns, anything?"

"There's been no time. Nobody's prepared. We'll hear what they have to say on the six o'clock news."

Nat went back into the kitchen, followed by his wife. Johnny was playing quietly on the floor. Only Jill looked anxious.

"I can hear the birds," she said. "Listen, Dad."

Nat listened. Muffled sounds came from the windows, from the door. Wings brushing the surface, sliding, scraping, seeking a way of entry. The sound of many bodies, pressed together, shuffling on the sills. Now and again came a thud, a crash, as some bird dived and fell. "Some of them will kill themselves that way," he thought, "but not enough. Never enough."

"All right," he said aloud. "I've got boards over the windows, Jill. The birds can't get in."

❷ He went and examined all the windows. His work had been thorough. Every gap

was closed. He would make extra certain, however. He found wedges, pieces of old tin, strips of wood and metal, and fastened them at the sides to reinforce the boards. His hammering helped to deafen the sound of the birds, the shuffling, the tapping, and more ominous—he did not want his wife or the children to hear it—the splinter of cracked glass.

"Turn on the wireless," he said, "let's have the wireless."

This would drown the sound also. He went upstairs to the bedrooms and reinforced the windows there. Now he could hear the birds on the roof, the scraping of claws, a sliding, jostling sound.

He decided they must sleep in the kitchen, keep up the fire, bring down the mattresses, and lay them out on the floor. He was afraid of the bedroom chimneys. The boards he had placed at the chimney bases might give way. In the kitchen they would be safe because of the fire. He would have to make a joke of it. Pretend to the children they were playing at camp. If the worst happened, and the birds forced an entry down the bedroom chimneys, it would be hours, days perhaps, before they could break down the doors. The birds would be imprisoned in the bedrooms. They could do no harm there. Crowded together, they would stifle and die.

He began to bring the mattresses downstairs. At sight of them his wife's eyes widened in apprehension. She thought the birds had already broken in upstairs.

> Muffled sounds came from the windows, from the door. Wings brushing the surface, sliding, scraping, seeking a way of entry.

◆ **Build Vocabulary**

furtively (fʉr´ tiv lē) *adv.*: Stealthily, so as to avoid being heard

imperative (im per´ ə tiv) *adj.*: Absolutely necessary; urgent

❸ "All right," he said cheerfully, "we'll all sleep together in the kitchen tonight. More cozy here by the fire. Then we shan't be worried by those silly old birds tapping at the windows."

He made the children help him rearrange the furniture, and he took the precaution of moving the dresser, with his wife's help, across the window. It fitted well. It was an added safeguard. The mattresses could now be laid, one beside the other, against the wall where the dresser had stood.

"We're safe enough now," he thought. "We're snug and tight, like an air-raid shelter. We can hold out. It's just the food that worries me. Food, and coal for the fire.
❹ We've enough for two or three days, not more. By that time . . ."

No use thinking ahead as far as that. And they'd be giving directions on the wireless. People would be told what to do. And now, in the midst of many problems, he realized that it was dance music only coming
❺ over the air. Not Children's Hour, as it should have been. He glanced at the dial. Yes, they were on the Home Service all right. Dance records. He switched to the Light program. He knew the reason. The usual programs had been abandoned. This only happened at exceptional times. Elections and such. He tried to remember if it had happened in the war, during the heavy raids on London. But of course. The B.B.C.[9] was not stationed in London during the war. The programs were broadcast from other, temporary quarters. "We're better off here," he thought; "we're better off here in the kitchen, with the windows and the doors boarded, than they are up in the towns. Thank God we're not in the towns."

At six o'clock the records ceased. The time signal was given. No matter if it scared the children, he must hear the news. There was a pause after the pips.[10] Then the an-

nouncer spoke. His voice was solemn, grave. Quite different from midday.

"This is London," he said. "A National
❻ Emergency was proclaimed at four o'clock this afternoon. Measures are being taken to safeguard the lives and property of the population, but it must be understood that these are not easy to effect immediately, owing to the unforeseen and unparalleled nature of the present crisis. Every householder must take precautions to his own building, and where several people live together, as in flats and apartments, they must unite to do the utmost they can to prevent entry. It is absolutely imperative that every individual stay indoors tonight and that no one at all remain on the streets, or roads, or anywhere withoutdoors.[11] The birds, in vast numbers, are attacking anyone on sight, and have already begun an assault upon buildings; but these, with due care, should be impenetrable. The population is asked to remain calm and not to panic. Owing to the exceptional nature of the emergency, there will be no further transmission from any broadcasting station until 7 A.M. tomorrow."

They played the National Anthem. Nothing more happened. Nat switched off the set. He looked at his wife. She stared back at him.

"What's it mean?" said Jill. "What did the news say?"

"There won't be any more programs tonight," said Nat. "There's been a breakdown at the B.B.C."

"Is it the birds?" asked Jill. "Have the birds done it?"

> ◆ **Literature and Your Life**
> ❼
> Has a state of emergency ever been declared in your community because of a natural calamity, such as a blizzard or a hurricane?

❽

---

9. B.B.C.: British Broadcasting Corporation.
10. pips *n.*: Beeping sounds that indicate the time.

11. withoutdoors *adv.*: Old-fashioned variation of outdoors.

The Birds ◆ 61

Customize for
Visual/Spatial Learners

The painting on this page should help these students appreciate the ominous mood of the story at this point. Encourage students to jot down in their notebooks a few words describing the mood of the painting, along with a few words describing the mood of the story at this point. Then have them compare the two moods. *Students should note that the moods of both the story and the painting are gloomy and threatening.*

Listening to Literature
Audiocassettes This is a good time to play the audiocassette recording of "The Birds," up to this point. Hearing the story will provide a good review, clarify unclear details, and build the suspense to this point.

"No," said Nat, "it's just that everyone's very busy, and then of course they have to get rid of the birds, messing everything up, in the towns. Well, we can manage without the wireless for one evening."

"I wish we had a gramophone,"[12] said Jill, "that would be better than nothing."

She had her face turned to the dresser backed against the windows. Try as they did to ignore it, they were all aware of the shuffling, the stabbing, the persistent beating and sweeping of wings.

"We'll have supper early," suggested Nat, "something for a treat. Ask Mammy. Toasted cheese, eh? Something we all like?"

---

12. gramophone (gram´ ə fōn´) *n.*: Phonograph; record player.

He winked and nodded at his wife. He wanted the look of dread, of apprehension, to go from Jill's face.

He helped with the supper, whistling, singing, making as much clatter as he could, and it seemed to him that the shuffling and the tapping were not so intense as they had been at first. Presently he went up to the bedrooms and listened, and he no longer heard the jostling for place upon the roof.

"They've got reasoning powers," he thought; "they know it's hard to break in here. They'll try elsewhere. They won't waste their time with us."

Supper passed without incident, and then, when they were clearing away, they

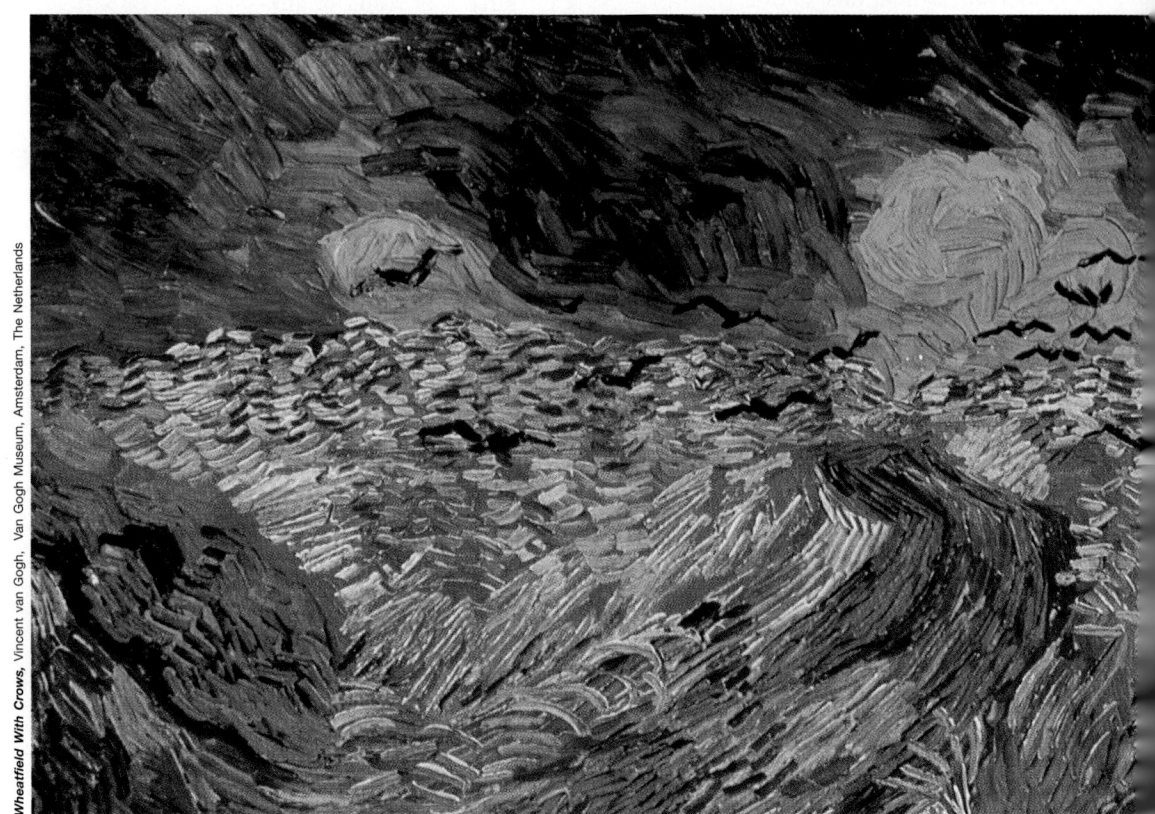

Wheatfield With Crows, Vincent van Gogh, Van Gogh Museum, Amsterdam, The Netherlands

62 ◆ Spine Tinglers

Humanities: Art

Wheatfield With Crows, 1890, by Vincent van Gogh.

Born in Holland, Vincent van Gogh (1853–1890) was a self-taught artist who struggled with loneliness and despair much of his short life. His great fame came only after his death.

Van Gogh worked in the Impressionist technique of dots and strokes of pure color. His use of thick strokes of color suited such ordinary sights as gnarled tree branches, cornfields, and the shape of the cypress tree for which he is known. After working in and around Paris for some years, van Gogh traveled to southern France in 1888, in search of the intense light and color of the south. He painted *Wheatfield With Crows* (19 ⅞ x 39 ½ inches) in July of 1890 when he was in Auvers. Critics have looked for symbolism in the crows, the sky, and the paths that seem to end abruptly without providing any exit from the field.

Use these questions for discussion:

1. Point out the details or the elements of this painting that might give it a feeling of menace. *The dark and stormy sky, the flock of birds circling or flying toward the viewer, and paths that don't lead out of the field create a disturbing and threatening feeling.*

2. How might Nat in "The Birds" respond to this scene? *Knowing the ways of birds and being able to recognize weather patterns, Nat could determine whether the elements in this scene were normal occurrences or really a threat to beware of.*

heard a new sound, droning, familiar, a sound they all knew and understood.

His wife looked up at him, her face alight. "It's planes," she said; "they're sending out planes after the birds. That's what I said they ought to do all along. That will get them. Isn't that gunfire? Can't you hear guns?"

❶ It might be gunfire out at sea. Nat could not tell. Big naval guns might have an effect upon the gulls out at sea, but the gulls were inland now. The guns couldn't shell the shore because of the population.

"It's good, isn't it," said his wife, "to hear the planes?" And Jill, catching her enthusiasm, jumped up and down with Johnny. "The planes will get the birds. The planes will shoot them."

Just then they heard a crash about two miles distant, followed by a second, then a third. The droning became more distant, passed away out to sea.

"What was that?" asked his wife. "Were they dropping bombs on the birds?"

"I don't know," answered Nat. "I don't think so."

He did not want to tell her that the sound they had heard was the crashing of aircraft. It was, he had no doubt, a venture on the part of the authorities to send out <u>recon-naissance</u> forces, but they might have known the venture was suicidal. What ❷ could aircraft do against birds that flung themselves to death against propeller and fuselage, but hurtle to the ground themselves? This was being tried now, he supposed, over the whole country. And at a cost. Someone high up had lost his head.

"Where have the planes gone, Dad?" asked Jill.

"Back to base," he said. "Come on, now, time to tuck down for bed."

It kept his wife occupied, undressing the children before the fire, seeing to the bedding, one thing and another, while he went round the cottage again, making sure that nothing had worked loose. There was no further drone of aircraft, and the naval guns had ceased. "Waste of life and effort," Nat said to himself. "We can't destroy enough of them that way. Cost too heavy. There's always gas. Maybe they'll try spraying with gas, mustard gas. We'll be warned first, of course, if they do. There's one thing, the best brains of the country will be on to it tonight."

◆ Build Vocabulary

reconnaissance (ri kän´ ə səns) *adj.*: Exploratory in nature, as when examining or observing to seek information

◀ **Critical Viewing** Think of a name for this painting that describes the feeling it conveys. ❸ [Describe]

The Birds ◆ 63

Lead less proficient readers to
understand that Nat has figured out
that the birds attack when the tide is
high and retreat when the tide is
low. Explain that in every twenty-four
hours there are two high tides and
two low tides, making two times a
day that the birds will attack and
retreat.

◆ **Critical Thinking**

❶ Apply Have students discuss
whether they think that most people
in our society share Nat's faith in science. Why do people place so much
trust in science? *Students will probably
respond that most people today do
share Nat's faith in science, because science has demonstrated the ability to
solve just about any problem.*

◆ **Reading Strategy**

❷ Nat and his family can rest while
the tide is out. Have students predict
what the birds will be doing during
this time. *They will be resting, feeding,
gathering their strength, and planning.*

◆ **Critical Thinking**

❸ Analyze What does Nat's constant planning reveal about an emergency? Is Nat the type of person students would want to be with if they
were faced with an emergency? *Nat's
constant planning reveals that he has
an analytical mind. Students will probably respond that Nat is the type of person they'd want to be with in the face
of an emergency, because he retains his
composure and comes up with solutions
to problems.*

❶ Somehow the thought reassured him. He
had a picture of scientists, naturalists,
technicians, and all those chaps they called
the back-room boys, summoned to a council; they'd be working on the problem now.
This was not a job for the government, for
the chiefs of staff—they would merely carry
out the orders of the scientists.

"They'll have to be ruthless," he thought.
"Where the trouble's worst they'll have to
risk more lives, if they use gas. All the livestock, too, and the soil—all contaminated.
As long as everyone doesn't panic. That's the
trouble. People panicking, losing their heads.
The B.B.C. was right to warn us of that."

Upstairs in the bedrooms all was quiet.
No further scraping and stabbing at the
windows. A lull in battle. Forces regroup-
ing. Wasn't that what they called it in the
old wartime bulletins? The wind hadn't
dropped, though. He could still hear it roaring in the chimneys. And the sea breaking
down on the shore. Then he remembered
the tide. The tide would be on the turn.
Maybe the lull in battle was because of the
tide. There was some law the birds obeyed,
and it was all to do with the east wind and
the tide.

He glanced at his watch. Nearly eight
o'clock. It must have gone high water an
hour ago. That explained the lull: the birds
attacked with the flood tide. It might not
work that way inland, upcountry, but it
seemed as if it was so this way on the
coast. He reckoned the time limit in his
head. They had six hours to go without at-
❷ tack. When the tide turned again, around
one-twenty in the morning, the birds would
come back . . .

There were two things he could do. The
first to rest, with his wife and the children,
and all of them snatch what sleep they
could, until the small hours. The second to
go out, see how they were faring at the
farm, see if the telephone was still working
there, so that they might get news from the
exchange.

He called softly to his wife, who had just
settled the children. She came halfway up
the stairs and he whispered to her.

"You're not to go," she said at once,
"you're not to go and leave me alone with
the children. I can't stand it."

Her voice rose hysterically. He hushed
her, calmed her.

"All right," he said, "all right. I'll wait till
morning. And we'll get the wireless bulletin
then too, at seven. But in the morning,
when the tide ebbs again, I'll try for the
farm, and they may let us have bread and
potatoes, and milk too."

His mind was busy again, planning
against emergency. They would not have
milked, of course, this evening. The cows
would be standing by the gate, waiting in
the yard, with the household inside, bat-
tened behind boards, as they were here at **❸**
the cottage. That is, if they had time to take
precautions. He thought of the farmer,
Trigg, smiling at him from the car. There
would have been no shooting party, not
tonight.

The children were asleep. His wife, still
clothed, was sitting on her mattress. She
watched him, her eyes nervous.

"What are you going to do?" she
whispered.

He shook his head for silence. Softly,
stealthily, he opened the back door and
looked outside.

It was pitch dark. The wind was blowing
harder than ever, coming in steady gusts,
icy, from the sea. He kicked at the step outside the door. It was heaped with birds.
There were dead birds everywhere. Under
the windows, against the walls. These were
the suicides, the divers, the ones with broken necks. Wherever he looked he saw dead
birds. No trace of the living. The living had
flown seaward with the turn of the tide. The
gulls would be riding the seas now, as they
had done in the forenoon.

In the far distance, on the hill where the
tractor had been two days before, some-

64 ◆ *Spine Tinglers*

Speaking and Listening Mini-Lesson

PANEL DISCUSSION
This mini-lesson supports the Speaking and
Listening activity in the Idea Bank on page
74.
Introduce the Concept Encourage students to discuss endangered animal species
and identify the issues that divide people on
the question of protecting animals. Then set
up a panel with three or four members.
Develop Background Have students find
out about specific bird species that are

endangered. Lead students to consider these
points:
• Birds can be threatened either by direct
 human action, such as hunting, or by
 human encroachment on their habitats.
• Without protection, animal species can
 become extinct.
• Humans can aid endangered species by
 passing laws, making others aware of the
 problem, and enforcing penalties for behavior that threatens the animals' welfare.

Apply the Information With this background, each panel member can become
familiar with one of these issues and can
develop arguments to express his or her
viewpoint. Remind students to include supporting facts and examples. Have the panel
present its views to the rest of the class.
Assess the Outcome Evaluate the panel
on the following points: the content of their
presentations, the strength of their arguments, and their presentation.

thing was burning. One of the aircraft that had crashed; the fire, fanned by the wind, had set light to a stack.

He looked at the bodies of the birds, and he had a notion that if he heaped them, one upon the other, on the windowsills they would make added protection for the next attack. Not much, perhaps, but something. The bodies would have to be clawed at, pecked, and dragged aside before the living birds could gain purchase on the sills and **④** attack the panes. He set to work in the darkness. It was queer; he hated touching them. The bodies were still warm and bloody. The blood matted their feathers. He felt his stomach turn, but he went on with his work. He noticed grimly that every windowpane was shattered. Only the boards had kept the birds from breaking in. He stuffed the cracked panes with the bleeding bodies of the birds.

When he had finished he went back into the cottage. He barricaded the kitchen door, made it doubly secure. He took off his bandages, sticky with the birds' blood, not with his own cuts, and put on a fresh bandage.

His wife had made him cocoa and he drank it thirstily. He was very tired.

"All right," he said, smiling, "don't worry. We'll get through."

He lay down on his mattress and closed his eyes. He slept at once. He dreamt uneasily, because through his dreams there ran a thread of something forgotten. Some **⑤** piece of work, neglected, that he should have done. Some precaution that he had known well but had not taken, and he could not put a name to it in his dreams. It was connected in some way with the burning aircraft and the stack upon the hill. He went on sleeping, though; he did not awake. It was his wife shaking his shoulder that awoke him finally.

"They've begun," she sobbed, "they've started this last hour. I can't listen to it any longer alone. There's something smelling bad too, something burning."

Then he remembered. He had forgotten to make up the fire. It was smoldering, nearly out. He got up swiftly and lit the lamp. The hammering had started at the windows and the doors, but it was not that he minded now. It was the smell of singed feathers. The smell filled the kitchen. He knew at once what it was. The birds were coming down the chimney, squeezing their way down to the kitchen range.

He got sticks and paper and put them on the embers, then reached for the can of paraffin.[13]

"Stand back," he shouted to his wife. "We've got to risk this."

He threw the paraffin onto the fire. The flame roared up the pipe, and down upon the fire fell the scorched, blackened bodies of the birds.

The children woke, crying. "What is it?" said Jill. "What's happened?"

Nat had no time to answer. He was raking the bodies from the chimney, clawing them out onto the floor. The flames still roared, and the danger of the chimney catching fire was one he had to take. The flames would send away the living birds from the chimney top. The lower joint was the difficulty, though. This was choked with the smoldering, helpless bodies of the birds caught by fire. He scarcely heeded the attack on the windows and the door: let them beat their wings, break their beaks, lose their lives, in the attempt to force an entry into his home. They would not break in. He thanked God he had one of the old cottages, with small windows, stout walls. Not like **⑦** the new council houses. Heaven help them up the lane in the new council houses.

"Stop crying," he called to the children. "There's nothing to be afraid of, stop crying."

---

13. **paraffin** (par´ ə fin) *n.:* Kerosene.

The Birds ◆ 65

◆ **Reading Strategy**
What do you predict will happen next inside the house? **⑥**

◆ **Critical Thinking**
④ Analyze How do the gruesome details in this passage add to the impact of the story? *The gruesome descriptions make the story even more disturbing and horrifying.*

◆ **Literary Focus**
⑤ Foreshadowing Ask students what they think Nat's dream of forgetting foreshadows. *The dream foreshadows that he has forgotten something important in real life.*

◆ **Reading Strategy**
⑥ Predict Students might answer: *Nat will have to find a way to build up the fire and kill the birds who are coming down the chimney.*

◆ **Reading Strategy**
⑦ Predict Ask students to predict what has happened to the people in the new council houses. *Students might answer: They have all been killed by birds that got into their houses.*

Comprehension Check ✓

1 Why does Nat encourage this bloodthirsty response to the birds' actions? *As long as the family can feel challenged and enthusiastic about beating the birds, they won't give up the fight, and they have a chance to survive.*

◆ **Critical Thinking**

2 **Analyze Character** Ask students to analyze how Nat's knowledge of birds helps him at this moment in the story. *He knows another type of bird has joined the attack, so he is able to stay one step ahead of the birds' strategy.*

He went on raking at the burning, smoldering bodies as they fell into the fire.

"This'll fetch them," he said to himself, "the draft and the flames together. We're all right, as long as the chimney doesn't catch. I ought to be shot for this. It's all my fault. Last thing, I should have made up the fire. I knew there was something."

Amid the scratching and tearing at the window boards came the sudden homely striking of the kitchen clock. Three A.M. A little more than four hours yet to go. He could not be sure of the exact time of high water. He reckoned it would not turn much before half-past seven, twenty to eight.

"Light up the Primus,"[14] he said to his wife. "Make us some tea, and the kids some cocoa. No use sitting around doing nothing."

That was the line. Keep her busy, and the children too. Move about, eat, drink; always best to be on the go.

He waited by the range. The flames were dying. But no more blackened bodies fell from the chimney. He thrust his poker up as far as it could go and found nothing. It was clear. The chimney was clear. He wiped the sweat from his forehead.

"Come on now, Jill," he said, "bring me some more sticks. We'll have a good fire going directly." She wouldn't come near him, though. She was staring at the heaped singed bodies of the birds.

"Never mind them," he said. "We'll put those in the passage when I've got the fire steady."

The danger of the chimney was over. It could not happen again, not if the fire was kept burning day and night.

"I'll have to get more fuel from the farm tomorrow," he thought. "This will never last. I'll manage, though. I can do all that with the ebb tide. It can be worked, fetching what we need, when the tide's turned. We've just got to adapt ourselves, that's all."

---

14. **Primus** (prī´ məs) *n.*: Small, portable stove.

They drank tea and cocoa and ate slices of bread and Bovril.[15] Only half a loaf left, Nat noticed. Never mind though, they'd get by.

"Stop it," said young Johnny, pointing to the windows with his spoon, "stop it, you old birds."

"That's right," said Nat, smiling, "we don't want the old beggars, do we? Had enough of 'em."

They began to cheer when they heard the thud of the suicide birds.

"There's another, Dad," cried Jill, "he's done for."

"He's had it," said Nat. "There he goes, the blighter."

This was the way to face up to it. This was the spirit. If they could keep this up, hang on like this until seven, when the first news bulletin came through, they would not have done too badly.

"Give us a cigarette," he said to his wife. "A bit of a smoke will clear away the smell of the scorched feathers."

"There's only two left in the packet," she said. "I was going to buy you some from the Co-op."

"I'll have one," he said. "t'other will keep for a rainy day."

No sense trying to make the children rest. There was no rest to be got while the tapping and the scratching went on at the windows. He sat with one arm round his wife and the other round Jill, with Johnny on his mother's lap and the blankets heaped about them on the mattress.

"You can't help admiring the beggars," he said; "they've got persistence. You'd think they'd tire of the game, but not a bit of it."

Admiration was hard to sustain. The tapping went on and on and a new rasping note struck Nat's ear, as though a sharper beak than any hitherto had come to take over from its fellows. He tried to remember the names of birds; he tried to think which

---

15. **Bovril** (bŏ´ vril) *n.*: Thick beef-flavored liquid used to make broth.

species would go for this particular job. It was not the tap of the woodpecker. That would be light and frequent. This was more serious, because if it continued long the wood would splinter as the glass had done. Then he remembered the hawks. Could the hawks have taken over from the gulls? Were there buzzards now upon the sills, using talons as well as beaks? Hawks, buzzards, kestrels, falcons—he had forgotten the birds of prey. He had forgotten the gripping power of the birds of prey. Three hours to go, and while they waited, the sound of the splintering wood, the talons tearing at the wood.

❸

> There was a soft patter on the floor of the children's bedroom. The birds had broken through . . .

Nat looked about him, seeing what furniture he could destroy to fortify the door. The windows were safe because of the dresser. He was not certain of the door. He went upstairs, but when he reached the landing he paused and listened. There was a soft patter on the floor of the children's bedroom. The birds had broken through . . . He put his ear to the door. No mistake. He could hear the rustle of wings and the light patter as they searched the floor. The other bedroom was still clear. He went into it and began bringing out the furniture, to pile at the head of the stairs should the door of the children's bedroom go. It was a preparation. It might never be needed. He could not stack the furniture against the door, because it opened inward. The only possible thing was to have it at the top of the stairs.

"Come down. Nat, what are you doing?" called his wife.

"I won't be long," he shouted. "Just making everything shipshape up here."

❹ He did not want her to come; he did not want her to hear the pattering of the feet in the children's bedroom, the brushing of those wings against the door.

At five-thirty he suggested breakfast, bacon and fried bread, if only to stop the growing look of panic in his wife's eyes and to calm the fretful children. She did not know about the birds upstairs. The bedroom, luckily, was not over the kitchen. Had it been so, she could not have failed to hear the sound of them up there, tapping the boards. And the silly, senseless thud of the suicide birds, the death and glory boys, who flew into the bedroom, smashing their heads against the walls. He knew them of old, the herring gulls. They had no brains. The black-backs were different; they knew what they were doing. So did the buzzards, the hawks . . .

❺

He found himself watching the clock, gazing at the hands that went so slowly round the dial. If his theory was not correct, if the attack did not cease with the turn of the tide, he knew they were beaten. They could not continue through the long day without air, without rest, without more fuel, without . . . His mind raced. He knew there were so many things they needed to withstand siege. They were not fully prepared. They were not ready. It might be that it would be safer in the towns after all. If he could get a message through on the farm telephone to his cousin, only a short journey by train upcountry, they might be able to hire a car. That would be quicker—hire a car between tides . . .

❻

His wife's voice, calling his name, drove away the sudden, desperate desire for sleep.

"What is it? What now?" he said sharply.

"The wireless," said his wife. "I've been watching the clock. It's nearly seven."

"Don't twist the knob," he said, impatient for the first time. "It's on the Home where it is. They'll speak from the Home."

◆ **Build Vocabulary**

fretful (fret′ fəl) *adj.*: Irritable and discontented

The Birds ◆ 67

Over and Above #13, 1964, Clarence H. Carter

They waited. The kitchen clock struck seven. There was no sound. No chimes, no music. They waited until a quarter past, switching to the Light. The result was the same. No news bulletin came through.

"We've heard wrong," he said. "They won't be broadcasting until eight o'clock."

They left it switched on, and Nat thought of the battery, wondered how much power was left in it. It was generally recharged when his wife went shopping in the town. If the battery failed they would not hear the instructions.

68 ◆ *Spine Tinglers*

▲ **Critical Viewing** What words would you use to describe the demeanor of this bird? [Describe] ❶

"It's getting light," whispered his wife. "I can't see it, but I can feel it. And the birds aren't hammering so loud."

She was right. The rasping, tearing sound grew fainter every moment. So did the shuffling, the jostling for place upon the step, upon the sills. The tide was on the turn. By eight there was no sound at all. Only the wind. The children, lulled at last

Humanities: Art

Over and Above, 1964, by Clarence H. Carter.

The cool blue and white shades and the rounded lines of this painting do little to offset the bird's threatening appearance: the reddish eyes look down menacingly, and the needle-sharp beak points downward menacingly as well, accentuated by its shadow. The size of the bird, too, adds to the feeling of danger the painting projects. The bird's head and shoulders dominate the painting, filling up almost the entire upper portion of the canvas.

Clarence H. Carter was born in Portsmouth, Ohio, in 1904. He studied at the Cleveland School of Art. His paintings are exhibited at major museums in the U.S., including the Philadelphia Museum of Art, the Cleveland Museum of Art, and, in New York, the Metropolitan Museum of Art and the Museum of Modern Art.

Use these questions for discussion:
1. How does the artist use color and shadow to create a threatening mood? *The bird is too cleanly white, and its red eyes*

seem hostile. Its sharp, curved beak appears threatening.

2. How does the title of the painting tie in with the story? *The birds fly over and above the humans, and they have set themselves up to reign over and above all others.*

3. Which of the paintings on these pages best illustrates the story as you imagined it? Give reasons for your answer. *Students' answers should be supported by reasons stressing similarities in theme, mood, or content.*

by the stillness, fell asleep. At half-past eight Nat switched the wireless off.

"What are you doing? We'll miss the news," said his wife.

"There isn't going to be any news," said Nat. "We've got to depend upon ourselves."

He went to the door and slowly pulled away the barricades. He drew the bolts and, kicking the bodies from the step outside the door, breathed the cold air. He had six working hours before him, and he knew he must reserve his strength for the right things, not waste it in any way. Food, and light, and fuel; these were the necessary things. If he could get them in sufficiency, they could endure another night.

He stepped into the garden, and as he did so he saw the living birds. The gulls had gone to ride the sea, as they had done before; they sought sea food, and the buoyancy of the tide, before they returned to the attack. Not so the land birds. They waited and watched. Nat saw them, on the hedgerows, on the soil, crowded in the trees, outside in the field, line upon line of birds, all still, doing nothing.

He went to the end of his small garden. The birds did not move. They went on watching him.

"I've got to get food," said Nat to himself. "I've got to go to the farm to find food."

He went back to the cottage. He saw to the windows and the doors. He went upstairs and opened the children's bedroom. It was empty, except for the dead birds on the floor. The living were out there, in the garden, in the fields. He went downstairs.

"I'm going to the farm," he said.

His wife clung to him. She had seen the living birds from the open door.

"Take us with you," she begged. "We can't stay here alone. I'd rather die than stay here alone."

He considered the matter. He nodded.

"Come on, then," he said. "Bring baskets, and Johnny's pram.[16] We can load up the pram."

---

16. pram *n.*: Baby carriage.

They dressed against the biting wind, wore gloves and scarves. His wife put Johnny in the pram. Nat took Jill's hand.

"The birds," she whimpered, "they're all out there in the fields."

"They won't hurt us," he said, "not in the light."

They started walking across the field towards the stile, and the birds did not move. They waited, their heads turned to the wind.

When they reached the turning to the farm, Nat stopped and told his wife to wait in the shelter of the hedge with the two children.

"But I want to see Mrs. Trigg," she protested. "There are lots of things we can borrow if they went to market yesterday; not only bread, and . . ."

"Wait here," Nat interrupted. "I'll be back in a moment."

The cows were lowing, moving restlessly in the yard, and he could see a gap in the fence where the sheep had knocked their way through, to roam unchecked in the front garden before the farmhouse. No smoke came from the chimneys. He was filled with misgiving. He did not want his wife or the children to go down to the farm.

"Don't gib[17] now," said Nat, harshly, "do what I say."

She withdrew with the pram into the hedge, screening herself and the children from the wind.

He went down alone to the farm. He pushed his way through the herd of bellowing cows, which turned this way and that, distressed, their udders full. He saw the car standing by the gate, not put away in the garage. The windows of the farmhouse were smashed. There were many dead gulls lying in the yard and around the house. The living birds perched on the group of trees behind the farm and on the roof of the house. They were quite still. They watched him.

Jim's body lay in the yard . . . what was left of it. When the birds had finished, the

---

17. gib (jib) *v.*: Hesitate.

The Birds ◆ 69

◆ Critical Thinking

❷ **Make Inferences** Ask students why Nat has decided that the family must rely on itself. *Suggested answer: He feels that either everyone else is dead or has given up. The family will get no help from outside.*

◆ Build Grammar Skills

❸ **Compound Sentences** Have students notice all the information about sea birds that is packed into this compound sentence. Why did du Maurier choose to include all the information in a single compound sentence, rather than in two separate sentences? *Students may note that providing all this information in a single sentence helps du Maurier create a striking contrast between the sea birds and the land birds, which are described in a series of short sentences.*

◆ Reading Strategy

❹ Encourage students to predict what the birds are waiting for. *They wait for the tide to turn so they can renew, and maybe finish, their attack.*

◆ *Literature and Your Life*

❺ Why do people generally want to avoid being alone when faced with a stressful situation like the one in this story? *People want to avoid being alone because they look to others for support and protection during difficult times.*

◆ Critical Thinking

❻ **Analyze Character** Nat still wants to protect his family, but something has changed. Ask students: How has he changed? What does he think he will find at the farm? *He believes the birds are winning and thinks everyone at the farm is dead.*

❶ Foreshadowing Students might answer: *Yes, although Nat is better prepared to withstand the birds' attacks, he can't fight them off forever. Sooner or later he too will succumb. Others might answer: No, the birds are not out to kill everyone. But they do intend to dominate the Earth. Nat's family may survive, but they will have to live in subjugation to the birds.*

❷ Comprehension Check ☑

What does Nat mean when he realizes the birds are gorged with food? *He means they have eaten their fill from their kills during the night.*

◆ **Critical Thinking**

❸ Analyze Why is the fact that the birds "are gorged with food" significant? *It is significant because being filled with food causes the birds to rest.*

cows had trampled him. His gun was beside him. The door of the house was shut and bolted, but as the windows were smashed it was easy to lift them and climb through. Trigg's body was close to the telephone. He must have been trying to get through to the exchange when the birds came for him. The receiver was hanging loose, the instrument torn from the wall. No sign of Mrs. Trigg. She would be upstairs. Was it any use going up? Sickened, Nat knew what he would find.

"Thank God," he said to himself, "there were no children."

◆ **Literary Focus** ❶
Do you think the deaths of everyone at the farm foreshadow a similar fate for Nat and his family? Why or why not?

He forced himself to climb the stairs, but halfway he turned and descended again. He could see her legs protruding from the open bedroom door. Beside her were the bodies of the black-backed gulls, and an umbrella, broken.

"It's no use," thought Nat, "doing anything. I've only got five hours, less than that. The Triggs would understand. I must load up with what I can find."

He tramped back to his wife and children.

"I'm going to fill up the car with stuff," he said. "I'll put coal in it, and paraffin for the Primus. We'll take it home and return for a fresh load."

"What about the Triggs?" asked his wife.

"They must have gone to friends," he said.

"Shall I come and help you, then?"

"No; there's a mess down there. Cows and sheep all over the place. Wait, I'll get the car. You can sit in it."

Clumsily he backed the car out of the yard and into the lane. His wife and the children could not see Jim's body from there.

"Stay here," he said, "never mind the pram. The pram can be fetched later. I'm going to load the car."

Her eyes watched his all the time. He believed she understood, otherwise she would have suggested helping him to find the bread and groceries.

70 ◆ Spine Tinglers

They made three journeys altogether, backwards and forwards between their cottage and the farm, before he was satisfied they had everything they needed. It was surprising, once he started thinking, how many things were necessary. Almost the most important of all was planking for the windows. He had to go round searching for timber. He wanted to renew the boards on all the windows at the cottage. Candles, paraffin, nails, tinned stuff; the list was endless. Besides all that, he milked three of the cows. The rest, poor brutes, would have to go on bellowing.

On the final journey he drove the car to the bus stop, got out, and went to the telephone box. He waited a few minutes, jangling the receiver. No good, though. The line was dead. He climbed on to a bank and looked over the countryside, but there was no sign of life at all, nothing in the fields but the waiting, watching birds. Some of them slept—he could see the beaks tucked into the feathers.

"You'd think they'd be feeding," he said to himself, "not just standing in that way."

Then he remembered. They were gorged with food. They had eaten their fill during the night. That was why they did not move this morning . . . ❷ ❸

No smoke came from the chimneys of the council houses. He thought of the children who had run across the fields the night before.

"I should have known," he thought; "I ought to have taken them home with me."

He lifted his face to the sky. It was colorless and gray. The bare trees on the landscape looked bent and blackened by the east wind. The cold did not affect the living birds waiting out there in the fields.

"This is the time they ought to get them," said Nat; "they're a sitting target now. They must be doing this all over the country. Why don't our aircraft take off now and spray them with mustard gas? What are all our chaps doing? They must know, they must see for themselves."

◆ **Workplace Skills Mini-Lesson**

SEEING A PROJECT THROUGH

This mini-lesson teaches the skills needed to take a project from start to completion.

Introduce the Concept Nat has a project to make his home as safe, well supplied, and impenetrable as possible. Have students work in groups to identify a work situation at home or on a part-time job in which they might have to plan and carry out a project.

Develop Background Have students list the steps required in carrying out a project. Guide them to include these steps on their list:

• Plan the project.
• Assign roles in carrying it out.
• Gather necessary materials.
• Execute the project.
• Stay "on task."

Apply the Information Have students tailor their lists to the specific task they have chosen. Encourage each student to choose a portion of the project for which he or she can be responsible.

Assess the Outcome Have students evaluate their plans of action. Be sure they have included all the steps necessary to carry out their projects to completion. Then encourage them to compare their plans to Nat's. Is there anything Nat could have done better?

He went back to the car and got into the driver's seat.

"Go quickly past that second gate," whispered his wife. "The postman's lying there. I don't want Jill to see."

He accelerated. The little Morris bumped and rattled along the lane. The children shrieked with laughter.

"Up-a-down, up-a-down," shouted young Johnny.

It was a quarter to one by the time they reached the cottage. Only an hour to go.

"Better have cold dinner," said Nat. "Hot up something for yourself and the children, some of that soup. I've no time to eat now. I've got to unload all this stuff."

He got everything inside the cottage. It could be sorted later. Give them all something to do during the long hours ahead. First he must see to the windows and the doors.

He went round the cottage methodically, testing every window, every door. He climbed on to the roof also, and fixed boards across every chimney, except the kitchen. The cold was so intense he could hardly bear it, but the job had to be done. Now and again he would look up, searching the sky for aircraft. None came. As he worked he cursed the inefficiency of the authorities.

"It's always the same," he muttered. "They always let us down. Muddle, muddle, from the start. No plan, no real organization. And we don't matter down here. That's what it is. The people upcountry have priority. They're using gas up there, no doubt, and all the aircraft. We've got to wait and take what comes."

He paused, his work on the bedroom chimney finished, and looked out to sea. Something was moving out there. Something gray and white amongst the breakers.

"Good old Navy," he said, "they never let us down. They're coming down-channel, they're turning in the bay."

He waited, straining his eyes, watering in the wind, towards the sea. He was wrong, though. It was not ships. The Navy was not there. The gulls were rising from the sea. The massed flocks in the fields, with ruffled feathers, rose in formation from the ground and, wing to wing, soared upwards to the sky.

◆ Reading Strategy
Predict what will happen next.

The tide had turned again.

Nat climbed down the ladder and went inside the kitchen. The family were at dinner. It was a little after two. He bolted the door, put up the barricade, and lit the lamp.

"It's nighttime," said young Johnny.

His wife had switched on the wireless once again, but no sound came from it.

"I've been all round the dial," she said, "foreign stations, and that lot. I can't get anything."

"Maybe they have the same trouble," he said, "maybe it's the same right through Europe."

She poured out a plateful of the Triggs' soup, cut him a large slice of the Triggs' bread, and spread their dripping upon it.

They ate in silence. A piece of the dripping ran down young Johnny's chin and fell on to the table.

"Manners, Johnny," said Jill, "you should learn to wipe your mouth."

The tapping began at the windows, at the door. The rustling, the jostling, the pushing for position on the sills. The first thud of the suicide gulls upon the step.

"Won't America do something?" said his wife. "They've always been our allies, haven't they? Surely America will do something?"

> The massed flocks in the fields, with ruffled feathers, rose in formation from the ground and, wing to wing, soared upwards to the sky.

The Birds ◆ 71

◆ **Critical Thinking**

❹ Interpret Ask students: Why does Nat keep looking for aircraft? Does he really believe they will come? *He has to force himself to keep hoping so he won't give up. He probably doesn't really believe it.*

◆ **Reading Strategy**

❺ Predict As the tide turns, the gulls will come to shore again, this time with the violence and strategy of a naval attack.

◆ **Critical Thinking**

❻ Infer What can students infer has happened to the rest of the broadcasting world? *Possible answer: They too have succumbed to the birds' attacks.*

◆ Critical Thinking

❶ Draw a Conclusion Nat has come to a conclusion about why the birds are attacking. What is it? Do students agree with it? *He believes they are attacking because their instincts, fueled by memories of human abuse of nature, now lead them to destroy the abusers. Students may agree because the attacks are so intelligent and well planned.*

◆ Reading Strategy

❷ Predict Have students discuss what is happening at the end of the story and make predictions about what will happen to Nat and his family. *Students may predict that Nat and his family will eventually be killed by the birds, because the birds will at some point find a way to get into the house.*

Reinforce and Extend

Answers
◆ Literature and Your Life

Reader's Response Most students will find it exciting and suspenseful because of the increasingly savage attacks by the birds and because of the ominous gatherings of birds that portend future attacks.

Thematic Focus Answers must involve situations, such as an animal rescue, in which the end result hangs in the balance until the last moment.

☑ Check Your Comprehension

1. There are more birds than usual, and the birds are more daring, with a gull actually diving down on the farmer.

2. A flock of birds had flown into the room through an open window and attacked the children.

3. Nat noticed that the birds were spreading out in formation in the sky in preparation for an attack. He wanted his daughter to get home safely without being injured by the birds.

4. The people were killed by the birds.

5. Nat brought a store of food and fuel into the house, boarded up all but one of the chimneys, and checked that the boards on the windows were secure.

Nat did not answer. The boards were strong against the windows, and on the chimneys too. The cottage was filled with stores, with fuel, with all they needed for the next few days. When he had finished dinner he would put the stuff away, stack it neatly, get everything shipshape, handy-like. His wife could help him, and the children too. They'd tire themselves out, between now and a quarter to nine, when the tide would ebb; then he'd tuck them down on their mattresses, see that they slept good and sound until three in the morning.

He had a new scheme for the windows, which was to fix barbed wire in front of the boards. He had brought a great roll of it from the farm. The nuisance was, he'd have to work at this in the dark, when the lull came between nine and three. Pity he had not thought of it before. Still, as long as the wife slept, and the kids, that was the main thing.

The smaller birds were at the window now. He recognized the light tap-tapping of their beaks and the soft brush of their wings. The hawks ignored the windows. They concentrated their attack upon the door. Nat listened to the tearing sound of splintering wood, and wondered how many million years of memory were stored in those little brains, behind the stabbing beaks, the piercing eyes, now giving them this instinct to destroy mankind with all the deft precision of machines. **❶**

"I'll smoke that last cigarette," he said to his wife. "Stupid of me, it was the one thing I forgot to bring back from the farm."

He reached for it, switched on the silent wireless. He threw the empty packet on the fire, and watched it burn. **❷**

Guide for Responding

◆ Literature and Your Life

Reader's Response Did you find this story exciting and suspenseful? Why or why not?

Thematic Focus Name at least two suspenseful situations from nature that you have either seen or heard about.

Group Activity The different types of birds in the story seem to have their own personalities and ways of behavior. With a small group, brainstorm for at least four personality traits of the gulls. Support each trait with an example of behavior from the story.

☑ Check Your Comprehension

1. According to the farmer, what was different about the birds this fall?
2. Why did a cry of terror come from the room in which the children slept?
3. Why did Nat ask the farmer to drive his daughter the rest of the way home after school?
4. What happened to the postman and the people who lived on the farm?
5. What preparations did Nat make just before the final attack of the birds was about to begin?

72 ◆ *Spine Tinglers*

Beyond the Selection

FURTHER READING

Other Works by Daphne du Maurier
Rebecca
Jamaica Inn
Don't Look Now (short stories)

Other Works on the Theme of Nature's Darker Side
"The Snows of Kilimanjaro," Ernest Hemingway

INTERNET
You and your students may find additional information about Daphne du Maurier and "The Birds" on the Internet. We suggest the following sites. Please be aware, however, that sites may have changed from the time we published this information.

The Daphne du Maurier Home Page is at **http://www. westwind. co.uk/westwind/cornwall/maurier.html**

For inside information about the making of the Alfred Hitchcock movie, "The Birds," visit **http://socrates.bodegabay.com/features/ birds.html**

We *strongly recommend* that you preview the sites before you send students to them.

Guide for Responding (continued)

◆ Critical Thinking

INTERPRET

1. Why are the birds so destructive? **[Analyze]**
2. How do the successive announcements on the BBC help create a sense of suspense? **[Analyze]**
3. At a certain point, the BBC is no longer broadcasting. What does this imply about conditions in the cities of England? **[Draw Conclusions]**
4. In the end, will Nat and his family survive the attacks? Why or why not? **[Speculate]**
5. What makes the birds suddenly attack people and try to kill them? **[Draw Conclusions]**

APPLY

6. Do you think that an animal population could suddenly turn against people? Why? **[Speculate]**

EVALUATE

7. Do you think the inconclusive ending of this story is effective? Why or why not? **[Evaluate]**

◆ Reading Strategy

MAKE PREDICTIONS

As you read "The Birds," you made **predictions** based on story details. Now focus on the end of the story. The words "The tapping began at the windows" signal the beginning of yet another assault by the birds. Keeping in mind the story details up to this point, what do you think will happen? Why?

◆ Build Grammar Skills

COMPOUND SENTENCES

In "The Birds," du Maurier frequently uses **compound sentences**—sentences that consist of two or more independent clauses.

Practice Add a clause to each sentence to form a compound sentence.

Example: The sky was gray

Answer: The sky was gray, and the wind was howling.

1. The birds swooped down
2. The sky darkened
3. The radio was turned on
4. He had prepared for this moment
5. The tapping sound grew louder

◆ Literary Focus

FORESHADOWING

Daphne du Maurier uses **foreshadowing**—hinting at events to come—to build suspense and create a sense of impending doom.

1. How is Nat's sighting of masses of gulls riding the sea a foreshadowing of possible disaster?
2. How does the BBC announcement of a national emergency foreshadow tragic events?

◆ Build Vocabulary

USING THE SUFFIX -ful

The word *fretful* in "The Birds" contains the suffix *-ful*. Add the suffix *-ful* to these words. Tell their meaning.

1. sorrow   2. teaspoon   3. help

USING THE WORD BANK

On a separate sheet of paper, match the word from the Word Bank to its synonym.

1. placid   a. gloomy
2. garish   b. urgent
3. reconaissance c. calm
4. sullen   d. exploratory
5. furtively   e. gaudy
6. imperative   f. stealthily

Beyond Literature

Media Connection

Alfred Hitchcock's *The Birds*
Imagine sitting in a dark movie theater watching flickering images of flocks of birds descending on an unsuspecting town. This was what it was like to watch Alfred Hitchcock's (1899–1980) classic tale of horror, *The Birds*, adapted from du Maurier's story. Released in 1963, Hitchcock's film is still regarded as one of the most terrifying movies ever made and has influenced many subsequent horror films. What do you think might have led Hitchcock to adapt du Maurier's story into a film?

The Birds ◆ 73

73

Idea Bank

Customizing for
Performance Levels

Following are suggestions for matching the Idea Bank topics with your students' performance levels:

Less Advanced Students: 1, 4, 7
Average Students: 2, 4, 6
More Advanced Students: 3, 5

Customizing for
Learning Modalities

Following are suggestions for matching Idea Bank topics with your students' learning modalities:

Visual/Spatial: 3, 6, 7
Auditory: 4, 5
Verbal Linguistic: 1, 2, 5

Writing Mini-Lesson

Refer students to the Writing Handbook, page 962, for instruction on the writing process, and page 964 for further information on Description.

Writer's Solution

Writing Lab CD-ROM

Have students complete the tutorial on Description. Follow these steps:

1. Have students use the Sensory Word Bin to help them gather details.
2. Students should draft on computer.
3. Have students use the Vague Adjectives Checker to aid revision.

You will need approximately 70 minutes of class time to complete the preceding steps.

Sourcebook

Have students use Chapter 1, Description (pp. 1–29) for additional support. This chapter includes in-depth instruction on descriptions of places (p. 6) and creating a main impression (p. 19).

*B*uild *Y*our *P*ortfolio

Idea Bank

Writing

1. **The Final Outcome** Will Nat and his family survive the birds' attack? Write an ending to the story.

2. **Public Service Announcement** Write an announcement for broadcast on the BBC describing government measures—such as military actions—to stop attacks of the birds.

3. **Book vs. Movie** Watch a videotape of Alfred Hitchcock's 1963 film version of "The Birds." Then write an essay in which you compare and contrast the short story with the movie.

Speaking and Listening

4. **Panel Discussion** In "The Birds," people try to protect themselves from birds. In real life, birds often need protection from people. With a small group, hold a panel discussion in which you discuss ideas on what can be done to protect birds and their habitats. **[Science Link]**

5. **Scene** With a small group, review the scene in which Nat tries to convince Mr. Trigg to take precautions against the birds. Act out a continuation of the scene with additional dialogue in which Nat becomes more persuasive.

Projects

6. **Multimedia Presentation** Give a multimedia presentation on any four birds mentioned in the story. For each bird, research size, distinguishing features, natural habitat, and habits. Include photos or drawings and, if possible, include a recording of sounds made by each. **[Science Link]**

7. **A Picture of Flight** Draw or paint a picture of a bird in flight. Use an encyclopedia or other reference book to find a picture to serve as a model. **[Art Link]**

74 ◆ *Spine Tinglers*

Writing Mini-Lesson

Bird's-Eye View of a Place

Imagine how different this story would be if it were told from a bird's-eye view! The action would be described from above, rather than below, and the perspective would be altered. Write a description of a familiar place as it would look to a bird overhead. Here are some tips to help you:

Writing Skills Focus: A Consistent Viewpoint

To make your bird's-eye view of a place clear, maintain a **consistent viewpoint.** As you write, remember that you are looking down on your scene. Wandering from this viewpoint will only confuse your readers.

Notice how du Maurier maintains the viewpoint of a person looking up in this passage.

Model From the Story

Then he saw the gannet, poised for the dive, above him in the sky. . . . Only the gannet remained. One single gannet above him in the sky.

Prewriting Choose a familiar place to describe. Then draw a rough sketch of the place as seen from above. Label the key details in the sketch. Your sketch will help you visualize the place from a bird's perspective.

Drafting Refer to your sketch as you draft your bird's-eye view. Include details that indicate a downward-looking perspective, and avoid making observations from a different point of view. For example, a bird in the sky would be able to see an entire basketball court at a glance. It wouldn't, however, be able to see the color of a person's eyes.

Revising Reread your bird's-eye view, checking for inconsistencies of viewpoint. Correct any passage that describes something from the ground up.

☑ ASSESSMENT OPTIONS

Formal Assessment, Selection Test, pp. 10–12, and Assessment Resources Software. The selection test is designed so that it can be easily customized to the performance levels of your students.
Alternative Assessment, p. 4, includes options for less advanced students, more advanced students, musical/rhythmic learners, verbal/linguistic learners, and visual/spatial learners.

PORTFOLIO ASSESSMENT

Use the following rubrics in the *Alternative Assessment* booklet to assess student writing:
The Final Outcome: Narrative Rubric, p. 89
Public Service Announcement: Description Rubric, p. 90
Book vs. Movie: Evaluation/Review Rubric, p. 97
Writing Mini-Lesson: Description Rubric, p. 90

Writing Process Workshop

Observation

You observe things all the time: an action-packed basketball game, the passing of a thunderstorm, the results of a laboratory experiment. When you describe an event that you've watched over a period of time, you are writing an **observation.** By using vivid details, you can re-create the event and make your readers feel as if they are witnessing it themselves.

The following skills, introduced in this section's Writing Mini-Lessons, will help you write an observation of any event.

Writing Skills Focus

▶ **Use precise details** to create a vivid picture. For example, tell whether the liquid in a test tube is beet red or carrot red. (See p. 12.)

▶ **Anticipate readers' questions** by thinking about what they'll want to know and providing it. (See p. 33.)

▶ **Use vivid verbs** rather than general ones—like *hover* rather than *fly*. (See p. 40.)

▶ **Maintain a consistent perspective.** In observing a game, for example, don't shift from a spectator's vantage point to a player's. (See p. 74.)

Hank Aaron uses all these skills as he observes the events leading up to his record-breaking homer.

MODEL FROM LITERATURE

from *I Had a Hammer* by Hank Aaron

Downing's first pitch was a change of pace that went into the dirt. ① The umpire, Satch Davidson, threw it out, and the first-base umpire, Frank Pulli, tossed Downing another one of the specially marked infrared balls. Downing rubbed it up and then threw his slider low and down the middle, which was not where he wanted it ② but which was fine with me. . . . The ball shot out ③ on a line over the shortstop, Bill Russell, who bent his knees as if he were going to jump up and catch it. ④

① This precise detail about the first pitch helps create tension.

② Aaron answers a question readers might ask: Did Downing get the pitch where he wanted it?

③ *Shot out* is a more vivid verb than *traveled.*

④ Aaron describes the whole scene from a batter's vantage point.

Establish Writing Guidelines
Review the following key characteristics of an observation:

- An observation describes an event the writer witnessed firsthand.
- The event is observed over a period of time.
- Most often, the details in an observation are presented in chronological order.
- Observations often focus on scientific phenomena, such as storms.

You may want to distribute the scoring rubric for Description (p. 90 in ***Alternative Assessment***) to make students aware of the criteria on which they will be evaluated before they begin. See the suggestions on page 77 for how you can customize the rubric to this workshop.

Refer students to the Writing Handbook, page 962, for instruction on the writing process, and page 964 for further information on descriptive writing.

Writer's Solution

Writers at Work Videodisc
To introduce students to the key elements and to show them how science-fiction writer Anne McCaffrey uses description in her writing, play the videodisc segment on Description (Ch. 1). Have students discuss how McCaffrey uses her observational skills in gathering details to include in her descriptions.

Play frames 335 to 10785

Writing Lab CD-ROM
If students have access to computers, have them work in the tutorial on Description to complete all or part of their observations. Follow these steps:
1. Students can review the interactive model of an observation.
2. Have students use the Word Bins activities to gather precise details.
3. Students can draft their observation on computer.
4. Have students use the revision checker for vague adjectives.

Sourcebook
Students can find additional support, including topic ideas, models, and graphic organizers, in the chapter on Description (pp. 1–29).

Cross-Curricular Connection: Science

Tell students that most scientists keep observation journals in which they record in great detail what they observe when conducting an experiment. The scientists will later refer back to their journal entries when putting together a report of their findings. Have students discuss how the way in which a scientist might record observations for his or her own use might differ from how a writer might record observations for a reading audience. *Students should note that a scientist might use his or her own type of shorthand and would be less concerned with using precise language than a writer would. In addition, scientists might include technical terms and data that wouldn't be included in a piece of writing targeted toward a general audience.*

Prewriting

You may want to have students work in small groups to brainstorm for additional topic ideas. Remind students that any event that takes place over a period of time can make a good topic for an observation.

Customize for
English Language Learners

Because these students may not have yet developed an awareness of the shades of meaning of various words in the English language, they will most likely need extra help in coming up with vivid verbs to use in their observations. Look over the verbs that students have listed and work with them to come up with ones that are more vivid.

 **Writer's Solution**

Writing Lab CD-ROM

Four Word Bin activities—sensory words, color words, place words, and character trait words—are included in the Gathering Details section of the tutorial on Description. Students can use any or all of the Word Bins to collect descriptive words for their observations. Students can save these words and later copy and paste them into their drafts.

Drafting

Encourage students to draft their observations in a single sitting, without pausing to labor over a specific word or to correct a grammatical error. Once students have completed a draft, they'll have an opportunity to go back into their work and make extensive revisions.

APPLYING LANGUAGE SKILLS: Using Vivid Verbs

A vivid verb describes an action more precisely than a general verb.

General Verb:
He <u>runs</u> down the highway.

Vivid Verb:
He <u>lopes</u> down the highway.

Notice how the vivid verb paints a picture of a man running with a long, swinging stride.

Practice On your paper, replace the general verb in each sentence with a more vivid one.

1. He [moves] across the basketball court.
2. She [walks] down the avenue.
3. The hawk [flies] on an updraft of warm air.

Writing Application As you draft your observation, use vivid verbs to describe actions. If you can't think of a vivid verb at the moment, mark the general verb you use and replace it when you revise your work.

Writer's Solution Connection
Writing Lab

To help you gather precise details for your observation, use the Sensory Word Bin Activities in the Writing Lab tutorial on Description.

Prewriting

Choose a Topic Come up with a topic by searching your memory for interesting events that you've recently witnessed. You can also choose one of the topic ideas listed here.

Topic Ideas

- The passing scene from a car or bus window
- A seasonal event or celebration
- A natural event, like a thunderstorm
- The behavior of a pet

Create a Chart of Vivid Verbs Across the top of your chart, jot down general verbs to describe your subject. Then, under each, list vivid verbs that convey the same idea. You can draw on these as you draft your observation.

General: Move	General: Fly
Lope	Glide
Stride	Soar

Develop Details by Anticipating Readers' Questions
If you're observing a thunderstorm, think of questions readers might ask about it:
▶ Where did it take place?
▶ How long did it last?
▶ How close did the lightning strike?
Answer each question by listing details you might include in your observation.

Science Writing Tip In a scientific observation, you answer many questions with precise measurements rather than general terms: An object is 3.6 meters tall, not just "tall."

Drafting

Keep a Consistent Perspective Don't confuse readers by observing a sports event from the stands in one paragraph and from the field in the next. Avoid this kind of mix-up by reminding yourself of your vantage point each time you begin a new paragraph. Then, as you write your observation, picture what you're seeing *from* that location.

Applying Language Skills

Using Vivid Verbs Explain to students that vivid verbs are especially important in an observation, because the focus of this type of writing is to capture an event that takes place over a period of time. The event is made up of a series of individual actions, each of which is described using an action verb. By using precise verbs to capture the individual actions, a writer enables readers to picture the events more clearly.

Answers

Suggested responses:

1. streaks, glides, charges
2. strolls, parades, saunters
3. soars, glides, hovers

 **Writer's Solution**

For additional instruction and practice, use the **Language Lab CD-ROM** lesson on Vivid Verbs and the practice page on Action Verbs, p. 11 in the *Writer's Solution Grammar Practice Book.*

Using Adverbs Discuss with students how the meaning of each of the example sentences changes if the adverb is removed. Then have students substitute other possible adverbs and discuss how the substitutions alter the meaning.

Answers

Suggested responses:
1. late, early
2. violently, suddenly

 **Writer's Solution**

For additional instruction and practice, use the practice pages on Adverbs, pp. 18–19 in the *Writer's Solution Grammar Practice Book.*

Mark Places to Use Precise Details Avoid pausing to fill in precise details. Just mark the place; you can go back and insert details like a player's name or uniform number later. Professional editors often use the abbreviation TC or TK, meaning that something is "to come."

Revising

Use a Checklist Go back to the Writing Skills Focus on the first page of the lesson and use the items as a checklist to evaluate and revise your observation.

▶ Have I used precise details?
Fill in the details that you didn't have time to look up or remember as you drafted.

▶ Have I used vivid verbs rather than general verbs?
Look for general verbs like move, fly, and go. If possible, replace them with more vivid and specific verbs.

▶ Have I anticipated and answered readers' questions?
Have a peer reviewer read your observation and jot down his or her unanswered questions.

▶ Have I maintained a consistent viewpoint?
Draw a crude picture of the scene you've observed, marking your vantage point with an X. In reviewing your observation, be sure that everything you described was viewed from position X.

REVISION MODEL

① crouched,
Suddenly the player by the net bent down, then leaped
②The top of the net was six feet high, and she rose about two feet above it.
high to reach the ball. She saw everyone below her. ③

① The writer uses a more vivid verb.
② This sentence includes a precise detail and answers a question readers might have: How high did she jump?
③ The writer deletes a confusing shift in perspective.

Publishing

▶ **Classroom** Share details of your observations with classmates and identify types of jobs that require observational skills.

▶ **School Newspaper** Create an Observation Column for your school's newspaper.

▶ **Internet** Post your writing to a message board in a news group.

APPLYING LANGUAGE SKILLS: Using Adverbs

Adverbs modify adjectives, verbs, and other adverbs, and they can help answer readers' questions:

When?
        adv   v
The umpire *finally* misses a call.

Where?
           v   adv
The batter practices *here* in the batting box.

How?
 v   adv
He grips the bat *wildly*.

To what extent?
         adv   adj
The pitcher is *very* dedicated.
        adj   adv
That pitcher hardly *ever* loses.

Practice On your paper, fill in adverbs to answer questions.

1. The storm was supposed to arrive _____ in the evening. (When in the evening?)
2. A lightning bolt struck _____, felling a tree. (Where did it strike?)

Writing Application Review your observation and find questions that are unanswered. Then answer these questions for readers by using adverbs.

Writer's Solution Connection Language Lab

For more practice with adverbs, complete the Language Lab Lesson on Problems with Modifiers.

Revising

You may want to have students work with peer reviewers to revise their observations. Have students use the revision checklist to guide their review. In addition, instruct them to offer specific, concrete suggestions for improvement, rather than simply offering general criticisms.

Writer's Solution

Writing Lab CD-ROM
The Vague Adjectives Revision Checker in the Revision section of the tutorial on Description identifies vague adjectives, such as *good* and *nice*, in students' papers and provides guidance to help students replace these adjectives with more precise ones.

Publishing

Tell students that even if they choose not to share their observations with a wider audience at this time, they may later want to incorporate what they've written into a longer piece of writing that they would want to share. For this reason, students should save what they've written and keep it in a place where they can easily find it at a later time.

Reinforce and Extend

Review the Writing Guidelines
After students have completed their papers, review the characteristics of an observation. Encourage students to come up with additional criteria for an effective observation based on what they learned through completing the assignment.

Connect to Literature Unit 7 ("Nonfiction") includes an example of an observation: Sally Ride's essay "Single Room, Earth View" (p. 559).

✓ ASSESSMENT		4	3	2	1
PORTFOLIO ASSESSMENT Use the rubric on Description in *Alternative Assessment* (p. 90) to assess students' writing. Add these criteria to customize the rubric to this assignment.	**Precise Details**	The writer consistently uses precise details to create a vivid picture for readers.	The writer uses precise details, but leaves out several key details.	The observation includes some, but far too few, precise details.	The observation includes too few details, and those that are included are vague.
	Vivid Verbs	The writer consistently uses vivid verbs.	The writer uses a mixture of vivid verbs and more general verbs.	The writer uses some, but very few, vivid verbs.	The writer consistently uses vague verbs.

Students will be familiar with various kinds of maps from their social studies textbooks. Point out that reading maps is a useful skill outside of school. They will have occasions to read road maps and street maps like the one in this lesson.

Customize for
Visual/Spatial Learners

Although visual/spatial learners should be successful in reading maps, other students may have difficulty getting oriented on a map. Directions like "Turn north" or "Make a left onto . . ." may not be clear. It's important to get oriented before trying to following directions. Suggest that it may help to turn the map so that the orientation of the map corresponds to the directions.

Apply the Strategy

Have students examine the map on this page, noting locations of sites, streets, etc. You might point out that in a city with numbered streets, they might have to infer the numbers of streets that are not shown. For instance, in this map there are no numbered streets between 14th Street and 17th Street in the section shown on this map.

Answers

1. This map will work. All of the desired locations are on this map.
2. A logical order for visiting the attractions is to start at the White House, then visit the National Aquarium, the Washington Monument, and the Lincoln Memorial. A second option is to follow this order in reverse.
3. Following the route starting at the White House, you would walk three blocks along E Street to 14th Street, and a half block on 14th Street to the National Aquarium. From the corner of 14th Street and Constitution Avenue, you would walk eight blocks to Henry Bacon Drive and one diagonal block from there to the Lincoln Memorial. The distance is approximately fifteen blocks.
4. A second walking tour might start at the Treasury Department and walk along 14th Street to the American Museum of Natural History.

78

Strategies for Success

When you read a work of literature or a reference work that's accompanied by maps, knowing how to read the map will enhance your understanding of the work. Knowing how to read a map is equally if not more important when you're visiting a new city or looking for a famous landmark. The type of map you'll use on such occasions is a street map, which often shows buildings, parks, and other landmarks, in addition to streets.

Identify Your Purpose Identify your purpose in looking at a street map. Are you looking for a specific landmark, a particular street, or do you want to know the general layout of a neighborhood? Do you want to get to a specific place from where you are? Knowing your purpose will help you focus on the part of the map that you need.

Get an Overview Once you've identified your purpose, determine whether the street map fits your needs. Does it show an entire city or just a section? Are all the streets shown on the map or only the major ones?

Then get familiar with the map. Which way is north on the map? Where do the names of the streets appear? How does the map indicate buildings or other landmarks?

Read the Map When you're in the city and you want to get from one place to another, start by finding your location on the map. You can then determine the direction you need to travel to get where you want to be.

Apply the Strategy

It's your first trip to our nation's capital. You want to plan a walking tour that includes the White House, Lincoln Memorial, National Aquarium, and Washington Monument.

1. Will this map suit your needs? Why or why not?
2. In what order will you visit the attractions? Why?
3. Approximately how many blocks will you walk to complete the tour?
4. Plan another walking tour for the next day. Write the directions and attractions in the order you will visit them.

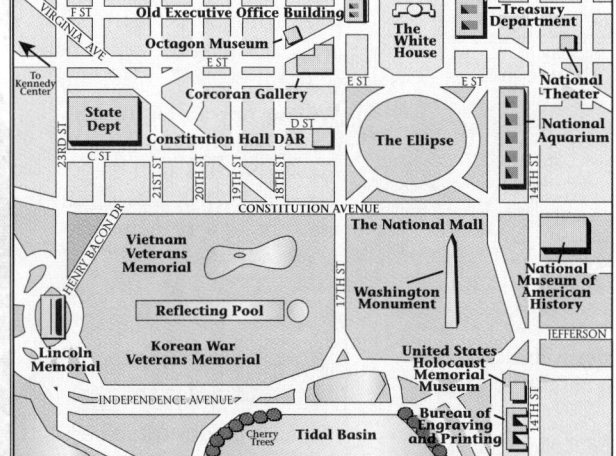

> ✔ Here are other situations in which a street map can be helpful:
> ▶ Meeting someone in an unfamiliar neighborhood
> ▶ Providing directions to your house
> ▶ Determining distances between places

PART 2 *It's a Mystery*

La Réponse Imprévue, René Magritte, Musées Royaux des Beaux-Arts de Belgique, Bruxelles-Koninklijke Musea voor Schone Kunsten van Belgie, Brussel

The selections in this section capture both imaginary and real-life mysteries. "The Red-headed League" provides students with an opportunity to see the world's most famous fictional detective, Sherlock Holmes, use his amazing powers of observation to solve a mystery. "The Listeners," "Beware: Do Not Read This Poem," and "Echo" may surprise your students by showing that a mystery can be captured as effectively in a poem as in a story or a drama. Finally, "Caucasian Mummies Mystify Chinese" captures a real-life mystery involving a recent discovery of caucasian mummies in China.

Customize for
Varying Student Needs
When assigning the selections in this part, keep in mind these factors:

"The Red-headed League"
• A long short story (18 pp.)
• Less proficient readers may need to read in sections
• Contains difficult vocabulary, long sentences, and unfamiliar expressions that may present a challenge to both less proficient readers and English Language Learners

"The Listeners"
• An accessible narrative poem with a mysterious mood that should capture students' interest

"Beware: Do Not Read This Poem"
• Contains abbreviations that may need to be explained to English Language Learners

"Echo"
• A short, accessible poem filled with vivid imagery

"Caucasian Mummies Mystify Chinese"
• A brief, high-interest article (26 pp.)

 Humanities: Art

The Unexpected Answer (La réponse imprévue), 1933, by René Magritte.

The Belgian painter René Magritte (1898–1967) was one of the leading Surrealist painters of the early twentieth century. Surrealism is an artistic movement that juxtaposes images that ordinarily do not belong together in order to create visual shock and to express concepts that cannot be explained—irrational connections such as those that occur in dreams. Magritte had a natural affinity for the surreal and rendered

his paintings of mysterious events, strange situations, and bizarre concepts in a precise, colorful, and often highly realistic style.

The Unexpected Answer poses a mystery on its very surface: We see a realistic-looking door with a strangely shaped hole in it. We might assume that some bizarre creature made the hole by rushing through the door in terror. The hole is not jagged, however, which could suggest that the door was made with the hole in it.

Have students link the painting to the

theme of Part 2 ("It's a Mystery") by answering the following questions:
1. If you were a detective coming upon this door, what questions would you ask about it? *Questions may include: Who or what made the hole? Was it running into the room or out of the room? Why is the hole so oddly shaped? Why is the hole not jagged? What lies beyond the door?*
2. Create the title for a mysterious story based on one of your questions. *Responses should indicate an element of mystery.*

Guide for Reading

OBJECTIVES

1. To read, comprehend, and interpret a story
2. To relate a story to personal experience
3. To identify key details in a mystery story
4. To understand the elements of a mystery story
5. To build vocabulary in context and learn the root *-spec-*
6. To develop skill in using coordinate adjectives
7. To use elaboration writing a detective story
8. To respond to the story through writing, speaking and listening, and projects

SKILLS INSTRUCTION

Vocabulary:
Word Roots: *-spec-*

Grammar:
Coordinate Adjectives

Literary Focus:
The Mystery

Reading Strategy:
Key Details

Writing:
Elaboration

Speaking and Listening:
Presenting a Summary; Grilling the Suspect (teacher edition)

PORTFOLIO OPPORTUNITIES

Writing: Observation Journal; Dramatic Scene; Cause-and-Effect Essay

Writing Mini-Lesson: Using Elaboration

Speaking and Listening: Presenting a Summary; Grilling the Suspect

Projects: The Science of Detection; Planning the Heist

More About the Author
In addition to being a doctor and world-famous writer of detective stories, Sir Arthur Conan Doyle was a prominent British patriot and historian. During World War I, he wrote a six-volume study titled *History of the British Campaign in France and Flanders.* He also sent books to British prisoners in Germany. Certain letters in these books, marked by tiny pinpricks, spelled out secret messages bearing news of the war. Sherlock Holmes would surely have approved.

Sir Arthur Conan Doyle
(1859–1930)

The Englishman Sir Arthur Conan Doyle is known for creating the world's most famous fictional detective, Sherlock Holmes.

This larger-than-life character has outlived his creator and now outwits criminals in the movies.

From Medicine to Mysteries

Perhaps it is no accident that the creator of the sharp-eyed, observant Holmes began his career as an eye doctor. In this profession, however, Doyle found little success and began writing stories to supplement his income. He probably modeled Sherlock Holmes, the hero of one of these stories, on a medical school professor who could diagnose a patient's illness from clues other doctors ignored.

The "Birth" of Sherlock Holmes After several rejections from publishers, Doyle sold his first detective novel in 1887. In this novel, *A Study in Scarlet*, he introduces readers to the brilliant Holmes and to Holmes's devoted companion, Dr. John Watson. Perhaps remembering his own medical background, Doyle writes in the voice of Dr. Watson and pretends that the good doctor is telling the story.

The "Death" of Sherlock Holmes Readers grew to love the odd detective who solved puzzling crimes. However, Doyle soon wearied of Holmes and killed off his own character in a story entitled "The Final Problem." The public would not stand for this outrage, however. Many readers wrote to Doyle, pleading with him to undo the death of Holmes. In the end, generous fees from publishers convinced Doyle to bring back the beloved detective. It seems as if he will never die again!

◆ Build Vocabulary

WORD ROOTS *-spec-*
In your Word Bank, you have the word *introspective*. This word is built on the root *-spec-*, which means "see" or "look." If you combine this root with *intro*, you have a word that means "looking inward." Therefore, an introspective person, like Sherlock Holmes, is one who looks within himself to find answers.

WORD BANK

singular	
avail	
hoax	
introspective	
vex	
conundrums	
astuteness	
formidable	

As you read "The Red-headed League," you will encounter the words on this list. Each word is defined on the page where it first appears. Preview the list before you read.

◆ Build Grammar Skills

COORDINATE ADJECTIVES
To describe Sherlock Holmes's many keen observations, Sir Arthur Conan Doyle uses numerous adjectives. Often, he uses more than one adjective before a noun, as in this example:

I . . . found him deep in conversation with a *very stout, florid-faced, elderly* gentleman with *fiery red* hair.

Adjectives are **coordinate** if they each separately modify the noun; they are not coordinate if the final adjective is thought of as part of the noun.

Coordinate: *stout, florid-faced, elderly* gentleman

Not Coordinate: *fiery red* hair

Prentice Hall Literature Program Resources

REINFORCE / RETEACH / EXTEND

Selection Support Pages
Build Vocabulary: Word Roots: *-spec-*, p. 18
Build Grammar Skills: Coordinate Adjectives, p. 19
Reading Strategy: Key Details, p. 20
Literary Focus: The Mystery, p. 21

Strategies for Diverse Student Needs, p. 5

Beyond Literature
Career Connection: Detective, p. 5

Alternative Assessment, p. 5

Formal Assessment Selection Test, pp. 13–15,

Assessment Resources Software

Writing and Language Transparencies
Graphic Organizer: Story Map, p. 84

Resource Pro CD-ROM
"The Red-headed League"—includes all resource material and customizable lesson plan

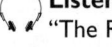 **Listening to Literature Audiocassettes**
"The Red-headed League"

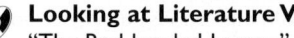 **Looking at Literature Videodisc**
"The Red-headed League"

The Red-headed League

◆ *Literature and Your Life*

CONNECT YOUR EXPERIENCE

A new student arrives in your school. Just a quick glance at him gives you clues to his personality: his clothes, shoes, and hairstyle; the way he carries himself; or any unusual habits, like cracking his knuckles. If you hear him speak, you get further clues about him.

This sizing up of people is part of the unpaid detective work of everyday life. As an amateur sleuth already, you'll want to read about the exploits of the world's greatest professional—Sherlock Holmes.

THEMATIC FOCUS: IT'S A MYSTERY

Notice the techniques that Holmes uses to solve the strange mystery of "The Red-headed League." How could you apply these techniques to mysteries that you encounter?

◆ Background for Understanding

LITERATURE

Sherlock Holmes, who is usually pictured wearing a cape and deer-stalker cap, is recognizable throughout the world. He's even recognized by people who've never read a Sherlock Holmes mystery. New Holmes adventures continually appear in the form of television productions and movies. Even Commander Data, the android from *Star Trek: The Next Generation,* has spent fun-filled hours pretending to be Sherlock Holmes.

Journal Writing Think about the qualities of a successful detective. Jot down your ideas in your journal.

◆ Literary Focus

THE MYSTERY

A **mystery** is a story of suspense that usually contains the following elements: a crime, a crime-solver, a criminal, suspects, and key details such as clues, alibis, and characters' possible reasons for committing a crime. In most mysteries, the crime-solver, or detective, is the hero, and the reader "roots for" him or her.

◆ Reading Strategy

KEY DETAILS

Readers of mysteries try to solve the crime along with—or even before—the detective. You do this by noting **key details**, pieces of information having a bearing on the crime. These key details are often clues to solving the mystery.

The following passage from the story contains a key detail that helps Holmes to solve the mystery of "The Red-headed League":

> " . . . I have a small pawn-broker's business
>
> . . . I used to be able to keep two assistants, but now I only keep one; and I would have a job to pay him but that he is willing to come for half wages so as to learn the business."

From this passage, you might conclude that the assistant's willingness to work for "half wages" is suspicious. As you read this story, locate other key details and jot them down. Refer to your list as you attempt to solve the mystery.

Guide for Reading ◆ 81

One-Minute Insight

The talents of supersleuth Sherlock Holmes are effectively revealed in this tightly woven tale of deceptive manipulation and criminal activity. The Red-headed League is a ploy through which master criminals position themselves in a strategic location to tunnel into an adjacent bank, intending to make off with £30,000 in French gold. Through clear deduction from the facts presented, Holmes sees through the scheme and brings in the authorities at the exact moment to catch the criminals "red-handed."

◆ Critical Thinking

❶ **Make Inferences** What can you infer about Holmes's and Watson's attitude toward crime-solving from this conversation? *Responses may include: They find it exciting, enjoyable, and rewarding. They welcome the insight it offers into the stranger side of human life and behavior.*

Customize for
More Advanced Students

Challenge these students by having them use the details on this page to make inferences about the role Jabez Wilson plays in the mystery plot. *Students may respond that Jabez Wilson is probably a victim whose seeking out a consultation with Holmes sets forth the details from which Holmes will reason and solve the mystery.*

🎞 Looking at Literature
Videodisc

To capture students' interest and motivate them to read "The Red-headed League," play Chapter 2 of the videodisc. In this segment, several contemporary mystery writers discuss their techniques for writing mysteries. Discuss the timeless appeal of mysteries. Why do they appeal to so many people?

Chapter 2

The Red-headed League

Sir Arthur Conan Doyle

I had called upon my friend, Mr. Sherlock Holmes, one day in the autumn of last year and found him in deep conversation with a very stout, florid-faced, elderly gentleman with fiery red hair. With an apology for my intrusion, I was about to withdraw when Holmes pulled me abruptly into the room and closed the door behind me.

"You could not possibly have come at a better time, my dear Watson," he said cordially.

"I was afraid that you were engaged."

"So I am. Very much so."

"Then I can wait in the next room."

"Not at all. This gentleman, Mr. Wilson, has been my partner and helper in many of my most successful cases, and I have no doubt that he will be of the utmost use to me in yours also."

The stout gentleman half rose from his chair and gave a bob of greeting, with a quick little questioning glance from his small, fat-encircled eyes.

"Try the settee,"[1] said Holmes, relapsing into his armchair and putting his finger tips together, as was his custom when in judicial moods. "I know, my dear Watson, that you share my love of all that is bizarre and outside the conventions and humdrum routine of everyday life. You have shown your relish for it by the enthusiasm which has prompted you to chronicle, and, if you will excuse my saying so, somewhat to embellish so many of my own little adventures.

"Your cases have indeed been of the greatest interest to me," I observed.

---

1. **settee** (se tē´) *n.*: Small sofa.

82 ◆ *Spine Tinglers*

Block Scheduling Strategies

Consider these suggestions to take advantage of extended class time:

- Have students complete the journal activity in Background for Understanding (p. 81). Then have them meet in small groups to discuss their entries and compare Sherlock Holmes with other fictional detectives that they have read about or seen in movies.

- Have small groups of students select portions of the story to act out. Then have students listen to the selection on audiocassette so that

they can compare their portrayals of the characters to the actors' portrayals.

- Have students write captions for the illustrations to create a storyboard of the story. Students can work in groups and compare their storyboards with those of other groups.

- Then have students complete the Writing Mini-Lesson (p. 101). Before they begin, have students find and discuss examples of elaboration in "The Red-headed League."

Humanities: Art

Illustrations for "The Red-headed League," by Sidney Paget.

These illustrations were created by the artist specifically for the story "The Red-headed League." Each illustration depicts characters from the story at a dramatic point in the plot.

Sidney Paget (1860–1908) was a British painter of portraits, landscapes, and town scenes. In addition, he worked as an illustrator for several London newspapers and

illustrated books by Sir Walter Scott as well as Sir Arthur Conan Doyle.

Use these questions for discussion:
1. How well does the illustrator depict the characters as Doyle described them? Back up your opinions with passages from the story. *Students should cite passages in the story that either do or do not support the illustrator's interpretations of the characters' appearances. For example, Mr. Jabez Wilson is shown on p. 83 being*

greeted by his employer, Duncan Ross, while Wilson's assistant, Vincent Spaulding, looks on.

2. Do you think that seeing the artist's interpretation of how the characters in the story might look adds to or detracts from the story? Explain. *Some students might think the illustrations help them make the characters "come alive"; others may prefer being left to imagine the appearances of the characters for themselves.*

"You will remember that I remarked the other day, just before we went into the very simple problem presented by Miss Mary Sutherland, that for strange effects and extraordinary combinations we must go to life itself, which is always far more daring than any effort of the imagination."

"A proposition which I took the liberty of doubting."

"You did, Doctor, but none the less you must come round to my view, for otherwise I shall keep on piling fact upon fact on you until your reason breaks down under them and acknowledges me to be right. Now, Mr. Jabez Wilson here has been good enough to call upon me this morning, and to begin a narrative which promises to be one of the most singular which I have listened to for some time. You have heard me remark that the strangest and most unique things are very often connected not with the larger but with the smaller crimes, and occasionally, indeed, where there is room for doubt whether any positive crime has been committed. As far as I have heard it is impossible for me to say whether the present case is an instance of crime or not, but the course of events is certainly among the most singular that I have ever listened to. Perhaps, Mr. Wilson, you would have the great kindness to recommence your narrative. I ask you not merely because my friend Dr. Watson has not heard the opening part but also because the peculiar nature of the story makes me anxious to have every possible detail from your lips. As a rule, when I have heard some slight indication of the course of events, I am able to guide myself by the thousands of other similar cases which occur to my memory. In the present instance I am forced to admit that the facts are, to the best of my belief, unique."

The portly client puffed out his chest with an appearance of some little pride and pulled a dirty and wrinkled newspaper from the inside pocket of his great coat. As he glanced down the

◆ **Build Vocabulary**

singular (sin´ gyə lər) *adj.*: Extraordinary; rare

advertisement column, with his head thrust forward and the paper flattened out upon his knee, I took a good look at the man and endeavored, after the fashion of my companion, to read the indications which might be presented by his dress or appearance.

I did not gain very much, however, by my inspection. Our visitor bore every mark of being an average commonplace British tradesman, obese, pompous, and slow. He wore rather baggy gray shepherd's check trousers, a not over-clean black frock coat, unbuttoned in the front, and a drab waistcoat with a heavy brassy Albert chain, and a square pierced bit of metal dangling down as an ornament. A frayed top hat and a faded brown overcoat with a wrinkled velvet collar lay upon a chair beside him. Altogether, look as I would, there was nothing remarkable about the man save his blazing red head, and the expression of extreme chagrin and discontent upon his features.

Sherlock Holmes's quick eye took in my occupation, and he shook his head with a smile as he noticed my questioning glances. "Beyond the obvious facts that he has at some time done manual labor, that he takes snuff,[2] that he is a Freemason,[3] that he has been in China, and that he has done a considerable amount of writing lately, I can deduce nothing else."

Mr. Jabez Wilson started up in his chair, with his forefinger upon the paper, but his eyes upon my companion.

"How, in the name of good fortune, did you know all that, Mr. Holmes?" he asked. "How did you know, for example, that I did manual labor? It's as true as gospel, for I began as a ship's carpenter."

"Your hands, my dear sir. Your right hand is quite a size larger than your left. You have

◆ *Literature and Your Life*

Sherlock Holmes is able to figure out information about his client from his appearance. What sorts of clues can clothing give about a person?

---

2. **snuff:** Powdered tobacco.
3. **Freemason:** Member of a secret society.

Cultural Connection

Detective stories are popular around the world, but they originated in the West—in the United States, England, and France. Perhaps this is no accident; detective stories are an exercise in deductive reasoning and these countries are steeped in the intellectual tradition of logic and rationality. Poe's detective character, Auguste Dupin, has a brilliant deductive mind. The French followed Poe with the first full-length detective novel, *The Lerouge Affair,* by Emile

Gaboriau. This was followed by *The Moonstone* by English author Wilkie Collins and Sir Arthur Conan Doyle's stories featuring Sherlock Holmes, another master of logic and reasoning. Other British authors, such as Dorothy Sayers, Agatha Christie, and P. D. James, have continued in a tradition of highly structured plots and intellectual, aristocratic detectives. American detective fiction, in contrast, developed a more dramatic, violent style with the works of

Dashiell Hammett and Raymond Chandler. The French, in turn, have left their own cultural stamp on the genre with George Simenon's Chief Inspector Maigret, who spends as much time pondering his suspects' personalities and psychology as he does following clues.

Ask students why they think detective stories are so popular. Which detective stories do they prefer? Have them give reasons for their preferences.

worked with it, and the muscles are more developed."

"Well, the snuff, then, and the Freemasonry?"

❺ "I won't insult your intelligence by telling you how I read that, especially as, rather against the strict rules of your order, you use an arc-and-compass breastpin."

"Ah, of course, I forgot that. But the writing?"

"What else can be indicated by that right cuff so very shiny for five inches, and the left one with the smooth patch near the elbow where you rest it upon the desk?"

"Well, but China?"

❻ "The fish that you have tattooed immediately above your right wrist could only have been done in China. I have made a small study of tattoo marks and have even contributed to the literature of the subject. That trick of staining the fishes' scales of a delicate pink is quite peculiar to China. When, in addition, I see a Chinese coin hanging from your watch-chain, the matter becomes even more simple."

Mr. Jabez Wilson laughed heavily. "Well, I never!" said he. "I thought at first that you had done something clever, but I see that there was nothing in it, after all."

❼ "I begin to think, Watson," said Holmes, "that I make a mistake in explaining. 'Omne ignotum pro magnifico,'[4] you know, and my poor little reputation, such as it is, will suffer shipwreck if I am so candid. Can you not find the advertisement, Mr. Wilson?"

"Yes, I have got it now," he answered with his thick red finger planted halfway down the column. "Here it is. This is what began it all. You just read it for yourself, sir."

I took the paper from him and read as follows:

To THE RED-HEADED LEAGUE:

On account of the bequest of the late Ezekiah Hopkins, of Lebanon, Pennsylvania, U. S A., there is now

❽
> ◆ **Reading Strategy**
> One type of clue in a mystery is written evidence. What does this piece of evidence reveal?

---

4. *Omne ignotum pro magnifico* (äm´ nä ig nō´ təm prō mag nē´ fē kō): Latin for "Whatever is unknown is magnified."

another vacancy open which entitles a member of the League to a salary of £4[5] a week for purely nominal services. All red-headed men who are sound in body and mind, and above the age of twenty-one years, are eligible. Apply in person on Monday, at eleven o'clock, to Duncan Ross, at the offices of the League, 7 Pope's Court, Fleet Street.

"What on earth does this mean?" I ejaculated after I had twice read over the extraordinary announcement.

❾ Holmes chuckled and wriggled in his chair, as was his habit when in high spirits. "It is a little off the beaten track, isn't it?" said he. "And now, Mr. Wilson, off you go at scratch and tell us all about yourself, your household, and the effect **❿** which this advertisement had upon your fortunes. You will first make a note, Doctor, of the paper and the date."

"It is *The Morning Chronicle* of April 27, 1890. Just two months ago."

"Very good. Now, Mr. Wilson?"

---

5. **£4:** Four pounds in British money—a large amount at the time in which the story is set.

The Red-headed League ◆ 85

Cross-Curricular Connection: Social Studies

With a population of about 7 million, London, the capital of Great Britain, is the eleventh largest city in the world today. In Sherlock Holmes's day, however, it was the largest. Even more so than today, the city was an international capital of art, science, manufacturing, finance, and trade.

Late nineteenth-century London was the center of the then vast British empire. Its ports handled ships that carried people and goods to and from such places as India, Hong Kong, and

Australia. It became the world's most populous city largely as a result of the Industrial Revolution, which began in the 1700's and continued through the 1800's. Scores of factories were built, creating a landscape of contrasts in which smokestacks rose up next to venerable old buildings.

Have students discuss why London is an ideal setting for Sherlock Holmes and his adventures.

"Well, it is just as I have been telling you, Mr. Sherlock Holmes," said Jabez Wilson, mopping his forehead; "I have a small pawnbroker's business at Coburg Square, near the City. It's not a very large affair, and of late years it has not done more than just give me a living. I used to be able to keep two assistants, but now I only keep one; and I would have a job to pay him but that he is willing to come for half wages so as to learn the business."

"What is the name of this obliging youth?" asked Sherlock Holmes.

"His name is Vincent Spaulding, and he's not such a youth, either. It's hard to say his age. I should not wish a smarter assistant, Mr. Holmes; and I know very well that he could better himself and earn twice what I am able to give him. But, after all, if he is satisfied, why should I put ideas in his head?"

❷ "Why, indeed? You seem most fortunate in having an employee who comes under the full market price. It is not a common experience among employers in this age. I don't know that your assistant is not as remarkable as your advertisement."

❸ "Oh, he has his faults, too," said Mr. Wilson. "Never was such a fellow for photography. Snapping away with a camera when he ought to be improving his mind, and then diving down into the cellar like a rabbit into its hole to develop his pictures. That is his main fault, but on the whole he's a good worker. There's no vice in him."

"He is still with you, I presume?"

"Yes, sir. He and a girl of fourteen, who does a bit of simple cooking and keeps the place clean—that's all I have in the house, for I am a widower and never had any family. We live very quietly, sir, the three of us; and we keep a roof over our heads and pay our debts, if we do nothing more.

"The first thing that put us out was that advertisement. Spaulding, he came down into the office just this day eight weeks, with this very paper in his hand, and he says:

" 'I wish to the Lord, Mr. Wilson, that I was a red-headed man.'

" 'Why that?' I asks.

" 'Why,' says he, 'here's another vacancy on the League of the Red-headed Men. It's worth quite a little fortune to any man who gets it, and I understand that there are more vacancies than there are men, so that the trustees are at their wits' end what to do with the money. If my hair would only change color, here's a nice little crib all ready for me to step into.'

" 'Why, what is it, then?' I asked. You see, Mr. Holmes, I am a very stay-at-home man, and as my business came to me instead of my having to go to it, I was often weeks on end without putting my foot over the doormat. In that way I didn't know much of what was going on outside, and I was always glad of a bit of news.

" 'Have you never heard of the League of the Red-headed Men?' he asked with his eyes open.

" 'Never.'

" 'Why, I wonder at that, for you are eligible yourself for one of the vacancies.'

" 'And what are they worth?' I asked.

" 'Oh, merely a couple of hundred a year, but the work is slight, and it need not interfere very much with one's other occupations.'

"Well, you can easily think that that made me prick up my ears, for the business has not been over-good for some years, and an extra couple of hundred would have been very handy.

◆ *Literature and Your Life*

When something is "too good to be true," it usually is. What seems suspicious about this club?

❹

" 'Tell me all about it,' said I.

" 'Well,' said he, showing me the advertisement, 'you can see for yourself that the League has a vacancy, and there is the address where you should apply for particulars. As far as I can make out, the League was founded by an American millionaire, Ezekiah Hopkins, who was very peculiar in his ways. He was himself red-headed, and he had a great sympathy for all red-headed men; so when he died it was found that he had left his enormous fortune in the hands of trustees, with instructions to apply the interest to the providing of easy berths to men whose hair is of that color. From all I hear it is splendid pay and very little to do.

❺

" 'But,' said I, 'there would be millions of red-headed men who would apply.'

" 'Not so many as you might think,' he answered. 'You see it is really confined to Londoners, and to grown men. This American had started from London when he was young, and he wanted to do the old town a good turn. Then, again, I have heard it is no use your applying if your hair is light red, or dark red, or anything but real bright, blazing, fiery red. Now, if you cared to apply, Mr. Wilson, you would just walk in; but perhaps it would hardly be worth your while to put yourself out of the way for the sake of a few hundred pounds.'

"Now, it is a fact, gentlemen, as you may see for yourselves, that my hair is of a very full and rich tint, so that it seemed to me that if there was to be any competition in the matter I stood as good a chance as any man that I had ever met. Vincent Spaulding seemed to know so much about it that I thought he might prove useful so I just ordered him to put up the shutters for the day and to come right away with me. He was very willing to have a holiday,[6] so we shut the business up and started off for the address that was given us in the advertisement.

❻

"I never hope to see such a sight as that again, Mr. Holmes. From north, south, east, and west every man who had a shade of red in his hair had tramped into the city to answer the advertisement. Fleet Street was choked with red-headed folk, and Pope's Court looked like a coster's orange barrow.[7] I should not have thought there were so many in the whole country as were brought together by that single advertisement. Every shade of color they were—straw, lemon, orange, brick, Irish-setter, liver, clay: but, as Spaulding said, there were not many who had the real vivid flame-colored tint. When I saw how many were waiting, I would have given it up in despair: but Spaulding would not hear of it. How he did it I could not imagine, but he pushed and pulled and butted until he got me through the crowd, and right up to the steps which led to the office. There was a double stream upon the stair, some going up in hope, and some coming back dejected: but we wedged in as well as we could and soon found ourselves in the office."

"Your experience has been a most entertaining one," remarked Holmes as his client paused and refreshed his memory with a huge pinch of snuff. "Pray continue your very interesting statement."

"There was nothing in the office but a couple of wooden chairs and a deal table, behind which sat a small man with a head that was even redder than mine. He said a few words to each candidate as he came up, and then he always managed to find some fault in them which would disqualify them. Getting a vacancy did

---

6. **holiday:** A day off from work; a vacation.
7. **coster's orange barrow:** Pushcart of a seller of oranges.

◆ *Literature and Your Life*

❹ Responses can include: *It is very uncommon for people, even eccentric millionaires, to pay others to do little or nothing. Also, it is suspicious that the bizarre criteria for belonging to the League fit Jabez Wilson so well.*

◆ **Critical Thinking**

❺ **Analyze** Summarize Mr. Wilson's description of the Red-headed League. Make special note of the facts that seem suspicious. *How would Spaulding know anything about Ezekiah Hopkins? How would he have heard that "it is splendid pay and very little to do"? Is Spaulding trying to lure Wilson into this situation, and if he is, does he have Wilson's best interest in mind?*

◆ **Reading Strategy**

❻ **Key Details** If students compare the text of the Red-headed League's advertisement to the information Spaulding gave Wilson, they will see that Spaulding does in fact know a great deal about the League. What is strange about this key detail? Elicit the following responses: *Spaulding seems to be the only one who is familiar with the League. Wilson, Holmes, and Watson all live in London, but none of them had ever heard of it.*

Customize for
Less Proficient Readers

Have these students read with a partner the passage in which Spaulding accompanies Wilson to answer the advertisement. Have them offer explanations for the assistant's behavior. *Students may point out that Spaulding shows great determination as he urges Jabez Wilson on and conducts him to the office. His actions suggest that he has reasons of his own for wanting Wilson to join the League.*

Customize for
More Advanced Students

Ask students to explain how the passage on this page contributes to the mystery. *Students may point out that Jabez Wilson provides a wealth of clues for the crime solver Students may also observe that careful listening plays an important part in Holmes's crime-solving technique. Holmes encourages Wilson to tell the whole story in his own words with little or no interruption.*

not seem to be such a very easy matter, after all. However, when our turn came the little man was much more favorable to me than to any of the others, and he closed the door as we entered, so that he might have a private word with us.

" 'This is Mr. Jabez Wilson,' said my assistant, 'and he is willing to fill a vacancy in the League.'

" 'And he is admirably suited for it,' the other answered. 'He has every requirement. I cannot recall when I have seen anything so fine.' He took a step backward, cocked his head on one side, and gazed at my hair until I felt quite bashful. Then suddenly he plunged forward, wrung my hand, and congratulated me warmly on my success.

"'It would be injustice to hesitate, said he. 'You will, however, I am sure, excuse me for taking an obvious precaution.' With that he seized my hair in both his hands, and tugged until I yelled with the pain. 'There is water in your eyes,' said he as he released me. 'I perceive that all is as it should be. But we have to be careful, for we have twice been deceived by wigs and once by paint. I could tell you tales of cobbler's wax which would disgust you with human nature.' He stepped over to the window and shouted through it at the top of his voice that the vacancy was filled. A groan of disappointment came up from below, and the folk all trooped away in different directions until there was not a red head to be seen except my own and that of the manager.

" 'My name,' said he, 'is Mr. Duncan Ross, and I am myself one of the pensioners upon the fund left by our noble benefactor. Are you a married man, Mr. Wilson? Have you a family?'

"I answered that I had not.

"His face fell immediately.

" 'Dear me!' he said gravely, 'that is very serious indeed! I am sorry to hear you say that. The fund was, of course, for the propagation and spread of the red-heads as well as for their maintenance. It is exceedingly unfortunate that you should be a bachelor.'

"My face lengthened at this, Mr. Holmes, for I thought that I was not to have the vacancy after all: but after thinking it over for a few minutes he said that it would be all right.

" 'In the case of another,' said he, 'the objection might be fatal, but we must stretch a point in favor of a man with such a head of hair as yours. When shall you be able to enter upon your new duties?'

" 'Well, it is a little awkward, for I have a business already,' said I.

" 'Oh, never mind about that, Mr. Wilson!' said Vincent Spaulding. 'I should be able to look after that for you.'

" 'What would be the hours?' I asked.

" 'Ten to two.'

"Now a pawnbroker's business is mostly done of an evening, Mr. Holmes, especially Thursday and Friday evening, which is just before pay-day: so it would suit me very well to earn a little in the mornings. Besides, I knew that my assistant was a good man, and that he would see to anything that turned up.

" 'That would suit me very well,' said I. 'And the pay?'

" 'Is £4 a week.'

" 'And the work?'

" 'Is purely nominal.'

" 'What do you call purely nominal?'

" 'Well, you have to be in the office, or at least in the building, the whole time. If you leave, you forfeit your whole position forever. The will is very clear upon that point. You don't comply with the conditions if you budge from the office during that time.'

" 'It's only four hours a day, and I should not think of leaving,' said I.

" 'No excuse will <u>avail</u>,' said Mr. Duncan Ross: 'neither sickness nor business nor anything else. There you must stay, or you lose your billet.'[8]

" 'And the work?'

" 'Is to copy out the Encyclopedia Britannica. There is the first volume of it in that press. You must find your own ink, pens, and blotting-

---

8. **billet** (bil′ it) *n*.: Position; job.

◆ **Build Vocabulary**

avail (ə vāl′) *v*.: Be of help

paper, but we provide this table and chair. Will you be ready tomorrow?'

" 'Certainly,' I answered.

" 'Then, good-bye, Mr. Jabez Wilson, and let me congratulate you once more on the important position which you have been fortunate enough to gain.' He bowed me out of the room, and I went home with my assistant, hardly knowing what to say or do, I was so pleased at my own good fortune.

◆ *Literature and Your Life*

If you were in Jabez Wilson's place, would you be suspicious of the nature of the work he is to perform? Why or why not?

"Well, I thought over the matter all day, and by evening I was in low spirits again: for I had quite persuaded myself that the whole affair must be some great <u>hoax</u> or fraud, though what its object might be I could not imagine. It seemed altogether past belief that anyone could make such a will, or that they would pay such a sum for doing anything so simple as copying out the Encyclopedia Britannica. Vincent Spaulding did what he could to cheer me up, but by bedtime I had reasoned myself out of the whole thing. However, in the morning I determined to have a look at it anyhow, so I bought a penny bottle of ink, and with a quill-pen, and seven sheets of foolscap paper,[9] I started off for Pope's Court.

"Well, to my surprise and delight, everything was as right as possible. The table was set out ready for me, and Mr. Duncan Ross was there to see that I got fairly to work. He started me off upon the letter A, and then he left me; but he would drop in from time to time to see that all was right with me. At two o'clock he bade me good-day, complimented me upon the amount that I had written, and locked the door of the office after me.

"This went on day after day, Mr. Holmes, and on Saturday the manager came in and planked

---

9. **foolscap paper:** Writing paper.

◆ **Build Vocabulary**

hoax (hōks) *n.*: Deceitful trick

down four golden sovereigns for my week's work. It was the same next week, and the same the week after. Every morning I was there at ten, and every afternoon I left at two. By degrees Mr. Duncan Ross took to coming in only once of a morning, and then, after a time, he did not come in at all. Still, of course, I never dared to leave the room for an instant, for I was not sure when he might come, and the billet was such a good one, and suited me so well, that I would not risk the loss of it.

"Eight weeks passed away like this, and I had written about Abbots and Archery and Armor and Architecture and Attica, and hoped with diligence that I might get on to the B's before very long. It cost me something in foolscap, and I had pretty nearly filled a shelf with my writings. And then suddenly the whole business came to an end."

◆ *Literature and Your Life*

⑤ Students may respond that they would be suspicious of such work. Copying the words from an encyclopedia by hand is a mindless task that serves no apparent purpose.

◆ **Reading Strategy**

⑥ **Key Details** Summarize Mr. Wilson's experience at the Red-headed League, stressing the points you think most significant. *He could not leave the room during his employment; he had to provide his own ink and paper; he was supervised at first and then not at all; his work was shelved; his employment ended abruptly.*

Customize for
Visual/Spatial Learners
Have students identify the character and incident pictured in the illustration. Ask: What can you tell about the character from his position? *Jabez Wilson reads the notice that the Red-headed League has been dissolved. He is literally taken aback by the notice.*

The Red-headed League ◆ 89

❶ Have students explain the note's message in their own words. Then have them explain why Jabez Wilson would be upset over this news.
Students may paraphrase the note by saying that the Red-headed League has been "shut down" or has "gone out of business." Jabez Wilson would be upset over this fact because it means that his source of extra income has disappeared.

Comprehension Check ☑

❷ After the League is dissolved, what circumstances lead Mr. Wilson to question its validity? *Wilson returns to the offices to find everyone gone. While speaking with the landlord, Wilson discovers that Mr. Ross was an alias for William Morris.*

◆ **Literary Focus**

❸ **The Mystery** Elicit the following responses: *The red-headed man who accepted Jabez Wilson into the League now emerges as a suspect. His abrupt disappearance and his use of false identities, or aliases, are the clues that point to him.*

◆ **Critical Thinking**

❹ **Make Inferences** What might be the "graver issues" that Holmes senses in Jabez Wilson's story?
Students may say that Holmes suspects that the Red-headed League was set up so that those behind it could prepare for or conceal a larger crime.

Customize for
Logical/Mathematical Learners
Some of Holmes's questions indicate that he is establishing a timeline of events related to the crime. Logical/mathematical learners can use the information Holmes gathers, together with other pieces of evidence that establish dates, to construct a graphic timeline. When students have completed the story, have them review their timelines. Is the timing of events consistent with Holmes's explanation of the crime?

"To an end?"

"Yes, sir. And no later than this morning. I went to my work as usual at ten o'clock, but the door was shut and locked, with a little square of cardboard hammered on to the middle of the panel with a tack. Here it is, and you can read for yourself."

He held up a piece of white cardboard about the size of a sheet of notepaper. It read in this fashion:

THE RED-HEADED LEAGUE
IS
DISSOLVED.
October 9, 1890.

Sherlock Holmes and I surveyed this curt announcement and the rueful face behind it, until the comical side of the affair so completely overtopped every other consideration that we both burst out into a roar of laughter.

"I cannot see that there is anything very funny," cried our client, flushing up to the roots of his flaming head. "If you can do nothing better than laugh at me, I can go elsewhere."

"No, no," cried Holmes, shoving him back into the chair from which he had half risen. "I really wouldn't miss your case for the world. It is most refreshingly unusual. But there is, if you will excuse my saying so, something just a little funny about it. Pray what steps did you take when you found the card upon the door?"

"I was staggered, sir. I did not know what to do. Then I called at the offices round, but none of them seemed to know anything about it. Finally, I went to the landlord, who is an accountant living on the ground floor, and I asked him if he could tell me what had become of the Red-headed League. He said that he had never heard of any such body. Then I asked him who Mr. Duncan Ross was. He answered that the name was new to him.

" 'Well,' said I, 'the gentleman at No. 4.'

" 'What, the red-headed man?'

" 'Yes.'

" 'Oh,' said he, 'his name was William Morris. He was a solicitor[10] and was using my

---

10. **solicitor:** Member of the legal profession.

room as a temporary convenience until his new premises were ready. He moved out yesterday.'

" 'Where could I find him?'

" 'Oh, at his new offices. He did tell me the address. Yes, 17 King Edward Street, near St. Paul's.'

"I started off, Mr. Holmes, but when I got to that address it was a manufactory of artificial kneecaps, and no one in it had ever heard of either Mr. William Morris or Mr. Duncan Ross."

"And what did you do then?" asked Holmes.

"I went home to Saxe-Coburg Square, and I took the advice of my assistant. But he could not help me in any way. He could only say that if I waited I should hear by post. But that was not quite good enough, Mr. Holmes. I did not wish to lose such a place without a struggle, so, as I had heard that you were good enough to give advice to poor folk who were in need of it, I came right away to you."

"And you did very wisely," said Holmes. "Your case is an exceedingly remarkable one, and I shall be happy to look into it. From what you have told me I think that it is possible that graver issues hang from it than might at first sight appear."

"Grave enough!" said Mr. Jabez Wilson. "Why, I have lost four pound a week."

"As far as you are personally concerned," remarked Holmes, "I do not see that you have any grievance against this extraordinary league. On the contrary, you are, as I understand, richer by some £30, to say nothing of the minute knowledge which you have gained on every subject which comes under the letter A. You have lost nothing by them."

"No, sir. But I want to find out about them, and who they are, and what their object was in playing this prank—if it was a prank—upon me. It was a pretty expensive joke for them, for it cost them two and thirty pounds."

"We shall endeavor to clear up these points for you. And, first, one or two questions, Mr.

Wilson. This assistant of yours who first called your attention to the advertisement—how long had he been with you?"

"About a month then."

"How did he come?"

"In answer to an advertisement."

"Was he the only applicant?"

"No, I had a dozen."

"Why did you pick him?"

"Because he was handy and would come cheap."

"At half-wages, in fact."

"Yes."

"What is he like, this Vincent Spaulding?"

"Small, stout-built, very quick in his ways. no hair on his face, though he's not short of thirty. Has a white splash of acid upon his forehead."

Holmes sat up in his chair in considerable excitement. "I thought as much," said he. **❺** "Have you ever observed that his ears are pierced for earrings?"

❻ "Yes, sir. He told me that a gypsy had done it for him when he was a lad."

"Hum!" said Holmes, sinking back in deep thought. "He is still with you?"

"Oh, yes, sir; I have only just left him."

"And has your business been attended to in your absence?"

"Nothing to complain of, sir. There's never very much to do of a morning."

"That will do, Mr. Wilson. I shall be happy to give you an opinion upon the subject in the course of a day or two. Today is Saturday, and I hope that by Monday we may come to a conclusion."

"Well, Watson," said Holmes when our visitor had left us, "what do you make of it all?"

"I make nothing of it," I answered frankly. "It is a most mysterious business."

"As a rule," said Holmes, "the more bizarre a thing is the less mysterious it proves to be. It is **❼** your commonplace, featureless crimes which are really puzzling, just as a commonplace face is the most difficult to identify. But I must be prompt over this matter."

"What are you going to do, then?" I asked.

"To smoke," he answered. "It is quite a three pipe problem, and I beg that you won't speak to me for fifty minutes." He curled himself up in his chair, with his thin knees drawn up to his hawk-like nose, and there he sat with his eyes closed and his black clay pipe thrusting out like the bill of some strange bird. I had come to the conclusion that he had dropped asleep, and indeed was nodding myself, when he suddenly sprang out of his chair with the gesture of a man who has made up his mind

and put his pipe down upon the mantelpiece.

"Sarasate[11] plays at the St. James's Hall this afternoon," he remarked. "What do you think, Watson? Could your patients spare you for a few hours?"

"I have nothing to do today. My practice is never very absorbing."

"Then put on your hat and come. I am going through the City first, and we can have some lunch on the way. I observe that there is a

---

11. Sarasate (sä rä sä′ tä): Spanish violinist and composer.

The Red-headed League ◆ 91

91

◆ **Critical Thinking**

❺ Make Inferences Why do you think Holmes is so excited when he hears this description of Spaulding? *Holmes has had previous knowledge or contact with Spaulding and knew his ears were pierced for earrings.*

Comprehension Check ☑

❻ How does Holmes know that Spaulding's ears are pierced? What fact does Holmes's knowledge reveal? *He recognizes Spaulding, based on Wilson's description. This reveals that Holmes has met or heard of Spaulding before.*

◆ **Literary Focus**

❼ The Mystery Why does Holmes say that more bizarre crimes are easier to figure out than "commonplace, featureless crimes"? *Students may recognize that a crime has not been committed as yet, that Holmes is solving a mystery as it unravels, and that nothing too out of the ordinary has taken place.*

◆ *Literature and Your Life*

❽ Point out the techniques that Holmes uses to help him concentrate. Tell students that people use many different devices to help them concentrate. Some take a walk or pace a room, while others prefer to sit still like Holmes. Have students describe the techniques that they use to focus their attention on a problem. Ask them why such devices are helpful. *Creative problem solving often is carried on accompanied by music and other activity that allows the facts to simmer. Writers and artists might clean house or play a game of tennis while the mind ponders a special problem to be solved. Have students discuss what they do when they have an idea to mull over.*

Customize for
Visual/Spatial Learners
Ask students to identify the character pictured in the illustration. How do they know who it is? *Sherlock Holmes is seated, puffing on his pipe, deep in thought as he sifts through the details of the case.*

❾ Clarification The City to which Holmes refers is the historic district in downtown London. In fact, this district is the site of the original "City of London," a small, centuries-old city around which modern London grew.

 Workplace Skills Mini-Lesson

Interviewing Skills

This mini-lesson is designed to help students explore various work situations that call for interviewing skills.

Introduce the Concept Remind students that Sherlock Holmes skillfully interviews both clients and suspects. Then point out that interviewing skills are essential for a wide variety of jobs.

Develop Background Help students brainstorm to name jobs that require interviewing skills. Possibilities include newspaper/television reporter, personnel manager, market researcher,

and psychologist. Discuss which kinds of questions elicit the most information from interviewees, establishing that yes-and-no questions are the least productive.

Apply the Information Have pairs of students choose one of the jobs and role-play an interview.

Assess the Outcome Have students use the Peer Assessment: Speaker/Speech sheet in *Alternative Assessment,* p. 111, to evaluate the interviews. Then ask students whether they developed an interest in jobs they had not previously considered.

91

◆ Build Grammar Skills

❶ Have students review the examples of coordinate adjectives and adjectives that are not coordinate on page 80. You might suggest that adjectives are coordinate only if it makes sense to place the word "and" between them. Then have them find (a) one example of coordinate adjectives and (b) two examples of adjectives that are not coordinate in the sentence here. *Coordinate: poky, little, shabby-genteel place; not coordinate: dingy two-storied brick houses; small railed enclosure.*

◆ Reading Strategy

❷ **Key Details** Responses may include the following: *Holmes is studying the pawnbroker's shop to determine if it is a likely target for a robbery. Holmes thumps the pavement to detect an underground hiding place. Holmes knocks on the door so that he can catch of glimpse of Wilson's assistant, whom he seemed to recognize from Wilson's description.*

◆ Critical Thinking

❸ **Identify Cause and Effect** Remind students that, as Holmes noted earlier, Jabez Wilson's jacket cuff was worn out as a result of all the writing he had been doing. Then ask: What might Holmes expect to learn from looking at the knees of Spaulding's trousers? *Students may say that Holmes wants to determine whether or not Spaulding had been doing any work that involved crawling or kneeling.*

---

good deal of German music on the program, which is rather more to my taste than Italian or French. It is <u>introspective</u>, and I want to introspect. Come along!"

❶ We traveled by the Underground as far as Aldersgate; and a short walk took us to Saxe-Coburg Square, the scene of the singular story which we had listened to in the morning. It was a poky, little, shabby-genteel place, where four lines of dingy two-storied brick houses looked out into a small railed–in enclosure, where a lawn of weedy grass and a few clumps of faded laurel bushes made a hard fight against a smoke-laden and uncongenial atmosphere. Three gilt balls and a brown board with "JABEZ WILSON" in white letters, upon a corner house, announced the place where our red-headed client carried on his business. Sherlock Holmes stopped in front of it with his head on one side and looked it all over, with his eyes shining brightly between puckered lids. Then he walked slowly up the street, and then down again to the corner, still looking keenly at the houses. Finally he returned to the pawnbroker's, and, having thumped vigorously upon the pavement with his stick two or three times, he went up to the door and knocked. It was instantly opened by a bright-looking, clean-shaven young fellow, who asked him to step in.

> **❷** ◆ **Reading Strategy**
> In this passage, Holmes is gathering key details that may be clues. See if you can identify those details.

"Thank you," said Holmes, "I only wished to ask you how you would go from here to the Strand."

"Third right, fourth left," answered the assistant promptly, closing the door.

"Smart fellow, that," observed Holmes as we walked away. "He is, in my judgment, the fourth smartest man in London, and for daring I am not sure that he has not a claim to be third. I have known something of him before."

◆ **Build Vocabulary**
introspective (in´ trə spek´ tiv) *adj.*: Causing one to look into one's own thoughts and feelings

---

"Evidently," said I, "Mr. Wilson's assistant counts for a good deal in this mystery of the Red-headed League. I am sure that you inquired your way merely in order that you might see him."

"Not him."

"What then?"

"The knees of his trousers."

"And what did you see?"

"What I expected to see."

"Why did you beat the pavement?"

❸ "My dear doctor, this is a time for observation, not for talk. We are spies in an enemy's country. We know something of Saxe-Coburg Square. Let us now explore the parts which lie behind it."

The road in which we found ourselves as we turned round the corner from the retired Saxe-Coburg Square presented as great a contrast to it as the front of a picture does to the back. It was one of the main arteries which conveyed the traffic of the City to the north and west. The roadway was blocked with the immense stream of commerce flowing in a double tide inward and outward, while the footpaths were black with the hurrying swarm of pedestrians. It was difficult to realize as we looked at the line of fine shops and stately business premises that they really abutted on the other side upon the faded and stagnant square which we had just quitted.

"Let me see," said Holmes, standing at the corner and glancing along the line, "I should like just to remember the order of the houses here. It is a hobby of mine to have an exact knowledge of London. There is Mortimer's, the tobacconist, the little newspaper shop, the Coburg branch of the City and Suburban Bank, the Vegetarian Restaurant, and McFarlane's carriage-building depot. That carries us right on to the other block. And now, Doctor, we've done our work, so it's time we had some play. A sandwich and a cup of coffee, and then off to violin land, where all is sweetness and delicacy and harmony, and there are no red-headed clients to <u>vex</u> us with their <u>conundrums</u>."

❹ My friend was an enthusiastic musician, being himself not only a very capable performer but a composer of no ordinary merit.

Beyond the Classroom

Community Connection

Historic Sites The City is what Londoners call the district in which Holmes foils a daring bank robbery. Deriving its name from the City of London—the original settlement that developed into modern London—this historic downtown area is as bustling today as it was during Sir Arthur Conan Doyle's lifetime.

Have students work in small groups to identify and research various old and his-

toric sites in their community. For example, students may focus on the oldest house, the oldest building, the oldest business, the birthplace of a famous person, or the site of a notable event. To gather ideas and information, they might consult commemorative plaques, interview longtime residents, or visit their local historical society.

Local Maps Sherlock Holmes declares that it is a hobby of his to have an exact knowledge of London. Have students put their knowledge of their community to work by making maps that they can present to newcomers to your school. In addition to information about their school and its outdoor facilities, the maps can include nearby points of interest such as shops, restaurants, and bus stops.

All the afternoon he sat in the stalls wrapped in the most perfect happiness, gently waving his long, thin fingers in time to the music, while his gently smiling face and his languid, dreamy eyes were as unlike those of Holmes, the sleuthhound, Holmes the relentless, keen-witted, ready-handed criminal agent, as it was possible to conceive. In his singular character the dual nature alternately asserted itself, and his extreme exactness and <u>astuteness</u> represented, as I have often thought, the reaction against the poetic and contemplative mood which occasionally predominated in him. The swing of his nature took him from extreme languor to devouring energy; and, as I knew well, **⑤** he was never so truly <u>formidable</u> as when, for days on end, he had been lounging in his armchair amid his improvisations and his black-letter editions. Then it was that the lust of the chase would suddenly come upon him, and that his brilliant reasoning power would rise to the level of intuition, until those who were unacquainted with his methods would look askance at him as on a man whose knowledge was not that of other mortals. When I saw him that afternoon so enwrapped in the music at St. James's Hall I felt that an evil time might be coming upon those whom he had set himself to hunt down.

"You want to go home, no doubt, Doctor," he remarked as we emerged.

"Yes, it would be as well."

"And I have some business to do which will take some hours. This business at Coburg Square is serious."

"Why serious?"

"A considerable crime is in contemplation. I have every reason to believe that we shall be in time to stop it. But today being Saturday

◆ **Build Vocabulary**

vex (veks) v.: Annoy

conundrums (kə nun′ drəmz) n.: Puzzling questions or problems

astuteness (ə stoot′ nis) n.: Shrewdness

formidable (fôr′ mə də bəl) adj.: Awe-inspiring

rather complicates matters. I shall want your help tonight."

"At what time?"

"Ten will be early enough."

"I shall be at Baker Street at ten."

"Very well. And, I say, Doctor, there may be some little danger, so kindly put your army revolver in your pocket." He waved his hand, turned on his heel, and disappeared in an instant among the crowd.

I trust that I am not more dense than my neighbors, but I was always oppressed with a sense of my own stupidity in my dealings with Sherlock Holmes. Here I had heard what he had heard, I had seen what he had seen, and yet from his words it was evident that he saw clearly not only what had happened but what **⑥** was about to happen, while to me the whole business was still confused and grotesque. As I drove home to my house in Kensington I thought over it all, from the extraordinary story

The Red-headed League ◆ 93

of the red-headed copier of the Encyclopedia down to the visit to Saxe-Coburg Square, and the ominous words with which he had parted from me. What was this nocturnal expedition, and why should I go armed? Where were we going, and what were we to do? I had the hint from Holmes that this smooth-faced pawnbroker's assistant was a formidable man—a man who might play a deep game. I tried to puzzle it out, but gave it up in despair and set the matter aside until night should bring an explanation.

It was a quarter past nine when I started from home and made my way across the Park, and so through Oxford Street to Baker Street. Two hansoms[12] were standing at the door, and as I entered the passage I heard the sound of voices from above. On entering his room I found Holmes in animated conversation with two men, one of whom I recognized as Peter Jones, the official police agent, while the other was a long, thin, sadfaced man, with a very shiny hat and oppressively respectable frock coat.

"Ha! our party is complete," said Holmes, buttoning up his pea-jacket and taking his heavy hunting crop from the rack. "Watson, I think you know Mr. Jones, of Scotland Yard? Let me introduce you to Mr. Merryweather, who is to be our companion in tonight's adventure."

"We're hunting in couples again, Doctor, you see," said Jones in his consequential way. "Our friend here is a wonderful man for starting a chase. All he wants is an old dog to help him to do the running down."

"I hope a wild goose may not prove to be the end of our chase," observed Mr. Merryweather gloomily.

"You may place considerable confidence in Mr. Holmes, sir," said the police agent loftily.

"He has his own little methods, which are, if he won't mind my saying so, just a little too theoretical and fantastic, but he has the makings of a detective in him. It is not too much to say that once or twice, as in that business of the Sholto murder and the Agra treasure, he has been more nearly correct than the official force."

"Oh, if you say so, Mr. Jones, it is all right," said the stranger with deference. "Still, I confess that I miss my rubber.[13] It is the first Saturday night for seven-and-twenty years that I have not had my rubber."

---

12. hansoms: Two-wheeled covered carriages for two passengers.

13. rubber: Card games.

"I think you will find," said Sherlock Holmes, "that you will play for a higher stake tonight than you have ever done yet, and that the play will be more exciting. For you, Mr. Merryweather, the stake will be some £30,000: and for you, Jones, it will be the man upon whom you wish to lay your hands."

"John Clay, the murderer, thief, smasher, and forger. He's a young man, Mr. Merryweather, but he is at the head of his profession, and I would rather have my bracelets on him than on any criminal in London. He's a remarkable man, is young John Clay. His grandfather was a royal duke, and he himself has been to Eton[14] and Oxford.[15] His brain is as cunning as his fingers, and though we meet signs of him at every turn, we never know where to find the man himself. He'll crack a crib[16] in Scotland one week, and be raising money to build an orphanage in Cornwall the next. I've been on his track for years and have never set eyes on him yet."

"I hope that I may have the pleasure of introducing you tonight. I've had one or two little turns also with Mr. John Clay, and I agree with you that he is at the head of his profession. It is past ten, however, and quite time that we started. If you two will take the first hansom, Watson and I will follow in the second."

Sherlock Holmes was not very communicative during the long drive and lay back in the cab humming the tunes which he had heard in the afternoon. We rattled through an endless labyrinth of gas-lit streets until we emerged into Farrington Street.

"We are close there now," my friend remarked. "This fellow Merryweather is a bank director, and personally interested in the matter. I thought it as well to have Jones with us also. He is not a bad fellow, though an absolute imbecile in his profession. He has one positive virtue. He is as brave as a bulldog and as tenacious as a lobster if he gets his claws upon anyone. Here

---

14. **Eton:** Famous British secondary school for boys.
15. **Oxford:** Oldest university in Great Britain.
16. **crack a crib:** Break into and rob a house.

---

we are, and they are waiting for us."

We had reached the same crowded thoroughfare in which we had found ourselves in the morning. Our cabs were dismissed, and, following the guidance of Mr. Merryweather, we passed down a narrow passage and through a side door, which he opened for us. Within there was a small corridor, which ended in a very massive iron gate. This also was opened, and led down a flight of winding stone steps, which terminated at another formidable gate. Mr. Merryweather stopped to light a lantern, and then conducted us down a dark, earth-smelling passage, and so, after opening a third door, into a huge vault or cellar, which was piled all round with crates and massive boxes.

"You are not very vulnerable from above," Holmes remarked as he held up the lantern and gazed about him.

"Nor from below," said Mr. Merryweather, striking his stick upon the flags which lined the floor. "Why, dear me, it sounds quite hollow!" he remarked, looking up in surprise.

"I must really ask you to be a little more quiet!" said Holmes severely. "You have already imperiled the whole success of our expedition. Might I beg that you would have the goodness to sit down upon one of those boxes, and not to interfere?"

The solemn Mr. Merryweather perched himself upon a crate, with a very injured expression upon his face, while Holmes fell upon his knees upon the floor and, with the lantern and a magnifying lens, began to examine minutely the cracks between the stones. A few seconds sufficed to satisfy him, for he sprang to his feet again and put his glass in his pocket.

"We have at least an hour before us," he remarked, "for they can hardly take any steps until the good pawnbroker is safely in bed. Then they will not lose a minute, for the sooner they do their work the longer time they will have for their escape. We are at present, Doctor—as no doubt you have divined—in the cellar of the City branch of one of the principal London banks. Mr. Merryweather is the chairman of directors, and he will explain to you that there are reasons why

---

❹ **Key Details** Why do you think Mr. Merryweather, a bank director, has been invited to go along? *If the crime is a theft involving the nearby bank, then no doubt Merryweather could be useful.*

◆ **Critical Thinking**

❺ **Compare and Contrast** Contrast what Holmes says about Jones's talents with what Jones has said about Holmes's ability. *Jones implies that Holmes cannot do the job without them. Holmes compliments Jones for his bravery and tenacity, but jokes with him about his inability to solve crimes.*

◆ **Reading Strategy**

❻ **Key Details** Predict where Holmes and the others are going, basing your answer on the buildings listed by Holmes on page 92. *Among the buildings mentioned is the Coburg branch of the City and Suburban Bank. The fact that Mr. Merryweather is directing them and opening the doors for them leads to the conclusion that they are in the bank.*

◆ **Build Grammar Skills**

❼ **Coordinate Adjectives** Call students' attention to the phrases *winding stone steps* and *dark, earth-smelling passage.* Have students identify the coordinate adjectives. *The coordinate adjectives are "dark, earth-smelling." The adjectives "winding" and "stone" are not coordinate.*

Comprehension Check ☑

❽ Ask students: What signs of the enemy's preparations did Holmes and the others find in the vault? *Mr. Merryweather tapped on the floor and discovered that the ground underneath was hollow. Holmes examined the cracks between the stones lining the floor and must have concluded that someone had cut through from below.*

◆ **Literary Focus**

The Mystery Have students summarize what they know about the criminal so far. Remind them that this information will help Holmes learn the motive for the crime and trap the criminal. Summaries should include: *The criminal's real name is John Clay. He is a cunning murderer, thief, and forger who has eluded the police for years. Posing as "Vincent Spaulding," he played a pivotal role in drawing Jabez Wilson into the Red-headed League.*

① Key Details Mr. Merryweather reveals that the amount of gold being stored in the bank is unusually large and that its presence is not a well-kept secret. These facts suggest that the criminal, John Clay, intends to steal the gold.

◆ Literary Focus

② The Mystery How does the description of their preparations heighten the suspense? *The author's description of the preparations adds to the suspense. The details about the necessity of being in total darkness, as well as the suggestion that they are about to come face to face with the criminal, build excitement.*

◆ Build Vocabulary

③ Word Roots: -spec- Point out that the word *inspector* contains the root *-spec-*, which means "look" or "see." Then explain that the suffix *-or*, as in *inventor*, means "someone who." Ask students: What, then, is an inspector? *An inspector is someone who inspects, or examines.*

◆ Critical Thinking

④ Identify Cause and Effect How does Watson's description of what he is feeling and hearing add to the suspense? *Watson represents the reader's presence in the story in the questions he asks of Holmes and his participation as narrator. Now he takes us to the final moments and in his description we hear the distinguishable breathing of Jones and Merryweather, feel his anticipation, and loss of reference to time.*

Customize for
Visual/Spatial Learners
Have students identify the characters and event pictured in the illustration. *Holmes apprehends John Clay, alias Spaulding, as he attempts to exit from the tunnel with his bank loot.*

---

the more daring criminals of London should take a considerable interest in this cellar at present."

"It is our French gold," whispered the director. "We have had several warnings that an attempt might be made upon it."

"Your French gold?"

"Yes. We had occasion some months ago to strengthen our resources and borrowed for that purpose 30,000 napoleons from the Bank of France. It has become known that we have never had occasion to unpack the money, and that it is still lying in our cellar. The crate upon

which I sit contains 2,000 napoleons packed between layers of lead foil. Our reserve of bullion is much larger at present than is usually kept in a single branch office, and the directors have had misgivings upon the subject."

"Which were very well justified," observed Holmes.

"And now it is time that we arranged our little plans. I expect that within an hour matters will come to a head. In the meantime, Mr. Merryweather, we must put the screen over that dark lantern."

"And sit in the dark?"

"I am afraid so. I had brought a pack of cards in my pocket, and I thought that, as we were a *partie carrée*,[17] you might have your rubber after all. But I see that the enemy's preparations have gone so far that we cannot risk the presence of a light. And, first of all, we must choose our positions. These are daring men, and though we shall take them at a disadvantage, they may do us some harm unless we are careful. I shall stand behind this crate, and do you conceal yourselves behind those. Then, when I flash a light upon them, close in swiftly. If they fire, Watson, have no compunction about shooting them down."

I placed my revolver, cocked, upon the top of the wooden case behind which I crouched. Holmes shot the slide across the front of his lantern and left us in pitch darkness—such an absolute darkness as I have never before experienced. The smell of hot metal remained to assure us that the light was still there, ready to flash out at a moment's notice. To me, with my nerves worked up to a pitch of expectancy, there

---

17. *partie carrée* (pär tē cä rā´): French for "group of four."

was something depressing and subduing in the sudden gloom, and in the cold dank air of the vault.

"They have but one retreat," whispered Holmes. "That is back through the house into Saxe-Coburg Square. I hope that you have done what I asked you, Jones?"

❸ "I have an inspector and two officers waiting at the front door."

"Then we have stopped all the holes. And now we must be silent and wait."

❹ What a time it seemed! From comparing notes afterwards it was but an hour and a quarter, yet it appeared to me that the night must have almost gone, and the dawn be breaking above us. My limbs were weary and stiff, for I feared to change my position; yet my nerves were worked up to the highest pitch of tension, and my hearing was so acute that I could not only hear the gentle breathing of my companions, but I could distinguish the deeper, heavier in-breath of the bulky Jones from the thin, sighing note of the bank director. From my position I could look over the case in the direction of the floor. Suddenly my eyes caught the glint of a light.

At first it was but a lurid spark upon the stone pavement. Then it lengthened out until it became a yellow line, and then, without any warning or sound, a gash seemed to open and a hand appeared; a white, almost womanly hand, which felt about in the center of the little area of light. For a minute or more the hand, with its ❺ writhing fingers, protruded out of the floor. Then it was withdrawn as suddenly as it appeared, and all was dark again save the single lurid spark which marked a chink between the stones.

◆ **Literary Focus**
❻ At this point in the story, the suspense reaches its height. What story elements contribute to the building of suspense?

Its disappearance, however, was but momentary. With a rending, tearing sound, one of the broad, white stones turned over upon its side and left a square, gaping hole, through which streamed the light of a lantern. Over the edge there peeped a clean-cut, boyish face,

which looked keenly about it, and then, with a hand on either side of the aperture, drew itself shoulder-high and waist-high, until one knee rested upon the edge. In another instant he stood at the side of the hole and was hauling after him a companion, lithe and small like himself, with a pale face and a shock of very red hair.

"It's all clear," he whispered. "Have you the chisel and the bags? Great Scott! Jump, Archie, jump, and I'll swing for it."

Sherlock Holmes had sprung out and seized the intruder by the collar. The other dived down the hole, and I heard the sound of rending cloth as Jones clutched at his skirts. The light flashed upon the barrel of a revolver, but Holmes's hunting crop came down on the man's wrist, and the pistol clinked upon the stone floor.

"It's no use, John Clay," said Holmes blandly. "You have no chance at all."

"So I see," the other answered with the utmost coolness. "I fancy that my pal is all right, though I see you have got his coattails."

"There are three men waiting for him at the door," said Holmes.

"Oh, indeed! You seem to have done the thing very completely. I must compliment you."

"And I you," Holmes answered. "Your redheaded idea was very new and effective."

"You'll see your pal again presently," said Jones. "He's quicker at climbing down holes than I am. Just hold out while I fix the derbies."[18]

"I beg that you will not touch me with your filthy hands," remarked our prisoner as the handcuffs clattered upon his wrists. "You may not be aware that I have royal blood in my veins. Have the goodness, also, when you address me always to say 'sir' and 'please.'"

"All right," said Jones with a stare and a snigger. "Well, would you please, sir, march upstairs, where we can get a cab to carry your Highness to the police station?"

"That is better," said John Clay serenely. He made a sweeping bow to the three of us

---

18. **derbies:** Handcuffs.

◆ **Literary Focus**
❺ **The Mystery** Why do you think that it is so effective to describe the criminal's hand as it first appears from the tunnel? *By describing the hand only, Doyle is withholding the identity of the criminal until just the right moment. It is important to know if he is armed or not, and if he suspects any trouble. It is with his hands that he had dug the tunnel and it is with his hand that he plans to take what he wants.*

◆ **Literary Focus**
❻ **The Mystery** Ask a volunteer to read this paragraph aloud. Then have students identify the details and phrases that help create a sense of excitement and suspense. Students may cite the following: *"... the hand, with its writhing fingers, protruded out of the floor"; "With a rending, tearing sound, one of the broad, white stones turned over upon its side ..."; "Over the edge there peeped a clean-cut boyish face...."*

◆ **Critical Thinking**
❼ **Draw Conclusions** Can you identify the two men who climb out of the tunnel? *Using the clues that are given, it appears to be Vincent Spaulding and Duncan Ross.*

Speaking and Listening Mini-Lesson

Summary
This mini-lesson supports the Speaking and Listening activity in the Idea Bank on page 101.

Introduce the Concept Tell students that fictional detectives are often called on to "reconstruct the crime." This is exactly what students will be doing when they deliver summaries of the events leading up to the arrest of John Clay.

Develop Background Before students prepare their summaries, have them consid-

er these guidelines:
• Summaries should be accurate. Going back over the source of information (in this case, the text of the story) will help ensure accuracy.
• Summaries cover main points. As students go back over the story, they will need to distinguish between more and less important events.
• Summaries should be clear. Students should make sure that they present the main events in chronological order.

Apply the Information Following these guidelines, students should be able to prepare and deliver brief oral summaries of the story. Remind them that since they will be playing Sherlock Holmes, they will want to use appropriate words and gestures when they speak.

Assess the Outcome Have students evaluate the summaries in terms of accuracy, conciseness, and clarity.

98

◆ Literary Focus

❶ The Mystery Invite students to sum up the case by identifying the crime-solver, the criminals, the crime, and the victims in the story. *Crime-solver: Sherlock Holmes; criminals: John Clay and his red-headed accomplice; crime: an attempted bank robbery; victims: the directors and owners of the bank and, to some extent, Jabez Wilson.*

◆ Build Vocabulary

❷ Word Roots: -spec- Point out that the word *suspected*, which in this case means "saw or supposed based on incomplete evidence," contains the root *-spec-*. Have students use this word in sentences of their own. *Students might generate such sentences as: Holmes suspected that Spaulding was digging a tunnel. I suspected that my sister had borrowed my camera.*

Comprehension Check ☑

❸ Have students summarize in their own words the connection among Spaulding's interest in working for the pawnbroker, his interest in photography, and the crime he was planning to commit. Summaries should include: *Spaulding knew that Jabez Wilson's house was close to the bank that held the gold; he planned to dig a tunnel from the house to the bank; his "hobby" provided him with an excuse for spending long periods of time in Wilson's cellar.*

and walked quietly off in the custody of the detective.

"Really, Mr. Holmes," said Mr. Merryweather as we followed them from the cellar, "I do not know how the bank can thank you or repay you. There is no doubt that you have detected and defeated in the most complete manner one of the most determined attempts at bank robbery that have ever come within my experience."

"I have had one or two little scores of my own to settle with Mr. John Clay," said Holmes. "I have been at some small expense over this matter, which I shall expect the bank to refund, but beyond that I am amply repaid by having had an experience which is in many ways unique, and by hearing the very remarkable narrative of the Red-headed League."

"You see, Watson," he explained in the early hours of the morning as we sat over a glass of whisky and soda in Baker Street, "it was perfectly obvious from the first that the only possible object of this rather fantastic business of

the advertisement of the League, and the copying of the Encyclopedia, must be to get this not over-bright pawnbroker out of the way for a number of hours every day. It was a curious way of managing it, but, really, it would be difficult to suggest a better. The method was no doubt suggested to Clay's ingenious mind by the color of his accomplice's hair. The £4 a week was a lure which must draw him, and what was it to them, who were playing for thousands? They put in the advertisement, one rogue has the temporary office, the other rogue incites the man to apply for it, and together

> **◆ Literary Focus**
> Here, the solution to the mystery is revealed to Watson—and to the reader. Holmes explains the criminal's motivation and methods, and the story comes to a close.

they manage to secure his absence every morning in the week. From the time that I heard of the assistant having come for half wages, it was obvious to me that he had some strong motive for securing the situation."

"But how could you guess what the motive was?"

"Had there been women in the house, I should have suspected a mere vulgar intrigue. That, however, was out of the question. The man's business was a small one, and there was nothing in his house which could account for such elaborate preparations, and such an expenditure as they were at. It must, then, be something out of the house. What could it be? I thought of the assistant's fondness for photography, and his trick of vanishing into the cellar. The cellar! There was the end of this tangled clue. Then I made inquiries as to this mysterious assistant and found that I had to deal with one of the coolest and most daring criminals in London. He was doing something in the cellar—something which took many hours a day for

98 ◆ Spine Tinglers

Speaking and Listening Mini-Lesson

Grilling the Suspect

This mini-lesson supports the Speaking and Listening activity in the Idea Bank on page 101.

Introduce the Concept Mention that police inspectors (or detectives, as they are called in the United States) "grill," or question, suspects to obtain confessions or further information about suspects' crimes.

Develop Background In preparation for this activity, have partners choose their roles. Then have the "Joneses" and the "Spauldings" meet in small groups to plan their strategies—either for convincing or tricking Spaulding into revealing information, or for evading Jones's questions. Group members might also discuss their characters and how they should speak and act.

Apply the Information Students should then be able to role-play the parts of Spaulding and Jones with their partners.

Assess the Outcome Have students evaluate their own role-playing and that of their partners. Remind them to give positive as well as constructive evaluations.

❸ months on end. What could it be, once more? I could think of nothing save that he was running a tunnel to some other building.

"So far I had got when we went to visit the scene of action. I surprised you by beating upon the pavement with my stick. I was ascertaining whether the cellar stretched out in front or behind. It was not in front. Then I rang the bell, and, as I hoped, the assistant answered it. We have had some skirmishes, but we had never set eyes upon each other before. I hardly looked at his face. His knees were what I wished to see. You must yourself have remarked how worn, wrinkled, and stained they were. They spoke of those hours of burrowing. The only remaining **❹** point was what they were burrowing for. I walked round the corner, saw that the City and Suburban Bank abutted on our friend's premises, and felt that I had solved my problem. When you drove home after the concert I called upon Scotland Yard and upon the chairman of the bank directors, with the result that you have seen."

"And how could you tell that they would make their attempt tonight?" I asked.

"Well, when they closed their League offices that was a sign that they cared no longer about Mr. Jabez Wilson's presence—in other words,

that they had completed their tunnel. But it was essential that they should use it soon, as it might be discovered, or the bullion might be removed. Saturday would suit them better than any other day, as it would give them two days for their escape. For all these reasons I expected them to come tonight." **❹**

"You reasoned it out beautifully," I exclaimed in unfeigned admiration. "It is so long a chain, and yet every link rings true."

"It saved me from ennui,"[19] he answered, yawning. "Alas ! I already feel it closing in upon me. My life is spent in one long effort to escape from the commonplaces of existence. These little problems help me to do so."

"And you are a benefactor of the race," said I.

He shrugged his shoulders. "Well, perhaps, after all, it is of some little use," he remarked. " 'L'homme c'est rien—l'oeuvre c'est tout,'[20] as Gustave Flaubert wrote to George Sand."[21]

---

19. **ennui** (än´ wē): Boredom.
20. **L'homme c'est rien—l'oeuvre c'est tout** (lum sä rēn lŧvr sä tōō): French for "Man is nothing—the work is everything."
21. **Gustave Flaubert** (gōōs täv´ flō bär´) . . . **George Sand:** Notable French novelists of the nineteenth century.

Guide for Responding

◆ *Literature and Your Life*

Reader's Response What did you think of the solution to the mystery? Was it a satisfying ending to the story?

Thematic Focus When have you used your powers of observation to solve real-life mysteries?

Role Play With a partner, act out a scene that takes place between Holmes and Watson a year after the story ends. Have them reflect back on the highlights of the case.

☑ Check Your Comprehension

1. Why does Jabez Wilson come to see Sherlock Holmes?
2. As a member of the Red-headed League, what job is Wilson given?
3. Whom does Holmes suspect is the master criminal?
4. Why do the criminals want Jabez Wilson out of the pawnbroker's shop?
5. What happens the night of the attempted burglary?

The Red-headed League ◆ 99

Comprehension Check ☑

❹ Are you satisfied by Holmes's explanation of the case? Were you able to predict some of the developments? *Holmes, having picked up on the clue of Spaulding, spending so much time in the cellar, sought first to determine in which direction he may have been burrowing. Once the investigation revealed the hollow space, he followed it to the bank. His clothing revealed that Spaulding had been on his knees for hours.*

Reinforce and Extend

Answers
◆ *Literature and Your Life*

Reader's Response Students may say the solution to the mystery was clever and satisfying once it became clear.

Thematic Focus Students' responses should identify specific situations in which their observations solved real-life mysteries, as, for example, in finding a lost set of car keys.

☑ Check Your Comprehension

1. Wilson thinks he is the victim of a fraud.
2. Wilson's job is to copy the Encyclopaedia Britannica.
3. Holmes suspects Vincent Spaulding, an employee of Jabez Wilson.
4. They want Wilson out of the shop so they can dig a tunnel from the pawnshop to the nearby bank.
5. Holmes, Watson, Mr. Jones of Scotland Yard, and the bank director wait for and surprise the criminals as they attempt to rob the bank.

Beyond the Selection

FURTHER READING

Other Works by Sir Arthur Conan Doyle
A Study in Scarlet
The Sign of Four
The Hound of the Baskervilles

Mysteries by Other Writers
"The Purloined Letter," Edgar Allan Poe
Murder on the Orient Express, Agatha Christie
Pudd'nhead Wilson, Mark Twain

INTERNET

You and your students may find additional information about Sir Arthur Conan Doyle and Sherlock Holmes on the Internet. We suggest the following site. Please be aware, however, that sites may have changed from the time we published this information. For information about Sherlock Holmes, go to **http://www.cs.cmu.edu/afs/andrew.emu.edu/usr18/mset/www/holmes.html**

We *strongly recommend* that you preview the site before you send students there.

◆ Build Grammar Skills

❶ Parallelism Have students identify parallel structures in this passage. Then ask how they help create a mood for the poem. *And his horse . . . champed; And a bird . . . flew up; And he smote—The repetition creates a sense of mystery; it also suggests inevitability.*

►Critical Viewing◄

❷ Explain The mood is mysterious and lonely. Students may say that the isolated, empty-but-lit house, shadowed by thick, dark trees and surrounded by black night, creates the feeling of mystery that characterizes the poem.

◆ Reading Strategy

❸ Use Your Senses Invite students to picture the "starred and leafy sky." Have them imagine they are looking up through the branches of a tree into a dark, starry-night sky. Then ask why the poet calls the sky "leafy." *When the Traveler looks up through the trees, he sees the pattern of leaves superimposed on the starry sky.*

Customize for
More Advanced Students
Challenge students to find the parallelism between lines 3–4 and lines 23–24, later in the poem. *Both passages refer first to how the horse ate grass from the ground. The earlier lines refer to the forest floor seen through the ferns, while the later lines refer to the sky seen through the leaves. The rhythms of the two passages are similar, as well.*

The *Listeners*

Walter de la Mare

Het Blind Huis, William Degouve de Nunques, State Museum, Kröller-Müller, Otterlo, The Netherlands

'Is there anybody there?' said the Traveler,
 Knocking on the moonlit door;
And his horse in the silence champed[1]
  the grasses
 Of the forest's ferny floor:

❶ 5 And a bird flew up out of the turret,
 Above the Traveler's head:
And he smote[2] upon the door again a
  second time;
 'Is there anybody there?' he said.
But no one descended to the Traveler;

10 No head from the leaf-fringed sill
Leaned over and looked into his gray eyes,
 Where he stood <u>perplexed</u> and still.
But only a host of <u>phantom</u> listeners
 That dwelt in the lone house then

15 Stood listening in the quiet of the moonlight
 To that voice from the world of men:
Stood <u>thronging</u> the faint moonbeams on
  the <u>dark</u> stair,
 That goes down to the empty hall,
Hearkening in an air stirred and shaken

20 By the lonely Traveler's call.

---

1. **champed** (champt) *v*.: Chewed.
2. **smote** (smōt) *v*.: Struck hard.

 Critical Viewing Does this painting convey the same feeling as "The Listeners"? Why or why not? [**Explain**]

◆ Build Vocabulary
perplexed (pər plekst´) *adj*.: Puzzled; full of doubt
thronging (throŋ´ iŋ) *v*.: Crowding into

Humanities: Art

Het Blinde Huis, 1892, by William Degouve de Nunques.

"The House of Mystery," or "The Blind House," glows like an orange jack-o'-lantern through the dark night. The house itself seems to possess a malevolent intelligence, while the single glowing window in the dark shadows on the left seems to have secret significance.

William Degouve de Nunques was a member of the Symbolist movement in painting, which favored paintings that suggested ideas and moods rather than imitating the visible world in a realistic way.

Use these questions for discussion:
1. Which details in the painting make it an appropriate illustration for the poem "The Listeners"? *Answers should include: the "moonlit door," the "dark turf," the "leaf-fringed sill," the "starred and leafy sky."*
2. How does the painting call attention to who or what is inside the house, rather than to its surroundings? *The surroundings are dark and barely visible, whereas the house is brightly colored and glowing.*

◆ **Critical Thinking**

❹ **Evaluate** Ask students what questions this passage prompts them to ask. *Who is "them"? What promise had the Traveler made?* Then invite them to imagine their own answers. *Students may say that "them" refers to people who are dead or gone away, or to people who are in the house but not responding to the Traveler.*

And he felt in his heart their strangeness,
  Their stillness answering his cry,
While his horse moved, cropping the dark
    turf,
  'Neath the starred and leafy sky;

❸

25 For he suddenly smote on the door, even
  Louder, and lifted his head:—

❹

'Tell them I came, and no one answered,
  That I kept my word,' he said.
Never the least stir made the listeners,
30   Though every word he spake[3]
Fell echoing through the shadowiness of
    the still house
From the one man left awake:
Ay, they heard his foot upon the stirrup
  And the sound of iron on stone,

❺

35 And how the silence surged softly backward,
  When the plunging hoofs were gone.

3. spake (spāk) *v.:* Spoke.

◆ **Critical Thinking**

❺ **Interpret** Ask students why the author ends the poem with an image of the listeners rather than with the Traveler. *Students may say that ending with the listeners gives an eerie, mysterious feeling; that focusing on ghosts is more interesting than focusing on a living man on horseback and therefore a better subject for a poem.*

Reinforce and Extend

Answers
◆ *Literature and Your Life*

Reader's Response Students should identify examples of "spookiness" and explain why or why not they were effective.

Thematic Focus The poet leaves out information about who the listeners are.

☑ **Check Your Comprehension**

1. The time is in the past when people traveled on horseback; the place is a castle or country home.
2. A traveler comes to an apparently deserted house, knocks on the door three times, says that he came and kept his promise, and gallops away. The mysterious listeners in the house do not respond.
3. Lines 27 and 28.

◆ **Critical Thinking**

1. The poem is like a dream in its presentation of a mysterious, ominous scene; it is different from a dream in its use of poetic devices and structure.
2. He probably wanted to focus the poem on the mysterious listeners rather than on the more everyday Traveler.
3. Knowing more would mean imagining less and therefore not experiencing an unsolvable mystery.
4. A puzzle has a definite solution, but this kind of mystery doesn't.

Guide for Responding

◆ *Literature and Your Life*

Reader's Response Did you find this poem spooky and chilling? Why or why not?

Thematic Focus What information does the poet leave out to increase the sense of mystery?

☑ **Check Your Comprehension**

1. Briefly describe the time and place in which the action of the poem occurs.
2. What happens in the poem?
3. Which two lines of the poem best explain why the Traveler comes to the house?

◆ **Critical Thinking**

INTERPRET
1. How is this poem like a dream? **[Analyze]**
2. Why do you think de la Mare called the poem "The Listeners" rather than "The Traveler"? **[Infer]**
3. Would knowing more about the characters lessen the poem's mystery? Explain. **[Synthesize]**

APPLY
4. What's the difference between a puzzle and a mystery like the one presented in this poem? **[Distinguish]**

The Listeners ◆ 105

Block Scheduling Strategies

Consider the following suggestions to take advantage of extended class time.

- Have students complete the journal activity in "Background for Understanding" (p. 105) and discuss their entries in small groups. Suggest they talk about why Escher's drawing is an appropriate illustration for the three poems.
- Have students listen to the poems on audio-cassette, visualizing the poems as they listen.
- With students, read Literature and Your Life (p. 105). Then brainstorm about dreams: What

is the experience of dreaming like? Why do dreams often come back to "haunt" you? Finally, have them read "The Listeners," and respond to Critical Thinking question 1, in which students are asked to compare the poem to a dream (p. 107).

- Invite students to work in small groups to answer the other Critical Thinking questions (pp. 107 and 109).

One-Minute Insight

Ishmael Reed's poem invites readers to consider the power of a poem to draw readers in and, by showing them frightening aspects of themselves, to disturb and even threaten them.

Comprehension Check ☑

❶ What situation does the poem set up? *The poet describes a TV thriller in which a woman's preoccupation with her own image takes over her life.*

◆ Critical Thinking

❷ Connect Ask students to explain how "the hunger" of a poem can be "legendary." *"Legendary" evokes the idea of stories or tales from a mysterious, distant past, suggesting that the "hunger of this poem" has been taking in victims since that far-off time.*

◆ Build Grammar Skills

❸ Parallelism Invite students to identify the parallelism in this passage and to describe its effect. *The poet repeats the phrase "back off from this poem," interspersed with the lines "it has drawn in yr___." The effect is to create a sense of menace. The parallelism also creates tension by repeating the contrasting words "drawn in" and "back off."*

◆ Critical Thinking

❹ Interpret Invite students to read this passage aloud in a tone of voice that expresses their interpretations of the poem. What meanings did the readers intend? What meanings did the listeners pick up? *Students should convey that this passage is the climax of the poem. Their reading should also convey the poem's sense of menace, as well as its driving, irresistible rhythm.*

Beware:
Do Not Read This Poem
Ishmael Reed

❶
```
        tonite, thriller was
        abt an ol woman, so vain she
        surrounded her self w/
           many mirrors
  5     It got so bad that finally she
        locked herself indoors & her
        whole life became the
           mirrors

        one day the villagers broke
 10     into her house, but she was too
        swift for them. she disappeared
           into a mirror
        each tenant who bought the house
        after that lost a loved one to
 15        the ol woman in the mirror:
           first a little girl
           then a young woman
           then the young woman/s husband
```
❷
```
        the hunger of this poem is legendary
 20     it has taken in many victims
        back off from this poem
        it has drawn in yr feet
```
❸
```
        back off from this poem
        it has drawn in yr legs
 25     back off from this poem
```

```
        it is a greedy mirror
        you are into this poem. from
           the waist down
        nobody can hear you can they?
 30     this poem has had you up to here
           belch
        this poem aint got no manners
        you cant call out frm this poem
        relax now & go w/ this poem
 35     move & roll on to this poem
```
❹
```
           do not resist this poem
           this poem has yr eyes
           this poem has his head
           this poem has his arms
 40        this poem has his fingers
           this poem has his fingertips
        this poem is the reader & the
           reader this poem
```

```
        statistic: the us bureau of missing persons reports
 45        that in 1968 over 100,000 people disappeared
           leaving no solid clues
              nor trace       only
        a space       in the lives of their friends
```

◆ Build Vocabulary

legendary (lej´ ən der´ ē) *adj.*: Based on legends, or stories handed down for generations

106 ◆ *Spine Tinglers*

Speaking and Listening Mini-Lesson

Oral Interpretation

This mini-lesson supports the Speaking and Listening activity in the Idea Bank on page 111.

Introduce the Concept Explain that oral interpretation is an oral presentation of literature in which the meaning is communicated vocally.

Develop Background Prepare students by having them listen to the audiocassette recording of the poem, paying attention to the reader's volume, speed, and tone of voice. Listen; then have students tell when they thought the reader was particularly effective and explain why.

Apply the Information Students should now develop their own oral interpretations of the poem. Encourage partners to give each other feedback and to modify their readings.

Assess the Outcome Invite students to perform their interpretations for another set of partners. Then, as a class, discuss how reading and hearing the poem affected students' understanding of and feelings about it. Ask: Which new ideas, if any, did you get from hearing the different oral interpretations?

Tropical Tree, 1990, Grimanesa Amoros, 75 x52", acrylic and mixed media on canvas, ©1997 Grimanesa Amoros/Licensed by VAGA, New York, NY

Echo

Henriqueta Lisboa
Translated by Hélcio Veiga Costa

Green parrot
let out a shrill scream.
Rock in sudden
anger, replied.

5 A great uproar
invaded the forest.
Thousands of parrots
screamed together
and rock echoed.

10 From all sides
strafing space
steely screams rained
and rained down.

Very piercing screams!
15 But no one died.

◆ **Build Vocabulary**
strafing (strāf´ ing) *v.*: Attacking with machine-gun fire

Guide for Responding

◆ *Literature and Your Life*
Reader's Response Which poem did you find more mysterious? Why?
Thematic Focus When Reed describes you as disappearing into his poem, what does he suggest about the mystery of reading? What is strange about the echoes in Lisboa's poem?

☑ Check Your Comprehension
1. How is Reed's poem like "the ol woman in the mirror"?
2. What happens in the poem "Echo"?

◆ Critical Thinking
INTERPRET
1. How would you describe the speaker's tone of voice in Reed's poem? **[Infer]**
2. What message is the speaker trying to convey when he says, "this poem is the reader & the / reader is this poem"? **[Interpret]**
3. How would "Echo" be different without the last line? **[Speculate]**
EXTEND
4. If you were setting these poems to music, what types of music would you choose? Explain. **[Music Link]**

Beware: Do Not Read This Poem/Echo ◆ 107

One-Minute Insight
Henriqueta Lisboa's "Echo" evokes the powerful, frightening qualities of natural phenomena, but suggests a contrast between the natural world, in which "no one died," with the even more violent human world.

◆ Reading Strategy
❺ Use Your Senses Invite students to picture the scene being described. *Students should describe the parrot, the trees, and the rock.*

❻ Clarification Point out that the poet is comparing the incident in the jungle to the results of an actual bombing raid, in which many people would have died.

Reinforce and Extend

Answers
◆ *Literature and Your Life*
Reader's Response Students may find the poetic license in "Beware: Do Not Read This Poem" makes it more mysterious; nevertheless, the images in "Echo" make that poem mysterious in a different sense.

Thematic Focus Reading can "swallow up" the reader, involving and transforming at once. The echoes in "Echo" seem to have substance in addition to sound.

☑ Check Your Comprehension
1. Like the old woman in the mirror, the poem swallows up the reader.
2. A green parrot screams and the scream is echoed by a rock. Then thousands of parrots scream, causing more echoes.

◆ Critical Thinking
1. The voice is tough and angry, but also humorous and sly.
2. He may be saying that the poem and the reader have merged for the moment because the poem has grabbed the reader's attention.
3. The poem would be more frightening and less humorous.
4. For "Beware . . . ," students might suggest music with a strong beat, to match the poem's tone. "Echo" could use shrill instrumental sounds, like high-pitched violins.

Answers

◆ Reading Strategy

1. Many images appeal to the sense of hearing: the Traveler's knocking; his words, which echo through the house; the plunging hoofs of his galloping horse; the silence that surges back when he's gone.
2. "Echo"; as you read the poem, you "hear" the cry and echo of first one, and then many parrots; these cries are mysterious.
3. (a) "Beware: Do Not Read This Poem"; (b) You are invited to see yourself disappear into the "greedy mirror" of the poem.

◆ Literary Focus

1. The poet uses imagery of touch to describe silence—it "surged softly backward"—and imagery of sight to describe the "phantom listeners"—"thronging the faint moonbeams on the dark stair."
2. Students may mention the sounds described in the poem, for example, the "knocking," the "plunging hoofs." Some may suggest using suspenseful music as well.
3. When you read, you mysteriously disappear into the words and lose awareness of yourself. The mirror imagery pictures this process.
4. The "shrill scream" of the single parrot and the "steely screams" of the many parrots have a disturbing, jarring effect.

◆ Build Grammar Skills

1. The two lines are parallel.
2. their strangeness, /Their stillness . . .
3. The following words are parallel: Stood listening / Stood thronging

◆ Build Vocabulary

1. He uses the word *smote*.
2. The word adds to the mystery because it is old-fashioned and therefore strange.
3. The symbols & and *w/* are poetic license.
4. The unusual symbols make the poem seem stranger.

Using the Word Bank

The detective entered the deserted house and stood in front of the mirror, <u>perplexed</u>. Deep inside the mysterious glass, he could see the <u>legendary</u> parrots, a species that had never existed. Hundreds of them were <u>thronging</u> a forest clearing, <u>strafing</u> the trees with their steely cries.

108

Guide for Responding *(continued)*

◆ Reading Strategy

USE YOUR SENSES

You have entered new, mysterious worlds by **using your senses.** In "The Listeners," for example, you have stood on both sides of a "moonlit door," waiting with the Traveler and with the "phantom listeners" he addresses.

1. Why is sound as important as sight in experiencing the world of "The Listeners"?
2. In which of the other two poems do you *hear* a mystery? Explain.
3. (a) Which of the poems asks you to picture yourself? (b) Describe the picture or pictures of yourself that you see.

◆ Build Grammar Skills

PARALLELISM

Usually, parallelism suggests that the world is regular, rational, predictable. In these poems, however, the images that the parallel groups of words describe are startling and offbeat. The result is that the repetitions can throw you off balance and disturb—not reassure—you.

> **Parallelism** is the repeated use of specific grammatical forms.

In this passage from "Beware: Do Not Read This Poem," notice how two different grammatical forms are repeated in alternate lines.

> back off from this poem
> it has drawn in yr feet
> back off from this poem
> it has drawn in yr legs . . .

Practice Identify the parallelism in the following excerpts from the poems.

1. this poem has his head / this poem has his arms
2. And he felt in his heart their strangeness, / Their stillness answering his cry . . .
3. Stood listening in the quiet of the moonlight/ To that voice from the world of man:/ Stood thronging the faint moonbeams on the dark stair, . . .

Writing Application Write an eight-line poem describing something interesting you recently observed. Include at least two examples of parallelism.

108 ◆ Spine Tinglers

◆ Literary Focus

IMAGERY

Poets use the picture-painting words called **imagery** to take you to mysterious places.

1. Explain how the imagery in "The Listeners" helps you hear "silence" and see invisible "listeners."
2. Would you use sound effects, music, or both if you were making a short film based on "The Listeners?" Give reasons for your answer.
3. Ishmael Reed compares reading to disappearing into "a greedy mirror." How does the mirror imagery help you to experience the strangeness of reading?
4. Find two examples of imagery in "Echo" and show how they create a feeling of uncertainty The poems in this section use imagery in a special way that gives you pictures of worlds that are haunted by mystery.

◆ Build Vocabulary

POETIC LICENSE AND VOCABULARY IN POEMS

Poetic license is a poet's freedom to violate rules of vocabulary and grammar to create literary effects. Poets like Walter de la Mare and Ishmael Reed use old-fashioned words, symbols, and abbreviations for specific purposes.

1. What old-fashioned word does de la Mare include in lines 5–7?
2. Does his use of this word make the poem seem more mysterious? Why or why not?
3. Identify two examples of poetic license in line 34 of "Beware: Do Not Read This Poem."
4. How does Reed's use of poetic license in line 34 make his poem seem more unusual or strange?

USING THE WORD BANK

On your paper, rewrite the following paragraph and fill in the blanks with words from the Word Bank.

The detective entered the deserted house and stood in front of the mirror, ___?___ . Deep inside the mysterious glass, he could see the ___?___ parrots, a species that had never existed. Hundreds of them were ___?___ a forest clearing, ___?___ the trees with their steely cries.

 Beyond the Selection

FURTHER READING

Other Works by the Authors
Best Stories of Walter de la Mare
Collected Poems, Walter de la Mare
New and Collected Poems of Ishmael Reed
Conjure, Ishmael Reed
Chattanooga, Ishmael Reed
Endearment, Henriqueta Lisboa
Godmother Moon, Henriqueta Lisboa

INTERNET

You may wish to direct students to the following address on the Internet for poems by de la Mare, in addition to "The Listeners": **http://ftp.lexmark.com/data/poem/poem2.html** Please be aware, however, that sites may have changed from the time we published this information.

We *strongly recommend* that you preview the site before you send students there.

Build Your Portfolio

 ## Idea Bank

Writing

1. **Comic Strip** Create a comic strip about a mysterious poem that swallows people. **[Art Link]**

2. **TV Review** Write a summary of a television program about a real-life mystery that is difficult to solve. Include a brief thumbs-up or thumbs-down review of the program. **[Media Link]**

3. **Dramatic Scene** Write a dramatic scene that takes place "in the lone house" of "The Listeners" after the Traveler has galloped away. Use your scene to answer some of the questions left unanswered by the poem. **[Performing Arts Link]**

Speaking and Listening

4. **Oral Interpretation** With a partner, take turns reading aloud Ishmael Reed's "Beware: Do Not Read This Poem." Before you begin, ask yourself questions like: Should different parts of the poem be read louder or softer, at different speeds, or with different tones of voice?

5. **Storytelling** Make up and tell a story involving the Traveler and the Listeners from "The Listeners," the old woman from "Beware: Do Not Read This Poem," and the parrot from "Echo."

Projects

6. **Multimedia Presentation** "Echo" is set in Brazil's tropical rain forest. Give a multimedia presentation on this environment, taking the class on a magical mystery tour through its wonders. **[Science Link; Technology Link]**

7. **Art Exhibit** In a corner of your classroom, display some of the "impossible" scenes drawn by the Dutch artist M. C. Escher. Include a blank notebook with the exhibit and invite your classmates to fill it with comments. **[Art Link]**

 ## Writing Mini-Lesson

Movie Summary

"Beware: Do Not Read This Poem" begins like an answer to the question, What happened in the television program *Thriller?* A **summary** like Reed's briefly outlines important events and leaves out unimportant ones. Choose a movie you recently saw, and write a summary of it for a friend. It does not have to be in lines of poetry, but it should follow a clear timeline.

Writing Skills Focus: Sequence of Events

Show a clear **sequence of events**—the order in which things happen—when summarizing a movie, telling a story, or explaining a process. Notice how Reed uses words that show time to help readers understand the sequence of events in a television program.

Model From the Poem

first a little girl

then a young woman

then the young woman's husband . . .

Prewriting Draw a timeline like this one, including the key events of the movie in chronological order:

1.   2.   3.   4.   5.

Refer to the timeline as you draft and revise your summary.

Drafting Use words that show time to help readers understand the sequence of events. Examples: *first, before, after, finally, one day, then, meanwhile, at the same time, later.*

Revising Read your summary aloud to classmates and ask them whether they understand the order of events. If not, see where you can insert time words to clarify the sequence.

 ### Idea Bank

Customizing for
Performance Levels
Following are suggestions for matching the Idea Bank topics with your students' performance levels:
  Less Advanced Students: 1, 4, 7
  Average Students: 2, 4, 6
  More Advanced Students: 3, 5

Customizing for
Learning Modalities
Following are suggestions for matching Idea Bank topics with your students' learning modalities:
  Visual/Spatial: 1, 6, 7
  Auditory: 4, 5
  Musical/Rhythmic: 4
  Verbal/Linguistic: 2, 3

 ### Writing Mini-Lesson

Refer students to the Writing Handbook, page 962, for instruction on the writing process, and page 964 for further information on Exposition.

Writer's Solution

Writing Lab CD-ROM
For additional support, use the tutorial on Exposition. Follow these steps:
1. Use the Timeline Activity to arrange the details for the summary chronologically.
2. While drafting, use the Transition Word Bin.
3. Use the Revision checker for transition words to aid revision.
You will need approximately 60 minutes of class time to complete these steps.

Sourcebook
Have students use Chapter 3, Exposition (pp. 62–95) for additional support. This chapter includes in-depth instruction on chronological order (p. 82).

✓ ASSESSMENT OPTIONS

Formal Assessment, Selection Test, pp. 16–18, and Assessment Resources Software. The selection test is designed so that it can be easily customized to the performance levels of your students. *Alternative Assessment,* p. 6, includes options for less advanced students, more advanced students, musical/rhythmic learners, verbal/linguistic learners, and visual/spatial learners.

PORTFOLIO ASSESSMENT
Use the following rubrics in the *Alternative Assessment* booklet to assess student writing:
Comic Strip: Narrative Rubric, p. 88
TV Review: Evaluation/Review Rubric, p. 97
Dramatic Scene: Drama Rubric, p. 102
Writing Mini-Lesson: Summary Rubric, p. 91

Guide for Reading

OBJECTIVES

1. To read, comprehend, and interpret a news article
2. To relate a news article to personal experience
3. To identify the main idea of a news article
4. To grasp the organization of facts in a news article
5. To build vocabulary in context and learn the suffix *-ist*
6. To develop skill in using the active and passive voice
7. To write a news feature with an attention-grabbing lead
8. To respond to a news article through writing, speaking and listening activities, and projects

SKILLS INSTRUCTION

Vocabulary:
Suffixes: *-ist*
Grammar:
Active and Passive Voice
Literary Focus:
News Article
Reading Strategy:
Main Idea

Writing:
Grabbing the Reader's Attention
Speaking and Listening:
Oral Presentation (teacher edition)
Critical Viewing:
Deduce; Draw Conclusions

PORTFOLIO OPPORTUNITIES

Writing: Book Jacket; Short Story; Travel Brochure
Writing Mini-Lesson: News Feature
Speaking and Listening: Group Discussion; Oral Presentation
Projects: Photo Essay; Costume Drawing

Keay Davidson (1953–)

With every passing day, technology opens new doors to the world of science, and Keay Davidson loves the challenge of sharing these advances with readers. As a science reporter and the author of two books and many magazine articles, Davidson tracks the latest on everything from the space program to tornadoes.

Space Program Launches Reporter While still in college, Davidson began work as a newspaper reporter. He held staff positions at three Georgia newspapers until moving to Florida in 1976 to take his first full-time reporting job. Davidson knew he'd found his true calling when, in 1979, he was assigned to cover science and the space program. In 1981, he moved to the West Coast to become a science reporter for the *Los Angeles Times*; then, in 1986, for the *San Francisco Examiner*.

Davidson doesn't limit his writing to newspapers, however; his articles have appeared in *National Geographic* and other magazines. He has co-authored a book, *Wrinkles in Time,* about new scientific theories on the origins of the universe.

In 1996, when the movie Twister *swept through theaters, Davidson introduced the science behind the special effects in* Twister: The Science of Tornadoes.

He also produced a special version of the book just for students.

Science: A Link Between Past and Present Archaeology has always fascinated Davidson, who is drawn by its emotional impact. When an archaeological discovery alters our understanding of that history—as with the Caucasian mummies in this article—its impact can extend beyond science to change even the way we see ourselves.

◆ Build Vocabulary

SUFFIXES: *-ist*

Early in this article, you learn that a Chinese archaeologist is responsible for finding several mysterious mummies. *Archaeologist* is one of several words in the article that end in the suffix *-ist*, which means "one who practices." Knowing the meaning of *-ist*, you can then determine that an archaeologist is a person who practices archaeology, the scientific study of ancient peoples and cultures.

WORD BANK

dogmas
parched
archaeologist
imperialist
subjugation
reconcile

As you read "Caucasian Mummies Mystify Chinese," you will encounter the words on this list. Each word is defined on the page where it first appears. Preview the list before you read. Notice other words that end in *-ist*.

◆ Build Grammar Skills

ACTIVE AND PASSIVE VOICE

Lively writing, the kind that keeps you moving through a news article, usually features verbs in the active voice. A verb is in the **active voice** when the subject of the sentence performs the action. A verb is in the **passive voice** when the action is performed on the subject. When the performer of an action is not known or is not important, the writer uses the passive voice.

Active Voice: Wang Binghua <u>found</u> the first of more than 100 mummies . . .

Passive Voice: They <u>were buried</u> in simple graves, roughly 6 feet deep . . .

As you read "Caucasian Mummies Mystify Chinese," notice how Davidson uses both the active and passive voice.

110 ◆ Spine Tinglers

Caucasian Mummies Mystify Chinese

◆ *Literature and Your Life*

CONNECT YOUR EXPERIENCE

How were the Egyptian pyramids built? Why—and how—were towering slabs of rock arranged in circles at Stonehenge? These so-called unsolved mysteries—discoveries or events for which we have no easy explanation—are popular subjects for books, articles, and television programs. Think about why both fictional and true-life unexplained phenomena are so popular.

Journal Writing Write about a real-life unsolved mystery you've read about or seen on television. Why did it capture your interest?

THEMATIC FOCUS: IT'S A MYSTERY

How does modern science help us solve ancient mysteries?

◆ Background for Understanding

SOCIAL STUDIES

This article explores the importance of the discovery of more than one hundred mummies in China. Are you surprised to hear the word *mummy* in connection with a place other than ancient Egypt? In fact, mummies have been found all over the world, including Europe, Peru, and Mexico. While mummification was a ritual way of preserving the dead in some cultures, mummies also form naturally in certain environments. Because people were often buried with their clothing, jewelry, tools, and even food, mummies and their burial sites can tell us much about how ancient peoples lived.

◆ Literary Focus

NEWS ARTICLE

The purpose of a **news article**, such as "Caucasian Mummies Mystify Chinese" is to inform you—the reader—by answering six basic questions, known as the five W's and H: *who, what, when, where, why,* and *how.*

The article's opening sentences, called the lead, are written to capture your attention, summarize the main points of the story, and answer as many of the six questions as possible. Notice as you read that the reporter goes on to provide details in the form of facts, as well as expert opinions that add authority and interest to the article.

◆ Reading Strategy

MAIN IDEA

Whether you are researching magazine articles or simply scanning a news story for information, finding the main idea is an important reading skill. At first glance, the **main idea**—the most important point—of a piece of writing is not always obvious. In a well-written news article, the main idea is usually presented in the lead paragraph. The body of the article, however, may provide additional important details.

An easy way to focus on the main idea as you read is to look for answers to the six questions *who, what, when, where, why,* and *how.* As you read this article, jot down answers to these questions in a chart like this:

Who?	
What?	
When?	
Where?	
Why?	
How?	

Preparing for Standardized Tests

Reading and Vocabulary The Reading Strategy focuses on the main idea. Identifying the main idea is a skill that is key to analyzing passages in tests of reading comprehension. Applying the strategy in this selection and reinforcing it with the Reading Strategy page in *Selection Support,* p. 27, will give students experience with this important skill.

Grammar and Language This Build Grammar Skills lesson provides opportunities for students to distinguish between the active and passive voice. Understanding when each voice is appropriate and being able to use active and passive voice effectively in their own writing will help students on essay sections of standardized tests. The Build Grammar Skills page on Active and Passive Voice, p. 27 in *Selection Support,* provides additional practice.

One-Minute Insight

Journalist Keay Davidson writes about the discovery, in a Chinese desert, of more than 100 "astoundingly well-preserved mummies . . . whose inexplicably blond hair and white skin" suggest that they were European, rather than Asian. This discovery is surprising because it contradicts a long-held belief that Chinese society evolved "on its own with little foreign input." The discovery is important because it demonstrates that even long-held beliefs about history are subject to change. It also demonstrates that we all come from a "global heritage"—that even societies that are far apart both geographically and culturally have traded ideas and customs from the dawn of history up until the present.

◆ Build Vocabulary

❶ Suffixes: -ist Point out that the word *scientist* contains the suffix *-ist*. Ask students: How does the suffix change the word *science*? *Because the suffix -ist means "a person who," scientist means "a person who practices science."*

◆ Critical Thinking

❷ Clarification Explain to students that the "ice man" was a man whose well-preserved, 5,000-year-old remains were discovered on September 19, 1991, in the high Alps between Austria and Italy. Ask students to consider why Davidson might consider this discovery less important than that of the Caucasian mummies. *Many more mummies were found in China; the Caucasian mummies suggest a link between two cultures previously believed totally separate. The discovery has encouraged scientists from the two cultures to work together.*

Customize for
English Language Learners

Difficult vocabulary, such as "societal evolution" and "The collaboration required delicate negotiations . . ." may prove challenging for English-language learners. Work with these students to make a list of these terms. Then, as a class, come up with simpler language that clarifies each challenging term.

Caucasian Mummies Mystify Chinese

Keay Davidson
from San Francisco Examiner

112 ◆ Spine Tinglers

Block Scheduling Strategies

Consider these suggestions to take advantage of extended class time:

- Have students complete the journal activity in Literature and Your Life (p. 111) and read their entries to a partner or a small group.
- Invite students to listen to all or part of the selection on audiocassette. Have them discuss how listening to a news story is similar to and different from reading it in the newspaper.
- Encourage students to research Keay Davidson on the Internet to locate some of his exciting scientific articles.

- Direct students to work in discussion groups to answer the Critical Thinking questions (p. 116).
- Have students complete the Writing Mini-Lesson (p. 117). Before students get started, encourage them to read a news feature in a newspaper or magazine or to listen to one on radio or television. Have them look for specific elements of news features in Davidson's article.

San Francisco—In dim light they appear to be sleeping, but they've been dead up to 4,000 years: more than 100 astoundingly well-preserved mummies unearthed in a Chinese desert, whose inexplicably blond hair and white skin could topple <u>dogmas</u> about early human history.

A former Stanford scientist is analyzing the mummies' DNA in hopes of answering haunting questions: Who are they? Where did they come from? And what on earth were these European-looking men, women and children doing in China's <u>parched</u> out-back 2,000 years before Jesus, when Europe was largely a dark forest? Sixteen years after the first mummies were found, the Chinese government has granted Western researchers their first close look at these faces from prehistory: a baby in colorful swaddling clothes; a 20-year-old girl with braided hair, found buried in a curled-up position with her hands by her chest, as if dozing; a man with a pigtail, scarlet-colored clothes and red, blue, and amber leg wrappings . . . .

The discovery—which could have far greater impact on our understanding of societal evolution than the lone, ancient "ice man" uncovered in the Alps in 1991—is described in an article by science writer Evan Hadingham in the April 1994 issue of *Discover* magazine. Based on the *Discover* article and *San Francisco Examiner* interviews with experts on genetics and Chinese history and culture, here's how the discoveries unfolded. In 1978 and 1979, Chinese archaeologist Wang Binghua found the first of <u>what would prove to be more than 100 mummies</u> in Xinjiang[1] Province. They had white skin, blond hair, long noses and skulls, and deep-set eyes—Caucasians,[2] perhaps from Northern Europe.

---

1. **Xinjiang** (zin jē ang´)
2. **Caucasian** (kô kā´ zhen) *adj*.: Belonging to one of the major geographical groups of human beings, including the native peoples of Europe, who are loosely called the *white race*, though their skin colors may vary.

◀ **Critical Viewing** What features of this mummy might help scientists to deduce facts about the man and his life? [Deduce]

Little Attention in the West

Only scanty press reports have reached the West, at least partly because of the region's isolation, Chinese bureaucratic inertia and the regime's suppression of foreign contacts, particularly after the Tiananmen Square massacre[3] of 1989.

Now the cloud of mystery is lifting thanks to an investigation organized by University of Pennsylvania China scholar Victor Mair, in collaboration with researchers in China, the United States and Italy. The collaboration required delicate negotiations with Chinese officials.

It would have been "absolutely unthinkable" for Chinese authorities to grant Westerners such access—including tissue samples from the mummies—only five years ago, Mair told *The Examiner*. "In the 1910s and 1920s, it was a game of the <u>imperialist</u> (Western) archaeologists to go in and take away important stuff—ancient manuscripts, artworks, paintings, statues . . . (Chinese officials are) very sensitive to that and they don't want to make the same situation recur," Mair said.

He also speculates that some Chinese officials may have initially hesitated to ballyhoo the find because they didn't know what to make of all those Caucasian faces. They date from a time when, according to regional histories and

---

3. **Tiananmen** (tyen´ an men´) **Square massacre:** The murder of approximately 3,000 pro-democracy demonstrators by Chinese soldiers in Beijing, the capital of China, on June 3, 1989.

◆ **Build Vocabulary**

dogmas (dôg´ məz) *n*.: Firmly-held beliefs or doctrines

parched (pärcht) *adj*.: Dried up by heat

archaeologist (är´ kē äl´ ə jist) *n*.: Person who practices the scientific study of the remains of ancient ways of life

imperialist (im pir´ ē əl ist) *adj*.: Here, describing a person from a country that seeks to dominate weaker countries

Caucasian Mummies Mystify Chinese ◆ 113

◆ **Literary Focus**
Notice how sections of the article are introduced with subheads that function like abbreviated lead statements.

◆ **Build Vocabulary**

❸ **Suffixes: -ist** Guide students to recognize that the word *archaeologist* contains the suffix *-ist*. Ask students: How does the suffix help you understand the meaning of the word? *Added to the two roots meaning* ancient *and* study, archaeologist *means "one who studies ancient peoples and cultures."*

▶**Critical Viewing**◀
❹ **Deduce** Student responses may include the following: *The man's physical features—skin, hair, nose, and deep-set eyes—and his western-style clothing suggest that he was Caucasian, rather than Asian. From this, scientists might deduce that he probably was a Northern European traveling or living in ancient China.*

◆ **Literary Focus**

❺ **News Article** Guide students to notice that each subhead provides a quick summary of the main idea of the section that follows it. The subhead shows what kinds of details will be discussed in the section.

◆ **Build Vocabulary**

❻ **Suffixes: -ist** Point out that the word *imperialist* contains the suffix *-ist*. When added to the root *empire,* the word becomes *imperialist,* which means someone from a powerful country who seeks to dominate a weaker country.

Customize for
Less Proficient Readers
Invite students to summarize the news article up to the end of the paragraph subheaded "Little Attention in the West." Summaries should include the following: *More than 100 well-preserved Caucasian mummies, dead for about 4,000 years, have been found in the Chinese desert. At first, China did little to publicize the discovery for three reasons: China, at the time, discouraged contact with foreign countries, the Chinese feared that Western researchers might take away important artifacts, and the discovery suggested that ancient Chinese culture had been influenced by European culture. Now, however, Chinese and Western scientists are working together to find out who these people were.*

Cross-Curricular Connection: Science

Today, scientists examine mummies from different cultures with "high-tech" techniques, including radiocarbon dating, DNA tests, and CT scanners. CT scanners are special X-ray machines with 3-D computer technology that allows scientists to look inside a mummy's body, as if peeling away one layer at a time, without actually destroying the mummy itself.

Have students discuss how state-of-the-art scientific technology helps scientists find information that would have been unavailable to them before the "technology explosion" that began not-so-many years ago. Based on the article, encourage them to evaluate the benefits of such technology. Has it led to useful knowledge or has it merely confused people and made life more complicated?

▲ **Critical Viewing** Find the Xinjiang province on the map. Based on its location, explain why Europeans might have settled in that particular part of China. **[Draw Conclusions]**

national pride, China was advancing—developing writing and metal artifacts and wheeled vehicles—without help from foreign meddlers.

Bodies' Condition Excellent

The mummies were unearthed at scattered burial sites in an approximately 500-mile-wide region of northwest China, between the so-called Celestial (Tian Shan) Mountains and the Taklimakan[4] Desert. They range in age from 2000 B.C. to 300 B.C., based largely on radiocarbon dating.

Where do they come from? At the University of Sassari in Italy, anthropological geneticist[5] Paolo Francalacci—who worked at Stanford until recently—hopes to determine the mummies' likely place of origin by comparing their DNA, or genetic material, with modern DNA from different societies.

"It will take time before we know anything (from the DNA analysis)," cautions

4. **Taklimakan** (täk li mä kän)
5. **anthropological geneticist:** One who studies the historical development of human beings through the examination of their genes.

Francalacci's Stanford colleague, Luigi Luca Cavalli-Sforza, a population geneticist. "It's a very tricky type of analysis. Old DNA is generally very damaged.

"What I find most surprising of all is that these mummies were in such perfect condition," Cavalli-Sforza said. Their European-looking features are "sufficient, I think, to say these people came from Northern Europe. . . . My guess is that these (people) were kind of 'scouts' (who) were, most probably, traveling east and maybe settled there (in Xinjiang)." He believes thousands of mummies may yet be found.

Why has it taken so long for the news to get Western scholars' attention? While Western news media trumpeted the 5,000-year-old "ice man" found in the Austrian and Italian Alps, they have ignored the Chinese find—almost . . . .

Poor Chinese public relations could be partly to blame. Mair suspects that in the late 1970s, Chinese scholars were so startled by the Caucasian mummies that they weren't sure what to do with them.

"I think it flummoxed them when they found these Caucasian people out there . . . it's not what they expected," he said. "They didn't know how to put it into any of their schemes for history; it just didn't make sense to them . . . ."

> ◆ **Reading Strategy**
> How does this question and those found elsewhere in the article help you gather information about the main idea?

Speaking and Listening Mini-Lesson

Oral Presentation

This mini-lesson supports the Speaking and Listening activity in the Idea Bank on page 117.

Introduce the Concept Have students develop criteria for effective oral presentations.

Develop Background Have students review these guidelines for a speech:

• The speaker should clearly state the purpose of the speech in the introduction.
• The introduction should grab the audience's attention.

• The speech should be tailored to the audience.
• Supporting information should be provided for each main idea.
• The speech should persuade the audience to accept the speaker's opinion.

Apply the Information Students can present their findings and persuade their colleagues of the importance of their find.

Assess the Outcome Have students evaluate oral presentations against the criteria and guidelines they discussed earlier.

Nagging Questions

In 1987, Mair happened to be touring China when he entered a museum in Urumqi[6] that displayed mummies of a man, woman and child—a family, as it appeared. They had died 3,000 years earlier, "yet the bodies looked as if they were buried yesterday," he said.

What left him "thunderstruck," though, was their faces: They were Caucasians, apparently of European origin. "The questions kept nagging at me: Who were these people? How did they get out here at such an early date?"

The April 1994 issue of *Discover* includes a gallery of color photos of the corpses. They include a man with a painted image of the sun—a religious symbol?—on the temple of his head; the baby in swaddling clothes, its eyes covered with stones—a burial ritual?; a woman in a tall, peaked hat,. . . and a woman wearing a fur-lined coat, leather mittens and a two-pointed hat that, according to Chinese archaeologists, indicates she might have had *two husbands*—a possible result of a shortage of females. They were buried in simple graves, roughly 6 feet deep, with mats at the bottom. Some graves contain artifacts hinting that the living mourned the dead: For example, a baby was buried

with a sort of milk bottle fashioned from a sheep's udder.

"This is my favorite story in the seven years that I've edited *Discover* . . . because we were able to publish something monumental before anyone else," said the magazine's editor, Paul Hoffman.

Traditionally, Chinese historians insist that their society evolved on its own with little foreign input. That view has played well in modern China, which resents its past subjugation to foreign imperialists.

But Mair says the traditional view is hard to reconcile with the discovery of so many Caucasians who lived in what is now the westernmost edge of China, thousands of years before Marco Polo.[7] "The archaeological, linguistic, and textual evidence forces me to conclude that China has both significantly influenced and been influenced by other civilizations throughout history and, indeed, prehistory," Mair said. . . .

7. **Marco Polo** (1254–1324): Italian traveler and trader considered to be the first European to cross the length of Asia.

◆ Build Vocabulary

subjugation (sub´ jə gā´ shən) *n*.: Enslavement

reconcile (rek´ ən sīl´) *v*.: Bring into agreement

6. **Urumqi** (ür üm chē)

Guide for Responding

◆ *Literature and Your Life*

Reader's Response As you read about the Caucasian mummies and the questions they raise for historians, what questions of your own come to mind? What else would you like to know about these ancient people and the way they lived?

Thematic Focus After reading "Caucasian Mummies Mystify Chinese," do you agree that real-life mysteries can be just as intriguing as those created by storytellers? Why or why not?

Journal Writing The archaeologists who discovered the mummies and the scientists who are analyzing them both play important roles. Explain which you

would find more interesting—working in the field as an archaeologist or using science and technology in the lab—and why.

☑ Check Your Comprehension

1. What is remarkable about the mummies' appearance?
2. Where do experts think the people found in the Chinese desert originally came from?
3. (a) What year were the first mummies unearthed? (b) Was the article written at the time the mummies were discovered?
4. What kind of tests are scientists using to analyze the mummies?

Caucasian Mummies Mystify Chinese ◆ 115

Beyond the Selection

FURTHER READING

Other Works by Keay Davidson
Twister: The Science of Tornadoes
Wrinkles in Time

Other Works About Ancient Mysteries
Caves, George Laycock
The Tomb of Tutankhamen,
Howard Carter

INTERNET

You may wish to direct students to the following addresses on the Internet: **http://achilles.net/~tedd/songs/icesong.html**
They will find information and a poetic tribute to the "ice man," referred to in the article. The address
http://www.archaelolgy.org/9609/newsbriefs /tarim.html
will lead students to the article "The Mummies' Threads," a study of garments worn by 3,000-year-old mummies in China. Be aware that Internet sites may have changed since we published this information. We *strongly recommend* that you preview sites before you send students to them.

Establish Writing Guidelines

Review the following key characteristics of a remembrance:

- A remembrance brings to life memorable people, places, or events from your past.

- When effective, a remembrance evokes for the reader many of the same sensory details that the writer recalls from experience.

- A remembrance includes both vivid descriptive details and your reflections about the person, place, or event you're recalling.

- It can be somewhat personal in nature, with much of the description focusing on your feelings and interpretations of external events.

You may want to distribute the scoring rubric for Description (p. 90 in *Alternative Assessment*) to make students aware of the criteria on which their work will be evaluated before they begin. For suggestions on how you can customize the rubric to this workshop, see page 120.

Refer students to the Writing Handbook, page 962, for instruction on the writing process, and page 964 for further information on Description.

 Writer's Solution

Writing Lab CD-ROM

If students have access to computers, have them work on the Tutorial on Description to complete all or part of their remembrances. Have students follow these steps:

1. Use the Self-Interview feature to help them focus on a topic for their remembrance.
2. Draft their remembrance on a computer.
3. Use the Word Bins to help them replace vague adjectives with precise ones.
4. Use the Self-Evaluation Checklist to help them revise.

Sourcebook

Students can find additional support, including topic ideas, inspirations, and graphic organizers, in the chapter on Description (pp. 1–29). The chapter includes a model of a remembrance (p. 4).

Remembrance

Writing Process Workshop

When you experience an exciting or frightening moment, you tend to remember it. For example, you may remember winning a big game or living through a dangerous weather event like this tornado. When you write about such an event, you are writing a **remembrance**. By giving a detailed, step-by-step account of the event, you help readers feel as if they are there sharing the memorable moment with you.

Re-create one of your most exciting or frightening experiences by writing a remembrance about it. The following skills, introduced in this section's Writing Mini-Lessons, will help you write your remembrance.

Writing Skills Focus

▶ **Grab readers' attention** immediately by starting with a striking description or gripping situation. An exciting opening always makes readers eager for more. (See p. 117.)

▶ **Offer elaboration** by providing vivid, colorful details that make your description precise and complete. (See p. 101.)

▶ **Provide a clear sequence of events.** Relate the details of your experience in order, so that readers are not confused about what happened first, next, and last. (See p. 109.)

In the following short piece, the author uses the above writing skills while describing a memorable encounter with a tornado.

WRITING MODEL

I've experienced some pretty bad weather, but last year's tornado was the first storm that ever struck fear in my heart.① First, the sky went from blue to black, and then the wind and rain began to whip furiously. ② I remember crouching at the window, staring in disbelief as our lawn furniture danced crazily through the air. ③

① The opening sentence grabs readers' attention.

② The author uses the words *first* and *then* to help show the order of events.

③ This colorful detail about the tornado makes it easy for readers to picture the scene clearly in their minds.

 Cross-Curricular Connection: Social Studies

Tell students that the remembrances of different people throughout history are often recorded in memoirs. Historians and other social scientists often use these first-person primary source documents to help complete a portrait of a particular event or place in time. For example, the details that a world leader or diplomat might recall about the day a nation goes to war would vary significantly from those recalled by someone in the military—or from the experience of a popular cultural figure or from an artist of the day. Have students discuss their unique "take" on the event, person, or place that inspires their remembrances. Ask them what details a historian reading their account a century from now might find revealing about the time and place in which they live. *Student responses should show an understanding that their remembrances need not resemble a journalistic, factual account of their topic. Rather, their writing should draw upon a memory that is heavily flavored by their personal point of view. A future historian might be able to read such a remembrance as representative of a young adult's perspective growing up in your students' community.*

Prewriting

Choose a Topic To find a topic, think about the scariest or most exciting moments in your life. Choose the one moment you feel would interest readers the most. The following suggestions may help you.

> ### Topic Ideas
> - A crucial victory for me
> - My brush with danger
> - How I survived a storm
> - My claim to fame

Elaborate a List of Details List as many details as you can that are related to the experience. Try to use colorful words and phrases to capture each detail. Look at these examples:

river flooded	helicopter rescue
piled sandbags	heavy rains
house floated away	sat on rooftop

Organize Events in Sequence Review your list. Think about the events that happened first, second, third, and so on. Number your notes accordingly. Don't be afraid to add new details that come to mind as you work.

3 river flooded	5 helicopter rescue
2 piled sandbags	1 heavy rains
6 house floated away	4 sat on rooftop

Drafting

Start With an Attention-Grabbing Beginning Begin your remembrance with remarkable details rather than dreary facts. Write something that will spark readers' curiosity about your experience. For example, you might dive right into the action, then go back and explain the events leading up to it; or you might begin with your reactions to the experience—for instance, "My heart beat wildy and I felt as if I'd explode!"

APPLYING LANGUAGE SKILLS: Using Precise Adjectives

As you're writing, use precise adjectives to enable readers to *see*, *hear*, *smell*, *feel*, and *taste* what you're describing. Look at this example:

General Adjective
I heard a loud noise.

Precise Adjective
I heard a thunderous noise.

Notice how the precise adjective helps you "hear" the noise better than the general adjective.

Practice On your paper, replace each italicized adjective with a more precise one.
1. We had a *bad* flood in our town.
2. The river did *big* damage to homes.
3. Workers made a *good* effort to help others.

Writing Application As you write your remembrance, use precise adjectives to describe people, places, and things. A thesaurus can help you find precise adjectives to replace general ones.

> ### Writer's Solution Connection
> ### Writing Lab
> To help you find precise adjectives for your remembrance, use the Sensory Word Bins activity in the Writing Lab tutorial on Narration.

Prewriting

You may want to have students work in small groups to brainstorm additional topic ideas. In fact, students who have known each other over a period of years may be able to suggest topics for one another. However, remind students that each individual should list his or her own details, even if the experience was a shared one. Indeed, the subjective quality of the details chosen will heighten the effectiveness of the remembrance.

Customize for
Visual/Spatial Learners
To help these students elaborate their list of details, have them form mental images and sketch the setting of the remembrance and its key figures. They can then label parts of their pictures with the appropriate descriptive words and phrases. This process should help students recall images that otherwise might be elusive to memory, whereas the focused action of sketching should help them make their details as precise as possible.

Customize for
Interpersonal Learners
These students may find it helpful to interview each other briefly in order to support whatever aspect of the prewriting requires it. For instance, a student who has difficulty organizing events in sequence could simply note the order that naturally springs to mind when orally recounting the memory to someone else.

Drafting

Encourage students to outline their remembrances and to begin at a particularly dramatic point. As students draft, they may realize that the reader might require certain additional background information—or that they can now recall details that don't fit into their planned sequence of events in an obvious way. Tell students that such departures from their prewriting plans are acceptable and are a natural by-product of writing about a topic from memory. They can handle such changes to their writing while drafting or, if they prefer, jot down some notes on the side and turn to them to use when revising their work.

Applying Language Skills
Using Precise Adjectives

Answers
Suggested responses:
1. devastating, catastrophic, cataclysmic
2. irreparable, lasting, major
3. valiant, commendable, strenuous

Writer's Solution

For additional instruction and practice, use the **Language Lab CD-ROM** units on Parts of Speech and Using Modifiers and practice in the *Writer's Solution Grammar Practice Book* (p.15).

Avoiding Fragments and Run-on Sentences (page 120)

Answers
Suggested responses:
1. The wet and weak house was about to topple.
2. A rescue helicopter hovered loudly overhead.
3. They lowered a ladder, and I then climbed up.

Writer's Solution

For additional instruction and practice, use the **Language Lab CD-ROM** lesson on Fragments and Run-on Sentences and the practice pages in the *Writer's Solution Grammar Practice Book* (pp. 62–65).

119

Revising

You may want to have students work with peer reviewers to revise their remembrances. Have peer reviewers use the revision checklist to guide their review. In addition, instruct them to offer specific, concrete suggestions for improvement, rather than simply offering general criticisms.

 **Writer's Solution**

Writing Lab CD-ROM

The Sentence Length Revision Checker in the Revision section of the tutorial on Description identifies both long and short sentences in the student's writing as well providing revision strategies. Not only will the readability of the remembrance benefit from more variation in sentence length, but students' attention may also be drawn to fragments and run-ons that require correction.

Publishing

In addition to the publishing ideas mentioned in the student text, your class may want to consider creating a "time capsule." Including objects and "artifacts" along with their writing and sealing the contents of the capsule for an audience in the "future" may underscore for students the ephemeral quality of their own memories—and the need to preserve them against the further erosion by time.

Reinforce and Extend

Review the Writing Guidelines
After students have completed their writing, review the characteristics of a remembrance. Encourage students to come up with additional criteria based on what they learned through completing the assignment.

Connect to Literature Unit 7 ("Nonfiction") includes an example of a remembrance: Rudolfo A. Anaya's "A Celebration of Grandfathers," page 576.

APPLYING LANGUAGE SKILLS: Avoiding Fragments and Run-on Sentences

A sentence fragment lacks a subject, a verb, or both and fails to express a complete thought.

Fragment: *Brave rescue workers.*

Correction: *Brave rescue workers saved the day.*

A run-on sentence has two or more main clauses incorrectly punctuated as a single sentence.

Run-on Sentence: *Rain fell, I waited.*

Correction: *Rain fell. I waited.*

Practice On your paper, correct these sentences.

1. The wet and weak house.
2. A rescue helicopter.
3. They lowered a ladder I climbed up.

Writing Application As you revise your remembrance, eliminate sentence fragments and run-on sentences.

Writer's Solution Connection
Language Lab

For more practice with sentence fragments and run-on sentences, complete the Language Lab activity on Fragments and Run-ons.

120 ◆ *Spine Tinglers*

Use Time Words to Sequence Events As you describe events, include time words to help show the order in which things happen. Here are a few words you might use:

Examples of Time Words				
first	later	afterward	soon	last
next	then	suddenly	when	finally

Revising

Use a Checklist Turn back to the Writing Skills Focus on the first page of the lesson. Use the skills as a checklist while revising your writing, in order to improve it. If you can't answer yes to the following questions, revise your work as necessary.

▶ Have I grabbed the readers' attention?

▶ Have I elaborated my ideas by using vivid details?

▶ Have I made the sequence of events clear?

REVISION MODEL

① *Rainwater crept up to my knees.*
∧ ~~There was lots of rain around me.~~ I helped pile
② *bulky canvas* ③ *two days*
∧ sandbags by the riverbank. The river flooded ∧. *later*

① The writer replaces the first sentence with a stronger attention-grabber.

② Additional details about the sandbags make it easier for readers to visualize them.

③ The author adds time words to make the sequence of events clearer.

Publishing

▶ **Classroom** Record your remembrance on tape. Set up a Listening Corner where classmates can listen to your story.

▶ **Library** Put your remembrance in a classroom book of memories and present it to the school or local library.

▶ **Other Classes** Visit other classes and share your remembrances orally. Answer questions listeners may have.

✓ ASSESSMENT		4	3	2	1
PORTFOLIO ASSESSMENT Use the rubric on Description in *Alternative Assessment* (p. 90) to assess students' writing. Add these criteria to customize the rubric to this assignment.	**Precise Adjectives**	The writer consistently uses precise adjectives.	The writer uses a mixture of precise adjectives and general adjectives.	The writer uses some, but very few, precise adjectives.	The writer consistently uses general adjectives.
	Precise Details	The writer consistently uses precise details to create a vivid picture for readers.	The writer uses precise details, but leaves out several key details.	The remembrance includes some, but far too few, precise details.	The remembrance includes too few details, and those that are included are vague.

Real-World Reading Skills Workshop

Using Visuals to Support Meaning

Strategies for Success

You may sometimes flip through a magazine looking quickly at the pictures to see whether you want to read the articles. You may not have realized, however, that you can use photographs and illustrations to enhance your understanding of and appreciation for literature and other writing. Pictures often help to reinforce what is in the written text and sometimes even provide information that extends beyond the text.

Use Your Experiences When you look at a picture, you recall all of your past experiences and ideas about the subject you are observing. Often you can use this personal knowledge to help make new inferences, or draw conclusions, about what you see. For example, if you see a picture of someone in a specific car and you know the cost of the car, you might make inferences about the economic status of the person in the car. Be careful about jumping to conclusions, however. You won't know for certain whether the person in the picture owns the car, or has achieved a certain economic status, unless it is directly stated in the text or caption.

Use Visual Clues in Combination With Text

To get the most from illustrations and photographs, always read the text and captions. Ask yourself: How do the illustrations relate to the written text? What information do the visuals provide that isn't in the text? How do the captions help me understand the visuals?

Apply the Strategy

The picture on this page is from an article about computer programs in local schools. You can make inferences about the school's program simply by combining what you are told in the caption and shown in the picture.

1. What can you infer about the computer class based solely on the picture?
2. What do you know about the class based solely on the caption?
3. What information about the class is contained in both the caption and the picture?
4. Do the picture and the caption make you want to learn more about the computer class at this school? Explain your answer.

Students learn how to access the Internet in computer class.

> ✔ Here are other situations in which visual clues may provide additional information:
> ▶ Textbooks
> ▶ Magazine articles
> ▶ Computer applications
> ▶ Internet Web sites

Real-World Reading Skills ◆ 121

Answers

1. Students might reply that the class is sparsely attended given the evident resources at students' disposal. One might infer, though, that those present are focused, serious individuals who give their complete attention to the computer screens in front of them.
2. One can infer that each computer is equipped with a modem and the necessary software for exploring the Internet. Furthermore, one can infer that the students are receiving some sort of instruction on how to use this.
3. The information in the photo and caption overlaps in that we know from both that those shown are students and that the class they are attending relates to computers. Point out that while the caption mentions the Internet, this information cannot be inferred from the photo alone.
4. Some students will respond positively, stating that both the photo and the caption point to an impressive program devoted to the Internet. Others may contend that the photo fails to capture the interest and excitement of going on-line.

Remind students that an interview consists of one person asking questions of another. They may interview someone formally if, for example, the person can provide information for the report. They may also engage in informal interviews by calling a person or an organization for information. For example, calling a business to find out what hours it's open is, in a sense, an informal interview.

Customize for
Bodily/Kinesthetic Learners

Remind these students that they need to focus on expressing themselves verbally over the telephone. As they prepare their questions, have them write out several key guidelines to help keep them on track with their interviews.

Apply the Strategy

Remind students of the importance of phrasing questions briefly and clearly for telephone interviews.

Answers

Suggested responses:

1. Appropriate questions could include "What are your impressions of our community?" "Which of your stories were your favorite to write?" and "Which writers have had the greatest influence on your writing?"
2. Questions could include "What was most memorable about the awards ceremony?" and "How did you feel when the governor introduced you at the ceremony?"
3. Students should request information about the measurements that correspond to sizes and about the procedure for exchanging items that don't fit.

Telephone Interviewing

Speaking and Listening Workshop

Conducting telephone interviews is a great way to gather information for your writing or to learn more about a work of literature. Following are some tips to help you become a successful telephone interviewer.

Plan Your Questions As with a face-to-face interview, you need to be prepared when you interview someone over the phone. Before making the call, list the specific things you want to find out. It helps to research your topic first so you can ask appropriate questions.

Prepare for Responses Interviewers must be ready to record their information quickly. As you listen to a response, take brief notes on important information only. Jot down key words and phrases that will help you remember the entire answer later. Don't try to write out a response word for word, unless you plan to use it as a direct quote. If you miss part of an answer, politely ask the speaker to repeat it. If you plan to tape the interview, first notify the person of your intention.

Tips for Telephone Interviewing

✔ *To have a successful telephone interview, follow these suggestions:*

▶ Be polite. Begin and end the call by thanking the person for his or her time.
▶ Speak directly into the mouthpiece, slowly and clearly.
▶ Hold or prop the phone securely against your ear so you hear answers clearly.

Apply the Strategies

Find a partner and role-play the following situations. Conduct each interview with your backs to one another, so you cannot see your partner as you talk. Take notes on the answers you receive. Later, you can switch roles and perform the scene again.

1. Your favorite author is in town, staying at a nearby hotel. You call for an interview for a class report. What questions do you have about the writer's work and about his or her visit to your community?
2. A teacher in your school is out of town, receiving the "Teacher of the Year" award from the governor. You call the teacher for an interview for your school newspaper. What do you ask about the ceremony and the award?
3. You are in charge of buying uniforms for the school band or football team. However, you can order by catalog only. What questions will you ask the manufacturer over the phone about the uniforms?

122 ◆ *Spine Tinglers*

 Workplace Skills Mini-Lesson

Telephone Polling

Interviewing or just talking to people on the telephone is an important skill in many work situations. For example, telemarketers call people to sell goods and services that may not be available from other sources. During political campaigns, callers poll randomly selected households to determine how favorably a candidate is being received in different demographic areas of a community.

Even in day-to-day office situations, people communicate with others by telephone. A person in advertising may need to contact the manufacturing division of a company to gather information about a product they will be marketing. The information they request and transmit must be clear, concise, and detailed.

Have students brainstorm to list a number of workplace situations in which telephone communication is central to the work. Then have them classify the situations in three groups which indicate where telephone work is most essential, somewhat necessary, and least important.

Extended Reading Opportunities

A good spine tingler will keep you on the edge of your seat. Following are just a few possibilities for extending your exploration of spine-tingling situations.

Suggested Titles

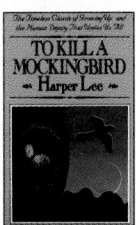

A Tale of Two Cities
Charles Dickens

This historical novel, set in London and Paris during the French Revolution, is filled with suspenseful plot twists such as false accusations, look-alike characters, and bitter people thirsting for revenge. At the center of it all is beautiful Lucy Manette—whose father wavers between sanity and madness after spending eighteen years in a French prison, and whose husband is later unjustly imprisoned and sentenced to die by the guillotine.

To Kill a Mockingbird
Harper Lee

This novel, set in the South in the early 1930's, is narrated by a strong-willed girl named Scout. Through Scout's narration, readers meet her older brother, Jem, and her beloved father, Atticus, a respected lawyer who defends an African American accused of attacking a white woman. Scout also recounts the chilling legend of Boo Radley, a neighborhood recluse, feared by all the children, who seems to be following Scout and her brother.

The Strange Case of Dr. Jekyll and Mr. Hyde
Robert Louis Stevenson

This is the story of a mild-mannered doctor who explores his dark side—with terrifying results. Fascinated with the idea of evil, the story's main character, Dr. Jekyll, develops a potion that changes him into the violent Mr. Hyde. Before long, however, Jekyll finds himself transforming into Hyde without the aid of the potion, leaving him, and terrified readers, to wonder which personality will finally win out.

Other Possibilites

Rebecca	Daphne du Maurier
Jurassic Park	Michael Crichton
The Adventures of Sherlock Holmes	Sir Arthur Conan Doyle
Buried in Ice: The Mystery of a Lost Arctic Expedition	Owen Beattie and John Geiger

Planning Students' Extended Reading

All of the works listed on this page are good choices for extending the theme of Spine Tinglers. Following is some information that may help you choose which to teach.

Customize for *Varying Student Needs*

When assigning the selections in this part to your students, keep in mind the following factors:

- *A Tale of Two Cities* is a challenging classic novel with a strong connection to world literature. Because of its length and difficulty level, you will want to allow several weeks to teach the novel.
- *To Kill a Mockingbird* is a contemporary classic with a high interest level. However, the novel does include some sensitive issues listed below.
- *The Strange Case of Dr. Jeckyll and Mr. Hyde* is a short, accessible novel with a plot that should be familiar to students.

Sensitive Issues *To Kill a Mockingbird* by Harper Lee uses the viewpoint of an innocent narrator to probe sensitive racial issues in the pre-World War II South. You may wish to use caution in recommending this book to readers for whom racial discrimination is a personally sensitive issue. On the other hand, the book provides an excellent basis for discussion of these issues as they occurred in the past and as they may now be different in the present.

Literature Study Guides Literature study guides are available for all three suggested titles. These guides include section summaries, discussion questions, and activities.

Resources for Teaching Novels, Plays, and Literature Collections

In addition to graphic organizers, teaching strategies, and transparencies that will be invaluable in teaching any of these novels, this booklet includes formal tests for *A Tale of Two Cities* and *The Strange Case of Dr. Jeckyll and Mr. Hyde.*

Customize for *Special Needs*

To meet the needs of your special needs students, you may want to consider using these titles from Globe Fearon's Pacemaker Classics series: *The Strange Case of Dr. Jeckyll and Mr. Hyde* and *A Tale of Two Cities.*

Planning Instruction and Assessment

Unit Objectives

1. To read selections in different genre that develop the theme of Challenges and Choices
2. To apply a variety of reading strategies, particularly literal comprehension strategies, appropriate for reading these selections
3. To recognize literary elements used in these selections
4. To increase vocabulary
5. To learn elements of grammar and usage
6. To write in a variety of modes and about situations based on the selections
7. To develop speaking and listening skills, by doing proposed activities

Meeting the Objectives

With each selection, you will find instructional material and portfolio opportunities through which students can meet these objectives. Further, you will find additional practice pages for reading strategies, literary elements, vocabulary, and grammar in the **Selection Support** booklet in the Teaching Resources box.

Setting Goals Work with your students at the beginning of the unit to set goals for unit outcomes. Plan what skills and concepts you wish students to acquire. You may individualize according to students' performance levels or learning modalities.

Portfolios You may have students keep portfolios of their work or of their work in progress. The activities and prompts on the Build Your Portfolio page of each selection provide opportunities for students to apply the concepts presented with the selection.

Human Achievement, Tsing-Fang Chen, Lucia Gallery, NYC

Humanities: Art

Human Achievement, by Tsing-Fang Chen.

This artwork celebrates human achievements in a number of areas: science, exploration, film, literature, music, art, philosophy, and athletics. The focal point, the realistically rendered face of Albert Einstein under his famous formula expressing the relationship between matter and energy, $e = mc^2$, may make students focus on the scientific achievements portrayed: the moon landing, the microscopes and beakers next to the hydrocarbon ring. You may want to call attention to the other images: Shakespeare's name and portrait, the masks from Noh theater, the violinist, the archaeological discovery of the archaeopteryx (an ancient reptilian feathered creature regarded as a link between dinosaurs and present-day birds), and the representations of systems of writing.

Have students link the art to the theme of Unit 2 ("Challenges and Choices") by answering the following questions:

1. What achievements and achievers does this artist celebrate? *Answers include achievements and achievers mentioned in this note.*
2. Choose one achievement represented here and explain the challenge met by the achiever. *Sample response: The scientific challenge is to explain how the components of physical life work.*

124

Challenges and Choices

An athlete challenges herself to be the best she can be. A powerful leader makes decisions that can affect an entire country. No matter who you are, life involves facing challenges and making choices. In these stories, poems, and essays, you'll see how people in many different situations deal with some of the challenges and choices life has to offer.

Assessing Student Progress

The following tools are available to measure the degree to which students meet the unit objectives:

Informal Assessment

The questions on the Guide for Responding sections are a first level of response to the concepts and skills presented with the selection. Students' responses are a brief informal measure of their grasp of the material. Their responses on this level can indicate where further instruction and practice are needed. You may then follow up with the practice pages in the *Selection Support* booklet.

You will find literature and reading guides in the *Alternative Assessment* booklet, which you may give students on an individual basis for informal assessment of their performance.

Formal Assessment

In the *Formal Assessment* booklet, you will find selection tests and a unit test.

Selection Tests The selection tests measure comprehension and skills acquisition for each selection or group of selections.

Unit Test The unit test, which calls on students to read a passage of literature they have not previously seen, applies the unit skills on a broader level. The Critical Reading section measures Unit Objectives 1, 2, and 3. The Vocabulary and Grammar section measures Objectives 4 and 5. The Essay section measures Objectives 1 and 6. Both the Critical Reading and Vocabulary and Grammar sections use formats similar to those found on many standardized tests, including the SAT.

◆ 125

Alternative Assessment

Portfolios As you review individual pieces or the collected work in students' portfolios, you will find assessment sheets available in the portfolio section of the *Alternative Assessment* booklet.

Scoring Rubrics You will find scoring rubrics for writing modes in the *Alternative Assessment* booklet. You can apply these to Writing Mini-Lessons and to Writing Process Workshop lessons.

Speaking and Listening The *Alternative Assessment* booklet contains assessment sheets for speaking and listening activities.

Learning Modalities The *Alternative Assessment* booklet contains activities that appeal to different learning styles. You may use these as an alternative measurement of students' growth.

Guide for Reading

OBJECTIVES

1. To read, comprehend, and interpret a preface to a biography
2. To relate a biographical preface to personal experience
3. To use interactive reading strategies
4. To identify anecdotes
5. To build vocabulary in context and learn the suffix *-ic*
6. To identify independent and subordinate clauses
7. To write an anecdote
8. To respond to the selection through writing, speaking and listening, and projects

SKILLS INSTRUCTION

Vocabulary:
Suffixes: *-ic*
Grammar:
Independent and Subordinate Clauses
Reading Strategy:
Using Interactive Strategies
Literary Focus:
Anecdote

Writing:
Showing, Not Telling
Speaking and Listening:
Panel Discussion (teacher edition)
Critical Viewing:
Infer; Describe

PORTFOLIO OPPORTUNITIES

Writing: Gettysburg Address; Newspaper Article; Character Profile
Writing Mini-Lesson: Anecdote
Speaking and Listening: Dramatic Scene; Panel Discussion
Projects: Timeline; Conflict Resolution

More About the Author
Carl Sandburg liked to take long walks, to watch movies, and to collect and sing folk songs. He had a deep, rich voice. He was a public figure who knew United States presidents and the actress Marilyn Monroe—she sent him her poems. He appeared on many television talk shows and won several prizes for his writing. Among Sandburg's awards was one from the NAACP, citing his civil rights work, and naming him a lifelong member. He looked at it every day. Sandburg's most cherished honor, however, was to have had at least twenty-four schools named after him.

Carl Sandburg (1878–1967)

Imagine finding one subject so interesting that you could write six books on it. Carl Sandburg was so fascinated with the life and times of Abraham Lincoln that he wrote a six-volume biography of our sixteenth president.

Sandburg believed that the Civil War was our nation's most desperate crisis and Abraham Lincoln our greatest leader.

Sandburg's admiration for Lincoln inspired true dedication—all together, he spent eighteen years researching and writing the enormous biography. The finished work included *Abraham Lincoln: The Prairie Years*, in two volumes, and *Abraham Lincoln: The War Years*, in four volumes. Sandburg's many years of hard work won him a Pulitzer Prize, as well as recognition for having written what many people consider the greatest historical biography of the 1900's.

A Varied Life Carl August Sandburg was born on January 6, 1878, in Galesburg, Illinois. At the age of thirteen he left school, and for the next seven years he held a variety of odd jobs, including porter, scene changer, truck handler, dishwasher, potter, and itinerant farm worker. After the Spanish-American War broke out in 1898, Sandburg served briefly in the United States Army in Puerto Rico. This experience caused the strong antiwar feelings that Sandburg would hold throughout his life.

A Prize-Winning Writer After returning from Puerto Rico, Sandburg enrolled in Lombard College, where he discovered literature. In 1914, while working as a journalist, Sandburg published a group of poems in a literary journal and gained his first recognition as a poet. This was the beginning of a writing career that would earn him two Pulitzer Prizes—one for his Lincoln biography in 1940 and another for his *Complete Poems* in 1951.

◆ Build Vocabulary

SUFFIXES: *-ic*

Early in this selection, Sandburg describes Lincoln as being "clothed with despotic power." Notice that the word *despotic* contains the adjective-forming suffix *-ic*, which means "like" or "pertaining to." If you know that the noun *despot* means "absolute ruler," you can figure out that *despotic* power means "unlimited power," like that held by an absolute ruler.

despotic
chattel
cipher
slouching
censure
gaunt
droll

WORD BANK

As you read the excerpt from "A Lincoln Preface," you will encounter the words on this list. Each word is defined on the page where it first appears. Preview the list before you read.

◆ Build Grammar Skills

INDEPENDENT AND SUBORDINATE CLAUSES

A clause is a group of words that contains both a subject and a verb. An **independent clause,** or *main clause,* can stand by itself as a complete sentence. A **subordinate clause** has a subject and a verb but cannot stand alone. It must be linked to an independent clause in order to make sense. Look at the following example from "A Lincoln Preface." The independent clause is in boldface, and the subordinate clause is in italics.

s   v   s   v
Greeley is so rotten *that nothing can be done with him.*

Subordinate clauses are usually introduced by **subordinating conjunctions,** such as *because, when, before, if, since,* and *while,* or by **relative pronouns,** such as *that, which, who,* and *whom.*

Prentice Hall Literature Program Resources

REINFORCE / RETEACH / EXTEND

Selection Support Worksheets
Build Vocabulary: Suffixes: *-ic*, p. 30
Build Grammar Skills: Independent Clauses and Subordinate Clauses, p. 31
Reading Strategy: Interactive Strategies, pp. 32–33
Literary Focus: Anecdote, p. 34

Strategies for Diverse Student Needs, p. 8

Beyond Literature Workplace Skills: Leadership, p. 8

Formal Assessment Selection Test, pp. 26–28, Assessment Resources Software

Alternative Assessment, p. 8

Writing and Language Transparencies
Personal Narrative, pp. 21–27

Resource Pro CD-ROM
from *A Lincoln Preface*—includes all resource material and customizable lesson plan

 Listening to Literature Audiocassettes
from *A Lincoln Preface*

from A Lincoln Preface

◆ *Literature and Your Life*

CONNECT YOUR EXPERIENCE

You may admire an athlete for her awesome ability and down-to-earth personality. You may look up to a relative for his kindness, strength, and humor. These people are heroes, and you appreciate them for their achievements or fine qualities. We are often inspired to pay tribute to our heroes in some way. Carl Sandburg, for example, wrote a six-volume biography of his hero, Abraham Lincoln.

Journal Writing Make a list of your heroes, jotting down the qualities that make each person heroic in your eyes. Think about ways in which you could pay tribute to the people on your list.

THEMATIC FOCUS: CHALLENGES AND CHOICES

Abraham Lincoln served as president during the bloodiest war in the history of the United States. Yet he faced the daily challenges and difficult choices of his presidency with compassion and humor, as you'll learn from this excerpt from his biography.

◆ Background for Understanding

HISTORY

Abraham Lincoln is remembered as one of our greatest presidents; yet at the time of his election in 1861, less than half the country supported him. One reason is that Lincoln was opposed to slavery—and many landowners in the southern United States still kept slaves. A month after his inauguration, eleven southern states had left the Union and declared themselves an independent Confederacy. Civil war broke out between the Union and the Confederacy.

Lincoln's background as a lawyer hardly prepared him to deal with a civil war, but he rose to the challenge and became the chief military strategist of the Union cause. Lincoln kept the Union states from splitting apart and eventually led them to victory in 1865. He had planned for the reconstruction of the southern states, but he was unable to complete those plans. Just six weeks after his second inauguration, Lincoln was assassinated by a supporter of the Confederacy, John Wilkes Booth.

◆ Literary Focus

ANECDOTE

If you want to describe a friend's sense of humor to someone who doesn't know her, you might relate an anecdote about a time when your friend said or did something funny. An **anecdote** is a brief story about an interesting, amusing, or strange event. In the following portrait of Abraham Lincoln, Carl Sandburg uses anecdotes to give readers a sense of what Lincoln was like.

Guide for Reading ◆ 127

Interest Grabber

Lincoln was a controversial figure in his own time—a hero to some and a villain to others. Today he is remembered by most as a principled man of great stature whose strong convictions saw the country through unprecedented troubled times. Ask students to brainstorm for and discuss a list of the qualities they associate with Lincoln. Then present the following Lincoln quotations from the piece:

I never had a policy. I have simply tried to do what seemed best each day....

I will violate the Constitution, if necessary....

Have students evaluate these statements and discuss whether they fit their impressions of Lincoln.

Customize for
Less Proficient Readers
To fully grasp the meanings of some of Sandburg's sentences that begin with the pronoun *he*, these students can use context clues or look back to previous paragraphs in order to identify the antecedents. Students can substitute proper names for the pronouns as they read.

Customize for
More Advanced Students
Students can compare their own prior knowledge of Lincoln and the Civil War period of American history with the picture Sandburg presents. Guide them to do research to verify the author's statements or to clarify their understanding of the anecdotes.

Customize for
English Language Learners
The long complex sentences in this selection may pose problems for English language learners. Have these students either paraphrase the sentences as needed or break them down into shorter sentences.

Customize for
Visual/Spatial Learners
Encourage these students to pause at descriptive passages to form the mental images the language suggests.

Preparing for Standardized Tests

Reading and Vocabulary The Reading for Success strategies will enable students to improve performance on the reading comprehension portions of standardized tests. Strategies such as setting a purpose and predicting engage readers with the text and help them retain what they have read. For additional practice, use the Reading for Success pages in **Selection Support,** pp. 32–33.

Grammar and Language Portions of some standardized tests require students to identify and correct sentence fragments. Students may be asked to determine whether a clause is an independent one and therefore can stand by itself as a complete sentence, as in the following:

Who was a member of General Lee's staff. *no*
Longstreet was a general in the Army of Northern Virginia. *yes*

The Build Grammar Skills lesson for this selection focuses on this topic. For additional practice, use the Build Grammar Skills page on Independent and Subordinate Clauses, p. 31, in **Selection Support.**

Lincoln Proclaiming Thanksgiving, Dean Cornwell, The Lincoln Museum, Fort Wayne, Indiana, a part of Lincoln National Corp.

❶ ▲ Critical Viewing What can you tell about Lincoln from this painting? [Infer]

When he was renominated, it was by the device of seating delegates from Tennessee, which gave enough added votes to seat favorable delegates from Kentucky, Missouri, Louisiana, Arkansas, and from one county in Florida. Until late in that campaign of 1864, he expected to ❷ lose the November election; military victories brought the tide his way; the vote was 2,200,000 for him and 1,800,000 against him. Among those who bitterly fought him politically, and accused him of blunders or crimes, were Franklin Pierce, a former president of the United States; Horatio Seymour, the Governor of New York;

 This information helps you achieve your **purpose** of gaining new knowledge about Lincoln.

Samuel F. B. Morse, inventor of the telegraph; Cyrus H. McCormick, inventor of the farm reaper; General George B. McClellan, a Democrat who had commanded the Army of the Potomac; and the Chicago *Times*, a daily newspaper. In all its essential propositions the Southern Confederacy had the moral support of powerful, respectable elements throughout the North, probably more than a million votes believing in the justice of the cause of the South as compared with the North.

While propagandas raged, and the war winds howled, he sat in the White House, the Stubborn Man of History, writing that the Mississippi was one river and could not belong to two countries, that the plans for railroad connec- ❸

130 ◆ *Challenges and Choices*

🎵 **Humanities: Art**

Lincoln Proclaiming Thanksgiving, by Dean Cornwell.

Abraham Lincoln issued the first annual Thanksgiving Proclamation in October of 1863. He set the date as the last Thursday in November to coincide with New England harvest traditions.

Dean Cornwell (1892–1960), of Louisville, Kentucky, was an illustrator. This picture is an oil painting rich not only in color but in the thoughtfulness it expresses. The painter makes us feel the presence of a living, thinking, beloved man. Use

these questions for discussion:
1. What might Lincoln be thinking about? *He has just signed the proclamation and may be pondering the difficult issues dividing the country. He may be wondering whether his efforts here will have a healing effect.*
2. What art elements add drama to the painting? *The use of shadows and dark, muted colors reflects the gloomy and serious times. The arch of the fireplace frames the clutter of papers and maps that the President is dealing with.*

❸ tion from coast to coast must be pushed through and the Union Pacific[4] realized.

His life, mind and heart ran in contrasts. When his white kid gloves broke into tatters while shaking hands at a White House reception, he remarked, "This looks like a general bustification." When he talked with an Ohio friend one day during the 1864 campaign, he mentioned one public man, and murmured, "He's a thistle! I don't see why God lets him live." Of a devious Senator, he said, "He's too crooked to lie still!" And of a New York editor, "In early life in the West, we used to make our shoes last a great while with much mending, and sometimes, when far gone, we found the leather so rotten the stitches would not hold. Greeley is so rotten that nothing can be done with him. He is not truthful; the stitches all tear out." As he sat in the telegraph office of the War Department, reading cipher dispatches, and came to the words, Hosanna and Husband, he would chuckle, "Jeffy D.,"[5] and at the words, Hunter and Happy, "Bobby Lee."[6]

> You can **predict**, based on this sentence, that Sandburg will now present contrasting sides of Lincoln's personality.

> You might **respond** with surprise to Lincoln's harsh remarks.

While the luck of war wavered and broke and came again, as generals failed and campaigns were lost, he held enough forces of the Union together to raise new armies and supply ❹ them, until generals were found who made war as victorious war has always been made, with terror, frightfulness, destruction, and valor and sacrifice past words of man to tell.

A slouching, gray-headed poet,[7] haunting the hospitals at Washington, characterized him as "the grandest figure on the crowded canvas of the

> ❺ Footnotes are useful if you have no **prior knowledge** about a certain reference.

drama of the nineteenth century—a Hoosier Michael Angelo."[8]

His own speeches, letters, telegrams and official messages during that war form the most significant and enduring document from any one man on why the war began, why it went on, and the dangers beyond its end. He mentioned "the politicians," over and again "the politicians," with scorn and blame. As the platoons filed before him at a review of an army corps, he asked, "What is to become of these boys when the war is over?"

He was a chosen spokesman: yet there were times he was silent; nothing but silence could at those times have fitted a chosen spokesman; in the mixed shame and blame of the immense wrongs of two crashing civilizations, with nothing to say, he said nothing, slept not at all, and wept at those times in a way that made weeping appropriate, decent, majestic. ❽

His hat was shot off as he rode alone one night in Washington; a son he loved died as he watched at the bed; his wife was accused of betraying information to the enemy, until denials from him were necessary; his best companion was a fine-hearted and brilliant son with a deformed palate and an impediment of speech; when a Pennsylvania Congressman told him the enemy had declared they would break into the city and hang him to a lamppost, he said he had considered "the violent preliminaries" to such a scene; on his left thumb was a scar where an ax had nearly chopped the thumb off when he was a boy; over one eye was a scar where he had been hit with a club in the hands of a man trying to steal the cargo off a Mississippi River flatboat; he threw a cashiered[9] officer out of his room in the White House, crying, "I can bear censure, but not insult. I never wish to see your face again."

---

8. **Michael Angelo:** Michelangelo (mik´ əl an´ jə lō), a famous Italian artist (1475–1564).
9. **cashiered** (ka shird´) v.: Dishonorably discharged.

◆ **Build Vocabulary**

cipher (sī´ fər) adj.: Code

slouching (slouch´ iŋ) adj.: Drooping

censure (sen´ shər) n.: Strong disapproval

---

4. **Union Pacific:** Railroad chartered by Congress in 1862 to form part of a transcontinental system.
5 **"Jeffy D":** Jefferson Davis (1808–1889) president of the Confederacy.
6. **"Bobbie Lee":** Robert E. Lee (1807–1870), commander in chief of the Confederate army.
7. **slouching . . . poet:** Walt Whitman (1819–1892).

from *A Lincoln Preface* ◆ 131

◆ **Reading for Success**

❹ **Respond** Ask students to respond to this characterization of war. Note that the generals referred to here were Grant, Sherman, and Sheridan. Sherman's view was to make war so horrible that the South would think twice before engaging in another.

Customize for
More Advanced Students

❺ These students may wish to read some of Walt Whitman's poems about this President he so admired. Suggest "O Captain, My Captain" and "When Lilacs Last in the Dooryard Bloomed," both of which were written in response to Lincoln's death.

❻ **Clarification** Point out that the Civil War produced a literary bonanza: thousands of participants wrote copiously about it, from the lowly soldiers in the field to the highest ranking officers.

◆ **Reading for Success**

❼ **Form a Mental Picture** Have students discuss this image of Lincoln. Ask whether it is consistent with other images they have of him.

◆ **Build Vocabulary**

❽ **Suffixes: -ic** Guide students to recognize that *majestic* means "characterized by majesty." Ask them to name other majestic things or ideas.

❾ **Clarification** William Wallace (Willy) Lincoln died of scarlet fever at the age of 11, in 1862. It broke Lincoln's heart. His "best companion" was his youngest son, Tad, 3 years younger than Willy. Tad died when he was 18.

Cross-Curricular Connection: Music

At the outbreak of World War II, American composer Aaron Copland (1900–1990) received a letter from conductor Andre Kostalanetz, who asked him to contribute to a "musical portrait gallery of great Americans." In response, Copland chose Abraham Lincoln as his subject. "A Lincoln Portrait" blends original music with familiar American folk tunes to accompany a spare and dramatic script based on Lincoln's own words. Invite students to listen to a recording of the piece and respond to it.

◆ *Literature and Your Life*

❷ Inform students that Lincoln's rise to the presidency was a rags-to-riches story in the fullest sense. Ask students to discuss whether such a story could happen today.

Reinforce and Extend

Customize for
Verbal/Linguistic Learners
These students may wish to read more of Lincoln's own words and compare his eloquent speeches with those of today's politicians. Refer them, for example, to the speeches Lincoln made during his debates with Stephen Douglas, to his inaugural addresses, and to the Gettysburg Address.

Answers
◆ *Literature and Your Life*

Reader's Response Students who appreciate Lincoln's humor may cite some of Lincoln's quips, such as the one about the devious Senator: "He's too crooked to lie still."

Thematic Focus Students may choose from people they know personally as well as from those they know through the media.

☑ **Check Your Comprehension**
1. He referred to Harriet Beecher Stowe.
2. Lincoln was willing to violate the Constitution in order to save the Union.
3. Lincoln's preference for this story reveals that he had a sense of humor about himself and didn't take himself too seriously.
4. Suggested answers include compassionate, humorous, humble, angry, driven, powerful.

Of men taking too fat profits out of the war, he said, "Where the carcass is there will the eagles be gathered together."

❶ An enemy general, Longstreet, after the war, declared him to have been "the one matchless man in forty millions of people," while one of his private secretaries, Hay, declared his life to have been the most perfect in its relationships and adjustments since that of Christ.

❷ Between the days in which he crawled as a baby on the dirt floor of a Kentucky cabin, and the time when he gave his final breath in Washington, he packed a rich life with work, thought, laughter, tears, hate, love.

With vast reservoirs of the comic and the droll, and notwithstanding a mastery of mirth and nonsense, he delivered a volume of addresses and letters of terrible and serious appeal, with import beyond his own day, shot through here and there with far, thin ironics, with paragraphs having raillery[14] of the quality of the Book of Job,[15] and echoes as subtle as the whispers of wind in prairie grass.

---

14. raillery (rāl′ ər ē) *n.*: Good-natured teasing.
15. Book of Job (jōb): Book of the Old Testament in which a man named Job is tested by God.

Perhaps no human clay pot has held more laughter and tears.

The facts and myths of his life are to be an American possession, shared widely over the world, for thousands of years, as the tradition of Knute or Alfred, Lao-tse or Diogenes, Pericles or Caesar,[16] are kept. This because he was not only a genius in the science of neighborly human relationships and an artist in the personal handling of life from day to day, but a strange friend and a friendly stranger to all forms of life that he met.

He lived fifty-six years of which fifty-two were lived in the West—the prairie years.

> **Respond** to Sandburg's appraisal of Lincoln as a great leader and a genius. In light of what you now know about Lincoln, do you agree with Sandburg?

---

16. Knute (knoot) **or Alfred, Lao-tse** (lou′ dzu′) **or Diogenes** (dī äj′ ə nēz), **Pericles** (per′ ə klēz) **or Caesar** (sē′ zer): Well-known thinkers and leaders from different eras and places.

◆ **Build Vocabulary**

droll (drōl) *adj.*: Comic and amusing in an odd way

Guide for Responding

◆ *Literature and Your Life*

Reader's Response Which anecdote about Abraham Lincoln revealed the most to you about his character?

Thematic Focus If you were to write a biography about someone who has faced many challenges and choices, who would it be?

Group Activity With a group, brainstorm for a list of people who have faced difficult challenges and made tough choices in their lives. Share your list with the class.

☑ **Check Your Comprehension**
1. To whom did Lincoln refer as "the little woman who wrote the book that made this great war"?
2. Why did Lincoln say he was willing to violate the Constitution?
3. According to Sandburg, Lincoln's favorite story about himself involves two Quaker women overheard talking. What does Lincoln's preference for this story reveal about his character?
4. Describe three personality traits that are revealed in Sandburg's portrait of Lincoln.

134 ◆ *Challenges and Choices*

Beyond the Selection

FURTHER READING
Other Works by the Author
Rootabaga Stories
The Complete Poems of Carl Sandburg

Other Works About Abraham Lincoln
With Malice Toward None, Stephen B. Oates
Lincoln, David Herbert Donald

INTERNET
You and your students may find additional information about Carl Sandburg and Lincoln on the Internet. We suggest the following sites. Please be aware, however, that sites may have changed from the time we published this information.

For information on Sandburg, go to **http://.alexia.lis.uiuc.edu/~roberts/carlpage.htm**

For a comprehensive look at Lincoln, see **http://www.netins.net/showcase/creative/lincoln.html**

We *strongly recommend* that you preview the sites before you send students to them.

Guide for Responding (continued)

◆ Critical Thinking

INTERPRET
1. What was Lincoln's most important goal during the Civil War? **[Interpret]**
2. How did Lincoln use "practical politics" to end slavery? **[Connect]**
3. How does Sandburg show that Lincoln "packed a rich life with work, thought, laughter, tears, hate, love"? **[Distinguish]**
4. How does Sandburg's use of anecdotes personalize his portrait of Lincoln? **[Analyze]**
5. In what ways does Sandburg describe Lincoln as a complex man? **[Analyze]**

EVALUATE
6. Do you think Lincoln was justified in violating the Constitution? Why or why not? **[Make a Judgment; Support]**

EXTEND
7. How does this portrait of Lincoln compare with other biographical works you have read about great leaders? **[Literature Link]**

◆ Build Vocabulary

USING THE SUFFIX -ic
The suffix -ic means "like" or "pertaining to." Define each of these words, incorporating the definition of -ic into each answer.

1. problematic
2. dramatic
3. poetic
4. artistic
5. patriotic

USING THE WORD BANK
On your paper, write the letter of the word that is a synonym of the vocabulary word given.
1. despotic: (a) fearful, (b) lonely, (c) tyrannical
2. chattel: (a) idle talk, (b) personal property, (c) loud noise
3. cipher: (a) code, (b) quiet, (c) lazy
4. slouching: (a) stumbling, (b) drooping, (c) struggling
5. censure: (a) disapproval, (b) disappointment, (c) hardship
6. gaunt: (a) weak, (b) thin and bony, (c) clumsy
7. droll: (a) serious, (b) cruel, (c) comic

◆ Reading for Success

INTERACTIVE READING STRATEGIES
Review the reading strategies and the notes showing how to interact with the text. Then apply them to answer these questions.
1. Based on your prior knowledge of Lincoln, which anecdotes surprised you?
2. Which words or phrases in the first paragraph helped you to form a mental picture of what the author is describing?
3. Do you agree with Sandburg's opinion of Lincoln? Explain.

◆ Literary Focus

Anecdote
"A Lincoln Preface" contains many **anecdotes,** or brief stories, that reveal Lincoln's personality.
1. Describe three anecdotes Sandburg uses to reveal Lincoln's character.
2. What does each anecdote illustrate?

◆ Build Grammar Skills

INDEPENDENT CLAUSES AND SUBORDINATE CLAUSES
Writers use independent and subordinate clauses to achieve sentence variety and to show supporting or modifying ideas.

Practice On your paper, write *I* for *independent* or *S* for *subordinate* for each clause in italic type. Indicate the subordinating conjunction or relative pronoun in the subordinate clauses.

An **independent,** or main, **clause** can stand alone as a sentence. A **subordinate clause** must be linked to a main clause using a subordinating conjunction or a relative pronoun.

1. *When he was renominated,* it was by the device of seating delegates from Tennessee . . .
2. His hat shot off *as he rode alone one night in Washington . . .*
3. *Whatever promise you make to those men,* I will perform it.
4. He is not truthful; *the stitches all tear out.*

Answers

◆ Critical Thinking

1. Lincoln's most important goal during the Civil War was to hold the country together.
2. "He manipulated the admission of Nevada as a state in the Union" in order to obtain votes for the Emancipation Proclamation.
3. Sandburg includes anecdotes that illustrate each of these qualities.
4. Sandburg portrays Lincoln as an active, thoughtful, sensitive, many-sided man.
5. Sandburg describes Lincoln as a man of contrasts. He could be angry and compassionate, sad and humorous. Also, he was a "man of the people" who exercised an almost despotic power.
6. Some students may argue that the end—the abolition of slavery—justified the means. Others may argue that it is never justifiable to violate the law.
7. Some students may point out that Sandburg's portrait conveys a more down-to-earth look at its subject than other biographies of famous leaders.

◆ Reading for Success

1. Students may have been most surprised by the idea of Lincoln's "almost despotic power."
2. The funereal images—"bells sobbed" and "cities wore crepe"—vividly portray the somber procession.
3. Students may respond to the warmth of Sandburg's portrait.

◆ Literary Focus

1. Answers might include Lincoln's willingness to violate the Constitution, his concern for the "boys" when the war ends, and his manipulation of Nevada's admission to the Union in order to win votes for the Emancipation Proclamation.
2. Lincoln's willingness to violate the Constitution shows his determination to save the Union; Lincoln's concern for the soldiers shows his caring and compassion; Lincoln's manipulation of Nevada's admission contradicts his reputation as "Honest Abe," but reveals his belief that rules should sometimes be bent to benefit an important cause.

◆ Build Vocabulary

Using the Suffix: -ic
1. Problematic: Having the nature of a problem—hard to solve or deal with
2. Dramatic: Connected with drama—full of action; vivid
3. Poetic: Of or like a poet or poetry—imaginative, creative
4. Artistic: Of art or artists—done skillfully or tastefully
5. Patriotic: Pertaining to a patriot—loyally supportive of one's country

Using the Word Bank
1. c 2. b 3. a 4. b 5. a
6. b 7. c

◆ Build Grammar Skills
1. S, *When;* 2. S, *as;* 3. S, *Whatever;* 4. I

 Writer's Solution

For additional instruction and practice, use the lesson in the **Language Lab CD-ROM** on combining sentences and the practice pages on Clauses (pp. 53–59) in the *Writer's Solution Grammar Practice Book.*

Idea Bank

Customizing for
Performance Levels

Following are suggestions for matching the Idea Bank topics with your students' performance levels:

Less Advanced Students: 1, 4, 6
Average Students: 2, 5
More Advanced Students: 3, 7

Customizing for
Learning Modalities

Following are suggestions for matching Idea Bank topics with your students' learning modalities:

Verbal/Linguistic: 1, 5, 7
Auditory: 4, 5
Bodily/Kinesthetic: 5, 7
Visual/Spatial: 6

Writing Mini-Lesson

Refer students to the Writing Handbook, page 962, for instruction on the writing process, and page 964 for further information on narration.

Writer's Solution

Writers at Work Videodisc

Have students view the videodisc segment on Narration (Ch. 2) featuring Isabel Allende to learn how Allende develops her stories and novels. Have students discuss how they can use techniques they've learned about in the video to come up with ideas for their anecdotes.

Play frames 10786 to 22536

Writing Lab CD-ROM

Have students complete the Tutorial on Narration. Follow these steps:

1. Have students look at the interactive model of an anecdote in the About Narration section.
2. Have students use the Story Line diagram to map out the events in their plot.
3. Have students draft their anecdotes on computer.

Allow about 70 minutes of class time for students to complete these steps.

Sourcebook

Have students use Chapter 2, Narration (pp. 30–61), for additional support. The chapter includes an annotated student model of an anecdote (p. 37).

Build Your Portfolio

 ## Idea Bank

Writing

1. **Gettysburg Address** According to legend, Lincoln drafted the Gettysburg Address on the back of an envelope. Find a copy of the Gettysburg Address. Then, on an envelope, jot down the key concepts and phrases that Lincoln may have written in a first draft of this address. **[Social Studies Link]**

2. **Newspaper Article** Write a brief news article describing the *who, what, where, when, why,* and *how* of Lincoln's death.

3. **Character Profile** Write a short profile of Lincoln, describing the traits, talents, and special skills that helped him succeed as president.

Speaking and Listening

4. **Dramatic Scene** With a partner or small group, enact one of the anecdotes Sandburg tells about Lincoln. **[Performing Arts Link]**

5. **Panel Discussion** Conduct a panel discussion on Lincoln's use of "practical politics" to end slavery with the passage of the Emancipation Proclamation. Panel members should prepare their remarks in advance. **[Social Studies Link]**

Projects

6. **Timeline** Create a timeline of the most significant events in Lincoln's life and presidency, including famous speeches and personal tragedies. **[Art Link; Social Studies Link]**

7. **Conflict Resolution** During a civil war, people are so close to issues that resolution is especially difficult. Choose a conflict in your school or community. Explain the conflict and the parties involved, and establish a step-by-step guide for resolving the conflict.

 ## Writing Mini-Lesson

Anecdote

By using anecdotes that reveal Lincoln's personality, Carl Sandburg helps readers feel that they know Lincoln as a flesh-and-blood person and not simply as a shadowy figure from history. You, too, can use anecdotes to bring life to characters and events in your writing. The following tips will show you how.

Writing Skills Focus: Showing, Not Telling

How can you make the descriptions in your anecdote interesting and effective? One way is by **showing, not telling.** This means that you use details in your writing to get your point across, rather than state the obvious. For example, in the first paragraph of "A Lincoln Preface," Carl Sandburg wants to convey the grief people experienced when Lincoln died. Rather than say, "People were sad," Sandburg writes:

. . . bells sobbed; cities wore crepe; people stood with hats off . . .

Keep in mind the technique of showing, not telling, as you plan, draft, and revise your anecdote.

Prewriting Choose a person, place, or event to describe in an anecdote. Then decide on your main point—to illustrate someone's bravery, for example. Jot down details that will help make this point without having to state it directly.

Drafting Weave the details into an anecdote—a mini-story with a beginning, middle, and end. You may decide to add quotations to your anecdote, an effective method for showing, not telling.

Revising Show your anecdote to a friend and ask that person to describe its main point. If the point isn't clear, try to add details that are more specific. You might also want to add a title that conveys your point without stating it outright.

✓ ASSESSMENT OPTIONS

Formal Assessment, Selection Test, pp. 26–28, and Assessment Resources Software. The selection test is designed so that it can be easily customized to the performance levels of your students. ***Alternative Assessment,*** p. 8, includes options for less advanced students, more advanced students, verbal/linguistic learners, musical/rhythmic learners, and visual/spatial learners.

PORTFOLIO ASSESSMENT
Use the following rubrics in the *Alternative Assessment* booklet to assess student writing:
Newspaper Article: Description Rubric, p. 90
Character Profile: Description Rubric, p. 90
Gettysburg Address: Summary Rubric, p. 91
Writing Mini-Lesson: Narrative Rubric, p. 89

PART 1 *For the Good of All*

The Promise, Paulette Peters, Museum of American Folk Art

For the Good of All ◆ 137

One-Minute Planning Guide

The selections in this section present many situations where challenges and choices are made. In "I Have a Dream," Martin Luther King, Jr., challenges Americans to live in harmony with one another. The speech is paired with lyrics to a song that pays tribute to Martin Luther King, Jr. The excerpt from *Rosa Parks: My Story* shows how one person's choice can have an impact on society. "There Is a Longing" presents a challenge to Native Americans to learn and become leaders in society. "I Hear America Singing" pays homage to Americans working together for the common good. The unit ends with "The Golden Kite, the Silver Wind," a story that illustrates cooperation is better than competition.

Customize for
Varying Student Needs

When assigning the selections in this part to your students, keep in mind the following factors:

"I Have a Dream"
- Students may need background of American civil rights movement

from *Rosa Parks: My Story*
- A first-person account of an incident that accelerated the civil rights movement in America

"There Is a Longing"
- Less proficient readers may benefit from jotting down key points as they read

"I Hear America Singing"
- Less proficient readers may need help in understanding symbolism of the word *song*

"The Golden Kite, the Silver Wind"
- Connection of story events to present-day reality may prove difficult for some students

 Humanities: Art

The Promise, by Paulette Peters.

This fabric collage, which includes among its various components quilted and solid pieces, embodies the notion of diverse parts harmonizing into a whole. The use of color throughout unifies the work, from the geometric block-by-block quilted sides, to the furrowed middle, to the representational landscape in the background—all in the same earth tones. Similarly, the silhouetted

people are mirrored by the shadows in the landscape and the border of the collage. In addition, the geometric portions of the work and the posture of the people in the foreground draw the viewer's eye to the trees, river, mountains, and sky beyond—the "promise" of the title.

Have students link the artwork to the theme of Part 1 ("For the Good of All") by answering the following questions:

1. Why do you think the artist called her work "The Promise"? *Sample response: The landscape might be viewed as holding out the promise of a better life.*
2. What might these images communicate about working together? *The group of people have to cooperate in order to reach their goal or to decide whether to continue toward it.*

Guide for Reading

OBJECTIVES

1. To read, comprehend, and interpret three poems and an excerpt from an autobiography
2. To relate poems and autobiography to personal experience
3. To respond to literature
4. To identify author's purpose
5. To build vocabulary in context and learn the root -cred-
6. To use the verbs *shall* and *will* correctly and effectively
7. To write a proposal for a school speaker
8. To respond to the work through writing, speaking and listening, and projects

SKILLS INSTRUCTION

Vocabulary: Word Roots: -cred-

Grammar: Use of *Shall* and *Will*

Reading Strategy: Respond

Literary Focus: Author's Purpose

Writing: Benefits of Proposed Ideas

Speaking and Listening: Interview (teacher edition)

Critical Viewing: Draw Conclusions; Analyze; Interpret

PORTFOLIO OPPORTUNITIES

Writing: The American Dream; The Song of America; Argument for the Defense

Writing Mini-Lesson: Proposal for a School Speaker

Speaking and Listening: Interview; Radio News Report

Projects: America in Poetry; Multimedia Presentation

More About the Authors

When **Dr. Martin Luther King, Jr.,** became the youngest-ever recipient of the Nobel Peace Prize, he donated the entire $54,000 prize to help the civil rights movement.

Rosa Parks left Montgomery in 1957 for Detroit, Michigan, after she and her husband lost their jobs. There she became an assistant to Representative John Conyers of Michigan.

Chief Dan George moved audiences with his dignified portrayal of an aged Indian chief in the 1970 film *Little Big Man.*

When critical and popular appreciation for **Walt Whitman's** *Leaves of Grass* was slow to come, Whitman wrote anonymous newspaper reviews of them in an attempt to provide a context for reading his bold work.

Martin Luther King, Jr. *(1929–1968)*

Dr. Martin Luther King, Jr., was one of the most dynamic civil rights leaders of the twentieth century. During the 1950's and 1960's, King organized nonviolent protests that helped to bring about equal rights for all Americans. His tireless efforts for civil rights inspired people of all races and earned King the 1964 Nobel Peace Prize.

Rosa Parks *(1913–)*

In 1955, Rosa Parks was arrested for breaking an unjust law. This incident, described in *Rosa Parks: My Story*, sparked a boycott that led to the end of segregation on the Montgomery bus system. Park's courageous action marked the start of the civil rights movement.

Chief Dan George *(1899–1981)*

Chief Dan George had many careers, including actor and writer. Chief of the Squamish Band of Burrard Inlet in British Columbia, Canada, he was deeply concerned about developing mutual respect between Native Americans and other North Americans.

Walt Whitman *(1819–1892)*

Walt Whitman, one of America's greatest poets, was a lover of democracy and a champion of the common individual. His expansive vision and spirit may be glimpsed in "I Hear America Singing."

◆ Build Vocabulary

WORD ROOTS: -cred-

Martin Luther King, Jr., expresses the dream that "this nation will rise up and live out the true meaning of its creed." The word *creed* comes from the root -cred-, which means "believe." Knowing the meaning of -cred- will help you determine that a creed is a statement of belief.

creed
oppression
oasis
exalted
prodigious
hamlet
complied
manhandled
determination
endurance

WORD BANK

As you read the selections, you will encounter the words on this list. Each word is defined on the page where it first appears. Preview the list before you read.

◆ Build Grammar Skills

USE OF *SHALL* AND *WILL*

Future time is expressed with *shall* or *will* and a main verb. At one time, the rule was that *shall* was used for the first person and *will* for the third person. Notice that Chief Dan George follows this rule:

First Person: I *shall* see our young braves ...

Third Person: They *will* be our new warriors ...

Now, however, that rule no longer applies. *Will* is always the appropriate helping verb to use to express future time. You can use *shall*, however, to express determination or formality, as in this statement from "I Have a Dream...."

Determination: ... all flesh *shall* see it.

138 ◆ Challenges and Choices

Prentice Hall Literature Program Resources

REINFORCE / RETEACH / EXTEND

Selection Support Pages
Build Vocabulary: Word Roots: -cred-, p. 35
Build Grammar Skills: Use of *Shall* and *Will*, p. 36
Reading Strategy: Respond, p. 37
Literary Focus: Author's Purpose, p. 38

Strategies for Diverse Student Needs, p. 9

Beyond Literature
Career Connection: Past and Present, p. 9

Formal Assessment Selection Test, pp. 29–31, Assessment Resources Software

Alternative Assessment, p. 9

Writing and Language Transparencies
Outline p. 96

Resource Pro CD-ROM
—includes all resource material and customizable lesson plan

 Listening to Literature Audiocassettes
"I Have a Dream," from *Rosa Parks: My Story*, "There Is a Longing ...," "I Hear America Singing"

Looking at Literature Videodisc
"I Have a Dream"

I Have a Dream ◆ *from* Rosa Parks: My Story
There Is a Longing ◆ I Hear America Singing

◆ *Literature and Your Life*

CONNECT YOUR EXPERIENCE

Think of a time when you were inspired by someone's words—in a speech, a work of writing, or even a conversation. Why were you moved? Often, as in these selections, we find inspiration in the words of people who challenge us to be the best we can be.

THEMATIC FOCUS: FOR THE GOOD OF ALL

Accepting our differences ... contributing to the good of all ... striving for success. These challenges, and the choices they require us to make, are reflected in the following selections.

◆ Background for Understanding

HISTORY

Civil rights are freedoms that people are entitled to as members of a society. For example, the freedom of speech guaranteed by the United States Constitution is a civil right. Some Americans, including African Americans and members of other ethnic minorities, have not always enjoyed such civil rights and have had to struggle for equality. That struggle—marked by demonstrations, marches, and legal challenges—is known as the civil rights movement. The movement, which began in the 1950's and was led by figures such as Martin Luther King, Jr., and Rosa Parks, has led to the passage of new laws aimed at protecting the civil rights of everyone.

Journal Writing Jot down your thoughts about why it is dangerous for Americans to take civil rights for granted.

◆ Literary Focus

AUTHOR'S PURPOSE

An **author's purpose** is his or her reason for writing. For example, an author's purpose for writing a humorous story might be to entertain readers. Other purposes include persuading readers or explaining how to do something. As you read each selection, determine the author's purpose by asking yourself what the author wants to accomplish. Observe the techniques the author uses to achieve his or her purpose, then decide whether the author is successful.

◆ Reading Strategy

RESPOND

Whenever you read a work of literature, you **respond** to it. What you read might bring you joy or sadness, thrills or inspiration. There is always a response. You can't help but respond because you bring your own unique experiences and memories to everything you read. As you read a story, a speech, or a poem, something the author presents touches you and triggers an emotional response.

Each of these four selections evokes a bold image of what America is and what it might become. As you read them, ask yourself how they relate to you personally. What is it in your experience or memory that connects you to them? Your questioning may evoke an emotional response.

Guide for Reading ◆ 139

Interest Grabber Play a brief passage from Dr. King's "I Have a Dream" speech. Have students describe the ideal circumstances of which Dr. King dreams. You might list key points on the board. Compare Dr. King's vision with the idea of "the American dream." Discuss why the pursuit of the American dream can be a controversial goal. Suggest that students consider how "the dream" is embodied in each of these selections.

Customize for
Less Proficient Readers
To help less proficient readers through these pieces, have them identify and analyze the authors' use of figurative language. Help them recognize how metaphors and similes can turn an idea into inspiring, soaring words that touch an audience. For instance, in the "I Have a Dream" speech, examine the impact of the metaphor of "jangling discords of our nation" turning into a "symphony of brotherhood."

Customize for
More Advanced Students
Challenge more advanced students to identify common attributes of the four writers in this grouping. For example, students might mention joy in life, inner strength, optimism, or a realistic view of obstacles. Have them find support in specific lines or phrases from the works.

Customize for
English Language Learners
Three of the pieces in this group were written to be heard. Have students listen to or deliver "I Have a Dream," "I Hear America Singing," and "There Is a Longing ..." to grasp their rhythmic qualities and the power of the imagery the authors use. To highlight the tension in the Parks excerpt, you might have students dramatize the bus scene.

Preparing for Standardized Tests

Reading and Vocabulary The Build Vocabulary lesson focuses on learning word meaning through the use of the root *-cred-*. Students can apply this knowledge to decode unfamiliar items on standardized tests. For additional practice, use the Build Vocabulary page in *Selection Support,* p. 35. Students can also apply the Literary Focus lesson to identify the author's purpose in comprehension passages on standardized tests. For more practice use the Literary Focus page in *Selection Support,* p. 38.

Grammar and Language Portions of some standardized tests require students to recognize the correct usage of verbs. Students may be asked to select the best verb form, as in the following:

We (shall, will) have lunch at noon. *will*
I vow that I (shall, will) reach my goal. *shall*

The Build Grammar Skills lesson for this selection focuses on this topic, and clarifies distinctions between these related verb forms. For additional practice, use the Build Grammar Skills page on *shall* and *will,* p. 36, in *Selection Support.*

One-Minute Insight

Dr. Martin Luther King, Jr.'s, "I Have a Dream" is one of the great speeches of the civil rights movement and one of the best known in American history. His elegant words and sermonlike cadence galvanized the nation. King blended simple words and images with biblical references and political realities to urge great numbers of people to find ways to join together to strive for change. The deeply persuasive tone of a preacher exhorting his people to embrace his ideal vision has universal appeal to those who hope to eliminate racial injustice.

❶ Clarification The ellipsis points that begin this piece indicate that it's an excerpt; some of it before the part given here was omitted.

◆ **Literary Focus**

❷ Author's Purpose Discuss the technique King uses to present his persuasive speech. *Students may observe that King's speech reflects a preaching style in which a preacher repeats simple phrases to form a bond with a congregation and to provide phrases they can recall and pass on to others.*

◆ **Literary Focus**

❸ Discuss King's use of biblical language in this paragraph. How does it advance his argument? *Using biblical language lends reverence and credibility to his ideas and gives them authority.*

▶**Critical Viewing**◀

❹ Draw Conclusions Students may conclude from the huge crowd of people that Dr. King's message was very important and that he had a great deal of support.

"I Have a Dream"

Martin Luther King, Jr.

140 · Challenges and Choices

Block Scheduling Strategies

Consider these suggestions to take advantage of extended class time:

- Students may complete the journal activity in Background for Understanding (p. 139) and discuss their entries in small groups.
- Have students listen to all or some of the selections on audiotape. Have them respond to the pieces. Discuss how listening to them adds to their appreciation of the messages.

- Suggest that students research the authors, the American civil rights movement, Native American rights, or the Montgomery bus boycott on the Internet either before or after they read.
- Have students work together to answer the Critical Thinking questions following the selections (pp. 142 and 146).
- Have students work in small groups to complete the Build Vocabulary activities (p. 148).

- Students may work individually or with a partner to complete the Writing Mini-Lesson (p. 149). Before students begin, have a class discussion on the key elements of a persuasive piece. Have students look for specific examples of these elements in the works in this set. Discuss how these elements appeal to readers or listeners.

❶ **❷** . . . I say to you today, my friends, that in spite of the difficulties and frustrations of the moment I still have a dream. It is a dream deeply rooted in the American dream.

I have a dream that one day this nation will rise up and live out the true meaning of its <u>creed</u>: "We hold these truths to be self-evident; that all men are created equal."

I have a dream that one day on the red hills of Georgia the sons of former slaves and the sons of former slaveowners will be able to sit down together at the table of brotherhood.

I have a dream that one day even the state of Mississippi, a desert state sweltering with the heat of injustice and <u>oppression</u>, will be transformed into an <u>oasis</u> of freedom and justice.

I have a dream that my four little children will one day live in a nation where they will not be judged by the color of their skin but by the content of their character.

I have a dream today.

I have a dream that one day the state of Alabama, whose governor's lips are presently dripping with the words of interposition and nullification,[1] will be transformed into a situation where little black boys and black girls will be able to join hands with little white boys and white girls and walk together as sisters and brothers.

I have a dream today.

❸ I have a dream that one day every valley shall be <u>exalted</u>, every hill and mountain shall be made low, the rough places will be made plains,

---

1. **Interposition** (in´ tər pə zish´ ən) **and nullification** (nul´ ə fi kā´ shən): Disputed doctrine that a state can reject federal laws considered to be violations of its rights.

◆ Build Vocabulary

creed (krēd) *n.*: Statement of belief

oppression (ə presh´ ən) *n.*: Keeping others down by the unjust use of power

oasis (ō ā´ sis) *n.*: Fertile place in the desert

exalted (eg zôlt´ əd) *v.*: Lifted up

◀ **Critical Viewing** What does this photograph tell you about the importance of Dr. King's message to those who heard his speech? [**Draw Conclusions**]

❹

CONNECTIONS TO TODAY'S WORLD

Years after his death, Martin Luther King, Jr., continues to touch the lives of millions of people throughout the world. Politicians, writers, musicians—people from all walks of life—continue to promote King's message of equality and harmony. The following song by the popular Irish rock band U2 was written as a tribute to King and his message.

One man come in the name of love
One man come and go
One man come, he to justify
One man to overthrow

Chorus:

In the name of love
What more in the name of love
In the name of love
What more in the name of love

One man caught on a barbed wire fence
One man he resist
One man washed on an empty beach
One man betrayed with a kiss |**❺**

(Chorus)

Early morning, April four
Shot rings out in the Memphis sky
Free at last
They took your life
They could not take your pride

(Chorus)

---

1. What emotion does this song evoke? Explain.
2. What message does the song convey? Support your answer.
3. How does the song's message relate to King's message in "I Have a Dream"?

I Have a Dream ◆ 141

Connections to Today's World

The lyrics of the song "Pride" by U2 represent just one of many responses to the assassination of Dr. Martin Luther King, Jr., on April 4, 1968. The song supports King's memory by comparing the sacrifice of his life to that of other martyrs for causes throughout the ages.

❺ Clarification Point out that the betrayal by a kiss refers to the betrayal of Jesus by Judas, a well-known part of the story of the death on a cross of Jesus of Nazareth.

Answers

1. Students should recognize the emotions of sadness and anger that underlie the words of the lyrics.
2. The song states that people have different purposes in life and that causes based on love outlive the people whose purposes may be thwarted by injustice or assassins.
3. The song validates King's dream in that it states that even death cannot destroy the causes King supported in life.

Customize for
Musical/Rhythmic Learners
The ideals of a movement reach many people through music. Have musical and rhythmic learners perform or play thematic songs to experience the emotional power of the lyrics and the unity of people singing together to express one idea. Guide them to find songs of the civil rights movement, such as "We Shall Overcome," songs with lyrics from Whitman, such as "I Sing the Body Electric," songs reflecting America's diversity, such as "This Land is Your Land," and songs about an ideal land, such as "Oleanna."

◆ *Literature and Your Life*
Martin Luther King, Jr., gave this speech on August 28, 1963. Ask students in what ways King is still an inspirational voice, and whether they think that his dream will ever come true.

Cross-Curricular Connection: Music

Popular music often captures the waves of emotion generated by significant events of a time. The song by U2 memorializes the life of Dr. Martin Luther King, Jr., just as the song "Turn, Turn" memorialized the words of Ecclesiastes used in the funeral service for President John F. Kennedy. Students may also remember the version of "Candle in the Wind" performed by British songwriter Elton John at the funeral service for Diana, Princess of Wales, in 1997.

Have students find song lyrics that refer to events or people in history. Ask them to plan a performance of the songs and to make a collage of the lyrics to display at the performance. Students may also choose to write lyrics of their own to commemorate a historical event.

◆ Critical Thinking

❶ Analyze Ask students why King includes these diverse geographical locations in this speech. Why are Georgia and Mississippi given last?
Students may say that the diverse locations make his speech more broadly American: the rural, urban, and industrial northeast, a Rocky Mountain state, and a Pacific state. He lists the southern sites last for contrast; he shows that his dreams must extend to places where freedom has not yet taken hold.

◆ Reading Strategy

❷ Respond Ask students why they think King mentioned these particular groups, and how his list might change if he were writing today.
Students may say that King mentioned those groups because they suffered persecution; today he might contrast other groups who have experienced discrimination, such as men and women or Christians and Muslims.

Looking at Literature
Videodisc To provide background and historical perspective for Martin Luther King's speech, play Chapter 3 of the videodisc. This segment features historical footage and background for the civil rights movement and King's role as one of its most important leaders. Discuss how the ideals and issues reviewed in this segment remain relevant today.

Chapter 3

Reinforce and Extend

Answers
◆ *Literature and Your Life*

Reader's Response King's speech inspires feelings of hope and enthusiasm for freedom.

Thematic Focus He challenges Americans to work for equal rights and freedom for all.

Group Activity One idea might be to start a multicultural feature in the school newspaper.

✓ Check Your Comprehension
1. King's dream is that one day Americans of all races, creeds, and religions will live together in peace and equality.

---

and the crooked places will be made straight, and the glory of the Lord shall be revealed, and all flesh shall see it together.[2]

This is our hope. This is the faith with which I return to the South. With this faith we will be able to transform the jangling discords of our nation into a beautiful symphony of brotherhood. With this faith we will be able to work together, to pray together, to struggle together, to go to jail together, to stand up for freedom together, knowing that we will be free one day.

This will be the day when all of God's children will be able to sing with new meaning "My country 'tis of thee, sweet land of liberty, of thee I sing. Land where my fathers died, land of the pilgrim's pride, from every mountainside, let freedom ring."

And if America is to be a great nation this must become true. So let freedom ring from the **❶** prodigious hilltops of New Hampshire. Let freedom ring from the mighty mountains of New York. Let freedom ring from the heightening

---

2. **every valley . . . all flesh shall see it together:** Refers to a biblical passage (Isaiah 40: 4 and 5).

Alleghenies of Pennsylvania!

Let freedom ring from the snowcapped Rockies of Colorado!

Let freedom ring from the curvaceous peaks of California!

But not only that: let freedom ring from Stone Mountain of Georgia!

Let freedom ring from every hill and molehill of Mississippi. From every mountainside, let freedom ring.

❶

When we let freedom ring, when we let it ring from every village and every hamlet, from every state and every city, we will be able to speed up that day when all of God's children, black men and white men, Jews and Gentiles, Protestants and Catholics, will be able to join hands and sing in the words of that old Negro spiritual, "Free at last! Free at last! Thank God almighty, we are free at last!"

❷

◆ Build Vocabulary
prodigious (prə dij′ əs) *adj.*: Wonderful; of great size
hamlet (ham′ lit) *n.*: Very small village

Guide for Responding

◆ *Literature and Your Life*

Reader's Response What kinds of feelings does Martin Luther King's speech stir in you?
Thematic Focus What does Martin Luther King challenge Americans to do?
Group Activity What can you do to foster tolerance and equality among students in your school? With a small group, brainstorm for practical ideas.

✓ Check Your Comprehension
1. In your own words, briefly state King's dream.
2. What are the roots, or sources, of this dream?
3. What will the hope of realizing his dream enable King to do?

◆ Critical Thinking

INTERPRET
1. Why does King mention the names of so many states in his speech? **[Infer]**
2. Explain the effect of repeating the phrase, "I have a dream." **[Analyze]**

EVALUATE
3. (a) To what degree do you think King's speech was persuasive? (b) What aspects of the speech made it so? **[Assess; Support]**

EXTEND
4. If you were to express King's dream in a drawing or painting, what images would you include? **[Art Link]**

---

2. The sources of King's dream are the Bible and the Declaration of Independence.
3. King will be able to return to the South and work toward brotherhood.

◆ Critical Thinking
1. Suggested response: King wants to suggest that civil rights are the concern of all Americans, no matter where they live.

2. Suggested response: When King repeats this phrase, he emphasizes his conviction and recalls the repetitions in a sermon.
3. (a) King's speech was highly persuasive. (b) King's repetition of the words "I have a dream" and his eloquent description of the positive results of the realized dream make the speech persuasive.

4. Drawings or paintings should contain images consistent with fostering equal rights for all people.

from Rosa Parks:
My Story

Rosa Parks (with Jim Haskins)

The Beginning, Artis Lane

3 ▲ Critical Viewing How does this picture reflect the ideal of equal rights for all people? [Analyze]

4 **5** When I got off from work that evening of December 1, I went to Court Square as usual to catch the Cleveland Avenue bus home. I didn't look to see who was driving when I got on, and by the time I recognized him, I had already paid my fare. It was the same driver who had put me off the bus back in 1943, twelve years earlier. He was still tall and heavy, with red, rough-looking skin. And he was still mean-looking. I didn't know if he had been on that route before—they switched the drivers around sometimes. I do **5**

from Rosa Parks: My Story ◆ 143

Develop Understanding

One-Minute Insight

Rosa Parks's small act of civil disobedience became a turning point for America. Heroism isn't always a great feat of power or physical prowess. A quiet act of inner strength can break new ground. Parks writes in the plain style of an ordinary person who, in retrospect, recognizes her impact but who never meant to be a symbol. The calm way she tells what happened on a Montgomery city bus in 1955 shows how her personal experiences and values led her to defy a law and act on her beliefs.

▶Critical Viewing◀

3 **Analyze** The picture reflects the ideal by showing both a white American and an African American seated in close proximity in the same area of a bus.

4 **Clarification** In 1955, Montgomery law said, "Every person operating a bus line shall provide equal accommodation . . . in such a manner as to separate the white people from the Negroes." Four days after Rosa Parks refused the driver's request to give up her seat to a white passenger, she was tried, found guilty, and fined. That day, the Montgomery bus boycott began and lasted for 381 days. Parks appealed the case, which was later dropped.

◆ **Literary Focus**

5 Discuss the author's purpose in giving this background information. *Parks foreshadows trouble, shows that she would have let this bus pass had she realized who the driver was, and shows she wasn't a rebel by nature.*

Beyond the Classroom

Community Connection
Institutions for Social Change Governmental agencies work to implement social policies that help people manage difficult life situations. However, in many communities, nongovernmental organizations, such as churches, synagogues, mosques, shelters, clubs, or civic groups, lead the way for social change. Have students investigate groups and organizations in your area that work for social change or that offer religious, community, or ethical direction. Have them share with the class what they learn about these local groups, such as who their clients are, what services they offer to them, and how they get financial support.

❶ **Clarify** Have students explain what "make it light" means. *It means to avoid having the full power of the law fall on her.* What does Rosa Parks realize at that moment? *She's tired of giving in to intimidation.*

◆ **Literary Focus**

❷ **Author's Purpose** Have students identify the purpose for which Parks may have included this paragraph. *Her purpose might be to show how unjustly African Americans were treated in the segregated South or to record in writing exactly what happened on that fateful day in 1955.*

◆ *Literature and Your Life*

❸ Invite students to relate to the feeling of "this is the last straw." Ask them to recall a situation in their own lives when they said "no" or stood up to a bully or for an ideal, even if it meant going against expectations. For example, a student may have stopped a neighbor from abusing a pet or argued with an authority who wrongly accused a friend of a violation.

◆ **Reading Strategy**

❹ **Respond** Invite students to respond to Rosa Parks's descriptions of how she felt. Ask questions such as these: Why did Parks "give permission" for her arrest? Why did she stay calm? Why did she remain on the bus? Do you think she showed courage?

know that most of the time if I saw him on a bus, I wouldn't get on it.

I saw a vacant seat in the middle section of the bus and took it. I didn't even question why there was a vacant seat even though there were quite a few people standing in the back. If I had thought about it at all, I would probably have figured maybe someone saw me get on and did not take the seat but left it vacant for me. There was a man sitting next to the window and two women across the aisle.

The next stop was the Empire Theater, and some whites got on. They filled up the white seats, and one man was left standing. The driver looked back and noticed the man standing. Then he looked back at us. He said, "Let me have those front seats," because they were the front seats of the black section. Didn't anybody move. We just sat right where we were, the four of us. Then he spoke a second time: "Y'all better make it light on yourselves and let me have those seats."

The man in the window seat next to me stood up, and I moved to let him pass by me, and then I looked across the aisle and saw that the two women were also standing. I moved over to the window seat. I could not see how standing up was going to "make it light" for me. The more we gave in and complied, the worse they treated us. ❶

I thought back to the time when I used to sit up all night and didn't sleep, and my grandfather would have his gun right by the fireplace, or if he had his one-horse wagon going anywhere, he always had his gun in the back of the wagon. People always say that I didn't give up my seat because I was tired, but that isn't true. I was not tired physically, or no more tired than I usually was at the end of a working day. I was not old, although some people have an image of me as being old then. I was forty-two. No, the only tired I was, was tired of giving in. ❷

The driver of the bus saw me still sitting there, and he asked was I going to stand up. I said, "No." He said, "Well, I'm going to have you arrested." Then I said, "You may do that." These were the only words we said to each other. I didn't even know his name, which was James Blake, until we were in court together. He got out of the bus and stayed outside for a few minutes, waiting for the police. ❸

As I sat there, I tried not to think about what might happen. I knew that anything was possible. I could be manhandled or beaten. I could be arrested. People have asked me if it occurred to me then that I could be the test case the NAACP[1] had been looking for. I did not think about that at all. In fact if I had let myself think too deeply about what might happen to me, I might have gotten off the bus. But I chose to remain. ❹

---

1. **NAACP:** *abbr.:* National Association for the Advancement of Colored People.

◆ **Build Vocabulary**

complied (kəm plīd´) *v.:* Carried out or fulfilled a request

manhandled (man´ han´ dəld) *v.:* Treated roughly

Beyond Literature

Social Studies Connection

The Struggle for Human Rights
Today, people in many countries throughout the world are denied basic human liberties. For example, although the constitution of China guarantees freedom of speech, anyone who criticizes the Communist government can be severely punished. This became all too clear in 1989 when thousands of university students crowded into Beijing's Tiananmen Square, holding demonstrations for democracy in China. Government troops broke up the demonstrations, killing hundreds of students in the process. Today, in China and elsewhere, the struggle for human rights continues. Do you think the passage of laws is enough to ensure human rights? Explain.

144 ◆ *Challenges and Choices*

Cross-Curricular Connection: Social Studies

After the Supreme Court upheld the separate-but-equal concept in *Plessy vs. Ferguson* (1896), segregation legislation, known as "Jim Crow laws," grew widespread. Although African Americans gained federal rights that had once been denied to them, state and local laws were passed to restrict them in many demeaning ways. So, despite the Emancipation Proclamation and Constitutional amendments, the way of life for many southern blacks did not improve until the civil rights protests of the 1950's and 1960's caused old restrictions to be abolished. Have students interview Americans who can remember life before the civil rights movement. Or show excerpts from the documentary *Eyes on the Prize* to help students learn more about the impact and abolition of Jim Crow laws.

One-Minute Insight Chief Dan George believes that Native Americans must ensure their survival and their standing in today's world by acknowledging their ancient heritage and pride in traditional values as they also work to embrace what is best of "the white man's success." Knowing that a smooth mix of old ways with the new won't be easy to achieve, George asks the sacred spirits for guidance to lead and inspire a new generation to become "the proudest segment of your society."

(5) ▲ Critical Viewing How has the artist combined Native American symbols with symbols of contemporary American society? What do you think was her purpose in doing so? [Interpret]

There Is a Longing . . .

Chief Dan George

(6)
There is a longing in the heart of my people
to reach out and grasp that which is
   needed
for our survival. There is a longing among
the young of my nation to secure for
   them selves
5 and their people the skills that will
provide them with a sense of worth and
purpose. They will be our new warriors.
Their training will be much longer and
more demanding than it was in olden days.
10 The long years of study will demand
more <u>determination</u>; separation from home
and family will demand <u>endurance</u>. But
   they
will emerge with their hand held forward,
not to receive welfare, but to grasp the
15 place in society that is rightly ours.

(7)
I am a chief, but my power to make war
is gone, and the only weapon left to me
is speech. It is only with tongue and speech
that I can fight my people's war.

20 Oh, Great Spirit![1] Give me back the courage
of the olden Chiefs. Let me wrestle with
my surroundings. Let me once again,
live in harmony with my environment.
Let me humbly accept this new culture
25 and through it rise up and go on. Like
the thunderbird[2] of old, I shall rise again
out of the sea; I shall grab the instruments
of the white man's success—his
education, his skills. With these new tools
30 I shall build my race into the proudest
segment of your society. I shall see our
young braves and our chiefs sitting in
the houses of law and government, ruling
and being ruled by the knowledge and
35 freedoms of *our* great land.

(8)
(9)

1. **Great Spirit:** For many Native Americans, the greatest power or god.
2. **thunderbird:** A powerful supernatural creature that was thought to produce thunder by flapping its wing and produce lightning by opening and closing its eyes. In the folklore of some Native American nations, the thunderbird is in constant warfare with the powers beneath the waters.

◆ **Build Vocabulary**

determination (dē tʉr′ mi nā′ shən) *n.:* Firm intention
endurance (en do͝or′ əns) *n.:* Ability to withstand hardship and stress and to carry on

from *Rosa Parks: My Story/There Is a Longing* ◆ 145

▶**Critical Viewing**◀

(5) Interpret The Native American woman is wearing traditional bead-work. The stars and stripes is a contemporary American symbol. The eagle is a symbol in both Native American and contemporary American cultures. The artist is showing that both Native Americans and contemporary American society are moving toward a common future.

(6) Clarification In this sentence, the author refers to survival of the values, culture, language, and traditions that define his people, not survival in terms of life or death.

◆ **Critical Thinking**

(7) Make Inferences Ask students what they can infer about the status or condition of Chief Dan George's people when he wrote this speech. *Students may suggest that the people have been stripped of their traditional defenses and cultural lifestyle.*

◆ **Literary Focus**

(8) Author's Purpose Discuss the author's purpose in this piece. Guide students to recognize that George uses the tone of a prayer, an invocation, or a plea for divine guidance so he can find the strength and wisdom to guide those who rely on him. It reveals his humility and his fervent hope for a secure future.

◆ **Build Grammar Skills**

(9) Use of *Shall* and *Will* Point out how the author's use of the verb form *shall* emphasizes the formality and determination in his remarks.

♪ Humanities: Art

We the People, by Kathy Morrow.
   Kathy Morrow, who created *We the People,* is an Anglo who grew up on Apache and Sioux reservations because her father organized and trained Native American police forces. Have students examine this piece and discuss these questions:

1. How does this work convey a sense of longing and determination? *Students may observe that*

the movement of the eagle seems to be toward a brighter, more ideal future.

2. What does the title of the painting suggest to you? *The title echoes the preamble to the Constitution of the United States ("We, the people of the United States of America . . ."), which assumes the unity of all its citizens under a single governing body.*

One-Minute Insight

In *Leaves of Grass*, Whitman describes "America's busy, teeming, intricate whirl." This poem celebrates his joyous view of the indomitable American spirit. People distinguish themselves by righteous hard work, take pride in tasks that build the future, and demonstrate an exuberance of skill and purpose that makes each one a vibrant contributor to the spirit of a proud nation.

❶ **Clarification** Whitman loved to attend the opera, which was very popular in his day. Living in New York, he was able to hear many of the great singers of that time. One night at the opera in 1848, he happened to meet someone from a New Orleans newspaper at intermission. The man hired Whitman to come to his southern city to work as a journalist for his paper. This trip inspired some of the poems in *Leaves of Grass*.

◆ **Reading Strategy**

❷ **Respond** Whitman found great inspiration in diversity and responded with joy to the purity of physical labor. If he were writing today, he might use occupations different from the ones he included then. Have students respond to the feeling Whitman creates in these lines.

Customize for
Visual/Spatial Learners
To help students gain a richer appreciation for the America Whitman describes, have them create a mural to fit the poem. They might draw or paint images of the workers Whitman mentions, or make a collage of people at modern jobs that echoes the mood and spirit of hard work.

Reinforce and Extend

Answers
◆ *Literature and Your Life*

Reader's Response Rosa Park's words could evoke a time when students felt they were treated unfairly; Chief Dan George's words might suggest a situation from which students felt themselves excluded; Walt

146

I Hear America Singing

Walt Whitman

I hear America singing, the varied carols I hear, I ❶
Those of mechanics, each one singing his as it should be blithe and strong,
The carpenter singing his as he measures his plank or beam,
The mason singing his as he makes ready for work, or leaves off work,
5 The boatman singing what belongs to him in his boat, the deckhand singing on the steamboat deck,
The shoemaker singing as he sits on his bench, the hatter singing as he stands, ❷
The wood-cutter's song, the ploughboy's on his way in the morning, or at noon intermission or at sundown,
The delicious singing of the mother, or of the young wife at work, or of the girl sewing or washing,
Each singing what belongs to him or her and to none else,
10 The day what belongs to the day—at night the party of young fellows, robust, friendly,
Singing with open mouths their strong melodious songs.

Guide for Responding

◆ *Literature and Your Life*

Reader's Response What personal feelings or experiences could you relate to the words of Rosa Parks, Chief Dan George, and Walt Whitman?
Thematic Focus In these selections, what challenges are faced by Rosa Parks, Native Americans, and American workers?

☑ **Check Your Comprehension**

1. What reason does Rosa Parks give for staying in her seat?
2. In "There Is a Longing," how will the speaker's people obtain a sense of worth and purpose?
3. What carols does the speaker hear in "I Hear America Singing"?

◆ **Critical Thinking**

INTERPRET
1. In "There Is a Longing," how do the "new warriors" the speaker wishes to see compare with the warriors of old? **[Compare and Contrast]**
2. Are the people really singing in "I Hear America Singing"? Explain. **[Interpret]**
EVALUATE
3. Why do you think that Rosa Parks's decision to remain seated on the bus was appropriate for a general civil rights test case? **[Make a Judgment]**
4. Has the speaker in "There Is a Longing" selected the best means for improving his people's lives? **[Assess]**
5. Would "I Hear America Singing" have been more or less effective if it had been written with a regular rhythm and rhyme scheme? **[Evaluate]**
APPLY
6. How do the ideas and issues in these three selections still hold true today? **[Synthesize]**

146 ◆ Challenges and Choices

Whitman's words might relate to an accomplishment for which students feel particularly satisfied.
Thematic Focus Rosa Parks must fight for her rights, Native Americans must learn new skills, and American workers must perform tasks for the good of society.

☑ **Check Your Comprehension**

1. She was tired of giving in to unfair treatment.
2. They will do so through study to obtain the essential skills needed to prosper in today's society.
3. He hears the sounds of various kinds of work.

◆ **Critical Thinking**

1. The new warriors fight for a sense of worth by learning the skills needed in modern society. The old warriors

fought military battles.
2. The people are celebrating, not singing. What is "heard" is the figurative "humming" of various kinds of work.
3. It was appropriate because it dealt with a basic, straightforward human right or fair treatment.
4. Yes, because speaking out for education and necessary skills training is the best way to help people get ahead.

(Answers continue on page 147.)

Coal (from America Today), Thomas Hart Benton, © The Equitable Life Assurance Society of the United States Collection. © T. H. Benton and R. P. Benton Testamentary Trusts/Licensed by VAGA, New York, NY

▲ **Critical Viewing** How does this painting capture the spirit of American workers celebrated in "I Hear America Singing"? [**Analyze**]

I Hear America Singing ◆ 147

Answers (continued)

5. Students might say it would have been less effective because the individuality of each worker's song might be lost.
6. Today, many people still seek equal rights, justice, and the education and skills necessary to earn a living and contribute to society.

▶**Critical Viewing**◀

❸ **Analyze** The painting captures the spirit of American workers by showing American factories steaming with activity and a coal miner working hard to contribute to a mighty and bustling society.

 Humanities: Art

Coal, 1920, by Thomas Hart Benton.
Thomas Hart Benton (1889–1975) felt that his greatest education came from the years he spent roaming the United States. In his art, he glorified hard work and the American thirst for progress.

This work is part of a series of murals that depicts contemporary America, done for the New School for Social Research in New York City. This vigorous mural shows the mining and industrial uses of coal and the workers who made this whole process possible. Benton used an innovative montage of images separated by stylized architectural elements, a technique that revolutionized mural design in America.
Use these questions for discussion:

1. What phrases and moods does the mural evoke? *Responses may include backbreaking work, fatigue, push for progress, a mix of manual and mechanical labor, modernization.*
2. Compare and contrast Benton's and Whitman's views of work. *Both glorified work and workers, both took pride in the diversity of American labor. Whitman romanticized work, while Benton depicted its more gritty, realistic images.*

 Beyond the Selection

FURTHER READING

Other Works by the Authors
Leaves of Grass, Walt Whitman
My Heart Soars, Chief Dan George
Quiet Strength, Rosa Parks

Other Works of Choice for the Good of All
"The Autobiography of Miss Jane Pittman," Jane Pittman
"I Will Fight No More Forever," Chief Joseph

INTERNET

The Internet provides excellent opportunities for students to gather more information for this group of selections. We suggest the following sites. Please be aware, however, that sites may have changed from the time we published this information. To learn more about Walt Whitman, visit **http:www. liglobal.com/walt**

The site at **http://www.blackhistory.eb.com** has links for Rosa Parks and Martin Luther King, Jr.

We *strongly recommend* that you preview the sites before you send students to them.

OBJECTIVES

1. To read, comprehend, interpret, and respond to a fable
2. To relate a fable to students' personal experience
3. To predict consequences of actions in a story
4. To identify the key characteristics of a fable
5. To build vocabulary in context and learn the word root *-clam-*
6. To develop skill in identifying and using action verbs and linking verbs
7. To write a public service campaign using an appropriate style
8. To respond to the work through writing, speaking and listening, and projects

SKILLS INSTRUCTION

Vocabulary: Word Roots: *-clam-*

Grammar: Action Verbs and Linking Verbs

Reading Strategy: Predict Consequences of Actions

Literary Focus: Fable

Writing: Use an Appropriate Style for the Medium

Speaking and Listening: Dramatization (teacher edition)

Critical Viewing: Infer

PORTFOLIO OPPORTUNITIES

Writing: Fable; Persuasive Letter; Science Report

Writing Mini-Lesson: Public Service Ad Campaign

Speaking and Listening: Dramatization; Improvisation

Projects: Science Report; Map

More About the Author

Ray Bradbury's childhood love for the stories of Edgar Allan Poe and Edgar Rice Burroughs grew into a lifelong passion for tales of adventure, horror, and fantasy. Bradbury is best known as a science fiction writer whose works, including this fable, often mirror his concern for the fate of society and the perils of unchecked technology. He has always looked to the future; he predicted interactive television and virtual reality years before their actual emergence.

Guide for Reading

Ray Bradbury (1920–)

Years before space travel became a reality or computers became common household appliances, science-fiction writers were exploring the possibilities of technology and stretching the limits of readers' imaginations. One of the most celebrated science-fiction writers is Ray Bradbury. Bradbury has written numerous collections of stories and has won many awards, including the World Fantasy Award for lifetime achievement and the Grand Master Award from the Science Fiction Writers of America.

An astronaut has even named a lunar landmark Dandelion Crater, after Bradbury's autobiographical novel Dandelion Wine.

A Science-Fiction Writer's Beginnings

Bradbury was born in Waukegan, Illinois, and spent his boyhood along the western shores of Lake Michigan. At an early age, he developed a love of horror movies, fantasy cartoons, and suspenseful stories by writers such as Edgar Allan Poe.

In 1932, Bradbury's family moved to Tucson, Arizona. Bradbury wrote his first stories there in Tucson, banging out tales of space travel on a six-dollar typewriter, a Christmas gift from his parents. A year later, the family moved to Los Angeles, California, where Bradbury has resided ever since.

In high school, Bradbury pursued his passion for science fiction and fantasy by founding and editing a quarterly publication called *Futuria Fantasia*. By this time, he was already writing at least one story a week. This rapid and disciplined pace has continued: Every morning between 9 and 11, Bradbury sits down at his typewriter and drafts 2,000 to 3,000 words of manuscript.

◆ Build Vocabulary

WORD ROOTS: *-clam-*

In this story you'll encounter the word *acclaimed,* which contains *-claim-*, a variation of the root *-clam-*, meaning "call out" or "shout." Considering that the prefix *ac-* means "to" or "toward," you might guess that *acclaimed* means "called out toward." This is close to the actual definition, "greeted with loud applause or approval."

WORD BANK

portents
vile
ravenous
acclaimed
pandemonium
spurn

As you read "The Golden Kite, the Silver Wind," you will encounter the words on this list. Each word is defined on the page where it first appears. Preview the list before you read.

◆ Build Grammar Skills

ACTION VERBS AND LINKING VERBS

Verbs can be categorized as either action verbs or linking verbs. **Action verbs** express physical or mental actions. They tell you what the subject of the sentence does. **Linking verbs** express a state of being and connect the subject to a word or words that rename or describe the subject. The most common linking verb is some form of the verb *be (am, is, are, was, were).*

Following are examples of both an action verb and a linking verb from the story.

Action Verb: They both *sat* thinking.

Linking Verb: Life *was* full of symbols and omens.

150 ◆ *Challenges and Choices*

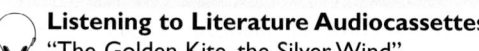

Prentice Hall Literature Program Resources

REINFORCE / RETEACH / EXTEND

Selection Support Pages
Build Vocabulary: Word Roots: *-clam-*, p. 39
Build Grammar Skills: Action Verbs and Linking Verbs, p. 40
Reading Strategy: Predict Consequence of Actions, p. 41
Literary Focus: Fable, p. 42

Strategies for Diverse Student Needs, p. 10

Beyond Literature
Cross-Curricular Connection: Social Studies, p. 10

Formal Assessment Selection Test, pp. 32–34, Assessment Resources Software

Alternative Assessment, p. 10

Writing and Language Transparencies
Cluster Organizer, p. 80

Resource Pro CD-ROM
"The Golden Kite, the Silver Wind"—includes all resource material and customizable lesson plan

Listening to Literature Audiocassettes
"The Golden Kite, the Silver Wind"

The Golden Kite, the Silver Wind

◆ Literature and Your Life

CONNECT YOUR EXPERIENCE

Have you and a friend ever tried to outdo each other? Maybe your rivalry focused on who had the better CD collection or who could perform the most daring feat. The two of you may have become consumed by your rivalry, but most likely, no one else was hurt as a result of it. In this story, a rivalry becomes so intense that it leads to widespread suffering.

Journal Writing Write about a rivalry that caused suffering on both sides.

THEMATIC FOCUS: FOR THE GOOD OF ALL

This story shows how the choices people make can hurt both themselves and their rivals. How can people rise to the challenge of making choices that are for the good of all?

◆ Background for Understanding

HISTORY

"The Golden Kite, the Silver Wind" was written during the Cold War, a period of intense rivalry between the United States and the former Soviet Union. During this time, the two countries competed for position as the world's leading nation. Each action by one country—an alliance, the placement of a weapon, the launching of a satellite—was countered by a reaction from the other country.

Because both countries had huge arsenals of nuclear weapons, many people feared that the rivalry between the superpowers could escalate into a nuclear war with the potential of destroying all life on Earth. As you read, think about how the events in the story might relate to the situation between the United States and the Soviet Union at the time of the Cold War.

◆ Literary Focus

FABLE

A **fable** is a brief story, often with animals as characters, that teaches a lesson. The lesson, or moral, is sometimes directly stated in a single sentence at the end of the fable. Other times, the actions and choices of the characters guide you to the moral of the story. In this fable, the actions of two rival cities provide a lesson about the advantages of cooperation versus competition.

◆ Reading Strategy

PREDICT CONSEQUENCES OF ACTIONS

In this story, a Chinese village takes a series of actions that in turn sparks reactions from a rival village. As you read, try to **predict the consequences** of each action by considering events that have already occurred along with what you have learned about the characters and their motivations. Then read on to see whether you were correct.

A chart like the one shown might help you. Write down the events as they happen. Before you read further, predict the consequence of that event. You will see a pattern develop that will lead you to the moral of the story.

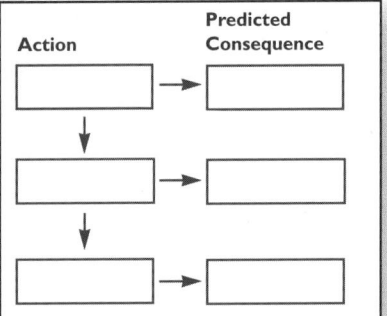

Interest Grabber Initiate a discussion of rivalry. Include questions like these: How do rivals behave toward one another? How far will rivals go to outdo one another? What kinds of outcomes can result from a rivalry? Students might answer these questions in terms of a real rivalry situation they know.

Point out that this story is about the unexpected results of actions taken by rivals.

Customize for
Less Proficient Readers
To help less proficient readers through this fable, have them follow along in their text as they listen to the recording of the selection.

Listening to Literature Audiocassettes

Customize for
English Language Learners
This fable uses figurative language and terms with which English language learners may be unfamiliar. To help these students, explain or clarify expressions such as "death rattled his cane in the outer courtyard," and "like a rusted machine, the city ground to a halt."

Customize for
Interpersonal Learners
In this fable, Ray Bradbury uses the relationships between a Mandarin and his daughter and between him and a neighboring Mandarin to convey a message. To enrich appreciation of the piece, have students focus on these characters and their roles, motivations, and interactions.

Guide for Reading ◆ 151

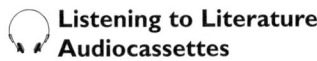

Preparing for Standardized Tests

Reading and Vocabulary The Build Vocabulary lesson focuses on learning word meaning through the use of the root *-clam-*. Students can apply this skill when working with verbal items on standardized tests. For additional practice, use the Build Vocabulary page in *Selection Support,* p. 39. The Reading Strategy lesson, Predict Consequences of Actions, is helpful in reading comprehension portions of standardized tests. For more practice, use the Reading Strategy page in *Selection Support*, p. 41.

Grammar and Language Portions of some standardized tests require students to understand the distinction between action verbs and linking verbs. Students may be asked to categorize a verb as one or the other, as in the following:

Kim *doused* the note with perfume. *action verb*
Her perfume *smelled* like lilacs. *linking verb*

The Build Grammar Skills lesson for this selection focuses on this topic. For additional practice, use the Build Grammar Skills page on Action Verbs and Linking Verbs, p. 40, in *Selection Support.*

This fable highlights the negative consequences of ever-rising competition as a mode of interaction. It symbolizes the behaviors of nations or groups that, from fear or arrogance, aggressively build up their defenses rather than try to work out their differences. On a literal level, the fable is about two rival towns that construct ever more complex walls to empower and protect themselves. As the competition escalates, both communities suffer unforeseen consequences.

►Critical Viewing◄

❶ Speculate Students might say that each ruler wants to prove that he is better than the other or rules over a more powerful realm.

Cultural Connection

This fable uses many symbols from Chinese culture. Acquaint students with some of them, such as the animals of the Chinese astrological calendar. Explain that over a twelve-year cycle, each year is named for an animal whose qualities and characteristics influence people born in that year. For instance, people born in 1982, the Chinese year of the dog, are believed to be gracious and responsible.

Have students find out more about the symbolic qualities associated with animals in China or in other cultures, for example, the industrious ant, the loyal boar, or the wise dragon. Discuss with students how different cultures ascribe different meanings to their symbols. For example, the rat in western culture is a symbol of deceit and betrayal; but in Chinese culture, the rat is considered a loving

The Golden Kite, the Silver Wind

Ray Bradbury

❶ ▲ Critical Viewing This story describes the rivalry between two Mandarins. Why might two rulers become involved in a case of one-upmanship? [Speculate]

Block Scheduling Strategies

Consider these suggestions to take advantage of extended class time:

- Students may complete the journal activity in Literature and Your Life (p. 151) and discuss their entries in small groups.
- Suggest that students research fables or the writings of Ray Bradbury on the Internet either before or after they read.
- Have students listen to all or part of the selection on audiotape. Have them discuss the theme of cooperation. Ask them whether lis-

tening to the story adds to their appreciation of it.

- Students can work in discussion groups to answer the Critical Thinking questions (p. 157).
- Have students complete the Writing Mini-Lesson (p. 158). Before students get started have a class discussion on the goals of public service announcements. Have students look for specific examples of appropriate styles for writing public service ads.

"In the shape of a *pig?*" cried the Mandarin.[1]

"In the shape of a pig," said the messenger, and departed.

"Oh, what an evil day in an evil year," cried the Mandarin. "The town of Kwan-Si, beyond the hill, was very small in my childhood. Now it has grown so large that at last they are building a wall."

"But why should a wall two miles away make my good father sad and angry all within the hour?" asked his daughter quietly.

"They build their wall," said the Mandarin, "in the shape of a pig! Do you see? Our own city wall is built in the shape of an orange. That pig will devour us, greedily!"

"Ah."

They both sat thinking.

Life was full of symbols and omens. Demons lurked everywhere, Death swam in the wetness of an eye, the turn of a gull's wing meant rain, a fan held *so*, the tilt of a roof, and, yes, even a city wall was of immense importance. Travelers and tourists, caravans, musicians, artists, coming upon these two towns, equally judging the <u>portents</u>, would say, "The city shaped like an orange? No! I will enter the city shaped like a pig and prosper, eating all, growing fat with good luck and prosperity!"

The Mandarin wept. "All is lost! These symbols and signs terrify. Our city will come on evil days."

"Then," said the daughter, "call in your stonemasons and temple builders. I will whisper from behind the silken screen and you will know the words."

The old man clapped his hands despairingly. "Ho, stonemasons!

Ho, builders of towns and palaces!"

The men who knew marble and granite and onyx and quartz came quickly. The Mandarin faced them most uneasily, himself waiting for a whisper from the silken screen behind his throne. At last the whisper came.

"I have called you here," said the whisper.

"I have called you here," said the Mandarin aloud, "because our city is shaped like an orange, and the <u>vile</u> city of Kwan-Si has this day shaped theirs like a <u>ravenous</u> pig—"

◆ Build Vocabulary

portents (pôr´ tentz) *n.*: Things that are thought to be signs of events to come; omens

vile (vil) *adj.*: Evil; wicked

ravenous (rav´ ə nəs) *adj.*: Greedily hungry

---

1. **Mandarin** (man´ de rin): A high official of China; here, the ruling leader.

The Nymph of the Lo River, Attributed to Ku K'ai-chih, Freer Gallery of Art, Smithsonian Institution, Washington, D.C.

The Golden Kite, the Silver Wind ◆ 153

Customize for
More Advanced Students

Have students focus on elements of setting, character, theme, and language in this piece that mark it as a fable. Ask students how and why the author of this fable makes the piece timeless and universal. *The author does so by using characters and plot that are straightforward and symbolize the dangers of competitiveness. His reason for doing so is to teach the moral lesson of those dangers to contemporary leaders.*

◆ **Literary Focus**

❷ **Fable** Point out that this fable begins with no introductory passage and no background details of any kind; characters just begin to speak. Why do you think Bradbury does this? *Fables are short and symbolic, so an author has no room for extraneous details. Bradbury lets characters' words and actions reveal the story.*

◆ **Reading Strategy**

❸ **Predict Consequences of Actions** Have students predict what the daughter will do. *From her hiding place behind the screen, the daughter will offer suggestions for the builders on how to deal with the situation.*

◆ **Critical Thinking**

❹ **Make Inferences** Ask students: What can you infer about the role of women or daughters in the Mandarin's society? Responses may include: *Women have less power and influence than men, and someone younger defers to his or her elders. Therefore, the Mandarin's daughter can advise her father only if she hides herself and lets him take credit for her ideas.*

♪ Humanities: Art

The Nymph of the Lo River (section of a handscroll), by Ku K'ai-chih.

To the ancient Chinese, the world was full of supernatural creatures. Places often had their own particular guardian spirit. For example, bodies of water often had a resident dragon, and a mountain might be home to a ki-lin, or Chinese unicorn. Some of these guardian spirits were benevolent, and might appear to people to give advice or warn of dangers. In this watercolor, the guardian of the Lo River has taken human form and is advising an official.

Use these questions for discussion:
1. What story setting can you infer from the details of the work of art? *The details of the figures and their clothing, as well as the way in which trees are rendered, suggest an East Asian locale of a time long ago.*
2. In what ways is the style of the work of art especially appropriate for a fable? *The uncluttered composition and the straightforward rendering of the figures and trees convey the basic truth about the subject just as a fable conveys a basic truth without resorting to great detail.*

153

Customize for
More Advanced Students

The Mandarin assumes that his daughter has left out of modesty and deference to him. Have students discuss other possible reasons for the daughter's sudden disappearance. *She may have left because she was ashamed of her idea, perhaps feared it would create more problems than it would help, or needed time alone to think of better solutions.*

Customize for
Verbal / Linguistic Learners

Point out examples of figurative language used in the selection. For instance, students might notice the simile "pleasure was like a winter flower" or the metaphor "a whisper that was a falling drop of rain." Encourage students to identify other uses of figurative language in this fable, and restate their meaning in other words.

◆ Build Vocabulary

Present the word *exclaim* as another word based on the root -clam-. Ask students what it means (*cry out*) and where they might substitute it for another verb in the fable. Challenge students to name other words based on -clam-, such as *proclamation*, *declaim*, or *clamor*, and substitute them in the fable where suitable.

◆ Reading Strategy

❶ Predict Consequences of Actions Predictions may express the idea that no matter what shape a new wall may take, the other village will find another shape to overcome it. Therefore, as each village devotes more time to rebuilding its walls, each will have less time for normal pursuits, such as maintaining homes, farms, and businesses.

Here the stonemasons groaned and wept. Death rattled his cane in the outer courtyard. Poverty made a sound like a wet cough in the shadows of the room.

"And so," said the whisper, said the Mandarin, "you raisers of walls must go bearing trowels and rocks and change the shape of *our* city!"

The architects and masons gasped. The Mandarin himself gasped at what he had said. The whisper whispered. The Mandarin went on: "And you will change our walls into a club which may beat the pig and drive it off!"

The stonemasons rose up, shouting. Even the Mandarin, delighted at the words from his mouth, applauded, stood down from his throne. "Quick!" he cried. "To work!"

When his men had gone, smiling and bustling, the Mandarin turned with great love to the silken screen. "Daughter," he whispered, "I will embrace you." There was no reply. He stepped around the screen, and she was gone.

Such modesty, he thought. She has slipped away and left me with a triumph, as if it were mine.

The news spread through the city; the Mandarin was acclaimed. Everyone carried stone to the walls. Fireworks were set off and the demons of death and poverty did not linger, as all worked together. At the end of the month the wall had been changed. It was now a mighty bludgeon with which to drive pigs, boars, even lions, far away. The Mandarin slept like a happy fox every night.

"I would like to see the Mandarin of Kwan-Si when the news is learned. Such pandemonium and hysteria; he will likely throw himself from a mountain! A little more of that wine, oh Daughter-who-thinks-like-a-son."

But the pleasure was like a winter flower; it died swiftly. That very afternoon the messenger rushed into the courtroom. "Oh, Mandarin, disease, early sorrow, avalanches, grasshopper plagues, and poisoned well water!"

The Mandarin trembled.

"The town of Kwan-Si," said the messenger, "which was built like a pig and which animal we drove away by changing our walls to a mighty stick, has now turned triumph to winter ashes. They have built their city's walls like a great bonfire to burn our stick!"

The Mandarin's heart sickened within him, like an autumn fruit upon an ancient tree. "Oh, gods! Travelers will spurn us. Tradesmen, reading the symbols, will turn from the stick, so easily destroyed, to the fire, which conquers all!"

"No," said a whisper like a snowflake from behind the silken screen.

"No," said the startled Mandarin.

"Tell my stonemasons," said the whisper that was a falling drop of rain, "to build our walls in the shape of a shining lake."

The Mandarin said this aloud, his heart warmed.

"And with this lake of water," said the whisper and the old man, "we will quench the fire and put it out forever!"

The city turned out in joy to learn that once again they had been saved by the magnificent Emperor of ideas. They ran to the walls and built them nearer to this new vision, singing, not as loudly as before, of course, for they were tired, and not as quickly, for since it had taken a month to rebuild the wall the first time, they had had to neglect

 ◆ Reading Strategy What do you think will be the consequence of this latest action? ❶

◆ Build Vocabulary

acclaimed (ə klāmd´) *v.*: Greeted with loud applause or approval; hailed

pandemonium (pan´ də mōn´ nē əm) *n.*: Wild disorder, noise, or confusion

spurn (spurn) *v.*: Reject in a scornful way

154 ◆ Challenges and Choices

🖐 Speaking and Listening Mini-Lesson

Dramatization

This mini-lesson supports the Speaking and Listening activity in the Idea Bank on page 158.

Introduce the Concept Point out that a dramatization, or performance of a story, can emphasize certain elements or interpretations. Divide the class into drama groups. Have groups discuss the effects they wish to create in dramatizing the written tale.

Develop Background Before groups begin working on their dramatizations, guide participants to consider these points:

• Convey ideas with actions as well as words.
• Convey emotions that fit the characters.
• Plan how to handle narration: Present it all, read selected passages, divide it among several readers, or replace it with dialogue.

Apply the Information Have each group

determine how members will participate. Some students can create a script; others can prepare costumes, props, backdrops, or sound effects. One student can direct the dramatization.

Assess the Outcome Have students discuss variations among the dramatizations and use the Peer Assessment form for a dramatic performance, p. 113 in *Alternative Assessment.*

business and crops and therefore were somewhat weaker and poorer.

There then followed a succession of horrible and wonderful days, one in another like a nest of frightened boxes.

"Oh, Emperor," cried the messenger, "Kwan-Si has rebuilt their walls to resemble a mouth with which to drink all our lake!"

"Then," said the Emperor, standing very close to his silken screen, "build our walls like a needle to sew up that mouth!"

❷ "Emperor!" screamed the messenger. "They make their walls like a sword to break your needle!"

The Emperor held, trembling, to the silken screen. "Then shift the stones to form a scabbard to sheathe that sword!"[2]

"Mercy," wept the messenger the following morn, "they have worked all night and shaped their walls like lightning which will explode and destroy that sheath!"

Sickness spread in the city like a pack of evil dogs. Shops closed. The population, working now steadily for endless months upon the changing of the walls, resembled Death himself, clattering his white bones like musical instruments in the wind. Funerals began to appear in the streets, though it was the middle of summer, a time when all should be tending and harvesting. The Mandarin fell so ill that he had his bed drawn up by the silken screen and there he lay, miserably giving his architectural orders. The voice behind the screen was weak now, too, and faint, like the wind in the eaves.

"Kwan-Si is an eagle. Then our walls must be a net for that eagle. They are a sun to burn our net. Then we build a moon to eclipse their sun!"

◆ **Literary Focus**
What is the lesson to be learned from the actions of the two Mandarins?

❸

Like a rusted machine, the city ground to a halt.

---
2. **scabbard** (skab′ ərd) **to sheathe** (shēth) **that sword!**: Case to hold the blade of the sword.

Rectangular box (detail), Avery Brundage Collection, Asian Art Museum of San Francisco

▲ **Critical Viewing** Based on this scene from an ancient Chinese box, make inferences about the setting and characters in this story. [Infer] ❹

At last the whisper behind the screen cried out:

"In the name of the gods, send for Kwan-Si!"

Upon the last day of summer the Mandarin Kwan-Si, very ill and withered away, was carried into our Mandarin's courtroom by four starving footmen. The two mandarins were propped up, facing each other. Their breaths fluttered like winter winds in their mouths. A voice said:

"Let us put an end to this."

The old men nodded.

"This cannot go on," said the faint voice. "Our people do nothing but rebuild our cities to a different shape every day, every hour. They have no time to hunt, to fish, to love, to be good to their ancestors and their ancestors' children."

"This I admit," said the mandarins of

❺

The Golden Kite, the Silver Wind ◆ 155

◆ **Critical Thinking**

❷ **Make Inferences** Bradbury describes the Mandarin as "standing very close to his silken screen." Have students decide what kind of leader the Emperor is, based on his behavior so far. *Students may infer that he lacks imagination and vision, has little skill dealing with problems, or finds the challenges of leadership so great that he must rely on a secret advisor for help. Other students may add that the Mandarin is enlightened because he takes advice from his daughter.*

◆ **Literary Focus**

❸ **Fable** Responses should include the idea that leaders who are so busy trying to outmaneuver each other will lose sight of their true task: to inspire and guide their people to lead productive lives. All the effort they spend on competing drains the vitality of their communities.

▶**Critical Viewing**◀

❹ **Infer** The setting is in an ornate building or palace in ancient China. The characters' clothing and proximity to the ornate table indicate that these people are important dignitaries.

◆ **Reading Strategy**

❺ **Predict Consequences of Actions** Have students predict what the Mandarins will do to end the conflict between their cities. *Students should predict that the Mandarins will find a way to stop the ridiculous escalation so that people's lives can return to normal, that they'll find a compromise that favors neither community.*

 Humanities: Art

Rectangular Box (detail), Late Ming Dynasty, early seventeenth century.

The Ming dynasty ruled China from A.D. 1368 to 1664. During that time, Chinese authority stretched into Mongolia, Korea, Southeast Asia, and the Ryukyu Islands.

Noteworthy is the fact that the Ming dynasty was a very creative period in the arts in China. Artists produced fine works in porcelain and bronze, and architects designed the imperial palace in the Forbidden City area of Beijing.

Use these questions for discussion:
1. What do the details of this work of art suggest about Chinese society of the time? *The orderly and formal posture of the figures, along with the ornate robes, suggest a polite and formal society.*

2. What incidents in the story might this work of art illustrate? *The work might illustrate the Mandarin's meeting with the stonemasons and builders or the meeting of the two rival mandarins.*

Idea Bank

Customizing for
Performance Levels

Following are suggestions for matching the Idea Bank topics with your students' performance levels:

Less Advanced Students: 1, 6
Average Students: 2, 4, 7
More Advanced Students: 3, 5

Customizing for
Learning Modalities

Following are suggestions for matching Idea Bank topics with your students' learning modalities:

Visual/Spatial: 7
Logical/Mathematical: 1, 3, 6
Verbal/Linguistic: 2
Interpersonal: 4, 5

Writing Mini-Lesson

Refer students to the Writing Handbook, page 962, for instruction on the writing process, and page 965 for further information on Persuasion. Have students use the Cluster Organizer, which is available on blackline master in *Writing and Language Transparencies,* p. 80, to help generate ideas for their public service ad campaign.

Writer's Solution

Writing Lab CD-ROM

Have students complete the Tutorial on Persuasion. Follow these steps:
1. Have students complete an Audience Profile.
2. Have students draft on computer. Allow 60 minutes of class time to complete these activities.

Sourcebook

Have students use Chapter 4, Persuasion (pp. 97–127), for additional support. The chapter includes a model of a public service announcement (p. 126).

Build Your Portfolio

Idea Bank

Writing

1. **Fable** Write a fable that, like "The Golden Kite, the Silver Wind," teaches a lesson about conflict or cooperation.

2. **Persuasive Letter** Think about a specific conflict in today's world that you want to see resolved. Write a persuasive letter to the two sides urging them to end the conflict. Point out the negative consequences of the conflict and suggest a resolution that will benefit both sides.

3. **Science Report** Like a kite and the wind, many animals and plants exist together in a way that is helpful to both. Find out more about helpful relationships in nature. Then prepare a research report on one such relationship. **[Science Link]**

Speaking and Listening

4. **Dramatization** With a small group of classmates, develop and present a dramatic production of Bradbury's story.

5. **Improvisation** With a partner, act out the development and resolution of a conflict between two people. Do not discuss with each other ahead of time who the people are and what the conflict is. **[Performing Arts Link]**

Projects

6. **Good Advice** Collect morals from other fables, along with short sayings that convey useful advice. Assemble your collection into an illustrated booklet.

7. **Map** Create a map that illustrates some aspect of the Cold War. For example, you might show the alliances each side formed. If possible, use photographs, diagrams, and other media to help present your findings. **[Social Studies Link]**

Writing Mini-Lesson

Public Service Ad Campaign

Create a series of advertisements that convey a message about the importance of resolving conflicts. Choose the medium—print, radio, television, and so on—through which the messages will be presented.

Writing Skills Focus: Use Appropriate Style for the Medium

When you whiz by a billboard on the highway, you don't have much time to read it. To work well, a billboard message must be short, eye-catching, and to the point. Other types of media lend themselves to other styles of communication. Dialogue, for example, works well in a radio ad. To make sure you get your message across, use an **appropriate style** for the medium.

Prewriting Brainstorm for a list of points you would like to make about conflicts and how to resolve them. For example, you might note how important it is for people to listen to one another to resolve conflicts. Review the list and choose the points you want to include in your campaign. Then identify the best way to convey these points through the medium you have chosen. For example, if you're preparing magazine ads, you'll need to find visuals to include.

Drafting Draft your ads, making sure that you follow the format appropriate to your medium. For example, if you're preparing print ads, you should write copy to accompany your visuals; if you're preparing television ads, create a brief script.

Revising Revise your campaign to make the best use of the medium you have chosen. If your ad is highly visual, for example, be sure that the verbs in your message work well with your images.

✓ ASSESSMENT OPTIONS

Formal Assessment, Selection Test, pp. 32–34, and Assessment Resources Software. The selection test is designed so that it can be easily customized to the performance levels of your students.
Alternative Assessment, p. 10, includes options for less advanced students, more advanced students, interpersonal learners, verbal/linguistic learners, logical mathematical learners, and kinesthetic learners.

PORTFOLIO ASSESSMENT
Use the following rubrics in the *Alternative Assessment* booklet to assess student writing:
Good Advice: Problem-Solution Rubric, p. 94
Fable: Narration: Fictional Narrative Rubric, p. 88
Persuasive Letter: Persuasion Rubric, p. 98
Writing Mini-Lesson: Persuasion Rubric, p. 98

Writing Process Workshop

Persuasive Speech

Abraham Lincoln and Martin Luther King, Jr., used their powers of persuasion to help our nation overcome tremendous challenges. Both are known for their rousing **persuasive speeches**—formal spoken presentations in which a speaker tries to convince an audience to act or think in a certain way. Follow in the footsteps of King and Lincoln by writing and presenting a persuasive speech on an issue that you believe is critical to today's generation.

The following skills, introduced in this section's Writing Mini-Lessons, will help you develop your speech.

Writing Skills Focus

▶ **Don't just tell listeners that they should accept your positions, show them why they should.** Provide anecdotes—brief stories—that illustrate why the cause for which you're arguing is right on target. (See p. 136.)

▶ **Mention the benefits of your ideas.** Tell listeners what they will gain by doing what you ask of them. (See p. 149.)

▶ **Use an appropriate style for your medium.** Take advantage of your personal contact with the audience. Write words that you can speak with emotion! (See p. 158.)

Martin Luther King, Jr., uses all these skills in the historic speech he delivered in Washington, D.C., in 1963.

MODEL FROM LITERATURE

from "I Have a Dream" by Martin Luther King, Jr.

When we let freedom ring, when we let it ring from every village and every hamlet, from every state and every city, ① we will be able to speed up that day when all of God's children, black men and white men, Jews and Gentiles, Protestants and Catholics, will be able to join hands and sing ② in the words of that old Negro spiritual, "Free at last! Free at last! Thank God almighty, we are free at last!" ③

① King adds to the impact of his speech by dramatizing, or showing, the situation that would occur if equal rights were to be realized.

② King explains how all people will benefit from equal rights.

③ By quoting a spiritual, King is able to let his speech "ring out" with emotion.

Writing Process Workshop ◆ 159

Cross-Curricular Connection: Performing Arts

Through movies and the theater—as well as perhaps their own background in drama—students may be familiar with the persuasive speeches that appear throughout Shakespeare's plays, such as *Julius Caesar* and *Henry V.* Explain that these dramatic speeches differ from Shakespeare's well-known soliloquies in that they feature a main character who is a real historical figure speaking to a group at a critical moment—not just speaking to himself or herself, or to the theater audience. Ask students what they can learn from these powerful pieces of writing that might apply to their own speeches. On the other hand, what important differences should be kept in mind between these fictional speeches and the actual ones they will be writing? *Students should respond that speeches such as that of Marc Anthony after Caesar's death feature many of the hallmarks of effective persuasion, including the repetition of key points. Shakespeare's characters often use well thought-out, logical arguments and appeal to their listeners' emotions by using a variety of strategies. However, Shakespeare's poetic, highly dramatic style may be inappropriate for discussing current events.*

Prepare and Engage

Establish Writing Guidelines
Before students begin, review the following key characteristics of a persuasive speech:

- A persuasive speech is a persuasive piece designed to be presented orally instead of in writing.

- When effective, a persuasive speech stirs the audience to reconsider their opinions.

- Persuasive speakers use a variety of techniques such as the repetition of key points to capture and hold the audience's attention.

You may want to distribute the scoring rubric for Persuasion (p. 98 in *Alternative Assessment*) to make students aware of the criteria on which their work will be evaluated before they begin. For suggestions on how you can customize the rubric to this workshop, see page 161.

Refer students to the Writing Handbook, page 962, for instruction on the writing process, and page 965 for further information on persuasive writing.

Writer's Solution

Writers at Work Videodisc
To introduce students to key elements and to show them how NBA writer Larry Weitzman uses persuasive writing, play the videodisc segment on Persuasion (Ch. 4). Ask students how to apply Weitzman's advice about how to choose appropriate words for a draft.

Play frames 33836 to 42938

Writing Lab CD-ROM
If your students have access to computers, you may want to have them work on the Tutorial on Persuasion to complete their remembrances. Have students follow these steps:
1. Make use of the interactive instruction on statistics, survey results, quotations, and examples.
2. Draft their persuasive speeches on the computer.
3. Respond to the Self-Evaluation Checklist to help them revise.

Sourcebook
Students can find additional support in the chapter on Persuasion (pp. 96–127). Included are sixteen topic ideas for persuasive speeches and in-depth instruction on considering an audience for persuasive writing.

Develop Student Writing

Prewriting

Advise students as they choose a topic that although they may select one about which they have "strong feelings," those emotions should be capable of being supported by facts and well-reasoned arguments. While everyone probably has opinions that feel "right," these may not be appropriate topics for a persuasive speech. Reassure students that whether their audience agrees or disagrees with them, it will be interested in the reasons for their opinions and the serious thought they have given to them.

Customize for
Logical/Mathematical Learners

To help these students gather evidence in statistical form, encourage them to critically evaluate the numbers—both those that support their argument and those that do not. Ask them to consider the source of their statistic, and to consider whether the statistic implies a cause-and-effect relationship or simply a correlation.

 **Writer's Solution**

Writing Lab CD-ROM

Have students make use of the interactive instruction on using library resources that can be found in the Gathering Evidence section of the Tutorial on Persuasion. Library catalogs, encyclopedias, magazine articles (found through the *Reader's Guide to Periodical Literature*)—as well as CD-ROMs and on-line services—are all covered. Once students have conducted their research, they can complete a Note Cards activity in the Organizing Evidence section that will help them find an order for their persuasive speech.

Writing Process Workshop

APPLYING LANGUAGE SKILLS: Active and Passive Voice

A verb in the active voice shows the subject doing an action. A verb in the passive voice shows the subject receiving an action.

Active Voice:
Workers <u>cut</u> the trees.

Passive Voice:
Trees <u>are cut</u> by workers.

Notice how the active voice makes writing more forceful and lively.

Practice Rewrite each sentence so the verb is in the active voice.

1. Medicinal plants are discovered by scientists in the rain forest.
2. Oxygen is produced by trees.
3. The rain forest can be saved by people who care.

Writing Application As you draft your speech, focus on using the active voice. Use the passive voice only when the performer of the action is unknown or unimportant.

Writer's Solution Connection Writing Lab

To help you come up with a topic, use the Inspirations in the Choosing a Topic section in the tutorial on Persuasion.

160 ◆ *Challenges and Choices*

Prewriting

Choose a Topic Think of a current issue about which you have strong feelings and which you think is especially important. Then clarify your position on that issue. If no ideas come to mind, try one of these topics.

> **Topic Ideas**
> - Why people should recycle
> - Why the nation should have a third political party
> - Why education is important
> - Why teenagers should do volunteer work

Gather Evidence to Support Your Position Once you've chosen an issue and clarified your position on that issue, gather evidence—facts, statistics, and so on—that you can use to support your position. If possible, try to think of anecdotes—brief stories—that you can use to illustrate your position. For example, if you are arguing for the need to preserve the rain forest, you might tell the story of a particular species that could be wiped out. Most likely, you'll need to conduct research either in the library or on the Internet to help you pull together the facts, statistics, and anecdotes you'll need. You might use an organizer like this one as you gather support.

Facts	Statistics	Anecdotes
Rain forest that is cut down cannot be replaced in our lifetimes.	Rain forests used to cover about 20% of Earth's surface; today, cover about 7%.	Trip to rain forest in Brazil showed me the tremendous diversity in the rain forest.

Technology Tip To use the Internet to gather information, come up with a few key words related to your topic. Then use a search engine to find information related to the key words.

List the Benefits In addition to gathering evidence to support your position, list benefits that will result from the course of action you're proposing.

Applying Language Skills
Using Active Voice Explain to students that understanding the effects of active and passive constructions is particularly important in speech writing. Passive constructions weaken the effect of a speech.

Answers
Suggested responses:
1. Scientists discover medical plants in the rain forest.
2. Trees produce oxygen.
3. People who care can save the rain forest.

 Writer's Solution

For additional instruction and practice, have students complete the lesson on Active and Passive Voice in the **Language Lab CD-ROM,** and practice page 76 in the *Writer's Solution Grammar Practice Book.*

Using Parallel Structure
Explain to students that a lack of clear parallel structure hampers an audience's ability to pick up on a speaker's emphasis. Supporting related ideas with parallel structure helps the listener retain the ideas.

Answers
Suggested response: Preserving the rain forest saves endangered species, protects native cultures, and helps prevent global warming.

Writer's Solution

For additional instruction and practice on how to make sentences form effective paragraphs, use the **Language Lab CD-ROM** lesson on Unity and Coherence in Paragraphs and the practice pages 128–130 in the *Writer's Solution Grammar Practice Book.*

160

Drafting

Write in the Style of Your Medium As you write, remember that you will eventually deliver the speech aloud. Use powerful words and phrases that you can stress as you talk to your listeners face to face. Also think how you might use visual aids to help persuade your audience. Adapt your text so that it mentions your visual aids.

Use an Organization That Will Help Convince Your Audience As you draft your speech, present your evidence in an order that will hold the interest of your audience and leave a strong impression in their minds. You may want to use an order-of-importance organization, beginning with less important points and leading up to your strongest arguments.

Revising

Add Evidence to Strengthen Your Argument Read through your first draft, looking for places in which you can add evidence to bolster your argument. If you find that you have little evidence to support a key point, you may need to go back and conduct additional research to gather more evidence.

Practice Reading Your Speech Aloud Working either on your own or with classmates, read your speech aloud several times. Make sure that your speech flows seamlessly from one point to the next. If it doesn't, add transition words to make stronger connections. Also, look for places in which you can improve the way your speech sounds by replacing a word or restructuring a sentence.

Publishing

Present Your Speech Deliver your speech to your class, keeping the following points in mind:

- ▶ Use the volume and tone of your voice to emphasize key points and keep your audience engaged.
- ▶ Use hand gestures where appropriate to support what you're saying.
- ▶ Look at all of your listeners. Try to avoid focusing on just one or two people.

APPLYING LANGUAGE SKILLS: Using Parallel Structure

Using parallel structure—the repeated use of the same grammatical structure—is an excellent way to drive home your main points in a speech. Look at this example from Martin Luther King's speech:

Parallel Structure:

Let freedom ring from the prodigious hilltops of New Hampshire. Let freedom ring from the mighty mountains of New York.

Practice Write a passage using parallel structure that states these ideas.

Preserving the Rain Forest:

1. Saves endangered species
2. Protects native cultures
3. Helps prevent global warming

Writing Application Review your speech and find places where you can use parallel structure to emphasize a key point or strengthen the sound of your speech.

Writer's Solution Connection

Writing Lab

For more instruction on parallel structure and revision, work through the Revision section of the tutorial on Persuasion.

Writing Process Workshop ◆ 161

Drafting

Students may find that as they draft their persuasive speeches, their writing reads more like a persuasive essay than a speech. Encourage students to add colloquial expressions and humor as appropriate, to make their writing more like a speech.

Revising

You may want to have students work with peer reviewers to revise their persuasive speeches. Have peer reviewers use the revision checklist to guide their review.

 **Writer's Solution**

Writing Lab CD-ROM
The interactive instruction on avoiding faulty logic and unreasonable appeals will help them critically examine their own arguments while revising.

Publishing

You can enhance students' presentation of their speeches by videotaping them and donating a copy of the tape to your school library. Students can develop an index of speakers and topics to accompany the videotape, thus transforming their speeches into a resource of information.

Reinforce and Extend

Review the Writing Guidelines After students have completed their writing, review the characteristics of a persuasive speech. Encourage students to come up with additional criteria based on what they learned through completing the assignment.

Connect to Literature Unit 5 ("Visions of the Future") includes an example of a persuasive speech—Nelson Mandela's "Glory and Hope" (p. 445). In this speech, Mandela exhorts his audience to move forward into the future.

✓ ASSESSMENT		4	3	2	1
PORTFOLIO ASSESSMENT Use the rubric on Persuasion in *Alternative Assessment* (p. 98) to assess students' writing. Add these criteria to customize the rubric to this assignment.	**Active Voice**	The writer consistently uses active voice.	The writer uses a mixture of active and passive voice.	The writer uses active voice only in a few cases where it is appropriate.	The writer consistently uses passive voice.
	Speech Writing	The writer consistently uses devices (repetition of key points, transitions, visual aids, humor) that support the spoken delivery of the text.	The writer includes some devices that support the spoken delivery of the text. The observation includes some, but far too few, precise details.	The writer includes few devices that support the spoken delivery of the text.	The writer includes no devices that support the spoken delivery of the text.

Guide for Reading

OBJECTIVES

1. To read, comprehend, and interpret poetry and a biographical sketch
2. To relate literature to personal experience
3. To generate questions to facilitate comprehension
4. To identify figurative language
5. To build vocabulary in context and learn the suffix -ly
6. To develop skill in using commas to separate items in a series
7. To use suitable criteria in writing an essay evaluating figurative language
8. To respond to the work through writing, speaking and listening, and projects

SKILLS INSTRUCTION

Vocabulary:
Suffixes: -ly
Grammar:
Commas in Series
Reading Strategy:
Generate Questions
Literary Focus:
Poems and Biographical Sketch

Writing: Use Correct Punctuation for Items in a Series
Speaking and Listening: Job Interview (teacher edition)
Critical Viewing: Compare and Contrast; Analyze

PORTFOLIO OPPORTUNITIES

Writing: Recipe; Dialogue; Job Description
Writing Mini-Lesson: Evaluating the Writer's Use of Figurative Language
Speaking and Listening: Job Interview; Group Discussion
Projects: Docudrama; Nutrition Report

More About the Author

In his poetry, **Robert Frost** displays his attachment to the farms, fields, and simple values of rural New England life. He was an impassioned botanist and naturalist who keenly observed details.

Born in St. Louis, **Maya Angelou** was raised by her grandmother in segregated Arkansas. The poem she read at Bill Clinton's first inauguration, "On the Pulse of Morning," earned her international recognition.

Marge Piercy is known for her many novels and volumes of poetry and for her commitment to feminism. Her poetry often conveys strong, angry messages and "a coherent vision of the world—as it is now and as it should be."

Robert Frost (1874–1963)

In January of 1961, when John F. Kennedy took the helm as president of the United States, he called on fellow New Englander Robert Frost—at the time probably America's most famous living poet—to recite two poems at the inauguration. Earlier in his career, Frost was not so well received in his native land. In 1912, unable to earn a living as a poet, he packed up his family and moved to England. After British editions of his poetry volumes *A Boy Will* (1913) and *North of Boston* (1914) won praise on both sides of the Atlantic, Frost returned to the United States a celebrity. (See p. 412 for more on Robert Frost.)

Maya Angelou (1928–)

Three decades after Frost's appearance at the Kennedy inauguration, President-elect Bill Clinton invited fellow Arkansan Maya Angelou to perform a poem for his inaugural ceremonies. In both her poetry and her nonfiction, Angelou draws on her own experience, frequently exploring the problems of poverty, racism, and sexism. (For more information on Maya Angelou, see p. 244.)

Marge Piercy (1936–)

The young Marge Piercy seemed an unlikely future writer. Born into economic hardship in Detroit, Michigan, Piercy was the first person in her family to attend college. It took her more than ten years to win recognition as a writer, during which time six of her novels were rejected for publication. Now even better known as a poet, Piercy's *To be of use* (1973), and many other highly praised verse collections have been published.

164 ◆ Challenges and Choices

◆ Build Vocabulary

SUFFIXES: -ly

The words *amicably* and *meticulously* end with the suffix -ly, which is often used to turn adjectives into adverbs of manner (adverbs that tell *how* or *in what manner*). If you know that the adjective *meticulous* means "very careful or thorough," you can figure out that *meticulously* must mean "in a very careful or thorough manner."

WORD BANK

As you read the three selections, you will encounter the words on this list. Each word is defined on the page where it first appears. Preview the list before you read.

| diverged |
| amicably |
| meticulously |
| specters |
| ominous |
| unpalatable |
| dallying |
| submerged |
| harness |

◆ Build Grammar Skills

COMMAS IN SERIES

A **comma** can make a big difference in the clarity of your writing. Separating three or more items in a series is one way that commas make writing clearer. Think about how the meaning of this sentence from "New Directions" would change if there were a comma after *meat*, or how confusing the meaning would be if there were no comma after *lard*:

> The next morning she left her house carrying the meat pies, lard, an iron brazier, and coals for a fire.

If the items in the series are already separated by conjunctions (such as *and* or *or*), commas are not necessary.

Prentice Hall Literature Program Resources

REINFORCE / RETEACH / EXTEND

Selection Support Pages
Build Vocabulary: Suffixes: -ly, p. 43
Build Grammar Skills: Commas in Series, p. 44
Reading Strategy: Generate Questions, p. 45
Literary Focus: Figurative Language, p. 46

Strategies for Diverse Student Needs, p. 11

Beyond Literature
Cross-Curricular Connection: Social Studies, p. 11

Formal Assessment Selection Test, pp. 35–37, Assessment Resources Software

Alternative Assessment, p. 11

Writing and Language Transparencies
Responding to Literature, pp. 45–51

Resource Pro CD-ROM
"The Road Not Taken," "New Directions," "To Be of Use"—includes all resource material and customizable lesson plan

Listening to Literature Audiocassettes
"The Road Not Taken," "New Directions," "To Be of Use"

The Road Not Taken
New Directions ◆ To be of use

◆ *Literature and Your Life*

CONNECT YOUR EXPERIENCE
Each one of us makes choices every day. Some choices can make a major difference in your future. Will you pursue a certain career path? Will you challenge yourself to try something new? Choices like these are explored in the following selections, which often compare these choices to forks in the road of life.

Journal Writing What choices or decisions that young people make could change their lives forever? Jot down some important choices that people often make before they are thirty.

THEMATIC FOCUS: PUTTING OURSELVES TO THE TEST
In these three selections, decision making plays an important role. Do the speakers think things through carefully? Do they take the easy path? You decide as you read each selection.

◆ Background for Understanding

HISTORY
In the early twentieth century, job opportunities were limited for many Americans—particularly for African Americans like Annie Johnson, the central figure in Maya Angelou's "New Directions." At the time when this episode takes place, the most common occupation for African American women was domestic labor—cleaning, child care, and other household work. For women who were also raising families of their own, caring for someone else's household was an extra burden. That's probably why Annie Johnson struck off in a "new direction."

◆ Literary Focus

FIGURATIVE LANGUAGE
Figurative language is language that means more than it says literally. When Marge Piercy tells us she loves people who "jump into work head first/without dallying in the shallows," she is using figurative language. Piercy does not mean literally that the people she loves best are deep-sea divers. Rather, she is expressing her admiration for people who take on challenges courageously.

◆ Reading Strategy

GENERATE QUESTIONS
One way to get a better understanding of what you read is to create questions based on the text and then see if you can answer them. To **generate questions**, begin with the common question words *who*, *what*, *where*, *when*, *why*, and *how*. For example, consider the opening sentence of "New Directions":

> In 1903 the late Mrs. Annie Johnson of Arkansas found herself with two toddling sons, very little money, a slight ability to read and add simple numbers.

From that sentence alone, you could generate the following questions:
* When did these events happen?
* Where did they happen?
* To whom did they happen?
* What situation did she find herself in?

Read to find the answers to these questions. Continue to generate questions about this selection and answer them as you read. Do the same for the poems.

Guide for Reading ◆ 165

Interest Grabber The selections in this group explore life decisions and their implications. Before students begin reading, engage their interest and get them thinking about the theme by completing this activity: Write the first few words of Frost's poem— "Two roads diverged . . ."—on the chalkboard. Either as a class or in small groups, have students create a poem of their own that begins with Frost's famous words. Have students take turns adding lines until the poem is complete. Have a volunteer read aloud the finished product. Then have students read Frost's poem and compare it to the one they've just created.

Customize for
Less Proficient Readers
These students may be confused by poetic syntax, particularly the word order Robert Frost uses. Help them rephrase lines in a more straightforward subject-verb order or work with them to paraphrase difficult passages.

Customize for
More Advanced Students
Encourage these students to discover the larger, more universal meaning of each piece in this grouping. For example, guide them to recognize that Frost's poem is not about a nature walk, but rather a way to approach decisions in one's life, and that Angelou's piece is more a prescription for living than a biographical sketch.

Customize for
English Language Learners
The two poems in this group include many examples of figurative language. Help English language learners recognize and understand the meanings of the similes, metaphors, and personification the poets use. To aid you in doing so, refer to the Literary Focus side-column notes that accompany the pieces.

Customize for
Interpersonal Learners
You may wish to have students discuss the meanings of the pieces in this selection in pairs or in small groups. Students can share their feelings and debate their responses and insights.

Preparing for Standardized Tests

Reading Tell students that learning how to answer questions in their minds is a key to performing well on standardized tests. The Reading Strategy, Generate Questions, that is taught with these selections helps students learn both to ask and to answer questions as they read. In a standardized test situation, students will be given a set of specific questions to answer—they won't be called on to ask their own questions.

However, they can apply the skill of reading to find answers to questions, which is an important part of the strategy of generating questions. Tell students that when they take a standardized test they should preview the questions that accompany a passage and read with the purpose of answering the questions. For additional practice in the reading strategy, use the Reading Strategy page in **Selection Support**, p. 45.

One-Minute Insight

Frost's poem is about much more than a walk in the woods. It's about what to do when faced with a crossroads in life—a time when there's an important decision to make. The speaker must decide whether to pursue a more conventional direction in his life or to resist conformity by following his individual desires and leading a less routine life. He chooses the less conventional path, and as he reflects back years later, he feels he's made the right decision.

▶Critical Viewing◀

❶ Compare and Contrast Students may observe that the photograph has a misty, dreamlike quality, while the poem is reflective and poignant.

◆ Critical Thinking

❷ Make Inferences Ask students to explain what Frost means in lines 2 and 3. *The poet wishes he didn't have to miss some of life's experiences by choosing one course over another.*

◆ Literary Focus

❸ Figurative Language Point out the personification in these lines, as the poet describes the "claim" of the road on the traveler. Ask students to explain the effect of the road's "better claim." *The poet expresses that a road can have needs; that in life, there are paths that need to be followed.*

◆ Critical Thinking

❹ Make Inferences Ask students to explain why Frost is "... telling this with a sigh...." Then ask why there is a pause at the end of line 18. *Students may say that the pause indicates the significance of his decision; that he is proud of his choice; or that he is still unsure of it.*

◆ Reading Strategy

❺ Generate Questions Students may ask "*What '... has made all the difference'?*" *Students should recognize the poet's meaning—that what is important is to choose your own path and not simply follow the more-traveled path.*

166

The Road Not Taken

Robert Frost

❶| ▲ Critical Viewing Compare and contrast the mood of this photograph with the mood of the poem. **[Compare and Contr**

166 ◆ Challenges and Choices

Block Scheduling Strategies

Consider these suggestions to take advantage of extended class time:

- Have students complete the journal activity in Literature and Your Life (p. 165) and discuss their entries in small groups.
- Have students listen to the two poems on the audiotape. Then have them read the two poems silently. Follow with a discussion of the ways in which an oral performance of a poem adds to its impact.
- Have students research the poems and other

works of Robert Frost, Marge Piercy, and Maya Angelou on the Internet either before or after they read.

- Students may work in discussion groups to answer the Reading Strategy and Figurative Language questions (p. 172).
- Have students complete the Writing Mini-Lesson (p. 173). Before students begin, use the Responding to Literature Transparency in ***Writing and Language Transparencies,*** pp. 45–51, to introduce this kind of writing.

Guide for Responding

◆ *Literature and Your Life*

Reader's Response Which of the speaker's feelings or experiences seem most relevant to your own life?

Thematic Response Think about the challenges and choices that the speaker faces. Would you say he has put himself to a test? Explain.

Journal Writing Describe a situation—real or fictional—similar to the one faced by this poem's speaker.

☑ Check Your Comprehension

1. (a) What two choices does the speaker face? (b) Which does he choose?
2. What is the speaker sorry he could not do?
3. What does he predict he will do in the future?

◆ Critical Thinking

INTERPRET

1. What sort of person does the speaker of this poem reveal himself to be? **[Classify]**
2. Assuming the speaker is the poet, to what decision in his life might the poem refer? Cite details to support your conclusion. **[Infer; Support]**
3. Why do you think the speaker expects to sigh when he recalls this incident in the future? **[Draw Conclusions]**

EVALUATE

4. Robert Frost once said that a poem "begins as a lump in the throat, a sense of wrong, a homesickness, a loneliness." Would you say that description applies in any way to this poem? Cite details to support your evaluation. **[Evaluate]**

APPLY

5. Do you think it is generally a good idea to choose a less traveled path in life? Explain your opinion. **[Hypothesize; Support]**

The Road Not Taken ◆ 167

Two roads diverged in a yellow wood,
❷ And sorry I could not travel both
And be one traveler, long I stood
And looked down one as far as I could
5 To where it bent in the undergrowth;

Then took the other, as just as fair,
❸ And having perhaps the better claim,
Because it was grassy and wanted
     wear;
Though as for that, the passing there
10 Had worn them really about the same,

And both that morning equally lay
In leaves no step had trodden black.
Oh, I kept the first for another day!
Yet knowing how way leads on to way,
15 I doubted if I should ever come back.

❹ I shall be telling this with a sigh
Somewhere ages and ages hence:
Two roads diverged in a wood, and I—
❺ I took the one less traveled by,
20 And that has made all the difference.

◆ Build Vocabulary

diverged (di vʉrjd′) *v.*: Branched out in different directions.

Reinforce and Extend

Answers
Reader's Response Students may note that they're frequently faced with decisions related to conformity.

Thematic Response Students will probably respond that he has put himself to the test because choosing not to conform is more difficult than choosing to conform.

☑ Check Your Comprehension

1. (a) He has to choose between two roads. (b) He chooses the less traveled road.
2. He is sorry he can't take both paths.
3. He will tell the story and note that taking the less-traveled road has "made all the difference."

◆ Critical Thinking

1. Suggested responses: hesitant, brave, nonconformist, thoughtful, poetic, philosophical, rueful
2. Students may feel it refers to becoming a poet and may cite biographical details about Frost's early difficulties in pursuing a career as a poet.
3. People feel some regret for what might have been, even when they think they made the right choice.
4. Students should recognize that Frost's remark indicates the significance he places on the emotional content of poetry.
5. Some students may say that being different helps you stand out from the pack. Others may say that being different can make people unhappy.

◆ Beyond the Classroom

Community Connection
At a Crossroads Point out to students that it's likely that in their lifetimes they'll need to make some key choices—tough decisions that will have profound effects on the course their lives will take. Discuss that, like most people, they'll face career decisions, decisions about where to live, and many other important and difficult personal decisions. Then explain that one need not blindly grope through life, approaching each turning point as if he or she were the first ever to do so. Tell students that we can benefit from the experiences of others.

Have students interview older family members or adults they know to find out about turning points in their lives. Have them ask these adults to describe the decisions they faced, the information or potential results they had to consider, and what they chose to do under the circumstances. They can ask the adults how they feel about the choice today, about whether they have any regrets. Students can share the results of their interviews with classmates.

One-Minute Insight

This piece is more than a biographical sketch of one woman's road from adversity to success. Like "The Road Not Taken," it is about choices. Annie Johnson faces a dilemma; she is temporarily a victim of circumstances, facing a tough road through life. She could give up, but she doesn't. Instead, she shows us that despite life's many obstacles, success follows those who are courageous, creative, and flexible in their decisions. She shows us that taking initiative can lift us out of dead-end paths.

◆ Reading Strategy

❶ Generate Questions Students might ask "What did William *not* tell Annie?" *They might question his character, his commitment to Annie and his children, his aspirations toward the ministry, and his true reasons for leaving.* Invite students to share their inferences about William's character.

◆ Critical Thinking

❷ Make Predictions Ask students to think about what Annie says about factory work in the area, about her cooking skills, and about what she saw ahead for herself when she "looked up the road." Then have them predict what she'll do to "cut [herself] a new path." *Students will most likely predict that Annie will pursue a cooking-related career.*

◆ Literary Focus

❸ Figurative Language Have students notice the personification Angelou uses here, in the phrase "to scare hungry away." *Hunger is personified as a pest one can chase away.*

◆ Reading Strategy

❹ Generate Questions After reading this paragraph, students might ask, "Why is Annie carrying the stones?" Ask a volunteer to explain her reasoning. *Students may say that she's testing whether she's strong enough to carry a heavy weight the long distance to each factory. Some may predict that she'll carry food, utensils, and pots that weigh about that much.*

New Directions

❀ Maya Angelou ❀

In 1903 the late Mrs. Annie Johnson of Arkansas found herself with two toddling sons, very little money, a slight ability to read and add simple numbers. To this picture add a disastrous marriage and the burdensome fact that Mrs. Johnson was a Negro.

❶ When she told her husband, Mr. William Johnson, of her dissatisfaction with their marriage, he conceded that he too found it to be less than he expected, and had been secretly hoping to leave and study religion. He added that he thought God was calling him not only to preach but to do so in Enid, Oklahoma. He did not tell her that he knew a minister in Enid with whom he could study and who had a friendly, unmarried daughter. They parted amicably, Annie keeping the one-room house and William taking most of the cash to carry himself to Oklahoma.

❷ Annie, over six feet tall, big-boned, decided that she would not go to work as a domestic and leave her "precious babes" to anyone else's care. There was no possibility of being hired at the town's cotton gin or lumber mill, but maybe there was a way to make the two factories work for her. In her words, "I looked up the road I was going and back the way I come, and since I wasn't satisfied, I decided to step off the road and cut

me a new path." She told herself that she ❷ wasn't a fancy cook but that she could "mix groceries well enough to scare hungry away ❸ and from starving a man."

She made her plans meticulously and in secret. One early evening to see if she was ready, she placed stones in two five-gallon pails and carried them three miles to the cotton gin. She rested a little, and then, discarding some rocks, she walked in the ❹ darkness to the saw mill five miles farther along the dirt road. On her way back to her little house and her babies, she dumped the remaining rocks along the path.

That same night she worked into the early hours boiling chicken and frying ham. She made dough and filled the rolled-out pastry with meat. At last she went to sleep.

The next morning she left her house carrying the meat pies, lard, an iron brazier,[1] and coals for a fire. Just before lunch she

---

1. **iron brazier** (brā´ zhər): Pan for holding burning charcoal or coals as a heat source for cooking; a portable barbecue.

◆ Build Vocabulary

amicably (am´ i kə blē) *adj.*: Agreeably

meticulously (mə tik´ yōō ləs lē) *adv.*: Very carefully and precisely

Beyond the Classroom

Career Connection
Filling a Need Like Levi Strauss, who made a fortune during the Gold Rush not by prospecting but by clothing the Forty-Niners, Annie Johnson found success by creating a job where one had not existed before. The ability to make oneself essential by creatively matching one's skills to a need one can identify is as valuable a skill in today's rapidly changing job market as it was in 1849 and in Annie Johnson's time.

Hold a class discussion in which students talk about any modern-day Annie Johnsons they know. Then have students work in pairs or small groups to brainstorm for a need in your school or community that they could imagine filling. Have them prepare a job description that explains how they would fill that need by providing a specific service or product.

New Directions

◆ Maya Angelou ◆

In 1903 the late Mrs. Annie Johnson of Arkansas found herself with two toddling sons, very little money, a slight ability to read and add simple numbers. To this picture add a disastrous marriage and the burdensome fact that Mrs. Johnson was a Negro.

When she told her husband, Mr. William Johnson, of her dissatisfaction with their marriage, he conceded that he too found it to be less than he expected, and had been secretly hoping to leave and study religion. He added that he thought God was calling him not only to preach but to do so in Enid, Oklahoma. He did not tell her that he knew a minister in Enid with whom he could study and who had a friendly, unmarried daughter. They parted amicably, Annie keeping the one-room house and William taking most of the cash to carry himself to Oklahoma.

Annie, over six feet tall, big-boned, decided that she would not go to work as a domestic and leave her "precious babes" to anyone else's care. There was no possibility of being hired at the town's cotton gin or lumber mill, but maybe there was a way to make the two factories work for her. In her words, "I looked up the road I was going and back the way I come, and since I wasn't satisfied, I decided to step off the road and cut me a new path." She told herself that she wasn't a fancy cook but that she could "mix groceries well enough to scare hungry away and from starving a man."

She made her plans meticulously and in secret. One early evening to see if she was ready, she placed stones in two five-gallon pails and carried them three miles to the cotton gin. She rested a little, and then, discarding some rocks, she walked in the darkness to the saw mill five miles farther along the dirt road. On her way back to her little house and her babies, she dumped the remaining rocks along the path.

That same night she worked into the early hours boiling chicken and frying ham. She made dough and filled the rolled-out pastry with meat. At last she went to sleep.

The next morning she left her house carrying the meat pies, lard, an iron brazier,[1] and coals for a fire. Just before lunch she

---

1. **iron brazier** (brā´ zhər): Pan for holding burning charcoal or coals as a heat source for cooking; a portable barbecue.

◆ Build Vocabulary

amicably (am´ i kə blē) *adj.*: Agreeably

meticulously (mə tik´ yōō ləs lē) *adv.*: Very carefully and precisely

Humanities: Art

Mill Hand's Lunch Bucket, 1978, by Romare Bearden.

Romare Bearden (1911–1988) was a leading modern artist and an important figure in the Harlem Renaissance movement in the late thirties. He used innovative photomontage, collage, and painting techniques to explore aspects of the African American experience. Bearden often worked with brilliant colors, as is apparent in this piece. He created a sense of depth by layering flat figures, interrupting them with curves, angles, patterns, and glimpses into other spaces.

This collage is from the Profile/Part I: The Twenties Series (Pittsburgh Memories). It depicts the inside of a house in which workers are eating. Outside the window, a factory is visible, its fumes filling the sky. Use these questions for discussion:

1. What is the mood in the house? How do you know? *It is somber; the figures are bent over, solemn faced, and do not seem to be interacting.*

2. What does Bearden imply about work for the mill hands? *By making the mill so much a part of the scene, Bearden suggests that the mill looms over people's lives in a mill town; it can be seen, heard, and smelled; here, it seems to blend with the interior of the house.*

◆ Literary Focus

❶ Figurative Language Have students notice the simile "looking like specters." Have them use context clues and their visual reasoning to determine what a specter is and to picture what these men look like. *They look like ghosts or apparitions.*

◆ Build Grammar Skills

❷ Commas in Series Point out the commas used to separate items in this series. Emphasize how the commas clarify the meaning of the sentence. Guide students to see the many ways to change its meaning by changing the position of some of the commas.

◆ *Literature and Your Life*

❸ Ask students to describe times in their lives that they made a decision that didn't work and then had to change their course of action. Point out that teachers, coaches, writers, builders, lawyers, and many others often need to revise plans. *Students may point to a time they began researching a topic for a report, had little success, and then had to choose another topic. They might recall times when they had to rethink a trip or party they were planning, a job they began, or a sports strategy that stopped working.*

◆ Literary Focus

❹ Figurative Language Students should note that the image of the path as a metaphor for a new way of life is here expanded to become a road one travels only as long as it leads to a promising future.

---

❶ appeared in an empty lot behind the cotton gin. As the dinner noon bell rang, she dropped the savors into boiling fat and the aroma rose and floated over to the workers who spilled out of the gin, covered with white lint, looking like <u>specters</u>.

Most workers had brought their lunches of pinto beans and biscuits or crackers, onions and cans of sardines, but they were tempted by the hot meat pies which Annie ladled out of the fat. She wrapped them in newspapers, which soaked up the grease, and offered them for sale at a nickel each. Although business was slow, those first days Annie was determined. She balanced her appearances between the two hours of activity.

So, on Monday if she offered hot fresh pies at the cotton gin and sold the remaining cooled-down pies at the lumber mill for three cents, then on Tuesday she went first to the lumber mill presenting fresh, just-cooked pies as the lumbermen covered in sawdust emerged from the mill.

For the next few years, on balmy spring days, blistering summer noons, and cold,

◆ Build Vocabulary

specters (spekʹ tərz) *n.*: Ghostly images; phantoms

ominous (ämʹ ə nəs) *adj.*: Threatening; menacing

unpalatable (un palʹ it ə bəl) *adj.*: Distasteful; unpleasant

---

wet, and wintry middays, Annie never disappointed her customers, who could count on seeing the tall, brown-skin woman bent over her brazier, carefully turning the meat pies. When she felt certain that the workers had become dependent on her, she built a stall between the two hives of industry and let the men run to her for their lunchtime provisions.

She had indeed stepped from the road which seemed to have been chosen for her and cut herself a brand-new path. In years that stall became a store where customers could buy cheese, meal, syrup, cookies, candy, writing tablets, pickles, canned goods, fresh fruit, soft drinks, coal, oil, and leather soles for worn-out shoes. **❷**

Each of us has the right and the responsibility to assess the roads which lie ahead, and those over which we have traveled, and if the future road looms <u>ominous</u> or unpromising, and the roads back uninviting, then we need to gather our resolve and, carrying only the necessary baggage, step off that road into another direction. If the new choice is also <u>unpalatable</u>, without embarrassment, we must be ready to change that as well. **❸**

> ### ◆ Literary Focus
> How does Angelou expand on the earlier image of the path to help us understand the figurative language in a broader context? **❹**

 Speaking and Listening Mini-Lesson

Job Interview

This mini-lesson supports the Speaking and Listening activity in the Idea Bank on page 173.

Introduce the Concept Tell students that a job interview is a meeting between an employer and a prospective candidate for a position. They will need to describe the position for which their candidate is applying. Then have students talk about the personality and skills Annie Johnson, Robert

Frost, or Marge Piercy would bring to a job. One student can record responses.

Develop Background Have students talk about the features of job interviews and identify the kinds of questions an employer might ask and the kinds of responses a prospective employee might give. Have them discuss all other aspects of the interview, such as promptness, honesty, and politeness and respect for one another.

Apply the Information Students can prepare the interviewers' questions in advance. Two group members can role-play the employer and candidate for employment, while other group members watch and record what happens.

Assess the Outcome Students can evaluate how well the candidate did and decide whether he or she should be hired. They can use the Peer Assessment: Speaker/Speech form in ***Alternative Assessment,*** p. 111.

To be of use
Marge Piercy

The people I love the best
jump into work head first
without dallying in the shallows
and swim off with sure strokes almost out
   of sight.
5 They seem to become natives of that
   element,
the black sleek heads of seals
bouncing like half-submerged balls.

I love people who harness themselves, an
   ox to a heavy cart,
who pull like water buffalo, with massive
   patience,
10 who strain in the mud and the muck to
   move things forward,
who do what has to be done, again and
   again.
I want to be with people who submerge
in the task, who go into the fields to harvest
and work in a row and pass the bags along,
15 who are not parlor generals and field
   deserters
but move in a common rhythm
when the food must come in or the fire be
   put out.

The work of the
   world is common as mud.
Botched, it smears the hands, crumbles to
   dust.
20 But the thing worth doing well done
has a shape that satisfies, clean and
   evident.
Greek amphoras[1] for wine or oil,
Hopi[2] vases that held corn, are put in
   museums
but you know they were made to be used.
25 The pitcher cries for water to carry
and a person for work that is real.

---

1. **amphoras** (am´ fər əz) *n.*: Tall jars that have a narrow neck and base and two handles, used by the ancient Greeks and Romans.
2. **Hopi** (hō´ pē) *n.*: Pueblo tribe of Indians in northeastern Arizona.

◆ **Build Vocabulary**

dallying (dal´ ē iŋ) *v.*: Wasting time; loitering

submerged (səb mɰrjd´) *adj.*: Covered with something; underwater

harness (här´ nis) *v.*: Attach, as with straps for pulling or controlling

Guide for Responding

◆ *Literature and Your Life*

Reader's Response Would you rather meet Annie Johnson or the speaker of this poem? Explain.

Thematic Response How do Annie Johnson and the speaker of this poem feel about challenges?

☑ **Check Your Comprehension**

1. Why does Annie Johnson have to find a source of income?
2. How does she earn a living?
3. In the first stanza of the poem, what kind of people does the speaker say she loves best?

◆ **Critical Thinking**

INTERPRET
1. Why do you think Annie Johnson chose not to pursue a factory job or a job as a domestic? **[Infer]**
2. What does Johnson's achievement suggest about the human spirit in general? **[Draw Conclusions]**
3. What kinds of values do lines 12–18 of the poem stress? **[Analyze]**

APPLY
4. How important is it for a person to feel he or she is useful? Explain. **[Defend]**

New Directions/To be of use ◆ 171

◆ **Beyond the Selection**

FURTHER READING

Other Works by the Authors
"Stopping by Woods on a Snowy Evening," Robert Frost
All God's Children Need Traveling Shoes, Maya Angelou
Breaking Camp, Marge Piercy

Other Works With the Theme of Putting Ourselves to the Test
Kon Tiki, Thor Heyerdahl
Black Boy, Richard Wright

INTERNET
The Internet provides excellent opportunities for students to learn more about the authors. We suggest the following sites. Please be aware, however, that sites may have changed from the time we published this information.
   To hear Robert Frost read his poetry, go to **http://www.town.hall.org.** To visit with Maya Angelou, try **http://www.bdd.com/athwk/.** Marge Piercy has a home page at **http://www. capecod.net/~tmpiercy/**
   We *strongly recommend* that you preview the sites before you send students to them.

Develop Understanding

One-Minute Insight This poem celebrates the nature of work and workers. The poet admires workers who display determination and strength, who plunge into tasks wholeheartedly, and who work cooperatively with others.

Customize for
English Language Learners
Help these students understand the meanings of the lines that contain figurative language in each stanza. Point out that the poem is not about swimming or diving, pulling, passing bags, or shaping pottery, but about approaching one's work earnestly and with vigor.

Customize for
More Advanced Students
Point out the water imagery in this poem. Have students discuss why the poet uses it. *Students might say that water, like work, is essential for life.*

◆ **Critical Thinking**

❺ **Make Inferences** Discuss that in these lines the poet makes the point that she admires people who are determined, steadfast, and diligent, no matter how difficult or unpleasant their task.

❻ **Clarification** Point out to students that a "parlor general" is one who talks but doesn't act, who leads from behind rather than by example. Discuss that a parlor general is similar to someone we might describe as a "backseat driver."

◆ **Reading Strategy**

❼ **Generate Questions** Students might be curious to know why the poet chose these particular containers to give as examples. They might wonder what each signifies. *Each is a vessel for holding something, is ideal for its purpose, and is aesthetically pleasing.*

(Answers are on page 172.)

Answers

◆ Literature and Your Life

Reader's Response Some students may choose to meet Annie Johnson, whom they feel they know as a person. Others may choose Marge Piercy because they agree with the ideas in her poem.

Thematic Response Both enjoy challenges.

☑ Check Your Comprehension

1. She is a single parent with two small children.
2. She sells meat pies to local factory workers.
3. She prefers those who jump in head first without dallying.

◆ Critical Thinking

1. Students should recognize that Johnson has a young family to raise singlehandedly and so cannot put in long hours away from home.
2. Suggested responses: It is resilient; it faces challenges; it flourishes in spite of hardship.
3. These lines stress the value of pitching in to do the work that must be done and working cooperatively with others to get it done.
4. Most students are likely to believe that feeling useful is important. They may cite examples mentioning the achievements, self-esteem, and contentment of people who feel useful.

◆ Literary Focus

1. Both show an independent streak; both show a desire to be different; both show a thoughtful approach to making important decisions in life.
2. The people in Piercy's poem are far less hesitant; Frost's speaker, though perhaps ultimately making a daring decision, remains somewhat uncertain about whether or not he did the right thing.

◆ Build Vocabulary

Using the Suffix -ly

1. amicably: in a friendly manner
2. meticulously: in a very careful or thorough manner
3. ominously: in a menacing or threatening manner
4. unpalatably: in an unacceptable manner

Guide for Responding (continued)

◆ Literary Focus

FIGURATIVE LANGUAGE

The writers of these selections use **figurative language** to help us envision the decisive point in a person's life. For example, Frost and Angelou both use the image of a road or path to convey the idea of a career or way of life.

1. Compare Frost's "less traveled" road with the "new path" that Johnson carves for herself. What similar approaches to life do these images convey?
2. Contrast the way Frost's speaker approaches the two roads and the way the people in Piercy's opening stanza approach the water. What different approaches to life does the figurative language convey?

◆ Build Vocabulary

USING THE SUFFIX -ly

The suffix -ly is often used to turn adjectives into adverbs. Use the suffix -ly to turn each of the four adjectives into an adverb. List and define the newly created adverbs in your notebook. Also use each adverb in a sentence.

1. amicable: friendly
2. meticulous: very careful or thorough
3. ominous: menacing; threatening
4. unpalatable: unacceptable

USING THE WORD BANK

Copy these statements into your notebook, then indicate whether each is true or false.

1. If a stream of traffic *diverged*, it probably moved into different lanes or in different directions.
2. If you and your friend part *amicably*, you are most likely in a bad mood.
3. If you clean your room *meticulously*, it is messy.
4. Some children dress as *specters* on Halloween.
5. A smile is usually an *ominous* expression.
6. Most chefs try to cook *unpalatable* meals.
7. Window shoppers seem to enjoy *dallying*.
8. Deep-sea divers use air tanks when *submerged*.
9. In Alaska, some people *harness* dogs to a sled.

◆ Reading Strategy

GENERATE QUESTIONS

Asking and answering **questions** about a selection can help you remember its details and understand it better. Jot down two or three questions you asked yourself while reading each of these selections; then explain how they helped you with your reading.

◆ Build Grammar Skills

COMMAS IN A SERIES

When you list three or more items in a series, separate them with **commas** to make your meaning clear.

Practice Copy the following sentences into your notebook, adding or deleting commas where needed.

1. Mrs. Annie Johnson had little education less money, and two small sons to raise by herself.
2. She had no desire to work as a domestic or at the cotton gin or in the saw mill.
3. She decided to turn ham chicken dough and lard into meat pies to sell to the factory workers.
4. The workers enjoyed the meat pies along with their pinto beans, and crackers, and sardines.

Beyond Literature

Career Connection

Choosing a Career Choosing a career is one of the most important decisions you will ever make. How can you make the right career choice? Consider your values or goals, your interests, and your abilities. For example, do you value working with others or working alone? Are you interested in artistic activities or in working outdoors? Are you good at fixing a bicycle or at solving math problems? If you're unsure about what you do best, don't worry. You have lots of time to learn and even to change your mind. Take a moment right now to jot down some of your interests, listing what you like about each.

Using the Word Bank

1. true; 2. false; 3. false;
4. true; 5. false; 6. false;
7. true; 8. true; 9. true

◆ Build Grammar Skills

1. Mrs. Annie Johnson had little education, less money, and two small sons to raise by herself.
2. correct
3. She decided to turn ham, chicken, dough, and lard

into meat pies to sell to the factory workers.
4. The workers enjoyed the meat pies along with their pinto beans and crackers and sardines.

✎ Writer's Solution

For additional instruction and practice, use the lesson in the **Language Lab CD-ROM** on Commas and the practice pages on Commas (pp. 100–101) in *The Writer's Solution Grammar Practice Book.*

Build Your Portfolio

Idea Bank

Writing

1. **Recipe** Write a recipe that Annie Johnson could have used in her new business. The recipe could be for the meat pies described in the selection or for something else that Johnson might have sold. **[Home Economics Link]**

2. **Dialogue** Write a dialogue between the speaker of either poem and Annie Johnson. Consider what either speaker would be likely to say to Johnson and how Johnson might respond.

3. **Job Description** Write a one-page job description that you think could apply to one of the three selections. **[Career Link]**

Speaking and Listening

4. **Job Interview** Working with another student, role-play a job interview that might take place between Annie Johnson or the speaker of either poem and a potential employer. **[Career Link]**

5. **Group Discussion** Marge Piercy once said that she wanted her poems to be useful. Of the three selections, which do you find most "useful"? Share your ideas in a small-group discussion.

Projects

6. **Docudrama** Working in a small group, video-tape an interview with a local businessperson, a teacher, or another professional to learn about the person's career. **[Career Link]**

7. **Nutrition Report** Would Annie Johnson's meals be popular with a health-conscious public today? Research the nutritional value and health-fulness of the ingredients in Johnson's meat pies, mentioned in the selection. Share your findings in an oral or written report. **[Health Link]**

Writing Mini-Lesson

Evaluation of Figurative Language

By using figurative language—such as the image of a road in Robert Frost's "The Road Not Taken"— writers hope to add clarity and color to their writing. Choose one of the selections and write an essay in which you evaluate the writer's use of figurative language.

Writing Skills Focus: Suitable Criteria for Effective Figurative Language

To help you evaluate the **effectiveness of figurative language**, answer the following questions:
- Does the figurative language work for you or does it leave you confused?
- What do you find interesting about the figurative language?
- When making comparisons, does the writer avoid using clichés, or trite, overused expressions?
- If the figurative language extends over several lines, does it remain logical and consistent?

Prewriting Choose a selection to evaluate, then list examples of figurative language in that selection. For each example, identify the basic comparison being stated or implied. Think about whether that comparison seems fresh and unusual.

Drafting State your reaction to the figurative language, then cite examples to support your reaction. Present the examples in some type of order— order of importance, for instance, or the order in which they appear in the work.

Revising Make sure you have offered enough examples to support all general statements about the selection. Check to see that your word choice is clear and precise and that your sentences flow logically and smoothly.

Idea Bank

Customizing for
Performance Levels
Following are suggestions for matching the Idea Bank topics with your students' performance levels:
Less Advanced Students: 1, 4, 6
Average Students: 2, 5
More Advanced Students: 3, 7

Customizing for
Learning Modalities
Following are suggestions for matching Idea Bank topics with your students' learning modalities:
Visual/Spatial: 6
Auditory: 4, 5
Verbal/Linguistic: 2, 4, 5, 7
Logical/Mathematical: 7

Writing Mini-Lesson

Refer students to the Writing Handbook, page 962, for instruction on the writing process, and page 966 for further information on Response to Literature.

Writer's Solution

Writers at Work Videodisc
Have students view the videodisc segment on Response to Literature (Ch. 7) featuring book reviewer Lawrence Chua to see how he evaluates a piece of literature. Have students discuss how to apply his techniques in writing their evaluation of figurative language.

Play frames 23797 to 32801

Writing Lab CD-ROM
Have students competed the Tutorial on Response to Literature. Follow these steps:
1. Have students look at the interactive model of a critical review in the About Response to Literature section.
2. Have students draft on computer, using the Evaluation Word Bin to come up with descriptive words to use in their evaluations.
Allow 70 minutes of class time for students to complete these steps.

Sourcebook
Have students use Chapter 7, Response to Literature (pp. 194–227), for additional support.

✓ ASSESSMENT OPTIONS

Formal Assessment, Selection Test, pp. 35–37, and Assessment Resources Software. The selection test is designed so that it can be easily customized to the performance levels of your students. *Alternative Assessment,* p. 11, includes options for less advanced students, more advanced students, interpersonal learners, verbal/linguistic learners, visual/spatial learners, and logical/mathematical learners.

PORTFOLIO ASSESSMENT
Use the following rubrics in the *Alternative Assessment* booklet to assess student writing:
Recipe: How-to/Process Explanation Rubric, p. 93
Dialogue: Narrative Rubric, p. 88
Job Description: Description Rubric, p. 90
Writing Mini-Lesson: Evaluation/Review Rubric, p. 97

OBJECTIVES

1. To read, comprehend, interpret, and respond to a fantasy
2. To relate a fantasy story to personal experience
3. To distinguish fantasy from reality to facilitate comprehension
4. To understand the elements of fantasy
5. To build vocabulary in context and learn the suffix -ity
6. To develop skill in using compound predicates
7. To write a travel brochure using a persuasive tone
8. To respond to the work through writing, speaking and listening, and projects

SKILLS INSTRUCTION

Vocabulary:
Suffixes: -ity

Grammar:
Compound Predicates

Reading Strategy:
Distinguish Fantasy From Reality

Literary Focus:
Fantasy

Writing: Using a Persuasive Tone

Speaking and Listening:
Dramatic Monologue (teacher edition)

Critical Viewing: Speculate; Support

PORTFOLIO OPPORTUNITIES

Writing: Police Report; Obituary; Real Estate Advertisement
Writing Mini-Lesson: Travel Brochure
Speaking and Listening: Dramatic Reading; Dramatic Monologue
Projects: Cultural Map of India; Report on Hinduism

More About the Author

R. K. Narayan (na-RAY-an) grew up in an orthodox Brahmin family. Raised by his grandmother, he was exposed to classical Indian tales and myths early in life. These were so woven into his consciousness that, he says, "subterranean murmurs" shaped his life and informed his writing. Narayan's style is lean and direct, echoing India's oral tradition. Readers should not expect logical explanations for everything he writes. According to Narayan, and consistent with Hindu beliefs, events just *are*. Without needing to know *why*, readers can immerse themselves in the journey of the story.

Guide for Reading

R. K. Narayan (1906-   )

If you could take all the swirling cultures, contradictions, and beauty of twentieth-century India and roll them up into one person, that person would probably resemble R. K. Narayan. In a career that has spanned more than sixty years, Narayan has written more than fifteen novels, as well as numerous collections of short stories, travel books, and essays. The sheer scope of his literary achievements has led at least one other writer to call him "the foremost Indian writer who writes in English."

A Novelist's Life Born in the major southern city of Madras, Narayan was one of nine children of a middle-class family. He attended Maharaja's College in the southern city of Mysore, but did not graduate until he was twenty-four. After briefly working as a teacher, he became a novelist. In 1935, he completed his first novel, *Swami and Friends*.

In his novels, legends, and short stories, Narayan skillfully combines traditional Western plots and themes with Indian subject matter to create works that are exotic yet accessible to Western readers. In 1958, Narayan was awarded the National Prize of the Indian Literary Academy, the nation's highest literary honor.

Universal Themes Most of Narayan's stories take place in the same fictional place, a town called Malgudi. While Malgudi is a distinctly southern Indian place, the tales that Narayan tells about it are universal. If you change the backdrop of any of Narayan's tales to a modern American town, you will find that the characters' struggles, plans, hopes, and dreams still apply. There is no aspect of the human experience about which Narayan has not written. It is this universal quality that makes his writing so special.

◆ Build Vocabulary

SUFFIXES: -ity

In this story, you will find the word *longevity* used by one of the characters. The suffix -ity, which means "state of" or "condition of," gives a clue to the meaning of the word *longevity*. You will recognize the base of the word is *long*. A way to define *longevity* would be "the *condition of* having a *long* life." In this story, one person appears to have a *longevity* of more than 500 years!

WORD BANK

sobriety
awry
literally
longevity
imperative
venture

As you read "Old Man of the Temple," you will encounter the words on this list. Each word is defined on the page where it first appears. Preview this list before you read and look for the words as they appear in the story.

◆ Build Grammar Skills

COMPOUND PREDICATES

In "Old Man of the Temple," R. K. Narayan uses compound predicates. A **compound predicate** consists of two or more verbs or verb phrases (a main verb plus a helping verb) that share the same subject. Compound predicates enable the writer to include a lot of action into a single sentence without having to repeat the subject.

$$\text{I took out my torch, got down, and walked about, but could see no one.}$$

As you read "Old Man of the Temple," notice the author's frequent use of compound predicates to describe the many actions of his characters while still keeping the story moving briskly.

174 ◆ Challenges and Choices

Prentice Hall Literature Program Resources

REINFORCE / RETEACH / EXTEND

Selection Support Pages
Build Vocabulary: Suffixes: -ity, p. 47
Build Grammar Skills: Compound Predicates, p. 48
Reading Strategy: Distinguish Fantasy From Reality, p. 49
Literary Focus: Fantasy, p. 50

Strategies for Diverse Student Needs, p. 12

Beyond Literature
Humanities Connection: Art, p. 12

Formal Assessment Selection Test, pp. 38–40, Assessment Resources Software

Alternative Assessment, p. 12

Writing and Language Transparencies
Descriptive and Observational Writing, pp. 17–20

Resource Pro CD-ROM
"Old Man of the Temple"—includes all resource material and customizable lesson plan

Listening to Literature Audiocassettes
"Old Man of the Temple"

Old Man of the Temple

◆ *Literature and Your Life*

CONNECT YOUR EXPERIENCE

You see a shadow dart behind a tree on a cold autumn evening, but when you reach the tree and look, there is nothing there—what could it be? Although this story takes place in a far-off land, the narrator's experience is universal: He sees something and cannot believe his eyes. It is this element of the mysterious that makes reading ghost stories so much fun.

THEMATIC FOCUS: PUTTING OURSELVES TO THE TEST

How would you react if you were suddenly confronted with something that you could not explain? Would you face the challenge and try to solve the mystery or would you choose to avoid it?

◆ Background for Understanding

CULTURE

"Old Man of the Temple" takes place near Malgudi, a fictional town. Though it is a make-believe place, Malgudi could be any one of thousands of rural southern Indian towns. Imagine a place where all but the largest roads are unpaved. Through the morning mist, you can see cattle roaming along the dirt paths and farmers tilling the fields before the sun rises too high and the day becomes too hot to work. It is a place where the ruins of temples hundreds of years old decay amidst the creeping, cobralike tendrils of tropical vines.

Journal Writing Be a "ghost writer" and think up a ghost for a story. Describe it and tell why it appears as it does.

◆ Literary Focus

FANTASY

"Old Man of the Temple" is a **fantasy**—a work of fiction that includes characters, places, or events that could not reasonably exist or happen. We enjoy fantasy because it lets our imaginations run wild. When we read fantasy, we suspend our disbelief in the impossible in order to enjoy the tale. Fantasy must, however, contain some elements of real life, if only to give perspective to the fantastical elements.

◆ Reading Strategy

DISTINGUISH FANTASY FROM REALITY

As this story begins, a man and his driver are driving down a lonely rural road at night. That much can be established. Very soon, however, it becomes more and more difficult to **distinguish fantasy from reality**—to tell what is real and what is not.

As you read, it may help to jot down which elements of the story are real and which are fantastic. To organize your information, make a chart with two columns, labeled "Real" and "Fantastic." Write down the elements of the story in the appropriate column.

Real	Fantastic

Guide for Reading ◆ 175

Interest Grabber

People all over the world hear, read, and tell scary stories to entertain, instruct, or warn. They respond to ripples of fear, unexplained mystery, and gruesome detail. The nature of ghosts varies. In some cultures, ghosts are dead ancestors, angry because they've been excluded from paradise. Some are upset over unfinished work. Others return to contact relatives, friends, or enemies. Hook students' interest in this story by writing the following passage on the chalkboard or reading it aloud:

> "Dead! Dead!" he said. "Don't talk nonsense. How can I be dead when you see me before you now? If I am dead how can I be saying this and that?"

Have students react to this passage, and make predictions about the kind of person the speaker is and whom he may be addressing.

Customize for
Less Proficient Readers

To help these students through this story, have them work in groups of three to read sections of dialogue aloud to each other. Different students can take the roles of the Talkative Man, Doss, and the old man, assuming a different voice for each character. In this way much of the story's confusion, as well as the transformation of Doss into the old man, might become more clear.

Customize for
English Language Learners

Because Narayan learned to speak and write in British English, some words in this story may confuse American English language learners. Help them by clarifying British expressions, such as *torch* for flashlight.

Customize for
Logical/Mathematical Learners

Have these students pay close attention to the explanations that the narrator offers for the story's fantastic events. Encourage them to come up with other possible explanations for what happens in the story and to share these explanations with the class.

✎ Preparing for Standardized Tests

Vocabulary Knowing that the suffix *-ity* means "state of" or "condition of" will be invaluable to your students when completing vocabulary sections of standardized tests. By using their knowledge of this suffix, students may often find that they can piece together the meaning of a word that at first seems unfamiliar. For example, the word *longevity* may be unfamiliar, but students most certainly are familiar with the word *long*. Students might then guess that the word *longevity* means "the state or condition of being long." This is probably close enough to the actual meaning of the word to help students come up with the correct multiple-choice answer for an item in an analogy, sentence completion, or synonym section of a standardized test.

One-Minute Insight

In this fantasy, the narrator, the Talkative Man, tells about an encounter he once had with a peculiar old man. The old man seems to live in a ruined temple, moving with no sense of time between past and present. The narrator soon realizes that the old man is a dead spirit who has become lost and has temporarily taken over the body of the Talkative Man's driver. Through the power of suggestion, he helps the old man regain his way. The author uses the device of this dead spirit to write about a timeless theme: people's inability to let go of the past.

Customize for
More Advanced Students

The Hindu world view holds that actions in the wide web of life determine future destiny. People may pass repeatedly through different forms from life to life, even between the human and animal worlds. When this regular cycle of rebirth and transmigration is not followed, the situation would most likely be considered "unnatural." Challenge students to look for elements in this tale that echo Narayan's Hindu beliefs.

Humanities: Architecture

The temple pictured here is located in the western part of India. The form of this Hindu temple resembles a melted candle. With their variety of forms and elaborate relief carvings of gods, goddesses, and demons, Hindu temples reflect Hinduism's beliefs in reincarnation and in a god of many forms and natures. Many Hindu temples in northern India have tall towers with curving sides that taper at the top. In southern India, Hindu temples have towers that rise in rectangular pyramids made of steplike blocks of stones.

Ask students to describe the features of the temple that mark it as northern or southern. *The tall towers with curving sides that taper near the top show a northern influence.*

176 ◆ Challenges and Choices

Block Scheduling Strategies

Consider these suggestions to take advantage of extended class time:

- Group students to share their journal writing ideas from the activity on page 175.
- Introduce students to the setting of the story by using the Humanities: Art page on Indian Temples in *Beyond Literature,* p. 12.
- Have students work in discussion groups to answer the Critical Thinking questions (p. 182).

- Before students complete the Writing Mini-Lesson (p. 183), discuss examples of persuasive tones that students may encounter in their lives. Identify key elements of persuasion and talk about how these elements influence an audience.

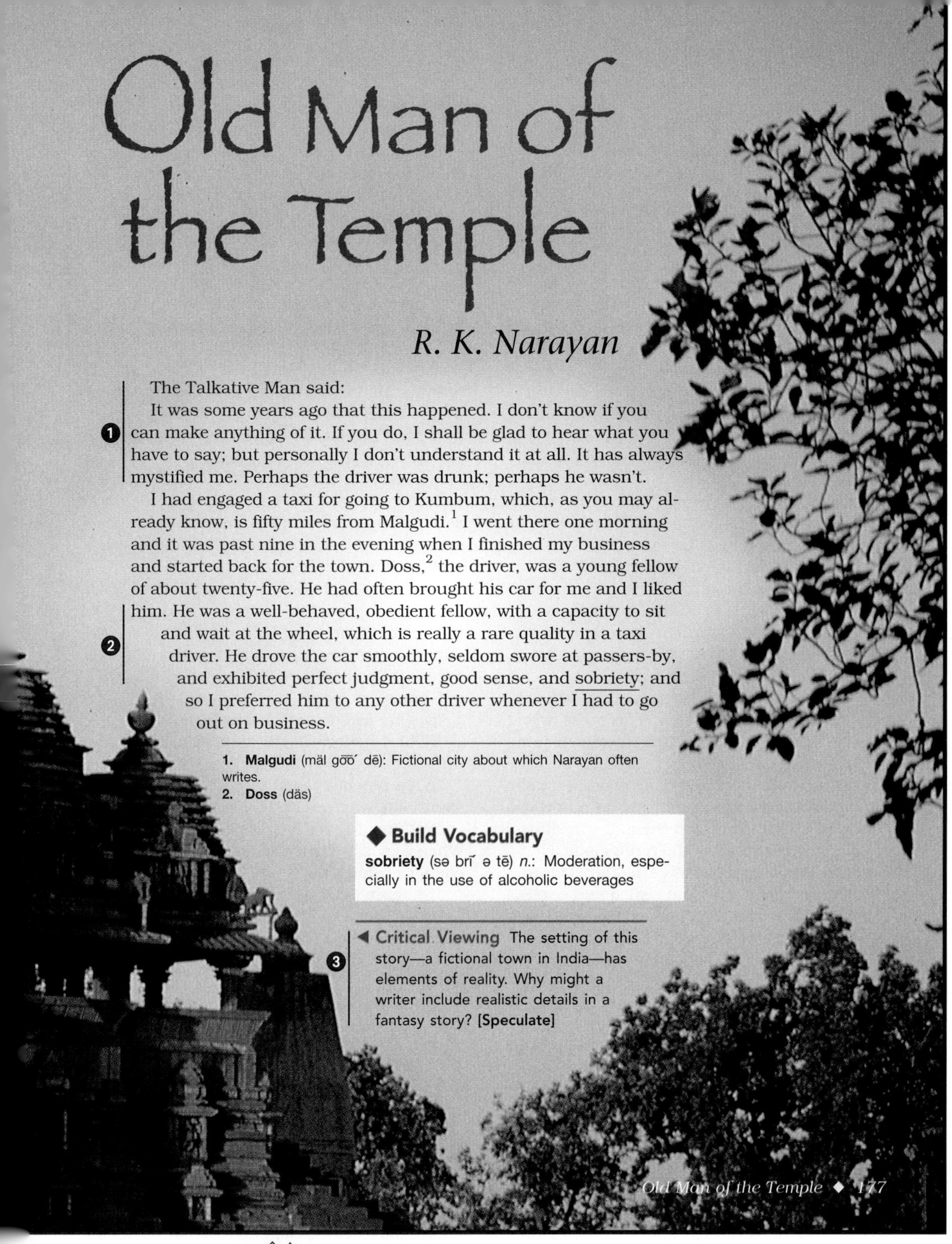

Old Man of the Temple

R. K. Narayan

The Talkative Man said:

1 It was some years ago that this happened. I don't know if you can make anything of it. If you do, I shall be glad to hear what you have to say; but personally I don't understand it at all. It has always mystified me. Perhaps the driver was drunk; perhaps he wasn't.

I had engaged a taxi for going to Kumbum, which, as you may already know, is fifty miles from Malgudi.[1] I went there one morning and it was past nine in the evening when I finished my business and started back for the town. Doss,[2] the driver, was a young fellow of about twenty-five. He had often brought his car for me and I liked him. 2 He was a well-behaved, obedient fellow, with a capacity to sit and wait at the wheel, which is really a rare quality in a taxi driver. He drove the car smoothly, seldom swore at passers-by, and exhibited perfect judgment, good sense, and sobriety; and so I preferred him to any other driver whenever I had to go out on business.

1. **Malgudi** (mäl go͞o´ dē): Fictional city about which Narayan often writes.
2. **Doss** (däs)

◆ Build Vocabulary

sobriety (sə brī´ ə tē) *n.*: Moderation, especially in the use of alcoholic beverages

3 ◄ Critical Viewing The setting of this story—a fictional town in India—has elements of reality. Why might a writer include realistic details in a fantasy story? **[Speculate]**

1 Clarification Narayan uses The Talkative Man as an engaging and recurring character. The Talkative Man's comment about making "anything of it" points to the Hindu world view of people's powerlessness to influence events. He implies that Hindu culture has no need to relate cause and effect. He presents the tale straightforwardly, as he recalls it, leaving interpretation to the reader.

◆ Build Vocabulary

2 The Suffix *-ity* Draw students' attention to the three words in this passage with the suffix *-ity: capacity, quality,* and *sobriety.* Discuss how the meanings of these words all relate to the concept of "condition." Explain that in fact the common function of *-ity* is to turn an adjective into a noun that names a "state" as shown by the words *sober* and *sobriety.* Note that in this case both the root and the suffix undergo a spelling change.

►Critical Viewing◄

3 Speculate Call students' attention to the picture of the Hindu temple on this page. Ask them how the picture affects their ideas about the setting of the story. Then ask: Can you imagine a setting without something realistic in it? *Students should note that even fantasy has to connect in some way with the real world in order for a writer to describe it and a reader to understand it.*

Cross-Curricular Connection: Social Studies

Despite its ancient civilization and strong cultural traditions, pre-British India had never been unified politically. This disunity, combined with the religious divisions between Hindus and Muslims, left India unable to resist the colonial urges of the European powers. In the 18th century, Great Britain established control over India, first through the commercial activities of the East India Company, and later by British parliamentary law. India became a formal member of the British Empire in 1876. British technology modernized transportation and communication, yet British disregard for Indian tradition and customs aroused resentment and fueled the rise of a nationalist movement.

India gained independence on August 15, 1947. Mohandas Gandhi (1869–1948) was the key figure in this struggle, which was characterized by his policy of nonviolent resistance. Have students find out more about Gandhi and his religious, social, and political efforts to bring independence to India. Students can view the British-Indian film "Gandhi" (1982) on video or read excerpts from his autobiography.

◆ **Literary Focus**

❶ Fantasy Elicit responses like these: *The paragraph gives the time of night, the name of the village, its approximate location along the road, the time of month, and describes the darkness that covered the town.* These items, though realistic, also establish a dark, lonely atmosphere, one in which the unexpected flourishes.

◆ **Reading Strategy**

❷ Distinguish Fantasy From Reality Point out the contradiction between the condition of the temple, as the narrator sees it, and Doss's explanation of what he has seen. Discuss how this contrast builds up expectation for a leap into fantasy. Ask students how this discrepancy may be important to the story. *Students may respond that finding out the cause of the discrepancy will become the focal point of the story.*

◆ *Literature and Your Life*

❸ The narrator has a choice to make. He can insist upon leaving or he can pursue this strange situation more deeply, as Doss asks. Ask students to give their reactions to this dilemma and tell what they might do, given a similar choice. *Students may respond that they would be curious to learn more about the situation.*

◆ **Critical Thinking**

❹ Analyze Have students explain what is happening in this passage. *The old man is making Doss see things that aren't really there, and finally taking possession of his body.*

◆ **Build Grammar Skills**

❺ Compound Predicates Have students identify the compound predicates in this paragraph and list each subject and its verbs. *I got, walked, opened, shook; he opened, assumed, rubbed.*

178

---

❶ It was about eleven when we passed the village Koopal,[3] which is on the way down. It was the dark half of the month and the surrounding country was swallowed up in the night. The village street was deserted. Everyone had gone to sleep; hardly any light was to be seen. The stars overhead sparkled brightly. Sitting in the back seat and listening to the continuous noise of the running wheels, I was half lulled into a drowse.

All of a sudden Doss swerved the car and shouted: "You old fool! Do you want to kill yourself?"

I was shaken out of my drowse and asked: "What is the matter?"

Doss stopped the car and said, "You see that old fellow, sir. He is trying to kill himself. I can't understand what he is up to."

I looked in the direction he pointed and asked, "Which old man?"

"There, there. He is coming towards us again. As soon as I saw him open that temple door and come out I had a feeling, somehow, that I must keep an eye on him."

I took out my torch, got down, and walked about, but could see no one. There was an old temple on the roadside. It was utterly in ruins; most portions of it were mere mounds of old **❷** brick; the walls were <u>awry</u>; the doors were shut to the main doorway, and brambles and thickets grew over and covered them. It was difficult to guess with the aid of the torch alone what temple it was and to what period it belonged.

"The doors are shut and sealed and don't look as if they had been opened for centuries now," I cried.

"No, sir," Doss said coming nearer. "I saw the old man open the doors and come out. He is standing there; shall we ask him to open them again if you want to go in and see?"

❸ I said to Doss, "Let us be going. We are wasting our time here."

---

3. **Koopal** (ko͞o päl´)

◆ **Literary Focus**
What realistic elements in this paragraph set the stage for the fantasy?

We went back to the car. Doss sat in his seat, pressed the self-starter, and asked without turning his head, "Are you permitting this fellow to come with us, sir? He says he will get down at the next milestone."

"Which fellow?" I asked.

Doss indicated the space next to him.

"What is the matter with you, Doss? Have you had a drop of drink or something?"

"I have never tasted any drink in my life. sir," **❹** he said, and added, "Get down, old boy. Master says he can't take you."

"Are you talking to yourself?"

"After all, I think we needn't care for these unknown fellows on the road," he said.

"Doss," I pleaded. "Do you feel confident you can drive? If you feel dizzy don't drive."

"Thank you, sir," said Doss. "I would rather not start the car now. I am feeling a little out of sorts." I looked at him anxiously. He closed his eyes, his breathing became heavy and noisy, and gradually his head sank.

"Doss, Doss," I cried desperately. I got down, walked to the front seat, opened the door, and shook him vigorously. He opened his eyes, as-**❺** sumed a hunched-up position, and rubbed his eyes with his hands, which trembled like an old man's.

"Do you feel better?" I asked.

"Better! Better! Hi! Hi!" he said in a thin, piping voice.

"What has happened to your voice? You sound like someone else," I said.

"Nothing. My voice is as good as it was. When a man is eighty he is bound to feel a few changes coming on."

"You aren't eighty, surely," I said.

"Not a day less," he said. "Is nobody going to move this vehicle? If not, there is no sense in **❻** sitting here all day. I will get down and go back to my temple."

"I don't know how to drive," I said. "And

◆ **Build Vocabulary**

awry (ə rī´) *adj.*: Not straight

Speaking and Listening Mini-Lesson

Dramatic Monologue

This mini-lesson supports the Speaking and Listening activity in the Idea Bank on page 183.

Introduce the Concept Ask students to contrast monologue and dialogue. *A monologue is a speech made by one character or person; a dialogue is a conversation between two people or characters.* Point out that in this story, the Talkative Man presents his tale as a monologue.

Develop Background Before students begin to write their monologues, have them discuss ways to make a monologue appealing. Lead them to consider these points:

• A monologue should reveal something of the character of the speaker.

• A monologue must be engaging so it won't feel like a flat lecture or droning speech.

Apply the Information With this background, students should be able to develop monologues. You might have them work in pairs to plan, write, revise, and rehearse their monologues before presenting it to the class. Divide the class into groups for presenting the monologues.

Assess the Outcome After the presentations, invite students to share insights they gained into the character of the old man based on the monologues. To evaluate the monologues, have students use the Peer Assessment: Dramatic Performance page in *Alternative Assessment*, p. 113.

unless you do it, I don't see how it can move."

"Me!" exclaimed Doss. **6** "These new chariots! God knows what they are drawn by, I never understand, though I could handle a pair of bullocks[4] in my time. May I ask a question?"

"Go on," I said.

"Where is everybody?"

"Who?"

7 "Lots of people I knew are not to be seen at all. All sorts of new fellows everywhere, and nobody seems to care. Not a soul comes near the temple. All sorts of people go about but not one who cares to stop and talk. Why doesn't the king ever come this way? He used to go this way at least once a year before."

"Which king?" I asked.

"Let me go, you idiot," said Doss, edging towards the door on which I was leaning. "You don't seem to know anything." He pushed me aside, and got down from the car. He stooped as if he had a big hump on his back, and hobbled along towards the temple. I followed him, hardly knowing what to do. He turned and snarled at me: "Go away, leave me alone. I have had enough of you."

"What has come over you, Doss?" I asked.

"Who is Doss, anyway? Doss, Doss, Doss. What an absurd name! Call me by my name or leave me alone. Don't follow me calling 'Doss, Doss.' "

4. **bullocks** (bōŏl′ əks) *n*.: Oxen; steer.

Leaf from a royal manuscript of the Shah-Jehan Nameh: A Procession in a Palace Courtyard, The Art Institute of Chicago

▲ Critical Viewing This painting shows a royal procession from the time of the old man's reminiscences. Point out details that illustrate the pageantry and lavishness associated with royalty in ancient India. **[Support]**

Old Man of the Temple ◆ 179

◆ **Reading Strategy**

6 **Distinguish Fantasy From Reality** To help students distinguish between fantasy and reality, ask who exclaims "Me!" and what clues help them know. *It seems as if Doss says it, but it's actually the voice of the old man speaking through Doss.* What does the speaker mean by "new chariots"? *He is referring to cars.*

◆ **Reading Strategy**

7 **Distinguish Fantasy From Reality** The conversation in this passage blends reality and fantasy. Ask students to identify these elements through clues the author gives to help them know which is which. *The old man describes observations of people that are realistic, and refers to a king, which would make sense in India's past. However, when the narrator wonders which king, the old man gets angry, thinking the narrator is ignorant not to know the king.*

▶**Critical Viewing**◀

8 **Support** Accept any details students can support, such as lavish dress, elaborate carpets on the ground, adornments on the elephants and horses, the playing of musical instruments, people standing as if in prayer, guards tending the gate.

 Cultural Connection

Views on Death Every culture has its own set of beliefs regarding death. For instance, Judaism teaches that a person's spirit lives on in the good deeds of the family and friends whose lives he or she influenced. Some Native Americans believe in "good" and "bad" deaths, depending on the circumstances of one's demise. Invite groups to read and report on tales from various cultures that explore what happens when people die.

Humanities: Art

Procession in a Palace Courtyard, leaf from a royal manuscript of the Shah-Jeh an Nameh, Mogul, mid-seventeenth century.

This watercolor shows the pageantry of a grand procession.

Use these questions for discussion:

1. What elements of this scene reflect old India? *Answers may include traditional clothing, separation of men and women, use of horses for transportation, architecture of wall and gateway.*

2. How is this picture related to this story? *It portrays the old man's memory of the annual royal processions that used to pass by the temple.*

Answers

◆ Critical Thinking

1. First, he cannot see the old man, and second, the temple from which Doss said the old man exited is in truth a pile of ruins.

2. The narrator reacts to Doss's transformation coolly. He cannot believe Doss is possessed.

3. The old man, through Doss, mentions "these new chariots" and "the king," which sound old-fashioned and out of place to the Talkative Man.

4. (a) His reaction to Doss's transformation implies that he is much more likely to follow reason than be led by his emotions. He cannot fully accept a supernatural explanation, instead saying "Perhaps the driver was drunk; perhaps he wasn't." (b) The narrator's words —in particular his command to the old man, "You ought not to be here anymore . . . because you are dead"—reveal him to be a logical person, more apt to try and solve a problem as though it were a puzzle than let his emotions carry him away.

5. The family is an example of an element from real life that must be included in a fantasy to give it perspective. Here, the family shows that the ghost is not merely a figment of Doss's or the narrator's imagination, and also adds another perspective of people who have encountered the ghost.

6. (a) The names of the characters and the temple is Indian, though the temple could be substituted for an old church in Western cultures. (b) Most of the elements of the setting are the Indian variations on universal places: a dark road, a vehicle (the taxi), a lonely ruin, an isolated house.

7. Students' responses should include specific points of comparison and contrast.

◆ Reading Strategy

1. Fantastic elements include the ghost, Doss's hallucination about the old man and the temple, Doss's possession by the ghost.

2. (a) The plot becomes fantastical just as the narrator is awakened by Doss's swerving to miss the old man. (b) We know because the narrator cannot see the old man, so the reader as well doubts his existence.

182

Guide for Responding (continued)

◆ Critical Thinking

INTERPRET

1. Why does the narrator find Doss's words about the old man unbelievable? **[Analyze]**

2. How does the narrator react to Doss's transformation? **[Analyze]**

3. Why is the narrator suspicious of what the old man says? Give examples. **[Interpret]**

4. (a) Is the narrator the type of person who would be more likely to be ruled by his feelings or by reason? (b) Why? **[Infer]**

5. What purpose does the introduction of the family at the end of the story serve? **[Connect]**

EVALUATE

6. (a) Which elements of this story are uniquely Indian? (b) Which are universal? **[Classify]**

EXTEND

7. (a) How does this story compare with other fantasies you have read or seen on film? (b) Which elements of the plot or characters are similar? (c) Which are different? **[Compare and Contrast]**

◆ Reading Strategy

DISTINGUISH FANTASY FROM REALITY

"Old Man of the Temple" contains both **realistic and fantastic elements.** If you made a chart while reading, refer to it to answer these questions.

1. Name two elements that are fantastic.

2. (a) At what point does the plot become fantastical? (b) How do you know?

◆ Literary Focus

FANTASY

In "Old Man of the Temple," **fantasy**—in this instance, the narrator's encounter with a ghost–is essential to the plot of the story. This encounter is what the Talkative Man wants to tell us about; without it there is no story.

1. Why is this story a fantasy?

2. How does the inclusion of fantastic elements make the story appealing?

3. What realistic elements of the story make it believable?

◆ Build Vocabulary

USING THE SUFFIX -ity

Knowing that the suffix -ity means "the state or condition of being . . . ," write definitions for the following words:

1. brutality   3. generosity
2. severity   4. individuality

USING THE WORD BANK

On your paper, write the word whose meaning is closest to that of the first word.

1. sobriety: (a) sadness, (b) loneliness, (c) moderation
2. awry: (a) angry, (b) crooked, (c) clever
3. literally: (a) actually, (b) scholarly, (c) differently
4. longevity: (a) height, (b) endurance, (c) duration
5. imperative: (a) essential, (b) unnecessary, (c) ruler
6. venture: (a) game, (b) risk, (c) skill

◆ Build Grammar Skills

COMPOUND PREDICATES

Compound predicates enable a writer to describe the many actions of a single character without having to repeat the subject.

Practice On your paper, write the following sentences. Underline the compound predicate in each.

1. He stooped, wiped the beads of perspiration off his forehead, and hobbled along towards the temple.

2. He drove the car smoothly, seldom swore at passers-by, and exhibited perfect judgment.

3. I dug the earth, burnt every brick, and put them one upon another, all single-handed.

Writing Application On your paper, combine each group of sentences into a single sentence, using a compound predicate.

1. The old man came out of the temple. He looked in all directions. He began to walk.

2. I was sitting in the back seat of the car. I was listening to the hum of the motor. I dozed off.

3. I saw an old man run in front of the car. But I didn't see where he went.

182 ◆ Challenges and Choices

◆ Literary Focus

1. This story is a fantasy because it contains elements that could not reasonably happen, in this instance, a ghost.

2. The fantastic elements make the story unpredictable, thus enticing the reader to continue reading.

3. Realistic elements of the story include the setting, the family at the end, the story the family tells, and the narrator's cool attitude.

◆ Build Vocabulary

Using the Suffix -ity

1. Cruelty, a savage act
2. The quality of being rigorous or unsparing in the treatment of others
3. The quality of being unselfish or gracious, a generous act
4. A trait that distinguishes one person or thing from others

Using the Word Bank

1. c 2. b 3. a 4. c 5. a
6. b

◆ Build Grammar Skills

Practice

1. stooped, . . . wiped, . . . and hobbled
2. drove, . . . swore, . . . and exhibited
3. dug, . . . burnt, . . . and put

(Answers continue on page 183.)

Build Your Portfolio

Idea Bank

Writing

1. **Police Report** Imagine that you are a police officer who has been summoned to the scene by the family in the story. Write a brief description of the scene and each character's version of the events. **[Career Link]**

2. **Obituary** What kind of person do you think the old man was when he was alive? Using information in the story and information that you make up, write an obituary for the old man.

3. **Real Estate Advertisement** With a group of classmates, create a real-estate advertisement to sell the temple ruins. **[Career Link]**

Speaking and Listening

4. **Dramatic Reading** With a few classmates, give a dramatic reading of the story. Remember that for drama to be interesting, the characters must be brought to life—so don't hesitate to overact a little! **[Performing Arts Link]**

5. **Dramatic Monologue** Write a monologue in which the old man relates the elements of the story from his point of view. Deliver your monologue to the class. **[Performing Arts Link]**

Projects

6. **Cultural Map of India** Using an atlas, encyclopedia, or other reference books as guides, draw a map of India and locate areas of the major religions and languages on the map. **[Social Studies Link]**

7. **Report on Hinduism** Southern India, where this story takes place, is overwhelmingly Hindu. Write a brief research report on Hinduism and explain how Hinduism enriches your understanding of this story. **[Social Studies Link]**

Writing Mini-Lesson

Travel Brochure

India, the country in which this story takes place, is so diverse that a visitor could spend a year there and still see less than half of what there is to see. Choose a particular city, area, or attraction—either abroad or close to home—and write a travel brochure about that place.

Writing Skills Focus: Using a Persuasive Tone

Besides giving information, a successful brochure uses a **persuasive tone** to entice people to visit a particular place. Look at the following passage from a travel brochure on India:

Model
Be sure to visit the Taj Mahal, the world's most romantic and beautiful tomb. You'll see in it the love that an emperor bore for the wife he buried there. Also, you'll be amazed that this domed white marble building, 313 feet high, is so symmetrical that it doesn't seem large at all.

Phrases like *world's most romantic and beautiful tomb* and *you'll be amazed* create a persuasive tone by appealing to a tourist's desire for an unforgettable vacation experience.

Prewriting Decide on a place to write about and the features you'll describe. Gather appealing details that will persuade your audience to visit the place.

Drafting Many qualities can make the tone of your brochure persuasive. For instance, vivid sensory descriptions will appeal to people's imagination and a sense of humor will spark interest and a friendly, receptive attitude.

Revising Reread your draft. Would you be persuaded to visit the place? Can you make your tone more persuasive and your speaker even more likable?

Old Man of the Temple ◆ 183

Writing Application
1. The old man came out of the temple, looked in all directions, and began to walk.
2. I was sitting in the back seat of the car, listening to the hum of the motor, and I dozed off.
3. I saw an old man run in front of the car, but didn't see where he went.

Writer's Solution

For additional instruction and practice use the practice pages on Sentence Parts (pp. 26–29) in the *Writer's Solution Grammar Practice Book*.

Idea Bank
Customizing for
Performance Levels
Following are suggestions for matching the Idea Bank topics with your students' performance levels:
    Less Advanced Students: 1, 4, 7
    Average Students: 2, 4, 6
    More Advanced Students: 3, 5

Customizing for
Learning Modalities
Following are suggestions for matching Idea Bank topics with your students' learning modalities:
    Verbal/Linguistic: 1, 4, 7
    Auditory: 4, 5
    Visual/Spatial: 6

Writing Mini-Lesson

Refer students to the Writing Handbook, page 962, for instruction on the writing process, and page 964 for further information on Description.

Writer's Solution

Writing Lab CD-ROM
Have students complete the Tutorial on Description. Follow these steps:
1. Have students look at the interactive model of a travel brochure in the About Description section.
2. Have students use the Sensory Word Bins to gather details.
3. Have students draft on computer.
4. Use the Vague Adjectives checker to aid revision.
Allow 100 minutes of class time to complete these activities.

Sourcebook
Have students use Chapter 1, Description (pp. 1–29), for additional support. The chapter includes a workplace writing model of a travel brochure (p. 8).

183

✓ ASSESSMENT OPTIONS

Formal Assessment, Selection Test, pp. 38–40, and Assessment Resources Software. The selection test is designed so that it can be easily customized to the performance levels of your students.
Alternative Assessment, p. 12, includes options for less advanced students, more advanced students, visual/spatial learners, intrapersonal learners, verbal/linguistic learners, and logical/mathematical learners.

PORTFOLIO ASSESSMENT
Use the following rubrics in the *Alternative Assessment* booklet to assess student writing:
Police Report: Description Rubric, p. 90
Obituary: Narrative Rubric, p. 89
Real Estate Advertisement: Drama Rubric, p. 102
Travel Brochure: Description Rubric, p. 90

OBJECTIVES

1. To read, comprehend, and interpret a myth
2. To relate a myth to students' personal experience
3. To predict outcomes to facilitate comprehension
4. To identify the personality traits of a hero
5. To build vocabulary in context and learn the root -mort-
6. To develop skill in using plural and possessive nouns
7. To write a speech of introduction
8. To respond to the work through writing, speaking and listening, and projects

SKILLS INSTRUCTION

Vocabulary: Word Roots: -mort-

Grammar: Possessive Nouns

Reading Strategy: Predict

Literary Focus: Hero in a Myth

Writing: Appealing to Your Audience

Speaking and Listening: Trial (teacher edition)

Critical Viewing: Draw Conclusions; Speculate; Support

PORTFOLIO OPPORTUNITIES

Writing: Review; Feature Article; Modern-Day Myth

Writing Mini-Lesson: Speech of Introduction

Speaking and Listening: Comic Skit; Trial

Projects: Mask; Map

More About the Author
Edith Hamilton was born in Dresden, Germany, of American parents. Hamilton's interest in Greek and Roman mythology can be traced to her childhood. When she was seven years old, her father began teaching her Latin, and soon after that, Greek. So it may not be surprising that late in life, after a successful career as an educator, she devoted her attention to the ancient Greeks and Romans and to the parallels between life then and now. At the age of ninety, Hamilton traveled to Athens, Greece, where she saw one of her translations of a Greek play performed at the Acropolis.

Guide for Reading

Edith Hamilton *(1867–1963)*

Edith Hamilton's long journey on Earth began soon after the Civil War and ended in the Space Age. Her heart went on an even longer journey—back to the worlds of ancient Greece and Rome—to find messages that modern people could apply to their lives.

Educator of Young Women

Hamilton started out not as a writer, but as a groundbreaking educator. After graduating from Bryn Mawr College, she studied for a year in Europe, becoming the first woman to attend classes at the University of Munich, where she had to sit by herself on the lecture platform, separated from the male students. Shortly after completing her studies, she helped found the Bryn Mawr School in Baltimore, the first college preparatory school for women. As the school's headmistress, Hamilton taught a generation of young women the lesson she had learned: not to limit their goals simply because they were not men.

A Late-Blooming Writer Although she made the Bryn Mawr School a success, Hamilton admitted later on that she had never really liked being headmistress. She left Bryn Mawr in 1922.

At an age when most people of her time would have considered retirement, Hamilton launched into what would become her true career.

She began to write articles on the subject closest to her heart: ancient Greece. These pieces proved so popular that Hamilton was persuaded to turn them into a book, which was called *The Greek Way*, published in 1930.

Her other books include *The Roman Way* (1932), *The Prophets of Israel* (1936), and *Mythology* (1942).

◆ Build Vocabulary

WORD ROOTS: -mort-

In this selection, you'll encounter the word *mortified*, which is based on the root -mort-, meaning "death."

By knowing the root, you might guess that the word *mortified* means to "feel dead." The actual meaning of the word is "deeply humiliated" or "wounded in self-respect."

WORD BANK

kindred
mortified
despair
wavering
revelry
deity
reconciled

As you read "Perseus," you will encounter the words on this list. Each word is defined on the page where it first appears. Preview the list before you read, and look for the words as they appear in the story.

◆ Build Grammar Skills

POSSESSIVE NOUNS

"Perseus" contains nouns in the **possessive case,** which shows ownership or kinship.

• The possessive case of singular nouns is formed by adding an apostrophe and -s:
   Athena's shield

• The possessive case of a singular proper noun ending in -s is formed by adding an apostrophe and an -s:
   Douglas's chart

• The possessive case of plural nouns ending in -s or -es is formed by adding an apostrophe:
   Terrible Sisters' island

• The possessive case of plural nouns that do not end in -s is formed by adding an apostrophe and an -s:
   fishermen's brothers

184 ◆ Challenges and Choices

Prentice Hall Literature Program Resources

REINFORCE / RETEACH / EXTEND

Selection Support Pages
Build Vocabulary: Word Roots: -mort-, p. 51
Build Grammar Skills: Possessive Nouns, p. 52
Reading Strategy: Predict, p. 53
Literary Focus: Hero in a Myth, p. 54

Strategies for Diverse Student Needs, p. 13

Beyond Literature
Cross-Curricular Connection: Art, p. 13

Formal Assessment Selection Test, p. 41–43, Assessment Resources Software

Alternative Assessment, p. 13

Writing and Language Transparencies
Biographical Profile, pp. 9–15

Resource Pro CD-ROM
"Perseus"—includes all resource material and customizable lesson plan

Listening to Literature Audiocassettes
"Perseus"

Perseus

◆ *Literature and Your Life*

CONNECT YOUR EXPERIENCE

Some people love to rise to difficult occasions, while others prefer to keep their lives on an even keel. Perseus, the main character in this selection, is the first sort of person—the type who thrives on grappling with thorny problems. Which sort are you?

THEMATIC FOCUS: PUTTING OURSELVES TO THE TEST

Perseus' passage from one peril to the next might make you wonder what you would do if you suddenly found yourself in his sandals, faced with the choice between taking on a highly dangerous mission or being viewed with scorn. What alternatives might you have in such a tight spot?

◆ Background for Understanding

CULTURE

"Perseus" takes place in a mythological world populated by Greek gods and goddesses. The cast of Greek gods you will meet in Perseus' story includes Zeus, the chief god, who fathered a number of human children; Athena, goddess of war and wisdom; and Hermes, the messenger god (whom you may know by his Roman name Mercury).

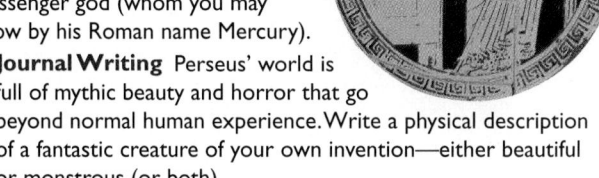

Journal Writing Perseus' world is full of mythic beauty and horror that go beyond normal human experience. Write a physical description of a fantastic creature of your own invention—either beautiful or monstrous (or both).

◆ Literary Focus

HERO IN A MYTH

Start with a brave young man who loves his mother. Add some sympathetic gods and a terrible monster. You now have the makings of a **hero in a myth**—a character who performs amazing feats in a tale involving supernatural beings and fantastic events. The hero in a myth is often aided by magical elements. Nevertheless, the hero must exhibit admirable qualities such as courage, loyalty, and fairness. As you read, think about how Perseus' good qualities make him worthy of the supernatural help he gets.

◆ Reading Strategy

PREDICT

"Perseus" begins with a prediction by an oracle (prophet) about a future event. When you read any work of literature, you too can **predict outcomes**—not by using supernatural powers, but by thinking about the world presented in the literature and about the logical consequences of the characters' actions. These factors help you narrow down many possible outcomes to the few most likely ones.

To help you predict outcomes in "Perseus," make a chart like this one.

Situation	Possible Outcome	Reasons for Prediction	Outcome

Guide for Reading ◆ 185

Interest Grabber Engage student interest by reading the following passage from the story aloud:

"... He was young and proud and keenly mortified. He stood up before them all and did exactly what the King had hoped he would do, declared that he would give him a present better than any there. He would go off and kill Medusa and bring back her head as his gift ... No one in his senses would have made such a proposal. Medusa was one of the Gorgons."

"... No man unaided could kill Medusa."

Urge students to use their imaginations to come up with ideas about what type of creature Medusa might be. Do they imagine that the character to whom the passage refers, Perseus, will be successful? Tell them they'll have to read the selection to find out.

Customize for
Less Proficient Readers
To help less proficient readers through the poetry sections, rephrase some of the archaic language and/or read sections aloud as students follow along in their book.

Customize for
More Advanced Students
Have students analyze why Edith Hamilton presents the myth both in prose and poetry. *She includes excerpts from another interpreter's version of the same myth.* Read aloud samples from both styles. Ask students to describe how they differ and how they complement one another.

Customize for
English Language Learners
There are several words in the myth that have multiple meanings. Examples include *visited upon, took ship, fair,* and *missile*. Help these students use context clues to understand the appropriate meaning of each confusing term or expression.

✎ Preparing for Standardized Tests

Reading and Vocabulary Vocabulary development will enable students to improve performance on the verbal portions of tests. The Build Vocabulary lesson focuses on the word root *-mort-*. Students can apply this skill to determine the meaning of words that appear on standardized tests. For example, recognizing the root meaning "death" will help students recognize and distinguish the meanings of words such as *mortuary, mortician, mortify,* and *moribund*. For additional practice, use the Build Vocabulary page in **Selection Support**, p. 51.

Grammar and Language Portions of some standardized tests require students to understand how to form the possessive case of singular and plural nouns. Students may be asked to choose the correct form from choices given, as in the following:

> The (athlete's, athletes') first discus throw was her best effort. *athlete's*

The Build Grammar Skills lesson for this selection focuses on this topic. For additional practice, use the Build Grammar Skills page on Possessive Nouns, p. 52 in **Selection Support**.

One-Minute Insight

In this myth as in others, the characters cannot escape their fates. Despite clever or elaborate plans, neither great heroes nor devious villains will alter their destinies. In the myth, a king, Acrisius, receives a prophecy that his daughter will one day have a son who will kill Acrisius. Acrisius takes a series of steps to prevent the prophecy from coming true, first imprisoning his daughter and later casting her out into the sea in a box once Acrisius discovers that she has had a son during her imprisonment. However, all of Acrisius's efforts fail as a result of divine intervention. First, Zeus visits his daughter Danaë while she is imprisoned and fathers a son, Perseus. Then the gods intervene to save Danaë and Perseus when they are cast into the sea. In the end, Perseus inadvertently kills Acrisius during an athletic contest, thereby fulfilling the prophecy.

❶ Clarification To enhance students' appreciation of the myth, keep a mythology anthology or dictionary on hand. Students can find out more about the gods, characters, and exotic locales mentioned in the story. A map of Greece and the region can also be useful. For instance, students can find out that *Argos* has been continually inhabited and is today a city in the Argolis region of the Peloponnese. They can learn that *oracles* are answers from the gods (or the places where such answers were given) to mortals' questions about the future. *Delphi* is the site of the temple of Apollo and his oracle, the most powerful one in Greece. It's located on Mount Parnassus in central Greece.

Customize for
Less Proficient Readers
Help students understand the character of Acrisius by guiding them to identify his predicament and discussing what he does and does not do about it.

PERSEUS

Edith Hamilton

King Acrisius[1] of Argos had only one child, a daughter, Danaë.[2] She was beautiful above all the other women of the land, but this was small comfort to the King for not having a son. ❶ He journeyed to Delphi to ask the god if there was any hope that some day he would be the father of a boy. The priestess told him no, and added what was far worse: that his daughter would have a son who would kill him.

The only sure way to escape that fate was for the King to have Danaë instantly put to death—taking no chances, but seeing to it himself. This Acrisius would not do. His fatherly affection was not strong, as events proved, but his fear of the gods was. They visited with terrible punishment those who shed the blood of <u>kindred</u>. Acrisius did not dare slay his daughter. Instead, he had a house built all of bronze and sunk underground, but with part of the roof open to the sky so that light and air could come through. Here he shut her up and guarded her.

> So Danaë endured, the beautiful,
> To change the glad daylight for brass-
>   bound walls.
> And in that chamber secret as the
>   grave
> She lived a prisoner. Yet to her came
> Zeus in the golden rain.

◆ **Build Vocabulary**
kindred (kin´ drid) *n.*: Relatives

1. **King Acrisius** (ə kris´ ē əs)
2. **Danaë** (dan´ ā ē)

186 ◆ Challenges and Choices

 Block Scheduling Strategies

Consider these suggestions to take advantage of extended class time:

• Start with an extended class discussion about Greek mythology. Have students share what they know about Greek gods and recount any myths they remember.

• Play all or part of the selection on audiocassette. Use the recording as the basis for a discussion about how the myth might be adapted into a television movie.

• Have students work in discussion groups to answer the Critical Thinking questions (p. 194).

• Students can work in groups to complete the Speaking and Listening activity that calls on them to conduct a mock trial (p. 195).

• Have students work on the *Writer's Solution Writing Lab* CD-ROM to complete the Writing Mini-Lesson (p. 195). Students should use the instruction and activities in the Tutorial on Exposition.

Customize for
Visual/Artistic Learners

Invite students to acquire fine art images of the characters in the myth and compare them with Hamilton's descriptions. Or, have them draw their own sketches based on the written descriptions.

◆ **Literary Focus**

❷ **Hero in a Myth** Have students discuss Acrisius' qualities and flaws and whether they think he is or is not a hero. *Students should recognize that Acrisius' behavior clearly reveals that he is not a hero.*

▶**Critical Viewing**◀

❸ **Draw Conclusions** Students' responses will vary, although some may point to the more intense action in this painting. In this depiction, Perseus hurtles toward the monster with much vigor, while both the sky and sea are violent and frightening. They may say that there is more of an emotional impact in this painting, pointing to the way Andromeda looks upward at Perseus. Her mouth is open, in terror; she is longing for his help.

Andromeda Liberated, Pierre Mignard. Louvre, Paris, France

As she sat there through the long days and hours with nothing to do, nothing to see except the clouds moving by overhead, a mysterious thing happened, a shower of gold fell from the sky and filled her chamber. How it was revealed to her that it was Zeus who had visited her in this shape we are not told, but she knew that the child she bore was his son.

For a time she kept his birth secret from her father, but it became increasingly difficult to do so in the narrow limits of that bronze house and finally one day the little boy—his name was Perseus—was discovered by his grandfather. "Your child!" Acrisius cried in great anger. "Who is his father?" But when Danaë answered proudly, "Zeus," he would not believe her. One thing only he was sure of, that the boy's life

❷

◄ **Critical Viewing** The man with the sword is Perseus as an adult. Judging from this painting, how do you think others perceive him? Cite details in the artwork to support your answer. **[Draw Conclusions]**

❸

Perseus ◆ 187

🗝 **Humanities: Art**

Perseus and Andromeda, c. 1580, by Paolo Veronese.

This piece of art illustrates the point in Perseus' adventures where, in the nick of time, he swoops down and kills the serpent to save Andromeda from certain death. Paolo Veronese (1528–1588), a northern Italian Renaissance painter, was born in Verona, where he learned his craft. Known for the pageantry and splendor of his work,

Veronese achieved success and recognition in his lifetime. He is considered by art historians to have been, next to Tintoretto, the most important Venetian painter of his time.

Use these questions for discussion:

1. What gifts is Perseus using in his effort to save Andromeda? *He is using Hermes' sword, Athena's shield, and the winged sandals the Hyperboreans gave him.*

2. What elements of the painting highlight Perseus' heroism? *Students can point to his focus on his task, his muscles, his position not only above the monster, but also above the city in the background. They can notice that the serpent is a terrifying creature that is threatening Andromeda with open jaws, and that she is chained and helpless.*

was a terrible danger to his own. He was afraid to kill him for the same reason that had kept him from killing her, fear of Zeus and the Furies who pursue such murderers. But if he could not kill them outright, he could put them in the way of tolerably certain death. He had a great chest made, and the two placed in it. Then it was taken out to sea and cast into the water.

In that strange boat Danaë sat with her little son. The daylight faded and she was alone on the sea.

> When in the carven chest the winds and
>   waves
> Struck fear into her heart she put her
>   arms,
> Not without tears, round Perseus tenderly
> She said, "O son, what grief is mine.
> But you sleep softly, little child,
> Sunk deep in rest within your cheerless
>   home,
> Only a box, brass-bound. The night, this
>   darkness visible,
> The scudding waves so near to your soft
>   curls,
> The shrill voice of the wind, you do not
>   heed,
> Nestled in your red cloak, fair little face."

❶ ┌─────────────────────┐
│ ◆ **Reading Strategy** │
│ Will Danaë and │
│ Perseus survive? On │
│ what do you base │
│ your prediction? │
└─────────────────────┘

Through the night in the tossing chest she listened to the waters that seemed always about to wash over them. The dawn came, but with no comfort to her for she could not see it. Neither could she see that around them there were islands rising high above the sea, many islands. All she knew was that presently a wave seemed to lift them and carry them swiftly on and then, retreating, leave them on something solid and motionless. They had made land; they were safe from the sea, but they were still in the chest with no way to get out.

Fate willed it—or perhaps Zeus, who up to now had done little for his love and his child—that they should be discovered by a good man, a fisherman named Dictys. He came upon the great box and broke it open and took the pitiful cargo home to his wife who was as kind as he. They had no children and they cared for Danaë and Perseus as if they were their own. The two lived there many years, Danaë content to let her son follow the fisherman's humble trade, out of harm's way. But in the end more trouble came. Polydectes,[3] the ruler of the little island, was the brother of Dictys, but he was a cruel and ruthless man. He seems to have taken no notice of the mother and son for a long time, but at last Danaë attracted his attention. She was still radiantly beautiful even though Perseus by now was full grown, and Polydectes fell in love with her. He wanted her, but he did not want her son, and he set himself to think out a way of getting rid of him.

There were some fearsome monsters called Gorgons who lived on an island and were known far and wide because of their deadly power. Polydectes evidently talked to Perseus about them; he probably told him that he would rather have the head of one of them than anything else in the world. This seems practically certain from the plan he devised for killing Perseus. He announced that he was about to be married and he called his friends together for a celebration, including Perseus in the invitation. Each guest, as was customary, brought a gift for the bride-to-be, except Perseus alone. He had nothing he could give. He was young and proud and keenly mortified. He stood up before them all and did exactly what the King had hoped he would do, declared that he would give him a present better than any there. He would go off and kill Medusa and bring back her head as his gift. Nothing could have suited the King better. No one in his senses would have made such a proposal. Medusa was one of the Gorgons, **❷**

───────────────────

3. **Polydectes** (pol i dek′ tēz)

Cultural Connection

The ancient Greeks were not the only people to have created a body of myths to explain historical events and natural phenomena, and to present ethical and moral lessons. Other cultures have their own elaborate myths that model behavior and make sense of the unexplainable. Although the names of the places, gods, heroes, and villains change from culture to culture, many of the tales and participants are remarkably similar.

Invite students to look further into the idea that similar myths show up in different cultures. They might start by examining Roman mythology, in which many of the same gods reappear, but with new names. They can find two myths to compare—one Roman and one Greek—that tell the same story. Or they can explore the myths of other cultures to identify similarities and differences.

Danae with young Perseus arriving on the island of Seripo,
Museo Archeologico, Ferrara, Italy.

▲ Critical Viewing   Do you think Zeus intervened
to save Perseus and Danaë? Why or why not?
[Speculate]

❸

And they are three, the Gorgons, each
with wings
And snaky hair, most horrible to mortals.
Whom no man shall behold and draw
again
The breath of life,

❹

for the reason that whoever looked at them
were turned instantly into stone. It seemed
that Perseus had been led by his angry pride
into making an empty boast. No man unaided
could kill Medusa.

But Perseus was saved from his folly. Two
great gods were watching over him. He took
ship as soon as he left the King's hall, not daring to see his mother first and tell her what he
intended, and he sailed to Greece to learn
where the three monsters were to be found. He
went to Delphi, but all the priestess would say
was to bid him seek the land where men eat

not Demeter's golden
grain, but only acorns.
So he went to Dodona,
in the land of oak
trees, where the talk-
ing oaks were which
declared Zeus's will
and where the Selli
lived who made their
bread from acorns.
They could tell him,
however, no more than
this, that he was under
the protection of the
gods. They did not
know where the Gor-
gons lived.

❺

When and how Her-
mes and Athena came
to his help is not told
in any story, but he
must have known
despair before they did so. At last, however, as
he wandered on, he met a strange and beautiful person. We know what he looked like from
many a poem, a young man with the first down
upon his cheek when youth is loveliest, carrying, as no other young man ever did, a wand of
gold with wings at one end, wearing a winged
hat, too, and winged sandals. At sight of him
hope must have entered Perseus' heart, for he
would know that this could be none other than
Hermes, the guide and the giver of good.

This radiant personage told him that before
he attacked Medusa he must first be properly
equipped, and that what he needed was in the
possession of the nymphs of the North. To find
the nymphs' abode, they must go to the Gray
Women who alone could tell them the way.
These women dwelt in a land where all was

◆ **Build Vocabulary**
mortified (môrt´ ə fīd´) *adj.*: Embarrassed
despair (di sper´) *n.*: Hopelessness

Perseus ◆ 189

❸ **Speculate** Students may contend that since Zeus had shown no
interest in Perseus previously, there's
no reason to think he was responsible. On the other hand, students may
know that the involvement of the
gods is a hallmark of myths and so
may believe that Zeus was indeed
responsible.

◆ **Reading Strategy**

❹ **Predict** Ask students to predict
what will happen when Perseus
attempts to kill the Gorgon. *Some
students may say that Perseus' excessive
pride will cause him to fail, while others
may say that he is the son of Zeus and
will succeed with divine help. Others
may note that whether or not Perseus
kills Medusa, he needs to live to kill his
grandfather, as prophesied.*

◆ **Build Grammar Skills**

❺ **Possessive Nouns** Have students identify the two cases of the
possessive form of a singular noun
shown in this passage. Guide them to
recognize that the possessive form of
a noun ending with an "s" needs an
apostrophe and an -s added.

Customize for
Visual/Spatial Learners
Point out that the scene appears on a
piece of cracked pottery. Tell students
that archaeologists study such art to
infer information about a culture. Ask
students to tell what they can infer
from the portrayal of Danaë and
young Perseus. *Students may observe
that the mother and child are very close,
suggesting their intimate bond. The welcoming figure may be the caring fisherman Dictys, who liberated the two from
the chest.*

Cross-Curricular Connection: Social Studies

Perseus travels to Greece to consult with the
priestesses at Delphi. Delphi was the site of the
most important temple and oracle of the god
Apollo. The word *oracle* stands for either the
place where someone can petition a god or goddess for an answer to a vexing problem or for
the answer itself. The answer would be given
through priests or priestesses who inhabited the
temple. A priest or priestess would give the

answer through an intricate ritual special to the
specific oracle. The oracle at Delphi is one of the
most thoroughly researched shrines of ancient
Greece.

Encourage students to locate the site of the
oracle at Delphi, and to research its history and
what historians and archaeologists have been able
to find out about its rituals and the role it played
in the culture of ancient Greece.

❶ Draw Conclusions Students can infer that the people are appreciative of what Perseus has done. Several are approaching him, some are bowing to him, one is hugging him, and another is kissing his hand. The presence of hovering angels completes the scene of adoration and gratefulness, and amazement at his accomplishment.

◆ Critical Thinking

❷ Draw Conclusions Hermes and Athena come to Perseus' aid. Have students explain why they do.
Students may say that since Perseus is the son of Zeus, the gods will conspire to see him through his tasks.

Customize for
Visual/Spatial Learners

Help students envision what Medusa looks like by having them describe the image of the Medusa on this page. Draw out their responses to include observation of the entwined snakes that form Medusa's hair as well as the shieldlike frame that suggests that the image is reflected in Athena's shield.

Critical Viewing ►
In addition to his gifts from the gods, what does Perseus need to slay Medusa?
[Draw Conclusions]
❶

dim and shrouded in twilight. No ray of sun looked ever on that country, nor the moon by night. In that gray place the three women lived, all gray themselves and withered as in extreme old age. They were strange creatures, indeed, most of all because they had but one eye for the three, which it was their custom to take turns with, each removing it from her forehead when she had had it for a time and handing it to another.

❷ All this Hermes told Perseus and then he unfolded his plan. He would himself guide Perseus to them. Once there Perseus must keep hidden until he saw one of them take the eye out of her forehead to pass it on. At that moment, when none of the three could see, he must rush forward and seize the eye and refuse to give it back until they told him how to reach the nymphs of the North.

He himself, Hermes said, would give him a sword to attack Medusa with—which could not be bent or broken by the Gorgon's scales, no matter how hard they were. This was a wonderful gift, no doubt, and yet of what use was a sword when the creature to be struck by it could turn the swordsman into stone before he was within striking distance? But another great deity was at hand to help. Pallas Athena stood beside Perseus. She took off the shield of polished bronze which covered her breast and held it out to him. "Look into this when you attack the Gorgon," she said. "You will be able to see her in it as in a mirror, and so avoid her deadly power."

Now, indeed, Perseus had good reason to hope. The journey to the twilight land was long, over the stream of Ocean and on to the very border of the black country where the Cimmerians dwell, but Hermes was his guide and he could not go astray. They found the Gray Women at last, looking in the wavering light like gray birds, for they had the shape of swans. But their heads were human and beneath their wings they had arms and hands. Perseus did just as Hermes had said, he held back until he saw one of them take the eye out

Speaking and Listening Mini-Lesson

Trial

This mini-lesson supports the Speaking and Listening activity in the Idea Bank on page 195.

Introduce the Concept Discuss with students the nature of an opening argument in a criminal trial. Invite students to share what they know about this kind of persuasive speech. If possible, invite a student or two to interview an attorney or law student to find out some of the specific features of an opening argument. Ask them to find out about opening arguments both for the prosecution and for the defense. Have them share their findings with the class.

Develop Background Divide students into groups and subdivide groups into teams of prosecuting attorneys and defense attorneys. You may wish to encourage students to argue a position they do not hold so that they can practice their skill at presenting a persuasive argument. One or more groups should be jurors.

Apply the Information Have the teams of attorneys present their arguments, first for the prosecution, then for the defense. Urge jurors to listen carefully and to take notes.

Assess the Outcome Have students evaluate their own and other groups' arguments for Acrisius' guilt or innocence. Ask the jury to weigh the facts and the logic and persuasiveness of each argument and come to a consensus if they can.

of her forehead. Then before she could give it to her sister, he snatched it out of her hand. It was a moment or two before the three realized they had lost it. Each thought one of the others had it. But Perseus spoke out and told them he had taken it and that it would be theirs again ❸ only when they showed him how to find the nymphs of the North. They gave him full directions at once; they would have done anything to get their eye back. He returned it to them and went on the way they had pointed out to him. He was bound, although he did not know it, to the blessed country of the Hyperboreans,[4] at the back of the North Wind, of which it is said: "Neither by ship nor yet by land shall one find the wondrous road to the gathering place of the Hyperboreans." But Perseus had Hermes with him, so that the road lay open to him, and he received that host of happy people who are always banqueting and holding joyful revelry. They showed him great kindness: they welcomed him to their feast, and the maidens dancing to the sound of flute and lyre paused to get for him the gifts he sought. These were three: winged sandals, a magic wallet which would always become the right size for what- ❹ ever was to be carried in it, and, most impor- tant of all, a cap which made the wearer invisible. With these and Athena's shield and Hermes' sword Perseus was ready for the Gor- gons. Hermes knew where they lived, and leav- ing the happy land the two flew back across Ocean and over the sea to the Terrible Sisters' island.

By great good fortune they were all asleep when Perseus found them. In the mirror of the bright shield he could see them clearly, crea- tures with great wings and bodies covered with

---

4. **Hyperboreans** (hī per bō´ rē anz)

◆ Build Vocabulary

wavering (wā´ ver iŋ) *adj.*: Flickering
revelry (rev´ əl rē) *n.*: Party

golden scales and hair a mass of twisting snakes. Athena was beside him now as well as Hermes. They told him which one was Medusa and that was important, for she alone of the three could be killed; the other two were im- ❺ mortal. Perseus on his winged sandals hovered above them, looking, however, only at the shield. Then he aimed a stroke down at Medusa's throat and Athena guided his hand. With a single sweep of his sword he cut through her neck and, his eyes still fixed on the shield with never a glance at her, he swooped low enough to seize the head. He dropped it into the wallet

◆ Literary Focus
What heroic qualities does Perseus exhibit through these actions? ❻

which closed around it. He had nothing to fear from it now. But the two other Gorgons had awakened and, horrified at the sight of their sister slain, tried to pursue the slayer. Perseus was safe; he had on the cap of darkness and they could not find him.

> So over the sea rich-haired Danaë's son,
> Perseus, on his winged sandals sped,
> Flying swift as thought.
> In a wallet of silver,
> A wonder to behold,
> He bore the head of the monster,
> While Hermes, the son of Maia,
> The messenger of Zeus,
> Kept ever at his side.

On his way back he came to Ethiopia and alighted there. By this time Hermes had left him. Perseus found, as Hercules was later to find, that a lovely maiden had been given up to be devoured by a horrible sea serpent. Her name was Andromeda and she was the daugh- ter of a silly vain woman,

> That starred Ethiop queen who strove
> To set her beauty's praise above
> The sea-nymphs, and their power
> offended.

◆ **Literary Focus**

❸ **Hero in a Myth** Ask students to explain how Perseus' actions in his encounter with the Gray Women show that he is a hero. *Students may say that after he carefully followed the instructions Hermes gave to him, he kept his word and returned the eye to the women.*

◆ **Reading Strategy**

❹ **Predict** Perseus was given three gifts during his stay with the Hyperboreans. Have students predict how he will use the sandals, the magic wallet, and the cap. *Students are likely to say that he'll use the sandals to flee from danger, the wallet to carry something, perhaps Medusa's head, and the hat to escape from another peril.*

◆ **Build Vocabulary**

❺ **Roots: -mort-** Have students use the context clues provided, and their understanding of the root -mort- to identify the meaning of the word *immortal. It means "living or lasting for- ever"; some students may recognize the prefix im- (not) and use this knowledge to help them know the meaning of immortal.*

◆ **Literary Focus**

❻ **Hero in a Myth** Responses can point to the way Perseus bravely and carefully followed the advice he was given and used each of his props to carry out the dangerous job of killing Medusa and then escaping the wrath of the other two Gorgons.

Cross-Curricular Connection: Science

The word *astronomy* derives from a combination of two Greek words, *astron,* which means "star," and *nomos,* which means "law." Although the ancient Greeks were not the first to study the stars, they were the first to systematically catalog them. Therefore, many of the names for stars and constellations come from the Greeks, names like Andromeda, Cassiopeia, and Cassiopeia's hus- band, Cepheus. There is also a constellation named for Perseus' grandson, Hercules.

Have students do research to find out more about the constellations named for Andromeda, Cassiopeia, Hercules, and Cepheus, or for other characters in Greek mythology. They can find out where in the sky to look for each and when dur- ing the year and night to find them. They can find out what each looks like and draw a picture of it. They'll learn, for instance, that Cassiopeia looks like points in a crown and that Cepheus looks more like a simple house with a roof than a king. Ask students who have telescopes to try to locate these constellations.

◆ Literature and Your Life

❶ Discuss with students the ways that the gods influenced mortals' behavior in Greek mythology, emphasizing the consequences of going against the gods' wishes or warnings. Then have students consider and talk about the influences on behavior in modern times. Ask them to discuss why people go against these influences, and what consequences await them.

▶Critical Viewing◀

❷ Support Perseus, using his winged sandals, is descending upon and preparing to kill the serpent that is threatening Andromeda.

◆ Reading Strategy

❸ Predict Students can predict that the oracle's prophesy will be carried out—that Perseus will kill Acrisius, his grandfather.

◆ Literature and Your Life

❹ Have students consider Perseus' decision to return to Argos and reconcile with Acrisius. Ask them if they think this was a hard or easy decision or if it was a smart one. Ask them to explain what they would have done had they been in Perseus' sandals.

🎵 Humanities: Art

Perseus and Andromeda, c. 1580, by Paolo Veronese.

Paolo Veronese (PAH oh loh vay roh NAY say) (1528–1588) painted in Venice toward the end of the Italian Renaissance. His real name was Cagliari but he was called Veronese because he was born in Verona. His work was popular for its depiction of historical subjects and myths.

This painting shows Perseus slaying the sea monster that is trying to kill Andromeda, who is chained to a rock by the sea.

Use the following for discussion:

1. What dramatic event is the focus of the painting? *Students should note that the serpent is within a short leap of devouring Andromeda, but Perseus's sword will behead it first.*
2. How does color contribute to the drama of the scene? *The blood red of Andromeda's garment flows toward the flamelike orange of Perseus's clothing, forming an arc above the threatening oranges of the serpent's mouth and eye.*

192 ◆ *Challenges and Choices*

She had boasted that she was more beautiful than the daughters of Nereus, the Sea-god. An absolutely certain way in those days to draw down on one a wretched fate was to claim superiority in anything over any <u>deity</u>; nevertheless people were perpetually doing so. In this case the punishment for the arrogance the gods detested fell not on Queen Cassiopeia,[5] Andromeda's mother, but on her daughter. The Ethiopians were being devoured in numbers by the serpent; and, learning from the oracle that they could be freed from the pest only if Andromeda were offered up to it, they forced Cepheus,[6] her father, to consent. When Perseus arrived the maiden was on a rocky ledge by the sea, chained there to wait for the coming of the monster. Perseus saw her and on the instant loved her. He waited beside her until the great snake came for its prey; then he cut its head off just as he had the Gorgon's. The headless body dropped back into the water; Perseus took Andromeda to her parents and asked for her hand, which they gladly gave him.

With her he sailed back to the island and his mother, but in the house where he had lived so long he found no one. The fisherman Dictys' wife was long since dead, and the two others, Danaë and the man who had been like a father to Perseus, had had to fly and hide themselves from Polydectes, who was furious at Danaë's refusal to marry him. They had taken refuge in a temple, Perseus was told. He learned also that the King was holding a banquet in the

---

5. **Queen Cassiopeia** (kas′ ē ō pē′ ə)
6. **Cepheus** (sē′ fəs)

◀ **Critical Viewing** What does Perseus prove by killing the sea monster? **[Support]**

 Beyond the Classroom

Community Connection

Local Hero Although it is not a given that if you do heroic deeds a statue will be built in your honor, many have been honored in such a fashion. Invite students to find out for which heroes there exist statues or monuments in your community. Have them identify the person, explain the reason for the honor, and describe the statue or monument. Ask them to explain why the memorial is located where it is and, perhaps, what other location would make as much sense. Alternately, students can identify heroes for whom there ought to be a memorial in your area. Have them describe what this statue or monument should look like and what inscription it might carry.

palace and all the men who favored him were gathered there. Perseus instantly saw his opportunity. He went straight to the palace and entered the hall. As he stood at the entrance, Athena's shining buckler on his breast, the silver wallet at his side, he drew the eyes of every man there. Then before any could look away he held up the Gorgon's head; and at the sight one and all, the cruel King and his servile courtiers, were turned into stone. There they sat, a row of statues, each, as it were, frozen stiff in the attitude he had struck when he first saw Perseus.

❸ ◆ **Reading Strategy**
How will the story end?

When the islanders knew themselves freed from the tyrant it was easy for Perseus to find Danaë and Dictys. He made Dictys king of the island, but he and his mother decided that they would go back with Andromeda to Greece and try to be <u>reconciled</u> to Acrisius, to see if the many years that had passed since he had put them in the chest had not softened him so that he would be glad to receive his daughter and grandson. When they reached Argos, however, they found that

❹

Acrisius had been driven away from the city, and where he was no one could say. It happened that soon after their arrival Perseus heard that the King of Larissa, in the North, was holding a great athletic contest, and he journeyed there to take part. In the discus-throwing when his turn came and he hurled the heavy missile, it swerved and fell among the spectators. Acrisius was there on a visit to the King, and the discus struck him. The blow was fatal and he died at once.

So Apollo's oracle was again proved true. If Perseus felt any grief, at least he knew that his grandfather had done his best to kill him and his mother. With his death their troubles came to an end. Perseus and Andromeda lived happily ever after. Their son, Electryon, was the grandfather of Hercules.

Medusa's head was given to Athena, who bore it always upon the aegis, Zeus's shield, which she carried for him.

◆ **Build Vocabulary**
deity (dē´ ə tē) *n.:* A god
reconciled (rek´ ən sīld) *adj.:* Became friends again

Guide for Responding

◆ *Literature and Your Life*

Reader's Response Which of Perseus' adventures would make the best action-adventure movie? Why?

Thematic Focus If you had been Perseus, would you have accepted King Polydectes' challenge to find a unique wedding present? Why or why not?

Group Discussion Perseus' grandfather, Acrisius, truly believed the prediction that his grandson would end up killing him. As a group, discuss what Acrisius could and should have done in response to this prediction: Was he at all justified in the actions he took? What alternatives did he have?

☑ Check Your Comprehension

1. (a) What prediction does the priestess make to Acrisius? (b) What two actions does Acrisius take to prevent the prophecy from coming true?
2. (a) Why does Perseus set out to kill Medusa? (b) What help does he receive from Hermes and Athena? (c) How does Perseus manage to kill Medusa?
3. How does Perseus eventually fulfill the priestess's prediction?

Perseus ◆ 193

◆ **Critical Thinking**
❺ **Draw Conclusions** The tale ends with Acrisius' accidental death. Have students explain why this ending is appropriate. *Students may say that the oracle's prophesy had to come true, Acrisius had to die at the hands of his grandson. They can point out that since Perseus came back with good intentions, not vengeance, and because he did not mean to kill Acrisius, his standing as a hero is intact.*

Reinforce and Extend

Answers
◆ *Literature and Your Life*

Reader's Response Students may argue in favor of Perseus' being cast to sea as a child, his killing of Medusa or Polydectus, or the death of Acrisius.

Thematic Focus Although some students may be inclined to respond that they would be more cautious than was Perseus, others would say that they too would have accepted the challenge.

☑ **Check Your Comprehension**
1. (a) He predicts that he will be killed by his grandson. (b) He hides his daughter Danaë away so that she will not meet men, and he then sends his daughter and grandson away to what he believes is certain death.
2. (a) He boasts that he will bring back the head of the Medusa as a gift. (b) Hermes gives him a sword that cannot be bent or broken, and Athena gives him a mirrored shield to help him avoid Medusa's power. (c) Perseus tricks the Old Gray Women into giving him a helmet of invisibility. He wears the helmet, which makes him invisible, and holds up the shield so that he sees only Medusa's reflection. He finds the Gorgons asleep and strikes off Medusa's head before she can wake up. He puts the head in his expandable wallet.
3. Acrisius has fled his home to escape the prophecy. Perseus participates in a discus-throwing contest in Larissa and hits Acrisius, who is in the audience.

  Beyond the Selection

FURTHER READING
Other Works by Edith Hamilton
Three Greek Plays
The Great Age of Greek Literature
Echo of Greece

Other Works With the Theme of Dangerous Challenges
The Odyssey, Homer
"The Golden Fleece," from Greek mythology
Undaunted Courage, Stephen E. Ambrose

LITERATURE CD-ROMS
Disc 2, Features 11 and 12, of the *Myths and Legends of Ancient Greece* **CD-ROM** contains an animated version of the Perseus myth. The entire myth is presented through audio and illustrations. This presentation is ideal for visual/spatial learners and less proficient readers.

Answers

◆ Critical Thinking

1. Acrisius is a cruel, selfish, uncaring character.
2. The fact that Perseus is Zeus's son leads the reader to believe that he is special, that he has stores of resourcefulness and courage as part of his birthright.
3. Sample reasons: on a whim, in recognition of his bravery and devotion to his mother, as a way of ridding the world of a monster
4. Students may predict that Perseus would have failed in his quest, or that he would be resourceful enough to find another way to complete his task.
5. The myth suggests that people cannot, whatever extreme actions they may take, escape their fate, although their fates may be fulfilled at a time, in a place, or by a method that is unexpected.
6. Most students will probably make the judgment that Acrisius deserves his fate.
7. In most cases students will cite works in which the characters were foiled in their efforts to control fate.

◆ Reading Strategy

1. Factors include that he is the central character in the myth; that he is a son of Zeus; that he is assisted by Athena and Hermes
2. (a) It has been predicted by an oracle; Acrisius' attempts to prevent the birth and to end the life of Perseus have been foiled in miraculous ways; he has merited punishment for his actions. (b) the coincidental nature of his death; his coincidental presence in an audience far from his home when Perseus' discus coincidentally happens to swerve into the audience

◆ Literary Focus

Students should cite Perseus' bravery, resourcefulness, devotion, loyalty, and selflessness.

◆ Build Vocabulary

1. condition of being deathless or living forever
2. person who takes care of the dead
3. involving death
4. cause to live or be remembered forever
5. place where dead bodies are stored

Guide for Responding (continued)

◆ Critical Thinking

INTERPRET
1. What is revealed about Acrisius' character through the actions he takes to escape fate? **[Infer]**
2. Why is it important that Perseus is Zeus's son? **[Infer]**
3. What might have led Athena and Hermes to help Perseus in his quest? **[Infer]**
4. What would have happened to Perseus if he had not received help from the gods? **[Predict]**
5. What does this myth suggest about people's ability to escape or control fate? Explain. **[Draw Conclusions]**

EVALUATE
6. Considering the actions he takes against Danaë and Perseus, does Acrisius deserve his fate? Why or why not? **[Make a Judgment]**

EXTEND
7. (a) What situations from other works of literature, movies, or real life can you recall in which someone tried to escape or control fate?
   (b) What were the outcomes? **[Literary Link]**

◆ Reading Strategy

PREDICT
An adventure-filled story like "Perseus" keeps you wondering what will happen next. If you made a **prediction** chart while reading, you might refer to it now to help you answer these questions:
1. What factors would allow you to predict that Perseus will succeed in his quest to kill Medusa?
2. The oracle's prophecy to Acrisius could have had several outcomes. (a) Why is Acrisius' death a logical outcome? (b) What aspects of his death could not have been predicted?

◆ Literary Focus

HERO IN A MYTH
The central character of "Perseus" is a good example of a **hero in a myth**, a character with admirable personality traits who performs amazing feats with the aid of supernatural elements.
What admirable personality traits does Perseus possess?

◆ Build Vocabulary

USING THE WORD ROOT -mort-
Knowing that the root -mort- means "dead," write definitions for the following words:

1. immortality   4. immortalize
2. mortician   5. mortuary
3. mortally

USING THE WORD BANK
On your paper, write the word whose meaning is closest to that of the first word:
1. deity: (a) goodness, (b) god, (c) generosity
2. mortified: (a) cleansed, (b) stiff, (c) humiliated
3. revelry: (a) party, (b) awakening, (c) disagreement
4. despair: (a) hopelessness, (b) ruin, (c) sacrifice
5. reconciled: (a) guessed, (b) became friends again, (c) forgotten
6. wavering: (a) greeting, (b) stumbling, (c) flickering
7. kindred: (a) relatives, (b) childhood, (c) hostility

◆ Build Grammar Skills

POSSESSIVE NOUNS
The **possessive case** of nouns indicates kinship and ownership. Determine whether each possessive noun is singular or plural and follow the appropriate rule to form the possessive case.

Practice In your notebook, write the following sentences. Use the correct form from the choices given in the parentheses:
1. The (oracles', oracle's) prophecy frightened Acrisius.
2. Perseus stole the Gray (Women's, Womens') eye.
3. Then he went to the (Gorgon's, Gorgons') island.
4. Looking at Medusa turned the (warriors, warriors') bodies into stone.
5. Perseus depended on the help of two (gods, gods').

Writing Application Write two or three paragraphs in which you summarize the key events of the myth of Perseus. Include at least five examples of nouns in the possessive case.

Using the Word Bank
1. b   2. c   3. a   4. a   5. b
6. b   7. a

◆ Build Grammar Skills
1. oracle's;   2. Women's;
3. Gorgons';   4. warriors';
5. gods

✎ Writer's Solution

For additional instruction and practice, use the lesson in the **Language Lab CD-ROM** on The Eight Parts of Speech: Nouns and the page on Apostrophes with Possessive Nouns, p. 112 in the *Writer's Solution Grammar Practice Book.*

*B*uild *Y*our *P*ortfolio

Idea Bank

Writing

1. **Review** Write a brief review of "Perseus" to appear an Internet Home Page. Citing details from the story, tell why people would or would not want to read the myth.

2. **Feature Article** Write a newspaper feature article on the life of Perseus. Decide the slant of your article: Is Perseus a brave, noble hero or merely a foolish young man with the great luck to have two gods on his side?

3. **Modern-Day Myth** Invent a modern-day "monster" and write a myth about a contemporary hero who destroys it. Include powerful helpers who come to the hero's aid.

Speaking and Listening

4. **Comic Skit** With a group of classmates, plan and perform a skit dramatizing the scene in which Perseus gets the eye from the three Gray Women. **[Performing Arts Link]**

5. **Trial** Imagine that Acrisius does not die, but he is brought to trial for his treatment of Danaë and Perseus. As a prosecuting attorney, present an opening argument to a jury of your classmates, accusing the king of intent to commit murder. **[Social Studies Link]**

Projects

6. **Mask** Using the medium of your choice, create a Medusa mask. Let your imagination fly; the only requirement is that you somehow suggest the snakes of Medusa's hair. **[Art Link]**

7. **Map** Draw a map showing Perseus' travels from the time of his birth until the end of the story. Illustrate your map with the various gods and monsters he meets. **[Art Link; Social Studies Link]**

Writing Mini-Lesson

Speech of Introduction

Imagine that you have been selected to deliver a speech introducing Perseus at a large public gathering to celebrate his achievements. Your speech will tell your audience something of Perseus' background and will go on to praise and describe his deeds. You will end by introducing the great man himself, who will then speak to the audience you have warmed up for him.

Writing Skills Focus: Appealing to Your Audience

Of all the forms of writing, speeches pay the most attention to the **audience.** The audience is right there, breathing along with the speaker, taking in his or her words—nodding, frowning, laughing, crying, cheering. A successful speechwriter consciously appeals to the audience in various ways—for example, by arousing people's emotions, amusing them, making them think, or holding their attention with a gripping story.

Prewriting List the important facts of Perseus' life—the belief that he is a son of Zeus, his being cast to sea by his cruel grandfather, his devotion to his mother, his victory over Medusa, and so on. Then look over the list to choose events and details that will appeal to your audience or excite their admiration for Perseus.

Drafting As you write your speech, draw on the information in your list to appeal to your audience. Organize the information in time order or group the details into categories by focusing on each of Perseus' character traits and citing details from his life that relate to each trait.

Revising Reread your draft. Have you used the most appealing material from Perseus' story? Have you used too many pieces of information—should your speech be shorter? Have you left out anything that could win over the audience?

Guide for Reading

More About the Author

In addition to his interest in poetry, **Yusef Komunyakaa** is a jazz aficionado. He has co-edited two volumes of *The Jazz Poetry Anthology*.

Lillian Morrison has written many poems about athletics. She has said, "I love rhythms, the body movement implicit in poetry, explicit in sports. . . ." In addition to writing poetry, Morrison collects folk rhymes. She has edited several volumes of oral verse.

Naomi Shihab Nye has twice traveled abroad as a participant in the Arts America Program. During her stay in Jerusalem, where her family moved to be near their Arab relatives, Nye came to appreciate the "intricate interweaving of cultures and prayers and songs and holidays."

Yusef Komunyakaa *(1947–)*

He won the 1994 Pulitzer Prize for poetry for his book *Neon Vernacular: New and Selected Poems*. He grew up in Bogalusa, Louisiana, and earned the Bronze Star in Vietnam, serving as reporter and editor of the military newspaper *The Southern Cross*. One of his eight books of poetry is entitled *Dien Cai Dau*, which is Vietnamese for "crazy." He now teaches at Indiana University.

These are facts about the life of Yusef Komunyakaa (yōō′ sef kō mən ya′ kä). What you really need to know about him to understand his poem "Slam, Dunk, & Hook" is that he likes "connecting the abstract to the concrete. There's tension in that. I believe the reader or listener should be able to enter the poem as a participant." That's what Komunyakaa does in "Slam, Dunk, & Hook," which is about basketball, but also about life on city streets.

Lillian Morrison *(1917–)*

Lillian Morrison has worked as a librarian and has written and compiled many books. She has published seven books of her own poetry, including *Whistling the Morning In*. She has put together several anthologies of poems about sports (including one revolving around basketball and entitled, coincidentally, *Slam Dunk*), along with collections of riddles, playground chants, and autograph sayings.

Naomi Shihab Nye *(1952–)*

Naomi Shihab Nye spent her teenage years in Jerusalem and has since worked as a visiting writer at several institutions, including the University of Texas. Her books of poems have received such awards as the Pushcart Prize and recognition by the American Library Association. She says, "For me poetry has always been a way of paying attention to the world. . . ."

◆ Build Vocabulary

SPECIALIZED VOCABULARY: JARGON

"Slam, Dunk, & Hook" and "The Spearthrower" use **jargon**, special vocabulary used in a particular occupation, sport, or other well-defined activity. For instance, the term *feint* in "Slam, Dunk, & Hook" refers to a pretended move meant to take an opponent off guard. The term is much older than basketball, for it originally came from swordplay. Look for other examples of sports jargon as you read these two poems.

WORD BANK

Before you read, preview this list of words from the poems.

metaphysical
jibed
feint
surge

◆ Build Grammar Skills

PREPOSITIONAL PHRASES
Prepositional phrases are groups of words beginning with prepositions and ending with nouns or pronouns. The introductory preposition is a word like *on, between,* or *from* that shows relationships; the noun or pronoun in the phrase is called the object of the preposition. In this example from "Slam, Dunk, & Hook," *on* is the preposition and *sneakers* is the object of the preposition:

> Fast breaks. Lay ups. With Mercury's
> Insignia *on our sneakers,*

Prepositional phrases act either as adjectives to describe nouns and pronouns or as adverbs to describe verbs, adjectives, and other adverbs.

Slam, Dunk, & Hook
The Spearthrower ◆ Shoulders

◆ *Literature and Your Life*

CONNECT YOUR EXPERIENCE

These poems are about the exhilaration of pure physical action trained on an important goal. As you read, experience the sensations described and imagine what it means to spend every ounce of your strength for something you want with all your heart.

THEMATIC FOCUS: PUTTING OURSELVES TO THE TEST

These poems show people meeting physical challenges in sports contests and in everyday life. Do you excel when you're striving for a definite goal—and therefore risking failure—or do you perform better when the pressure is off?

Journal Writing Write three sentences describing your impressions of an athletic contest you saw recently. Try to make your readers see what you saw and hear what you heard.

◆ Background for Understanding

SPORTS

The title "The Spearthrower" refers not to the athlete who actually hurls the javelin but rather to the poet who sends her "signed song" of praise for women athletes into the "bullying dark" of athletic events formerly dominated by men. In associating the poet with the athlete, Morrison follows a tradition from ancient Greece, where poets sang songs honoring Olympic athletics.

The title "Slam, Dunk, & Hook" refers to various moves made by basketball players. A *slam-dunk* is a powerful leap in which a player's hands rise above the basket and push the ball through. A *hook shot* is a curving toss from under and to the side of the basket.

◆ Literary Focus

THEME IN POETRY

The surface of each of these poems vividly describes physical action, but underneath that surface is a **theme,** an idea about life that sits at the center of the poem. If the lines, images, and rhythms in the poem are its body, then the theme is its heart, its driving force.

In poetry, as in other literature, theme can be hinted at sideways or stated directly. In "The Spearthrower" and "Shoulders," the themes are stated directly. On the other hand, in "Slam, Dunk, & Hook," the theme is implied; there seems to be much more than a game at stake.

◆ Reading Strategy

FORM MENTAL IMAGES

A poet writes words that makes your mind's eye see pictures. **Forming mental images** of a poem means turning the poet's words into pictures by applying your own experiences.

For example, when you see Komunyakaa's basketball players "poised in midair" like "storybook sea monsters," will you picture fearsome dragons with great wings or just long necks and sleepy eyes lifting out of the ocean?

When you read "Shoulders," how might you picture someone "stepping gently"? In light, tiptoeing steps or in heavy, slow steps?

When you form mental images as you read a poem, what you see will be based on your own experiences and imaginings—your life, your reading, your viewing, your dreams. In this way you collaborate with the poet; you find your way into the poem's world, and the poem finds its way into yours.

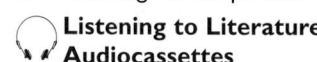
Guide for Reading ◆ 197

**Interest Grabber** Write the words "Poetry" and "Sports" on the chalkboard. Ask students what the two have in common. Most likely, your students will respond that sports and poetry have little in common. Next, have students brainstorm to come up with images describing exciting moments from sporting events. List all of the images on the board under the word "Sports." When you've finished, point out that all of these images could serve as the starting points for poems. Finally, tell students that the poems they're about to read capture the excitement of sports through vivid images like the ones they've just listed.

Customize for
Less Proficient Readers
To help these students appreciate the poems and picture the images the poems include, have them follow along in their book as they listen to the recordings of the poems.

🎧 **Listening to Literature Audiocassettes**

Customize for
More Advanced Students
Guide students to be on the lookout for the fresh images, interesting phrases, and unusual juxtapositions of words the poets use. Have them list examples in their journal.

Customize for
English Language Learners
These students may be unfamiliar with the sports jargon in the first two poems—such as "fast breaks," "lay ups," "dunk," "drive to the inside," "laps," "clear the highest bar." Pair English language students with native speakers who know the terms and expressions and can explain them.

📀 **Looking at Literature Videodisc** To provide background and insight into the author of "Shoulders," play Chapter 4 of the videodisc. In this interview with the writer, Naomi Shihab Nye describes why she writes and where she finds ideas for writing. Discuss how Nye's comments enrich the meaning of the poem. In particular, discuss how "Shoulders" fits Nye's criteria of "making connections" in her writing.

Chapter 4

Preparing for Standardized Tests

Vocabulary Students may sometimes encounter jargon in reading passages on standardized tests. For example, a test may include a section from a science essay that includes a number of specialized terms. Point out to students that although they may be unfamiliar with such terms, they can usually determine their meaning from the context in which they are used, or by breaking down the unfamiliar words into parts. Help students practice using context clues and/or word parts to determine the meaning of jargon by writing the following passage on the board:

> The doctor was relieved when the *echocardiogram* revealed nothing abnormal about the patient's heart.

Point out that the context makes it clear that an *echocardiogram* is a device used to test for abnormalities in the heart. The way in which the device works and its purpose are also evident in the structure of the word: *echo* indicates that the device uses sound waves; and *cardio* indicates that it relates to the heart.

Yusef Komunyakaa's poem focuses on the empowering nature of basketball. The poem describes the sport's physical action—fast breaks, corkscrewing, dunking balls—and leads into an example of how the sport provided a vehicle for an athlete to purge his grief and anger over the death of his mother.

Customize for
English Language Learners
These students may need help to interpret the meaning of some of the compound words the poet uses, such as *footwork, storybook, roundhouse,* and *backboard.* Invite classmates to explain the meanings of these words.

Customize for
Bodily/Kinesthetic Learners
Have these students act out the physical movements described by the poets—dribbling, fast breaking, feinting, corkscrewing, and so on. They can also demonstrate how the man in "Shoulders" carries his son across the street.

◆ **Reading Strategy**

❶ **Form Mental Images** Guide students to notice how the poet uses onomatopoeia and alliteration to help readers form mental images, such as in the line *Swish of strings like silk,* which describes the successful result of a 10-foot shot that hit nothing but net.

Slam, Dunk, & Hook

Yusef Komunyakaa

Fast breaks. Lay ups. With Mercury's[1]
Insignia[2] on our sneakers,
We outmaneuvered the footwork
❶ Of bad angels. Nothing but a hot
5 Swish of strings like silk
Ten feet out. In the roundhouse[3]
Labyrinth[4] our bodies
Created, we could almost
Last forever, poised in midair
10 Like storybook sea monsters.
A high note hung there
A long second. Off
The rim. We'd corkscrew
Up & dunk balls that exploded
15 The skullcap of hope & good
Intention. Bug-eyed, lanky,
All hands & feet . . . sprung rhythm.
We were metaphysical when girls
Cheered on the sidelines.
20 Tangled up in a falling,
Muscles were a bright motor
Double-flashing to the metal hoop
Nailed to our oak.
When Sonny Boy's mama died

---

1. **Mercury's:** Mercury was the Roman god of travel.
2. **insignia** (in sig´ nē ə) *n.:* Emblems or badges; logos.
3. **roundhouse** *n.:* Area on the court beneath the basket.
4. **labyrinth** (lab´ ə rinth) *n.:* Maze.

Block Scheduling Strategies

Consider these suggestions to take advantage of extended class time:

• Play the audiocassette recording of all or part of the poems. Have students discuss how the readings bring the poems to life.

• Have students work in discussion groups to answer the Build Vocabulary and Build Grammar Skills questions (p. 202).

• Interested students may practice reading the poems aloud, rehearse by presenting them to small groups, and then present the oral (or choral) readings to the class.

• Have students complete the Writing Mini-Lesson (p. 203). Before students get started have a class discussion on the characteristics and goals of sports editorials. Invite a few students to read aloud one sports editorial that they like from a newspaper or a sports magazine. Have students identify and discuss the techniques the writers use.

❷ **Theme in Poetry** Focus students' attention on these lines. Ask them to tell what the poet implies about what basketball can offer in addition to wins and losses. Invite them to share personal experiences with the healing powers of sports. *Students may say that athletics has the capability of helping people cope with grief and other of life's challenges.*

♦ **Literary Focus**

❸ **Theme in Poetry** Guide students to notice how the repetition of the first line of the poem triggers a restatement of the theme. Elicit from students how the last six lines allude to the power of basketball to elevate participants to do more than win or lose a game.

▶**Critical Viewing**◀

❹ **Connect** The art illustrates a drive to inside moving toward a shot that could become a slam dunk. The image perfectly captures the poem's phrase "...we could almost/Last forever, poised in midair/Like storybook sea monsters."

25 He played nonstop all day, so hard
Our backboard splintered.
Glistening with sweat, we jibed
& rolled the ball off our
❷ Fingertips. Trouble
30 Was there slapping a blackjack
Against an open palm.
Dribble, drive to the inside, feint,
& glide like a sparrow hawk.
Lay ups. Fast breaks.
35 We had moves we didn't know
We had. Our bodies spun
❸ On swivels of bone & faith,
Through a lyric slipknot
Of joy, & we knew we were
40 Beautiful & dangerous.

Night Games, Ernie Barnes, The Company of Art, Los Angeles

♦ **Build Vocabulary**

metaphysical (met′ ə fiz′ i kəl) *adj.*: Spiritual; beyond the physical

jibed (jībd) *v.*: Stopped short and turned from side to side

feint (fānt) *v.*: Pretended move to catch the opponent off guard

❹ ▲ Critical Viewing Relate details in this painting to lines in the poem "Slam, Dunk, & Hook." [Connect]

Slam, Dunk, & Hook ♦ 199

Humanities: Art

Night Game, by Ernie Barnes.
Ernie Barnes studied art history and painting before becoming a professional football player. When his athletic career ended and he became an artist, he "put all the violence and power [he] had felt on the field into [his] paintings."

This painting shows a pick-up basketball game at night in an old-fashioned outdoor neighborhood court. Guide students to notice the orange basketball that appears as if a moon in a tempestuous sky, and point out its orange glow upon the players' arms and legs.

Use these questions for discussion:
1. In addition to the nighttime setting, what else do you notice about the setting? *It takes place in a run-down, makeshift court in an inner city. Since three players are shoeless, the court's surface may be dirt or grass.*
2. How would you describe the appearance of the players and the nature of their game? *The elongated, ghostly appearance of the upward-reaching players, their disregard for typical sports clothing and gear, and their complete focus makes it seem as if their play transcends a mere game.*

One-Minute Insight

Like "Slam, Dunk, & Hook," this poem is about athletics. It describes the grace and beauty of the physical action of women's track and field events. The poem captures how women athletes overcome great obstacles to perform amazing feats of prowess and in doing so serve as an inspiration to fans.

◆ Literary Focus

❶ Theme in Poetry Guide students to see how the language the poet uses has the feel of a wish, even a prayer. Refer to the several lines that begin "that the . . ." and include an athletic achievement.

▶ Critical Viewing◀

❷ Infer She may be thinking about throwing the javelin farther than any spear has yet been thrown.

Customize for
More Advanced Students

Ask students why they think the poet uniformly uses lines that are short and simple. Ask them to tell whom they think the last line addresses. *Students can point to the urgency of her message; they can say that the last line is a directive for all women athletes and all those who agree with her that women's sports needs support.*

◆ Literature and Your Life

Invite students to share stories about real-life groundbreakers, in sports or in other fields, whom they know personally or whom they've read about or have seen in the movies or on television. Discuss what characteristics and personality traits these people have in common.

The Spearthrower

Lillian Morrison

She walks alone
to the edge of the park
and throws into
the bullying dark
5 her javelin
of light,
her singing sign
her signed song
❶ that the runner may run
10 far and long

her quick laps
on the curving track,
that the sprinter surge
and the hurdler leap,
15 that the vaulter soar,
clear the highest bar,
and the discus fly
as the great crowds cry
to their heroines
20 Come on!   ❶

◆ Build Vocabulary
surge (sɜrj) *v.*: Increase suddenly; speed up

◀ **Critical Viewing** Based on the young woman's expression, what might her feelings be at this moment? [Infer]   ❷

200 ◆ Challenges and Choices

◆ Speaking and Listening Mini-Lesson

Sportscast
This mini-lesson supports the Speaking and Listening activity in the Idea Bank on page 203.

Introduce the Concept Have students form groups based on the sporting event about which they wish to do a sportscast. Ask them to discuss features and characteristics of effective sportscasting and to note pitfalls to avoid. Guide groups to agree on a suitable setting for their event and how to share the tasks.

Develop Background Before students prepare their sportscasts, have them discuss the rules and components of their sport, elements to highlight, and any background their target audience may need or want. Have them talk about when in the event to provide play-by-play, when to be quiet, and when to provide background information, explanations of what's happening or what's to come, analysis, or summary.

Apply the Information Have groups present their sportscasts. Encourage them to prepare handouts for classmates that briefly identify the nature of the events they'll be covering.

Assess the Outcome Have students evaluate their own and other presentations for clarity, accuracy, thoroughness, emphasis, excitement, and entertainment.

Shoulders

Naomi Shihab Nye

A man crosses the street in rain,
stepping gently, looking two times north
   and south,
because his son is asleep on his shoulder.

5   No car must splash him.
   No car drive too near to his shadow.

❸ This man carries the world's most sensitive
      cargo
   but he's not marked.
   Nowhere does his jacket say FRAGILE,
   HANDLE WITH CARE.

10   His ear fills up with breathing.
❹   He hears the hum of the boy's dream
   deep inside him.

   We're not going to be able
   to live in the world
15   if we're not willing to do what he's doing
❺   with one another.

   The road will only be wide.
   The rain will never stop falling.

Guide for Responding

◆ Literature and Your Life

Reader's Response Which images in these poems were clearest to you? Why?

Thematic Focus Do the subjects of these poems succeed in meeting their challenges? Explain.

☑ Check Your Comprehension

1. In "Slam, Dunk, & Hook," what did the players outmaneuver, according to lines 3–4?
2. What did Sonny Boy do when his mother died?
3. In "The Spearthrower," what specific athletic events are mentioned?
4. What do the great crowds cry, and to whom?
5. In "Shoulders," where are the father and child?
6. What does the father take care to prevent?

◆ Critical Thinking

INTERPRET

1. In "Slam, Dunk, & Hook," what does playing basketball help the neighborhood boys to do? **[Infer]**
2. Why might the basketball players be both "beautiful" and "dangerous"? **[Explain]**
3. In "The Spearthrower," what "signed song" does the poet throw? **[Explain]**
4. In "Shoulders," what is the double meaning of the poem's title? (Hint: Think of where the father is walking.) **[Interpret]**

EVALUATE

5. How well does Yusef Komunyakaa capture the actual feel of a basketball game? **[Assess]**

EXTEND

6. What sort of music would you choose to accompany each of these poems? **[Music Link]**

Beyond the Selection

FURTHER READING

Other Works by the Authors
Magic City, Yusef Komunyakaa
The Sidewalk Racer, Lillian Morrison
Hugging the Jukebox, Naomi Shihab Nye

Other Works With the Theme of Putting Ourselves to the Test
"Susan Butcher," Bill Littlefield
"John Henry," Traditional
"Charge of the Light Brigade," Alfred, Lord Tennyson

INTERNET

You and your students may find additional information about the poets on the Internet. We suggest the following sites. Please be aware, however, that sites may have changed from the time we published this information.

For quotations and poems by Naomi Shihab Nye go to **http://vac.tamu.edu/~xo75bb/naomi/**

For information about Yousef Komunyakaa, go to **http://www.indiana.edu/~mfawrite/komunyak.htm/**

We *strongly recommend* that you preview the sites before you send students to them.

Develop Understanding

One-Minute Insight This poem, by Naomi Shihab Nye, describes a scene in which a man, carrying a sleeping child on his shoulder, carefully crosses a street in the rain. The poet urges us to treat what is important and one another with the same care with which the man carries his "sensitive cargo."

◆ Literary Focus

❸ **Theme in Poetry** Ask students to tell what the poet is referring to in her description of "the world's most sensitive cargo." *On one level, the "cargo" is the helpless child; on another level, it refers to all people and to any object, idea, or principle one holds dear.*

◆ Reading Strategy

❹ **Form Mental Images** Have students use the poet's description to picture how the man is holding the child. *The child's head is nuzzled in the man's neck, his mouth by the man's ear.*

◆ Critical Thinking

❺ **Analyze** Ask students to reread the final six lines, which state the poet's theme. Have them paraphrase their meaning. *Students' responses should include the idea that despite ever-present difficult circumstances, we should treat one another with care and sensitivity.*

Reinforce and Extend

Answers

◆ Literature and Your Life

Reader's Response Some students will choose the images of the athletes in the first two poems if they are familiar with the sport or event; other students might more easily picture the man and child in "Shoulders."

Thematic Focus The basketball players succeed; the outcomes for the women athletes and the man in the street are left unresolved.

(Answers continue on page 202.)

201

Answers (continued)

☑ Check Your Comprehension

1. They outmaneuver "the footwork of bad angels."
2. He played basketball nonstop until he splintered the backboard.
3. Events include running long races; sprinting (shorter races); hurdles; pole vaulting; discus throwing.
4. They shout "Come on" to the athletes.
5. They are on a busy street in the rain; the child is on the father's shoulders.
6. He prevents a car from overlapping even his son's shadow.

◆ Critical Thinking

1. It helps them sometimes to stay out of trouble; it gives them success and a reason to go on.
2. Their grace and speed make them beautiful; their power and single-minded fierceness make them dangerous.
3. The poet "throws" her poem.
4. There are the father's sheltering shoulders and the dangerous shoulders of the highway.
5. Most students will say that the "feel" of the basketball game is effectively captured in images such as the "hot swish" shots, dunked balls, and glistening bodies.
6. Students' choices should reflect the different moods of each poem.

◆ Reading Strategy

1. Some students may mention Sonny Boy's splintering the backboard; others might cite the sea monsters.
2. She creates the image of a solitary figure surrounded by darkness with one shaft of light spearing the darkness.
3. Answers should take note of the width of the road and the rain.

◆ Build Vocabulary

1. (a) Dribble—to move while bouncing the ball; drive to the inside—passing down the basketball court to just below the basket; fast breaks—rapid shifts and turns. (b) that of a fast-moving, exciting, changeable game
2. Terms include javelin, laps, springer, hurdler, vaulter, discus.

Using the Word Bank
feint, jibed, metaphysical, surge

Guide for Responding (continued)

◆ Reading Strategy

FORM MENTAL IMAGES

Now that your mind has provided pictures to match the poets' words, you may find the poems sticking with you in a new way. In "Slam, Dunk, & Hook," for example, you may have pictured a worn, yellow backboard breaking in half from the intense pounding of a boy who had just lost his mother.

1. Which image in "Slam, Dunk, & Hook" creates the most vivid picture in your mind?
2. What picture does the poet create of herself in the opening lines of "The Spearthrower"?
3. The final image of "Shoulders" is a road. Describe what you see in your own words.

◆ Build Vocabulary

USING SPORTS JARGON

Jargon is special vocabulary used in the context of an occupation, sport, or other well-defined activity. Writing that uses too much jargon can be almost impossible to understand. However, when used well—in a limited way and for a clear purpose—certain kinds of jargon can add a contemporary liveliness to writing.

1. (a) What do the following terms mean: "Dribble," "drive to the inside," "Fast breaks"? (b) What impression of basketball do these words create?
2. Find five terms specific to track-and-field competition in "The Spearthrower."

USING THE WORD BANK

On your paper, rewrite the following paragraph and fill in the blanks with words from the Word Bank.

As we sat in the bleachers, we saw the center _____?_____ left, then pass the ball to the right, confusing the player guarding her. The player who caught the ball then _____?_____, looking for a teammate closer to the basket. The moment was almost _____?_____, as she found an opening that allowed her to _____?_____ past the guard and make her shot. Two points!

◆ Literary Focus

THEME IN POETRY

A poem uses sensory images, figurative language, sound devices, even its title, to communicate a **theme,** or central idea about life. Sometimes the theme in a poem is a familiar insight; at other times, it's a new idea. At still other times, the theme is more a feeling brought to the reader's attention.

1. The speaker in "Slam, Dunk, & Hook" says "We outmaneuvered the footwork/Of bad angels." What does that line suggest about the role of basketball in the street life of the neighborhood kids?
2. How does the "spearthrower" (that is, the poet who sings of women athletes) enable the runner to run and the discus to fly?
3. What idea about life is Nye expressing when she talks about the road always being wide and the rain always falling?

◆ Build Grammar Skills

PREPOSITIONAL PHRASES

All three poets use prepositional phrases to add details and complexity to descriptions.

Practice Use two or more prepositional phrases to add details to each of the following sentences:

> **Prepositional phrases** are groups of words beginning with a preposition and ending with a noun or pronoun.

1. André shot the basketball.
2. The ball rose and then hit the backboard.
3. Mala heard the starting gun and surged forward.
4. She crossed the finish line.
5. Her speed impressed her opponents.
6. The mother carried her child.
7. She walked slowly.
8. People moved to let her pass.

◆ Literary Focus

1. It suggests that playing basketball may keep some kids out of serious trouble.
2. She write poems in praise of the athletes, and by making their worthiness more public she is securing their place in American culture, thus making more events for women more likely.
3. She is expressing the idea that life is dangerous and unpredictable and larger than any individual.

◆ Build Grammar Skills

Sample answers:

1. With his heart in his mouth, André shot the basketball high into the air.
2. The ball rose over their heads toward the ceiling and then hit the backboard with a thunk.
3. In her starting blocks, Mala heard the starting gun and surged forward like a greyhound.
4. With her arms high in the air, she crossed the finish line of the marathon.
5. Her speed in the sprint impressed her opponents at the track meet.
6. The mother of twins carried her sick child to the doctor's office.

(Answers continue on page 203.)

Build Your Portfolio

Idea Bank

Writing

1. **Poem** Write a poem about your favorite individual or team sport. Your poem should create a vivid picture of the sport, particularly the way the players move. **[Physical Education Link]**

2. **Description** Take the three sentences you wrote in your journal describing a sports event and turn them into two paragraphs describing that event more fully.

3. **Story** Write a short story explaining how the father in "Shoulders" ended up walking along the busy highway in the rain carrying his sleeping child. Write from the father's point of view.

Speaking and Listening

4. **Oral Interpretation** With several other students perform an oral reading of "Slam, Dunk, & Hook." Plan who will read which section or line of the poem. If possible, memorize the poem and include actions. **[Performing Arts Link]**

5. **Sportscast** Choose one of the track-and-field events in "The Spearthrower" and do a sportscast describing the contest from start to finish. **[Performing Arts Link; Career Link]**

Projects

6. **Painting/Drawing** In your favorite visual medium, recreate the scene described in "Shoulders." Try to make your work convey a strong feeling. **[Art Link]**

7. **Multimedia Presentation** Give a multimedia presentation focusing on some aspect of women's athletic competitions: for example, a biography of one outstanding athlete or an exciting current topic. Include photographs and/or drawings, recordings, and videotapes if feasible.

Writing Mini-Lesson

Sports Editorial

Write an editorial—a brief piece of writing that presents one side of an issue on a sports-related topic. For example, you might focus on a question such as: Do you think women's sports should get more media coverage? Would you like to see your city build a new sports arena?

> #### Writing Skills Focus: Anticipation of Questions
>
> To make sure your editorial persuades as many readers as possible, try to **anticipate questions** from readers who might disagree with you. Take a hard look at your opinion, and imagine how opponents might question it. Then, answer these questions as well as you can. For example, in writing an editorial arguing for increased funding of the school district's sports programs, you might anticipate such questions as: "Why should sports programs be funded when arts programs are cut back?" An answer might be: "Neither should be cut back. The district should propose a bond issue to raise money for its needs."

Prewriting Choose a sports-related issue and take a position. Then jot down questions and opposing viewpoints.

Drafting Write your editorial by stating the issue clearly and expressing your opinion reasonably. (Often, an editorial writer refers to himself or herself as "this writer.") Work in the questions you anticipated—and your answers.

Revising Show your editorial to several people. Try to find at least one reader who disagrees with you. Ask if your opinion sounds fair and if you have answered all objections effectively. If you hear a point that you should have raised, add it to your editorial.

Slam, Dunk, & Hook/The Spearthrower/Shoulders ◆ 203

✓ **ASSESSMENT OPTIONS**

Formal Assessment, Selection Test, pp. 44–46, and Assessment Resources Software. The selection test is designed so that it can be easily customized to the performance levels of your students.
Alternative Assessment, p. 14, includes options for less advanced students, more advanced students, musical/rhythmic learners, verbal/linguistic learners, and visual/spatial learners.

PORTFOLIO ASSESSMENT
Use the following rubrics in the *Alternative Assessment* booklet to assess student writing:
Poem: Poetry Rubrick, p. 101
Description: Description Rubric, p. 90
Story: Narrative Rubric, p. 88
Writing Mini-Lesson: Persuasion Rubric, p. 98

Answers *(continued)*

7. She walked slowly home in the rain with her dog.
8. People moved to the side of the walk to let her pass.

 Writer's Solution

For additional instruction and practice, use the practice page on prepositional phrases (p. 41) in the *Writer's Solution Grammar Practice Book.*

 Idea Bank
Customizing for
Performance Levels
Following are suggestions for matching the Idea Bank topics with your students' performance levels:
    Less Advanced Students: 1, 4, 7
    Average Students: 2, 4, 6
    More Advanced Students: 3, 5

Customizing for
Learning Modalities
Following are suggestions for matching Idea Bank topics with your students' learning modalities:
    Visual/Spatial: 1, 6, 7
    Auditory: 4, 5
    Verbal/Linguistic: 2, 3

 Writing Mini-Lesson
Refer students to the Writing Handbook, page 962, for instruction on the writing process, and page 965 for further information on Persuasion.

 Writer's Solution

Writing Lab CD-ROM
Have students complete the Tutorial on Persuasion. Follow these steps:
1. Have students complete an Audience Profile.
2. Have students draft on computer.
3. Use the Vague Adjectives Checker to aid revision.
Allow approximately 60 minutes of class time to complete these activities.

Sourcebook
Have students use Chapter 4, Persuasion (pp. 96–127), for additional support.

Establish Writing Guidelines

Review the following key characteristics of a persuasive essay:

- A persuasive essay is a piece of writing that aims to convince an audience to take action or accept a position.
- A persuasive essay logically presents compelling evidence for its position.

You may want to distribute the scoring rubric for Persuasion (p. 98 in **Alternative Assessment**) to make students aware of the criteria on which their work will be evaluated. For suggestions on how you can customize the rubric, see page 206.

Refer students to the Writing Handbook, page 962, for instruction on the writing process, and page 965 for further information on persuasive writing.

 Writer's Solution

Writers at Work Videodisc

To introduce students to key elements and to show them how the NBA's Larry Weitzman uses persuasive writing, play the videodisc segment on Persuasion (Ch. 4). Ask students what the different types of writing required by Weitzman's job have in common and which elements of each they might use in their persuasive essays.

Play frames 33836 to 42938

Writing Lab CD-ROM

If your students have access to computers, they may work on the Tutorial on Persuasion to complete their persuasive essays. Have students follow these steps:

1. Review the interactive model of a persuasive essay.
2. Use the interactive instruction on detecting bias in sources while they are gathering evidence.
3. Draft on the computer.
4. Use the interactive instruction on avoiding faulty logic and unreasonable appeals.
5. Use the Self-Evaluation Checklist to help them make revisions.

Sourcebook

Students can find additional support in the chapter on Persuasion (pp. 96–127). Included is extensive instruction on avoiding faulty logic and unreasonable appeals.

Persuasive Essay

Writing Process Workshop

As the literature in this section reveals, writing can challenge us to look at things in new ways. One type of writing that can change the way we think is the **persuasive essay**. A persuasive essay is a short piece of writing that attempts to convince an audience to think or act in a certain way.

Develop a persuasive essay in which you convince readers to accept your position on an issue about which you care. The following skills, introduced in this section's Writing Mini-Lessons, will help you develop your persuasive essay.

Writing Skills Focus

▶ **Make effective use of figurative language**—language that means more than it says literally. (See p. 173.)

▶ **Appeal to your audience** by stirring their emotions, making them laugh, making them think, or keeping them in suspense. (See p. 195.)

▶ **Anticipate readers' questions.** Think about questions or objections that people may have to your arguments and try to address them. (See p. 203.)

▶ **Use a persuasive tone** in your writing in order to make people want to read on and to convince them to accept your point of view. (See p. 183.)

Maya Angelou uses all these skills as she argues for an individual's right to make his or her own choices in life.

MODEL FROM LITERATURE

from "New Directions" by Maya Angelou

① Angelou effectively uses the figurative image of a road to mean life.

② Words like *ominous* and *unpromising* appeal to readers' emotions.

③ Angelou persuades readers to "step off that road."

④ Angelou answers a question readers may ask: What if our new choice is also bad?

Each of us has the right and the responsibility to assess the roads which lie ahead, and those over which we have traveled, ① and if the future road looms ominous or unpromising, and the roads back uninviting, ② then we need to gather our resolve and, carrying only the necessary baggage, step off that road into another direction. ③ If the new choice is also unpalatable, without embarrassment, we must be ready to change that as well. ④

204 ◆ Challenges and Choices

 Workplace Skills Mini-Lesson

Proposals

Essayists are not the only people who benefit professionally from their persuasive writing skills. Tell students that in order to excel at many jobs, they may be required to write formal proposals or memos persuading their colleagues or supervisors to take a particular course of action. Ask students to suggest why companies might prefer to have proposals for new projects or policies in writing as opposed to having ideas discussed in meetings or similar forums. How might such pro-

posals differ from other kinds of persuasive essays with which students are familiar?

Suggested answers include: companies might prefer written proposals because they are easy to distribute; it is clear who the author of an idea is and not open to dispute later; it's easy to check on the validity and reliability of the evidence presented when it is documented. Such proposals might differ from other persuasive essays in that the writer knows the intended audience quite well and may be able to leave out certain types of background information.

Prewriting

Choose a Topic Think of issues that are important to you. If nothing springs to mind, you may want to browse through magazines and newspapers to help spark ideas. Another option is to choose one of the following topics.

> ### Topic Ideas
> - Students should wear school uniforms.
> - The country needs a female president.
> - Paying taxes should be voluntary.
> - Colleges should accept all applicants.

Anticipate Readers' Questions Once you've chosen your topic, decide on the position that you will present in your essay. Then list potential objections and questions about that position. For example, if your essay presents an argument in favor of all schools having computers, you might list these questions:

Sample Questions
▶ Who will pay for the computers?
▶ What if classrooms aren't big enough?
▶ What if all teachers can't teach the use of computers?

Gather Strong Evidence Using the questions and objections you listed as a starting point, gather evidence—facts, statistics, and reasons—to support your argument. This may require research, either in the library or on the Internet.

Plan Your Use of Figurative Language List examples of figurative language you might use in your essay. For example, you may come up with objects and events to compare to aspects of your topic. Look over the ideas you come up with, and evaluate the effectiveness of each one. Check off the examples that work best.

Example:
A computer is
▶ a ticket to the train ride of success
▶ a key to opening future's door
▶ like air that we need to breathe

Drafting

Appeal to Your Audience As you write, always keep your readers in mind. Use formal, respectful language, and address each concern you think your readers may have.

APPLYING LANGUAGE SKILLS: Avoiding Double Comparisons

A **double comparison** occurs when *more* and *-er* or *most* and *-est* are used with the same modifier.

Incorrect:
Computers are <u>more better</u> than typewriters.

Correct:
Computers are <u>better</u> than typewriters.

Practice Rewrite each sentence to avoid a double comparison.
1. Schools are the most best places for computers.
2. Work can be done more faster on a computer.
3. Students who use computers are more better prepared for future careers

Writing Application As you draft your persuasive essay, avoid using double comparisons.

Writer's Solution Connection Language Lab

For additional instruction and practice in avoiding double comparisons, complete the Language Lab lesson on Forms of Comparisons.

Prewriting

Students are asked to anticipate reader's questions as they plan their persuasive essays. Point out that different audiences will typically have different types of questions they feel need to be answered. As a starting point, use the student text's example regarding a school's need for computers. Discuss how an essay with that argument might be tailored for a PTA group, fellow students, or for a school's administration. Encourage students to identify the audience for their essays with the same precision.

Customize for *Verbal/Linguistic Learners*
To help these students extend their use of figurative language, have them evaluate and categorize the types of figurative language on their lists of ideas. Similes compare two things by using the words "like" or "as" whereas metaphors omit these words and make the comparison more directly. Personification compares a thing to the qualities or attributes of a person. Verbal/linguistic learners can determine whether their lists of phrases achieve an appropriate balance between these different types, not favoring one too heavily over the others.

 Writer's Solution

Writing Lab CD-ROM
Have students complete the Audience Profile and the Purpose Profile activities, both of which can be found in the Prewriting section of the Tutorial. Students answer questions to help them focus their persuasive essays before they prepare the draft. Then, students can refer to these profiles at any point during the drafting process if they are concerned about wandering off track.

Applying Language Skills
Avoiding Double Comparisons Explain to students that the temptation to overstate their case when writing their persuasive essays might cause them unwittingly to commit the error of using double comparisons.

Answers
Suggested responses:
1. Schools are the best place for computers.
2. Work can be done faster on a computer.
3. Students who use computers are better prepared for future careers.

 Writer's Solution

Use the **Language Lab CD-ROM** lesson, Double and Illogical Forms of Comparison.

Applying Language Skills
Avoiding Faulty Logic Explain to students that if readers notice in a persuasive essay even one instance of faulty logic it can undermine the credibility of the entire text.

Answers
1. This item contains overgeneralization. While using computers can *help* lead *some* people to success, this does not automati-

cally imply that the reverse is true.
2. The inclusion of the word "everyone" creates an overgeneralization.
3. The word "make" is a red flag for faulty cause-and-effect reasoning. There is no causal relationship between computers and native intelligence.

 Writer's Solution

For additional practice, complete the practice exercises in the Critical Thinking Skills section of the *Writer's Solution Grammar Practice Book*, p. 165.

Drafting

As they draft their persuasive essays, students may find that they have omitted specific evidence that would strengthen their claims. Without interrupting the drafting process, students can note areas for research "follow-up" that they can conduct while revising their essays.

Revising

You may want to have students work with peer reviewers to revise their persuasive essays. Reviewers should use the revision checklist to guide their review. Reviewers should not simply debate the writer's position if they happen to disagree with it.

 Writer's Solution

Writing Lab CD-ROM

The Vague Adjectives Highlighter and the Interactive Self-Evaluation Checklist in the Revision section of the Tutorial on Persuasion can help in the revision stage of students' drafts.

Publishing

To supplement the publishing ideas in the student edition, students may consider sending their essays to a specifically targeted audience of decision-makers or fellow activists.

Reinforce and Extend

Review the Writing Guidelines
After students have completed their writing, review the characteristics of a persuasive essay. Encourage students to come up with additional criteria.

Connect to Literature Unit 5 ("Visions of the Future") includes an example of a persuasive essay: Bryan Wooley's "To the Residents of A.D. 2029" (p. 434).

APPLYING LANGUAGE SKILLS: Avoiding Faulty Logic

Never use poor reasoning in your arguments. For example, avoid making overgeneralizations—broad statements for which there are exceptions—and presenting questionable cause-and-effect sequences when one event is not clearly caused by another.

Practice Explain why each item is or is not an example of faulty logic.

1. People who don't have computers become failures for life.
2. In a few years, everyone will have a computer.
3. Computers make you smart.

Writing Application Review the arguments in your persuasive essay. Remove any faulty logic you find.

Writer's Solution Connection Writing Lab

To help you complete all stages of writing your persuasive essay, use the instruction and activities in the Tutorial on Persuasion.

Present Strong Support for Your Argument Use the evidence you've gathered to support each point you make. Your argument is only as strong as the support you offer.

Use a Persuasive Tone Carefully choose your words and phrases to make readers eager to agree with your views. When discussing computers, for example, you might mention the "lightning speed" and the "amazing accuracy" of the machines.

Revising

Hold a Peer Conference Share your draft with a classmate and get some feedback. Use the comments as guidelines for revising your essay. Ask your peer these questions:

▶ How effective is my figurative language?
▶ Have I anticipated all my readers' questions?
▶ How well have I appealed to my audience?
▶ How persuasive is the tone in my writing?

REVISION MODEL

① one of the keys to the future

Computers are very ~~important~~. They make it ②~~possible~~ for

②easy

people all over the globe to communicate with one another in

③ Not everyone has computer access today, but in just
a few years virtually everyone will.

an instant. People who haven't developed computer skills

④ If you're one of those people, I urge you to turn on a

will fall behind. computer and start developing your skills.

① The writer adds a figure of speech (figurative language) to capture the importance of computers.
② A simple change of wording makes this sentence even more persuasive.
③ The writer adds a sentence to address a possible objection.
④ The writer directly addresses a segment of his audience.

Publishing

▶ **Classroom** Invite classmates to read your persuasive essay. Encourage them to share their opinions.
▶ **Newspaper** Send your essay to your school or local newspaper as a Letter to the Editor.
▶ **Internet** Post your essay on a bulletin board or class Web site. See what responses you receive.

✓ ASSESSMENT		4	3	2	1
PORTFOLIO ASSESSMENT Use the rubric on Persuasion in **Alternative Assessment** (p. 98) to assess students' writing. Add these criteria to customize the rubric to this assignment.	**Avoiding Faulty Logic**	The writer consistently uses sound reasoning in argumentation.	The writer occasionally uses logic that is questionable.	The writer noticeably employs such examples of faulty reasoning as circular arguments and overgeneralizations.	The writer consistently uses faulty logic throughout the piece.
	Figurative Language	The writer consistently uses figurative language in ways that are both appropriate and effective.	The writer includes figurative language that is occasionally effective.	The writer includes figurative language that at times impedes the sense and purpose of the essay.	The writer attempts to include figurative language that does not make sense, or avoids using figurative language.

Real-World Reading Skills Workshop

Challenge the Text

Strategies for Success

A famous humorist once said, "All I know is what I read in the papers." The person really meant that you shouldn't believe something simply because it's in print. You have to challenge the text and decide whether or not the writer's statements are reliable.

Separate Facts From Opinions

Whenever you read a statement, first decide whether it is a provable fact or just a personal opinion. You can check a fact with a reliable source such as an encyclopedia or textbook. A personal opinion, on the other hand, only reflects someone's likes and dislikes, which can't be proved right or wrong. However, in an effective piece of writing, the writer will back up his or her opinions with facts. When you come across a writer's opinions, check to see whether they're supported by facts.

Consider the Writer's Background

Another consideration to keep in mind when evaluating a writer's opinions is the writer's background or level of expertise on the subject he or she is addressing. Ask yourself: What education or experience does the writer have that is related to the topic? What does the author gain if I accept the opinion?

Look for Faulty Reasoning

Another thing to look out for is writing that lacks logic. For example, a writer might ask you to believe something simply because everyone else does. Or an author may jump to conclusions without offering enough evidence. Whenever you read a statement, ask yourself, Does this make sense to me?

BILLY NEDER FOR CLASS PRESIDENT!!

Why should you vote for Billy Neder?

- He's a capable person who really understands what students need!

- He's had experience as class president three years in a row.

- He's good at math. So he'd make a great school leader!

- His father is our town mayor. Mayor Neder says, "Billy is your best candidate."

Apply the Strategy

Read the poster carefully. Then complete each item below.

1. Find an example of a provable fact. How could you go about proving it?
2. Find an example of a personal opinion. Is it a statement that you would challenge? Why?
3. Find an example of an expert opinion. How reliable do you feel it is? Why?
4. Find an example of faulty reasoning. Why doesn't the statement make sense?

✔ Here are other situations in which challenging the text is important:
▶ Reading a newspaper editorial
▶ Reading a scientific report
▶ Reading a government proposal

Introduce the Strategy

Regardless of students' personal interests (sports, the arts, politics, or science), a perusal of a daily newspaper will show that coverage of that field is not limited to objective reporting but nearly always includes much opinionated commentary. Point out to students that developing strategies to challenge texts will benefit them in many ways, both in and outside of school.

Customize for
Logical/Mathematical Learners

Ask these students to pretend that they have been hired as political consultants to the "Billy Neder Campaign." Their first task is to revise the poster so that each statement's logic is unassailable—apparently Billy feels each of these points deserves to be mentioned. Have these students generate "evidence" that would support even the most faulty instances of reasoning such as "He's good at math, so he'd make a great school leader." They can report their findings and recommendations to the class after the text has been thoroughly challenged.

Apply the Strategy

Have students read the poster once before examining it critically. Ask: Is Billy Neder the sort of person they would vote for? Why or why not? You may want to take a quick poll to determine the strength of Billy's support in class before applying the text-challenging strategies. Afterward, conduct a second poll and assess the results. Point out the degree to which student opinions have changed, and ask whether a politician such as Billy would applaud the sort of reading skills they are learning.

Answers

1. The facts relating to Billy's tenure as class president and his father's as mayor should be matters of public record and thus easily proven by checking past school and local newspapers.

2. The sentence "He's a capable person who really understands what students need!" actually contains two personal opinions that the writer ties together, perhaps believing that doing so gives them the semblance of fact. Students may want to challenge one or both of these claims. What exactly is meant by the word "capable," and who are the students whose needs he understands?

3. The mayor's recommendation can be considered an expert opinion because he is a professional politician. However, because he is also Billy's father, students may question its reliability because of the inherent bias of the source.

4. The statement "He's good at math, so he'd make a great school leader" is clearly an example of faulty reasoning. The statement does not make sense because it assumes some kind of relationship between math proficiency and the "people skills" necessary for leadership.

207

Speaking and Listening Workshop

Resisting Persuasion

How easily can you be persuaded to do something? Some people can be persuaded without much effort. But as a responsible listener, you should resist easy persuasion. You should evaluate *what* is said, not *how* it is said.

Listen for Loaded Language Loaded language can play on your emotions and trigger a response in you. For example:

"Don't be a baby! All the really cool kids are trying out for the team."

Ignore Empty Promises Listen carefully to the way certain statements are worded. You may find that certain words and phrases can trick you into believing things that aren't really true. For example:

"These sneakers are like having a new pair of feet! They can make you a fast runner! They're something else!"

Tips for Resisting Persuasion

✔ *If you want to resist persuasion and make responsible decisions, follow this plan:*
- ▶ Ignore loaded words that trigger emotions.
- ▶ Be on the lookout for empty promises.
- ▶ Ask yourself, What is *really being said?*

Apply the Strategies

With a partner, role-play these situations. Work out a conversation that shows your attempts to resist persuasion.

1. A salesperson tries to persuade you to buy the most expensive sunglasses in the store. How does the salesperson use loaded words and make empty promises? What do you say to resist the persuasion?
2. A friend wants you to sign a petition supporting a cause with which you don't agree. What arguments does the friend give? What empty promises and loaded words are used? How do you answer?

208 ◆ Challenges and Choices

 Speaking and Listening Mini-Lesson

Career Connection
Consumer Affairs Advocacy At all levels of government as well as in the nonprofit, private sector, there are numerous consumer advocacy groups whose goal is to prevent fraudulent claims in advertising and marketing. In areas that range from consumer goods to health care related items, specialists are constantly reviewing flamboyant claims made in commercials or though mail order advertisements. Often the agencies that employ such advocates are instrumental in passing legislation that regulates the claims that can be made on a product's packaging.

Students who are able to analyze persuasive arguments and teach others appropriate strategies of resistance may consider future employment in such a field. Interested students can invite a consumer affairs advocate to speak before the class and perhaps add to the list of strategies presented here.

Extended Reading Opportunities

The challenges that life brings and the choices we make in meeting those challenges have been the basis for many works of literature. Following are a few possibilities through which you can further explore challenges and choices.

Suggested Titles

The Old Man and the Sea
Ernest Hemingway

This novel tells of a man's heroic struggle with nature. The battle begins when the old fisherman Santiago hooks a giant marlin after going months without a catch. The old man puts up a fierce effort to conquer the huge and powerful fish, fighting exhaustion, hunger, injury, and even a pack of sharks. This story, told in Hemingway's lean, straightforward style, is a timeless tale of courage and adventure.

The Miracle Worker
William Gibson

This moving play is based on the true story of Helen Keller, who was left blind, deaf, and unable to speak following an illness when she was an infant. The title refers to Helen's teacher, Annie Sullivan, a young woman determined to meet the challenge of helping Helen to communicate. This play, Gibson's most famous, inspired an Academy Award-winning movie.

Rosa Parks: My Story
Rosa Parks
with Jim Haskins

One of the pivotal moments of the American civil rights movement occurred on December 1, 1955, when Rosa Parks, an African American, chose not to give up her seat to a white rider on a bus in Montgomery, Alabama. Through this memoir, readers get a first-hand account of that dramatic event and its aftermath, as well as biographical information about one of the leaders of the civil rights movement.

Other Possibilities

Of Mice and Men	John Steinbeck
Lyddie	Katherine Paterson
Zlata's Diary: A Child's Life in Sarajevo	Zlata Filipovic
River Thunder	Will Hobbs

Planning Students' Extended Reading

All of the works listed on this page are good choices for extending the theme of Challenges and Choices. Following is some information that may help you choose which to teach.

Customize for
Varying Student Needs

When assigning the selections in this part to your students, keep in mind the following factors:

- *The Old Man and the Sea* is a classic work of one man's heroic struggle with nature. This book may present a challenge to some readers.

- *The Miracle Worker* presents the riviting true story of the relationship between deaf and blind Helen Keller and her teacher Annie Smith. The play does include some sensitive issues listed below.

- *Rosa Parks: My Story* is the account of one woman's courage in the civil rights movement. However, the autobiography does have sensitivity issues listed below.

Sensitive Issues *The Miracle Worker* deals frankly with blindness and deafness. If you have physically challenged students, you may want to assess those students' sensitivity to such a story before assigning the play to them. However, it may be that such students will feel optimistic after reading how Helen Keller overcame a dual disability to lead an exciting and full life.

Rosa Parks: My Story takes the reader back to the blossoming of the civil rights movement during the 1950's. You may wish to use caution in recommending this book to readers for whom racial discrimination is a personally sensitive issue. However, the book may be an excellent tool for discussing the civil rights movement and how society has changed since the 1950's.

Literature Study Guides

Literature study guides are available for all three suggested titles. These guides include section summaries, discussion questions, and activities.

Resources for Teaching Novels, Plays, and Literature Collections

In addition to graphic organizers, teaching strategies, and transparencies that will be invaluable in teaching any of these works, this booklet includes formal tests for *The Old Man and the Sea,* *The Miracle Worker,* and *Rosa Parks: My Story*

Planning Instruction and Assessment

Unit Objectives

1. To read selections in different genre that develop the theme of Moments of Discovery
2. To apply a variety of reading strategies, particularly literal comprehension strategies, appropriate for reading these selections
3. To recognize literary elements used in these selections
4. To increase vocabulary
5. To learn elements of grammar and usage
6. To write in a variety of modes and about situations based on the selections
7. To develop speaking and listening skills, by doing proposed activities

Meeting the Objectives

With each selection, you will find instructional material and portfolio opportunities through which students can meet these objectives. Further, you will find additional practice pages for reading strategies, literary elements, vocabulary, and grammar in the **Selection Support** booklet in the Teaching Resources box.

Setting Goals Work with your students at the beginning of the unit to set goals for unit outcomes. Plan what skills and concepts you wish students to acquire. You may individualize according to students' performance levels or learning modalities.

Portfolios You may have students keep portfolios of their work or of their work in progress. The activities and prompts on the Build Your Portfolio page of each selection provide opportunities for students to apply the concepts presented with the selection.

Thunderhead, 1933, Frederick Phillips, Atlas Galleries, Chicago, Illinois

Frederick Philips '93

UNIT 3

Moments of Discovery

Any insight can be a moment of discovery—children learning about nature, a woman musing on past generations, a man realizing that certain human qualities go beyond culture. Whether big or small, the moments of discovery in these selections teach people something about themselves, others, and the world around them.

◆ *211*

Assessing Student Progress

The following tools are available to measure the degree to which students meet the unit objectives:

Informal Assessment

The questions on the Guide for Responding sections are a first level of response to the concepts and skills presented with the selection. Students' responses are an informal measure of their grasp of the material. You may follow up with the practice pages in the *Selection Support* booklet.

You will find literature and reading guides in the *Alternative Assessment* booklet, which you may give students for informal assessment.

Formal Assessment

In the *Formal Assessment* booklet, you will find selection tests and a unit test.

Selection Tests The selection tests measure comprehension and skills acquisition for each selection.

Unit Test The unit test, which calls on students to read a passage of literature they have not previously seen, applies the unit skills on a broader level. The Critical Reading section measures Unit Objectives 1, 2, and 3. The Vocabulary and Grammar section measures Objectives 4 and 5. The Essay section measures Objectives 1 and 6. Both the Critical Reading and Vocabulary and Grammar sections use formats similar to those of many standardized tests, including the SAT.

Alternative Assessment

Portfolios As you review individual pieces or the collected work in students' portfolios, you will find assessment sheets available in the portfolio section of the *Alternative Assessment* booklet.

Scoring Rubrics You will find scoring rubrics for writing modes in the *Alternative Assessment* booklet. You can apply these to Writing Mini-Lessons and to Writing Process Workshop lessons.

Speaking and Listening The *Alternative Assessment* booklet contains assessment sheets for speaking and listening activities.

Learning Modalities The *Alternative Assessment* booklet contains activities that appeal to different learning styles. You may use these as an alternative measurement of students' growth.

Humanities: Art

Thunderhead, 1933, by Frederick Philips.

Students should know that a thunderhead is a cloud that is full of electrical charges and will generate lightning. At first glance, the painting seems to be a fairly realistic rendering of a thundercloud watched by a girl. There are some bizarre details to discover, however: the fact that the cloud seems to contain a sliver of moon, and the unseen light that causes the shadows in the painting.

Help students link the painting with the theme of Unit 3 ("Moments of Discovery") by answering the following questions:

1. What does the girl seem to feel about the coming storm, and how can you tell? *Her body language suggests that she is fascinated by it.*
2. Why might she feel this way? *She may never have seen a cloud like this one before.*
3. What might the girl discover from watching the cloud? *She might discover that she is not afraid of storms; she might discover a new moon hidden in the cloud; she might discover different shapes inside the cloud.*

The Reading for Success page in each unit presents a set of problem-solving procedures to help readers understand authors' words and ideas on multiple levels. Good readers develop a bank of strategies which they can draw from as needed.

Unit 3 introduces strategies for constructing meaning. It is important for students to go beyond the literal comprehension level in order to apply higher-level critical thinking skills. The strategies for constructing meaning help readers achieve a higher level of reading comprehension—making inferences and drawing conclusions, interpreting, identifying relationships, and comparing and contrasting.

These strategies for constructing meaning are modeled with "Children in the Woods." Each green box shows an example of the thinking process involved in applying one of these strategies.

How to Use the Reading for Success Page

- Introduce the strategies for constructing meaning, presenting each as a problem-solving procedure. Be sure students understand what each strategy involves and under what circumstances to apply it.

- Before students read the essay, have them preview it, looking at the annotations in the green boxes that model the strategies.

- To reinforce these strategies after students have read "Children of the Woods," have students complete the Reading for Success page in *Selection Support,* pp. 61–62. This page gives students an opportunity to read a selection and practice strategies for constructing meaning by writing their own annotations.

Reading for Success

Strategies for Constructing Meaning

In order to understand a piece of writing fully, you must do more than simply comprehend the writer's words. You have to go a step further and put the words and ideas together in your own mind, so that they have meaning for you. Constructing meaning is particularly important when you are reading any kind of nonfiction—from short essays to lengthy textbooks. Use these strategies to help you construct meaning:

Make inferences.

Writers don't always tell you everything directly. You have to make inferences to arrive at ideas that writers suggest but don't say. You make an inference by considering the details that the writer includes or doesn't include. Think about what this choice of details tells you about the author's values or purpose in writing. Sometimes it's also helpful to "read between the lines." This means looking beyond the literal meaning of the words to obtain a full picture of what the author means.

Draw conclusions.

A conclusion is a general statement that you can make and explain by reasons, or support with details from the text. Making a series of inferences can lead you to draw a conclusion.

Interpret what you read.

Interpreting what you read, or explaining it in your own words, will help make the information your own. When you interpret, you also explain the importance of what the author is saying.

Identify relationships.

To fully understand the information presented to you, you need to examine the relationships between ideas and events. Writers might show these relationships among ideas in a text: sequence, or when events happen relative to one another; greater or lesser importance; and cause and effect.

Compare and contrast.

Compare and contrast ideas in the work with other ideas in the same work, or with ideas that are already familiar to you. For example, you might look for ways in which an experience described in an essay is similar to something you've done, or different from anything you've experienced or heard of.

As you read the following essay by Barry Lopez, look at the notes along the sides. These notes demonstrate how to apply these strategies to a work of literature.

Reading Strategies: Support and Reinforcement

Appropriate Reading Strategies Students are given a reading strategy to apply while reading each selection in this book. The strategies taught within each unit build from the group of strategies taught in the Reading for Success feature in that unit. As a result, skills such as contrasting and drawing conclusions are taught with selections later in this unit.

Reading Prompts To encourage application of the given reading strategy, there are occasional prompts, within green boxes, at appropriate and significant points.

In addition, there are red boxes prompting application of the Literary Focus concept and maroon boxes prompting students to connect an event in the selection with their lives.

Using the Boxed Annotations and Prompts

The material in the green, red, and maroon boxes along the sides of selections is intended to help students apply the literary element and the reading strategy and to make a connection with their lives.

You may use the boxed material in these ways:

- Have students pause when they come to a prompt and respond to it before they continue.

- Urge students to read through the selection ignoring the boxes. After they have read the selection completely, have them go back and review the selection, responding to the prompts.

Children in the Woods

Barry Lopez

MODEL

When I was a child growing up in the San Fernando Valley in California, a trip into Los Angeles was special. The sensation of movement from a rural area into an urban one was sharp. On one of these <u>charged</u> occasions, walking down a sidewalk with my mother, I stopped suddenly, caught by a pattern of sunlight trapped in a spiraling imperfection in a windowpane. A stranger, an elderly woman in a cloth coat and a dark hat, spoke out spontaneously, saying how remarkable it is that children notice these things.

> **Compare and contrast** this experience with a similar one from your own childhood.
>
> 1

I have never forgotten the texture of this incident. Whenever I recall it I am moved not so much by any sense of my young self but by a sense of responsibility toward children, knowing

◀ **Critical Viewing** How might a child's discoveries during a walk in the woods be different from those of an adult? [Compare and Contrast]   ❷

◆ Build Vocabulary

charged (chärjd) *adj.*: Tensely expectant; intense

Children in the Woods 215

Block Scheduling Strategies

Consider these suggestions to take advantage of extended class time:

• Before students read, have a class discussion in which students share experiences in which they've learned something important from observing nature.

• After students have finished reading, coordinate with a science teacher to take students on a walk similar to the one described in Lopez's essay. Have students keep an observation journal during the walk. The journal will

help students to complete the Writing Mini-Lesson (p. 220), which asks them to create a field guide.

• Guide students to complete the Writing Mini-Lesson (p. 220). Before students get started, lead a class discussion on the use of sensory details in the essay. Have students make an observation chart listing the five senses and, if possible, a sensory detail for each sense. Ask: What do these precise details add to the essay?

Develop Understanding

One-Minute Insight

In this personal essay, the author, Barry Lopez, asserts that the most important thing we can teach a child—and learn ourselves—is that everything in the natural world, including humankind, fits together perfectly, making an interrelated whole that is much bigger than the sum of its parts. Lopez demonstrates that the best way to teach this concept to children is to take them walking in the woods. In doing so, we should refrain from lecturing or even speaking too much, and set an example by expressing awe at the wonders of nature found there. By encouraging children to notice and appreciate nature, adults can guide them to discover "how wonderfully all this fits together."

Customize for *Visual/Spatial Learners*

The photograph on this page can serve as an invaluable aide to help these students picture the events and details in the essay. Have students identify as many details as they can, including the types of vegetation found in the photograph. Then have them compare the details in the photograph to the details they'll later encounter in the essay.

◆ Reading for Success

❶ **Compare and Contrast** Ask students if they can recall something said by an adult when they were children that made a positive lasting impression on them. Ask students: How is the author's experience similar to something you experienced as a child? How is it different?

▶Critical Viewing◀

❷ **Compare and Contrast** Students may say that children are more likely to notice and wonder at details that adults dismiss as unimportant. Students may also say that children are more likely to wander off a path to explore.

❶ Make Inferences Discuss with students the details that lead to the inference that Lopez loves nature and is knowledgeable about plants and animals. Point out that his ability to name so many of the species native to the region demonstrates his knowledge of nature, while his decision to live in "relatively undisturbed country" speaks to his love of nature.

◆ Reading for Success

❷ Make Inferences From this passage, have students make inferences about Lopez's attitude toward children. *Students can infer that Lopez likes children because he often has children as visitors and he is very concerned about teaching them the right things about nature. He doesn't want to destroy children's natural interest in the world around them by telling them too much.*

◆ Reading for Success

❸ Identify Relationships Have students make a time line for this paragraph that indicates how the author's relationship with his "students"—the children he takes for walks—has changed over the years. *Students' time lines should show that the author has gone from saying too much (naming all the plants and animals they saw) to saying less, and finally to only answering questions or calling attention to interesting phenomena.*

▶Critical Viewing◀

❹ Assess Most students will agree with the author. Some may point out that observation is an essential part of science, and that the purpose of science is to describe and explain the world around us.

how <u>acutely</u> I was affected in that moment by that woman's words. The effect, for all I know, has lasted a lifetime.

> From the details in this passage, you can **infer** that the author loves nature and is knowledgeable about plants and animals.

Now, years later, I live in a rain forest in western Oregon, on the banks of a mountain river in relatively undisturbed country, surrounded by 150-foot-tall Douglas firs,[1] delicate deer-head orchids, and clearings where wild berries grow. White-footed mice and mule deer, mink and coyote move through here. My wife and I do not have children, but children we know, or children whose parents we are close to, are often here. They always want to go into the woods. And I wonder what to tell them.

In the beginning, years ago, I think I said too much. I spoke with an encyclopedic knowledge of the names of plants or the names of birds passing through in season. Gradually I came to say less. After a while the only words I spoke, beyond answering a question or calling attention quickly to the slight difference between a sprig of red cedar and a sprig of incense cedar,[2] were to <u>elucidate</u> single objects.

I remember once finding a fragment of a raccoon's jaw in an alder thicket. I sat down alongside the two children with me and encouraged them to find out who this was—with only the three teeth still intact in

1. **Douglas firs:** Tall evergreen trees of the pine family.
2. **sprig of red cedar . . . incense cedar:** Twigs from two types of trees of the pine family.

a piece of the animal's maxilla[3] to guide them. The teeth told by their shape and placement what this animal ate. By a kind of visual <u>extrapolation</u> its size became clear. There were other clues, immediately present, which told, with what I could add of climate and terrain, how this animal lived, how its broken jaw came to be lying here. Raccoon, they surmised. And tiny tooth marks along the bone's broken edge told of a mouse's hunger for calcium.

3. **maxilla** (mak sil´ ə) *n.*: Upper jaw.

▲ **Critical Viewing** Do you agree with the author that discoveries children make in nature can help them understand the world around them? **[Assess]**

◆ **Build Vocabulary**

acutely (ə kyoot´ lē) *adv.*: Sharply

elucidate (i loo´ sə dāt´) *v.*: Explain

extrapolation (ik strap´ ə lā´ shən) *n.*: Conclusions drawn by speculation on the basis of facts

◆ **Beyond the Classroom**

Career Connection

Biologist/Botanist Students who show particular interest in this essay may have an interest in biology—the branch of science that studies animals, or botany—the branch of science that studies plants.

Whether as curators for natural-history museums, writers of field guides, college professors, or experts on water and land pollution, biologists and botanists study the living world. Biology and botany may well be the leading sciences for the future since they focus on problems that all living creatures face, such as the threatened environment.

Encourage interested students to gather information about these careers and the education and preparation necessary to pursue them. When students share their findings, have them discuss how taking walks in the woods with Barry Lopez could encourage a child to aspire to a career in biology or botany.

Community Connection

Local Features Encourage students to visit places in their community where they can explore nature. Advise them to clear their minds and sharpen their senses so that they will notice the sorts of things that Lopez mentions in his essay: fragrances, bird songs, animal tracks, and so on. Suggest they take younger students along and practice the approach Lopez supports for introducing children to nature.

We set the jaw back and went on.

If I had known more about raccoons, finer points of osteology,[4] we might have guessed more: say, whether it was male or female. But what we deduced was all we needed. Hours later, the maxilla, lost behind us in the detritus of the forest floor, continued to effervesce. It was tied faintly to all else we spoke of that afternoon.

In speaking with children who might one day take a permanent interest in natural history—as writers, as scientists, as film-makers, as anthropologists[5]—I have sensed that an extrapolation from a single fragment of the whole is the most invigorating experience I can share with them. I think children know that nearly anyone can learn the names of things; the impression made on them at this level is fleeting. What takes a lifetime to learn, they comprehend, is the existence and substance of myriad relationships: it is these relationships, not the things themselves, that ultimately hold the human imagination.

The brightest children, it has often struck me, are fascinated by metaphor—with what is shown in the set of relationships bearing on the raccoon, for example, to lie quite beyond the raccoon. In the end, you are trying to make clear to them that everything found at the edge of one's senses—the high note of the winter wren, the thick perfume of propo-

lis that drifts downwind from spring willows, the brightness of wood chips scattered by beaver—that all this fits together. The inde-structibility of these associations conveys a sense of permanence that nurtures the heart, that cripples one of the most insidious of human anxi-eties, the one that says, you do not belong here, you are unnecessary.

> From this passage, you can **infer** that the author is con-cerned about peo-ple's relationships with nature.

Whenever I walk with a child, I think how much I have seen disappear in my own life. What will there be for this person when he is my age? If he senses something ineffable in the landscape, will I know enough to encour-age it?—to somehow show him that, yes, when people talk about violent death, spiri-tual exhilaration, compassion, futility, final causes, they are drawing on forty thousand years of human meditation on *this*—as we embrace Douglas firs, or stand by a river across whose undulating back we skip stones, or dig out a ca-mas bulb,[6] biting down into a taste so much wilder than last night's potatoes.

> You might **interpret** this paragraph as: I want children to know that interaction with nature is at the core of much of human philosophy.

The most moving look I ever saw from a child in the woods was on a

---

6. **camas** (kam´ əs) **bulbs:** Underground buds of a sweet and edible American plant.

---

4. **osteology** (äs´ tē äl´ ə jē) n.: Study of the structure and function of bones.
5. **anthropologists** (an´ thrə päl´ ə jists) n.: Special-ists in the study of mankind, especially the cultures of mankind.

◆ Build Vocabulary

detritus (di trīt´ əs) n.: Debris

effervesce (ef´ ər ves´) v.: To be lively

myriad (mir´ ē əd) adj.: Countless; innumerable

insidious (in sid´ ē əs) adj.: Treacherous in a sly, tricky way

ineffable (in ef´ ə bəl) adj.: Too overwhelming to be expressed in words

Children in the Woods 217

◆ Critical Thinking

⑤ Interpret Ask students to explain in which way they think the raccoon's jaw "continued to effer-vesce." What do they think was the topic of conversation? *Suggested response: The raccoon's jaw inspired a continuing discussion about how every-thing in nature is interrelated and inter-dependent.*

◆ Reading Strategy

⑥ Compare and Contrast Have students compare and contrast Lopez's attitude toward children to that of teachers they have known. *Students may recall teachers who have taught them by leading them to make their own discoveries.*

◆ Build Grammar Skills

⑦ Forms of Adjectives Have stu-dents identify the adjective in this sentence and explain why the superlative form is used. *"Brightest" is the superlative form of bright. The chil-dren to whom the sentence refers are being compared to all children.*

Customize for
Less Proficient Readers

⑧ Lopez's use of sophisticated lan-guage may make this sentence diffi-cult for students to understand. Have less proficient readers work in groups to break the sentence down into its parts, identify the key ideas, then restate these ideas in their own words.

◆ *Literature and Your Life*

⑨ Draw students' attention to the author's statement about disappear-ing species and changing landscape. Ask students what experiences they have had with disappearing wildlife or with other environmental concerns. How do these experiences help them understand and appreciate the essay? *Their own experiences make what the author says more meaningful.*

Speaking and Listening Mini-Lesson

Teaching Children
This mini-lesson supports the Speaking and Listening activity in the Idea Bank on page 220.
Introduce the Concept Have students discuss "how-to" demonstrations they have seen or heard.
Develop Background Before students begin, have them discuss the best way to teach young children how to do something.
  Lead students to consider these points:
• Show, don't tell.

• Begin with a clear statement of the purpose.
• Tailor your message to your audience.
• Present the steps in a logical order.
• Use note cards and visual aids.
• Summarize the steps in the conclusion.
• Leave time for questions and answers.

Apply the Information With this background, students should be able to teach young children about a favorite topic.

Assess the Outcome Use the bullet points listed here as a checklist to assess performance.

217

mud bar by the footprints of a heron.[7] We were on our knees, making handprints beside the footprints. You could feel the creek vibrating in the silt and sand. The sun beat down heavily on our hair. Our shoes were soaking wet. The look said: I did not know until now that I needed someone much older to confirm this, the feeling I have of life here. I can now grow older, knowing it need never be lost.

The quickest door to open in the woods for a child is the one that leads to the smallest room, by knowing the name each thing is called. The door that leads to the cathedral is marked by a hesitancy to speak at all, rather to encourage by example a sharpness of the senses. If one speaks it should only be to say, as well as one can, how wonderfully all this fits together, to indicate what a long, fierce peace can derive from this knowledge.

7. **heron** (her´ ən): Wading bird with a long neck, long legs, and a long, tapered bill.

Guide for Responding

Literature and Your Life

Reader's Response Would you like to explore the woods, beaches, or parks near your home with someone like Barry Lopez? Explain.

Thematic Focus How does "Children in the Woods" illustrate moments of discovery?

Journal Entry Describe a situation—real or imagined—where you helped another person discover something about the natural world.

☑ Check Your Comprehension
1. What happened to the author as a child in Los Angeles?
2. Where does the author live?
3. List three of the activities that took place on walks in the woods.
4. What, according to the author, is more important for children to know about nature than the names of plants and animals?

Beyond the Selection

FURTHER READING

Other Works by Barry Lopez
Of Wolves and Men
Arctic Dreams: Imagination and Desire in a Northern Landscape

Other Works About the Natural World
"The Heron," Theodore Roethke
Teaching a Stone to Talk, Annie Dillard
Earth Shine, Anne Morrow Lindbergh

INTERNET

The Internet provides an alternative means of discovering and exploring today's world. The following site sponsored by Discovery Channel provides guided, interactive tours in history, technology, science, nature, and exploration.

To reach the Discovery Channel site, go to **http://www.discovery.com**

We *strongly recommend* that you preview the site before you send students to it.

Guide for Responding (continued)

◆ Critical Thinking

INTERPRET
1. Why is the author concerned about what he tells children? **[Interpret]**
2. Why did the author change the way he told children about nature? **[Draw Conclusions]**
3. Why does the author use the method he does to teach children about nature? **[Infer]**
4. What do children gain from an understanding of relationships in nature? **[Analyze]**

APPLY
5. How could you apply Barry Lopez's ideas to teach art to children? **[Apply]**

EXTEND
6. How might an understanding of the relationships among the parts of a whole be useful in the following careers: auto mechanic, businessperson, wheat farmer, doctor? **[Career Link]**

◆ Reading for Success

STRATEGIES FOR CONSTRUCTING MEANING
Review the reading strategies and the notes showing how to construct meaning from what you read. Then apply the strategies to do the following:
1. For the paragraph that starts "In the beginning" on p. 216, compare and contrast the way Lopez dealt with children in the past with the way he deals with them now.
2. Explain how the children's inference about the raccoon bone is based on details they observed.
3. Draw inferences about the author's character from the paragraph beginning on p. 217 that starts: "The most moving look I ever saw...."

◆ Literary Focus

CENTRAL IDEA AND SUPPORT
The **central idea** of this essay is the main point that Barry Lopez wants to convey.
1. State the central idea of "Children in the Woods" in your own words.
2. List three supports from the essay and explain how they illustrate the central idea.

◆ Build Vocabulary

USING THE PREFIX *extra-*
Use the meaning of the prefix *extra-* to explain the meaning of the following terms:
1. extraterrestrial (*terra* means "earth")
2. extraordinary

USING THE WORD BANK
On your paper, write the word from the Word Bank that answers each question.
1. What does a carbonated drink do when you open the can?
2. If you didn't understand a point someone made, what might you ask them to do?
3. What do scientists get when they use facts to help them draw conclusions?
4. What is the atmosphere at an awards ceremony a few seconds before the winner is announced?
5. What would you find scattered around a junkyard?
6. How might someone experience a bad headache?
7. How might you describe a disease that is deadly but very hard to detect?
8. How many stars are in the sky?
9. How could you describe a feeling so strong you can't put it into words?

◆ Build Grammar Skills

FORMS OF ADJECTIVES
Different **forms of an adjective** are used to describe one (positive), two (comparative), or more than two (superlative) things.

Practice On your paper, write the comparative and superlative forms of the following adjectives:
1. happy   2. exciting   3. tricky

Writing Application Write the following paragraph, filling each blank with the correct form of the listed adjective:

My cat has ___?___ (long) whiskers. In fact, she has the ___?___ (long) whiskers I've ever seen. She is ___?___ (outgoing) than most cats and is even ___?___ (friendly) than many dogs. I think she is the ___?___ (good) cat in the world.

Children in the Woods ◆ 219

◆ Build Vocabulary

Using the Prefix *extra-*
1. Something that is extraterrestrial comes from outside the planet Earth.
2. Something that is extraordinary is out of the ordinary, or special.

Using the Word Bank
1. effervesce;   2. elucidate;
3. extrapolation;   4. charged;
5. detritus;   6. acutely;
7. insidious;   8. myriad;
9. ineffable

◆ Build Grammar Skills

Practice
1. happier, happiest
2. more exciting, most exciting
3. trickier, trickiest

Writing Application
long, longest, more outgoing, friendlier, best

◆ Writer's Solution

For additional instruction and practice, use the lesson in the **Language Lab CD-ROM** on the Eight Parts of Speech. For additional support, use the pages on Degrees of Comparison, pp. 88–89 in the *Writer's Solution Grammar Practice Book.*

Answers
◆ Critical Thinking

1. He knows that anything he says may leave a lasting impression.
2. He was not emphasizing what was really important—the relationships among living things and their surroundings.
3. By concentrating on one object, rather than on the names of many objects, children are able to determine how it relates to the other objects they see, and come to understand that all things are connected.
4. They construct meaning from what they see, and also come to understand that they, too, are a part of the natural world.
5. Suggested response: Instead of telling them technical details, let them experiment and make discoveries about color and design for themselves.
6. Accept all logical responses.

◆ Reading for Success

1. Instead of lecturing, he now elicits information to guide discovery.
2. The size and shape of the teeth suggest the type of food the animal ate. The size of the piece of jaw indicates the size of the animal. The location where the bone was found suggests the habitat of the animal. Marks on the jawbone indicate the behavior and nutritional needs of mice.
3. Suggested response: The author enjoys playing with children and is not afraid of looking undignified. He is aware of sensory details in his environment. He is also sensitive to the feedback children need from adults.

◆ Literary Focus

1. Suggested response: The best way to help a child learn about the world is to facilitate his or her process of discovery.
2. Students may cite the anecdotes about observing the pattern of sunlight, teaching children about the woods, finding the raccoon bone, or making handprints.

Idea Bank

Customizing for
Performance Levels

Following are suggestions for matching the Idea Bank topics with your students' performance levels:

Less Advanced Students: 1, 7
Average Students: 2, 4, 5
More Advanced Students: 3, 6

Customizing for
Learning Modalities

Following are suggestions for matching Idea Bank topics with your students' learning modalities:

Verbal Linguistic: 1, 2, 3
Auditory: 4, 5
Visual/Spatial: 6, 7
Bodily/Kinesthetic: 4, 5

Writing Mini-Lesson

Refer students to the Writing Handbook, page 962, for instruction on the writing process, and page 964 for further information on Description. You may also use the writing process models of Descriptive and Observational Writing, pp. 17–20 in *Writing and Language Transparencies.*

Writer's Solution

Writers at Work Videodisc

Have students view the videodisc segment (Ch. 1) featuring science-fiction writer Anne McCaffrey. Have students discuss how she uses detailed descriptions to help readers understand any world—real or fictional.

Play frames 335 to 10785

Writing Lab CD-ROM

Have students complete the Tutorial on Description. Follow these steps:

1. Use the Word Bins to gather sensory words and color words.
2. Have students draft on computer.
3. View the video clip on revising to see an example of how a description is made more precise.
4. Have students use the interactive instruction on offering constructive criticism to aid in peer review.

Allow 120 minutes of class time to complete these steps.

Sourcebook

Have students use Chapter 1, Description (pp. 1–29), for additional support. The chapter includes a model of an observation (p. 5).

Build Your Portfolio

Idea Bank

Writing

1. **Poem** Write a poem about an important discovery about nature.

2. **Dialogue** Write a realistic dialogue between a curious child and a parent or teacher. In the dialogue, show how the adult guides the child to find an answer.

3. **Persuasive Essay** Drawing on Barry Lopez's ideas and your own, write a persuasive essay about teaching children about nature. You may choose to support techniques and ideas that are similar to Lopez's, or you might take a different approach.

Speaking and Listening

4. **Teaching Children** Select a topic that you are good at and that interests you. Keeping Barry Lopez's ideas in mind, decide how to teach young children about your topic. When you have finished preparing, teach your lesson to a child or small group of children. **[Career Link]**

5. **Dramatization** With a small group, dramatize one of the scenes from the essay. Add details and dialogue to help bring the scene to life.

Projects

6. **Relationship Map** Prepare a graphic organizer that shows the relationships among the living things that inhabit a nearby wood, park, or vacant lot. Embellish your graphic organizer with drawings or photographs. **[Science Link]**

7. **Rain-Forest Presentation** The woods that Barry Lopez describes are part of a temperate rain forest. Prepare a presentation on temperate rain forests. Include a world map that shows where temperate rain forests are located. **[Science Link]**

Writing Mini-Lesson

Field Guide

In "Children in the Woods," Barry Lopez vividly describes the woods around his home. You can also teach people about the wildlife you see each day by creating a field guide that focuses on five living things in or near your home. A field guide provides detailed descriptions of and information about particular types of wildlife or wildlife specific to a region.

Writing Skills Focus: Specific Examples

To help readers perceive important details, your field guide needs **specific examples.** A specific example, such as "a two-inch long gray centipede" is more useful and vivid than a vague example like "a bug." Notice how Lopez uses specific examples in this excerpt.

Model From the Essay

Now, years later, I live in a rain forest in western Oregon . . . surrounded by 150-foot-tall *Douglas firs*, delicate *deerhead orchids*, and clearings where wild berries grow. *White-footed mice* and *mule deer*, *mink* and *coyote* move through here.

Prewriting Brainstorm for a list of animals that live near your home. From your list, select the subjects for your field guide. Gather information about each animal.

Drafting Provide specific examples that show what the animals look like and how they behave. For example, if you are describing the feeding habits of rabbits, tell exactly which plants they eat.

Revising Have a classmate read your field guide and list questions that are left unanswered. Use the question to guide your revisions.

✓ ASSESSMENT OPTIONS

Formal Assessment, Selection Test, pp. 51–53, and Assessment Resources Software. The selection test is designed so that it can be easily customized to the performance levels of your students.
Alternative Assessment, p. 15, includes options for less advanced students, more advanced students, verbal/linguistic learners, interpersonal learners, and visual/spatial learners.

PORTFOLIO ASSESSMENT
Use the following rubrics in the *Alternative Assessment* booklet to assess student writing:
Poem: Poetry Rubric, p. 101
Dialogue: Narrative Rubric, p. 89, or Drama Rubric, p. 102
Persuasive Essay: Persuasion Rubric, p. 98
Writing Mini-Lesson: Description Rubric, p. 90

PART **1** *Finding Our Identity*

My Judy, Mabel Martin Davidson

Finding Our Identity ◆ 221

 Humanities: Art

My Judy, by Mabel Martin Davidson.

As students look at the painting, read them the following lines from Andrew Marvell's seventeenth-century poem "The Garden": "Annihilating all that's made/To a green thought in a green shade." Ask them what a "green thought" might be—how it feels to be in a space like the one shown here.

Help students link the art to the theme of Part 1 ("Finding Our Identity") by answering the following questions:

1. Would you rather be outdoors or indoors when you want some time to think by yourself? Why? *Students who prefer being outdoors may cite the tranquillity of nature; students who prefer being indoors may cite complete security.*

2. How do you think her surroundings affect the girl's mood? *Most students will probably feel that the green surroundings make the girl feel serene.*

3. Imagine that this girl is a character in a story. What is she like, and why does she go to this place? *Sample response: She is a very quiet girl who feels confused in large groups of people and so has been coming to her own secret place.*

One-Minute Planning Guide

The selections in this section explore identity. "Rules of the Game" presents the struggle of a young girl with immigrant parents to become who she is. "Checkouts" presents a teenage girl and boy who discover each other but are too timid to express their feelings. The song lyrics to "Both Sides Now" asserts the wisdom of life's discoveries. "Fifteen" explores the discovery of someone unique. "Sympathy" and "Caged Bird" present discoveries about the nature of freedom. "We never know how high we are" tells of the discovery of great personal potential. In the excerpt from *In My Place,* Charlayne Hunter-Gault describes self-discovery under trying circumstances.

Customize for
Varying Student Needs
When assigning the selections in this part, keep in mind these factors:

"Rules of the Game"
- A touching story of a young girl's quest for identity in San Francisco's Chinatown
- Less proficient readers may need help discerning the central theme of this selection

"Checkouts"
- A contemporary story of first love; students may identify with the main characters

"Fifteen"
- The discovery of an injured motorcylist leads to self-discovery
- Less proficient readers may need help with the theme

"Sympathy"
- A poem that uses the metaphor of a caged bird to make a discovery about freedom

"Caged Bird"
- This poem contrasts a caged bird with a free bird to make a discovery about freedom
- Help students to understand the worth of freedom to the unfree

"We never know how high we are"
- A little poem with a big message about human potential

from *In My Place*
- This autobiographical piece tells of quest for an education in the face of racial prejudice
- Help students with background on the quest for civil rights in America

221

Guide for Reading

OBJECTIVES

1. To read, comprehend, and interpret a story
2. To relate a story to personal experience
3. To contrast characters in a story
4. To identify generational conflict
5. To build vocabulary in context and investigate the origins of words from French
6. To identify clauses in complex sentences
7. To write a proposal, using clear and logical organization, to change the rules of a game
8. To respond to the story through writing, speaking and listening, and projects

SKILLS INSTRUCTION

Vocabulary: Word Origins: Words From French

Grammar: Complex Sentences

Reading Strategy: Contrasting Characters

Literary Focus: Generational Conflict

Writing: Clear and Logical Organization

Speaking and Listening: Dialogue (teacher edition)

Critical Viewing: Support

PORTFOLIO OPPORTUNITIES

Writing: Notes for a Magazine Article; Letter; Extension

Writing Mini-Lesson: Proposal to Change the Rules of a Game

Speaking and Listening: Radio Commentary; Dialogue

Projects: Chess Set; Game

More About the Author

Amy Tan grew up in the United States, but when she went to China for the first time in 1987, she said, "As soon as my feet touched China, I became Chinese."

The story "Rules of the Game" is imaginary, but the feelings it portrays are true. Tan finds that writing fiction helps her to portray emotional truth.

Amy Tan (1952–)

Like Waverly, the nine-year-old chess champion in this story, Amy Tan was something of a child prodigy, displaying literary promise at the ripe age of eight. Born in Oakland, California, she grew up in the San Francisco Bay area, the setting of her acclaimed first novel, *The Joy Luck Club*, from which "Rules of the Game" comes.

> *Tan has said that writing the novel helped her discover "how very Chinese" she was.*

A Chinese American Writer As a young woman, Tan supported herself as a technical writer, and she played the piano and wrote fiction for relaxation. Through writing, she discovered her own ethnic identity. Tan has said in interviews that she had tried to minimize her ethnicity when she was younger. All that changed when she began to write about the rich but painful intersection of two cultures in Chinese American women.

Cultural Tug of War In 1985, Tan wrote "Rules of the Game," which she later included in *The Joy Luck Club*, a novel that weaves together the stories of four Chinese mothers and their American-born daughters. *The Joy Luck Club* was made into a popular film, with Tan collaborating on the screenplay. Tan's later novels include *The Kitchen God's Wife* (1991) and *The Hundred Secret Senses* (1995).

◆ Build Vocabulary

WORD ORIGINS: WORDS FROM FRENCH

In this story the words *etiquette* ("proper behavior"), *souvenirs* ("reminders"), and *tournament* ("contest") all come from French. Many chess terms, as well, come from French. *Checkmate* is a French derivative of the Persian phrase *shah mat*, which means, literally, "The king is dead." *Pawn*, which refers to the lowliest chesspiece, comes from the French word *pion*, meaning "assistant." As you read "Rules of the Game," look for other words that might have come from French.

WORD BANK

pungent
benevolently
retort
prodigy
malodorous
concessions

Before you read, preview this list of words from the story.

◆ Build Grammar Skills

COMPLEX SENTENCES

To describe a tense relationship between two strong people, Amy Tan begins "Rules of the Game" with a complex sentence:

> I was six when my mother taught me the art of invisible strength.

A **complex sentence** is made up of one independent clause, which can stand by itself as a complete sentence (*I was six ...*), and at least one subordinate clause, which cannot stand by itself as a sentence (*...when my mother taught me the art of invisible strength*).

As you read "Rules of the Game," notice Amy Tan's use of complex sentences to show the highly charged tug of war between a mother and daughter.

222 ◆ Moments of Discovery

Prentice Hall Literature Program Resources

REINFORCE / RETEACH / EXTEND

Selection Support Pages
Build Vocabulary: Word Origins: Words From French, p. 64
Build Grammar Skills: Complex Sentences, p. 65
Reading Strategy: Contrast Characters, p. 66
Literary Focus: Generational Conflict, p. 67

Strategies for Diverse Student Needs, p. 16

Beyond Literature
Cross Curricular Connection: Performing Arts, p. 16

Formal Assessment Selection Test, pp. 54–56, Assessment Resources Software

Alternative Assessment, p. 16

Writing and Language Transparencies
Letter to the Editor, pp. 41–44

Resource Pro CD-ROM
"Rules of the Game"—includes all resource material and customizable lesson plan

Listening to Literature Audiocassettes
"Rules of the Game"

Rules of the Game

◆ *Literature and Your Life*

CONNECT YOUR EXPERIENCE

In "Rules of the Game," a generational tug of war is complicated by a conflict between Chinese and American cultures. No matter what your cultural background, however, the battle of wills that takes place in this selection should be familiar to you.

THEMATIC FOCUS: FINDING OUR IDENTITY

In this story you get one point of view—that of the child seeking independence—but there is another side as well. How would you feel if you were a parent watching your child reject the values you have lived by?

Journal Writing In your journal, examine a cultural or generational conflict you know about.

◆ Background for Understanding

CULTURE

Chess, which plays a central role in Tan's story, is believed to have evolved from a game first played in India in the sixth century. It was known as *chaturanga,* a name that referred to the four divisions of an army of the period: elephants, horses, chariots, and foot soldiers. The game spread to Persia (the present Iran), and after conquering Persia in the seventh century, Arab invaders introduced chess to other lands around the Mediterranean Sea. During the Middle Ages, games of chess became part of courtship rituals between knights and ladies. Today, chess is played by people of all ages and cultural backgrounds around the world.

◆ Literary Focus

GENERATIONAL CONFLICT

Generational conflict exists when beliefs and values change from one generation to another. The "generation gap" becomes even wider, however, when parents have a cultural background that is different from the one in which they are raising their children. In "Rules of the Game," a Chinese mother and her American-born daughter, Waverly, are locked in a battle of wills.

◆ Reading Strategy

CONTRAST CHARACTERS

The first sentence of this story sets up the battle of wills that the story plays out. On one side, there is American-born Waverly, a young girl; on the other, her Chinese mother. Throughout the story, you will see these two characters engaged in conflict, with high stakes for each. In order to follow the story, you need to understand the way the writer is contrasting these two adversaries.

To fully explore the contrast between Waverly and Mrs. Jong, it may help you to develop a chart like the one shown. Use it to keep track of each character's traits, needs, and principal actions.

	Waverly	Mrs. Jong
Background	Born in the U.S.	Born in China
Significant Actions		
Significant Statements		
Personality Traits		
Hopes		

Guide for Reading ◆ 223

Rules of the Game

from

The Joy Luck Club
Amy Tan

I was six when my mother taught me the art of invisible strength. It was a strategy for winning arguments, respect from others, and eventually, though neither of us knew it at the time, chess games.

❶ "Bite back your tongue," scolded my mother when I cried loudly, yanking her hand toward the store that sold bags of salted plums. At home, she said, "Wise guy, he not go against wind. In Chinese we say, Come from South, blow with wind—poom!—North will follow. Strongest wind cannot be seen."

❷ The next week I bit back my tongue as we entered the store with the forbidden candies. When my mother finished her shopping, she quietly plucked a small bag of plums from the rack and put it on the counter with the rest of the items.

My mother imparted her daily truths so she could help my older brothers and me rise above our circumstances. We lived in San Francisco's Chinatown. Like most of the other Chinese children who played in the back alleys of restaurants and curio shops,[1] I didn't think we were poor. My bowl was always full, three five-course meals every day, beginning with a soup full of mysterious things I didn't want to know the names of.

We lived on Waverly Place, in a warm, clean, two-bedroom flat that sat above a small Chinese bakery specializing in steamed pastries and dim sum.[2] In the early morning, when the alley was still quiet, I could smell fragrant red beans as they were cooked down to a pasty sweetness. By daybreak, our flat was heavy with the odor of fried sesame balls and sweet curried chicken crescents. From my bed, I would listen as my father got ready for work, then locked the door behind him, one-two-three clicks.

At the end of our two-block alley was a small sandlot playground with swings and slides well-shined down the middle with use. The play area was bordered by wood-slat benches where old-country people sat cracking roasted watermelon seeds with their golden teeth and scattering the husks to an impatient gathering of gurgling pigeons. The best playground, however, was the dark alley itself. It was crammed with daily mysteries and adventures. My brothers and I would peer into the medicinal herb shop, watching old Li dole out onto a stiff sheet of white paper the right amount of insect shells, saffron-colored[3] seeds and <u>pungent</u> leaves for his ailing customers. It was said that he once cured a woman dying of an ancestral curse that had eluded the best of American doctors. Next to the pharmacy was a printer who specialized in gold-embossed wedding invitations and festive red banners.

Farther down the street was Ping Yuen Fish

❸

---

1. **curio** (kyoor′ ē ō′) **shops:** Shops that sell unusual or rare items.
2. **dim sum** (dim′ tsoom): Shells of dough filled with meat and vegetables and served as a light meal.
3. **saffron-colored:** Orange-yellow.

Block Scheduling Strategies

Consider these suggestions to take advantage of extended class time:

- Have students read Background for Understanding (p. 223) and discuss what other facts they know about chess.
- Instruct students to work in pairs to create a Contrast Characters Chart like the one on page 223. One student can write down Waverly's traits, and the other can write Mrs. Jong's.

- Have students work in pairs to discuss and complete the Critical Thinking questions on page 232.
- Encourage students to work in groups to create the Idea Bank Dialogue on page 233. Students may enjoy taping or videotaping their dialogues.
- Ask students to complete the Writing Mini-Lesson on page 233. Encourage them to work in small groups to create comparison-contrast charts before they write.

Market. The front window displayed a tank crowded with doomed fish and turtles struggling to gain footing on the slimy green-tiled sides. A hand-written sign informed tourists, "Within this store, is all for food, not for pet." Inside, the butchers with their bloodstained white smocks deftly gutted the fish while customers cried out their orders and shouted, "Give me your freshest," to which the butchers always protested, "All are freshest." On less crowded market days, we would inspect the crates of live frogs and crabs which we were warned not to poke, boxes of dried cuttlefish, and row upon row of iced prawns, squid, and slippery fish. The sanddabs made me shiver each time; their eyes lay on one flattened side and reminded me of my mother's story of a careless girl who ran into a crowded street and was crushed by a cab. "Was smash flat," reported my mother.

At the corner of the alley was Hong Sing's, a four-table cafe with a recessed stairwell in front that led to a door marked "Tradesmen." My brothers and I believed the bad people emerged from this door at night. Tourists never went to Hong Sing's, since the menu was printed only in Chinese. A Caucasian[4] man with a big camera once posed me and my playmates in front of the restaurant. He had us move to the side of the picture window so the photo would capture the roasted duck with its head dangling from a juice-covered rope. After he took the picture, I told him he should go into Hong Sing's and eat dinner. When he smiled and asked me what they served, I shouted, "Guts and duck's feet and octopus gizzards!" Then I ran off with my friends, shrieking with laughter as we scampered across the alley and hid in the entryway

---

4. **Caucasian** (kô kā´ zhən) adj.: Person of European ancestry.

◆ **Build Vocabulary**

pungent (pun´ jənt) adj.: Producing a sharp sensation of smell

---

grotto[5] of the China Gem Company, my heart pounded with hope that he would chase us.

My mother named me after the street that we lived on: Waverly Place Jong, my official name for important American documents. But my family called me Meimei,[6] "Little Sister," I was the youngest, the only daughter. Each morning before school, my mother would twist and yank on my thick black hair until she had formed two tightly wound pigtails. One day, as she struggled to weave a hard-toothed comb through my disobedient hair, I had a sly thought.

I asked her, "Ma, what is Chinese torture?" My mother shook her head. A bobby pin was wedged between her lips. She wetted her palm and smoothed the hair above my ear, then pushed the pin in so that it nicked sharply against my scalp.

"Who say this word?" she asked without a trace of knowing how wicked I was being. I shrugged my shoulders and said, "Some boy in my class said Chinese people do Chinese torture."

"Chinese people do many things," she said simply. "Chinese people do business, do medicine, do painting. Not lazy like American people. We do torture. Best torture."

My older brother Vincent was the one who actually got the chess set. We had gone to the annual Christmas party held at the First Chinese Baptist Church at the end of the alley. The missionary ladies had put together a Santa bag of gifts donated by members of another church. None of the gifts had names on them. There were separate sacks for boys and girls of different ages.

One of the Chinese parishioners had donned a Santa Claus costume and a stiff paper beard with cotton balls glued to it. I think the only children who thought he was the real thing were too young to know that Santa Claus

---

5. **entryway grotto** (grät´ ō) n.: The entryway resembled a cave.
6. **Meimei** (mā´ mā´)

◆ **Build Vocabulary**

❹ **Word Origins** Point out to students that the word *menu* in this passage is not only of French origin, but is *borrowed* from French. Explain that borrowed words are words taken from another language without being changed. Challenge students to find another word borrowed from French in this passage. *The word* cafe *is borrowed from French.*

◆ **Build Grammar Skills**

❺ **Complex Sentences** Have students identify the independent clause and subordinate clause in this sentence. Ask them how the sentence reflects the relationship between Waverly and Mrs. Jong. *Independent clause: "I had a sly thought"; subordinate clause: "as she struggled to weave a hard-toothed comb through my disobedient hair"; Mrs. Jong struggles to subdue Waverly's hair, and Waverly rebels, just as she rebels against her mother's efforts to subdue her in other ways.*

◆ **Literary Focus**

❻ **Generational Conflict** The attitude of the characters in this passage points to a generational conflict as well as a cultural one. Ask students to explain how a sense of generational conflict is conveyed in this passage. *Waverly Jong seems ready to criticize and question, a characteristic of youth, whereas her mother seems to defend her people and their ways while criticizing the Americans of her new surroundings. This loyalty to old ways is characteristic of her generation.*

✛ **Beyond the Classroom**

Community Connection
Ethnic Communities Point out to students that in San Francisco, where Waverly lives, Chinatown is a large community filled with Chinese stores and restaurants. Many other cities contain Chinatowns, and most cities have other ethnic communities as well. Discuss the contribution of these communities to their towns and cities, and talk about the customs and traditions they foster.

❶ Analyze Character Ask students to explain what Waverly reveals about her character by her approach to the Christmas presents. *She reveals that she is cunning and strategic in her attempt to garner a valuable gift.*

◆ **Reading Strategy**

❷ Contrast Characters Mrs. Jong's attitude toward the chess set differs significantly from her children's. Mrs. Jong is too proud, too conscious of her own self-worth, to have her family accept an item that is clearly not good enough for someone else. In contrast, the children are pleased to get a game that looks like fun, even if it is second-hand.

◆ **Reading Strategy**

❸ Contrast Characters This family scene illustrates a difference between Waverly and her mother. Ask: How do Mrs. Jong's and Waverly's activities in this passage reveal a difference between the two characters? *Mrs. Jong is preparing a traditional meal; Waverly is learning a game played more often by males than females, and seems disinterested in her mother's work.*

was not Chinese. When my turn came up, the Santa man asked me how old I was. I thought it was a trick question; I was seven according to the American formula and eight by the Chinese calendar. I said I was born on March 17, 1951. That seemed to satisfy him. He then solemnly asked if I had been a very, very good girl this year and did I believe in Jesus Christ and obey my parents. I knew the only answer to that. I nodded back with equal solemnity.

Having watched the other children opening their gifts, I already knew that the big gifts were not necessarily the nicest ones. One girl my age got a large coloring book of biblical characters, while a less greedy girl who selected a small box received a glass vial of lavender toilet water. The sound of the box was also important. A ten-year-old boy had chosen a box that jangled when he shook it. It was a tin globe of the world with a slit for inserting money. He must have thought it was full of dimes and nickels, because when he saw that it had just ten pennies, his face fell with such undisguised disappointment that his mother slapped the side of his head and led him out of the church hall, apologizing to the crowd for her son who had such bad manners he couldn't appreciate such a fine gift.

As I peered into the sack, I quickly fingered the remaining presents, testing their weight, imagining what they contained. I chose a heavy, compact one that was wrapped in shiny silver foil and a red satin ribbon. It was a twelve-pack of Life Savers and I spent the rest of the party arranging and rearranging the candy tubes in the order of my favorites. My brother Winston chose wisely as well. His present turned out to be a box of intricate plastic parts; the instructions on the box proclaimed that when they were properly assembled he would have an authentic miniature replica of a World War II submarine.

Vincent got the chess set, which would have been a very decent present to get at a church Christmas party except it was obviously used and, as we discovered later, it was missing a

black pawn and a white knight. My mother graciously thanked the unknown benefactor, saying, "Too good. Cost too much." At which point, an old lady with fine white, wispy hair nodded toward our family and said with a whistling whisper, "Merry, merry Christmas."

When we got home, my mother told Vincent to throw the chess set away. "She not want it. We not want it," she said, tossing her head stiffly to the side with a tight, proud smile. My brothers had deaf ears. They were already lining up the chess pieces and reading from the dog-eared instruction book.

I watched Vincent and Winston play during Christmas week. The chess board seemed to hold elaborate secrets waiting to be untangled. The chessmen were more powerful than Old Li's magic herbs that cured ancestral curses. And my brothers wore such serious faces that I was sure something was at stake that was greater than avoiding the tradesmen's door to Hong Sing's.

"Let me! Let me!" I begged between games when one brother or the other would sit back with a deep sigh of relief and victory, the other annoyed, unable to let go of the outcome. Vincent at first refused to let me play, but when I offered my Life Savers as replacements for the buttons that filled in for the missing pieces, he relented. He chose the flavors: wild cherry for the black pawn and peppermint for the white knight. Winner could eat both. As our mother sprinkled flour and rolled out small doughy circles for the steamed dumplings that would be our dinner that night, Vincent explained the rules, pointing to each piece. "You have sixteen pieces and so do I. One king and queen, two bishops, two knights, two castles, and eight pawns. The pawns can only move forward one step, except on the first move. Then they can move two. But they can only take men by moving crossways like this, except in the beginning, when you can move ahead and take another pawn."

Cross-Curricular Connection: Art

Explain to students that though Waverly's brother's chess pieces were made of plastic, the carving of chess pieces is an art that has been practiced all over the world for hundreds of years. Chess sets have been created in materials such as ivory, fine wood, glass, porcelain, silver, gold, and jewels. Chess sets made in different countries have very different looks: some Indian sets have kings and queens riding on elephants, while an Italian set made in the nineteenth century portrays the king as Neptune and the pawns as fishes. Students might enjoy researching decorative chess sets and presenting oral reports on them, along with pictures to show the class.

"Why?" I asked as I moved my pawn. "Why can't they move more steps?"

"Because they're pawns," he said.

"But why do they go crossways to take other men. Why aren't there any women and children?"

"Why is the sky blue? Why must you always ask stupid questions?" asked Vincent. "This is a game. These are the rules. I didn't make them up. See. Here. In the book." He jabbed a page with a pawn in his hand. "Pawn. P-A-W-N. Pawn. Read it yourself."

My mother patted the flour off her hands. "Let me see book," she said quietly. She scanned the pages quickly, not reading the foreign English symbols, seeming to search deliberately for nothing in particular.

"This American rules," she concluded at last. "Every time people come out from foreign country, must know rules. You not know, judge say, Too bad, go back. They not telling you why so you can use their way go forward. They say, Don't know why, you find out yourself. But they knowing all the time. Better you take it, find out why yourself." She tossed her head back with a satisfied smile.

I found out about all the whys later. I read the rules and looked up all the big words in a dictionary. I borrowed books from the Chinatown library. I studied each chess piece, trying to absorb the power each contained.

I learned about opening moves and why it's important to control the center early on; the shortest distance between two points is straight down the middle. I learned about the middle game and why tactics between two adversaries are like clashing ideas; the one who plays better has the clearest plans for both attacking and getting out of traps. I learned why it is essential in the endgame[7] to have foresight, a mathematical understanding of all possible moves, and patience; all weaknesses and advantages become evident to a strong adversary and are obscured to a tiring opponent. I discovered that

Chess Mates, 1992, Pamela Chin Lee, Courtesy of the artist

▲ **Critical Viewing** Based on details in the painting, who do you think is winning this chess game? Why? **[Support]** ❺

for the whole game one must gather invisible strengths and see the endgame before the game begins.

I also found out why I should never reveal "why" to others. A little knowledge withheld is a great advantage one should store for future use. That is the power of chess. It is a game of secrets in which one must show and never tell.

I loved the secrets I found within the sixty-four black and white squares. I carefully drew a handmade chessboard and pinned it to the wall next to my bed, where at night I would stare for hours at imaginary battles. Soon I no longer lost any games or Life Savers, but I lost my adversaries. Winston and Vincent decided they were more interested in roaming the streets after school in their Hopalong Cassidy[8] cowboy hats.

---

7. **endgame** (end´ gām´): Final stage of a chess game in which each player has only a few pieces left on the board.

8. **Hopalong Cassidy:** Character in cowboy movies during the 1950's.

Rules of the Game ◆ 227

Rules of the Game ◆ 227

◆ Critical Thinking

❹ **Interpret** Mrs. Jong seems to be speaking about chess, but she is really making a much broader statement. Ask students to explain what advice she is giving Waverly. *She is saying that Waverly must find out the rules of life herself in order to succeed. No one can tell her the rules or explain why they exist.*

▶Critical Viewing◀

❺ **Support** The expressions of the chess players, rather than the positions of the pieces on the board (which are not clear enough to make out) reveal that the girl has the upper hand. The man looks a little upset and is concentrating hard; the girl looks confident and pleased with herself.

◆ Reading Strategy

❻ **Contrast Characters** Here Waverly shows she shares one of her mother's character traits. Ask: How are Waverly and her mother revealed to be similar? *They both like to have power over others by withholding information.*

🎵 **Humanities: Art**

Chess Mates, 1992, by Pamela Chin Lee.

Pamela Chin Lee draws on her Chinese heritage in this painting of a chess game. Although the two figures in the painting are playing a competitive game, their relaxed body positions suggest a friendly relationship between the two. The word "mates" in the title, by playing on the chess term, *mate,* suggests a combination of friendliness and competition.

Use these questions for discussion:

1. Which figure in the painting is emphasized? Why? *The figure of the man is larger and more*
central in the painting, making the girl's apparent victory more interesting and surprising. Or one might argue that the girl's moving a piece is the central action of the painting, making her role more important.*

2. How does this painting reflect what happens in "Rules of the Game"? *The story, like the painting, focuses on a young girl who learns to beat older, male opponents at chess.*

227

◆ Build Vocabulary

❶ Word Origins Point out that the word "advantage" is from the French word *avant*, meaning "before." Explain that its present meaning derives from its original meaning because an advantage involves knowledge that you have *before* someone else has it.

◆ *Literature and Your Life*

❷ Ask students to explain the generational conflict that is going on in this passage. Have them identify the causes of the conflict and the results. Students who want to pursue the topic further can meet with partners or small groups to discuss experiences they have had similar to Waverly's. *The conflict is caused by the younger character having more expertise in a particular area than the parent. The parent feels inadequate, but wants to appear helpful and to participate in the child's experience. The child finds the parent's attempts annoying and inadvertently hurts the parent's feelings.*

◆ Literary Focus

❸ Generational Conflict Ask students: Is Waverly really embarrassed to be seen with her mother? *Students may say that Waverly is not embarrassed simply to be seen with her mother, but she is embarrassed by the way her mother is acting.*

◆ Literary Focus

❹ Generational Conflict Waverly is upset because her mother does not seem to be expressing her pride in an appropriate manner. Similarly, Mrs. Jong is furious because Waverly appears to be embarrassed by her, not just her behavior. Point out to students that different generations may have different ideas about correct behavior in public, and even different notions about what words such as *embarrassment* mean. Ask students if they would be embarrassed if they were Waverly. Make the point that Waverly, herself, is not doing anything embarrassing. Why, then, should she feel embarrassed? Lead a brief discussion about why children sometimes find their parents embarrassing. *Students may say they don't want to feel like children. If they think their parents act strangely or differently, they are afraid people will judge them by judging their parents.*

---

❶ gathered. I went to school, then directly home to learn new chess secrets, cleverly concealed advantages, more escape routes.

But I found it difficult to concentrate at home. My mother had a habit of standing over me while I plotted out my games. I think she thought of herself as my protective ally. Her lips would be sealed tight, and after each move I made, a soft "Hmmmmph" would escape from her nose.

❷ "Ma, I can't practice when you stand there like that," I said one day. She retreated to the kitchen and made loud noises with the pots and pans. When the crashing stopped, I could see out of the corner of my eye that she was standing in the doorway. "Hmmmmph!" Only this one came out of her tight throat.

My parents made many concessions to allow me to practice. One time I complained that the bedroom I shared was so noisy that I couldn't think. Thereafter, my brothers slept in a bed in the living room facing the street. I said I couldn't finish my rice; my head didn't work right when my stomach was too full. I left the table with half-finished bowls and nobody complained. But there was one duty I couldn't avoid. I had to accompany my mother on Saturday market days when I had no tournament to play. My mother would proudly walk with me, visiting many shops, buying very little. "This my daughter Wave-ly Jong," she said to whoever looked her way.

❸ One day, after we left a shop I said under my breath, "I wish you wouldn't do that, telling everybody I'm your daughter." My mother stopped walking. Crowds of people with heavy bags pushed past us on the sidewalk, bumping into first one shoulder, then another.

"Aiii-ya. So shame be with mother?" She grasped my hand even tighter as she glared at me.

I looked down. "It's not that, it's just so obvious. It's just so embarrassing."

"Embarrass you be my daughter?" Her voice was cracking with anger.

"That's not what I meant.

That's not what I said."

"What you say?"

I knew it was a mistake to say anything more, but I heard my voice speaking. "Why do you have to use me to show off? If you want to show off, then why don't you learn to play chess." My mother's eyes turned into dangerous black slits. She had no words for me, just sharp silence.

I felt the wind rushing around my hot ears. I jerked my hand out of my mother's tight grasp and spun around, knocking into an old woman. Her bag of groceries spilled to the ground.

"Aii-ya! Stupid girl!" my mother and the woman cried. Oranges and tin cans careened down the sidewalk. As my mother stooped to help the old woman pick up the escaping food, I took off.

I raced down the street, dashing between people, not looking back as my mother screamed shrilly, "Meimei! Meimei!" I fled down an alley, past dark curtained shops and merchants washing the grime off their windows. I sped into the sunlight, into a large street crowded with tourists examining trinkets and souvenirs. I ducked into another dark alley, down another street, up another alley. I ran until it hurt and I realized I had nowhere to go, that I was not running from anything. The alleys contained no escape routes.

My breath came out like angry smoke. It was cold. I sat down on an upturned plastic pail next to a stack of empty boxes, cupping my chin with my hands, thinking hard. I imagined my mother, first walking briskly down one street or another looking for me, then giving up and returning home to await my arrival. After two hours, I stood up on creaking legs and slowly walked home.

◆ Build Vocabulary

concessions (kən sesh´ ənz) *n.*: Things given or granted as privileges

> **◆ Literary Focus**
> What makes Waverly upset at her mother's behavior? Why is her mother's voice "cracking with anger"?
> **❹**

230 ◆ *Moments of Discovery*

🎭 Speaking and Listening Mini-Lesson

Dialogue

This mini-lesson supports the Speaking and Listening activity in the Idea Bank on page 233.

Introduce the Concept Remind students that in a dialogue two or more characters trade thoughts, opinions, and ideas. The tone of a dialogue is conversational.

Develop Background Lead students to consider these questions:

• How would each character's feelings have changed in the years since the conflict?

• Would the characters be likely to be able to express their real feelings years later?

Apply the Information Pairs can write their dialogues, each student taking one part. Remind them to keep their dialogues consistent with the personalities of the characters.

Assess the Outcome Have students perform their dialogues for the class. Have students assess the performances, focusing on whether the characterizations are consistent and believable.

The alley was quiet and I could see the yellow lights shining from our flat like two tiger's eyes in the night. I climbed the sixteen steps to the door, advancing quietly up each so as not to make any warning sounds. I turned the knob; the door was locked. I heard a chair moving, quick steps, the locks turning—click! click! click!—and then the door opened.

"About time you got home," said Vincent. "Boy, are you in trouble."

He slid back to the dinner table. On a platter were the remains of a large fish, its fleshy head still connected to bones swimming upstream in vain escape. Standing there waiting for my punishment, I heard my mother speak in a dry voice.

"We not concerning this girl. This girl not have concerning for us."

Nobody looked at me. Bone chopsticks[11] clinked against the insides of bowls being

---

11. **chopsticks** (chäp´ stiks´): Two small sticks of wood, bone, or ivory, held together in one hand and used as utensils for eating, cooking, and serving food.

emptied into hungry mouths.

I walked into my room, closed the door, and lay down on my bed. The room was dark, the ceiling filled with shadows from the dinnertime lights of neighboring flats.

In my head, I saw a chessboard with sixty-four black and white squares. Opposite me was my opponent, two angry black slits. She wore a triumphant smile. "Strongest wind cannot be seen," she said.

Her black men advanced across the plane, slowly marching to each successive level as a single unit. My white pieces screamed as they scurried and fell off the board one by one. As her men drew closer to my edge, I felt myself growing light. I rose up into the air and flew out the window. Higher and higher, above the alley, over the tops of tiled roofs, where I was gathered up by the wind and pushed up toward the night sky until everything below me disappeared and I was alone.

I closed my eyes and pondered my next move.

Guide for Responding

◆ *Literature and Your Life*

Reader's Response The story ends without a final showdown. Who do you think will eventually win the "game"—Waverly or her mother? Why?

Thematic Focus Why do you think Waverly seems so angry with her mother?

Group Discussion As a group, consider games and sports that have complicated rules and strategies—for example, football, tennis, or Monopoly. Collaborate on a list of rules and strategies from various games that can be extended beyond the game to daily life—to the family, school, workplace, or political scene, for example.

☑ Check Your Comprehension

1. How does Waverly start playing chess?
2. Explain how she progresses from losing to her brothers at chess to being compared with Bobby Fischer in *Life* magazine.
3. Describe what happens between Waverly and Mrs. Jong at the market.
4. What happens when Waverly returns home after the incident at the market?
5. How does the story end?

Rules of the Game ◆ 231

Beyond the Selecton

FURTHER READING

Other Works by Amy Tan
The Moon Lady

Other Works About Generational Conflict
Racing the Sun, Paul Pitts
Soul Daddy, Jacqueline Roy

INTERNET

You and your students may find additional information on chess and Amy Tan on the Internet. We suggest the following sites. Please be aware, however, that sites may have changed from the time we published this information.

Kids Chess Network, Inc. is at **www.infochess.com**

A charming short story by Amy Tan, "The Chinese Siamese Cat," with color illustrations, can be accessed at the address **http://www.tampines. org.sh/story1/html**

We *strongly recommend* that you preview the sites before you send students to them.

◆ Critical Thinking

1. She manipulates her mother into buying treats for her in the store.
2. (a) She pretends to be weaker than she is. Meanwhile she grows stronger by studying chess all the time. (b) She pretends not to want things she does want, manipulating her mother. She tries to keep her feelings secret.
3. Superficially about chess, the story is also about strategies in relationships.
4. The battle of wills between parents and children is universal. The weapons Waverly and her mother use—misdirection, haranguing, guilt—are also universal. The strong family values and respect for tradition of Chinese culture provide the special circumstances of the Jongs' battle.
5. Answers may include nearly any "maturation" story, including *The Adventures of Huckleberry Finn*.

◆ Reading Strategy

1. Waverly is younger and born in America; her daily life is steeped in American culture.
2. She wants her to have opportunities for success, probably by "fitting into" American culture and playing by its "rules."
3. Both are strong-willed, focused individuals, very intelligent, very proud.

◆ Literary Focus

1. She probably feels her mother is trying to steal some of her own success. She is also embarrassed by the way her mother calls attention to both of them.
2. Mrs. Jong knows what it means to lose a parent and lose a culture; she knows how hard it will be for Waverly to fit into an alien society.

◆ Build Vocabulary

reules: rules
circonstances: circumstances
solennité: solemnity
Sample sentences:
1. Rules are necessary in games.
2. Waverly cannot fully appreciate the circumstances her mother found herself in when she was a young girl in China.
3. An air of solemnity often surrounds the playing of chess.

Using the Word Bank
1. a   2. b   3. b   4. c   5. b   6. c

◆ Critical Thinking

INTERPRET

1. How does Waverly show that she understands the use of strategy even before she starts playing chess? **[Analyze]**
2. Mrs. Jong gives Waverly rules of behavior in the form of Chinese sayings. (a) How does Waverly use these rules to win at chess? (b) How does she use them in her struggle with her mother? **[Connect]**
3. Why do you think Amy Tan called this story "Rules of the Game"? **[Connect]**

EVALUATE

4. Which elements of the struggle between Waverly and her mother are universal, and which are uniquely Chinese American? **[Assess]**

EXTEND

5. What other stories can you think of in which a child uses success in some activity to outgrow a parent? **[Literature Link]**

◆ Reading Strategy

CONTRAST CHARACTERS

"Rules of the Game" develops conflict between two strong characters who are both similar to and different from each other.
1. Why is Waverly in a better position than her mother to understand "American rules"?
2. What does Mrs. Jong want for her daughter that she doesn't have herself?
3. In what ways are Waverly and Mrs. Jong more alike than they admit?

◆ Literary Focus

GENERATIONAL CONFLICT

The cultural conflict in "Rules of the Game" heightens the **generational conflict** between a mother and her daughter.
1. What does Waverly resent about her mother's behavior when they are shopping together?
2. What might Mrs. Jong feel that her child does not yet understand?

◆ Build Vocabulary

Here are the original French words from which some of the English words in the story evolved. Write the English equivalent of each word, along with a sentence using the English word.
1. *reules*   2. *circonstances*   3. *solemnité*

USING THE WORD BANK

On your paper, write the word whose meaning is closest to that of the first word.
1. concessions: (a) things granted, (b) large meetings, (c) secrets
2. retort: (a) foolish deed, (b) clever reply, (c) old wisdom
3. malodorous: (a) evil-minded, (b) bad-smelling, (c) beautiful-sounding
4. prodigy: (a) young child, (b) large amount, (c) talented person
5. pungent: (a) sweet-tasting, (b) sharp-smelling, (c) witty
6. benevolently: (a) wealthily, (b) attractively, (c) in a kind way

◆ Build Grammar Skills

COMPLEX SENTENCES

In a complex sentence, the subordinate clause is usually introduced by a subordinating conjunction, such as *when, as, because, who, which, that,* or *if.*

> A **complex sentence** consists of one independent clause and at least one subordinate clause.

Practice On your paper write the following sentences from "Rules of the Game." Underline the independent clause in each sentence once and the subordinate clause twice.
1. The next week I bit back my tongue as we entered the store with the forbidden candies.
2. When we got home, my mother told Vincent to throw the chess set away.
3. I came back to the park and approached a man who was observing the game.
4. As her men drew closer to my edge, I felt myself growing light.

◆ Build Grammar Skills

Practice
1. The next week I bit back my tongue <u>as we entered the store with the forbidden candies.</u>
2. <u>When we got home,</u> my mother told Vincent to throw the chess set away.
3. I came back to the park and approached a man <u>who was observing the game.</u>
4. <u>As her men drew closer to my edge,</u> I felt myself growing light.
5. My mother placed my first trophy next to a new plastic chess set <u>that the neighborhood Tao society had given to me.</u>

✎ Writer's Solution

For additional instruction and practice, use the lesson in the **Language Lab CD-ROM** on Sentence Style and the practice page in the *Writer's Solution Grammar Practice Book* on The Four Structures of Sentences, p. 57.

Build Your Portfolio

Idea Bank

Writing

1. **Notes for a Magazine Article** Imagine that you are a journalist developing a feature article on chess prodigy Waverly Jong. Write notes about a visit to her home in Chinatown. Focus particularly on your impressions of Waverly and her mother. **[Career Link]**

2. **Letter** Write a letter from Mrs. Jong to her daughter expressing how she feels after the incident in the market.

3. **Extension** Write an extension of "Rules of the Game," telling what happens the following day in the Jong household.

Speaking and Listening

4. **Radio Commentary** Imagine that you are a radio announcer describing a national chess tournament in which Waverly Jong is a finalist. Set the scene for your listeners, focusing on Waverly and her opponent. **[Media Link]**

5. **Dialogue** With another classmate, create a dialogue between Waverly and her mother that takes place years after the events in this story, when Waverly is grown up.

Projects

6. **Chess Set** Design your own chess set. You can draw or paint your design or use modeling clay to sculpt your chess pieces. Label each figure. **[Art Link]**

7. **Game** Work with a partner to invent a game with its own rules, board, and pieces. Once you decide how your game is to be played, make a model of it with your partner. Then teach your game to your classmates and have a tournament.

Writing Mini-Lesson

Proposal to Change the Rules of a Game

Choose a sport or game with which you are familiar and think about how you might change the rules. Write a proposal meant to persuade some official body to adopt the rule change you suggest.

Writing Skills Focus: Clear and Logical Organization

Organize your proposal either subject by subject or feature by feature. In **subject by subject** organization, you discuss all the features of one subject (in this case, the current rules of your game, and where they are inadequate) and then the features of the other subject (in this case, the new rules you are proposing and how they would improve the game). If you organize **feature by feature,** you focus on each of the failings of the current rules and how your new rules would improve the situation in each case.

Prewriting Write down the rules you wish to change, and then list all their disadvantages. Next to each disadvantage, write how your new rules would correct the problem.

Drafting Decide how you want to organize your proposal. If you want to go subject by subject, present all the qualities of one subject first, then all the qualities of the next subject. If, on the other hand, you want to go feature by feature, discuss each aspect of your subjects in turn.

Use transitions such as *in contrast, instead of, on the one hand . . . on the other hand,* to highlight the differences between your two subjects.

Revising Reread your draft. Are the advantages of your new system over the old system clear? If you were an official of the sport or game, would you be persuaded to consider the ideas in the proposal?

Rules of the Game ◆ 233

Idea Bank

Customizing for
Performance Levels
Following are suggestions for matching the Idea Bank topics with your students' performance levels:
  Less Advanced Students: 1
  Average Students: 2, 4, 6
  More Advanced Students: 3, 5, 7

Customizing for
Learning Modalities
Following are suggestions for matching Idea Bank topics with your students' learning modalities:
  Visual/Spatial: 6
  Verbal/Linguistic: 1, 2, 3, 4
  Logical/Mathematical: 7
  Interpersonal: 5

Writing Mini-Lesson
Refer students to the Writing Handbook, page 962, for instruction on the writing process, and page 965 for further information on Persuasion. You may also use the writing process models for a Letter to the Editor in *Writing and Language Transparencies,* pp. 41–44, to guide students through the writing process.

Writer's Solution

Writing Lab CD-ROM
Have students use the Tutorial on Persuasion to help them complete the mini-lesson. Follow these steps:
1. Have students review the audio-annotated model of a position paper.
2. Suggest that students complete the Audience Profile.
3. Direct students to play the video clip on persuading a diverse audience.
4. Have students draft their proposals on computer.
You will need about 60 minutes to complete these steps.

Sourcebook
Have students use Chapter 4, Persuasion (pp. 96–127), for additional support.

✓ ASSESSMENT OPTIONS

Formal Assessment, Selection Test, pp. 54–56, and Assessment Resources Software. The selection test is designed so that it can be easily customized to the performance levels of your students. *Alternative Assessment,* p. 16, includes options for less advanced students, more advanced students, intrapersonal learners, musical/rhythmic learners, verbal/linguistic learners, and visual/spatial learners.

PORTFOLIO ASSESSMENT
Use the following rubrics in the *Alternative Assessment* booklet to assess student writing:
Notes for a Magazine Article: Summary Rubric, p. 91
Letter: Expression Rubric, p. 87
Extension: Fictional Narrative Rubric, p. 88
Writing Mini-Lesson: How-to/Process Explanation Rubric, p. 93

Guide for Reading

OBJECTIVES

1. To read, comprehend, and interpret a story and a poem
2. To relate a story and a poem to personal experience
3. To relate to personal experience to enhance understanding of a story and a poem
4. To identify irony
5. To build vocabulary in context and learn the suffix *-ment*
6. To develop skill in identifying and using pronouns and antecedents
7. To write a scene from a teen soap opera, keeping the audience in mind
8. To respond to the story and poem through writing, speaking and listening, and projects

SKILLS INSTRUCTION

Vocabulary:
Suffixes: *-ment*

Grammar:
Pronouns and
Antecedents

Reading Strategy:
Relate to Personal
Experience

Literary Focus:
Irony

Writing: Keeping
the Audience in
Mind

**Speaking and
Listening:** Oral
Story (teacher
edition)

Critical Viewing:
Analyze

PORTFOLIO OPPORTUNITIES

Writing: Classified Advertisement, Job Evaluation, Love Poem

Writing Mini-Lesson: Scene From a Teen Soap Opera

Speaking and Listening: Television News Report, Oral Story

Projects: Audio Montage, Historic Homes

Cynthia Rylant (1954–)

Quiet, thoughtful characters who are isolated in some way from their peers are this author's specialty. She has said, "I don't want to deal with the people who have what they want. I want to deal with people who don't have what they want, to show their lives too." Rylant, who grew up in a West Virginia mountain town, discovered a love of good writing in college English classes. She never thought about becoming a writer herself, however, until she took a job as a librarian and began reading lots of children's books.

Since publishing her first book, *When I Was Young in the Mountains*, in 1982, Rylant has produced a wide range of literary works—picture books, poetry, short stories, and novels. In 1993, her novel *Missing May* won the Newbery Award.

William Stafford (1914– 1993)

Reading a poem by William Stafford is like having a conversation with the poet. According to commentator Robert Bly, Stafford's poems are "spoken like a friend over coffee."

Stafford grew up in Kansas but spent his later years teaching and writing in Oregon. He didn't publish his first book, *West of Your City*, until he was forty-six. Throughout the remainder of his life, however, he produced a large volume of work. He wrote a poem every day and published numerous collections, including *Traveling in the Dark*, which won the National Book Award in 1962.

His writing earned Stafford the respect of important public figures. In fact, when Stafford died, the governor of Oregon called him "an Oregon treasure."

◆ Build Vocabulary

SUFFIXES: -ment

In "Checkouts," a girl admires a boy's dishevelment. Someone who is disheveled is untidy, and *dishevelment* refers to the condition of being untidy. The suffix *-ment* means "the state of or condition of." Added to a verb, it changes the verb into a noun. For example, adding *-ment* to the verb *disappoint* creates the noun *disappointment*.

WORD BANK

intuition
reverie
shards
harried
brazen
dishevelment
perverse
articulate
lingered
demure

As you read these selections, you will encounter the words on this list. Each word is defined on the page where it first appears. Preview the list before you read.

◆ Build Grammar Skills

PRONOUNS AND ANTECEDENTS

A **pronoun** takes the place of a noun in a sentence. Without pronouns, writers would have to repeat nouns, making long, unwieldy sentences. The noun that a pronoun replaces is the pronoun's **antecedent**. Every pronoun should have a clear antecedent. In this sentence, an arrow points from one pronoun to its antecedent.

Her parents wrote up the *list* and handed *it* to her.

At the beginning of "Checkouts," the author uses a pronoun that does not have an antecedent. As you read, think about why the author might have done so.

234 ◆ Moments of Discovery

Checkouts ◆ Fifteen

◆ Literature and Your Life

CONNECT YOUR EXPERIENCE
You get on the school bus and sit alone instead of taking a seat next to someone you don't know. You can't go to a concert because you came down with a bad case of the flu. Missed opportunities for new adventures occur just about every day. In these two selections, young people experience lost opportunities for different reasons.

Journal Writing Write about a missed opportunity in your life. Imagine what might have happened if you had seized the opportunity.

THEMATIC FOCUS: FINDING OUR IDENTITY
In "Checkouts," a girl falls in love. In "Fifteen," a boy chances upon a riderless motorcycle. These opportunities for new experiences lead the two teenagers to discoveries about themselves.

◆ Background for Understanding

CULTURE
In "Checkouts," the main character is compared to "a Tibetan monk in solitary meditation." Tibet, once an independent nation north of the Himalaya Mountains, is now part of China. Its people are devout Buddhists. Buddhist monks live in seclusion, devoting their time to various spiritual pursuits, including meditation. Meditation involves clearing the mind of all thoughts to achieve a state of perfect calmness. In "Checkouts," the main character achieves this state by grocery shopping!

◆ Literary Focus

IRONY
Irony is a literary technique in which the outcome is different from what the reader or the characters expect or from what might logically be expected. For example, "Checkouts" follows a seemingly predictable story line about a budding relationship between a boy and a girl, but the outcome of this relationship turns out to be different from what readers might expect.

◆ Reading Strategy

RELATE TO PERSONAL EXPERIENCE
One of the great things about literature is that it allows you to travel to places you've never been and explore experiences you've never had. Even though you may never have had exactly the same experiences presented in a work, you will most likely have had some of the feelings that the characters experience, know people like the characters, or had experiences that are in some ways similar to those presented in the selection. As you read, look for these types of connections. Doing so will help you become more involved in what you read and help you to understand and appreciate the characters and events.

Guide for Reading ◆ 235

In class, have five students form a "talk-show" panel to briefly discuss their opinions about what can happen when people fall in love or develop a strong infatuation at first sight. Then open up the discussion to "call-in" comments and questions from the class. Wrap up the activity and explain that "Checkouts" describes one course that love at first sight can take.

Customize for
Less Proficient Readers
Because most of the action in Rylant's story takes place in the minds of the characters, these students might find the story hard to follow. Have them use a two-column chart to help them track each change in the boy's and the girl's outlooks.

Customize for
More Advanced Students
Challenge these students to critically evaluate the story based on these criteria: Is it entertaining? Is is believable? What universal message or insights does it convey? As students read, they should gather information to support their evaluations. When they've finished, have them share their evaluations with the rest of the class, and use the evaluations to stimulate a class discussion.

Customize for
English Language Learners
There are several vocabulary words, in addition to the ones defined in the text, that may be unfamiliar to these students. Pair students with native English speakers to define and write sentences for the following additional words: *impulse, sifting, unfocused,* and *fetishes* from context.

Preparing for Standardized Tests

Grammar Grammar and usage sections of standardized tests, including the ACT, sometimes call on students to revise sentences that contain errors in pronoun-antecedent agreement. For example, students might encounter sentences like these:

> Jill studies biology, a course you need in order to prepare for medical school.
> Each nation has their own culture.

The Build Grammar Skills lesson accompanying these selections teaches how to identify pronouns and antecedents—the first step in learning about pronoun-antecedent agreement. After students have completed the activities on page 242, extend their learning by having them correct the previous examples. Look for the following corrections:

> Jill studies biology, a course *she* needs in order to prepare for medical school.
> Each nation has *its* own culture.

In this story, a girl and a boy fall in love at first sight—but never actually meet! Readers might expect such a missed opportunity to give a story a sad ending, but in "Checkouts," the plot takes a different turn. For both characters, the missed opportunity leads to new opportunities, not only for friendships and romance, but also for self-discovery. Students will easily relate to this story—a familiar one to many teenagers.

Customize for
English Language Learners
Assure these students that the girl did not actually lie on the floor and beg her parents not to move—she just felt like doing those things.

◆ *Literature and Your Life*
❶ Ask students who have moved to a new town or entered a new school to share their experiences with the class. What makes it difficult to be a newcomer? How can others make it easier on newcomers? *Students should acknowledge that having to gain acceptance from others is probably the biggest challenge faced by newcomers. Other children can help newcomers by recognizing their situation and reaching out to them.*

◆ **Critical Thinking**
❷ **Evaluate** Point out that in this passage the author gives away an important plot element that will follow. Ask students why Rylant might have used this technique of directly stating a plot development at the beginning of a story. Ask what effect the statement had on them. *Students might say that the suddenness and boldness of the narrator's declaration at the beginning of the story raises their interest. They might sense a conflict and be curious to see how it unfolds.*

◆ **Critical Thinking**
❸ **Synthesize** If the girl likes grocery shopping because it lets her "think and relax and wander," what other activities might she enjoy for the same reason? *Students might suggest going for walks, browsing in the library, or other activities that take little concentration.*

Checkouts

Cynthia Rylant

❶ Her parents had moved her to Cincinnati, to a large house with beveled glass windows[1] and several porches and the *history* her mother liked to emphasize. You'll love the house, they said. You'll be lonely at first, they admitted, but you're so nice you'll make friends fast. And as an impulse tore at her to lie on the floor, to hold to their ankles and tell them she felt she was dying, to offer anything, anything at all, so they might allow her to finish growing up in the town of her childhood, they firmed their mouths and spoke from their chests and they said, It's decided.

❷ They moved her to Cincinnati, where for a month she spent the greater part of every day in a room full of beveled glass windows, sifting through photographs of the life she'd lived and left behind. But it is difficult work, suffering, and in its own way a kind of art, and finally she didn't have the energy for it anymore, so she emerged from the beautiful house and fell in love with a bag boy at the supermarket. Of course, this didn't happen all at once, just like that, but in the sequence of things that's exactly the way it happened.

❸ She liked to grocery shop. She loved it in the way some people love to drive long country roads, because doing it she could think and relax and wander. Her parents wrote up the list and handed it to her and off she went without complaint to perform what they regarded as a great sacrifice of her time and a sign that she was indeed a very ❹ nice girl. She had never told them how much she loved grocery shopping, only that she was "willing" to do it. She had an <u>intuition</u> which told her that her parents were not

---

1. **beveled** (bev´ əld) **glass:** Glass having angled or slanted edges.

◆ **Build Vocabulary**

intuition (in´ tōō wish´ ən) *n.:* Knowledge of something without reasoning

❺ ▶ **Critical Viewing** The girl in this story relaxes by grocery shopping. How can performing everyday activities help a person to relax? [Analyze]

236 ◆ Moments of Discovery

 Block Scheduling Strategies

Consider these suggestions to take advantage of extended class time:

• Have pairs of students take turns performing the role-playing activity in Literature and Your Life (p. 240).

• Play the recording of "Fifteen" in **Listening to Literature.** Have students analyze the structure of the poem and the poet's choice of words based on what they hear.

• Invite students to meet in small groups to talk about how they were able to relate "Checkouts"

and "Fifteen" to their own personal experiences.

• Have students prepare and perform the Oral Story activity in the Idea Bank (p. 243). Use the Speaking and Listening Mini-Lesson at the bottom of page 238 to facilitate this activity.

• Divide the class into teams to debate whether or not motorcyclists, such as the one in "Fifteen," should be required to wear helmets. See the activity in *Alternative Assessment,* p. 17.

◆ **Reading Strategy**

❹ **Relate to Personal Experience** Point out that most people keep some of their thoughts secret, even from those closest to them. Ask students how the experience of secret likes and dislikes can add to a reader's enjoyment of the story. *Similar personal experiences help a reader identify with a character.*

▶**Critical Viewing**◀

❺ **Analyze** Because everyday activities tend to be routine and repetitive, they require little concentration, thereby allowing a person to daydream. In addition, a person may feel less stressed when doing something productive.

Customize for
Visual/Spatial Learners
Encourage these students to use the art on this page to help them picture the story's setting. What details are included in the art that are not included in the story? *There are numerous details, including the price listings and the stacks of food, that are in the art but not mentioned in the story.*

Food City, 1967, Richard Estes, Akron Art Museum, Akron, Ohio, © Richard Estes / Licensed by Vaga, New York, NY / Courtesy of Marlborough Gallery, NY

Checkouts ◆ 237

Cross-Curricular Connection: Art and Architecture

The only detail mentioned about the house in Cincinnati is the "beveled glass windows." Explain that beveled windows have a sloping rather than a flat edge where they meet the frame. Because most modern homes have plain windows, beveling suggests an older style of architecture.

Students may be interested in finding out more about older styles of architecture found in American houses:

• New England or Cape Cod houses are made of wood with small rooms and sloping roofs.

• Southern Colonial houses are large with high-

pitched roofs, columns in front, and porches.

• Georgian houses are square or rectangular, made of brick, with a central hall and many tall windows.

• Victorian houses have elaborate designs and large rooms. They were most popular in the late 1800's.

Have students choose a style of architecture to research and report on. Suggest that picturing the girl in "Checkouts" in a particular type of house might help make the story more real for them.

◆ Literary Focus

❶ Irony The situation is ironic because you'd expect her to be mad at the boy for dropping the mayonnaise, not to fall in love with him.

Connections to Today's World

About the Author

Grammy Award-winning musician **Joni Mitchell** was born Roberta Joan Anderson in Fort McLeod, Alberta, Canada in 1943. She won fame as a folk singer, composer, and lyricist in the 1960's. "Both Sides Now" was a mammoth best-selling hit, as were her songs "The Circle Game" and "Woodstock."

Customize for
English Language Learners

The figurative language and allusions in these lyrics may be difficult for these students to comprehend. Help them understand lines such as "Bows and flows of angel hair," "feathered canyons," and "Moons and Junes and Ferris wheels." Invite them to share figurative expressions they know in their native language.

◆ *Literature and Your Life*

Find a recording of "Both Sides Now" in a personal music collection or in your local library. Play the recording for the class. Ask students to compare the experience of hearing the song sung to that of reading the lyrics on paper.

Answers

1. The speaker discovers her perspectives change.
2. Students may feel that looking at something from "both sides" can help you understand it or reveal that there is much that you still don't understand.
3. Some students may mention particular experiences that help them relate to the song. Others may say that they have not experienced similar feelings.

↑ safe for sharing such strong, important facts about herself. Let them think they knew her.

Once inside the supermarket, her hands firmly around the handle of the cart, she would lapse into a kind of <u>reverie</u> and wheel toward the produce. Like a Tibetan monk in solitary meditation, she calmed to a point of deep, deep happiness; this feeling came to her, reliably, if strangely, only in the supermarket.

> **◆ Literary Focus**
> **❶** Why is the description of how the girl fell in love ironic?

Then one day the bag boy dropped her jar of mayonnaise and that is how she fell in love.

He was nervous—first day on the job—and along had come this fascinating girl, standing in the checkout line with the unfocused stare one often sees in young children, her face turned enough away that he might take several full

◆ Build Vocabulary

reverie (rev´ ər ē) *n.*: Dreamy thought of pleasant things

CONNECTIONS TO TODAY'S WORLD
Both Sides Now

Joni Mitchell

The girl in this story is intrigued by the fact that the bag boy contrasts sharply with the world in which she lives. As songwriter Joni Mitchell notes in this Grammy-winning song, the type of interest that Rylant's character takes can help lead a person toward a more complete view of the world.

Bows and flows of angel hair
And ice cream castles in the air
And feathered canyons everywhere
I've looked at clouds that way

5 But now they only block the sun
They rain and snow on everyone
So many things I could have done
But clouds got in my way

I've looked at clouds from both sides now
10 From up and down, and still somehow
It's clouds' illusions I recall
I really don't know clouds at all

Moons and Junes and Ferris wheels
The dizzy dancing way you feel
15 As every fairy tale comes real
I've looked at love that way

But now it's just another show
You leave them laughing when you go
And if you care don't let them know
20 Don't give yourself away

I've looked at love from both sides now
From give and take, and still somehow
It's love's illusions I recall
I really don't know love at all

25 Tears and fears and feeling proud
To say I love you, right out loud
Dreams and schemes and circus crowds
I've looked at life that way

But now old friends are acting strange
30 They shake their heads, they say I've changed
Something's lost, but something's gained
In living every day

I've looked at life from both sides now
From win and lose, and still somehow
35 It's life's illusions I recall
I really don't know life at all

1. What discovery does the speaker of this song make about herself?
2. How does the speaker's discovery relate to the experiences of Rylant's characters?
3. Have you ever experienced feelings like the ones expressed in this song? Explain.

238 ◆ *Moments of Discovery*

Speaking and Listening Mini-Lesson

Oral Story

This mini-lesson supports the Speaking and Listening activity in the Idea Bank on page 243.

Introduce the Concept Have students discuss stories they have told or heard in the past. What makes some stories interesting and others boring?

Develop Background Have students reread the story, jotting down the parts they want to include. Remind them to look for ways to add humor. Then have them consider these questions:

• Who is your audience? How might you tell the

story differently to a parent and to a friend?
• What should you do if you sense that you are losing your listener's attention?

Apply the Information Have students develop and perform their oral stories for the class.

Assess the Outcome Have students assess one another's performances, focusing on whether the performances are entertaining and true to Rylant's story. You might use the Peer Assessment form for Oral Interpretation, p. 112, in *Alternative Assessment.*

looks at her as he packed sturdy bags full of food and the goods of modern life. She interested him because her hair was red and thick, and in it she had placed a huge orange bow, nearly the size of a small hat. That was enough to distract him, and when finally it was her groceries he was packing, she looked at him and smiled and he could respond only by busting her jar of mayonnaise on the floor, shards of glass and oozing cream decorating the area around his feet.

She loved him at exactly that moment, and if he'd known this perhaps he wouldn't have fallen into the brown depression he fell into, which lasted the rest of his shift. He believed he must have looked the jackass in her eyes, and he envied the sureness of everyone around him: the cocky cashier at the register, the grim and harried store manager, the bland butcher, and the brazen bag boys who smoked in the warehouse on their breaks. He wanted a second chance. Another chance to be confident and say witty things to her as he threw tin cans into her bags, persuading her to allow him to help her to her car so he might learn just a little about her, check out the floor of the car for signs of hobbies or fetishes and the bumpers for clues as to beliefs and loyalties.

But he busted her jar of mayonnaise and nothing else worked out for the rest of the day.

Strange, how attractive clumsiness can be. She left the supermarket with stars in her eyes, for she had loved the way his long nervous fingers moved from the conveyor belt to the bags, how deftly (until the mayonnaise) they had picked up her items and placed them in her bags. She had loved the way the hair kept falling into his eyes as he leaned over to grab a box or a tin. And the tattered brown shoes he wore with no socks. And the left side of his collar turned in rather than out.

The bag boy seemed a wonderful contrast to the perfectly beautiful house she had been forced to accept as her home, to the *history* she hated, to the loneliness she had become used to, and she couldn't wait to come back for more of his awkwardness and dishevelment.

Incredibly, it was another four weeks before they saw each other again. As fate would have

it, her visits to the supermarket never coincided with his schedule to bag. Each time she went to the store, her eyes scanned the checkouts at once, her heart in her mouth. And each hour he worked, the bag boy kept one eye on the door, watching for the red-haired girl with the big orange bow.

Yet in their disappointment these weeks there was a kind of ecstasy. It is reason enough to be alive, the hope you may see again some face which has meant something to you. The anticipation of meeting the bag boy eased the girl's painful transition into her new and jarring life in Cincinnati. It provided for her an anchor amid all that was impersonal and unfamiliar, and she spent less time on thoughts of what she had left behind as she concentrated on what might lie ahead. And for the boy, the long and often tedious hours at the supermarket which provided no challenge other than that of showing up the following workday . . . these hours became possibilities of mystery and romance for him as he watched the electric doors for the girl in the orange bow.

And when finally they did meet up again, neither offered a clue to the other that he, or she, had been the object of obsessive thought for weeks. She spotted him as soon as she came into the store, but she kept her eyes strictly in front of her as she pulled out a cart and wheeled it toward the produce. And he, too, knew the instant she came through the door—though the orange bow was gone, replaced by a small but bright yellow flower instead—and he never once turned his head in her direction but watched her from the corner of his vision as he tried to swallow back the fear in his throat.

It is odd how we sometimes deny ourselves

◆ Build Vocabulary

shards (shärdz) *n.*: Broken pieces

harried (har´ ēd) *adj.*: Worried

brazen (brā´ zən) *adj.*: Shamelessly bold

dishevelment (di shev´ əl ment) *n.*: A state of being untidy

◆ Critical Thinking

❷ Deduce Ask students what this passage tells them about the boy's personality. Which details in the passage show this character trait? *Readers might infer that the boy is shy because he drops the jar of mayonnaise when the girl smiles at him.*

◆ Literary Focus

❸ Irony Have students explain why this passage is ironic. *The passage is ironic because "awkwardness and dishevelment" might be considered negative rather than positive qualities. The boy probably wouldn't imagine himself valued for such qualities.*

◆ Build Vocabulary

❹ Suffixes: -ment Point out the word "disappointment" in this passage. Ask students how they would figure out the meaning of this word if they were unfamiliar with it. *The suffix -ment forms a noun out of a verb. Thus* disappointment *means "the condition of being disappointed."*

◆ Critical Thinking

❺ Interpret Ask students to paraphrase this passage. *The girl's preoccupation with the bag boy gives her something to hope for and keeps her from missing her home town.*

◆ Critical Thinking

❻ Infer Ask students what this passage tells them about the girl's personality. Which details in the passage show this character trait? *Students can infer that the girl is shy because she doesn't look at the boy while she is in the market.*

 Beyond the Classroom

Career Connection

Explain to students that it is important for them to be aware of their own interests and skills when considering job opportunities. Having a job that is well-suited to one's interests and abilities can make the difference between frustrating drudgery and a rewarding career.

Point out the passage in the story in which the bag boy's job is described: ". . . the long and often tedious hours at the supermarket . . ." Review with the class that the boy eventually ". . . made a desperate search for something better . . ."

Lead a discussion in which students consider the differences a job one likes or dislikes can make in a person's life. They might consider why most people are more successful at jobs they enjoy.

To help students determine what jobs might be appropriate for them, have them create "interest inventories" in which they note their own interests, likes, and dislikes. Have them match their interests with possible jobs—either part-time for the present or full-time for future careers.

239

One-Minute Insight

Emily Dickinson's poem speaks of the human fear of achieving greatness. According to the speaker, we impose limitations on ourselves because life seems safer in a cage than outside.

◆ Critical Thinking

❶ Interpret Ask the class to discuss their interpretation of these lines. *Students will probably interpret the lines to mean that we don't know our true potential until we are asked to meet new challenges.*

◆ *Literature and Your Life*

❷ Encourage students to cite examples from life that either support or contradict Dickinson's assertion that people are capable of exceeding their expectations of themselves. *Students may cite acts of heroism in rescuing others from fires or other disasters.*

◆ Build Vocabulary

❸ Levels of Diction Have students work with partners to rephrase these lines in informal diction. *Suggested paraphrase: Heroic acts would be everyday occurrences if people didn't limit themselves through fear.* **Ask students:** Why didn't Emily Dickinson just come out and state this idea plainly? *Students may think that the elevated diction in this stanza heightens the point Dickinson is expressing and serves to make the reader think more about the ideas in the stanza.*

Bubbles, Watercolor, 39" x 29". Courtesy of South Burdick.

248 ◆ *Moments of Discovery*

Humanities: Art

Bubbles, by Scott Burdick.

Scott Burdick attended the American Academy of Art in Chicago and studied Life Drawing and Oil Painting under Bill Parks. He has received several awards for his art, including the 1996 Silver Medal of Honor from the American Watercolor Society.

In this painting, a young woman is waving a bubble wand, creating a whole spectrum of dazzling colors around her. Her body position and facial expression suggest feelings of joy and freedom.

Use these questions for discussion:

1. How does the picture of the girl suggest the mood of Emily Dickinson's poem? *Accept reasonable responses: The girl's pose and manner suggest that her "stature touches the sky."*

2. If the girl in the painting could read "We never know how high we are," what do you think she would say in response? *Accept reasonable responses: She might agree with the poem; she might say that her purpose in life is to enjoy herself, not to be a hero.*

We never know how high we are

Emily Dickinson

1   We never know how high we are
    Till we are asked to rise
2   And then if we are true to plan
    Our statures touch the skies—
    The Heroism we recite
3   Would be a normal thing
    Did not ourselves the Cubits[1] warp
    For fear to be a King—

---

1. **Cubits** (kyo͞o′ bitz): Ancient measure of the length of the arm from the end of the middle finger to the elbow.

◆ Build Vocabulary

warp (wôrp) v.: Bend or twist out of shape; distort

Customize for
Less Proficient Readers
Let students know that the first two lines, which are relatively straightforward, contain the main idea of the entire poem. Suggest that students read pairs of lines with a partner, and help each other relate each pair of lines of the poem to the first two.

Customize for
Musical / Rhythmic Learners
Play the audiocassette recording of this poem, encouraging students to notice the rhythms and rhymes. Point out that the last word in each second line is emphasized by the rhyme and the shortness of the line.

Guide for Responding

◆ Literature and Your Life

Reader's Response What, if anything, has ever made you feel like a caged bird?

Thematic Focus What discovery does the speaker make in each poem?

Role Play With another student, create a dialogue between the caged bird and the free bird. Explore how they would feel toward each other and whether they would have any feelings in common.

☑ Check Your Comprehension

1. What does the caged bird want to do?
2. Of what does the free bird in Angelou's poem think?
3. According to Dickinson's poem, what happens when we are asked to rise to an occasion?

◆ Critical Thinking

INTERPRET

1. What might the cage represent in Dunbar's poem? **[Analyze]**
2. Compare and contrast the bird images used by Dunbar and Angelou. **[Compare and Contrast]**
3. Does Dickinson feel that people are capable of acting better than they do, or that they do not give themselves credit for the good things they actually accomplish? **[Distinguish]**

APPLY

4. Explain how a human being could be the equivalent of a caged bird or a free bird. **[Generalize]**

EXTEND

5. Is Dickinson more likely to see people as caged birds or free birds? **[Literature Link]**

We never know how high we are ◆ 249

Cross-Curricular Connection: Mathematics/Social Studies

The poem mentions an archaic unit of measure, the cubit (line 7). Ask students to find out what a cubit is and how long it is. *It is an ancient unit of measurement based on the length from the elbow to the tip of the forefinger; about 18–21 inches.* Challenge students to discover other old or obscure units of measurement. Have them list or chart what each unit measured, where and when it was used, and what the measurement was based on (for example, a part of the body). Units may measure length, weight, area, volume, or

other quantities. Examples might include hectares, hecatombs, furlongs, fathoms, and others. Before students begin, ask them to state possible sources of information. *Dictionary, encyclopedia, math books*

Discuss why Emily Dickinson used the archaic term "cubit" in her poem. *It is an example of elevated diction. Because the obscure term is not used in ordinary speech, it captures the attention and imagination of the reader.*

Reinforce and Extend

Answers

◆ Literature and Your Life

Reader's Response Students may identify feelings of fear that have made them feel like a caged bird.

Thematic Focus The speaker in "Sympathy" discovers the feeling of being a caged bird. In "Caged Bird," the speaker discovers the feeling of the free bird. In Dickinson's poem, the speaker discovers the contrast between what people are capable of and what they do.

☑ Check Your Comprehension

1. The caged bird wants to break through its bars to freedom.
2. The free bird thinks of trade winds and fat worms.
3. We meet the challenge "if we are true to plan."

◆ Critical Thinking

1. The cage might represent slavery or discrimination.
2. Dunbar's caged bird has bloody and broken wings and prays for freedom; Angelou uses images of both free and caged birds to create a contrast.
3. Dickinson indicates that people can and do rise to greatness, but often don't give themselves credit for their accomplishments.
4. Some people are restricted by circumstances from achieving their dreams; others rise above any limitations to accomplish their goals.
5. The poem suggests that people fear greatness, and therefore see themselves as caged birds.

249

from In My Place

Charlayne Hunter-Gault

On January 9, 1961, I walked onto the campus at the University of Georgia to begin registering for classes. Ordinarily, there would not have been anything unusual about such a routine exercise, except, in this instance, the officials at the university had been fighting for two and a half years to keep me out. I was not socially, intellectually, or morally undesirable. I was Black. And no Black student had ever been admitted to the University of Georgia in its 176-year history. Until the landmark *Brown* v. *Board of Education* decision that in 1954 declared ❶ separate but equal schools unconstitutional, the university was protected by law in its exclusion of people like me. In applying to the university, Hamilton Holmes and I were making one of the first major tests of the court's ruling in Georgia, and no one was sure just how hard it would be to challenge privilege. It would take us two and a half years of fighting our way through the system and the courts, but finally, with ❷ the help of the NAACP[1] Legal Defense and Educational Fund, Inc., and with the support of our family and friends, we won the right that should have been ours all along. With the ink barely dry on the court order of three days before, Hamilton Holmes and I walked onto the campus and into history.

We would be greeted by mobs of white students, who within forty-eight hours would hurl epithets, burn crosses and Black effigies, and fi-❸ nally stage a riot outside my dormitory while, nearby, state patrolmen ignored the call from university officials to come and intervene. Tear gas would disperse the crowd, but not before I got word in my dorm room, now strewn with glass from a rock through my window, that Hamilton

---

1. **NAACP** *abbr.*: National Association for the Advancement of Colored People.

◆ Build Vocabulary

epithets (ep´ ə thetz) *n.*: Abusive words or phrases; slurs

effigies (ef´ ə gēz) *n.*: Crude figures or dummies representing hated people or a group

disperse (dis pʉrs´) *v.*: Drive off or scatter in different directions

4 Analyze Students may mention determination, courage, self-confidence, and compassion.

Humanities: Photography

Ask students to summarize what the photograph shows: a young African American woman, apparently from the 1950's or 1960's, being photographed and observed by onlookers as she walks on a university campus. Tell students that the photograph shows Charlayne Hunter-Gault as a student.

Use the following questions to discuss the photograph:
1. What might Hunter-Gault be thinking in the photograph? *She appears determined to ignore the attention she is drawing.*
2. Compare and contrast the photograph of Hunter-Gault with the experience of reading her story. In what ways can a picture show you more than a piece of writing, and in what ways might it be more limited? *A photograph can make an action seem more real and can include many small details; a photograph cannot show you people's thoughts.*

4 ▲ Critical Viewing What character traits enable people to maintain their dignity in the face of discrimination? **[Analyze]**

from *In My Place* ◆ 251

Speaking and Listening Mini-Lesson

Dramatic Monologue

This mini-lesson supports the Speaking and Listening activity in the Idea Bank on page 254.

Introduce the Concept Explain that a dramatic monologue is performed by one actor who reveals to the audience the thoughts and feelings of the character she or he is portraying.

Develop Background Have students meet in groups to discuss the concerns

Charlayne would have had. Suggest they consider these points:
• What did Charlayne expect to happen?
• What did she think was the worst thing that could happen?
• Was she sure about how she would react, or did she grapple with self-doubt?

Apply the Information After the group discussions, students should have gathered the ideas they need to prepare their monologues.

Assess the Outcome Suggest students perform their monologues for partners or trade written monologues. Partners should check that:
• facts in the monologue don't contradict facts in the selection
• the character reveals her true thoughts and feelings
• the tone is honest and compelling.

❶ **Commonly Confused Words**
Write on the chalkboard the words *accept* and *except*. Ask students: Which of these words could you substitute for the word *but* in this sentence? *Students should choose "except."*

◆ **Reading Strategy**

❷ **Draw Conclusions** Have students explain why Hunter-Gault's dream would have been impossible to fulfill in the South of earlier years. Ask them to cite evidence for their conclusions. *The dream would have been impossible because she would not have been able to get the proper education, and she would probably not have been given a job in journalism. As evidence, students should cite school segregation and the Jim Crow laws.*

❸ **Clarification** Tell students that the name Jim Crow comes from a nineteenth-century minstrel song that was used by white entertainer Thomas D. Rice (d. 1860) in a song-and-dance act that stereotyped blacks.

Reinforce and Extend

Answers
◆ *Literature and Your Life*

Reader's Response Students may admit that they wouldn't have been able to stand up to the threats.

Thematic Focus People fear change and often do terrible things attempting to prevent it.

☑ **Check Your Comprehension**
1. Officials wanted the school to remain segregated.
2. Students yelled epithets, burned crosses, and staged a riot.
3. She stayed in order to fulfill her dream of becoming a journalist.

◆ **Critical Thinking**
1. Students may say that bigotry and discrimination is a mind-set that is difficult to change.
2. She needed courage, determination, and moral strength.
3. People draw courage from knowing that their actions can benefit others as well as themselves.
4. For Dunbar the dream is a prayer that makes life livable.
5. Yes. She rose to heroic height.

252

---

and I were being suspended for our own safety. It might have been the end of the story but for the fact that the University of Georgia was now the lead case in a series of events that would become Georgia's entry into the Civil Rights Revolution. And we—like the legions of young Black students to follow in other arenas—were now imbued with an unshakable determination to take control of our destiny and force the South to abandon the wretched Jim Crow laws[2] it had perpetuated for generations to keep us in our place.

The newfound sense of mission that now motivated us evolved for me out of a natural desire to fulfill a dream I had nurtured from an early age. With a passion bordering on obsession, I wanted to be a journalist, a dream that would have been, if not unthinkable, at least undoable in the South of my early years. But no one ever told me not to dream, and when the time came to act on that dream, I would not let anything stand in the way of fulfilling it.

---

2. Jim Crow laws: Upholding or practicing discrimination against African Americans. Jim Crow was a derogatory name given to African Americans from the title of a nineteenth-century minstrel song.

◆ **Build Vocabulary**
imbued (im byōōd´) *v.*: Inspired
perpetuated (pur pech´ ōō wāt id) *v.*: Caused to continue indefinitely; prolonged

---

Guide for Responding

◆ *Literature and Your Life*

Reader's Response If you had faced the obstacles Hunter-Gault did, would you have pursued your dream or given it up?

Thematic Focus What unfortunate discovery about people can you make from Hunter-Gault's difficulties during her early days at the University of Georgia?

☑ **Check Your Comprehension**
1. Why did the officials at the University of Georgia try to prevent Hunter-Gault from enrolling there?
2. How were Hunter-Gault and Hamilton Holmes treated by the other students at the university during their first two days?
3. Why did the author stay at the university, despite all the difficulties she faced?

◆ **Critical Thinking**

INTERPRET
1. What various reasons could account for the white students' violent reaction to Hunter-Gault's attempt to attend college with them? **[Analyze]**
2. What qualities did Hunter-Gault need in order to succeed in her mission? **[Draw Conclusions]**
APPLY
3. Hunter-Gault speaks of a "newfound sense of mission." How can a sense of pursuing a larger purpose, as well as her own personal goals, give someone strength? **[Relate]**
EXTEND
4. The author says, "No one ever told me not to dream." What might Paul Laurence Dunbar tell her about dreaming? **[Literature Link]**
5. Does Hunter-Gault's commitment to her dream fulfill Dickinson's idea of heroic behavior? **[Literature Link]**

 Beyond the Selection

FURTHER READING

Other Works by the Authors
The Paul Laurence Dunbar Reader
The Poems of Emily Dickinson
I Know Why the Caged Bird Sings,
Maya Angelou

Other Works About Dreams and Discovery
Coming of Age in Mississippi, Anne Moody
The Thread That Runs So True, Jesse Stuart
Notes of a Native Son, James Baldwin

INTERNET

You and your students may find additional information about the authors on the Internet. We suggest the following site. Please be aware, however, that sites may have changed from the time we published this information.

For a description of Emily Dickinson's homestead and links to other Dickinson sites, go to **http://www-astro.phas-u.mass.edu/local/ amherst/walking-tour/dickinson.html**

We *strongly recommend* that you preview the sites before you send students to them.

Guide for Responding (continued)

◆ Reading Strategy

DRAW CONCLUSIONS

The poems and essay in this group of selections encourage you to **draw conclusions** about the value of dreaming in human life.

1. What conclusion can you draw from Dunbar's and Angelou's poems about how the dream of freedom affects the caged bird? What evidence led you to this conclusion?
2. What can you conclude from Dickinson's poem about who is responsible for a life falling short of its potential?
3. Hunter-Gault's pursuit of her dream led her to risk physical danger. What conclusion can you draw from this circumstance about her commitment to her dream?

◆ Build Vocabulary

USING LEVELS OF DICTION

Dunbar, Angelou, Dickinson, and Hunter-Gault all use different **levels of diction** to express their feelings about the importance of dreams and aspirations.

1. Find two examples of old-fashioned or elevated levels of diction in "Sympathy." What impression of the speaker do such words create in your mind?
2. Emily Dickinson is known for mixing levels of diction in her writing. Find one example of a simpler word choice and one example of a more elevated word choice in her poem.

USING THE WORD BANK

On your paper, write the word whose meaning is closest to that of the first word:

1. warp: (a) hit, (b) distort, (c) time
2. disperse: (a) scatter, (b) steal, (c) scold
3. perpetuated: (a) made happen, (b) prolonged, (c) honored
4. effigies: (a) speeches, (b) tombs, (c) dummies
5. keener: (a) sharper, (b) tastier, (c) better looking
6. imbued: (a) painted, (b) placed, (c) inspired
7. epithets: (a) books, (b) slurs, (c) legends

◆ Literary Focus

SYMBOL

A **symbol** is something that suggests a significance beyond its literal meaning. All writers, but particularly poets, use symbols to give their writing another dimension.

1. In "Sympathy," what might the bird's beating his wing on the cage bars symbolize in human life?
2. In "Caged Bird," the free bird "dares to claim the sky" and then "names the sky his own." Literally, this means the bird flies up, but what human experience might this action symbolize?
3. Dickinson says, "We never know how high we are / Till we are asked to rise." What might *height* and *rising* symbolize here?

◆ Build Grammar Skills

COMMONLY CONFUSED WORDS: *ACCEPT* AND *EXCEPT*

Accept is a verb that means "to receive" or "to agree to." **Except** can be a preposition or conjunction meaning "but" or a verb meaning "to leave out."

Practice On your paper, rewrite the following sentences, choosing the correct word to complete each:

1. Many white students could not (accept, except) Charlayne Hunter-Gault when she enrolled at the University of Georgia.
2. (Accept, Except) for her race, Hunter-Gault was not that different from many of the students attending the university.
3. The university officials tried to (accept, except) the new student from the requirement that freshmen live in the dormitory.
4. Pioneers like Hunter-Gault made it easier for the next generation to (accept, except) integration.
5. Formerly all-white schools like the University of Georgia were forced to (accept, except) African American students.

◆ Reading Strategy

1. The dream of freedom makes the constraints of being caged all the more painful.
2. People impose their own limitations on themselves.
3. Her dream was stronger than her fear of physical danger.

◆ Build Vocabulary

Using Levels of Diction

1. "Alas" and "opes" are examples of old-fashioned diction. They define the speaker as literate and thoughtful.
2. The first line is simple: "We never know how high we are." The last two lines are more elevated: "Did not ourselves the Cubits warp/For fear to be a King."

Using the Word Bank

1. b 2. a 3. b 4. c 5. a 6. c
7. b

◆ Literary Focus

1. The bird's beating wing can symbolize the struggle against oppression. It is also an image of the physical violence that people are subjected to in civil strife.
2. In naming the sky his own, the bird asserts his freedom. He can travel anywhere he wishes.
3. "Height" and "Rising" can mean assuming responsibility or taking initiative. These words can also mean acting courageously in a crisis.

◆ Build Grammar Skills

1. accept; 2. Except; 3. except;
4. accept; 5. accept

 Writer's Solution

For additional instruction and practice, use the lesson in the **Language Lab CD-ROM** on Formal and Informal English in the Choosing Words unit.

Idea Bank
Customizing for
Performance Levels

Following are suggestions for matching the Idea Bank topics with your students' performance levels:

    Less Advanced Students: 1, 4, 7
    Average Students: 2, 4, 6
    More Advanced Students: 3, 5

Customizing for
Learning Modalities

Following are suggestions for matching Idea Bank topics with your students' learning modalities:

    Kinesthetic: 4
    Auditory: 4, 5, 7
    Visual/Spatial: 6
    Musical/Rhythmic: 7

Writing Mini-Lesson

Refer students to the Writing Handbook, page 962, for instruction on the writing process, and page 965 for further information on Creative Writing.

Writer's Solution

Writing Lab CD-ROM

Have students complete the Tutorial on Creative Writing. Follow these steps:

1. Have students use the poetry topic wheel to see words and images to help spark song ideas.
2. Encourage students to use the tips on how to keep their purpose focused.
3. Have students draft their poems on computer.

Allow approximately 70 minutes of class time for students to complete these steps.

Sourcebook

Have students use Chapter 6, Creative Writing (pp. 162–193), for additional support. The chapter includes a model of song lyrics (p. 169).

Build Your Portfolio

Idea Bank

Writing

1. **Editorial** Write an editorial for the student newspaper at the University of Georgia at the time of Charlayne Hunter-Gault's enrollment. Try to persuade the students at the university to change their behavior toward the new African American students. **[Media Link]**

2. **Letter** Write a letter from Dunbar to Angelou expressing his reaction to her poem. Is he flattered or angered that she borrowed symbols and images from his poem?

3. **Dialogue** Imagine that Emily Dickinson meets one of the African American writers in this group. Write a dialogue between them, discussing whether people are better or worse than they think they are.

Speaking and Listening

4. **Choral Reading** With other students, stage a choral reading of "Sympathy" and "Caged Bird." **[Performing Arts Link]**

5. **Dramatic Monologue** Imagine that you are the young Charlayne Hunter-Gault on the night before her first day at the University of Georgia. Prepare and perform a monologue expressing her feelings as she faces this crisis.

Projects

6. **Multimedia Presentation** Prepare a multimedia presentation on some facet of the civil rights movement. Include photographs, newspaper and magazine stories, audiotapes or videotapes in your presentation. **[Social Studies Link]**

7. **Music** Find or compose music that contrasts the songs of the caged bird and the free bird. Play or perform your music for the class. **[Music Link]**

Writing Mini-Lesson

Song Honoring a Hero

Charlayne Hunter-Goult was a hero to many of the people of her time. Think of a modern-day hero, and write words to a song celebrating this person. If you are musically inclined, you can set your words to music, or you can find an already existing melody and write appropriate words for it. In writing your song honoring a hero, the following may help you.

> #### Writing Skills Focus: Clear and Consistent Purpose
>
> If you define a **clear and consistent purpose,** your song of praise will be focused and effective. Following are a few of the purposes you might consider:
>
> ##### Possible Purposes:
> - To entertain listeners with a great story
> - To make listeners admire the hero
> - To teach a lesson about life
> - To praise an unsung everyday hero

Prewriting Decide on your purpose, then brainstorm for the qualities that make the hero admirable. Refer to your purpose as you accumulate information, to help you decide which qualities to emphasize in your song of praise.

Drafting Because you are writing a kind of poem, rather than a prose description, you will have to be more selective and use fewer words, which will have greater impact. Feel free to use figures of speech, such as similes, metaphors, and symbols.

Revising Read your song of praise out loud to see whether it is concise and flows smoothly. Make sure that your song accomplishes the purpose you set out to achieve.

✓ ASSESSMENT OPTIONS

Formal Assessment, Selection Test, pp. 60–62, and Assessment Resources Software. The selection test is designed so that it can be easily customized to the performance levels of your students.

Alternative Assessment, p. 18, includes options for less advanced students, more advanced students, visual/spatial learners, intrapersonal learners, logical/mathematical learners, and bodily/kinesthetic learners.

PORTFOLIO ASSESSMENT

Use the following rubrics in the *Alternative Assessment* booklet to assess student writing:

Editorial: Persuasion Rubric, p. 98
Letter: Expression Rubric, p. 87
Dialogue: Narrative Rubric, p. 88
Writing Mini-Lesson: Poetry Rubric, p. 101

Writing Process Workshop

Comparison-and-Contrast Essay

Without even realizing it, we're always making comparisons. For example, as you read the selections in this section, you probably saw similarities and differences in the ways in which the characters addressed the theme of finding one's identity.

A **comparison-and-contrast essay** is a brief written exploration of the similarities and differences between two (or more) things. Using the skills listed below—which were introduced in this section's Writing Mini-Lessons—write a comparison-and-contrast essay on a topic that interests you.

Writing Skills Focus

▶ **Give specific examples** to show precisely how your two subjects are alike and different. (See p. 220.)

▶ **Use a clear and logical organization** to make it easy for readers to follow your comparison. (See p. 233.)

▶ **Keep your audience in mind.** Provide details to clarify any topics or terms they won't recognize. (See p. 243.)

▶ **Have a clear and consistent purpose** for writing. Make your purpose clear to your audience. (See p. 254.)

The poet Maya Angelou uses these skills as she compares and contrasts a free bird with a caged bird.

MODEL FROM LITERATURE

from "Caged Bird" by Maya Angelou

A free bird leaps
on the back of the wind
and floats downstream
till the current ends ①
and dips his wing
in the orange sun rays
and dares to claim the sky.

But a bird that stalks
down his narrow cage ②
can seldom see through
his bars of rage
his wings are clipped and
his feet are tied
so he opens his throat to sing. ③

① The poet gives specific examples of the free bird's actions, contrasting them with the caged bird's actions in the second verse.

② The poet organizes her details by describing each bird in a separate stanza.

③ Readers can sense Angelou's purpose: to compare and contrast freedom and slavery.

Writing Process Workshop ◆ 255

Prepare and Engage

Establish Writing Guidelines

Before students begin, review the following key characteristics of a comparison-and-contrast essay:

• A comparison-and-contrast essay presents a writer's conclusions gained from analyzing the similarities and differences between two or more subjects.

• When effective, a comparison-and-contrast essay displays the writer's familiarity with his or her subjects.

You may want to distribute the scoring rubric for Comparison/Contrast (p. 96 in *Alternative Assessment*) to make students aware of the criteria on which their work will be evaluated. For suggestions on how you can customize the rubric to this workshop, see page 257.

Refer students to the Writing Handbook, page 962, for instruction in the writing process, and page 964 for information on expository writing.

 ### Writer's Solution

Writers at Work Videodisc

To show students how journalist Gene Bryan Johnson uses expository writing, play the videodisc segment on Exposition (Ch. 3). Ask students to explain how Johnson's contention that "Expository writing makes things clear" is relevant to the comparison-and-contrast essay. *The technique of comparing a familiar item to an unfamiliar one is a clear way to convey new information to readers.*

Play frames 22539 to 32284

Writing Lab CD-ROM

If your students have access to computers, they may work in the Tutorial on Exposition to complete their essays. Have students follow these steps:

1. Use a Topic Wheels activity to generate ideas for a comparison-and-contrast essay.
2. Draft comparison-and-contrast essays on the computer.
3. Respond to the Self-Evaluation Checklist to help judge the effectiveness of their essays.

Sourcebook

Students can find additional support, including topic ideas and models, in the chapter on Exposition (pp. 62–95).

 ## Cross-Curricular Connection: Science

Students may be aware that for many years evolutionary biologists and paleontologists compared and contrasted prehistoric dinosaurs with present-day reptiles in order to provide the public with information about a phenomenon that can no longer be experienced directly. Recently, however, many notable scientists have written essays that contend that dinosaurs have much more in common with birds in behavior and appearance.

Ask students why scientists often try to explain their findings and theories by presenting them in terms of other, more familiar ideas.

Students might respond that a comparison-and-contrast organization suits scientific topics because the main endeavor of science is to compare the known with the unknown.

Does the more recent comparison of dinosaurs to birds invalidate comparisons of dinosaurs to reptiles, or simply offer an alternative? *The ways in which some scientists now believe that reptiles are different from dinosaurs is perhaps what enabled the former to survive extinction, showing that a comparison of dinosaurs to reptiles is far from being outdated or invalid.*

Introduce the Strategy

Tell students that consumer reports can be found in many places, from evening television news broadcasts to specialized magazines and newsletters that contain little else.

Explain that reading strategies are crucially important in making use of such reports because unscrupulous manufacturers, trade associations masquerading as impartial agencies, and journalists with conflicts-of-interest may all treat what seems to be a legitimate consumer report as a branch of advertising and marketing. Consumers must be on guard or risk being taken in by what appears to be a well-intentioned, objective report.

Apply the Strategy

Ask students to note the four areas the report covers. *Price, longevity, arch support, and foot injuries.* Have them apply the three strategies provided—considering the source, answering their questions, and reviewing the date of findings—to each of these four areas in turn. Discuss which areas of the report, if any, should be taken more seriously than others.

Answers

1. Many students will detect bias in the report due to its source—one of the companies whose products are being evaluated. For example, Bounce sneakers are conveniently left out when the writer tallies the number of complaints related to foot injuries.
2. The number of users' complaints is not given for Bounce sneakers, nor are we told how these foot injuries were sustained or by what type of users.
3. Answers to this question will most likely fall into two camps. Those who value a basketball sneaker for its durability will choose the Bounce brand. Those who value arch support to accommodate the impact of constant jumping will prefer Cushy.
4. Many students will say they would buy Bounce sneakers for walking because they last as long or longer than the other brands yet cost less than Cushy sneakers.
5. Many students may conclude that Bounce sneakers offer the most benefits because of their durability. In addition, their mid-range price could make them appear to be the best dollar value.

Real-World Reading Skills Workshop

Strategies for Success

Before you buy a product, it's wise to comparison-shop by checking out two or more competing brands. One way to do this is to read a consumer report—an evaluation of competing products written after the products were tested. Here's what to look for in your reading:

Consider the Source Most consumer reports are written by people who have no ties to any of the companies whose products they evaluate. Some reports, however, are written by people hired by a particular manufacturer. Naturally, their judgment may be biased. Always check the source of a report before deciding how reliable the findings are.

Answer Your Questions Before reading a report, think of questions you have about each brand. For example: How much does it cost? How long will it last? What are its benefits? What are its dangers? Then, as you read, look for the answer to each question. If you don't find all your answers, read another report on the same product.

Look at the Date Note the date that a report was written. A year-old report can be inaccurate today. Companies often make changes in their products. An item may now contain new ingredients or offer a different guarantee, for example. Always look for the most recent information.

SNEAKERS REPORT 6/27/93
from *Bounce Company Annual Report*

Dynamo Sneakers are the least expensive on the market. They retail for only $19.99, compared to $29.99 for Bounce Sneakers and $38.99 for Cushy Sneakers.

Of the three brands, Bounce was found to last longest for basketball use — the average life being 8 months. For walking only, both Bounce and Cushy had an average life of 12 months, compared to Dynamo's 7.

Cushy is the only sneaker of the three to offer an air-filled cushion under the arch of the foot. Both Dynamo and Bounce have plain rubber arch supports.

Last year, there were 54 complaints of foot injuries by Cushy users, compared to 38 for Dynamo.

Apply the Strategy

Imagine you want to buy sneakers. Use the consumer report to help you decide.

1. Do you feel the report is reliable? Why or why not?
2. What information about users' complaints is not given?
3. Which brand would you buy for basketball? Why?
4. Which brand would you buy for walking? Why?
5. Which brand do you feel offers the most benefits? Why?

> ✔ A consumer report can also be helpful if you are
> ▶ planning to start a business
> ▶ advertising a product
> ▶ inventing a new product

Cross-Curricular Connection: Social Studies

Throughout history people have gathered, often in international forums, to discuss a particular crisis and propose solutions to it. After World War II, for example, diplomats and world leaders met to formulate and implement changes in the way international affairs were conducted. Their goal was to prevent another war on a global scale, and one of their solutions that is still with us is the United Nations. Students may also be familiar with gatherings that have addressed common problems relating to public health or the environment. Such conferences often divide their efforts between carefully delineating the problem and offering thoughtful solutions to it. Ask students how the backgrounds and perspectives of such representatives may influence the types of solutions that they propose. *A particular economic and cultural background might affect someone's beliefs, limiting the type of solutions proposed. A politically neutral country, such as Switzerland, is not apt become involved in politics.*

PART *2* *Learning About Ourselves and Others*

Sunday School Boys (detail), 1990, Jonathan Green, Oil on canvas. 23" x 23", Courtesy of the artist

Learning About Ourselves and Others ◆ 259

The selections in this section provide examples of people learning about themselves and others. In "The Interlopers," two feuding parties learn too late that they like each other. In "The Rug Merchant," James Michener relates a true story of what he learned through his dealings with a delightful salesperson. "Combing" reveals discoveries made by simple actions. "Women" is a tribute to the women of a past generation. "maggie and milly and molly and may" is a humorous verse about self-discovery by E. E. cummings. The poem "Astonishment" ponders why we are who we are living here and now.

Customize for
Varying Student Needs
When assigning the selections in this part to your students, keep in mind the following factors:

"The Interlopers"
• This story holds student interest and rewards the reader with a surprise ending

"The Rug Merchant"
• A delightful study in persistance
• Students may need background information on cultures of the Middle East

"Combing"
• A poem which shows how a simple act can span generations of tradition

"Women"
• The sacrifices of women of an earlier generation are highlighted in this poem

"maggie and milly and molly and may"
• Students will enjoy this humorous piece about finding ourselves

"Astonishment"
• This poem asks why we are who we are living at this particular time and place.
• Perhaps this poem could spark a serious discussion about the mysteries of life

 Humanities: Art

Sunday School Boys, 1990, by Jonathan Green.
Born in 1955 in South Carolina, Jonathan Green graduated in 1982 from the School at the Chicago Art Institute. He uses the media of oil and acrylic paints to create a rich portrait of African American life.

Sunday School Boys depicts a group of African American boys attending a church service. Students will notice that the boys don't seem to have faces.

Help the students link the art to the theme of Part 2 ("Learning About Ourselves and Others")

by answering the following questions:
1. In what ways are the boys alike? In what ways are they different? *They appear to be around the same age and size. Their skin color is different.*
2. What do you think the artist meant to express about these young people by barely giving them faces in this painting? *Sample response: The artist may be suggesting that their identities are just emerging—that young people's similarities may be more apparent than their differences, which emerge over time.*

259

Pr

1. To
sh
2. To
3. To
4. To
5. To
th
6. To
be
7. To
for
8. To
sp

Voca
Roo

Grar
Cor
Cor
Betw

Read
Cau

Liter
Cor

Writ
Peace

Writ
Spea
Argu

Proj
Prese

Mo
He
as
sibl
and
the
nur
sto
Ro
Sho
rea
bo
Alic
wro
pe
ing

wil
a B
of
co

One-Minute Insight

This story points out that an ongoing feud between two individuals or families not only fuels feelings of hatred and bitterness, but has the power to destroy both feuding parties. "The Interlopers" begins at the climax of a generations-long feud, when two of the feuding individuals find themselves face to face in the forest. As they are about to destroy each other, however, a tree crashes down and traps them. During the time that they're trapped, they eventually agree to reconcile. As the story ends, however, it appears that their decision has come too late, as they're about to be devoured by a pack of wolves. Written in the early part of this century, the story resonates today when not only individuals, but nations, still cannot put an end to their feuding, failing to recognize that the inability to reconcile can lead to tragedy.

❶ Clarification The word *interloper* is made of the prefix *inter-* (between or among) and the root word *lope* (to run or leap along). The original meaning of the word is "to interfere with another's trading rights or privileges." The word has developed a more general meaning as well—"to intrude in the affairs of others."

◆ Critical Thinking

❷ Analyze Character Traits Ask students what they can infer about Ulrich's character. *At this point, students will probably suggest that Ulrich is ruthless and dangerous—someone it would be a mistake to anger.*

The ❶ Interlopers

Saki

 In a forest of mixed growth somewhere on the eastern spurs of the Carpathians,[1] a man stood one winter night watching and listening, as though he waited for some beast of the woods to come within the range of his vision, and, later, of his rifle. But the game for whose presence he kept so keen an outlook was none that figured in the sportsman's calendar as lawful and proper for the chase: Ulrich von Gradwitz[2] patrolled the dark forest in quest of a human enemy.

The forest lands of Gradwitz were of wide extent and well stocked with game; the narrow strip of <u>precipitous</u> woodland that lay on its outskirt was not remarkable for the game it harbored or the shooting it afforded, but it was the most jealously guarded of all its owner's territorial possessions. A famous lawsuit, in the days of his grandfather, had wrested it from the illegal possession of a neighboring family of petty landowners; the dispossessed party had never acquiesced in the judgment of the Courts, and a long series of poaching affrays[3] and similar scandals had embittered the relationships between the families for three generations. The neighbor feud had grown into a personal one since Ulrich had come to be head of his family; if there was a man in the world whom he detested and wished ill to it

---

1. **Carpathians** (kär pā′ thē ənz): Mountains in central Europe.
2. **Ulrich von Gradwitz** (ŏŏl′ rik fôn gräd′ vitz)
3. **poaching affrays** (pōch′ iŋ ə frāz′): Disputes about hunting on someone else's property.

◆ Build Vocabulary

precipitous (pri sip′ ə təs) *adj.*: Steep; sheer

marauders (mə rôd′ ərz) *n.*: Raiders; people who take goods by force

---

Block Scheduling Strategies

Consider these suggestions to take advantage of extended class time:

- Invite students to find out more about Saki by doing research on the Internet.
- Ask students to work in small groups to develop a creative sentence for each item in Word Bank (p. 260) before students read. Groups can share their sentences.
- Have students work with partners to fill in the Cause-and-Effect chart on page 261.

- After students have read the story, you may wish to play all or part of the audiocassette recording for reinforcement.
- Have students work on the Writing Mini-Lesson on page 269. Direct attention to the "Passage With Elaboration," pointing out that details not in the original story were added in order to elaborate. Remind students that they can add their own details as long as the story remains unified and coherent.

❸ was Georg Znaeym,[4] the inheritor of the quarrel and the tireless game-snatcher and raider of the disputed border-forest. The feud might, perhaps, have died down or been compromised if the personal ill will of the two men had not stood in the way; as boys they had thirsted for one another's blood, as men each prayed that misfortune might fall on the other, and this wind-scourged winter night Ulrich had banded together his foresters to watch the dark forest, not in quest of four-footed quarry, but to keep a lookout for the prowling thieves whom he suspected of being afoot from across the land boundary. The roebuck[5] which usually kept in the sheltered hollows during a storm wind, were running like driven things tonight, and there was movement and unrest among the creatures that were wont to sleep through the dark hours. Assuredly there was a disturbing element in the forest, and Ulrich could guess the quarter from whence it came.

He strayed away by himself from the watchers whom he had placed in ambush on the crest of the hill, and wandered far down the steep slopes amid the wild tangle of undergrowth, peering through the tree trunks and listening through the whistling and skirling of the wind and the restless

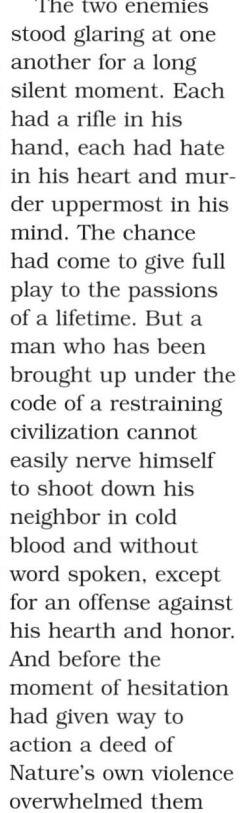

beating of the branches for sight or sound of the <u>marauders</u>. If only on this wild night, in this dark, lone spot, he might come across Georg Znaeym, man to man, with none to witness—that was the wish that was uppermost in his thoughts. And as he stepped round the trunk of a huge beech he came face to face with the man he sought. **❹**

The two enemies stood glaring at one another for a long silent moment. Each had a rifle in his hand, each had hate in his heart and murder uppermost in his mind. The chance had come to give full play to the passions of a lifetime. But a man who has been brought up under the code of a restraining civilization cannot easily nerve himself to shoot down his neighbor in cold blood and without word spoken, except for an offense against his hearth and honor. And before the moment of hesitation had given way to action a deed of Nature's own violence overwhelmed them both. A fierce shriek of the storm had been answered by a splitting crash over their heads, and ere they could leap aside a mass of falling beech tree had thundered down on them. Ulrich von Gradwitz found himself stretched on the ground, one arm numb beneath him and the other held almost as helplessly in a tight tangle of forked branches, while both legs were pinned beneath the fallen mass. His heavy shooting-boots had saved his feet from

---

4. **Georg Znaeym** (gā´ ôrg znä´ im)
5. **roebuck** (rō´ buk´) *n.*: Male deer.

The Interlopers ◆ 263

◆ *Literature and Your Life*

❸ Point out that the result of the lawsuit was unsatisfactory to Georg Znaeym. Ask students if this situation—one in which a disagreement is settled by an outside party to the dissatisfaction of one of the individuals—is familiar to them. Discuss the problems such a settlement can cause. *Students may give examples such as an umpire's decision in a ball game, a teacher's decision regarding a disagreement between two students, a parent's decision regarding a disagreement between two siblings. Such decisions leave one party angry and bitter, and may lead to further animosity and even violence.*

◆ **Critical Thinking**

❹ Infer Ask students why they think Znaeym was there. *Some students may think, as Gradwitz does, that Znaeym is out hunting. They should also entertain the possibility that Znaeym hopes to kill Gradwitz, as Gradwitz hopes to kill Znaeym.*

Customize for
Less Proficient Readers
The stage has been set for a confrontation between the men. Have students summarize what has happened up to this point and predict what will happen next.

Cross-Curricular Connection: Science

Wolves have long been fodder for imagination. Folk tales, fairy tales, and legends make use of wolves as bad and threatening characters. As children, students might have heard the stories of "The Three Little Pigs," "Little Red Riding Hood," and "The Boy Who Cried 'Wolf'." Students will discover that wolves also play a key role in Saki's story, surrounding the characters and threatening to bring about their destruction. Have students conduct research to learn more about wolves, keeping in mind the following question: "Do wolves deserve the negative portrayal they have received in literature?" Students can use science books, encyclopedias, the Internet, or other resources to find out more about the habits and habitats of these animals. Have students share what they have learned about wolves.

◆ Critical Thinking

❶ Interpret Ask students: Why does Georg conclude his taunt with the words "There's real justice for you"? Ask a volunteer to read the sentence, accenting the word *real*.

Students should recognize that the use of the word justice was a calculated choice on Georg's part because Georg never believed that the courts were fair to his family. By emphasizing the word real, *Georg is saying that this would be justice at last.*

◆ Critical Thinking

❷ Interpret What does the posturing in this passage reveal to students about the two characters?

Students should note that the posturing reveals the two men's stubbornness and the intensity of their hatred for each other.

◆ Reading Strategy

❸ Identify Causes and Effects Elicit the following response: *Both men are bluffing; each wants the other to believe that his death is just around the corner.*

◆ Build Grammar Skills

❹ *Between* and *Among* Point out the use of the prepositional phrase *between us.* Ask students to explain why Saki used the word *between* rather than *among.* *The word* between *is used when referring to two people; in this case* us *refers to Ulrich and Georg.*

▶ Critical Viewing ◀

❺ Analyze Students may suggest that unexpected and dangerous encounters would occur in such a bleak setting. They may find the trail of footsteps ominous.

---

being crushed to pieces, but if his fractures were not as serious as they might have been, at least it was evident that he could not move from his present position till someone came to release him. The descending twigs had slashed the skin of his face, and he had to wink away some drops of blood from his eyelashes before he could take in a general view of the disaster. At his side, so near that under ordinary circumstances he could almost have touched him, lay Georg Znaeym, alive and struggling, but obviously as helplessly pinioned down as himself. All round them lay a thick-strewn wreckage of splintered branches and broken twigs.

Relief at being alive and exasperation at his captive plight brought a strange <u>medley</u> of pious thank-offerings and sharp curses to Ulrich's lips. Georg, who was nearly blinded with the blood which trickled across his eyes, stopped his struggling for a moment to listen, and then gave a short, snarling laugh.

❶ "So you're not killed, as you ought to be, but you're caught, anyway," he cried; "caught fast. Ho, what a jest, Ulrich von Gradwitz snared in his stolen forest. There's real justice for you!"

And he laughed again, mockingly and savagely.

"I'm caught in my own forest land," retorted Ulrich. "When my men come to release us you will wish, perhaps, that you were in a better plight than caught poaching on a neighbor's land, shame on you."

Georg was silent for a moment; then he answered quietly:

❷ "Are you sure that your men will find much to release? I have men,

> ◆ **Reading Strategy**
> **❸** Why do Georg and Ulrich tell each other about how their men will find them?

too, in the forest tonight, close behind me, and *they* will be here first and do the releasing. When they drag me out from under these branches it won't

264 ◆ Moments of Discovery

---

need much clumsiness on their part to roll this mass of trunk right over on the top of you. Your men will find you dead under a fallen beech tree. For form's sake I shall send my <u>condolences</u> to your family."

❷ "It is a <u>useful hint</u>," said Ulrich fiercely. "My men had orders to follow in ten minutes' time, seven of which must have gone by already, and when they get me out—I will remember the hint. Only as you will have met your death poaching on my lands I don't think I can decently send any message of condolence to your family."

❹ "Good," snarled Georg, "good. We fight this quarrel out to the death, you and I and our foresters, with no cursed interlopers to come between us. Death and damnation to you, Ulrich von Gradwitz."

> ◆ **Build Vocabulary**
> **medley** (med′ lē) *n.*: Mixture of things not usually found together
> **condolence** (kən dō′ ləns) *n.*: Expression of sympathy with a grieving person
> **languor** (laŋ′ gər) *n.*: Lack of vigor; weakness

▼ **Critical Viewing** What kinds of encounters or incidents might occur in this setting? **[Analyze] ❺**

Career Connection

Forestry "The Interlopers" takes place in a heavily wooded area. A tree falls and the fate of the characters hangs in the balance. If this story were set in modern times and the setting were a public forest, a forester might have rescued the men. Do students know what else foresters do besides rescuing people and warning them about starting forest fires? Have students who are interested in forestry research the specific duties of

foresters. Suggest they find out what kind of education and preparation one needs to have a career in forestry. Have students share their findings with the class or with an interested group.

Community Connection

Setting Boundaries Remind students that the plot of "The Interlopers" is based on a boundary dispute. Have students discuss how people in your community mark the boundaries of their property. Some ques-

tions students might consider include:

• How do the boundary markings of residential buildings differ from commercial buildings?

• What parts of apartment buildings are considered public, and what parts are private?

• How do individuals mark the boundaries of the land around their homes?

• Who marks the legal boundaries of property?

"The same to you, Georg Znaeym, forest-thief, game-snatcher."

Both men spoke with the bitterness of possible defeat before them, for each knew that it might be long before his men would seek him out or find him; it was a bare matter of chance which party would arrive first on the scene.

Both had now given up the useless struggle to free themselves from the mass of wood that held them down; Ulrich limited his endeavors to an effort to bring his one partially free arm near enough to his outer coat pocket to draw out his wine flask. Even when he had accomplished that operation it was long before he could manage the unscrewing of the stopper or get any of the liquid down his throat. But what a heaven-sent draft it seemed! It was an open winter, and little snow had fallen as yet, hence the captives suffered less from the cold than might have been the case at that season of the year; nevertheless, the wine was warming and reviving to the wounded man, and he looked across with something like a throb of pity to where his enemy lay, just keeping the groans of pain and weariness from crossing his lips.

❻ "Could you reach this flask if I threw it over to you?" asked Ulrich suddenly; "there is good wine in it, and one may as well be as comfortable as one can. Let us drink, even if tonight one of us dies." **❻**

"No, I can scarcely see anything; there is so much blood caked round my eyes," said Georg, "and in any case I don't drink wine with an enemy." **❼**

Ulrich was silent for a few minutes, and lay listening to the weary screeching of the wind. An idea was slowly forming and growing in his brain, an idea that gained strength every time that he looked across at the man who was fighting so grimly against pain and exhaustion. In the pain and languor that Ulrich himself was feeling the old fierce hatred seemed to be dying down.

> ◆ **Literary Focus**
> What do you think motivates Ulrich's change of heart? Does this change reflect an internal or external conflict? **❽**

"Neighbor," he said presently, "do as you please if your men come first. It was a fair compact. But as for me, I've changed my mind. If my men are the first to come you shall be the first to be helped, as though you were my guest. We have quarreled like devils all our lives over this stupid strip of forest, where the trees

◆ **Critical Thinking**

❻ Infer Ask students: How does Ulrich's offer of wine signal a change in attitude and hint at a possible end to the conflict? *Students should recognize that the offer represents the first time one of the characters makes a positive gesture toward the other.*

◆ **Critical Thinking**

❼ Compare and Contrast Draw students' attention to the fact that Ulrich offers Georg wine but Georg rebuffs the gesture. Ask: "Why is there such a difference in each man's attitude?" *Students should recognize that Ulrich is in a better position to be magnanimous because the court decision was in his family's favor. Legally, Georg is trespassing on Ulrich's property, so he would probably have too much pride to make the first peace offer.*

◆ **Literary Focus**

❽ Conflict Ulrich recognizes that he and Georg face possible death, and when people are about to die, they often want to make amends for past wrongs. This change reflects an internal conflict because the conflict is between Ulrich and his own past feelings.

The Interlopers ◆ 265

 Workplace Skills Mini-Lesson

Resolving Conflicts

Introduce the Concept Most students are aware that unresolved conflicts between people can result in bad feelings and loss of friendship. Point out that in "The Interlopers" that result was destined to be permanent, because both men were about to lose their lives.

Develop Background In the workplace, unresolved conflicts can also have serious results. Ask students to suggest what some

of these results might be. *defective products, loss of customers, loss of job* Lead students to recognize the following:

- A worker should try to talk to a peer about resolving a problem before involving a supervisor.
- Often both parties must make compromises in order to settle a disagreement.
- Each party should try to see the situation from the other person's point of view.

Apply the Information Have students work in small groups to discuss how they might handle this situation: "A co-worker has been taking extended lunch breaks, leaving you with extra work to do."

Assess the Outcome Have students evaluate their own and other groups' resolutions of the conflict, using the criteria outlined earlier in this lesson.

◆ **Build Grammar Skills**

❶ *Between* and *Among* Direct students' attention to the phrase *among the forester folk.* Ask them to explain why *among* is the correct preposition to use. *Among is used when there are more than two entities, and folk refers to many people.*

◆ **Literary Focus**

❷ **Conflict** Ask students: How does this passage relate to the central conflicts of the story? *Students should note that Georg's response to Ulrich's peace offering resolves both the external conflict between them and Georg's internal conflict as well.*

◆ **Critical Thinking**

❸ **Analyze Character** Remind students that this is the second time Georg has referred to *interlopers.* Ask students why this word is significant to him. *Georg believes that interlopers (the court) were responsible for his family losing its land.*

◆ **Critical Thinking**

❹ **Predict** Have students predict how the story will end. *Many students will predict that the two men will be saved and that the story will end happily. They'll soon find out that this isn't the case.*

can't even stand upright in a breath of wind. Lying here tonight, thinking, I've come to think we've been rather fools; there are better things in life than getting the better of a boundary dispute. Neighbor, if you will help me to bury the old quarrel I— I will ask you to be my friend."

Georg Znaeym was silent for so long that Ulrich thought, perhaps, he had fainted with the pain of his injuries. Then he spoke slowly and in jerks.

❶ ❷ "How the whole region would stare and gabble if we rode into the market square together. No one living can remember seeing a Znaeym and a von Gradwitz talking to one another in friendship. And what peace there would be among the forester folk if we ended our feud tonight. And if we choose to make peace among our people there is none other to interfere, no interlop-❸ ers from outside . . . You would come and keep the Sylvester night beneath my roof, and I would come and feast on some high day at your castle . . . I would never fire a shot on your land, save when you invited me as a guest; and you should come and shoot with me down in the marshes where the wildfowl are. In all the countryside there are none that could hinder if we willed to make peace. I never thought to have wanted to do other than hate you all my life, but I think I have changed my mind about things too, this last half-hour. And you offered me your wine flask . . . Ulrich von Gradwitz, I will be your friend."

For a space both men were silent, turning over in their minds the wonderful changes that this dramatic reconciliation would bring about. In the cold, gloomy forest, with the wind tearing in fitful gusts through the naked branches and whistling round the tree trunks, they lay and waited for the help that would now bring release and <u>succor</u> to both parties. And each ❹ prayed a private prayer that his men might be the first to arrive, so that he might be

266 ◆ *Moments of Discovery*

Speaking and Listening Mini-Lesson

Persuasive Argument
This mini-lesson supports the Speaking and Listening activity in the Idea Bank on page 269.

Introduce the Concept In a persuasive argument, one person (or group) tries to convince another that he (or they) is right by building up arguments that lead to a strong final point. Arguing as Ulrich or Georg, students should try to anticipate each other's arguments.

Develop Background Before students develop their arguments, discuss what makes an argument strong. Lead students to consider these points:

• Arguments should be based on facts, not opinions.

• Each opinion should be backed up by factual evidence.

• Arguments should be presented in a reasonable tone of voice rather than an emotional tone.

Apply the Information Using this background, students should be able to develop and present strong arguments to support their stands as owners of the property.

Assess the Outcome Have students listen to the arguments for each side and choose which side presented the stronger case based on the criteria presented in *Develop Background.*

the first to show honorable attention to the enemy that had become a friend.

Presently, as the wind dropped for a moment, Ulrich broke silence.

◆ Reading Strategy
⑤ How do both men feel about each other now? How do you think the story will end?

④

"Let's shout for help," he said; "in this lull our voices may carry a little way."

"They won't carry far through the trees and undergrowth," said Georg, "but we can try. Together, then."

The two raised their voices in a prolonged hunting call.

"Together again," said Ulrich a few minutes later, after listening in vain for an answering halloo.

"I heard something that time, I think," said Ulrich.

"I heard nothing but the pestilential wind," said Georg hoarsely.

There was silence again for some minutes, and then Ulrich gave a joyful cry.

"I can see figures coming through the wood. They are following in the way I came down the hillside."

Both men raised their voices in as loud a shout as they could muster.

"They hear us! They've stopped. Now they see us. They're running down the hill toward us," cried Ulrich.

"How many of them are there?" asked Georg.

"I can't see distinctly," said Ulrich; "nine or ten."

"Then they are yours," said Georg; "I had only seven out with me."

"They are making all the speed they can, brave lads," said Ulrich gladly.

"Are they your men?" asked Georg. "Are they your men?" he repeated impatiently as Ulrich did not answer.

"No," said Ulrich with a laugh, the idiotic chattering laugh of a man unstrung with hideous fear.

"Who are they?" asked Georg quickly, straining his eyes to see what the other would gladly not have seen.

"*Wolves.*"

◆ Build Vocabulary
succor (suk´ ər) *n.*: Aid; help; relief

Guide for Responding

◆ *Literature and Your Life*

Reader's Response With whom did you sympathize: Ulrich, Georg, neither, or both? Why?

Thematic Focus What did Ulrich and Georg discover about themselves and each other while they were trapped under the fallen tree?

Journal Entry When Ulrich and Georg finally ended their conflict, it was too late. List some benefits that might have been achieved by ending the conflict years earlier.

☑ Check Your Comprehension

1. What is Ulrich doing in the forest?
2. What has kept the feud between the families going for three generations?
3. Why don't Ulrich and Georg shoot each other when they meet in the forest?
4. How do the two men become trapped?

The Interlopers ◆ 267

Beyond the Selection

FURTHER READING

Other Works by Saki
The Story-teller: Thirteen Tales by Saki
"The Open Window"
"Sredni Vashtar"

Other Works About Discovery Through Catastrophe
Flight #116 Is Down, Caroline B. Cooney
Changes in Latitudes, Will Hobbs

INTERNET

You and your students many find additional information about Saki on the Internet. We recommend the following site. Please be aware, however, that the site may have changed from the time we published this information. For information about Saki, go to: **http://www.crl.com/%7Esubir/saki/bio.html**

We *strongly recommend* that you preview this and related sites before you send students to them.

◆ Reading Strategy
⑤ Identify Causes and Effects
The men feel that they are no longer enemies and each is eager to show his goodwill toward the other. Some students may predict a happy ending, while others may suspect that the plot will turn in a different direction.

Listening to Literature Audiocassettes The point at which the men call out and wait for a response is a good moment to play the final portion of the audiocassette recording. The dialogue, made up of short, abrupt sentences, emphasizes the urgency the men feel. Hearing the final word "wolves" read aloud will add to the effect of Saki's surprise ending.

Customize for
More Advanced Students
The change in attitude between the men can be seen in the words and phrases they use to address each other. Have students make a list of words that shows the progression from animosity to acceptance. *Students' lists will likely include words such as "forest-thief," "game-snatcher" then "enemy," "neighbor," "friend," "guest."*

Reinforce and Extend

Answers
◆ *Literature and Your Life*
Reader's Response Responses should be supported by facts from the story.

Thematic Focus They discovered that what they had been feuding over didn't matter and that they would be much better off being friends.

☑ Check Your Comprehension

1. Ulrich is patrolling the forest, looking for his enemy, Georg.
2. Georg's family had never acquiesced to the decision of the courts, which awarded the land to Ulrich's family. That fact, and subsequent poaching episodes, has kept the feud going.
3. They don't shoot each other because they were brought up under a code of a restraining civilization which teaches that murder is wrong.
4. They are trapped by a huge beech tree that falls upon them when a stormy wind blows the tree down.

Answers

◆ Critical Thinking

1. Ulrich and Georg share a stubborn streak, which won't let them give up the feud. Both share an enjoyment of the outdoors and hunting. Ulrich, however, is a wealthy landowner while Georg is of lesser social status.
2. Ulrich is angry at Georg in principle. Ulrich cannot stand to have Georg trespass on any part of his land, even if the land in question is virtually worthless, especially after the courts had decided in Ulrich's family's favor long ago.
3. Georg does not agree with the judge's decision, which long ago awarded the land to Ulrich's family. Therefore, Georg feels he is hunting on his own land.
4. They probably realized that when compared to having a tree fall upon them, the feud seems ridiculous.
5. Accept any of these answers: Each man regards the other as an interloper; the court is an interloper; the wolves are interlopers.
6. Students will speculate on the nature of the two men's newfound friendship and on how people react to it.
7. Students may point to any of many "trouble spots" around the globe, such as the Middle East or Northern Ireland, and may point to the role of international organizations such as the United Nations in brokering a settlement.

◆ Build Grammar Skills

1. between; 2. among;
3. among; 4. between; 5. among

◆ Literary Focus

1. The feud between Ulrich and Georg. This is an external conflict.
2. Ulrich's and Georg's struggles to free themselves from the fallen tree. This is an external conflict.
3. Both characters' deliberations over whether or not to become friends. This is an internal conflict.

◆ Reading Strategy

One *cause* is the tree falling on the men; its *effect* is that they begin to mend their feud. A second *cause* is that no one comes to rescue the men; its *effect* will be that they will be eaten by the wolves.

Guide for Responding (continued)

◆ Critical Thinking

INTERPRET

1. List ways in which Ulrich and Georg are alike, and ways in which they are different. **[Compare and Contrast]**
2. Why is Ulrich so angry at Georg for trespassing on a small and nearly worthless piece of land? **[Infer]**
3. Why doesn't Georg consider himself a poacher? **[Infer]**
4. Why do Ulrich and Georg end their feud when they find themselves trapped under the fallen tree? **[Infer]**
5. An interloper is someone who intrudes into the affairs of others. Give two interpretations of the story's title. **[Interpret]**

APPLY

6. Describe how the story might have continued if the two men had been rescued. **[Speculate]**

EXTEND

7. Disputes over land often occur among nations. What are some territorial disputes among nations in today's world? How might these disputes be resolved? **[Social Studies Link]**

◆ Build Grammar Skills

COMMONLY CONFUSED WORDS: BETWEEN AND AMONG

Between is used to show a relationship between two items at a time. *Among* is used to show a relationship among more than two items at a time.

Practice In your notebook, write the word that correctly completes each sentence.

1. Chris and I have only two dollars (between, among) us.
2. She stood (between, among) the other actors on stage.
3. He was the only child (between, among) a roomful of adults.
4. Let's keep this a secret (between, among) you and me.
5. There was a dispute (between, among) several of the people in the crowd.

◆ Literary Focus

CONFLICT

A **conflict** is a struggle between opposing forces. An **external conflict** pits characters against each other or against the forces of nature. An **internal conflict** pits a character against himself or herself.

Find an example of each of the following types of conflict in "The Interlopers" and explain the nature of the conflict.

1. A character in conflict with another character
2. A character in conflict with nature
3. A character in conflict with himself

◆ Reading Strategy

IDENTIFY CAUSES AND EFFECTS

Every conflict has both **causes** and **effects**. For example, the conflict between Ulrich's and Georg's grandfathers was caused by both men's desire for the same piece of land. One effect of this conflict is that Ulrich and Georg are now enemies. Identify two other causes and effects in the story.

◆ Build Vocabulary

USING THE WORD ROOT -dol-

The root -*dol*- means "pain." Read the definitions of the following words that contain -*dol*-. Then, on a separate sheet of paper, write a sentence that contains each word.

1. In*dol*ent means "avoiding the pain of work; lazy."
2. *Dol*eful means "full of sadness."

USING THE WORD BANK

In your notebook, write sentences as described below using one word from the Word Bank.

1. Write the lead sentence of a news article describing a robbery.
2. Describe the site of a rock-climbing expedition.
3. Tell what a group of rescue workers did for flood victims.
4. Write the first line of a letter to a friend who has lost an elderly family member.
5. Tell how you would feel after spending a week in bed with the flu.
6. Write the menu description for a special salad.

◆ Build Vocabulary

Using the Word Root -dol-
Sample sentences:
1. The indolent student consistently forgot his homework.
2. From her doleful expression we could tell the news was bad.

Using the Word Bank
Sentences should use the following words:
1. marauders; 2. precipitous;
3. succor; 4. condolence;
5. languor; 6. medley

 **Writer's Solution**

For additional instruction and practice, use the page on Common Usage Problems in the *Writer's Solution Grammar Practice Book,* p. 93.

Build Your Portfolio

 ## Idea Bank

Writing

1. **Last Letter** Write a letter Ulrich or Georg might have written before the wolves closed in, telling how the members of both families should treat each other from now on.

2. **Happy Ending** Write a new ending for "The Interlopers" in which the two men are saved. Describe how the two former enemies announce their newly discovered friendship.

3. **Peaceful Speech** Imagine that you had been a friend of both Ulrich's and Georg's grandfathers when the feud began. Write a brief speech directed toward one of the two men in which you try to bring about a reconciliation.

Speaking and Listening

4. **Persuasive Argument** Form two groups of three students. One group will represent Ulrich and the other, Georg. Have each group present an argument including reasons why the person they represent is entitled to the disputed piece of land.

5. **Performance** Prepare a dramatic interpretation of the story to perform for the class. **[Performing Arts Link]**

Projects

6. **Real-Estate Advertisement** Create a magazine advertisement announcing that the disputed piece of land is for sale. In your ad, describe the property, give a price, and tell whom a buyer should contact. **[Career Link]**

7. **Presentation on Wolves** Create a multimedia presentation on wolves that includes information on where they live, how they raise their young, how they form packs, and how they hunt. Include photos, drawings, film clips, or audio recordings in your presentation. **[Science Link; Art Link]**

Writing Mini-Lesson

News Story

"Nature's own violence" spells doom for Ulrich and Georg when a huge tree crashes down upon them. Imagine that you are a reporter assigned to write a news story about the freak accident and its terrible aftermath. Keep the following in mind as you write.

Writing Skills Focus: Elaboration for Understanding

Elaboration is the development of ideas and details to make a piece of writing precise and complete. In a strong news story, the writer uses elaboration to answer the questions *who, what, when, where, why,* and *how.* Facts, statistics, sensory details, and quotations are types of elaboration that work well in news stories.

Prewriting Organize your story according to the three main parts of a news story:
1. The **headline** is the first thing a reader sees. Compose a short headline that grabs the reader's attention.
2. The **lead** is the first paragraph of a news story. Put your most important information here.
3. The **body** provides details on information presented in the lead. Elaborate most in this section.

Drafting Begin your news story with a striking statement about the accident that will capture your readers' attention. Then tell your story, following news-story organization. As you write, ask yourself what your readers will find interesting or what they'll need to know, and elaborate on those aspects of the story.

Revising Read your story aloud to a classmate and ask if any part of the story is unclear or requires further elaboration. Use the classmate's suggestions to guide you in making revisions.

The Interlopers ♦ 269

 ## Idea Bank

Customizing for
Performance Levels
Following are suggestions for matching the Idea Bank topics with your students' performance levels:
Less Advanced Students: 1, 6
Average Students: 2, 4, 5
More Advanced Students: 3, 7

Customizing for
Learning Modalities
Following are suggestions for matching Idea Bank topics with your students' learning modalities:
Verbal/Linguistic: 4, 5
Visual/Spatial: 6, 7

 ## Writing Mini-Lesson

Refer students to the Writing Hand-book, page 962, for instruction on the writing process, and page 964 for further information on Exposition. You may also use the writing process models for a cause-and-effect essay in *Writing and Language Transparencies,* pp. 37–40, to guide students through the writing process.

 Writer's Solution

Writers at Work Videodisc
Before students begin writing have them view the videodisc segment featuring radio news journalist Gene Bryan Johnson (Ch. 3) to learn valuable insights to help them put together their news reports. Discuss with students the techniques that Johnson uses that they can use in writing their news reports.

Play frames 22539 to 32284

Writing Lab CD-ROM
Have students complete their news stories using the Tutorial on Exposition. Follow these steps:
1. Have students use the chain-of-events organizer to help organize their details.
2. Have students draft on computer.
3. Have students use the revision checkers for language variety and transition words to help them revise.
You'll need about 90 minutes of class time to have students complete these steps.

✓ ASSESSMENT OPTIONS

Formal Assessment, Selection Test, pp. 63–65, and Assessment Resources Software. The selection test is designed so that it can be easily customized to the performance levels of your students.
Alternative Assessment, p. 19, includes options for less advanced students, more advanced students, visual/spatial learners, verbal/linguistic learners, logical/mathematical learners, and bodily/kinesthetic learners.

PORTFOLIO ASSESSMENT
Use the following rubrics in the *Alternative Assessment* booklet to assess student writing:
Last Letter: Expression Rubric, p. 87
Happy Ending: Narrative Rubric, p. 88
Peaceful Speech: Persuasion Rubric, p. 98
Writing Mini-Lesson: Description Rubric, p. 90

OBJECTIVES

1. To read, comprehend, interpret, and respond to an essay
2. To relate an essay to students' personal experience
3. To make inferences about character in an essay
4. To identify characterization in essays
5. To build vocabulary in context and learn the word root *-vis-*
6. To use *like* and *as/as if* correctly
7. To write a Letter of Complaint
8. To respond to the essay through writing, speaking and listening, and projects

SKILLS INSTRUCTION

Vocabulary: Word Roots: *-vis-*

Grammar:
Correct Use of *Like* and *As/As If*

Reading Strategy:
Make Inferences About Characters

Literary Focus:
Characterization in Essays

Writing: Clear Explanation of the Problem

Speaking and Listening:
Dramatic Monologue (teacher edition)

Critical Viewing: Deduce

PORTFOLIO OPPORTUNITIES

Writing: Sales Catalog; Dramatic Scene; Short Story

Writing Mini-Lesson: Letter of Complaint

Speaking and Listening: Conversation; Dramatic Monologue

Projects: Design a Rug; Report on Afghanistan

More About the Author

Michener said that when he was a boy his family was so poor that they didn't even have enough money to buy Christmas presents. As a wealthy and successful writer, Michener still showed little interest in material things, and gave away more than $100 million to charity.

Although James Michener did not care to talk about his own writing, he did try to help young writers improve their skills. He urged them to enrich their stories with more detail. "I say, 'Where does [the story] take place? How old is [the hero]? What are [his or her] backgrounds?' If they're not answering those questions, they're not good at storytelling."

Guide for Reading

James Michener (1907–   )

This globe-trotting American writer began life as a foundling child in Doylestown, Pennsylvania. He was adopted by Mabel Michener and raised as a Quaker. After graduating from Swarthmore College, he worked as a book editor until he joined the navy during World War II. His experiences in the Pacific would set Michener on a new course after the war, when the editor stopped working on other people's manuscripts and started creating his own. Michener wrote eighteen related sketches called *Tales of the South Pacific* (1947), a work that won him a Pulitzer Prize. The book was soon adapted into a very popular musical by Richard Rodgers and Oscar Hammerstein; this play, *South Pacific,* was later turned into a film and has become an American classic.

Portraits of Lands and Cultures

This first work propelled Michener into a long and productive career as a portraitist of other lands and people. Two of his novels, *The Bridges at Toko-Ri* (1953) and *Sayonara* (1954), were set in Japan—both also were turned into films, as was his best-selling *Hawaii* (1959). Michener has also written about the Holy Land in *The Source* (1965), Spain in *Iberia* (1968), and South Africa in *The Covenant* (1980). He ranged ever farther afield in *Space,* a 1983 novel about the American space effort.

Michener has also found inspiration close to home. *Centennial* (1974) covers centuries of life in Colorado, while *Chesapeake* (1978) does the same for Maryland's Eastern Shore region. In *Texas* (1985), Michener hardly left his own backyard, since he has resided in Austin for many years.

◆ Build Vocabulary

WORD ROOTS: *-vis-*

In this selection, you will find the word *improvised* used twice to describe two very different things. What these improvised things have in common is that they are hastily put together, not planned ahead of time. Literally, *improvised* means "unforeseen"; the word is based on the Latin root *-vis-*, which means "see." In this case, it is preceded by the prefixes *im-* and *pro-*, which mean "not" and "before," respectively. Some other *-vis-* words you may know are *vision, invisible,* and *revise* (literally, "to see again").

improvised
laden
encompassed
impose
ingeniously

WORD BANK

Before you read, preview this list of words from the story. In your notebook, write the words you think you already know and their meanings.

◆ Build Grammar Skills

CORRECT USE OF *LIKE* AND *AS/AS IF*

Because he is telling a story that involves the passage of time as well as some complex human interactions, James Michener often uses subordinate clauses introduced by conjunctions. Take a look at one of his sentences, which includes a subordinate clause introduced by the conjunction *as:*

> In time the rugs arrived, just *as* Muhammed Zaqir *had predicted they would.*

Notice that Michener does not write "... just *like* Muhammed Zaqir had predicted they would," because *like* is a preposition, not a conjunction, and must not be used to introduce clauses.

270 ◆ *Moments of Discovery*

Prentice Hall Literature Program Resources

REINFORCE / RETEACH / EXTEND

Selection Support Pages
Build Vocabulary: Word Roots: *-vis-*, p. 80
Build Grammar Skills: Correct Use of *Like* and *As/As If,* p. 81
Reading Strategy: Make Inferences About Characters, p. 82
Literary Focus: Characterization in Essays, p. 83
Strategies for Diverse Student Needs, p. 20
Beyond Literature
Cross-Curricular Connection: Social Studies, p. 20

Formal Assessment Selection Test, p. 66–68, Assessment Resources Software

Alternative Assessment, p. 20

Writing and Language Transparencies
Business Letter, pp. 53–56

Resource Pro CD-R⊘M
"The Rug Merchant"—includes all resource material and customizable lesson plan

⌒ **Listening to Literature Audiocassettes**
"The Rug Merchant"

The Rug Merchant

◆ *Literature and Your Life*

CONNECT YOUR EXPERIENCE

Sometimes you make decisions and then find yourself unmaking them. You believe you have sized someone up, and then you discover that a bit more measuring tape is called for. That is what happens to someone in "The Rug Merchant."

Journal Writing How do you decide whether or not you like and trust someone? Write down the chief standards that you use to size up a new acquaintance as someone you would like to know.

THEMATIC FOCUS: LEARNING ABOUT OURSELVES AND OTHERS

Sometimes making discoveries about other people makes you see yourself in a new way too. Why do you think people are often reluctant to change their views about a person?

◆ Background for Understanding

CULTURE

People in central and western Asia invented carpets over a thousand years ago as coverings for earthen floors in dwellings and mosques. Most Oriental rugs are made of sheep's wool, but the finest are made of silk, which has a more supple texture than wool and can be made to produce glowing colors. Different designs are associated with different regions in Asia: Most have abstract or geometric patterns, although some include representational images—for example, people, plants, and animals.

◆ Literary Focus

CHARACTERIZATION IN ESSAYS

The setting is a hotel in the Middle East. A thin man, with a smile that never leaves his face, rides up on a camel, walks into a room, and throws dozens of beautiful rugs on the floor. These and many other details—what the man says, how he behaves, what other people say about him—will be added to his **characterization,** the act of creating and developing a character. Writers create and develop characters through **characterization.** What a character says, how he or she behaves, and what other people say about that character are all elements of characterization.

◆ Reading Strategy

MAKE INFERENCES ABOUT CHARACTERS

The rug merchant who walks into James Michener's room leaves his rugs and says, "No necessity to buy. I leave here. You study, you learn to like." His actions and words suggest either that he is hopelessly naive or that he has a sixth sense about who can be trusted. Michener uses such details to help you draw your own conclusions—**make inferences**—about what the character is like.

As you read, it may help to note any details that allow you to make inferences. To organize your information, make a chart like the one shown here.

Appearance (inference)	Words (inference)	Actions (inference)

Guide for Reading ◆ 271

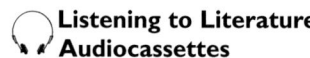
 Preparing for Standardized Tests

Reading The reading strategy taught with this selection—making inferences—is one of the main skills tested in critical reading sections of standardized tests. To help students apply what they learn to a standardized test format, have them recast the questions in the Reading Strategy section on page 278 in the form of multiple-choice questions. Their questions should have a clear answer, but the distracters they include should be close enough to the answer to challenge people taking the test. For more practice, use the Reading Strategy page in **Selection Support,** p. 82.

Grammar and Language Portions of some standardized tests may require students to use *like* and *as/as if* correctly. Students may be asked to select the correct word to complete a sentence, as in the following:

She did the job (like, as) she was told to. *as*

The Build Grammar Skills lesson for this selection focuses on this topic. For additional practice, use the Build Grammar Skills page on *Like and As,* p. 81, in **Selection Support.**

One-Minute Insight This essay shows how people of varied backgrounds can bridge a cultural gap. At first, Muhammad Zaqir and James Michener are at cross-purposes. Zaqir wants to sell rugs, and Michener refuses to consider buying. Over a few days, a change takes place: As the men talk, they decide to trust each other. Their trust is based on their growing faith, and not on contracts. Michener trusts Zaqir to see that the rugs arrive, and Zaqir trusts Michener to honor his promise to pay.

The concept of establishing trust that is highlighted in this story is probably one that students will be able to related to personal experience.

❶ Clarification Explain to students that *Herat* is a city in Afghanistan, near Iran. Have students locate Herat on a map to see where the story takes place. See p. 20 in **Beyond Literature**.

❷ Clarification Explain to students that *Koranic* refers to the Koran, the sacred scripture of Islam. One such symbol is the *Mihrab* (MEE-hrobb), or prayer niche, which appears on all Islamic prayer rugs.

◆ **Reading Strategy**

❸ Make Inferences About Characters Ask students: Why does Muhammad Zaqir rush out, leaving his rugs behind with Michener? What can you infer about his character from this detail? *Lead students to recognize the shrewdness of Zaqir's sales methods. He knows that further talk would produce more resistance on Michener's part. He also knows that the beautiful rugs would "sell themselves."*

The Rug Merchant

from *The World Is My Home: A Memoir*

James Michener

❶ I once made a long trip over the Dasht-i-Margo, the desert in Afghanistan, to the ancient city of Herat,[1] where I lodged in a former mosque with earthen floors. I had been in my improvised quarters only a few minutes when a very thin, toothy man with longish black hair and a perpetual smile entered and started throwing onto the dirt floor twenty or thirty of the most enchantingly beautiful Persian rugs I had ever seen. Their designs were miraculous—intri-❷ cate interweavings of Koranic symbols framed in geometric patterns that teased the eye—but their colors were also sheer delight: reds, yellows, greens and especially dark blues that were radiant.

They made my room a museum, one rug piled atop another, all peeking out at me, and when they were in place and the smiling man was satisfied with his handiwork—I supposed that this was a service of the so-

1. **Herat** (he rät´)

called hotel—to my amazement he handed me a scrap of paper on which was written in pencil in English: "MUHAMMAD ZAQIR, RUG MERCHANT, HERAT."

Aware at last of how I had been trapped, I protested: "No! No! No rugs!" but without relaxing his smile the least bit he said in English: "No necessity to buy. I leave here. You study, you learn to like," and before I could ❸ protest further he was gone. I ran out to make him take back his rugs, for I wanted none of them, but he was already leading his laden camel away from the old mosque.

I assumed he had learned from the hotel manager that I was to be in Herat for five days, and it was obvious that he felt confident that within that period he could wear

◆ **Build Vocabulary**

improvised (im´ prə vīzd) *adj.*: Put together on the spur of the moment

laden (lād´ ən) *adj.*: Burdened

272 ◆ *Moments of Discovery*

Block Scheduling Strategies

Consider these suggestions to take advantage of extended class time:

• Have students complete the journal activity in Literature and Your Life (p. 271) and discuss their entries in small groups.

• Direct students to research James Michener on the Internet before or after they read the selection.

• Invite students to listen to all or part of the selection on audiocassette. Have them discuss how the spoken version of the merchant's dialogue compares to their silent reading of it. Would they read the merchant's dialogue in the same way or differently? Suggest they give their own readings in groups.

• Have student volunteers act out scenes from the selection.

• Have students use the *Writer's Solution Writing Lab* CD-ROM tutorial on Practical and Technical Writing to complete the Writing Mini-Lesson (p. 279). Encourage students to make use of the letter template included in the tutorial.

►Critical Viewing◄

❹ Deduce Students might look at the abundance of rugs, the way the merchant is displaying one, and his expression—which seems to say the beauty of the rug speaks for itself— to deduce that he is proud of his rugs.

Customize for
Visual/Spatial Learners
The photographs on this page and on the next pages can be invaluable aides in helping these students picture the story's setting and characters. Take the time to discuss such details as the physical appearance of the man and his rugs (p. 273) and to explore what the mule (pp. 274–275) reveals about the setting.

❹ ▲ **Critical Viewing** Do you think the carpet dealer is proud of his rugs? Explain. **[Deduce]**

Humanities: Photography

The photograph shows a rug dealer, like Zaqir, holding a rug at the Grand Bazaar in Istanbul, Turkey. Zaqir gets rugs from many places, including Iran and China. The rugs are still handmade, as they have been for hundreds of years. Rug-weaving is often a family art; a large rug, like the one shown above, might take a family several generations to complete.

The dyes used in the rug are also handmade, from traditional recipes that use natural ingredients like crushed flowers and ground-up insects. The patterns may show birds, plants, and other realistic objects, or they may be abstract.

Use these questions for discussion:
1. What accounts for the fascination that these rugs have for Michener? *The complex designs and richness and variety of color make these rugs especially attractive.*
2. What conclusions might students draw from the fact that one rug like this may take several people many years to make? *The enormous amount of time and effort that goes into the making of such rugs is one of the factors that makes them so precious to the people who value them. It is also an indication of the importance of the craft in these cultures.*

❶ Clarification *Meshed* is a city in Iran. *Bukhara* (Boo-KHA-rah) and *Samarkand* are cities in what is now Uzbekistan but, when this essay was written, were still part of the Soviet Union. All three cities are famous for their carpets.

◆ **Reading Strategy**

❷ Make Inferences About Characters Ask students how they think Zaqir knows that Michener lives in Pennsylvania. *He probably found out from the owner of the hotel.* What can students infer about Zaqir from this fact? *Students might say that he is wily, intelligent, or resourceful.*

◆ **Build Grammar Skills**

❸ Like and As/As If Ask students to identify the subordinate clause in this sentence. Have them explain why the phrase "as if" is used in the sentence instead of "like." *The subordinate clause "the rugs were of little value" is preceded by "as if" rather than "like" because "as if" is a subordinating conjunction, while "like" is a preposition.*

◆ **Reading Strategy**

❹ Make Inferences About Characters Ask students why they think Zaqir keeps coming back, even after Michener has made it clear that he doesn't want any rugs. What character trait does this imply? *Students should recognize that Zaqir is persistent. Also, they might infer that he has learned from experience that this strategy works.*

◆ **Critical Thinking**

❺ Infer Ask students why Zaqir tells Michener, "you have a fine eye." *Some may say that Zaqir really does admire Michener's taste. Others may say he is flattering Michener because he knows that complimenting people makes them more likely to buy his rugs.*

me down and persuade me to buy a rug. He started on the evening of that first day; he came back after supper to sit with me in the shadowy light cast by a flickering lamp. He said: "Have you ever seen lovelier rugs? That one from my friend in Meshed. Those two from the dealer in Bukhara. This one from a place you know, maybe? Samarkand."

When I asked him how he was able to trade with such towns in the Soviet Union[2] he shrugged: "Borders? Out here we don't bother," and with a sweep of his hand that encompassed all the rugs he said: "Not one woven in Afghanistan," and I noted the compelling pronunciation he gave that name: Ahf-han-ee-stahn.

He sat for more than an hour with me that evening, and next day he was back before noon to start his serious bargaining: "Michener-sahib,[3] name German perhaps?" I told him it was more likely English, at which he laughed: "English, Afghans, many battles, English always win but next day you march back to India, nothing change." When I corrected him: "I'm not English," he said: "I know. Pennsylvania. Three, four, maybe five of your rugs look great your place Pennsylvania."

"But I don't need rugs there. I don't really want them."

"Would they not look fine Pennsylvania?" and as if the rugs were of little value, he kicked the top ones aside to reveal the glowing wonders of those below.

When he returned that second night he got down to even more serious business:

---

2. Soviet Union: The Union of Soviet Socialist Republics consisted of fifteen republics strictly controlled by the country's central government until independence movements in 1991.
3. Michener-sahib (sä´ ib): Mr. Michener.

◆ **Build Vocabulary**
encompassed (en kum´ pəst) *v.:* Surrounded

"The big white and gold one you like, six hundred dollars." On and on he went, and when it was clear that I had no interest whatever in the big ones, he subtly covered them over with the smaller six-by four-foot ones already in the room; then he ran out to his camel to fetch seven or eight of the size that I had in some unconscious way disclosed I might consider, and by the end of that session he knew that I was at least a possible purchaser of four or five of the handsome rugs.

"Ah, Michener-sahib, you have fine eye. That I ❺

 Cross-Curricular Connection: Social Studies

The setting of this essay is a hotel room in Herat, Afghanistan. Afghanistan is located in south-central Asia, and is bordered by Iran on the west, Pakistan on the south and east, and Turkmenistan, Uzbekistan, and Tajikistan to the north. A narrow panhandle 150 miles long, the Vakhan, extends eastward to touch China. The Vakhan, a mountainous area in the Pamirs, served in the past as a buffer between Russian Turkistan, British India, and China. In the 1980's, the Vakhan was occupied by the Soviet Union.

Herat is located on the Harirud river in northwestern Afghanistan. Unlike most of the country, which is mountainous, the area around Herat is relatively flat, and is one of Afghanistan's richest agricultural areas. Several ancient cities existed near or at the site of modern Herat, including one built by Alexander the Great in the fourth century B.C. In the fifteenth century, Herat was the capital of Persia and a center of science and culture. Later, Herat became known for its beautiful carpets, which typically featured animals chasing one another and fighting among coiled vines and stylized flowers.

Encourage interested students to find out more about the history of Afghanistan and Herat. Challenge them to find out when Herat permanently became part of Afghanistan. *The city switched between Persian and Afghan control several times before becoming part of Afghanistan in 1863.*

one from China, silk and wool, look at those tiny knots." Then he gave me a lesson in rug making; he talked about the designs, the variation in knots, the wonderful compactness of the Chinese variety, the dazzling colors of the Samarkand. It was fascinating to hear him talk, and all the while he was wearing me down.

◆ Literary Focus
6 What does Zaqir's persistence and sales technique suggest about his understanding of people?

He was a persistent rascal, always watching till he saw me return to my mosque after work, then pouncing on me.

On the third day, as he sat drinking tea with me while our chairs were perched on his treasury of rugs, four and five deep at some places and covering the entire floor, he knocked down one after another of my objections: "You can't take them with you? No traveler can. I send them to you, camel here, ship Karachi, train New York, truck to your home Pennsylvania." Pasted onto the pages of his notebook were addresses of buyers from all parts of the world to whom he had shipped his rugs, and I noticed that they had gone out from Meshed in Iran, Mazar-e-Sharif in Afghanistan and Bukhara[4] in Russia; apparently he really moved about with his laden camel. But he also had, pasted close to the shipping address, letters from his customers proving that the rugs had finally reached their new owners. In our dealings he seemed to me an honest man.

On that third night, when it began to look as if I might escape without making a purchase even though I had shown an interest in six rugs, he hammered at me regarding payments: "Now, Michener-sahib, I can take American dollars, you know."

"I have no American dollars." Rapidly he ran through the currencies that he would accept, British, Indian, Iranian, Pakistani, Afghani, in that descending order, until I had to stop him with a truthful statement: "Muhammad, my friend, I have no money, none of any kind," and before the last word had been uttered he cried: "I take traveler's checks, American Express, Bank

4. **Bukhara** (bü kär´ ə)

◆ Literary Focus
6 Characterization in Essays Zaqir has learned from his experience as a merchant that the more he talks to potential customers, the more likely they are to buy from him. He probably has also learned that people find it difficult to turn down a likable salesperson after they get to know him or her.

◆ Reading Strategy
7 Make Inferences About Characters Ask students what they can infer about Zaqir from the way in which he deals with the objections raised by Michener. *Students may say that Zaqir's prompt answers to the objections and his familiarity with the route from Herat to Pennsylvania reflect the merchant's experience and his resourcefulness.*

◆ Build Grammar Skills
8 *Like* and *As/As If* Ask students to identify the subordinate clause in this sentence and to explain the function of the phrase "as if." Have them explain why it would be incorrect to substitute "like" for "as if." *The subordinate clause is "I might escape without making a purchase." "As if" is a subordinating conjunction. "Like" would be incorrect because it is a preposition.*

◆ Critical Thinking
9 Interpret Ask students to suggest why Michener now addresses Zaqir as "my friend." *Students may say that Michener feels close to Zaqir after the hours they have spent together, or that he wants to emphasize that he is telling the truth about his lack of funds.*

Beyond the Classroom

Career Connection

Sales In this essay, James Michener paints a word-portrait of a master seller. Muhammad Zaqir succeeds at his profession in part because he has knowledge and enthusiasm for his product, and can communicate them to potential customers, and also because he is very persistent and a good strategist.

Suggest that students set up informal interviews with local salespeople. The students should go to their interviews with written lists of questions about approaches to selling and the skills required. Students can meet after their interviews and compare findings. Have them compare and contrast the skills that salespeople in their community use with ones Zaqir uses. Students could also use the interviews to judge whether their own personalities would be suited to a career in sales. What would they sell? Is there a product about which they are as enthusiastic and knowledgeable as Zaqir is about his rugs? What sales techniques would be appropriate for selling that product?

❶ Make Inferences About Characters Elicit responses such as the following: *At this point in the essay Zaqir has gotten to know Michener to the point that he judges him trustworthy. Zaqir is an experienced salesman and he is confident he can trust his own abilities as an accurate judge of character.*

Customize for
English Language Learners
Help these students appreciate Michener's pun on the word "draw." Explain that "draw a check" is another way of saying "write a check" or "make out a check." In this case, the person is literally drawing a check, in the sense of drawing a picture.

◆ Critical Thinking

❷ Evaluate Characters Ask students to predict whether Michener will get his rugs or not. On what evidence do they base their predictions? *Students will probably predict that Michener will get the rugs. Some may base their predictions simply on the fact that Michener has presented Zaqir as a charming person. Some may be convinced by the letters from other customers or by the fact that Zaqir trusted Michener with his rugs.*

❸ Clarification Explain that *Karachi* (kah-RAH-tchee) is a city in Pakistan, *Istanbul* a city in Turkey, *Trieste* (tree-ESS-tay) in Italy, and *Marseilles* (mar-SAY) in France. Let students locate these cities on a world map to see that Zaqir has shipped rugs all over the world.

America in California," and then I had to tell him the sad news: "Muhammad, friend. I have no traveler's checks. Left them all locked up in the American embassy in Kabul. Because there are robbers on the road to Meshed."

"I know. I know. But you are an honest man, Michener-sahib. I take your personal check."

When I said truthfully that I had none, he asked simply: "You like those six rugs?"

"Yes, you have made me appreciate them. I do."

With a sweeping gesture he gathered the six beauties, rolled them deftly into a bundle and thrust them into my arms: "You take them. Send me a check when you get to Pennsylvania."

> ◆ **Reading Strategy**
> What inference can you make about Zaqir based on his willingness to wait for payment for the rugs?

"You would trust me?"

"You look honest. Don't I look honest?" And he picked up one of his larger rugs, a real beauty, and showed me the fine knots: "Bukhara. I got it there, could not pay. I send the money when I sell. Man in Bukhara trusts me. I trust you."

I said I could not <u>impose</u> on him in that way. Something might happen to me or I might prove to be a crook, and the discussion ended, except that as he left me he asked: "Michener, if you had the money, what rugs would you take with you?" and I said "None, but if you could ship them, I'd take those four," and he said: "Those four you shall have. I'll find a way."

Next day he was back in the mosque right after breakfast with an astonishing proposal: "Michener-sahib, I can let you have those four rugs, special price, four hundred fifty dollars." Before I could repeat my inability to pay, he said: "Bargain like this you never see again. Tell you what to do. You write me a check."

When I said, distressed at losing such a bargain: "But I really have no blank checks," he said: "You told me yesterday. I believe you.

But draw me one," and from his folder he produced a sheet of ordinary paper and a pencil. He showed me how to draw a copy of a blank check, bearing the name of the bank, address, amount, etc.—and for the first time in my life I actually drew a blank check, filled in the amount and signed it, whereupon Muhammad Zaqir placed it in his file, folded the four rugs I had bought, tied them with string and attached my name and address.

He piled the rugs onto his camel, and then mounted it to proceed on his way to Samarkand.

Back home in Pennsylvania I started to receive two different kinds of letters, perhaps fifteen of each. The following is a sample of the first category:

> I am a shipping agent in Istanbul and a freighter arrived here from Karachi bringing a large package, well wrapped, addressed to you in Pennsylvania. Upon receipt of your check for $19.50 American I will forward the package to you.

From Karachi, Istanbul, Trieste, Marseilles and heavens knows where else I received a steady flow of letters over a three-year period, and always the sum demanded was less than twenty dollars, so that I would say to myself: "Well, I've invested so much in it already, I may as well risk a little more." And off the check would go, with the rugs never getting any closer. Moreover, I was not at all sure that if they ever did reach me they would be my property, for my unusual check had never been submitted for payment, even though I had forewarned my local bank: "If it ever does arrive, pay it immediately, because it's a debt of honor."

The second group of letters explained the long delay:

> I am serving in Kabul as the Italian ambassador and was lately in Herat where a rug merchant showed me that remark-

---

 **Speaking and Listening Mini-Lesson**

Dramatic Monologue

This mini-lesson supports the Speaking and Listening activity in the Idea Bank on page 279.

Introduce the Concept Explain that "The Rug Merchant" is written in the *first person;* that is, the narrator uses the pronoun *I* to refer to himself. In "The Rug Merchant," the author is the narrator. Therefore, the story is told from the author's *point of view.* Make sure students understand that their mono-

logues will be told in the first person from Zaqir's point of view.

Develop Background Since the selection doesn't state what Zaqir is thinking or feeling, students will have to make *inferences* in order to prepare their monologues. Lead them to consider the following points:

• They can use what Zaqir says to infer what he might be thinking or feeling.

• They can use Zaqir's actions and other evidence to make inferences about his

thoughts and feelings.

Apply the Information Have students use this background to prepare and perform their monologues for groups. They can use their inferences about Zaqir to determine what he would say and how he would say it.

Assess the Outcome Have students assess their own monologues and those of their group on the basis of how consistent they are with Michener's characterization of Zaqir.

able check you gave him for something like five hundred dollars. He asked me if I thought it would be paid if he forwarded it and I assured him that since you were a man of good reputation it would be. When I asked him why he had not submitted it sooner, he said: "Michener-sahib a good name. I show his check everybody like you, sell many rugs."

These letters came from French commercial travelers, English explorers, Indian merchants, almost anyone who might be expected to reach out-of-the-way Herat and take a room in that miserable old mosque.

In time the rugs arrived, just as Muhammad Zaqir had predicted they would, accompanied by so many shipping papers they were a museum in themselves. And after my improvised check had been used as an advertisement for nearly five years, it too came home to roost and was honored. Alas, shortly thereafter the rugs were stolen, but I remember them vividly and with longing. Especially do I remember the man who spent four days ingeniously persuading me to buy.

◆ **Build Vocabulary**

impose (im pōz´) v.: Put to some trouble
ingeniously (in jēn´ yəs lē) adv.: Cleverly

Beyond Literature

Media Connection

Michener and Hollywood "The Rug Merchant" comes from James Michener's autobiography, *The World Is My Home: A Memoir.* The book is well named, because Michener has visited countless places all over the world. Many of Michener's visits have blossomed into books with titles a travel agent would love: *Tales of the South Pacific, Hawaii, Caravans, Chesapeake, Poland, Texas, Alaska,* and *Caribbean.* Because Michener's books often relate fascinating histories and describe exotic lands, Hollywood producers have snapped them up and turned them into screenplays for feature films and television movies. Films based on Michener's works include *The Bridges at Toko-Ri, Caravans, Hawaii, Return to Paradise, Sayonara,* and *South Pacific.* Television movies and series include *Centennial, Dynasty,* and *Space.* Incidentally, *Space* names one of the few places Michener hasn't visited.

ACTIVITY Rent a video of a James Michener movie. Share your opinion of it with your classmates.

Guide for Responding

◆ *Literature and Your Life*

Reader's Response Would you have bought the rugs if you had been in James Michener's place? Why or why not?
Thematic Focus What did the rug merchant do that surprised you most?
Role Play With a partner, role play an interaction between a persuasive salesperson and a reluctant customer.

☑ **Check Your Comprehension**

1. List five offers the rug merchant made during his visit to Michener.
2. What did Michener learn from the rug merchant?
3. Michener didn't have any money with him. How did he pay for the rugs?
4. (a) How long did it take the rugs to reach Michener in Pennsylvania? (b) What had the rug merchant been doing during that time?

The Rug Merchant ◆ 277

Beyond the Selection

FURTHER READING

Other Works by James Michener
Tales of the South Pacific
Hawaii
The Source
Centennial
Texas
Iberia

INTERNET

You may find additional information about Michener on the Internet. We suggest the following site. Please be aware, however, that the site may have changed from the time we published this information.

The James Michener Home Page is at **http://www.jamesmichener.com/**

The site includes links to articles on Michener and an interactive map showing his settings.

We *strongly recommend* that you preview the site before you send students to it.

Answers

◆ Critical Thinking

1. Students might say that Michener likes Zaqir or that Zaqir's persistance makes him difficult to refuse.
2. Zaqir shows his honesty by being willing to leave his rugs with Michener and by showing shipping labels from other satisfied and trusting individuals. Zaqir is a rascal when he refuses to take "no" for an answer and returns to Michener day after day.
3. Students might say that Michener discovers that Zaqir is honest, likeable, and persistent.
4. Michener will never forget Zaqir's persistent sales pitch nor his honesty and trust.
5. The essay suggests that in Zaqir's culture people are more trusting of one another and conduct business in less formal ways than in Michener's culture.
6. This essay teaches that persistence and flexibility pay off in a sales career.

◆ Reading Strategy

1. Zaqir is a trusting individual.
2. The fact that Michener pays the amounts shows that he likes Zaqir very much.

◆ Literary Focus

1. Students might say that Zaqir is honest, persistent, congenial, and trusting. Actions and words cited must be consistant with the students' impression.
2. Some students will say that Zaqir is a believable human being, while others might say that Zaqir's extremely persistent behavior makes him seem like an overdrawn or unrealistic character.

◆ Build Vocabulary

Using the Word Root -vis-
1. visitation: The act of going to see someone.
2. invisibility: The quality of being unable to be seen.
3. envision: To imagine or see in the mind.

Using the Word Bank
1. b 2. a 3. c 4. a 5. b

◆ Build Grammar Skills

1. . . . the rugs just as a loving father. . . .

Guide for Responding (continued)

◆ Critical Thinking

INTERPRET
1. Why do you think Michener continues his discussions with Zaqir even though he does not want to buy any rugs? **[Infer]**
2. Explain how Zaqir can strike Michener as both "an honest man" and "a rascal." **[Classify]**
3. What do you think Michener discovers about Zaqir in the course of their dealings? **[Infer]**
4. Why does Michener say that he will remember Zaqir? **[Draw Conclusions]**

APPLY
5. What does the essay suggest about the differences between Zaqir's culture and Michener's culture? **[Generalize]**

EXTEND
6. What could this essay teach someone about how to succeed as a salesperson? **[Career Link]**

◆ Reading Strategy

MAKE INFERENCES ABOUT CHARACTERS
By choosing a few crucial details, Michener shows us a great deal about a man he met only four times, but who continued to be part of his life for years to come.
1. What inference can you make about Zaqir's character based on his creation of the blank check?
2. What does Michener's willingness to pay the amounts demanded over the course of five years enable you to infer about his feelings for Zaqir?

◆ Literary Focus

CHARACTERIZATION IN ESSAYS
In "The Rug Merchant," James Michener weaves a portrait of an actual human being that is almost as vivid as any of his beautiful rugs.
1. State your single strongest impression of Zaqir and the actions or words that contribute to this impression.
2. Do you find Zaqir a believable, real-life human being or a fantastic but not convincing character? Explain.

◆ Build Vocabulary

USING THE WORD ROOT -vis-
Knowing that the Latin root -vis- means "see," write definitions for the following words.
1. visitation   2. invisibility   3. envision

USING THE WORD BANK
On your paper, write the word whose meaning is closest to that of the first word.
1. laden: (a) spoon, (b) burdened, (c) abandoned
2. improvised: (a) unplanned, (b) entertaining, (c) careful
3. encompassed: (a) directed, (b) ruled over, (c) included
4. ingeniously: (a) cleverly, (b) dishonestly, (c) stupidly
5. impose: (a) arrange, (b) bother, (c) stand

◆ Build Grammar Skills

CORRECT USE OF LIKE AND AS/AS IF
As can be used either as a preposition to introduce prepositional phrases or as a subordinating conjunction to introduce subordinate clauses. **Like** can be used as a preposition but not as a conjunction.

Used as Prepositions
Correct: It looks like spring.
My role as Hamlet was fun.

Used as Conjunctions
Correct: I did it just as you told me to do.

Incorrect: I did it just like you told me to.

Practice On your paper, rewrite each incorrect sentence correctly. If a sentence has no errors, write "correct."
1. He bent over the rugs just like a loving father bends over his child.
2. The rugs glowed like embers in a fireplace.
3. Zaqir returned, like Michener knew he would.
4. The rug merchant used the check as if it were cash.
5. Zaqir used the check like cash.

2. correct
3. . . . returned, as Michener knew. . . .
4. correct
5. correct

Build Your Portfolio

 ## Idea Bank

Writing

1. **Sales Catalog** Imagine that you are creating a sales catalog for Zaqir's rugs. Review the descriptions of the rugs in the essay, and then write a brief description of four different rugs, mentioning the patterns, colors, and type of weaving seen in each. **[Career Link]**

2. **Dramatic Scene** Based on one of Zaqir's visits to Michener, write a short dramatic scene that consists entirely of their conversation.

3. **Short Story** Imagine that Michener and Zaqir meet years later, after the rugs have come to Michener and been stolen. Write a story that sets forth the circumstances that bring them together again. What do they have to say to each other?

Speaking and Listening

4. **Conversation** Role-play a phone conversation between Michener and one of the many people who receive his rugs.

5. **Dramatic Monologue** Perform a dramatic monologue in the character of Zaqir, in which you express what Zaqir feels after he leaves Michener's hotel with the improvised check.

Projects

6. **Design a Rug** Design and draw a rug of your own. You may conduct research to get ideas for your rug or base your design on Michener's descriptions of Zaqir's rugs **[Art Link]**

7. **Report on Afghanistan** Assemble information about Afghanistan, including a map showing its location in Asia, facts about its land and people, photographs, and any objects you can find. **[Social Studies Link]**

 ## Writing Mini-Lesson

Letter of Complaint

Imagine a problem that might arise over the purchase of a rug or another household item. Suppose the item arrives damaged, or it is not the one you purchased. Write a letter of complaint attempting to address this problem. As you write, the following may help you.

> #### Writing Skills Focus: Clear Explanation of the Problem
>
> In order to succeed, a letter of complaint should contain a **clear explanation of the problem** at hand. The language should be direct and concise. If time or cause-effect relationships are involved, they should be clearly indicated.

Prewriting Make a list of all the important circumstances of the problem you are seeking to solve. Do not overload the letter with too much detail, but do provide enough information so that your reader knows what you expected to happen and how the result has fallen short. It may help you to list a chain of causes and effects in chronological order before you write. This will enable you to see whether you have your circumstances in clear order and whether you need more information.

Drafting State your problem clearly and firmly and include all the relevant information. Try to strike the right tone—emphasize the importance and justice of your complaint without insulting or irritating the reader. Finally, ask that a particular action (a refund or replacement, for example) be taken to resolve your problem.

Revising Reread your draft. Have you stated the problem as clearly and briefly as possible? Do you need to add any important details? Ask yourself how it would strike you, if you were on the receiving end of the letter. Look for ways to make your writing appeal to the reader and still do justice to your complaint.

Guide for Responding ♦ 279

 ## Idea Bank

Customizing for *Performance Levels*
Following are suggestions for matching the Idea Bank topics with your students' performance levels:
Less Advanced Students: 1, 4
Average Students: 2, 5, 6
More Advanced Students: 3, 7

Customizing for *Learning Modalities*
Following are suggestions for matching Idea Bank topics with your students' learning modalities:
Visual/Spatial: 1, 6, 7
Verbal/Linguistic: 2, 3, 5
Auditory: 4, 5
Logical/Mathematical: 7
Interpersonal: 4

 ## Writing Mini-Lesson

Refer students to the Writing Handbook, page 962, for instruction on the writing process, and page 966 for further information on Practical and Technical Writing. You may also use the Business Letter transparencies in *Writing and Language Transparencies*, pp. 53–56, to guide students through the writing process.

 ### Writer's Solution

Writing Lab CD-ROM
Have students use the tutorial on Practical and Technical Writing to complete their letters. Follow these steps:
1. Have students write their letters using the letter shell template. Doing so will ensure that they use proper letter format.
2. Have students use the Self-Evaluation Checklist to help them revise.

Allow 70 minutes of class time for students to complete these steps.

Sourcebook
Have students use Chapter 8, Practical and Technical Writing (pp. 228–262), for additional support.

Guide for Reading

OBJECTIVES

1. To read, comprehend, and interpret four poems
2. To relate poems to personal experience
3. To interpret meaning of poems
4. To identify moments of insight
5. To build vocabulary in context and learn words with multiple meanings
6. To use reflexive and intensive pronouns correctly
7. To write a journal entry using elaboration to add emotional depth
8. To respond to poems through writing, speaking and listening, and projects

SKILLS INSTRUCTION

Vocabulary:
Words With Multiple Meanings

Grammar:
Reflexive and Intensive Pronouns

Reading Strategy:
Interpret Meaning

Literary Focus:
Moment of Insight

Writing:
Elaboration to Add Emotional Depth

Speaking and Listening: Oral Interpretation (teacher edition)

Critical Viewing: Describe; Compare; Draw Conclusions

PORTFOLIO OPPORTUNITIES

Writing: Postcard; Poem; Dialogue
Writing Mini-Lesson: Journal Entry
Speaking and Listening: Oral Interpretation; Television Interview
Projects: Multimedia Presentation; Photo Essay

More About the Authors

Gladys Cardiff is the poetry editor of *Third Coast Magazine*, a magazine that publishes contemporary poetry and fiction.

Alice Walker was active in the civil rights movement of the 1950's, as a voter-registration worker in Georgia and as a Head Start teacher in Mississippi.

After World War I, **E. E. Cummings** lived in Paris, where he painted and wrote poetry. Later, he lived in New York City's Greenwich Village until his death.

Wisława Szymborska (vees-WAH-vah sheem-BOR-skah) said, when she learned that she had won the Nobel Prize, "I am very happy, stunned, and frightened. I'm afraid I will not have a quiet life now." In Poland, her collections of poetry sell out as quickly as they are printed.

Gladys Cardiff (1942–   )

According to Gladys Cardiff, "Combing" is one of the few poems she has written that did not require revision.

Born in Montana, where her Cherokee father and Irish/Welsh mother taught school on a Blackfoot reservation, Cardiff grew up in Seattle, Washington, and received a bachelor's degree and a master's degree in creative writing from the University of Washington.

Alice Walker (1944–   )

The youngest of eight children, this author thought she had been born into the wrong family because she always seemed to need more peace and quiet than the others. From the time she was eight, she kept a journal and wrote poems.

Walker was born in Eatonton, Georgia. As a child, she attended all-black schools and had many teachers who encouraged her love of reading and writing. Walker has written poetry, short stories, novels, and nonfiction. One of her best-known novels—*The Color Purple*—was made into an acclaimed motion picture.

E. E. Cummings (1894–1962)

Readers expect playful, lyrical, eccentric poems from this individualist New England poet. Born in Boston, Massachusetts, and nurtured in its rich literary tradition, Cummings graduated from Harvard University. Serving in Europe during World War I, Cummings was briefly imprisoned because his unusual printing in his letters home led the censors to believe he was a spy.

Wisława Szymborska (1923–   )

"Question authority" might be the motto of this contemporary Polish poet. In "Astonishment," she uses the word *why* eight times. During World War II, when the Nazis closed Polish secondary schools and universities, Szymborska attended school illegally.

Today, the poet lives quietly in Poland, giving few interviews and letting her poetry speak for her. In 1996, she was awarded the Nobel Prize for Literature.

◆ Build Vocabulary

WORDS WITH MULTIPLE MEANINGS

Poets play with words, and words that have more than one meaning particularly lend themselves to play. For example, in "Women," Alice Walker uses the word *stout* to mean "sturdy," but it can also mean "courageous" or "heavyset"—definitions that could also work in the context of the poem.

WORD BANK

intent
plaiting
stout
languid

Before you read, preview this list of words from the poems.

◆ Build Grammar Skills

REFLEXIVE AND INTENSIVE PRONOUNS

A **reflexive pronoun** indicates that the subject is doing something to, for, or on behalf of itself:

For whatever we lose (like a you or a me)
it's always *ourselves* we find in the sea

Intensive pronouns draw attention to a person or thing and usually come right after the word. An intensive pronoun is not really needed in the sentence:

How they knew what we/ *Must* know/
Without knowing a page/ Of it/ *Themselves.*

280 ◆ *Moments of Discovery*

Prentice Hall Literature Program Resources

REINFORCE / RETEACH / EXTEND

Selection Support Pages
Build Vocabulary: Words With Multiple Meanings, p. 84
Build Grammar Skills: Reflexive and Intensive Pronouns, p. 85
Reading Strategy: Interpret Meaning, p. 86
Literary Focus: Moment of Insight, p. 87

Strategies for Diverse Student Needs, p. 21

Beyond Literature
Humanities Connection: Art, p. 21

Formal Assessment Selection Test, pp. 69–71, Assessment Resources Software

Alternative Assessment, p. 21

Writing and Language Transparencies
Reflective Essay, pp. 5–8

Resource Pro CD-ROM
"Combing," "Women," "maggie and milly and molly and may," "Astonishment"

Listening to Literature Audiocassettes
"Combing," "Women," "maggie and milly and molly and may," "Astonishment"

Combing ◆ Women
◆ maggie and milly and molly and may ◆
Astonishment

◆ *Literature and Your Life*

CONNECT YOUR EXPERIENCE
Throughout our lives, we make discoveries that help us define and redefine who we are. Each of the poems that follows presents such a discovery. You may find that the discoveries or the poems' speakers lead you to personal discoveries of your own.

Journal Writing Start writing an entry about anything you like. Keep writing for five to ten minutes. Don't change the subject. Explore every idea you have about the subject. See if your exploration leads you to any personal discoveries.

THEMATIC FOCUS: LEARNING ABOUT OURSELVES AND OTHERS
These poems exemplify different ways of exploring one's identity—through family connections, nature, and an appreciation of the world around us. What are other ways of exploring identity?

◆ Background for Understanding

HISTORY
In "Women," the speaker expresses her admiration for the African American women of her mother's generation, who fought for the desegregation of public schools in the South. Until the mid-1950's, these schools were segregated, which means there were separate schools for white students and black students. In 1954, the United States Supreme Court ruled that separate schools for black students and white students created a system that was inherently unequal. Many southern states and local school districts forcibly resisted the federal government's attempts to integrate their schools.

◆ Literary Focus

MOMENT OF INSIGHT
Poets use specific images to explore ideas and feelings. As the poet writes, these specific images may lead to a **moment of insight**, a fresh new thought that arises from the poet's musings. Very specific details add up to a general insight into life, often expressed at the end of a poem.

◆ Reading Strategy

INTERPRET MEANING
The speakers of these poems describe moments of insight about life. You will be better prepared to understand the insight if you try to **interpret the meaning** behind the poets' words. Three practices will help you interpret the meaning of a poem. First, use sensory images—those you can see, hear, taste, touch, or smell—to form a picture in your mind of what is being described. Second, ask yourself why the poet has chosen these specific images. Third, connect what is being said to your own experience.

Guide for Reading ◆ 281

Preparing for Standardized Tests

Reading and Vocabulary Portions of some standardized tests require students to interpret a passage from literature. The reading strategy for this selection—interpret meaning—will enable students to improve performance on such portions. The Build Vocabulary lesson focuses on mastering words with multiple meanings. Students will be able to apply this skill when working with reading comprehension and verbal reasoning items on standardized tests. For more practice, use the Build Vocabulary page in **Selection Support,** p. 72.

Grammar and Language Portions of some standardized tests require students to use reflexive and intensive pronouns correctly. Students may be asked to select the correct pronoun to complete a sentence, as in the following:

    I bought (me, myself) a new pair of shoes.
    myself

The Build Grammar Skills lesson for this selection focuses on this topic. For additional practice, use the Build Grammar Skills page on Reflexive and Intensive Pronouns in **Selection Support,** p. 73.

281

One-Minute Insight In these poems, the speaker expresses a moment of insight in which an important aspect of personal identity is suddenly revealed. In "Combing," the speaker discovers her bond with other women in her family. In "Women," the speaker recognizes that her way has been paved by African American women of previous generations. These two poems explore clues that lead to moments of self-discovery.

▶Critical Viewing◀

❶ Describe, Compare Students may find the mood of the painting is warm and reflective, like the mood of the poem.

◆ **Reading Strategy**

❷ Interpret Meaning Ask students: What are the "orange/Parings"? Suggest they use the sensory image in the poem to form a picture in their minds before they answer. Then ask why they think the poet chose this particular image. *The orange parings are the red-headed daughter's curls. The word "parings" helps the reader visualize exactly what the curls look like.*

◆ **Reading Strategy**

❸ Interpret Meaning Ask students to interpret the meaning of "... Sitting/Before the oven I hear/The orange coils tick/The early hour ..." Advise them to form a mental picture and try to relate the lines to their own experience. *Students may imagine the speaker dried her hair by sitting before an open oven whose electrical coils glowed orange. Most students have seen heating elements glowing orange in blow-dryers, toasters, or space heaters. Some may have noticed that electrical heating elements tick as they heat up.*

Customize for
Less Proficient Readers
These students may find it helpful to make a chart or drawing showing the four generations to which the speaker refers: the speaker, the speaker's daughter, the speaker's mother, and the speaker's great-grandmother.

282

Combing

Gladys Cardiff

Woman Combing Girl's Hair (detail), Malcolm T. Liepke

▲ **Critical Viewing** What words would you use to describe the mood of the painting? Would you use the same words to describe the mood of the poem? [Describe; Compare]

Bending, I bow my head
And lay my hand upon
Her hair, combing, and think
How women do this for
5   Each other. My daughter's hair
Curls against the comb,
Wet and fragrant—orange
Parings. Her face, downcast,
Is quiet for one so young.

10   I take her place. Beneath
My mother's hands I feel
The braids drawn up tight
As a piano wire and singing,
Vinegar-rinsed. Sitting
15   Before the oven I hear
The orange coils tick
The early hour before school.

She combed her grandmother
Mathilda's hair using
20   A comb made out of bone.
Mathilda rocked her oak wood
Chair, her face downcast,
Intent on tearing rags
In strips to braid a cotton
25   Rug from bits of orange
And brown. A simple act,

Preparing hair. Something
Women do for each other,
Plaiting the generations.

◆ **Build Vocabulary**
Intent (in tent´) *adj.*: Firmly fixed; concentrated
Plaiting (plāt´ in) *v.*: Braiding

282 ◆ Moments of Discovery

Block Scheduling Strategies

Consider these suggestions to take advantage of extended class time:

• Guide students to complete the journal activity in Literature and Your Life (p. 281) and discuss their entries in small groups.

• Have students work in discussion groups to answer the Critical Thinking questions (p. 285).

• Direct students to work on the Poem in the Idea Bank (p. 287). Have them perform a role-play with partners to get ideas about what a woman described in "Women" might say.

• Allow students to use library, Internet, or other school resources to gather information for the Multimedia Presentation and Photo Essay projects in the Idea Bank (p. 287).

• Encourage students to write a sequel to "maggie and milly and molly and may" in which each of the girls makes a new discovery. This activity is described in greater detail in **Alternative Assessment,** p. 21.

Women

Alice Walker

They were women then
My mama's generation
4 | Husky of voice—<u>Stout</u> of
Step
5 **5** | With fists as well as
Hands
6 | How they battered down
Doors
And ironed
10 Starched white
Shirts
How they led
Armies
Headragged Generals
15 **7** | Across mined
Fields

Booby-trapped | **7**
Ditches
20 To discover books
Desks
A place for us | **8**
How they knew what we
Must know
Without knowing a page |
25 Of it | **9**
Themselves.

◆ Build Vocabulary

Stout (stout) *adj.*: Sturdy; forceful

The Quiltmakers, Paul Goodnight, Color Circle Art Publishing, Inc.

▲ **Critical Viewing** Draw conclusions about the artist's attitude toward these women. Is it similar to the one expressed by Alice Walker? [Draw Conclusions] **10**

Cross-Curricular Connection: Social Studies

The greater students' understanding of the civil rights movement, the better they will relate to Alice Walker's poem, "Women." Have students use the library, the Internet, or interviews with adults to find out more about the fight for integration of schools and for equal rights for black people. To help students research women who played important roles in the civil rights movement, write on the chalkboard key names and terms for them to look up: Rosa Parks, Ella Baker, Fannie Lou Hamer, Bernice Johnson Reagon, Eleanor Holmes Norton, and *Brown v. Board of Education of Topeka* (the 1954 case in which the Supreme Court ruled that segregation in public schools is unconstitutional). Have students present reports to the class based on their research. Ask them to explain how their research added to their appreciation or understanding of the poem.

◆ Build Vocabulary

4 Words With Multiple Meanings *Sturdy* or *forceful* could be substituted for the word *stout* in this line. Ask students to explain how the other meanings of *stout*—*courageous* and *heavyset*—enrich the poem, as well. *Students may answer that* heavyset *creates a visual image of some of the women, while* courageous *adds meaning to the line.*

◆ Critical Thinking

5 Infer Ask students: "What does the word *fists* tell about what these women were like?" *They were ready to fight for what they wanted.*

◆ Reading Strategy

6 Interpret Meaning Ask students to consider the underlying meaning of the phrase, "battered down doors." *"Battered down" could mean "overcame"; the word* doors *could mean unjust laws that closed off equal opportunities to African Americans.*

◆ Reading Strategy

7 Interpret Meaning Ask students which words in this passage have meanings underlying the obvious ones. What do these words mean in the poem? *Answers should include: "Armies" (civil rights workers); "Generals" (civil rights leaders); "mined/Fields" and "Booby-trapped/Ditches" (dangerous situations).*

◆ Critical Thinking

8 Evaluate How would students evaluate the character of the women on the basis of what they were fighting for? *They were fighting for the rights of all African Americans, especially African American children, and not just for their own rights. They were unselfish as well as courageous.*

◆ Build Grammar Skills

9 Reflexive and Intensive Pronouns Review with students why the pronoun *themselves* is intensive rather than reflexive. *The purpose of the pronoun here is emphasis.*

▶Critical Viewing◀

10 Draw Conclusions Students may conclude that the artist, like Alice Walker, sees the women as powerful and determined.

283

◆ Critical Thinking

1. It connects the three stanzas and the four generations.
2. stout, fists, battered, led, Generals
3. You can discover what brings you pleasure, fear, and comfort.
4. She finds all the possibilities in life astonishing.
5. Students might say that the mothers in "Women" are very similar to other mothers who want the best for their children.
6. She draws on her awareness of different species and the cosmos to point out how many things inspire astonishment.

◆ Reading Strategy

1. (a) Students may say they could see the speaker combing a child's red hair, see an older woman braiding a child's hair as she sat by a stove, see the same woman combing an even older woman's hair as she rocked in a wooden rocker tearing rags into strips. (b) The images help a reader understand the connections between the women.
2. Students may say that they thought of how hard life was for these women and what courage they had to face what they did.
3. Each discovery, and the girl's reaction to it, revealed something about her personality.
4. (a) Students may say they recalled how they sometimes ask questions that have no answers. (b) Students may say that the strategy helped them understand why the author asked so many questions.

◆ Literary Focus

1. The moment of insight is how smart these women were to understand what they themselves had not experienced.
2. "It is always ourselves we find in the sea."
3. It is in the last stanza, which is shorter than the other three.
4. Students may identify the most meaningful moment of insight as the one that "hit closest to home."
5. Sample answer: the discovery of the dog in "Astonishment," and the speaker's accompanying realization of how preoccupied she has been with her thoughts.

Guide for Responding *(continued)*

◆ Reading Strategy

To truly appreciate these poems, you had to go beyond the literal meaning of the words and **interpret** the poet's deeper **meaning**. To do so, you may have used sensory images to form a picture in your mind, asked yourself questions about the poet's decisions, or related the poem to your own experience.

1. (a) What images did you have in your mind while reading "Combing"? (b) How did they add to your understanding of the poem?
2. Describe your thinking as you read "Women."
3. In "maggie and milly and molly and may," why did the poet tell what each girl found at the beach?
4. (a) What strategy or strategies did you use to help you interpret meaning while reading "Astonishment"? (b) How helpful was the strategy?

◆ Literary Focus

MOMENT OF INSIGHT

Poets sometimes write to discover what they think. The point at which it becomes clear just what the poet is thinking is the **moment of insight**. In "Combing," for example, a woman combing her daughter's hair is reminded of her own mother and the times when she used to comb hair. Then she has a moment of insight: Combing hair is something the women in her family have always done for one another. It connects various generations. The reader is prepared for this moment of insight by everything the poet has written up to that point.

1. What moment of insight do you experience along with the speaker in Alice Walker's poem "Women"?
2. What words does E. E. Cummings use to express the moment of insight in "maggie and milly and molly and may"?
3. How is the moment of insight set off structurally in "Combing"?
4. Which moment of insight meant the most to you? Explain why.
5. Which moment of insight came as the greatest surprise to you? Explain why.

◆ Build Vocabulary

WORDS WITH MULTIPLE MEANINGS

Give two definitions of the italicized word in each sentence and explain how the multiple meanings of the word add to the meaning of the sentence.
1. The king sent his *stoutest* soldiers into battle.
2. The sharp-tongued talk-show host offered some *fresh* opinions on the subject.

USING THE WORD BANK

Write the word from the Word Bank that is an antonym for each of the following words.
1. sturdy
2. unbraiding
3. distracted
4. weak

◆ Build Grammar Skills

REFLEXIVE AND INTENSIVE PRONOUNS

myself	ourselves
yourself	yourselves
herself, himself, itself	themselves

The words in the box can be either **reflexive** or **intensive pronouns**. When the subject of a sentence performs an action to, for, or on behalf of the pronoun, it is a reflexive pronoun—it *reflects* back to the subject. When the pronoun is used to emphasize a noun or another pronoun, it is intensive—it makes the noun or pronoun more *intense*.

Practice On your paper, write the reflexive or intensive pronoun and label it correctly.
1. The speaker describes herself in the act of combing her daughter's hair.
2. The mothers understood what kind of education their children needed even though they themselves had had little schooling.
3. Take E. E. Cummings's advice and look for yourself in the sea.
4. In "Astonishment," the speaker asks herself many questions.

Writing Application Write two sentences—one in which you use *myself* as an intensive pronoun and one in which you use *myself* as a reflexive pronoun.

◆ Build Vocabulary

Using Words With Multiple Meanings

1. sturdiest, most courageous; suggests that the soldiers had two advantages: physical stamina and courage
2. new, rude; suggests that the host has new ideas but may express them in an offensive manner

Using the Word Bank

1. languid; 2. plaiting; 3. intent; 4. stout

◆ Build Grammar Skills

1. herself—reflexive
2. themselves—intensive
3. yourself—reflexive
4. herself—reflexive

Writing Application

Answers may be similar to the following:
Intensive: I wrote it myself.
Reflexive: I describe myself in my poem.

 Writer's Solution

For additional instruction and practice, use the page on Reflexive and Intensive Pronouns in the *Writer's Solution Grammar Practice Book*, p. 8.

Build Your Portfolio

 Idea Bank

Writing

1. **Postcard** Imagine that you have taken a trip to the seashore. Write a postcard to a friend describing one thing you experienced at the shore and telling why it was significant to you.

2. **Poem** Write a poem in which the speaker is one of the women described in "Women." What moment of insight about her child might she have? **[Social Studies Link]**

3. **Dialogue** Suppose that the speaker of "Combing" and the speaker of "Astonishment" were to meet. Write a dialogue in which the two talk about the search for identity.

Speaking and Listening

4. **Oral Interpretation** With two classmates, prepare an oral reading of "Combing." Work together to get the right speed and inflection for the whole poem. **[Performing Arts Link]**

5. **Television Interview** With a partner, prepare an interview for a television documentary about the civil rights movement. **[Media Link; Social Studies Link]**

Projects

6. **Multimedia Presentation** Create a multimedia presentation about the sea. Choose a specific part of the world to portray, and conduct research to discover what kind of plant and animal life you would find there. **[Science Link]**

7. **Photo Essay** Prepare a photo essay of mothers and daughters. Try to include mothers and daughters of all ages and backgrounds. Write captions that reflect your response to each photo. **[Art Link]**

 Writing Mini-Lesson

Journal Entry

Poetry is one way of exploring ideas and feelings. Another way is through journal writing. Write a journal entry in which you describe an experience that led you to a moment of insight. Keep the following point in mind as you develop your journal entry.

Writing Skills Focus: Elaboration to Add Emotional Depth

Among the most common pieces of advice given to aspiring writers is, "Show, don't tell." In your journal entry, include details that will help readers *feel* what you are describing. If you were scared, for example, you might describe sweaty palms or trembling hands. If you were happy, you might describe your light heart or the bounce in your step.

Prewriting Start by jotting down experiences that led you to important discoveries. Then choose one of these experiences as your topic. Next, note the details of that experience. Finally, arrange your details in the order in which they occurred.

Drafting Using your notes as a starting point, recount the experience. Include the details that give emotional depth to your description. Spell out the moment of insight near the end of your journal entry.

Revising Read over your journal entry, crossing out any details that do not specifically lead to the moment of insight. Notice whether there are places where you might use intensive pronouns to emphasize your main idea.

 Idea Bank

Customizing for
Performance Levels
Following are suggestions for matching the Idea Bank topics with your students' performance levels:
    Less Advanced Students: 1, 4
    Average Students: 2, 5, 7
    More Advanced Students: 3, 6

Customizing for
Learning Modalities
Following are suggestions for matching Idea Bank topics with your students' learning modalities:
    Visual/Spatial: 1, 6, 7
    Auditory: 4, 5
    Logical/Mathematical: 7
    Intrapersonal: 3
    Musical/Rhythmic: 2

 Writing Mini-Lesson

Refer students to the Writing Handbook, page 962, for instruction on the writing process, and page 964 for further information on Description. You may also use the transparencies for a Reflective Essay in *Writing and Language Transparencies*, pp. 5–8, to guide students through the writing process.

✎ Writer's Solution

Writing Lab CD-ROM
Have students use the Tutorial on Description to complete their journal entries. Follow these steps:
1. Use the sensory word bins for gathering details.
2. Have students draft on computer.
3. Use the Vague Adjectives Checker to aid revision.

Sourcebook
Have students use Chapter 1, Description (pp. 1–29), for additional support. The chapter includes an annotated student model of a remembrance (p. 24).

✓ ASSESSMENT OPTIONS

Formal Assessment, Selection Test, pp. 69–71, and Assessment Resources Software. The selection test is designed so that it can be easily customized to the performance levels of your students.
Alternative Assessment, p. 21, includes options for less advanced students, more advanced students, logical/mathematical learners, interpersonal learners, visual/spatial learners, and verbal/linguistic learners.

PORTFOLIO ASSESSMENT
Use the following rubrics in the *Alternative Assessment* booklet to assess student writing:
Postcard: Expression Rubric, p. 87
Poem: Poetry Rubric, p. 101
Dialogue: Drama Rubric, p. 102
Writing Mini-Lesson: Expression Rubric, p. 87

Revising

You may want to have students work with peer reviewers to revise their problem-and-solution essays. Reviewers should use the revision checklist to guide their review.

 Writer's Solution

Writing Lab CD-ROM

The Transition Words Revision Checker in the Revision section of the Tutorial on Exposition can help students make sure that their essay flows smoothly from one idea to another.

Publishing

Students may wish to contact organizations that are interested in what young adults think about today's problems. Perhaps one of these groups might decide to reprint the essay in a newsletter or other official publication for its members. A good source for locating such organizations is *The Encyclopedia of Associations*, which can be found in any library.

Reinforce and Extend

Review the Writing Guidelines
After students have completed their writing, review the characteristics of a problem-and-solution essay. Encourage students to come up with additional criteria based on what they learned through completing the assignment.

Connect to Literature Unit 5 ("Visions of the Future") includes an example of a problem-and-solution essay: from Bill Gates's *The Road Ahead* (p. 385).

APPLYING LANGUAGE SKILLS: Adverb Clauses

Adverb clauses are subordinate clauses that modify a verb, adjective, adverb, or verbal by telling *where, when, in what manner, to what extent, under what condition,* or *why.*

Examples:
Why: We need to raise money because the swings are old.

When: We can buy new swings after money is raised.

Practice Add an adverb clause to answer each question in parentheses.
1. We need a new seesaw _____. (*Why?*)
2. We can install the new seesaw _____. (*When?*)
3. Our kids need a better park _____. (*Why?*)
4. We can make the park safer _____. (*When?*)

Writing Application Review your problem-and-solution essay. See where you can add adverb clauses to answer the question *Why? When?* or *Where?*

Elaborate to Add Emotional Depth As you write, offer details to help readers understand the seriousness or urgency of the problem. Help your audience see that the problem must be dealt with immediately. Then offer details to convince readers that your solution will indeed work.

Revising

Use a Peer Reviewer Have a peer review your essay and answer the following questions.
► Does the essay clearly explain the problem and its causes in the first paragraph? How could the explanation of the problem be improved?
► Does the essay present a clear, detailed explanation of the solution? What, if any, details should be added or deleted?
► Does the essay convey the importance of the problem? If not, what can be done to make the essay more convincing?

Use your classmate's responses to these questions to help you revise. If any of the classmate's comments were unclear, be sure to ask for clarification.

REVISION MODEL

① *playground is in serious need of repair.*

② *The landing area beneath the slides is strewn with gravel. The seesaw is about to fall apart.*

The Oak Street Park is in bad shape. Swings are broken

③ *Children may easily be hurt on them.*

and splintered.

① The writer explains the problem more clearly.
② The writer adds details to help readers better understand the problem.
③ The writer adds this statement to stress the importance of the problem.

Publishing

Publish Your Essay in a School or Local Newspaper If you have a creative solution to an important problem, share it. If your essay focuses on a school issue, see if you can get the essay published in the school newspaper. If it focuses on a local or national issue, try one of your local newspapers.

290 ◆ *Moments of Discovery*

☑ ASSESSMENT		4	3	2	1
PORTFOLIO ASSESSMENT Use the rubric on Problem-Solution in *Alternative Assessment* (p. 94) to assess students' writing. Add these criteria to customize the rubric to this assignment.	**Adverb Clauses**	The writer consistently and effectively uses adverb clauses to add important information.	The writer occasionally uses adverb clauses effectively.	The writer uses some adverb clauses, but they are not always clear in meaning.	The writer consistently uses adverb clauses that are flawed in meaning or construction.
	Elaborating for Emotional Depth	The writer consistently provides elaboration that engages readers' emotions.	The writer occasionally elaborates to add emotional depth in an appropriate manner.	The writer rarely elaborates to add emotional depth, and the elaboration is only sometimes effective.	The writer avoids elaborating to add emotional depth, or consistently does so in a heavy-handed manner.

Real-World Reading Skills Workshop

Reading for Specific Information

Strategies for Success

Suppose you need information on a specific topic, such as the planet Mars. You have a general science book that covers many topics: plants, animals, the solar system, and so on. How can you find the specific information you seek? Follow this strategy:

Check the Table of Contents In the front of the book, skim the chapter titles for a reference to your specific topic. The table of contents might indicate a more general topic that is related to your topic. For example, a science book might have a chapter entitled "Our Solar System."

Check the Index Many books have an index at the back. This alphabetical listing of topics is much more detailed than a table of contents. Look for your topic. If you can't find it, look for it listed under another heading in the index.

Use Subheads and Captions Within a chapter itself, scan the pages for subheads and picture captions that refer to your topic. Also, look for key words that may be boldfaced or italicized in the text.

Apply the Strategy

Use the table of contents and the index to answer these questions.

1. Which chapter would probably have information on an oasis? Which page?

2. Which chapter would probably have information on the North Pole? Which page?

3. Which chapter would probably have information on prairie dogs? Which page?

4. Which chapter would probably have information on toucans? Which page?

✔ *You may also find specific information in*
  ▶ Newspapers
  ▶ Textbooks
  ▶ Magazines

Introduce the Strategy

To demonstrate the importance of this workshop's strategies, ask students to name the different types of writing that may require research of some sort and, therefore, necessitate the skill of reading for specific information. *Student responses may include various types of expository writing, reports, persuasive writing, and research papers.* You may want to follow up this question by asking students what academic subjects other than Language Arts often call on them to read for specific information. *Student responses may include social studies, math, science, and foreign languages.*

Point out that the situations and subjects they have mentioned relate to school alone, and that in the "real world" this skill is often necessary in the workplace and crucial to many professions. Ask students what sort of jobs might require a person to scan large reference volumes looking for specific information. *Answers include lawyers researching laws or past cases, doctors looking up the details of a specific disease or drug, or accountants searching government documents relating to tax rules and regulations.*

Customize for
English Language Learners

Many of the items shown in the index may present challenges in vocabulary for these students. In order to grasp the strategies provided, these students may require having particular words such as *Mars* and *solar system* explained, so that they can follow the examples offered.

Apply the Strategy

Explain to students that an index is not only more detailed than a table of contents but also structured quite differently. Students who may expect to find in an index an alphabetical listing of every item covered in a book will soon find that only major categories are alphabetized, with subtopics alphabetized in turn within each category. Ask students what major categories or topics the indexer of *Our World* has chosen as headings. *Birds, Desert, Prairie dogs, Prairies, Tundra* Point

out that devising such indexes is an art as well as science, and that a good indexer tries to anticipate readers' needs. For example, when answering question three in the student text, ask students why "Prairie dogs" is given its own heading in the index whereas the specific birds mentioned are not. *Encourage students to speculate here, since the actual book is unavailable. Answers may include that prairie dogs are covered in greater depth than other animals, or perhaps page 74 includes an illustration of a prairie dog along with a caption.*

Answers

1. "The Desert" chapter, page 1, would probably have the information.

2. "The Frozen Tundra" chapter would have the information, possibly on page 91 under "climate," although it is difficult to say because the index does not list specific geographical places under the heading "Tundra."

3. The "Prairies" chapter, page 72, would have the information.

4. The "Rain Forest" chapter, page 53, would have the information.

Introduce the Strategy

To establish a real-world context for the speaking and listening skills presented here, invite students to briefly share incidents from their own experiences where such strategies were followed—or not followed. Ask what the immediate and long-term results of certain types of behavior were. *Students' responses should include examples of avoiding a particular business because its customers are treated rudely or the services it provides are not useful.*

Customize for
Interpersonal and Verbal/Linguistic Learners

These students may enjoy working together to observe and then list specific phrases, gestures, and body language that facilitate the application of the strategies. After applying the strategies themselves, encourage them to take notes based on what they observe with the other role-playing teams. You may want to wrap up the workshop by having these students present their findings to the class.

Apply the Strategy

1. Coach the students playing the business person to listen for the specifics of the customer's situation. Encourage both students to come up with creative ways to honor such policies and also adapt to the specific situation. One such resolution might involve a store manager, who can ensure that both the policy and the customer's needs are being addressed.

2. Coach both students to consider the different options available. Does the stock clerk already know when the item will be back in stock, and can someone in sales notify the customer by phone when it is? Or, if the customer's need is more urgent, can the CD be placed on special order?

3. The open-ended nature of this scenario allows for many different ways of playing it out; encourage students to explore these variations while always keeping the strategies in mind. For example, a homeowner may need the service being offered, but the schedules may not be completely compatible. In this case the worker should aim for achieving a compromise that works for both parties.

Speaking and Listening Workshop — Conducting Business

You probably don't realize it, but there are many situations in which you conduct business—even at this stage of your life. Returning a defective product to the store, ordering an item that is out of stock, requesting information about a product you are interested in buying, and recruiting customers for a service you offer—such as babysitting or lawn mowing—are all forms of conducting business. In all these instances, there are guidelines you can follow that will help you get the best results.

Be Polite Whether you are making a complaint, requesting information, or offering a service, be polite and respectful. People will be more inclined to listen to what you have to say and to respond favorably.

Be Specific State your needs clearly. If you are returning a product, do you want an exchange, a refund, or a different item? If you are offering a service, what are your hours and fees?

Tips for Conducting Business

✔ *If you want to conduct business in a successful way, follow these strategies:*
  ▶ *Be polite and respectful*
  ▶ *Be specific about your complaint*
  ▶ *Be precise about what you want or what you are offering*

Apply the Strategies

With a partner, role-play these situations. Work out a conversation in which you conduct business in the best possible way. Later, switch roles with your partner.

1. You are returning a sweater that is too big for you. The sweater was a gift, so you don't have a receipt.
2. You want to buy a CD that is out of stock at your local record store.
3. You are interested in doing yard work and are available every Saturday and every other Sunday.

292 ◆ *Moments of Discovery*

Beyond the Classroom

Career Connection
Customer Service Representative Students who enjoyed applying the strategies in the role of the business person may want to consider a career as a customer service representative. Point out that such jobs are becoming increasingly necessary for companies to conduct business effectively. Often such an employee receives extensive training, and is called upon not only to take orders, but to respond to customer questions and concerns. Have students discuss occasions in which they have interacted with customer service representatives. In what ways did these professionals apply or expand upon the strategies provided here? *Students may respond that customer service representatives combine a polite attitude with an upbeat, cheerful tone of voice. If they do not immediately have the specific information requested, they can help the customer by searching a computer database, or by transferring the customer to a representative with greater expertise.*

Extended Reading Opportunities

Stories in which characters make discoveries about themselves and the world around them have always been popular with readers. Following are just a few possibilities that explore characters' moments of discovery.

Suggested Titles

Great Expectations
Charles Dickens

Set in nineteenth-century England, this classic novel traces the passage of a boy called Pip into adulthood. Along the way, he encounters many memorable characters, including a pair of escaped convicts, a wealthy old woman who hasn't left her house since being jilted on her wedding day, and a beautiful young girl who captures his heart. Through a series of adventures, Pip makes many discoveries about himself, the people close to him, and the society in which he lives.

When the Legends Die
Hal Borland

This is the story of a young man who discovers his identity and cultural heritage as he struggles with the challenges of nature. After his father kills another brave, Thomas Black Bull and his parents flee the Ute reservation in southwestern Colorado to live in the wilderness. There they follow the old ways of Native Americans—hunting, fishing, and fighting for survival. Life is good until Thomas's parents die and he is left on his own.

The House on Mango Street
Sandra Cisneros

This book, a mixture of poetry and prose, tells the story of Esperanza Cordero, a young girl living in Chicago. Through her neighbors on Mango Street, Esperanza makes many discoveries about life as she explores questions such as: Should a girl get married or pursue her education? How does writing help people express their ideas and solve their problems? Why is growing up so confusing?

Other Possibilities

I Heard the Owl Call My Name	Margaret Craven
China Boy	Gus Lee
Sisters/Hermanas	Gary Paulsen

All of the works listed on this page are good choices for extending the theme of Moments of Discovery. Following is some information that may help you choose which to teach.

Customize for
Varying Student Needs

When assigning the selections in this part to your students, keep in mind the following factors:

- *Great Expectations* is the classic story of the adventures of a young boy in his passage into adulthood. Because this novel is lengthy, you may want to allow a few weeks to teach it.

- *When the Legends Die* is the story of Thomas Black Bull, a young boy who discovers his Native American identity and cultural heritage through living in the wilderness with his parents. This novel can serve as a stepping stone to discussion about the importance of respecting others' cultural heritage.

- *The House on Mango Street* is the story of Esperanza Cordero, a young girl growing up in Chicago. In this novel, Esperanza explores questions of interest to students, such as why is growing up so confusing.

Literature Study Guides Literature study guides are available for all three suggested titles. These guides include section summaries, discussion questions, and activities.

Resources for Teaching Novels, Plays, and Literature Collections In addition to graphic organizers, teaching strategies, and transparencies that will be invaluable in teaching any of these works, this booklet includes formal tests for *Great Expectations, When Legends Die,* and *The House on Mango Street.*

Great Expectations, by Charles Dickens, can be found in the **Literature Library** for *Prentice Hall Literature, Timeless Voices, Timeless Themes.*

The *Prentice Hall Literature* **Study Guide** provides support for teaching the novel, including the following:
Author Background
Historical Background
Synopses of Plot, Character, Setting and Theme
Literary Elements and Techniques
Chapter-by-Chapter Analysis
Essays and Imaginative Writing Assignments
Guidelines for Dealing with Provocative Themes
Bibliography
Blackline Masters
Tests

Planning Instruction and Assessment

Unit Objectives

1. To read selections in different genre that develop the theme of "The Lighter Side"
2. To apply a variety of reading strategies, particularly literal comprehension strategies, appropriate for reading these selections
3. To recognize literary elements used in these selections
4. To increase vocabulary
5. To learn elements of grammar and usage
6. To write in a variety of modes and about situations based on the selections
7. To develop speaking and listening skills, by doing proposed activities

Meeting the Objectives

With each selection, you will find instructional material and portfolio opportunities through which students can meet these objectives. Further, you will find additional practice pages for reading strategies, literary elements, vocabulary, and grammar in the **Selection Support** booklet in the Teaching Resources box.

Setting Goals Work with your students at the beginning of the unit to set goals for unit outcomes. Plan what skills and concepts you wish students to acquire. You may individualize according to students' performance levels or learning modalities.

Portfolios You may have students keep portfolios of their work or of their work in progress. The activities and prompts on the Build Your Portfolio page of each selection provide opportunities for students to apply the concepts presented with the selection.

Scientist's Hobby: Failure #18 of the Anti-Gravity Pack, 1992, Bruce Widdows, Courtesy of George Adams Gallery, New York

Humanities: Art

Scientist's Hobby: Failure #18 of the Anti-Gravity Pack, 1992, by Bruce Widdows.

Students may have a little difficulty interpreting the artwork, since the dog appears to be aloft—hardly the "failure" referred to in the title. Point out that the machine attached to the dog's back seems to be stalling or wobbling, as indicated by the lines drawn around it. Encourage students to find funny details in the painting—such as the bone on the fishing pole, the camera man with his old-fashioned home-movie camera recording the historic experiment, the little platform the scientist has nailed to his roof, and the dog's eager expression.

Help students link the artwork to the theme of Unit 4 ("The Lighter Side") by answering the following questions:

1. How does the title add to the humor of the artwork? *The title helps create the idea of a persistent inventor who has tried and failed 18 times to defy gravity. The title also gives the invention a scientific-sounding name.*

2. Artists often take situations that might be serious in real life and make them funny by exaggerating them or adding silly elements. How does the artist do this here? *The dog is probably going to fall about 20 feet to the ground, which would be a serious situation. However, the fact that this is failure #18, the silly looking anti-gravity pack, the earnestness of the inventor and camera man, and the cartoonlike style of the art all make the situation funny rather than serious.*

294

UNIT 4

The Lighter Side

Whats so funny? It might be an animal trainer teaching 5,000 flies how to "act." It might be a tongue-in-cheek reminiscence by a famous comedian. It might be an outlandish poem told in "nonsense" language. Check out these stories, essays, poems, and more. You're sure to find something to make you smile.

◆ 295

Assessing Student Progress

The following tools are available to measure the degree to which students meet the unit objectives:

Informal Assessment

The questions on the Guide for Responding sections are a first level of response to the concepts and skills presented with the selection. Students' responses are a brief informal measure of their grasp of the material. Their responses on this level can indicate where further instruction and practice are needed. You may then follow up with the practice pages in the *Selection Support* booklet.

You will find literature and reading guides in the *Alternative Assessment* booklet, which you may give students on an individual basis for informal assessment of their performance.

Formal Assessment

In the *Formal Assessment* booklet, you will find selection tests and a unit test.

Selection Tests The selection tests measure comprehension and skills acquisition for each selection or group of selections.

Unit Test The unit test applies the unit skills on a broader level. The Critical Reading section measures Unit Objectives 1, 2, and 3. The Vocabulary and Grammar section measures Objectives 4 and 5. The Essay section measures Objectives 1 and 6.

Alternative Assessment

Portfolios As you review individual pieces or the collected work in students' portfolios, you will find assessment sheets available in the portfolio section of the *Alternative Assessment* booklet.

Scoring Rubrics You will find scoring rubrics for writing modes in the *Alternative Assessment* booklet. You can apply these to Writing Mini-Lessons and to Writing Process Workshop lessons.

Speaking and Listening The *Alternative Assessment* booklet contains assessment sheets for speaking and listening activities.

Learning Modalities The *Alternative Assessment* contains activities that appeal to different learning styles. You may use these to as an alternative measurement of students' growth.

OBJECTIVES

1. To read, comprehend, and interpret a story
2. To relate a story to personal experience
3. To use interactive reading strategies
4. To identify point of view
5. To build vocabulary in context and learn the word root -scrut-
6. To develop skill in pronoun-antecedent agreement
7. To write a character profile conveying a main impression
8. To respond to the story through writing, speaking and listening, and projects

SKILLS INSTRUCTION

Vocabulary: Word Roots: -scrut-
Grammar: Pronoun and Antecedent Agreement
Reading for Success: Interactive Reading Strategies
Literary Focus: Point of View

Writing: Main Impression
Speaking and Listening: Performance (teacher edition)
Critical Viewing: Analyze; Hypothesize

PORTFOLIO OPPORTUNITIES

Writing: One More Daydream; Written Recommendation; Diary Entry
Writing Mini-Lesson: Character Profile
Speaking and Listening: Performance; Panel Discussion
Projects: Daydream Illustrations; Report on Dreaming

More About the Author

James Thurber once wrote, "You can fool too many of the people too much of the time." He came to be recognized for his drawings almost as much as his writing, though he originally thought little of his artwork. Only after another New Yorker magazine writer took some of Thurber's crumpled "doodles" from a wastebasket and submitted them for publication did Thurber consider himself an artist as well as a writer.

Guide for Reading

James Thurber (1894–1961)

When you read some of James Thurber's work, you may find yourself asking, "Is this fiction or nonfiction?"

In both his writing and his cartoonlike drawings, Thurber liked to blur the line between the real and the not-so-real.

Many of his essays, for example, are composed of little stories, and his memoirs contain obvious fiction.

There's no question, however, that "The Secret Life of Walter Mitty" is pure fiction. This amusing fantasy became an instant classic when it first appeared in 1939. It was reprinted by *Reader's Digest* and was also made into a popular movie.

A Lifetime of Writing A native of Columbus, Ohio, James Thurber began his writing career as a reporter for the *Columbus Evening Dispatch*. It was through his later work on *The New Yorker* magazine, however, that he became well known as a humorous writer and cartoonist.

During his lifetime, Thurber wrote more than twenty volumes of plays, stories, essays, fables, reminiscences, and verse. Even after losing his vision in the early 1940's, he continued to write until his death in 1961. Thurber received honorary degrees from Williams College and Yale University and, in 1960, won the Antoinette Perry award for the theatrical review *A Thurber Carnival*.

◆ Build Vocabulary

WORD ROOTS: -scrut-

At one point in "The Secret Life of Walter Mitty," Thurber describes the main character as being "inscrutable." You can figure out the meaning of *inscrutable* if you know the meaning of the word root from which it is derived. *Inscrutable* comes from the word root -scrut-, which means "to search or examine." *Inscrutable* literally means "not able to be searched or examined," or "not easily understood."

rakishly
hurtling
distraught
haggard
insolent
insinuatingly
cur
cannonading
derisive
inscrutable

WORD BANK

Before you read, preview this list of words from the story.

◆ Build Grammar Skills

PRONOUN AND ANTECEDENT AGREEMENT

You will notice that the pronouns Thurber uses agree with their **antecedents**—the words they replace—in gender (masculine, feminine, or neuter) and number (singular or plural). Notice the pronouns in this example:

Walter Mitty reached in a pocket and brought out the gloves. He put them on.

The pronoun *he*—masculine and singular—agrees with its antecedent, *Walter Mitty*, which is masculine and singular. The pronoun *them*, plural and neuter, agrees with its antecedent, *gloves*, which is plural and neuter.

296 ◆ The Lighter Side

The Secret Life of Walter Mitty

◆ Literature and Your Life

CONNECT YOUR EXPERIENCE

You're relaxing on a park bench on a warm summer day. Suddenly, you're someone else—a movie star accepting an award or a basketball superstar slam-dunking the winning basket. Then, you're you again; you were daydreaming. "The Secret Life of Walter Mitty" is about a man whose frequent, adventurous daydreams will amuse and entertain you.

Journal Writing Can daydreaming ever help a person achieve his or her goals? Explore your answer to this question in a journal entry.

THEMATIC FOCUS: THE LIGHTER SIDE

A very tall man folds himself into a compact car. A tiny girl is pulled along by a huge dog on a leash. The contrasts in situations like these can make you smile. Contrast plays an important part in "The Secret Life of Walter Mitty," where the differences between Walter Mitty's real life and his secret life provide some amusing moments.

◆ Background for Understanding

SCIENCE

The human mind works both logically and randomly. As the psychologist William James noted around the turn of the century, a person's thoughts often form an unorganized and seemingly unconnected series of insights, memories, and reflections. A single incident, for example, can stimulate an almost endless flow of thoughts. In "The Secret Life of Walter Mitty," the title character's thoughts often jump back and forth between his fantastic imaginings and the realities of his life.

The Man With Three Masks,
John Rush, Courtesy of the artist

◆ Literary Focus

POINT OF VIEW

Point of view is the perspective from which a story is told. "The Secret Life of Walter Mitty" is not told by Walter Mitty himself, but it is told in such a way that you the reader know his thoughts and feelings. This is called the **limited third person** point of view. The words *third person* indicate that the narrator is "outside" of the story, and the word *limited* means that the narrator reveals the thoughts and feelings of only one character. By telling the story from the point of view of one character, the author encourages you to sympathize with this character. You know what this character thinks and feels in a way you never can with people in real life.

Guide for Reading ◆ 297

Preparing for Standardized Tests

Reading and Vocabulary Developing reading comprehension skills will help students to improve their performance on both reading comprehension and vocabulary items on the verbal portions of standardized tests. The Reading for Success strategies will help students interact with texts so as to improve their comprehension. For additional practice, use the Reading for Success pages in **Selection Support,** pp. 90–91.

Grammar and Language Portions of some standardized tests require students to select a

pronoun that agrees with an antecedent in a given sentence. Students may be asked to select the correct pronoun to complete sentences such as the following:

Jane and Linda borrowed Ralph's bat, wishing they had brought (her, their) own. *their*

The Build Grammar Skills lesson for this selection focuses on agreement between pronouns and antecedents. For additional practice, use the Build Grammar Skills page in **Selection Support,** p. 89.

The Reading for Success page in each unit presents a set of problem-solving procedures to help readers understand authors' words and ideas on multiple levels. Good readers develop a bank of strategies from which they can draw as needed.

Unit 4 introduces interactive reading strategies that give readers an approach for comprehending text on a personal level—reading purposefully, asking questions, reading between the lines, clarifying, and anticipating the unexpected.

These interactive reading strategies are modeled with "The Secret Life of Walter Mitty." Each green box shows an example of the thinking process involved in applying one of these strategies.

How to Use the Reading for Success Page

- Introduce the interactive reading strategies, presenting each as a problem-solving procedure. Be sure students understand what each strategy involves and under what circumstances to apply it.

- Before students read the story, have them preview it, looking at the annotations in the green boxes that model the strategies.

- To reinforce these strategies after students have read "The Secret Life . . .," have students do the Reading for Success pages in *Selection Support,* pp. 90–91. This activity gives students an opportunity to read a selection and practice interactive reading strategies by writing their own annotations.

Reading for Success

Interactive Reading Strategies

To get the most out of many things in life, you have to get involved. This rule is as true in reading as it is in playing sports or visiting new places. By interacting with what you read, you'll read more effectively. You'll better understand and remember what you read. Use these strategies to interact with what you're reading.

Set a purpose for your reading.

You might read a short story for enjoyment, or read a biography to learn about a noteworthy individual. Giving yourself a purpose focuses your thoughts. For example, for "The Secret Life of Walter Mitty," your purpose might be to find out what is Walter Mitty's "secret life."

Ask questions.

As you read, question what's going on in the story or article. For example, ask *why* a character behaves as he does or *what* caused an event to happen. Then search the text for answers as you read on.

Read between the lines.

Authors don't always state everything directly; sometimes they just suggest ideas. When you "read between the lines," you look beyond the words to find out what else the author means.

Clarify.

If you come to a passage you don't understand, pause to clarify the meaning of what you're reading. You may have to read back or ahead to figure out an unclear situation, or you may have to go outside the text to find out what something means.

Expect the unexpected.

From many years of reading, you've come to expect stories to develop in a certain way. However, sometimes authors will play with your expectations. Be prepared.

As you read "The Secret Life of Walter Mitty," look at the notes along the sides. The notes demonstrate how to apply these strategies to your reading.

Reading Strategies: Support and Reinforcement

Appropriate Reading Strategies Students are given a reading strategy to apply in reading each selection. For example, students focus on asking questions to help them follow an author's argument, or expect the unexpected in a piece of fiction that intends to surprise. For each selection a strategy is suggested that is appropriate to the selection.

Reading Prompts To encourage application of the given reading strategy, there are occasional prompts, within green boxes, at appropriate and significant points.

In addition, there are red boxes prompting application of the Literary Focus concept and maroon boxes prompting students to connect with their lives.

Using the Boxed Annotations and Prompts The material in the green, red, and maroon boxes along the sides of selections is intended to help students apply the literary element and the reading strategy and to make a connection with their lives.

You may use the boxed material in several ways:

- Have students pause when they come to a box and respond to its prompt before they continue reading.

- Urge students to read through the selection ignoring the boxes. After they have read the selection completely, they may go back and review the selection, responding to the prompts.

The Secret Life of Walter Mitty

James Thurber

"We're going through!" The Commander's voice was like thin ice breaking. He wore his full-dress uniform, with the heavily braided white cap pulled down rakishly over one cold gray eye. "We can't make it, sir. It's spoiling for a hurricane, if you ask me." "I'm not asking you, Lieutenant Berg," said the Commander. "Throw on the power lights! Rev her up to 8,500! We're going through!" The pounding of the cylinders increased: ta-pocketa-pocketa-pocketa-*pocketa-pocketa*. The Commander stared at the ice forming on the pilot window. He walked over and twisted a row of complicated dials. "Switch on No. 8 auxiliary!" he shouted. "Switch on No. 8 auxiliary!" repeated Lieutenant Berg. "Full strength in No. 3 turret!" shouted the Commander. "Full strength in No. 3 turret!" The crew, bending to their various tasks in the huge, hurtling eight-engined Navy hydroplane,[1]

---

1. **hydroplane** (hī′ drə plān) *n.*: Seaplane.

◆ **Build Vocabulary**

rakishly (rāk′ ish lē) *adv.*: With a careless, casual look; dashing

hurtling (hurt′ liŋ) *adj.*: Moving swiftly and with great force

looked at each other and grinned. "The Old Man'll get us through," they said to one another. "The Old Man ain't afraid of Hell!". . .

"Not so fast! You're driving too fast!" said Mrs. Mitty. "What are you driving so fast for?"

> This abrupt shift in the action is a reminder to **expect the unexpected.**

"Hmm?" said Walter Mitty. He looked at his wife, in the seat beside him, with shocked astonishment. She seemed grossly unfamiliar, like a strange woman who had yelled at him in a crowd. "You were up to fifty-five," she said. "You know I don't like to go more than forty. You were up to fifty-five." Walter Mitty drove on toward Waterbury in silence, the roaring of the SN202 through the worst storm in twenty years of Navy flying fading in the remote, intimate airways of his mind. "You're tensed up again," said Mrs. Mitty. "It's one of your days. I wish you'd let Dr. Renshaw look you over."

> This paragraph **clarifies** what was happening in the opening paragraph of the story—Walter Mitty was daydreaming.

Walter Mitty stopped the car in front of the building where his wife went to have her hair done. "Remember to get those overshoes while I'm having my

The Secret Life of Walter Mitty ◆ 299

MODEL

Develop Understanding

One-Minute Insight In this famous story, James Thurber creates for readers a vivid image of an ineffectual, "hen-pecked" husband who suffers from a complete inability to cope with the world around him. Feeling powerless and picked-on by everyone—from parking-lot attendants to police officers to anonymous passersby—Mitty retreats into a daydream world where he becomes dashing, powerful, and in control—the opposite of his real-world self. To get back at his "tormentors," he gives them subservient roles in his dreams.

This story is so famous that a person who daydreams all the time can be called a "Walter Mitty." The question the story poses for readers is: Is it good or bad to be a Walter Mitty? Is he comic or tragic—or maybe both?

◆ Critical Thinking

❶ Infer Ask students: What sort of person is the Commander? Which details give you this information? *Students should grasp that the Commander is an authoritative person with nerves of steel. He knows what to do in an emergency; his subordinates obey him, have faith in him, and admire his courage.*

Comprehension Check ☑

❷ Ask students what they can tell about the real Walter Mitty from this passage. *Walter Mitty is a quiet, unassuming man who is nagged by his wife.*

◆ Critical Thinking

❸ Infer Ask students to describe how Mrs. Mitty treats her husband. *She bosses him around; she treats him like a child; she doesn't treat him with respect.*

---

❶ Analyze The masks represent different "faces" people put on to protect themselves from other people. Like Walter Mitty's daydreams, the masks shield the inner person from a hostile outside world.

◆ **Reading for Success**

❷ Expect the Unexpected Have students trace the action of the gloves in this passage. Ask them to explain how each action differs. *Mitty dislikes putting the gloves on for his wife, but obeys the policeman. In his daydream, however, the gloves unexpectedly become an acceptable part of his genteel costume.*

◆ **Critical Thinking**

❸ Infer Ask students: How do people treat Walter Mitty in his daydreams? *They treat him with respect and admiration.*

◆ **Build Grammar Skills**

❹ Pronoun and Antecedent Agreement Ask students to identify the antecedent of the pronoun "him" in this passage. What is the gender and number of this pronoun? *The antecedent of "him" is Renshaw. It is masculine and singular.*

◆ **Reading for Success**

❺ Clarify Ask students which words clarify where Mitty is as he comes out of his daydream. *We know from the words "parking-lot attendant" that Mitty is in a parking lot.*

The Man With Three Masks, John Rush, Courtesy of the artist

▲ **Critical Viewing** Analyze the significance of the mask in this painting. Why does the man hold one mask up to his face and have other masks nearby? [Analyze]

❶

hair done," she said. "I don't need overshoes," said Mitty. She put her mirror back into her bag. "We've been all through that," she said, getting out of the car. "You're not a young man any longer." He raced the engine a little. "Why don't you wear your gloves? Have you lost your gloves?" Walter Mitty reached in a pocket and

> By **reading between the lines**, you can infer that Mrs. Mitty thinks her husband is helpless.

❷

brought out the gloves. He put them on, but after she had turned and gone into the building and he had driven on to a red light, he took them off again. "Pick it up, brother!" snapped a cop as the light changed, and Mitty hastily pulled on his gloves and lurched ahead. He drove around the streets aimlessly for a time, and then he drove past the hospital on his way to the parking lot.

. . . "It's the millionaire banker, Wellington McMillan," said the pretty nurse. "Yes?" said Walter Mitty, removing his gloves slowly. "Who has the case?" "Dr. Renshaw and Dr. Benbow, but there are two specialists here, Dr. Remington from New York and Mr. Pritchard-Mitford from London. He flew over." A door opened down a long, cool corridor and Dr. Renshaw came out. He looked distraught and haggard. "Hello, Mitty," he said. "We're having the devil's own time with McMillan, the millionaire banker and close personal friend of Roosevelt. Obstreosis of the ductal tract.[2] Wish you'd take a look at him." "Glad to," said Mitty.

In the operating room there were whispered introductions: "Dr. Remington, Dr. Mitty. Mr. Pritchard-Mitford, Dr. Mitty." "I've read your book on streptothricosis,"

❷

❸

> This paragraph, like the first, provides details to meet your **purpose**—to find out what Walter Mitty's secret life is.

---

2. obstreosis of the ductal tract: Thurber has invented this and other medical terms.

🎭 **Humanities: Art**

The Man With Three Masks, by John Rush.
John Rush (1948–) considers the greatest single influence on his art to be Michaelangelo, who shaped his figure design. In this painting, a conservatively dressed man holds a mask up to his face. The masks in the background suggest that he will try them on as well.

Because a mask often symbolizes the "face" a person presents to the world, perhaps hiding or masking his real self, the painting is fitting to discuss in connection with Walter Mitty, whose inner self so differs from the self he shows to the world.

Use these questions for discussion:
1. What symbolic meanings might the man and the masks have in this painting? *Students may say that the man represents a person's real self; the masks, ways in which the person would like others to see him.*
2. If the man is Walter Mitty, what might the masks represent? *The masks might represent the characters Mitty imagines himself to be— or the faces Mitty presents to his wife, while the man is the "real" Mitty, whose imagination takes him on wild adventures.*

said Pritchard-Mitford, shaking hands. "A brilliant performance, sir." "Thank you," said Walter Mitty. "Didn't know you were in the States, Mitty," grumbled Remington. "Coals to Newcastle,[3] bringing Mitford and me up here for tertiary." "You are very kind," said Mitty. A huge, complicated machine, connected to the operating table, with many tubes and wires, began at this moment to go pocketa-pocketa-pocketa. "The new anesthetizer is giving way!" shouted an intern. "There is no one in the East who knows how to fix it!" "Quiet, man!" said Mitty, in a low, cool voice. He sprang to the machine, which was now going pocketa-pocketa-queep-pocketa-queep. He began fingering delicately a row of glistening dials. "Give me a fountain pen!" he snapped. Someone handed him a fountain pen. He pulled a faulty piston out of the machine and inserted the pen in its place. "That will hold for ten minutes," he said. "Get on with the operation." A nurse hurried over and whispered to Renshaw, and Mitty saw the man turn pale. "Coreopsis has set in," said Renshaw nervously. "If you would take over, Mitty?" Mitty looked at him and at the craven figure of Benbow, who drank, and at the grave, uncertain faces of the two great specialists. "If you wish," he said. They slipped a white gown on him; he adjusted a mask and drew on thin gloves; nurses handed him shining . . .

"Back it up, Mac! Look out for that Buick!" Walter Mitty jammed on the brakes. "Wrong lane, Mac," said the parking-lot attendant, looking at Mitty closely. "Gee. Yeh," muttered Mitty. He began cautiously to back out of the

---

3. **coals to Newcastle:** The proverb "bringing coals to Newcastle" means bringing things to a place unnecessarily—Newcastle, England, was a coal center and so did not need coal brought to it.

lane marked "Exit Only." "Leave her sit there," said the attendant. "I'll put her away." Mitty got out of the car. "Hey, better leave the key." "Oh," said Mitty, handing the man the ignition key. The attendant vaulted into the car, backed it up with insolent skill, and put it where it belonged.

> This paragraph might prompt the **question**, "Why is Walter Mitty treated this way in his real life?"

They're so cocky, thought Walter Mitty, walking along Main Street; they think they know everything. Once he had tried to take his chains off, outside New Milford, and he had got them wound around the axles. A man had had to come out in a wrecking car and unwind them, a young, grinning garageman. Since then Mrs. Mitty always made him drive to a garage to have the chains taken off. The next time, he thought, I'll wear my right arm in a sling; they won't grin at me then. I'll have my right arm in a sling and they'll see I couldn't possibly take the chains off myself. He kicked at the slush on the sidewalk. "Overshoes," he said to himself, and he began looking for a shoe store.

When he came out into the street again, with the overshoes in a box under his arm, Walter Mitty began to wonder what the other thing was his wife had told him to get. She had told him, twice, before they set out from their house for Waterbury. In a way he hated these weekly trips to town—he was always getting something wrong.

◆ Build Vocabulary

distraught (di strôt') *adj.*: Extremely troubled; confused; distracted

haggard (hag' ərd) *adj.*: Having a wild, worn look, as from sleeplessness

insolent (in' sə lənt) *adj.*: Boldly disrespectful in speech or behavior

The Secret Life of Walter Mitty ◆ 301

◆ Build Grammar Skills

❶ Pronoun and Antecedent Agreement Ask students to identify the antecedent of the pronoun *he* in this passage. Why does Thurber choose a masculine singular pronoun? *The antecedent is "defendant." The masculine singular pronoun was chosen because the antecedent is masculine and singular.*

◆ Reading for Success

❷ Set a Purpose Ask students how this passage further fulfills their reading purpose—to find out about Mitty's secret life. What new information does this passage give the reader? *The passage indicates the Mitty would like to be like the movie hero who rescues a fair "damsel in distress." The "lovely, dark-haired girl" contrasts sharply with Mrs. Mitty.*

◆ Reading for Success

❸ Read Between the Lines Challenge students to read between the lines to figure out why Mitty goes to the smaller A&P farther up the street, and why he doesn't use the words "puppy biscuit." *Mitty goes to the smaller store because he wants to be noticed as little as possible, and doesn't use the words "puppy biscuit" because he thinks the women on the street were making fun of him for saying these words.*

◆ Literary Focus

❹ Point of View Ask students to see Walter Mitty in this scene from Mrs. Mitty's point of view. Through Walter Mitty's eyes, she is a nagging, annoying wife. How might Mitty appear through his wife's eyes? *Students may think that Mrs. Mitty looks down on her husband or that he annoys her. Some may feel that she is just trying to protect Walter from his own incompetence.*

❺ Clarification Explain that *Liberty* magazine was a popular publication with articles of general interest, similar to *Reader's Digest*. Early during World War II, German's military use of air power was considered a revolutionary strategy.

302

Kleenex, he thought, Squibb's, razor blades? No. Toothpaste, toothbrush, bicarbonate, carborundum, initiative and referendum?[4] He gave it up. But she would remember it. "Where's the what's-its-name?" she would ask. "Don't tell me you forgot the what's-its-name." A newsboy went by shouting something about the Waterbury trial.

. . . "Perhaps this will refresh your memory." The District Attorney suddenly thrust a heavy automatic at the quiet figure on the witness stand. "Have you ever seen this before?" Walter Mitty took the gun and examined it expertly. "This is my Webley-Vickers 50.80," he said calmly. An excited buzz ran around the courtroom. The Judge rapped for order. "You are a crack shot with any sort of firearms, I believe?" said the District Attorney, insinuatingly. "Objection!" shouted Mitty's attorney. "We have shown that the defendant could not have fired ❶ the shot. We have shown that he wore his right arm in a sling on the night of the fourteenth of July." Walter Mitty raised his hand briefly and the bickering attorneys were stilled. "With any known make of gun," he said evenly, "I could have killed Gregory Fitzhurst at three hundred feet *with my left hand*." Pandemonium broke loose in the courtroom. A woman's scream rose above the bedlam and suddenly a lovely, dark-haired girl was in Walter Mitty's arms. The Dis- ❷ trict Attorney struck at her savagely. Without rising from his chair, Mitty let the man have it

> When you **clarify** that cur means "a mean, ugly dog," you can appreciate the humor here.

on the point of the chin. "You miserable cur!" . . .

"Puppy biscuit," said Walter Mitty. He stopped walking and the buildings of Waterbury rose up out of the misty courtroom and surrounded ❸ him again. A woman who was passing laughed. "He said 'Puppy biscuit,'" she said to her companion. "That man said 'Puppy biscuit' to himself." Walter Mitty hurried on. He went into an

---

4. carborundum (kär´ bə run´ dəm), **initiative** (i nish´ ē ə tiv) **and referendum** (ref ə ren´ dəm): Thurber is purposely making a nonsense list; carborundum is a hard substance used for scraping, initiative is the right of citizens to introduce ideas for laws, and referendum is the right of citizens to vote on laws.

A. & P., not the first one he came to but a smaller one farther up the street. "I want some biscuit for small, young dogs," he said to the clerk. "Any special brand, sir?" The greatest pistol shot in the world thought a moment. "It says 'Puppies Bark for It' on the box," said Walter Mitty. ❸

His wife would be through at the hairdresser's in fifteen minutes, Mitty saw in looking at his watch, unless they had trouble drying it; sometimes they had trouble drying it. She didn't like to get to the hotel first; she ❹ would want him to be there waiting for her as usual. He found a big leather chair in the lobby, facing a window, and he put the overshoes and the puppy biscuit on the floor beside it. He picked up an old copy of *Liberty* and sank down into the chair. "Can Germany Conquer the World Through the Air?" Walter Mitty ❺ looked at the pictures of bombing planes and of ruined streets.

. . . "The cannonading has got the wind up in young Raleigh,[5] sir," said the sergeant. Captain Mitty looked up at him through tousled hair. "Get him to bed," he said wearily. "With the others. I'll fly alone." "But you can't, sir," said the sergeant anxiously. "It takes two men to handle that bomber and the Archies[6] are pounding hell out of the air. Von Richtman's circus[7] is between here and Saulier." "Somebody's got to get that

> Look at the footnote to **clarify** the meaning of "Von Richtman's circus."

ammunition dump," said Mitty. "I'm going over. Spot of brandy?" He poured a drink for the

---

5. **has got the wind up in young Raleigh:** Has made young Raleigh nervous.
6. **Archies:** Slang term for antiaircraft guns.
7. **Von Richtman's circus:** German airplane squadron.

◆ Build Vocabulary

insinuatingly (in sin´ yo͞o āt´ iŋ lē) *adv.*: Hinting or suggesting indirectly; implying

cur (kʉr) *n.*: Mean, contemptible person; mean, ugly dog

cannonading (kan´ ən ād´ iŋ) *n.*: Continuous firing of artillery

---

302 ◆ The Lighter Side

Speaking and Listening Mini-Lesson

Performance

This mini-lesson supports the Speaking and Listening activity in the Idea Bank on page 306.

Introduce the Concept Explain that the students will work in groups to create scripts and rehearse a skit that reflects the dialogue, action, and mood of a daydream in the story.

Develop Background Groups should take into account the following:

• A script should include dialogue, stage directions, and props, if possible. It could also include narration.

• Casting need not follow the story's gender specifications. Students may be narrators, or supply sound effects as needed ("pocketa-pocketa-pocketa," for example).

Apply the Information Groups should work cooperatively to produce their scripts, rehearse, and then give their performance.

Assess the Results Invite students to discuss how the performances succeeded in capturing the daydreams. You might have students use the Peer Assessment form for a Dramatic Performance, p. 113, in *Alternative Assessment*.

New Orleans Fantasy (detail), Max Papart, Nahan Galleries, New York

▶Critical Viewing◀
❻ Hypothesize Students may answer that Walter Mitty's daydreams reflect whatever has embarrassed or humiliated him most recently. Therefore, a daydream about being a graceful trapeze artist might result after Mitty had done something clumsy.

❻ ▲ **Critical Viewing** Describe a situation that might make Walter Mitty daydream about being a circus performer. **[Hypothesize]**

The Secret Life of Walter Mitty ◆ 303

Humanities: Art

New Orleans Fantasy (detail), 1985, by Max Papart.

In this lithograph, a colorfully dressed acrobat swings from a trapeze. While Walter Mitty never imagines himself an acrobat in the story, the freedom and daring represented by the trapeze artist characterize Mitty's fantasies. Max Papart (1911–1985) was a French lithographer whose fanciful style is represented in this painting. He studied art in Marseilles, but traced his greatest influence to the works of surrealist painters he encountered at an exhibit in Paris in 1938. He later settled in New Orleans and credited his grandson with giving his work a lighter palette and a new gaiety.

Use the following questions for discussion:

1. What associations do you have with the words *trapeze artist*, or a picture, like this one, of an acrobat on a trapeze? *Most students will associate words such as* daring, balance, graceful, breathtaking, *and so on.*

2. What introduction can you suggest for a Walter Mitty-like fantasy about being a trapeze artist? *Sample response: "A gasp arose form the audience as they beheld the great Mitzini prepare to execute his most daring feat—hundreds of feet above the arena, with no net."*

303

Idea Bank

Customizing for
Performance Levels

Following are suggestions for matching the Idea Bank topics with your students' performance levels:

Less Advanced Students: 1, 6
Average Students: 2, 4, 5
More Advanced Students: 3, 7

Customizing for
Learning Modalities

Following are suggestions for matching Idea Bank topics with your students' learning modalities:

Verbal/Linguistic: 1, 2, 5
Intrapersonal: 3
Visual/Spatial: 6
Auditory: 4, 5
Bodily/Kinesthetic: 4

Writing Mini-Lesson

Refer students to the Writing Handbook, page 962, for instruction on the writing process, and page 964 for further information on description. You may also use the models of a Biographical Profile, pp. 9–15 in *Writing Language Transparencies,* to guide students through the writing process.

Writer's Solution

Writers at Work Videodisc

Have students view the videodisc segment (Ch. 1) featuring Anne McCaffrey to see how she uses her imagination to create description in her stories. Have students discuss how storytelling can help them write their character profiles.

Play frames 335 to 10785

Writing Lab CD-ROM

Have students complete the Tutorial on Description. Follow these steps:

1. Have students use the Word Bins to gather character trait words.
2. Play the video clip of a character profile.
3. Have students draft on computer.
4. Use the Interactive Self-Evaluation Checklist to evaluate their drafts.

Allow approximately 75 minutes to complete these steps.

Sourcebook

Have students use Chapter 1, Description (pp. 1–29), for additional support. The chapter includes a model of a character profile (p. 7).

Build Your Portfolio

Idea Bank

Writing

1. **One More Daydream** Make up another daydream for Walter Mitty that is true to Mitty's personality.

2. **Written Recommendation** Should Walter Mitty stop daydreaming and take control of his life or should he keep daydreaming to add some happiness to his days? Write a recommendation in which you suggest to Walter Mitty what he should do.

3. **Diary Entry** Write a diary entry about a day with Walter Mitty from Mrs. Mitty's point of view. In Mrs. Mitty's own voice, tell how she feels when her husband seems preoccupied.

Speaking and Listening

4. **Performance** With a group of classmates, act out one of Walter Mitty's daydreams. Rehearse the scene by reading the parts aloud until they seem natural. **[Performing Arts Link]**

5. **Panel Discussion** Are daydreams of little consequence, or might they lead the daydreamer to a possible future career or to an idea for a fantastic new invention? With a small group of classmates, hold a panel discussion on the value of daydreams.

Projects

6. **Daydream Illustrations** James Thurber drew illustrations for many of his written works. Draw an illustration for each of Walter Mitty's five daydreams. Write titles for your illustrations and display them in class. **[Art Link]**

7. **Report on Dreaming** Prepare a written report on the latest scientific facts and theories about dreaming. **[Science Link]**

Writing Mini-Lesson

Character Profile

Walter Mitty imagines himself as a variety of fearless characters who take bold action. Imagine a character who does great things, like discovering the cure for a disease or breaking an Olympic record. Write a character profile that clearly describes that character.

Writing Skills Focus: Main Impression
Your character profile should convey a **main impression** of the character. Is this person incredibly brilliant? If so, include details to show his or her brilliance and avoid details that do not relate to it. Notice how Thurber conveys the main impression of a bold and decisive "Commander" Mitty.

Model From the Story
"We can't make it, sir. It's spoiling for a hurricane, if you ask me." "I'm not asking you, Lieutenant Berg," said the Commander. "Throw on the power lights! Rev her up to 8,500! We're going through!"

Prewriting To create a main impression, decide upon the chief character trait you want to convey. Then jot down details that support the trait. These might include physical description, actions, achievements, spoken words, ideas, thoughts, and feelings.

Drafting Decide on the most effective order for presenting your details. For example, you might use this order: (1) Physical Description, (2) Thoughts and Feelings, (3) Words and Actions. Write your draft, elaborating on those details.

Revising Show your character profile to a classmate and ask that person to describe the chief character trait. If the trait isn't clear, provide additional details that support the trait and eliminate those that don't.

✓ ASSESSMENT OPTIONS

Formal Assessment, Selection Test, pp. 76–78, and Assessment Resources Software. The selection test is designed so that it can be easily customized to the performance levels of your students.

Alternative Assessment, p. 22, includes options for less advanced students, more advanced students, interpersonal learners, visual/spatial learners, intrapersonal learners, and logical/mathematical learners.

PORTFOLIO ASSESSMENT

Use the following rubrics in the *Alternative Assessment* booklet to assess student writing:
One More Daydream: Narrative Rubric, p. 88
Written Recommendation: Description Rubric, p. 90
Diary Entry: Expression Rubric, p. 87
Writing Mini-Lesson: Description Rubric, p. 90

PART 1 *Everyday Humor*

Man Prepared to Jump/Fly, Fred Hilliard, Stock Illustration Source, Inc.

One-Minute Planning Guide

The selections in this section focus on humorous situations in everyday life. In the short play "The Inspector-General," the title character has an encounter that readers will find humorous—even though the Inspector-General does not. "Go Deep to the Sewer" is comedian Bill Cosby's tongue-in-cheek remembrance of childhood sports. In "Fly Away" an animal trainer describes his most challenging assignment—training hundreds of flies to "perform" in a movie. "An Entomological Study of Apartment 4A" is a writer's amusing account of what she learns about the various insects she finds in her apartment. The section ends with two cartoons by Gary Larson that take a bug's eye view of the world.

Customize for
Varying Student Needs
When assigning the selections in this section to your students, keep in mind the following factors:

"The Inspector-General"
- Satire provides the humor in this selection
- Setting (Russia in the late 1800's) may be unfamilar to students
- Play can be read aloud in class

"Go Deep to the Sewer"
- Brief, easy-to read article
- High-interest plot will appeal to virtually all students

"Fly Away"
- High interest—provides inside look at one aspect of the film industry

"An Entomological Study of Apartment 4A"
- Contains interesting scientific facts about insects
- Some specialized vocabulary

from "The Far Side"
- "The Far Side" cartoons will be familiar to many students

 ## Humanities: Art

Man Prepared to Jump/Fly by Fred Hilliard.

In the *Man Prepared to Jump/Fly,* the humor of the situation will probably be easier for students to grasp. Encourage students to note particularly silly touches, such as the birds shackled to the man's head, legs, and arms; his headgear; the expectant poses of man and birds alike; the fact that the man's eyes are closed while the birds' eyes are open; and the tentative wording ("Jump/Fly") of the title.

Help students link this art to the theme of Part 1 ("Everyday Humor") by answering the following questions:
1. What "everyday" details can you find in this picture, and how do they add to its humor? *The leashes and collars represent ordinary implements put to a humorous use. Also, the idea that the man is prepared for his experiment to end up being a jump rather than a flight has a certain everyday, common-sense feeling to it.*
2. Compare this art to the one on pages 294–295. Which do you find funnier, and why? *Students who find this work funnier are likely to cite the number and sizes of the birds and the way they are strapped onto the hopeful "flier." Students who find the other work funnier may cite details such as the bone on the fishing pole, the title, and the contraption attached to the dog.*
3. This art makes light of what serious situation? *The art makes light of the human desire to fly, the hope of the inventor, and the likelihood that he will fail.*

307

OBJECTIVES

1. To read, comprehend, and interpret a play
2. To relate a play to personal experience
3. To read between the lines
4. To identify irony
5. To build vocabulary in context and learn the word root *-nym-*
6. To recognize and correct double negatives
7. To write an ad that includes necessary background information
8. To respond to the play through writing, speaking and listening, and projects

SKILLS INSTRUCTION

Vocabulary: Word Roots: *-nym-*
Grammar: Double Negatives
Reading Strategy: Read Between the Lines
Literary Focus: Irony

Writing: Necessary Background
Speaking and Listening: Speech to Town Officials (teacher edition)
Critical Viewing: Speculate; Connect

PORTFOLIO OPPORTUNITIES

Writing: Advice Column; Letter to the Czar; Dialogue
Writing Mini-Lesson: Ad for a New Inspector-General
Speaking and Listening: Speech to Town Officials; Performance
Projects: Report on Russian Life; Multimedia Report

More About the Author
Anton Chekhov became interested in the theater in his high-school days, often organizing and acting in amateur performances of both serious and comic plays. One of the plays he staged was *The Inspector-General,* a hugely popular comedy written in 1835 by the great Russian writer Nikolai Gogol. Chekhov's own play titled *The Inspector-General* was inspired by this earlier work, in which the citizens of a small town go to ridiculous lengths to contend with a surprise visit from a government inspector.

Guide for Reading

Anton Chekhov (1860–1904)

Life was hard for the majority of people who lived in Russia in the 1800's. Until 1861, most Russians were serfs—people bound to the service of a small group of wealthy land-owning nobles. The serfs had few rights and were forced to work long hours in the fields for little money. Those who challenged Russia's rigid social structure were dealt with harshly, often being sent into icy exile in Siberia.

Anton Chekhov vividly captured the harsh realities of nineteenth-century Russian life in his writing.

A Physician and Writer The grandson of a serf who had purchased his freedom, Chekhov grew up in a small Russian coastal town. He later moved to Moscow, where he attended medical school. While studying medicine, he began writing humorous sketches and short stories for publication in various newspapers. After Chekhov graduated from medical school, writing became his major focus, though he practiced medicine on a part-time basis throughout his life.

Accomplishments as a Writer Chekhov wrote more than 1,000 short stories during his lifetime. He also wrote several critically acclaimed plays, including *The Seagull* (1896), *Uncle Vanya* (1899), and *The Three Sisters* (1901). Although he did not become famous outside of Russia until after his death, he is now regarded as one of the finest playwrights and short-story writers the world has ever produced.

◆ Build Vocabulary

WORD ROOTS: *-nym-*
In "The Inspector-General" you will find the word *anonymous,* which contains the word root *-nym-,* meaning "name." Ano*nym*ous literally means "without a *name*" or "with no known or acknowledged name." What other words can you think of that contain the root *-nym-?*

WORD BANK

incognito
anonymous
trundle
valet
buffet

As you read "The Inspector-General," you will encounter the words on this list. Each word is defined on the page where it first appears. Preview the list before you read.

◆ Build Grammar Skills

DOUBLE NEGATIVES
People don't always speak in grammatically correct sentences. It's not surprising, then, that the dialogue in Chekhov's play includes sentences with grammatical errors. For example, the driver of a horse cart uses a pair of double negatives when describing the habits of the inspector-general:

[He] *Don't* want *no one* to see him, *don't* want *no one* to know who he is.

A **double negative** is the use of two negative words when only one is correct. This example can be corrected by changing each *no one* to *anyone.*

308 ◆ *The Lighter Side*

 Prentice Hall Literature Program Resources

REINFORCE / RETEACH / EXTEND

Selection Support Pages
Build Vocabulary: Word Roots: *-nym-*, p. 93
Build Grammar Skills: Double Negatives, p. 94
Reading Strategy: Read Between the Lines, p. 95
Literary Focus: Irony, p. 96

Strategies for Diverse Student Needs, p. 23

Beyond Literature
Community Connection: Local Services, p. 23

Formal Assessment Selection Test, pp. 79–81, Assessment Resources Software

Alternative Assessment, p. 23

Writing and Language Transparencies
Cluster Organizer, p. 80

Resource Pro CD-ROM
"The Inspector-General"—includes all resource material and customizable lesson plan

Listening to Literature Audiocassettes
"The Inspector-General"

The Inspector-General

◆ Literature and Your Life

CONNECT YOUR EXPERIENCE
Sometimes people hide their identities or pretend to be someone else. Maybe they are trying to impress someone or are playing a practical joke. Often their charade doesn't have the effect they've planned. The results can be embarrassing, even humorous. "The Inspector-General" captures such a situation.

THEMATIC FOCUS: EVERYDAY HUMOR
Although the character in Chekhov's play feels humiliated when his charade backfires, the situation is humorous because he seems to be getting what he deserves.

Journal Writing Jot down your memories of humorous movies or television programs you have seen involving failed schemes of unlikeable characters.

◆ Background for Understanding

HISTORY
From the 1500's until the Marxist revolution of 1917, Russia was ruled by czars—iron-fisted emperors who held tight control over virtually every aspect of Russian life. To keep a close eye on local officials throughout Russia's vast landscape, the czars employed people in the position of inspector-general. The inspectors-general were charged with observing how local schools, courts, hospitals, and so on were functioning. Because of people's resentment of the czar's absolute authority, the inspectors-general were often unpopular among the public.

◆ Literary Focus

IRONY
When a literary work such as Chekhov's takes a surprising turn, it creates **irony**—a contrast between an expected outcome and an actual outcome. Several kinds of irony are used in literature. In **verbal irony** a word or phrase is used to suggest the opposite of its usual meaning. In **dramatic irony** there is a contradiction between what a character thinks and what the reader knows is true. In **irony of situation**, an event occurs that directly contradicts the expectations of the characters or of the reader. Writers often use irony to create humor.

◆ Reading Strategy

READ BETWEEN THE LINES
Writers often withhold key pieces of information to keep readers guessing or make them uncertain about the outcome of a work. For example, a writer might not immediately reveal a character's identity. Instead, it is left up to the reader to piece together the character's identity based on what the character says or does, or details of his or her appearance. When you use information that the writer does provide to draw conclusions about missing details, you are **reading between the lines.**

In "The Inspector-General," a traveler begins asking his driver questions about the inspector-general. Chekhov doesn't say why he is asking these questions, but you can come up with the answer by reading between the lines. Pay close attention to the types of questions the traveler asks, and note the details of his behavior. What do these details reveal about the traveler's motives?

Preparing for Standardized Tests

Reading and Vocabulary Learning to make inferences will help students improve their performance on reading comprehension items on standardized tests. The Reading Strategy focuses on reading between the lines, a form of making inferences. Students can apply this skill when working with verbal reasoning items on standardized tests. For additional practice, use the Reading Strategy page in *Selection Support*, p. 95.

Grammar and Language Portions of some standardized tests require students to demonstrate their mastery of standard English grammar, including the correct use of negatives. Students may be asked to select the correct word or phrase to complete a sentence:

She didn't see (anyone, no one). *anyone*

The Build Grammar Skills lesson will help students learn to use negatives correctly by identifying and correcting double negatives. For additional practice, use the Build Grammar Skills page on Double Negatives, p. 94, in *Selection Support.*

 **Interest Grabber** Ask students to imagine that they are writers for a TV sitcom. Invite them to continue this story idea: Kim knows that her nosy younger brother Lee likes to listen in on her phone conversations. One day, Kim decides to get back at her brother. . . .

Ask volunteers to share their ideas. Then tell students that the play they are about to read deals with a somewhat similar situation. Encourage them to look for ways in which a "snoop" gets what he deserves.

Customize for
Less Proficient Readers
Less proficient readers may not be familiar with the print conventions used in plays. Pointing out examples, explain that stage directions are printed in italics; the names of characters appear in capital letters when they are not part of the dialogue.

Customize for
More Advanced Students
To help more advanced students appreciate the many ironies that contribute to the play's humor, have them make a chart with three headings: *Verbal Irony, Dramatic Irony,* and *Irony of Situation.* Have the students find as many examples of each type of irony as they can in the selection. For example, the driver is using verbal irony when he says "he's a blessing from heaven" in response to the traveler's question about the inspector-general's job performance. Dramatic irony occurs when the traveler says that "no one knows he's coming," while the reader knows otherwise. Irony of situation occurs when the inspector-general realizes that his plans to maintain secrecy have failed.

Customize for
English Language Learners
For these students, point out and correct examples of nonstandard grammar, including double negatives, in the play's dialogue.

One-Minute Insight Brimming with sly ironies, this one-act play shows what happens when the tables are turned on a self-satisfied fellow who takes pride in his own craftiness. Traveling "incognito," Pyotr Pavlovich Posudin questions the driver of a cart he has hired about what the locals think of their new government inspector. As the driver divulges that they know all about his habit of sneaking around, it becomes increasingly clear to the audience that the driver knows that the traveler and the inspector-general are one and the same. The fact that the "traveler" is much slower to catch on only adds to the ironic humor, proving that he is not nearly as clever as he thinks and that the joke is on him.

❶ **Clarification** Students may wonder why Chekhov writes "the little town of N__" instead of providing the name of the town. Explain that indicating a place in this way is an old-fashioned literary convention. Originally, this convention acted as a handy abbreviation or served to conceal names to protect the innocent. Later, this convention was used to add a touch of realism to fiction.

◆ **Critical Thinking**

❷ **Infer** What can you conclude about the traveler from this piece of information? *Responses might include: He is a self-important and self-absorbed person; he cares more about himself than about anyone or anything else.*

The Inspector-General

Anton Chekhov

⁂

The curtain goes up to reveal falling snow and a cart facing away from us. Enter the STORYTELLER, *who begins to read the story. Meanwhile, the* TRAVELER *enters. He is a middle-aged man of urban appearance, wearing dark glasses and a long overcoat with its collar turned up. He is carrying a small traveling bag. He climbs into the cart and sits facing us.*

⁂

❶ STORYTELLER *[The Inspector-General].* In deepest incognito, first by express train, then along back roads, Pyotr Pavlovich Posudin[1] was hastening toward the little town of N____, to which he had been summoned by an anonymous letter. "I'll take them by surprise," he thought to himself. "I'll come down on them like a thunderbolt out of the blue. I can just imagine their faces when they hear who I am." *[Enter the* DRIVER, *a peasant, who climbs onto the cart, so that he is sitting with his back to us, and the cart begins to* trundle *slowly away from us.]* And when he thought to himself for long enough, he fell into conversation with the driver of the cart. What did he talk about? About himself, of course. *[Exit the* STORYTELLER.*]* ❷

TRAVELER. I gather you've got a new inspector-general in these parts.

DRIVER. True enough.

TRAVELER. Know anything about him? *[The* DRIVER *turns and looks at the* TRAVELER, *who turns his coat collar up a little higher.]*

DRIVER. Know anything about him? Of course we do! We know everything about all of them up there! Every last little clerk—we know the color of his hair and the size of his boots! *[He turns back to the front, and the* TRAVELER *permits himself a slight smile.]*

TRAVELER. So, what do you reckon? any good, is he? *[The* DRIVER *turns around.]*

DRIVER. Oh, yes, he's a good one, this one.

TRAVELER. Really?

DRIVER. Did one good thing straight off.

TRAVELER. What was that?

DRIVER. He got rid of the last one. Holy terror he was! Hear him coming five miles off! Let's say he's going to this little town. Somewhere like we're going, say. He'd let all the world

---

1. **Pyotr Pavlovich Posudin** (pyō′ tr päv lō′ vich pō sū′ dən)

◆ **Build Vocabulary**

incognito (in käg′ ni tō′) *adv., adj.:* With true identity unrevealed or disguised

anonymous (ə nän′ ə məs) *adj.:* Without a known or acknowledged name

trundle (trun′ dəl) *v.:* To roll along; to rotate

♦ **Build Vocabulary**

❸ Word Roots: -nym- Ask students to suppose that the letter that the driver describes is unsigned. What word could they use to describe both the letter and its sender? *anonymous*

▶**Critical Viewing**◀

❹ Speculate Students may say that life would be cold, dreary, and uneventful in this sort of setting.

Valmondois Sous la Neige, Maurice de Vlaminck

know about it a month before. So now he's on his way, say, and it's like thunder and lightning coming down the road. And when he gets where he's going, he has a good sleep. He has a good eat and drink, and then he starts. Stamps his feet, shouts his head off. Then he has another good sleep, and off he goes.

TRAVELER. But the new one's not like that?

DRIVER. Oh, no. The new one goes everywhere on the quiet. Creeps around like a cat. Don't want no one to see him, don't want no one to know who he is. Say he's going into this town down the road here. Someone there ❸ sent him a letter on the sly, let's say. "Things going on here you should know about." Something of that kind. Well, now, he creeps out of his office, so none of them up there see him go. He hops on a train just like

▲ **Critical Viewing** What might life be like in a ❹ setting such as this one? [Speculate]

anyone else, just like you or me. When he gets off, he don't go jumping into a cab or nothing fancy. Oh, no. He wraps himself up from head to toe so you can't see his face, and he wheezes away like an old dog so no one can recognize his voice.

> ♦ **Literary Focus**
> Why is this description of the new inspector-general ironic?

TRAVELER. Wheezes? That's not wheezing! That's the way he talks! So I gather. I ❻

DRIVER. Oh, is it? But the tales they tell about him. You'd laugh till you burst your tripes![2]

TRAVELER [*sourly*]. I'm sure I would.

♦ **Literary Focus**

❺ Irony Students may point out that there seems to be a contrast between appearance and reality here. The driver is supposedly describing the new inspector-general, yet his description very closely matches the traveler.

♦**Reading Strategy**

❻ Read Between the Lines Ask students: Why does the traveler add "So I gather"? *The traveler realizes that his comments about the wheezing gave away the fact that he knows quite a bit about the new inspector-general. He adds these words to "cover up."*

Customize for
Bodily/Kinesthetic Learners
The stage directions in *The Inspector-General* include gestures and facial expressions that help reveal the characters' feelings and motives. Bodily/kinesthetic learners can help classmates appreciate this aspect of the comedy by performing a version that captures these important nonverbal details.

The Inspector-General ♦ 311

Humanities: Art

Valmondois Sous La Neige, by Maurice de Vlaminck.

Maurice de Vlaminck was born in Paris in 1876. In the early 1900's, he belonged to a group of artists dubbed the *Fauves*—meaning "wild beasts"—because of their bold use of color. De Vlaminck later turned to painting evocative landscapes in rich, dark colors.

Use these questions for discussion:

1. Notice that the central point of interest is the road. What would be down the road if this were an illustration for *The Inspector-General?*

What other detail would you add? *The town of N_ would be down the road. A horse and cart with a driver and passenger could be added.*

2. You can read between the lines in art as well as in literature. Imagine that people are looking out of the windows as the inspector-general rides by. Using details from the play, what might they be saying or thinking? *Students might answer along these lines: "There goes that sneaky inspector, thinking no one knows who he is . . ."*

◆ Critical Thinking

1. The traveler wants to know whether the people of the town know anything about the inspector-general and whether the arrival of the inspector-general will surprise everyone.
2. Based on what the driver says, the inspector-general is secretive and sneaky, but is not clever enough to pull off a surprise inspection.
3. Both inspectors-general are alike in that they both take their duties seriously. They are different in many ways. The old inspector-general, for example, was very boisterous and outgoing. In contrast, the new inspector-general is quiet and secretive.
4. Students will probably say that the driver is wiser. The driver is intelligent enough to see through the disguise of the inspector-general.
5. Students may say that a good inspector-general should be honest and forthright and treat people fairly.

◆ Reading Strategy

1. Students may have caught on when the traveler makes an indignant response to the driver's remark about the way the inspector-general "wheezes."
2. Students may have noticed that the traveler pulls his coat up to hide his face, just as the inspector-general is said to do. Students may also cite that the traveler hides his bag when the driver says that the inspector-general carries vodka in a bag.
3. The driver matches the inspector-general's characteristics to the traveler's actions.
4. Students may say that the driver was sure from the beginning because he describes the inspector-general exactly and notes how the town was warned by telegraph of the inspector-general's arrival.

◆ Literary Focus

1. The driver considers the inspector-general "good" because he is easily "found out." This means that the inspector-general is bad at doing his job.
2. The inspector-general's efforts at anonymity don't work. The driver knows who the traveler is.

314

Guide for Responding (continued)

◆ Critical Thinking

INTERPRET
1. Why does the traveler question the driver about the inspector-general? **[Infer]**
2. How would you characterize the inspector-general based on the driver's description of him? Support your answer. **[Analyze]**
3. In what ways are the old and new inspectors-general alike? In what ways are they different? **[Compare and Contrast]**

EVALUATE
4. Who do you think is the wiser person, the traveler or the driver? Why? **[Make a Judgment]**

EXTEND
5. Based on this play, what lessons can be learned about how to perform effectively in a job as an inspector-general? **[Career Link]**

◆ Reading Strategy

READ BETWEEN THE LINES
In "The Inspector-General," Chekhov withholds a key piece of information: the traveler's identity. By **reading between the lines**—piecing together key details—you can figure out that the the traveler is in fact the inspector-general.
1. When did you first realize that the traveler was the inspector-general?
2. What details led you to this conclusion?
3. What evidence is there that the driver is aware of the traveler's identity?
4. Do you think the driver was aware of the traveler's identity from the beginning? Explain.

◆ Literary Focus

IRONY
The fact that the driver is aware of the traveler's identity is an example of **irony**, a contrast between an expected outcome and an actual outcome.
1. Why is the driver's remark that the inspector-general is "a good one" an example of verbal irony?
2. Why are the results of the traveler's attempts to hide his identity an example of irony of situation?

◆ Build Vocabulary

USING THE WORD ROOT -nym-
The word root -nym- means "name." Using the clues in parentheses, define each word.
1. pseudonym (*pseudo-* = "false")
2. antonym (*ant-* = "opposite")
3. synonym (*syn-* = "together")

USING THE WORD BANK
In your notebook, complete each sentence with a word from the Word Bank.
1. The heavy trucks slowly ___?___ along the bumpy road.
2. An ___?___ donor gave $10,000 to the hospital fund.
3. The ___?___ pressed the pants of the hotel guest.
4. The ___?___ featured delicious main courses and desserts.
5. Traveling ___?___, the spy checked into the motel under a false name.

◆ Build Grammar Skills

DOUBLE NEGATIVES
A **double negative** is the use of two negative words when only one is correct. Double negatives are not acceptable in standard written English.

Practice In your notebook, rewrite each sentence, correcting any double negatives.
1. At first, the traveler thinks that nobody knows nothing about him.
2. He doesn't think that no one can figure out who he is.
3. There's not nothing particularly special about the friendly driver.
4. The fellow who runs the buffet isn't doing nothing but getting ready for the inspector-general.
5. In the end, the traveler doesn't say nothing but "Turn around!"

Writing Application Sometimes double negatives are used in dialogue to capture the way certain people actually speak. Write a brief passage of dialogue between two characters who occasionally use double negatives. Then write out how you'd correct each double negative.

◆ Build Vocabulary

1. A pseudonym is a false name.
2. The antonym of a word is opposite it in meaning.
3. Together, synonyms provide a group of reasonable substitutes for a given word.

Using the Word Bank
1. trundle; 2. anonymous;
3. valet; 4. buffet;
5. incognito

◆ Build Grammar Skills

A way to correct each sentence is shown here.
1. ...nobody knows <u>anything</u> about him.
2. He doesn't think that <u>anyone</u> can...
3. There's nothing particularly special (<u>Delete *not*</u>)
4. The fellow who runs the buffet isn't doing <u>anything</u>...
5. In the end, the traveler doesn't say <u>anything</u>...

✎ Writer's Solution

For additional instruction and practice, use the lesson in the **Language Lab CD-ROM** on Problems with Modifiers and the Negative Sentences page in the *Writer's Solution Grammar Practice Book*, p. 92

Build Your Portfolio

 Idea Bank

Writing

1. **Advice Column** Write an advice column directed toward the inspector-general, providing advice on how he can improve his job performance. **[Career Link]**

2. **Letter to the Czar** Assume the role of the inspector-general and write a letter to the czar explaining why you did not follow through with your planned inspection.

3. **Dialogue** Imagine that the Russian czar has summoned the inspector-general to explain why he did not complete his inspection. Create a dialogue that might take place on such an occasion.

Speaking and Listening

4. **Speech to Town Officials** Putting yourself in the role of the inspector-general, deliver a speech to town officials on a subject of community interest. **[Community Link]**

5. **Performance** With a partner, read aloud the parts of the driver and the traveler, paying close attention to the tone of voice and style of delivery that seem to work best for both characters. **[Performing Arts Link]**

Projects

6. **Report on Russian Life** Conduct research to learn about what life was like in Russia during the hundreds of years when czars ruled. Present your findings to the class. **[Social Studies Link]**

7. **Multimedia Report** Identify examples of irony in movies or television programs. Then put together a multimedia presentation in which you show these examples and explain their effect. **[Media Link]**

 Writing Mini-Lesson

Ad for a New Inspector-General

Pretend that you're the Russian czar, and have just fired the inspector-general for failing to inspect the town. Write a newspaper ad to find a new inspector-general.

> **Writing Skills Focus:**
> **Necessary Background**
>
> In any piece of writing, it's essential to provide readers with **background information** they'll need. In a story, for example, readers need background information on the characters and setting. Make sure your ad contains all necessary background so that potential job candidates have enough information to decide whether or not to apply for the job.

Prewriting A newspaper ad for a job contains the following four types of information. Jot down notes on the information you will include for each.
1. **Job Description** Gives the job title and explains the duties of the job.
2. **Applicant Qualifications** Tells what experience and educational background are necessary.
3. **Job Benefits** Gives the salary and other rewards.
4. **Contact Information** Indicates whom to contact for a job interview.

Drafting Refer to your notes as you draft your ad. Devote a short paragraph to each of the four types of information. To attract qualified job applicants, begin your ad with an attention-grabbing first sentence, such as "Do you love to travel to exciting places?"

Revising Have a classmate read your ad to see whether any of the information is unclear or insufficient. If problems exist, add more background information where needed.

The Inspector-General ◆ 315

OBJECTIVES

1. To read, comprehend, and interpret two personal narratives
2. To relate a personal narrative to personal experience
3. To recognize situational humor
4. To identify a humorous remembrance
5. To build vocabulary in context and learn about sports jargon
6. To develop skill in using adjective clauses
7. To write a humorous personal narrative with a strong introduction
8. To respond to these humorous remembrances through writing, speaking and listening, and projects

SKILLS INSTRUCTION

Vocabulary:
Specialized
Vocabulary: Sports
Jargon

Grammar:
Adjective Clauses

Reading Strategy:
Recognize
Situational Humor

Literary Focus:
Humorous
Remembrance

Writing: Strong
Introduction

**Speaking and
Listening:**
Stand-up Comic
Monologue
(teacher edition)

Critical Viewing:
Connect; Compare;
Speculate

PORTFOLIO OPPORTUNITIES

Writing: Sports Report; Résumé; Dramatic Scene

Writing Mini-Lesson: Humorous Personal Narrative

Speaking and Listening: Stand-up Comic Monologue; Interview

Projects: Research Report; Multimedia Biography

More About the Authors

The character of Fat Albert, who appears briefly in the narrative, is one of **Bill Cosby's** most popular creations. Not only did Cosby write a book about Albert, he created a television cartoon show based on the character, which won awards for its education value.

Ralph Helfer is the animal trainer who first developed the "Affection Training" method for training wild animals. This method uses affection and positive rewards for good behavior, but no punishment for misbehavior.

Guide for Reading

Bill Cosby (1937–)

One of the most popular and influential entertainers in the United States, Bill Cosby has been breaking new ground for decades and making people laugh while doing it. The son of a navy cook and a domestic worker, Cosby grew up in the housing projects of Philadelphia. He left high school to join the navy but soon regretted that choice and eventually earned his high-school diploma through a correspondence course. He cut short his studies at Temple University to pursue stand-up comedy in the coffeehouses of Philadelphia in the early 1960's. His career as a comedian soon went national.

In 1965, he became the first African American performer to star in a prime-time television drama when he played the role of tennis coach and undercover agent Alexander Scott in the action series *I Spy*, a role for which he won an Emmy award. Cosby's greatest success came with his extremely popular television situation comedy, *The Cosby Show*, which ran from 1984 to 1992. Cosby has written a number of books, including *The Wit and Wisdom of Fat Albert, Fatherhood, Time Flies*, and *Childhood*.

Ralph Helfer (1937–)

One of the leading animal trainers in the world, Ralph Helfer has persuaded animals to do what directors want them to do in more than 5,000 movies and television programs. In his book *The Beauty of the Beasts*, Helfer explains that his work as a stuntman and wild-animal trainer has led to his being "clawed by lions, attacked by bears, bitten by poisonous snakes, and nearly suffocated by pythons." Helfer and his trained animals have won 18 PATSY awards for the best animal performances on the screen. He is the founder of Marineworld/Africa USA.

◆ Build Vocabulary

SPECIALIZED VOCABULARY: SPORTS JARGON

Jargon refers to special language that comes from a particular activity, such as a profession, sport, or art. Much of the fun of reading "Go Deep to the Sewer" comes from Bill Cosby's inventive use of sports jargon, beginning with the title. "Go deep to . . ." is an expression that refers to the far edges of the playing field. For example, in football the expression "goes deep" refers to a wide receiver going out for a long pass.

lateral
yearned
decoy
interpretation
skeptical

WORD BANK

Before you read, preview this list of words from the selections.

◆ Build Grammar Skills

ADJECTIVE CLAUSES

Writers use adjective clauses to add key descriptive details to a sentence. An **adjective clause** is a subordinate clause (a group of words that contains a subject and a verb but cannot stand on its own) that modifies a noun or pronoun in another clause. Look at Cosby's first sentence:

> The essence of childhood, of course, is play,
> adjective clause 1—modifies *play*
> which my friends and I did endlessly on streets
> adjective clause 2—modifies *streets*
> that we reluctantly shared with traffic.

Adjective clauses are introduced by the relative pronouns *who, whom, whose, which,* and *that* and the subordinating conjunctions *where, when,* and *why*.

316 ◆ *The Lighter Side*

Prentice Hall Literature Program Resources

REINFORCE / RETEACH / EXTEND

Selection Support Pages
Build Vocabulary: Specialized Vocabulary: Sports Jargon, p. 97
Build Grammar Skills: Adjective Clauses, p. 98
Reading Strategy: Recognize Situational Humor, p. 99
Literary Focus: Humorous Remembrance, p. 100

Strategies for Diverse Student Needs, p. 24

Beyond Literature
Workplace Skills: Acting Responsibly, p. 24

Formal Assessment Selection Test, pp. 82–84, Assessment Resources Software

Alternative Assessment, p. 24

Writing and Language Transparencies
Personal Narrative, pp. 21–27

Resource Pro CD-ROM
"Go Deep to the Sewer," "Fly Away"—includes all resource material and customizable lesson plan

 Listening to Literature Audiocassettes
"Go Deep to the Sewer," "Fly Away"

Go Deep to the Sewer ◆ Fly Away

◆ Literature and Your Life

CONNECT YOUR EXPERIENCE

Life gives some people lemons, and they make lemonade. Life gives other people lemons, and they make big meringue pies to toss so that others will laugh. Maybe you are one of those lucky individuals who can find something funny in most experiences—even difficult ones. These two selections focus on the lighter side of personal experiences.

THEMATIC FOCUS: EVERYDAY HUMOR

Think about how these humorous memoirs might inspire you to see the lighter side of some of your own experiences.

Journal Writing Jot down a list of entertaining tales from your life.

◆ Background for Understanding

PERFORMING ARTS

Ralph Helfer originally used a method of animal training that involved making the animal fear the trainer, often by punishing misbehavior. After following this method for years and being injured and threatened by the animals he was trying to train, Helfer decided to develop a new system, which he called "affection training." The trainer who practices affection training wins the animal's confidence and loyalty rather than its fear by displaying love, patience, and understanding. Helfer says, "Instead of dealing with my animals physically, I deal with them emotionally." He argues that animals trained through fear remain dangerous to work with and explains that he has not been injured by an animal since he began to use the affection-training method.

◆ Literary Focus

HUMOROUS REMEMBRANCE

A **humorous remembrance** is a memoir that looks at the past through glasses that, if not exactly rose-colored, have great comic eyebrows attached. Such a remembrance communicates what is funny about the writer's past experience, as in "Fly Away," or finds something funny in an experience that may have had its painful moments, as in "Go Deep to the Sewer."

◆ Reading Strategy

RECOGNIZE SITUATIONAL HUMOR

You read something that makes you laugh. Why? Sometimes you get the verbal humor—funny-sounding words or clever puns, or you respond to a character with a wacky attitude toward life. Sometimes you **recognize situational humor:** You see what is laughable about a particular set of circumstances. Much of the humor in "Go Deep to the Sewer" and "Fly Away" is situational, arising from actions that take place in wildly inappropriate settings or with unusual props. As you read these memoirs, look for each humorous situation and note what makes each one comic. Use a graphic organizer such as the one shown to capture your observations.

What Is Being Done?	Who Is Doing it?
Where?	Using What?

Guide for Reading ◆ 317

Interest Grabber Hook students' interest by asking them to describe some of the funniest moments from movies or television shows that feature Bill Cosby, or some of the most amazing moments from movies or television shows that include performances by wild animals. After students have recounted some special moments, point out that the selections will give a behind-the-scenes look at both Bill Cosby and animal performances. The first selection is written by Bill Cosby about his boyhood, and the second is written by an animal trainer who trains wild animals to act in movies.

Customize for
Less Proficient Readers
Less advanced students might benefit from listing and defining the sports jargon throughout "Go Deep to the Sewer," such as *huddle, downs,* and *right fielder,* as they read.

Customize for
More Advanced Students
More advanced students might enjoy singling out humorous sections of the pieces and analyzing why they are funny. Have them discuss whether the author uses exaggeration or satire, or juxtaposes events in a surprising manner.

Customize for
English Language Learners
Humor can be difficult to understand when it is in an unfamiliar language. Have groups of students act out the humorous scenes of "Go Deep to the Sewer" and explain the humorous scenes of "Fly Away."

Customize for
Bodily/Kinesthetic Learners
Bodily/kinesthetic learners might gain a greater appreciation of the events Bill Cosby describes if they act out the movements in the football and stickball games. Encourage them to read the selection carefully and, if necessary, make a diagram showing the players' moves. Then they can demonstrate the action for the class.

 Preparing for Standardized Tests

Reading and Vocabulary The Build Vocabulary lesson focuses on jargon, or specialized words, that have to do with sports. Students can apply what they learn about jargon when working on vocabulary items on standardized tests. For additional practice, use the Build Vocabulary page in *Selection Support,* p. 97.

Grammar and Language Many standardized tests include portions in which obtaining the correct answer requires that a student be able to identify what noun or pronoun is modified by an adjective clause. For example, a question may hinge on understanding a sentence like the following:

Fruit flies, <u>which are well known to fans of bananas,</u> were used by T. H. Morgan in his genetics experiments. (fruit flies, fans, bananas, T. H. Morgan, experiments) *fruit flies*

The Build Grammar Skills lesson for this selection focuses on adjective clauses. For additional practice, use the Build Grammar Skills page on Adjective Clauses, p. 98, in *Selection Support.*

One-Minute Insight

This personal narrative describes the games that Bill Cosby used to play as a boy. As he looks back with a fond, self-mocking eye toward his past, Bill Cosby paints a funny and heartwarming picture of what it was like to grow up on the streets of Philadelphia.

►Critical Viewing◄

❶ Connect The painting depicts two young boys, obviously friends, sitting on the stoop of a city dwelling. Thus, the painting captures the essence of an urban setting and also emphasizes the bond of friendship between youngsters like those described by Cosby.

Young Brothers in the Hood by Tom McKinney.

This piece of art shows two young boys sitting on the stoop of a city apartment building. Either of the boys could easily be Bill Cosby as a boy or one of his friends.

Discuss the art with questions like the following:

1. What can you tell about how these two boys feel about each other, based on the way the artist positions them? *They are close friends, as indicated by the way they sit close together, legs and arms touching.*

2. What details in the painting make it a good illustration for Cosby's personal narrative? *The setting for the painting is urban, the boys' expressions and body positions indicate that they are relaxed and having a good time. The boy on the left has a mischievous expression on his face, as Cosby might have had when responding to his mother's warnings about cars.*

Young Brothers in the Hood, Tom McKinney

318   The Lighter Side

Block Scheduling Strategies

Consider these suggestions to take advantage of extended class time:

- Introduce students to the Cosby piece by discussing with them the Build Vocabulary section (p. 316) featuring sports jargon. Ask for examples of sports jargon that have entered general use, such as "He's out in left field," meaning that he's bewildered.

- Have students complete the journal activity on page 317. Encourage them to refer to their journal entries to write a Stand-up Comic Monologue (p. 329).

- Students can work in pairs to create the role-playing television Interview from the Idea Bank on page 329. Pairs can audiotape or videotape their interviews and show them to the class.

- As students begin the Writing Mini-Lesson (p. 329), encourage them to write strong introductions and then exchange introductions with a partner. Partners can evaluate the strength of each other's introductions.

Go Deep to the Sewer

Bill Cosby

The essence of childhood, of course, is play, which my friends and I did endlessly on streets that we reluctantly shared with traffic. As a daring receiver in touch football, I spent many happy years running up and down those asphalt fields, hoping that a football would hit me before a Chevrolet did.

My mother was often a nervous fan who watched me from her window.

"Bill, don't get run over!" she would cry in a moving concern for me.

"Do you see me getting run over?" I would cleverly reply.

And if I ever *had* been run over, my mother had a seat for it that a scalper[1] would have prized.

Because the narrow fields of those football games allowed almost no lateral movement, an end run was possible only if a car pulled out and blocked for you. And so I worked on my pass-catching, for I knew I had little chance of ever living my dream: taking a handoff and sweeping to glory along the curb, dancing over the dog dung like Red Grange.

The quarterback held this position not because he was the best

---

◀ **Critical Viewing** How does this painting help you picture the setting and the characters in Cosby's essay? [Connect]

1. **scalper** (skalp´ ər) *n*.: Person who buys tickets and sells them later at higher than regular prices.

◆ **Build Vocabulary**
lateral (lat´ ər əl) *adj*.: Sideways

◆ **Beyond the Classroom**

Career Connection

Football-Related Careers Explain to students that Red Grange was a football player who played for the University of Illinois and the Chicago Bears. Professional football began in western Pennsylvania in the nineteenth century but didn't become popular until the 1950's. By 1958 three million people had attended NFL (National Football League) games. The AFL (American Football League) was formed in 1959, and the two leagues merged in 1970, agreeing to play a championship game that became known as the Super Bowl.

Students who might like to pursue a career linked to professional football have numerous job opportunities to explore. Encourage interested students to research one or more of the following possibilities: coach, trainer, team physician, ticket manager, radio or television play-by-play announcer, and public relations director. For each job title, students could write a summary that includes a job description as well as the required education and training.

❶ Compare Like Cosby's essay, this photograph depicts a youngster playing stickball, without a real baseball bat or uniform. In contrast with the essay, the photograph shows a park scene rather than an urban street scene.

Customize for
More Advanced Students
More advanced students might benefit from determining how the city setting of this narrative affects the humor of the writer's memories. Ask students how the humor might change if the narrative were set in the country. *Much of the humor depends on the street setting and the threat of game disruption or even death by automobile. Changing the setting would have a significant effect on the specific type of humor.*

320   *The Lighter Side*

passer but because he knew how to drop to one knee in the huddle and diagram plays with trash.

"Okay, Shorty," Junior Barnes would say, "this is you: the orange peel."

"I don' wanna be the orange peel," Shorty replied. "The orange peel is Albert. I'm the gum."

"But let's make 'em *think* he's the orange peel," I said, "an' let 'em think Albert's the manhole."

"Okay, Shorty," said Junior, "you go out ten steps an' then cut left behind the black Oldsmobile."

"I'll sorta go *in* it first to shake my man," said Shorty, "an' then, when he don' know where I am, you can hit me at the fender."

"Cool. An' Arnie, you go down to the corner of Locust an' fake takin' the bus. An' Cos, you do a zig out to the bakery. See if you can shake your man before you hit the rolls."

"Suppose I start a fly pattern to the bakery an' then do a zig out to the trash can," I said.

"No, they'll be expecting that."

I spent most of my boyhood trying to catch passes with the easy grace of my heroes at Temple;[2] but easy grace was too hard for me. Because I was short and thin, my hands were too small to catch a football with arms extended on the run. Instead, I had to stagger backwards and smother the ball in my chest. How I <u>yearned</u> to grab the ball in my hands while striding smoothly ahead, rather than receiving it like someone who was catching a load of wet wash. Often, after a pass had bounced off my hands, I returned to the quarterback and glumly said, "Jeeze, Junior, I don' know what

---

2. **Temple:** Temple University in Philadelphia, Pennsylvania.

◀ **Critical Viewing** Compare and contrast the details in this photograph with those in Cosby's essay. [Compare]

happened." He, of course, knew what had happened: he had thrown the ball to someone who should have been catching it with a butterfly net.

Each of these street games began with a quick review of the rules: two-hand touch, either three or four downs, always goal-to-go, forward passing from anywhere, and no touchdowns called back because of traffic in motion. If a receiver caught a ball near an oncoming car while the defender was running for his life, the receiver had guts, and possibly a long excuse from school.

I will never forget one particular play from those days when I was trying so hard to prove my manhood between the manholes. In the huddle, as Junior, our permanent quarterback, dropped to one knee to arrange the garbage offensively, I said, "Hey, Junior, make me a <u>decoy</u> on this one."

Pretending to catch the ball was what I did best.

"What's a decoy?" he said.

"Well, it's—"

"I ain't got time to learn. Okay, Eddie, you're the Dr Pepper cap an' you go deep toward New Jersey."

"An' I'll fool around short," I said.

"No, Cos, you fake goin' deep an' then buttonhook at the DeSoto. An' Harold, you do a zig out between 'em. *Somebody* get free."

Moments later, the ball was snapped to him and I started sprinting down the field with my defender, Jody, who was matching me stride for stride. Wondering if I would be

◆ **Literary Focus**
What view of his childhood is Cosby presenting here?

◆ **Build Vocabulary**

yearned (yūrnd) *v.:* Longed for; desired

decoy (dē′ koi) *n.:* Person used to lure others into a trap

321

Comprehension Check ☑️

❶ What does the writer mean by "unlimited time"? Why is it "almost enough"? *He means time as it is measured in childhood, when a day can seem to last forever. It is "almost enough" because time passes even for children, and they grow up.*

◆ Literary Focus

❷ Humorous Remembrance
Ask students how Cosby uses exaggeration to make this scene humorous. *He claims that the ball could be "seen only on radar screens," which makes the image of playing at night even funnier.*

◆ Build Grammar Skills

❸ Adjective Clauses Ask students to locate the two adjective clauses in this passage and tell how they add to the writer's description. *The two clauses are "when you connected with a Spaldeen in stickball" and "where it might gently bop somebody's mother sitting on a stoop." The clauses give facts and add humorous details.*

◆ Reading Strategy

❹ Recognize Situational Humor
The use of manhole covers and cars as bases is funny because they are so different from what ballplayers usually use.

---

able to get free for a pass sometime within the next hour, I stopped at the corner and began sprinting back to Junior, whose arm had been cocked for about fifteen seconds, as if he'd been posing for a trophy. Since Eddie and Harold also were covered, and since running from scrimmage was impossible on that narrow field, I felt that this might be touch football's first eternal play: Junior still standing there long after Eddie, Harold, and I had dropped to the ground, his arm still cocked as he tried to find some way to pass to himself.

❶ But unlimited time was what we had and it was almost enough for us. Often we played in the street until the light began to fade and the ball became a blur in the dusk. If there is one memory of my childhood that will never disappear, it is a bunch of boys straining to find a flying football in the growing darkness of a summer night.

There were, of course, a couple of streetlamps on our field, but they were useful only if your pattern took you right up to one of them to make your catch. The rest of the field was lost in the night; and what an adventure it was to refuse to surrender to that night, to hear the quarterback cry "Ball!" and then stagger around in a kind of gridiron blindman's buff.

"Hey, you guys, dontcha think we should call the game?" said Harold one summer evening.

"Why do a stupid thing like that?" Junior replied.

"'Cause I can't see the ball."

"Harold, that don't make you special. Nobody can see the ball. But y' *know* it's up there."

❷ And we continued to stagger around as night fell on Philadelphia and we kept looking for a football that could have been seen only on radar screens.

One day last year in a gym, I heard a boy say to his father, "Dad, what's a Spal*deen?*"

This shocking question left me

depressed, for it is one thing not to know the location of the White House or the country that gave its name to Swiss cheese, but when a boy doesn't know what a Spal*deen* is, our educational system has failed. For those of you ignorant of basic American history, a Spal*deen* was a pink rubber ball with more bounce than can be imagined today. Baseball fans talk about the lively ball, but a lively baseball is a sinking stone compared to a Spal*deen,* which could be dropped from your eye level and bounce back there again, if you wanted to do something boring with it. And when you connected with a Spal*deen* in stickball, **❸** you put a pink rocket in orbit, perhaps even over the house at the corner and into another neighborhood, where it might gently bop somebody's mother sitting on a stoop.

I love to remember all the street games that we could play with a Spal*deen.* First, of course, was stickball, an organized version of which is also popular and known as baseball. The playing field was the same rectangle that we used for football: it was the first rectangular diamond. And for this game, we had outfield walls in which people happened to live and we had bases that lacked a certain uniformity: home and second were manhole covers, and first and third were the fenders of parked cars.

> ◆ **Reading Strategy**
> What makes the lack of uniformity in the bases humorous? **❹**

One summer morning, this offbeat infield caused a memorable <u>interpretation</u> of the official stickball rules. Junior hit a two-sewer shot and was running toward what should have been third when third suddenly drove away in first. While the bewildered Junior tried to arrive safely in what had become a twilight zone, Eddie took my throw from center field and tagged him out.

"I'm not out!" cried Junior in outrage. "I'm right here on third!"

And he did have a point, but so did

322   *The Lighter Side*

Speaking and Listening Mini-Lesson

Stand-up Comic Monologue

This mini-lesson supports the Speaking and Listening activity in the Idea Bank on p. 329.

Introduce the Concept Have students talk about what aspects of material and delivery make stand-up comic routines they have seen on television funny. Suggest that they list these key points and use them in developing their own routines. These points can serve as criteria for assessing their monologues.

Develop Background Encourage students to think of an incident in their own lives that would make a funny subject for a routine. Have them consider these questions:

- Will my audience find the incident amusing?
- How can I use situational humor, exaggeration, and self-mockery to make the routine funnier?

Apply the Information As students draft their monologues, remind them to include

an introduction and a final punch line. Encourage them to use peer reviewers to help them revise their work. After writing the final draft, students can rehearse and then present their routines to the class.

Assess the Outcome Have students judge the effectiveness of each monologue by discussing how humorous the content was and whether the delivery technique added to the humor.

Eddie, who replied, not without a certain logic of his own, "But third ain't *there* anymore."

In those games, our first base was as mobile as our third; and it was a floating first that set off another lively division of opinion on the day that Fat Albert hit a drive over the spot from which first base had just driven away, leaving us without a good part of the right field foul line. The hit would have been at least a double for anyone with movable legs, but Albert's destination was first, where the play might have been close had the right fielder hit the cutoff man instead of a postman.

❺ "Foul ball!" cried Junior, taking a guess that happened to be in his favor.

"You're out of your mind, Junior!" cried Albert, an observation that often was true, no matter what Junior was doing. "It went

right over the fender!"

"What fender?"

"If that car comes back, you'll *see* it's got a fender," said Albert, our automotive authority.

However, no matter how many pieces of our field drove away, nothing could ever take away the sweetness of having your stick connect with a Spal*deen* in a magnificent *whoppp* and drive it so high and far that it bounced off a window with a view of New Jersey and then caromed back to the street, where Eddie would have fielded it like Carl Furillo[3] had he not backed into a coal shute.

❻

---

3. **Carl Furillo** (kärl fər il′ ō): Baseball player for the Brooklyn Dodgers in the 1950's.

◆ **Build Vocabulary**

interpretation (in tʉr′ prə tā′ shən) *n.*: Explanation

Guide for Responding

◆ *Literature and Your Life*

Reader's Response Would you enjoy playing stickball and football under the circumstances Bill Cosby describes? Why or why not?

Thematic Focus If you were telling someone about this selection, which part would you single out as the funniest?

☑ **Check Your Comprehension**

1. What obstacles did Cosby and his friends face when they played their games?
2. What did Junior the quarterback use to diagram plays for his team?
3. What did the young Bill Cosby dream of doing?
4. Why does Eddie insist that Junior is out after his "two-sewer shot"?

◆ **Critical Thinking**

INTERPRET

1. Why do you think the boys kept playing football long past daylight? **[Infer]**
2. What does their ability to deal with unusual obstacles in playing their games suggest about the boys' attitude toward life? **[Draw Conclusions]**
3. How do you think Bill Cosby really felt as a boy about the fact that he couldn't catch passes the way he wanted to? **[Analyze]**
4. (a) What does Cosby mean when he says "The essence of childhood, of course, is play, ... "?
   (b) Do you agree with him? **[Make a Judgment]**

EXTEND

5. What life skills do you think Cosby and his playmates developed in playing football and stickball on the streets of Philadelphia? **[Career Link]**

Go Deep to the Sewer ◆ 323

◆ **Build Vocabulary**

❺ **Specialized Vocabulary: Sports Jargon** Ask students what a *foul ball* is and why Junior would want to call the hit a foul. *A foul ball is a ball that is out of bounds. Junior wanted to call a fair ball a foul ball because the hit was good for the opposition.*

◆ **Reading Strategy**

❻ **Recognize Situational Humor** Have students determine how the situation in this passage adds to the humor. *The author sets up a great hit and a fine fielding move — and then has the fielder fall down a coal chute, ending a dramatic passage with a highly comic moment.*

Reinforce and Extend

Answers

◆ *Literature and Your Life*

Reader's Response Some students might appreciate the adventure of playing these sports under difficult circumstances; others might not.

Thematic Focus Responses may include humorous details such as the parts about the quarterback making diagrams with trash.

☑ **Check Your Comprehension**

1. Obstacles included traffic, pedestrians, oddly shaped playing areas, and changing conditions on the street.
2. He used trash.
3. He dreamed of being a star football player.
4. Junior isn't safe on base because third base had driven away.

◆ **Critical Thinking**

1. Suggested response: They truly loved playing the game.
2. They are adaptable and know they have to make things happen for themselves.
3. He was probably frustrated, upset, and embarrassed.
4. (a) Children need more than anything else to play and pretend.
   (b) Most students will agree that children need opportunities to play.
5. Students may suggest that the games built the following skills: creativity; good motor coordination; awareness of surroundings; and coping with adversity.

Beyond the Selection

FURTHER READING

Other Works by Bill Cosby
Fatherhood
Time Flies
Childhood

Other Humorous Memoirs
If Life Is a Bowl of Cherries, What Am I Doing in the Pits? Erma Bombeck
My World, and Welcome to It, James Thurber
Mama's Bank Account, Kathryn Forbes

INTERNET

You and your students may find additional information about Bill Cosby on the Internet. We suggest the following site. Please be aware, however, that the site may have changed from the time we published this information.

The Bill Cosby Home Page is located at **http://www.iconn.net/sadick/cosby.html**

We *strongly recommend* that you preview the site before you send students to it.

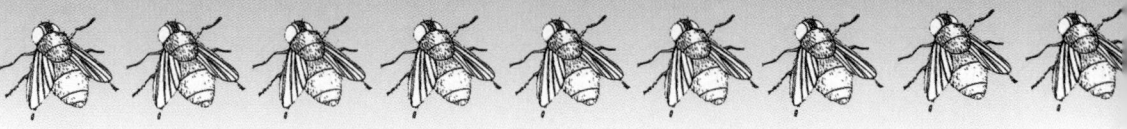

▲ Critical Viewing After reading the selection, what other challenges can you think of that might be faced by people in the film industry who work with animals? [Speculate] **①**

With everything set, I opened the small door of the fly house. Hiding the gas capsule in the palm of my hand and reaching inside, I broke it open, closed the door, and waited for fifteen seconds. To everybody's amazement, the buzzing stopped. Next, I opened the door and scooped out three or four handfuls of flies. I shook them out as one would when counting a pound of peanuts. Putting the little sleeping flies all over the "body," I began to dramatically count the last few: "Five-thousand twenty, five-thousand twenty-one, five-thousand **②**

twenty-one . . . that makes it half!" **②**

I told everyone to hold still, then I gave the flies a verbal cue: "Okay guys—Jack, Bill, Mary—come on, up and at 'em!"

Slowly the flies started to awaken, then move around. In a few moments the whole mass of them was swarming all over the "thing," but they were still too drowsy to fly, as my professor friend had told me they would be.

"Okay, roll!" yelled the director. The camera rolled on the fly swarm, and I shot a look at the crew. They appeared to be in

shock. Then, having gotten enough footage, the director shouted, "Okay, Ralph, *now!*"

My great moment.

"Okay, group," I said to the flies. "Get ready: on the count of three, all of you take off."

The crew, absolutely bug-eyed (forgive the pun), was hypnotized.

"One," I counted. They looked from the flies to me.

"Two."

"Three!" I yelled, clapping my hands and stamping my foot at the same time. Five thousand twenty-one flies flew up, up, around and around. The camera hummed, until the director, rousing himself from his amazed state, said, "Cut!"

❸

◆ Literary Focus
How does Helfer signal here that the high point of his narrative is approaching?

The entire crew was silent for a moment, and then they burst into applause and delighted laughter.

"You did it, you really did it!" said the director, slapping me heartily on the back. "I'm not even going to ask you how. I don't even want to know. But if I ever need a trained *anything,* you're the man I'll call!"

Straight-faced, I said, "Well, actually, I've recently trained 432 flies to form a chorus line on my arm, and on cue they all kick a leg at the same time."

The director, poker-faced, looked straight at me. "Which one?" he asked.

"Which one what?"

"Which leg?"

"The left one, of course!"

We all broke up laughing and headed home.

❹

❺

Guide for Responding

◆ *Literature and Your Life*

Reader's Response What surprised you the most about Helfer's achievement?

Thematic Focus What, if any, humorous experiences does this selection bring to mind? Why?

Group Discussion As the use of computer-generated images in movies grows more realistic, "live" effects like the one Helfer describes are becoming rare. With a group of classmates, discuss what has been gained and lost with the increasing use of computers to create special effects in movies and television.

☑ Check Your Comprehension

1. What was Helfer asked to do?
2. What plan did he develop?
3. What happened at the shoot?
4. How did the director and crew react?

◆ Critical Thinking

INTERPRET

1. Why do you think Helfer kept the tranquilizer capsule hidden at the shoot? **[Infer]**
2. What does the way Helfer planned and executed the effect suggest about his skills as an animal trainer? **[Draw Conclusions]**
3. Why does Helfer pretend to count out the number of flies? **[Analyze]**
4. How do you think Helfer feels about his achievement? **[Infer]**

EVALUATE

5. Should Helfer have revealed his secret to the director? Why or why not? **[Make a Judgment]**

EXTEND

6. From what Helfer tells about his work, what skills do you think being an animal trainer requires? **[Career Link]**

Fly Away ◆ 327

Beyond the Selection

FURTHER READING

Other Humorous Memoirs
Innocents Abroad, Mark Twain
All Creatures Great and Small, James Herriot
"Surely You're Joking, Mr. Feynman!" Richard Feynman
The Grass Is Always Greener Over the Septic Tank, Erma Bombeck

INTERNET

You and your students may find additional information about flies on the Internet. We suggest the following site. Please be aware, however, that the site may have changed from the time we published this information. Students can find out more about flies and their behavior at **http://www.ento.vt.edu/Facilities/OnCampus/idlab/id/id-flies. html**

We *strongly recommend* that you preview the site before you send students to it.

Reinforce and Extend

Answers
◆ *Literature and Your Life*

Reader's Response Students may be surprised that nothing went wrong and the flies flew away on cue.

Thematic Focus Students may describe a time when something was accomplished in an unlikely fashion, or when a scheme went utterly awry.

Group Discussion Students may note that computers can create spectacular effects, but that the fun of figuring out how the film-makers created an illusion has been lost.

☑ Check Your Comprehension

1. He was asked to make 5,000 flies swarm on a dummy and then take off on cue.
2. He would take newly hatched flies to the shoot, tranquilize them for a few minutes with a harmless gas, and let them fly away when the gas wore off.
3. Everything happened according to his plan. Helfer added some "touches"—sprinkling flies on the dummy to make it seem that he had counted out the exact number and pretending to give a verbal cue to make them fly away.
4. They were amazed and amused.

◆ Critical Thinking

1. He wanted people to think he had really trained the flies.
2. It suggests that he is very thorough, knows animals, and is quite a showman.
3. He does it to make it seem as if he is even more in control of the events than he actually is, and to add drama.
4. He is proud, and perhaps even a little smug.
5. Students may think that Helfer should not have revealed it, because the trick is so simple that the director will get annoyed that no one on his staff thought of it.
6. Skills that are needed include resourcefulness, patience, attention to detail, knowledge, and ability to analyze a situation quickly.

◆ Reading Strategy

1. The inappropriateness of the items he uses makes it funny.
2. Cosby's description of his ineptitude, such as his mentioning of catching a pass as if he were "catching a load of wet wash," is amusing.
3. Humor is provided by the details about streetlamps, and being unable to see the ball while playing.
4. The irregularity and mobility of such bases as manhole covers and automobile fenders is funny.
5. The pinpoint perfection is funnier because it presents the absurd illusion that Helfer had actually trained the flies.
6. This is funny because it seems as if Helfer can actually keep track of each one of the thousands of flies.
7. Because the reader knows Helfer's secret, the audience's awe and amazement seems humorously out of proportion.

◆ Build Vocabulary

Using Sports Jargon

Students' examples may be similar to the following:

a. "touchdowns called back because of traffic in motion": The touchdowns were ruled invalid because of moving vehicles.
b. "the first rectangular diamond": Baseball is usually played on a square field called a diamond.
c. "two-sewer shot": The equivalent of a two-base hit, which allows the hitter to go to second base, when the bases are manhole covers.
   1. Someone might *slam-dunk* a crumpled candy wrapper into a waste basket.
   2. A patient in a doctor's waiting room might be considered *on deck*.
   3. A house painter seeing a storm brewing might say "let's *punt*," stopping his or her progress and letting the storm take the offensive.

Using the Word Bank

1. a   2. b   3. b   4. c

◆ Literary Focus

1. Some serious elements include the boys' poverty and the potential danger of playing in the street.
2. Helfer communicates pride with a tinge of ludicrousness.
3. Some students may prefer Cosby's

Guide for Responding (continued)

◆ Reading Strategy

RECOGNIZE SITUATIONAL HUMOR

Both selections build their effects around **situational humor**—circumstances that combine actions, people, and settings in funny, and often improbable, ways.

1. In Cosby's memoir, what makes Junior's diagramming plays in trash funnier than if he had used a chalkboard?
2. What is amusing about the way Cosby describes his attempts at catching passes?
3. What details provide the humor in Cosby's description of playing ball after dusk?
4. What is funny about the bases Cosby describes in the boys' stickball game?
5. What makes the pinpoint perfection of Helfer's flies funnier than the antics of trained seals would be?
6. Helfer pretends to count the sleeping flies. Why is this funny?
7. How does the audience reaction to Helfer's achievement add to the humor of the situation?

◆ Build Vocabulary

USING SPORTS JARGON

In his memoir Bill Cosby uses **jargon**—the special language from a particular activity—for comic effect. He takes terms from baseball and football and combines them with features of street life to create some memorable phrases.

Find three examples of Cosby's playful use of sports jargon in "Go Deep to the Sewer." Define each example.

Explain how each of the following examples of sports jargon might be used in everyday speech.

1. slam dunk   3. punt
2. on deck

USING THE WORD BANK

On your paper write the word whose meaning is closest to that of the first word.

1. skeptical: (a) questioning, (b) vague, (c) angry
2. yearned: (a) stretched, (b) longed, (c) remembered
3. decoy: (a) charming, (b) lure, (c) rot
4. lateral: (a) exact, (b) one-sided, (c) sideways

◆ Literary Focus

HUMOROUS REMEMBRANCE

A **humorous remembrance** focuses on the lighter side of an event from the writer's past.

1. What serious elements enter into Cosby's humorous remembrance?
2. What overall impression of his work does Helfer communicate in his remembrance?
3. Cosby's remembrance strings together a series of experiences that make up his memory of childhood play. Helfer's memoir focuses on one particularly remarkable job experience. Which piece do you find more appealing, and why?

◆ Build Grammar Skills

ADJECTIVE CLAUSES

Adjective clauses enable writers to add information—facts, details, comments, and so on—to describe more fully a person, place, thing, or event in their writing.

> An **adjective clause** is a subordinate clause that modifies a noun or pronoun.

Practice On your paper, write the following sentences from the selections. Draw one line under the adjective clause in each, and draw an arrow to the noun or pronoun that the clause modifies.

1. My mother was often a nervous fan who watched me from her window.
2. We walked over to a cage that was being heated by a special infrared lamp.
3. I love to remember all the street games that we could play with a Spal*deen*.
4. I went to work, first converting an old box in which we'd been keeping crickets . . .
5. I will never forget one particular play from those days when I was trying so hard to prove my manhood between the manholes.

Writing Application Write a paragraph describing a humorous experience from your childhood. Use at least three adjective clauses in your paragraph.

---

essay because it resonates with their own experiences. Others may prefer Helfer's essay because the idea of trained flies is appealingly bizarre.

◆ Build Grammar Skills

1. who watched me from her window; modifies *fan*
2. that was being heated by a special infrared lamp; modifies *cage*
3. that we could play with a Spaldeen; modifies *games*
4. in which we'd been keeping crickets; modifies *box*
5. when I was trying so hard to prove my manhood between the manholes; modifies *days*

✒ Writer's Solution

For additional instruction and practice, use the lesson in the **Language Lab CD-ROM** on Varying Sentence Structure. Also use the practice pages on Adjective Clauses (pp. 53–54) in the *Writer's Solution Grammar Practice Book.*

Build Your Portfolio

Idea Bank

Writing

1. Sports Report Think of a sport with which you are familiar. Then imagine the sport being played in an inappropriate area with comic possibilities—for example, volleyball in your school cafeteria. Write a "serious" sports report describing such a game.

2. Résumé Imagine that you are an animal trainer, and create a résumé for yourself listing and briefly describing your education or training and your job experiences. **[Career Link]**

3. Dramatic Scene Write a dramatic scene based on one of the selections. Create dialogue and stage directions actors could use to perform the scene. **[Performing Arts Link]**

Speaking and Listening

4. Stand-up Comic Monologue Bill Cosby's memoir first began as part of his stand-up comedy routine. Take an incident or situation in your own life that has comic potential, and write a two-minute monologue emphasizing the funny aspects of that experience.

5. Interview With another student, role-play a television interview with Ralph Helfer, discussing some of his more entertaining experiences training animals. **[Media Link]**

Projects

6. Research Report Do some research on current methods of training animals, and report your findings to the class.

7. Multimedia Biography Prepare a multimedia biography of Bill Cosby. Include photographs as well as video or audio recordings.

Writing Mini-Lesson

Humorous Personal Narrative

Choose a memorable experience and write a **humorous narrative** about it. Try to start off on the right note, catching your readers' attention and making them smile in anticipation of your story. The following may help you get your narrative rolling.

Writing Skills Focus: Strong Introduction

As both Bill Cosby and Ralph Helfer show you, the first few sentences of a humorous personal narrative set the tone for the whole story. Writing a **strong introduction** will win over your readers and make them want to smile with you. You can try a number of strategies for writing a strong introduction. For example, Ralph Helfer plunges right into his story with some dialogue:

Model From the Story

"I need 5,000 trained flies. Can you do it? Yes or no!" The voice at the other end of the phone was insistent.

Prewriting Think of the funniest and most memorable aspects of the incident you've chosen. Jot down the details that come to mind. Then list some ways in which you might exaggerate these details.

Drafting Decide on your strategy for writing a strong introduction: whether you want to try writing dialogue, stating your main idea, posing a question to your readers, flashing back from the outcome of the incident, or offering a piece of advice. Then relate your experience, following basic chronological order, making sure to include the funniest details and actions you can remember.

Revising Reread your draft. Have you included amusing details and actions? Is the opening likely to capture your readers' attention? Will your introduction make them want to read further?

Go Deep to the Sewer/Fly Away ◆ 329

Customizing for *Performance Levels*

Following are suggestions for matching the Idea Bank topics with your students' performance levels:

Less Advanced Students: 1, 5
Average Students: 2, 4, 6
More Advanced Students: 3, 7

Customizing for *Learning Modalities*

Following are suggestions for matching Idea Bank topics with your students' learning modalities:

Interpersonal: 5
Logical/Mathematical: 6
Auditory: 4, 5, 7
Visual/Spatial: 7

Writing Mini-Lesson

Refer students to the Writing Handbook, page 962, for instruction on the writing process, and page 964 for further information on narration.

 Writer's Solution

Writers at Work Videodisc

Have students view the videodisc segment on Narration (Ch. 2) featuring writer Isabel Allende to see how she draws upon her memories when she writes. Have students discuss how personal experiences can be the inspiration for fiction as well as nonfiction.

Play frames 10786 to 22536

Writing Lab CD-ROM

Have students complete the Tutorial on Narration. Follow these steps:
1. Have students use the Story Wheel activity to spark ideas for writing.
2. Suggest using the Photo Storyboard activity to help students plan their narrative.
3. Have students draft on computer. Allow about 70 minutes to complete these steps.

Sourcebook

Have students use Chapter 2, Narration (pp. 30–61), for additional support. The chapter includes a model from literature of a personal narrative (p. 35) and an annotated student model of a personal narrative (p. 56). It also includes tips on starting a narrative (p. 50).

✓ ASSESSMENT OPTIONS

Formal Assessment, Selection Test, pp. 82–84, and Assessment Resources Software. The selection test is designed so that it can be customized to the performance levels of your students. *Alternative Assessment,* p. 24, includes options for less advanced students, more advanced students, bodily/kinesthetic learners, visual/spatial learners, interpersonal learners, and logical/mathematical learners.

PORTFOLIO ASSESSMENT

Use the following rubrics in the *Alternative Assessment* booklet to assess student writing:
Sports Report: Technical Description/Explanation Rubric, p. 108
Résumé: Résumé and Cover Letter Rubric, p. 107
Dramatic Scene: Drama Rubric, p. 102
Writing Mini-Lesson: Narrative Based on Personal Experience Rubric, p. 89

Guide for Reading

OBJECTIVES

1. To read, comprehend, and interpret a feature article
2. To relate a feature article to personal experience
3. To set a purpose for reading
4. To identify the elements of a feature article
5. To build vocabulary in context and learn the prefix *micro-*
6. To identify participial phrases
7. To write a letter to an expert using an appropriate level of formality
8. To respond to a feature article through writing, speaking and listening, and projects

SKILLS INSTRUCTION

Vocabulary:
Prefixes: *micro-*

Grammar:
Participial Phrases

Reading Strategy:
Set a Purpose for Reading

Literary Focus:
Feature Article

Writing: Level of Formality

Speaking and Listening:
Dialogue (teacher edition)

PORTFOLIO OPPORTUNITIES

Writing: Animal Organizer; Bug Story; Public Relations Campaign

Writing Mini-Lesson: Letter to an Expert

Speaking and Listening: Oral Report; Dialogue

Projects: Insect Survey; Pet Arthropod

More About the Author
Patricia Volk was born in New York City in 1943. Her fiction often focuses on urban women with wry senses of humor that help them survive the emotional upheavals they face. Of her comic novel, *White Light,* one critic said that her "delightful urban sensibility, a quirky sense of humor and a light touch ... are enough to put this book in the winner's circle."

Patricia Volk (1943–)

Patricia Volk's quirky sense of humor can be seen in her short stories, novels, and articles. Volk's amusing tone is also a key element in her written advertisements, many of which have won awards. The selection you're about to read is a feature article, not an advertisement, but it may influence how you think, just as an ad does.

Don't be surprised if "An Entomological Study of Apartment 4A" makes you want to purchase a can of bug spray.

Beginnings as a Writer Initially, Volk's focus was on the visual arts, rather than on writing. She worked as an art director at several advertising agencies, as well as magazines such as *Seventeen* and *Harper's Bazaar*. Within a few years, however, her passion for writing began to reveal itself, and in 1988, she became a full-time writer.

Writing Reveals the Writer
Volk's experiences and background are reflected in her writing. You can see her artistic training in the vivid descriptions and delightful details that are sprinkled throughout her work. In addition, her keen appreciation for the everyday humor of modern urban life reflects the fact that she has spent almost all of her life in New York City.

◆ Build Vocabulary

PREFIXES: *micro-*

In this article, Patricia Volk describes bugs as "microcosms." The word *microcosm* contains the prefix *micro-*, which means "small." Because *-cosm-* means "world" or "universe," *microcosm* literally means "little world." By referring to bugs as *microcosms*, Volk means that they are like miniature versions of the world. By examining such miniature versions, you can gain an understanding of the larger world.

WORD BANK

| microcosms |
| metaphors |
| poignant |
| malevolence |
| immortalized |

As you read "An Entomological Study of Apartment 4A," you will encounter the words on this list. Each word is defined on the page where it first appears. Preview the list before you read.

◆ Build Grammar Skills

PARTICIPIAL PHRASES

A **participial phrase** consists of a participle—a verb form that acts as an adjective to modify a noun or pronoun—and the words that complete or modify its meaning. In this sentence from "An Entomological Study of Apartment 4A," the italicized words, beginning with the past participle *stacked*, make up a participial phrase that modifies *hall*:

Sorkin greets me in a hall *stacked six feet high with drawers of Pyraustinae, a moth.*

Participial phrases enable writers to include additional descriptions. As you read the article, keep an eye out for participial phrases.

330 ◆ The Lighter Side

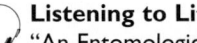
Prentice Hall Literature Program Resources

REINFORCE / RETEACH / EXTEND

Selection Support Pages
Build Vocabulary: Prefixes: *micro-*, p. 101
Build Grammar Skills: Participial Phrases, p. 102
Reading Strategy: Set a Purpose for Reading, p. 103
Literary Focus: Feature Article, p. 104

Strategies for Diverse Student Needs, p. 25

Beyond Literature
Cross-Curricular Connection: Science, p. 25

Formal Assessment Selection Test, pp. 85–87, Assessment Resources Software

Alternative Assessment, p. 25

Writing and Language Transparencies
Business Letter, pp. 53–56

Resource Pro CD-ROM
"An Entomological Study of Apartment 4A"—includes all resource materials and customizable lesson plan

Listening to Literature Audiocassettes
"An Entomological Study of Apartment 4A"

An Entomological Study of Apartment 4A

◆ Literature and Your Life

CONNECT YOUR EXPERIENCE

Often, we're fascinated by creatures that repel us. Even if you can't bear to look at that many-legged thing that just scurried under the stove, you still want to know what it is. This natural curiosity inspired Patricia Volk to collect the bugs she found in her apartment and take them to an expert for identification. This article is the result of her adventures.

Journal Writing By making light of the problem of having bugs in her apartment, Patricia Volk was able to learn new and interesting things about these unwelcome guests. In your journal, examine how a different approach to a problem—perhaps a less serious approach—can lead to a rewarding solution.

THEMATIC FOCUS: EVERYDAY HUMOR

Patricia Volk's approach to the bugs in her city apartment gives us a lighter look at an everyday annoyance.

◆ Background for Understanding

SCIENCE

In everyday speech, the words *bug* and *insect* are used to refer to many different types of animals. In science, however, referring to a spider as a *bug* or an *insect* is highly inaccurate. In fact, it's worse than calling a cat a *dog*. Insects are six-legged animals such as ants, bees, butterflies, fleas, grasshoppers, beetles, termites, and cockroaches. Insects also include true bugs, which, as Volk points out in her article, "have a modified beaklike mouth." Spiders, mites, and ticks—all of which have eight legs—are not insects.

◆ Literary Focus

FEATURE ARTICLE

The purpose of a **feature article**, such as "An Entomological Study of Apartment 4A," is to entertain readers or to provide information on a subject of interest. Feature articles, which appear in newspapers or magazines, are often human-interest stories, which means that they focus on some interesting aspect of a person or group of individuals. These articles are designed to interest readers in a subject and to evoke an emotional response to the subjects' achievements, problems, or ideas.

◆ Reading Strategy

SET A PURPOSE FOR READING

As a feature article, "An Entomological Study of Apartment 4A" is full of useful and interesting material. To get the most out of what you read, **set a purpose** for reading before you begin and then read to achieve your purpose. For example, if your purpose is to gather information for an extra-credit science report, you might focus on obtaining useful facts. If your primary purpose is to amuse yourself, you might look for a funny event or fascinating fact that you could share with others.

To help you set and achieve a purpose for reading this article, make a table similar to the one that follows. As you read, fill in the table with notes about the article that fulfill your purpose.

My Purpose	Items That Will Help Me Achieve My Purpose	Details That Achieve My Purpose

Guide for Reading ◆ 331

Get students interested in the selection by asking them, "What is the most disgusting bug you have ever seen?" Encourage students to share their experiences with "gross" insects, spiders, ticks, or any other creepy crawly creatures, by inviting them to talk about bugs they have encountered on hikes, camping trips, and other outdoor excursions. Ask what size and color the bugs were, how they behaved, and what else made them fascinating, "gross," or annoying. Then ask students why they think some people feel afraid of, or disgusted by, bugs, while others find them fascinating or fun.

Customize for
Less Proficient Readers
If possible, bring an insect-killing product to class. Show it to the students and let them discuss the product's helpful and harmful features. Make sure they understand that the author of this essay has lots of insects in her apartment as a result of not wanting to use harmful insecticides. She is visiting an *entomologist,* an insect expert, to learn how to safely get rid of the bugs in her apartment.

Customize for
More Advanced Students
Challenge more advanced students to list alphabetically the insect names the author mentions and to use their prior knowledge of spelling and pronunciation to figure out how to pronounce the names properly. Have them write out the pronunciations phonetically, separating the syllables with spaces and printing the accented syllables in uppercase letters.

Customize for
English Language Learners
You may want to help English language learners to translate difficult vocabulary and pronounce insect names.

Customize for
Visual/Spatial Learners
Encourage students to find pictures of insects and make an insect display, labeling each "specimen" with its correct name. Invite students to present their displays to the class.

 Preparing for Standardized Tests

Reading and Vocabulary Understanding the meaning of prefixes will help students to remember definitions of familiar words and to infer the meanings of unfamiliar words that they encounter on the verbal portions of standardized tests—both reading comprehension and vocabulary items. The Build Vocabulary lesson focuses on learning word meaning through the use of the prefix *micro-*. Students can apply this skill when working with verbal reasoning items on standardized tests. For additional practice, use the Build Vocabulary page in **Selection Support,** p. 101.

Grammar and Language The Build Grammar Skills lesson for this selection focuses on participial phrases. Being able to identify participial phrases and the words they modify will help students improve their scores on the verbal portions of standardized tests. For additional practice, use the Build Grammar Skills page on Participial Phrases, p. 102, in **Selection Support.**

One-Minute Insight

This feature article takes a light-hearted, humorous approach to a problem that frustrates many: the proliferation of bugs and other insect life in city apartments. The author consults a renowned entomologist to find help in her search for a natural way to control insect life. While it doesn't solve her problem, the visit gives her a new appreciation for the diversity and mystery of the insect world. Readers will learn many fascinating facts about insects—but they may also develop a new sense of our connection to nature and its creatures.

◆ **Critical Thinking**

❶ **Analyze Characters** Ask students what kind of person would go to an entomologist rather than an exterminator to find help in getting rid of bugs in her home. *Students may say this person would be intelligent, interested in learning about any topic, or a creative problem solver.*

◆ **Reading Strategy**

❷ **Set a Purpose for Reading** Possible purposes for reading might be to learn more about insects, to find out how to get rid of bugs, or to enjoy the author's humor. Allow students to choose their own purposes, but encourage them to choose one that will sustain them throughout the entire article.

❸ **Clarification** Explain that there actually is a scientific difference between insects and bugs. The word *bug* refers to a category of insects that have particular features, such as a mouth with a long feeding tube, a pair of thin, delicate back wings, and a pair of front wings that cross and overlap. Some examples of real bugs are bedbugs, aphids, and water bugs.

An Entomological Study of Apartment 4A

Patricia Volk

L ouis Sorkin has a prominent fore-head, gently rounded abdomen and powerful bandy legs. During the day, he can be found in the entomology department of the American Museum of Natural History. Sorkin, a senior scientific assistant, has agreed to identify the insects that have been calling my home home since we asked Fred, the building pest control operator, to stop spraying.

"God bless you," Fred used to say at the door, as if we might be seeing each other for the last time.

"What's in this stuff, anyway?" I said to him one day. Malathion, a controversial pesticide, was on the list.

Normally I admire bugs, which happens to be the scientific name for insects that have a modified beaklike mouth. As a child, I collected them in glass cigar tubes my father brought home from his restaurant. Bugs are <u>microcosms</u> and microcosms are <u>metaphors</u>. But something was eating grooves in my favorite brown hat. A black crawly thing with more legs than the

Rockettes had staked out the north bed-room wall. There was a fauna in the freezer and a bug as shiny as patent leather had moved into the water gauge of our electric coffee maker. Darkest of all, there were definite signs of wildlife in the back-room closet a former tenant had jury-rigged into a shower. Whatever it was, it was big.

What I'm hoping Louis N. Sorkin will tell me is what eats what and whether biological warfare is an apartment possibility. California used Australian ladybugs to get rid of cottony-cushion scale. The Mormons lucked out when sea gulls saved them from the locusts. Could my pests have natural enemies on the food chain, something besides the Tokay gecko that barks at night and looks like a Tokay gecko?

◆ **Build Vocabulary**

microcosms (mī´krə käz´əms) *n.:* Little worlds
metaphors (met´ə fôrz´) *n.:* Figures of speech in which things are spoken of as if they were something else

332 ◆ The Lighter Side

Block Scheduling Strategies

Consider these suggestions to take advantage of extended class time:

• Have students complete the journal activity in Literature and Your Life (p. 331). Then, in small groups, have them discuss the extent to which a "good attitude" can help people cope. Is a "good attitude" more helpful in some situations than in others? Which ones? Why?

• Invite students to look at the Reading Strategy feature (p. 331) and to make a chart setting their purposes for reading.

• With students, read the Background for Understanding (p. 331). Then invite students to choose insects from the feature article on which to report. Students might make formal oral reports, bring in pictures, or actually collect live or dead insects.

• Invite students to work in small groups to answer the Critical Thinking questions (p. 337).

Sorkin greets me in a hall stacked six feet high with drawers of Pyraustinae, a moth. We scuttle into a room crammed with journals, papers and boxes of stoppered vials. On the wall, a sign reads, "Feeling Lousy?" Sorkin's desk is littered with dental tools, mail, baby food jars and mugs with spoons—roach heaven.

6 I hand him my hat. He tweezes something off the brim and puts it under his microscope.

"This is a shed skin of one of the dermestid beetles in the larval stage," he says. "I think this one is the Anthrenus species. They've been grazing along it here . . . here . . . they like wool. In New York City, they live under the parquet[1] floor. Hair is a very good food source for them."

"What do they eat on hair?"

"The hair itself. It's protein."

I empty two shopping bags filled with takeout containers and hand over the freezer specimen.

It turns out that it's an immature German cockroach, which means, Sorkin says, it could have been found anywhere. Of my 21 specimens, 11 are German cockroaches. This comes as a big surprise because some look like black dots, some are pear-shaped with pale dorsal banding and some look like greasy pecan shells. Sorkin explains that roaches have a three-stage metamorphosis, going from egg to wingless nymph to adult. During the nymph stage, they molt up to seven times.

"German cockroaches are called Belgian cockroaches in Germany," Sorkin says, scratching his arm. I scratch mine too. "They're also called steam-bugs, shiners and Yankee settlers."

---

1. **parquet** (pär kā´) **floor:** Wooden floor in which the pieces of wood fit together to form a pattern.

He studies a bug I found in my colander under the grapes.

"Oh! Otiorhynchus ovatus! A strawberry root weevil. It's an outdoor weevil that sometimes comes into homes as it migrates."

"How would it get into a fourth-floor apartment?"

"They crawl."

7 "Would it eat my roaches?"

"It would starve."

I show him an arachnid that has spun a web in its container. Maybe it eats strawberry root weevils.

8 "This is a jumping spider. Normally it would be outside."

Sorkin peers into the container with the north-wall stalker.

"A house centipede!" His mustache twitches. "This is a neat animal! Chilopoda have their front legs modified to inject venom. They're predators. They live on roaches and spiders and probably other centipedes."

Bingo! A natural roach enemy. "So if I introduce more Chilopods, they'll get rid of the roaches?"

"Not completely. You'd have to isolate your apartment. If you could keep them from gaining access through cracks and wall voids and holes around pipes and the door to the hallway, yeah, you could have a really insect-free zone."

The phone rings. It rings all day. Louis Sorkin is the 911 of insect emergencies. If you open your safe and bugs fly in your face or you need to know whether New Mexican centipedes produce cyanide, Sorkin's your man.

He studies two flies I found on the bathroom windowsill. There's no masking his disgust.

An Entomological Study of Apartment 4A ◆ *333*

Cross-Curricular Connection: Science

There are more than 800,000 known species of insects, divided into a number of orders. Insects include beetles, moths, butterflies, wasps, ants, bees, flies, mosquitoes, cockroaches, grasshoppers, and true bugs. Fossil records reveal that this amazing form of animal life first appeared on earth about 400 million years ago. All insects have six legs and a segmented body composed of a head; a thorax that includes three pairs of jointed legs and, in most insects, one or two pairs of wings; and an abdomen. Insects have a complicated relationship with people. On the one hand, insects carry disease, infest food, and destroy crops. On the other hand, they pollinate plants, kill and eat pests harmful to people, and serve as a source of food in some parts of the world.

Have students identify their own questions about insects, based on the information in the feature article, and do research to find the answers.

◆ **Critical Thinking**

4 Interpret After directing students' attention to the definitions of *microcosm* and *metaphor*, ask them to put this sentence into their own words. Lead them to unlock the meaning of the sentence by asking: In what way is a bug a "little world"? For what could a "little world" be a metaphor? *A bug is a microcosm, or little world, in that all the complexities of life can be seen in this little creature; a microcosm is a metaphor in the sense that we say, "You can see the whole world in a little bug." Because we cannot literally "see the whole world" in a bug, we would be speaking metaphorically.*

◆ **Critical Thinking**

5 Evaluate Ask students whether they find this passage humorous. Lead them to identify the elements of humor here. *Students might say that the author uses exaggeration ("more legs than the Rockettes," "fauna," "wildlife"); and personification, or talks about the bugs as if they were people ("staked out," "moved into"). They may think the humor stems from using a light tone to speak of a problem some would consider very serious.*

◆ **Build Vocabulary**

6 Prefixes: *micro-* Point out that the word *microscope* contains the prefix *micro-*. Ask students: How does knowing the prefix help you understand the meaning of the word? *The prefix micro- means "small." A scope is an instrument for seeing. Therefore, the word microscope means "an instrument for seeing small objects."*

Comprehension Check ☑

7 Why is the author asking this question? What does the answer mean? *Her original purpose in visiting Sorkin was to find a type of animal that would live in her apartment and eat the roaches and other annoying insects, so that she would not need to use insecticides. Sorkin's answer indicates that the weevil would not eat the roaches.*

8 Clarification Explain that a spider is an *arachnid*—not an insect—because a spider has eight legs and an insect, six.

"These are a little moldy or fungus-y. They look like houseflies, *Musca domestica*."

He checks a dust ball from under our bed for dust mites, which spend their days with their mouths open, waiting for scales to drop from our skin.

"Can't see much here."

"Is it true that there are things that live on our eyelids?"

"There are two species of certain follicle mites around the nose and forehead."

❶ "What's the reason for us to have them?"

"They're just there. Demidex folliculorum. They feed on the material in the hair follicles and usually don't cause any trouble whatsoever. Hold your skin tight like this"—Sorkin pulls his forehead to the side with four fingers—"and push it with a 3-by-5 card and look at what you pushed on a slide, you might even find them."

I try it, but even with magnification of 200, nothing shows up. Maybe moisturizer kills them.

Sorkin checks sweepings from the backroom closet shower.

"This is an American cockroach. You also have the shed skin of what looks like another Anthrenus species and an Odd beetle. The reason it has that name is because the male and female don't look alike. So you've got three different things in here."

On deck is my strangest bug. It suspends itself in liquid, like a peanut in pudding.

"Oh yeah." Sorkin recognizes it instantly. "This is a tortoise beetle. When they're alive they're sometimes gold-colored."

"How did it get in the apartment?"

"Flew."

Sorkin helps me load the containers back into the shopping bag. I head home thinking about the high drama that goes on behind

the kitchen pegboard and wondering about the strawberry root weevil. What compelled it to climb four stories to a place where it would find nothing to eat? A strawberry root weevil entering an apartment is a suicidal gesture . . . .

The next morning, while I'm getting coffee, a juvenile roach heads for the food processor. Although I can do 3.8 m.p.h. on the treadmill and the fastest roach in the world can only go 2.9, I'm no match for it. In the sink, there's a mature female that looks like she's carrying a purse. She died with her egg case stuck in her. Before Sorkin, I never would have found this poignant. Sipping coffee, I gaze at the ceiling. That's when it hits me: I've neglected my prime bug habitat.

Back at the museum, Sorkin rotates a new container with hundreds of insects and insect fragments I've retrieved from our glass ceiling fixture.

"There's . . . a hover fly . . . a spotted cucumber beetle . . . staphylinid beetles . . . a carabid stink beetle . . . ichneumon wasps . . . leaf hoppers . . . a ladybird beetle . . . a fungus beetle . . . a silverfish . . . mirid plant bugs . . . a chironomid midge . . . drugstore beetles . . . and . . . more dermestids. All these insects are attracted to light and they fly in. Then they die and the dermestids eat them."

"How do the dermestids know they're in there?"

"They smell them."

◆ Build Vocabulary

poignant (poin´ yənt) *adj.*: Drawing forth compassion; moving

malevolence (mə lev´ ə ləns) *n.*: Bad or evil feelings or intentions

334 ◆ *The Lighter Side*

334

CONNECTIONS TO TODAY'S WORLD

A poem might make you smile and a story can set you chuckling, but a cartoon can really crack you up—especially if it's a cartoon by Gary Larson. In his popular cartoons from *The Far Side*, Larson has poked fun at humans, animals, birds, and even bugs.

THE FAR SIDE By GARY LARSON

"Think about it, Ed. ... The class Insecta contains 26 orders, almost 1,000 families, and over 750,000 described species — but I can't shake the feeling we're all just a bunch of bugs."

THE FAR SIDE By GARY LARSON

"Shoot! Drain's clogged. ... Man, I hate to think what might be down there."

1. Do you think these cartoons are funny? Point out specific details to support your answer.
2. In what ways do these cartoons poke fun at the way people perceive nature? How does this technique make the cartoons funny?

I ask Sorkin about my most surprising insect encounter:

"One night, I was making guacamole and when I put in the chili powder it started to move. How could insects live on something so hot?"

"Oh, cigarette beetles are very common in dried pepper. They do quite well. Some insects feed on insecticide."

I follow Sorkin to another room. He points to a heap of black molts from his tarantula (they would make terrific earmuffs), then lifts the lid off a plastic tray. There it is, ready to pounce, a furry ball of

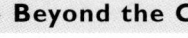

malevolence. Sorkin shows me a jar of preserved insects saved at the 100th anniversary dinner of the New York Entomological Society. There's a cerambycid larva as big as a parsnip, giant meal worms and a black thing the size of a small hamburger.

"This is a belostomadid, or true water bug, from Thailand. The body has a Gorgonzola cheese flavor."

Sorkin's personal favorite is grubs over easy.

"Tastes like bacon," he says.

"Are bugs kosher?"[2] ❺ ❻

---

2. **kosher** (ko´ shər) *adj.*: Fit to eat according to Jewish dietary laws.

An Entomological Study of Apartment 4A ◆ 335

◆ **Build Grammar Skills**

❺ **Participial Phrases** Have students identify in this sentence the participial phrase and the noun it modifies. *The participial phrase is "saved at the 100th anniversary dinner of the New York Entomological Society," which modifies "insects."*

❻ **Clarification** Explain that the word *kosher* refers to foods that Jewish people who closely follow the traditions of Judaism are allowed to eat. Pork products, such as bacon, are not kosher. The question is humorous because we know the author is not really planning to eat grubs, whether they are kosher or not.

Connections to Today's World

In "An Entomological Study of Apartment 4A," we learn about bugs from the viewpoint of Patricia Volk. In these cartoons, the bugs are the ones doing the talking.
1. Most students will find the cartoons funny. They might support this by citing details such as the exasperated posture of the insect in the shower or the bizarre and varied forms of the insects at a cocktail party.
2. The bugs say things that people commonly say in similar situations. Thus, the ironies of situation and speech in the cartoons are especially humorous.

🏰 Beyond the Classroom

Career Connection

Journalism Although many journalists report on specific news events, feature writers, such as Patricia Volk, focus on topics of "human interest." For this feature article, she interviewed a fascinating person with a wide store of knowledge about a topic that would interest many readers as much as it interested Volk herself. While "hard news" is almost always covered in a straightforward, objective style, feature writing allows the author to bring in humor, personal experience, observations, and opinions.

Have students who might be interested in journalism careers read a variety of feature articles in newspapers and magazines. They might also explore book-length works of journalists such as Calvin Trillin, Ellen Willis, and Jimmy Breslin. Encourage students to interview subjects of their choice and write feature articles of their own to see if they would enjoy a career similar to Patricia Volk's. Students should also research the kind of preparation and education most journalists have in their backgrounds. You might mention that Volk studied at the Creative Writing Center at Columbia University.

Idea Bank
Customizing for
Performance Levels
Following are suggestions for matching the Idea Bank topics with your students' performance levels:
   Less Advanced Students: 1, 4
   Average Students: 2, 5, 6
   More Advanced Students: 3, 7

Customizing for
Learning Modalities
Following are suggestions for matching Idea Bank topics with your students' learning modalities:
   Verbal/Linguistic: 2, 3, 4, 5, 7
   Visual/Spatial: 6, 7
   Logical/Mathematical: 1, 6
   Interpersonal: 5

 Writing Mini-Lesson
Refer students to the Writing Handbook, page 962, for instruction on the writing process, and page 966 for further information on practical and technical writing. You may also use the Business Letter models in Writing and Language Transparencies, pp. 53–56, to guide students through the writing process.

 Writer's Solution

Writers at Work Videodisc
Have students view the videodisc segment (Ch. 8) featuring registered nurse Glo Simon to see how she uses technical writing in her work. Have students discuss why accuracy is important in practical and technical writing.

Play frames 34430 to 43977

Writing Lab CD-ROM
Have students compete the Tutorial on Practical and Technical Writing. Follow these steps:
1. Use the Note Cards Activity for practical writing.
2. Have students draft on computer.
3. Use the Interactive Self-Evaluation Checklists to aid revision.

Sourcebook
Have students use Chapter 8, Practical and Technical Writing (pp. 228–262), for additional support. The chapter includes an annotated student model of a letter requesting information (p. 257).

Build Your Portfolio

Idea Bank

Writing

1. **Animal Organizer** In the article, Volk mentions many different types of animals. Prepare a chart that sorts the animals into the following categories: "Insects," "Arachnids," "Chilopods," and "Other." Write a descriptive paragraph for each category. **[Science Link]**

2. **Bug Story** Write a humorous story about a real or imagined incident that involves insects or spiders.

3. **Public Relations Campaign** Patricia Volk's article deals with a misunderstood and underappreciated form of life—the bug. Select a different creature that has a "bad reputation." Write a plan for improving that creature's image.

Speaking and Listening

4. **Oral Report** Prepare and present an oral report on common house and garden pests in your area. Use visual aids to enhance your report.

5. **Dialogue** Write a humorous dialogue between Patricia Volk and one or more of the bugs in her apartment. Practice your dialogue with a partner, then perform it for the class. **[Performing Arts Link]**

Projects

6. **Insect Survey** Take a census of the insects in your home or in a small outdoor area. Report your finding in the form of a bar graph or pie chart. **[Math Link]**

7. **Pet Arthropod** Prepare an illustrated manual that explains how to take care of an arthropod pet, such as a caterpillar, spider, praying mantis, cricket, or ant colony. **[Science Link; Art Link]**

Writing Mini-Lesson

Letter to an Expert

Imagine that you want to ask entomologist Louis Sorkin to identify and provide information about an interesting insect that you found. Write a letter in which you request information from the insect expert.

Writing Skills Focus: Level of Formality

When writing a letter, it is important to use the right **level of formality**. A letter to a stranger may seem rude if it is too informal; a letter to a friend may seem cold or awkward if it is too formal. When in doubt, err on the side of formality. It is better to be considered a little too proper than to be considered impolite.

Tips for Your Letter

- Include your address and the date.
- Address the recipient with the appropriate title and last name.
- Get to the point quickly.
- Avoid slang.
- Be polite—say "thank you."
- End with a formal closing, such as *Sincerely* or *Very truly yours*.

Prewriting List insects that you've found inside or outside of your home. Choose one that interests you. Then jot down the questions that you would like to ask about it.

Drafting In the body of your letter, identify who you are, tell why you're interested in the insect, then ask the questions you have. Be straightforward and use the appropriate level of formality.

Revising Make sure that your letter contains a heading, inside address, salutation, body, closing, and signature. If you are not certain about the standard form of a business letter, consult a grammar book.

✓ ASSESSMENT OPTIONS

Formal Assessment, Selection Test, pp. 85–87, and Assessment Resources Software. The selection test is designed so that it can be easily customized to the performance levels of your students.
Alternative Assessment, p. 25, includes options for less advanced students, more advanced students, musical/rhythmic learners, verbal/linguistic learners, and visual/spatial learners.

PORTFOLIO ASSESSMENT
Use the following rubrics in the *Alternative Assessment* booklet to assess student writing:
Animal Organizer: Description Rubric, p. 90
Bug Story: Narrative Based on Personal Experience Rubric, p. 89, or Fictional Narrative Rubric, p. 88
Public Relations Campaign: How-to/Process Explanation Rubric, p. 93
Writing Mini-Lesson: Business Letter/Memo Rubric, p. 106

Writing Process Workshop

Letter to an Author

As you read the selections in this section, questions may have come to mind that you'd like to ask one or more of the authors. Maybe you'd like to learn more about Bill Cosby's childhood or ask Ralph Helfer about how he learned so much about flies. Choose an author in this section or in another part of the book whose work captured your interest. Then write a letter to that author praising his or her work, offering constructive criticism, or asking questions. Don't be surprised if you get a reply—many authors answer letters from their readers.

The following skills, introduced in this section's Writing Mini-Lessons, will help you write a letter to an author.

Writing Skills Focus

▶ **Start with a strong introduction.** Grab the author's attention and interest in your opening sentence. (See p. 329.)

▶ **Give necessary background information** in your letter. Tell the author a little about yourself. Also, don't forget to identify the work that you read. (See p. 315.)

▶ **Offer your main impression** of the author's work. Explain why you liked or disliked it. (See p. 306.)

▶ **Maintain a level of formality.** Be polite and always show respect. Don't use slang in your letter. (See p. 338.)

Notice how the writer uses these skills in this model.

WRITING MODEL

Dear Mr. Helfer:

    If my handwriting is shaky, it's because I'm still laughing after reading your story "Fly Away." ① It was the funniest thing I've ever read! I think you have a tremendous sense of humor ② ③. . . .

    I'm a high-school freshman who loves teaching his dog to do tricks. ④ Would you be interested in a partner after I finish school?

Sincerely,
Daryl Drew

① The writer tries to capture the author's interest with an amusing opening line.

② Notice that although the writer uses a personal tone, he avoids using slang.

③ The writer makes it clear that his main impression of the author's work is favorable.

④ The writer gives some useful background information about himself.

Writing Process Workshop ◆ 339

Beyond the Classroom

Workplace Connection

Editor Explain to students that the word *editor* can have many different meanings. Some editors work for book publishing companies. One type of book editor helps to choose which books the company will publish and then works with authors to make their books as good as possible. In the course of working with an author on a book, the editor reads the manuscript at many stages. After each reading, the editor communicates, often by letter, responses to the work in progress and suggestions for revision. Ask students how an editor's responses to an author's work differ from a student's responses in a letter to an author. *Students should note that an editor's purpose is to suggest revisions and guide the author's work, while a student's is simply to share his or her response to an author's work.*

Prepare and Engage

Establish Writing Guidelines

Review the following key characteristics of a letter to an author:

• A letter to an author is one way of responding to literature.

• The writer of a letter to an author may praise the author's work.

• The writer may ask questions about the work or offer constructive criticism.

You may want to distribute the scoring rubric for Response to Literature (p. 103 in the ***Alternative Assessment*** booklet) to make students aware of the criteria on which they will be evaluated. See the suggestions on page 341 for how you can customize the rubric to this workshop.

Writing and Language Transparencies

To help students understand the letter format, you might find it helpful to use the transparencies for Writing Process Model 10: Business Letter (pp. 45–51).

Writer's Solution

Writers at Work Videodisc

To provide guidance in responding to literature, play the videodisc segment featuring book reviewer Lawrence Chua (Ch. 7). Have students discuss what they can learn from Chua to apply to their letters

Play frames 23797 to 32801

Writing Lab CD-ROM

If your students have access to computers, you may want to have them work in the tutorial on Response to Literature to complete all or part of their letters. Follow these steps:

1. Invite students to view the Audio-annotated Model from Literature of a letter to an author.

2. Suggest students draft their letter in the Letter Shell.

3. Encourage students to use the Language Variety Checker to help them eliminate repeated words.

4. Direct students to the Interactive Self-Evaluation Checklist to help them revise.

Sourcebook

Students can find additional support in the chapter on Response to Literature (pp. 194–227).

Develop Student Writing

Prewriting

Remind students to choose works to which they had strong responses. You may have students work in small groups to discuss recently read selections that made a strong impact on them.

Customize for
Less Proficient Writers

These students may find it helpful to organize their background information on a chart with five headings: My Age/Grade, My Interests, When I Read the Work, Where I Read the Work, and Other Works I've Read by the Author. They can refer to their charts to choose the information they'd like to provide about themselves in their letters.

Customize for
English Language Learners

Because these students may not yet have developed a strong sense of English sentence structure, help them organize their reactions by providing the following format to fill in:

I liked _____ best because _____.

I liked _____ least because _____.

They can use their completed sentences in their letters. Remind them to give constructive criticism if they decide to include what they liked least.

Drafting

Remind students that the purpose of their prewriting activities is to help them as they draft their letters. Encourage students to refer to and use any notes, lists, or charts they made in the prewriting stage. Also remind them that, as they draft their letters, they may decide to change or add to the ideas they formed in the prewriting stage.

Applying Language Skills

Avoiding Run-on Sentences

Answers
Suggested responses:
1. The characters were unusual, and they behaved strangely.
2. The story was great because it was different and fresh.
3. The ending was clever. My friends and I were all fooled.

APPLYING LANGUAGE SKILLS: Avoiding Run-on Sentences

A **run-on sentence** joins two or more sentences together incorrectly.

Incorrect:
I liked your book, it made me laugh.

Correct:
I liked your book. It made me laugh.

A run-on sentence can be corrected by breaking it into smaller sentences. You can also rewrite it as a compound sentence by adding a comma and a coordinating conjunction such as *and, but,* or *or.*

Practice On your paper, correct each run-on sentence.

1. The characters were unusual, they behaved strangely.
2. The story, it was different and fresh, was great.
3. The ending was clever, I was fooled, so were my friends.

Writer's Solution Connection
Writing Lab

To help you follow the proper format, draft your letter in the Letter Shell in the tutorial on Response to Literature.

Prewriting

Choose an Author Look over the table of contents of this book and recall which selections you've read. Choose a selection by a living author that sparked an especially strong reaction in you.

Jot Down Your Reactions Once you've chosen a selection, jot down your reactions to it. Note what you liked most, what you liked least, and why.

Make a List of Questions Continue gathering your thoughts by coming up with as many questions as you can about the selection.

> ### Examples of Questions
> 1. Who inspired the main character?
> 2. How does the story relate to your experience?
> 3. How did you come up with the idea for the story?

Plan Your Background Information Once you've collected your ideas about the selection, think about the background information you'd like to provide about yourself. For example, you might mention:
- ▶ Your age or grade level
- ▶ Your personal interests
- ▶ When and where you read the author's work
- ▶ Other works you've read by the same author

Drafting

Create a Strong Beginning Authors are likely to get hundreds—even thousands—of letters from readers. As a result, it's important that the first sentence of your letter grabs the author's interest and curiosity. Don't start by simply giving your name or asking a general question such as, "How are you?" Instead, try one of these approaches:

> ### Approaches to Beginning a Letter
> ▶ Start with a strong statement about how much you liked the work.
> ▶ Start by describing the lasting impact the work has had on you.
> ▶ Immediately connect the work to an important personal experience.
> ▶ Use a humorous opening to grab the author's interest.

 Writer's Solution

For additional instruction and practice, use the **Language Lab CD-ROM** lesson on Fragments and Run-on Sentences and the Recognizing Run-ons and Correcting Run-ons pages in the *Writer's Solution Grammar Practice Book* (pp. 64–65).

Avoiding Misplaced Modifiers
Answers
Suggested responses:
1. The story, which made me laugh out loud, is based on the author's personal experiences.
2. On my computer, I wrote a story with a surprise ending.
3. I watched the hawk soaring gracefully above the treetops as it disappeared from view.

Writer's Solution

For additional instruction and practice, use the **Language Lab CD-ROM** lesson on Problems with Modifiers and the Misplaced Modifiers page (p. 66) in the *Writer's Solution Grammar Practice Book.*

Use an appropriate level of formality and the appropriate format Remember that you're writing a letter to an established author. Avoid using slang and jargon that you might use in a letter to one of your friends. In addition, be sure to follow appropriate letter format.

Offer Your Main Impression Don't make the author wonder whether or not you liked his or her work. State your feelings clearly and directly.

Revising

Strengthen Your Main Impression Revise your letter, looking for places where you can strengthen your main impression by replacing a vague adjective with a more specific one or by adding details.

Add Background About Yourself A letter to an author is an excellent way for an author to get to know readers. Add details about your interests and experiences that in some way relate to the work.

REVISION MODEL

Dear Mr. Cosby:

① *I've always enjoyed watching your program on television, but*
∧I never knew you were a talented writer until I read your

essay "Go Deep to the Sewer." I could relate to the characters
② *because my friends and I used to play football in a parking lot when*
  I was younger.
in the essay.∧I thought your descriptions of the rules of the

                                              hilarious
games you played were ③∧funny. . . .

① *The writer strengthens the opening sentence.*
② *The writer clarifies this statement by adding personal background.*
③ *The writer replaces "funny" with a more precise adjective.*

Publishing

Send Your Letter The best way for your letter to reach the author is for you to send it to the author's publisher or agent. You can find information and addresses in the acknowledgements section of this book.

Use E-Mail Instead of sending your letter through the mail, you may want to use e-mail. Browse the Internet to see whether there is a Web site through which you can reach the author. If not, direct your e-mail to the publisher or agent.

APPLYING LANGUAGE SKILLS: Avoiding Misplaced Modifiers

A **misplaced modifier** modifies the wrong word in a sentence.

Incorrect:
At age ten, you were my favorite author.

Correct:
You were my favorite author when I was ten.

Practice On your paper, rewrite each sentence to eliminate a misplaced modifier.

1. The story is based on the author's personal experiences, which made me laugh out loud.
2. I wrote a story on a computer with a surprise ending.
3. Soaring gracefully above the treetops, I watched the hawk disappear from view.

Writing Application Check your letter carefully for misplaced modifiers. If you find any, revise your sentences.

Writer's Solution Connection Language Lab

For additional instruction and practice, complete the lesson on Misplaced Modifiers.

Revising

You may want to have students work with peer reviewers to revise their letters. Have peer reviewers list vague adjectives in their partners' letters. Then the two partners can work together to come up with more vivid adjectives or more details to add in order to strengthen the main impression of their letters.

Writer's Solution

Writing Lab CD-ROM
The Language Variety Checker in the Revision section of the tutorial on Response to Literature highlights words used four or more times. Students can use it to revise their drafts to use fewer repeated words.

Publishing

Encourage students to mail their letters. Assure them that most letters mailed to the publisher of an author's books and marked with the author's name are actually delivered to the author, and that many authors do read and respond to letters from readers.

Reinforce and Extend

Review the Writing Guidelines
After students have completed their letters, review main skills for writing a letter to an author (see Literary Skills Focus, p. 339). Suggest students check their own letters to make sure they have used each skill.

Connect to Literature Unit 7 ("Nonfiction") includes an example of a response to literature: Steve Gietschier's book review of *In These Girls, Hope Is a Muscle*. Unit 7 ("Visions of the Future") contains an essay in the form of a formal letter to a stranger: Bryan Wooley's "To the Residents of A.D. 2029."

✓ ASSESSMENT		4	3	2	1
PORTFOLIO ASSESSMENT Use the rubric on Response to Literature in **Alternative Assessment** (p. 103) to assess students' writing. Add these criteria to customize the rubric to this assignment.	**Strong Introduction**	The writer uses lively language and a fresh, original approach to grab the author's interest.	The opening paragraph is well written and uses lively language, but the approach is not original.	The writer uses lively language, but the approach is not original and includes grammatical errors.	The language is dull, and/or the opening sentences contain several errors.
	Main Impression	The writer states his or her main impression clearly and gives reasons and examples to back up this statement.	The writer clearly states his or her main impression but doesn't back it up well.	The writer's main impression of the author's work is unclear.	The writer neglects to state his or her main impression of the author's work.

Most students have probably read a novel or other longer work of literature. Discuss with the class the differences between reading a longer work and reading a shorter one, such as a short story or poem. Students should note that, in a longer work of literature, the author creates a "world" in which the reader can "live," or become absorbed, for the time it takes to read the work—even when the reader is not actively reading.

Customize for
Logical/Mathematical Learners

These students may have more success reading a novel or other extended work of literature if they keep a chart on which they indicate their goals and progress; briefly summarize the changes that occur in character, plot, and setting during each reading session; and note page numbers of passages they particularly enjoyed and to which they would like to return.

Apply the Strategy

Have students examine the chapter listings for the first half of the novel *Lord of the Flies*. Point out that a chapter listing provides information about chapter titles and the length of chapters. This information is useful in looking back at what has already been read and in planning how to read the remainder of the book. Invite students to make predictions based on the chapter headings and write them down so they can check, as they read, whether their predictions were accurate or whether a character or the plot changed in an unexpected way.

Reading Novels and Other Extended Works

Real-World Reading Skills Workshop

Strategies for Success

This book is filled with brief literary works—short stories, articles, essays, poems. Most of the selections can be read in one sitting. A novel, a full-length play, or an in-depth work of nonfiction, on the other hand, is more likely to be read over an extended period of time. In addition, extended works are likely to involve many more characters, settings, and events than shorter works do. As a result, you should approach reading longer works somewhat differently from shorter works.

Plan Your Reading An extended work may take several days or even weeks to complete. Before you start, plan your times for reading. Set goals for how much you want to read at each sitting. Try to read every day if possible. Don't let too much time elapse between readings, or you may forget important details that you read earlier.

Notice Changes That Occur In a brief work of literature, there is usually not enough time for major changes to take place. In a longer work, on the other hand, many things may change as time goes on. As you read, ask yourself questions such as: *How much time passes from one chapter to the next? What new settings are introduced? How do the main characters change by the end of the work?*

Appreciate Details A short-story writer or a poet does not have much time or space for elaborate detail. A novelist or a biographer does, however. As you read, take time to enjoy descriptive passages about a setting or character. Do not "race over" those parts in order to get to the plot.

Apply the Strategy

Use the chapter listings for the first half of the novel *Lord of the Flies* to answer these questions.

1. Approximately how many pages per day will you have to read in order to complete the first five chapters of *Lord of the Flies* in three days?
2. Which two chapters might you plan to read on the same day?
3. What is the setting of the book? How can you tell?

✔ *Here are several situations in which you may apply the skills for reading a novel:*
▶ *Reading a novel for a school assignment*
▶ *Reading a novel for summer pleasure*
▶ *Reading a nonfiction book while working on a paper*

Answers
1. Because Chapter 1 begins on page 7 and Chapter 6 begins on page 95, there are eighty-eight pages in the first five chapters (95−7=88). This means that you would have to read approximately thirty pages a day to complete the first five chapters in three days (88 ÷ 3=29.3).
2. Chapters 2 and 3 are short—twelve pages and ten pages, respectively—so you might plan to read them on the same day. Alternatively, Chapters 3 (ten pages) and 4 (eighteen pages) together would complete a day's quota of pages.
3. Students may say that the setting is a tropical island, as indicated by chapter titles that refer to a shell and huts on a beach.

PART 2 Out of the Ordinary

Spotted Dogs on Tree, © Dave Cutler, Stock Illustration Source, Inc.

Outlandish characters and bizarre situations provide the humor in this section. "Macavity: The Mystery Cat," "Problems With Hurricanes," and "Jabberwocky" are three poems that will amuse students with flamboyant characters and their out of the ordinary advantures. "Talk" is a humorous folk tale from Africa in which animals and inanimate objects suddenly have a lot to say. The section ends with "One Ordinary Day with Peanuts," a chillingly funny tale in which a man is revealed to be not at all what he seems.

Customize for
Varying Student Needs

When assigning the selections in this section to your students, keep in mind the following factors:

"Macavity: The Mystery Cat"
• Amusing narrative poem
• Connection to long-running Broadway play

"Problems with Hurricanes"
• Short, accessible poem

"Jabberwocky"
• Contains invented words that may present a challenge to both less proficient readers and English Language Learners

"Talk"
• Accessible folk tale from Africa
• Students will find story amusing

"One Ordinary Day with Peanuts"
• Less proficient readers and English Language Learners may need help understanding surprise ending.

♪ Humanities: Art

Spotted Dogs on Tree by Dave Cutler.
   One type of humor involves taking things out of their normal context (for example, strapping birds onto someone's body to help him fly or using a bone and fishing pole to get a dog to fly). In this artwork, a tree has spotted dogs at the ends of its branches, rather than the leaves one would expect. Encourage students to notice that the dogs appear to be growing from the ends of the branches like leaves, rather than perching on the branches like animals. Point out the fact that the dogs on the right side of the tree have triangular blue spots and the ones on the left side have round red spots, while the larger animal on the ground has red and blue spots.

   Help students link the art to the theme of Part 2 ("Out of the Ordinary") by answering the following questions:
1. How many "out-of-the-ordinary" things can you find in this picture? *Out-of-the-ordinary things include the fact that dogs are in the tree, that the dogs appear to dan-* *gle or grow from the branches rather than sit on them, and that half the dogs have red circular spots and the other half have blue triangular spots, while the one dog on the ground has both kinds of spots.*
2. What idea is the artist expressing by making each of the dogs in the tree look a little different from the rest? *The artist may be expressing the idea that recognizing that something is out of the ordinary doesn't mean that you've said all you can say about it.*

343

One-Minute Insight "Problems With Hurricanes" is comical when it warns the reader to beware of flying fruit, but the poet may be speaking symbolically when he says that the greatest danger is from "the fury of the wind," but "mangoes/And all such beautiful/sweet things."

◆ **Build Grammar Skills**

❶ Parts of Speech Determined by Function Ask: How can you tell *campesino* is a noun. *It is preceded by the article "A" and followed by the verb "looked."*

◆ **Reading Strategy**

❷ Contrast the Serious and the Ridiculous Ask students to identify the serious and ridiculous elements in these lines. *Lines 3-5 sound serious; then the reader is surprised by the list of fruits. The visual image of fruits "flying into town like projectiles" is absurd.*

Looking at Literature Videodisc To provide background on hurricanes and motivate students to read the poem, play Chapter 6 of the videodisc. This segment focuses on the destruction caused by Hurricane Andrew in 1992. Discuss why people are both fascinated with and fearful of hurricanes.

Chapter 6

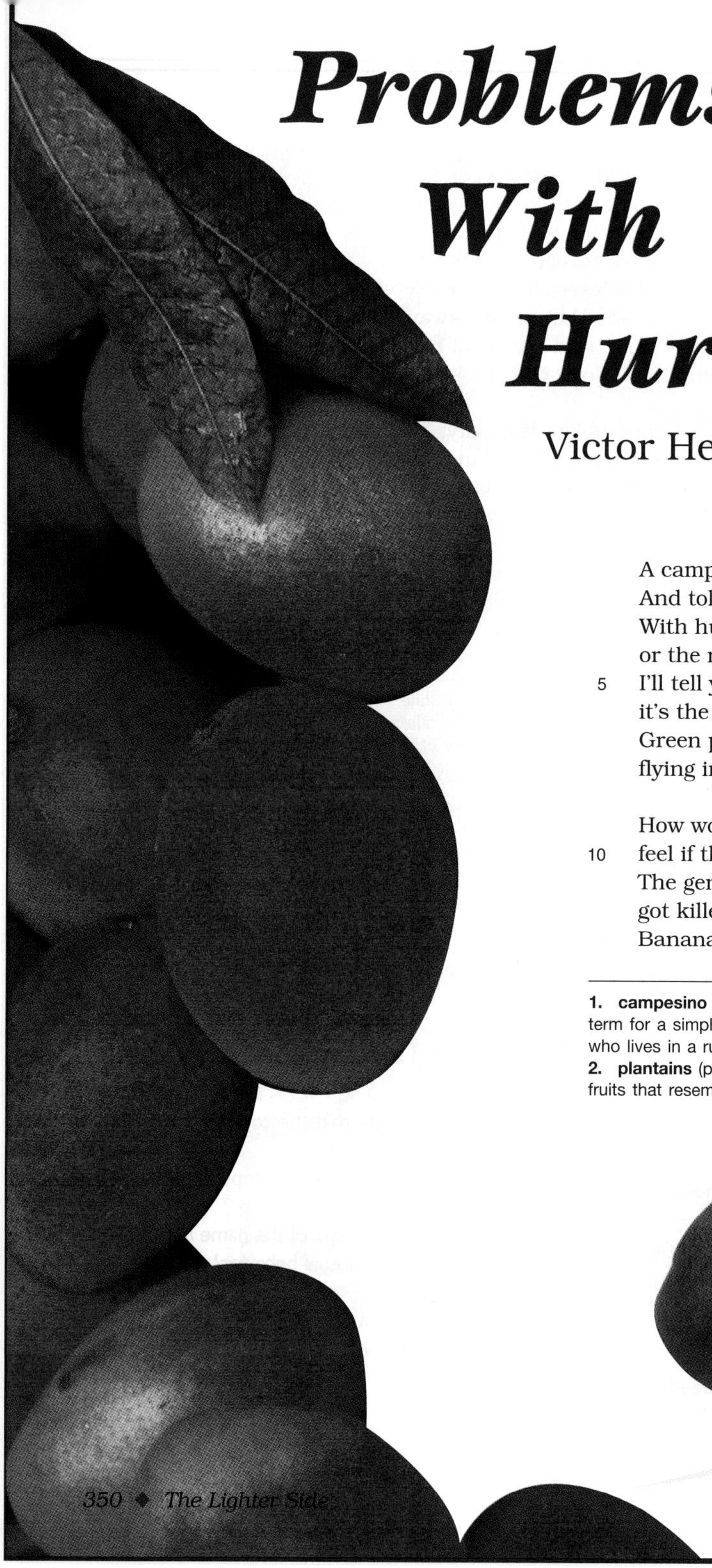

Problems With Hurricanes

Victor Hernández Cruz

A campesino[1] looked at the air ❶
And told me:
With hurricanes it's not the wind
or the noise or the water.
5 I'll tell you he said: ❷
it's the mangoes, avocados
Green plantains[2] and bananas
flying into town like <u>projectiles</u>.

How would your family
10 feel if they had to tell   ❸
The generations that you
got killed by a flying
Banana.

---

1. **campesino** (käm´ pe sē nô) *n.*: Spanish term for a simple farmer or another person who lives in a rural area.
2. **plantains** (plan´ tins) *n.*: Starchy tropical fruits that resemble bananas.

350 ◆ *The Lighter Side*

Speaking and Listening Mini-Lesson

Oral Report
This mini-lesson supports the Speaking and Listening activity on page 355.

Introduce the Concept Explain that the more one knows about a topic, the more he or she can enjoy a piece of literature related to it. Sharing information through an oral report, a formal verbal presentation of information and often conclusions drawn from that information, benefits their classmates as well as themselves.

Develop Background Discuss the skills students must use in developing a report: note-taking, outlining, and fact-checking are among the most important. If students write their reports, revising will be critical.

Apply the Information Have students research their topics, organize their materials, and prepare their reports. Encourage them to practice aloud. Urge students to learn their material well enough so that they can speak comfortably.

Assess the Outcome Evaluate each report on the breadth of factual information presented and on the logical organization of the information. Have students comment on how the information they learned from their own and others' reports enriched their appreciation of the poems. Use the following pages from *Alternative Assessment:* Self-Assessment: Speech, p. 110; Peer Assessment: Speaker/Speech, p. 111.

Death by drowning has honor
15 If the wind picked you up
and slammed you
Against a mountain boulder **❹**
This would not carry shame
But
20 to suffer a mango smashing
Your skull
or a plantain hitting your **❺**
Temple at 70 miles per hour
is the ultimate disgrace.

25 The campesino takes off his hat—
As a sign of respect
toward the fury of the wind **❻**
And says:
Don't worry about the noise
30 Don't worry about the water
Don't worry about the wind—
If you are going out
beware of mangoes **❼**
And all such beautiful **❽**
35 sweet things.

◆ **Build Vocabulary**

projectiles (prə jek´ tilz) *n.*: Objects that are
hurled through the air

Problems With Hurricanes ◆ 351

Customize for
Less Proficient Readers
These students might find "Problems With
Hurricanes" easier to read and comprehend if
it were punctuated in a more traditional way
and if quotation marks were used to set off the
words spoken by the campesino. Give them
copies of the poem on which they can insert
quotation marks and punctuation. You might
pair them with more advanced students for
this activity.

◆ **Critical Thinking**

❸ Analyze Ask students to
describe the tone of these lines and
give reasons for their choices.
*Students may say the tone is light,
humorous, joking, facetious, and so on.
Reasons might include: The image of a
flying banana is funny; the question is
so ridiculous, the speaker cannot be serious.*

◆ **Critical Thinking**

❹ Analyze Have students decide if
they agree that the deaths described
in these lines are honorable and give
reasons for their opinions. *Students
may say these deaths are honorable
because they are caused by powerful
forces of nature.*

◆ **Critical Thinking**

❺ Analyze Have students explain
why being killed by a mango or a
plantain is disgraceful. *A piece of fruit
is not usually considered forceful or dangerous—certainly not a lethal weapon.*

◆ **Reading Strategy**

**❻ Contrast the Serious and the
Ridiculous** Ask students: When
someone says, "I take off my hat to
you," what is the person's meaning?
Why does the campesino take off his
hat? What is ridiculous about the gesture? *Taking off one's hat is a sign of
respect. The campesino takes off his hat
because he doesn't want to insult the
wind with what he says. The gesture is
ridiculous because the wind can't understand it.*

◆ **Literary Focus**

❼ Humorous Diction Ask students: What makes "beware of mangoes" a humorous choice of words?
*The phrase "beware of _____" usually
has a serious danger as its third word;
the choice of mangoes seems absurd.*

◆ **Reading Strategy**

**❽ Contrast the Serious and the
Ridiculous** What is ridiculous about
the idea that we should beware of
beautiful sweet things? *These things
are not usually dangerous.* What is serious about it? *There can be hidden dangers in love or in beautiful objects.*

Answers

◆ Reading Strategy

1. In "Jabberwocky" what is most serious is the battle between the hero and the monster, while what is most ridiculous is the invented language. In "Macavity: The Mysterious Cat," what is most serious is the language and details about crime and crimefighters, while what is most ridiculous is the application of this language to a cat. In "Problems With Hurricanes" what is most serious is the death and destruction that hurricanes cause, while what is most ridiculous is the deaths by flying tropical fruit.

2. Students who find "Jabberwocky" the most serious may cite as support the love of language reflected in the poem. Students who find "Macavity" the most serious may cite its cat lovers' understanding of cats. Students who cite "Problems With Hurricanes" may cite the serious messages that the last seven lines may convey.

3. In "Macavity: The Mystery Cat" students may cite the contrast between the actions of the cat and those of a human; in "Problems With Hurricanes" students would likely cite the dangers posed by flying fruit; in "Jabberwocky" the humor arises from the serious events told in nonsense language.

◆ Literary Focus

1. Words and phrases include "the Hidden [Paw]," "master criminal," "defy the Law," "bafflement of Scotland Yard," "scene of crime," "fiend," "monster of depravity," "footprints," "file of Scotland Yard's," "looted," "jewel-case is rifled," "Foreign Office," "Treaty's gone astray," "deceitfulness," "alibi," "agents," and "the Napoleon of Crime." The words and phrases contribute to humor because they are ridiculous when applied to a cat.

2. Most students are likely to feel that in "Jabberwocky" the humor comes primarily from diction; in "Problems With Hurricanes" it comes primarily from situation; and in "Macavity" it comes from a nearly equal combination of both.

Guide for Responding (continued)

◆ Reading Strategy

CONTRAST THE SERIOUS AND THE RIDICULOUS

In all three poems, a combination of **serious** and **ridiculous** details are used to create humor.

1. Sum up what is most serious and most ridiculous in each of the three poems.
2. Of the three, which poem do you think is the most serious? Why?
3. Using details from one or more of the poems as examples, explain why combining serious and ridiculous details creates humor.

◆ Literary Focus

HUMOROUS DICTION

In all three poems, **diction**, or word choice, helps achieve humor. In "Jabberwocky," readers delight in the silly sounds of invented words like *galumphing*. In "Macavity," there is a humorous contrast between the formal diction of the speaker and the actual identity of Macavity and the nature of his activities. In "Problems With Hurricanes," there are humorous contrasts between serious phrases like "ultimate disgrace" and unexpected phrases like "flying banana."

1. Find at least three words and phrases in "Macavity" that seem typical of mystery or crime fiction. How do these contribute to the humor?
2. Does diction play an equally strong role in creating the humor in all three poems? Explain.

Beyond Literature

Science Connection

Hurricanes The campesino in "The Problem With Hurricanes" says "Don't worry about the water,/Don't worry about the wind," but that is exactly what you should worry about when a hurricane approaches. The winds of a hurricane swirl at 75 miles per hour or more. As a hurricane approaches land, strong winds and heavy rains form huge ocean waves called storm surges that can cause severe flooding. Most hurricane activity occurs along the Gulf of Mexico and the Atlantic coast. What kinds of storms do you get in your area?

◆ Build Vocabulary

USING PORTMANTEAU WORDS

Chortled, combining *chuckle* and *snort*, is still widely used today. It is one of the best known **portmanteau words**—invented words formed by blending two words into one—used in "Jabberwocky."

1. Complete the origins of these portmanteau words coined for "Jabberwocky":
   a. *mimsy* = miserable + ?
   b. *burbled* = gurgled + ?
2. Use a dictionary, if necessary, to explain the origins of these portmanteau words: (a) smog, (b) brunch, (c) motel.

USING THE WORD BANK

In your notebook, complete each sentence with a word from the Word Bank.

1. The magician seemed to perform ___?___, for it looked like her assistant was floating in air.
2. Bullets and darts are types of ___?___.
3. Lions and tigers are part of the ___?___ family.
4. The poem was written in invented language, to the ___?___ of many readers.
5. Store the food in the ___?___.
6. The sinner had engaged in many forms of ___?___.
7. Jack, ___?___ with glee and mischief as he hid in the corner, observed the outcome of his practical joke.
8. Cary Grant was an actor of great sophistication and ___?___.

◆ Build Grammar Skills

PART OF SPEECH FROM FUNCTION

Though you cannot be sure of the meanings of the invented words in "Jabberwocky," you can usually figure out the part of speech of each word from its function.

Practice In your notebook, indicate the part of speech of each numbered word below. Also, explain why you think the word is that part of speech.

And as in (1) *uffish* though he stood,
The (2) *Jabberwock*, with eyes of flame,
Came (3) *whiffling* through the (4) *tulgey* wood,
And (5) *burbled* as it came!

◆ Build Vocabulary

Portmanteau Words

1. (a) flimsy; (b) bubbled
2. (a) smog = smoke + fog
   (b) brunch = breakfast + lunch
   (c) motel = motor(car) + hotel

Using the Word Bank

1. levitation; 2. projectiles;
3. feline; 4. bafflement;
5. larder; 6. depravity;
7. chortling; 8. suavity

◆ Build Grammar Skills

1. *uffish*: adjective; modifies *thought* and ends in *-ish*, a common adjective ending
2. *Jabberwock*: noun; names something after *the* and begins with capital letter, indicating a proper noun
3. *whiffling*: verb (verbal); shows action and ends in *-ing*, common verb ending
4. *tulgey*: adjective; modifies *wood*

5. *burbled*: verb; shows action and ends in *-ed*, a common verb ending

 **Writer's Solution**

For additional instruction and practice, use the lesson in the **Language Lab CD-ROM** on the Eight Parts of Speech and the practice page (p. 25) on Reviewing Parts of Speech in the *Writer's Solution Grammar Practice Book*.

Build Your Portfolio

 Idea Bank

Writing

1. Wanted Poster Create a wanted poster for Macavity, in which you list his crimes and describe his appearance and habits. **[Art Link]**

2. News Report Write a newspaper article reporting the events of any one of the poems. If you choose "Jabberwocky," clarify unfamiliar words.

3. Rewrite for Another Setting Rewrite "Jabberwocky" or "Macavity" with a more contemporary American setting or "Problems With Hurricanes" with a new setting.

Speaking and Listening

4. Choral Reading Working in a small group, prepare a choral reading of one of the poems. You might alternate reading stanzas or certain groups of lines, and you might read certain lines or parts as a group. **[Performing Arts Link]**

5. Oral Report Using science books or other factual sources, research the properties of looking-glasses, or mirrors; the behavior of cats; or the causes and effects of hurricanes. Present your findings in an oral report. **[Science Link]**

Projects

6. Glossary Working with a classmate, create an alphabetical glossary that defines and illustrates the use of each invented word in "Jabberwocky."

7. Farm Report Find out more about weather conditions and foods grown in Puerto Rico. Present your findings in a report that might appear in a farmers' magazine. Try to include information maps, charts, photographs, and other visuals. **[Social Studies Link; Science Link]**

 Writing Mini-Lesson

Fantastic Poem

All three poems are unusual, to say the least. In fact, they might qualify as **fantasy**—writing that knowingly breaks the rules of reality. Write your own out-of-this-world poem about a fantastic creature or event.

Writing Skills Focus: Precise Details

When you write about something unfamiliar to readers, you need to provide **precise details** so that your readers understand what you're talking about. Look at this example:

Vague: It had a big bump on its face.

More Precise: It had a bulbous pimple on its snout.

Most Precise: It had a bulbous purple pimple on a green snout as long as an alligator's.

Include precise details in your poem to help readers picture what you're describing.

Prewriting List precise details that you might use to describe the out-of-this-world creature or event. Choose details that you think will help you achieve an overall mood—humorous, eerie, or the like. If you plan to write a poem with a rhyme scheme, compile a list of rhyming words.

Drafting Write either a free-verse poem—one without regular rhythm or rhyme scheme—or one with a regular rhythm and rhyme scheme. Create an image of the creature, using precise details that contribute to your overall mood.

Revising Read your poem aloud to be sure you have achieved your desired effect. Check to see whether you have used precise details that convey the appearance or character of the out-of-this-world creature or the fantastic nature of the event.

Macavity: The Mystery Cat/Problems With Hurricanes/Jabberwocky ◆ 355

 Idea Bank

Customizing for
Performance Levels
Following are suggestions for matching the Idea Bank topics with your students' performance levels:
Less Advanced Students: 1, 4
Average Students: 2, 5, 6
More Advanced Students: 3, 7

Customizing for
Learning Modalities
Following are suggestions for matching Idea Bank topics with your students' learning modalities:
Interpersonal: 4
Auditory: 4, 5
Visual/Spatial: 6

 Writing Mini-Lesson

Refer students to the Writing Handbook, page 962, for instruction on the writing process, and page 965 for further information on creative writing. Have students use the Cluster Organizer in **Writing and Language Transparencies,** p. 80, to organize their precise details.

 Writer's Solution

Writers at Work Videodisc
Have students view the videodisc segment on Creative Writing (Ch. 6) featuring Grant Moran to see how he uses his imagination in his work. Have students discuss how they can tap their imaginations to write a fantastic poem.

Play frames 12243 to 21791

Writing Lab CD-ROM
Have students complete the Tutorial on Creative Writing. Follow these steps:
1. Use the Video Tips on Gathering Details.
2. Use the Interactive Self-Evaluation Checklist for Poetry to aid revision.

Sourcebook
Have students use Chapter 6, Creative Writing (pp. 162–193), for additional support. The chapter includes indepth instruction on Gathering Details (p. 179).

Guide for Reading

1. To read, comprehend, and interpret a story
2. To relate a story to personal experience
3. To recognize illogical situations
4. To identify the characteristics of a humorous folk tale
5. To build vocabulary in context and learn about the prefix *re-*
6. To identify adverb clauses
7. To write a book-jacket blurb, maintaining a clear and consistent purpose
8. To respond to the story through writing, speaking and listening, and projects

SKILLS INSTRUCTION

Vocabulary:
Prefixes: *re-*

Grammar:
Adverb Clauses

Reading Strategy:
Recognize Illogical Situations

Literary Focus:
Humorous Folk Tale

Writing: Clear and Consistent Purpose

Speaking and Listening:
Dramatic Reading (teacher edition)

PORTFOLIO OPPORTUNITIES

Writing: Sequel; News Report; Humorous Folk Tale

Writing Mini-Lesson: Book-Jacket Blurb

Speaking and Listening: Dramatic Reading; Interview

Projects: Storyboard; Multimedia Report

More About the Author
In 1967, Harold Courlander published his novel *The African,* a highly respected work that developed a wide readership. The book clearly illustrates Courlander's in-depth knowledge of the African culture.

Harold Courlander (1908–)

Harold Courlander has had a long, distinguished career as a builder of bridges between different cultures. "I have always had a special interest in using fiction and nonfiction narration to bridge communications between other cultures and our own," he has said.

Courlander has studied and written about numerous cultures—African, West Indian, Native American, and African American. His long list of publications includes a number of folk-tale collections as well as books on the literature and music of other cultures. The settings for his novels range from eighteenth-century Africa to rural Mississippi to the Hopi people before the arrival of the Europeans. In addition, Courlander has compiled and edited several albums of folk music from recordings he made in his research in the field. Regarding folk tales, Courlander has said, "Folk tales as such have no special meaning for me unless they convey human values, philosophical outlook, cultural heritage . . . ."

George Herzog (1901–1984)

Born in Budapest, Hungary, George Herzog pioneered in the field of ethnomusicology, which is the study of music for its cultural values and social significance. During his long career, Herzog founded programs of ethnomusicological studies at various American universities. He also taught courses in linguistics and cultural anthropology—the study of the customs of different ethnic groups—and introduced American students to the study of folk music as an academic discipline. Herzog published numerous books on folk music, including the music of Native American and West African cultures.

◆ Build Vocabulary

PREFIXES: *re-*

In this story, the word *refrain* uses the prefix *re-*, which means "back" or "again." *Refrain* puts the prefix *re-* together with the root *-frain-*, based on the Latin word *frenere*, which means "to curb." So the word *refrain* means "to hold oneself back."

You already know many words that start with the prefix *re-*: *return, renew, reflect, redo, rethink, rewrite, review,* and *revise*, to name just a few. See if you can add more words to this list. Keep your eyes open; there is one more *re-* word in the story.

ford
refrain
scowling

WORD BANK
As you read "Talk," you will encounter the words on this list. Each word is defined on the page where it first appears. Preview the list before you read.

◆ Build Grammar Skills

ADVERB CLAUSES

"Talk" tells an action-packed story at a galloping pace, due in part to the use of adverb clauses to help describe what is going on. An **adverb clause** is a subordinate clause that modifies a verb, an adjective, or an adverb in another clause. Adverb clauses clarify actions in other clauses by telling *where, when, why, how, to what extent,* or *under what conditions* the actions occur. Adverb clauses are introduced by conjunctions, such as *when, where, because, since, if, as,* and *why.* For example:

The man *became* angry, *because his dog had never talked before,* . . .

In this example, *because* introduces an adverb clause that explains why the man became angry.

Prentice Hall Literature Program Resources

REINFORCE / RETEACH / EXTEND

Selection Support Pages
Build Vocabulary: Prefixes: *re-*, p. 109
Build Grammar Skills: Adverb Clauses, p. 110
Reading Strategy: Recognize Illogical Situations, p. 111
Literary Focus: Humorous Folk Tale, p. 112

Strategies for Diverse Student Needs, p. 27

Beyond Literature
Cross-Curricular Connection: Social Studies, p. 27

Formal Assessment Selection Test, pp. 91–93, Assessment Resources Software

Alternative Assessment, p. 27

Writing and Language Transparencies
Sunburst Organizer, p. 64

Resource Pro CD-ROM
"Talk"—includes all resource material and customizable lesson plan

Listening to Literature Audiocassettes
"Talk"

Talk

◆ Literature and Your Life

CONNECT YOUR EXPERIENCE

Your breakfast muffin somersaults out of your hands and lands jam-side-down on the floor. Then your jacket wrestles with you and wins. They may be called "inanimate objects," but too often they seem to have mischievous little minds of their own. You'd love to yell at them, but you'd feel silly talking to things that can't talk back. "Talk" is an African folk tale that whimsically nudges this idea a step further into "What if?" territory.

THEMATIC FOCUS: OUT OF THE ORDINARY

This funny folk tale makes light of human beings' sense of superiority to the rest of the things on this planet. How would you react if you discovered that your possessions had minds of their own?

◆ Background for Understanding

GEOGRAPHY

"Talk" is set on the west coast of Africa, in the country now known as the Republic of Ghana, whose capital is Accra. Many of the story's details reflect the everyday reality of life there. The first character in the story is a "country man" (more than 65 percent of the population in Ghana is rural) who sets out to dig yams, one of the staples of the diet of rural Ghanaians. This country man owns a cow. Among the other characters in the story are a fisherman and a weaver, common occupations in Ghana, a country known for its beautiful hand-woven cloths. A river figures prominently in "Talk"—more than half of Ghana's landmass is occupied by the Volta River basin, which is filled with streams, marshes, and lagoons.

◆ Literary Focus

HUMOROUS FOLK TALE

A **folk tale** is an anonymous story passed down by word of mouth from one generation to the next. Whether they are heroic or humorous, folk tales express the beliefs and values of the cultures that create them. Folk tales typically present simple characters and far-fetched situations. Meant to entertain and to instruct, such stories often use humor or exaggeration to appeal to their audiences.

◆ Reading Strategy

RECOGNIZE ILLOGICAL SITUATIONS

A cartoon coyote races over a cliff edge and treads thin air for a few seconds before the gravity of his situation sinks in. You know that this could not possibly happen in real life. You automatically check each new event you see or hear against your experience of life and your understanding of the laws of nature. This checking-out process enables you to **recognize illogical situations** when you see them—like the coyote running on empty air or the first bit of chat in "Talk."

Illogical situations can make a work of fantasy more fantastic and entertaining. On the other hand, illogical situations can distract you from a story that otherwise seems to be realistic. Keep track of the illogical situations you come across in "Talk" by jotting down what happens each time; why it is illogical; and what, if anything, each illogical situation adds to the story.

Situation	Why Illogical	Adds What to Story?

Interest Grabber Some of the elements that make this folk tale humorous are the same ones that make us laugh at jokes—especially those of the type called "shaggy dog" stories. Ask students if they've heard any good jokes lately. Invite them to share a few appropriate jokes. Then discuss what makes people laugh at jokes.

Elicit from students that outlandish situations, repetition of silly acts or words, ironic dialogue, "double takes," and one character's false sense of superiority over another all contribute to the humor of jokes. Tell students to watch for these same elements as they read "Talk."

Customize for
Less Proficient Readers
Since this story contains a great deal of repetition, less proficient readers may feel comfortable reading parts aloud. Pair a less proficient reader with a more fluent reader. Have the less proficient reader read the parts of the story that repeat the telling of what the objects and animals say while the more fluent reader reads the rest of the tale.

Customize for
More Advanced Students
One of the characteristics that makes this tale humorous is its fast pace. Have these students keep track of words (e.g., *breathlessly*) and phrases (e.g., *chasing a gazelle*) that communicate the impression of speed.

Customize for
English Language Learners
This story begins with a farmer digging up a yam. Be sure these students know what a yam is and why it must be dug up. In the U.S., the word *yam* often refers to a sweet potato. You might bring in a yam to show to the students.

Customize for
Logical / Mathematical Learners
To keep track of the action, these students might make a flow chart—a diagram showing the steps in a sequence. A flow chart will help them record the order and details of character interactions.

Preparing for Standardized Tests

Reading and Vocabulary Being able to figure out unfamiliar words gives students an advantage when taking standardized tests that feature comprehension or vocabulary items. One of the most common and useful prefixes for students to know is *re-*. Students might be asked to identify a word that is most nearly the *opposite* as, in the following:

   replenish (a) add (b) furnish
   (c) deplete (d) remove *(c) deplete*

The Build Vocabulary lesson focuses on learning word meaning through the use of the prefix *re-*. For additional practice, use the Build Vocabulary

page in *Selection Support,* p. 109.

Grammar and Language Some standardized tests ask students to differentiate between complete sentences and fragments. Students sometimes mistakenly assume that adverb clauses, particularly those that begin with *because,* are complete sentences because they contain a subject and verb. The Build Grammar Skills lesson focuses on adverb clauses and their correct use in a sentence. For additional practice, use the Build Grammar Skills page on Adverb Clauses, p. 110, in *Selection Support.*

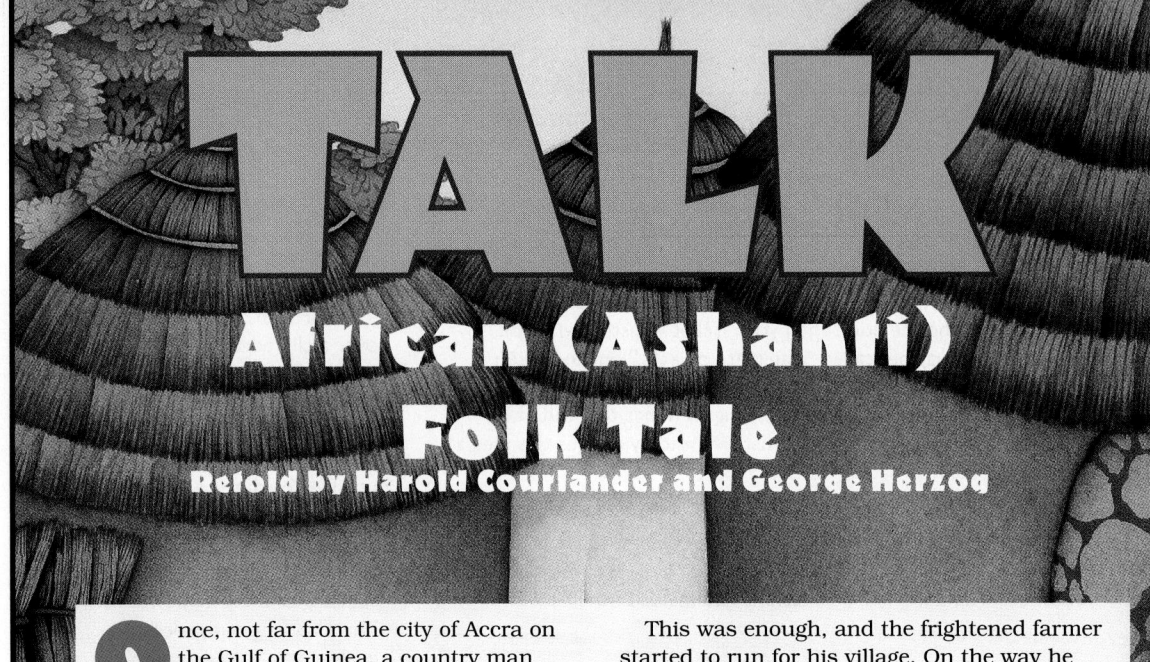

TALK
African (Ashanti) Folk Tale
Retold by Harold Courlander and George Herzog

To enjoy this folk tale, the reader must temporarily accept the illogical and humorous premise that objects and animals can speak. The real humor stems from everyone's enjoyment of a good put-down—a chance to make fun of someone who thinks herself or himself superior to others. In the folk tale, beginning with the farmer who digs up the talking yam, each character makes fun of the previous one's fear, then is frightened himself. Perhaps readers love stories like this because they let us know that the "chiefs" among us are no better than everyone else.

◆ **Critical Thinking**

❶ **Interpret** Ask students to read the yam's lines in the tone they think the yam would use. Of what human failing is the yam accusing the farmer? *The yam is annoyed because the farmer was too lazy to weed his garden, but now wants the harvest.*

◆ **Reading Strategy**

❷ **Recognize Illogical Situations** Ask students to identify the illogical situation. *It is that inanimate objects (and animals) can talk.*

◆ **Literary Focus**

❸ **Humorous Folk Tale** Ask students why it is funny that the farmer asks the cow, "Did you say something?" What does the question imply about the farmer? *It is funny because even though the farmer can't imagine that a yam can talk, he assumes that the cow can talk. This implies that the farmer is stupid.*

◆ **Build Grammar Skills**

❹ **Adverb Clauses** Ask students to find the adverb clause in this sentence. *The adverb clause is "because his dog had never talked before."*

◆ **Literary Focus**

❺ **Humorous Folk Tale** Ask students why it is funny that the farmer puts down the branch gently. *The farmer's action is funny because he is obeying a branch.*

Once, not far from the city of Accra on the Gulf of Guinea, a country man went out to his garden to dig up some yams to take to market. While he was digging, one of the yams said to him, "Well, at last you're here. You never weeded me, but now you come around with your digging stick. Go away and leave me alone!"

The farmer turned around and looked at his cow in amazement. The cow was chewing her cud and looking at him.

"Did you say something?" he asked.

The cow kept on chewing and said nothing, but the man's dog spoke up. "It wasn't the cow who spoke to you," the dog said. "It was the yam. The yam says leave him alone."

The man became angry, because his dog had never talked before, and he didn't like his tone besides. So he took his knife and cut a branch from a palm tree to whip his dog. Just then the palm tree said, "Put that branch down!"

The man was getting very upset about the way things were going, and he started to throw the palm branch away, but the palm branch said, "Man, put me down softly!"

He put the branch down gently on a stone, and the stone said, "Hey, take that thing off me!"

This was enough, and the frightened farmer started to run for his village. On the way he met a fisherman going the other way with a fish trap on his head.

"What's the hurry?" the fisherman asked.

"My yam said, 'Leave me alone!' Then the dog said, 'Listen to what the yam says!' When I went to whip the dog with a palm branch the tree said, 'Put that branch down!' Then the palm branch said, 'Do it softly!' Then the stone said, 'Take that thing off me!'"

"Is that all?" the man with the fish trap asked. "Is that so frightening?"

"Well," the man's fish trap said, "did he take it off the stone?"

"Wah!" the fisherman shouted. He threw the fish trap on the ground and began to run with the farmer, and on the trail they met a weaver with a bundle of cloth on his head.

"Where are you going in such a rush?" he asked them.

"My yam said, 'Leave me alone!'" the farmer said. "The dog said, 'Listen to what the yam says!' The tree said, 'Put that branch down!' The branch said, 'Do it softly!' And the stone said, 'Take that thing off me!'"

"And then," the fisherman continued, "the fish trap said, 'Did he take it off?'"

358 ◆ *The Lighter Side*

Speaking and Listening Mini-Lesson

Dramatic Reading

This mini-lesson supports the Speaking and Listening activity in the Idea Bank on page 361.

Introduce the Concept Point out that a dramatic reading is an expressive oral presentation of a work of literature.

Develop Background As students prepare to do their dramatic reading, encourage them to consider these points:

• Determine how many people will make for an optimum reading; a narrator and at least two other individuals are probably necessary.

• Decide on a tone for each reader. For example, the narrator can be either objective or humorous.

Apply the Information Have each group practice its reading and then perform it for the class.

Assess the Outcome Have students evaluate their own and other groups' dramatic readings by discussing their appropriateness of tone and projected humor. Have students use the Peer Assessment guide for Oral Interpretation, p. 112, in *Alternative Assessment*.

"That's nothing to get excited about," the weaver said. "No reason at all."

"Oh, yes it is," his bundle of cloth said. "If it happened to you you'd run too!"

"Wah!" the weaver shouted. He threw his bundle on the trail and started running with the other men.

They came panting to the <u>ford</u> in the river and found a man bathing. "Are you chasing a gazelle?" he asked them.

The first man said breathlessly, "My yam talked at me, and it said, 'Leave me alone!' And my dog said, 'Listen to your yam!' And when I cut myself a branch the tree said, 'Put that branch down!' And the branch said, 'Do it softly!' And the stone said, 'Take that thing off me!'"

6 The fisherman panted. "And my trap said, 'Did he?'"

The weaver wheezed. "And my bundle of cloth said, 'You'd run too!'"

"Is that why you're running?" the man in the river asked.

"Well, wouldn't you run if you were in their position?" the river said.

The man jumped out of the water and began to run with the others. They ran down the main street of the village to the house of the chief. The chief's servant brought his stool out, and he came and sat on it to listen to their com-
7 plaints. The men began to recite their troubles.

"I went out to my garden to dig yams," the farmer said, waving his arms. "Then everything began to talk! My yam said, 'Leave me alone!' My dog said, 'Pay attention to your yam!' The tree said, 'Put that branch down!' The branch said, 'Do it softly!' And the stone said, 'Take it off me!'"

"And my fish trap said, 'Well, did he take it off?'" the fisherman said.

"And my cloth said, 'You'd run too!'" the weaver said.

"And the river said the same," the bather said hoarsely, his eyes bulging.

The chief listened to them patiently, but he couldn't <u>refrain</u> from <u>scowling</u>. "Now this is really a wild story," he said at last. "You'd better all go back to your work before I punish you for disturbing the peace." **8**

So the men went away, and the chief shook his head and mumbled to himself, "Nonsense like that upsets the community."

"Fantastic, isn't it?" his stool said. "Imagine, a talking yam!" **9**

◆ **Build Vocabulary**

ford (förd) *n.:* Shallow place in a river that can be crossed

refrain (ri frān´) *v.:* To hold back

scowling (skoul´ iŋ): Contracting the eyebrows and frowning to show displeasure

Guide for Responding

◆ *Literature and Your Life*

Reader's Response Which situation in "Talk" struck you as the funniest? Why?

Thematic Focus "Talk" comes to us from western Africa. Does its humor span the gap between two different cultures? Do you think most Americans would find "Talk" funny? Why or why not?

Group Activity As a group, come up with three stories or movies in which objects or animals talk to human beings. (You might think of other folk tales,

fairy tales, or fantasies.) Compare them with what happens in "Talk." Are the objects in other stories meant to be funny? How do people react when the objects start to speak?

☑ **Check Your Comprehension**

1. What happens when the country man goes out to dig up some yams to take to market?
2. What upsets each man who joins the country man?
3. (a) What does the chief say to them? (b) Who gets the last word?

Talk ◆ 359

◆ **Beyond the Selection**

FURTHER READING

Other Works by Harold Courlander
The African

Other Works About Humans' Sense of Superiority
Wish You Were Here, Rita Mae Brown and Sneaky Pie Brown
Catnap, Carole Nelson Douglas
"St. Dragon and the George," Gordon Dickson

INTERNET

To find additional information about African folk tales on the Internet, go to the following site. Please be aware, however, that the site may have changed from the time we published this information.

An extensive bibliography of illustrated tales from Africa, along with a synopsis of each tale, is at **http://www.prairienet.org/infoctr/cpl/ afbktlss.html**

We *strongly recommend* that you preview the site before you send students to it.

◆ **Literary Focus**

6 Humorous Folk Tale Ask students to describe the effect of repetition in the folk tale. How would the story be affected if it began when all the men approach the chief, so that each of their stories is told only once? *Repetition creates humor. The story would not be funny if each of the men's stories was told only once.*

◆ **Build Vocabulary**

7 Prefixes: re- Draw students' attention to the word *recite*. Have them identify the prefix (*re-*) and the base word (*cite*). If necessary, explain the meaning of *cite* (to say or quote). Ask: "How does knowing the meaning of the prefix *re-* help you to know the meaning of *recite*?" *The prefix re- means "back" or "again," so recite means "to say or quote back."*

◆ **Critical Thinking**

8 Make Inferences Ask students: "What is the chief's attitude toward the men? Which two words in this passage help you know this?" *The chief feels superior to the men. The words "patiently" and "scowling" are clues to his superior attitude.*

◆ **Critical Thinking**

9 Evaluate The tale ends with the words of the stool. Ask students to explain whether this is a good place to end the story. *Possible responses: Yes, because the chief is left "holding the bag"; no, because it would be interesting to see how the chief responds to his stool.*

Reinforce and Extend

Answers
◆ *Literature and Your Life*

Reader's Response Students should give reasons for their choices.

Thematic Focus Students might feel that the humor spans the cultural gap and is funny to Americans because of the easily understood situations and character traits.

☑ **Check Your Comprehension**

1. A yam speaks to him.
2. Each man is upset by animals and inanimate objects speaking to him.
3. (a) The chief says that the men's story is wild and that they should go back to work. (b) The chief's stool has the last word.

Critical Thinking

1. (a) The fisherman is calm because he thinks the story is too incredible to have really happened. (b) When the fish trap speaks to him, he realizes that the story is true.
2. Perhaps they feel that they have been taken for granted or even mistreated.
3. Such a report would indicate that the world is undergoing a major fundamental change.
4. The story ridicules people's skepticism and feelings of superiority.
5. Suggested response: The chief should have asked for proof of the story rather than dismissing it as nonsense.
6. Perhaps the chief might ask the stool why it is talking.
7. For each story, students should explain what is repeated and give logical reasons for indicating one repetition as better.

Build Vocabulary

Using the Prefix re-
1. To grow again.
2. To make fresh or sound again.
3. Something that makes the mind or body fresh again.
4. To make fresh again; to revive.

Using the Word Bank
1. b   2. c   3. c

Reading Strategy

1. It is illogical that inanimate objects, plants, and animals talk to each man.
2. Students should support their opinions with logical arguments.
3. The chief's reaction to the men is logical in that it is appropriate for someone who doesn't believe what is being said.

Literary Focus

1. The characters are not developed as well as other characters in this textbook. They are simply identified.
2. The folk tale seems to project an image of a culture that values community and the wisdom of its leader.

Build Grammar Skills

1. While the country man was digging (when)

Guide for Responding *(continued)*

◆ Critical Thinking

INTERPRET
1. (a) Why is the fisherman so calm when the farmer tells his crazy story? (b) Why does he get so upset when his fish trap speaks to him? **[Analyze]**
2. What reason might the objects and animals have for speaking all of a sudden? **[Deduce]**
3. Why would the report of objects and animals speaking upset the whole community? **[Infer]**
4. What aspects of human nature does the story hold up to ridicule? **[Draw Conclusions]**

APPLY
5. What do you think the chief should have said to the men who came rushing in to him? **[Modify]**
6. What might the chief say when his stool talks back to him? **[Hypothesize]**

EXTEND
7. The plot of "Talk" develops by repeating variations on an incident several times. Identify one other story that uses repetition as noticeably as "Talk" does. Which repetition do you like better? **[Literature Link]**

◆ Build Vocabulary

USING THE PREFIX re-
Knowing that the prefix re- means "back" or "again," write definitions for the following words.
1. regenerate   3. recreation
2. renovation   4. refresh

USING THE WORD BANK
On your paper, write the word whose meaning is most nearly *opposite* that of the first word.
1. scowling: (a) frowning, (b) smiling, (c) resting
2. ford: (a) icy canal, (b) shallow underwater spot, (c) deep underwater spot
3. refrain: (a) continue, (b) stop, (c) begin

◆ Reading Strategy

RECOGNIZE ILLOGICAL SITUATIONS
"Talk" builds a series of **illogical situations**. If you made a chart while reading the story, refer to it to answer these questions.
1. What is illogical about what happens to each man in "Talk"?
2. Does the use of illogical situations grow funnier or less funny as the story goes on?
3. Is the chief's reaction to the men logical or illogical? Explain.

◆ Literary Focus

HUMOROUS FOLK TALE
"Talk" is a **humorous folk tale** that uses simple characters and a far-fetched situation to make a point about human nature.
1. How are the characters in "Talk" different from characters in other stories in this book?
2. What image of its culture does the folk tale seem to project?

◆ Build Grammar Skills

ADVERB CLAUSES
Adverb clauses allow writers to explain *when, where, how,* and *why* events happen.

> An **adverb clause** is a subordinate clause that modifies a verb, an adjective, or an adverb.

Practice On your paper, write the following sentences. Underline the adverb clauses in each and indicate what it tells about the word it modifies.
1. While the country man was digging, one of his yams began to talk to him.
2. Wouldn't you run if you were in their position?
3. When I went to whip the dog, the tree told me to put the branch down.
4. You had better all go back to work before I punish you for disturbing the peace.
5. Wherever the first man ran, he found talking objects.

2. if you were in their position (why)
3. When I went to whip the dog (when)
4. before I punish you for disturbing the peace (why)
5. Wherever the first man ran (where)

✎ Writer's Solution

For additional instruction and practice, use the lesson in the **Language Lab CD-ROM** on Varying Sentence Structure. You may also use the Adverb Clauses page (p. 55) in the *Writer's Solution Grammar Practice Book.*

Build Your Portfolio

 ## Idea Bank

Writing

1. Sequel Imagine what several of the characters in "Talk" do next and write a sequel to this story.

2. News Report Prepare a news report describing what happens in "Talk" from the point of view of the nonhumans. **[Media Link]**

3. Humorous Folk Tale Think of your school as a community, with its own culture, customs, and values. Write a humorous folk tale set in your school using simple characters and a far-fetched situation.

Speaking and Listening

4. Dramatic Reading Work with other students to give a dramatic reading of the story. Exercise your creativity in bringing the nonhuman characters to life. **[Performing Arts Link]**

5. Interview Imagine that a famous television interviewer or talk show host is conducting an interview with one of the nonhuman characters in "Talk." With another student, role-play this situation. **[Media Link]**

Projects

6. Storyboard Create a storyboard for a cartoon of "Talk." First decide on the events you think should be shown. Then draw a series of pictures illlustrating these situations, with a caption under each. **[Art Link]**

7. Multimedia Report "Talk" is set in West Africa, near the Gulf of Guinea. Prepare a report about this region. Include as much multimedia material as you can find—a map; photographs of people, land, and art; tapes of voices and music; and actual art objects and cloths, if you can find them.

 ## Writing Mini-Lesson

Book-Jacket Blurb

A **book-jacket blurb** is a combination summary and advertisement, telling potential readers enough about a book to whet their interest without giving away the whole story—all in about 300 words or less. Choose a novel or nonfiction book that you have read recently and write a book-jacket blurb to entice readers to buy it.

Writing Skills Focus: Clear and Consistent Purpose

If you define a **clear and consistent purpose** for yourself each time you write, your writing will stay on course and be focused, clear, and forceful. Make a list of possible writing purposes, and then choose the one that seems most effective.

Possible Purposes:
- to amuse readers
- to arouse curiosity
- to appeal to a sense of adventure
- to inform

Prewriting Once you have decided on your purpose, determine which aspects of your book you want to emphasize in the blurb. For example, if you want to amuse your readers, think about some of the funniest moments in the book. Make a list of the examples you want to include.

Drafting Again, think of your purpose as you write. If you want to amuse your readers, be as funny as the book is. If you quote directly from the book, be sure your quotation is accurate.

Revising Pretend that you are a reader who knows nothing about the book, and decide what impression you would get from this blurb. If necessary, rewrite your blurb until you have struck the note you want.

 ## Idea Bank

Customizing for
Performance Levels
Following are suggestions for matching the Idea Bank topics with your students' performance levels:
- Less Advanced Students: 1, 4
- Average Students: 2, 5, 6
- More Advanced Students: 3, 7

Customizing for
Learning Modalities
Following are suggestions for matching Idea Bank topics with your students' learning modalities:
- Verbal/Linguistic: 1, 2, 3, 7
- Interpersonal: 4, 5
- Visual/Spatial: 6, 7
- Auditory: 7

 ## Writing Mini-Lesson

Refer students to the Writing Handbook, page 962, for instruction on the writing process, and page 965 for further information on persuasion. Have students use the Sunburst Organizer in **Writing and Language Transparencies,** p. 64, to arrange their prewriting examples.

🖋 *Writer's Solution*

Writers at Work Videodisc
Have students view the videodisc segment (Ch. 4) featuring National Basketball Association writer Larry Weitzman to see how he makes a piece of persuasive writing compelling. Have students discuss the technique of persuasive writing.

Play frames 33836 to 42938

Writing Lab CD-ROM
Have students compete the Tutorial on Persuasion. Follow these steps:
1. Use the Purpose Profile to focus writing.
2. Have students draft on the computer.
3. Use the Proofreading Checklist to aid revision.

Sourcebook
Have students use Chapter 4, Persuasion (pp. 96–127), for additional support. The chapter includes indepth instruction on avoiding faulty logic and unreasonable appeals (pp. 118–119).

✓ ASSESSMENT OPTIONS

Formal Assessment, Selection Test, pp. 91–93, and Assessment Resources Software. The selection test is designed so that it can be easily customized to the performance levels of your students.
Alternative Assessment, p. 27, includes options for less advanced students, more advanced students, musical/rhythmic learners, verbal/linguistic learners, and visual/spatial learners.

PORTFOLIO ASSESSMENT
Use the following rubrics in the ***Alternative Assessment*** booklet to assess student writing:
Sequel: Fictional Narrative Rubric, p. 88
News Report: Summary Rubric, p. 91
Humorous Folk Tale: Narrative Based on Personal Experience Rubric, p. 89
Writing Mini-Lesson: Persuasion Rubric, p. 98

Jackson's stock in trade is looking for—and finding—the menacing shadows that lurk just beneath the surface of ordinary experience. In this story, she chronicles what appears to be an ordinary day in the life of a character. His actions seem quite ordinary up to the last moment, when the author unleashes a final surprise. Only then will we be able to answer the question, "Just what is 'ordinary'?"

◆ Critical Thinking

❶ Make Judgments Ask students to identify what is odd about the way in which Mr. Johnson makes his way uptown. *Students should point out that the opening scene suggests that Mr. Johnson is headed for work until he begins to wander at random, which is apparently part of his daily routine.*

One Ordinary Day, With Peanuts

SHIRLEY JACKSON

Mr. John Philip Johnson shut his front door behind him and came down his front steps into the bright morning with a feeling that all was well with the world on this best of all days, and wasn't the sun warm and good, and didn't his shoes feel comfortable after the resoling, and he knew that he had undoubtedly chosen the precise very tie which belonged with the day and the sun and his comfortable feet, and, after all, wasn't the world just a wonderful place? In spite of the fact that he was a small man, and the tie was perhaps a shade vivid, Mr. Johnson <u>irradiated</u> this feeling of well-being as he came down the steps and onto the dirty sidewalk, and he smiled at people who passed him, and some of them even smiled back. He stopped at the newsstand on the corner and bought his paper, saying "*Good* morning" with real conviction to the man who sold him the paper and the two or three other people who were lucky enough to be buying papers when Mr. Johnson skipped up. He remembered

to fill his pockets with candy and peanuts, and then he set out to get himself uptown. He stopped in a flower shop and bought a carnation for his buttonhole, and stopped almost immediately afterward to give the carnation to a small child in a carriage, who looked at him dumbly, and then smiled, and Mr. Johnson smiled, and the child's mother looked at Mr. Johnson for a minute and then smiled too.

When he had gone several blocks uptown, Mr. Johnson cut across the avenue and went along a side street, chosen at random; he did not follow the same route every morning, but preferred to pursue his eventful way in wide detours, more like a puppy than a man intent upon business. It happened this morning that halfway down the block a moving van was parked, and the furniture from an

◆ Build Vocabulary

irradiated (ir rā´ dē āt´ id) *v*.: Gave out; radiated

Block Scheduling Strategies

Consider these suggestions to take advantage of extended class time:

• To introduce students to the mood of the story, invite them to share their journal entries (p. 363). Discuss the sort of things that keep them especially busy on frenzied days.

• Have students in small groups use the Reading Strategy questions (p. 363) as a guideline for discussion of characters' actions in the story.

• Use a map of New York City to locate the details of the story setting.

• To make sure students understand the theme of the story, discuss with them the Critical Thinking questions on page 372.

• To provide students with an opportunity to demonstrate understanding of the story in writing, use the Writing Mini-Lesson (p. 373). Discuss how the guidelines can be used to plan Mr. Johnson's day as a crabby, disagreeable troublemaker.

upstairs apartment stood half on the sidewalk, half on the steps, while an amused group of people <u>loitered</u>, examining the scratches on the tables and the worn spots on the chairs, and a **②** harassed woman, trying to watch a young child and the movers and the furniture all at the same time, gave the clear impression of <u>endeavoring</u> to shelter her private life from the people staring at her belongings. Mr. Johnson **③** stopped, and for a moment joined the crowd, and then he came forward and, touching his hat civilly, said, "Perhaps I can keep an eye on your little boy for you?"

The woman turned and glared at him distrustfully, and Mr. Johnson added hastily, "We'll sit right here on the steps." He beckoned to the little boy, who hesitated and then responded agreeably to Mr. Johnson's genial smile. Mr. Johnson brought out a handful of peanuts from his pocket and sat on the steps with the boy, who at first refused the peanuts on the grounds that his mother did not allow him to accept food from strangers; Mr. Johnson said that probably his mother had not intended peanuts to be included, since elephants at the circus ate them, and the boy considered, and then agreed solemnly. They sat on the steps cracking peanuts in a comradely fashion, and Mr. Johnson said, "So you're moving?"

"Yep," said the boy.

"Where you going?"

"Vermont."

"Nice place. Plenty of snow there. Maple sugar, too; you like maple sugar?"

"Sure."

"Plenty of maple sugar in Vermont. You go- **④** ing to live on a farm?"

"Going to live with Grandpa."

"Grandpa like peanuts?"

"Sure."

"Ought to take him some," said Mr. Johnson, reaching into his pocket. "Just you and Mommy going?"

"Yep."

◆ Build Vocabulary

loitered (loit´ erd) v.: Hung about; lingered

endeavoring (en dev´ er iŋ) v.: Trying; attempting

"Tell you what," Mr. Johnson said. "You take some peanuts to eat on the train."

The boy's mother, after glancing at them frequently, had seemingly decided that Mr. Johnson was trustworthy, because she had devoted herself wholeheartedly to seeing that the movers did not—what movers rarely do, but every housewife believes they will—crack a leg from her good table, or set a kitchen chair down on a lamp. Most of the furniture was loaded by now, and she was deep in that nervous stage when she knew there was something she had forgotten to pack—hidden away in the back of a closet somewhere, or left at a neighbor's and forgotten, or on a clothesline— and was trying to remember under stress what it was.

"This all, lady?" the chief mover said, completing her dismay.

Uncertainly, she nodded.

"Want to go on the truck with the furniture, sonny?" the mover asked the boy, and laughed. The boy laughed too and said to Mr. Johnson, "I guess I'll have a good time at Vermont."

"Fine time," said Mr. Johnson, and stood up. "Have one more peanut before you go," he said to the boy.

The boy's mother said to Mr. Johnson, "Thank you so much; it was a great help to me."

"Nothing at all," said Mr. Johnson gallantly. "Where in Vermont are you going?"

The mother looked at the little boy accusingly, as though he had given away a secret of some importance, and said unwillingly, "Greenwich."

"Lovely town," said Mr. Johnson. He took out a card, and wrote a name on the back. "Very good friend of mine lives in Greenwich," he said. "Call on him for anything you need. His wife makes the best doughnuts in town," he added soberly to the little boy.

"Swell," said the little boy.

"Goodbye," said Mr. Johnson.

He went on, stepping happily with his new-shod feet, feeling the warm sun on his back and on the top of his head. Halfway down the **⑤** block he met a stray dog and fed him a peanut. At the corner, where another wide avenue

One Ordinary Day, With Peanuts ◆ 365

◆ *Literature and Your Life*

❷ Call attention to the description of moving day and the nervous woman. Have students recall a time when they've had their hands full. How can having an audience add to the general confusion of trying to organize and keep track of details? *Students may recount moving day experiences or similarly hectic circumstances that drew a crowd of onlookers.*

◆ Reading Strategy

❸ Question Characters' Actions Ask students to explain why, while Mr. Johnson's behavior seems nice, it is out of the ordinary. Would they leave the child with Mr. Johnson if they were the parent? Why, or why not? *Students should grasp that most people know that children are taught not to talk to strangers, and therefore would not make such an offer. Most parents would never leave a child with a stranger, no matter how ingratiating his manner.*

◆ Build Grammar Skills

❹ Capitalization of Proper Nouns Have students identify the proper nouns that are capitalized in this portion of the dialogue. Ask them to explain why these nouns should be capitalized. *The proper nouns are Vermont—a specific place; Grandpa—a specific person; Mommy—a specific person.*

◆ Critical Thinking

❺ Make Comparisons Ask students how the description of Mr. Johnson plodding along lazily and aimlessly helps to emphasize the hectic pace of modern life. *Mr. Johnson steps "happily," enjoying the whole wide world from his head right down to his new shoes; around him, people are "hurrying," "frowning," "clattering."*

Cross-Curricular Connection: Music

Part of the tension of the story is derived from the city setting. Invite students to brainstorm for features of the setting based on information from the story and their own experiences. Write their ideas on the chalkboard. Challenge students to take the list they have generated and use it to create a city "symphony" of sound. Suggest that they decide on a theme. For example, they could reflect city noises of morning, afternoon, and evening; a walking tour uptown; or the events of Jackson's story. They can use the theme to create an outline and then collect and create appropriate sounds to record on audiotape. Encourage students to use their ingenuity to find instruments and objects that mimic city sounds that can be combined with natural sounds of squealing brakes, honking horns, sirens, bells, and so on. One sound could be repeated regularly to create a rhythm.

◆ Critical Thinking

❷ **Analyze Characters** "... risking suspicious displeasure," Mr. Johnson takes the woman's arm; later he tries out "his winning smile" on her. Ask students what these actions reveal about Mr. Johnson and his motives. *Students should be aware of Mr. Johnson's calculated, self-conscious actions that are meant to get a particular response and that suggest prior experience in similar situations.*

◆ *Literature and Your Life*

❸ Mr. Johnson gets in the way of the woman hurrying to work and further annoys her by making conversation. Ask students to describe situations in which they have had to try not to be rude to well-meaning people taking up their time. *Students can recall irritating and awkward delays brought on by do-gooders.*

◆ Reading Strategy

❹ **Question Characters' Actions** Students will probably believe that he offers to pay her for her time so that she will stay around—he probably has some good deed he wants to perform and needs the time.

Comprehension Check ☑

❺ How does this scene reinforce the idea that Mr. Johnson is not acting entirely spontaneously? *Mr. Johnson is looking in the crowd for a certain kind of person. He is able to size people up and anticipate how they will react to him. His actions suggest that he has done this sort of thing before, rather than relying solely on chance encounters.*

---

❶ faced him, Mr. Johnson decided to go on uptown again. Moving with comparative laziness, he was passed on either side by people hurrying and frowning, and people brushed past him going the other way, clattering along to get somewhere quickly. Mr. Johnson stopped on every corner and waited patiently for the light to change, and he stepped out of the way of anyone who seemed to be in any particular hurry, but one young lady came too fast for him, and crashed wildly into him when he stooped to pat a kitten which had run out onto the sidewalk from an apartment house and was now unable to get back through the rushing feet.

"Excuse me," said the young lady, trying frantically to pick up Mr. Johnson and hurry on at the same time, "terribly sorry."

The kitten, regardless now of danger, raced back to its home. "Perfectly all right," said Mr. Johnson, adjusting himself carefully. "You seem to be in a hurry."

"Of course I'm in a hurry," said the young lady. "I'm late."

She was extremely cross and the frown between her eyes seemed well on its way to becoming permanent. She had obviously awakened late, because she had not spent any extra time in making herself look pretty, and her dress was plain and unadorned with collar or brooch, and her lipstick was noticeably crooked. She tried to brush past Mr. Johnson, but, risking her suspicious displeasure, he took her arm and said, "Please wait."

❷ "Look," she said ominously, "I ran into you and your lawyer can see my lawyer and I will gladly pay all damages and all inconveniences suffered therefrom but please this minute let me go because *I am late.*"

"Late for what?" said Mr. Johnson; he tried his winning smile on her but it did no more than keep her, he suspected, from knocking him down again.

"Late for work," she said between her teeth. ❸ "Late for my employment. I have a job and if I am late I lose exactly so much an hour and I cannot really afford what your pleasant conversation is costing me, be it *ever* so pleasant."

"I'll pay for it," said Mr. Johnson. Now these

366 ◆ The Lighter Side

were magic words, not necessarily because they were true, or because she seriously expected Mr. Johnson to pay for anything, but because Mr. Johnson's flat statement, obviously innocent of irony, could not be, coming from Mr. Johnson, anything but the statement of a responsible and truthful and respectable man.

"What *do* you mean?" she asked.

"I said that since I am obviously responsible for your being late I shall certainly pay for it."

"Don't be silly," she said, and for the first time the frown disappeared. "I wouldn't expect you to pay for anything—a few minutes ago I was offering to pay *you.* Anyway," she added, almost smiling, "it *was* my fault."

"What happens if you don't go to work?"

She stared. "I don't get paid."

"Precisely," said Mr. Johnson.

"What do you mean, precisely? If I don't show up at the office exactly twenty minutes ago I lose a dollar and twenty cents an hour, or two cents a minute or. . . " She thought. ". . . Almost a dime for the time I've spent talking to you."

Mr. Johnson laughed, and finally she laughed, too. "You're late already," he pointed out. "Will you give me another four cents worth?"

"I don't understand why."

"You'll see," Mr. Johnson promised. He led her over to the side of the walk, next to the buildings, and said, "Stand here," and went out into the rush of people going both ways. Selecting and considering, as one who must make a choice involving perhaps whole years of lives, he estimated the people going by. Once he almost moved, and then at the last minute thought better of it and drew back. Finally, from half a block away, he saw what he wanted, and moved out into the center of the traffic to intercept a young man, who was hurrying, and dressed as though he had awakened late, and frowning.

"Oof," said the young man, because Mr.

> ◆ **Reading Strategy**
> Why might Mr. Johnson offer to pay for the young woman's time? ❹

❺

◆ Build Vocabulary

ominously (äm´ ə nəs lē) *adv.*: In a threatening way

Speaking and Listening Mini-Lesson

Dramatic Scene

This mini-lesson supports the Speaking and Listening activity in the Idea Bank on page 373.

Introduce the Concept Remind students that Miss Kent and Mr. Adams are total strangers who have been brought together by odd circumstances. Their conversation might be a bit stiff.

Develop Background Student pairs should decide what part of Mr. Adams's and Miss Kent's experience they want to depict. They might discuss the peculiarity of Mr. Johnson's behavior or

where they want to go. In any case, their dialogue should reflect two people meeting for the first time.

Apply the Information Student pairs can work together to create a dramatic scene, practice the dialogue, and perform it for the rest of the group.

Assess the Outcome To evaluate the dramatic scenes, have students use the Peer Assessment page for a Dramatic Performance, in *Alternative Assessment* (p. 113).

Johnson had thought of no better way to intercept anyone than the one the young woman had unwittingly used upon him. "Where do you think you're going?" the young man demanded from the sidewalk.

"I want to speak to you," said Mr. Johnson ominously.

The young man got up nervously, dusting himself and eyeing Mr. Johnson. "What for?" he said. "What'd *I* do?"

"That's what bothers me most about people nowadays," Mr. Johnson complained broadly to the people passing. "No matter whether they've done anything or not, they always figure someone's after them. About what you're going to do," he told the young man.

❻ "Listen," said the young man, trying to brush past him, "I'm late, and I don't have any time to listen. Here's a dime, now get going."

"Thank you," said Mr. Johnson, pocketing the dime. "Look," he said, "what happens if you stop running?"

"I'm late," said the young man, still trying to get past Mr. Johnson, who was unexpectedly clinging.

"How much you make an hour?" Mr. Johnson demanded.

❼ "A communist, are you?" said the young man. "Now will you please let me—"

"No," said Mr. Johnson insistently, "*how* much?"

"Dollar fifty," said the young man. "And *now* will you—"

"You like adventure?"

The young man stared, and, staring, found himself caught and held by Mr. Johnson's genial smile; he almost smiled back and then repressed it and made an effort to tear away. "I got to *hurry*," he said.

"Mystery? Like surprises? Unusual and exciting events?"

"You selling something?"

▶ Critical Viewing This scene is filled with anonymous people moving about. What might Mr. Johnson think about these people? [Speculate]

❽

One Ordinary Day, With Peanuts ◆ 367

◆ **Critical Thinking**

❻ **Evaluate** Ask students what the man and woman could have done to avoid having to hurry so much. *Students may suggest time-saving strategies that will help the people plan ahead, such as getting up earlier or finding quicker transportation to work.*

❼ **Clarification** The young man accuses Mr. Johnson of being a communist, a label with negative connotations. Explain that at the time the story was written, opposition to communism in the United States was extreme, and any allusion to communist doctrine—even the idea that wealth should be shared—could be construed as traitorous.

▶Critical Viewing◀

❽ **Speculate** Students may say that Mr. Johnson considers everyone on the street to be possible targets of his goodwill. The more people, the more possibilities.

Humanities: Art

Photographs of crowded city streets are used to illustrate the story. Have students look at the street scenes and discuss the following questions:

1. How do the photographs help you imagine what it is like to get caught up in the pace of the city? *Photographs show real-life scenes that help verify the hectic pace alluded to throughout the story, as well as the familiar, "ordinary" events that are portrayed.*

2. Point out the details in the photographs that give clues to the time period of the story.

Students should refer to the clothing of the women—e.g., the kerchiefs on their heads—and the models of the vehicles, which suggest the 1950's.

3. What feelings do you get about being on city streets as you look at the photographs? *Encourage students to describe how they respond to the hustle and bustle of the crowded streets shown in the photographs.*

367

►Critical Viewing◄

❶ Infer The photograph depicts a crowded sidewalk on a busy street lined with tall buildings; people are moving in different directions, going about their business. Students can use these clues to infer that the setting is a large city, rather than a small city or town.

Customize for
Less Proficient Readers
Have students summarize the events of the scene on pages 367–368 to underscore the dynamic of Mr. Johnson's behavior and how people respond to him. Summaries should include the following: *Mr. Johnson knocks the man down; they argue; the man tries to get away by giving Mr. Johnson a dime; Mr. Johnson prevents him from leaving and starts asking questions; the man still tries half-heartedly to get away, but Mr. Johnson persuades him further and then leads him over to the girl and gives them both money.*

❶ ▲ **Critical Viewing** Based upon this photograph, what can you infer about the setting of this story? [Infer]

"Sure," said Mr. Johnson. "You want to take a chance?"

The young man hesitated, looking longingly up the avenue toward what might have been his destination and then, when Mr. Johnson said, "I'll pay for it," with his own peculiar convincing emphasis, turned and said, "Well, okay. But I got to *see* it first, what I'm buying."

Mr. Johnson, breathing hard, led the young man over to the side where the girl was standing; she had been watching with interest Mr. Johnson's capture of the young man and now, smiling timidly, she looked at Mr. Johnson as though prepared to be surprised at nothing.

Mr. Johnson reached into his pocket and took out his wallet. "Here," he said, and handed a bill to the girl. "This about equals your day's pay."

"But no," she said, surprised in spite of herself. "I mean, I *couldn't*."

"Please do not interrupt," Mr. Johnson told her. "And *here*," he said to the young man, "this will take care of *you*." The young man accepted the bill dazedly, but said, "Probably counterfeit," to the young woman out of the side of his mouth. "Now," Mr. Johnson went on, disregarding the young man, "what is your name, miss?"

"Kent," she said helplessly. "Mildred Kent."

"Fine," said Mr. Johnson. "And you, sir?"

"Arthur Adams," said the young man stiffly.

"Splendid," said Mr. Johnson. "Now, Miss Kent, I would like you to meet Mr. Adams. Mr. Adams, Miss Kent."

Miss Kent stared, wet her lips nervously, made a gesture as though she might run, and said, "How do you do?"

Mr. Adams straightened his shoulders,

368 ◆ *The Lighter Side*

 Humanities: Photography

Media Connection
New York City streets are especially crowded, even when compared to those of other big cities around the country. Have students look at the photographs that illustrate this story and discuss the following questions:
1. How do the photographs help you visualize what it is like for Mr. Johnson to stop people in the crowd? *Students can see that moving against the flow, stopping to bend down, or stepping in front of people would be disruptive.*
2. How would the story be different in a small-town setting? *People's activities and reactions to Mr. Johnson, as well as Mr. Johnson's attention-getting methods, would be different in a quieter, more leisurely atmosphere.*

scowled at Mr. Johnson, made a gesture as though he might run, and said, "How do you do?"

"Now *this*," said Mr. Johnson, taking several bills from his wallet, "should be enough for the day for both of you. I would suggest, perhaps, Coney Island[1]—although I personally am not fond of the place—or perhaps a nice lunch somewhere, and dancing, or a matinee,[2] or even a movie, although take care to choose a really *good* one; there are *so* many bad movies these days. "You might," he said, struck with an inspiration, "visit the Bronx Zoo, or the Planetarium.[3] Anywhere, as a matter of fact," he concluded, "that you would like to go. Have a nice time."

As he started to move away, Arthur Adams, breaking from his dumbfounded stare, said, "But see here, mister, you *can't* do this. Why—how do you know—I mean, *we* don't even know—I mean, how do you know we won't just take the money and not do what you said?"

You've taken the money," Mr. Johnson said. "You don't have to follow any of my suggestions. You may know something you prefer to do—perhaps a museum, or something."

"But suppose I just run away with it and leave her here?"

"I know you won't," said Mr. Johnson gently, "because you remembered to ask *me* that. Goodbye," he added, and went on.

As he stepped up the street, conscious of the sun on his head and his good shoes, he heard from somewhere behind him the young man saying, "Look, you know you don't *have* to if you don't want to," and the girl saying, "But unless *you* don't want to. . ." Mr. Johnson smiled to himself and then thought that he had better hurry along; when he wanted to he could move very quickly, and before the young woman had gotten around to saying, "Well, *I* will if *you* will," Mr. Johnson was several blocks away and had already stopped twice, once to

---

1. **Coney Island:** Famous beach area and amusement park in Brooklyn, one of the five boroughs of New York City.
2. **matinee:** Here, an afternoon performance of an on- or off-Broadway show.
3. **Planetarium:** The Hayden Planetarium, adjoining the American Museum of Natural History in New York City.

help a lady lift several large packages into a taxi and once to hand a peanut to a seagull. By this time he was in an area of large stores and many more people and he was buffeted constantly from either side by people hurrying and cross and late and sullen. Once he offered a peanut to a man who asked him for a dime, and once he offered a peanut to a bus driver who had stopped his bus at an intersection and had opened the window next to his seat and put out his head as though longing for fresh air and the comparative quiet of the traffic. The man wanting a dime took the peanut because Mr. Johnson had wrapped a dollar bill around it, but the bus driver took the peanut and asked ironically, "You want a transfer, Jack?"

On a busy corner Mr. Johnson encountered two young people—for one minute he thought they might be Mildred Kent and Arthur Adams—who were eagerly scanning a newspaper, their backs pressed against a storefront to avoid the people passing, their heads bent together. Mr. Johnson, whose curiosity was insatiable, leaned onto the storefront next to them and peeked over the man's shoulder; they were scanning the "Apartments Vacant" columns.

Mr. Johnson remembered the street where the woman and her little boy were going to Vermont and he tapped the man on the shoulder and said amiably, "Try down on West Seventeen. About the middle of the block, people moved out this morning."

"Say, what do you—" said the man, and then, seeing Mr. Johnson clearly, "Well thanks. Where did you say?"

"West Seventeen," said Mr. Johnson. "About the middle of the block." He smiled again and said, "Good luck."

"Thanks," said the man.

"Thanks," said the girl, as they moved off.

"Goodbye," said Mr. Johnson.

He lunched alone in a pleasant restaurant,

◆ Build Vocabulary

buffeted (buf´ it ed) *v.*: Jostled; knocked about

insatiable (in sā´ shə bəl) *adj.*: Unable to be satisfied

One Ordinary Day, With Peanuts ◆ 369

◆ Build Grammar Skills

❷ **Capitalization of Proper Nouns** Have students identify the proper nouns in this passage. *Mr. Johnson is a specific person. Coney Island, the Bronx Zoo, and the Planetarium are specific places in New York City.*

◆ Critical Thinking

❸ **Interpret** Ask students why Mr. Johnson has to reassure Arthur and Mildred before he can leave. *Arthur doesn't trust Mr. Johnson and feels certain that there must be strings attached to his actions. Arthur's confusion is evidence of the extraordinary quality of Mr. Johnson's behavior.*

◆ Reading Strategy

❹ **Question Characters' Actions** Ask students if they can explain why the bus driver asks Mr. Johnson if he wants a transfer. What would the students like to ask Mr. Johnson at this point in the story? *The bus driver is suspicious of Mr. Johnson's actions. He can't believe that someone would give away even a peanut without wanting something in return. Students may want to know if Mr. Johnson has some hidden motive for his actions.*

◆ Build Grammar Skills

❺ **Capitalization of Proper Nouns** Ask students to find the proper noun in the clause and explain why it is capitalized. *"Apartments Vacant" is a heading or title.*

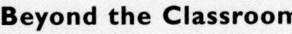

Beyond the Classroom

Community Connection

Working People Many people in the story are on their way to work, but not all city jobs are performed in offices or factories. A number of people mentioned in the story are on the street doing their jobs: newsstand operator, florist, movers, bus driver, cab driver. Record students responses as they discuss the workers they encounter during a typical day or week in their own community. Are students surprised by how many people they depend on to keep things running smoothly?

Suggest students interview men and women who work in their community. Each interview should include one or two questions about pressures on the job and how the person interviewed copes with them.

Career Connection

Service Workers and Volunteers In this story, Mr. Johnson spends his day helping anyone he finds who is in need. People who need help in the real world do not have to depend on chance meetings with eccentric people, however. Have students find out about helping hands in the community. What philanthropic organizations are active? What kinds of services do they provide? Students can call the volunteer bureau, the Red Cross, the county hospital, and local churches and charities to find out what they do and how their programs are staffed.

◆ Literary Focus

❶ Surprise Ending Apparently Mr. Johnson is wrapping up his day, since the story is reaching its end. Ask students how the story might end. Have them conjecture about what the surprise could be. *Students will probably think a surprise is in store. Accept all speculations about what could happen.*

◆ *Literature and Your Life*

❷ Mr. Johnson has trouble getting a taxi, which can be nearly impossible at the busiest times of the day. Have students describe finding transportation in hectic public places. *Students can share their own, or others', experiences riding on crowded buses, or being caught in a traffic jam when they need to be somewhere.*

❸ Clarification Point out that Mr. Johnson has been walking uptown all day—from lower Manhattan toward upper Manhattan—so he must go downtown to get home. The cab that Mr. Johnson hailed was actually heading in the opposite direction when it stopped to pick him up.

◆ Build Grammar Skills

❹ Capitalization of Proper Nouns Ask students to identify the proper nouns in the words spoken by Mr. Johnson. *The proper nouns are Vulcan—the name of a specific horse; Wednesday—a specific day of the week.*

◆ Reading Strategy

❺ Question Characters' Actions Students should conclude that Mr. Johnson's behavior here is consistent with the way he has been acting all day, freely giving out money and supposedly sound advice with nothing expected in return and nothing apparently to gain.

---

where the food was rich, and only Mr. Johnson's excellent digestion could encompass two of their whipped-cream-and-chocolate-and-rum-cake pastries for dessert. He had three cups of coffee, tipped the waiter largely, and went out into the street again into the wonderful sunlight, his shoes still comfortable and fresh on his feet. Outside he found a beggar staring into the windows of the restaurant he had left and, carefully looking through the money in his pocket, Mr. Johnson approached the beggar and pressed some coins and a couple of bills into his hand. "It's the price of the veal cutlet lunch plus tip," said Mr. Johnson. "Goodbye."

After his lunch he rested; he walked into the nearest park and fed peanuts to the pigeons. It was late afternoon by the time he was ready to start back downtown, and he had refereed two checker games and watched a small boy and girl whose mother had fallen asleep and awakened with surprise and fear which turned to amusement when she saw Mr. Johnson. He **❶** had given away almost all of his candy, and had fed all the rest of his peanuts to the pigeons, and it was time to go home. Although the late afternoon sun was pleasant, and his shoes were still entirely comfortable, he decided to take a taxi downtown.

He had a difficult time catching a taxi, be- **❷** cause he gave up the first three or four empty ones to people who seemed to need them more; finally, however, he stood alone on the corner and—almost like netting a frisky fish—he **❸** hailed desperately until he succeeded in catching a cab which had been proceeding with haste uptown and seemed to draw in towards Mr. Johnson against its own will.

"Mister," the cab driver said as Mr. Johnson climbed in, "I figured you was an <u>omen</u>, like. I wasn't going to pick you up at all."

"Kind of you," said Mr. Johnson ambiguously.

"If I'd of let you go it would of cost me ten bucks," said the driver.

"Really?" said Mr. Johnson.

"Yeah," said the driver. "Guy just got out of the cab, he turned around and give me ten

bucks, said take this and bet it in a hurry on a horse named Vulcan,[4] right away."

"Vulcan?" said Mr. Johnson, horrified. "A fire sign[5] on a Wednesday?" **4**

"What?" said the driver. "Anyway, I said to myself if I got no fare between here and there I'd bet the ten, but if anyone looked like they needed the cab I'd take it as an omen and I'd take the ten home to the wife."

"You were very right," said Mr. Johnson heartily. "This is Wednesday, you would have lost your money. Monday, yes, or even Saturday. But never never never a fire sign on a Wednesday. Sunday would have been good, now."

"Vulcan don't run on Sunday," said the driver.

"You wait till another day," said Mr. Johnson. "Down this street, please, driver. I'll get off on the next corner."

"He *told* me Vulcan, though," said the driver.

"I'll tell you," said Mr. Johnson, hesitating with the door of the cab half open. "You take that ten dollars and I'll give you another ten dollars to go with it, and you go right ahead and bet that money on any Thursday on any horse that has a name indicating. . . let me see, Thursday . . . well, grain. Or any growing food."

> ◆ **Reading Strategy**
> Do the actions in this paragraph seem consistent with Mr. Johnson's personality, past behavior, and remarks? **5**

"Grain?" said the driver. "You mean a horse named, like, Wheat or something?"

"Certainly," said Mr. Johnson. "Or, as a matter of fact, to make it even easier, any horse whose name includes the letters C, R, L. Perfectly simple."

"Tall corn?" said the driver, a light in his eye. "You mean a horse named, like, Tall Corn?"

"Absolutely," said Mr. Johnson. "Here's your money."

"Tall Corn," said the driver. "Thank *you*, mister."

"Goodbye," said Mr. Johnson.

---
4. **Vulcan:** Also the name of the Roman god of fire.
5. **fire sign:** Term borrowed from astrology but referring here to Vulcan.

370 ◆ The Lighter Side

 Speaking and Listening Mini-Lesson

Retold Story

This mini-lesson supports the Speaking and Listening activity in the Idea Bank on page 373.

Introduce the Concept In retelling a story for young children, the language and imagery in the story will be different from the original.

Develop Background Suggest that students work together to summarize the main events of the story. Then individuals, pairs, or small groups can develop ideas for telling the story to a child. Simplified language, clear descriptions, a variety of voices and tones, and sound effects will bring the story to life.

Apply the Information Students can work on their own to create an engaging

version of the story appropriate for young children. They can then share it with the class.

Assess the Outcome Evaluate the retold stories on how well they followed the plot, how easy they were to understand, and how clearly they conveyed the characters and setting. What storytelling techniques were particularly effective?

He was on his own corner and went straight up to his apartment. He let himself in and called "Hello?" and Mrs. Johnson answered from the kitchen, "Hello, dear, aren't you early?"

"Took a taxi home," Mr. Johnson said. "I remembered the cheesecake, too. What's for dinner?"

Mrs. Johnson came out of the kitchen and kissed him; she was a comfortable woman, and smiling as Mr. Johnson smiled. "Hard day?" she asked.

"Not very," said Mr. Johnson, hanging his coat in the closet. "How about you?"

"So-so," she said. She stood in the kitchen doorway while he settled into his easy chair and took off his good shoes and took out the paper he had bought that morning. "Here and there," she said.

"I didn't do so badly," Mr. Johnson said. "Couple young people."

"Fine," she said. "I had a little nap this afternoon, took it easy most of the day. Went into a department store this morning and accused the woman next to me of

◆ Literary Focus
What is surprising about these details?
6

shoplifting, and had the store detective pick her up. Sent three dogs to the pound—*you* know, the usual thing. Oh, and listen," she added, remembering.

"What?" asked Mr. Johnson.

"Well," she said, "I got onto a bus and asked the driver for a transfer, and when he helped someone else first I said that he was impertinent, and quarreled with him. And then I said why wasn't he in the army, and I said it loud enough for everyone to hear, and I took his number and I turned in a complaint. Probably got him fired." **7**

"Fine," said Mr. Johnson. "But you do look tired. Want to change over tomorrow?" **8**

"I *would* like to," she said. "I could do with a change."

"Right," said Mr. Johnson. "What's for dinner?"

"Veal cutlet."

"Had it for lunch," said Mr. Johnson. **9**

◆ Build Vocabulary

omen (ō´ mən) *n.*: Sign foretelling a future event, either good or evil

impertinent (im purt´ ən ənt) *adj.*: Rude; impolite

Guide for Responding

◆ *Literature and Your Life*

Reader's Response Were you surprised by the story's ending? Why or why not?

Thematic Response Think about the humor that the story contains. In what way is the humor achieved by what is out of the ordinary in the story?

Journal Entry Jot down some details from an ordinary day in your life that turned out not to be so ordinary.

☑ Check Your Comprehension

1. What does Mr. John Philip Johnson do for the woman who is moving to Vermont?
2. What does Mr. Johnson do for Mr. Adams and Miss Kent?
3. What does Mr. Johnson keep in his pocket and hand out to various people he meets?
4. According to what she tells her husband when he gets home, how did Mrs. Johnson spend her day?
5. What do the couple decide they will do on the next day?

One Ordinary Day, With Peanuts ◆ *371*

Beyond the Selection

FURTHER READING

Other Works by Shirley Jackson
"The Lottery"
"The Haunting of Hill House"
We Have Always Lived in the Castle

Other Works With Surprise Endings
"An Occurrence at Owl Creek Bridge," Ambrose Bierce
"The Piece of String," Guy de Maupassant

INTERNET

Students may find out more about Shirley Jackson on the Internet. We suggest the following site. Please be aware, however, that the site may have changed from the time we published this information. For more about Jackson's life and work, visit **http://host2.omnimag.com/darkecho/ archives/jackson.html**

We *strongly recommend* that you preview the site before you send students to it.

◆ Literary Focus

6 **Surprise Ending** From the dialogue, students should infer that Mrs. Johnson has evidently spent the day harassing people, causing trouble, and being unpleasant with the same single-mindedness that Mr. Johnson used to be helpful and friendly.

◆ Critical Thinking

7 **Make Inferences** Ask students what this scene reveals about how the Johnsons spend their time. *The Johnsons' routine is carefully calculated to elicit specific responses from those they encounter. Successfully manipulating people and situations is their only purpose.*

◆ Literary Focus

8 **Surprise Ending** Ask students what this conversation implies. *The roles of Mr. and Mrs. Johnson—the nice person and the mean person—are interchangeable. Tomorrow, Mr. Johnson might torment the very people he helped today.*

◆ Reading Strategy

9 **Question Characters' Actions** Ask the class why Mr. Johnson says this. *Mr. Johnson is being rude to his wife because he has already taken on his new role.*

Reinforce and Extend

Answers
◆ *Literature and Your Life*

Reader's Response Most students may have thought that a surprise awaited them at the end of the story but may find the actual surprise unexpected.

Thematic Focus The humor in the story is based on the unexpected results of seemingly ordinary behavior.

☑ Check Your Comprehension

1. He keeps an eye on her boy and gives her the name of a friend of his in Vermont.
2. He introduces the two and, interrupting their busy days, sends them off to spend a relaxing day together.
3. He has peanuts.
4. She has spent the day irritating people.
5. They will switch roles.

Establish Writing Guidelines

Before students begin, review the following key characteristics of a critical evaluation:

- A critical evaluation of a literary work discusses various elements in the work, such as plot, character, setting, and writing style.

- It expresses the writer's opinions about elements in the work.

- The writer's opinions are backed up with specific examples from the work.

- The writer may make a recommendation to readers.

You may want to distribute the scoring rubric for Critical Review (p. 104 in **Alternative Assessment**) to make students aware of the criteria on which they will be evaluated before they begin. See the suggestions on page 376 for how you can customize the rubric to this workshop.

 Writer's Solution

Writers at Work Videodisc

Play the segment featuring book reviewer Lawrence Chua (Ch. 7), and discuss how Chua evaluates the works he reviews. What criteria does he use?

Play frames 23797 to 32801

Writing Lab CD-ROM

If your students have access to computers, you may want to have them work in the tutorial on Response to Literature to complete all or part of their critical evaluations. Follow these steps:

1. Suggest students use the Evaluation Word Bin to help them choose precise adverbs and adjectives in their critical evaluations.
2. Have students draft on computer.
3. Remind students to use the Interactive Self-Evaluation Checklist to help them judge the effectiveness of their critical evaluations.

Sourcebook

Students can find additional support in the chapter on Response to Literature (pp. 194–227).

374

Critical Evaluation

Writing Process Workshop

When you're deciding whether or not to see a new movie, you probably look at television or newspaper reviews of the movie to see what the critics think. A movie review is one type of **critical evaluation**—a written or spoken examination of what is and is not effective in a literary work, television program, or movie. Most often, a critical evaluation includes a brief summary of the work and makes a recommendation to readers or viewers.

Try your hand at writing a critical evaluation of one of the selections in this section. The following skills, introduced in this section's Writing Mini-Lessons, will help you.

Writing Skills Focus

▶ **Have a clear and consistent purpose** for writing. Keep your purpose in mind as you develop and write your evaluation. (See p. 361.)

▶ **Follow the criteria** for writing a critical evaluation: Explain what you did and did not like about the piece, support your points, summarize key events in the selection, and make a recommendation. (See p. 373.)

▶ **Offer precise details** about the work so that readers understand exactly what you are saying. (See p. 355.)

In the following model, the writer applies all the above skills in a critical evaluation of Shirley Jackson's "One Ordinary Day, With Peanuts."

① The writer includes a summary of the story.

② This passage gives an indication of the writer's purpose.

③ The writer provides specific details to support her opinion of the story.

WRITING MODEL

In Shirley Jackson's short story "One Ordinary Day, With Peanuts," a man spends his day helping strangers. ① First, he shares peanuts with a boy about to move to Vermont . . .

Jackson's story is quite entertaining ② because of the carefree nature of its main character and its clever surprise ending. ③

374 ◆ *The Lighter Side*

 Beyond the Classroom

Workplace Connection

Film Critic Tell students that most newspapers and many magazines publish reviews of movies that help readers decide which ones they might like to see. Movie reviews may also be broadcast as part of a radio or television program. Film critics see many movies and choose to review those they think would most interest their audiences—the readers of their particular publications, the viewers of their television show, or radio listeners. A film critic employs many of the same writing strategies used by a student writing a critical review of a work of literature. Lead a class discussion comparing the skills a film critic must develop with those used in writing a critical review of a work of literature. *Suggested response: Like the writer of a critical review of a literary work, a film critic would be careful to gear the language of a review to his or her intended audience, use precise evaluative modifiers, use language variety, revise, and proofread carefully.*

Prewriting

Choose a Topic To which selection in this section did you have the strongest reaction? That selection will make the best topic for a critical evaluation. If necessary, scan the Table of Contents or flip through the book to spark your memory.

Clarify Your Opinion Once you've chosen your selection, collect your thoughts about it. Create a chart like this one, listing what you liked about the selection and what you didn't like about it.

What I Liked	What I Didn't Like

Identify Your Purpose Look over your list of likes and dislikes. Decide whether you will or will not recommend the work to readers.

Follow the Criteria Begin by jotting down a brief summary of the selection. After summarizing the story events, go back and check off those that are most important. Cross out those that you feel are minor. Then number the most important events according to the order in which they occurred in the story. After listing your opinions, jot down details from the story that will help support each opinion.

Drafting

Follow the Criteria Using the details you've gathered, begin drafting your evaluation. Start with a paragraph that reveals your overall opinion of the selection. Follow with a brief summary of the key details. Then elaborate on your opinion of the work. End with a recommendation to readers.

Offer Precise Details It's not enough to simply say that you found a story humorous, you must back up your opinions. Explain *why* you found the story humorous, and cite specific examples of details that contribute to the humor.

Applying LANGUAGE SKILLS: Direct Quotations

In your evaluation, include **direct quotations**, word-for-word passages taken directly from the selection. Place quotation marks before and after each quotation you use. If you quote a passage of ten lines or longer, indent the entire passage and set it off from the text that introduces it and follows it up.

Practice In your notebook, add quotation marks before and after each direct quotation.

1. William Least Heat Moon writes, Nameless, Tennessee, was a town of maybe ninety people if you pushed it . . .
2. The old people I remember from my childhood were strong in their beliefs, recalls Rudolfo Anaya.

Writing Application As you draft your critical evaluation, make sure that you use the necessary punctuation marks when using a direct quotation.

Writer's Solution Connection Writing Lab

Use the Evaluation Word Bin activity in the tutorial on Response to Literature to help you come up with words to express your opinions.

Prewriting

Suggest that students copy the titles in the table of contents for Part 2 of Unit 4 and rate each title on a scale of one to ten based on the strength of their reactions to the work. Then they can choose from the titles that were ranked the highest.

Customize for
More Advanced Students

Let these students know that a critical review can compare and contrast two or more works, rather than focus on only one. Suggest that they vary the writing assignment by choosing another work they have read by the same author or a different author's work that is related in some way to the work from Part 2 ("of the Ordinary"). The two works could be related by theme, plot, character, setting, or style. The writer should show why he or she preferred one work to the other.

Customize for
Interpersonal Learners

Suggest that students who work better with others than on their own choose partners or form a small literary discussion group. Have each student create a "What I Liked/What I Didn't Like" chart and make a copy for each group member. Then the group can discuss the entries on each member's chart to help clarify their ideas and purpose.

 **Writer's Solution**

Writing Lab CD-ROM
A Chain of Events graphic organizer for plot is included in the Gathering Details section of the tutorial on Response to Literature. Completing this chart will help students gather and organize their details.

Drafting

Suggest that students who are having trouble beginning their drafts use their prewriting notes to make an outline; then use the outline to guide their drafts.

Applying Language Skills
Direct Quotations
Answers
1. William Least Heat Moon writes, "Nameless, Tennessee, was a town of maybe ninety people if you pushed it. . ."
2. "The old people I remember from my childhood were strong in their beliefs," recalls Rudolfo Anaya.

 **Writer's Solution**

For additional instruction and practice, use the **Language Lab CD-ROM** lesson on Quotation

Marks and the Quotation Marks with Direct Quotations pages in the *Writer's Solution Grammar Practice Book* (pp. 106–107).

Degree of Comparison
Answers
1. longer; 2. best; 3. cleverest; 4. stranger

 **Writer's Solution**

For additional instruction and practice, use the practice pages on Degrees of Comparison (pp. 88–89) and Clear Comparisons (pp. 90–91) in the *Writer's Solution Grammar Practice Book.*

Revising

Suggest students add to their check-lists the following questions:

- Have I used the most precise adjectives and adverbs possible?
- Have I used quotations as examples to back up my opinions?
- Have I punctuated quotations correctly?

Publishing

Suggest that students create a class literary magazine in which they publish their opinions of works read in and out of class. Interested students can organize a group of editors to work on the magazine, soliciting critical reviews from other students, editing the reviews, organizing them into a magazine-type layout, and making copies for "subscribers."

Reinforce and Extend

Review the Writing Guidelines
After students have completed their writing, review the characteristics of a critical review. Have students reread the Writing Skills focus on page 339, and be sure they have addressed each point in their work. Encourage students to discuss what they have learned about responding to literature from this assignment.

Connect to Literature Unit 7 ("Nonfiction") includes Steve Gietschier's review of the book *In These Girls, Hope Is a Muscle.*

Applying Language Skills: Degree of Comparison

Use the **comparative degree** when comparing two things and the **superlative degree** when comparing three or more things.

Comparative:
Carroll's poem is funnier than Eliot's.

Superlative:
Jackson's story is the funniest piece of all.

Practice On your paper, write the correct form of each word in brackets.

1. "Macavity" is a [long] poem than "Jabberwocky."
2. "Talk" is the [good] folk tale I ever read.
3. Jackson is the [clever] author of them all.
4. The ending was [strange] than I thought it would be.

Writing Application Review your critical evaluation. Check to be sure you used the correct degrees of comparison in your writing.

Writer's Solution Connection Language Lab

For more instruction and practice, complete the lesson on Forms of Comparison.

376 ◆ *The Lighter Side*

Use Strong Evaluative Modifiers Present your opinions as forcefully and clearly as possible by using precise adjectives to either praise or criticize the work. Look at these examples:

Mild Praise	High Praise	Mild Disapproval	Strong Disapproval
readable	stimulating	slow moving	painfully boring
factual	honest	inconsistent	biased

Revising

Use a Checklist Use the following checklist to help you revise your critical evaluation.

- ▶ Have you clearly expressed your opinion of the work?
- ▶ What can you do to strengthen your support for your opinion?
- ▶ Have you summarized the selection in a way that will enable readers to follow what you're talking about?

Use a Model Look at the revisions made in this paragraph from a review of *The Miracle Worker*, written by Susana Seaton, a student at Long Beach High School in Long Beach, Mississippi. Notice that Susana deletes a redundant passage and clarifies the last sentence by replacing a weak phrase with a strong adjective.

REVISION MODEL

I recently saw a movie version of William Gibson's play *The Miracle Worker*. This is a story of Helen Keller. The movie was very effective—the acting was terrific, and the final scene of the "miracle" at the water pump brought tears to my eyes, and the movie was not maudlin and very emotional. Helen Keller's problems made my own troubles seem less insignificant. than what they are.

Publishing

Create a Class Publication With some classmates, create a class magazine of literary reviews.

✓ ASSESSMENT		4	3	2	1
PORTFOLIO ASSESSMENT Use the rubric on Critical Review in *Alternative Assessment* (p. 104) to assess students' writing. Add these criteria to customize the rubric to this assignment.	**Opinions and Support**	The writer clearly expresses opinions about the work and supports every opinion with at least one detail from the work.	The writer clearly expresses opinions about the work but neglects to support some opinions.	The writer's opinions are not always clearly expressed, and the writer neglects to support any opinions.	The writer's opinion is unclear or unsupported by details in the work.
	Precise Adjectives and Adverbs	The writer consistently uses precise adjectives and adverbs.	The writer uses a mixture of precise adjectives and adverbs and more general modifiers.	The writer uses some, but very few, precise adjectives and adverbs.	The writer consistently uses general or vague adjectives and adverbs.

Real-World Reading Skills Workshop

Judging a Writer's Purpose

Strategies for Success

Whenever you read, try to determine the author's purpose in writing. Doing so will help you to respond more critically to the work. For example, if you know that an author's purpose is to persuade, you won't want to accept everything that the writer says at face value. In order to persuade, a writer may leave out certain facts and choose others that will spark the reader's emotions.

Ask yourself the following questions to determine a writer's purpose. Note that sometimes a piece of writing may have more than one purpose. For instance, an article that provides information may also advance a certain point of view.

Does the writer want to inform me?
Many times, a writer's goal is to educate readers by sharing information on a topic. For example, the purpose of an encyclopedia article is to give you facts about a subject. A news report is meant to inform you about a recent event.

Does the writer wish to persuade me?
Sometimes writers want to convince readers to agree with their opinion on an issue. A newspaper editorial is an example of writing that tries to persuade. Writers might even urge readers to take some kind of action. For example, a campaign speech urges people to vote for a particular candidate.

Does the writer want to entertain me?
In some cases, a writer's only purpose is to amuse you. A humorous novel or a joke book is meant to make you laugh. A horror story aims to give you a good scare, which is another way of entertaining you.

Apply the Strategy

A newspaper contains many kinds of writing with different purposes. Read the description of each newspaper feature below. Explain whether the purpose of each is most likely to *inform, persuade,* or *entertain.* Then point out any additional purposes that each may have.

1. Front-page news article on a war that has broken out overseas
2. Comic strips and cartoons
3. Letter to the editor that explains the need for a new traffic light in town
4. Humorous column about the annoyances of spring cleaning
5. Weather forecast
6. Advertisement for a sale on shoes

✔ Here are situations in which judging a writer's purpose can be helpful:
  ▶ Reading a pamphlet you've been handed on the street
  ▶ Browsing through a magazine for an article to read
  ▶ Looking in the library for a good book

Real-World Reading Skills Workshop ◆ 377

Answers
Suggested responses:
1. The purpose is to inform.
2. The main purpose is to entertain. Additional purposes may be to inform or persuade.
3. The main purpose is to persuade, but the article may also inform.
4. The main purpose is to entertain, but the article may also be intended to inform or persuade.
5. The purpose is to inform. Some forecasts are also intended to entertain.
6. The main purpose is to persuade. In achieving this purpose, the ad may also inform and entertain.

377

Remind students that "body language" means the way people communicate in ways other than speech. Motions, body position, and facial expression are examples of body language. Body language is so strong that sometimes it even contradicts what a person is saying, and the listener gets the body-language message rather than the spoken one. For example, if you ask a friend for a favor, and the answer is "Sure," but your friend sighs before speaking and rolls his or her eyes upward, you get a very different message.

Customize for
Bodily/Kinesthetic Learners
Have students who communicate well with their bodies pantomime messages in body language for the class to "translate." Have them model good body language by role-playing conversations in which each person's body language supports his or her words. You may also want them to demonstrate a situation in which a person's body language is inconsistent with his or her words—for example, an unconvincing liar claiming that the dog ate his or her homework.

Apply the Strategy

Have students read over the situations they will role-play. Encourage them to think about the impression they would want to make and how their body language could help support that impression.

Answers
Suggested responses:
1. Students should make direct eye contact to support the impression that they are honest and trustworthy. They should smile to show they are friendly and easy to get along with.
2. Students should stand straight and have excellent posture, indicating they are upstanding citizens. They should look at their audience to show that they are sincere.
3. Students should smile and assume an informal body position to indicate that they are friendly and relaxed. Too serious a facial expression or an overly formal posture could make the new student nervous.

Speaking and Listening Workshop — Body Language

You speak with more than just your mouth—the rest of your body sends out messages, too. People are influenced by the way you sit, stand, and look as you speak. Your "body language" is an important part of communicating with others.

Posture Counts When you talk on the phone with friends, you might be lying on your bed or slumped in a chair. But in a formal face-to-face conversation, you can't be so casual. It is important to sit or stand straight as you speak. Otherwise, the other person may feel that you lack respect or aren't really interested in the conversation.

Maintain Eye Contact In a face-to-face conversation, it is always important to maintain good eye contact. Looking away can annoy or confuse the other person. Your body language may make you appear to be more interested in something else you see.

378 ◆ *The Lighter Side*

Tips for Using Good Body Language

✔ *If you want to make a good impression when speaking in a formal situation, follow these suggestions:*

▶ Stand or sit up straight. Don't slouch or hunch over as you speak and listen.
▶ Maintain good eye contact. Don't look away from the person with whom you are speaking.
▶ Wear a smile. A friendly face helps to ensure a friendly conversation.

Apply the Strategies

With a partner, role-play these situations. Use good body language as you speak and listen. Later, switch roles and perform each situation again.
1. You are being interviewed for a summer job—perhaps as a camp worker, a baby sitter, or a sales clerk.
2. The town mayor is honoring you for being an outstanding citizen. You are asked to say a few words after being presented with an award.
3. You meet a new student in the school cafeteria. During lunch, you tell the student about school, your town, and your interests.

 ### Workplace Skills Mini-Lesson

Job Interview
One of the most significant situations in which good body language is of utmost importance is the job interview. Usually, an applicant for a job is meeting the interviewer for the first time. In addition to information on the job application, and before the applicant even gets a chance to speak to the interviewer, the applicant's body language makes the first—and possibly even the strongest—impression. Have students list the personal qualities they would want to convey to the interviewer and indicate how body language could communicate each quality. For example, leaning slightly forward and making direct eye contact would indicate that the applicant is a good listener and would take direction well.

$\mathcal{E}$xtended Reading Opportunities

Everyone can use a laugh now and then. Following are just a few possibilities for extending your exploration of the lighter side.

Suggested Titles

The Prince and the Pauper
Mark Twain

In this social satire, set in sixteenth-century England, a young prince and a London street beggar exchange identities. Twain uses both understatement and exaggeration to describe the confusing events that follow. The amusing twists and turns of the plot ultimately reveal a deeper message—that it is wrong to judge people by their outward appearances, and that anyone can be a king.

Alice's Adventures in Wonderland
Lewis Carroll

In this fanciful story, a young girl falls down a rabbit hole and finds herself in a strange country where nothing seems to make sense. At times she grows huge as a giant; at other times she shrinks to the size of a mouse. Along the way, Alice meets an assortment of extraordinary characters, including a talking rabbit, a sleepy doormouse, and a grinning Cheshire cat. More than just a children's story, this book uses satire and symbolism to poke fun at society.

Childhood
Bill Cosby

In this entertaining book, funnyman Bill Cosby shares humorous reminiscences from his own childhood. He recalls getting scolded for his bad manners, acting up in school, suffering through crushes on girls, and playing sports on the streets of Philadelphia. Each tale is told in the sidesplitting style that has secured for Cosby his place as one of the country's best-loved comedians.

Other Possibilities

The Little Prince	Antoine de St. Exupery
The Pigman and Me	Paul Zindel
She Loves You: A Curious Tale Concerning a Miraculous Intervention	Elaine Segal

---

Planning Students' Extended Reading

All of these works are good choices for extending the theme of "The Lighter Side." Following is some information that will help you choose which to teach.

Customize for
Varying Student Needs

When assigning the selections in this part to your students, keep in mind the following factors:

- *The Prince and the Pauper* is a classic work of literature with a plot with which students may already be familiar. Twain's language and writing style may present a challenge to your less proficient readers.

- *Alice's Adventures in Wonderland* is a classic children's story. If you choose to assign this work, encourage students to focus on how Carroll uses satire to poke fun at society.

- *Childhood* is a book of reminiscences by a well-known figure that should be interesting and accessible to all of your students.

Resources for Teaching Novels, Plays, and Literature Collections

This booklet includes graphic organizers, teaching strategies, and transparencies that you can use in teaching any of these works.

Customize for
Special Needs

To meet the needs of your special needs students, you may want to consider using the version of *The Prince and the Pauper* in Globe Fearon's Pacemaker Classics series.

Planning Instruction and Assessment

Unit Objectives

1. To read selections in different genres that develop the theme of Visions of the Future.
2. To apply a variety of reading strategies, particularly literal comprehension strategies, appropriate for reading these selections
3. To recognize literary elements used in these selections
4. To increase vocabulary
5. To learn elements of grammar and usage
6. To write in a variety of modes and about situations based on the selections
7. To develop speaking and listening skills, by doing proposed activities

Meeting the Objectives

With each selection, you will find instructional material and portfolio opportunities through which students can meet these objectives. Further, you will find additional practice pages for reading strategies, literary elements, vocabulary, and grammar in the **Selection Support** booklet in the Teaching Resources box.

Setting Goals Work with your students at the beginning of the unit to set goals for unit outcomes. Plan what skills and concepts you wish students to acquire. You may individualize according to students' performance levels or learning modalities.

Portfolios You may have students keep portfolios of their work or of their work in progress. The activities and prompts on the Build Your Portfolio page of each selection provide opportunities for students to apply the concepts presented with the selection.

Humanities: Art

Untitled.

Help students understand that the art here depicts about three levels of an infinite iteration. The "big picture" represents a computer network. Each computer within that network displays another image of the network. Each computer within that image of the network displays another image of the network, in which each computer displays an image of the network—and so on, by implication, to infinity.

Help students link this artwork to the theme of Unit 5 ("Visions of the Future") by answering the following questions:

1. What view of the future does this picture suggest to you? *It suggests a world linked by an infinite number of computers, in which computerization seems to generate still more computerization.*
2. Do you feel that this picture presents a primarily positive or negative attitude toward computers? Explain. *Students*

interpreting the picture in a positive light should point to the versatility and power of computers and the way in which they allow us to extend our own capabilities. Students seeing a negative attitude should point to the slightly eerie mood of the picture, as well as the fact that it seems separate from the human world.

UNIT 5

Visions of the Future

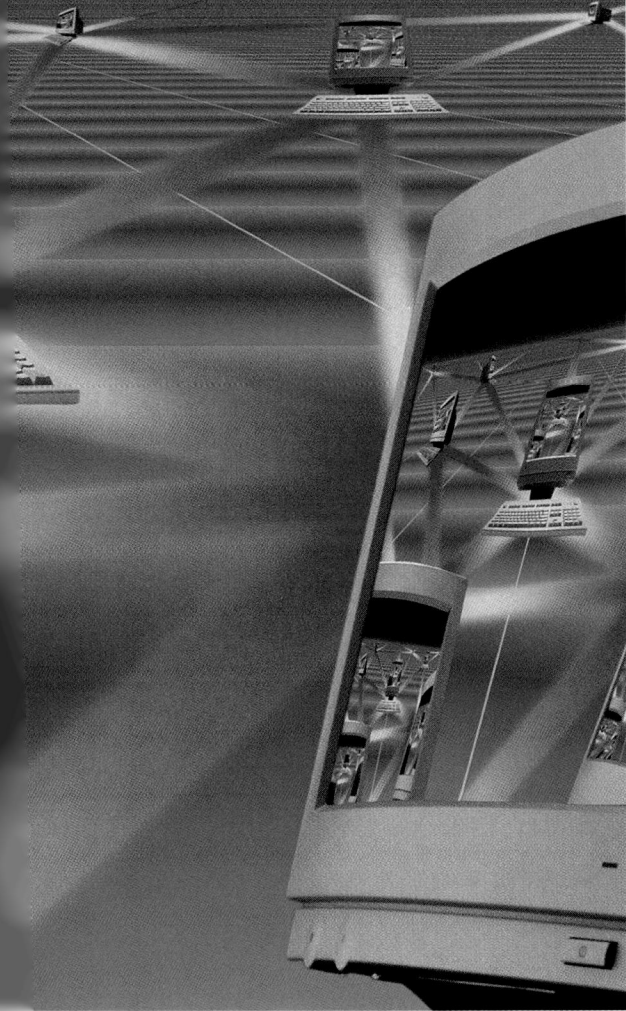

People have always tried to imagine the future. Some have worried that today's human carelessness will produce the problems of tomorrow. Others have looked toward the future with hope and optimism. Still others have imagined inventions and developments beyond our wildest dreams. As you read these selections, ask yourself how each writer's vision compares with your own.

◆ *381*

Assessing Student Progress

The following tools are available to measure the degree to which students meet the unit objectives:

Informal Assessment

The questions on the Guide for Responding sections are a first level of response to the concepts and skills presented with the selection. Students' responses are a brief informal measure of their grasp of the material. Their responses on this level can indicate where further instruction and practice are needed. You may then follow up with the practice pages in the **Selection Support** booklet.

You will find literature and reading guides in the **Alternative Assessment** booklet, which you may give students on an individual basis for informal assessment of their performance.

Formal Assessment

In the **Formal Assessment** booklet, you will find selection tests and a unit test.

Selection Tests The selection tests measure comprehension and skills acquisition for each selection or group of selections.

Unit Test The unit test applies the unit skills on a broader level. The Critical Reading section measures Unit Objectives 1, 2, and 3. The Vocabulary and Grammar section measures Objectives 4 and 5. The Essay section measures Objectives 1 and 6.

Alternative Assessment

Portfolios As you review individual pieces or the collected work in students' portfolios, you will find assessment sheets available in the portfolio section of the **Alternative Assessment** booklet.

Scoring Rubrics You will find scoring rubrics for writing modes in the **Alternative Assessment** booklet. You can apply these to Writing Mini-Lessons and to Writing Process Workshop lessons.

Speaking and Listening The **Alternative Assessment** booklet contains assessment sheets for speaking and listening activities.

Learning Modalities The **Alternative Assessment** contains activities that appeal to different learning styles. You may use these to as an alternative measurement of students' growth.

Guide for Reading

OBJECTIVES

1. To read, comprehend, and interpret an essay
2. To relate an essay to personal experience
3. To use strategies for reading critically
4. To identify expository writing
5. To build vocabulary in context and learn the word root *-simul-*
6. To develop skill in ensuring pronouns agree with indefinite pronoun antecedents
7. To write a letter for a time capsule using a clear beginning, middle, and end
8. To respond to the essay through writing, speaking and listening, and projects

SKILLS INSTRUCTION

Vocabulary:
Word Roots: *-simul-*

Grammar:
Pronoun Agreement With Indefinite Pronoun Antecedents

Reading for Success:
Strategies for Reading Critically

Literary Focus:
Expository Writing

Writing:
Clear Beginning, Middle, and End

Speaking and Listening:
Oral Report (teacher edition)

Critical Viewing
Evaluate; Apply

PORTFOLIO OPPORTUNITIES

Writing: Interview Questions; Description of the Future; Business Proposal

Writing Mini-Lesson: Letter for a Time Capsule

Speaking and Listening: Role Play; Oral Report

Projects: Multimedia Presentation; Advertising Campaign

More About the Author
When William H. Gates and Paul G. Allen founded Microsoft in April 1975, Gates was not yet twenty years old! Today, he is the CEO of an international company that has offices in forty-eight countries and distributes software in thirty languages. Much of Gates's success can be attributed to his ability to recognize the needs of consumers and to guide the company to develop products that meet those needs.

Bill Gates (1955–)

With a fortune of $23.9 billion as of January 1997, Bill Gates is "the richest man in the world, and maybe the smartest," according to *Newsweek* magazine. This world-famous businessman is the chief executive officer and co-founder of Microsoft Corporation, the world's largest computer software company.

A Computer Genius Gates's fascination with computers began in the eighth grade. He and his friend Paul Allen taught themselves the computer language BASIC and began writing programs. One of Gates's early programs created schedules for students—it even contained extra instructions that ensured Gates a spot as one of the few boys in a class full of girls. In high school, Gates spent the summers working as a computer programmer. He and Paul Allen also invented a way to use a new microprocessor chip to analyze and graph traffic data.

Envisioning the Future Although Gates and Allen's Traf-O-Data machine was not a huge success, they continued to believe in the importance of microprocessors. The two teenagers realized something that computer manufacturers did not: Microprocessors would improve rapidly and could become the "brains" of small, powerful computers.

In 1975, Gates and Allen wrote the first version of BASIC for a microcomputer. By doing so, they made it possible for other programs to be written. The two friends soon started their own company, which has grown into a corporation with more than 21,000 employees and $8 billion a year in sales.

Looking Forward Gates's ability to envision a future with inexpensive computing power enabled him to build a software empire. In his book *The Road Ahead*, Gates examines the future of computer technology.

◆ Build Vocabulary

WORD ROOTS: *-simul-*
In this excerpt from *The Road Ahead*, Bill Gates describes a television program from his childhood during which a man spun ten plates simultaneously on the noses of ten dogs. The word *simultaneous* contains the word root *-simul-*, which means "same." Thus, events that are simultaneous happen at the same time. What other words can you think of that contain the root *-simul-*?

simultaneously
capacious
precursors
infrared
parlance

WORD BANK
As you read *The Road Ahead,* you will encounter the words on this list. Each word is defined on the page where it first appears. Preview this list before you read.

◆ Build Grammar Skills

PRONOUN AGREEMENT WITH INDEFINITE PRONOUN ANTECEDENTS
A **pronoun** must agree in number (singular or plural) and gender with its antecedent, the word to which it refers. When the antecedent is a singular indefinite pronoun—a word like *anyone* or *someone*—a writer must use gender-neutral pronouns. In this example *his or her,* which is gender-neutral and singular, refers to the indefinite singular antecedent *anyone.*

The message could be . . . read later by *anyone,* at *his* or *her* convenience.

It would be incorrect to use the word *their* in place of *his or her* in the above sentence. Because *their* is plural, it would not agree with the singular antecedent.

382 ◆ *Visions of the Future*

from The Road Ahead

◆ *Literature and Your Life*

CONNECT YOUR EXPERIENCE

Technology changes at an astounding pace. Computers that seem cutting-edge when new don't have enough processing power, memory, or features a few years later. A video game that once impressed you may now seem slow and unexciting. In this essay, Bill Gates takes you on a tour of the technological innovations that will replace today's groundbreaking technology.

THEMATIC FOCUS: VISIONS OF THE FUTURE

Having a vision of the future has helped Bill Gates achieve tremendous success. As you read this selection, you may be inspired to begin developing your own vision of the future that might one day help you establish a successful career.

Journal Writing In your journal, speculate about the kinds of technology that will exist twenty years in the future. How will this technology affect your life?

◆ Background for Understanding

TECHNOLOGY

The Internet consists of tens of thousands of computer networks that are connected to one another via telephone lines and that follow an agreed-upon set of rules for communication. These networks belong to commercial organizations, educational institutions, governmental agencies, or not-for-profit organizations. (This is why Internet addresses contain the suffixes *.com, .edu, .gov,* or *.org.*)

Through the Internet, people can access "pages" of information. These pages may include text, graphics, sounds, programs, and "links" to other pages. In *The Road Ahead,* Bill Gates envisions a new Internet service—the delivery of high-quality video programming when the customer wants it.

◆ Literary Focus

EXPOSITORY WRITING

The Road Ahead is an example of **expository writing,** writing that informs or explains something by presenting information. Expository writing usually contains details, examples, and facts conveyed in an informative tone. A newspaper article on a current event, a chapter in a history book, an entry in an encyclopedia—all these are examples of expository writing. As you read this essay, notice how the author uses facts to share information and to support his opinions. Use a graphic organizer like this one to note each of Gate's opinions and to list the facts he uses to back it up.

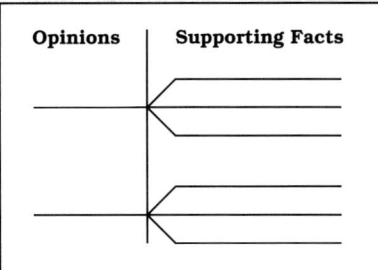

Opinions	Supporting Facts

Preparing for Standardized Tests

Reading The Reading for Success strategies for reading critically will help students' performance on the reading comprehension portions of standardized tests. Questions on these tests often require students to identify an author's purpose and to evaluate a writer's message. For additional practice, use the Reading for Success pages in **Selection Support,** pp. 119–120.

Grammar and Language Grammar items in the verbal portions of standardized tests may require students to provide the correct gender-neutral pronoun when the antecedent is indefinite. For example:

> Everyone had to turn in (his or her, their) locker key before summer vacation. *his or her*

The Build Grammar Skills lesson focuses on this topic. For additional practice, use the Build Grammar Skills page on Pronoun Agreement in **Selection Support,** p. 118.

 **Interest Grabber** Tell students to imagine that all the computers in their city or town ceased to function early this morning. Have them brainstorm for a list of ways in which their lives would be affected. Be sure students recognize the extent to which computers play a role in today's society. For example, computers often synchronize traffic lights at intersections, ring up purchases in stores, control bank transactions, monitor the vital signs of hospital patients, control the systems of an automobile, and so on. Tell students that they will read about additional applications for computer technology in the future.

Customize for
Less Proficient Readers

This selection contains a lot of information for the reader to process. To ensure comprehension, these students might pause at the end of each paragraph to summarize what they have read and state the author's ideas in their own words.

Customize for
More Advanced Students

Suggest that students keep this question in mind as they read and discuss it afterward: Does the author present opinions as facts and, if so, where?

Customize for
English Language Learners

Because the essay contains specialized communications vocabulary that may prove difficult for these students, have them listen to the audiocassette recording of the selection as they read, and remind them to use the notes at the bottom of the page for definitions of technical terms.

Listening to Literature
Audiocassettes

Customize for
Verbal/Linguistic Learners

Have students jot down a few interesting new words and note in their journals how they might use the words in conversation or in writing.

Guide for Reading

OBJECTIVES

1. To read, comprehend, and interpret a story
2. To relate a story to personal experience
3. To identify relevant details
4. To understand the elements of science fiction
5. To build vocabulary in context and learn the prefix *circum-*
6. To develop skill in using contractions
7. To write directions for operating a simple machine based on clear explanation of procedures
8. To respond to the story through writing, speaking and listening, and projects

SKILLS INSTRUCTION

Vocabulary:
Prefixes: *circum-*

Grammar:
Contractions

Reading Strategy:
Identify Relevant Details

Literary Focus:
Science Fiction

Writing: Clear Explanation of Procedures

Speaking and Listening:
Discussion of a Concept (teacher edition)

Critical Viewing:
Compare and Contrast; Extend

PORTFOLIO OPPORTUNITIES

Writing: Diary Entry; Newspaper Story; Title Memo

Writing Mini-Lesson: Directions for Operating a Simple Machine

Speaking and Listening: Discussion of a Concept; Performance

Projects: Poster; History of Computers

More About the Author

Isaac Asimov pioneered several concepts that have become mainstays of science fiction. Through his many stories and novels about robots, for example, he formulated a "code" of robot behavior that other writers learned from and followed. Briefly, the code states that a robot must place the safety of human beings above its own. Asimov also coined the term *robotics*—meaning the science of robots—in his fictional works.

Isaac Asimov (1920–1992)

When asked what he would do if a doctor gave him six months to live, Isaac Asimov replied, "Type faster." One noteworthy fact about this writer is the amazing amount of material he produced. During his last thirty years, he wrote a book about every six weeks.

Child Prodigy Asimov came to the United States from Russia when he was three years old. By the time he entered first grade, he had already taught himself to read. Realizing that his parents could not read English, he had asked the neighborhood children to tell him the sound of each letter of the alphabet. Then he began sounding out words himself. As a child, Asimov spent most of his time in his parents' candy store reading library books and pulp magazines (printed on cheap pulp paper, these magazines contained sensational stories of crime and love).

The Young Storyteller Growing up, Asimov wished for permanent reading material. Books had to be returned to the library, and magazines returned to the racks to be sold. At age eleven, Asimov decided to write his own books, which would make up his personal library.

Literary Achievements During his life, Isaac Asimov wrote more than 470 books on a wide variety of subjects, including science, history, Shakespeare, and the Bible, but he is best known as a writer of science fiction.

Isaac Asimov is considered one of the "founding fathers" of science fiction.

His most famous works include *I Robot, The Foundation Trilogy, Fantastic Voyage* (which was made into a movie), and short stories like "Nightfall" and "The Machine That Won the War."

◆ Build Vocabulary

PREFIXES: *circum-*

The word *circumvent* in this story begins with the prefix *circum-*, which means "around." Once you know this prefix, you can determine that *circumvent* refers to getting around something. It actually means "to go around; to avoid."

WORD BANK
erratic
grisly
imperturbable
oracle
surcease
subsidiary
circumvent

As you read "The Machine That Won the War," you will encounter the words on this list. Each word is defined on the page where it first appears. Preview this list before you read.

◆ Build Grammar Skills

CONTRACTIONS

A **contraction** is a shortened form of a word in which an apostrophe replaces the missing letter or letters. Contractions help a writer say things in a shorter, less formal way. Contractions can be used to make the character's words sound like everyday speech, as in these examples from "The Machine That Won the War."

He said, "*I'll* (I will) miss it after a grisly fashion."

And now *we're* (we are) alive and *it's* (it is) the Denebians who are shattered and destroyed.

392 ◆ Visions of the Future

Prentice Hall Literature Program Resources

REINFORCE / RETEACH / EXTEND

Selection Support Pages
Build Vocabulary: Prefixes: *circum-*, p. 122
Build Grammar Skills: Contractions, p. 123
Reading Strategy: Identify Relevant Details, p. 124
Literary Focus: Science Fiction, p. 125

Strategies for Diverse Student Needs, p. 30

Beyond Literature
Cross-Curricular Connection: Science: *Fact and Fiction,* p. 30

Formal Assessment Selection Test, p.104–106, Assessment Resources Software

Alternative Assessment, p. 30

Writing and Language Transparencies
Process Analysis, pp. 29–32

Resource Pro CD-ROM
"The Machine That Won the War"—includes all resource material and customizable lesson plan

Listening to Literature Audiocassettes
"The Machine That Won the War"

The Machine That Won the War

◆ Literature and Your Life

CONNECT YOUR EXPERIENCE
Your everyday life is more dependent on computers than you may think. Computers track purchases in stores, banking transactions, and library records. Sometimes, as in this story, computers are used for important military applications.

THEMATIC FOCUS: FANTASTIC IDEAS
In this futuristic story, a computer is used to defend Earth against invaders from another solar system. As you read, think about this: If you had to make an important decision, would you rely on a computer for help?

◆ Background for Understanding

TECHNOLOGY
The small, personal computers you are familiar with had not yet been invented when Isaac Asimov wrote this story. Instead, computers were big, cumbersome machines like the ENIAC shown here. Solving problems on such computers required the setting of thousands of cables and switches by hand. Other early computers were called UNIVAC, EDVAC, MANIAC, and BINAC. Perhaps Asimov was thinking of these machines when he named the computer in "The Machine That Won the War." The name he uses is Multivac.

◆ Literary Focus

SCIENCE FICTION
This story is **science fiction**, a form of literature in which the writer creates settings, characters, and situations that are not found in reality. The setting might be an altered present, an alternative past, or a possible future. All these changes to time or reality are based on real science, but the writer makes free use of imagination. As you read, notice details that tell you this story is set in the future.

Journal Writing Choose a science-fiction movie, television series, or book that you like. List details—such as characters, vehicles, and machines—that are not found in reality.

◆ Reading Strategy

IDENTIFY RELEVANT DETAILS
At the beginning of the story, a character says, "It's hard to remember when we weren't at war with Deneb, and it seems against nature now to be at peace and to look at the stars without anxiety." This mention of the stars is a **relevant,** or important, **detail** that causes you to realize that the war was not between countries on Earth, and you realize that the story is set in the future. Throughout the story, Asimov uses such details to describe this future world. Look at this example:

> We hadn't reached the point where manned vessels had had to take over and where interstellar warps could swallow up a planet clean, if aimed correctly.

Even though you don't know what an interstellar warp is, you know that it's dangerous if it can "swallow up a planet clean." Recognizing relevant details like this will help you understand and appreciate the story.

Guide for Reading ◆ 393

One-Minute Insight

How much credit does a giant computer known as Multivac deserve for Earth's victory in a ten-year-long war with a world called Deneb? That is the question that three veterans of the war probe in this story. As Henderson, Jablonsky, and Swift each reveal the secret ways in which they tampered with, "corrected," and ultimately disregarded the mighty computer's data, it becomes clear that Multivac is not quite the hero most people believe it to be. The three men's revelations prove that the computer is no match for the complex and unpredictable human mind.

Customize for
Visual / Spatial Learners

Have these students carefully examine the illustration on these two pages. Discuss this futuristic scene and what it suggests about the story. Use the following questions:

1. What is going on in the scene? *Space craft are firing weapons at each other.*
2. When and where is the action depicted in this picture taking place? *It is happening in the distant future in outer space.*
3. Based upon this illustration, what do you think the story is about? *The story is probably about a war, or about the threat of war, in the future.*

394   Visions of the Future

Block Scheduling Strategies

Consider these suggestions to take advantage of extended class time:

- To introduce students to this selection, hold a science-fiction panel discussion in which students discuss the characteristics of the genre. Ask students to explore the common elements of science-fiction movies and science-fiction television programs they've seen.

- To familiarize students with the author, invite them to research Isaac Asimov on the Internet, either before or after they read.

- To reinforce what students have learned about science fiction from the selection, have students meet in groups, complete the Group Activity in the Guide for Responding (p. 399).

- Students can work in discussion groups to answer the Reading Strategy and Literary Focus questions on relevant details and science fiction, respectively (p. 400).

- Have students complete the Writing Mini-Lesson (p. 401). Before students begin writing their directions for operating a simple machine, have a class discussion in which students can brainstorm for examples of everyday machines they have used.

The Machine That Won the War

Isaac Asimov

The celebration had a long way to go and even in the silent depths of Multivac's underground chambers, it hung in the air.

If nothing else, there was the mere fact of isolation and silence. For the first time in a decade, technicians were not scurrying about the vitals of the giant computer, the soft lights did not wink out their <u>erratic</u> patterns, the flow of information in and out had halted.

It would not be halted long, of course, for the needs of peace would be pressing. Yet now, for a day, perhaps for a week, even Multivac might celebrate the great time, and rest.

Lamar Swift took off the military cap he was wearing and looked down the long and empty main corridor of the enormous computer. He sat down rather wearily in one of the technician's swing-stools, and his uniform, in which he had never been comfortable, took on a heavy and wrinkled appearance.

He said, "I'll miss it all after a <u>grisly</u> fashion. It's hard to remember when we weren't at war with Deneb, and it seems against nature now to be at peace and to look at the stars without anxiety."

The two men with the Executive Director of the Solar Federation were both younger than Swift. Neither was as gray. Neither looked quite as tired.

John Henderson, thin-lipped and finding it hard to control the relief he felt in the midst of triumph, said, "They're destroyed! They're destroyed! It's what I keep saying to myself over and over and I still can't believe it. We all talked so much, over so many years, about the menace hanging over Earth and all its worlds, over every human being, and all the time it was true, every word of it. And now we're alive and it's the Denebians who are shattered and destroyed. They'll be no menace now, ever again."

"Thanks to Multivac," said Swift, with a quiet glance at the <u>imperturbable</u> Jablonsky, who through all the war had been Chief Interpreter of science's <u>oracle</u>. "Right, Max?"

Jablonsky shrugged. He said, "Well, that's what *they* say." His broad thumb moved in the direction of his right

◆ Build Vocabulary

erratic (er at′ ik) *adj.*: Irregular; random

grisly (griz′ lē) *adj.*: Horrifying; gruesome

imperturbable (im′ pər tʉr′ bə bəl) *adj.*: Unable to be excited or disturbed

oracle (ō′ rə kəl) *n.*: Source of knowledge or wise counsel

The Machine That Won the War 395

Cross-Curricular Connection: Math

The number system we use every day is called the *decimal system*. It uses 10 digits—0 through 9—and place values that go up by multiples of 10 to represent any possible number. Computers, however, store and process numbers, as well as words, pictures, and sounds, using the *binary system*.

The prefix *bi-* means "two." The binary system uses two digits—0 and 1—and place values that go up by multiples of 2 to express numbers. Thus the number 9 in the binary system is 1001. (The rightmost place stands for 1's; the next place stands for 2's; the next stands for 4's; and the next stands for 8's. Thus 1001 can be read as "one 8 plus one 1=9.")

- Write the following numbers and their binary "translations" on the board:
  1=0001
  2=0010
  3=0011
  4=0100

  5=0101
Challenge students to continue through the number 9. *6=0110; 7=0111; 8=1000; 9=1001*

- Have students research why computers use the binary system. *The two digits—0 and 1—correspond to the two electrical states—"off" and "on"—produced in computer circuits.*

395

CONNECTIONS TO TODAY'S WORLD

OBJECTIVES

1. To read, comprehend, and interpret a teleplay
2. To relate a teleplay to personal experience
3. To respond to a teleplay through writing, speaking and listening, and projects

SKILLS INSTRUCTION

Speaking and Listening:
Dramatic Performance (teacher edition)

Thematic Connection:
Fantastic Ideas

Critical Viewing:
Infer; Draw Conclusions; Predict

PORTFOLIO OPPORTUNITIES

Writing: Television Listing; Description of a Future Invention
Speaking and Listening: Dramatic Performance
Projects: Internet Research

More About *Star Trek*

The enormously popular television show *Star Trek* has had several incarnations. It began as a science-fiction show created by Gene Roddenberry in 1968 about the starship *Enterprise*. The *Enterprise* was captained by James T. Kirk and staffed by, among others, the impassive Mr. Spock (half-human and half-Vulcan, a race without human emotions), the resourceful engineer Scotty, and the excitable Dr. McCoy. Although the original *Enterprise* had a five-year mission to go "where no man has gone before," the show ran only three years. However, many loyal fans called "Trekkies" watched the show in reruns. While interest in *Star Trek* grew, the show inspired fan clubs, conventions, spin-off books, and magazines. The popularity of the canceled show eventually led to several movies and a number of television sequels, the first of which was *Star Trek: The Next Generation*. According to physicist David Allen Batchelor, Ph.D., "Generally, *Star Trek* is . . . more faithful to science than any other science-fiction series ever shown on television," despite its occasional mistakes and inaccuracies.

Thematic Connection

FANTASTIC IDEAS

Years before the first astronaut ventured into space, science-fiction writers were transporting readers to distant planets and introducing technological wonders that seemed possible only in the imagination. Amazingly, many of the events, settings, and inventions that science-fiction pioneers such as H. G. Wells and Jules Verne brought to life in their stories and novels have become a reality only decades later. At the same time, science-fiction has continually grown in popularity and has extended beyond literature to movies and television. Contemporary writers such as Isaac Asimov and Arthur C. Clarke have continued to stretch the boundaries of readers' imaginations, exploring such possibilities as permanent space stations and colonies on other planets. Meanwhile, millions of viewers have flocked to theaters to see *Star Wars* and other movies in which human heroes battle alien creatures far into the future and deep in space.

Of all the science-fiction stories to be presented either in print or on film, the *Star Trek* series may be the most popular. The original *Star Trek* television series that first aired in 1968 has been adapted into several successful movies and has inspired a variety of spinoff series, including *Star Trek: The Next Generation*. The selection that follows is a portion of a script from the television series *Star Trek: The Next Generation*. Like the science-fiction stories in this section, the episode is set in space in the future. As you read, try to imagine which, if any, of the fantastic devices described in the selection—such as a transporter that can "beam" a person from one place to another in a matter of seconds—will someday become a reality.

402 ◆ *Visions of the Future*

Interest Grabber Most of your students will probably be familiar with *Star Trek: The Next Generation*. They might enjoy taking a poll to find out who has seen the show; the spin-offs, such as *Deep Space 9*; the original series; and each of the movies.

Since some students may *not* be familiar with the show, invite resident "Trekkies" to summarize the high points by asking, "What does a first-time viewer/reader need to know to get the most out of the show?"

Customize for
English Language Learners
Alert these students to the made-up words they will encounter. You may have English language learners raise their hand when each term arises so that you can explain the term.

Customize for
Logical/Mathematical Learners
These students might enjoy finding out which aspects of the show are based in science and which are totally imaginary. Use the Internet section of Beyond the Teleplay (p. 409) in the teacher edition.

STAR TREK: THE NEXT GENERATION

Data's Day

Story by **Harold Apter**

Teleplay by **Harold Apter and Ronald D. Moore**

In this episode, the crew of the starship Enterprise makes contact with one of the ships of their fiercest enemies, the Romulans, the warlike inhabitants of a distant planet. At the beginning of this segment, Vulcan Ambassador T'Pel of the Federation (an alliance of planets that includes Earth) is about to be beamed aboard the Romulan ship for a negotiation session. Her mission is to negotiate with the enemy Romulans to restore full diplomatic relations between the Federation and the Romulan Empire.

❶

❷

[*The image of* MENDAK, *a Romulan Admiral, comes on the screen. His attitude is neutral . . . a shrewd negotiator careful not to give anything away.*]

CAST

PICARD, Captain of the *USS Enterprise*
RIKER, First Officer
DATA, an android
BEVERLY, Dr. Crusher, Ship's Doctor
GEORDI, Engineering Officer
WORF, Security Officer
O'BRIEN, Transporter Operator
T'PEL, Vulcan Ambassador
MENDAK, A Romulan Admiral

ABBREVIATIONS

EXT.: Exterior
INT.: Interior
V.O.: Voice-over
O.S.: Offscreen

MENDAK: I am Admiral Mendak.

T'PEL: There is no established protocol for a meeting of this nature. The logical course is for me to transport aboard your ship and begin the negotiations.

❸

MENDAK: [*noncommittal*] Yes . . . [*looks at* PICARD] Captain, I note your defensive systems have been activated.

[PICARD *glances at* WORF *and receives a quick nod in return.*]

PICARD: As are yours, Admiral.

MENDAK: [*smiles*] It was not meant as an accusation . . . [*to* T'PEL] Indeed, I salute your show of strength. Ambassador, we are honored by your presence. You may transport aboard at your convenience.

T'PEL: The honor is mine.

[*The view screen returns to*

Data's Day ◆ 403

One-Minute Insight This episode focuses on two major themes. The first is logic and deductive reasoning. Data takes Sherlock Holmes's motto to heart: "Once you have eliminated the impossible, whatever remains, however improbable, must be the truth." Based on this principle, Data, an android whose brain is really a computer, questions a fact that everyone else had taken for granted—and solves the mystery.

The other major theme of the episode is maintaining peace. Both Captain Picard and the Romulans must decide when to present a strong front and when to back down.

Thematic Connection

❶ Fantastic Ideas Ask students what aspects of this situation tell us that this is a science-fiction program, rather than a realistic show. *Students should identify the following elements: the starship; the existence of nonhuman races (Romulans and Vulcans); the ability to transport people by "beaming"; and reference to the Federation, "an alliance of planets that includes Earth."*

◆ Background for Understanding

❷ Point out to students that, although many scientists agree that life may exist in other solar systems, it is unlikely that so many distant races would have humanoid shapes, as the Romulans and Vulcans do. The transporter, which beams people aboard the *Enterprise*, is purely imaginary. According to today's physics, it seems unlikely that a person's atoms could be taken apart and then reassembled exactly as before.

Comprehension Check ✓

❸ What is T'Pel proposing? *Students should realize that T'Pel, an ambassador for the Federation, is proposing to board an enemy warship to begin peace negotiations.*

Beyond the Classroom

Community Connection
Planetarium Although many of the scientific details in *Star Trek* are simply imaginary, others do reflect what scientists know about our universe. One way for students to get a sense of the vastness of the universe is at a planetarium. Most planetariums offer shows about stars, planets, and other features of space, as well as exhibits and guided tours from which visitors can learn more about astronomy and physics.

If possible, arrange a field trip for your class to a local planetarium or science museum. If this is not feasible, encourage interested students to attend on their own and then report back to the class. In either case, you might work as a class to identify questions of interest before the trip and then arrange for a report or discussion afterward, both to see how those questions were answered and to identify any new questions that might have arisen.

❶ Draw Conclusions The expression is appropriate because Data is actually a computerized robot fabricated to resemble a human being.

◆ Critical Thinking

❷ Draw Conclusions Ask students what conclusions they draw from the fact that the material left behind by the ambassador does not match the genetic record of the ambassador herself. *Students should conclude that the material left behind was not actually from the ambassador's own body—that the material may have been planted or may have been from another person.*

❸ Clarification Invite students to recognize that Data has his own theory of "the discrepancy," but that he encourages Beverly to present her theory first. Ask them why Data might choose to proceed this way and whether, based on their own experience, they think he is right to do so. *Students may say that Data is being cautious, or that he thinks Beverly will be more likely to believe him if she comes up with the idea herself. Some students may say Data is being tactful.*

◆ Critical Thinking

❹ Make Inferences Invite students to infer where the "second" transporter signal has come from and why. *Students should infer that it came from the Romulans, as some kind of hostile trick, possibly to kidnap Ambassador T'Pel.*

❺ Clarification Make sure students understand that, although there is no realistic physics behind the notion of "subspace," this speech is an important explanation for the plot. If Romulan transporters can imitate those of the *Enterprise*, that means that the Romulans could have been running their transporter secretly, at the same time that the *Enterprise* was running its transporter—thus capturing T'Pel from the *Enterprise* transporter.

▲ **Critical Viewing** This picture of Data shows a face with a blank—though perhaps slightly pleasant—stare. Why is this expression an appropriate one for Data? [**Draw Conclusions**]

BEVERLY: Now, the breakdown of the organic material found on the Transporter pad should be identical. [*beat as she reads screen*] Mitochondrial structure fits all general parameters . . . no change in the nucleotide bases . . .

[*The test stops and the two screens highlight sections of the genetic code that are different.*]

BEVERLY: [*frowns*] There's a slight discrepancy in the base pair sequence.

[*She runs another test . . . the screens then stop on another section of code that's different.*]

BEVERLY: [*to* DATA] Chemically, these are identical . . . however, the organic sample from the Transporter is showing numerous single-bit errors . . . like replicated material.

DATA: Can you postulate an explanation for the discrepancy?

BEVERLY: I'd say the DNA was either mutated by the Transporter during the rematerialization process . . .

DATA: [*he expected this*] A supposition not supported by the Transporter records.

BEVERLY: Or these aren't the remains of the Ambassador.

[*On their reactions . . .*]

FADE OUT.

FADE IN:

INT. READY ROOM

[DATA, GEORDI, RIKER and PICARD.]

DATA: [*to* PICARD] The only abnormality found during my investigation was a temporary increase in the matter to energy signal ratio. This fluctuation was well within operating parameters and would normally not invite further consideration. However, due to the circumstances, I decided to investigate the possibility that a *second* Transporter signal had caused the fluctuation. Although this was highly improbable, it was the only remaining theory.

RIKER: A second transporter signal? From where?

DATA: From the Devoras.

GEORDI: Romulan transporters operate on similar subspace frequencies to our own. With minor adjustments they could be made to simulate our own transporter carrier wave.

PICARD: So they beamed the Ambassador off our own pad.

DATA: While simultaneously a small amount of genetically similar material was left in the Ambassador's place.

RIKER: To make us believe she died as a result of the "malfunction."

DATA: Yes, sir.

Although the safest course of action would be to contact Starfleet for instructions, Picard decides to confront the Romulans. Enterprise's crew sets a course to intercept the Devoras and prepares for battle. Closing in, the Enterprise hails the Devoras and opens up a communications channel.

ON VIEWSCREEN—INTERCUT AS NEEDED

[MENDAK's *image appears.*]

MENDAK: Captain Picard, you agreed to leave the Neutral Zone without—

PICARD: [*firm*] Admiral Mendak, you are holding our Ambassador captive.

[*A wisp of a smile plays about* MENDAK's *lips . . . he seems to enjoy this a little.*]

MENDAK: I can assure you . . . there is no one being held captive aboard this ship.

PICARD: We know about the Transporter "malfunction" and that you are holding Ambassador T'Pel.

[MENDAK *waits for a beat . . . then nods to someone o.s.*]

WORF: Captain, Romulan Warbird decloaking to starboard!

EXT. SPACE—THE ENTERPRISE & ROMULANS

[*Another Romulan ship decloaks and now two Romulans are facing the Enterprise.*]

INT. MAIN BRIDGE

[*As before. Intercut with Viewscreen.*]

MENDAK: I suggest you leave . . . now.

[PICARD *will not be moved.*]

PICARD: It is my responsibility to protect the lives of Federation citizens. I will not permit this abduction to succeed.

[MENDAK *isn't taking him seriously yet.*]

MENDAK: Captain, you're not going to start an incident which might—

PICARD: [*final*] I am prepared to take whatever action is necessary to obtain the Ambassador's return.

[MENDAK *takes* PICARD's *measure for a moment.* MENDAK *finally sees that* PICARD *means business.*]

MENDAK: Fortunately . . . I'm not ready to start a war today . . .

[MENDAK *gestures to someone o.s. and Ambassador* T'PEL *moves into view, wearing a Romulan uniform. There are shocked reactions around the Bridge.*]

RIKER: T'Pel?

T'PEL: Sub-Commander Selok, actually.

[*It's all clear to* PICARD *now.*]

PICARD: A spy.

MENDAK: A patriot, Captain . . . she has

Data's Day ◆ 407

Critical Thinking

6 Make Judgments Invite students to give their opinions about Picard's course of action, which is not "the safest." Why do they think he is choosing this course, and what do they believe will be the outcome? *Students will probably say that Picard is acting out of concern for T'Pel's safety and perhaps also out of anger at the Romulans. Students may predict a battle, a heroic rescue of T'Pel, or a new plot twist.*

Critical Thinking

7 Compare and Contrast Ask students to identify the differences between Picard's and Mendak's reactions. What does this reveal about their characters? *Students may say that Picard is upset but firm, whereas Mendak is amused. They may conclude that Picard is earnest and concerned for the welfare of others, whereas Mendak is arrogant, not taking the lives of others seriously.*

Literature and Your Life

8 Ask students, based on what they know about dealing with bullies, whether they approve or disapprove of Picard's reaction. Invite them to explain their answers. *Some students may applaud Picard's willingness to take a firm stand in order to protect T'Pel; others may be concerned that his actions might start a war.*

Critical Thinking

9 Analyze Characters What do Mendak's words tell students about his character? *Students may conclude that while Mendak is presumably an evil bully, he is completely in control of his emotions and capable of making rational decisions.*

Critical Thinking

10 Evaluate a Scene's Effectiveness Invite students to give their opinion of this revelation. What do they think it means? Were they surprised? Would they have preferred a different outcome? *Students should realize that Sub-Commander Selok is a spy. Encourage students to explain why they were or were not surprised, and to explain why they did or did not like the revelation.*

❶ Predict Some students will say that future technological developments will enable such a ship to be built, while others might believe that such technology will probably never be available.

❷ Clarification Invite students to explain this phrase, which is roughly equivalent to "You win some, you lose some."

❸ Clarification Invite students to explain Data's reference to the analogy, which suggests that although Picard has conceded this round to the Romulans, he has not given up the "game"—the contest for control of the universe, or the effort to make peace in the universe.

Reinforce and Extend

Answers
Literature and Your Life

Reader's Response Students' reasons should include references to the text.

Thematic Focus Some students may say that based upon the growth in complexity of current technology, some things, such as the starship and the phaser, might become realities.

✓ **Check Your Comprehension**
1. Ambassador T'Pel seems to have been killed in a transporter accident.
2. Data discovers that the Romulan transporter had beamed the Ambassador off the *Enterprise*.
3. She is Romulan Sub-Commander Selok.

◆ Critical Thinking
1. The Romulans are devious people who will do almost anything to gain an advantage over an opponent. The fact that the Romulans plant a spy on board the *Enterprise* and lie about the transporter incident illustrates this.
2. The Romulans lie about the transporter incident and accuse Picard of staging the "accident" in order to prevent peace negotiations. The crew of the *Enterprise* care about the safety of T'Pel and try to rescue her.

(Answers continue on p. 409.)

408

▲ **Critical Viewing** The *USS Enterprise* explores the outer reaches of space at warp speed. Do you think that such a technologically advanced ship will ever be built? Why or why not? **[Predict]** ❶

performed her service to the Empire with distinction.

T'PEL/SELOK: [*smiles*] Thank you for your . . . help, Captain.

MENDAK: You can see now that we are not holding one of your citizens . . . and we thank you for returning our sister to us. [*voice hardens*] But my patience has limits . . . the game is over. I expect you to leave peacefully. Now.

[*The transmission ends.*]

WORF: Sir, long-range scanners show three more Romulan ships moving into this sector.

[PICARD *takes that in . . . looks at* RIKER.]

❷ **RIKER:** [*quiet*] Some days you get the bear, some days the bear gets you.

[PICARD *sees the only rational course of action.*]

PICARD: Reverse course . . . take us back to Federation territory, warp six. Engage.

EXT. SPACE – THE ENTERPRISE & ROMULANS

[*The Enterprise turns and moves away.*]

INT. MAIN BRIDGE

[*As before . . . push in on* DATA.]

DATA [V.O.]: Captain Picard once drew an analogy between life and a chess game . . . he said that the loss of a single piece does not concede the game itself.

[DATA *glances over his shoulder at the others on the Bridge. People are returning to normal business. The Red Alert indicators turn off.*]

408 ◆ Visions of the Future

 Speaking and Listening Mini-Lesson

Dramatic Performance
This mini-lesson supports the Speaking and Listening activity in the Idea Bank on page 409.
Introduce the Concept Have students list the materials they will need to prepare to make a dramatic presentation. They can decide whether to use simple costumes or props, how to set up the space to indicate the starship, whether they want to use sound effects and music, and so on. They should also decide who will play each part.

Develop Background Discuss what makes a dramatic presentation effective; for example: speaking loudly, clearly, and with expression; using appropriate gestures; having lines memorized; knowing where and when to move.

Apply the Information Encourage students to set goals for rehearsal, to rehearse, and to present their scenes in class.

Assess the Outcome To evaluate the performances, have students use the Peer Assessment: Dramatic Performance page in *Alternative Assessment,* p. 113.

Guide for Responding

◆ Literature and Your Life

Reader's Response After reading this script, would you like to see the episode? Why or why not?

Thematic Focus Do you believe that the types of events and technological wonders depicted in this episode might become a reality? Why or why not?

☑ Check Your Comprehension

1. What happens when Ambassador T'Pel attempts to beam aboard the Romulan ship?
2. What important discovery does Data make?
3. What is T'Pel's true identity?

◆ Critical Thinking

INTERPRET

1. Based on their actions in this selection, how would you characterize the Romulans? Support your answer. **[Analyze]**
2. How does the Romulans' behavior contrast with that of the *Enterprise* crew? Support your answer. **[Compare and Contrast]**
3. What details and events in this selection help to build suspense or interest in the outcome? Explain. **[Support]**
4. Why is the ending surprising? **[Analyze]**

EXTEND

5. How might this episode be different if it had been written as a short story, rather than in the form of a television script? **[Literature Link]**

Thematic Connection

FANTASTIC IDEAS

Like the science-fiction stories in this section, this episode from *Star Trek: The Next Generation*, presents a vision of the future in which humans inhabit space colonies and travel effortlessly from planet to planet.

1. Compare and contrast the details of the setting of this episode with those of one of the science-fiction stories in this section. What are the similarities? What are the differences?
2. What is it about science-fiction television programs, movies, and stories that attracts audiences? Support your answer.

Idea Bank

Writing

1. **Television Listing** Write a brief summary of this episode to appear as a listing in a television guide. Describe the events in a way that will entice viewers to watch the program.
2. **Description of a Future Invention** This episode is filled with technological wonders, such as transporters that can "beam" people from one spaceship to another. Use your imagination to dream up some other technological wonder that might be invented in the distant future. Then write a detailed description of this invention.

Speaking and Listening

3. **Dramatic Performance** With a group of classmates, assume the roles of the various characters in this episode and act it out for your classmates. Try to deliver your lines in a way that fits the characters and captures their emotions. **[Performing Arts Link]**

Projects

4. **Internet Research** The Internet is filled with Web sites that feature information about *Star Trek*. Do some exploring to see what you can learn about this amazingly popular series. Share your findings with your classmates. **[Technology Link]**

Data's Day ◆ 409

 Beyond the Selection

FURTHER READING

Other Works With the Theme of the Future
Dhalgren, Samuel Delany
The Dispossessed, Ursula LeGuin
Valentine Pontifex, Robert Silverberg

INTERNET

You and your students may find additional information about *Star Trek* on the Internet. We suggest the following site. Please be aware, however, that the site may have changed from the time we published this information.

For a fascinating article about how scientists view *Star Trek*, go to **http://www.gstc.nasa.gov/education/just_for_fun/startrek/html**

We *strongly recommend* that you preview the site before you send students to it.

409

Guide for Reading

OBJECTIVES

1. To read, comprehend, and interpret poems
2. To relate poems to personal experience
3. To recognize a poet's purpose
4. To identify alliteration
5. To build vocabulary in context and learn the suffix -ous
6. To develop skill in using commonly confused words: lie, lay
7. To write a poem using brevity and clarity
8. To respond to the poems through writing, speaking and listening, and projects

SKILLS INSTRUCTION

Vocabulary:
Suffixes: -ous

Grammar:
Commonly Confused Words: Lie and Lay

Reading Strategy:
Recognize a Poet's Purpose

Literary Focus:
Alliteration

Writing:
Brevity and Clarity

Speaking and Listening:
Panel Discussion (teacher edition)

PORTFOLIO OPPORTUNITIES

Writing: Diary Entry; Poem; Short Story
Writing Mini-Lesson: Poem to a Future Generation
Speaking and Listening: Panel Discussion; Oral Interpretation
Projects: Bumper Stickers; Job Expo

More About the Authors

The terrain, the people, and his own experiences of his native New England countryside all enrich **Robert Frost's** poetry.

Richard Brautigan was born in Tacoma, Washington. In the late 1950's, he moved to San Francisco, where he was "discovered" by Kurt Vonnegut, who introduced his work to a major publisher.

While **Sara Teasdale** led an unhappy life, she enjoyed success as a poet. Her first volume of poems (1907) established her reputation, and in 1918 her book *Love Songs* won the Columbia University Poetry Society prize, forerunner of the Pulitzer Prize for poetry.

Edwin Muir's philosophical poetry reflects the poet's search for meaning in life. Frequent themes are those of time and immortality, love and death.

Robert Frost (1874–1963)

The title of his poem "Fire and Ice" could well describe two different views of this poet. Witty and warm to some, he appeared cold and biting to others. All agreed, however, that Frost put poetry first in his life. The result was a large body of work that made him the most popular American poet of his time. Frost won four Pulitzer Prizes. (See page 164 for more on Robert Frost.)

Sara Teasdale (1884–1933)

Sara Teasdale's poetry—much of it on the subject of love—was rooted in her own experience. Because of difficulties with her personal relationships, Teasdale had a sad life, and she often expressed her sadness through poetry. She once commented that "poems are written because of a state of emotional irritation" and that the poem "free[s] the poet from an emotional burden."

Richard Brautigan (1935–1984)

With the 1967 publication of his novel *Trout Fishing in America*, this writer became a chief spokesperson of the hippie generation. Ironically, Brautigan was actually a product of the beat generation that preceded the hippies by more than a decade. Nevertheless, in his writing Brautigan was definitely a free spirit.

Edwin Muir (1887–1959)

A prolific writer who produced many volumes of poetry and several novels, Edwin Muir had visions of the future that were rooted in his past. He spent his first fourteen years on a farm in the Orkney Islands north of the Scottish mainland, and much of his imagery comes from this place.

◆ Build Vocabulary

SUFFIXES: -ous

Sara Teasdale describes "wild plum trees in tremulous white." The word *tremulous* is related to the word *tremble.* The suffix *-ous* means "full of" or "characterized by." Added to the base form of a word, it becomes an adjective. So *tremulous* means "characterized by trembling" or "quivering."

WORD BANK

perish
suffice
tremulous
covenant
confounds
steeds
archaic

As you read these poems, you will encounter the words on this list. Each word is defined on the page where it first appears. Preview the list before you read.

◆ Build Grammar Skills

COMMONLY CONFUSED WORDS: LIE AND LAY

In "The Horses," Edwin Muir describes unused objects using two different but related verbs:

The tractors lie about our fields.
...ploughs, long laid aside.

The verb *lie* means "to be in a reclining position." It is never followed by a direct object. The verb *lay* means "to place" or "to put down." It may be followed by a direct object. Confusion sometimes occurs because the past tense of *lie* is *lay.* Become familiar with the principal parts:

lie, lying, lay, (has) lain
lay, laying, laid, (has) laid

410 ◆ Visions of the Future

Prentice Hall Literature Program Resources

REINFORCE / RETEACH / EXTEND

Selection Support Pages
Build Vocabulary: Suffixes: -ous, p.126
Build Grammar Skills: Lie and Lay, p. 127
Reading Strategy: Recognize a Poet's Purpose, p.128
Literary Focus: Alliteration, p.129

Strategies for Diverse Student Needs, p. 31

Beyond Literature
Career Connection: Computers in the Workplace, p. 31

Formal Assessment Selection Test, pp. 107–109,

Assessment Resources Software

Alternative Assessment, p. 31

Writing and Language Transparencies
Sunburst Organizer, p. 64

Resource Pro CD-ROM
—includes all resource material and customizable lesson plan

Listening to Literature Audiocassettes
"Fire and Ice," "There Will Come Soft Rains," "All Watched Over by Machines of Loving Grace," "The Horses"

Fire and Ice ◆ All Watched Over by Machines of Loving Grace ◆ There Will Come Soft Rains ◆ The Horses

◆ Literature and Your Life

CONNECT YOUR EXPERIENCE

Is the world heading toward a gloomy destruction or a golden age of harmony? You may have seen movies or read books about future worlds with very different views of the future. Some are frightening; some are enticing; some are thought-provoking. As you'll discover in the following selections, poets, also, have used their craft to explore visions of the future.

Journal Writing Write about a story you have read or a movie you have seen about a future world. Describe your feelings about this world.

THEMATIC FOCUS: FANTASTIC IDEAS

These poems present fantastic ideas that may prompt you to think about the direction in which our world is moving.

◆ Background for Understanding

HISTORY

In "There Will Come Soft Rains," Sara Teasdale mentions "the war," but she does not specify which war. The poet and her husband both opposed World War I (1914–1918), even though their position was not a popular one.

World War I, called the Great War at the time, was the first war fought with machine guns, which could spit out 600 to 700 bullets per minute. The war pitted Germany against France, England, and Russia. When soldiers left their trenches to charge the enemy, they could be sure that large numbers of them would be brutally cut down by machine-gun fire. The impersonality of this type of warfare horrified many.

◆ Literary Focus

ALLITERATION

Alliteration is the repetition of a consonant sound at the beginning of a word. Poets use alliteration to emphasize certain words, and to create sounds and musical effects. The first two lines of "Fire and Ice" begin, "Some say." The repetition of the s sound creates the effect of whispering and adds a sense of slyness to the poem.

◆ Reading Strategy

RECOGNIZE A POET'S PURPOSE

These poems are like wake-up calls. Each poet's purpose is to call attention to a situation or an attitude that the poet finds troubling or worthy of thought. Learning to recognize a poet's purpose will help you better understand a poem.

One thing that will help you **recognize a poet's purpose** is to look for the meaning behind the words. Notice if a word seems startling, surprising, or jarring. Ask yourself, "Why has the poet chosen that word?" The answer may lead you to the poet's purpose. Using a graphic organizer like this one, note each word or detail that jars you or sparks your emotions. Next to each word, jot down its effect.

Key Words		Effects
_____	→	_____
_____	→	_____
_____	→	_____

Preparing for Standardized Tests

Reading and Vocabulary The Building Vocabulary lesson focuses on learning the adjective suffix -ous. Practice with determining word meanings and parts of speech by recognizing suffixes will improve students' scores on vocabulary and reading comprehension items. For additional practice, use the Build Vocabulary page on the suffix -ous in **Selection Support,** p. 126.

Grammar and Language Standardized tests often require students to complete a sentence by choosing the correct word from a pair of commonly confused words, as in the following:

The cat (lay, laid) in the sun. *lay*
The seal (lies, lays) on the beach. *lies*

The Build Grammar Skills lesson focuses on the correct use of lie and lay. For additional practice, use the Build Grammar Skills page on lie and lay in **Selection Support,** p. 127.

One-Minute Insight

In "Fire and Ice," Frost contemplates the end of the world, linking two means of physical destruction with powerful, potentially destructive emotions. The alliteration and repetition of the s sound adds a sinister quality to the poem. "All Watched Over by Machines of Loving Grace" presents a less sinister, but still disturbing, vision of the future. Although the future Brautigan depicts is peaceful, the poet suggests that humans have surrendered control of their destiny to benevolent machines.

◆ **Critical Thinking**

❶ **Interpret** Point out that Frost is speaking about the world, but he might also have a message for the individual. Ask: On a personal level, how can the fire of desire be destructive? *Responses can include that desire can lead to jealousy, envy, resentment, and deceit.*

◆ **Reading Strategy**

❷ **Recognize a Poet's Purpose** Ask students to define the word *suffice*, eliciting that it means "to be just good enough, but not the best." The word *suffice* might not seem a strong enough verb for writing about the end of the world. Ask students why they think Frost chooses that word. *Frost purposely uses understatement in order to create a shocking effect and grab the reader's attention.*

▶ **Critical Viewing** ◀

❸ **Apply** In the illustration, fire is represented by red-hot lava, and ice by a wind-sculpted iceberg. Students may say love, anger, and resentment are linked with fire, and fear and detachment with ice.

◆ **Reading Strategy**

❹ **Recognize a Poet's Purpose** Ask students: Why does Brautigan choose the word *mammals*, rather than *humans* or *animals*? *Elicit from students that mammals includes both animals and humans. Brautigan may be implying that humans are in complete harmony with nature, and therefore not differentiated from other mammals.*

Fire and Ice

Robert Frost

Some say the world will end in fire,
Some say in ice.
❶ From what I've tasted of desire
I hold with those who favor fire.
5 But if it had to perish twice,
I think I know enough of hate
To say that for destruction ice
Is also great
❷ And would suffice.

▲ **Critical Viewing** Aside from desire and hate, what other human conditions can you associate with fire and ice? **[Apply]**

◆ **Build Vocabulary**
perish (per´ ish) v.: Die
suffice (sə fis´) v.: To be enough

412   *Visions of the Future*

Block Scheduling Strategies

Consider these suggestions to take advantage of extended class time:

• Since poems are meant to be heard, have students first listen to them on audiocassette. Then have students read them silently. Before the class discusses the poems, have volunteers read them aloud.

• Have students work with partners to complete the Literary Focus activity (p. 417). Encourage students to find and share additional examples of alliteration.

• Encourage students to draft the Diary Entry, Poem, or Short Story, as suggested in the Idea Bank (p. 418). When students have completed their drafts, allow them to confer quietly with a peer reviewer about their work and obtain feedback for revision.

• As an enrichment project, have groups of students create posters displaying one of the poems, along with accompanying photographs.

All Watched Over by Machines of Loving Grace

Richard Brautigan

I like to think (and
the sooner the better!)
of a cybernetic¹ meadow
where mammals and computers
5   live together in mutually
programming harmony
like pure water
touching clear sky.

I like to think
(right now, please!)
10   of a cybernetic forest
filled with pines and electronics

where deer stroll peacefully
past computers
as if they were flowers
15   with spinning blossoms.
I like to think
  (it has to be!)
of a cybernetic ecology
where we are free of our labors
and joined back to nature,
20   returned to our mammal
brothers and sisters,
and all watched over
by machines of loving grace.

---

1. **cybernetic** (sī′ bər net′ ik) *adj.:*
Having to do with computers.

Guide for Responding

◆ Literature and Your Life

Reader's Response How do the views of these two poets compare with your own views of the future? Explain.

Thematic Focus How do these poets connect a vision of the future with the past?

☑ **Check Your Comprehension**

1. What is the subject of "Fire and Ice"?
2. What two things does the speaker of "All Watched Over by Machines of Loving Grace" want to see living in harmony?

◆ Critical Thinking

INTERPRET

1. How might the "fire" of desire bring an end to the world? **[Speculate]**
2. In what way is ice a fitting metaphor for hatred? **[Interpret]**
3. Why does Brautigan say "machines of loving grace" to describe computers? **[Infer]**

APPLY

4. Compare your own experiences with computers with Brautigan's vision of the future. **[Relate]**

Fire and Ice/All Watched Over by Machines of Loving Grace ◆ 413

◆ Literary Focus

❺ Alliteration Ask students: What beginning consonant sound is prevalent in lines 11–15 and what is the effect of the alliteration? *The p sound is prevalent. It begins the words pines, peacefully, and past. Because the sound begins the word peacefully in this poem, we associate it with peacefulness within the context of the poem. Students might also note the internal p sound in computer. It seems to connect computers with the idea of peacefulness.*

◆ Critical Thinking

❻ Synthesize Ask students: What does the speaker of the poem mean when he says "it has to be!"? *Students should note that this is the third parenthetical remark in the poem, with each remark becoming stronger. The speaker hopes fervently for the world he describes, because he fears the alternatives.*

Reinforce and Extend

Answers

◆ Literature and Your Life

Reader's Response Pessimistic students might agree with Frost, while optimistic students might agree with Brautigan.

Thematic Focus The poets describe the future in terms of familiar images from the past.

☑ **Check Your Comprehension**

1. It is the end of the world.
2. The speaker wants to see mammals and computers living in harmony.

◆ Critical Thinking

1. Suggested response: Passions sometimes make people fight one another. Greed for land and material possessions could cause a world war.
2. Hatred is sometimes expressed in cold behavior.
3. Suggested response: Brautigan foresees a time when computers assist animals and people to such a degree as to seem alive and intrinsically benevolent.
4. Responses should include instances in which computers have either helped students or made things more complicated.

One-Minute Insight

"There Will Come Soft Rains" and "The Horses" both deal with the aftermath of war. Despite its beautiful, serene images of nature, "There Will Come Soft Rains" is a pessimistic poem; it states that humans could kill themselves off in war, and nothing would care. "The Horses" is more optimistic. It implies that some force cares about humans, and that humans can redeem themselves from past mistakes and live in harmony with themselves and nature.

◆ **Critical Thinking**

❶ **Make Inferences** Ask: What kind of picture does Teasdale paint in the first six lines? *Responses can include: She paints a peaceful, beautiful picture of unspoiled nature; she paints a picture of a warm spring season when the world is at peace.*

◆ **Reading Strategy**

❷ **Recognize a Poet's Purpose** Ask students why they think Teasdale did not mention war until line 7. *Students should grasp that, by painting a peaceful picture and then suddenly introducing the concept of war, the poet takes the reader by surprise, emphasizing the horror of war in contrast with the peacefulness of the scene described in the earlier lines.*

◆ **Reading Strategy**

❸ **Recognize a Poet's Purpose** Point out that Teasdale repeats the words *not one* three times. Ask students why they think she does this. *By repeating the phrase three times, Teasdale drives home the idea that absolutely no part of creation—plant or animal—is going to miss people if they are so foolish as to annihilate themselves.*

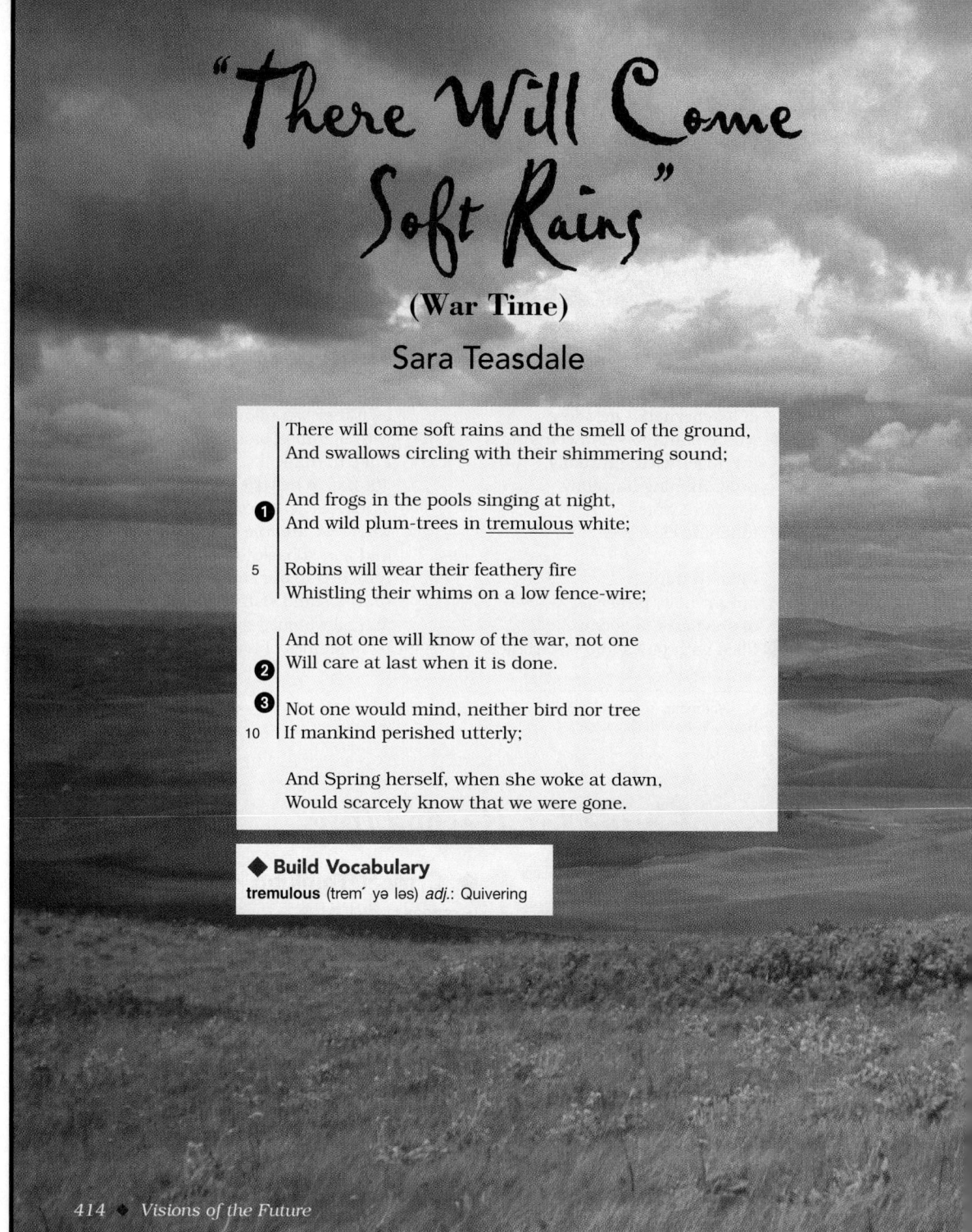

"There Will Come Soft Rains"

(War Time)

Sara Teasdale

There will come soft rains and the smell of the ground,
And swallows circling with their shimmering sound;

❶ And frogs in the pools singing at night,
And wild plum-trees in <u>tremulous</u> white;

5 Robins will wear their feathery fire
Whistling their whims on a low fence-wire;

❷ And not one will know of the war, not one
Will care at last when it is done.

❸ Not one would mind, neither bird nor tree
10 If mankind perished utterly;

And Spring herself, when she woke at dawn,
Would scarcely know that we were gone.

◆ **Build Vocabulary**

tremulous (trem´ yə ləs) *adj.*: Quivering

414 ◆ *Visions of the Future*

Speaking and Listening Mini-Lesson

Panel Discussion

This mini-lesson supports the first Speaking and Listening activity in the Idea Bank on page 418.

Introduce the Concept Explain that a panel discussion differs from a debate in that there are no sides. Each person on the panel speaks as an individual with his or her own personal views. A moderator controls the discussion.

Develop Background Remind students that not everyone feels the same about the role of computers in our lives. Have students determine their own opinions about how computers effect our lives. Students might freewrite in their journals or talk over their ideas with partners.

Apply the Information Have students form groups of three or four panel members and a moderator. The moderator should introduce the panel members and

have a prepared question to get the discussion started.

Assess the Outcome Evaluate the panelists using criteria similar to the following: supported position with facts, details, and logic; presented ideas clearly; answered the moderator's question; responded appropriately to other panelists' views; participated to the best of his or her ability; demonstrated an understanding of the topic; prepared for the activity.

The Horses

Edwin Muir

Barely a twelvemonth after
The seven days war that put the world to sleep,
4| Late in the evening the strange horses came.
By then we had made our <u>covenant</u> with silence,
5 But in the first few days it was so still
We listened to our breathing and were afraid.
On the second day
The radios failed; we turned the knobs; no answer.
On the third day a warship passed us, heading north,
10 Dead bodies piled on the deck. On the sixth day
A plane plunged over us into the sea. Thereafter
Nothing. The radios dumb;
5| And still they stand in corners of our kitchens,
And stand, perhaps, turned on, in a million rooms
15 | All over the world. But now if they should speak,
6| If on a sudden they should speak again,
If on the stroke of noon a voice should speak,
We would not listen, we would not let it bring
That old bad world that swallowed its children quick
20 At one great gulp. We would not have it again.
7| Sometimes we think of the nations lying asleep,
Curled blindly in impenetrable sorrow,
And then the thought <u>confounds</u> us with its strangeness.

The tractors lie about our fields; at evening
25 They look like dank sea-monsters couched and waiting.
We leave them where they are and let them rust:
'They'll moulder away and be like other loam.'[1]
We make our oxen drag our rusty ploughs,
8| Long laid aside. We have gone back
30 | Far past our fathers' land.
    And then, that evening

◆ **Build Vocabulary**

covenant (kuv´ ə nənt) *n*.: Agreement; pact
confounds (kən foundz´) *v*.: Bewilders; confuses

1. **loam** (lōm) *n*.: Dark, rich soil.

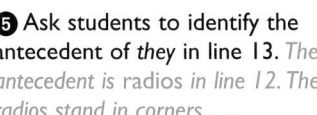

◆ **Critical Thinking**

❷ **Interpret** Ask: What do the horses and tractors represent? *The horses represent the natural world. The tractors represent the world of machines.*

◆ **Build Vocabulary**

❸ **Suffixes: -ous** Ask: What part of speech is the word *fabulous*? To what noun is *fabulous* related? What is the meaning of *fabulous* in this context? *The word fabulous is an adjective related to the word fable. Here, it means "fabled," or "imaginary."*

◆ **Critical Thinking**

❹ **Interpret** Ask students the meaning of: ". . . sent/By an old command. . ." and ". . . that long-lost archaic companionship." *The old command might be the command of God that gave humans dominion over all the animals; it might be the horses' instinct to serve humans.*

◆ **Critical Thinking**

❺ **Interpret** Ask: What is "free servitude"? Why can it "pierce our hearts"? *"Free servitude" means willing or voluntary servitude. We are moved by the horses' selfless sacrifice of freedom.*

◆ **Critical Thinking**

❻ **Predict** Ask students what they predict for the future. Will people make the same mistakes that led them into war? *Accept all responses that are supported by logical reasons.*

416

❶ Late in the summer the strange horses came.
We heard a distant tapping on the road,
A deepening drumming; it stopped, went on again
35 And at the corner changed to hollow thunder.
We saw the heads
Like a wild wave charging and were afraid.
❷ We had sold our horses in our fathers' time
To buy new tractors. Now they were strange to us
40 As fabulous <u>steeds</u> set on an ancient shield
❸ Or illustrations in a book of knights.
We did not dare go near them. Yet they waited,
Stubborn and shy, as if they had been sent
❹ By an old command to find our whereabouts
45 And that long-lost <u>archaic</u> companionship.
In the first moment we had never a thought
That they were creatures to be owned and used.
Among them were some half-a-dozen colts
Dropped in some wilderness of the broken world,
50 Yet new as if they had come from their own Eden.[2]
Since then they have pulled our ploughs and borne our loads,
❺ But that free servitude still can pierce our hearts.
❻ Our life is changed; their coming our beginning.

---

2. **Eden:** In the Bible, the garden where life began with Adam and Eve; paradise.

◆ **Build Vocabulary**
steeds (stēdz) *n.*: Horses
archaic (är kā´ ik) *adj.*: Seldom-used; old-fashioned

 Guide for Responding

◆ *Literature and Your Life*

Reader's Response What do *you* think nature's attitude toward humans is? Explain.
Thematic Focus What kind of future do these poems envision?

☑ **Check Your Comprehension**

1. According to "There Will Come Soft Rains," how does nature feel about humans?
2. In "The Horses," what has happened to the world?

416 ◆ *Visions of the Future*

◆ **Critical Thinking**

INTERPRET
1. What is the theme of "There Will Come Soft Rains"? **[Interpret]**
2. In "The Horses," in what way are the horses associated with rebirth and renewal? **[Associate]**
3. What role will the horses serve in the future? Support you answer. **[Speculate]**
APPLY
4. How might "There Will Come Soft Rains" be different if it had been written in the age of nuclear weapons? **[Connect]**

☆ **Beyond the Selection**

FURTHER READING
Other Works by Robert Frost
"Mending Wall," "Birches," "The Death of the Hired Man," *A Boy's Will, North of Boston*
Other Works by Richard Brautigan
"Xerox Candy Bar," "Yes, the Fish Music," "Karma Repair Kit: Item 1-4, " *The Return of the Rivers*
Other Works by Sara Teasdale
"Night," *Love Songs, Flame and Shadow*
Other Works by Edwin Muir
The Voyage, The Labyrinth

INTERNET
You and your students may find additional information about the authors on the Internet. We suggest the following site. Please be aware, however, that the site may have changed from the time we published this information.
For information about Robert Frost, go to **http://www.pro-net.co.uk/home/catalyst/RF/**
We *strongly recommend* that you preview the site before you send students to it.

Guide for Responding (continued)

◆ Reading Strategy

RECOGNIZE THE POETS' PURPOSE

All these poems have a similar purpose: The poets want to warn readers to consider the possible impact of present events and developments on the future. You can **recognize the poets' purposes** by looking carefully at their choice of words and details. For example, Edwin Muir contrasts images of total devastation with images of the primitive beauty of horses to lead readers to think about the negative effects and destructive potential of technology.

1. "There Will Come Soft Rains" describes the world after a devastating war. Why doesn't the poet describe war itself?
2. What do you think is Teasdale's purpose? Why?
3. In "All Watched Over by Machines of Loving Grace," how does the phrase "cybernetic meadow" help you recognize the poet's purpose?

◆ Build Grammar Skills

COMMONLY CONFUSED WORDS: LIE AND LAY

Study the use of **lie** and **lay** in the following sentences.

Lie: I always *lie* on my side to get to sleep.
She *lay* awake for hours worrying.
The cows *have lain* under that tree all day.

Lay: *Lay* your clothes on the bed.
Workers *laid* our new carpet yesterday.
I *have laid* the baby in the cradle.

Practice On your paper, write the correct form of the verb for each sentence.

1. In "Fire and Ice," the poet (lies, lays) out two different scenarios of the end of the world.
2. In "All Watched Over by Machines of Loving Grace," the poet pictures deer strolling by computers that (lie, lay) in the grass.
3. In "There Will Come Soft Rains," the reader can almost picture frogs singing their songs on logs (lying, laying) in a pond.
4. In "The Horses," dead bodies (lay, laid) on the deck of a ship.

◆ Literary Focus

ALLITERATION

Poets may use **alliteration**—the repetition of consonant sounds at the beginning of words—to help create a mood by emphasizing certain sounds. For example, in the first stanza of "There Will Come Soft Rains," the *s* sound seems to whisper, emphasizing the peaceful nature of the scene.

1. What other alliteration creates a peaceful sound in "There Will Come Soft Rains"?
2. What feeling does "feathery fire" create?
3. Find two examples of alliteration in "Fire and Ice" and explain their effect.

◆ Build Vocabulary

USING THE SUFFIX -ous

Make an adjective out of each of these words by adding the suffix -ous, meaning "full of" or "characterized by." Then, in your notebook, complete each sentence by adding one of the new words.

    a. peril **b.** courage **c.** mischief **d.** clamor

1. The mayor made a ___?___ decision to take an unpopular stand.
2. The ___?___ kittens unwound a whole ball of yarn.
3. After a ___?___ voyage, the passengers gave thanks for reaching land safely.
4. The ___?___ crowd forcefully demanded an end to the unjust policy.

USING THE WORD BANK

On your paper, write the letter of the correct synonym for each first word.

1. covenant: (a) church, (b) argument, (c) agreement
2. suffice: (a) be helpful, (b) be enough, (c) be wrong
3. steeds: (a) rewards, (b) cattle, (c) horses
4. confounds: (a) irritates, (b) surprises, (c) confuses
5. tremulous: (a) quivering, (b) huge, (c) emotional
6. archaic: (a) curved, (b) simple, (c) old-fashioned

Fire and Ice/All Watched Over . . ./There Will Come Soft Rains/The Horses ◆ 417

◆ Build Grammar Skills

1. lays; 2. lie; 3. lying; 4. lay

Writer's Solution

For additional information and practice, use the practice pages (pp. 11–14) in the *Writer's Solution Grammar Practice Book.*

◆ Build Vocabulary

1. courageous;
2. mischievous; 3. perilous;
4. clamorous

Using the Word Bank
1. c 2. b 3. c 4. c 5. a
6. c

Answers
◆ Literature and Your Life

Reader's Response Some may say that nature is indifferent to humans; others might point out that some animals fear humans.

Thematic Focus "There Will Come Soft Rains" envisions the annihilation of humans. "The Horses" envisions a future in which humans, because of destruction caused by war, will have to "start over again" by turning to nature for help.

☑ Check Your Comprehension

1. Nature wouldn't miss humans.
2. The world has been nearly totally destroyed by war.

◆ Critical Thinking

1. The theme is the insignificance of human beings.
2. The horses represent the beginning of humans' reconnection to nature and their feelings.
3. Suggested response: The horses will help humans survive by doing strenuous tasks. They will also help humans gain purpose in their lives through their relationship with the horses.
4. In the age of nuclear weapons, all of nature might meet the same terrible fate as humans.

◆ Reading Strategy

1. Describing war would put the emphasis on war, and the poet's point is that nature is indifferent to humans' destructive activity.
2. Teasdale's purpose is to warn people about the destructive power of war and to remind people of humans' relative insignificance.
3. It combines computers and nature in the same place.

◆ Literary Focus

1. The *w* sound in "when she woke" and "whistling their whims" is a soft, gentle sound.
2. The *f* sound of "feathery fire" creates a feeling of motion, imitating the sound of ruffling feathers.
3. The *s* sound in "Some say" creates a jarring mood. The *f* sound in "favor fire" creates a somewhat gentle feeling of inevitability.

417

Idea Bank

Writing Mini-Lesson

Refer students to the Writing Handbook, page 962, for instruction on the writing process, and page 965 for further information on Creative Writing.

Writer's Solution

Writers at Work Videodisc

Have students view the videodisc segment (Ch. 6) featuring Grant Moran to hear his views on creative writing. Have students discuss the role of the imagination in creative writing.

Play frames 12243 to 21791

Writing Lab CD-ROM

Have students complete the Tutorial on Creative Writing. Follow these steps:

1. Have students play the audio-annotated slide show about using vivid images.
2. Have students draft on the computer.
3. Have students use the Interactive Self-Evaluation Checklist for Poetry.

Allow approximately 90 minutes of class time to complete these steps.

Sourcebook

Have students use Chapter 6, Creative Writing (pp. 162–193), for additional support. The chapter includes Tips for Using Sound Devices in a Poem or Song Lyrics (p. 183).

Build Your Portfolio

Idea Bank

Writing

1. **Diary Entry** Poet Richard Brautigan envisions a future when computers can improve people's lives. Write a diary entry for a day—in the present or future—that is enriched by computers.

2. **Poem** Write a poem of your own that expresses a vision of the future. Your vision can be either one that people should strive for or one that should be avoided.

3. **Short Story** Write a short story based on "The Horses" that takes the speaker twenty years into the future. Show what has happened to the relationship between horses and humans.

Speaking and Listening

4. **Panel Discussion** With a group, hold a panel discussion with a moderator and several people with different points of view. Debate the question: Computers—hope of the future or scourge of the present? **[Technology Link]**

5. **Oral Interpretation** Prepare a dramatic reading of "Fire and Ice." Work on using tone of voice and facial expressions to emphasize meaning. **[Performing Arts Link]**

Projects

6. **Bumper Stickers** Design a bumper sticker with an anti-war slogan based on the ideas in "There Will Come Soft Rains." **[Art Link]**

7. **Job Expo** With a group, research jobs related to the computer profession. Present your findings in a Job Expo for your class. Write short blurbs describing several kinds of jobs. Draw pictures or cut photos from magazines to illustrate the jobs. Group members can be available at the Job Expo to answer questions. **[Career Link]**

418 ◆ *Visions of the Future*

Writing Mini-Lesson

Poem to a Future Generation

These poems make readers think about the present by describing the future. In "There Will Come Soft Rains," for example, the poet emphasizes the destructiveness of war by imagining a future in which all humans have been destroyed. Write a short poem that does the opposite by describing one or more good qualities of today's world for people living in the future.

> **Writing Skills Focus:
> Brevity and Clarity**
>
> In your poem, strive for **brevity** and **clarity**. Brevity means stating your thoughts in as few words as possible. Clarity means making sure those words create clear images.
>
> For example, "Fire and Ice" is only nine lines long, but it conveys a powerful message. That's because Frost focused his poem on two clear one-word images—fire and ice—that are easy to picture and that stir up many associations in readers' minds.

Prewriting Start by deciding on the message that you'd like to convey. Then brainstorm to create a list of images from the present that will help you convey your message. Try to come up with images that are clear and brief and will spark an association in your readers' minds.

Drafting Put your images together in a way that will give a clear picture of the present to the future generation. Use as few words as possible to present each image.

Revising Have a classmate read your poem and underline any words that do not create a clear picture or do not seem necessary. Revise your poem to eliminate these words.

✓ ASSESSMENT OPTIONS

Writing Process Workshop

Process Explanation

If you've ever tried to program a VCR or bake a cake, you know how important it can be to have a clear, easy-to-follow explanation of how to perform a process. Think of a process that you know well—for example, how to throw a baseball or how to log onto the Internet. Then write a clear explanation of that process that will help readers to perform the process even if they have no prior knowledge of your topic.

The following skills, introduced in this section's Writing Mini-Lessons, will help you write your **process explanation**.

Writing Skills Focus

▶ **Provide a clear beginning, middle, and end** to your writing. Identify the process you are explaining, give all the necessary information, and make the end result clear. (See p. 390.)

▶ **Explain all procedures clearly.** Present the steps of the process in the order in which they occur. Also, avoid leaving out important details of any of the steps. (See p. 401.)

▶ **Be brief and precise** in your writing. Don't add unnecessary information. (See p. 418.)

Bill Gates uses all these skills as he explains how computer servers will help people in the future.

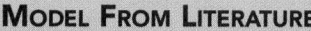

MODEL FROM LITERATURE

from *The Road Ahead* by Bill Gates

Movies, TV shows, and other kinds of digital information will be stored on "servers," which are computers with capacious disks. ① If you ask to see a particular movie, check a fact, or retrieve your electronic mail, your request will be routed by switches to the server or servers storing that information. ② The digitalized data will be retrieved from the server and routed by switches back to your television, personal computer, or telephone. ③

① Gates begins by explaining what a server is and then goes on to explain how it works.

② The author offers a clear explanation of how a server operates.

③ Gates's process explanation is clear and to the point.

Cross-Curricular Connection: Science

Tell students that a lab report is really a process explanation in which a student explains, step by step, how he or she conducted an experiment. The writer of a lab report, like the writer of a process explanation, should use clear and specific language, headings and numbers to make the report easier to follow, and diagrams or other illustrations to help clarify the experiment.

You might explain that, in the professional world, the results of a scientific experiment are not accepted until the experiment has been repeated several times by different experi-

menters and has yielded the same results. Therefore, a professional scientist's lab report really is a process explanation for other scientists to follow when they repeat an experiment. Discuss with the class how a professional scientist's audience differs from a student's, and whether this difference should affect their writing. *A professional scientist can assume that his audience will understand technical terms, while a student should use easy-to-understand language or explain each technical term used.*

Prepare and Engage

Establish Writing Guidelines
Before students begin, review the following key characteristics of a process explanation:

- A process explanation offers a step-by-step explanation of how to do something.

- A good process explanation is clear and specific.

- The writer of a process explanation often uses headings, labels, or numbers to make the steps of the process clear.

- The writer may also include diagrams and illustrations to help clarify the process.

You may want to distribute the scoring rubric for a How-to/Process Explanation (p. 93 in **Alternative Assessment**) before students begin, to make them aware of the criteria on which they will be evaluated. See the suggestions on page 421 for how you can customize the rubric to this workshop.

Writer's Solution

Writers at Work Videodisc
To help students see how the ability to write a process explanation can apply to a career, play the segment featuring nurse Glo Simon (Ch. 8).

Play frames 34430 to 43977

Writing Lab CD-ROM
If your students have access to computers, you may want to have them work in the tutorial on Practical and Technical Writing to complete all or part of their process explanations. Follow these steps:
1. Have students use a Chain of Events organizer to map out their ideas.
2. Have students draft on computer.
3. Advise students to use the Vague or Imprecise Word Bins to replace vague, imprecise words with ones that are more exact.
4. Direct students to the Guidelines for Peer Revision for tips on helpful techniques for working with a peer reviewer.

Sourcebook
Students can find additional support in the chapter on Practical and Technical Writing (pp. 228–262).

Real-World Reading Skills Workshop

Strategies for Success

Whether you're in school taking a test or at home using a brand-new appliance, you can't begin until you read the directions. You need to review the directions carefully so you'll succeed at the task that faces you. Follow these tips:

Read Slowly Enough to Notice Each Word If you're about to take a test, you may be eager to get started. If you read the directions too quickly, however, you may answer questions the wrong way. Take the reading time you need so every word registers.

Notice the Order of Steps Directions often are given in more than one sentence. There may be several steps for you to follow. Before you do anything else, read all the directions through once. Then go back and reread any parts you do not understand clearly. If there is someone who can clarify the meaning, ask that person for help.

Look at Helpful Drawings or Diagrams New appliances, such as a VCR or an answering machine, usually come with diagrams as part of the directions. Study the drawings carefully. Match up the pieces or the features illustrated in the diagrams with the actual pieces or features.

How to Read Your Outgoing Message

1. Hold down the ANNOUNCE button for 2 seconds until you hear a beep.

2. Speak in a normal voice about 12 inches from the machine. Ask callers to leave their name, phone number, and message.

3. Press the STOP button when you finish your message. The machine will beep once.

4. Press the ANNOUNCE button to hear your outgoing message. If you wish to replace it with another recorded message, repeat steps 1 through 3.

Apply the Strategy

Did the manufacturer provide clear directions? Read the directions for recording an outgoing message. Then answer these questions.

1. What is the first thing you must do to record an outgoing message?
2. How far away from the machine should you stand while speaking?
3. What do you do after you finish recording your message?
4. At which two times will the machine beep?
5. How do you record a new message?

> ✔ Here are other situations in which reading directions is important:
> ▶ Operating the alarm on a clock radio
> ▶ Using a cookbook to prepare a meal
> ▶ Taking a test in school
> ▶ Using a new computer

PART *2* *Reaching for Tomorrow*

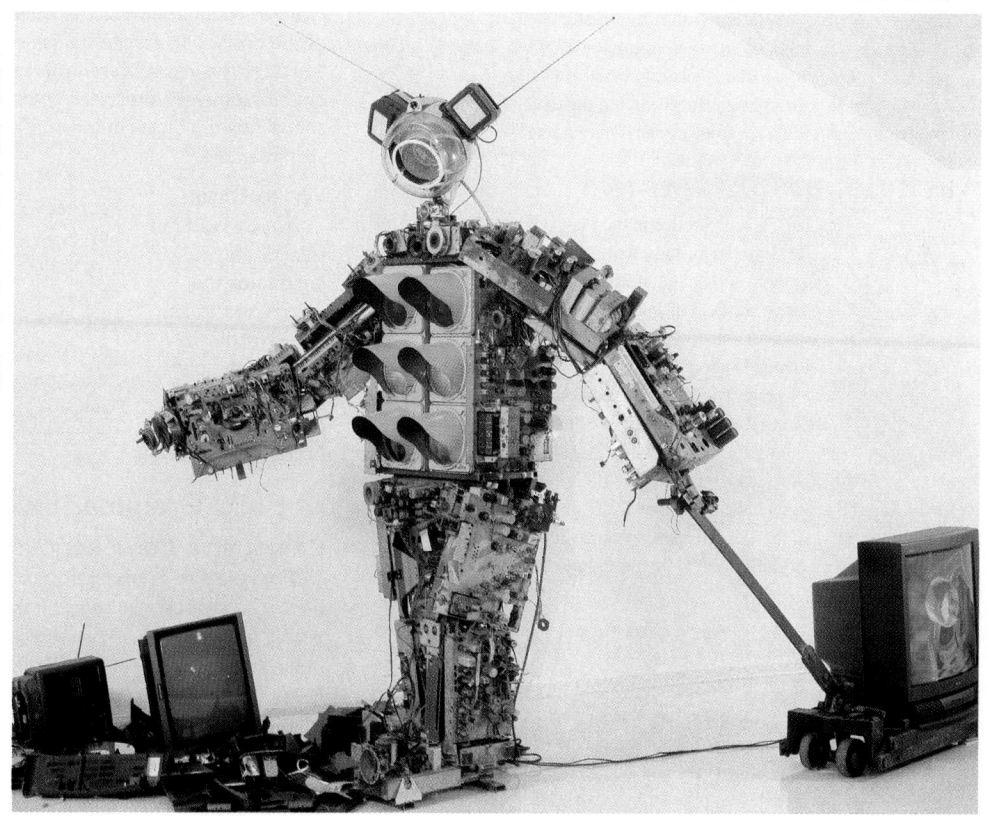

SYS Cop, 1994, Nam June Park, Carl Solway Gallery

Humanities: Art

SYS Cop, 1994, by Nam June Park.
This photograph shows a robot hauling a computer monitor, almost like a human being pulling a piece of luggage through an airport. Tell students that the word *robot* comes from the Czech word for "work"; the name and the concept of the robot were first introduced to the world in *R.U.R,* a 1921 play by the Czech writer Karel Capek, who criticized scientific progress and the loss of human individuality by imagining

the creation of mechanized beings who take over the world.
Help students link this art to the theme of Part 2 ("Reaching for Tomorrow") by answering the following questions:
1. What roles do you think robots will play in tomorrow's world? *Robots are likely to perform more and more jobs regarded as too dangerous or tedious for humans; as they become more sophisticated, they will be able to do higher-level jobs.*

2. Do you agree with the idea that the growth of technology points toward a less human tomorrow? *Students agreeing with this idea should cite our increasing dependence on robots, computers, and other machines. Students disagreeing should argue that humans will always design and control the technology, so that it simply enables them to expand the limits of human possibility.*

423

Guide for Reading

More About the Authors
   Arthur C. Clarke's strong belief in the benefits of space exploration helped promote the idea in the United States in the 1960's.
   Orion magazine has called **Rachel Carson's** *Silent Spring* "as important to stirring up the American conscience as Tom Paine's *Common Sense,* Upton Sinclair's *The Jungle,* and Harriet Beecher Stowe's *Uncle Tom's Cabin.*"
   In addition to essays and novels, **Bryan Woolley** writes short stories that are humorous, heartwarming, and sincere, and that capture the best of his home state, Texas.

Arthur C. Clarke (1917–)

For more than fifty years, Arthur C. Clarke has been turning out exceptional works of fiction and nonfiction. Born in Somerset, England, he wrote his first science-fiction stories while in the air force during World War II. Of more than fifty works, Clarke's most famous is his collaboration with film director Stanley Kubrick on the screenplay for *2001: A Space Odyssey.* Equally distinguished is Clarke's non-fiction. In a 1945 essay, he predicted the development of communications satellites long before they were a reality.

Rachel Carson (1907–1964)

Rachel Carson enrolled in the Pennsylvania College for Women to study writing. A lifelong love of science and nature, however, caused her to change her field of study to marine biology. She was later able to pursue both fields by writing eloquently about nature.
   Carson's widely praised book *The Sea Around Us* came out of her years as a biologist and editor at the United States Fish and Wildlife Service. Her most significant work, however, was *Silent Spring,* a chilling and well-documented warning about the dangers of pesticides. Before her book, few people understood the dangers of pollution or the interconnectedness of all life.

Bryan Woolley (1937–)

Born in Texas, Bryan Woolley has been a teacher, a journalist, and a novelist. His novel *November 22,* about the events in Dallas on the day President John F. Kennedy was assassinated, was praised by *Texas Monthly* as an outstanding book about Texas. In 1979, the author wrote "To the Residents of A.D. 2029," about his concerns for the present and his hopes for the future.

424 ◆ Visions of the Future

◆ Build Vocabulary

WORD ROOTS: -ann-
   In "If I Forget Thee, Oh Earth . . . ," you will come across the word *perennial.* It builds on the root -ann-, which comes from *annum,* the Latin word for "year." In *perennial,* the *a* has been changed to *e* because of the addition of the prefix *per-. Perennial* means "through the years." Perennial flowers blossom year after year, whereas annual flowers blossom for only one year, then die.

WORD BANK
   As you read the selections, you will encounter the words on this list. Each word is defined on the page where it first appears. Preview the list before you read.

purged
pyre
perennial
blight
moribund
postulated
beleaguered
schism

◆ Build Grammar Skills

CORRELATIVE CONJUNCTIONS
   Correlative conjunctions are pairs of conjunctions used to link words of equal rank. In "To the Residents of A.D. 2029," the line "As long as we *both* as a race *and* as a crowd of individuals" contains the correlative conjunctions *both . . . and,* which link the words *race* and *crowd.*

Common Correlative Conjunctions
both . . . and
either . . . or
neither . . . nor
not only . . . but / but also
whether . . . or

"If I Forget Thee, Oh Earth . . ."
◆ *from* Silent Spring ◆
To the Residents of A.D. 2029

◆ *Literature and Your Life*

CONNECT YOUR EXPERIENCE

Perhaps you are aware of local dangers to the environment and of individuals or groups that are seeking to correct them. In these readings, the authors encourage readers to think about environmental problems and their solutions.

Journal Writing In your journal, list what you consider to be environmental dangers and number them from most to least threatening.

THEMATIC FOCUS: REACHING FOR TOMORROW

These selections encourage you to reach for tomorrow by looking at present-day problems. As you read, you may find yourself wondering: What can I do to prevent future environmental tragedies?

◆ Background for Understanding

SCIENCE

Recent concerns about the atmosphere revolve around the ozone layer, which shields the Earth from 95 to 99 percent of the sun's harmful ultraviolet rays. Since the mid-1970's, some scientists have been concerned about a breakdown in the ozone layer caused by the use of CFCs found in aerosol sprays and refrigerants. Environmental scientists are closely monitoring the thinning ozone layer.

◆ Literary Focus

EXHORTATION

An **exhortation** is an urgent appeal or warning. In "If I Forget Thee, Oh Earth . . . ," Arthur C. Clarke—without actually stating it in words—is urging readers to pay attention to problems on Earth before the planet becomes unlivable.

An exhortation may be fiction or nonfiction. The warning may be stated or implied. To be effective, however, exhortation must be presented in a way that readers will hear it.

◆ Reading Strategy

DISTINGUISH BETWEEN FACT AND OPINION

In his essay, Bryan Woolley states, "Parts of our land are overcrowded, parts neglected, parts abused, parts destroyed." He also says, "Our present disrespect for the natural world is our most serious stupidity to date." Only the first statement is a fact. The second is an opinion. It may be based on fact, but the author has drawn a conclusion that may or may not be justified.

When you read, it is important to **distinguish between fact and opinion.** Facts can be tested for accuracy. Opinions cannot. You must decide whether there is sufficient evidence to support the opinion before deciding whether or not you agree with it.

Make a chart like the one shown. As you read, record at least one fact and one opinion from each selection.

Selection	Fact	Opinion

Guide for Reading ◆ 425

 Preparing for Standardized Tests

Reading and Vocabulary The ability to distinguish between fact and opinion, the focus of the Reading Strategy for this selection, will improve student performance on critical reading sections on standardized tests. In addition, achievement tests in science and history often require students to read a passage and assess possible conclusions, which requires the ability to tell fact from opinion, as well as the ability to draw conclusions from facts.

Writing and Grammar An appreciation for correlative conjunctions may help students to state their ideas more concisely in the essay portions of standardized tests and to answer usage questions correctly. It will also help them when dealing with word or logic problems such as the following:

Object A is larger than B, but smaller than C. Neither B nor A is smaller than D. List objects A, B, C, and D from smallest to largest. *D, B, A, C*

The Build Grammar Skills lesson focuses on correlative conjunctions. For additional practice, use the Build Grammar Skills page in **Selection Support,** p. 131.

Arthur C. Clarke's story is a grim portrait of life among the sole survivors of a nuclear holocaust on Earth—the residents of a moon colony who struggle to keep alive the memory of their home planet until future generations can return to it. The title of the story refers to an oath made by the Jews conquered by Nebuchadnezzar and exiled to Babylon in 597 B.C.: "If I forget thee, O Jerusalem, let my right hand forget her cunning. . . ."

The story provides an alarming warning to readers that if we do not protect our Earth, it is conceivable that people could someday be forced into exile in space and be left with only memories of what life on Earth was like.

Customize for
Visual/Spatial Learners
The photograph on this page can serve as a valuable aid to helping these students place themselves in the story's setting.

◆ **Reading Strategy**

❶ **Distinguish Between Fact and Opinion** Ask students what facts about Marvin's life they learn from the story's opening paragraph. Then ask if they have any opinions yet about what such a life would be like. Facts include that Marvin is ten years old and has never been Outside, that the people live in a controlled environment, and that their colony is divided into levels for different purposes. Some students may think that such a life would be exciting and interesting. Others may think it stifling or scary.

"If I Forget Thee, Oh Earth . . ."
Arthur C. Clarke

❶ When Marvin was ten years old, his father took him through the long, echoing corridors that led up through Administration and Power, until at last they came to the uppermost levels of all and were among the swiftly growing vegetation of the Farmlands. Marvin liked it here: it was fun watching the great, slender plants creeping with almost visible eagerness toward the sunlight as it filtered down through the plastic domes to meet them. The smell of life was everywhere, awakening inexpressible longings in his heart: no longer was he breathing the dry, cool air of the residential levels, purged of all smells but the faint tang of ozone.[1] He wished he could stay here for a little while, but Father would not let him. They went onward until they had reached the entrance to the Observatory, which he had never visited: but they did not stop, and Marvin knew with a sense of rising excitement that there could be only one goal left. For the first time in his life, he was going Outside.

There were a dozen of the surface vehicles, with their wide balloon tires and pressurized cabins, in the great servicing chamber. His father must have been expected, for they were led at once to the little scout car waiting by the huge circular door of the airlock. Tense with expectancy,

---

1. **ozone** (ō´ zōn) *n.*: Form of oxygen with a sharp odor.

◆ **Build Vocabulary**
purged (pʉrjd) *v.*: Cleansed; emptied

426   *Visions of the Future*

Block Scheduling Strategies

Consider these suggestions to take advantage of extended class time:

- Have students complete the journal activity in Literature and Your Life (p. 425) and share their lists of environmental dangers in a class discussion.

- To link the Build Vocabulary lesson to the selection, have students research common annual and perennial plants in their area and find out how they have been affected by recent changes in the environment.

- Students may search for environmental action sites on the Internet. They can start with the National Wildlife Federation site mentioned in the Internet section of Beyond the Selection (p. 433) in the teacher edition.

- Divide the class into small groups to work on the Writing Mini-Lesson (p. 439). Have each group select an environmental issue to research. Within each group, individual students can select different research sources to search for facts and statistics.

Marvin settled himself down in the cramped cabin while his father started the motor and checked the controls. The inner door of the lock slid open and then closed behind them: he heard the roar of the great air pumps fade slowly away as the pressure dropped to zero. Then the "Vacuum" sign flashed on, the outer door parted, and before Marvin lay the land which he had never yet entered.

He had seen it in photographs, of course: he had watched it imaged on television screens a hundred times. But now it was lying all around him, burning beneath the fierce sun that crawled so slowly across the jet-black sky. He stared into the west, away from the blinding splendor of the sun—and there were the stars, as he had been told but had never quite believed. He gazed at them for a long time, marveling that anything could be so bright and yet so tiny. They were intense unscintillating points, and suddenly he remembered a rhyme he had once read in one of his father's books:

> Twinkle, twinkle, little star,
> How I wonder what you are.

Well, *he* knew what the stars were. Whoever asked that question must have been very stupid. And what did they mean by "twinkle"? You could see at a glance that all the stars shone with the same steady, unwavering light. He abandoned the puzzle and turned his attention to the landscape around him.

They were racing across a level plain at almost a hundred miles an hour, the great balloon tires sending up little spurts of dust behind them. There was no sign of

◀ **Critical Viewing** From the moon, Earth looks like a big blue-and-white marble. How do photographs like this one convey the preciousness and fragility of our home planet? **[Analyze]**

the Colony: in the few minutes while he had been gazing at the stars, its domes and radio towers had fallen below the horizon. Yet there were other indications of man's presence, for about a mile ahead Marvin could see the curiously shaped structures clustering round the head of a mine. Now and then a puff of vapor would emerge from a squat smokestack and would instantly disperse.

They were past the mine in a moment: Father was driving with a reckless and exhilarating skill as if—it was a strange thought to come into a child's mind—he were trying to escape from something. In a few minutes they had reached the edge of the plateau on which the Colony had been built. The ground fell sharply away beneath them in a dizzying slope whose lower stretches were lost in shadow. Ahead, as far as the eye could reach, was a jumbled wasteland of craters, mountain ranges, and ravines. The crests of the mountains, catching the low sun, burned like islands of fire in a sea of darkness: and above them the stars still shone as steadfastly as ever.

There could be no way forward—yet there was. Marvin clenched his fists as the car edged over the slope and started the long descent. Then he saw the barely visible track leading down the mountainside, and relaxed a little. Other men, it seemed, had gone this way before.

Night fell with a shocking abruptness as they crossed the shadow line and the sun dropped below the crest of the plateau. The twin searchlights sprang into life, casting blue-white bands on the rocks ahead, so that there was scarcely need to check their speed. For hours they drove through valleys and past the foot of mountains whose peaks seemed to comb the stars, and sometimes they emerged for a moment into the sunlight as they climbed over higher ground.

"If I Forget Thee, Oh Earth . . ." ◆ 427

One-Minute Insight In this passage from Rachel Carson's landmark book, Carson sounds the warning about how the indiscriminate use of pesticides threatens our environment. Although this may seem strange to students who have grown up knowing about the dangers of pesticides and other pollutants, people at the time this was written resisted the idea that chemicals meant to improve the quality of human life could actually be harming it. In the tradition of many writers who have a controversial or unpleasant lesson to teach, Rachel Carson introduces her ideas in the form of a fable. This gentle approach allows readers to distance themselves from uncomfortable ideas and to consider them objectively. In addition, the mysterylike qualities of the excerpt spark readers' interest and encourage them to read on.

Looking at Literature Videodisc To provide a contemporary context to the dangers posed by DDT, play Chapter 7 of the videodisc. This segment describes the dangers to the environment still posed by DDT. Have students brainstorm for possible solutions to the problems described. With what other thraets to the environment are they most concerned?

Chapter 7

430 ◆ *Visions of the Future*

Customize for
More Advanced Students
The opening of *Silent Spring* unfolds almost like a mystery story: The writer creates a vivid setting, then provides numerous details that outline a sinister turn of events, although we are not told what is behind this ominous change. Have your more advanced students jot down notes as they read the excerpt as a detective might, or an investigator with the EPA. Are there many *different* valid theories that would account for the various calamities? When they are finished reading the selection, have these students share their "crime scene" notes with the rest of the class. As a follow-up activity, they can read *Silent Spring* in its entirety to evaluate the writer's theories by determining if she accounts adequately for all the evidence she presents.

from Silent Spring

Rachel Carson

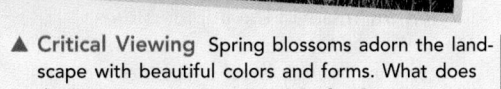

▲ **Critical Viewing** Spring blossoms adorn the landscape with beautiful colors and forms. What does the spring represent to you? **[Relate]** ❶

There was once a town in the heart of America where all life seemed to live in harmony with its surroundings. The town lay in the midst of a checkerboard of prosperous farms, with fields of grain and hillsides of orchards where, in spring, white clouds of bloom drifted above the green fields. In autumn, oak and maple and birch set up a blaze of color that flamed and flickered across a backdrop of pines. Then foxes barked in the ❷

from *Silent Spring* ◆ *431*

Customize for *Visual/Spatial Learners*

Encourage these students to consider how the photographs on this page contribute to the persuasive power of this selection. Students should note that the photographs capture the beauty of the environment and help readers to appreciate what would be lost if the environment were damaged.

Customize for *Less Proficient Readers*

Lead students to understand that Carson isn't referring to one specific town, but instead is capturing the qualities that characterize many towns throughout our nation and our world.

▶Critical Viewing◀

❶ **Relate** Have students describe the details of spring they observe in the photograph. Do they witness similar details themselves each spring, or are there other recurring phenomena in your locality? *Students may reply that spring means a thaw of winter snow and ice, the resultant floods or other natural disasters, the renewed appearance of wildlife and human social activity, a new sports season, and so on.*

◆ **Literary Focus**

❷ **Exhortation** Ask students how the author begins to create a sense of danger in the very first paragraph of her essay. *She describes details of an ordinary spring day in a typical American town, but the sentences are all in the past tense, suggesting that the town no longer exists. She hints that something terrible has happened to the town.*

 Cross-Curricular Connection: Science

The publication of Rachel Carson's *Silent Spring* in 1962 helped mobilize an entire generation of Americans to take action on behalf of the environment. One of the most significant achievements of this growing movement was the banning of the pesticide DDT, a substance as toxic as it was widespread.

Have students research other outcries against similar agricultural practices, such as that concerning Alar in 1989. Students with an interest in science should make a short presentation to the class on the scientific merits of such environmental and public health "crusades." Ask: Have there ever been relatively harmless practices that the media sensationalized or oversimplified? Have students discuss the potential outcome if *no* farmers attempted to protect or alter the produce they bring to market.

hills and deer silently crossed the fields, half hidden in the mists of the fall mornings.

Along the roads, laurel, viburnum and alder, great ferns and wildflowers delighted the traveler's eye through much of the year. Even in winter the roadsides were places of beauty, where countless birds came to feed on the berries and on the seed heads of the dried weeds rising above the snow. The countryside was, in fact, famous for the abundance and variety of its bird life, and when the flood of migrants was pouring through in spring and fall people traveled from great distances to observe them. Others came to fish the streams, which flowed clear and cold out of the hills and contained shady pools where trout lay. So it had been from the days many years ago when the

❶

▲ **Critical Viewing:** The aerial spraying of crops kills pests. However, this practice also has harmful side effects. What do you think these might be? **[Hypothesize]** ❷

first settlers raised their houses, sank their wells, and built their barns.

Then a strange <u>blight</u> crept over the area and everything began to change. Some evil spell had settled on the community: mysterious maladies swept the flocks of chickens; the cattle and sheep sickened and died. Everywhere was a shadow of death. The farmers spoke of much ❸

◆ **Build Vocabulary**

blight (blīt) *n.:* Something that destroys or prevents growth

432 ◆ *Visions of the Future*

illness among their families. In the town the doctors had become more and more puzzled by new kinds of sickness appearing among their patients. There had been several sudden and unexplained deaths, not only among adults but even among children, who would be stricken suddenly while at play and die within a few hours.

There was a strange stillness. The birds, for example—where had they gone? Many people spoke of them, puzzled and disturbed. The feeding stations in the backyards were deserted. The few birds seen anywhere were <u>moribund</u>; they trembled violently and could not fly. It was a spring without voices. On the mornings that had once throbbed with the dawn chorus of robins, catbirds, doves, jays, wrens, and scores of other bird voices there was now no sound; only silence lay over the fields and woods and marsh.

On the farms the hens brooded, but no chicks hatched. The farmers complained that they were unable to raise any pigs—the litters were small and the young survived only a few days. The apple trees

◆ **Build Vocabulary**
moribund (môr′ ə bund′) *adj.*: Dying

were coming into bloom but no bees droned among the blossoms, so there was no pollination and there would be no fruit.

The roadsides, once so attractive, were now lined with browned and withered vegetation as though swept by fire. These, too, were silent, deserted by all living things. Even the streams were now lifeless. Anglers no longer visited them, for all the fish had died.

In the gutters under the eaves and between the shingles of the roofs, a white granular powder still showed a few patches; some weeks before it had fallen like snow upon the roofs and the lawns, the fields and streams.

No witchcraft, no enemy action had silenced the rebirth of new life in this stricken world. The people had done it themselves.

This town does not actually exist, but it might easily have a thousand counterparts in America or elsewhere in the world. I know of no community that has experienced all the misfortunes I describe. Yet every one of these disasters has actually happened somewhere, and many real communities have already suffered a substantial number of them. A grim specter has crept upon us almost unnoticed, and this imagined tragedy may easily become a stark reality we all shall know.

◆ **Literary Focus**
What words heighten the impact of the warning at the end of this paragraph?

◆ **Reading Strategy**
❹ **Distinguish Between Fact and Opinion** Facts supporting the statement that the birds were moribund, or dying, include observations that the birds "trembled violently and could not fly," as well as the sudden silence replacing the usual "dawn chorus" of bird song.

Comprehension Check ☑
❺ What might be the source of the "white granular powder" that has fallen on lawns, fields, and streams? Have students look at the photo on page 432 for a hint. *It might be pesticides sprayed from airplanes.*

◆ **Literary Focus**
❻ **Exhortation** The words *grim specter, crept, unnoticed, tragedy,* and *stark reality* heighten the impact of the warning in this paragraph.

Reinforce and Extend

Answers
◆ *Literature and Your Life*
Reader's Response Some students may say that it is effective. Others may say that it is misleading in a work of nonfiction.

Thematic Focus She wants them to reach for a future in which the environment is protected.

☑ **Check Your Comprehension**
1. People were dying unexpectedly. The few birds seen anywhere were sickly. Other answers are possible.
2. She writes, "The people had done it themselves."

◆ **Critical Thinking**
1. They are humans, other animals, and plants.
2. She makes the point that all life is interconnected.
3. Some students may say that the composite picture emphasizes the importance of the problem. Others might feel that combining disparate facts is a form of exaggeration.

Guide for Responding

◆ *Literature and Your Life*

Reader's Response Is Carson's technique of describing environmental problems in a fictional town effective? Explain.

Thematic Focus For what kind of tomorrow does Rachel Carson want readers to reach?

☑ **Check Your Comprehension**
1. Name two symptoms of the environmental problem Rachel Carson describes.
2. According to Carson, who had caused the problem?

◆ **Critical Thinking**

INTERPRET
1. Rachel Carson describes sickness in three main categories of living things. What are they? **[Classify]**
2. What point does she make by dealing with all three categories? **[Draw Conclusions]**
EVALUATE
3. Is Rachel Carson's exhortation made more or less effective by the composite picture she paints? Explain. **[Make a Judgment]**

from *Silent Spring* ◆ 433

Beyond the Selection

FURTHER READING

Other Works by Rachel Carson
The Sea Around Us
The Sense of Wonder
The Edge of the Sea

Other Works About the Environment
50 Simple Things Kids Can Do to Save the Earth, John Jauna
The New Complete Guide to Environmental Careers, The Environmental Careers Organization

INTERNET
You and your students may find additonal information about protecting the environment on the Internet. We suggest the following site. Please be aware, however, that the site may have changed from the time we published this information.
Visit the Web site of the National Wildlife Federation at **http://www.nwf.org**
We *strongly recommend* that you preview the site before you send students to it.

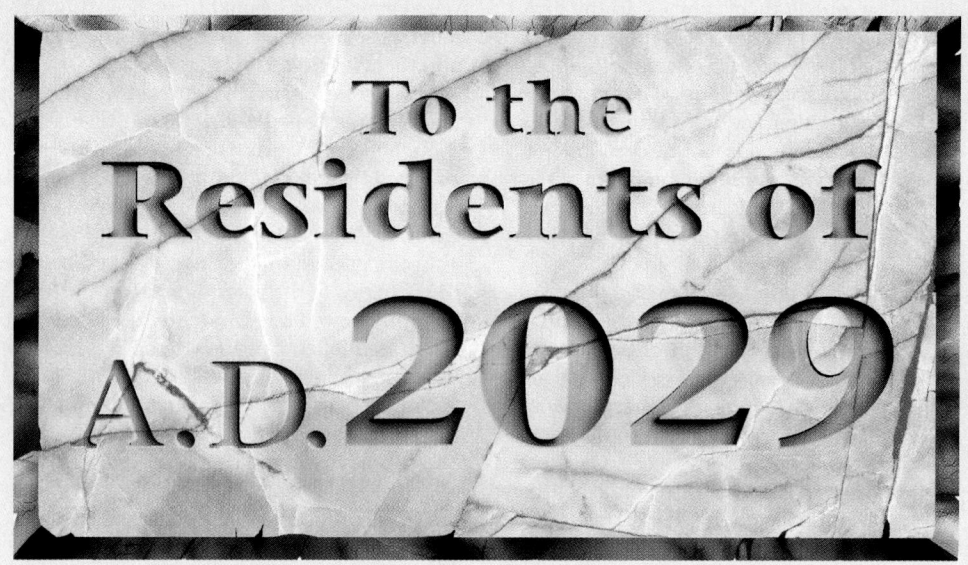

To the Residents of A.D. 2029

Bryan Woolley

Every writer's secret dream has been fulfilled for me. I know, as surely as anyone can know such things, that my works will be read fifty years from now. Well, one work, anyway.

This is because Collin County is about to dedicate a new courthouse and jail in McKinney, and somewhere in the vicinity of that structure the Collin County Historical Commission is going to bury a time capsule that will be opened in A.D. 2029, assuming that somebody's still around then, and that he can read. And I've been asked to contribute something to the capsule, probably because Mrs. Elisabeth Pink—the lady responsible for its contents—and I knew each other slightly long ago, in an era that by 2029 will be known as Prehistory. My contribution, Mrs. Pink's letter says, "could be either on our current status or what you think the future will hold."

I wish I could report to the future that our current status is hunky-dory, that we live in the Golden Age of something or other. Until recently it was possible for Americans to believe that. There's no doubt that in the twentieth

century, at least, the people of the United States have enjoyed the highest standard of living that the world has known up to this point in history. We've had so much of everything, in fact, that we've thought our supplies of the essentials of life—land, food, air, water, fuel— would last forever, and we've been wasteful. Sometimes we've even been wasteful of human life itself.

Lately, though, a sense of decline has set in. We've begun to realize that we're in trouble. We've poured so much filth into our water that much of it is undrinkable, and no life can live in it. Even the life of the ocean, the great mother of us all, is threatened. Scientists say the last wisp of pure, natural air in the continental United States was absorbed into our generally polluted atmosphere over Flagstaff, Arizona, several years ago. Parts of our land are overcrowded, parts neglected, parts abused, parts destroyed. We continue to depend on unrenewable

Cultural Connection: The Legacy of the Land

Bryan Woolley uses the device of the time capsule to deliver an important message to a future generation about the world it will inherit. Many Native Americans believe that the Earth is in fact a treasure that we lease from—or hold as a keepsake for—our children. That is, we can make no claim to owning it, for it is a timeless resource that transcends the notion of private property.

Have students research how this philosophy surfaces in the lifestyle, myths, and values of various Native American peoples across North America. These students can then compare and contrast their findings with Woolley's "four wishes" for the inheritors of the world he fears his generation is destroying.

▲ **Critical Viewing** Pollution damages the water, air, and land. What can be done to prevent pollution? [Discuss]

To the Residents of A.D. *2029* ◆ *435*

◆ Critical Thinking

❶ Identify Evidence Ask students what examples Woolley gives of people turning dreams into reality. *Europeans dreamed of another land across the ocean and then went and found it. Jules Verne dreamed of traveling under the sea and to the moon and inspired other people to make the dreams come true.*

◆ Literary Focus

❷ Exhortation Suggested response: *Appealing to readers as one race of human beings reminds us that we are all in the same boat and share in the fate of the Earth, so we must work together to save ourselves. Appealing to readers as a crowd of individuals recognizes that each of us has unique individual abilities to improve conditions in our society and that we must each decide as an individual to join in the struggle.*

▶ Critical Viewing ◀

❸ Speculate Answers may include that an appreciation of nature calms the emotions and enriches the human experience, allowing human beings to deal with one another more compassionately. Some students may reply more practically, that our respect for the natural world is repaid many times over in the food, material for clothing and shelter, and other resources that we are provided by it.

resources—petroleum; natural gas, and coal—for most of the fuel that heats and cools our homes; runs our industry, agriculture, and business; and propels our transportation. We've suddenly discovered that those resources are disappearing forever. Without usable land, air, water, and fuel, food production would be impossible, of course. In addition, the United States and the Soviet Union are at this moment trying to make treaties that we hope will keep us from destroying all life and the possibility of life if we decide to destroy each other before the fuel runs out.

So I would classify the current status that Mrs. Pink mentions as shaky, which makes the outlook for the future—even so near a future as A.D. 2029—uncertain.

An uncertain future is no new thing, of course. The future has always existed only in the imagination, a realm of hope and dread with which we can do little more than play games. But the games sometimes become serious. The Europeans <u>postulated</u> another land across the ocean for centuries and then came and found it. Jules Verne traveled un-der the sea and to the moon in his mind many years before we could make the machines to catch up with him. If, as we say, Necessity is the mother of Invention, then Desire is the father of Possibility.

Because of man's amazing record of making his dreams come true, I refuse to be pessimistic about the future, despite the frightening aspects of the present. As long as we—both as a race and as a crowd of individuals—retain our capacity for dreaming, we also keep the possibility of doing. And when doing becomes necessary, we invent a means to do so. Especially when we're in danger, as we are now.

Some of our present dangers surely will be around in 2029, for they're part of being human. We're too far from solving poverty, disease, and probably even war to be done with them in another half-century. Collin County probably will still need its courts and its jail—maybe more courts and a newer, stronger jail.

> **◆ Literary Focus**
> Why is the appeal to us "as a race and as a crowd of individuals" effective?

436 ◆ Visions of the Future

Speaking and Listening Mini-Lesson

Speech

This mini-lesson supports the Speaking and Listening activity in the Idea Bank on page 439.

Introduce the Concept Ask students to recall speakers they have heard. Why were some better or more memorable than others? With students, develop a checklist of speech-giving rules such as the following:
- Speak clearly and loudly.
- Make eye contact with the audience.

- Vary your tone of voice, volume, body language, and facial expression.

Develop Background Help students brainstorm for a list of environmental issues. Maga-zines, books, and local newspapers will help identify issues.

Apply the Information Students should research information to include in their speeches. They may record their speeches and listen for areas to improve.

Assess the Outcome Have students evaluate their speeches, using the checklist that they developed in the Introduce the Concept step. You may also want to distribute the Self-Assessment: Speech page and the Peer Assessment: Speaker/Speech page in *Alternative Assessment,* pp. 110 and 111.

But if my generation and my sons' generation do what we must to prolong the possibility of survival and the likelihood of this being read, most of the problems about which I'm worrying may seem quaint. If so, they'll be replaced by others that will seem as serious to those who gather to open the time capsule as mine do to me. Golden Ages exist only in retrospect, never for those who are trying to cope with them. ❸

So for the beleaguered residents of 2029 I wish four things:

—A deeper understanding of history, to better avoid repeating the errors of the past, for if each generation keeps on inventing its own mistakes, some of the old ones will have to be thrown out.

—A healing of the <u>schism</u> between man and

The Light Touches All and Forgets-Me-Not, from "Painterly Photography" by Elizabeth Murray

▲ **Critical Viewing:** How can respect for wildflowers and other parts of nature improve the quality of human life? **[Speculate]**

the rest of nature. Our present disrespect for the natural world is our most serious stupidity to date. We must realize that man can't long outlive the other living creatures.

—A wider and more profound appreciation of beauty. Music, poetry, pictures, and stories feed the soul as surely as wheat and meat and rice feed the body, and the soul of America is malnourished. ❹

—A sense of humor. If man ever stops laughing at himself, he can no longer endure life, nor will he have reason to.

◆ **Build Vocabulary**

postulated (päs´ chə lāt´ ed) v.: Claimed

beleaguered (bi lē´ gərd) adj.: Worried; tormented

schism (siz´ əm) n.: Split or division

Guide for Responding

◆ Literature and Your Life

Reader's Response Do you take a pessimistic or an optimistic view of the future? Why?

Thematic Focus What gives the author hope for tomorrow?

Group Activity In a small group, discuss the four things the author wishes for the future. Draw up a group list of four wishes for the future.

☑ Check Your Comprehension

1. Why is the author guaranteed an audience in fifty years?
2. Name two environmental problems mentioned by the author.
3. According to the author, what makes the future uncertain?

◆ Critical Thinking

INTERPRET

1. Identify at least two pessimistic signs for the future that Bryan Woolley mentions in his essay. **[Analyze]**
2. What specific evidence does he mention to support his statement that human beings have a record of making dreams come true? **[Support]**

EVALUATE

3. Does the author present a convincing argument for an optimistic view of the future? Explain. **[Assess]**

EXTEND

4. If society were to take the author's warning seriously, what would be three good career choices for the future? **[Career Link]**

To the Residents of A.D. *2029* ◆ 437

◆ Literature and Your Life

❹ Ask students if they agree or disagree with Woolley's opinion that "the soul of America is malnourished" because we lack appreciation for beauty in music, poetry, pictures, and stories. Have them give evidence from their own lives to support or discredit this opinion.

Reinforce and Extend

Answers
◆ Literature and Your Life

Reader's Response Help students to identify how much of their opinions are informed by fact.

Thematic Focus The record of human beings for achieving their dreams gives him hope for the future.

☑ Check Your Comprehension

1. The essay is being buried in a time capsule.
2. Problems include air pollution, water pollution, and dependence on fossil fuels.
3. The shaky status of the present makes the future uncertain.

◆ Critical Thinking

1. Suggested responses: The "last wisp of pure, natural air" has already left us, with other resources apparently soon following; we continue to be dependent on fossil fuels; we are still unable to solve the problems of poverty and disease.
2. He mentions Europeans' discovery of America as well as the reality of underwater travel and space travel predicted by Jules Verne.
3. Some students may agree that humans are good problem solvers, but others may claim that a strong track record in the past is no guarantee for the future.
4. Students may suggest the following careers: environmental scientist; historian; artist; comedian.

Beyond the Selection

FURTHER READING

Other Works by Bryan Woolley
The Edge of Texas and Other Texas Stories
The Bride Wore Crimson and Other Stories
Some Sweet Day (story collection)

Other Works About Looking to the Future
Future Shock, Alvin Toffler
"In the Mountains of Mourning," Lois McMaster Bujold
Beggars in Spain, Nancy Kress
"None So Blind," Joe Haldeman

INTERNET

You and your students may find additonal information about time capsules on the Internet. We suggest the following site. Please be aware, however, that the site may have changed from the time we published this information.

For interesting tips on time capsules, visit **http://burgh.com/business/ capsules/index. htm**

We *strongly recommend* that you preview the site before you send students to it.

◆ Reading Strategy

1. Sample response: There was much illness among farmers' families.
2. Sample response: "A grim specter has crept upon us."
3. Suggested responses: (a) the many deaths of animals and humans; (b) disagree: the author does not provide any statistics to prove that the death rate has gone up, merely that some deaths are mysterious; agree: the sheer fact that the deaths are often inexplicable is what is so ominous.
4. Suggested response: Two facts deal with our dependence on nonrenewable resources and the ability of Jules Verne to write about technology ahead of his time—both can be verified by an examination of documents or books in the public record; two opinions are that people cannot endure life without laughter and that the ability to dream leads to change—both are opinions because he roots them more in a personal view of human nature than on historical record and actual incidents.

◆ Literary Focus

1. The setting and plot are based in scientific reality.
2. By placing many instances of poisoning in one place, she heightens the importance of the events, intensifying the power of her warning.
3. (a) He uses humans' record of making their dreams come true. (b) It makes his essay a warning with hope.

◆ Build Vocabulary Skills

1. every year
2. happening every other year
3. hundredth anniversary celebration
4. happening every half year

Using the Word Bank

1. beleaguered, moribund; 2. blight, perennial; 3. pyre; 4. postulated; 5. schism, purged

◆ Build Grammar Skills

1. Endangered species include both animals and plants.
2. Neither the parents nor the children conserved electricity.
3. Either cut down on fuel consumption or be prepared to pay higher fuel prices.
4. Nuclear weapons kill both directly and indirectly.

Guide for Responding (continued)

◆ Reading Strategy

DISTINGUISH BETWEEN FACT AND OPINION

In these selections, the authors use both facts and opinions to try to persuade readers to adopt a certain outlook on environmental issues. Before deciding whether or not you agree with the outlook, you must **distinguish between fact and opinion.** A **fact** is a statement that can be proved true or false. An **opinion** is an expression of someone's belief. It cannot be proved true or false. If you made a chart, use it to answer these questions.

1. What is one fact mentioned in the chapter from "Silent Spring"?
2. What is one opinion expressed in that chapter?
3. (a) What facts support this opinion? (b) Do you agree with this opinion? Explain.
4. Identify two facts and two opinions in Bryan Woolley's essay, and explain what makes each a fact or an opinion.

◆ Literary Focus

EXHORTATION

In these selections, each author has written an **exhortation**—an urgent appeal or warning—to get you to think about problems that could cause the end of life on Earth as you know it. In "If I Forget Thee, Oh Earth . . . ," the warning is implied in a work of fiction. In nonfiction, the warning may be stated or it may be implied by the facts and ideas the author chooses to emphasize.

1. How does Arthur C. Clarke make his science-fiction story believable enough for you to take it seriously as an exhortation?
2. Rachel Carson creates a fictional place to show many examples of the dangers of pesticides. What effect does this have on her warning?
3. (a) What argument for an optimistic outlook does Bryan Woolley use in his exhortation? (b) What is the effect of his positive outlook?

◆ Build Vocabulary

USING THE WORD ROOT -ann-

In "If I Forget Thee, Oh Earth . . . ," the glow of dying atoms emanating from Earth is a *perennial* reminder of the mistakes of the past. *Perennial* comes from the Latin root *-ann-*, meaning "year." Use your knowledge of prefixes and suffixes to write the correct definition of each word.

1. annually   3. centennial
2. biannual   4. semiannual

USING THE WORD BANK

On your paper, rewrite these sentences, filling in each blank with a word from the Word Bank.

1. The ___?___ politician pleaded with his colleagues to revive the ___?___ bill he had proposed.
2. Brown spots on the shrubs warned of a ___?___ in the ___?___ garden.
3. The holy man had been cremated on a ___?___.
4. The police ___?___ that the burglar would return.
5. The leader of the ___?___ wished that she had ___?___ all opposition from her group.

◆ Build Grammar Skills

CORRELATIVE CONJUNCTIONS

Correlative conjunctions are pairs of conjunctions used to link words of equal rank. Common correlative conjunctions include *both . . . and, not only . . . but/but also, either . . . or, neither . . . nor, whether . . . or.*

Writing Application Combine each pair of sentences into one sentence by using correlative conjunctions.

1. Endangered species include animals. Endangered species also include plants.
2. The parents did not conserve electricity. The children did not conserve electricity.
3. Cut down on fuel consumption. If you don't, be prepared to pay higher fuel prices.
4. Nuclear weapons kill directly. They also kill indirectly.

---

4. Nuclear weapons kill both directly and indirectly.

✎ Writer's Solution

For additional instruction and practice, use the lesson in the **Language Lab CD-ROM** on Varying Sentence Structure. For additional instruction and practice, use the practice page on different kinds of conjunctions, p. 23, in the *Writer's Solution Grammar Practice Book.*

Build Your Portfolio

Idea Bank

Writing

1. **Bumper Sticker Slogan** Create an original bumper sticker to promote an environmental cause that you support. Remember to get your idea across in as few words as possible.

2. **Memo** As a descendant of Marvin in "If I Forget Thee, Oh Earth ... ," you have just returned from an advance exploration of Earth. Write a memo explaining what members of the Colony need to do to prepare for a return.

3. **Poem** Rachel Carson extols the beauties of the natural world. Write a poem that does the same. Focus on an aspect of nature you enjoy.

Speaking and Listening

4. **Speech** Prepare a speech about an environmental issue that concerns you. Think about what effect you want to have on your audience, and choose and organize information that will help you achieve that effect. **[Science Link]**

5. **Storytelling** Imagine you are one of the Colonists in "If I Forget Thee, Oh Earth...." Tell your child a story about growing up on Earth, especially as it contrasts with life in the Colony.

Projects

6. **Poster** Create a poster contrasting the image Rachel Carson describes at the beginning of *Silent Spring* with an image that represents the second scene she describes. Include a title or a slogan that sums up the message of your poster. **[Art Link]**

7. **Time Capsule** Prepare a time capsule with several items from the present that would represent your era accurately to someone opening the capsule in fifty years. **[Social Studies Link]**

Writing Mini-Lesson

Environmental Report

Rachel Carson's book *Silent Spring* had an enormous impact on the way many people viewed pest control, in large part due to its well-documented facts. Prepare your own report on an environmental issue. Be sure to include enough pertinent facts to support your main idea.

Writing Skills Focus: Elaboration to Prove a Point

Your report will be more convincing if you **elaborate** with facts and statistics **to prove your point.** Notice how Rachel Carson elaborates on her general statement, "Everywhere was a shadow of death."

> The farmers spoke of much illness among their families. In the town the doctors had become more and more puzzled by new kinds of sickness appearing among their patients.

Gather the facts and statistics you will use before you start writing. When revising, be sure every general statement is supported by facts.

Prewriting Choose an environmental issue on which to focus your report. Then collect facts and statistics, either firsthand or from reference books. Use note cards to record each fact and its source. Put your note cards in an order that makes sense to you and prepare an outline from the cards.

Drafting Write a strong introduction, body, and conclusion for your environmental report. As you write, back up each of your statements with facts.

Revising Have a classmate read your draft and point out areas where a lack of facts or statistics weakens your main point. If necessary, conduct additional research to support your statements.

Idea Bank

Customizing for *Performance Levels*
Following are suggestions for matching the Idea Bank topics with your students' performance levels:
- Less Advanced Students: 1, 7
- Average Students: 2, 4, 6
- More Advanced Students: 3, 5

Customizing for *Learning Modalities*
Following are suggestions for matching Idea Bank topics with your students' learning modalities:
- Visual/Spatial: 1, 6, 7
- Auditory: 4, 5
- Logical/Mathematical: 4
- Verbal/Linguistic: 2, 3, 4, 5

Writing Mini-Lesson

Refer students to the Writing Handbook, page 962, for instruction on the writing process, and page 960 for further information on Research Writing.

You may want to use the Cause-and-Effect Essay models in *Writing and Language Transparencies,* pp. 37–40, to guide students through the writing process.

Writer's Solution

Writing Lab CD-ROM
Have students complete the Tutorial on Research Writing. Follow these steps:
1. Have students complete the K-W-L chart to outline the information they wish to include in their reports.
2. Have students complete the interactive instruction activities on note taking and on evaluating facts and opinions.
3. Have students draft on computer.
4. Have students use the revision checkers on transitions to revise their drafts.

Allow approximately 120 minutes of class time to complete these steps.

Sourcebook
Have students use Chapter 5, Research Writing (pp. 130–161), for additional support. The chapter includes an annotated student model of a research paper (pp. 155–156).

✓ ASSESSMENT OPTIONS

Formal Assessment, Selection Test, pp. 110–112, and Assessment Resources Software. The selection test is designed so that it can be easily customized to the performance levels of your students. ***Alternative Assessment,*** p. 32, includes options for less advanced students, more advanced students, intrapersonal learners, verbal/linguistic learners, and interpersonal learners.

PORTFOLIO ASSESSMENT
Use the following rubrics in the ***Alternative Assessment*** booklet to assess student writing:
Bumper Sticker Slogan: Persuasion Rubric, p. 98
Memo: Business Letter/Memo Rubric, p. 106
Poem: Poetry Rubric, p. 101
Writing Mini-Lesson: Research Report/Paper Rubric, p. 99

Guide for Reading

More About the Authors

Both Nelson Mandela and Shu Ting write against a backdrop of political turmoil. For years, South Africa's system of apartheid kept the different races living apart from one another and gave all privileges and rights to the minority white population. Before, during, and after his long incarceration, **Nelson Mandela** pressured the South African government to end apartheid and create a more democratic state.

Shu Ting is a member of a group of poets in China who work through their art to achieve democracy in that country. Both selections are inspired by the writers' struggles, hopes, and dreams for a better future.

Shu Ting (1952–)

Shu Ting uses poetry to express her personal feelings—even though the Communist government of China has condemned such expression as anti-communist.

Shu Ting began writing poetry in 1979. Her works were well received. While still in her twenties, Shu Ting gained nationwide fame as a poet. During the 1980's, she became known as one of the "Misty Poets" of China. The term derives from a government literary critic's appraisal of an anti-communist poem by poet Gu Chen as "misty." The writings of the Misty Poets have fueled—and continue to fuel —a ceaseless struggle for democracy in China. The poem "Gifts," with Shu Ting's characteristic gentle touch and concern for others, bears a personal message for the future.

Nelson Mandela (1918–)

Considered a living testament to the strength of the human spirit, Nelson Mandela emerged from a twenty–seven-year prison term to become the first black president of South Africa.

Mandela was born in a country whose white government maintained a strict policy of apartheid, or legal discrimination against blacks. In 1944, Mandela began protesting apartheid. Twenty years later, after several arrests, he was sentenced to life in prison for acts of sabotage.

Mandela remained in prison until 1990. After his release, he continued to fight for equal rights for all South Africans. In 1991, apartheid was finally abolished and, in 1993, Mandela and South African president F. W. de Klerk shared the Nobel Peace Prize. The next year Mandela was elected president. "Glory and Hope" is his inaugural address.

◆ Build Vocabulary

SUFFIXES: *-logy*

In "Glory and Hope," Nelson Mandela speaks of an *ideology*. If you know that the suffix *-logy* means "the study, science, or theory of," you can figure out that *ideology* means "the study of ideas," or, more specifically, "the ideas on which a political, economic, or social system is based."

| pinions |
| hieroglyphics |
| confer |
| pernicious |
| ideology |
| chasms |
| covenant |
| inalienable |

WORD BANK

As you read the selections, you will encounter the words on this list. Each word is defined on the page where it first appears. Preview the list before you read.

◆ Build Grammar Skills

SUBJECT AND VERB AGREEMENT

Verbs must **agree** in number (singular or plural) with their subjects. In this example from "Glory and Hope," notice how verb endings change to match a singular or a plural subject.

...the grass turns (singular) green and the

flowers bloom (plural).

In the example, the singular verb *turns* agrees with the singular subject *grass*, and the plural verb *bloom* agrees with the plural subject *flowers*.

Prentice Hall Literature Program Resources

REINFORCE / RETEACH / EXTEND

Selection Support Pages
Build Vocabulary: Suffixes: *-logy*, p. 134
Build Grammar Skills: Subject and Verb Agreement, p. 135
Reading Strategy: Evaluate the Writer's Message, p. 136
Literary Focus: Tone, p. 137

Strategies for Diverse Student Needs, p. 33

Beyond Literature
Cross-Curricular Connection: Social Studies, p. 33

Formal Assessment Selection Test, pp. 113–115, Assessment Resources Software

Alternative Assessment, p. 33

Writing and Language Transparencies
Cluster Organizer, p. 80

Resource Pro CD-ROM
"Glory and Hope," "Gifts"—includes all resource material and customizable lesson plan

Listening to Literature Audiocassettes
"Glory and Hope," "Gifts"

Gifts ◆ Glory and Hope

◆ *Literature and Your Life*

CONNECT YOUR EXPERIENCE

A television newscast shows angry demonstrators chanting for freedom in a distant land. As you watch, you may not feel that what you're seeing affects you personally. Yet as these selections show, freedom is a concern shared by all people throughout the world.

THEMATIC FOCUS: REACHING FOR TOMORROW

Will people of all races and nationalities learn to respect each other and enjoy freedom in the future? These selections convey hope for a peaceful future.

Journal Writing List three things you can do today to help achieve freedom and peace for tomorrow.

◆ Background for Understanding

CULTURE

Apartheid, which means "apartness" in the Afrikaans language, is the policy of segregation and discrimination that was once practiced against nonwhites by the South African government. Under apartheid, housing, education, and transportation were segregated by law.

Apartheid became law in South Africa in 1948. Opposition to the policy grew—both inside and outside the country. In 1986, the governments of many nations, including the United States, reduced trade with South Africa in order to help end apartheid. The policy was finally abolished in 1991.

◆ Literary Focus

TONE

Tone is the attitude a writer takes toward an audience or subject. The tone of a literary work might be formal, informal, playful, or serious. The author's word choice is a key to understanding the tone of a piece. As you read, notice each writer's choice of words. How do the words contribute to the tone of each piece?

◆ Reading Strategy

EVALUATE THE WRITER'S MESSAGE

A writer's message is the idea that he or she wants to communicate. In his inaugural address, for example, Nelson Mandela has a message of hope for the people of South Africa.

You **evaluate a writer's message** by first identifying the message and then judging whether the message is valid, clearly reasoned out, and well-supported. You can evaluate a message without necessarily agreeing or disagreeing with it.

As you read these selections, first identify the message in each. Then evaluate each writer's message.

Guide for Reading ◆ 441

Today's students may be too young to remember apartheid or the events in Tiananmen Square—historical events that dramatically impacted the lives of these writers. As a result, you may want to set the stage for students' reading by having groups research one or both of the events as a homework assignment before reading the selection. If possible, the groups should locate photographs and video footage that they can show to classmates as they share what they have learned through their research. Follow with a class discussion about what it might have been like to live through the events. Then tell students that they're about to read the works by two writers who did live through the events.

Customize for
Less Proficient Readers

Remind these students that a speech is meant to be heard. Have them follow along in their texts as they listen to the recording of Mandela's speech. Ask: How is listening to the speech different from reading it?

Listening to Literature Audiocassettes

Customize for
More Advanced Students

Point out that an effective speech writer establishes a compelling rhythm to keep the audience's attention. One technique for doing this is repetition of words and sentence structures. Challenge advanced students to find examples of this technique in Mandela's speech. For example, Mandela often uses phrases in a series, separated by commas. Also, the driving rhythm of the three short sentences beginning with "Let there be . . ." toward the end of the speech bring the speech to its climax.

Customize for
English Language Learners

Mandela occasionally uses an inverted word order common to formal oratory in which objects and verbs come before subjects. Make students aware of these unusual sentence structures so that they do not hinder reading comprehension. Point out examples such as "All this we owe. . . ."

Preparing for Standardized Tests

Grammar and Language Standardized tests often include sections in which students are called on to identify errors in sentences. Problems with subject-verb agreement—the skill addressed in the Build Grammar Skills section—are among the errors most often included in these sentences. Following is a sample of what a test item might look like. Write the item on the board and have students try to come up with the correct answer. D

<u>None</u> of the <u>councilman's</u> <u>suggestions</u>
  A   B   C

<u>was adopted</u> at <u>last night's</u>
    D   E

meeting.

For additional practice, use the Build Grammar Skills page on Subject and Verb Agreement, p. 135, in *Selection Support.*

One-Minute Insight Nelson Mandela's inaugural speech is designed to lead his listeners out of the past toward a brighter, more democratic future. He reminds his listeners of past struggles but turns their attention to the challenges that lie ahead and the glories that await once those challenges are met.

Shu Ting's message is one of self-sacrifice for a greater good. Using a pond, sunlight, and birds as metaphors, she describes a journey from "hardship and failure to a future of warmth and light."

▶**Critical Viewing**◀

❶ **Connect** Discuss students' dreams for a better future before having them determine an image from nature that might illustrate those dreams. *Students' imagery should support and shed light on their "dreams."*

◆ **Reading Strategy**

❷ **Evaluate the Writer's Message** The pond in this poet's vision does not just stand there beautiful and inert; it has a job to do. Ask: Why isn't the pond unhappy at being destroyed? *It has sacrificed itself so that it could climb up and nourish roots and leaves.*

◆ **Reading Strategy**

❸ **Evaluate the Writer's Message** Ask students why the bird's pinions are "blood-stained," and what the hieroglyphics will mean. *Students may answer that the blood stains indicate a violent struggle; the hieroglyphics may chronicle the history of the struggle for democracy.*

◆ **Critical Thinking**

❹ **Evaluate Word Choice** Have students consider the title of the poem and these last lines. Ask: Does the word *gift* connote something positive or negative? How does it fit the author's message and the tone of the poem? *It has a positive connotation and is used here to indicates the poet's positive feelings toward the world around her. The title refers not only to what she has received from Earth, but also what she intends to give to others.*

442

Gifts *Shu Ting*

My dream is the dream of a pond
Not just to mirror the sky
But to let the willows and ferns
Suck me dry.
5   I'll climb from the roots to the veins,
And when leaves wither and fade
I will refuse to mourn
Because I was dying to live.   ❷

My joy is the joy of sunlight.
10 In a moment of creation
I will leave shining words
In the pupils of children's eyes
Igniting golden flames.
Whenever seedlings sprout
15 I shall sing a song of green.
I'm so simple I'm profound!

My grief is the grief of birds.
The Spring will understand:
Flying from hardship and failure
20 To a future of warmth and light.
There my blood-stained <u>pinions</u>
Will scratch <u>hieroglyphics</u>   ❸
On every human heart
For every year to come.

25 Because all that I am   ❹
Has been a gift from earth.

▲ **Critical Viewing** Relate this photograph to the first stanza of the poem. What image from nature could illustrate your "dream"? [Connect] ❶

◆ **Build Vocabulary**

pinions (pin′ yənz) *n.:* The last bony sections of a bird's wings

hieroglyphics (hī′ ər ō′ glif′ iks) *n.:* Pictures or symbols that represent words or ideas

442 ◆ *Visions of the Future*

Block Scheduling Strategies

Consider these suggestions to take advantage of extended class time:
- To ensure that students understand the Literary Focus concept of tone, read aloud portions of speeches, poems, and essays, asking students the tone of each piece.
- As you review the information in Background for Understanding (p. 441), ask students to share any knowledge they have about the recent history of South Africa. Have them compare and contrast this history with the history of civil rights in the United States. Then, after reading Mandela's speech, ask students if they can name any similar speeches in U.S. history that have inspired hope.
- After students do the Build Vocabulary activity (p. 446), brainstorm for additional words with the suffix *-logy*.
- Have students complete the Writing Mini-Lesson (p. 447). Before they write, brainstorm for a list of additional transition words: *especially, ever more, greater, in particular,* and so on.

Glory and Hope

by Nelson Mandela

Your majesties, your royal highnesses, distinguished guests, comrades and friends: Today, all of us do, by our presence here, and by our celebrations in other parts of our country and the world, <u>confer</u> glory and hope to newborn liberty.

Out of the experience of an extraordinary human disaster that lasted too long must be born a society of which all humanity will be proud.

Our daily deeds as ordinary South Africans must produce an actual South African reality that will reinforce humanity's belief in justice, strengthen its confidence in the nobility of the human soul and sustain all our hopes for a glorious life for all.

All this we owe both to ourselves and to the peoples of the world who are so well represented here today.

To my compatriots, I have no hesitation in saying that each one of us is as inti-

▲ **Critical Viewing** How do you think Mandela felt when this picture was taken? [Interpret] **8**

mately attached to the soil of this beautiful country as are the famous jacaranda trees of Pretoria and the mimosa trees of the bushveld.[1]

Each time one of us touches the soil of this land, we feel a sense of personal renewal. The national mood changes as the seasons change. **9**

We are moved by a sense of joy and exhilaration when the grass turns green and the flowers bloom.

That spiritual and physical oneness we

◆ Build Vocabulary

confer (kən fʉr´) v.: To give

---
1. **bushveld** (bŏŏsh´ velt) n.: Southern African grassland with abundant shrubs and thorny vegetation.

Gifts/Glory and Hope ◆ 443

◆ Literary Focus

5 Tone Ask students to explain what sets this opening paragraph apart from ordinary speech. How does it affect the tone of the speech? Why is this tone appropriate? *The entire paragraph is one sentence with structure, wording, and word order that is unusual for ordinary conversation— "all of us" is the subject, and "do . . . confer," separated by two prepositional phrases, is the verb; this elevates the tone of the speech to very formal; the tone is appropriate because Mandela is speaking to an audience that includes many heads of state.*

◆ Build Vocabulary

6 Suffixes: -logy Point out the word *society*, which has the same root as the word *sociology*. Ask: Based on your knowledge of the meaning of suffixes, what would you guess *sociology* means? *It means the study of societies or human relationships*

◆ Reading Strategy

7 Evaluate the Writer's Message Ask students to explain which two groups of people Mandela is addressing in this part of his speech. What is he saying to each? What is his purpose in each case? *He is promising dignitaries from other countries that, now that apartheid has been abolished, a democratic government can work successfully in South Africa. He is also calling upon his fellow South Africans to work to establish a democratic and peaceful way of life.*

▶Critical Viewing◀

8 Interpret Suggested response: *Mandela probably felt great joy in the knowledge that South Africa was at last a country of equal rights for all people. He undoubtedly also felt pride in being elected the first president of a free South Africa.*

◆ Build Grammar Skills

9 Subject and Verb Agreement This complex sentence contains the same verb used twice, once with a singular subject and once with a plural subject. Ask: What are the verbs in this sentence? What happens to this regular verb when it is used with a singular subject? *The verbs are changes and change; the verb adds an -s when used with a singular subject.*

 Beyond the Classroom

Career Connection

Security Forces Because of the threat of violence, South Africa had to have security forces present at all polling places during its first democratic election. Have students consider situations in which security forces are put to work in the United States—at concerts, huge sporting events, political rallies, and so on. Discuss the qualities that might make someone a good member of a security force; for example, fitness and steady nerves.

Community Connection

Suffrage: The Right to Vote Americans tend to take elections for granted, but 1994 was the first time voters of all races could vote in South Africa. Point out that until 1920, women could not vote in the United States. As late as the 1960's, people struggled and died to gain voting rights for African Americans in the South. Ask students to express their opinion about the importance of the right to vote.

443

Evaluate the Writer's Message

1. Suggested response: Mandela's message is that South Africa must now become a society that is a model of freedom and justice for all.
2. Suggested response: Mandela supports his message by citing what happens when such values are not adhered to. Freedom and justice were the very rights South Africa's blacks were denied under apartheid.
3. Suggested response: The poet's message concerns giving the gifts of her ideas and feelings to future generations. Everyone is capable of leaving similar gifts by simply expressing his or her ideas and feelings to others or by living in accordance with one's ideals. Shu Ting's message appears in a poem that is "emotionally logical" and internally consistent, two strong sources of support for the validity of her message.

◆ Literary Focus

1. "Glory and Hope" has a formal tone. The opening acknowledgment of dignitaries and the sophisticated vocabulary contribute to the tone. The primary intended audience of "Gifts" consists of ordinary people who live in China. With this in mind, Shu Ting's down-to-earth, cautious optimism is well suited to her audience.
2. Mandela tailors his writing for his audience by openly acknowledging the members of his audience. He uses a sophisticated vocabulary featuring abstract concepts and ideas to communicate the status and hopes of South Africa to world leaders and ordinary citizens alike. Shu Ting tailors her writing for her audience by using a personal and gentle style. She draws analogies from nature to communicate her message in an intimate way.
3. The intended audience of "Glory and Hope" consists of world leaders, distinguished guests, and the people of South Africa on a solemn occasion—therefore, Mandela's tone is appropriate, particularly its triumphant note. Shu Ting's poem, on the other hand, cannot afford to use such an upbeat tone, as the struggle of her

446

Guide for Responding (continued)

◆ Reading Strategy

EVALUATE THE WRITER'S MESSAGE

You **evaluate** a writer's message by examining his or her reasoning and support and by judging the validity of the message.
1. What is Nelson Mandela's message?
2. How does he support his message?
3. Evaluate Shu Ting's message in "Gifts."

◆ Literary Focus

TONE

The **tone**, or writer's attitude toward his or her audience and subject, is quite different in each of these selections. That difference is not merely because one is a speech and the other a poem. An additional difference is the intended audience for each selection.
1. What is the tone of each selection?
2. What words, phrases, or passages does each writer use to convey the tone?
3. Is the tone appropriate for each piece? Explain.

Beyond Literature

History Connection

Today's South Africa The ending of apartheid in 1991 began a new era of freedom and equality in South Africa. South African schools began to admit students of all races. Health care ceased to be provided on a racial basis. Imports and exports began to flow freely into and out of the nation, and once again, South African athletes were permitted to participate in international sporting events. Despite problems such as a high unemployment rate and the unequal distribution of certain services, many South Africans are now optimistic about the future.
Activity Use the Internet or the library to find more information about South Africa today.

◆ Build Vocabulary

USING THE SUFFIX -logy

Remembering that the suffix -logy means "the study, science, or theory of," write definitions for the following words:
1. zoology
2. sociology
3. biology

USING THE WORD BANK

On a separate sheet of paper, write the word or words from the Word Bank that complete each statement.
1. To give is to _____?_____.
2. _____?_____ rights cannot be taken away.
3. A destructive system of ideas is a _____?_____ _____?_____.
4. A solemn agreement is a _____?_____.
5. _____?_____ are sections of birds' wings.
6. _____?_____ are picture writings.
7. Beautiful _____?_____ are gorgeous gorges.

◆ Build Grammar Skills

SUBJECT AND VERB AGREEMENT

A **verb** form should always **agree** with its **subject** in number.

Practice In your notebook, rewrite each sentence, correcting any errors in subject-verb agreement.
1. Words of freedom comes from the lips of Nelson Mandela.
2. Shu Ting, one of the Misty Poets, write of personal feelings.
3. People throughout South Africa listens to Mandela's speech.
4. Shu Ting, like other poets, want to leave a message for future generations.
5. All people who believe in freedom rejoices in the transformation of South Africa.

---

people has to this day largely *not* been won. Her emotionalism is appropriate in the face of so much uncertainty.

◆ Build Vocabulary

1. study of animals; 2. study of society; 3. study of life

Using the Word Bank
1. confer; 2. Inalienable;
3. pernicious ideology;
4. covenant; 5. Pinions;
6. Hieroglyphics; 7. chasms

◆ Build Grammar Skills

1. Words of freedom <u>come</u> ....
2. Shu Ting, one of the Misty Poets, <u>writes</u> ....
3. People throughout South Africa <u>listen</u> ....
4. Shu Ting, like other poets, <u>wants</u> ....
5. All people who believe in freedom <u>rejoice</u> ....

✒ Writer's Solution

For additional instruction and practice, use the lesson in the **Language Lab CD-ROM** on Subject-Verb Agreement, and use the practice pages on subject and verb agreement, pp. 82–84, in the *Writer's Solution Grammar Practice Book*.

*B*uild *Y*our *P*ortfolio

 ## Idea Bank

Writing

1. **Letter to Nelson Mandela** Write a letter to Nelson Mandela in which you share which parts of his speech you found most inspiring. **[Social Studies Link]**

2. **Futuristic Essay** Write an essay in which you present your vision of human rights in the future. **[Social Studies Link]**

3. **Radio News Report** Write a radio news report about Mandela's speech. Include a brief summary, as well as background material on Mandela. **[Career Link]**

Speaking and Listening

4. **Oral Interpretation** With a small group, read aloud "Glory and Hope," with each group member reading a section of the speech. **[Performing Arts Link]**

5. **Panel Discussion** Hold a panel discussion on the kind of world you would like to leave to future generations. Discuss important issues such as human rights and the environment. **[Social Studies Link]**

Projects

6. **Multimedia Presentation** Give a multimedia presentation on South Africa. Discuss the geography, climate, and history of the nation. If possible, provide relevant photos or audio and video recordings. **[Social Studies Link; Media Link]**

7. **Poster** Design a poster that expresses in words and pictures the concept of a better world in the future. **[Art Link]**

 ## Writing Mini-Lesson

Speech for a Historic Figure

In his speech "Glory and Hope," Nelson Mandela presents a memorable message on the future of South Africa Choose another historic figure from the past or present, and write a speech for that person.

Writing Skills Focus: Transitions to Show Importance

Present a clear and easy-to-follow speech by using **transitions to show importance**. Transitions—such as *first, more importantly, better, best,* and *least*—show a clear relationship among ideas. Notice how Nelson Mandela uses the transition "not least" to indicate the important role of an individual.

Model From the Speech

We deeply appreciate the role . . . leaders have played. . . . Not least among them is my Second Deputy President, the Honorable F. W. de Klerk.

Prewriting After choosing the historic figure, determine the purpose of your speech. For example, if you're writing a speech for a scientist, the purpose might be to explain a new scientific discovery.

Drafting Organize your ideas using transitions to show the relative importance of each. You can arrange your ideas from least important to most important or do the reverse.

Revising Read your speech aloud and listen to how it sounds. If your ideas are not logically organized, rearrange them using transitions to show importance.

Gifts/Glory and Hope ◆ 447

Customizing for
Performance Levels
Following are suggestions for matching the Idea Bank topics with your students' performance levels:
    Less Advanced Students: 1, 4, 7
    Average Students: 2, 3, 4
    More Advanced Students: 5, 6

Customizing for
Learning Modalities
Following are suggestions for matching Idea Bank topics with your students' learning modalities:
    Visual/Spatial: 6, 7
    Auditory: 4, 5
    Logical/Mathematical: 2, 6
    Verbal/Linguistic: 1, 2, 3, 4, 5

 ## Writing Mini-Lesson

Refer students to the Writing Handbook, page 962, for instruction on the writing process, and page 965 for further information on persuasion.

Have students use the Cluster Organizer in *Writing and Language Transparencies,* p. 80, to help organize their prewriting ideas.

 ### Writer's Solution

Writer's at Work Videodisc
Have students view the videodisc segment (Ch. 4) featuring National Basketball Association writer Larry Weitzman talking about starting a draft. Have students discuss how to express excitement in a subject.

Play frames 33836 to 42938

Writing Lab CD-ROM
If students choose a persuasive focus for their speeches, have them complete the Tutorial on Persuasion. Follow these steps:
1. Have students use the Pros-and-Cons chart to gather evidence.
2. Have students draft on the computer.
3. Use the Transition Word Bin. Allow 90 minutes of class time to complete these steps.

Sourcebook
Have students use Chapter 4, Persuasion (pp. 96–127), for additional support. The chapter includes a model of a persuasive speech (p. 104).

☑ ASSESSMENT OPTIONS

Formal Assessment, Selection Test, pp. 113–115, and Assessment Resources Software. The selection test is designed so that it can be easily customized to the performance levels of your students. *Alternative Assessment,* p. 33, includes options for less advanced students, more advanced students, musical/rhythmic learners, verbal/linguistic learners, and visual/spatial learners.

PORTFOLIO ASSESSMENT
Use the following rubrics in the *Alternative Assessment* booklet to assess student writing:
Letter to Nelson Mandela: Expression Rubric, p. 87
Futuristic Essay: Persuasion Rubric, p. 98
Radio News Report: Summary Rubric, p. 91
Writing Mini-Lesson: Persuasion Rubric, p. 98

Revising

You might advise students that, even though their time is limited, it can be best used by quickly scanning their essays three separate times, one for each type of revision: clarifying main points, adding missing details, and correcting errors in grammar and spelling. If any time is left, they can go through their essays once more to replace vague words with more vivid or precise ones.

 Writer's Solution

Writing Lab CD-ROM

The Proofreading Checklist in the Revising and Editing section of the Tutorial on Practical and Technical Writing pinpoints errors students may make in their drafts so that they can check for those errors when revising.

Publishing

Students may reserve a section of their portfolios for successful test essays. That way, the essays of which they are most proud will be available to be shared when the opportunity arises.

Reinforce and Extend

Review the Writing Guidelines

After students have completed their papers, review the characteristics of an essay for a test. Encourage students to come up with additional time-saving tips that might help classmates improve their performance on essay tests.

APPLYING LANGUAGE SKILLS: Varying Sentence Length and Structure

Length: As you write, alternate long sentences with short sentences.

Some people say computers rule us whether we're awake or asleep. They're right.

Structure: Start some sentences with a noun or pronoun. Start others with a phrase or transition.

Computers are great now. In the future, they'll be even greater.

Practice Rewrite this passage to establish better sentence variety.

We have a computer at home. We also have computers in school. I enjoy using computers. I know how to play many computer games. I also know a variety of programs.

Writing Application Varying sentence length and structure will add to the effectiveness of any test essay. Try to establish variety as you write, because you may not have time to make revisions later.

Writer's Solution Connection Language Lab

For additional practice, complete the lesson on Varying Sentence Structure.

Use Transitions to Show Importance As you draft your essay, introduce new ideas and details with transition words that show relative importance. You may either place your most important ideas first or save them for last. Your transitions will tell readers the importance of each idea or detail.

Revising

Allow Time for Revisions Because you're pressured for time, it's tempting to skip the revision stage when writing a test essay. Doing so is a mistake, however. When drafting your essay, you may leave out important words or details that you won't notice unless you read over your writing. Allow a few minutes to review your writing quickly. Focus on the following points:

▶ Be sure that your main points are clear.
  If your main points are not evident, or if they are not clearly worded, go back and rephrase them.
▶ Look for any missing details.
  If you haven't included at least two or three details to support each main point, add new details.
▶ Correct errors in grammar and spelling.
  Your teacher will have a more favorable response to your essay if it is free of such errors.

Publishing

▶ **Share Your Work** A successful test essay demonstrates how much you've learned about an area of study. Others may also benefit from your efforts. You may want to share your essay with people close to you—friends or family members.

✓ ASSESSMENT		4	3	2	1
PORTFOLIO ASSESSMENT Use the rubric on the appropriate type of essay in *Alternative Assessment* to assess students' writing. Add these criteria to customize the rubric to this assignment.	**Main Ideas**	The writer provides a well-written thesis statement in an introductory paragraph and at least two main ideas that logically support the thesis.	The writer provides a thesis statement in an introductory paragraph and at least one main idea that supports the thesis.	The writer provides a thesis statement in an introductory paragraph, but doesn't adequately develop it.	The writer fails to provide a clear thesis statement, and it is unclear which sentences express main supporting ideas.
	Supporting Details	Each of the writer's main ideas is clearly and logically supported by at least two details.	One or more of the writer's main ideas are clearly and logically supported by only one detail.	Not all of the writer's main ideas are logically supported by details.	The writer fails to back up the main ideas in the essay with supporting details.

Real-World Reading Skills Workshop

Recognizing Key Words

Strategies for Success

Whenever you read a passage, it's important to look at each word. Some words are more important than others, however. Those words are **key words.** Without them, the meaning of the entire passage would be lost. Follow these tips for recognizing key words in your reading:

Find the Subject and Verb A sentence cannot be complete without a subject and a verb. The subject names whom or what the sentence is about. The verb tells what the subject does. In the sentence *The telephone rang loudly,* the key words are *telephone* (subject) and *rang* (verb). Focusing on these two words will help you to understand the essence of the sentence.

Look for Instruction Words When you read directions, as on a test, the key words include verbs that give commands. (The subject *you,* which does not appear, is understood.) For example, read these directions: *Print your name and then sign it directly below.* The two command verbs are *print* and *sign.* Without those key words, you wouldn't know what to do.

Look for Signal Words Writers often use signal words that indicate the importance of ideas (*most importantly,* for example) or explain the relationships among ideas (*in contrast, after, as a result,* and so on). These words are crucial to recognize because they help you to follow the writer's main points.

Test Directions

1. Do nothing until you read through these directions completely.

2. Print your full name in the upper left corner of your paper, last name first.

3. Print today's date in the upper right corner.

4. Fold your paper vertically down the middle.

5. Unfold the paper and number your paper from 1 to 10.

6. Ignore directions 2 to 5 above and put down your pen.

Apply the Strategy

Read the test directions on the paper. Then answer these questions.

1. What are the key verbs in directions 1 to 6?
2. Can you find any key subjects in the test directions? If so, what are they?
3. What are the key descriptive words in directions 1 to 6? What nouns or verbs do they describe?
4. If you took this test, would you do any writing or folding? Why?

✔ Here are some other situations in which recognizing key words can be helpful:
► Reading a contract you plan to sign
► Reading a science or social studies textbook
► Reading an instruction manual
► Reading an encyclopedia article

451

Introduce the Strategy

Ask students if they have ever skimmed a piece of writing without reading every single word. What kind of material do they find useful to skim rather than read thoroughly? Have students try skimming a passage from one of their books and discuss which words they noticed more than others. Mention that successful readers develop a skill for picking out *key words* to note whenever they are reading, but especially when they are reading quickly.

Customize for
English Language Learners

Because these students may not yet be sufficiently familiar with the language to distinguish key words in applying the strategy, you might copy this page for them and help them highlight the key words in the Test Directions. Suggest that this technique may be helpful with other reading material as well, but be sure to remind students to highlight only on copies—never on actual book pages.

Apply the Strategy

Have students read the Test Directions on this page, noting the key words as they read. Remind them that they will not be ready to answer the questions below until they have read the directions thoroughly. Students who use this technique will find these directions very easy to follow!

Answers

1. The key verbs are *Do* and *read* (#1), *Print* (#2), *Print* (#3), *Fold* (#4), *Unfold* and *number* (#5), *Ignore* and *put* (#6).
2. There are no subjects, because all sentences are imperative. The understood subject of each sentence is *you.*
3. The key descriptive words are *completely* (#1), *upper left* and *first* (#2), *today's* and *upper right* (#3), *vertically* (#4), *from 1 to 10* (#5), and *above* (#6).
4. If students took this test, they would do nothing, following the directions in #6: "Ignore directions 2 to 5 above and put down your pen."

Introduce the Strategy

Remind students that directions are usually given in short sentences in chronological order. The person giving directions will often use time-order transition words, such as *first, next, then,* and *finally* or *last.* Suggest that listening carefully for these words can be helpful in remembering the sequence of tasks being described.

Customize for
Visual/Spatial Learners

These students may have difficulty keeping long, involved oral directions straight in their minds. Suggest that, as soon as they find they are losing track of the directions they are being given, they politely ask the person giving the directions to pause while they get pencil and paper to take notes. If students number their notes, write neatly, and underline or highlight important words, they will have a visual record to which they can refer when it comes time to carry out the directions.

Apply the Strategy

Have partners alternate being the person who gives directions and the one who carries them out. You might coach students beforehand, mentioning that the purpose of the role-playing activity is not to "stump your partner" by giving impossible-to-follow directions, but to work cooperatively, one partner giving clear, organized directions and the other listening carefully and carrying them out successfully. However, it might be fun to experiment by challenging one partner to carry out deliberately jumbled, impossible directions given by the other.

Speaking and Listening Workshop

Following Oral Directions

In the course of a day, you probably hear many kinds of directions. Your teachers may explain how to do a homework assignment. Your parents may describe a household chore for you to do. It's important that you listen closely to the directions so that you'll be able to do the job correctly.

Listen for Important Words Once a student stayed up all night writing an essay for class. Imagine his surprise the next day when the teacher said, "I didn't ask you to *write* an essay. I told you to *read* one!"

When directions are spoken, pay careful attention to the verbs, or command words. What verbs do you find in these directions?

> *Please collect the dirty dishes that are on the table. Scrape off any food into the garbage container, and then place the dishes in the dishwasher. Then sweep and mop the floor.*

When directions are spoken, also listen closely for the nouns. Look again at the directions above. What nouns do you find?

452 ◆ *Visions of the Future*

Tips for Following Oral Directions

✔ *If you want to succeed at following oral directions, heed these helpful hints:*

▶ Listen carefully to the speaker's words. Try to pick out the key verbs and nouns.

▶ Don't do anything to distract your listening, such as gazing out a window.

▶ Keep your eyes on the speaker. He or she may use gestures to emphasize certain words.

▶ Repeat the directions to yourself before following them. Ask questions if necessary.

Apply the Strategies

With a partner, role-play these situations. After your partner gives you the directions, see how well you can carry them out.

1. Your gym teacher tells you a series of exercises to follow to help you keep physically fit.

2. Your acting coach describes a scene in which you play a certain type of character in a particular situation.

3. An airline flight attendant gives you instructions on what to do in case of an emergency landing.

4. The neighbor who has hired you as a baby sitter gives you instructions for taking care of the children.

Workplace Skills: Mini-Lesson

Taking Direction

Taking direction well is an important skill in almost any job for which students may be hired, now or in the future. Explain that even people like teachers, doctors, and business executives are often given important directions either by people who supervise them or by a colleague who may be an expert in a certain field. Suggest students watch TV shows about doctors, lawyers, or detectives and note when and by whom the main characters are given directions by other characters on the show. After several days of watching and note-taking, students can meet in groups to discuss what they saw. *Students should notice that even the main characters have supervisors who tell them what to do, or they ask for other characters' advice in carrying out certain tasks. They should also note the important words in the directions given on the show.*

Extended Reading Opportunities

People have always tried to imagine what life might be like in the future. Following are just a few possibilities through which you can explore visions of the future.

Suggested Titles

Farenheit 451
Ray Bradbury

This book is set in a time when firemen *start* fires—fires that burn books. Guy Montag is a fireman who enjoys his job and never thinks of questioning the system. Then he meets a teenage girl who tells him of a time when people were not afraid to think for themselves. Suddenly Montag realizes that he can no longer blindly accept the laws of his society.

The Time Machine
H. G. Wells

In this classic science-fiction tale, written more than one hundred years ago, H. G. Wells provides a grim view of the future. The story focuses on an inventor who travels into the future in a time machine he has built. On his travels, he views the progressive destruction of society and even life itself, eventually witnessing a time when giant crabs are the only surviving life form, and the sun and the Earth are dying.

Dragonsong
Anne McCaffrey

Set in the imaginary world of Pern, *Dragonsong* tells the story of Menolly, a young musician. When the laws of her society prevent Menolly from developing her musical talents, she wanders away from her home and discovers a group of rare and enchanting fire lizards. Menolly's relationship with the fire lizards and her unshakeable love for her music are the basis of this fantasy story.

Other Possibilities

Star Crossing: How to Get Around in the Universe	Judith Herbst
A Man on the Moon: The Voyages of the Apollo Astronauts	Andrew Chaikin
River Rats	Caroline Stevermer

Planning Students' Extended Reading

All of these works are good choices for extending the theme of "Visions of the Future." Following is some information that will help you choose which to teach:

Customize for
Varying Student Needs

When assigning the selections in this part to your students, keep in mind the following factors:

- *Fahrenheit 451* is the best-known work by popular science-fiction novelist Ray Bradbury. The book should be interesting and accessible to most students.

- *The Time Machine* is a science-fiction classic. However, it is probably the most challenging of the three suggested titles.

- *Dragonsong* is a fantasy novel with a female protagonist. It is written in a style that should be accessible to most students.

Resources for Teaching Novels, Plays, and Literature Collections

This booklet includes graphic organizers, teaching strategies, and transparencies that you can use in teaching any of these works.

Customize for
Special Needs

To meet the needs of your special needs students, you may want to consider using the version of *The Time Machine* in Globe Fearon's Pacemaker Classics series.

Planning Instruction and Assessment

Unit Objectives

1. To read selections in different genres that develop the theme of "Short Stories"
2. To apply a variety of reading strategies, particularly literal comprehension strategies, appropriate for reading these selections
3. To recognize literary elements used in these selections
4. To increase vocabulary
5. To learn elements of grammar and usage
6. To write in a variety of modes and about situations based on the selections
7. To develop speaking and listening skills, by doing proposed activities

Meeting the Objectives

With each selection, you will find instructional material and portfolio opportunities through which students can meet these objectives. Further, you will find additional practice pages for reading strategies, literary elements, vocabulary, and grammar in the **Selection Support** booklet in the Teaching Resources box.

Setting Goals Work with your students at the beginning of the unit to set goals for unit outcomes. Plan what skills and concepts you wish students to acquire. You may individualize according to students' performance levels or learning modalities.

Portfolios You may have students keep portfolios of their work or of their work in progress. The activities and prompts on the Build Your Portfolio page of each selection provide opportunities for students to apply the concepts presented with the selection.

Reading, 1973, Billy Morrow Jackson, Wichita Art Museum, Wichita, Kansas

Humanities: Art

Reading, 1973, by Billy Morrow Jackson.

Billy Morrow Jackson received his bachelor's degree in Fine Arts from Washington University and his master's from the University of Illinois, where he painted several murals and taught for many years before his retirement in 1987. Jackson paints chiefly in oils and watercolors.

Elicit from students that the young woman reading on the steps is probably sitting in a classroom building. The painting is full of secrets—what goes on behind the various doors, what is upstairs and downstairs, what the reader is reading.

Help students link this painting with the focus of Unit 6 ("Short Stories") by answering the following questions:

1. Imagine that the girl on the steps is a character in a story. Why is she sitting on the steps—is she waiting for someone? Does she like being there, or would she rather be outside? *Suggested response: This spot on the steps is one of her favorite places; it's very quiet and surprisingly private. She likes being indoors, especially since the weather outside is cold.*

2. What is the girl reading—a book for pleasure or something for her homework? *Suggested response: She is reading a novel for her pleasure. She had some time and had just started the book, which is by one of her favorite writers.*

UNIT **6**

Short Stories

A short story is a brief visit to an imaginary world. This world could be nineteenth-century Paris, the American Southwest, or the swamp country of South Carolina. Wherever you travel, you will meet fictional characters who deal with problems that are surprisingly real: for example, how to win someone's love or how to treat a younger brother. As you live through these problems with the characters, you may gain insights into your own life and into the world around you.

◆ 455

OBJECTIVES

1. To read, comprehend, and interpret a short story
2. To relate a story to personal experience
3. To use strategies for reading fiction to read for success
4. To analyze plot
5. To build vocabulary in context and learn the prefix *de-*
6. To develop skill in identifying sentence fragments
7. To write a thank-you letter using elaboration to make writing personal
8. To respond to the story through writing, speaking and listening, and projects

SKILLS INSTRUCTION

Vocabulary:
Prefixes: *de-*

Grammar:
Sentence Fragments

Reading for Success: Strategies for Reading Fiction

Literary Focus:
Plot

Writing:
Elaboration to Make Writing Personal

Speaking and Listening:
Monologue (teacher edition)

Critical Viewing:
Analyze; Connect

PORTFOLIO OPPORTUNITIES

Writing: Letter of Appreciation; Sequel; Surprise Ending

Writing Mini-Lesson: Thank-You Letter

Speaking and Listening: Play; Monologue

Projects: Comic Book; Multicultural Gifts

More About the Author

O. Henry wrote more than 200 pieces of fiction. His works are known for their surprise endings and their focus on the ironies of fate and coincidence. He had great sympathy for the weaknesses of human nature and wrote in the everyday language of ordinary people.

Guide for Reading

O. Henry (1862–1910)

William Sydney Porter, alias O. Henry, began his writing career under difficult circumstances: He was serving time in prison. Little in Porter's early life indicates that he was destined to become one of America's greatest short-story writers.

Wandering Toward Writing

Born in Greensboro, North Carolina, Porter dropped out of school at the age of sixteen to work at his uncle's drugstore. In 1882, he left to seek his fortune in Texas. He worked at a ranch, then at a general land office, and later at the First National Bank in Austin. By the time of his marriage in 1887, he had started writing sketches, some of which were published. Encouraged by this success, Porter started a humorous weekly in 1894. This venture failed, but Porter was firmly set on a writing career. He moved to Houston, where he worked for the *Houston Post* as a reporter, columnist, and cartoonist.

From Convict to Toast of the Town

In February 1896, Porter was indicted for embezzling bank funds. Although he had a chance of being pardoned, Porter chose to flee to Honduras. He returned to Texas when he learned his wife was dying. After her death, he was arrested, convicted, and sent to prison in Ohio. While serving his sentence, which was shortened to three years and three months for good behavior, Porter began writing short stories about life in the southwestern United States and Central America, drawing upon his experiences in Texas and Honduras. These stories were extremely popular with magazine readers. When he was released from prison, W. S. Porter became O. Henry.

O. Henry moved to New York City in 1902, and soon was writing stories at a rapid rate. For many of these stories, including "The Gift of the Magi," O. Henry drew upon his experiences and observations to depict the lives, loves, and losses of everyday people in New York City.

◆ Build Vocabulary

PREFIXES: *de-*

In "The Gift of the Magi," you will encounter the word *depreciate*, which means "to reduce in value." This word is derived from a Latin word meaning "price" and contains the prefix *de-*, which in this case means "down." When something depreciates, its price goes down.

The prefix *de-* has several other meanings. In addition to "down," it can also mean "away from," as in the word *deviate*, or "undo," as in *defrost*. As you read the story, look for other words that contain this versatile prefix.

WORD BANK

instigates
depreciate
cascade
chaste
meretricious
ravages
discreet

Before you read, preview this list of words from the story.

◆ Build Grammar Skills

SENTENCE FRAGMENTS

A **sentence fragment** is an incomplete sentence written as a sentence. Fragments lack a subject, a verb, or both, or don't express a complete thought. Avoid fragments in formal writing. However, in pieces of creative writing, sentence fragments can be used intentionally to add emphasis, to create the illusion of people talking to themselves, or to capture in dialogue how people actually speak. This story begins with the following fragment.

One dollar and eighty-seven cents.

The fragment lacks both a subject (in this case, *she*) and a verb (in this case, *had*). To make this a complete sentence, you would add the words *she* and *had* to form this sentence: She had one dollar and eighty-seven cents.

456 ◆ Short Stories

Prentice Hall Literature Program Resources

REINFORCE / RETEACH / EXTEND

Selection Support Pages
Build Vocabulary: Prefixes: *de-*, p. 138
Build Grammar Skills: Sentence Fragments, p. 139
Reading for Success: Strategies for Reading Fiction, pp. 140–141
Literary Focus: Plot, p. 142

Strategies for Diverse Student Needs, p. 34

Beyond Literature
Cross-Curricular Connection: Math, p. 34

Formal Assessment Selection Test, pp. 120–122,

Assessment Resources Software

Alternative Assessment, p. 34

Writing and Language Transparencies
Reflective Essay, pp. 5–8

Resource Pro CD-ROM
"The Gift of the Magi"—includes all resource materials and customizable lesson plan

Listening to Literature Audiocassettes
"The Gift of the Magi"

The Gift of the Magi

◆ Literature and Your Life

CONNECT YOUR EXPERIENCE

Quivering with excitement, you tear off the wrapping paper on your birthday gift. You open the box—and your spirits sink. Your gift is a lopsided sweater, made by an inexperienced knitter in your least favorite color. Hiding your disappointment, you thank the giver enthusiastically. After all, it's the thought that counts.

Gifts are sometimes less appropriate or more meaningful than they first appear. In this story, a husband and wife discover the unexpected problems and joys of giving gifts.

THEMATIC FOCUS: WORKING TOWARD A GOAL

As this story shows, a person may strive toward a goal with the best of intentions, only to find that his or her effort was misdirected. How can people redirect their efforts in such a situation?

Journal Writing In your journal, describe an incident—real or imagined—in which someone tried to do something nice but had his or her plans go awry. Explain what, if anything, the person did to fix problems resulting from his or her actions.

◆ Background for Understanding

ECONOMICS

When you read a story that was written more than ten years ago, you will find that prices or amounts of money seem ridiculously low. This is because the United States has experienced inflation over the years. Inflation is a continual increase in most or all major prices throughout an economy. Although the causes of inflation are hotly debated, the effects are clear: The purchasing power of a unit of currency goes down. In the story, which was written at the beginning of the twentieth century, $32 is a month's rent for Della and Jim. Today, $32 would not even pay for a night in an inexpensive motel.

◆ Literary Focus

PLOT

The events in a story make up its **plot,** which is traditionally divided into five parts: *exposition, rising action, climax, falling action,* and *resolution.* The exposition provides background information and sets the scene for the conflict—a struggle between opposing people or forces that drives the action of the story. The introduction of the conflict marks the beginning of the rising action, in which the conflict intensifies until it reaches the high point, or climax, of the story. After the climax, the action falls to a resolution. The resolution shows how the situation turns out and ties up loose ends.

As you read the story, jot down events associated with the different parts of the plot on a diagram like this one.

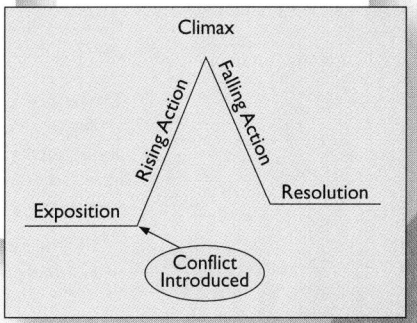

Climax
Rising Action
Falling Action
Exposition
Resolution
Conflict Introduced

To have some fun and to lead students into the story, encourage them to bring in examples of the most unusual or worst gifts they've ever received. Have them show the gifts to their classmates and describe how they reacted when they received them. Then lead into a discussion about gifts that at first disappointed them but later took on a special meaning. Finally, have students share experiences in which they've gotten a gift they've always wanted, only to discover for one reason or another that the gift wasn't quite what they expected. Tell students that the story they're about to read focuses on some surprising twists relating to a young couple's efforts to find special gifts for each other.

Customize for
Less Proficient Readers

To help these students apply the strategies for reading fiction, you may want to work closely with them, reading passages of the story aloud and discussing each of the prompts.

Customize for
More Advanced Students

"The Gift of the Magi" has a traditionally structured plot. These students may enjoy comparing and contrasting the plot of this story with that of other stories they have read. Suggest they meet in a group to fit plot events from other stories into a diagram similar to the one on page 457.

Customize for
English Language Learners

Make sure these students understand the reference to the Magi in the title of the story. Some students may not be familiar with the biblical story of the three kings, or wise men, who brought gifts to the infant Jesus. Latino students can share their custom of celebrating The Day of the Kings, on the sixth of January.

Customize for
Interpersonal Learners

These students may enjoy reading the story aloud to one another in a small group, pausing occasionally to share their responses as the conflicts of the plot intensify and are finally resolved.

Preparing for Standardized Tests

Reading The Strategies for Reading Fiction will help students deal with reading comprehension passages on standardized tests. Questions on these tests often ask students to make inferences or draw conclusions from the material they read. Help students practice these strategies by using the boxed prompts with "The Gift of the Magi." For additional practice, use the Reading for Success pages in *Selection Support,* pp. 140–141.

Grammar Standardized tests require students to recognize sentence errors such as fragments,

as in questions such as the following in the PSAT Improving Sentences format: That <u>being the tape I bought</u> at the flea market. *(C)*

    (A) being the tape I bought

    (B) being the tape that I bought

    (C) is the tape I bought

The Build Grammar Skills lesson for this selection focuses on this topic. For additional practice, use the Build Grammar Skills page on Sentence Fragments, p. 139, in *Selection Support.*

Strategies for Reading Fiction
The Reading for Success page in each unit presents a set of problem-solving procedures to help readers understand authors' words and ideas on multiple levels. Good readers develop a bank of strategies from which they can draw as needed.

Unit 6 introduces strategies for reading fiction. Students who learn to enjoy reading fiction are building a habit that will bring a lifelong source of entertainment and understanding. Based on research into techniques good readers use when reading fiction, the strategies outlined on this page will help students become more involved in their reading of stories and novels, and will increase their enjoyment, understanding, and appreciation of fiction.

The strategies are modeled on "The Gift of the Magi." Each green box shows an example of the thinking process involved in applying one of these strategies.

How to Use the Reading for Success Page

• Introduce the strategies for reading fiction, presenting each as a problem-solving procedure. Be sure students understand what each strategy involves and under what circumstances to apply it.

• Before students read the story, have them preview it, looking at the annotations in the green boxes that model the strategies.

• To reinforce these strategies after students have read "The Gift of the Magi," have students do the Reading for Success pages in *Selection Support*, pp. 140–141. These pages give students an opportunity to read a selection and practice these strategies by writing their own annotations.

Reading for Success

Strategies for Reading Fiction

Fiction, which includes novels and short stories, is literature of the imagination. The characters and events are made up by the author. Fiction can be strongly based on real people and events or may be wildly inventive. The following strategies will help you get more out of the fiction you read.

Predict.
As the events of the story unfold, try to figure out what will happen next. Look for hints in the story that suggest things to come. As you read on, you will see if your predictions are correct.

Identify with the characters and the situation.
Although characters in fiction aren't real people, they do have thoughts and feelings like we do. Try to identify with characters by putting yourself in their situation and thinking about how you'd respond.

Picture the action in your mind.
When you use your imagination and the details the author provides, a story will reel out in your mind like a movie. With practice, you will find that reading a story can be better than watching a movie—the casting is always exactly to your taste, and there are no limits on the costumes, scenery, or special effects.

Question.
Stories are more interesting when you ask questions about characters and events. Why does a character act in a certain way? What does something really mean? As you read, look for the answers to your questions.

Make inferences.
Writers do not tell you everything directly. To truly appreciate the characters and the situation, you need to "read between the lines" and look beyond what the words state to what they imply. For example, you can make inferences about a character's personality based on his or her actions.

Draw conclusions.
Try to piece together the details and the inferences you make to draw conclusions about a story's theme—the author's central message about life or human nature. You may also draw conclusions about what you think of the author or whether you like a particular type of story.

As you read the following short story, notice the notes along the side. The notes demonstrate how to apply these strategies to your reading.

Reading Strategies: Support and Reinforcement
Appropriate Reading Strategies Students are given a reading strategy to apply in reading each selection. For example, students will be prompted to picture the action in their minds as they read an action-filled story. In other selections a strategy is suggested that is appropriate to the selection.
Reading Prompts To encourage application of the given reading strategy, there are occasional prompts, within green boxes, at appropriate and significant points. In addition, there are red boxes prompting application of the Literary Focus concept and maroon boxes prompting students to connect with their lives.

Using the Boxed Annotations and Prompts
The material in the green, red, and maroon boxes along the sides of selections is intended to help students apply the literary element and the reading strategy and to make a connection with their lives.

You may use the boxed material in either of these ways:

• Have students pause when they come to a box and respond to its prompt before they continue reading.

• Urge students to read through the selection ignoring the boxes. After they have read the selection completely, they may go back and review the selection, responding to the prompts.

The Gift of the Magi

MODEL

O. Henry

One dollar and eighty-seven cents. That was all. And sixty cents of it was in pennies. Pennies saved one and two at a time by bulldozing the grocer and the vegetable man and the butcher until one's cheeks burned with the silent imputation of parsimony[1] that such close dealing implied. Three times Della counted it. One dollar and eighty-seven cents. And the next day would be Christmas.

> To **identify** with Della's problem, recall a time you worked very hard to accomplish something but fell short of your goal.

There was clearly nothing to do but flop down on the shabby little couch and howl. So Della did it. Which <u>instigates</u> the moral reflection that life is made up of sobs, sniffles, and smiles, with sniffles predominating.

While the mistress of the home is gradually subsiding from the first stage to the second, take a look at the home. A furnished flat[2] at $8 per week. It

> The narrative voice in the story is mocking, condescending, and opinionated. **Question** why the author chose to tell the story in this way.

◆ Build Vocabulary

instigates (in´ stə gāts´) v.: Urges on; stirs up

---

1. **silent imputation** (im pyoo tā´ shən) **of parsimony** (pär´ sə mō´ nē): Silent accusation of stinginess.
2. **flat** (flat) n.: Apartment.

The Gift of the Magi   459

This classic story of self-sacrificing love—and its ironic consequences—has been a favorite for generations. The narrative follows the actions of a young woman named Della, who wants to buy her husband a special Christmas gift but has virtually no money. She solves her problem by selling her hair, so that she can buy a chain for her husband's pocket watch. Ironically, her husband has sold his pocket watch in order to buy her a special present— a set of combs! The story's ironic ending is likely to spur spirited discussion and debate among your students about the wisdom—or foolishness—of the young couple, each of whom sacrifices a most-prized possession for the other.

◆ Literature and Your Life

Tell students that a gold pocket watch like this plays an important part in this story. Ask students to relate the importance of a family heirloom like this one to their own feelings about a favorite possession. *Students may mention their own family heirlooms, as well as souvenirs from special vacations or events, special gifts from relatives and friends, or things they have made themselves.*

Customize for
English Language Learners

These students may be confused by the metaphorical use of the word *bulldozing*. Describe how a bulldozer works and ask in what way a customer looking for a bargain might feel like a bulldozer.

◆ Literary Focus

❶ Plot Ask students what important background information they learn about Della and Jim in the first few paragraphs of the story. *They don't have much money; they have to scrimp to pay their bills and save for little extras.*

◆ Block Scheduling Strategies

Consider these suggestions to take advantage of extended class time:

- Have students conduct research on the Internet to learn more about O. Henry and his works.
- Use the activities in **Daily Language Practice** for Week 11. Write the sentences on the chalkboard and have students correct the errors.
- Students may work together in small groups to analyze the plot of "The Gift of the Magi" and answer the Literary Focus questions on page 465.

- Give students time to work on their scripts, rehearse their roles, or plan sets and costumes as they prepare the Speaking and Listening activity in the Idea Bank (p. 466).
- Have students complete the Writing Mini-Lesson (p. 466). Before they get started, have them work in pairs to discuss a special gift and why they liked it. As one partner talks, the other should ask questions to help the speaker think of ways to make the letter more personal.

◆ Build Vocabulary

❶ Prefixes: de- Have students find the word in this passage with the prefix *de-*. *description* Tell them that the root in this word, *-scribe-*, means "write." Have students explain how the meaning of the prefix contributes to the meaning of the word. *The meaning of* description *is "the act of writing down."*

◆ Literary Focus

❷ Plot Ask students to explain the conflict that is being set up in this part of the exposition. *Della wants to buy a special Christmas gift for Jim, but she has only $1.87, and it's already Christmas Eve, so she has to decide what to do.*

◆ Build Grammar Skills

❸ Sentence Fragments Have students identify the three sentence fragments in this passage and correct them. Point out that fragments can be long or short, but they do not express a complete thought on their own. *Fragments: "Only $1.87 to buy a present for Jim."—"Her Jim."—"Something fine and rare and sterling—something just a little bit near to being worthy of the honor of being owned by Jim." Possible corrections: "She had only $1.87 to buy a present for Jim, her Jim." "She wanted to buy something fine and rare and sterling—something just a little bit near to being worthy of the honor of being owned by Jim."*

Discuss with students the effect the writer may have wished to create by using fragments. *Students may suggest that the fragments reflect the way the character's thoughts are trying to piece together a solution to a seemingly unsolvable problem.*

---

❶ did not exactly beggar description,[3] but it certainly had that word on the lookout for the mendicancy squad.[4]

In the vestibule below was a letter-box into which no letter would go, and an electric button from which no mortal finger could coax a ring. Also appertaining thereunto was a card bearing the name "Mr. James Dillingham Young."

The "Dillingham" had been flung to the breeze during a former period of prosperity when its possessor was being paid $30 per week. Now, when the income was shrunk to $20, the letters of "Dillingham" looked blurred, as though they were thinking seriously of contracting to a modest and unassuming D. But whenever Mr. James Dillingham Young came home and reached his flat above he was called "Jim" and greatly hugged by Mrs. James Dillingham Young, already introduced to you as Della. Which is all very good.

> From the description of Jim's name, you can **infer** that Jim's loss of income has taken its toll on his self-confidence.

Della finished her cry and attended to her cheeks with the powder rag. She stood by the window and looked out dully at a gray cat walking a gray fence in a gray backyard. Tomorrow would be Christmas Day, and she had only $1.87 with which to buy Jim a present. She had been saving every penny she could for months, **❷** with this result. Twenty dollars a week doesn't **❸** go far. Expenses had been greater than she had calculated. They always are. Only $1.87 to buy a present for Jim. Her Jim. Many a happy hour she had spent planning for something nice for him. Something fine and rare and sterling—

---

3. **beggar description:** Resist description.
4. **mendicancy** (men′ di kən′ sē) **squad:** Police who arrested beggars.

◆ Build Vocabulary

depreciate (di prē′ shē āt) *v.*: Reduce in value

cascade (kas kād′) *n.*: Waterfall

---

something just a little bit near to being worthy of the honor of being owned by Jim.

There was a pier glass[5] between the windows of the room. Perhaps you have seen a pier glass in an $8 flat. A very thin and very agile person may, by observing his reflection in a rapid sequence of longitudinal strips, obtain a fairly accurate conception of his looks. Della, being slender, had mastered the art.

Suddenly she whirled from the window and stood before the glass. Her eyes were shining brilliantly, but her face had lost its color within twenty seconds. Rapidly she pulled down her hair and let it fall to its full length.

Now, there were two possessions of the James Dillingham Youngs in which they both took a mighty pride. One was Jim's gold watch that had been his father's and his grandfather's. The other was Della's hair. Had the Queen of Sheba[6] lived in the flat across the airshaft, Della would have let her hair hang out the window some day to dry just to depreciate Her Majesty's jewels and gifts. Had King Solomon been the janitor, with all his treasures piled up in the basement, Jim would have pulled out his watch every time he passed, just to see him pluck at his beard from envy.

So now Della's beautiful hair fell about her rippling and shining like a cascade of brown waters. It reached below her knee and made itself almost a garment for her. And then she did it up again nervously and quickly. Once she faltered for a minute and stood still while a tear or two splashed on the worn red carpet.

On went her old brown jacket; on went her

> **By reading between the lines,** you can tell that Della loves and honors her husband. The qualities that Della wants in a gift for Jim reflect her regard for him.

> **Ask yourself** why Della is acting in this way. What is she thinking?

---

5. **pier** (pir) **glass:** Tall mirror.
6. **Queen of Sheba:** In the Bible, the beautiful queen who visited King Solomon to test his wisdom.

 Workplace Skills Mini-Lesson

Looking for a Job

Introduce the Concept Tell students that if Della were living today, she could earn extra money by getting a temporary or part-time job.

Develop Background Have students discuss ways in which teenagers today can find temporary or part-time work. Suggest that often the best way to find a job is by spreading the word that you're looking for work by talking to people, handing out fliers, or posting a notice on a bulletin board.

Apply the Information Have students think of skills they might be able to use in a job after school or in the summer. Have them make fliers that might be distributed in the neighborhood or posted on a bulletin board. Encourage them to be creative in designing and writing their fliers.

Assess the Outcome Have students meet in groups to discuss prospective employers' possible reactions to the fliers. (Students should consider the appeal of the design and the clarity of the information presented in evaluating the fliers.)

Customize for
Visual/Spatial Learners

The artwork on this page can serve as an invaluable aid to help these students envision the story's setting. Have them point out details in the painting that help capture the time and place of O. Henry's story.

Customize for
Visual/Spatial Learners

Have these students describe the mood of the picture. Ask students to evaluate whether this mood fits the scene in the story in which Della goes to Madame Sofronie's shop to sell her hair. *Students may say that the scene looks too pleasant for such a sad event as the cutting of Della's beautiful hair.*

◆ **Literary Focus**

❹ **Plot** Tell students that Della's decision to cut her hair begins the rising action of the plot. Ask how they can tell she is feeling conflict about her decision. *Tears splash on the carpet as she prepares to leave for the haircutter's shop.*

▶**Critical Viewing**◀

❺ **Analyze** Students may say that she might have felt afraid, nervous, confused, self-conscious, or embarrassed.

 old brown hat. With a whirl of skirts and with the brilliant sparkle still in her eyes, she fluttered out the door and down the stairs to the street.

Where she stopped the sign read: "Mme. Sofronie. Hair Goods of All Kinds." One flight up

▲ **Critical Viewing** How do you think Della felt as she approached Madame Sofronie's shop? **[Analyze]** ❺

Della ran, and collected herself, panting. Madame, large, too white, chilly, hardly looked the "Sofronie." ❹

🎼 **Humanities: Art**

Hairdresser's Window, 1907, by John Sloan.

This piece of art illustrates a turn-of-the-century street scene outside a hairdresser's window, much like the one Della might have encountered on her way to sell her hair.

John Sloan began his career doing illustrations for a Philadelphia newspaper. He was a leading member of the so-called Ashcan School of painters who captured the gritty details of everyday life in large American cities.

Use these questions for discussion:

1. Judging from their facial expression and focus on the window, what might the people in the crowd be saying and thinking? *They may be wondering what the hairdresser is going to do and how it will turn out; they may be calling out to the girl or teasing her; the women may be wondering if they should have their hair done.*

2. What reasons might the hairdresser have for working in front of the window? *It may be a way of advertising for her services or of getting fresh air.*

461

"Will you buy my hair?" asked Della.

"I buy hair," said Madame. "Take yer hat off and let's have a sight at the looks of it."

Down rippled the brown cascade.

"Twenty dollars," said Madame, lifting the mass with a practiced hand.

"Give it to me quick," said Della.

Oh, and the next two hours tripped by on rosy wings. Forget the hashed metaphor. She was ransacking the stores for Jim's present.

She found it at last. It surely had been made for Jim and no one else. There was no other like it in any of the stores, and she had turned all of them inside out. It was a platinum fob chain[7] simple and chaste in design, properly proclaiming its value by substance alone and not by meretricious ornamentation—as all good things should do. It was even worthy of The Watch. As soon as she saw it she knew that it must be Jim's. It was like him. Quietness and value—the description applied to both. Twenty-one dollars they took from her for it, and she hurried home with the 87 cents. With that chain on his watch Jim might be properly anxious

❶ | Put yourself in Della's place by remembering a time when you did something considerate for someone you cared about.

From the way Della thinks about her husband in this passage and earlier in the story, you can **conclude** that she is loving, proud, and anxious to please him.

Carved Tortoiseshell Comb, mid 19th century, England or France, Cooper-Hewitt National Design Museum

---

7. **fob** (fäb) **chain:** Small chain connecting a watch to its pocket.
8. **Coney Island:** Beach and amusement park in Brooklyn, New York

---

about the time in any company. Grand as the watch was he sometimes looked at it on the sly on account of the old leather strap that he used in place of a chain. **❷**

When Della reached home her intoxication gave way a little to prudence and reason. She got out her curling irons and lighted the gas and went to work repairing the ravages made by generosity added to love. Which is always a tremendous task, dear friends—a mammoth task.

Within forty minutes her head was covered with tiny, close-lying curls that made her look wonderfully like a truant schoolboy. She looked at her reflection in the mirror long, carefully, and critically.

"If Jim doesn't kill me," she said to herself, "before he takes a second look at me, he'll say I look like a Coney Island[8] chorus girl. But what could I do—oh! what could I do with a dollar and eighty-seven cents?" **❸**

At 7 o'clock the coffee was made and the frying-pan was on the back of the stove hot and ready to cook the chops.

Jim was never late. Della doubled the fob chain in her hand and sat on the corner

---

▲ **Critical Viewing** How do you think Della might have felt about an elaborate, expensive comb like this one? [Connect] **❹**

◆ Build Vocabulary

chaste (chāst) *adj.*: Pure or clean in style; not ornate

meretricious (mer′ ə trish′ əs) *adj.*: Attractive in a cheap, flashy way

ravages (rav′ ij iz) *n.*: Ruins; devastating damages

✎ Cross-Curricular Connection: Social Studies

New York City, the probable setting for this story, has long been a place where people representing the extremes of wealth and poverty have lived in close proximity. O. Henry was part of a group of American writers, including Stephen Crane and Theodore Dreiser, who observed and described these urban extremes. There were few economic opportunities for poor young women of the time, whose job opportunities were limited to the drudgery of housework, sewing in sweatshops, or other low-paying jobs such as shop assistants.

Have students investigate the working conditions in early twentieth century urban areas like New York. Then discuss how a life of poverty might be easier or more difficult in a busy urban setting where people from all social levels live close together.

of the table near the door that he always entered. Then she heard his step on the stair away down on the first flight, and she turned white for just a moment. She had a habit of saying little silent prayers about the simplest everyday things, and now she whispered: "Please God, make him think I am still pretty."

The door opened and Jim stepped in and closed it. He looked thin and very serious. Poor fellow, he was only twenty-two—and to be burdened with a family! He needed a new overcoat and he was without gloves.

Jim stopped inside the door, as immovable as a setter at the scent of quail. His eyes were fixed upon Della, and there was an expression in them that she could not read, and it terrified her. It was not anger, nor surprise, nor disapproval, nor horror, nor any of the sentiments that she had been prepared for. He simply stared at her fixedly with that peculiar expression on his face.

Della wriggled off the table and went for him.

"Jim, darling," she cried, "don't look at me that way. I had my hair cut off and sold it because I couldn't have lived through Christmas without giving you a present. It'll grow out again—you won't mind, will you? I just had to do it. My hair grows awfully fast. Say 'Merry Christmas!' Jim, and let's be happy. You don't know what a nice—what a beautiful, nice gift I've got for you."

"You've cut off your hair?" asked Jim, laboriously, as if he had not arrived at that patent fact yet even after the hardest mental labor.

"Cut it off and sold it," said Della. "Don't you like me just as well, anyhow? I'm me without my hair, ain't I?"

Jim looked about the room curiously.

> **You can infer that** Della is impractical—Jim obviously needs a warm coat and gloves. **You may also conclude** from these details and others earlier in the story that Della and Jim are struggling financially.

> **Ask yourself questions** about what Jim thinks about Della's new hairstyle, then **predict** how he is going to behave.

❺

❻

"You say your hair is gone?" he said, with an air almost of idiocy.

"You needn't look for it," said Della. "It's sold, I tell you—sold and gone, too. It's Christmas Eve, boy. Be good to me, for it went for you. Maybe the hairs of my head were numbered," she went on with a sudden serious sweetness, "but nobody could ever count my love for you. Shall I put the chops on, Jim?"

Out of his trance Jim seemed quickly to wake. He enfolded his Della. For ten seconds let us regard with <u>discreet</u> scrutiny some inconsequential object in the other direction. Eight dollars a week or a million a year—what is the difference? A mathematician or a wit would give you the wrong answer. The Magi brought valuable gifts, but that was not among them. This dark assertion will be illuminated later on.

Jim drew a package from his overcoat pocket and threw it upon the table.

"Don't make any mistake, Dell," he said, "about me. I don't think there's anything in the way of a haircut or a shave or a shampoo that could make me like my girl any less. But if you'll unwrap that package you may see why you had me going a while at first."

White fingers and nimble tore at the string and paper. And then an ecstatic scream of joy; and then, alas! a quick feminine change to hysterical tears and wails, necessitating the immediate employment of all the comforting powers of the lord of the flat.

For there lay The Combs—the set of combs, side and back, that Della had worshipped for

---

> **Picture** the conversation between Della and Jim as a scene from a movie. Imagine how Jim's stunned surprise makes him move and speak. Envision Della trying to hide her anxiety by speaking too fast and too cheerfully.

> In response to Jim's mysterious statement, you might ask the question: What is in the package?

❼

❽

❾

◆ Build Vocabulary

discreet (dis krēt´) *adj.*: Tactful; respectful

◆ **Literary Focus**

❺ **Plot** Tell students that the tension of the plot continues to rise at this point in the story, as Della waits for Jim to come home. Ask how O. Henry draws out the suspense of the rising action in this passage. *He describes Della's reaction to hearing Jim's footsteps on the stairs and has her whisper a little prayer that Jim will not be angry at her or love her less for cutting her hair.*

◆ **Literary Focus**

❻ **Plot** Tell students that the climax, or high point of tension in the story, begins here. Ask what question Della and the reader are waiting to find the answer to. *How will Jim react to the fact that Della has cut her hair?*

◆ **Reading for Success**

❼ **Draw Conclusions** Tell students that in this passage O. Henry begins to hint at the resolution and the message of the story. Have students predict what the story's message will be. *The value of a gift does not depend on how much money one has to spend on it, but upon the amount of love that went into the giving.*

◆ **Literary Focus**

❽ **Plot** Tell students that the climax, or high point of tension, ends here, as we wait to see what is in the package. Ask students if they might predict what is in the package. *Students should note from Jim's behavior that the gift is something that is—at least for now—inconsequential.*

Comprehension Check ☑

❾ Why does Della start crying when she opens her gift from Jim? *Her gift is a set of beautiful combs for her hair, but she can't use them because she has cut and sold her hair to buy Jim's gift.*

 Speaking and Listening Mini-Lesson

Monologue

This mini-lesson supports the Speaking and Listening activity in the Idea Bank on page 466.

Introduce the Concept Tell students that some of the Strategies for Reading Fiction are crucial for preparing a monologue, a first-person retelling of a story from one character's point of view.

Develop Background Before students begin writing the monologue, have them explore techniques needed to retell a story from one character's point of view. Lead students to consider these points:

• The writer must identify with one character and his or her situation.

• The writer must make inferences about what a character is really thinking.

• The writer should try to picture the character's life in his or her mind.

Apply the Information Have students reread the story, imagining that they are either Della or Jim. As they read, have them pause during important parts of the story and freewrite what might be going through the character's mind. Have students use their freewriting notes to write their monologues. Have students present their monologues in small groups.

Assess the Outcome Use the Peer Assessment: Dramatic Performance page in *Alternative Assessment*, p. 113, for students to evaluate the monologues.

❶ Predict Ask students if they can predict what Jim will say next. *Some students may already have guessed that Jim has sold his watch to get money to buy Della's combs.*

◆ **Literary Focus**

❷ Plot Tell students that this part of the story marks the falling action, or resolution, as all of our questions have been answered. Ask students if they found the resolution satisfying, or if they wish the story had been told differently. *Some students may wish there was more explanation of what becomes of the characters. Others may appreciate the economy of the author in concluding the story so effectively.*

◆ **Critical Thinking**

❸ Evaluate Characters Ask students in what way Jim and Della are foolish and in what way they are wise. *They are foolish to buy expensive gifts they can't afford and, in the end, can't even use. They are wise because they give gifts from the heart, based on their understanding of what the other person yearns for, and they sacrifice some of their own desires in hopes of making someone else happy.*

Reinforce and Extend

Answers

◆ *Literature and Your Life*

Reader's Response Most students would say that they would have appreciated the gifts.

Thematic Focus Students should explain the importance to them of the thought or the cost of the gift.

☑ **Check Your Comprehension**

1. The story takes place on Christmas Eve in a city (probably New York City) around the turn of the century.
2. Jim and Della prize Jim's watch and Della's long hair.
3. Della sells her hair.
4. Jim sells his watch to buy the combs for Della's hair.
5. Jim had bought her the expensive combs she had yearned for to wear in her hair.
6. The watch fob is currently as useless to him as the combs are to Della.

464

---

long in a Broadway window. Beautiful combs, pure tortoise shell, with jeweled rims—just the shade to wear in the beautiful vanished hair. They were expensive combs, she knew, and her heart had simply craved and yearned over them without the least hope of possession. And now, they were hers, but the tresses that should have adorned the coveted adornments were gone.

> From Della's reaction, you can **infer** that she is devastated that she cannot use the combs but is grateful for Jim's thoughtfulness.

But she hugged them to her bosom, and at length she was able to look up with dim eyes and a smile and say: "My hair grows so fast, Jim!"

And then Della leaped up like a little singed cat and cried, "Oh, oh!"

Jim had not yet seen his beautiful present. She held it out to him eagerly upon her open palm. The dull precious metal seemed to flash with a reflection of her bright and ardent spirit.

"Isn't it a dandy, Jim? I hunted all over town to find it. You'll have to look at the time a hundred times a day now. Give me your watch. I want to see how it looks on it."

❶ Instead of obeying, Jim tumbled down on the couch and put his hands under the back of his head and smiled.

"Dell," said he, "let's put our Christmas presents away and keep 'em a while. They're too nice to use just at present. I sold the watch to get the money to buy your combs. And now suppose you put the chops on."

The Magi, as you know, were wise men—wonderfully wise men—who brought gifts to the Babe in the manger. They invented the art of giving Christmas presents. Being wise, their gifts were no doubt wise ones, possibly bearing the privilege of exchange in case of duplication. And here I have lamely related to you the uneventful chronicle of two foolish children in a flat who most unwisely sacrificed for each other the greatest treasures of their house. But in a last word to the wise of these days let it be said that of all who give gifts these two were the wisest. Of all who give and receive gifts, such as they are wisest. Everywhere they are wisest. They are the magi.

> To **identify** with the situation, in which both "perfect" presents turn out to be useless, recall how you felt in a situation in which what you expected and what actually happened were very different.

❶

❷

❸

Guide for Responding

◆ *Literature and Your Life*

Reader's Response If you were Jim or Della, how would you feel about the gift you received?

Thematic Focus Is giving a special gift a worthy goal? Explain your answer.

Journal Writing In the story, Della and Jim sell their most prized possessions to buy the "perfect" gift for each other. Think of a person to whom you would like to give a special gift. In your journal, describe the gift you would like to give and explain why the gift would be perfect for the recipient.

☑ **Check Your Comprehension**

1. What is the setting of the story?
2. At the beginning of the story, what possessions do Jim and Della prize the most?
3. What does Della do to get money for Jim's present?
4. What does Jim do to get money for Della's present?
5. Why is Jim particularly sorry that Della cut her hair?
6. Why does Jim react as he does when he sees Della's gift to him?

Beyond the Selection

FURTHER READING

Other Works by O. Henry
"The Ransom of Red Chief"
"After Twenty Years"
"The Last Leaf"

Other Works With the Theme of Working It Out
"Christmas Day in the Morning," Pearl S. Buck
"Thank You, M'am," Langston Hughes
"Then He Goes Free," Jessamyn West

INTERNET

You and your students may find additional information about O. Henry on the Internet. We suggest the following site. Please be aware, however, that the site may have changed from the time we published this information.

Students interested in reading more stories by O. Henry can visit the on-line short stories available at **http://www. bookwire.com/boldtype/ohenry/read.article$2307**

We *strongly recommend* that you preview the site before you send students there.

Guide for Responding (continued)

◆ Critical Thinking

INTERPRET
1. How do Della and Jim feel toward each other? Give evidence from the story to support your answer. **[Support]**
2. Why does the author describe Della and Jim as "two foolish children in a flat who most unwisely sacrificed for each other the greatest treasures of their house"? **[Infer]**
3. What does the author mean by "Of all who give and receive gifts, such as they are wisest. . . .They are the magi." **[Interpret]**
4. In your own words, state the central message of "The Gift of the Magi." **[Draw Conclusions]**

EVALUATE
5. Did Della and Jim do the right thing? Explain. **[Make a Judgment]**

APPLY
6. In your opinion, is it possible to be foolish and wise at the same time? Why or why not? **[Generalize]**
7. If you were either Jim or Della, how would you feel about the gift you received? **[Apply]**

◆ Build Vocabulary

USING THE PREFIX: *de-*
The prefix *de-* means "down," "away from," or "undo." Define each of the following words, incorporating the definition of *de-* into each answer.

1. demerit
2. delegate
3. deform

USING THE WORD BANK
In your notebook, write the word from the Word Bank that most closely matches the meaning of the words below.

1. waterfall   4. gaudy   6. cheapen
2. pure   5. damage   7. provoke
3. tactful

◆ Reading for Success

STRATEGIES FOR READING FICTION
Apply the reading strategies and notes showing how to read fiction to answer these questions.
1. What can you conclude about Jim and Della from the descriptions in the second through fifth paragraphs of the story?
2. What can you infer about Della's mood from the following sentence: "She stood by the window and looked out dully at a gray cat walking a gray fence in a gray backyard"?
3. How might the information in the paragraph on p. 460 starting "Now there were two possessions . . ." have helped you predict the ending?

◆ Literary Focus

PLOT
The **plot** of a story is a series of related events. It usually begins with an *exposition*. Then the *conflict* is introduced. The action intensifies during the *rising action*. The *climax*, or high point of the story, is followed by the *falling action*, which leads to the *resolution* and the tying up of loose ends.
1. What happens during the story's exposition?
2. What is the conflict in the story?
3. At what point is the climax reached?
4. How is the conflict resolved?

◆ Build Grammar Skills

SENTENCE FRAGMENTS
A **sentence fragment** lacks a subject, a verb, or both, or doesn't express a complete thought. Sentence fragments are not acceptable in formal writing except when used for special effect.

Practice In your notebook, list five sentence fragments from the story.

Writing Application Rewrite the following paragraph, correcting the sentence fragments.

Birthday party tomorrow. Have to get a gift. Fast. But what? A T-shirt? Which is always what people get when they don't know what to buy. Boring. Stuffed animal? Nah. Too dumb. CD? Might work!

◆ Build Grammar Skills
Students should explain why each of their excerpts is a fragment.

Writing Application
Suggested response:
There's a birthday party tomorrow. I have to get a gift, and I need to get it fast. But what should I get? Should I buy a T-shirt? That's what people always get when they don't know what to buy. A T-shirt would be *boring*. Shall I buy a stuffed animal? No, that would be too cutesy. I think a CD might work.

✒ Writer's Solution
For additional instruction and practice, use the lesson in the **Language Lab CD-ROM** on Sentence Style, and on the pages on Fragments in the *Writer's Solution Grammar Practice Book*, pp. 62–63.

Answers

◆ Critical Thinking
1. They love each other. Each sacrifices a prized possession to buy a gift for the other.
2. Della and Jim are foolish because they give up prized possessions to buy each other gifts they no longer need.
3. The Magi were wise men who gave gifts to the infant Jesus. Della and Jim give each other the precious gift of love.
4. Giving in a spirit of love is more valuable than any material gift.
5. Jim and Della did the right thing because they had the right intentions.
6. As Jim and Della demonstrate, it is possible to do a foolish thing for wise reasons.
7. Either character would be touched by the other's generosity.

◆ Reading for Success
Strategies for Reading Fiction
1. They are poor, proud, and in love.
2. The bleak scenery reflects Della's sad, depressed mood.
3. Students may have inferred that these possessions play a part in upcoming events.

◆ Literary Focus
1. The author introduces Della, describes the apartment, and provides background information about the watch and the hair.
2. There are a number of conflicts in the story, including Della's lack of money to buy a suitable present for Jim, and Della's mixed feelings about selling her hair.
3. The climax occurs when Della discovers the coveted combs.
4. The conflict is resolved when Della's present to Jim turns out to be as useless as his present to her.

◆ Build Vocabulary
Prefixes: de-
1. A demerit is a fault that *down*grades something.
2. A delegate is sent *away from* home to be a representative.
3. When something is deformed, its original or proper shape is *undone*.

Using the Word Bank
1. cascade; 2. chaste; 3. discreet; 4. meretricious; 5. ravages; 6. depreciate; 7. instigate

465

Idea Bank

Customizing for
Performance Levels

Following are suggestions for matching the Idea Bank topics with your students' performance levels:

Less Advanced Students: 1, 4, 6
Average Students: 2, 4, 7
More Advanced Students: 3, 5, 7

Customizing for
Learning Modalities

Following are suggestions for matching Idea Bank topics with your students' learning modalities:

Verbal/Linguistic: 1, 2, 3
Bodily/Kinesthetic: 4, 5
Auditory: 4, 5
Visual/Spatial: 6, 7

Writing Mini-Lesson

Refer students to the Writing Handbook, page 962, for instruction on the writing process, and page 966 for further information on practical and technical writing.

Writer's Solution

Writing Lab CD-ROM

Have students use the Tutorial on Practical and Technical Writing to compose their thank-you letters. The tutorial will illustrate to students the correct format for a letter. Follow these steps:

1. Students can use the Letter Shell to help them format their letters correctly.
2. Have students use the Revision Checker for Pronouns and Antecedents to revise their letter for clarity.

Allow approximately 60 minutes of class time to complete these steps.

Sourcebook

Have students use Chapter 8, Practical and Technical Writing (pp. 228–262), for additional support. The chapter includes an annotated student model of a letter, p. 257.

Build Your Portfolio

Idea Bank

Writing

1. **Letter of Appreciation** Write a letter of appreciation to someone whose thoughtfulness you regard as a treasured gift.

2. **Sequel** Even though the central conflict is resolved at the end of this story, readers may still wonder what happens next. Write a sequel that tells what happened to Della, Jim, the combs, and the watch.

3. **Surprise Ending** Write a story of your own with a surprise ending. Keep in mind that a good surprise ending is unexpected but not completely off-the-wall.

Speaking and Listening

4. **Play** With a small group of classmates, act out the story of "The Gift of the Magi." You may use the existing stage version of the story, which you can find in a library, or create a version of your own. **[Performing Arts Link]**

5. **Monologue** Assume the role of either Della or Jim and retell "The Gift of the Magi." Practice and revise your retelling until it is convincing, then perform your monologue for an audience. **[Performing Arts Link]**

Projects

6. **Comic Book** Create a comic-book version of "The Gift of the Magi." Illustrate all important plot events in the story. **[Art Link]**

7. **Multicultural Gifts** With a small group of classmates, find out about a gift-giving occasion in a culture other than your own. Share your findings in a multimedia report. **[Social Studies Link; Technology Link]**

Writing Mini-Lesson

Thank-You Letter

When people give you a gift or do something thoughtful for you, it's good manners to thank them. Think of a special gift that you received. Then write a thank-you letter expressing your appreciation.

Writing Skills Focus: Elaboration to Make Writing Personal

Make your thank-you letter more meaningful by **elaborating to make your writing personal.** Include details explaining *why* you like a gift and why it is meaningful to you. Share news regarding the gift and people of interest to the giver in your letter.

Model

Dear Abuelo,

I just love the snorkeling equipment you sent me for my birthday. When I saw the purge valve on the snorkel, I had to laugh. I must've made a real impression on you two summers ago when I tried to clear my old-fashioned snorkel and ended up inhaling what felt like half the bay.

I'm *really* looking forward to using my new equipment when we visit you and Abuela in December. Thanks to you, I won't have to surface every 30 seconds and pour out the water in my snorkel!

Prewriting Make a list of the reasons you like the gift, and think of other news you want to share.

Drafting As you write your letter, include personal details, such as features of the gift that particularly impress you, the way the gift makes you feel, and news about family and friends.

Revising Rework your letter, adding extra details and personal touches.

✓ ASSESSMENT OPTIONS

Formal Assessment, Selection Test, pp. 120–122, and Assessment Resources Software. The selection test is designed so that it can be easily customized to the performance levels of your students.

Alternative Assessment, p. 34, includes options for less advanced students, more advanced students, verbal/linguistic learners, visual/spatial learners, and logical/mathematical learners.

PORTFOLIO ASSESSMENT

Use the following rubrics in the **Alternative Assessment** booklet to assess student writing:

Letter of Appreciation: Expression Rubric, p. 87
Sequel: Fictional Narrative Rubric, p. 88
Surprise Ending: Fictional Narrative Rubric, p. 88
Writing Mini-Lesson: Expression Rubric, p. 87

PART 1
$\mathcal{P}$lot, $\mathcal{C}$haracter, and $\mathcal{P}$oint of View

One-Minute Planning Guide

The short stories in this section exemplify the literary elements of plot, point of view, and character. In "Sonata for Harp and Bicycle," a series of suspenseful plot twists lead to the solution of a mystery. In "The Scarlet Ibis," a young narrator poignantly reveals conflicting feelings about his physically challenged brother. Both "Blues Ain't No Mockin Bird" and "Uncle Marcos" feature memorable central characters who have a lasting impact on the lives of the people around them.

Customize for
Varying Students Needs
When assigning the selections in this section to your students, keep in mind the following factors:

"Sonata for Harp and Bicycle"
- Contains difficult vocabulary, long sentences, and unfamiliar expressions that may present a challenge to less proficient readers and English language learners
- Eerie ghost story will appeal to many students

"The Scarlet Ibis"
- Moving story about the relationship between brothers will appeal to many students

"Blues Ain't No Mockin Bird"
- Dialect may need to be explained to English language learners

"Uncle Marcos"
- Cultural details may be unfamiliar to some students
- Elements of magical realism may require some explanation

In a Village Near Paris, 1909, Lyonel Feininger, The University of Iowa Museum of Art, ©1997 Artists Rights Society (ARS), New York, VG Bild Kinst, Bonn

Plot, Character, and Point of View ◆ 467

♪ Humanities: Art

In a Village Near Paris, 1909, by Lyonel Feininger.

Born in New York City, Lyonel Feininger (1871–1956) began living in Germany as an adolescent when his parents, who were musicians, were touring that country. He began to paint in his thirties; his most famous works followed the Cubist style, creating layers upon layers with flat, hard-edged surfaces in vibrantly transparent colors. In the 1920's, Feininger became an influ-ential member of the German Bauhaus school, which combined art and technology.

In a Village Near Paris, a relatively early painting by Feininger, suggests his later use of vibrant color but does not yet show the Cubist influence. Encourage students to imagine various circumstances for the scene in the painting. Help them link the painting to the focus of Part 1 by answering the following questions:

1. Choose one of the people in this paint-ing, and imagine where he or she is going. *Suggested response: The small man on the left is taking a manuscript to a news-paper; he is hoping to publish his first story.*

2. Imagine that you could see this painting from another point of view—from inside one of the buildings or from high above. What would you see? *Suggested response: From above, the scene would look like pink channels between dark buildings, with small, dark figures moving through.*

Guide for Reading

OBJECTIVES

1. To read, comprehend, and interpret a short story
2. To relate a story to personal experience
3. To predict story events
4. To identify rising action and climax
5. To build vocabulary in context and learn words from myths
6. To develop skill in using commas before interrogative elements
7. To write a newspaper report on a strange occurrence using dramatic effects
8. To respond to the story through writing, speaking and listening, and projects

SKILLS INSTRUCTION

Vocabulary:
Word Origins:
Words From Myths
Grammar:
Commas Before
Interrogative
Elements
Reading Strategy:
Predict
Literary Focus:
Rising Action and
Climax

Writing: Dramatic
Effects
**Speaking and
Listening:** Planning
a Debate (teacher
edition)
Critical Viewing:
Speculate; Deduce;
Distinguish; Predict

PORTFOLIO OPPORTUNITIES

Writing: Memo; Continuation; Evaluation
Writing Mini-Lesson: Newspaper Report
on a Strange Occurrence
Speaking and Listening: Talk Show
Interview; Debate
Projects: Mystery Timeline; Illustration

Joan Aiken (1924–)

Unexplained mysteries, weird noises in the night, and eerie occurrences are all things you're likely to find in a Joan Aiken story. Aiken, the daughter of poet Conrad Aiken and sister of two other writers, was born in England.

> *During her childhood, the family lived in a creepy old house, an experience that helped to foster Aiken's fascination with mystery and the unexplained.*

An Early Start Aiken began writing when she was five years old and published her first story at age sixteen. "Writing," she has said, "is just the family trade." After working as a features editor for a magazine, a copywriter for a large London advertising agency, and with the United Nations in London, Aiken decided to devote herself exclusively to writing. The result has been an immense output of novels, poems, plays, and stories.

Words of Wit In addition to her interest in the mysterious, Aiken is also known for her wit. Many of her stories are humorous and imaginative, as are the titles of her books. Her first collection of short stories, for example, was called *All You Ever Wanted*. It was followed by another volume entitled *More Than You Bargained For*.

Like many writers, Aiken sometimes uses personal experiences in her stories. "Sonata for Harp and Bicycle" takes place in London, where Aiken has a home. The main character, Jason, is an advertising copywriter, a job that Aiken once held. As you read, you'll see evidence of Aiken's wit, as well as her flair for telling a spooky tale.

◆ Build Vocabulary

WORD ORIGINS: WORDS FROM MYTHS

Myths are fictional tales that explain the actions of gods or the causes of natural phenomena. Many English words come from myths. For example, the word *tantalizingly*, which appears in "Sonata for Harp and Bicycle," comes from the name Tantalus, a king in Greek mythology. He enraged the gods and was punished by being able to see but never reach water and food. Thus, *tantalizingly* means "done in a teasing manner by promising something and then withholding it."

encroaching
tantalizingly
furtive
menacing
reciprocate
ardent
gossamer
preposterous
engendered
improbably

WORD BANK

Before you read, preview this list of words from the story.

◆ Build Grammar Skills

COMMAS BEFORE INTERROGATIVE ELEMENTS

One use of the **comma** is to indicate a pause before a short **interrogative element**—a word or group of words that poses a question—at the end of a sentence. Notice how a comma sets off the question in each of these examples from "Sonata for Harp and Bicycle."

. . . but there is the liberty of the individual to be considered, *don't you think?*

You wouldn't be much loss, *would you?*

As you read the selection, look for other examples of sentences with final interrogative elements set off by commas.

More About the Author

Joan Aiken's best critics have been her own children. She used to read her books to them as she was writing and ask for their comments. Aiken has always said that books for young people should not sugarcoat the facts that life is hard and that evil and hardship do exist. Nevertheless, she likes to give her stories happy endings, in which good ultimately wins out over evil.

Prentice Hall Literature Program Resources

REINFORCE / RETEACH / EXTEND

Selection Support Pages
Build Vocabulary: Words From Myths, p. 143
Build Grammar Skills: Commas Before Interrogative Elements, p. 144
Reading Strategy: Predict, p. 145
Literary Focus: Rising Action and Climax, p. 146

Strategies for Diverse Students Needs, p. 35

Beyond Literature
Music Connection: Sonata, p. 35

Formal Assessment Selection Test, pp. 123–125,

Assessment Resources Software

Alternative Assessment, p. 35

Writing and Language Transparencies
Descriptive and Observational Writing, pp. 17–20

Resource Pro CD-ROM
"Sonata for Harp and Bicycle"—includes all resource material and customizable lesson plan

Listening to Literature Audiocassettes
"Sonata for Harp and Bicycle"

Sonata for Harp and Bicycle

◆ Literature and Your Life

CONNECT YOUR EXPERIENCE

Someone starts behaving in a strange, unpredictable way. Something disappears without explanation. Real-life mysteries happen all the time. Some people may ignore the mystery. Others might wonder about it but not try to solve it. Certain people, however, will always try to solve a mystery—even if there's danger involved.

Journal Writing In your journal, explore your answer to this question: Why do people love a mystery?

THEMATIC FOCUS: WORKING TOWARD A GOAL

In this story, a young copywriter stumbles into a mysterious situation and feels compelled to get to the bottom of it—even though others advise him against it.

◆ Background for Understanding

MUSIC

A sonata (sə nät′ ə), derived from the Italian word *suonare*, "to sound," is a musical composition for one or two instruments. Sonatas composed after 1750 contain several movements, or parts, and are written for a keyboard instrument alone or for another solo instrument (a flute, for example) and a piano.

The movements of a sonata are related to one another thematically. In a typical sonata, the first movement is lively, the second is slow, and the optional third movement is graceful and lively.

◆ Literary Focus

RISING ACTION AND CLIMAX

The most exciting part of a story is the **rising action**—the part that makes you want to keep reading. The rising action is the portion of the plot that builds to the **climax**—or high point of interest. In "Sonata for Harp and Bicycle," the rising action includes a complicated and puzzling mystery that fuels suspense.

◆ Reading Strategy

PREDICT

To **predict** is to guess what will happen based upon what you already know. As you read "Sonata for Harp and Bicycle," make predictions by looking for examples of *foreshadowing*—clues about future events that the author provides.

For example, the first sentence of the story, in which a new employee is told that "no one is allowed to remain in the building after five o'clock" is a clue. It might lead you to guess that something unusual or dangerous occurs in the building after five o'clock. While you read "Sonata for Harp and Bicycle," stay one step ahead of the plot by continually updating and revising your predictions.

Use a chart like this to help you. In one column, record clues you find. Jot down a prediction beside each clue. Then note what actually happens.

Clue	Prediction	What Actually Happens

**Interest Grabber** Tell your students that Aiken's story is about an advertising copywriter who goes to work at a company in which all the employees are hurried out of the building each evening at five o'clock. When the new employee asks why this is the case, he is told that it is a secret that will not be revealed to him until he has been with the company a long time. Not surprisingly, the copywriter is overwhelmed by curiosity. Hold a contest to see which student can come closest to predicting what will happen in the story based on the information you've given. Why are the employees rushed out each night? What will the new employee do to satisfy his curiosity?

Customize for
Less Proficient Readers
To help students utilize the reading strategy, have them complete the Reading Strategy page (p.145) in Selection Support, as they read.

Customize for
More Advanced Students
The climactic scene in the story is described as "bright as the picture on a Salvador Dali calendar." Before students read the story, encourage your more advanced students to research Dali and his work. Have them bring in examples of Dali's paintings. When the class has finished reading, have the students share what they've learned about Dali and connect his work to the story.

Customize for
English Language Learners
These students may be unfamiliar with business terms relating to office buildings and the advertising business. Before they read, explain to them the meanings of such words as *intercom, filing cabinet, switchboard, service entrance, copywriter,* and *layout.*

Customize for
Musical/Rhythmic Learners
Tell students that the sounds of harp music and a bicycle bell help create the atmosphere of this story. Have them bring in a bicycle bell and a recording of harp music (from the library). Demonstrate these sounds for the class, and ask musical learners to close their eyes and tell what feeling the sounds evoke for them.

 Preparing for Standardized Tests

Grammar and Language Many standardized tests include items in which a portion of a sentence is underlined and students are given five ways of phrasing the underlined portion. The answers provide different ways of changing the underlined portion. Write the following test item (on comma usage) on the chalkboard, and have the class try to come up with the correct answer:

Emily Dickinson is one of the most inspirational poets <u>in all of American literature isn't she?</u>

(A) in all of American literature isn't she?
(B) in all of American literature, isn't she.
(C) in all of American literature, isn't she?
(D) in all of American literature isn't she!
(E) in all of American literature. Isn't she?

Explain that (C) is correct because a comma should be used to set off a short interrogative element. For more practice on commas and interrogative elements, use the Build Grammar Skills practice on page 480 and the Build Grammar Skills page in *Selection Support* (p.144).

469

One-Minute Insight This intriguing story combines elements of mystery, romance, and the supernatural. It features a clever, resourceful hero who challenges the absurdly bureaucratic rules of his office and the long-established fears of his co-workers by visiting the office building after dark—after finding that all of the employees are rushed out of the building at five o'clock for a reason that is kept secret. In the process, he uses his problem-solving skills to rid the building of two ghosts who are lovers and to ensure a final triumph for love in the end. Students will enjoy the skill with which Joan Aiken uses visual and musical imagery to build suspense, as well as the touches of humor and romance that lighten this modern-day ghost story.

Customize for
Visual/Spatial Learners
The illustrations for this selection provide ideal material for building background for these students. Ask students to preview all of the pictures. Use these questions to spark discussion:

1. Based on the illustrations, where does the story take place? *It takes place in London, England.*

2. What might you predict about the story from the night-time and misty outdoor scenes? *Students may predict that the story either takes place mostly at night or involves something mysterious.*

3. What can you infer about the story from the painting of the office scene (p. 477)? *The story might take place in an office building and involve two co-workers.*

Listening to Literature Audiocassettes Like most ghost stories, this is a gripping story to hear read aloud. As a result, you may want to play all or part of the recording of the selection on the audio-cassette. You might, for example, play the portion of the story up to the point when Jason is about to enter the Grimes Buildings after hours. Students can then read the rest of the story.

Sonata for Harp and Bicycle

Joan Aiken

470 ◆ *Short Srories*

Block Scheduling Strategies

Consider these suggestions to take advantage of extended class time:

• Bring in a recording of a sonata performed on the harp and play it for students to build background for the story.

• Hold a class discussion in which students compare and contrast Aiken's story to other ghost stories they've heard or read.

• Have groups of students complete the Speaking and Listening activities on page 481 and perform their finished products for the class.

• If you have access to computers, devote a 90-minute block of time to having students complete the Writing Mini-Lesson (p. 481) in the *Writer's Solution Writing Lab CD-ROM* tutorial on Exposition. The tutorial provides a wealth of instructional options and activities to help students improve their writing skills.

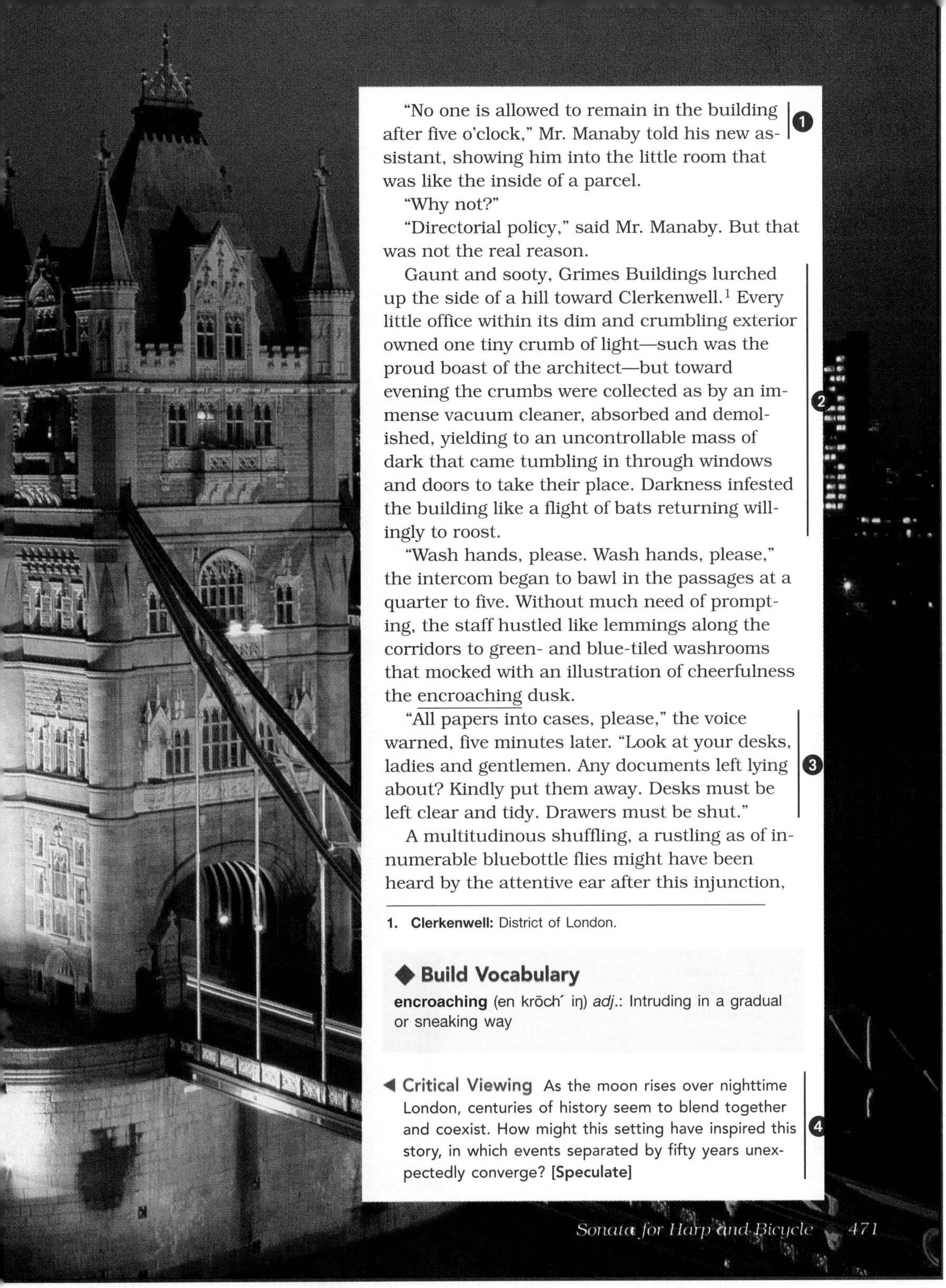

"No one is allowed to remain in the building after five o'clock," Mr. Manaby told his new assistant, showing him into the little room that was like the inside of a parcel.

"Why not?"

"Directorial policy," said Mr. Manaby. But that was not the real reason.

Gaunt and sooty, Grimes Buildings lurched up the side of a hill toward Clerkenwell.[1] Every little office within its dim and crumbling exterior owned one tiny crumb of light—such was the proud boast of the architect—but toward evening the crumbs were collected as by an immense vacuum cleaner, absorbed and demolished, yielding to an uncontrollable mass of dark that came tumbling in through windows and doors to take their place. Darkness infested the building like a flight of bats returning willingly to roost.

"Wash hands, please. Wash hands, please," the intercom began to bawl in the passages at a quarter to five. Without much need of prompting, the staff hustled like lemmings along the corridors to green- and blue-tiled washrooms that mocked with an illustration of cheerfulness the encroaching dusk.

"All papers into cases, please," the voice warned, five minutes later. "Look at your desks, ladies and gentlemen. Any documents left lying about? Kindly put them away. Desks must be left clear and tidy. Drawers must be shut."

A multitudinous shuffling, a rustling as of innumerable bluebottle flies might have been heard by the attentive ear after this injunction,

---

1. **Clerkenwell:** District of London.

◆ **Build Vocabulary**

encroaching (en krōch´ iŋ) *adj.*: Intruding in a gradual or sneaking way

---

◀ **Critical Viewing** As the moon rises over nighttime London, centuries of history seem to blend together and coexist. How might this setting have inspired this story, in which events separated by fifty years unexpectedly converge? [Speculate]

Sonata for Harp and Bicycle 471

◆ **Literary Focus**

❶ **Rising Action and Climax**
The story's rising action begins immediately with Manaby's statement. Have students try to guess what the story's climax might involve based on the story's opening line. *Students will probably guess that the climax will involve a revelation about something that occurs in the building after five o'clock.* Have students discuss how Aiken immediately creates suspense through the story's opening line. *The opening line immediately draws readers into the story, making them wonder why no one is allowed in the building after five o'clock.*

◆ **Reading Strategy**

❷ **Predict** Ask students what clues they can find in this passage that something spooky will happen in the building. Students might cite the "uncontrollable mass of dark" or the final sentence: "Darkness infested the building like a flight of bats returning willingly to roost."

◆ *Literature and Your Life*

❸ Ask students how they might feel about working in a place where impersonal commands were given to everyone over the intercom to leave immediately at five o'clock every day. *Some students might resent the intrusion into their personal freedom; some might be curious or frightened; others might simply welcome the chance to leave work promptly.*

▶ **Critical Viewing** ◀

❹ **Speculate** The blend of modern buildings and the centuries-old bridge might have inspired the author to blend the past and present in her story.

Workplace Skills Mini-Lesson

Dealing With Rules in the Workplace

Introduce the Concept Tell students that the rule requiring all employees to leave the Grimes Buildings at precisely five o'clock is an unusual one, but that most workplaces have certain rules employees are expected to follow.

Develop Background Tell students that workplaces might have rules about the following:

- when and how workers start and end shifts
- if employees must work nights or weekends
- how employees must dress and speak to customers or associates

Gather Information Have students interview the manager at a local fast-food restaurant or retail store to find out the company's most important rules for employees and the consequences of breaking the rules.

Discuss the Findings Have the class discuss the rules they discovered and how such rules would affect their decision to work for a company.

Customize for
Musical/Rhythmic Learners

Have these students point out descriptive phrases that help them imagine how the end of the workday sounds. Then ask what feelings the sounds convey. *Words and phrases such as "multitudinous shuffling," "rustling as of innumerable bluebottle flies," "slammed," and "staccato-voiced" create a busy, rushed feeling, while "the first faint notes of St. Paul's" and the "louder chimes of St. Bidduoph's-on-the-Wall" create a peaceful feeling.*

◆ Critical Thinking

❶ Analyze Ask students why Jason raises the question about the company policy of not allowing anyone to remain in the building after 5 P.M. What does the questioning imply about what kind of person Jason is? *Jason raises the question because he just cannot get himself to shrug off a most unusual policy. His insistent questioning shows that he is a curious person who cannot let a such a peculiar mystery remain unsolved.*

◆ Reading Strategy

❷ Predict Ask students if they think Jason will obey Miss Golden's warning to stop asking questions. *Students can predict that Jason will not stop, because he is curious and Miss Golden's terrified reaction will only increase his curiosity. If he listened to her, there would be no story.*

◆ Reading Strategy

❸ Predict Jason is flirting with her by asking what she wants for her birthday. The narrator tells us directly that Miss Golden is attracted to Jason, even though she doesn't realize it yet. The two will probably fall in love.

as the employees of Moreton Wold and Company thrust their papers into cases, hurried letters and invoices into drawers, clipped statistical abstracts together and slammed them into filing cabinets, dropped discarded copy into wastepaper baskets. Two minutes later, and not a desk throughout Grimes Buildings bore more than its customary coating of dust.

"Hats and coats on, please. Hats and coats on, please. Did you bring an umbrella? Have you left any shopping on the floor?" At three minutes to five the homegoing throng was in the lifts[2] and on the stairs; a clattering, staccato-voiced flood darkened momentarily the great double doors of the building, and then as the first faint notes of St. Paul's[3] came echoing faintly on the frosty air, to be picked up near at hand by the louder chimes of St. Biddulph's-on-the-Wall, the entire premises of Moreton Wold stood empty.

❶ "But why is it?" Jason Ashgrove, the new copywriter, asked his secretary one day. "Why are the staff herded out so fast? Not that I'm against it, mind you; I think it's an admirable idea in many ways, but there is the liberty of the individual to be considered, don't you think?"

❷ "Hush!" Miss Golden, the secretary, gazed at him with large and terrified eyes. "You mustn't ask that sort of question. When you are taken onto the Established Staff you'll be told. Not before."

"But I want to know now," Jason said in discontent. "Do you know?"

"Yes, I do," Miss Golden answered <u>tantalizingly</u>. "Come on, or we shan't have finished the Oat Crisp layout by a quarter to." And she stared firmly down at the copy in front of her, lips folded, candyfloss hair falling over her face, lashes hiding eyes like peridots,[4] a girl with a secret.

---

2. **lifts** (lifts) *n.*: British term for elevators.
3. **St. Paul's:** Famous church in London.
4. **peridots** (per´ ə däts´) *n.*: Yellowish-green gems.

◆ Build Vocabulary
tantalizingly (tan´ tə līz´ iŋ glē) *adv.*: In a teasing or tormenting way

Jason was annoyed. He rapped out a couple of rude and witty rhymes which Miss Golden let pass in a withering silence.

"What do you want for your birthday, Miss Golden? Sherry? Fudge? Bubble bath?"

"I want to go away with a clear conscience about Oat Crisps," Miss Golden retorted. It was not true; what she chiefly wanted was Mr. Jason Ashgrove, but he had not realized this yet.

> **◆ Reading Strategy**
> Do you think the relationship between Miss Golden and Jason will grow into a loving one?
> **❸**

Humanities: Photography

Portrait of a Place

Photography is used in travel brochures and posters to promote tourism to places all over the globe. Indeed, many travel brochures are photographic portraits of the places they promote.

To attract visitors to a particular place, travel agencies provide potential visitors with photographs that show off the best features of a given destination. A poor photograph—such as a drearily lit photo of a castle—can turn tourists away.

London, the setting of "Sonata for Harp and Bicycle," is a popular vacation destination, with tourists flocking to see such landmarks as Westminster Abbey, Buckingham Palace, Big Ben, and London Bridge. Have students examine with the eye of a travel agent the photographs illustrating this selection. Use these questions for discussion:

1. Which photo or photos do you think would encourage tourism? Why? *The photos of London Bridge and the Houses of Parliament taken at night would encourage*

tourism. *The illumination of London Bridge highlights its architectural features, and the nighttime photo of the Houses of Parliament captures a historical ambiance.*

2. Which photo or photos do you think would turn tourists away? Why? *The photo of the Houses of Parliament taken on a foggy day would turn tourists away. The scene appears drab and dreary.*

"Come on, don't tease! I'm sure you haven't been on the Established Staff all that long," he coaxed her. "What happens when one is taken on, anyway? Does the Managing Director have us up for a confidential chat? Or are we given a little book called *The Awful Secret of Grimes Buildings*?"

Miss Golden wasn't telling. She opened her drawer and took out a white towel and a cake of rosy soap.

"Wash hands, please! Wash hands, please!"

Jason was frustrated. "You'll be sorry," he said. "I shall do something desperate."

4

"Oh no, you mustn't!" Her eyes were large with fright. She ran from the room and was back within a couple of moments, still drying her hands.

"If I took you out for a coffee, couldn't you give me just a tiny hint?"

▼ **Critical Viewing** Londoners are accustomed to the sound of Big Ben, the bell in the Clock Tower of the Houses of Parliament, pictured here. This story also mentions the chimes of St. Paul's and St. Biddulph's-on-the-Wall. Why might a city build so many public timepieces? **[Deduce]**

5

Sonata for Harp and Bicycle ◆ 473

❶ **Predict** Have students identify the clues and make predictions based on them. *The clues are "fire escape" and "a bicycle and a harp." Students might predict that Jason will climb a fire escape. He might find someone riding a bicycle and someone playing a harp.*

❷ **Clarification** Tell students that the phrase "the bombed areas" refers to the fact that London was bombed repeatedly by German planes during World War II, in the 1940's. Portions of the city had to be rebuilt in the 1950's.

Customize for
Musical/Rhythmic Learners

❸ Suggest that a group of students get together and try to reproduce and record the sounds described in this passage. They can use musical instruments or any other objects—such as a bicycle bell—for sound effects. Play the recording for the class as a volunteer reads this passage aloud.

◆ **Literary Focus**

❹ **Rising Action and Climax** Ask students what questions are in their minds as Jason begins climbing the fire escape to enter the office building at night. Students may ask the following questions: *What will he find there? Is he in danger? Will he survive?*

◆ **Critical Thinking**

❺ **Speculate** Ask students why burglars might avoid the Grimes Buildings. *The mystery of the building might be common knowledge in the neighborhood. They may be afraid to find out why everyone is forced to leave at five o'clock and why there are no lights on in the building.*

◆ **Critical Thinking**

❻ **Deduce** Ask students what kind of bell Jason hears? *Most students will deduce from the title of the selection and the mentioning earlier in the story that "a bicycle bell tinkled its tiny warning," that the bell is a bicycle bell.*

Side by side Miss Golden and Mr. Ashgrove ran along the green-floored passages, battled down the white marble stairs among the hundred other employees from the tenth floor, the nine hundred from the floors below.

He saw her lips move as she said something, but in the clatter of two thousand feet the words were lost.

◆ **Reading Strategy**
❶ This paragraph contains clues to what will happen later in the story.

"—fire escape," he heard, as they came into the momentary hush of the carpeted entrance hall. And "—it's to do with a bicycle. A bicycle and a harp."

"I don't understand."

❷ Now they were in the street, chilly with the winter dusk smells of celery on carts, of swept-up leaves heaped in faraway parks, and cold layers of dew sinking among the withered evening primroses in the bombed areas. London lay about them wreathed in twilit mystery and fading against the barred and smoky sky. Like a ninth wave the sound of traffic overtook and swallowed them.

"Please tell me!"

But, shaking her head, she stepped onto a scarlet homebound bus and was borne away from him.

Jason stood undecided on the pavement, with the crowds dividing around him as around the pier of a bridge. He scratched his head, looked about him for guidance.

❸ An ambulance clanged, a taxi hooted, a drill stuttered, a siren wailed on the river, a door slammed, a brake squealed, and close beside his ear a bicycle bell tinkled its tiny warning.

A bicycle, she had said. A bicycle and a harp.

Jason turned and stared at Grimes Buildings.

Somewhere, he knew, there was a back way in, a service entrance. He walked slowly past the main doors, with their tubs of snowy chrysanthemums, and up Glass Street. A tiny <u>furtive</u> wedge of darkness beckoned him, a snicket, a hacket, an alley carved into the thickness of the building. It was so narrow that at any moment, it seemed, the overtopping

walls would come together and squeeze it out of existence.

Walking as softly as an Indian, Jason passed through it, slid by a file of dustbins,[5] and found the foot of the fire escape. Iron treads rose into the mist, like an illustration to a Gothic[6] fairy tale.

He began to climb.

❹ When he had mounted to the ninth story he paused for breath. It was a lonely place. The lighting consisted of a dim bulb at the foot of every flight. A well of gloom sank beneath him. The cold fingers of the wind nagged and fluttered at the tails of his jacket, and he pulled the string of the fire door and edged inside.

Grimes Buildings were triangular, with the street forming the base of the triangle, and the fire escape the point. Jason could see two long passages coming toward him, meeting at an acute angle where he stood. He started down the left-hand one, tiptoeing in the cavelike si-❺ lence. Nowhere was there any sound, except for the faraway drip of a tap. No night watchman would stay in the building; none was needed. Burglars gave the place a wide berth.

Jason opened a door at random; then another. Offices lay everywhere about him, empty and forbidding. Some held lipstick-stained tissues, spilled powder, and orange peels; others were still foggy with cigarette smoke. Here was a Director's suite of rooms—a desk like half an acre of frozen lake, inch-thick carpet, roses, and the smell of cigars. Here was a conference room with scattered squares of doodled blotting paper. All equally empty.

He was not sure when he first began to notice the bell. Telephone, he thought at first, and then he remembered that all the outside lines were disconnected at five. And this bell, any-❻ way, had not the regularity of a telephone's double ring: there was a tinkle, and then silence; a long ring, and then silence; a whole volley of rings together, and then silence.

Jason stood listening, and fear knocked against his ribs and shortened his breath. He

---

5. **dustbins:** British term for garbage cans.
6. **Gothic:** Mysterious.

▲ **Critical Viewing** Like fog, the mood of a story may blur the boundaries between reality and fantasy. How does the mood of this story make it difficult to tell where reality ends and fantasy begins? [Distinguish]

❼

knew that he must move or be paralyzed by it. He ran up a flight of stairs and found himself with two more endless green corridors beckoning him like a pair of dividers.

Another sound now: a waft of ice-thin notes, riffling up an arpeggio[7] like a flurry of snowflakes. Far away down the passage it

---

7. **arpeggio** (är pej′ ō) *n.*: Notes of a chord played one after the other instead of together.

echoed. Jason ran in pursuit, but as he ran the music receded. He circled the building, but it always outdistanced him, and when he came back to the stairs he heard it fading away to the story below.

He hesitated, and as he did so heard again the bell; the bicycle bell. It was approaching him fast, bearing down on him, urgent, menacing. He could hear the pedals, almost see the shimmer of an invisible wheel. Absurdly, he was

◆ **Build Vocabulary**

furtive (fur′ tiv) *adj.*: Preventing observation; sneaky

menacing (men′ is iŋ) *v.*: Threatening

Sonata for Harp and Bicycle ◆ 475

 Cross-Curricular Connection: Social Studies

London, England, is the setting for "Sonata for Harp and Bicycle." Its centuries-old palaces, government buildings, and cathedrals create a palpable impression of an unbroken historical tradition not unfelt by visitors to the city. London's history stretches back through the ages, tracing its beginnings as a Roman outpost to the year A.D. 43. Later, during the Middle Ages (400 to 1500), Germanic tribes, most notably the Angles and Saxons, continually attacked the city. In 1066, the French nobleman William the Conqueror invaded England and was crowned king. Many of London's familiar landmarks, such as Westminster Abbey and London Bridge, were built during this period.

Throughout the years, London has had to endure many additional trials. Bubonic plague and the Great Fire of London struck in the 1600's, while merciless bombing exacted a terrible toll during World War II. Through it all, however, London has managed not only to survive but to prosper.

A city with so many tangible links to the distant past—with stone edifices that seem to whisper secrets through the millennia—seems a likely spot for a ghost or two to haunt. Discuss with students the attributes that make London an ideal setting for "Sonata for Harp and Bicycle."

◆ Literary Focus

❶ Rising Action and Climax
Whoever is holding Jason is invisible, and may therefore be a ghost. On the basis of the reference to the song, students may conclude that it is the ghost of someone who proposed marriage to his girlfriend, but is still waiting for her answer.

❷ Clarification Tell students that the ghost's dialogue here represents a bit of comic relief in the midst of the rising action. Ask students if they can recall an old song featuring a bicycle, a girl named Daisy, and a boyfriend waiting for Daisy's answer. *The dialogue is an allusion to the song A Bicycle Built for Two.*

◆ Build Grammar Skills

❸ Commas Before Interrogative Elements Ask students to explain why there is a comma after the word *distinguished*. *It indicates a pause before the short interrogative element "don't you think" at the end of the sentence.* Read the sentence aloud so that students can hear the pause in the sentence.

◆ Literary Focus

❹ Rising Action and Climax Ask students what they think Berenice means when she says that Jason is doomed. *Students should gather that something terrible happens to people after having seen "The Wailing Watchman."*

---

reminded of the insistent clamor of an ice-cream vendor, summoning children on a sultry Sunday afternoon.

> **◆ Literary Focus**
> ❶ The action of the story is accelerating. Who or what is holding Jason?

There was a little fireman's alcove beside him, with buckets and pumps. He hurled himself into it. The bell stopped beside him, and then there was a moment while his heart tried to shake itself loose in his chest. He was looking into two eyes carved out of expressionless air; he was held by two hands knotted together out of the width of dark.

❷ "Daisy, Daisy?" came the whisper. "Is that you, Daisy? Have you come to give me your answer?"

Jason tried to speak, but no words came.

"It's not Daisy! Who are you?" The sibilants[8] were full of threat. "You can't stay here. This is private property."

He was thrust along the corridor. It was like being pushed by a whirlwind—the fire door opened ahead of him without a touch, and he was on the openwork platform, clutching the slender railing. Still the hands would not let him go.

"How about it?" the whisper mocked him. "How about jumping? It's an easy death compared with some."

Jason looked down into the smoky void. The darkness nodded to him like a familiar.[9]

"You wouldn't be much loss, would you? What have you got to live for?"

Miss Golden, Jason thought. She would miss me. And the syllables Berenice Golden lingered in the air like a chime. Drawing on some unknown deposit of courage he shook himself loose from the holding hands and ran down the fire escape without looking back.

Next morning when Miss Golden, crisp, fragrant, and punctual, shut the door of Room 492 behind her, she stopped short of the hat-pegs with a horrified gasp.

---
8. **sibilants** (sib´ əl əntz) *n.*: Hissing sounds.
9. **a familiar:** A spirit.

"Mr. Ashgrove, your hair!"

"It makes me look more distinguished, don't ❸ you think?" he said.

It had indeed this effect, for his impeccable dark cut had turned to a stippled silver which might have been envied by many a diplomat.

"How did it happen? You've not—" her voice sank to a whisper—"*you've not been in Grimes Buildings after dark?*"

"Miss Golden—Berenice," he said earnestly. "Who was Daisy? Plainly you know. Tell me the story."

"Did you see him?" she asked faintly.

"Him?"

"William Heron—The Wailing Watchman. ❹ Oh," she exclaimed in terror, "I can see you did. Then you are doomed—doomed!"

"If I'm doomed," said Jason, "let's have coffee, and you tell me the story quickly."

"It all happened over fifty years ago," said Berenice, as she spooned out coffee powder with distracted extravagance. "Heron was the night watchman in this building, patrolling the corridors from dusk to dawn every night on his bicycle. He fell in love with a Miss Bell who taught the harp. She rented a room—this room—and gave lessons in it. She began to reciprocate his love, and they used to share a picnic supper every night at eleven, and she'd stay on a while to keep him company. It was an idyll,[10] among the fire buckets and the furnace pipes.

"On Halloween he had summoned up the courage to propose to her. The day before he had told her he was going to ask her a very important question, and he came to the Buildings with a huge bunch of roses and a bottle of wine. But Miss Bell never turned up.

"The explanation was simple. Miss Bell, of course, had been losing a lot of sleep through her nocturnal romance, and so she used to take a nap in her music room between seven and ten, to save going home. In order to make

---
10. **idyll** (ī´ dəl) *n.*: Romantic scene, usually in the country.

◆ Build Vocabulary
reciprocate (re sip´ rə kāt) *v.*: Return

Speaking and Listening Mini-Lesson

Planning a Debate
This mini-lesson supports the Speaking and Listening activity in the Idea Bank on page 481.

Introduce the Concept Tell students that they will hold a debate on a real-life mystery. Also tell them that debates have a formal structure and that usually the audience votes on which side has presented the best evidence.

Develop Background Tell students that debates have the following form:
- Each side makes a statement telling why its members believe its position is right.
- The FOR side gives a piece of evidence.
- The AGAINST side rebuts, or offers opposing evidence.
- The AGAINST side gives new evidence.
- The FOR side rebuts this evidence.

Apply the Information Have two groups select a real-life mystery, choose sides on the mystery, research it, and debate.

Assess the Outcome Have the class vote on which side presented the most convincing case. In addition, evaluate each side on its adherence to debate format.

sure that she would wake up, she persuaded her father, a distant relative of Graham Bell,[11] to attach an alarm-waking fixture to her telephone which called her every night at ten. She was too modest and shy to let Heron know that she spent those hours in the building, and to give him the pleasure of waking her himself.

"Alas! On this important evening the line failed, and she never woke up. The telephone was in its infancy at that time, you must remember.

5

---

11. **Graham Bell:** Alexander Graham Bell (1847–1922), the inventor of the telephone.

"Heron waited and waited. At last, mad with grief and jealousy, having called her home and discovered that she was not there, he concluded that she had betrayed him; he ran to the fire escape, and cast himself off it, holding the roses and the bottle of wine.

"Daisy did not long survive him but pined away soon after. Since that day their ghosts

6

▼ **Critical Viewing** After the other workers have fled, Berenice and Jason remain behind to change the ending of the ghosts' story. Do you think they will succeed in their mission? [Predict] **7**

Office at Night, 1940, Edward Hopper, Walker Art Center, Minneapolis, Minnesota

Sonata for Harp and Bicycle ◆ 477

◆ **Critical Thinking**

5 Draw Conclusions Ask students to use the statement that "the telephone was in its infancy" and the earlier mention of the "bombed areas" to determine approximately when the incident of the night watchman—alluded to as happening over fifty years ago—occurred. *Because the mention of "bombed areas" alludes to areas of London still damaged by bombing not many years after the bombing raids during World War II (1939–1945) occurred, the present time in the story is approximately 1950. That information, along with the fact that the telephone was invented by Alexander Graham Bell in 1876, leads to the conclusion that the night-watchman incident probably occurred about the year 1900.*

◆ **Critical Thinking**

6 Make Judgments Ask students what conclusion William Heron draws when his love does not show up on time. Then ask how the tragedy might have been avoided if he had stopped to think more clearly. *Heron jumped off the fire escape because he jumped to conclusions! If he had stopped to think instead, he might have come up with other possible reasons for Daisy's delay, including illness, trouble with her family, accident, or oversleeping.*

▶**Critical Viewing**◀

7 Predict Because of the light tone the author uses throughout the story, students should predict that the story will have a happy ending; that Jason and Berneice will succeed.

 Humanities: Art

Office at Night, 1940, by Edward Hopper.
   In a setting similar to the one in the story, a man and his secretary work late at the office in this painting by Hopper.
   Edward Hopper was one of the great American realists of his time. He is famous for his oil paintings of urban and small-town scenes that express a sense of loneliness and detachment. Point out Hopper's dramatic use of light and shadow, the geometric patterns made by figures and objects,

and the stark absence of details that could distract the viewer from the essential elements of the painting.
   Use these questions for discussion:
1. What purpose might the artist have had for exaggerating the intense yellow glare in the room? **Suggested response:** *It creates an eerie glow and atmosphere, increased by the focus on the window shade and its cord, which seem to be blowing in the wind.*

2. Does this scene match the way you envision Jason's office in the story? Why or why not? *Have students point out descriptive details in the story that match or do not match the details in the painting.*

◆ Literary Focus

❶ Rising Action and Climax Ask students why the tension increases dramatically at this point in the story. *Since Jason has seen the ghost, we wonder whether he will leap from the fire escape and die within five days or whether he will think of a plan to avoid his fate.*

◆ Reading Strategy

❷ Predict Based on Jason's judgment of the ghosts as "inefficient" and his words "We must not begrudge our new-found happiness to others," students should predict that Jason is planning to bring the two ghosts together at last.

Comprehension Check ☑

❸ Why does the ghost of Miss Bell answer the phone in Jason's office? *That is the room in which she was sleeping the night her alarm failed to go off; her ghost is still sleeping there.*

◆ Reading Strategy

❹ Predict Ask students if they can guess what is in the canvas-covered bundle that Jason is slipping the straps of over his shoulders. *Because Jason mentioned earlier that he has to "see an old R.A.F. friend," some students may be able to predict that the bundle is a parachute that Jason intends to use if he is pushed off the fire escape.*

---

have haunted Grimes Buildings, he vainly patrolling the corridors on his bicycle, she playing her harp in the room she rented. *But they never meet.* And anyone who meets the ghost of William Heron will himself, within five days, leap down from the same fatal fire escape."

She gazed at him with tragic eyes.

"In that case we must lose no time," said Jason, and he enveloped her in an embrace as prompt as it was <u>ardent.</u> Looking down at the <u>gossamer</u> hair sprayed across his pin-stripe, he added, "Just the same it is a <u>preposterous</u> situation. Firstly, I have no intention of jumping off the fire escape—" here, however, he repressed a shudder as he remembered the cold, clutching hands of the evening before— "and secondly, I find it quite nonsensical that those two inefficient ghosts have spent fifty years in this building without coming across each other. We must remedy the matter, Berenice. We must not begrudge our new-found happiness to others."

> **◆ Reading Strategy**
> ❷ What do you think Jason plans to do to "remedy the matter"?

He gave her another kiss so impassioned that the electric typewriter against which they were leaning began chattering to itself in a frenzy of enthusiasm.

"This very evening," he went on, looking at his watch, "we will put matters right for that unhappy couple and then, if I really have only five more days to live, which I don't for one moment believe, we will proceed to spend them together, my bewitching Berenice, in the most advantageous manner possible."

She nodded, spellbound.

"Can you work a switchboard?" he added. She nodded again. "My love, you are perfection itself. Meet me in the switchboard room then,

> **◆ Build Vocabulary**
> **ardent** (är´ dənt) *adj.*: Passionate
> **gossamer** (gäs´ ə mər) *adj.*: Light, thin, and filmy
> **preposterous** (pri päs´ tər əs) *adj.*: Absurd
> **engendered** (in jen´ dərd) *v.*: Produced
> **improbably** (im präb´ ə blē) *adv.*: Unlikely to happen

478 ◆ Short Stories

at ten this evening. I would say, have dinner with me, but I shall need to make one or two purchases and see an old R.A.F.[12] friend. You will be safe from Heron's curse in the switchboard room if he always keeps to the corridors."

"I would rather meet him and die with you," she murmured.

"My angel, I hope that won't be necessary. Now," he said, sighing, "I suppose we should get down to our day's work."

Strangely enough the copy they wrote that day, although <u>engendered</u> from such agitated minds, sold more packets of Oat Crisps than any other advertising matter before or since.

That evening when Jason entered Grimes Buildings he was carrying two bottles of wine, two bunches of red roses, and a large canvas-covered bundle. Miss Golden, who had concealed herself in the switchboard room before the offices closed for the night, eyed these things with surprise.

"Now," said Jason, after he had greeted her, "I want you first to ring our own extension."

"No one will reply, surely?"

"I think she will reply."

Sure enough, when Berenice rang Extension 170 a faint, sleepy voice, distant and yet clear, whispered, "Hullo?"

"Is that Miss Bell?"

"Yes." ❸

Berenice went a little pale. Her eyes sought Jason's and, prompted by him, she said formally, "Switchboard here, Miss Bell. Your ten o'clock call."

"Thank you," the faint voice said. There was a click and the line went blank.

"Excellent," Jason remarked. He unfastened his package and slipped its straps over his shoulders. "Now plug into the intercom." ❹

Berenice did so, and then said, loudly and clearly, "Attention. Night watchman on duty, please. Night watchman on duty. You have an urgent summons to Room 492. You have an urgent summons to Room 492." The intercom echoed and reverberated through the empty

---

12. R.A.F.: Royal Air Force.

Beyond the Classroom

Career Connection

Advertising The main character in this story is an advertising copywriter, just as the author herself once was. A copywriter's job is to make a product sound appealing, by using words loaded with positive connotations and by persuading people that they want and need the product. The images chosen for an ad must be eye-catching and appealing.

Have students choose magazine ads they find appealing. Have them analyze which loaded words and images in the ads make them so appealing.

Invite students who are interested in a career as an advertizing copywriter or graphics designer to do library or Internet research on the topic. Encourage them to find a detailed job description as well as a list of qualifications for the position.

corridors, then coughed itself to silence.

"Now we must run. You take the roses, sweetheart, and I'll carry the bottles."

Together they raced up eight flights of stairs and along the passages to Room 492. As they neared the door a burst of music met them— **❺** harp music swelling out, sweet and triumphant. Jason took a bunch of roses from Berenice, opened the door a little way, and gently deposited them, with a bottle, inside the door. As he closed it again Berenice said breathlessly, "Did you see anyone?"

"No," he said. "The room was too full of music." She saw that his eyes were shining.

They stood hand in hand, reluctant to move away, waiting for they hardly knew what. Suddenly the door opened again. Neither Berenice nor Jason, afterward, would speak of what they saw but each was left with a memory, bright as the picture on a Salvador Dali[13] calendar, of a bicycle bearing on its saddle a harp, a bottle of

---

13. **Salvador Dali** (sal´ və dôr´ dä´ lē): Modern artist (1904–1989) famous for his unusual pictures.

wine, and a bouquet of red roses, sweeping <u>improbably</u> down the corridor and far, far away.

◆ Literary Focus
The story has reached its climax. Describe what is happening. **❻**

"We can go now," Jason said.

He led Berenice to the fire door, tucking the bottle of Médoc in his jacket pocket. A black wind from the north whistled beneath them as they stood on the openwork platform, looking down.

"We don't want our evening to be spoiled by the thought of a curse hanging over us," he said, "so this is the practical thing to do. Hang onto the roses." And holding his love firmly, Jason pulled the rip cord of his R.A.F. friend's parachute and leaped off the fire escape. **❼**

A bridal shower of rose petals adorned the descent of Miss Golden, who was possibly the only girl to be kissed in midair in the district of Clerkenwell at ten minutes to midnight on Halloween.

Guide for Responding

◆ *Literature and Your Life*

Reader's Response If you were in Jason's place, would you try to solve the mystery of the Grimes Buildings? Why or why not?

Thematic Focus What is Jason's goal? Does he accomplish it?

Group Discussion With a group, discuss mysteries you've heard about or experienced. Were any of the mysteries ever solved?

☑ Check Your Comprehension

1. Why does Jason first sneak into the Grimes Buildings after five P.M.?
2. How do the bicycle, the fire escape, and the harp relate to the buildings' secret?
3. What is Jason's plan for helping Daisy Bell and William Heron?
4. How does Jason avoid the fate that awaits anyone who sees Heron's ghost?

Sonata for Harp and Bicycle ◆ 479

Beyond the Selection

FURTHER READING

Other Works by Joan Aiken
A Creepy Company: Ten Tales of Terror
A Fit of Shivers: Tales for Late at Night
Give Yourself a Fright: Thirteen Stories of the Supernatural

Other Works About Working It Out
Best Ghost Stories of Algernon Blackwood, Algernon Blackwood
The Woman in White, Wilkie Collins

INTERNET
You and your students may find additional information about Joan Aiken on the Internet. We suggest the following site. Please be aware, however, that the site may have changed from the time we published this information. Tell students to visit **http://ocean.st.usm.edu/~dajones/findaids/ai ken.htm**

We *strongly recommend* that you preview the site before you send students to it.

479

Answers

◆ Critical Thinking

Interpreting

1. Suggested response: Neither thieves nor anyone else is brave enough to go into the building after five o'clock.
2. Suggested response: She is in love with Jason.
3. Suggested response: Attempting to solve the romantic problems of William and Daisy brings Jason and Berenice closer together.
4. Answers should touch upon the fact that decisions made too hastily might be wrong because they could be based upon faulty information. Also, before making any decision, emotions of the moment should be allowed to cool down. Only then can a rational decision be made. Of course, you should stress to students that suicide is *never* the right decision, and that no matter how overwhelming a problem or crisis might seem, there are professional counselors who can help a person get through a crisis situation.
5. Answers should include the fact that, through their own love, Jason and Berenice are able to work together to reunite William and Daisy and to end the haunting of the Grimes Buildings.
6. Suggested response: The harp is the instrument that Daisy Bell teaches, while the bicycle is the vehicle that William Heron uses on his rounds. Therefore, the harp and the bicycle are symbols of the two ghostly lovers. Both the harp and the bicycle make sounds that are described in the text. For the fifty years that the ghosts are apart, those sounds are separate, making separate "music." Once the ghosts are together, the harp and bicycle also come together. The harp and bicycle now play "music" together, as if in one musical composition, or sonata. In a sense, the harp and bicycle—along with the united lovers—"make beautiful music together."

◆ Reading Strategy

1. It predicts Jason's first encounter with the ghost of William Heron in the Grimes Buildings.
2. It predicts the coming together of the ghosts of Daisy Bell and William Heron.
3. It predicts Jason and Berenice falling in love.

480

Guide for Responding (continued)

◆ Critical Thinking

INTERPRET
1. Why don't the Grimes Buildings need a night watchman? **[Speculate]**
2. Why does Berenice Golden agree to meet Jason in the Grimes Buildings after dark? **[Infer]**
3. In what way does love beget, or lead to, love in this story? **[Draw Conclusions]**

APPLY
4. What lesson do the circumstances of William Heron's death teach about the process of making decisions? **[Generalize]**
5. How do the events of this story support the saying that "love conquers all"? **[Apply]**

EVALUATE
6. Explain, using examples from the story, why the title "Sonata for Harp and Bicycle" is appropriate for this selection. **[Evaluate]**

◆ Reading Strategy

PREDICT
When you make **predictions,** you piece together clues in the text to try to guess what will happen next. What event in Aiken's story does each of these excerpts help you predict?
1. "... close beside his ear a bicycle bell tinkled its tiny warning."
2. "Daisy, Daisy?" came the whisper. "Is that you, Daisy? Have you come to give me your answer?"
3. Miss Golden, Jason thought. She would miss me. And the syllables Berenice Golden lingered in the air like a chime.

◆ Literary Focus

RISING ACTION AND CLIMAX
In a literary work, the events that build up to the **climax**—or high point of the story—are called the **rising action**.
1. At what point in the story does the rising action begin? Explain.
2. What is the climax of the story? Support your answer.

◆ Build Vocabulary

USING WORDS FROM MYTHS
Use the clues below to match each word with the letter of its definition.

CLUES FROM GREEK MYTHOLOGY
Echo: nymph who pines away until only her voice remains
Hercules: son of Zeus, known for his strength
Narcissus: beautiful youth in love with his reflection
Titan: one of a race of giant deities

1. echo _____?_____   **a.** powerful or courageous
2. herculean _____?_____   **b.** of great size
3. narcissism _____?_____   **c.** repetition of a sound
4. titanic _____?_____   **d.** self-love

USING THE WORD BANK
Copy each word from the Word Bank; then write the letter of its synonym.

1. encroaching   **a.** passionate
2. tantalizingly   **b.** frightening
3. furtive   **c.** created
4. menacing   **d.** delicate
5. reciprocate   **e.** teasingly
6. ardent   **f.** unlikely
7. gossamer   **g.** secretive
8. preposterous   **h.** intruding
9. engendered   **i.** nonsensical
10. improbably   **j.** return

◆ Build Grammar Skills

COMMAS BEFORE INTERROGATIVE ELEMENTS
A **comma** is used to set off a short **interrogative element** (a word or group of words that poses a question) at the end of a sentence.
Practice On a sheet of paper, rewrite the following sentences, adding commas where needed.
1. The story was suspenseful wasn't it?
2. You like tales of the supernatural don't you?
3. You know another good story by Joan Aiken do you?
4. What's it about anyway?
5. You'd love to see the movie wouldn't you?

◆ Literary Focus
1. The rising action begins after Jason reenters the building.
2. The climactic moment is when the two ghosts are finally united and fly away on a bicycle bearing on its saddle a harp, a bottle of wine, and a bouquet of red roses.

◆ Build Vocabulary
1. c   2. a   3. d   4. b

Using the Word Bank
1. h   2. e   3. g   4. b   5. j
6. a   7. d   8. i   9. c   10. f

◆ Build Grammar Skills
1. The story was suspenseful, wasn't it?
2. You like tales of the supernatural, don't you?
3. You know another story by Joan Aiken, do you?
4. What's it about, anyway?
5. You'd love to see the movie, wouldn't you?

 **Writer's Solution**

For additional instruction and practice, use the lesson on commas in the **Language Lab CD-ROM** and the practice pages on commas (pp. 100–103) in the *Writer's Solution Grammar Practice Book.*

Build Your Portfolio

 Idea Bank

Writing

1. **Memo** Imagine you're designing the sets for a stage production of "Sonata for Harp and Bicycle." Write a memo to the producer describing your ideas for the sets.

2. **Continuation** Write a continuation of the story in which you tell what happens next to Jason and Berenice.

3. **Evaluation** Joan Aiken has said, "A flat or unsatisfactory ending is the worst sin a writer can commit." Evaluate how well Aiken followed her own advice, citing examples from the story.

Speaking and Listening

4. **Talk-Show Interview** Develop and perform a talk-show interview featuring Berenice, Jason, the two ghosts, and the host of the program. Plan the interview so that the two pairs of guests tell what happened at the Grimes Buildings from their own perspectives. **[Media Link]**

5. **Debate** Choose a real-life mystery that has been a subject of controversy—for example, the question of whether there is life on other planets. With a group of classmates, stage a debate that explores the two sides of the controversy.

Projects

6. **Mystery Timeline** Research a famous real-life mystery and create a timeline that outlines the facts and details of the mystery. Present the timeline to the class. **[Social Studies Link]**

7. **Illustration** The Grimes Buildings featured a "dim and crumbling exterior" and, every evening, "darkness infested the building." Create a painting or illustration that captures this eerie scene. **[Art Link]**

 Writing Mini-Lesson

Newspaper Report on a Strange Occurrence

Using your imagination or drawing from real-life stories you've heard, think of a strange or mysterious occurrence that would capture people's interest. Then write a newspaper story that provides a detailed account of the occurrence.

Writing Skills Focus: Dramatic Effects

Dramatic effects are story elements designed to create excitement and suspense. These might include an opening statement that heightens curiosity, a surprise ending, or a bizarre setting, as in this model:

Model From the Story

> It was a lonely place. The lighting consisted of a dim bulb at the foot of every flight. A well of gloom sank beneath him. The cold fingers of the wind nagged and fluttered at the tails of his jacket.

Prewriting Start by creating a timeline that outlines the main details leading up to and following the occurrence. Look over your timeline and determine the events and details that will have the strongest dramatic impact on your audience. Feature these in your report.

Drafting Start your report with a dramatic opening statement that will grab your audience's attention. For example, you might begin with the outcome of events, then go back and explain the events leading up to it. Also, try to come up with an ending that will leave your readers thinking.

Revising Have a classmate read your report and make suggestions for what you can do to make it more engaging. How can you improve the beginning? What gripping details can you add?

 Idea Bank

Customizing for *Performance Levels*

Following are suggestions for matching the Idea Bank topics with your students' performance levels:
    Less Advanced Students: 2, 7
    Average Students: 1, 4, 5
    More Advanced Students: 3, 6

Customizing for *Learning Modalities*

Following are suggestions for matching the Idea Bank topics with your students' learning modalities:
    Verbal/Linguistic: 1, 2, 4, 5
    Logical/Mathematical: 3
    Auditory: 4, 5
    Visual/Spatial: 6, 7

 Writing Mini-Lesson

Refer students to the Writing Handbook, page 962, for instruction on the writing process, and page 964 for further information on exposition.

Writer's Solution

Writing Process Transparencies
Have students use the Story Map in *Writing and Language Transparencies*, p. 83, to organize the events they'll include in their reports.

Writers at Work Videodisc
Have students view the videodisc segment (Ch. 3) featuring radio journalist Gene Bryan Johnson. Have students discuss how they can use his techniques to help them write their newspaper reports.

Play frames 22539 to 32284

Writing Lab CD-ROM
Have students complete the Tutorial on Exposition. Follow these steps:
1. Have students use the Timeline to organize their ideas.
2. Students can draft on computer.
3. Have students use the revision checkers for transitions and language variety.

Sourcebook
Have students use Chapter 3, Exposition (pp. 62–95), for additional support.

✓ ASSESSMENT OPTIONS

Formal Assessment, Selection Test, pp. 123–125, and Assessment Resources Software. The selection test is designed so that it can be easily customized to the performance levels of your students. *Alternative Assessment,* p. 35, includes options for less advanced students, more advanced students, logical/mathematical learners, visual/spatial learners, verbal/linguistic learners, bodily/kinesthetic learners, and musical/rhythmic learners.

PORTFOLIO ASSESSMENT
Use the following rubrics in the *Alternative Assessment* booklet to assess student writing:
Memo: Business Letter/Memo Rubric, p. 106
Continuation: Fictional Narrative Rubric, p. 88
Evaluation: Evaluation/Review Rubric, p. 97
Writing Mini-Lesson: Fictional Narrative Rubric, p. 88; Narrative Based on Personal Experience Rubric, p. 89

OBJECTIVES

1. To read, comprehend, and interpret a short story
2. To relate a story to personal experience
3. To identify with a character
4. To identify point of view
5. To build vocabulary in context and learn irregular plurals: -x to -ces words
6. To develop skill in using infinitives and infinitive phrases
7. To write a character sketch
8. To respond to the story through writing, speaking and listening, and projects

SKILLS INSTRUCTION

Vocabulary:
Irregular Plurals: -x to -ces

Grammar:
Infinitives and Infinitive Phrases

Reading Strategy:
Identify With a Character

Literary Focus:
Point of View

Writing:
Character Sketch

Speaking and Listening: Eulogy; Skit (teacher edition)

Critical Viewing:
Infer; Relate

PORTFOLIO OPPORTUNITIES

Writing: Journal Entry; Essay About a Symbol; Analysis of the Theme
Writing Mini-Lesson: Character Sketch
Speaking and Listening: Eulogy; Skit
Projects: Travel Brochure; Map

More About the Author
James Hurst's first artistic enterprise was studying to become a lyric baritone. He published his first story, "August Snow," at age thirty-five, in 1957, in the literary magazine *Prairie Schooner*. Since then, he has published in such prestigious journals as *The Transatlantic Review,* as well as in popular magazines like *Mademoiselle.* "The Scarlet Ibis" remains his most popular and widely read story, frequently anthologized in literature textbooks. About the story, Hurst wrote:

[The ibis] must be destined to die as Doodle was to die.... If the ibis had been back in a mangrove swamp, would it have died? Could not Doodle in another society have survived?

---

*G*uide for Reading

James Hurst (1922–)

James Hurst is no stranger to either the quiet beauty of a coastal swamp or the deadly fury of a hurricane.

Like the main character of this story, Hurst grew up on a farm in coastal North Carolina, a region known for both its tranquil landscapes and its violent storms.

A Man of Many Talents Hurst has done a lot more than write. He studied chemical engineering at North Carolina State College, served in the army during World War II, studied opera at New York's prestigious Juilliard School of Music, and eventually took a job in a New York bank. Hurst's career at the bank lasted for thirty-four years.

Career as a Writer While working at the bank, Hurst devoted his evenings to writing and published short stories in a variety of small magazines. Published in *The Atlantic* magazine in 1960, "The Scarlet Ibis" is by far Hurst's most popular and successful story.

About the Story One of the qualities that makes "The Scarlet Ibis" such a powerful story is Hurst's use of symbols—objects, people, or ideas that have an underlying meaning. The story's central symbol is a scarlet ibis, a type of bird rarely seen in the United States. When asked why he chose the ibis, Hurst wrote, "The ancient Egyptians worshipped the ibis because they believed it destroyed the crocodiles. . . . I wanted the bird to represent [the character of] Doodle [the younger brother of the story's narrator]— not Doodle's physical self, but his spirit." As you read the story, think about the ways in which the ibis symbolizes Doodle's spirit.

◆ Build Vocabulary

IRREGULAR PLURALS: -x to -ces
This selection contains the word *vortex,* which often refers to the center of a situation. The word has an unusual plural: *vortices.* To form the plural, you must change the e to i and the -x to -ces. Words that form the plural in this way—for example, *appendix* and *index*—often have two acceptable plurals. This is true of the plural of *vortex,* which can be written as either *vortices* or *vortexes.*

imminent
iridescent
vortex
infallibility
entrails
precariously
evanesced

WORD BANK
The words in this list are from this story. Before you read, jot down the definition of any words you recognize. Then check to see whether you're right.

◆ Build Grammar Skills

INFINITIVES AND INFINITIVE PHRASES
The story contains many **infinitives**—verb forms that come after the word *to* and act as nouns, adjectives, or adverbs. Infinitives are often part of an **infinitive phrase,** which is an infinitive with modifiers, complements, or a subject, all acting together as a single part of speech. Look at these examples:

Infinitive as a Noun: the grindstone begins *to turn . . .*

Infinitive Phrase as a Noun: its song seems *to die up in the leaves . . .*

Infinitive Phrases as Adjectives and Modifying Someone: I wanted more than anything else someone *to race to Horsehead Landing,* someone *to box with,* and someone *to perch with in the top fork of the great pine . . .*

REINFORCE / RETEACH / EXTEND

Selection Support Pages
Build Vocabulary: Irregular Plurals: -x to -ces, p. 147
Build Grammar Skills: Infinitives and Infinitive Phrases, p. 148
Reading Strategy: Identify With a Character, p. 149
Literary Focus: Point of View, p. 150

Strategies for Diverse Student Needs, p. 36

Beyond Literature
Cross-Curricular Connection: Science, p. 36

Formal Assessment Selection Test, pp. 126–128,

Assessment Resources Software

Alternative Assessment, p. 36

Writing and Language Transparencies
Descriptive and Observational Writing, pp. 17–20

Resource Pro CD-ROM
"The Scarlet Ibis"—includes all resource materials and customizable lesson plan

Listening to Literature Audiocassettes
"The Scarlet Ibis"

The Scarlet Ibis

◆ Literature and Your Life

CONNECT YOUR EXPERIENCE
Relationships can be very complicated. Sometimes your best pal can also be your biggest pain in the neck. This type of two-sided relationship often occurs among brothers and sisters. The narrator of this story has a range of conflicting feelings toward his younger brother. Although his brother is his closest companion, the narrator is embarrassed by him and places tremendous demands on him.

THEMATIC FOCUS: FACING CONFLICTS
As you read this story, you'll discover what happens as the narrator tries to work through his conflicting feelings toward his brother.

◆ Background for Understanding

SCIENCE
Found mostly in the tropics of South America, the scarlet ibis is a wading bird with long legs, a long, slender neck, and a wingspan of more than three feet. Bright scarlet in color with black-tipped wings, the scarlet ibis is strikingly beautiful.

These exquisite birds rarely appear in the United States except in Florida. As a result, the discovery of a scarlet ibis in this story's setting, a cotton farm in coastal North Carolina, is an unexpected and dramatic sight.

Journal Writing Jot down how you think you would react if a scarlet ibis or some other type of rare bird suddenly landed in your backyard or on your block. Would you find any special meaning in the event?

◆ Literary Focus

POINT OF VIEW
The **point of view** is the vantage point from which a story is told. Almost all stories are told either from a **third-person point of view**, in which the narrator does not participate in the action, or from a **first-person point of view**, in which the narrator is one of the characters and refers to himself or herself as "I." "The Scarlet Ibis" is told from a first-person point of view. By using the first-person point of view, Hurst makes readers feel as if they are a part of the action and enables them to experience firsthand how the events make the narrator feel.

◆ Reading Strategy

IDENTIFY WITH A CHARACTER
Authors who write in the first person invite you to walk through the story in the shoes of one of the characters. To take advantage of this opportunity, try to **identify with the character** by putting yourself in the character's place and thinking about how you would respond if you experienced the situations and events that the character experiences.

As you read "The Scarlet Ibis," use a chart like the one shown to help you identify with the story's narrator. List key events from the story in one column and record the narrator's reaction to each event. Then note what you might have said, done, or thought in a similar situation.

Story Event	How the Narrator Reacted	How I Might Have Reacted

Guide for Reading ◆ 483

 Preparing for Standardized Tests

Grammar and Language Standardized tests often include sections in which students are called on to identify errors in sentences. Split infinitives—a skill addressed in the Build Grammar Skills section—are among the types of errors often found in these sentences. Following is a sample of what a test item might look like. Write the item on the chalkboard and have students try to come up with the correct answer.

When the announcement came that the train
      (A)
was about to leave,
      (B)
passengers began to rapidly move toward the
      (C)   (D)   (E)
loading platform.

Explain that the correct answer is *(D)*, because the phrase *to rapidly move* contains a split infinitive. For more practice, use the Build Grammar Skills page on Infinitives and Infinitive Phrases, p. 148, in **Selection Support**.

This story poignantly reveals how cruelty and selfishness can be closely linked with love. Toward the beginning of the story, the narrator recounts his disappointment when his brother was born with severe physical disabilities. He then goes on to describe how, motivated by pride and self-interest, he pushed his brother, Doodle, to exceed expectations by learning to walk. Not satisfied by his brother's accomplishment and afraid that he would be embarrassed by having a brother who was different from other children, the narrator pushes Doodle to learn how to swim and to run. Frustrated by Doodle's lack of progress, the narrator abandons Doodle in a storm, and Doodle collapses and dies. Only when Doodle is dead does the narrator discover the depths of his feelings for his brother.

◆ Literary Focus

❶ Point of View Ask students to determine from what point of view this story is told and to explain how they know. *The story is told from a first-person point of view, which is clear from the word "our" at the very end of the paragraph.*

Customize for
English Language Learners

❷ Students who come from countries or cultures where the seasons are not similar to those in the temperate United States may need assistance with this passage. Explain that spring represents childhood; summer, youth; autumn, maturity; and winter, old age. Point out that this passage indicates that the events that the narrator describes happened long ago, when the narrator was young. If time permits, you may want to ask volunteers to describe what seasons are like in their countries of origin. Have the class as a whole discuss how different patterns of seasons might affect the way seasons represent character traits in the literature of different cultures.

The Scarlet Ibis

James Hurst

It was in the clove of seasons, summer was dead but autumn had not yet been born, that the ibis lit in the bleeding tree. The flower garden was stained with rotting brown magnolia petals and ironweeds grew rank amid the purple phlox. The five o'clocks by the chimney still marked time, but the oriole nest in the elm was untenanted and rocked back and forth like an empty cradle. The last graveyard flowers were blooming, and their smell drifted across the **❶** cotton field and through every room of our house, speaking softly the names of our dead. **❶**

It's strange that all this is still so clear to me, now that the summer has long since fled and time has had its way. A grindstone stands where the bleeding tree stood, just outside the kitchen **❷** door, and now if an oriole sings in the elm, its song seems to die up in the leaves, a silvery dust. The flower garden is prim, the house a gleaming white, and the pale fence across the

484 ◆ Short Stories

Block Scheduling Strategies

Consider these suggestions to take advantage of extended class time:

- Remind students to fill out a chart like the one shown in the Reading Strategy (p. 483). You may wish to distribute the Grid graphic organizer, p. 75, in *Writing and Language Transparencies*.

- Use the *Daily Language Practice* for Week 13. You may use the transparency on p. 113 in *Writing and Language Transparencies* or write the sentences on the chalkboard.

- Instruct students to work in groups to answer

the Critical Thinking questions (p. 494).

- Have students work on the Writing Mini-Lesson (p. 495). They can divide into groups based on the character about whom they choose to write. Encourage students to brainstorm for details in groups during prewriting, to draft alone and to revise with partners.

- Invite pairs of students to prepare the Skit in the Speaking and Listening activity (p. 495).

- Allow students to explore the topic of aquatic birds by reading the Beyond Literature feature (p. 493) and finding answers to its questions.

❸ yard stands straight and spruce. But sometimes (like right now), as I sit in the cool, green-draped parlor, the grindstone begins to turn, and time with all its changes is ground away—and I remember Doodle.

Doodle was just about the craziest brother a boy ever had. Of course, he wasn't a crazy crazy like old Miss Leedie, who was in love with President Wilson and wrote him a letter every day, but was a nice crazy, like someone you meet in your dreams. He was born when I was six and was, from the outset, a disappointment. He seemed all head, with a tiny body which was red and shriveled like an old man's. Everybody ❹ thought he was going to die—everybody except Aunt Nicey, who had delivered him. She said he would live because he was born in a caul[1] and cauls were made from Jesus' nightgown. Daddy had Mr. Heath, the carpenter, build a little mahogany coffin for him. But he didn't die, and when he was three months old Mama and Daddy decided they might as well name him. They named him William Armstrong, which was like tying a big tail on a small kite. Such a name sounds good only on a tombstone.

I thought myself pretty smart at many things, like holding my breath, running, jumping, or climbing the vines in Old Woman Swamp, and I wanted more than anything else someone to race to Horsehead Landing, someone to box with, and someone to perch with in the top fork of the great pine behind the barn, where across the fields and swamps you could see the sea. I ❺ wanted a brother. But Mama, crying, told me that even if William Armstrong lived, he would never do these things with me. He might not, she sobbed, even be "all there." He might, as long as he lived, lie on the rubber sheet in the center of the bed in the front bedroom where the white marquisette curtains billowed out in the afternoon sea breeze, rustling like palmetto fronds.[2]

---

1. **caul:** (kôl) *n.*: Membrane enclosing a baby at birth.
2. **palmetto fronds:** Palm leaves.

It was bad enough having an invalid brother, but having one who possibly was not all there was unbearable, so I began to make plans to kill him by smothering him with a pillow. However, one afternoon as I watched him, my head poked between the iron posts of the foot of the bed, he looked straight at me and grinned. I skipped through the rooms, down the echoing halls, shouting, "Mama, he smiled. He's all there! He's all there!" and he was.

When he was two, if you laid him on his stomach, he began to try to move himself, straining terribly. The doctor said that with his weak heart this strain would probably kill him, but it didn't. ❻ Trembling, he'd push himself up, turning first red, then a soft purple, and finally collapse back onto the bed like an old worn-out doll. I can still see Mama watching him, her hand pressed tight across her mouth, her eyes wide and unblinking. But he learned to crawl (it was his third winter), and we brought him out of the front bedroom, putting him on the rug before the fireplace. For the first time he became one of us.

As long as he lay all the time in bed, we called him William Armstrong, even though it was formal and sounded as if we were referring to one of our ancestors, but with his creeping around on the deerskin rug and beginning to talk, something had to be done about his name. It was I who renamed him. When he crawled, he crawled backwards, as if he were in reverse and couldn't change gears. If you called him, he'd turn around as if he were going in the other direction, then he'd back right up to you to be picked up. Crawling backward made him look like a doodle-bug, so I began to call him Doodle, and in time even Mama and Daddy thought it was a better name than William Armstrong. Only Aunt Nicey disagreed. She said caul babies should be treated with special respect since they might turn out to be saints. Renaming my brother was perhaps the kindest thing I ever did for him, because nobody expects much from someone called Doodle.

 Beyond the Classroom

Community Connection

Local Wildlife The narrator of "The Scarlet Ibis" refers, throughout the story, to the birds and other animals that live in his area. Invite students to find out more about the birds and animals native to your area. Students might visit a local wildlife preserve and report back to the class. You might also invite someone from a local conservation organization to talk to the class about area wildlife.

Local Vegetation The narrator also refers to the flowers and plants that grow in his region. Encourage students to research flowers and plants in their area. Have them find books on botany in the library, check with local nursery or agricultural organizations, or search the Web on the Internet to find information.

Discuss with students how the descriptions of fauna and flora add to the story.

◆ *Literature and Your Life*

1 Many students will say they identify with the narrator's frustration at having to take care of a fragile sibling. They may also say that they, like the narrator, would still love their brother and would want to share favorite activities with him.

◆ **Literary Focus**

2 **Point of View** Invite students to imagine how this passage might be different if a third-person narrator were telling the story. What might readers miss? What would they gain? *Students might speculate that a third-person narrator would not involve them so deeply in the character's feelings. A third-person narrator might offer a more objective view that would be less judgmental of the character than he is of himself.*

◆ **Critical Thinking**

3 **Evaluate** Ask students if the narrator seems like a real person to them. *Students may say that the narrator seems like a real person because of the way he teases his brother. Some students may find it hard to accept the older brother's cruelty.*

Although Doodle learned to crawl, he showed no signs of walking, but he wasn't idle. He talked so much that we all quit listening to what he said. It was about this time that Daddy built him a go-cart and I had to pull him around. At first I just paraded him up and down the piazza, but then he started crying to be taken out into the yard and it ended up by my having to lug him wherever I went. If I so much as picked up my cap, he'd start crying to go with me and Mama would call from wherever she was, "Take Doodle with you."

He was a burden in many ways. The doctor had said that he mustn't get too excited, too hot, too cold, or too tired and that he must always be treated gently. A long list of don'ts went with him, all of which I ignored once we got out of the house. To discourage his coming with me, I'd run with him across the ends of the cotton rows and careen him around corners on two wheels. Sometimes I accidentally turned him over, but he never told Mama. His skin was very sensitive, and he had to wear a big straw hat whenever he went out. When the going got rough and he had to cling to the sides of the go-cart, the hat slipped all the way down over his ears. He was a sight. Finally, I could see I was licked. Doodle was my brother and he was going to cling to me forever, no matter what I did, so I dragged him across the burning cotton field to share with him the only beauty I knew, Old Woman Swamp. I pulled the go-cart through the saw-tooth fern, down into the green dimness where the palmetto fronds whispered by the stream. I lifted him out and set him down in the soft rubber grass beside a tall pine. His eyes were round with wonder as he gazed about him, and his little hands began to stroke the rubber grass. Then he began to cry.

"For heaven's sake, what's the matter?" I asked, annoyed.

◆ *Literature and Your Life*

1 How would you feel if you had to take a brother like Doodle everywhere you went?

"It's so pretty," he said. "So pretty, pretty, pretty."

After that day Doodle and I often went down into Old Woman Swamp. I would gather wildflowers, wild violets, honeysuckle, yellow jasmine, snakeflowers, and water lilies, and with wire grass we'd weave them into necklaces and crowns. We'd bedeck ourselves with our handiwork and loll about thus beautified, beyond the touch of the everyday world. Then when the slanted rays of the sun burned orange in the tops of the pines, we'd drop our jewels into the stream and watch them float away toward the sea.

There is within me (and with sadness I have watched it in others) a knot of cruelty borne by the stream of love, much as our blood sometimes bears the seed of our destruction, and at times I was mean to Doodle. One day I took him up to the barn loft and showed him his casket, telling him how we all had believed he would die. It was covered with a film of Paris green[3] sprinkled to kill the rats, and screech owls had built a nest inside it.

2

Doodle studied the mahogany box for a long time, then said, "It's not mine."

"It is," I said. "And before I'll help you down from the loft, you're going to have to touch it."

"I won't touch it," he said sullenly.

"Then I'll leave you here by yourself," I threatened, and made as if I were going down.

Doodle was frightened of being left. "Don't go leave me, Brother," he cried, and he leaned toward the coffin. His hand, trembling, reached out, and when he touched the casket he screamed. A screech owl flapped out of the box into our faces, scaring us and covering us with Paris green. Doodle was paralyzed, so I put him on my shoulder and carried him down the ladder, and even when we were outside in the bright sunshine, he clung to me, crying, "Don't leave me. Don't leave me."

3

---

3. **Paris green:** Poisonous green powder.

Two Boys in a Punt, N. C. Wyeth, Courtesy of Dr. and Mrs. William A. Morton, Jr.

▲ Critical Viewing Doodle and his brother spend many hours exploring Old Woman Swamp. What can you tell about the brothers' relationship from this illustration and the details in the story? [Infer] ❹

The Scarlet Ibis ◆ 487

Build Grammar Skills

1 Infinitives and Infinitive Phrases Ask students to identify the infinitives in this passage and to explain how they function. *The infinitives are to teach, to walk, and to haul. They act as nouns.*

◆ Critical Thinking

2 Interpret Ask students: Why is the narrator's pride in Doodle both wonderful and terrible? *The narrator's pride in Doodle is wonderful because it motivates him to want to teach Doodle to walk; it is terrible because it makes the narrator act meanly to Doodle—he is going to get Doodle to walk whether he likes it or not.*

◆ Critical Thinking

3 Infer Ask students why they think that the picture of the two brothers as old men "never failed to make [Doodle] try again." *Students may speculate that Doodle is ashamed of the idea of being an old man in a go-cart. Some may think Doodle is motivated by the humor in the mental image his brother paints for him.*

◆ Reading Strategy

4 Identify With a Character Ask students if they have ever prepared a surprise for someone. Have them put themselves in the narrator's place. How would they feel during the time leading up to the surprise? How would they feel at the moment the surprise is revealed? *Students may say they would be bursting with impatience to present the surprise, and that when they finally did present it, they would feel proud, excited, satisfied.*

When Doodle was five years old, I was embarrassed at having a brother of that age who couldn't walk, so I set out to teach him. We were down in Old Woman Swamp and it was spring and the sick-sweet smell of bay flowers hung everywhere like a mournful song. "I'm going to teach you to walk, Doodle," I said.

He was sitting comfortably on the soft grass, leaning back against the pine. "Why?" he asked.

I hadn't expected such an answer. "So I won't have to haul you around all the time."

"I can't walk, Brother," he said.

"Who says so?" I demanded.

"Mama, the doctor–everybody."

"Oh, you can walk," I said, and I took him by the arms and stood him up. He collapsed onto the grass like a half-empty flour sack. It was as if he had no bones in his little legs.

"Don't hurt me, Brother," he warned.

"Shut up. I'm not going to hurt you. I'm going to teach you to walk." I heaved him up again, and again he collapsed.

This time he did not lift his face up out of the rubber grass. "I just can't do it. Let's make honeysuckle wreaths."

"Oh yes you can, Doodle," I said. "All you got to do is try. Now come on," and I hauled him up once more.

It seemed so hopeless from the beginning that it's a miracle I didn't give up. But all of us must have something or someone to be proud of, and Doodle had become mine. I did not know then that pride is a wonderful, terrible thing, a seed that bears two vines, life and death. Every day that summer we went to the pine beside the stream of Old Woman Swamp, and I put him on his feet at least a hundred times each afternoon. Occasionally I too became discouraged because it didn't seem as if he was trying, and I would say, "Doodle, don't you *want* to learn to walk?"

He'd nod his head, and I'd say, "Well, if you don't keep trying, you'll never learn." Then I'd paint for him a picture of us as old men, white-haired, him with a long white beard and me still pulling him around in the go-cart. This never failed to make him try again.

Finally one day, after many weeks of practicing, he stood alone for a few seconds. When he fell, I grabbed him in my arms and hugged him, our laughter pealing through the swamp like a ringing bell. Now we knew it could be done. Hope no longer hid in the dark palmetto thicket but perched like a cardinal in the lacy toothbrush tree, brilliantly visible. "Yes, yes," I cried, and he cried it too, and the grass beneath us was soft and the smell of the swamp was sweet.

With success so <u>imminent</u>, we decided not to tell anyone until he could actually walk. Each day, barring rain, we sneaked into Old Woman Swamp, and by cotton-picking time Doodle was ready to show what he could do. He still wasn't able to walk far, but we could wait no longer. Keeping a nice secret is very hard to do, like holding your breath. We chose to reveal all on October eighth, Doodle's sixth birthday, and for weeks ahead we mooned around the house, promising everybody a most spectacular surprise. Aunt Nicey said that, after so much talk, if we produced anything less tremendous than the Resurrection,[4] she was going to be disappointed.

At breakfast on our chosen day, when Mama, Daddy, and Aunt Nicey were in the dining room, I brought Doodle to the door in the go-cart just as usual and had them turn their backs, making them cross their hearts and hope to die if they peeked. I helped Doodle up, and when he was standing alone I let them look. There wasn't a sound as Doodle walked slowly across the room and sat down at his place at the table. Then Mama began to cry and ran over to him, hugging him and kissing him. Daddy hugged him too, so I went to Aunt Nicey, who was thanks praying in the doorway, and began to waltz her around. We danced together quite well until she came down on my big toe with her brogans, hurting me so badly I thought I was crippled for life.

Doodle told them it was I who had taught him

---

4. **the Resurrection:** (res´ e rek´ shen): The rising of Jesus Christ from the dead after his death and burial.

488 ◆ *Short Stories*

Speaking and Listening Mini-Lesson

Eulogy

This mini-lesson supports the Speaking and Listening activity in the Idea Bank on page 495.

Introduce the Concept Explain that a eulogy is a speech given in honor of someone who has died. Usually, a eulogy is given at a funeral or memorial service. Like all speeches, a eulogy consists of an attention-getting introduction, an information-presenting body, and a wrapping-up conclusion. The body of a eulogy typically consist of anec-

dotes that highlight the deceased's positive qualities. Have students talk about why people give eulogies at funerals.

Develop Background Before students begin to write their eulogies, work as a class to list the information about Doodle that should be included in such a speech. Prompt students with questions like these:
• Who will be at Doodle's funeral?
• What kinds of stories or facts about Doodle might comfort them?

Apply the Information With this background, students should be able to write their eulogies. Encourage volunteers to deliver their eulogies to the class.

Assess the Outcome The eulogies can be assessed using the following criteria: Did the speaker speak clearly? Was the eulogy clearly organized? Was the content appropriate? Did the content reflect an understanding of the story?

to walk, so everyone wanted to hug me, and I began to cry.

"What are you crying for?" asked Daddy, but I couldn't answer. They did not know that I did it for myself; that pride, whose slave I was, spoke to me louder than all their voices, and that Doodle walked only because I was ashamed of having a crippled brother.

Within a few months Doodle had learned to walk well and his go-cart was put up in the barn loft (it's still there) beside his little mahogany coffin. Now, when we roamed off together, resting often, we never turned back until our destination had been reached, and to help pass the time, we took up lying. From the beginning Doodle was a terrible liar and he got me in the habit. Had anyone stopped to listen to us, we would have been sent off to Dix Hill.

My lies were scary, involved, and usually pointless, but Doodle's were twice as crazy. People in his stories all had wings and flew wherever they wanted to go. His favorite lie was about a boy named Peter who had a pet peacock with a ten-foot tail. Peter wore a golden robe that glittered so brightly that when he walked through the sunflowers they turned away from the sun to face him. When Peter was ready to go to sleep, the peacock spread his magnificent tail, enfolding the boy gently like a closing go-to-sleep flower, burying him in the gloriously iridescent, rustling vortex. Yes, I must admit it. Doodle could beat me lying.

Doodle and I spent lots of time thinking about our future. We decided that when we were grown we'd live in Old Woman Swamp and pick dog-tongue for a living. Beside the stream, he planned, we'd build us a house of whispering leaves and the swamp birds would be our chickens. All day long (when we weren't gathering dog-tongue) we'd swing through the cypresses on the rope vines, and if it rained we'd huddle beneath an umbrella tree and play stickfrog. Mama and Daddy could come and live with us if they wanted to. He even came up with the idea that he could marry Mama and I could marry

Daddy. Of course, I was old enough to know this wouldn't work out, but the picture he painted was so beautiful and serene that all I could do was whisper Yes, yes.

Once I had succeeded in teaching Doodle to walk, I began to believe in my own infallibility and I prepared a terrific development program for him, unknown to Mama and Daddy, of course. I would teach him to run, to swim, to climb trees, and to fight. He, too, now believed in my infallibility, so we set the deadline for these accomplishments less than a year away, when, it had been decided, Doodle could start to school.

That winter we didn't make much progress, for I was in school and Doodle suffered from one bad cold after another. But when spring came, rich and warm, we raised our sights again. Success lay at the end of summer like a pot of gold, and our campaign got off to a good start. On hot days, Doodle and I went down to Horsehead Landing and I gave him swimming lessons or showed him how to row a boat. Sometimes we descended into the cool greenness of Old Woman Swamp and climbed the rope vines or boxed scientifically beneath the pine where he had learned to walk. Promise hung about us like the leaves, and wherever we looked, ferns unfurled and birds broke into song.

That summer, the summer of 1918, was blighted. In May and June there was no rain

◆ **Reading Strategy**
The narrator becomes even more determined to help Doodle after his success with walking. Would you have felt the same way? Why or why not?

◆ **Build Vocabulary**

imminent (im′ ə nent) *adj.*: Likely to happen soon

iridescent (ir′ ə des′ ənt) *adj.*: Having shifting, rainbowlike colors

vortex (vôr′ teks) *n.*: Center of a situation, which draws in all that surrounds it

infallibility (in fal′ ə bil′ ə tē) *n.*: Condition of being unable to fail

The Scarlet Ibis ◆ 489

◆ **Critical Thinking**

❺ **Make Judgments** Ask students if they agree with the narrator that he doesn't deserve praise because his actions were motivated by pride.
Some students may agree that the narrator acted more out of selfishness than love. Others may think the motivation is not as important as the outcome—Doodle will be much happier now that he can walk.

◆ **Critical Thinking**

❻ **Analyze** Ask students why they think Doodle tells such good "lies."
Students may say that Doodle likes to imagine himself as being able to fly because he has only just learned to walk. Dependent on his brother, he imagines a boy whom even peacocks and sunflowers obey.

◆ **Build Vocabulary**

❼ **Irregular Plurals: -x to -ces** Ask students to identify the word ending in *x*. *vortex* Then ask how that word forms its plural. *vortices*

◆ **Reading Strategy**

❽ **Identify With a Character** Students who agree may say that having one success would lead them to believe that even more successes are possible. Students who don't agree may say that it would make them fearful of pushing their luck.

◆ *Literature and Your Life*

❾ Invite students to describe how the narrator and Doodle are feeling at this point. Ask them to use their own experience to explain why the characters feel this way. *Students may say that, because of their previous success, and because spring is the season of hope, both boys are feeling hopeful about their plans.*

 Beyond the Classroom

Career Connection
Special Education In this story, the narrator works closely with his physically challenged brother, teaching him to walk and to perform other physically challenging tasks. Special-education teachers, physical therapists, and a range of other special-education specialists work with children—and, in some cases, adults—who have similar physical disabilities resulting from birth defects (as in Doodle's case), from accidents, from stroke, or from degenerative diseases.

Invite interested students to interview a special-education teacher or specialist at your school or in your community. Encourage them to ask such questions as:
• Why did you choose this field?
• What training and study did you need?
• What are your greatest challenges?
• What are your greatest rewards?
Encourage students to report back to the class on what they find out.

▶Critical Viewing◀

❶ Relate Students might say they would feel awed, frightened, or excited to see a scarlet ibis.

Customize for
Bodily/Kinesthetic Learners

❷ These students will gain a better understanding of the setting and mood of this passage if they act it out. Encourage them to choreograph a dance that shows the action in the scene, or to read the passage as dramatically (but seriously) as possible, using gestures to emphasize meaning.

Customize for
More Advanced Students

❸ Ask students where they have heard the phrase "clove of seasons" before in the story. What purpose does the repetition serve? *The phrase appears in the first sentence of the story. The repetition signals that now the narrator will get to the main part of the story—the part he set out to tell at the beginning.*

◆ Literary Focus

❹ Point of View Students may say that the narrator is so caught up in getting Doodle to be a "normal," physically active boy that he fails to pay attention to medical warning signs, such as Doodle's turning red or collapsing from exhaustion. In addition, the narrator fears having a brother who is different. He is determined to have a "normal" brother, even if Doodle doesn't care about being normal himself.

Scarlet Ibis, John James Audubon, New-York Historical Society

❶ ▲ Critical Viewing Like its relative—the sacred ibis of Egypt—the scarlet ibis lives in swampy areas and uses its long bill to probe in mud and shallow water for food. How would you react if this exotic bird showed up in *your* back yard? [Relate]

and the crops withered, curled up, then died under the thirsty sun. One morning in July a hurricane came out of the east, tipping over the oaks in the yard and splitting the limbs of the elm trees. That afternoon it roared back out of ❷ the west, blew the fallen oaks around, snapping their roots and tearing them out of the earth like a hawk at the <u>entrails</u> of a chicken. Cotton bolls were wrenched from the stalks and lay like green walnuts in the valleys between the rows, while the cornfield leaned over

uniformly so that the tassels touched the ground. Doodle and I followed Daddy out into the cotton field, where he stood, shoulders sagging, surveying the ruin. When his chin sank down onto his chest, we were frightened, and Doodle slipped his hand into mine. Suddenly Daddy straightened his shoulders, raised a giant knuckly fist, and with a voice that seemed to rumble out of the earth itself began cursing heaven, hell, the weather, and the Republican Party. Doodle and I, prodding each other and giggling, went back to the house, knowing that everything would be all right. ❷

And during that summer, strange names were heard through the house: Chateau Thierry, Amiens, Soissons, and in her blessing at the supper table, Mama once said, "And bless the Pearsons, whose boy Joe was lost at Belleau Wood."[5]

So we came to that clove of seasons. School ❸ was only a few weeks away, and Doodle was far behind schedule. He could barely clear the ground when climbing up the rope vines and his swimming was certainly not passable. We decided to double our efforts, to make that last drive and reach our pot of gold. I made him swim until he turned blue and row until he couldn't lift an oar. Wherever we went, I purposely walked fast, and although he kept up, his face turned red and his eyes became glazed. Once, he could go no further, so he collapsed on the ground and began to cry.

"Aw, come on, Doodle," I urged. "You can do it. Do you want to be different from everybody else when you start school?"

◆ Literary Focus
What more do you learn about the narrator through his words and actions toward Doodle? ❹

5. **Château Thierry:** (sha to tye re´), **Amiens** (a myan´), **Soissons** (swä sôn´), . . . **Belleau** (belo´) **Wood:** Places in France where battles were fought during World War I.

490 ◆ Short Stories

 Humanities: Art

The Scarlet Ibis, by John James Audubon.
This illustration represents the lovely bird, the name of which appears in the title of the story.
John James Audubon was one of the first artists ever to study and paint the birds of the United States. Audubon could not find an American publisher for his first collection of colored engravings of American birds, but the British edition of *Birds of America* brought him fame and fortune when it appeared from 1826 to 1838.

Use these questions for discussion:
1. What qualities of the scarlet ibis might have made it seem exotic or surprising to the characters in the story? *The bird's brilliant red color; its long, thin neck; and its distinctive, curved beak might have seemed exotic.*
2. How is the bird in this picture like Doodle? *It is fragile, otherworldly, unusual, with its own special beauty.*

"Does it make any difference?"

5 "It certainly does," I said. "Now, come on," and I helped him up.

As we slipped through dog days, Doodle began to look feverish, and Mama felt his forehead, asking him if he felt ill. At night he didn't sleep well, and sometimes he had nightmares, crying out until I touched him and said, "Wake up, Doodle. Wake up."

6 It was Saturday noon, just a few days before school was to start. I should have already admitted defeat, but my pride wouldn't let me. The excitement of our program had now been gone for weeks, but still we kept on with a tired doggedness. It was too late to turn back, for we **7** had both wandered too far into a net of expectations and had left no crumbs behind.

Daddy, Mama, Doodle, and I were seated at the dining-room table having lunch. It was a hot day, with all the windows and doors open in case a breeze should come. In the kitchen Aunt Nicey was humming softly. After a long silence, Daddy spoke. "It's so calm, I wouldn't be surprised if we had a storm this afternoon."

"I haven't heard a rain frog," said Mama, who believed in signs, as she served the bread around the table.

"I did," declared Doodle. "Down in the swamp."

"He didn't," I said contrarily.

"You did, eh?" said Daddy, ignoring my denial.

"I certainly did," Doodle reiterated, scowling at me over the top of his iced-tea glass, and we were quiet again.

Suddenly, from out in the yard, came a strange croaking noise. Doodle stopped eating, with a piece of bread poised ready for his mouth, his eyes popped round like two blue buttons. "What's that?" he whispered.

I jumped up, knocking over my chair, and had reached the door when Mama called, "Pick up the chair, sit down again, and say excuse me."

By the time I had done this, Doodle had excused himself and had slipped out into the yard. He was looking up into the bleeding tree. "It's a great big red bird!" he called.

The bird croaked loudly again, and Mama and Daddy came out into the yard. We shaded our eyes with our hands against the hazy glare of the sun and peered up through the still leaves. On the topmost branch a bird the size of a chicken, with scarlet feathers and long legs, was perched <u>precariously</u>. Its wings hung down loosely, and as we watched, a feather dropped away and floated slowly down through the green leaves.

"It's not even frightened of us," Mama said.

"It looks tired," Daddy added. "Or maybe sick."

Doodle's hands were clasped at his throat, and I had never seen him stand still so long. "What is it?" he asked.

Daddy shook his head. "I don't know, maybe it's—"

At that moment the bird began to flutter, but **8** the wings were uncoordinated, and amid much flapping and a spray of flying feathers, it tumbled down, bumping through the limbs of the bleeding tree and landing at our feet with a thud. Its long, graceful neck jerked twice into an S, then straightened out, and the bird was still. A white veil came over the eyes and the long white beak unhinged. Its legs were crossed and its clawlike feet were delicately curved at rest. Even death did not mar its grace, for it lay on the earth like a broken vase of red flowers, and we stood around it, awed by its exotic beauty.

"It's dead," Mama said.

"What is it?" Doodle repeated.

"Go bring me the bird book," said Daddy.

I ran into the house and brought back the bird book. As we watched, Daddy thumbed through its pages. "It's a scarlet ibis," he said, pointing to a picture. "It lives in the tropics—South America to Florida. A storm must have brought it here."

◆ Build Vocabulary

entrails (en´ trālz) *n.*: Internal organs, specifically intestines

precariously (prē ker´ ē əs lē) *adv.*: Insecurely

The Scarlet Ibis ◆ 491

◆ Critical Thinking

5 Contrast Ask students to contrast the narrator's and Doodle's feelings about being "different from everybody else." Invite them to suggest reasons for the contrast. *Students should note that the narrator is concerned, not only about being "different" himself, but also about having a brother who is "different," whereas Doodle doesn't understand the importance of being like others. Students might speculate that the narrator can, in fact, be like others, whereas Doodle has long ago accepted that he is different.*

◆ Critical Thinking

6 Analyze Invite students to explain what the narrator wants to be proud of. *Students might suggest that he wants to be proud of his own ability to accomplish difficult tasks, or that he wants to be proud of having a "normal" brother.*

Customize for
Less Proficient Readers

7 Students may have difficulty understanding the metaphor and allusion in this passage. Explain that the two boys have not walked into a literal net, but a situation that is like a net. Their expectations, like a net, trap Doodle and his brother into a course of action that will end in disaster. Point out that the phrase "had left no crumbs behind" may refer to folk tales, such as "Hansel and Gretel," in which the characters leave a trail of crumbs in order to find their way back. Ask students what the phrase about crumbs means. *It means that the narrator and Doodle cannot find their way back from the bad situation that they are in.*

◆ Build Grammar Skills

8 Infinitives and Infinitive Phrases Ask students to identify the infinitive and to tell how it is used. *The infinitive to flutter is used as a noun.*

Cross-Curricular Connection: Social Studies

World Conflicts World War I forms part of the background for the story. World War I was fought by the Allies —primarily France, Britain, Russia, and the United States—and the Central Powers—Germany, Turkey, and the Austro-Hungarian empire. Today, the war is generally viewed as a conflict over territory. The German empire was determined to establish itself as the major military power in Europe and to challenge Britain's naval superiority. The Allies, on the other hand, were committed to maintaining their economic superiority as well as their extensive colonial holdings in Africa and Asia.

Ask students why the author included details about the war in the story. One possible answer is that it makes the story seem more real by placing the events in a historical time period.

Suggest that students consult an atlas or an encyclopedia to find a map of France that shows the location of the town mentioned in the story.

❶ **Interpret** Ask students what they think it means that Doodle is the most affected and saddened by the ibis's death. *Students might say that Doodle identifies with the ibis. Like the ibis, Doodle has been feeling sick and weak. Also, he is different from those around him.*

◆ **Critical Thinking**

❷ **Analyze** Ask students what these actions reveal about Doodle. *Students might note that he is compassionate, identifies with the ibis, is inventive (because he thinks of the string), and is determined (he doesn't give up even though it is difficult for him to dig).*

◆ **Reading Strategy**

❸ **Identify With a Character** Some students may identify with Doodle's compassion and sympathy. Others may identify with the narrator's less intense concern or with Mama's fear of disease.

◆ **Reading Strategy**

❹ **Identify With a Character** Ask students with which character they now identify more—Doodle or the narrator. Even if students say they identify with neither, encourage them to try to put themselves in each character's place. *Some students may identify with the narrator because they understand the experience of feeling let down by another person. Other students may identify with Doodle, relating to his need for approval.*

Sadly, we all looked back at the bird. A scarlet ibis! How many miles it had traveled to die like this, in *our* yard, beneath the bleeding tree.

"Let's finish lunch," Mama said, nudging us back toward the dining room.

"I'm not hungry," said Doodle, and he knelt down beside the ibis.

"We've got peach cobbler for dessert," Mama tempted from the doorway.

Doodle remained kneeling. "I'm going to bury him."

"Don't you dare touch him," Mama warned. "There's no telling what disease he might have had."

"All right," said Doodle. "I won't."

Daddy, Mama, and I went back to the dining-room table, but we watched Doodle through the open door. He took out a piece of string from his pocket and, without touching the ibis, looped one end around its neck. Slowly, while singing softly "Shall We Gather at the River," he carried the bird around to the front yard and dug a hole in the flower garden, next to the petunia bed. Now we were watching him through the front window, but he didn't know it. His awkwardness at digging the hole with a shovel whose handle was twice as long as he was made us laugh, and we covered our mouths with our hands so he wouldn't hear.

> ◆ **Reading Strategy**
> With whose response toward the ibis do you most strongly identify? Why?

When Doodle came into the dining room, he found us seriously eating our cobbler. He was pale and lingered just inside the screen door. "Did you get the scarlet ibis buried?" asked Daddy.

Doodle didn't speak but nodded his head.

"Go wash your hands, and then you can have some peach cobbler," said Mama.

"I'm not hungry," he said.

"Dead birds is bad luck," said Aunt Nicey, poking her head from the kitchen door. "Specially *red* dead birds!"

As soon as I had finished eating, Doodle and I hurried off to Horsehead Landing. Time was short, and Doodle still had a long way to go if he was going to keep up with the other boys when he started school. The sun, gilded with the yellow cast of autumn, still burned fiercely, but the dark green woods through which we passed were shady and cool. When we reached the landing, Doodle said he was too tired to swim, so we got into a skiff and floated down the creek with the tide. Far off in the marsh a rail was scolding, and over on the beach locusts were singing in the myrtle trees. Doodle did not speak and kept his head turned away, letting one hand trail limply in the water.

After we had drifted a long way, I put the oars in place and made Doodle row back against the tide. Black clouds began to gather in the southwest, and he kept watching them, trying to pull the oars a little faster. When we reached Horsehead Landing, lightning was playing across half the sky and thunder roared out, hiding even the sound of the sea. The sun disappeared and darkness descended, almost like night. Flocks of marsh crows flew by, heading inland to their roosting trees, and two egrets, squawking, arose from the oyster-rock shallows and careened away.

Doodle was both tired and frightened, and when he stepped from the skiff he collapsed onto the mud, sending an armada of fiddler crabs rustling off into the marsh grass. I helped him up, and as he wiped the mud off his trousers, he smiled at me ashamedly. He had failed and we both knew it, so we started back home, racing the storm. We never spoke (What are the words that can solder cracked pride?), but I knew he was watching me, watching for a sign of mercy. The lightning was near now, and from fear he walked so close behind me he kept stepping on my heels. The faster I walked, the faster he walked, so I began to run. The rain was coming, roaring through the pines, and then, like a bursting Roman candle, a gum tree ahead of us was shattered by a bolt of lightning. When the deafening peal of thunder had

---

 Speaking and Listening Mini-Lesson

Skit

This mini-lesson supports the Speaking and Listening activity in the Idea Bank on page 495.

Introduce the Concept Explain that a skit is a short, informal drama. Like any drama, a skit requires actors to deliver dialogue, to gesture, and to move. The staging for a skit is minimal: in general there are few props and no sets, costumes, or special

effects. As a class, discuss why the narrator might have hidden the story of Doodle's death from his mother, as well as why he might now be telling her the story.

Develop Background Encourage pairs of students to explore the issues involved in their skit by considering these questions:

• How does the narrator feel about Doodle's death? How does the mother feel?

• How will the mother probably react when she first hears the truth? How will the narrator feel about her reaction?

Apply the Information Encourage students to rehearse their skit and then present it to the class.

Assess the Outcome Students can use the Peer Assessment: Dramatic Performance page in *Alternative Assessment*, p. 113, to evaluate the skits.

died, and in the moment before the rain arrived, I heard Doodle, who had fallen behind, cry out, "Brother, Brother, don't leave me! Don't leave me!"

❹ The knowledge that Doodle's and my plans had come to naught was bitter, and that streak of cruelty within me awakened. I ran as fast as I could, leaving him far behind with a wall of rain dividing us. The drops stung my face like nettles, and the wind flared the wet glistening leaves of the bordering trees. Soon I could hear his voice no more.

I hadn't run too far before I became tired, and the flood of childish spite evanesced as well. I stopped and waited for Doodle. The sound of rain was everywhere, but the wind had died and it fell straight down in parallel paths like ropes hanging from the sky. As I waited, I peered through the downpour, but no one came. Finally I went back and found him huddled beneath a red nightshade bush beside the road. He was sitting on the ground, his face buried in his arms, which were resting on his drawn-up knees. "Let's go, Doodle," I said.

He didn't answer, so I placed my hand on his forehead and lifted his head. Limply, he fell backwards onto the earth. He had been bleeding from the mouth, and his neck and the front of his shirt were stained a brilliant red.

"Doodle! Doodle!" I cried, shaking him, but there was no answer but the ropy rain. He lay **❺** very awkwardly, with his head thrown far back, making his vermilion neck appear unusually long and slim. His little legs, bent sharply at the knees, had never before seemed so fragile, so thin.

I began to weep, and the tear-blurred vision in red before me looked very familiar. "Doodle!" I screamed above the pounding storm and threw my body to the earth above his. For a long long time, it seemed forever, I lay there crying, sheltering my fallen scarlet ibis from the heresy[6] of rain.

---

6. **heresy** (her´ e se): Idea opposed to the beliefs of a religion or philosophy.

Guide for Responding

◆ Literature and Your Life

Reader's Response How did the end of the story make you feel? Why?

Thematic Focus How else might the narrator have resolved his conflicting feelings about Doodle?

☑ Check Your Comprehension

1. How does Doodle disappoint his brother?
2. What motivates the narrator to teach Doodle to walk?
3. What other plans does he make for Doodle?
4. Summarize the circumstances leading to Doodle's death.

Beyond Literature

Science Connection

Sea Birds The scarlet ibis is only one of a myriad of types of sea birds found in North America. Birds of the Pacific coast include the black oystercatcher and the western gull. Birds of the Atlantic coast include the American oystercatcher and the common tern. In winter, the southern coasts are home to certain varieties of ducks, geese, and other birds that nest in the Arctic during the summer. Some birds, such as the great blue heron, usually live in inland waters but sometimes nest near the ocean in order to hunt for fish along the coasts. What birds live in your area? Do any of them live near water?

◆ Build Vocabulary

evanesced (ev ə nest´) v.: Faded away

The Scarlet Ibis ◆ 493

◆ Critical Thinking

❺ Interpret Ask students what point the narrator seems to be making with this description of Doodle.

Students should see that the narrator is comparing Doodle to the scarlet ibis: His head is thrown back; his neck is vermillion and appears "unusually long and slim"; his legs are bent at the knees and appear fragile and thin.

Reinforce and Extend

Answers

◆ Literature and Your Life

Reader's Response Most students will react with sadness and somber reflection.

Thematic Focus Students will probably respond that the narrator could have tried to better understand Doodle and relate to him on his own terms.

☑ Check Your Comprehension

1. Doodle is a disappointment to his brother because the narrator wanted someone to race with, someone to box with, and someone to share his world in a physical way. He is also disappointed at having a brother for whom he must care constantly.
2. He is tired of hauling Doodle around everywhere, he's embarrassed at having a brother of that age who can't walk, and he believes he'll be proud that he was able to teach Doodle to walk.
3. He plans to teach Doodle to run, to swim, to climb trees, to fight.
4. Doodle and his brother are returning home from the swamp, and Doodle is exhausted from his day of exercise. Frightened by the lightning and thunder, he begs his brother not to leave him, but the narrator, disappointed in Doodle's physical performance, runs away as fast as he can. Soon the narrator stops, waits, and calls to Doodle; then he doubles back. He finds Doodle huddled on the ground, dead.

Beyond the Selection

FURTHER READING

Other Works by James Hurst
"August Snow"
"Once There Came a Cobra"
"The Summer of Two Figs"

Other Works About Family and Conflict
Arilla Sundown, Virginia Hamilton
Very Far Away From Anywhere Else, Ursula LeGuin
A Wind in the Door, Madeleine L'Engle

INTERNET

For students who wish to find out more about coastal North Carolina, the setting of the story, we suggest the following site. Please be aware, however, that the site may have changed from the time we published this information.
http://sunsite.unc.edu/nc/regionalinfo.html
We *strongly recommend* that you preview the site before you send students to it.

◆ Critical Thinking

1. (a) Doodle looks up to and depends on his brother. (b) He is disappointed at having such a brother, and is bothered by the inconvenience it causes him; at the same time, he develops a special kind of love for him.

2. On the surface, the narrator is motivated by selfishness and pride. It is, however, also reasonable to infer that the narrator acted out of boredom, brotherly affection, or even curiosity.

3. Doodle doesn't always just go along with his brother. He has a rich imaginary life. He responds to the ibis differently from the way others do.

4. Doodle and the ibis are different—out of place where they "land" and extremely difficult for others to "identify" or understand. Both die as a result of a storm, and both die in similar positions.

5. The death of the fragile ibis foreshadows the death of Doodle.

6. Students may judge that the narrator is directly responsible for Doodle's death because he drove him too strenuously and abandoned him in the storm. On the other hand, they may point out that Doodle's condition made his death a constant possibility.

7. The passage of time allows people the opportunity to reflect on and gain a greater appreciation for the meaning of past events.

◆ Reading Strategy

1. Students may say that they might have, like the narrator, attempted to teach Doodle to do new things.

2. Students' responses will probably center on the importance of attempting to deal with others with understanding and patience.

◆ Literary Focus

1. It makes it feel as if the narrator is speaking directly to the reader.

2. The story gains time and distance. Although the narrator is still haunted by that long-ago summer, he is able to lay it out in all its complexity.

3. Students may say that the story would reveal less about Doodle's relationship with his brother.

Guide for Responding (continued)

◆ Critical Thinking

INTERPRET

1. (a) What is Doodle's attitude toward his brother? (b) How would you describe the narrator's attitude toward Doodle? **[Analyze]**

2. Why does the narrator set such demanding goals for Doodle? **[Infer]**

3. In what ways does Doodle show that he has his own unique personality? **[Support]**

4. How is Doodle like the scarlet ibis? **[Compare]**

5. How does the appearance of the scarlet ibis hint at the outcome of the story? **[Analyze]**

EVALUATE

6. Do you think that the narrator is to blame for Doodle's death? Why or why not? **[Make a Judgment]**

APPLY

7. The story opens with the narrator, now an adult, remembering events from long ago. How does the passage of time change people and their feelings about past events? **[Apply]**

◆ Reading Strategy

IDENTIFY WITH A CHARACTER

To fully appreciate the narrator's experiences, try to put yourself in his place and think about what you would have done and how you would have felt.

1. If you were in the narrator's place, how do you think you might have treated Doodle? Why?

2. What can you learn from the narrator's experiences that you can apply to your relationships?

◆ Literary Focus

POINT OF VIEW

Point of view is the vantage point from which a story is told. This story is told from a first-person point of view—the narrator is one of the characters.

1. How does Hurst's use of the first-person point of view make you feel like part of the story?

2. What is the effect of having the narrator look back at the events years after they happened?

3. How might the story be different if it were told from the mother's or the father's point of view?

◆ Build Vocabulary

USING IRREGULAR PLURALS

Remembering that some words become plural by changing -x to -ces, change the following words from singular to plural. Use a dictionary to help you.

1. index   2. appendix   3. apex   4. matrix

USING THE WORD BANK

On your paper, write the word from the Word Bank that best completes each sentence.

1. Several of Liam's friends were swept into the ____?____ of his tragedy.

2. We admired the ____?____ skin of the trout.

3. We credited Ms. Chang, who never seemed to make a mistake, with ____?____.

4. The headlights revealed the ____?____ of a dead animal on the highway.

5. Our memories of the house ____?____ over time.

6. The darkening sky told us that a storm was ____?____.

◆ Build Grammar Skills

INFINITIVES AND INFINITIVE PHRASES

An **infinitive** is the form of the verb that comes after the word *to* and acts as a noun, adjective, or adverb. An infinitive that appears with modifiers, a complement, or a subject and acts as a single part of speech is called an **infinitive phrase.** When you write, be careful not to split infinitives by inserting an adverb between the word *to* and the verb.

    Incorrect: He began to *rapidly break away from the pack.*

    Correct: He rapidly began *to break away from the pack.*

Practice Identify the infinitives and infinitive phrases in each item and tell what they modify.

1. He began to try to move himself.

2. Doodle wanted to follow his brother everywhere.

3. Doodle still had a long way to go if he was going to keep up with his older brother.

Writing Application In your notebook, rewrite the following sentences to eliminate split infinitives.

1. I began to affectionately call him Doodle.

2. His hands began to steadily stroke the grass.

3. People thought he was going to soon die.

◆ Build Vocabulary

Irregular Plurals

1. indexes, indices
2. appendixes, appendices
3. apexes, apices
4. matrixes, matrices
5. helixes, helices

Using the Word Bank

1. vortex   4. entrails
2. iridescent   5. evanesced
3. infallibility   6. imminent

◆ Build Grammar Skills

Practice

1. to haul you around
2. to try to move himself
3. to go; to keep up with the other boys

Writing Application

1. Affectionately, I began to call him Doodle.

2. His hands began steadily to stroke the grass.

3. People thought he was going to die soon.

◆ Writer's Solution

For additional instruction and practice, use the *Writer's Solution Grammar Practice Book,* pp. 48–49 (Infinitives and Infinitive Phrases).

*B*uild *Y*our *P*ortfolio

Idea Bank

Writing

1. **Journal Entry** Put yourself in the place of the narrator. How would you have felt on the night of Doodle's death? Write a journal entry describing your feelings about your brother's death.

2. **Essay About a Symbol** Write a brief essay explaining how the scarlet ibis serves as the story's central symbol. (A symbol is an object, person, or idea that has an underlying meaning.) Support your ideas with details from the story.

3. **Analysis of the Theme** In a brief paper, analyze the story's theme. Tell the lessons the story teaches that readers can apply to their lives. Use details from the story for support.

Speaking and Listening

4. **Eulogy** Prepare and deliver a eulogy—a speech in honor of someone who has died—that the narrator might have presented at Doodle's funeral. **[Performing Arts Link]**

5. **Skit** Imagine that the narrator didn't tell his mother about the actual events of Doodle's death until years later. With a partner, act out the conversation that could have taken place when the narrator made this revelation.

Projects

6. **Travel Brochure** The story's setting—coastal North Carolina—is an area of striking natural beauty. Gather information, along with maps and photographs, of the region. Use the materials you gather to create a travel brochure to attract tourists. **[Career Link]**

7. **Map** Create a map of the story's setting. Base your map on the details Hurst provides. Label the spots where key events in the story take place.

Writing Mini-Lesson

Character Sketch

Create a character sketch of the narrator or his brother, Doodle, based on what you learn from the story. In your sketch, present the key personality traits of the character you chose. Use the following tips to help you present each personality trait.

Writing Skills Focus: Elaborate by Providing Details

As you develop your character sketch, elaborate on your main points by providing details to support each point and further explanations to deepen the reader's understanding. For example, rather than just saying that Doodle was physically challenged, explain the physical limitations he had. Where possible, quote brief passages from the story that point out these limitations. In addition, extend the reader's understanding of Doodle's physical limitations by pointing out how they affected his personality.

Prewriting Choose which character you will focus on and review the story to gather details about that character. Based on his actions in the story, try to draw as many conclusions as you can about his personality. Take notes on the main points you want to make about your character.

Drafting Begin with an introduction that makes a few generalizations about the character. Then elaborate on each generalization in a paragraph in which you cite details and events from the story for support.

Revising Look over your character sketch to make sure that you have provided enough information to support and explain each of the generalizations you made. If necessary, further elaborate on one or more of the character's traits.

The Scarlet Ibis ◆ 495

Guide for Reading

More About the Authors

Toni Cade Bambara was not only an author but also a dedicated community leader. In 1970, she edited and published *The Black Woman*, an anthology that included works by Nikki Giovanni and Alice Walker. In 1980, Bambara published her first novel, *The Salt Eaters*. Bambara has also written screenplays, including *Tar Baby*, which is based on Toni Morrison's novel.

Isabel Allende's exile from Chile marked the beginning of her writing career. Allende states: "I wanted to survive the terrible experience of exile, and I wanted to keep alive the memory of the past—the house that I lost ... the friends that were scattered all around the world."

Toni Cade Bambara

(1939–1995)

This writer's interest in her African American heritage comes through clearly in her writing, which often centers on the emerging identity of the black woman. She has said, "I write because I really think I've got hold of something, that if I share it, might save somebody else some time, might lift someone's spirits, or might enable someone to see more clearly." Bambara's cultural identity is even evident in her name. She adopted the name Bambara after finding the word on a sketchbook of her great-grandmother's. It is the name of an African tribe known for its textiles.

Bambara wrote two collections of short stories—*Gorilla, My Love,* where "Blues Ain't No Mockin Bird" first appeared, and *The Sea Birds Are Still Alive*—as well as a novel, *The Salt Eaters.*

Isabel Allende (1942–)

Recalling her early years, Isabel Allende has said, "I had a very lonely life when I was a child but very interesting—only adults around me . . . a very extravagant family." Allende grew up in Chile, where she lived with her grandparents. Her uncle was the former Chilean president Salvador Allende. In 1973, Salvador Allende's government was overthrown by General Augusto Pinochet—a ruthless dictator whose brutality toward his people attracted worldwide attention and led to his removal from power. Isabel Allende fled to Venezuela, where she lived in exile for a time before moving to California.

Allende's first novel, *The House of the Spirits,* was inspired by her extravagant family. Two of its main characters, Esteban and Clara, are based on her grandparents. Allende's other books include *Of Love and Shadows, Eva Luna, The Stories of Eva Luna, The Infinite Plan,* and *Paula.*

◆ Build Vocabulary

PREFIXES: *dis-*
Some words in these stories begin with the prefix *dis-*, which means "opposite." Knowing this, you can figure out the meaning of *dishonest, disappear, discover,* and other words with this prefix.

WORD BANK
As you read these stories, you will encounter the words on this list. Each word is defined on the page where it first appears. Preview the list before you read.

lassoed
formality
pallid
vanquished
fetid
impassive
disconsolately
unrequited

◆ Build Grammar Skills

POSSESSIVE NOUNS
In these stories, you will see many **possessive nouns**—nouns that show ownership, belonging, or another close relationship. The chart shows how to form possessive nouns.

Rules for Possessive Forms of Nouns	Examples
To form the possessive of singular nouns, add an apostrophe and s.	• our neighbor's yard • a pirate's mustache
To form the possessive of plural nouns that end in s, just add an apostrophe.	• the twins' bicycle • the folks' bed
To form the possessive of plural nouns that do not end in s, add an apostrophe and s.	• people's groceries

496 ◆ *Short Stories*

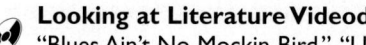

Blues Ain't No Mockin Bird
◆ Uncle Marcos ◆

◆ *Literature and Your Life*

CONNECT YOUR EXPERIENCE

Certain people from our childhoods become etched in our memories forever. It may be because of their unique personality traits or the lessons they taught us. In these stories, you'll meet two memorable characters who have left an indelible impression on the stories' narrators.

Journal Writing Write a brief description of a memorable person from your childhood.

THEMATIC FOCUS: APPRECIATING OTHERS

The narrators of these stories show great admiration for the characters they portray. Others in the stories do not share this attitude. Why do people have different perspectives toward others?

◆ Background for Understanding

LANGUAGE

"Blues Ain't No Mockin Bird" is written in dialect—a way of speaking that is common to people in a particular region or group. Dialect affects pronunciation, word choice, and sentence structure. You'll notice, for example, that the characters in Bambara's story don't pronounce the g on the ends of -ing words. Bambara's use of dialect makes her story sound informal and intimate, as if it were being related orally.

LITERATURE

Imagine a world in which people can rise up and float in the air, it can rain continuously for years, and a person can be born with the tail of a pig. These fantastic details capture how a group of writers—mostly from Latin America—stretch the boundaries of reality in their works. The authors, who include Isabel Allende, practice a style of writing known as "magical realism," in which fantastic details are blended with realistic ones to stretch the boundaries of readers' imaginations.

◆ Literary Focus

DIRECT AND INDIRECT CHARACTERIZATION

If you say that your friend is loyal, you're using **direct characterization.** If you tell a story that demonstrates your friend's loyalty without stating it directly, you're using **indirect characterization.** Allende and Bambara don't just say their characters are interesting or eccentric; they show you through the characters' own words and actions and through the way other characters respond to them.

◆ Reading Strategy

MAKE INFERENCES ABOUT CHARACTERS

In "Blues Ain't No Mockin Bird," Granny and Granddaddy Cain have a confrontation with photographers who are filming a documentary. When one photographer asks, "Mind if we shoot a bit around here?" Granny replies, "I do indeed." Based on what she says, you can **make an inference**—a reasonable conclusion based on the details the author provides—that she values her privacy and that she will not be pushed around.

In "Uncle Marcos," Clara remembers the time her uncle serenaded a woman with a barrel organ, accompanied by a parrot. From this, you can infer that Uncle Marcos is romantic and unpredictable.

When you read, look deeper than the actual words on the page and ask yourself what the author is implying about the characters as he or she describes their words and actions.

Guide for Reading ◆ 497

◆ Preparing for Standardized Tests

Reading The ability to make inferences—the Reading Strategy taught with these stories—is one of the main skills tested in Critical Reading sections of standardized tests. To introduce students to this skill and to alert them to how the skill is treated in standardized tests, have them read the opening paragraph of "Uncle Marcos." Then write the following question on the chalkboard:

What type of person was Uncle Marcos and how did Clara feel about him?

(A) Uncle Marcos was an unusual person with an adventurous spirit, who made a strong impression on Clara.
(B) Uncle Marcos was a professional hunter who was Clara's main role model.
(C) Uncle Marcos was a self-centered individual who didn't get along with Clara.
(D) Uncle Marcos was an adventurous person who had a falling out with Clara.
(E) Uncle Marcos was a bizarre individual whom Clara had once feared.

Lead students to the best answer, *(A)*. For additional practice, use the Reading Strategy page in *Selection Support,* p. 153.

Blues Ain't No Mockin Bird

Toni Cade Bambara

Bambara's story explores the issue of people's right to privacy. It focuses on the actions of a rural African American grandmother and grandfather who object when a camera crew shows up to capture documentary footage of their family. When the crew refuses to heed the grandmother and grandfather's wishes, the grandfather smashes the camera with his hand. The story raises a question that is especially relevant in today's world: Does the media have the right to capture people's lives without their permission?

Customize for
Visual/Spatial Learners
Have these students infer traits of character from the linocut illustration on this page. (A linocut is a print made from a design cut into the surface of a linoleum block.) Have them look for these traits in the character of Granny as they read. *The sharp angles and bold lines of the figure suggest strong determination and iron fortitude. The clothing suggests a field laborer, the hat to shield the sun and the pin to anchor clothing practically and simply.*

Sharecropper, Elizabeth Catlett, Courtesy Evan Tibbs Collection

498 ◆ *Short Stories*

◈ **Block Scheduling Strategies**

Consider these suggestions to take advantage of extended class time:

• After students have read "Blues Ain't No Mockin Bird" silently, have them listen to the audiocassette. Have them discuss how listening to the dialect affects their understanding of the characters.

• To help students focus on a main impression for their magazine feature (p. 514), suggest they form a mental picture of the person and make a quick sketch of how that person appears to them. Their sketch should help them flesh out details of their subject.

• Have students work in small groups to discuss the Thematic Focus activity on page 497. Then have the groups meet to share their conclusions.

• Students may work with a partner to determine answers to the Critical

Thinking questions on pages 503 and 512. Have them put aside questions that they can't agree on and discuss them with another pair of students.

• Encourage students to choose one of the writing activities in the Idea Bank (p. 514) and plan their response.

498

The puddle had frozen over, and me and Cathy went stompin in it. The twins from next door, Tyrone and Terry, were swingin so high out of sight we forgot we were waitin our turn on the tire. Cathy jumped up and came down hard on her heels and started tap-dancin. And the frozen patch splinterin every which way underneath kinda spooky. "Looks like a plastic spider web," she said. "A sort of weird spider, I guess, with many mental problems." But really it looked like the crystal paperweight Granny kept in the parlor. She was on the back porch, Granny was, making the cakes drunk. The old ladle dripping rum into the Christmas tins, like it used to drip maple syrup into the pails when we lived in the Judson's woods, like it poured cider into the vats when we were on the Cooper place, like it used to scoop butter-milk and soft cheese when we lived at the dairy.

"Go tell that man we ain't a bunch of trees."

"Ma'am?"

"I said to tell that man to get away from here with that camera." Me and Cathy look over toward the meadow where the men with the station wagon'd been roamin around all mornin. The tall man with a huge camera <u>lassoed</u> to his shoulder was buzzin our way.

"They're makin movie pictures," yelled Tyrone, stiffenin his legs and twistin so

the tire'd come down slow so they could see.

"They're makin movie pictures," sang out Terry.

"That boy don't never have anything original to say," say Cathy grown-up.

By the time the man with the camera had cut across our neighbor's yard, the twins were out of the trees swingin low and Granny was onto the steps, the screen door bammin soft and scratchy against her palms. "We thought we'd get a shot or two of the house and everything and then—"

"Good mornin," Granny cut him off. And smiled that smile.

"Good mornin," he said, head all down the way Bingo does when you yell at him about the bones on the kitchen floor. "Nice place you got here, aunty. We thought we'd take a—"

"Did you?" said Granny with her eye-brows. Cathy pulled up her socks and giggled.

"Nice things here," said the man, buzzin his camera over the yard. The pecan barrels, the sled, me and Cathy, the flowers, the printed stones along the driveway, the trees, the twins, the tool-shed.

"I don't know about the thing, the it, and the stuff," said Granny, still talkin with her eyebrows. "Just people here is what I tend to consider."

Camera man stopped buzzin. Cathy giggled into her collar.

◆ **Build Vocabulary**

lassoed (las´ ōd) v.: Wrapped around

◀ Critical Viewing As you read, compare Granny with the woman in the illustration. [**Compare and Contrast**]

❶

❷

❸

❹

Blues Ain't No Mockin Bird ◆ 499

◆ **Reading Strategy**

❶ **Make Inferences About Characters** Point out that the author's purpose in telling about the old ladle is more than mere descrip-tion. It is the author's indirect way of letting readers know the family has moved around a lot. Ask students what inference they can make about Granny and her family, based on this information. *Students may infer that Granny has trouble getting along with people. This will become relevant as the story progresses.*

▶Critical Viewing◀

❷ **Compare and Contrast** Lead students to see that the sharply angular lines and planes in the linocut create the impression of strength and pride. Granny demonstrates these traits, and could also be dressed in this simple, utilitarian clothing.

◆ **Critical Thinking**

❸ **Make Inferences** Direct stu-dents' attention to Granny's response to the camera man. Ask: Why does she cut off his words with "Good mornin"? Responses can include: *She wants him to realize that he is being impolite and disrespectful by not having enough courtesy to say "hello" or intro-duce himself; she wants him aware that he has not asked for or received her permission to film her property.*

◆ **Literary Focus**

❹ **Indirect Characterization** By enumerating the "things" in the yard, what does the narrator reveal about the camera man's attitude toward the family? *Students should note that he views the things and the people as objects, material for his film.*

 Humanities: Art

Sharecropper, by Elizabeth Catlett.

This linocut (p. 498) portrays an African American woman who is a sharecropper, possibly similar to Granny.

Elizabeth Catlett was born in 1919 in Washington, D.C. Catlett's paintings and sculp-tures are exhibited in major museums including the Metropolitan Museum of Art in New York and the National Museum of American Art in Washington, D.C. Catlett has stated that she wants to "present black people in their beauty

and dignity for ourselves and others to under-stand and enjoy."

Use this question for discussion: What details in the picture remind you of Granny? *Granny is an older woman so her hair is probably white like that of the woman in the picture. Both Granny and the woman are African Americans. The woman's clothing is clasped with a safety pin, which might be an indication of poverty. We know that Granny and her family are poor because they are recipients of food stamps.*

◆ **Literary Focus**

❶ Indirect Characterization
Students should recognize that Granny's facial expression (unsmiling), her manner of speaking (through her teeth), her actions (stepping off the porch toward the men), and her words all indicate that Granny does not want the men on her property.

◆ **Critical Thinking**

❷ Analyze a Character's Motive
Ask students why Granny doesn't answer Tyrone and Terry when they say, "Did he jump?" *Granny stares them down, making the point that their lively interest in the story is not so different from the photographer's interest in the man on the bridge—or from the interest the men in the yard have in Granny and her family.*

◆ **Build Grammar Skills**

❸ Possessive Nouns Direct attention to the word *Granny's*. Ask: Why does *Granny's* end in an apostrophe and *s*? *Granny's is a singular possessive noun. It indicates that story belongs to Granny.*

Comprehension Check ☑

❹ Why does the family move often?
Granny gets hurt by or fed up with people who don't respect her and needs to get away.

"Mornin, ladies," a new man said. He had come up behind us when we weren't lookin. "And gents," discoverin the twins givin him a nasty look. "We're filmin for the county," he said with a smile. "Mind if we shoot a bit around here?"

"I do indeed," said Granny with no smile. Smilin man was smiling up a storm. So was Cathy. But he didn't seem to have another word to say, so he and the camera man backed on out the yard, but you could hear the camera buzzin still. "Suppose you just shut that machine off," said Granny real low through her teeth, and took a step down off the porch and then another.

> ◆ **Literary Focus**
> How does Bambara use indirect characterization to tell you how Granny feels about having the photographers on her property?

"Now, aunty," Camera said, pointin the thing straight at her.

"Your mama and I are not related."

Smilin man got his notebook out and a chewed-up pencil.

"Listen," he said movin back into our yard, "we'd like to have a statement from you . . . for the film. We're filmin for the county, see. Part of the food stamp campaign. You know about the food stamps?"

Granny said nuthin.

"Maybe there's somethin you want to say for the film. I see you grow your own vegetables," he smiled real nice. "If more folks did that, see, there'd be no need—"

Granny wasn't sayin nuthin. So they backed on out, buzzin at our clothesline and the twins' bicycles, then back on down to the meadow. The twins were danglin in the tire, lookin at Granny. Me and Cathy were waitin, too, cause Granny always got somethin to say. She teaches steady with no let-up. "I was on this bridge one time," she started off. "Was a crowd cause this man was goin to jump, you understand. And a minister was there and the police and some other folks. His woman was there, too."

"What was they doin?" asked Tyrone.

"Tryin to talk him out of it was what they was doin. The minister talkin about how it was a mortal sin, suicide. His woman takin bites out of her own hand and not even knowin it, so nervous and cryin and talkin fast."

"So what happened?" asked Tyrone.

"So here comes . . . this person . . . with a camera, takin pictures of the man and the minister and the woman. Takin pictures of the man in his misery about to jump, cause life so bad and people been messin with him so bad. This person takin up the whole roll of film practically. But savin a few, of course."

"Of course," said Cathy, hatin the person. Me standin there wonderin how Cathy knew it was "of course" when I didn't and it was *my* grandmother.

After a while Tyrone say, "Did he jump?"

"Yeh, did he jump?" say Terry all eager. And Granny just stared at the twins till their faces swallow up the eager and they don't even care any more about the man jumpin. Then she goes back onto the porch and lets the screen door go for itself. I'm lookin to Cathy to finish the story cause she knows Granny's whole story before me even. Like she knew how come we move so much and Cathy ain't but a third cousin we picked up on the way last Thanksgivin visitin. But she knew it was on account of people drivin Granny crazy till she'd get up in the night and start packin. Mumblin and packin and wakin everybody up sayin, "Let's get on away from here before I kill me somebody." Like people wouldn't pay her for things like they said they would. Or Mr. Judson bringin us boxes of old clothes and raggedy magazines. Or Mrs. Cooper comin in our kitchen and touchin everything and sayin how clean it all was. Granny goin crazy, and Granddaddy Cain pullin her off the people, sayin, "Now, now, Cora." But next day loadin up the truck,

---

🎭 **Speaking and Listening Mini-Lesson**

Monologue
This mini-lesson supports the Speaking and Listening activity in the Idea Bank on page 514.

Introduce the Concept Point out to students that a monologue is a speech by a character that usually reveals the traits or personality of that character. Have students discuss how the camera man might feel if he has to explain his questionable actions to someone in authority.

Develop Background Before the camera man talks to his boss, he needs to plan his words very carefully. Suggest that students consider these points:

• Assume that the camera man does not lie. How would he shape his story?

• What details would he emphasize and what details would he try to "slide in"?

• How would he end his monologue?

Apply the Information Using these questions, students can plan and develop their monologue. Have them practice their monologues. Remind them that voice inflections and facial expressions contribute to the overall effect. Have students present their monologues to the class.

Assess the Outcome Have the rest of the class determine whether "the camera man" gets to keep his or her job! Have students use the Peer Assessment sheet for Dramatic Performance in *Alternative Assessment,* p. 113, to assess the monologues.

⑤ with rocks all in his jaw, madder than Granny in the first place.

"I read a story once," said Cathy soundin like Granny teacher. "About this lady Goldilocks who barged into a house **⑥** that wasn't even hers. And not invited, you understand. Messed over the people's groceries and broke up the people's furniture. Had the nerve to sleep in the folks' bed."

"Then what happened?" asked Tyrone. "What they do, the folks, when they come in to all this mess?"

"Did they make her pay for it?" asked Terry, makin a fist. "I'd've made her pay me."

⑦ I didn't even ask. I could see Cathy actress was very likely to just walk away and leave us in mystery about this story which I heard was about some bears.

"Did they throw her out?" asked Tyrone, like his father sounds when he's bein extra nasty-plus to the washin-machine man.

"Woulda," said Terry. "I woulda gone upside her head with my fist and—"

"You woulda done whatcha always do—go cry to Mama, you big baby," said Tyrone. So naturally Terry starts hittin on Tyrone, and next thing you know they tumblin out the tire and rollin on the ground. But Granny didn't say a thing or send the twins home or step out on the steps to tell us about how we can't afford to be fightin amongst ourselves. She didn't say nuthin. So I get into the tire to take my turn. And I could see her leanin up against the pantry table, staring at the cakes she was puttin up for the Christmas sale, mumblin real low and grumpy and holdin her forehead like it wanted to fall off and mess up the rum cakes.

Behind me I hear before I can see Grand daddy Cain comin through the woods in his field boots. Then I twist around to see the shiny black oilskin cuttin through what little left there was of yellows, reds, and oranges. His great white head not quite round cause of this

bloody thing high on his shoulder, like he was wearin a cap on sideways. He takes the shortcut through the pecan grove, and the sound of twigs snapping overhead and underfoot travels clear and cold all the way up to us. And here comes Smilin and Camera up behind him like they was goin **⑧** to do somethin. Folks like to go for him sometimes. Cathy say it's because he's so tall and quiet and like a king. And people just can't stand it. But Smilin and Camera don't hit him in the head or nuthin. They just buzz on him as he stalks by with the chicken hawk slung over his shoulder, squawkin, drippin red down the back of the oilskin. He passes the porch and stops a second for Granny to see he's caught the hawk at last, but she's just starin and mumblin, and not at the hawk. So he nails the bird to the toolshed door, the hammerin crackin through the eardrums. And the bird flappin himself to death and droolin down the door to paint the gravel in the driveway red, then brown, then black. And the two men movin up on tiptoe like they was invisible or we were blind, one.

"Get them persons out of my flower bed, Mister Cain," say Granny moanin real low like at a funeral.

"How come your grandmother calls her husband 'Mister Cain' all the time?" Tyrone whispers all loud and noisy and from the city and don't know no better. Like his mama, Miss Myrtle, tell us never mind the formality as if we had no better breeding than to call her Myrtle, plain. And then this awful thing—a giant hawk—come wailin up over the meadow, flyin low and tilted and screamin, zigzaggin through the pecan grove, breakin branches and hollerin, snappin past the clothesline, flyin every which way, flyin into things reckless **⑨** with crazy.

◆ Build Vocabulary

formality (fôr malʹ ə tē) *n.*: Established rules or customs

Blues Ain't No Mockin Bird ◆ 501

◆ Reading Strategy

⑤ Make Inferences About Characters Ask students: What does this paragraph tell you about Granny's sense of pride and about the relationship between her and her husband? *Students should suggest that Granny's pride is reflected by her refusal to accept people's old clothes and her outrage when people seem surprised that her house is well cared for. Her husband's willingness to move whenever she feels the need shows his love, respect, and loyalty.*

◆ Critical Thinking

⑥ Compare and Contrast How does Cathy's rendition of the story of the three bears differ from the traditional telling of the tale? *Students should note that the traditional tale focuses on Goldilocks and not on the feelings of the bears.*

◆ Reading Strategy

⑦ Make Inferences About Characters If Cathy walked away without finishing the story, whom would she be imitating? *Granny* Why does the narrator call her "Cathy actress"? *The narrator indicates that Cathy is acting the part of Granny.*

◆ Background for Understanding

⑧ Language You might want to point out two examples of dialect: "they was" instead of "they were" and "Cathy say" instead of "Cathy says."

◆ Critical Thinking

⑨ Make Comparisons Ask: Who, in the story, does the male hawk remind you of? Why? *The male hawk can be compared to Granddaddy because Granddaddy is protective of Granny, just as the male hawk is protective of his mate.*

Customize for
English Language Learners
These students may be unfamiliar with the story "Goldilocks and the Three Bears," referenced on this page. Have a native speaker share the story.

Beyond the Classroom

Career Connection
Photography The camera man in "Blues Ain't No Mockin Bird" was interested in getting pictures of Granny's residence. Some photographers take pictures that document a place or event; others, who consider photography an art form, are much more concerned with the composition of the work. Have interested students discuss what makes a photograph a work of art. In addition, students might investigate what kind of training someone needs to become a professional photographer.

Community Connection
Local Interest The camera man and his partner tell Granny that they are doing a story for the county. Sometimes a community will choose to film a documentary that will highlight special features and accomplishments of its citizens. Have students suggest a list of local-interest stories that might be done for their community. Then have them work in small groups to plan a documentary. Their plan should include what its purpose would be, what they would include in the film, how they would approach the subject.

◆ Critical Thinking

❶ Make Inferences Granddaddy kills the male hawk. Ask: Why does he do this? *Responses can include: This is Granddaddy's way of taking charge of the situation; he's trying to protect his family from the angry hawk; he wants to put the hawk out of its misery; he wants the two men to understand that he is on his own property and is a force to be reckoned with.*

◆ *Literature and Your Life*

❷ Have students relate to Granddaddy's method of handling the intruders. *Students will likely indicate that Granddaddy's way of dismissing the men was quite abrupt, although their own way may also have been abrupt.*

❸ Clarification Point out that the narrator often refers to the two men as "Smilin" and "Camera." You might point out that the narrator is making objects of the men in the same way the men are making objects of Granny and her family.

---

❶ "He's come to claim his mate," say Cathy fast, and ducks down. We all fall quick and flat into the gravel driveway, stones scrapin my face. I squinch my eyes open again at the hawk on the door, tryin to fly up out of her death like it was just a sack flown into by mistake. Her body holdin her there on that nail, though. The mate beatin the air overhead and clutchin for hair, for heads, for landin space.

The camera man duckin and bendin and runnin and fallin, jigglin the camera and scared. And Smilin jumpin up and down swipin at the huge bird, tryin to bring the hawk down with just his raggedy ole cap. Granddaddy Cain straight up and silent, watchin the circles of the hawk, then aimin the hammer off his wrist. The giant bird fallin, silent and slow. Then here comes Camera and Smilin all big and bad now that the awful screechin thing is on its back and broken, here they come. And Granddaddy Cain looks up at them like it was the first time noticin, but not payin them too much mind cause he's listenin, we all listenin, to that low groanin music comin from the porch. And we figure any minute, somethin in my back tells me any minute now, Granny gonna bust through that screen with somethin in her hand and murder on her mind. So Granddaddy say above the buzzin, but quiet, "Good day, gentlemen." Just like that. Like he'd invited them in to play cards and they'd stayed too long and all the sandwiches were gone and Reverend Webb was droppin by and it was time to go.

❷ They didn't know what to do. But like Cathy say, folks can't stand Granddaddy tall and silent and like a king. They can't neither. The smile the men smilin is pullin the mouth back and showin the teeth. Lookin like the wolf man, both of them. Then Granddaddy holds his hand out—this huge hand I used to sit in when I was a baby and he'd carry me through the house to my mother like I was a gift

on a tray. Like he used to on the trains. They called the other men just waiters. But they spoke of Granddaddy separate and said, The Waiter. And said he had engines in his feet and motors in his hands and couldn't no train throw him off and couldn't nobody turn him round. They were big enough for motors, his hands were. He held that one hand out all still and it gettin to be not at all a hand but a person in itself.

"He wants you to hand him the camera," Smilin whispers to Camera, tiltin his head to talk secret like they was in the jungle or somethin and come upon a native that don't speak the language. The men start untyin the straps, and they put the camera into that great hand speckled with the hawk's blood all black and crackly now. And the hand don't even drop with the weight, just the fingers move, curl up around the machine. But Granddaddy lookin straight at the men. They lookin at each other and everywhere but at Granddaddy's face.

"We filmin for the county, see," say Smilin. "We puttin together a movie for the food stamp program . . . filmin all around these parts. Uhh, filmin for the county."

"Can I have my camera back?" say the tall man with no machine on his shoulder, but still keepin it high like the camera was still there or needed to be. "Please, sir."

Then Granddaddy's other hand flies up like a sudden and gentle bird, slaps down fast on top of the camera and lifts off half like it was a calabash[1] cut for sharing.

"Hey," Camera jumps forward. He gathers up the parts into his chest and everything unrollin and fallin all over. "Whatcha tryin to do? You'll ruin the film." He looks down into his chest of metal reels and things like he's protectin a kitten from the cold.

❸

---

1. **calabash** (kal′ ə bash) *n*.: Large gourdlike fruit.

502 ◆ *Short Stories*

Cross-Curricular Connection: Science

Two hawks, one male and one female, play a central role in "Blues Ain't No Mockin Bird." Discuss what students know about hawks in real life. Some simple facts are the following:

- Hawks are birds of prey.
- The female is usually larger than the male.
- Some hawks remain mates for life.

Suggest that students try to correlate hawk facts with the story. For instance, students might want to consider the following questions:

- Could the hawks stand not only for Granny and Granddaddy, but also for the men who "preyed" on the family?
- Could Granny be considered larger than Granddaddy because the story revolves around her?

Have interested students find out more about hawks and suggest other ways that the habits of hawks can be applied to the story.

502

"You standin in the misses' flower bed," say Granddaddy. "This is our own place."

The two men look at him, then at each other, then back at the mess in the camera man's chest, and they just back off. One sayin over and over all the way down to the meadow, "Watch it, Bruno. Keep ya fingers off the film." Then Granddaddy picks up the hammer and jams it into the oilskin pocket, scrapes his boots, and goes into the house. And you can hear the squish of his boots headin through the house. And you can see the funny shadow

④
⑤
◆ Reading Strategy
What do you think is going through the men's minds as they back off?

he throws from the parlor window onto the ground by the string-bean patch. The hammer draggin the pocket of the oilskin out so Granddaddy looked even wider. Granny was hummin now—high not low and grumbly. And she was doin the cakes again, you could smell the molasses from the rum.

"There's this story I'm goin to write one day," say Cathy dreamer. "About the proper use of the hammer."

"Can I be in it?" Tyrone say with his hand up like it was a matter of first come, first served.

"Perhaps," say Cathy, climbin onto the tire to pump us up. "If you there and ready."

◆ **Build Grammar Skills**

❹ **Possessive Nouns** Point out the possessive noun *camera man's.* Ask students how this compound possessive noun would be different if there were more than one man. *The possessive noun would be* camera men's.

◆ **Reading Strategy**

❺ **Make Inferences About Characters** Responses can include: *The men realize they have underestimated the family and that Granddaddy is willing to fight to protect his turf; the men might also think that Granddaddy is a little crazy, since they probably were frightened by his killing the hawks.*

Guide for Responding

◆ *Literature and Your Life*

Reader's Response What character from the story would you most like to meet? Why?

Thematic Focus If you were a character in the story, how would your perspective of the filmmakers compare with Granny's?

Journal Entry In your journal, jot down whether or not you think that the filmmakers had the right to film the Cains. Support your opinion.

☑ **Check Your Comprehension**

1. Why are the photographers filming in the area?
2. How does Granny react toward the pair of photographers?
3. What story does Cathy tell?
4. What does Granny ask Granddaddy to do?
5. Describe Granddaddy's behavior toward the photographers.

◆ **Critical Thinking**

INTERPRET

1. What is the cameraman's attitude toward the Cain family? **[Infer]**
2. (a) What is the main point of Granny's story about the man who attempted suicide? (b) How does the story help explain Granny's behavior? **[Draw Conclusion]**
3. (a) What does the killing of the hawk's mate reveal about Granddaddy? (b) How does Granddaddy's action prepare you for what he does later in the story? **[Analyze]**
4. How do the two hawks resemble Granny and Granddaddy?
5. What do you think is the story's theme, or central message? Support your answer. **[Infer]**

EVALUATE

6. Is Granddaddy's treatment of the photographers justified? Explain. **[Make a Judgment]**

EXTEND

7. If you were to pursue a career as a reporter or photographer, what could you learn from this story that you could apply to your work? **[Career Link]**

Reinforce and Extend

Answers

◆ *Literature and Your Life*

Reader's Response Students may be most impressed with Granddaddy, or they may find Granny interesting in spite of how intimidating she is.

Thematic Focus Most students will share Granny's perspective, given the narrator's sympathetic portrayal.

☑ **Check Your Comprehension**

1. They are attempting to gather information on food stamp recipients.
2. Granny is angry and tells the man to turn off the camera.
3. She tells the story of "Goldilocks and the Three Bears."
4. She tells him to get the photographers out of her flower garden.
5. He is not overtly hostile, but his commanding presence intimidates them into not crossing him.

◆ **Critical Thinking**

1. The camera man has a condescending attitude toward the family.
2. (a) Her story points out that people like the county filmmakers would rather get a story than show concern for real people's problems. (b) It helps explain how angry she is when people like the filmmakers come around.
3. (a) It reveals that he is a man of decisive action. (b) We are not surprised that he will somehow protect his wife, family, and home from the filmmakers.
4. They have a close relationship—the second hawk comes to the rescue of the first, just as Granddaddy would come to the rescue of Granny.
5. Students' responses will center on the importance of family and protecting one's family against intruders.
6. Most students will judge Granddaddy's actions favorably, given the sympathetic way his family and their situation is portrayed.
7. Students will probably contend that the story shows the importance of being sensitive to their subjects' feelings and situations.

503

One-Minute Insight In "Uncle Marcos" the main character is an eccentric, laughed at by some, but loved by many, especially his niece Clara. Uncle Marcos impresses his community with his daring adventures in courtship, flight, rebirth, and clairvoyance. Through Clara's eyes Uncle Marcos earns the immortality he has gained only sporadically in his lifetime. The story conveys an important message about how individuals can be misjudged or underappreciated by some people but beloved by others.

◆ Literary Focus

❶ Direct and Indirect Characterization Draw attention to the description of Uncle Marcos as an explorer leaning on a rifle. This description is an example of direct characterization. However, the comparison of him with the Virgin is an example of indirect characterization. Ask: What does the author want the reader to infer from this comparison? *Readers should infer that one Uncle Marcos is no ordinary man but one with extraordinary powers.*

◆ *Literature and Your Life*

❷ Ask students to think about people who have become legends in their own families. Tell students that the author shares such family legends in the selection they are about to read.

►Critical Viewing◄

❸ Speculate Such a person might be bold, courageous, imaginative, optimistic, and persistant.

Looking at Literature Videodisc To provide background and insight into the author of "Uncle Marcos," Isabel Allende, play Chapter 8 of the videodisc. In this interview, Allende discusses *The House of Spirits,* the novel from which "Uncle Marcos" is taken, and the real-life Uncle Marcos. Discuss why it is important for writers to use real-life experiences and people as the basis for their writing.

Chapter 8

Uncle Marcos

❶
❷ . . . It had been two years since Clara had last seen her Uncle Marcos, but she remembered him very well. His was the only perfectly clear image she retained from her whole childhood, and in order to describe him she did not need to consult the daguerreotype[1] in the drawing room that showed him dressed as an explorer leaning on an old-fashioned double-barreled rifle with his right foot on the neck of a Malaysian tiger, the same triumphant position in which she had seen the Virgin standing between plaster clouds and pallid angels at the main altar, one foot on the vanquished devil. All Clara had to do to see her uncle was close her eyes and there he was, weather-beaten and thin, with a pirate's mustache through which his strange, sharklike smile peered out at her. It seemed impossible that he could be inside that long black box that was lying in the middle of the courtyard.

---

1. **daguerreotype** (də ger´ ō tip´) *n.:* Early type of photograph.

◆ Build Vocabulary

pallid (pal´ id) *adj.:* Pale

vanquished (van´ kwisht) *adj.:* Defeated

❸ ► **Critical Viewing** In this story, a man tries to build a flying machine. What character traits might you find in someone who attempts such a feat? [Speculate]

504 ◆ *Short Stories*

Cultural Connection

Point out that while many North American family units are limited to parents and children, an extended family is typical of many cultures, including Hispanic. In addition to parents and children, it often includes grandparents, aunts, uncles, cousins, and even close family friends (*compadres*) living in the same house or neighborhood. Even when they do not live in the same house, but far away like Uncle Marcos, they often visit and depend upon one another.

Find examples in the selection that show how family members depend upon one another.

Ask students whom they would like to live with if they could create their own extended family.

Customize for
Visual/Spatial Learners
Have students examine the figure propelling the bicycle-like flying machine. Suggest that they infer details about the character from what he looks like and what he is doing. *Students should observe that he looks determined, calm, proud; he is apparently daring and original to be flying such a craft.*

Customize for
Logical/Mathematical Learners
Ask these students whether the craft pictured here has the capacity for flight. They may need to research information on aerodynamics in order to respond. Have them report their conclusions to the class.

from
The House of the Spirits
Isabel Allende

Uncle Marcos from *The House of the Spirits* ◆ 505

Humanities: Art

Proposal for a Flying Machine

This 1877 engraving illustrates a one-person flying machine. In the story "Uncle Marcos," Marcos attempts a trip in a flying machine. His machine is described as "a bird of prehistoric dimensions, with the face of a furious eagle, wings that moved, and a propeller on its back" (p. 507).

Ask:

• How does this picture match the description of Marcos's flying machine? *The machine in the*

picture does resemble a huge bird, and the wings apparently move.

• How is the machine in the picture different from Marcos's? *There is no face on this machine or propeller on its back.*

• Does the man in the picture fulfill your vision of Uncle Marcos? Why or why not? *Students might say that the man in the picture does not have a "pirate's mustache" or a "strange, sharklike smile." However, he does look like he could pose with a tiger he has just shot.*

◆ Build Grammar Skills

① **Possessive Nouns** Point out the possessive noun *Nivea's.* Ask why the noun is possessive. *It indicates that Nivea owns the house.*

◆ Critical Thinking

② **Interpret** Ask: What does Severo mean when he says that Uncle Marcos's manners are those of a cannibal? *Responses can include: Severo means that Uncle Marcos does not bother with the rituals of politeness and does as he pleases; also, he picks up unfamiliar animals on his travels and brings them home; he misuses household appliances and dresses any way he wishes.*

◆ Build Grammar Skills

③ **Possessive Nouns** Ask students to identify the two plural possessive nouns in the passage. *ladies', relatives'* Have a volunteer spell the singular possessive form of each word. *lady's, relative's*

◆ Critical Thinking

④ **Make Inferences** Ask: How does Antonieta feel toward Marcos? How do you know? *Antonieta does not like him, is embarrassed by his attention, and thinks his method of courtship is ridiculous. The reader knows this because she quickly marries someone else and moves far away.*

Customize for
Less Proficient Readers
Have these students summarize Marcos's plan to win the hand of Antonieta. *He played the military march and waltz on the barrel organ beneath her window and had his parrot screech out her name.*

---

① Each time Uncle Marcos had visited his sister Nivea's home, he had stayed for several months, to the immense joy of his nieces and nephews, particularly Clara, causing a storm in which the sharp lines of domestic order blurred. The house became a clutter of trunks, of animals in jars of formaldehyde,[2] of Indian lances and sailor's bundles. In every part of the house people kept tripping over his equipment, and all sorts of unfamiliar animals appeared that had traveled from remote lands only to meet their death beneath Nana's irate broom in the farthest corners of the house. **②** Uncle Marcos's manners were those of a cannibal, as Severo put it. He spent the whole night making incomprehensible movements in the drawing room; later they turned out to be exercises designed to perfect the mind's control over the body and to improve digestion. He performed alchemy[3] experiments in the kitchen, filling the house with <u>fetid</u> smoke and ruining pots and pans with solid substances that stuck to their bottoms and were impossible to remove. While the rest of the household tried to sleep, he dragged his suitcases up and down the halls, practiced making strange, high-pitched sounds on savage instruments, and taught Spanish to a parrot whose native language was an Amazonic dialect. During the day, he slept in a hammock that he had strung between two columns in the hall, wearing only a loincloth that put Severo in a terrible mood but that Nivea forgave because Marcos had convinced her that it was the same costume in which Jesus of Nazareth had preached. Clara remembered perfectly, even though she had been only a tiny child, the first time her Uncle Marcos came to the house after one of his voyages. He settled in as if he planned to stay forever. After a short time, bored with having to appear at ladies' gatherings where the mistress of the house played the piano, with playing cards, and **③** with dodging all his relatives' pressures to pull himself together and take a job as a clerk in Severo del Valle's law practice, he bought a

---

2. **formaldehyde** (fôr mal´ də hīd´) *n.:* Solution used as a preservative.
3. **alchemy** (al´ kə mē) *n.:* Early form of chemistry, with philosophic and magical associations.

---

barrel organ and took to the streets with the hope of seducing his Cousin Antonieta and entertaining the public in the bargain. The machine was just a rusty box with wheels, but he painted it with seafaring designs and gave it a fake ship's smokestack. It ended up looking like a coal stove. The organ played either a military march or a waltz, and in between turns of the handle the parrot, who had managed to learn Spanish although he had not lost his foreign accent, would draw a crowd with his piercing shrieks. He also plucked slips of paper from a box with his beak, by way of selling fortunes to the curious. The little pink, green, and blue papers were so clever that they always divulged the exact secret wishes of the customers. Besides fortunes there were little balls of sawdust to amuse the children. The idea of the organ was a last desperate attempt to win the hand of Cousin Antonieta after more conventional means of courting her had failed. Marcos thought no woman in her right mind could remain <u>impassive</u> before a barrel-organ serenade. He stood beneath her window one evening and played his military march and his waltz just as she was taking tea with a group of female friends. Antonieta did not realize the music was meant for her until the parrot called her by her full name, at which point she appeared in the window. Her reaction was not what her suitor had hoped for. Her friends offered to spread the news to every salon[4] in the city, and the next day people thronged the downtown streets hoping to see Severo del Valle's brother-in-law playing the organ and selling little sawdust balls with a motheaten parrot, for the sheer pleasure of proving that even in the best of families there could be good reason for embarrassment. In the face of this stain to the family reputation, Marcos was forced to give up organ grinding and resort to less conspicuous ways of winning over **④**

---

4. **salon** (sə län´) *n.:* Regular gathering of distinguished guests that meets in a private home.

◆ Build Vocabulary
fetid (fet´ id) *adj.:* Rancid; rank; smelly
impassive (im pas´ iv) *adj.:* Showing no emotion

---

506 ◆ *Short Stories*

 Cross-Curricular Connection: Music

When Marcos tried to impress Cousin Antonieta, he purchased a barrel organ. The barrel organ is also called a piano organ. It belongs to a larger group of organs known as hand organs. Barrel organs were popular with street musicians. They were easy to play—all one had to do was to crank the handle. Have interested students find out more about the barrel organ. Some questions they might consider are the following:

- Marcos could play only two songs on his barrel organ. Is that unusual or is it the norm?
- Do people still play the barrel organ?
- How does a barrel organ compare to church organs or more modern organs?

If possible, have students make a diagram of the inner workings of a barrel organ.

his Cousin Antonieta, but he did not renounce his goal. In any case, he did not succeed, because from one day to the next the young lady married a diplomat who was twenty years her senior; he took her to live in a tropical country whose name no one could recall, except that it suggested negritude,[5] bananas, and palm trees, where she managed to recover from the memory of that suitor who had ruined her seventeenth year with his military march and his waltz. Marcos sank into a deep depression that lasted two or three days, at the end of which he announced that he would never marry and that he was embarking on a trip around the world. He sold his organ to a blind man and left the parrot to Clara, but Nana secretly poisoned it with an overdose of cod-liver oil, because no one could stand its lusty glance, its fleas, and its harsh, tuneless hawking of paper fortunes and sawdust balls.

◆ **Literary Focus**
What does the fact that Uncle Marcos's "deep depression" lasted only a few days tell you about his character?

That was Marcos's longest trip. He returned with a shipment of enormous boxes that were piled in the far courtyard, between the chicken coop and the woodshed, until the winter was over. At the first signs of spring he had them transferred to the parade grounds, a huge park where people would gather to watch the soldiers file by on Independence Day, with the goosestep they had learned from the Prussians. When the crates were opened, they were found to contain loose bits of wood, metal, and painted cloth. Marcos spent two weeks assembling the contents according to an instruction manual written in English, which he was able to decipher thanks to his invincible imagination and a small dictionary. When the job was finished, it turned out to be a bird of prehistoric dimensions, with the face of a furious eagle, wings that moved, and a propeller on its back. It caused an uproar. The families of the oligarchy[6] forgot all about the barrel organ, and Marcos became the star attraction of the season. People took Sunday outings to see the bird; souvenir vendors and strolling photographers made a fortune. Nonetheless, the public's interest quickly waned. But then Marcos announced that as soon as the weather cleared he planned to take off in his bird and cross the mountain range. The news spread, making this the most talked-about event of the year. The contraption lay with its stomach on terra firma,[7] heavy and sluggish and looking more like a wounded duck than like one of those newfangled airplanes they were starting to produce in the United States. There was nothing in its appearance to suggest that it could move, much less take flight across the snowy peaks. Journalists and the curious flocked to see it. Marcos smiled his immutable[8] smile before the avalanche of questions and posed for photographers without offering the least technical or scientific explanation of how he hoped to carry out his plan. People came from the provinces to see the sight. Forty years later his greatnephew Nicolás, whom Marcos did not live to see, unearthed the desire to fly that had always existed in the men of his lineage. Nicolás was interested in doing it for commercial reasons, in a gigantic hot-air sausage on which would be printed an advertisement for carbonated drinks. But when Marcos announced his plane trip, no one believed that his contraption could be put to any practical use. The appointed day dawned full of clouds, but so many people had turned out that Marcos did not want to disappoint them. He showed up punctually at the appointed spot and did not once look up at the sky, which was growing darker and darker with thick gray clouds. The astonished crowd filled all the nearby streets, perching on rooftops and the balconies of the nearest houses and squeezing into the park. No political gathering managed to attract so many people until half a century later, when the first Marxist candidate attempted, through strictly democratic channels, to become President. Clara would remember this holiday as long as she lived. People dressed in their spring best, thereby getting a

---

5. **negritude** (neg′ rə tood′) *n.*: Blacks and their cultural heritage.
6. **oligarchy** (äl′ i gär′ kē) *n.*: Government ruled by a few.

7. **terra firma** (ter′ a fur′ ma) *n.*: Firm earth; solid ground.
8. **immutable** (im myoot′ ə bəl) *adj.*: Never changing.

Uncle Marcos from *The House of the Spirits* ◆ 507

Customize for
More Advanced Students
Point out several of the unexplained allusions on this page. The mountain range Clara refers to is the Andes, which stretches along the entire west coast of South America. It is the second highest after the Himalayas of India and Tibet. At its widest part it is about 500 miles across.

The Marxist candidate to whom the author refers is her uncle, Salvador Allende, who was president of Chile from 1970 to 1973.

◆ **Literary Focus**

❺ Indirect Characterization
Students should recognize that Marcos does not take anything seriously for very long and is ready to move on from setbacks quickly.

Comprehension Check ☑

❻ What does Marcos do to become the star attraction of the season?
Marcos puts together a very crude "airplane."

❼ Clarification Be sure students are aware that the "gigantic hot-air sausage" with advertisements is a dirigible or blimp.

◆ **Build Vocabulary**

❽ Prefixes: *dis-* The word *disappoint* begins with the prefix *dis-*, meaning "the opposite of." Direct attention to the two uses of *appointed*, one in the beginning of the same sentence and one in the following sentence, which seem to emphasize the possibility that Marcos might *dis*appoint on the appointed day at the appointed spot.

◆ **Critical Thinking**

❾ Infer Ask: Why will Clara remember this holiday as long as she lives? *Responses can include: Clara loves her uncle very much, and it is a moment of triumph for him. This is one of the few things he has ever done that has brought him positive attention.*

Cross-Curricular Connection: Social Studies

Chile
Chile is the southernmost country of South America, lying between the snow-capped peaks of the Andes Mountains and the Pacific Ocean. Chile has a long history of political upheaval, beginning in 1817 when it won its independence from the Spanish, who had controlled the country since the sixteenth century. In 1976, Salvador Allende Gossens became president of Chile. Allende was the first Marxist to be democratical- ly elected to head any country in the Western Hemisphere. In 1973, the military, led by General Augusto Pinochet Ugarte, forcibly took over Allende's government and arrested his supporters. Reports suggested that Allende had committed suicide during the coup, although many believe he was assassinated. Pinochet became the military dictator of the new government. In 1989, he allowed democratic elections to be held, but retained control of the military.

◆ **Build Grammar Skills**

❶ Possessive Nouns Have students identify the three possessive nouns in the sentence. *mechanic's, racer's, explorer's* Ask them to explain how these nouns help them understand Marcos better. *The three nouns emphasize that Marcos is a man of many roles. He has the tools of the trade of a mechanic, a racer, and an explorer.*

◆ **Critical Thinking**

❷ Infer Clara continues to watch the horizon. Ask: Why does no one else look for Marcos? *Only Clara watches for Marcos because she is the only one who has faith in his endeavors and truly cares about him.*

◆ *Literature and Your Life*

❸ What comment on human nature is the author making? Do you agree that this is a typical public reaction to an important event? Can you think of any parallels in recent news reports? *Students are apt to give examples of stories that dominate the media for a long time, such as the trial of a celebrity or the suspicious crash of an airliner. However, unless there are new developments in a story, interest wanes quickly.*

◆ **Critical Thinking**

❹ Evaluate How does the word *ignorant* in this sentence achieve a humorous effect? Is it more ridiculous to suggest that Uncle Marcos reached the moon than to speculate that he disappeared into outer space?

◆ **Reading Strategy**

❺ Make Inferences About Characters Clara doesn't weep as the rest of the family does because she has faith that her uncle is still flying and that he will return.

---

step ahead of the official opening of the season, the men in white linen suits and the ladies in the Italian straw hats that were all the rage that year. Groups of elementary-school children paraded with their teachers, clutching flowers for the hero. Marcos accepted their bouquets and joked that they might as well hold on to them and wait for him to crash, so they could take them directly to his funeral. The bishop himself, accompanied by two incense bearers, appeared to bless the bird without having been asked, and the police band played happy, unpretentious music that pleased everyone. The police, on horseback and carrying lances, had trouble keeping the crowds far enough away from the center of the park, where Marcos waited dressed in mechanic's overalls, with huge racer's goggles and an explorer's helmet. He was also equipped with a compass, a telescope, and several strange maps that he had traced himself based on various theories of Leonardo da Vinci and on the polar knowledge of the Incas.[9] Against all logic, on the second try the bird lifted off without mishap and with a certain elegance, accompanied by the creaking of its skeleton and the roar of its motor. It rose flapping its wings and disappeared into the clouds, to a send-off of applause, whistlings, handkerchiefs, drumrolls, and the sprinkling of holy water. All that remained on earth were the comments of the amazed crowd below and a multitude of experts, who attempted to provide a reasonable explanation of the miracle. Clara continued to stare at the sky long after her uncle had become invisible. She thought she saw him ten minutes later, but it was only a migrating sparrow. After three days the initial euphoria that had accompanied the first airplane flight in the country died down and no one gave the episode another thought, except for Clara, who continued to peer at the horizon.

After a week with no word from the flying uncle, people began to speculate that he had gone so high that he had disappeared into

---

9. **Leonardo da Vinci** (le ə när' do də vin' che) . . . **Incas:** Leonardo da Vinci (1452–1519) was an Italian painter, sculptor, architect, and scientist. The Incas were Native Americans who dominated ancient Peru until the Spanish conquest.

508 ◆ *Short Stories*

---

outer space, and the ignorant suggested he would reach the moon. With a mixture of sadness and relief, Severo decided that his brother-in-law and his machine must have fallen into some hidden crevice of the cordillera,[10] where they would never be found. Nivea wept disconsolately and lit candles to San Antonio, patron of lost objects. Severo opposed the idea of having masses said, because he did not believe in them as a way of getting into heaven, much less of returning to earth, and he maintained that masses and religious vows, like the selling of indulgences, images, and scapulars,[11] were a dishonest business. Because of his attitude, Nivea and Nana had the children say the rosary,[12] behind their father's back for nine days. Meanwhile, groups of volunteer explorers and mountain climbers tirelessly searched peaks and passes, combing every accessible stretch of land until they finally returned in triumph to hand the family the mortal remains of the deceased in a sealed black coffin. The intrepid traveler was laid to rest in a grandiose funeral. His death made him a hero and his name was on the front page of all the papers for several days. The same multitude that had gathered to see him off the day he flew away in his bird paraded past his coffin. The entire family wept as befit the occasion, except for Clara, who continued to watch the sky with the patience of an astronomer. One week after he had been buried, Uncle Marcos, a bright smile playing behind his pirate's

◆ **Reading Strategy**

What inference can you make about what Clara believes concerning her uncle and his fate?

---

10. **cordillera** (kor' dil yer'ə) *n.:* System or chain of mountains.
11. **indulgences, images, and scapulars** (skap' yə lərz): Indulgences are pardons for sins, images are pictures or sculptures of religious figures, and scapulars are garments worn by Roman Catholics as tokens of religious devotion.
12. **say the rosary:** Use a set of beads to say prayers.

◆ **Build Vocabulary**

disconsolately (dis kän' sə lit lē) *adv.:* Unhappily

Beyond the Classroom

Career Connection

Aerodynamics In order to be able to fly successfully, Marcos needed some knowledge of aerodynamics, which is the study of forces that act on an object as it moves through the air. Before building their first plane, the Wright brothers studied aerodynamics. Today, aircraft manufacturers use aerodynamics when they design new planes. Interested students might investigate how aerodynamics affects the flight of a plane. In addition, students might like to find out if there are any kinds of flight that do not involve aerodynamics.

Community Connection

Flight Instruction For Marcos and the Wright brothers, a knowledge of aerodynamics helped them through their first flights. But how does someone learn to fly today? Have interested students find out where, in your community, someone can learn to fly. Some questions students might consider include the following:

- What kind of requirements must a person meet in order to take lessons?
- How long does it generally take someone to get a pilot's license? Is learning to fly expensive?

Have students report their findings to the class.

mustache, appeared in person in the doorway of Nivea and Severo del Valle's house. Thanks to the surreptitious[13] prayers of the women and children, as he himself admitted, he was alive and well and in full possession of his faculties, including his sense of humor. Despite the noble lineage of his aerial maps, the flight had been a failure. He had lost his airplane and had to return on foot, but he had not broken any bones and his adventurous spirit was intact. This confirmed the family's eternal devotion to San Antonio, but was not taken as a warning by future generations, who also tried to fly, although by different means. Legally, however, Marcos was a corpse. Severo del Valle was obliged to use all his legal ingenuity to bring his brother-in-law back to life and the full rights of citizenship. When the coffin was pried open in the presence of the appropriate authorities, it was found to contain a bag of sand. This discovery ruined the reputation, up till then untarnished, of the volunteer explorers and mountain climbers, who from that day on were considered little better than a pack of bandits.

Marcos's heroic resurrection made everyone forget about his barrel-organ phase. Once again he was a sought-after guest in all the city's salons and, at least for a while, his name was cleared. Marcos stayed in his sister's house for several months. One night he left without saying goodbye, leaving behind his trunks, his books, his weapons, his boots, and all his belongings. Severo, and even Nivea herself, breathed a sigh of relief. His visit had gone on too long. But Clara was so upset that she spent a week walking in her sleep and sucking her thumb. The little girl, who was only seven at the time, had learned to read from her uncle's storybooks and been closer to him than any other member of the family because of her prophesying powers. Marcos maintained that his niece's gift could be a source of income and a good opportunity for him to cultivate his own clairvoyance.[14] He believed that all human beings possessed this

13. **surreptitious** (sur´ əp tish´ əs) *adj.*: Secretive.
14. **clairvoyance** (kler voi´ əns) *n.*: Ability to perceive things that are not in sight or can't be seen.

ability, particularly his own family, and that if it did not function well it was simply due to a lack of training. He bought a crystal ball in the Persian bazaar, insisting that it had magic powers and was from the East (although it was later found to be part of a buoy from a fishing boat), set it down on a background of black velvet, and announced that he could tell people's fortunes, cure the evil eye, and improve the quality of dreams, all for the modest sum of five centavos.[15] His first customers were the maids from around the neighborhood. One of them had been accused of stealing, because her employer had misplaced a valuable ring. The crystal ball revealed the exact location of the object in question: it had rolled beneath a wardrobe. The next

15. **centavos** (sen ta´ vos) *n.*: Brazilian currency equal to l/100 of a cruzeiro.

▼ **Critical Viewing** This sketch of a helicopter by Italian artist and inventor Leonardo da Vinci predates the first working helicopters by about 450 years. What do you think Uncle Marcos would have thought of Leonardo da Vinci? **[Speculate]** ❽

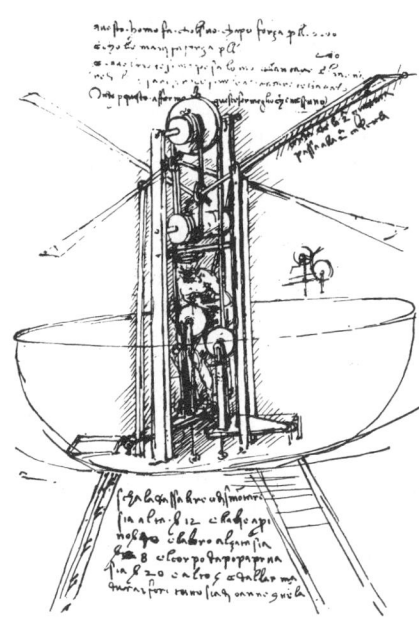

Uncle Marcos from *The House of the Spirits* ◆ 509

◆ **Reading Strategy**

❻ **Make Inferences About Characters** Does Uncle Marcos believe that he owes his survival to the prayers of the women and children? Why does he say he believes this? *Students should observe that Marcos will do just about anything to please an audience.*

◆ **Critical Thinking**

❼ **Make Comparisons** Point out that the family members and Clara differ in their reaction to Marcos's departure. Ask students why they think the reactions are so different. *The family members, other than Clara, find it difficult to put up with Marcos and his idiosyncrasies for very long. Clara loves her uncle and seems to have a gift for prophesying, so she might have a precognition of his death.*

▶**Critical Viewing**◀

❽ **Speculate** Students might think that Marcos would have admired and emulated da Vinci's phenomenal creativity.

Humanities: Autobiography

The House of the Spirits

Allende's novel, *The House of the Spirits,* begins as Alba, the granddaughter of Clara, writes from exile to keep alive the memory of her past. It is not difficult to see that that character of Alba is based on the author herself. "When I left Chile," says Allende, "I didn't dare tell my grandfather.... I couldn't find the words." Years later when her grandfather, nearly a hundred years old, telephoned to tell her that he was dying, "I wanted to tell my grandfather that I was never going to forget him, he would never die, just as my grandmother had never died.... And I started writing a letter, telling him the same things he had told me when I was a child." The letter, never sent, evolved into *The House of the Spirits.*

◆ Reading Strategy

❶ Make Inferences About Characters Students should realize that the ladies would be embarrassed if they thought that other people knew that they believed that Marcos and his niece had special powers.

Comprehension Check ☑

❷ Why do Marcos and Clara abandon their business? *They realize that they have too much power over people and that they might be responsible for a person's doing something foolish in order to change a prediction that Marcos and Clara made.*

◆ Reading Strategy

❸ Make Inferences About Characters Ask students to infer details about Clara's character from this passage. *Clara is very intelligent because she can tell all the stories about her uncle; she is interested in a variety of topics, from the customs of foreigners to antidotes for snake bites; she has an unusual ability to remember things because she knows words from Indian dialects.*

---

day there was a line outside the front door of the house. There were coachmen, storekeepers, and milkmen; later a few municipal employees and distinguished ladies made a discreet appearance, slinking along the side walls of the house to keep from being recognized. The customers were received by Nana, who ushered them into the waiting room and collected their fees. This task kept her busy throughout the day and demanded so much of her time that the family began to complain that all there ever was for dinner was old string beans and jellied quince.[16] Marcos decorated the carriage house with some frayed curtains that had once belonged in the drawing room but that neglect and age had turned to dusty rags. There he and Clara received the customers. The two divines wore tunics "color of the men of light," as Marcos called the color yellow. Nana had dyed them with saffron powder, boiling them in pots usually reserved for rice and pasta. In addition to his tunic, Marcos wore a turban around his head and an Egyptian amulet around his neck. He had grown a beard and let his hair grow long and he was thinner than ever before. Marcos and Clara were utterly convincing, especially because the child had no need to look into the crystal ball to guess what her clients wanted to hear. She would whisper in her Uncle Marcos's ear, and he in turn would transmit the message to the client, along with any improvisations of his own that he thought pertinent. Thus their fame spread, because all those who arrived sad and bedraggled at the consulting room left filled with hope. Unrequited lovers were told how to win over indifferent hearts, and the poor left with foolproof tips on how to place their money at the dog tracks. Business grew so prosperous that the waiting room was always packed with people, and Nana began to suffer dizzy spells from being on her feet so many hours a day. This time Severo had no need to intervene to put a stop to his brother-in-law's venture, for both Marcos and

> **◆ Reading Strategy**
> What can you infer about the motives of the ladies who didn't want to be recognized?

---

16. quince (kwins): Golden or greenish-yellow hard apple-shaped fruit.

510 ◆ Short Stories

Clara, realizing that their unerring guesses could alter the fate of their clients, who always followed their advice to the letter, became frightened and decided that this was a job for swindlers. They abandoned their carriage-house oracle and split the profits, even though the only one who had cared about the material side of things had been Nana.

Of all the del Valle children, Clara was the one with the greatest interest in and stamina for her uncle's stories. She could repeat each and every one of them. She knew by heart words from several dialects of the Indians, was acquainted with their customs, and could describe the exact way in which they pierced their lips and earlobes with wooden shafts, their initiation rites, the names of the most poisonous snakes, and the appropriate antidotes for each. Her uncle was so eloquent that the child could feel in her own skin the burning sting of snakebites, see reptiles slide across the carpet between the legs of the jacaranda[17] room divider, and hear the shrieks of macaws behind the drawing-room drapes. She did not hesitate as she recalled Lope de Aguirre's search for El Dorado,[18] or the unpronounceable names of the flora and fauna her extraordinary uncle had seen; she knew about the lamas who take salt tea with yak lard and she could give detailed descriptions of the opulent women of Tahiti, the rice fields of China, or the white prairies of the North, where the eternal ice kills animals and men who lose their way, turning them to stone in seconds. Marcos had various travel journals in which he recorded his excursions and impressions, as well as a collection of maps and books of stories and fairy tales that he kept in the trunks he stored in the junk room at the far end of the third courtyard.

---

17. jacaranda (jak′ a ran′ da): Type of tropical American tree.
18. Lope de Aguirre's (lo′ pā *the* ə gir′ es) . . . **El Dorado:** Lope de Aguirre was a Spanish adventurer (1510–1561) in colonial South America who searched for a legendary country called El Dorado, which was supposedly rich in gold.

◆ Build Vocabulary
unrequited (un ri kwit′ id) *adj.*: Not returned; not reciprocated

510

CONNECTIONS TO TODAY'S WORLD

The spirit of Uncle Marcos is alive and well! Just about every day, people come up with new inventions with the potential to change how we live. One organization that drives many of the important inventions that are made is NASA. The sketch below shows a proposal for a new type of satellite that would collect information about the sun's rays.

1. What important information is captured in this sketch?
2. In what ways might the person or people who came up with this idea be similar to Uncle Marcos?

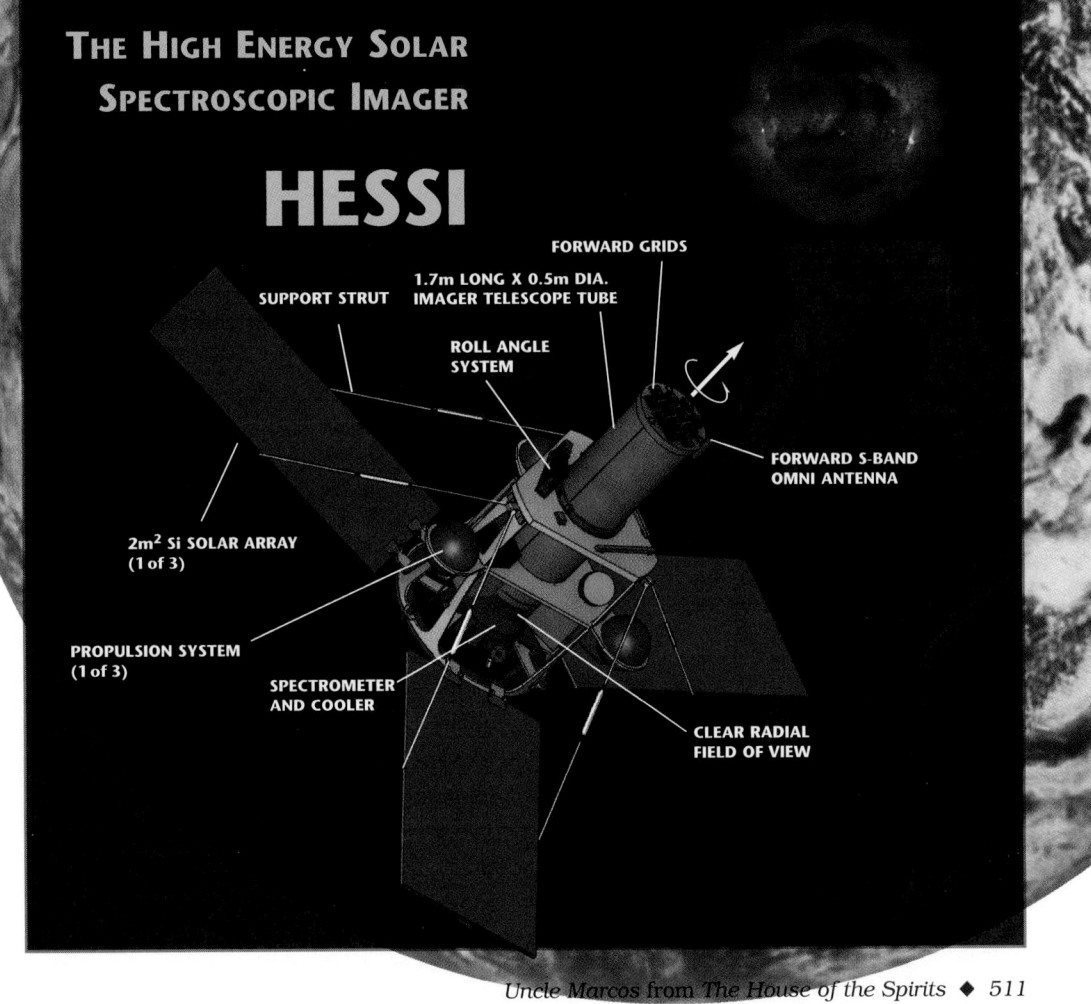

THE HIGH ENERGY SOLAR SPECTROSCOPIC IMAGER

HESSI

FORWARD GRIDS

SUPPORT STRUT

1.7m LONG X 0.5m DIA. IMAGER TELESCOPE TUBE

ROLL ANGLE SYSTEM

FORWARD S-BAND OMNI ANTENNA

2m² Si SOLAR ARRAY (1 of 3)

PROPULSION SYSTEM (1 of 3)

SPECTROMETER AND COOLER

CLEAR RADIAL FIELD OF VIEW

Uncle Marcos from The House of the Spirits ◆ 511

Connections to Today's World

Lead students to see that if Uncle Marcos lived today, this is the type of invention he might have developed. In addition, he probably would have wanted to travel into outer space or communicate via satellite with people on the other side of the world.

Answers

1. The sketch shows the shape and major functioning units of the Spectroscopic Imager.
2. The person who designed the Imager is probably creative, bold, and inventive, as was Uncle Marcos.

 Cross-Curricular Connection: Science

Satellites

There are two kinds of satellites, natural and artificial. A natural satellite is a moon that orbits a planet, just like our moon circles earth. An artificial satellite is a manufactured object that orbits a planet. Sent into space to orbit the Earth or other planets, such artificial satellites can have a variety of purposes. For example, weather satellites transmit pictures of cloud formations to help scientists study the weather, while communications satellites relay television programs between distant places on Earth.

Satellites remain in orbit for different lengths of time, dependent upon their orbital speed and distance from Earth. For example, a low-orbiting satellite can brush air particles in Earth's outer atmosphere, causing it to slow down, fall from orbit, and burn up in the atmosphere.

Invite interested students to research the history of satellites and to report their findings to the class. Students should include pictures of satellites in their reports.(A good encyclopedia has them.) Ask students which satellites look as if Uncle Marcos designed them.

◆ **Reading Strategy**

❶ **Make Inferences About Characters** Have students infer Marcos's relationship to his companion travelers. *Uncle Marcos must have been loved and appreciated by the other passengers.*

Reinforce and Extend

Answers

◆ *Literature and Your Life*

Reader's Response Many students will wish to accompany him on his flight, it being the focus of the story.

Thematic Focus Many students will share Clara's appreciative view of Uncle Marcos because he is portrayed sympathetically.

☑ **Check Your Comprehension**

1. Sample words include *eccentric, adventurous, strange, weird, dramatic, quixotic, charismatic, bothersome, impractical.*
2. The adventure seemed doomed from the start. It wasn't likely that such a contraption would actually work.
3. Clara, who had a gift for clairvoyance, would guess what the customers would want to hear and whisper the response into her uncle's ear.

◆ **Critical Thinking**

1. Students should note that most of the characters are contemptuous of Uncle Marcos and skeptical of his projects, while Clara is sympathetic and understanding.
2. Clara, unlike the other characters, is able to develop a bond with her uncle. She is not judgmental.
3. Uncle Marcos, in his own way, is courtly and understanding of others. One piece of evidence is how the other passengers on the ship forced the captain to take care of Marcos's body after he died.
4. She is embarrassed by his behavior and rejects his advances.
5. Students may believe that Uncle Marcos would be good at a creative occupation such as an artist or advertising director.
6. Students may come away from the story with an appreciation for the incredible possibilities of life, as well as for the benefits of marching to the beat of one's own drummer.

512

From there they were hauled out to inhabit the dreams of his descendants, until they were mistakenly burned half a century later on an infamous pyre.

Now Marcos had returned from his last journey in a coffin. He had died of a mysterious African plague that had turned him as yellow and wrinkled as a piece of parchment. When he realized he was ill, he set out for home with the hope that his sister's ministrations and Dr. Cuevas's knowledge would restore his health and youth, but he was unable to withstand the sixty days on ship and died at the latitude of Guayaquil,[19] ravaged by fever and hallucinating about musky women and hidden treasure. The captain of the ship, an Englishman by the name of Longfellow, was about to throw him overboard wrapped in a flag, but Marcos, de- ❶ spite his savage appearance and his delirium, had made so many friends on board and seduced so many women that the passengers prevented him from doing so, and Longfellow was obliged to store the body side by side with the vegetables of the Chinese cook, to preserve it from the heat and mosquitoes of the tropics until the ship's carpenter had time to improvise a coffin. At El Callao[20] they obtained a more appropriate container, and several days later the captain, furious at all the troubles this passenger had caused the shipping company and himself personally, unloaded him without a backward glance, surprised that not a soul was there to receive the body or cover the expenses he had incurred. Later he learned that the post office in these latitudes was not as reliable as that of far-off England, and that all his telegrams had vaporized en route. Fortunately for Longfellow, a customs lawyer who was a friend of the del Valle family appeared and offered to take charge, placing Marcos and all his paraphernalia in a freight car, which he shipped to the capital to the only known address of the deceased: his sister's house. . . .

---

19. **Guayaquil** (gwī ä kēl´): Seaport in western Ecuador.

20. **El Callao** (kə yä´ ō): Seaport in western Peru.

Guide for Responding

◆ *Literature and Your Life*

Reader's Response Which adventure would you most like to share with Uncle Marcos? Why?

Thematic Focus If you were a character in this story, how would you feel about Uncle Marcos?

Journal Writing Jot down your memories of an eccentric person you've encountered. What made the person eccentric? What sort of impression did the person make upon you?

☑ **Check Your Comprehension**

1. What four words could you use to describe Uncle Marcos?
2. Why was it easy for the townspeople to believe that Uncle Marcos had died in a plane crash?
3. How did Uncle Marcos and Clara tell fortunes?

◆ **Critical Thinking**

INTERPRET

1. What is each character's attitude toward Uncle Marcos? **[Interpret]**
2. How do the other characters' attitudes toward Uncle Marcos differ from Clara's? **[Compare and Contrast]**
3. Severo says: "Uncle Marcos's manners were those of a cannibal." What evidence from this story refutes Severo's claim? **[Support]**
4. What does Cousin Antonieta think of Uncle Marcos's method of courtship? **[Infer]**

EXTEND

5. What kind of job do you think Uncle Marcos would be good at? Explain. **[Career Link]**

APPLY

6. What lessons can be learned from Uncle Marcos and his approach to life? **[Apply]**

Beyond the Selection

FURTHER READING

Other Works by the Authors
Gorilla, My Love, Toni Cade Bambara
The Sea Birds Are Still Alive, Toni Cade Bambara
Eva Luna, Isabel Allende
The House of the Spirits, Isabel Allende

Other Works With the Theme of Perspectives of People
"The Handsomest Drowned Man in the World," Gabriel García Márquez
"The Most Dangerous Game," Richard Connell

INTERNET

For more information about the authors, we suggest the following Internet site. Please be aware, however, that sites may have changed from the time we published this information.

For Toni Cade Bambara, go to **http://www. inmotionmagazine.com/bambara.html**

We *strongly recommend* that you preview the site before you send students it.

Guide for Responding (continued)

◆ Reading Strategy

MAKE INFERENCES ABOUT CHARACTERS
Based on the characters' actions in this story, you can **make inferences,** or draw conclusions, about their personalities.

1. How does the photographer in "Blues Ain't No Mockin Bird" feel about the people he is filming? Support your answer.
2. In "Uncle Marcos," what details might lead you to infer that Marcos enjoys having an audience for his adventures?
3. What evidence supports the inference that Clara is an unusual child?

◆ Literary Focus

DIRECT AND INDIRECT CHARACTERIZATION
Characterization refers to a writer's revelations of a character's personality traits. In **direct characterization,** a writer simply states a fact about a character. In **indirect characterization,** a writer implies facts about a character by showing you what the character says or does and how other characters react to him or her. Notice Bambara's use of indirect characterization in this passage:

> "Nice things here," said the man, buzzin his camera over the yard. The pecan barrels, the sled, me and Cathy, the flowers, the printed stones along the driveway, the trees, the twins, the toolshed.

The man's actions show that he thinks the people have about the same importance as the things. You can infer that the man is insensitive and rude. If Bambara had simply said, "The man was insensitive and rude," she would have been using direct characterization.

1. Find an example of indirect characterization for two of the characters in each story.
2. For each example, rewrite it as direct characterization.
3. Which method do you think is more effective: indirect characterization or direct characterization? Explain your answer.

◆ Build Vocabulary

USING THE PREFIX *dis-*
In your notebook, write each sentence, completing it with a word that uses the prefix *dis-* with the italicized word.

1. The twins *agreed* to let Cathy and the narrator swing in the tire, but they ___?___ about when.
2. Granny demanded *respect*, but the cameraman treated her with ___?___.
3. Uncle Marcos exercised with *graceful* movements, but sometimes his behavior seemed ___?___ to Severo.
4. Uncle Marcos wanted only to *please* Cousin Antonieta, but he managed to ___?___ her instead.

USING THE WORD BANK
In your notebook, write the letter of the word or words closest in meaning to the first word.

1. lassoed: (a) loosened, (b) raced toward, (c) wrapped around
2. formality: (a) established customs, (b) casual attitude, (c) honesty
3. vanquished: (a) disappeared, (b) defeated, (c) cleaned
4. fetid: (a) fresh, (b) sweet, (c) smelly
5. impassive: (a) emotionless, (b) excited, (c) fair
6. disconsolately: (a) slowly, (b) unhappily, (c) quickly
7. unrequited: (a) not returned, (b) unreasonable, (c) not quiet

◆ Build Grammar Skills

POSSESSIVE NOUNS
Possessive nouns show ownership, belonging, or another close relationship. Review the chart on p. 496 to see how to form possessive nouns.

Practice In your notebook, change each underlined phrase into the correct possessive form.

1. the picture *of Uncle Marcos:* ___?___ picture
2. the curiosity *of the townspeople:* the ___?___ curiosity
3. the rudeness *of the cameraman:* the ___?___ rudeness
4. the argument *of the twins:* the ___?___ argument
5. the dignity *of Granddaddy Cain:* ___?___ dignity

Blues Ain't No Mockin Bird/Uncle Marcos from *The House of the Spirits* ◆ 513

Answers

◆ Reading Strategy
1. Students should point out that the condescending way the photographer treats the family indicates his contempt toward them.
2. Students may point out that Uncle Marcos's propensity for staying several months at a time indicates his enjoyment at having an audience for his tales of adventure.
3. Clara, unlike the others in her family, seems to understand and appreciate her uncle; she also appears to have the gift of prophesy.

◆ Literary Focus
1. Students' examples of indirect characterization should involve implied facts about the character based on what he or she says or what other characters say about him or her.
2. Students' rewritten characterizations should be stated directly.
3. Students' responses should show an appreciation for the literary benefits of each type of characterization.

◆ Build Vocabulary

Using the Prefix *dis-*
1. disagreed
2. disrespect
3. disgraceful
4. displease

Using the Word Bank
1. c 2. a 3. b 4. c
5. a 6. b 7. a

◆ Build Grammar Skills

Practice
1. Uncle Marcos's
2. the townspeople's
3. the camera man's
4. the twins'
5. Granddaddy Cain's

 **Writer's Solution**

For additional instruction and practice, use the practice page on Apostrophes With Possessive Nouns in the *Writer's Solution Grammar Practice Book,* p. 112.

Idea Bank

Customizing for
Performance Levels

Following are suggestions for matching the Idea Bank topics with your students' performance levels:

Less Advanced Students: 1, 5, 7
Average Students: 2, 6
More Advanced Students: 3, 4

Customizing for
Learning Modalities

Following are suggestions for matching Idea Bank topics with your students' learning modalities:

Verbal/Linguistic: 4, 5
Interpersonal: 4
Visual/Spatial: 6, 7

Writing Mini-Lesson

Refer students to the Writing Handbook, page 962, for instruction on the writing process, and page 964 for further information on description.

Writing Process Transparencies
To help student with their magazine profiles, use the Writing Process Model 2: Biographical Profile on pp. 17–20 of *Writing and Language Transparencies*.

Writer's Solution

Writing Lab CD-ROM
Have students complete the Tutorial on Description. Follow these steps:
1. Have students do the Self-Interview activity to help them select a topic for their magazine feature.
2. Have them draft on computer.
3. Have students use the Self-Evaluation Checklist to help them revise.

Allow approximately 30 minutes of class time to complete these steps.

Sourcebook
Have students use Chapter 1, Description (pp. 1–29), for additional support. The chapter includes a model of a character profile, p. 7.

Build Your Portfolio

Idea Bank

Writing

1. **Letter** Suppose you were there the day Uncle Marcos took off in his airplane. Write a letter to a friend describing the event and what you thought of it.

2. **Character Sketch** What type of person do you think Clara became as an adult? Use your imagination to create a character sketch describing what Clara is like as an adult.

3. **Persuasive Essay** Write a persuasive essay that answers this question: Do the news media have the right to intrude in people's lives in order to get a story?

Speaking and Listening

4. **Debate** Sometimes imaginative and adventurous people like Uncle Marcos are seen as irresponsible. With three classmates, debate whether colorful characters make an important contribution to family life and to society. Two people in your group will take the pro side, and two will take the con side. **[Social Studies Link]**

5. **Monologue** Put yourself in the place of the cameraman in "Blues Ain't No Mockin Bird." Explain to your boss what happened to your camera. **[Career Link]**

Projects

6. **Illustrated Report** Bambara's title refers to a type of music called the blues. Research this type of music and gather photographs, illustrations, and recordings, if possible. Present your findings to the class. **[Music Link]**

7. **Illustration** Illustrate a scene from one of the stories using your favorite art medium. Add a caption and display your work in class. **[Art Link]**

Writing Mini-Lesson

Magazine Feature

These stories feature amazing characters, brought to life through vivid details. Picture an amazing person you know or have read about and write a magazine feature about that person.

Writing Skills Focus:
Main Impression

As you write, focus your magazine feature on a **main impression**—in this case, what makes the person truly amazing. Include details that support the main impression and avoid details that do not support it. In this example, Isabel Allende includes only those details that show Uncle Marcos is unusual.

Model From the Story

While the rest of the household tried to sleep, he dragged his suitcases up and down the halls, practiced making strange, high-pitched sounds on savage instruments, and taught Spanish to a parrot whose native language was an Amazonic dialect.

Prewriting Decide on your main impression and list details that support it. Consider these categories: physical appearance, personality traits, activities, talents, and goals.

Drafting Using your prewriting notes, write about your amazing person. For each characteristic you mention, give an example that shows how the person exhibits that characteristic. Look through magazines for models of feature articles to help you write your own feature.

Revising Give your feature to a peer for review. See if your reviewer can accurately state the main impression. If not, look for places where greater detail or clearer description is needed. Discard any details that do not contribute to the main impression.

✓ ASSESSMENT OPTIONS

Formal Assessment, Selection Test, pp. 129–131, and Assessment Resources Software. The selection test is designed so that it can be easily customized to the performance levels of your students.
Alternative Assessment, p. 37, includes options for less advanced students, more advanced students, visual/spatial learners, verbal/linguistic learners, and intrapersonal learners.

PORTFOLIO ASSESSMENT
Use the following rubrics in the *Alternative Assessment* booklet to assess student writing:
Letter: Expression Rubric, p. 87
Character Sketch: Description Rubric, p. 90
Persuasive Essay: Persuasion Rubric, p. 98
Writing Mini-Lesson: Description Rubric, p. 90

Writing Process Workshop

Personal Narrative

Like the writers in this unit, we all have tales to tell. In fact, if you look back on your own life so far, you're likely to find many events and experiences that would make great stories. Bring one of these experiences to life by writing a **personal narrative**—a true story about a memorable experience or event from your life. Include your personal feelings about the event you're describing to enable your readers to connect with your narrative. The following skills, introduced in this section's Writing Mini-Lessons, will help you write your personal narrative.

Writing Skills Focus

▶ **Elaborate to make your writing personal** by providing details that capture how the experience affected you. (See p. 466.)

▶ **Provide vivid details** to help readers picture the people, setting, and events in your narrative. (See p. 495.)

▶ **Give a main impression** of the experience and its impact on you. (See p. 514.)

▶ **Create dramatic effects**, such as a suspenseful beginning or a surprise ending. (See p. 481.)

Author James Hurst uses several of these skills in this passage from "The Scarlet Ibis."

MODEL FROM LITERATURE

from "The Scarlet Ibis" by James Hurst

It was bad enough having an invalid brother, but having one who possibly was not all there was unbearable, so I began to make plans to kill him by smothering him with a pillow. ① However, one afternoon as I watched him, my head poked between the iron posts of the foot of the bed, he looked straight at me and grinned. ② I skipped through the rooms, down the echoing halls, shouting, "Mama, he smiled. He's all there! He's all there!" and he was. ③

① Details about the narrator's feelings provide vivid insights into his personality.

② The writer introduces a dramatic twist that grabs the reader's interest.

③ The events are described through vivid details that create a picture in the reader's mind.

Establish Writing Guidelines
Before students begin, review the following key characteristics of a personal narrative:
- A personal narrative is a true story about a memorable experience or period in the writer's life.
- The writer's feelings about events shape the way the story is told, and the way people and places are described.

You may want to distribute the scoring rubric for Narration (p. 89 in *Alternative Assessment*) to make students aware of the criteria on which they will be evaluated. See the suggestions on page 517 for how you can customize the rubric for this workshop.

 Writer's Solution

Writers at Work Videodisc
To introduce students to the key elements and show them how Isabel Allende uses them in her narrative writing, play the videodisc segment on Narration (Ch. 2). Have students discuss how Allende sees a book as a bridge, as well as how she views lies and the truth in narrative writing.

Play frames 10786 to 22536

Writing Lab CD-ROM
If your students have access to computers, you may want to have them work on the tutorial on Narration to complete all or part of their personal narratives. Follow these steps:
1. Have students review the interactive model of a personal narrative.
2. Encourage students to use the Word Bins to gather sensory details of setting and character traits as they draft on the computer and as they revise.
3. Have students use a Transition Word Bin to add transitions to their drafts.
4. Suggest students use the Self-Evaluation checklist.

Sourcebook
Students can find additional support, in the chapter on Narration (pp. 30–61).

 **Cross-Curricular Connection: Social Studies**

Tell students that personal narratives often revolve around a particular theme, such as civil rights, cultural identity, or immigration. People often write personal narratives about an important incident that helped shape their identity. Discuss personal narratives that touch on historic events and situations, such as from *Rosa Parks: My Story* and from *In My Place.* You may also want to discuss books that students are likely to have read previously, such as *Farewell to Manzanar,* which deals with the internment of Japanese-Americans during World War II, and *Little House on the Prairie,* which describes pioneer life. Have students discuss some pivotal moments in their lives that might make appropriate topics for a personal narrative.

515

Develop Student Writing

Prewriting

Remind students that knowing who their audience will be is as important as having a clear purpose. For instance, if a student is writing a personal narrative about a ski vacation for people who may not have skied before, he or she should explain such things as the grading system of trails, what a mid-mountain lodge is, and so on.

Customize for
English Language Learners

To help students acquire vocabulary for describing settings and people, collect pictures from magazines and help students label the scenes and people with appropriate adjectives. One source of adjectives is the Character Traits Word Bin that is found on page 51 of the *Writer's Solution Sourcebook;* you will probably want to modify this list according to your students' proficiency with English and to provide additional adjectives. You may wish to write the labels on removable sticky notes so that students can move the labels if they change their minds. Students can refer to the labeled pictures as they write their personal narratives.

Customize for
Less Proficient Writers

Encourage these students make a plot diagram before they begin drafting. The diagram should include the exposition, conflict and rising action, climax, and resolution. Have them refer to the diagram while drafting.

Drafting

Remind students to make their writing personal and dramatic as they draft. They might find it helpful to imagine that they are writing to a close friend who they want to impress.

APPLYING LANGUAGE SKILLS: Active and Passive Voice

A verb in the **active voice** shows the subject performing an action. A verb in the **passive voice** shows the subject receiving an action.

Active Voice:
I <u>chased</u> the thief.

Passive Voice:
The thief <u>was chased</u> by me.

Notice how the active voice makes writing more forceful and lively.

Practice Rewrite each sentence so that the verb is in the active voice.

1. The chase was joined by the police.
2. The wallet was dropped by the thief.
3. I was excited by this sudden surprise.

Writing Application As you draft your personal narrative, write most of your sentences using the active voice. Use the passive voice only when the performer of the action is unknown or unimportant.

Writer's Solution Connection
Writing Lab

To help you choose a topic, use the Sunburst Diagram activity in the Choosing a Topic section in the tutorial on Narration.

516 ◆ *Short Stories*

Prewriting

Choose a Topic Choose a memorable experience from your life on which to base your personal narrative. If no ideas come to mind, try the following suggestions.

- Look through your journal or scrapbook.
- Ask a family member to recall interesting moments from your life.
- Think about some of your "firsts"—your first pet, first trip, or first day in a new school, for example.

Plan Your Story Details Once you've chosen your topic, write detailed notes that answer the following questions: *Who* else was involved in the experience or event? *Where* and *when* did it take place? *What* happened first, next, and last? *Why* was the experience memorable? *How* did the experience make me feel?

Consider Your Purpose The purpose of most narratives is to entertain, but narratives can have other purposes as well. Decide what effect you want your narrative to have on your readers. Here are some tips for achieving different purposes.

To amuse:	• Use exaggeration • Emphasize the absurdity or silliness of a situation
To teach a lesson:	• Show clear causes and effects • Use precise language
To frighten:	• Create dark, eerie settings • Use suspenseful language

Drafting

Use Elaboration to Make Your Writing Personal As you draft your narrative, offer enough details so that readers can connect in a personal way with your narrative. Make them feel as if only you—and no other writer—could have told this particular story. Remember to share your personal feelings about the narrative's events.

Create Dramatic Effects Look for ways to make your narrative as interesting or exciting as possible. For example, you might begin with details that will grab readers' interest and arouse their curiosity. Later, add details that will heighten their curiosity. Even if your narrative doesn't have a surprise ending, make the ending one that readers will find memorable.

Applying Language Skills
Active and Passive Voice

Answers

1. The police joined the chase.
2. The thief dropped the wallet.
3. This sudden surprise excited me.

Writer's Solution

For additional instruction and practice, have students complete the Language **Lab CD-ROM** lesson on Active and Passive Voice and the practice pages on Active and Passive Voice, pp. 76–77, in the *Writer's Solution Grammar Practice Book.*

Using Pronouns

Answers

1. There was a loud noise on *my* block.
2. *I* ran outside to see what it was.
3. A neighbor called to my sister and *me.*
4. A friend of *mine* came over to help.

Writer's Solution

For additional instruction and practice, have students complete the practice pages on The Cases of Pronouns, pp. 78–80, in the *Writer's Solution Grammar Practice Book.*

Revising

Use a Checklist Go back to the Writing Skills Focus on the first page of this lesson, and use the items as a checklist to evaluate and revise your personal narrative. Ask yourself:

▶ Are my characters, setting, and events detailed enough?
Have one or more peers read your narrative. If they have questions about the content, add clarifying details.

▶ Is my writing personal enough?
Consider details you can add to make your narrative sound more like you.

▶ Have I given a main impression?
Find those places where you have expressed your feelings about your experience. Decide whether you need to elaborate on those feelings.

▶ Does my work contain dramatic elements?
Discuss with a peer whether your narrative is exciting. Add details that will further heighten readers' interest.

REVISION MODEL

Below is a revised paragraph from a personal narrative by Kileen Cheng, a student at Westwood High School in Round Rock, Texas. Notice that Kileen adds a sentence to increase suspense and to make a smoother transition into the story. She also replaces a vague word with one that is precise and adds details about the setting to help explain why the room had a relaxing effect on her.

After what seemed like an eternity, we finally arrived.
Minutes later, we were on our way to the hospital. My mom

and I easily found his room. I hesitantly opened the door and

crept ₂
~~went~~ inside. The room was rather small, with a low ceiling, and
was crowded with
~~had lots of~~ flowers of all different colors, shapes, and sizes.
The flowers added a warm glow and a feeling of home. The fresh fragrance
They helped me relax, and the whole atmosphere made me forget

momentarily about life's complications.

Publishing

▶ **Personal Drama** Together with classmates, act out a staged version of your narrative.

▶ **Magazine** Submit your personal narrative to a magazine that publishes true stories.

APPLYING LANGUAGE SKILLS: Using Pronouns

In a personal narrative, you often use the **pronouns** *I, me, my,* and *mine.*

I ran home quickly.

The dog chased Bob and me.

It bit my pants.

The dog wasn't mine.

Notice the pronoun form used in each sentence.

Practice On your paper, choose the correct pronoun to complete each sentence.

1. There was a loud noise on (my, mine) block.
2. (Me, I) ran outside to see what it was.
3. A neighbor called to my sister and (I, me).
4. A friend of (my, mine) came over to help.

Writing Application As you revise your personal narrative, check to see whether you have used the correct pronouns in your sentences. If you find any errors, correct them before making your final copy.

Writer's Solution Connection
Writing Lab

For more instruction on pronouns and revision, work through the Revision section of the tutorial on Narration.

Revising

You may want to have students work with peer editors to revise their personal observations. Have peer reviewers use the revision checklist to review. Tell the peer reviewers to offer specific, concrete suggestions for improvement rather than general criticism.

Writer's Solution

Writing Lab CD-ROM
Have students use the revision checkers for style in the Revising and Editing section of the tutorial on Narration. Students can use revision tools to check for passive voice, language variety, and clear links between pronouns and antecedents.

Publishing

Students who do not wish to share their personal observations with a larger audience at this time should be encouraged to save them. Most college applications include an essay about an experience that has affected the applicant in some way. A graded personal narrative can serve as a handy reference for style and content while writing such an essay.

Reinforce and Extend

Review the Writing Guidelines
After students have completed their papers, review the characteristics of a personal narrative. Encourage students to come up with additional criteria for an interesting short story based on what they learned through completing the assignment.

Connect to Literature Unit 3 ("Moments of Discovery") includes an example of a personal narrative: Charlene Hunter-Gault's essay from *In My Place* (p. 250).

✓ ASSESSMENT		4	3	2	1
PORTFOLIO ASSESSMENT Use the rubric on Narrative Based on Personal Experience in the **Alternative Assessment** booklet (p. 89) to assess the students' writing. Add these criteria to customize the rubric to this assignment.	**Active and Passive Voice**	Almost all of the verbs are in the active voice.	Active-voice verbs dominate, though there may be one or two instances of the weak-passive.	Verbs are generally in the active voice, but there are more than a few instances of the weak-passive.	Passive-voice verbs dominate the narrative, rendering it weak and ineffective.
	Elaboration	The narrative is filled with specific details and thoughts that make it an intensely personal experience for the reader.	The narrative uses specific details and thoughts that interest but do not completely envelop the reader.	The narrative offers enough details to make it readable, though there is definitely the sense that something is missing.	The narrative is general and vague and uses little or no specific details or thoughts. It could have been written by anyone.

517

Real-World Reading Skills Workshop

Strategies for Success

Recognizing the main ideas in a short story can help you to appreciate that story more. In the same way, spotting the main ideas in a nonfiction article will help you to better understand the article and enjoy it more.

Check the Lead Sentence In an article, each paragraph may contain its own main idea, which is often stated in the lead sentence—or first sentence—of the paragraph. As you read the rest of the paragraph, you'll find details to support the main idea.

Look at the End of the Article The end of an article sometimes summarizes the main ideas that were discussed previously. When you read an article, study the last paragraph carefully. Do you find earlier ideas being repeated? If so, they probably are main ideas.

Draw Your Own Conclusion Sometimes in an article, a main idea is not stated directly. Instead, you must make inferences about the main idea based on details that are provided. If you can't find a main idea in any sentence, ask yourself: What is the point of the paragraph? To what do all the details lead? Your answer will be the main idea.

Apply the Strategy

How well can you recognize main ideas? Read the article entitled "How Our Government Works." Then see if you can answer these questions.

1. What is the main idea of the first paragraph? Which sentence states the idea?
2. Is the main idea stated directly in the second paragraph? If so, where?
3. What is the main idea of the third paragraph? Is it stated directly?
4. Does the article summarize its main ideas? If so, where?

How Our Government Works

Our government has three branches, and each is affected by the other two. The legislative branch makes our laws. This branch includes the Senate and House of Representatives.

The executive branch exists to see that our laws are carried out. This branch is headed by the President.

The judicial branch interprets and explains our laws. This branch is made up of all our judges, including the Supreme Court. We need all three branches — the legislative, executive, and judicial — in order for our society to function.

✔ Here are other situations in which recognizing main ideas can be helpful:
► Reading a news story in the newspaper
► Reading a scientific research paper
► Reading a biographical sketch
► Reading an information sheet about a club

PART 2 *Setting and Theme*

Opened Door, Rose Weinstock

One-Minute Planning Guide

The short stories in this section illustrate the literary elements of setting and theme. Setting plays a major role in "The Man to Send Rain Clouds," in which Pueblo and Christian beliefs collide in the Southwest, and in "The Invalid's Story," which describes an unpleasant situation that occurs in the close quarters of a train compartment. In "The Necklace," an ironic twist of fate changes a woman's life, and in "The Harvest" some boys discover that there is usually more to a person than meets the eye.

Customize for
Varying Student Needs
When assigning the selections in this section to your students, keep in mind the following factors:

"The Man to Send Rain Clouds"
• Social studies connection
• Religious references may require explanation for some students

"The Invalid's Story"
• English language learners may need extra help in understanding the humorous misunderstandings that occur in the story

"The Necklace"
• Setting and time period may be unfamiliar to some students
• Long, complex sentences may present a challenge for less proficient readers and English language learners
• Short sentences and familiar words make this story accessible to most students

---

Humanities: Art

Opened Door by Rose Weinstock.
A New Yorker, Rose Weinstock is known for her finely detailed realist oil paintings. She studied at Wellesley College and the National Academy of Design.

Encourage students to look for signs that this very realistic work is a painting, not a photograph: for example, the slightly softer edges, particularly on the steps.

Help students link this painting to the focus of Part 2 ("Setting and Theme") by answering the following questions:

1. Is the mood of this painting comfortable or sinister, inviting or frightening—and why? *Students who find the mood comfortable or inviting could stress the beauty or old-fashioned charm of the entryway. Students who find it sinister or frightening could stress the heavy shadows around the doorway and the fact that the interior is completely in the dark.*

2. Name three very different kinds of stories that could conceivably take place in the house shown here. *Sample answer: This house could serve as the setting for a story about a close-knit family, a story about a haunting, and a story about time travel.*

519

Guide for Reading

OBJECTIVES

1. To read, comprehend, and interpret stories
2. To relate stories to personal experience
3. To use the senses to picture characters and settings
4. To identify setting
5. To build vocabulary in context and learn the suffix *-ous*
6. To develop skill in punctuating dialogue
7. To write a eulogy focusing on tone
8. To respond to the story through writing, speaking and listening, and projects

SKILLS INSTRUCTION

Vocabulary:
Suffixes: *-ous*

Speaking and Listening:
Dramatic Reading; Persuasive Speech (teacher edition)

Grammar:
Punctuating Dialogue

Reading Strategy:
Use Your Senses

Critical Viewing:
Relate; Support; Predict

Literary Focus:
Setting

Writing: Tone

PORTFOLIO OPPORTUNITIES

Writing: Suggestion Letter; Essay; Research
Writing Mini-Lesson: Eulogy
Speaking and Listening: Dramatic Reading; Persuasive Speech
Projects: Map; Diagram

More About the Authors

On the Laguna Pueblo reservation where she grew up, **Leslie Marmon Silko** was educated through high school by the Bureau of Indian Affairs. She attended the University of New Mexico and graduated *magna cum laude* in 1969. She has taught at the Navajo Community College in Arizona and at the University of New Mexico.

Mark Twain began his successful writing career with a collection of stories, *The Celebrated Jumping Frog of Calaveras County*. As his fame as a writer and lecturer grew, he traveled widely, publishing his first travel book, *The Innocents Abroad*, in 1869. Twain's great contribution to American literature rests on his sense of humor, which is evident even in this story about the death of the main character's friend.

Leslie Marmon Silko

(1948–)

Storytelling has been an important part of Leslie Marmon Silko's life practically from the day she was born. Raised on the Laguna Pueblo reservation in New Mexico, she grew up listening to tribal stories told by her great-grandmother and great-aunts. Drawing upon elements from the traditional tales she heard as a child, Silko has forged a successful career as a writer.

In her stories, novels, and poems, Silko explores what life is like for Native Americans in today's world. Many of her works, including "The Man Who Sends Rain Clouds," capture the contrast between traditional values and beliefs and the elements of modern-day life.

Mark Twain (1835–1910)

Born Samuel Langhorne Clemens, this great American humorist grew up in the river town of Hannibal, Missouri. Though Twain traveled and lived all over the United States, it is the great Mississippi River that runs through the heart of his life and work.

As a young man, he learned the trade of the riverboat pilot and took his pen name from a sounding cry used on Mississippi steamboats: 'By the mark—twain,' which means the water is two fathoms deep. Although Twain worked as a printer, prospector, reporter, editor, and lecturer, writing was his true calling. He was the best-known and most successful author of his generation. Some of his most popular works include *Tom Sawyer*, *The Adventures of Huckleberry Finn*, and *Life on the Mississippi*.

◆ Build Vocabulary

SUFFIXES: *-ous*

Prodigious. Deleterious. Ominous. Judicious. These words have two things in common: They all appear in "The Invalid's Story," and they all are many-syllabled words ending with the suffix *-ous*, which means "full of." For instance, *prodigious* combines *prodigy*, meaning "a marvel or wonder," with *-ous*; *prodigious* means "wonderful" or "amazing." In Twain's story, the word *prodigious* refers to a mistake. Fortunately for the reader, this prodigious mistake leads to a humorous story.

cloister
pagans
perverse
prodigious
deleterious
ominous
judicious
placidly
desultory

Word Bank

Before you read, preview this list of words from the stories.

◆ Build Grammar Skills

PUNCTUATING DIALOGUE

Both of these stories rely heavily on **dialogue**—conversation involving at least two speakers. Follow these rules for punctuating the dialogue:
- Use quotation marks before and after a speaker's exact words.
- Begin a new paragraph each time the speaker changes.
- Use commas to separate quotations from words that identify the speaker—no matter where those words appear in the sentence. The comma always appears before the quotation marks.
- When a paragraph ends while a character is still speaking, quotation marks do not appear at the end of that paragraph. However, they do appear at the beginning of the new paragraph.

 Prentice Hall Literature Program Resources

REINFORCE / RETEACH / EXTEND

Selection Support Pages
Build Vocabulary: Suffixes: *-ous*, p. 155
Build Grammar Skills: Punctuating Dialogue, p. 156
Reading Strategy: Use Your Senses, p. 157
Literary Focus: Setting, p. 158

Strategies for Diverse Student Needs, p. 38

Beyond Literature
Cross-Curricular Connection: Social Studies, p. 38

Formal Assessment Selection Test, pp. 132–134, Assessment Resources Software

Alternative Assessment, p. 38

Writing and Language Transparencies
Biographical Profile, pp. 9–15

Resource Pro CD-ROM
—includes all resource material and customizable lesson plan

Listening to Literature Audiocassettes
"The Man to Send Rain Clouds," "The Invalid's Story"

Literature CD-ROM
The History of American Literature: Part I, Disc 2 Feature 9

The Man to Send Rain Clouds
◆ The Invalid's Story ◆

◆ *Literature and Your Life*

CONNECT YOUR EXPERIENCE

At some time, everyone has to deal with the loss of a loved one. People cope with this in different ways. They may try to preserve the loved one's memory, or they may look to fulfill the person's last wishes. These stories present two very different sets of circumstances surrounding a person's death and others' responses to it.

THEMATIC FOCUS: FACING CONFLICTS

As these stories reveal, dealing with death can involve working out difficult and sometimes unexpected issues and situations.

◆ Background for Understanding

CULTURE

"The Man to Send Rain Clouds" explores the traditions of the Pueblo Indians. The Pueblos have lived in the southwestern United States for nearly 3,000 years. They first came into contact with Europeans when the Spanish arrived in the 1500's. During the twentieth century, the Pueblos have incorporated many aspects of the industrial world into their lives. Nevertheless, they have tried to maintain their ancient traditions and beliefs—including the view that if they keep themselves in harmony with the natural world, nature will give them what they need, such as sufficient rainfall for their crops. The Pueblos' balancing of modern ways with their own customs and views provides the central conflict in Silko's story.

Journal Writing Jot down what you know about the Pueblo people and other Native American cultures.

◆ Literary Focus

SETTING

In each of these stories, events grow out of the **setting**—the place and time of the action. In some stories, the setting simply provides a backdrop for the actions and characters. In other stories—including these—the setting shapes the characters' actions.

In addition to time and place, a story's setting includes the **cultural background** against which the action takes place: the customs, ideas, values, and beliefs of the society in which it occurs. The cultural background for "The Man to Send Rain Clouds" consists of the customs and beliefs of the Pueblo people.

◆ Reading Strategy

USE YOUR SENSES

A dry wintry desert waiting for rain. A stifling boxcar with a smelly package. The setting of each story gives your senses a real workout. As you read each one, **use your senses** to picture the setting and the characters in your mind.

Draw from your own experiences to see, hear, smell, taste, or feel what each author describes. For example, when Twain describes a piece of cheese with an overpowering odor, search your memory to recall when you've smelled especially pungent cheese, and try to re-create the sensation in your mind.

Use a graphic organizer like this one to help you record key details appealing to each sense.

Sights	Sounds	Smells	Tastes	Physical Sensations

Guide for Reading ◆ 521

One-Minute Insight

In each story, death provides a context for the author to explore life. In Leslie Marmon Silko's story, the death of Teofilo, an elderly Native American, serves as a backdrop to illuminate the actions, reactions, and interactions of the living. Characters lead their lives according to sets of rules and systems of belief dictated by cultural conventions that have developed over centuries but may be enriched and redefined through changing influences. The funeral rites for Teofilo provide such an enriching and redefining moment, as Native American tradition is combined with Christian tradition.

◆ **Literary Focus**

❶ **Setting** Have students identify physical features of the setting that are revealed in the paragraph. *Students can describe the landscape: a shallow, sandy canyon spotted with stands of cottonwoods and edged by snowy peaks; the trees are bare and a thin winter sun is shining.*

◆ **Critical Thinking**

❷ **Make Inferences** Have students visualize what Leon and Ken are doing. Ask: Why are Leon and Ken painting the old man's face? Why does Leon smile? *Students should infer that Leon and Ken are performing a ritual of their culture, and that Leon smiles because the ritual has been performed to his satisfaction.*

◆ **Critical Thinking**

❸ **Analyze** Ask students how Leon manages, in this passage, to keep the truth from Father Paul without actually lying. *Students should cite sentences such as "Everything is O.K. now," and ". . . he won't do that any more now."*

The Man to Send Rain Clouds

Leslie Marmon Silko

They found him under a big cottonwood tree. His Levi jacket and pants were faded light blue so that he had been easy to find. The big cottonwood tree stood apart from a small grove of winterbare cottonwoods which grew in the wide, sandy arroyo. He had been dead for a day or more, and the sheep had wandered and scattered up and down the arroyo. Leon and his brother-in-law, Ken, gathered the sheep and left them in the pen at the sheep camp before they returned to the cottonwood tree. Leon waited under the tree while Ken drove the truck through the deep sand to the edge of the arroyo. He squinted up at the sun and unzipped his jacket—it sure was hot for this time of year. But high and northwest the blue mountains were still in snow. Ken came sliding down the low, crumbling bank about fifty yards down, and he was bringing the red blanket.

❶ Before they wrapped the old man, Leon took a piece of string out of his pocket and tied a small gray feather in the old man's long white hair. Ken gave him the paint. Across the brown wrinkled forehead he drew a streak of white and along the high cheekbones he drew a strip of blue paint. He paused and watched Ken throw pinches of corn meal and pollen into the wind that fluttered the small gray feather. Then Leon painted with yellow under the old man's broad nose, and finally, when he had painted green across the chin, he smiled.

"Send us rain clouds, Grandfather." They laid the bundle in the back of the pickup and covered it with a heavy tarp before they started back to the pueblo.

They turned off the highway onto the sandy pueblo road. Not long after they passed the store and post office they saw Father Paul's car coming toward them. When he recognized their faces he slowed his car and waved for them to stop. The young priest rolled down the car window.

"Did you find old Teofilo?" he asked loudly.

Leon stopped the truck. "Good morning, Father. We were just out to the sheep camp. Everything is O.K. now."

"Thank God for that. Teofilo is a very old man. You really shouldn't allow him to stay at the sheep camp alone."

"No, he won't do that any more now."

"Well, I'm glad you understand. I hope I'll be seeing you at Mass[1] this week—we missed you last Sunday. See if you can get old Teofilo to come with you." The priest smiled and waved at them as they drove away.

Louise and Teresa were waiting. The table was set for lunch, and the coffee was boiling on the black iron stove. Leon looked at Louise and then at Teresa.

"We found him under a cottonwood tree in the big arroyo near sheep camp. I guess he sat down to rest in the shade and never got up again." Leon walked toward the old man's bed. The red plaid shawl had been shaken and spread carefully over the bed, and a new brown flannel shirt and pair of stiff new Levi's were arranged neatly beside the pillow. Louise held the screen door open while Leon and Ken

---

1. **Mass** (mas): Church service celebrated by Roman Catholics.

522 ◆ *Short Stories*

Block Scheduling Strategies

Consider these suggestions to take advantage of extended class time:

- Use the activities in *Daily Language Practice* for Week 6. You may dictate the passages to students, or you may use the transparency and have students correct the passages in groups.
- To enhance their understanding of the characters' use of feathers, cornmeal, and other rituals described in the story, have students research Pueblo culture.
- Be sure to focus on tone in your approach to

teaching the Writing Mini-Lesson on page 533. Point out that the word *eulogy* comes from Greek and means "good words." Discuss the tone that a eulogy can take: sad, serious, and even joyful. Before students begin writing, discuss circumstances that would warrant the various moods they have identified.

- Mark Twain was one of America's greatest humorists. Interested students could read other works by Twain and analyze his use of humor to explore serious topics.

Feast Day, San Juan Pueblo, 1921, William Penhallow Henderson, National Museum of American Art, Smithsonian Institution

▲ **Critical Viewing** In this tale of the Southwest, Native American customs clash with and then harmonize with customs brought by Spanish and Mexican missionaries. How do the ideas in the painting and the story connect with your own experience of old ways and new ways? **[Relate]** ❹

carried in the red blanket. He looked small and shriveled, and after they dressed him in the new shirt and pants he seemed more shrunken.

It was noontime now because the church bells rang the Angelus.[2] They ate the beans with hot bread, and nobody said anything until after Teresa poured the coffee.

Ken stood up and put on his jacket. "I'll see about the gravediggers. Only the top layer of soil is frozen. I think it can be ready before dark."

Leon nodded his head and finished his coffee. After Ken had been gone for a while, the neighbors and clanspeople came quietly to embrace Teofilo's family and to leave food on the

table because the gravediggers would come to eat when they were finished.

The sky in the west was full of pale yellow light. Louise stood outside with her hands in the pockets of Leon's green army jacket that was too big for her. The funeral was over, and the old men had taken their candles and medicine bags[3] and were gone. She waited until the body was laid into the pickup before she said anything to Leon. She touched his arm, and he noticed that her hands were still dusty from the corn meal that she had sprinkled around the old man. When she spoke, Leon could not hear her.

❺
❻

❼

---

2. **Angelus** (an´ jə ləs): Bell rung at morning, noon, and evening to announce a prayer.

3. **medicine bags:** Bags containing objects that were thought to have special powers.

The Man to Send Rain Clouds ♦ 523

 Humanities: Art

Feast Day, San Juan Pueblo, 1921, by William Penhallow Henderson.

Henderson's painting illustrates the presence of Christianity in a Native American community. The dark church evokes an air of mystery and secrecy. In contrast, the villagers are gathering for their feast day in a circle of warmth and light. Have students study the painting and discuss the following questions:
1. How does the painting evoke the Christian influence on, and the Christian ties to, the community? *The church has a strong presence in the village scene, although it is separated from the main square by trees and buildings.*
2. How does the artist use composition, light, and shadow to express the gulf between the two cultures? *The church is hidden in shadow, but the village square is bathed in light; all pathways to the church appear to be physically blocked; the figure on the left side of the church may be a priest, left out of the festivities.*

▶Critical Viewing◀
❹ **Relate** Invite students to share examples of blending cultures from their own lives or experiences. Some may practice religious ceremonies or maintain family traditions, customs, or language in conjunction with the demands and conventions of modern American life.

◆ **Reading Strategy**
❺ **Use Your Senses** Ask students how the senses of sight and touch are used to let the reader "feel" the weather. *Students can identify the author's use of color (pale yellow sky) and how clothing and posture make the reader feel the chill of the late winter afternoon.*

Comprehension Check ☑
❻ What kind of a funeral has just taken place? Students should infer that Teofilo's funeral has been a Pueblo Indian ritual.

◆ **Critical Thinking**
❼ **Draw Conclusions** Ask students why Louise sprinkled corn meal around the body? *Students should realize that sprinkling corn meal is a Native American funeral custom, perhaps done so that the deceased is not hungry in the next life.*

Customize for
Less Proficient Readers
To help these students understand the cross-cultural aspects of this story, have them keep a journal as they read the story, jotting down details that reveal the customs and beliefs that are of Native American origin and the customs and beliefs that are of Christian origin. Ask students to cite an example from the story in which the two sets of customs and beliefs harmonize. *An example is the Christian sprinkling of holy water done as part of the Native American nourishment of the deceased.*

Customize for
Visual/Spatial Learners
Have these students draw or paint one of the scenes in "The Man to Send Rain Clouds" that appeals to them visually. They might choose old Teofilo's face as it is painted by Leon and Ken, or Leon and Father Paul walking "down the hill to the graveyard" when "only half of the sun was

523

One-Minute Insight It may be said that death permeates Mark Twain's comic story in a very physical way. The narrator tells of the train trip he takes to bring the body of his newly deceased friend to his final resting place. The narrator and a railway expressman suffer intolerably from what they believe is the odor of the decomposing corpse. They struggle in a foul-smelling railway express car to maintain an unbearable and, as it happens, unnecessary vigil over a dead body, according to the parameters and conventions of civilized society. The vigil is unnecessary because the coffin has been mistakenly replaced by a box of guns, and the foul smell is emanating from a piece of Limburger cheese.

◆ Critical Thinking

❶ Infer Ask students what Twain is implying about his health in this opening sentence. Why is the sentence humorous? *Twain is implying that he is in poor health, old before his time. The statement is humorous because Twain pokes fun at marriage, implying with tongue in cheek that being married makes one miserable.*

◆ Reading Strategy

❷ Use Your Senses Ask students how the winter setting is an appropriate backdrop for the narrator's grief. What feeling do students get from reading the passage? *Students may say that the desolate winter landscape matches the feeling of loss and sorrow.*

Comprehension Check ☑

❸ What is in the box the narrator believes to be a coffin? How did the boxes get switched? *Make sure students understand that the coffin got switched with a shipment of guns, and the person delivering the guns has the coffin with the body inside.*

THE Invalid's Story
Mark Twain

❶ I seem sixty and married, but these effects are due to my condition and sufferings, for I am a bachelor, and only forty-one. It will be hard for you to believe that I, who am now but a shadow, was a hale, hearty man two short years ago—a man of iron, a very athlete!—yet such is the simple truth. But stranger still than this fact is the way in which I lost my health. I lost it through helping to take care of a box of guns on a two-hundred-mile railway journey one winter's night. It is the actual truth, and I will tell you about it.

I belong in Cleveland, Ohio. One winter's night, two years ago, I reached home just after dark, in a driving snowstorm, and the first thing I heard when I entered the house was that my dearest boyhood friend and schoolmate, John B. Hackett, had died the day before, and that his last utterance had been a **❷** desire that I would take his remains home to his poor old father and mother in Wisconsin. I was greatly shocked and grieved, but there was no time to waste in emotions; I must start at once. I took the card, marked "Deacon Levi Hackett, Bethlehem, Wisconsin," and hurried off through the whistling storm to the railway station. Arrived there I found the long white-pine box which had been described to me; I fastened the card to it with some tacks, saw it put safely aboard the express car, and then ran

◆ Build Vocabulary
prodigious (prə dij′ əs) *adj.*: Enormous
deleterious (del′ ə tir′ ē əs) *adj.*: Injurious; harmful to health or well-being

526 ◆ Short Stories

into the eating room to provide myself with a sandwich and some cigars. When I returned, presently, there was my coffin-box *back again,* apparently, and a young fellow examining around it, with a card in his hands, and some tacks and a hammer! I was astonished and puzzled. He began to nail on his card, and I rushed out to the express car, in a good deal of a state of mind, to ask for an explanation. But no—there was my box, all right, in the express car; it hadn't been disturbed. [The fact is that without my suspecting it a prodigious mistake had been made. I was carrying off a box of *guns* which that young fellow had come to the station to ship to a rifle company in Peoria, Illinois, and *he* had got my corpse.] Just then the **❸** conductor sang out "All aboard," and I jumped into the express car and got a comfortable seat on a bale of buckets. The expressman was there, hard at work—a plain man of fifty, with a simple, honest, good-natured face, and a breezy, practical heartiness in his general style. As the train moved off a stranger skipped into the car and set a package of peculiarly mature and capable Limburger cheese[1] on one end of my coffin-box—I mean my box of guns. That is to say, I know *now* that it was Limburger cheese, but at that time I never had heard of the article in my life, and of course was wholly ignorant of its character. Well, we sped through the wild night, the bitter storm raged on, a cheerless misery stole over me, my heart went down, down, down! The old expressman made

1. **Limburger cheese:** Cheese with a strong odor.

Speaking and Listening Mini-Lesson

Dramatic Reading
This mini-lesson supports the Speaking and Listening activity in the Idea Bank on page 533.
Introduce the Concept Students will practice reading expressively and energetically to give a dramatic reading of the story.
Develop Background Discuss what voice students attribute to the narrator and the expressman. Suggest that students visualize the demeanor and body language of each character as they practice different ways to express each character's words.

Apply the Information Using the information developed in the background discussion, students can first practice giving a dramatic reading of the story and then actually perform the dramatic reading for the class. Students may want to record their reading on audiocassette.

Assess the Outcome Have students critique the presentations. What made the funniest dramatic reading effective? How did the readers' interpretation of the characters' voices enhance the humor and absurdity of the tale?

a brisk remark or two about the tempest and the arctic weather, slammed his sliding doors to, and bolted them, closed his window down tight, and then went bustling around, here and there and yonder, setting things to rights, and all the time contentedly humming "Sweet By and By" in a low tone, and flatting a good deal. Presently I began to detect a most evil and searching odor stealing about on the frozen air. This depressed my spirits still more, because of course I attributed it to my poor departed friend. There was something infinitely saddening about his calling himself to my remembrance in this dumb, pathetic way, so it was hard to keep the tears back. Moreover, it

◆ Reading Strategy
What senses can you use to experience this description? How can an "odor" be "searching"?

distressed me on account of the old express-man, who, I was afraid, might notice it. However, he went humming tranquilly on, and gave no sign; and for this I was grateful. Grateful, yes, but still uneasy; and soon I began to feel more and more uneasy every minute, for every minute that went by that odor thickened up the more, and got to be more and more gamy and hard to stand. Presently, having got things arranged to his satisfaction, the expressman got some wood and made up a tremendous fire in his stove. This distressed me more than I can tell, for I could not but feel that it was a mistake. I was sure that the effect would be deleterious upon my poor departed friend. Thompson—the expressman's name was Thompson, as I found out in the course of the night—now went poking around his car, stopping up whatever stray cracks he could find, remarking that it didn't make any difference what kind of a night it was outside, he calculated to make us comfortable, anyway. I said nothing, but I believed he was not choosing the right way. Meantime he was humming to himself just as before; and meantime, too, the

▼ Critical Viewing Examine this painting of a railway station in 1874. How difficult do you think it was to get from one place to another at this time in history? What details in the painting support your ideas? [Support]

Sacramento Railroad Station, 1874, William Hahn, The Fine Arts Museum of San Francisco

The Invalid's Story ◆ 527

◆ Reading Strategy
❹ Use Your Senses The sense of hearing detects the music while the sense of smell detects the odor. Have students discuss how a bad odor seems to fill a space as if trying to get into every corner. Students may suggest that they can picture the odor—using the sense of sight—as if it were a floating, dark cloud.

▶Critical Viewing◀
❺ Support Students will probably say that getting from one place to another was very difficult in 1874. The painting shows that people had to rely on horse-drawn carriages to get to the train station. Horses, which have to be fed and cared for, traveled much more slowly than automobiles travel. In addition, people walking toward their train at the station had to watch out for horses crossing their path. The trunk in the foreground clearly shows that most nineteenth-century luggage wasn't easy to handle.

◆ Build Vocabulary
❻ Suffixes: -ous Point out that the word *tremendous* literally means "full of trembling." Though it has come to refer to size, its original meaning is more closely connected to one's reaction when encountering something big.

◆ Critical Thinking
❼ Analyze Cause and Effect Ask students how a warm fire might affect the smell coming from the cheese. How does this description heighten the humor of the story? *A warm fire might make the cheese softer and more moist, thereby increasing the odor coming from the cheese. The description heightens humor by focusing on the misconception that the corpse, rather than Limburger cheese, is the cause of the odor.*

 Humanities: Art

Sacramento Railroad Station, 1874, by William Hahn.

William Hahn's painting gives a dynamic and detailed glimpse of the rigors of transportation and the ordeal of travel in the late 1800's.

1. How does the depiction of the station help to show how the boxes could have been switched? *Students may say that the confusion and disorganization depicted make it easy to see*

how the mix-up occurred. Nowadays, improved methods of labeling, tracking, and handling serve to help prevent such a problem.

2. What would this station scene be like in winter? *Have students list details that would be added to a winter scene, such as slush, snow, and sleighs.*

◆ **Critical Thinking**

❶ **Draw Conclusions** Ask students whether moving the box will solve the problem. Have them give reasons for their answers. *Students may say that the smell of the cheese will be overwhelming no matter where it is located in the railway car; others may point out that the two men will not be able to move the box of guns in any case because it is too heavy.*

◆ **Critical Thinking**

❷ **Draw Conclusions** Ask students why Thompson changes the titles he gives to the corpse. *Each time the odor becomes discernibly more unbearable, Thompson raises the rank of the corpse.*

◆ **Critical Thinking**

❸ **Draw Conclusions** Ask students how the increasing strength of the odor correlates with the powers that Thompson attributes to the corpse? *As the odor becomes more powerful, Thompson attributes greater powers to the corpse.*

❹ **Clarification** Explain to students that carbolic acid, also known as phenol, is an aromatic organic compound that may be used as a disinfectant or antiseptic.

◆ **Critical Thinking**

❺ **Compare and Contrast** Ask students how the men would have been dressed if the story were set in the present, and how modern, cold-weather gear might have affected the story. *Students may suggest that the men today, in down jackets, perhaps, would have been better equipped to withstand the cold when they were forced outside the railway car.*

◆ **Critical Thinking**

❻ **Speculate** Ask students if they think a person's health, today, could be permanently shattered by an illness caused by being chilled outside a railroad car. *Students might say that more advanced medical care can now cure many illnesses that, during the nineteenth century, were often fatal.*

experiences of this night: and he got to referring to my poor friend by various titles—sometimes military ones, sometimes civil ones; and I noticed that as fast as my poor friend's effectiveness grew, Thompson promoted him accordingly—gave him a bigger title. Finally he said:

"I've got an idea. Suppos'n' we buckle down to it and give the Colonel a bit of a shove toward t'other end of the car?—about ten foot, say. He wouldn't have so much influence, then, don't you reckon?"

I said it was a good scheme. So we took in a good fresh breath at the broken pane, calculating to hold it till we got through: then we went there and bent over that deadly cheese and took a grip on the box. Thompson nodded "All ready," and then we threw ourselves forward with all our might: but Thompson slipped, and slumped down with his nose on the cheese, and his breath got loose. He gagged and gasped, and floundered up and made a break for the door, pawing the air and saying hoarsely, "Don't hender me!—gimme the road! I'm a-dying; gimme the road!" Out on the cold platform I sat down and held his head awhile, and he revived. Presently he said:

"Do you reckon we started the Gen'rul any?" I said no: we hadn't budged him.

"Well, then, *that* idea's up the flume. We got to think up something else. He's suited wher' he is, I reckon; and if that's the way he feels about it, and has made up his mind that he don't wish to be disturbed, you bet he's a-going to have his own way in the business. Yes, better leave him right wher' he is, long as he wants it so; becuz he holds all the trumps, don't you know, and so it stands to reason that the man that lays out to alter his plans for him is going to get left."

But we couldn't stay out there in that mad storm; we should have frozen to death. So we went in again and shut the door, and began to suffer once more and take turns at the break in the window. By and by, as we were starting away from a station where we had stopped a moment Thompson pranced in cheerily, and exclaimed:

"We're all right, now! I reckon we've got the Commodore this time. I judge I've got the stuff here that'll take the tuck out of him."

It was carbolic acid. He had a carboy[6] of it. He sprinkled it all around everywhere; in fact he drenched everything with it, rifle-box, cheese and all. Then we sat down, feeling pretty hopeful. But it wasn't for long. You see the two perfumes began to mix, and then—well, pretty soon we made a break for the door; and out there Thompson swabbed his face with his bandanna and said in a kind of disheartened way:

"It ain't no use. We can't buck agin *him*. He just utilizes everything we put up to modify him with, and gives it his own flavor and plays it back on us. Why. Cap, don't you know, it's as much as a hundred times worse in there now than it was when he first got a-going. I never *did* see one of 'em warm up to his work so, and take such a dumnation interest in it. No, sir, I never did, as long as I've ben on the road: and I've carried a many a one of 'em, as I was telling you."

We went in again after we were frozen pretty stiff; but my, we couldn't *stay* in, now. So we just waltzed back and forth, freezing, and thawing, and stifling, by turns. In about an hour we stopped at another station; and as we left it Thompson came in with a bag, and said—

"Cap, I'm a-going to chance him once more—just this once; and if we don't fetch him this time, the thing for us to do, is to just throw up the sponge and withdraw from the canvass.[7] That's the way *I* put it up."

He had brought a lot of chicken feathers, and dried apples, and leaf tobacco, and rags, and old shoes, and sulphur, and asafetida,[8] and one thing or another: and he piled them on a breadth of sheet iron in the middle of the floor, and set fire to them.

When they got well started. I couldn't see,

---

6. **carboy** (kär´ boi´) *n*.: Large glass bottle enclosed in basketwork to prevent it from breaking.
7. **withdraw from the canvass** (kan´ vəs): Give up the attempt.
8. **asafetida** (as´ ə fet´ ə də) *n*.: Bad-smelling substance from certain plants, used as medicine.

530 ◆ *Short Stories*

myself, how even the corpse could stand it. All that went before was just simply poetry to that smell—but mind you, the original smell stood up out of it just as sublime as ever—fact is, these other smells just seemed to give it a better hold: and my, how rich it was! I didn't make these reflections there—there wasn't time—made them on the platform. And breaking for the platform, Thompson got suffocated and fell: and before I got him dragged out, which I did by the collar, I was mighty near gone myself. When we revived, Thompson said dejectedly:

"We got to stay out here, Cap. We got to do it. They ain't no other way. The Governor wants to travel alone, and he's fixed so he can outvote us."

And presently he added:

"And don't you know, we're *pisoned*. It's *our* last trip, you can make up your mind to it. Typhoid fever is what's going to come of this. I feel it a-coming right now. Yes, sir, we're elected, just as sure as you're born.

We were taken from the platform an hour later, frozen and insensible, at the next station, and I went straight off into a virulent fever, and never knew anything again for three weeks. I found out, then, that I had spent that awful night with a harmless box of rifles and a lot of innocent cheese; but the news was too late to save *me*; imagination had done its work, and my health was permanently shattered; neither Bermuda nor any other land can ever bring it back to me. This is my last trip; I am on my way home to die.

❻

Guide for Responding

◆ *Literature and Your Life*

Reader's Response Did you find the story entertaining? Why or why not?

Thematic Focus What conflict do the narrator and Thompson face in this story?

Journal Writing Explain why you did or did not find this story humorous.

☑ Check Your Comprehension

1. What is the purpose of the narrator's journey?
2. Describe the mistake the narrator makes at the station. How does he complicate the mistake?
3. What makes the narrator and Thompson so uncomfortable?
4. What steps do they take to correct this problem?
5. What happens to the narrator in the end?

◆ Critical Thinking

INTERPRET

1. (a) Contrast what the narrator and Thompson believe to be true with what is really true.
   (b) How does this contrast contribute to the story's humor? **[Compare and Contrast]**
2. Thompson's description of the corpse's powerful odor makes it sound as if the corpse is deliberately trying to smell bad. How does this attitude add to the story's humor? **[Analyze]**
3. How would the characters' experience have been different if they'd known the source of the odor? **[Speculate]**
4. (a) Find at least three places in the story where the narrator exaggerates details. (b) How does the use of exaggeration contribute to the story's humor? **[Analyze]**

APPLY

5. How would the story be different if it were set in today's world? **[Connect]**

EXTEND

6. Would this story make a good movie? Why or why not? **[Media Link]**

The Invalid's Story ◆ 531

Beyond the Selection

FURTHER READING

Other Works by Leslie Marmon Silko
Ceremony
Yellow Woman and a Beauty of the Spirit

Other Works by Mark Twain
The Celebrated Jumping Frog of Calaveras County and Other Sketches
Great Short Works of Mark Twain

Other Works Related by Theme
"The Cremation of Sam McGee," Robert Service

INTERNET

For more information, see these Internet sites. Please be aware, however, that sites may have changed from the time we published this information.

For "The Man to Send Rain Clouds," visit **http://english.cla.umn.edu/lkd/vjg/Authors/LeslieMarmonSilko**

For "The Invalid's Story," visit **http://www.literature.org/works/Mark-Twain**

We *strongly recommend* that you preview the sites before you send students to them.

Reinforce and Extend

Answers

◆ *Literature and Your Life*

Thematic Focus They try to alleviate the horrible odor in the railway car. (They think the odor is from a dead body, but it's not.)

☑ Check Your Comprehension

1. The purpose is to bring his deceased friend's body to his parents in Wisconsin.
2. The narrator mistakes a box of rifles for a coffin. He complicates the mistake by not realizing that Limburger cheese is brought onto the train.
3. The intense smell makes them uncomfortable.
4. They break a pane of glass, walk in and out of the car, smoke cigars, sprinkle carbolic acid, and burn various materials to try to mask the odor.
5. The narrator contracts an illness as a result of the wintry weather and believes he is going to die.

◆ Critical Thinking

1. (a) They believe that the foul smell is from a decomposing corpse when in reality it is from a piece of Limburger cheese. (b) This adds to the humor by contributing to dramatic irony, a situation in which what the characters believe is true is different from what the reader knows is true.
2. The attitude that the corpse is trying to smell bad adds to the humor through irony. It is ironic that a dead person is seen as making conscious decisions.
3. If the characters had known the source, they would have probably enclosed the Limburger cheese in a container that would have stopped the odor from emanating.
4. (a) Examples of exaggeration include suggesting that the corpse has been dead for two or three years, saying the odor is a hundred times worse, and saying Typhoid fever will result. (b) Exaggeration magnifies humorous elements.
5. Suggested response: Today, the Limburger cheese probably would have been packaged in a way to preclude the escape of odors. Therefore, some other source of a foul odor would have been needed.
6. Student responses should reflect an understanding of the story.

Answers

◆ Literary Focus

1. The Native American funeral rites affect the action of the story in that the funeral of Teofilo incorporates both Native American and Christian rituals.
2. The desert dictates the need for water to alleviate the thirst of the deceased. It is also responsible for the wish for rain clouds.
3. They are in a claustrophobic railway express car that they share with a large box and a smelly (though unseen) cheese, with cold weather raging outside.
4. The relatively small space and closed environment of the car make the smell of the cheese more overpowering, pushing the men to try various solutions and finally escape into the dangerous cold air.

◆ Build Vocabulary

Using the Suffix -ous
1. melodious = full of melody; pleasing to hear.
2. prestigious = full of prestige, or renown.
3. riotous = full of disorder or confusion.

Using the Word Bank
1. c 2. a 3. b 4. c 5. a
6. c 7. a 8. b 9. b

◆ Reading Strategy

1. Suggested response: Silko appeals most to the senses of sight and touch. She describes the rugged details of the Southwest landscape, including the changing colors of the mountains and the sky. She also describes the textures of soil, structures, and clothing.
2. Students might choose the Native American funeral rites or the sprinkling of the holy water.
3. Students might choose the image of Thompson burying his face in his handkerchief and rocking his body or the image of the burning materials whose smells seemed to give the original smell "a better hold."

◆ Build Grammar Skills

Thompson shook his head. "Cap, how long ago did you say the General left this vale of tears for a better place?"

"Just a few days ago."

"Well, I'm impressed—the General seems to have got himself a jim-dandy head start in the smelling business. He is a real go-getter, he is."

"Mr. Thompson, I'm afraid I don't find this very funny."

"Neither do I, Cap."

Guide for Responding (continued)

◆ Literary Focus

SETTING

In both these stories, **setting**—the time, place, and culture in which the story unfolds—strongly influences the action. In fact, if you took the stories out of their settings, the central conflict in each would disappear, the characters would have no reason to behave as they do, and the story would evaporate altogether.

1. In "The Man to Send Rain Clouds," what aspects of the Native American culture affect the action, and how?
2. Why is the desert setting important in the action?
3. In "The Invalid's Story," describe the physical environment in which the narrator and Thompson sit.
4. What factors in this environment drive the action of the story?

◆ Build Vocabulary

USING THE SUFFIX -ous

Add the suffix -ous, meaning "full of," to each of the following words to create a new word. Define each new word.
1. melody + -ous =
2. prestige + -ous =
3. riot + -ous =

USING THE WORD BANK

On your paper, write the word or words closest in meaning to that of the first word.
1. deleterious: (a) delaying, (b) tasty, (c) harmful
2. cloister: (a) religious retreat, (b) group, (c) injury
3. judicious: (a) legal, (b) prudent, (c) imaginative
4. desultory: (a) romantic, (b) evil, (c) random
5. placidly: (a) quietly, (b) coldly, (c) politely
6. pagans: (a) aliens, (b) villains, (c) nonbelievers
7. ominous: (a) threatening, (b) dishonest, (c) dark
8. prodigious: (a) inventive, (b) enormous, (c) joyous
9. perverse: (a) untidy, (b) persisting in error, (c) on the other side

◆ Reading Strategy

USE YOUR SENSES

Each of these stories is filled with images, or word pictures, that appeal to various senses and help you picture in your mind the setting, the characters, and the events.

1. In "The Man to Send Rain Clouds," which two senses would you say Silko appeals to most? Support your answer.
2. List two images that especially stand out in Silko's story. Explain your answer.
3. While most stories use images of sight, sound, and sensation, "The Invalid's Story" is one of the few stories to play almost exclusively to the sense of smell. Find two images in the story that most vividly capture the smell of the cheese. Explain why each image is effective.

◆ Build Grammar Skills

PUNCTUATING DIALOGUE

When you **punctuate dialogue**, signal a change in speaker with a new paragraph and a new set of quotation marks.

When you write dialogue, being careful to use correct punctuation will help your readers keep track of who is saying what and when.

Practice On your paper, rewrite the following exchange of dialogue, adding correct punctuation.

Thompson shook his head. Cap, how long ago did you say the General left this vale of tears for a better place? Just a few days ago. Well I'm impressed—the General seems to have got himself a jim-dandy head start in the smelling business. He is a real go-getter, he is. Mr. Thompson, I'm afraid I don't find this very funny. Neither do I, Cap.

Writing Application Recall a conversation that you had in the past few days. Then re-create the conversation in writing. Follow the rules for punctuating dialogue.

✒ **Writer's Solution**

For additional instruction and practice, use the lesson in the **Language Lab CD-ROM** on Writing Dialogue and the practice pages on Quotation Marks with Direct Quotations (pp. 106–107) in the *Writer's Solution Grammar Practice Book.*

Build Your Portfolio

Idea Bank

Writing

1. **Suggestion Letter** Assume the role of the narrator in "The Invalid's Story," and write to the railroad company encouraging changes in their baggage-handling policies.

2. **Essay** Write a brief essay in which you explain what Silko's story reveals about Pueblo culture. Support your points with details from the story. You might point out, for example, what the story suggests about the Pueblo attitude toward nature.

3. **Research** Conduct research to learn more about either Pueblo culture or about railroad travel during the late 1800's. Present your findings in a written report. **[Social Studies Link]**

Speaking and Listening

4. **Dramatic Reading** With another classmate, prepare and deliver a dramatic reading of "The Invalid's Story." Use body language to emphasize the characters' misery.

5. **Persuasive Speech** "The Man to Send Rain Clouds" captures how the Pueblos have preserved their cultural heritage. Prepare and deliver a persuasive speech about why it is important for people to preserve their cultural heritages.

Projects

6. **Map** Create a map charting the route of the train in Twain's story. Include labels showing where events from the story might have occurred. **[Social Studies Link]**

7. **Diagram** Centuries ago, the Pueblos developed a sophisticated system for irrigating their land. Through research, find out about this system, and create a diagram illustrating how it works. **[Science Link]**

Writing Mini-Lesson

Eulogy

When someone dies, one way of dealing with your sense of loss is to express your feelings for the person in a formal speech called a eulogy. Write a eulogy in memory of a relative, someone else you knew well, or perhaps a public figure. As you write, the following may help you.

Writing Skills Focus: Tone

Tone refers to the attitude a writer projects toward his or her subject. The tone of a piece of writing can be sarcastic or respectful, affectionate or angry. When you write, think about the attitude you want to communicate toward your subject, and find words that express that attitude. Look at this passage from "The Man to Send Rain Clouds."

> Leon turned to look up at the high blue mountains in the deep snow that reflected a faint red light from the west. He felt good because it was finished, and he was happy about the sprinkling of the holy water; now the old man could send them big thunder-clouds for sure.

Notice that this description of Teofilo's burial has a peaceful, hopeful tone.

Prewriting Make a list of words to describe the person you are honoring that create the tone you want to project. Use your imagination to come up with incidents from the character's life that support your attitude toward him or her.

Drafting Begin your eulogy with a statement that sums up the attitude you wish to convey. Follow with details that support the statement.

Revising Review your draft, eliminating any language that strikes a wrong note and adding details that will strengthen the tone.

The Man to Send Rain Clouds/The Invalid's Story ◆ 533

Idea Bank
Customizing for *Performance Levels*

Following are suggestions for matching the Idea Bank topics with your students' performance levels:

Less Advanced Students: 1
Average Students: 2, 4, 6
More Advanced Students: 3, 5, 7

Customizing for *Learning Modalities*

Following are suggestions for matching Idea Bank topics with your students' learning modalities:

Verbal/Linguistic: 1, 2, 3
Auditory: 4, 5
Interpersonal: 4
Logical/Mathematical: 5
Visual/Spatial: 6, 7

Writing Mini-Lesson

Refer students to the Writing Handbook, page 962, for instruction on the writing process, and page 964 for further information on narration.

Writing Process Transparencies
To guide students in writing their eulogies, use the Writing Process Model 2: Biographical Profile in *Writing and Language Transparencies,* pp. 9–15.

Writer's Solution

Writing Lab CD-ROM
Have students complete the Tutorial on Narration. Follow these steps:
1. Use the Character Trait word bins for details about the subject of the eulogy.
2. Have students draft on computer.
3. Use the Proofreading Checklist to aid revision.

Allow approximately 90 minutes of class time to complete these steps.

Sourcebook
Have students use Chapter 2, Narration (pp. 30–61), for additional support. The chapter includes a model of a firsthand biography (p. 34).

✓ ASSESSMENT OPTIONS

Formal Assessment, Selection Test, pp. 132–134, and Assessment Resources Software. The selection test is designed so that it can be easily customized to the performance levels of your students. *Alternative Assessment,* p. 38, includes options for less advanced students, more advanced students, verbal/linguistic learners, bodily/kinesthetic learners, and visual/spatial learners.

PORTFOLIO ASSESSMENT

Use the following rubrics in the *Alternative Assessment* booklet to assess student writing:
Suggestion Letter: Business Letter/Memo Rubric, p. 106
Essay: Technical Description/Explanation Rubric, p. 108
Research: Research Report/Paper Rubric, p. 99
Writing Mini-Lesson: Expression Rubric, p. 87

Guide for Reading

Guy de Maupassant
(1850–1893)

Perhaps the best-known short-story writer in the world, Guy de Maupassant is known for his realistic stories that capture the surprising and sometimes unfortunate twists and turns of life. In "The Necklace," a middle-class woman's dreams of becoming part of the social elite suddenly turn into a nightmare.

Maupassant was raised in northern France. As a young man, he served in the Franco-Prussian War, gathering experiences that would later appear in some of his stories. When the war ended, he took a job as a government clerk and devoted his spare time to writing. Maupassant became the literary apprentice of the well-known writer Gustave Flaubert, who introduced him to other illustrious writers of the day. Although Maupassant became quite successful and wealthy, his later years were shadowed by ill health and depression.

Tomás Rivera (1935–1984)

Born in Crystal City, Texas, Tomás Rivera soon joined what he called the "migrant labor stream" that travels throughout the farmlands of the United States. Faced with the challenge of alternating schooling with work in the fields, Rivera pursued his education tirelessly. His persistence paid off, as he eventually earned a Ph.D. in Spanish Literature.

Rivera's concern for the education of minorities led him to a career as an educator, limiting the time he could devote to his writing. Nevertheless, he has become one of the most renowned Mexican American authors in the United States. His work most often focuses on the experiences of migrant farm workers, as in "The Harvest." Why do you think writers like Rivera so often focus their work on subjects closely tied to their experiences?

◆ Build Vocabulary

WORD ROOTS: -ject-

Have you ever dreaded an *injection* or *rejected* an offer? These words are formed from the root *-ject-*, which means "to throw." In "The Necklace," you'll encounter the word *dejection*. Given the fact that the prefix *de-* means "down," the root *-ject-* means "to throw," and the suffix *-tion* means "the state of being," what do you think *dejection* means? See how the meaning you come up with fits the word's context in the story.

déclassé
rueful
resplendent
disheveled
profoundly
harrowed
astutely

WORD BANK

As you read these stories, you will encounter the words on this list. Each word is defined on the page where it first appears. Preview the list before you read.

◆ Build Grammar Skills

PARTICIPIAL PHRASES

A **participial phrase** is a participle (a form of a verb that acts as an adjective) accompanied by its modifiers and complement. The entire phrase acts as an adjective, modifying a noun or pronoun. By using participial phrases, writers can pack a sentence with precise details. Look at this example from "The Necklace":

> She washed the dishes, *wearing down her pink nails on greasy casseroles and the bottoms of saucepans.*

The italicized words make up the entire participial phrase, which modifies the subject *She*. The participle in this phrase is *wearing*.

534 ◆ *Short Stories*

The Necklace ◆ The Harvest

◆ *Literature and Your Life*

CONNECT YOUR EXPERIENCE
Think of a time when a simple or surprising discovery had a lasting impact on your life. Both of these stories capture the lasting impact of a character's discovery. Watch for the moment of discovery, and think about how the discovery changes each character's world.

Journal Writing Jot down your memories of an important discovery that had a lasting impact on your life.

THEMATIC FOCUS: LEARNING ABOUT OURSELVES AND OTHERS
As these two stories illustrate, some discoveries are pleasant and enriching, while others can be very unpleasant. Consider how we can learn from both types of discoveries.

◆ Background for Understanding

CULTURE
Tomás Rivera and the characters in "The Harvest" share an identity with close to one million migrant workers throughout the United States. Migrant workers move from region to region, harvesting and processing crops. Often, they are poorly paid, and they sometimes cannot qualify for unemployment compensation and disability insurance. Many migrant workers are children, and their periodic uprooting makes it difficult for them to obtain an education. Tomás Rivera faced this obstacle, and his concern with the migrant workers with whom he grew up is reflected in both his writing and his work as an educator.

◆ Literary Focus

THEME
The **theme** of a literary work is the insight about life that it communicates. Sometimes the theme of a work is stated directly. More often, however, the theme is conveyed indirectly through the experiences of the characters, through the events and setting of the work, or through the use of literary devices, such as irony and symbols. For example, if a story shows a character finding that he has more in common with someone than expected, the story's theme might be an insight about the feelings that all people share.

◆ Reading Strategy

DRAW CONCLUSIONS
In determining the theme of most stories, you usually need to **draw conclusions**—to piece together details in the story and make decisions about the underlying meaning of these details. For example, if a story depicts a character who makes a tough decision, you might piece together what you know about the character to draw conclusions about why he made his decision. As you read these stories, use the details that the authors provide to draw conclusions about why the characters act as they do. Then try to draw conclusions about how the characters' actions might relate to the themes of the stories. You might use a chart like the one shown.

Character's Actions	Related Character Traits	Reasons for the Actions	What This Suggests About Theme

Engage students' interest in these stories by asking the following question: About how many times a day do you think you look in the mirror? Discuss with the class why we care so much about our physical appearance, when it has so little to do with what we are really like inside. Can a very beautiful or handsome person be dishonest or mean inside? Can an ordinary-looking person be intelligent, generous, and kind?

Suggest that, while we do care about appearances, we are often fooled by them, as are some of the characters in both stories students are about to read.

Customize for
Less Proficient Readers
Preview the vocabulary in the Word Bank with these students. Review the use of context clues to determine the meaning of unfamiliar words and suggest that students use this strategy as they read. Practice on the second paragraph of "The Necklace," which includes these potentially unfamiliar words: *wretched, caste, innate, suppleness, humble, peers.*

Customize for
More Advanced Students
Have students consider how they feel about Madame Loisel as they read "The Necklace." To what extent are their opinions inspired by events in the story? To what extent are they influenced by the author's directly expressed opinions about her?

Customize for
English Language Learners
Dialect in "The Harvest" may prove unfamiliar. Preview these idiomatic expressions and slang before students read: *It never fails, I reckon, this ain't, by hisself, catch on, I bet you.*

Customize for
Logical/Mathematical Learners
Challenge these students to convert francs to dollars to find out how much money Madame Loisel spent on her dress and how much the couple paid for the new necklace. Considering that the story was written in the nineteenth century, have them estimate how much money was spent in terms of today's economy.

 Preparing for Standardized Tests

Reading and Vocabulary The Reading Strategy lesson for this selection focuses on drawing conclusions. The ability to draw conclusions is helpful not only on the reading portions of standardized tests but also in achievement tests in specific subjects, such as science, which often present data and then ask students to formulate or defend hypotheses. For additional practice, use the Reading Strategy page in *Selection Support,* p. 161.

Grammar and Language The Build Grammar Skills lesson for this selection reviews participial phrases. Students can use this skill when asked to

correct any errors, if any, in a sentence:
Written by Rivera, the critics thought the story was wonderful. *(B)*

(A) Written by Rivera, the critics thought the story was wonderful.

(B) The critics thought the story, written by Rivera, was wonderful.

(C) The critics thought the story was wonderful, written by Rivera.

For additional practice, use the Build Grammar Skills page, p. 160, in *Selection Support.*

The Necklace

Guy de Maupassant

◆ **Critical Thinking**

❶ **Make Judgments** Ask students how they judge the young woman's choice of a husband. What were her reasons for marrying him? *Students may say that the words "slipped into marriage" imply that the woman did not marry for love, but because she felt that she would be unable to find a richer husband.*

❷ **Clarification** Students should understand that at the time and place in which this story is set, women had no standing in society other than that bestowed on them by marriage. Being beautiful and charming, this character felt she deserved a "better" marriage.

◆ **Critical Thinking**

❸ **Analyze Characters** Maupassant contrasts Madame Loisel with her husband throughout this opening section. Ask: How can you tell that it is only Madame Loisel who notices the three-day-old cloth on the table? *Madame Loisel is the one who is discontented; her husband loves the simple fare she serves.*

❶ She was one of those pretty, charming young women who are born, as if by an error of Fate, into a petty official's family. She had no dowry,[1] no hopes, not the slightest chance of being appreciated, understood, loved, and married by a rich and distinguished man; so she slipped into marriage with a minor civil servant at the Ministry of Education.

Unable to afford jewelry, she dressed simply: ❷ but she was as wretched as a déclassé, for women have neither caste nor breeding—in them beauty, grace, and charm replace pride of birth. Innate refinement, instinctive elegance, and suppleness of wit give them their place on the only scale that counts, and these qualities make humble girls the peers of the grandest ladies.

She suffered constantly, feeling that all the attributes of a gracious life, every luxury, should rightly have been hers. The poverty of her rooms—the shabby walls, the worn furniture, the ugly upholstery—caused her pain. All these things that another woman of her class would not even have noticed, tormented her and made her angry. The very sight of the little Breton girl who cleaned for her awoke rueful thoughts and the wildest dreams in her mind. She dreamt of thick carpeted reception rooms with Oriental hangings, lighted by tall, bronze torches, and with two huge footmen in knee breeches made drowsy by the heat from the stove, asleep in the wide armchairs. She dreamt of great drawing rooms upholstered in old silks, with fragile little tables holding priceless knickknacks, and of enchanting little sitting rooms redolent of perfume, designed for tea-time chats with intimate friends—famous, sought-after men whose attentions all women longed for.

When she sat down to dinner at her round table with its three-day-old cloth, and watched her husband opposite her lift the lid of the soup tureen and exclaim, delighted: "Ah, a good home-made beef stew! There's nothing better . . ." she would visualize elegant dinners with gleaming silver amid tapestried walls peopled by knights and ladies and exotic birds in a fairy forest; she would think of exquisite dishes served on gorgeous china, and of gallantries whispered and received with sphinx-like smiles[2] while eating the pink flesh of trout or wings of grouse. ❸

She had no proper wardrobe, no jewels, nothing. And those were the only things that she loved—she felt she was made for them. She would have so loved to charm, to be envied, to be admired and sought after.

---

1. **dowry** (dou´ rē) *n.*: Property that a woman brought to her husband at marriage.

2. **gallantries whispered and received with sphinx** (sfiŋks)-**like smiles**: Flirtatious compliments whispered and received with mysterious smiles.

Block Scheduling Strategies

Consider these suggestions to take advantage of extended class time:

- Have students listen to "The Necklace" on the audiocassette. Discuss how hearing the story clarifies their understanding of the main character and her problems.
- Use the activities for Week 14 in *Daily Language Practice,* p. 32, or the transparency in *Writing and Language Transparencies,* p. 113.
- Students might enjoy researching information about Maupassant on the Internet.

As you review the information in Background for Understanding (p. 535), have students discuss what they already know or have read about migrant workers.

- Students may work in pairs or small groups to answer the Critical Thinking questions (pp. 541 and 545).
- Direct students to complete the Writing Mini-Lesson (p. 547). Afterward, they can form groups to read one another's work and identify the climax and resolution of each scene.

She had a rich friend, a schoolmate from the convent she had attended, but she didn't like to visit her because it always made her so miserable when she got home again. She would weep for whole days at a time from sorrow, regret, despair, and distress.

Then one evening her husband arrived home looking triumphant and waving a large envelope.

"There," he said, "there's something for you."

She tore it open eagerly and took out a printed card which said:

"The Minister of Education and Madame Georges Ramponneau[3] request the pleasure of the company of M. and Mme. Loisel[4] at an evening reception at the Ministry on Monday, January 18th."

Instead of being delighted, as her husband had hoped, she tossed the invitation on the table and muttered, annoyed:

"What do you expect me to do with that?"

"Why, I thought you'd be pleased, dear. You never go out and this would be an occasion for you, a great one! I had a lot of trouble getting it. Everyone wants an invitation; they're in great demand and there are only a few reserved for the employees. All the officials will be there."

She looked at him, irritated, and said impatiently:

"I haven't a thing to wear. How could I go?"

It had never even occurred to him. He stammered:

"But what about the dress you wear to the theater? I think it's lovely. . . ."

He fell silent, amazed and bewildered to see that his wife was crying. Two big tears escaped from the corners of her eyes and rolled slowly toward the corners of her mouth. He mumbled:

"What is it? What is it?"

But, with great effort, she had overcome her

◆ **Reading Strategy**
④ What conclusion can you draw about Madame Loisel on the basis of her reaction to this invitation?

---

3. **Madame Georges Ramponneau** (ma dam′ zhôrzh ram pə nō′)
4. **Loisel** (lwa zel′)

---

misery; and now she answered him calmly, wiping her tear-damp cheeks:

"It's nothing. It's just that I have no evening dress and so I can't go to the party. Give the invitation to one of your colleagues whose wife will be better dressed than I would be."

He was overcome. He said:

"Listen, Mathilde,[5] how much would an evening dress cost—a suitable one that you could wear again on other occasions, something very simple?"

She thought for several seconds, making her calculations and at the same time estimating how much she could ask for without eliciting an immediate refusal and an exclamation of horror from this economical government clerk.

At last, not too sure of herself, she said:

"It's hard to say exactly but I think I could manage with four hundred francs."

He went a little pale, for that was exactly the amount he had put aside to buy a rifle so that he could go hunting the following summer near Nanterre, with a few friends who went shooting larks around there on Sundays.

However, he said:

"Well, all right, then. I'll give you four hundred francs. But try to get something really nice."

As the day of the ball drew closer, Madame Loisel seemed depressed, disturbed, worried—despite the fact that her dress was ready. One evening her husband said:

"What's the matter? You've really been very strange these last few days."

And she answered:

"I hate not having a single jewel, not one stone, to wear. I shall look so dowdy.[6] I'd almost rather

---

5. **Mathilde** (ma tēld′)
6. **dowdy** (dou′ dē) *adj.*: Shabby.

◆ **Build Vocabulary**

déclassé (dā′ klä sā′) *adj.*: Lowered in social status

rueful (rōō′ fəl) *adj.*: Feeling sorrow or regret

The Necklace ◆ 537

◆**Reading Strategy**

④ Draw Conclusions Elicit responses such as the following: *Although Madame Loisel wishes for an eventful and grand social life, she is too vain and concerned with appearances to attend the reception in her old clothes.*

◆**Reading Strategy**

⑤ Draw Conclusions Ask students what conclusion they can draw about Madame Loisel's husband from this passage. *Students should recognize that her husband is generous and cares about his wife's happiness.*

⑥ Clarification Explain that the franc is the official currency of France. Madame Loisel is asking for an amount equivalent to the cost of a hunting rifle—perhaps a few hundred dollars in today's money.

◆**Reading Strategy**

⑦ Draw Conclusions Ask students what conclusions they can draw about how Madame Loisel feels about her husband. Does she show the same concern for him that he shows for her? *Madame Loisel shows her lack of concern for her husband's feelings by complaining about her lack of jewelry after he has sacrificed his own pleasure to buy her a dress.*

Speaking and Listening Mini-Lesson

Improvisation

This mini-lesson supports the Speaking and Listening activity in the Idea Bank (p. 547).

Introduce the Concept Explain that an improvisation is a dramatic performance that the actors make up as they go along. The actors must stay in character; they cannot stop to discuss what to do. This means that each actor in an improvisation must pay careful attention. His or her responses must make

sense in light of what the others are doing and also suggest the direction in which he or she would like to proceed.

Develop Background After students have formed pairs, you may wish to give them time to confer as individual pairs or in groups of several pairs. Have them consider:

• How will Madame Loisel break the news?
• How will her husband react? Why?
• How will Madame Loisel respond? Why?

Apply the Information Set an appropriate time limit for the improvisations, then have each pair perform for the class.

Assess the Outcome Have students assess how well the improvisations reflected the actions and feelings of the characters. Did they present their viewpoints clearly? Did they convey meaning and emotion through gestures, facial expressions, and the way they spoke their lines?

◆ Critical Thinking

❶ Analyze Characters Point out Madame Loisel's reactions as she moves from pearls and gold to diamonds. Ask: What does Madame Loisel really desire? *She desires the life of comfort and beauty that the diamond necklace represents.*

◆ Build Grammar Skills

❷ Participial Phrases This paragraph is enlivened by four participial phrases that describe Madame Loisel. Ask students to locate each phrase, name the participle in each, and identify the word the phrases modify. Students might also identify two participles that modify the word *she,* but are not parts of phrases. *"carried away"—carried; "intoxicated with pleasure"—intoxicated; "forgetting everything . . ."—forgetting; "floating in a cloud of happiness . . ."—floating. All modify the word she. The word enraptured is also a participle modifying she, and the word formed is a participle modifying cloud.*

◆ Literary Focus

❸ Theme Remind students of Madame Loisel's insistence on looking the part of an upper-class lady. *Despite Madame Loisel's appearance at the party, her underlying reality has more to do with her shabby wrap than with her fancy gown and jewels.*

◆ Critical Thinking

❹ Compare and Contrast Ask students: What is Madame Loisel's fear as the evening ends? What is her husband's fear? What does this say about them? *Madame Loisel fears that her one taste of the good life will be her last; her husband is afraid he'll be tired at work the next day. He is practical and concerned with making a living; she is vain and selfish.*

---

not go to the party."

He suggested:

"You can wear some fresh flowers. It's considered very chic[7] at this time of year. For ten francs you can get two or three beautiful roses."

That didn't satisfy her at all.

"No . . . there's nothing more humiliating than to look poverty-stricken among a lot of rich women."

Then her husband exclaimed:

"Wait—you silly thing! Why don't you go and see Madame Forestier[8] and ask her to lend you some jewelry. You certainly know her well enough for that, don't you think?"

She let out a joyful cry.

"You're right. It never occurred to me."

The next day she went to see her friend and related her tale of woe.

Madame Forestier went to her mirrored wardrobe, took out a big jewel case, brought it to Madame Loisel, opened it, and said:

"Take your pick, my dear."

Her eyes wandered from some bracelets to a pearl necklace, then to a gold Venetian cross set with stones, of very fine workmanship. She tried on the jewelry before the mirror, hesitating, unable to bring herself to take them off, to give them back. And she kept asking:

"Do you have anything else, by chance?"

"Why yes. Here, look for yourself. I don't know which ones you'll like."

❶ All at once, in a box lined with black satin, she came upon a superb diamond necklace, and her heart started beating with overwhelming desire. Her hands trembled as she picked it up. She fastened it around her neck over her high-necked dress and stood there gazing at herself ecstatically.

Hesitantly, filled with terrible anguish, she asked:

"Could you lend me this one—just this and nothing else?"

"Yes, of course."

She threw her arms around her friend's neck, kissed her ardently, and fled with her treasure.

The day of the party arrived. Madame Loisel was a great success. She was the prettiest woman

---

7. **chic** (shēk) *n.:* Fashionable.
8. **Forestier** (fô rə styā´)

538 ◆ Short Stories

---

there—resplendent graceful, beaming, and deliriously happy. All the men looked at her, asked who she was, tried to get themselves introduced to her. All the minister's aides wanted to waltz with her. The minister himself noticed her.

She danced enraptured—carried away, intoxicated with pleasure, forgetting everything in this triumph of her beauty and the glory of her success, floating in a cloud of happiness formed by all this homage, all this admiration, all the desires she had stirred up—by this victory so complete and so sweet to the heart of a woman. ❷

When she left the party, it was almost four in the morning. Her husband had been sleeping since midnight in a small, deserted sitting room, with three other gentlemen whose wives were having a wonderful time.

He brought her wraps so that they could leave and put them around her shoulders—the plain wraps from her everyday life whose shabbiness jarred with the elegance of her evening dress. She felt this and wanted to escape quickly so that the other women, who were enveloping themselves in their rich furs, wouldn't see her.

Loisel held her back.

"Wait a minute. You'll catch cold out there. I'm going to call a cab."

But she wouldn't listen to him and went hastily downstairs. Outside in the street, there was no cab to be found; they set out to look for one, calling to the drivers they saw passing in the distance.

They walked toward the Seine,[9] shivering and miserable. Finally, on the embankment, they found one of those ancient nocturnal broughams[10] which are only to be seen in Paris at night, as if they were ashamed to show their shabbiness in daylight.

It took them to their door in the Rue des Martyrs, and they went sadly upstairs to their apartment. For her, it was all over. And he was ❹

◆ **Literary Focus**
What insight about life is suggested by the contrast between Madame Loisel's beautiful dress and the "plain wraps of her everyday life"? ❸

---

9. **Seine** (sān): River flowing through Paris.
10. **broughams** (brōoms) *n.:* Horse-drawn carriages.

 Cross-Curricular Connection: Music

Madame Loisel dances merrily to a waltz, a dance in three-quarter time. Despite the fact that it was considered scandalous, since the man and woman maintained close contact throughout the dance, the waltz became very popular in Europe during the eighteenth century. By the nineteenth century, when this story is set, it was well established. The most famous waltzes of the time were those by Johann Strauss (1804–1849) and his son Johann the Younger (1825–1899).

If possible, play samples of Strauss waltzes—such as the *Blue Danube* or *Tales from the Vienna Woods*—for the class as they imagine the elegantly dressed guests dancing at the party, Madame Loisel among them.

The New Necklace, 1910, William McGregor Paxton, Museum of Fine Arts, Boston

⑤ ▲**Critical Viewing** Imagine Mathilde trying on piece after piece of her wealthy friend's jewelry. What can you tell about her personality from this behavior? **[Infer]**

④ thinking that he had to be at the Ministry by ten.

She took off her wraps before the mirror so that she could see herself in all her glory once more. Then she cried out. The necklace was gone; there was nothing around her neck.

Her husband, already half undressed, asked: "What's the matter?"

She turned toward him in a frenzy:

"The . . . the . . . necklace—it's gone."

He got up, thunderstruck.

"What did you say? . . . What! . . . Impossible!"

And they searched the folds of her dress, the folds of her wrap, the pockets, everywhere. They didn't find it.

◆ **Build Vocabulary**

resplendent (ri splen´ dent) *adj*: Shining brightly

He asked:

"Are you sure you still had it when we left the ball?"

"Yes. I remember touching it in the hallway of the Ministry."

"But if you had lost it in the street, we would have heard it fall. It must be in the cab."

"Yes, most likely. Do you remember the number?"

"No. What about you—did you notice it?"

"No."

They looked at each other in utter dejection. Finally Loisel got dressed again.

"I'm going to retrace the whole distance we covered on foot," he said, "and see if I can't find it."

And he left the house. She remained in her evening dress, too weak to go to bed, sitting crushed on a chair, lifeless and blank.

Her husband returned at about seven o'-clock. He had found nothing. **⑥**

He went to the police station, to the newspapers to offer a reward, to the offices of the cab companies—in a word, wherever there seemed to be the slightest hope of tracing it.

She spent the whole day waiting, in a state of utter hopelessness before such an appalling catastrophe.

Loisel returned in the evening, his face lined and pale; he had learned nothing.

"You must write to your friend," he said, "and tell her that you've broken the clasp of the necklace and that you're getting it mended. That'll give us time to decide what to do."

She wrote the letter at his dictation.

By the end of the week, they had lost all hope.

Loisel, who had aged five years, declared: "We'll have to replace the necklace."

The next day they took the case in which it had been kept and went to the jeweler whose name appeared inside it. He looked through his ledgers:

"I didn't sell this necklace, madame. I only supplied the case."

Then they went from one jeweler to the next, trying to find a necklace like the other, racking their memories, both of them sick with worry and distress.

In a fashionable shop near the Palais Royal,

The Necklace ◆ 539

 Humanities: Art

The New Necklace, 1910, by William McGregor Paxton.

In this painting, a richly clothed woman shows a necklace to a woman who is more plainly dressed.

William McGregor Paxton (1869–1941) was an American artist best known for his portraits of upper-class life. In this painting, the details—elegant tapestries, beautiful gowns, and fine furniture—combine to suggest the world to which Madame Loisel aspires.

Use these questions for discussion:

1. If these women were Madame Loisel and Madame Forestier, which would you identify as Madame Loisel? *The contrasting clothing and attitudes of the two women, and the artist's use of light and shadow, suggest that the figure standing on the right is Madame Loisel.*

2. What does the painting suggest about the two women's attitudes toward the necklace? *The seated woman seems to be holding the necklace carelessly, whereas the standing woman is reaching for it with great care. This suggests that the seated woman is accustomed to wealth, but the other woman is in awe of it.*

they found a diamond necklace which they decided was exactly like the other. It was worth 40,000 francs. They could have it for 36,000 francs.

They asked the jeweler to hold it for them for three days, and they stipulated that he should take it back for 34,000 francs if the other necklace was found before the end of February.

Loisel possessed 18,000 francs left him by his father. He would borrow the rest.

*H*e borrowed, asking a thousand francs from one man, five hundred from another, a hundred here, fifty there. He signed promissory notes,[11] borrowed at exorbitant rates, dealt with usurers and the entire race of moneylenders. He compromised his whole career, gave his signature even when he wasn't sure he would be able to honor it, and horrified by the anxieties with which his future would be filled, by the black misery about to descend upon him, by the prospect of physical privation and moral suffering, went to get the new necklace, placing on the jeweler's counter 36,000 francs.

When Madame Loisel went to return the necklace, Madame Forestier said in a faintly waspish tone:

"You could have brought it back a little sooner! I might have needed it."

She didn't open the case as her friend had feared she might. If she had noticed the substitution, what would she have thought? What would she have said? Mightn't she have taken Madame Loisel for a thief?

Madame Loisel came to know the awful life of the poverty-stricken. However, she resigned herself to it with unexpected fortitude. The crushing debt had to be paid. She would pay it. They dismissed the maid; they moved into an attic under the roof.

She came to know all the heavy household chores, the loathsome work of the kitchen. She washed the dishes, wearing down her pink nails

---

11. **promissory** (präm´ i sôr´ē) **notes:** Written promises to pay back borrowed money.

on greasy casseroles and the bottoms of saucepans. She did the laundry, washing shirts and dishcloths which she hung on a line to dry; she took the garbage down to the street every morning, and carried water upstairs, stopping at every floor to get her breath. Dressed like a working-class woman, she went to the fruit store, the grocer, and the butcher with her basket on her arm, bargaining, outraged, contesting each sou[12] of her pitiful funds.

Every month some notes had to be honored and more time requested on others.

Her husband worked in the evenings, putting a shopkeeper's ledgers in order, and often at night as well, doing copying at twenty-five centimes a page.

And it went on like that for ten years.

After ten years, they had made good on everything, including the usurious rates and the compound interest.

Madame Loisel looked old now. She had become the sort of strong woman, hard and coarse, that one finds in poor families. Disheveled, her skirts askew, with reddened hands, she spoke in a loud voice, slopping water over the floors as she washed them. But sometimes, when her husband was at the office, she would sit down by the window and muse over that party long ago when she had been so beautiful, the belle of the ball.

How would things have turned out if she hadn't lost that necklace? Who could tell? How strange and fickle life is! How little it takes to make or break you!

Then one Sunday when she was strolling along the Champs Elysées[13] to forget

◆ Literary Focus
What insight about the effect of hardship on one's character does this description of Madame Loisel suggest?

---

12. **sou** (s$\overline{oo}$) *n.*: Former French coin, worth very little; the centime (sän tēm´), mentioned later, was also of little value.
13. **Champs Elysées** (shän zä lē zā´): Fashionable street in Paris.

◆ Build Vocabulary
disheveled (di shev´ əld) *adj.*: Disarranged and untidy
profoundly (prō found´ lē) *adj.*: Deeply and intensely

⬥ Workplace Skills Mini-Lesson

Organizational Skills

Loisel is hired to put other people's account books in order. In order to do so, he needs not only accounting ability but also organizational skills.

Introduce the Concept Point out that many student jobs require organizational skills. A good baby sitter, for example, knows how to organize children's time, put their toys and clothing away neatly, and keep track of how much he or she is

charging per hour and how many hours have been worked.

Develop Background Mention that a good student also needs to be organized. Review ways of organizing information: alphabetizing, organizing figures from least to greatest or greatest to least, listing things in categories, and so on.

Apply the Information Have students do an accounting of the money Loisel owes. Have students make up names of the

people to whom Loisel owes money while creating the list that tells how much he owes each one. The total should equal 18,000 francs.

Assess the Outcome Have volunteers describe how they organized their lists. Did they use alphabetical order? Did they organize by amount owed? Discuss which means of organizing seemed most useful.

the week's chores for a while, she suddenly caught sight of a woman taking a child for a walk. It was Madame Forestier, still young, still beautiful, still charming.

Madame Loisel started to tremble. Should she speak to her? Yes, certainly she should. And now that she had paid everything back, why shouldn't she tell her the whole story?

She went up to her.

"Hello, Jeanne."

The other didn't recognize her and was surprised that this plainly dressed woman should speak to her so familiarly. She murmured:

"But . . . madame! . . . I'm sure . . . You must be mistaken."

"No, I'm not. I am Mathilde Loisel."

Her friend gave a little cry.

"Oh! Oh, my poor Mathilde, how you've changed!"

"Yes, I've been through some pretty hard times since I last saw you and I've had plenty of trouble—and all because of you!"

"Because of me? What do you mean?"

"You remember the diamond necklace you lent me to wear to the party at the Ministry?"

"Yes. What about it?"

"Well, I lost it."

"What are you talking about? You returned it to me."

"What I gave back to you was another one just like it. And it took us ten years to pay for it. You can imagine it wasn't easy for us, since we were quite poor . . . Anyway, I'm glad it's over and done with."

Madame Forestier stopped short.

"You say you bought a diamond necklace to replace that other one?"

"Yes. You didn't even notice then? They really were exactly alike."

And she smiled, full of a proud, simple joy.

Madame Forestier, profoundly moved, took Mathilde's hands in her own.

"Oh, my poor, poor Mathilde! Mine was false. It was worth five hundred francs at the most!

Guide for Responding

◆ *Literature and Your Life*

Reader's Response Do you feel sorry for Madame Loisel? Why or why not?

Thematic Focus Do you think Madame Loisel discovered anything about herself as a result of her ordeal? Explain.

Journal Writing Write about what you would have done if you were in Madame Loisel's place.

☑ Check Your Comprehension

1. What explanation does Madame Loisel give for being upset about the special invitation?
2. What happens to spoil Madame Loisel's triumph at the party?
3. What happens to Madame Loisel in the ten years she works to pay off the cost of the necklace?

◆ Critical Thinking

INTERPRET

1. Do you think the author wants us to sympathize with Madame Loisel's unhappiness at the beginning of the story? Why or why not? **[Infer]**
2. How are the things that Madame Loisel values different from what her husband values? **[Compare and Contrast]**
3. (a) How does Madame Loisel change during the course of the story? (b) What causes her to change? **[Analyze]**
4. What symbolic meaning does the necklace have for Madame Loisel? **[Interpret]**
5. In what way is the ending of the story ironic, or surprising? **[Interpret]**

EXTEND

6. What does the story show you about life in middle-class French society in the late nineteenth century? **[Social Studies Link]**

The Necklace ◆ 541

◆ Reading Strategy

❹ **Draw Conclusions** Mesdames Loisel and Forestier were schoolmates at one time. Ask: Why is Madame Forestier still young, beautiful, and charming when Madame Loisel is not? *Unlike Madame Loisel, she has known a life without cares.*

◆ Reading Strategy

❺ **Drawing Conclusions** Ask students what they can conclude about how Madame Forestier's failure to recognize Madame Loisel makes Madame Loisel feel. *Madame Forestier's failure to recognize Madame Loisel would confirm for Madame Loisel that her outward appearance reflects the hardships she has had to bear. We know from details earlier in the story how important appearances are to Madame Loisel; therefore, she would feel hurt and possibly ashamed.*

◆ *Literature and Your Life*

❻ Point out that with these words, Madame Loisel discovers just what she has lost—something worth far more than the cost of the replacement necklace. Ask: How would you feel if your world were shaken by a discovery of this sort? *Students may say that they would feel foolish, disconcerted, amazed, horrified, and so on.*

Reinforce and Extend

Answers

◆ *Literature and Your Life*

Reader's Response Some students may feel sorry for Madame Loisel because she unnecessarily lost so much of her life to spartan living conditions and hard labor.

Thematic Focus Some students may feel that Madame Loisel realizes how vain and empty her earlier values had been; others may feel that she misses her earlier life.

☑ Check Your Comprehension

1. She has nothing suitable to wear.
2. She loses her friend's necklace.
3. She becomes stronger and coarser, having to struggle to survive.

◆ Critical Thinking

1. The author shows some sympathy for the fact that Madame Loisel is trapped in a boring, hopeless life. On the other hand, he shows her petulance and self-centeredness.
2. Madame Loisel values the outward appearance of being wealthy and desir-able. Her husband values the fundamental elements of life, such as a hearty meal or a good job.
3. The necklace symbolizes Madame Loisel's acceptance as a member of society's upper class.
4. The ending is ironic in that the very necklace that Madame Loisel values as beautiful and expensive forces her to become a common working woman, takes away her youth and beauty, and turns out to be a worthless fake.
5. The type of life a person led depended greatly upon his or her social status.

One-Minute Insight Focusing on the lives of migrant farm workers and their families, "The Harvest" describes on the curiosity of a group of young men who notice that an old man, Don Trine, who seems peculiar to them, goes on mysterious walks. Convinced that following Don Trine will lead them to buried treasure, the boys follow him and later return to the place where he ended his walk. Only one boy discovers what Don Trine's treasure is—a connection to the earth and a love for the land.

❶ Clarification In the world of migrant farm workers, the end of the growing season marks the end of the work cycle. Most return to a home base for the winter until the growing season begins again.

❷ Clarification We might "hold a wake" over someone who has just died; it is another word for the vigil people often hold over the dead before burial. A "wake over the earth" implies that the earth is dead, as indeed it may seem at the end of a harvest.

◆ Critical Thinking

❸ Interpret Ask students why Don Trine's walks attract so much attention. *Students may say that his behavior is unusual, and to the boys, any unusual behavior is suspicious.*

Customize for
Less Proficient Readers
❹ Because this passage is set in an unusual way, students may have difficulty with it. Ask students: What's going on in this passage? *Elicit the idea that people are talking about Don Trine.* Point out that the words people speak are set off by quotation marks. Ask students why the author did not use paragraph indents to mark where a new speaker starts or identify the specific speakers with words like "Raoul said" or "Pedro asked." *Lead students to realize that the individual speakers are not important here; the author wants to create a sense of gossip buzzing around the farm.*

The Harvest

Tomás Rivera

The end of September and the beginning of October. That was the best time of the year. First, because it was a sign that the work was coming to an end and that the return to Texas would start. Also, because there was something in the air that the folks created, an aura of peace and death. The earth also shared that feeling. The cold came more frequently, the frosts that killed by night, in the morning covered the earth in whiteness. It seemed that all was coming to an end. The folks felt that all was coming to rest. Everyone took to thinking more. And they talked more about the trip back to Texas, about the harvests, if it had gone well or bad for them, if they would return or not to the same place next year. Some began to take long walks around the grove. It seemed like in these last days of work there was a wake over the earth. It made you think.

That's why it wasn't very surprising to see Don Trine take a walk by himself through the grove and to walk along the fields every afternoon. This was at the beginning, but when some youngsters asked him if they could tag along, he even got angry. He told them he didn't want anybody sticking behind him.

"Why would he want to be all by hisself, anyway?"
"To heck with him: it's

his business."
"But, you notice, it never fails. Every time, why, sometimes I don't even think he eats supper, he takes his walk. Don't you think that's a bit strange?"
"Well, I reckon. But you saw how he got real mad when we told him we'd go along with him. It wasn't anything to make a fuss over. This ain't his land. We can go wherever we take a liking to. He can't tell us what to do."
"That's why I wonder, why'd he want to walk by hisself?"

And that's how all the rumors about Don Trine's walks got started. The folks couldn't figure out why or what he got out of taking off by himself every afternoon. When he would leave,

Farmworker de Califas, Tony Ortega, Courtesy of the artist

Humanities: Art

Farmworker de Califas, by Tony Ortega.
Working under a burning sun, the subject of this painting typifies the struggle of farm laborers everywhere.
Use these questions to stimulate discussion:
1. How does Ortega's use of color help you sense how the farm worker feels? *He paints ribbons of color like fire that let you know how hot the field must be.*

2. Does the author fully describe the setting in the story? How does this painting add to your experience of the story? *Students may say that there is little description in the story; therefore, the painting provides a visual image of the setting.*

and somebody would spy on him, somehow or other he would catch on, then take a little walk, turn around and head right back to his chicken coop. The fact of the matter is that everybody began to say he was hiding the money he had earned that year or that he had found some buried treasure and every day, little by little, he was bringing it back to his coop. Then they began to say that when he was young he had run around with a gang in Mexico and that he always carried around a lot of money with him. They said, too, that even if it was real hot, he carried a belt full of money beneath his undershirt. Practically all the speculation centered on the idea that he had money.

"Let's see, who's he got to take care of? He's an old bachelor. He ain't never married or had a family. So, with him working so many years . . . Don't you think he's bound to have money? And then, what's that man spend his money on? The only thing he buys is his bit of food every Saturday. Once in a while, a beer, but that's all."
"Yeah, he's gotta have a pile of money, for sure. But, you think he's going to bury it around here?"
"Who said he's burying anything? Look, he always goes for his food on Saturday. Let's check close where he goes this week, and on Saturday, when he's on his errand, we'll see what he's hiding. Whadda you say?"
"Good'nuff. Let's hope he doesn't catch on to us."
That week the youngsters closely watched

◆ Build Vocabulary

harrowed (har´ ōd) *v.*: Broken up and leveled by a harrow, a frame with spikes or disks, drawn by a horse or tractor

◀ **Critical Viewing** The bright colors in this painting capture the heat of the day and the energetic labors of the farm workers in the fields. Does this image capture the setting of the story as you imagine it? [Evaluate]

Don Trine's walks. They noticed that he would disappear into the grove, then come out on the north side, cross the road then cross the field until he got to the irrigation ditch. There he dropped from sight for a while, then he reappeared in the west field. It was there where he would disappear and linger the most. They noticed also that, so as to throw people off his track, he would take a different route, but he always spent more time around the ditch that crossed the west field. They decided to investigate the ditch and that field the following Saturday.

When that day arrived, the boys were filled with anticipation. The truck had scarcely left and they were on their way to the west field. The truck had not yet disappeared and they had already crossed the grove. What they found they almost expected. There was nothing in the ditch, but in the field that had been harrowed after pulling the potatoes they found a number of holes.

"You notice all the holes here? The harrow didn't make these. Look, here's some foot prints, and notice that the holes are at least a foot deep. You can stick your arm in them up to your elbow. No animal makes these kind of holes. Whadda you think?"
"Well, it's bound to be Don Trine. But, what's he hiding? Why's he making so many holes? You think the landowner knows what he's up to?"
"Naw, man. Why, look, you can't see them from the road. You gotta come in a ways to notice they're here. What's he making them for? What's he using them for? And, look, they're all about the same width. Whadda you think?"
"Well, you got me. Maybe we'll know if we hide in the ditch and see what he does when he comes here."
"Look, here's a coffee can. I bet you this is what he digs with."

> ◆ **Reading Strategy**
> What conclusion would you draw about Don Trine from his mysterious behavior?

The Harvest ◆ 543

◆ **Critical Thinking**

5 Interpret The rumors about Don Trine get more elaborate as time goes on. Ask: Why do most of the rumors center on money? *The migrant workers in the story have very little money and probably dream of having more.*

▶ **Critical Viewing** ◀

6 Evaluate Students may find that the setting in the painting gives the impression of late harvest, just as the story does.

◆ **Reading Strategy**

7 Draw Conclusions Don Trine's movements certainly indicate a desire to be secretive about whatever he is doing. Students may say that he is a very private person and seems to be hiding something.

Customize for
Visual/Spatial Learners
The scenes that describe people spying on Don Trine as he walks are quite vivid and humorous. Students might like to choose one of the spying scenes and illustrate it.

543

◆ Reading Strategy

1. She is petty and self-centered and obsessed with material things. She cannot appreciate her husband's love for her.
2. The story makes such values seem hollow and ultimately unsatisfying, and the people who live by them, small and miserable.
3. Most people don't bother thinking about others; most people are incapable of imagining someone whose values are different.
4. Suggested response: Nature can nourish and revive the human spirit.

◆ Literary Focus

1. This statement suggests that life is too complex for most people, including Madame Loisel, to understand. Her own values undermined her, putting her in a position to be destroyed by a bit of bad luck.
2. Suggested response: Living wholly for material values shrinks your spirit and leaves you open to the fickleness of fortune.
3. Suggested response: Human beings are deeply connected to nature and need to acknowledge their kinship, although many people do not recognize this need.

◆ Build Vocabulary

1. eject; 2. trajectory; 3. projectile

Using the Word Bank
1. a   2. a   3. b   4. b   5. c   6. c
7. b

◆ Build Grammar Skills

1. participial phrase: *Dancing all night;* word modified: *Madame Loisel*
2. participial phrase: *reaching desperately through her clothing;* word modified: *she*
3. participial phrase: *confounding all the workers;* word modified: *mystery*
4. participial phrase: *sifting the soil through his fingers;* word modified: *boy*

Guide for Responding (continued)

◆ Reading Strategy

DRAW CONCLUSIONS

By piecing together what you know about the characters in these stories, you can **draw conclusions** about the reasons for their actions. You can then use your understanding of their behavior to draw broader conclusions about human nature.

1. What conclusion can you draw about Madame Loisel from her response to the invitation her husband brings home?
2. Many of the characters in "The Necklace" place a high value on material goods. What conclusion can you draw about such values on the basis of this story? Explain.
3. What conclusion can you draw about human nature from the fact that most of the workers are satisfied with speculating about Don Trine's afternoon walk, as opposed to trying to understand it?
4. What conclusion can you draw about the importance of nature to the human spirit from the ending of Rivera's story?

◆ Literary Focus

THEME

Both these stories convey important **themes,** or general insights, related to human values. In both stories, the themes are conveyed indirectly through the characters' comments and actions.

1. Toward the end of "The Necklace," Madame Loisel thinks, "How strange and fickle life is! How little it takes to make or break you!" What does this statement suggest about the complexity of life?
2. Considering Madame Loisel's feelings at the beginning of the story, along with the events that occur in the aftermath of the ball and the surprising twist that occurs at the end, what would you say is the theme of "The Necklace"? Support your answer.
3. Using the last two paragraphs as a clue, what do you think is the theme of "The Harvest"? Support your answer.

◆ Build Vocabulary

USING THE WORD ROOT *-ject-*

Complete each sentence with one of the words containing the root *-ject-,* which means "to throw."

   a. trajectory   **b.** eject   **c.** projectile

1. When his engines went out, the pilot had to _____?_____.
2. Based on its_____?_____, the players could tell the ball would miss the basket.
3. Without regard for people's safety, he hurled a _____?_____ into the crowd.

USING THE WORD BANK

On your paper, write the word that comes closest in meaning to the first word.
1. astutely: (a) cleverly, (b) grandly, (c) thriftily
2. resplendent: (a) beautiful, (b) wealthy, (c) sturdy
3. profoundly: (a) slowly, (b) deeply, (c) quietly
4. déclassé: (a) decorated, (b) lowered in social status, (c) tardy
5. harrowed: (a) mad, (b) frightened, (c) plowed
6. rueful: (a) amused, (b) sweet, (c) regretting
7. disheveled: (a) attractive, (b) messy, (c) rusty

◆ Build Grammar Skills

PARTICIPIAL PHRASES

In both stories, the writers use **participial phrases**—groups of words consisting of a participle modified by an adverb or adverb phrase or accompanied by a complement—to pack sentences with details about the characters and their actions.

Practice Identify the participial phrases and the words they modify in the following sentences.
1. Dancing all night, Madame Loisel forgot her cares.
2. At home she looked for the necklace, reaching desperately through her clothing.
3. Don Trine's walks were a mystery confounding all the workers.
4. The boy, sifting the soil through his fingers, suddenly understood what Don Trine felt.

✎ Writer's Solution

For additional instruction and practice, use the lesson in the **Language Lab CD-ROM** on Misplaced Modifiers and the practice pages on Participles and Participial Phrases (pp. 44–45) in the *Writer's Solution Grammar Practice Book.*

Build Your Portfolio

Idea Bank

Writing

1. **Character Sketch** Write a character sketch of Monsieur Loisel, based on his actions and the comments of the narrator in "The Necklace."

2. **Different Point of View** By the end of "The Harvest," you have a clear sense of Don Trine's character and motivations. Rewrite the story using Trine as your first-person narrator.

3. **Essay About the Use of Irony** Irony, the contrast between an expected outcome and an actual outcome or between appearance and reality, plays a key role in "The Necklace." Review the story, looking for examples of irony. Then write an essay in which you discuss the role of irony in the story. Use passages from the story to support your points.

Speaking and Listening

4. **Improvisation** With another student, improvise a conversation between Madame Loisel and her husband after she returns from meeting her old friend ten years later.

5. **Debate** With a group of classmates, stage a debate on the issue of whether or not Madame Loisel deserved her fate.

Projects

6. **Illustration** Illustrate one of the scenes from "The Necklace," using any medium you like. Share your illustration with the class. **[Art Link]**

7. **Music** Find Mexican music to accompany a reading of "The Harvest." Share your music with the class, and explain why you chose it. **[Music Link]**

Writing Mini-Lesson

Scene for a Television Drama

Drama began thousands of years ago as stories were acted out around the campfire. Today we continue to watch stories being acted out around a cool, electronic campfire—the television. Imagine one of the stories you have read so far turned into a television drama. What would the final, climactic scenes of the drama be like?

Writing Skills Focus: Climax and Resolution

Every story—whether told as narrative or acted out as drama—reaches a high point of interest called a **climax**. The climax is the point at which the audience's tension and involvement peak. The climax usually takes the form of a confrontation between the main character and someone else or an action sequence involving the main character doing something like winning a race, surviving an earthquake, facing down a hostile crowd. Following the climax, the **resolution** shows how the drama's central conflict will be resolved.

Prewriting Choose one of the stories you have read in this book and write its climax and resolution as a scene for a television drama. Note the actions that you believe make up the climax and resolution of this story.

Drafting Turn the narration of the story's climax and resolution into dialogue (conversation) and stage directions. Review dramatic format (you might look at the plays in this book). Include instructions to the camera person, indicating close-ups and wide shots.

Revising After you have written your scene for a television drama, ask a friend to read it to see if it makes sense. Read it over yourself, and make any changes needed to clarify or enliven the action.

The Necklace/The Harvest ◆ 547

Idea Bank

Customizing for
Performance Levels

Following are suggestions for matching the Idea Bank topics with your students' performance levels:
Less Advanced Students: 1, 7
Average Students: 2, 4, 6
More Advanced Students: 3, 5

Customizing for
Learning Modalities

Following are suggestions for matching Idea Bank topics with your students' learning modalities:
Verbal/Linguistic: 1, 2, 3, 5
Interpersonal: 4
Visual/Spatial: 6
Musical/Rhythmic: 7

Writing Mini-Lesson

Refer students to the Writing Handbook, page 962, for instruction on the writing process, and page 965 for further information on Creative Writing.

Writing and Language Transparencies Use the Story Map transparency, p. 83, to illustrate the concepts of *climax* and *resolution*. To reinforce these concepts, have students identify the climax and resolution in familiar stories and movies.

Writer's Solution

Writing Lab CD-ROM

Have students use the tutorial on Creative Writing. Follow these steps:
1. View the video tips on using props and sets to aid in gathering details for the scene.
2. While drafting on computer, use the interactive instructions on stage directions.
3. Fill out the self-evaluation checklist for drama to aid in revision.
4. For further assistance with revision, review the audio-annotated student model of a dramatic scene. Allow approximately 90 minutes of class time to complete these steps.

Sourcebook

Have students use Chapter 6, Creative Writing (pp. 163–193), for additional support. This chapter includes a model from literature of a dramatic scene (p. 166), tips for writing dialogue (p. 182), and an annotated student model of a dramatic scene (pp. 187–188).

✓ ASSESSMENT OPTIONS

Formal Assessment, Selection Test, pp. 135–137, and Assessment Resources Software. The selection test is designed so that it can be easily customized to the performance levels of your students.
Alternative Assessment, p. 39, includes options for less advanced students, more advanced students, verbal/linguistic learners, logical/mathematical learners, visual/spatial learners, interpersonal learners, and bodily/kinesthetic learners.

PORTFOLIO ASSESSMENT

Use the following rubrics in the *Alternative Assessment* booklet to assess student writing:
Character Sketch: Description Rubric, p. 90
Poem: Poetry Rubric, p. 101
Fairy Tale: Narrative: Fictional Narrative Rubric, p. 88
Writing Mini-Lesson: Drama Rubric, p. 102

Revising

Tell students that revising is a vital step in the writing process because it takes a rough piece of work and polishes it. Tell them that when revising a short story it is good to look for ways to strengthen the plot, round out the characters, and sharpen the setting. Remind peer reviewers that their job is to offer specific, concrete suggestions for improvement rather than just general criticisms.

Publishing

Tell students that if they choose not to share their short story with a wider audience at this time, they may want to incorporate it later into a longer piece of writing. For example, they may want to expand the short story into a novel, or perhaps use it as a chapter in a novel. For this reason they should save what they've written.

Reinforce and Extend

Review the Writing Guidelines
After students have completed their papers, review the characteristics of a short story. Encourage students to come up with additional criteria for an interesting short story based on what they learned through completing the assignment.

Connect to Literature Unit 6 ("Short Stories") includes nine examples of short stories emphasizing elements such as plot, character, setting, point of view, and theme.

APPLYING LANGUAGE SKILLS: Subject and Verb Agreement With Collective Nouns

A **collective noun** names a group. It may be singular, where the group acts as a single unit, or plural, where the group acts as separate parts. Singular collective nouns take a singular verb. Plural collective nouns take a plural verb.

Singular: The class is on a field trip.

Plural: The class are writing their stories.

Practice Write each sentence, using the verb that agrees with the collective noun.

1. The crowd (has, have) stayed together.
2. The group (is, are) now spreading out.
3. The army (is, are) charging as a single unit.
4. The crowd (has, have) run to their homes.

Writing Application Review your story draft to make sure that any collective nouns you have used agree with their verbs. If not, correct the verb.

Include a Climax and Resolution Toward the end of your story, give a vivid description of the climax—the moment when the excitement and drama reach their highest point. Then provide a resolution that tells how everything turns out.

Revising

Use a Checklist Review the Writing Skills Focus on the first page of this lesson, and use the items as a checklist to evaluate and revise your short story. Ask yourself:

▶ Does my writing have a distinct tone?
Have one or more peers review your draft. Ask them to identify the tone of your writing. If they do not identify the tone you intended, consider how you might add, change, or remove details to achieve your desired tone.

▶ Does my story have a clear climax and resolution?
Have your peers identify the highest emotional point of your story. Then have them describe how the conflict turns out. If they are unsure of what your climax or resolution is, consider ways to make it clearer.

Work With a Peer Reviewer After reviewing your own work, have a peer make additional suggestions for revising your story. Have your peer reviewer keep these questions in mind:

1. How are the characters introduced, and how well are they developed? What makes them believable? How can they be improved?
2. How entertaining is the story? How can it be made more entertaining?
3. How clearly is the main conflict presented? How can it be made clearer?
4. How realistic is the dialogue? How can it be improved?

Publishing

Present Your Narrative to a Live Audience Reading your narrative aloud to a group is a great way to share it with others. Take time to practice beforehand—either alone in front of the mirror or with another person. Then, when presenting your narrative, read slowly and clearly and make eye contact with your audience. Vary the volume and tone of your voice for emphasis, and when you read dialogue, try to take on the personalities of the different characters.

✓ ASSESSMENT		4	3	2	1
PORTFOLIO ASSESSMENT Use the scoring rubric for Fictional Narrative in ***Alternative Assessment*** (p. 88) to assess students' writing. Add these criteria to customize the rubric to this assignment.	**Dialogue**	The dialogue is completely natural and makes the characters seem alive. It is punctuated correctly.	The dialogue is realistic but needs some fleshing out. For the most part, it is punctuated correctly.	The dialogue is adequate though not fully developed. Punctuation is inconsistent.	Dialogue is nonexistent or completely unnatural. It is not punctuated correctly at all.
	Collective Nouns	All verbs agree with their subjects.	Most verbs agree with their subjects.	Few verbs agree with their subjects.	No verbs agree with their subjects.

Real-World Reading Skills Workshop

Strategies for Success

A short story is not meant to be objective, so it's acceptable for a story writer to reveal a specific opinion through his or her writing. Other types of writing, however, *are* meant to be objective. Yet writers sometimes have a bias—a leaning toward a specific position. How can you recognize bias while reading?

Look for Loaded Words Loaded words are used to trigger a positive or a negative emotion in you. For example, politicians who cut budgets might call themselves "thrifty." In contrast, they might call opponents who increase funding for certain projects "reckless spenders." Look for vocabulary that unfairly creates bias.

Watch Out for Stereotyping
Stereotypes label all members of a group with the same qualities, ignoring the individual differences among them. For example, the argument that "all politicians are crooks" is stereotyping and creates bias.

Beware of Slanted Arguments A slanted argument promotes only one side of an issue and intentionally omits facts that go against that side. For example, a politician might urge you to vote for him because he showed up for work one hundred days in a row—but he might not tell you that he missed eighty days during the year.

> ✔ Here are other situations in which to watch for bias in your reading:
> ▶ A letter to the editor of a newspaper
> ▶ A petition that is being circulated
> ▶ A copy of a campaign speech
> ▶ A newspaper ad asking for your support

Vote NO for Rec Center

The teenagers in our town are asking for a new recreation center. I say we vote NO on their demand. First, teens are noisy and blast their boom boxes way too loudly. Where are the type of mature youths that we used to be? Last year, more than fifty of our teens were arrested for creating disturbances. Few of these irresponsible troublemakers have any regard for neatness or responsibility. They don't deserve a new rec center.

Apply the Strategy

Read the newspaper editorial. Then answer the questions that follow.

1. What loaded vocabulary appears in the article? Which words create a positive emotion? Which words create a negative emotion?

2. What examples of stereotyping do you find in the editorial? How does each example create bias?

3. What slanted arguments can you detect in the article? For each argument, what facts may the writer have left out in order not to hurt his case?

Speaking and Listening Workshop

Oral Storytelling

Long before people recorded stories in written form, they shared them orally. Whenever you share a story aloud with friends, you are carrying on a tradition that originated several centuries ago. Here are some tips to help you become a skilled storyteller.

Know Your Story Well Before you tell a story, read it to yourself several times or go over the details in your mind. Know all the characters and story events. If the story is long or complicated, jot down some notes to help you remember key details.

Speak With Emotion As you tell your story, be enthusiastic. Be as excited about the story as you want your audience to be. When there is dialogue between characters, try to give each speaker a distinct voice. Speak clearly and slowly so that listeners will understand you.

Use Your Body Good storytellers don't use their voices alone. They use their entire bodies. Before speaking, plan gestures or motions to make with your arms, legs, or head. Practice until these movements look natural. Animated movements will help make your story come alive.

Tips for Oral Storytelling

✔ If you want to be an effective storyteller, follow these strategies:
  ▶ Look directly at your audience.
  ▶ Speak clearly and with emotion.
  ▶ Use your body to act out the story.

Apply the Strategies

Be a storyteller in each situation below. Take the time necessary to prepare before sharing your story with classmates.

1. You are a cave dweller who has just had an exciting encounter. It might have been with an animal, such as a bear or lion, or with some other danger, like fire. Share your experience with your cave family.

2. You are a candidate for the neighborhood Liar's Club. To become a member, you must tell a whopping tall tale filled with impossible characters and events. Spin the most outrageous story you can imagine.

3. You are a clown hired to entertain at a children's birthday party. You have been asked to tell a familiar tale, such as "The Three Little Pigs" or "Hansel and Gretel." Retell the story, pretending your audience is a group of young children.

552 ◆ Short Stories

Cross-Curricular Connection: Science

Great discoveries in science, such as the discovery of gravity, the heliocentric Solar System, atomic energy, or Darwin's theory of Evolution, often have interesting and exciting stories behind them. Explain to students how such discoveries never occur in a vacuum and often involve intrigue, politics, and competitive races between two or more parties to be the first to make the discovery. For example, tell them how Galileo was forced by the Vatican under penalty of excommunication to renounce his heliocentric theory, or how Darwin published The Origin of Species early because he became aware that another naturalist had made the same discoveries and was on the verge of publishing his theory first.

Extended Reading Opportunities

For ages, people have created stories in an attempt to understand and share their experiences. Great writers from many different time periods and cultures have penned short stories. Following are just a few possibilities for extending your exploration of short stories.

Suggested Titles

The Short Stories of Isaac Bashevis Singer
Isaac Bashevis Singer

Singer—a Yiddish novelist, short-story writer, critic, and journalist—was born in Poland and emigrated to the United States in 1935 to pursue a career as a writer. In Singer's realistic stories, the forces of good and evil often collide. The forty-seven stories in this collection show the great compassion in Singer's writing, as well as his skillful blending of Jewish culture with other world cultures.

The Joy Luck Club
Amy Tan

This book tells the stories of four Chinese mothers and their American-born daughters. Each chapter focuses on one woman's story—a mother growing up in China long ago or a daughter living in modern-day San Francisco. Combined into a novel, these interwoven stories explore the difficulties that can result when two cultures meet head-on, as well as the fierce love that mothers and daughters share, no matter what their backgrounds.

21 Great Stories
Abraham H. Lass and Norma L. Tasman, editors

This collection features the work of twenty masterful storytellers. Within this volume, you'll find a wide range of styles. Stories by James Thurber and Mark Twain will amuse you. A mystery by Sir Arthur Conan Doyle will stump you. Two tales of terror by Edgar Allan Poe will chill you. Other great writers represented in this book include Ray Bradbury, Guy de Maupassant, Jack London, John Steinbeck, and James Joyce.

Other Possibilities

Across the Sea of Stars — Arthur C. Clarke, editor
Alfred Hitchcock's Ghostly Gallery — Alfred Hitchcock, editor
Cat Encounters: A Cat Lover's Anthology — Seon Manley and Lewis Gogo, editors

Planning Students' Extended Reading

All of these works are good choices for students' exploration of the short story genre. Following is some information that will help you choose which to teach.

Customize for
Varying Student Needs

When assigning the selections in this part to your students, keep in mind the following factors:

- The stories in *The Short Stories of Isaac Bashevis Singer* are easy to read and have themes that should be accessible and meaningful to all students.
- *The Joy Luck Club* contains stories that should not present difficulties for students of any performance levels. The stories may be especially meaningful for students whose parents moved her from other countries.
- *21 Great Stories* includes stories that range in level of difficulty. This collection is ideal for more advanced students.

Sensitive Issues Some of the stories in *21 Great Stories* contain language and subject matter that you may not find appropriate. We *strongly recommend* that you preview the stories before assigning them to students.

Resources for Teaching Novels, Plays, and Literature Collections This booklet includes graphic organizers, teaching strategies, and transparencies that you can use in teaching any of these works.

Planning Instruction and Assessment

Unit Objectives

1. To develop skill in reading nonfiction
2. To apply a variety of reading strategies, particularly literal-comprehension strategies, appropriate for reading these selections.
3. To recognize literary elements used in these selections
4. To increase vocabulary
5. To learn elements of grammar and usage
6. To write in a variety of modes and about situations based on the selections
7. To develop speaking and listening skills, by doing proposed activities

Meeting the Objectives

With each selection, you will find instructional material and portfolio opportunities through which students can meet these objectives. Further, you will find additional practice pages for reading strategies, literary elements, vocabulary, and grammar in the **Selection Support** booklet in the Teaching Resources box.

Setting Goals Work with your students at the beginning of the unit to set goals for unit outcomes. Plan what skills and concepts you wish students to acquire. You may individualize according to students' performance levels or learning modalities.

Portfolios You may have students keep portfolios of their work or of their work in progress. The activities and prompts on the Build Your Portfolio page of each selection provide opportunities for students to apply the concepts presented with the selection.

Street Reflections, 1988, Robert Vickery, oil on canvas, 16 x 20 inches, signed lower left: "Robert Vickery '88" ©1997 Robert Vickery/Licensed by VAGA, New York, NY

Humanities: Art

Street Reflections, 1988, by Robert Vickery.

Elicit as full a description of the art as possible: multiple reflections of people walking down a city street, with someone wearing glasses, possibly the artist, reflected closer up on the right. Encourage students to imagine the painter as re-creating images reflected in a window, including the reflection of the person in glasses (possibly himself) who stands facing the window.

Help students link the artwork to the focus of Unit 7 ("Nonfiction") by answering the following questions:

1. Nonfiction is writing that focuses on real life—it "reflects" the real world, often adding the dimension of the writer's perspective. In what way has the painter done something comparable in his work? *The painting literally presents "reflections" of daily life on a certain street; the multiple images and the close-up of the person in glasses add the personal perspective, something you wouldn't see in a straightforward photograph of the same scene.*

2. Why do you think the artist chose to include a close-up of one face, when most of the people in the painting are virtually faceless pedestrians? *The artist may be commenting about the difference between the anonymous crowd and the individual observer.*

554

Nonfiction

If fiction takes you on imaginative flights of fancy, nonfiction brings you back down to Earth. Nonfiction includes true stories about real people, places, and experiences. It also includes practical writing that informs you about something and persuasive writing that urges you to think or act in a certain way. On the following pages, you'll find many different types of nonfiction— from a reflective essay to a diary entry to a transcript of a radio news feature. Although all are different, each one in some way reflects real life.

◆ 555

Assessing Student Progress

The following tools are available to measure the degree to which students meet the unit objectives:

Informal Assessment

The questions on the Guide for Responding sections are a first level of response to the concepts and skills presented with the selection. Students' responses are a brief informal measure of their grasp of the material. Their responses on this level can indicate where further instruction and practice are needed. You may then follow up with the practice pages in the *Selection Support* booklet.

You will find literature and reading guides in the *Alternative Assessment* booklet, which you may give students on an individual basis for informal assessment of their performance.

Formal Assessment

In the *Formal Assessment* booklet, you will find selection tests and a unit test.

Selection Tests The selection tests measure comprehension and skills acquisition for each selection or group of selections.

Unit Test The unit test applies the unit skills on a broader level. The Critical Reading section measures Unit Objectives 1, 2, and 3. The Vocabulary and Grammar section measures Objectives 4 and 5. The Essay section measures Objectives 1 and 6.

Alternative Assessment

Portfolios As you review individual pieces or the collected work in students' portfolios, you will find assessment sheets available in the portfolio section of the Alternative Assessment booklet.

Scoring Rubrics You will find scoring rubrics for writing modes in the Alternative Assessment booklet. You can apply these to Writing Mini-Lessons and to Writing Process Workshop lessons.

Speaking and Listening The *Alternative Assessment* booklet contains assessment sheets for speaking and listening activities.

Learning Modalities The *Alternative Assessment* contains activities that appeal to different learning styles. You may use these as an alternative measurement of students' growth.

Guide for Reading

More About the Author
Sally Kristen Ride was born and raised in Los Angeles. She credits her physics teacher at Westlake Girls' High School with inspiring her to pursue science as a career. Her specialty is laser physics. She worked on a variety of projects for NASA and married a fellow astronaut before going on her first mission in 1983.

Sally Ride (1951–)

She might have become a professional tennis player, a science teacher, or a writer. What Sally Ride chose to be, however, was an astronaut.

Reaching for the Stars Ride's determination, competitive spirit, and academic excellence have enabled her to achieve her goals and to serve as a role model for others. Although best known for her scholarly pursuits, she is also a talented athlete. As a youngster, she ranked eighteenth nationally on the junior tennis circuit.

In 1973, Ride received degrees in English literature and physics from Stanford University. She then went on to earn graduate degrees from Stanford. In 1978, she read about NASA's call for astronauts in the Stanford University newspaper. She was one of more than 8,000 candidates to apply to the space program. Twenty-nine men and six women were accepted—including Sally Ride.

In June 1983, Sally Ride became the first American woman in space.

Ride was preparing for her third space mission when the space shuttle *Challenger* exploded shortly after liftoff in January 1986, killing all seven crew members. The accident put a temporary halt to shuttle missions, and as a result Ride didn't return to space. She did, however, play a key role on the Presidential Commission investigating the accident.

After NASA In 1987, Ride retired from NASA. Since then, she has worked as a science teacher and a writer. She is currently a professor of physics at the University of California at San Diego and Director of the California Space Institute, and is the author of several books on space.

◆ Build Vocabulary

WORD ROOTS: *-nov-*
In this essay, Sally Ride describes how seeing the Earth from space led her to "assume the role of a novice geologist." The word *novice* contains the word root *-nov-*, which means "new." A novice is someone who is new to an activity. In this case, Ride, who is a physicist, is a beginner at the science of geology. What other words can you think of in which the word root *-nov-* appears?

WORD BANK

articulate
surreal
ominous
novice
muted
eddies
subtle
eerie
diffused
extrapolating

As you read this essay, you will encounter the words on this list. Pair up with a classmate, and work together to write definitions for as many of the words as you can. As you read, check to see if you're right.

◆ Build Grammar Skills

CORRECT USE OF *ITS* AND *IT'S*
Although they are pronounced the same way, the posessive pronoun *its* and the contraction *it's* mean very different things. *Its*, which means "belonging to it," does not contain an apostrophe. The contraction *it's* (short for "it is") does contain an apostrophe. To avoid confusing the two words, substitute the words *it is* into the sentence. If the resulting sentence is correct, the contraction *it's* is the correct choice. Look at these examples from Ride's essay:

It's (it is) more than 22,000 miles lower . . .

In *its* light, we see ghostly clouds . . .

As you read the essay, pay attention to the way *its* and *it's* are used.

Prentice Hall Literature Program Resources

REINFORCE / RETEACH / EXTEND

Selection Support Pages
Build Vocabulary: Word Roots: *-nov-*, p. 163
Build Grammar Skills: Correct Use of *Its* and *It's*, p. 164
Reading for Success Strategies: Strategies for Reading Nonfiction, pp. 165–166
Literary Focus: Observation, p. 167

Strategies for Diverse Student Needs, p. 40

Beyond Literature
Cross-Curricular Connection: Science, p. 40

Formal Assessment Selection Test, pp. 142–144, Assessment Resources Software

Alternative Assessment, p. 40

Writing and Language Transparencies
Descriptive and Observational Writing, pp. 17–20

Resource Pro CD-ROM
"Single Room, Earth View"—includes all resource materials and customizable lesson plan

 Listening to Literature Audiocassettes
"Single Room, Earth View"

Single Room, Earth View

◆ Literature and Your Life

CONNECT YOUR EXPERIENCE

At street level, a city can be a confusing place. An orange-and-white barricade blocks the street for no apparent reason. You take a shortcut through a park—and find yourself lost in an unexpected spot.

From the viewing deck of a tall building, you can see the layout of the city. With your new perspective you understand things that baffled you before. You can see that the barricade protects a parade route, and that the path through the park bends in an odd way.

In this essay, you will experience what it's like to look down on the entire Earth, as Sally Ride describes her view from space.

THEMATIC FOCUS: OBSERVATIONS

How can observing places and situations from different perspectives give you a better understanding of the world around us?

Journal Writing Record your memories of a time when you looked at something from a new perspective.

◆ Background for Understanding

HISTORY

During her training as an astronaut, Sally Ride was a member of the support crew for the second and third space shuttle flights. Her turn to fly came on June 18, 1983, when she served as a flight engineer and mission specialist aboard the shuttle *Challenger*—the same shuttle that would explode shortly after liftoff three years later. Ride was the first American woman in space. Interestingly, her historic mission took place twenty years and two days after Soviet cosmonaut Valentina Tereshkova became the first woman in space.

◆ Literary Focus

OBSERVATION

In an **observation,** a writer describes an event he or she saw firsthand and watched over an extended period of time. The writer includes a lot of details and chooses vivid, precise words to re-create the event for the reader. Observations often focus on scientific phenomena, such as the behavior of a wild animal or the outcome of a laboratory experiment. In this essay, astronaut Sally Ride, a trained scientist, relays her observations of Earth's surface from the space shuttle. As you read, note the systematic, precise way in which she describes what she observed.

Guide for Reading ◆ 557

The Reading for Success page in each unit presents a set of problem-solving procedures to help readers understand authors' words and ideas on multiple levels. Good readers develop a bank of strategies from which they can draw as needed.

Unit 7 introduces strategies for reading nonfiction. Many students who do quite well at reading fiction find themselves at a loss in social studies or science classes because they lack the skills needed to read nonfiction successfully. It's important to recognize that reading nonfiction sometimes requires a different approach from that used to read fiction. Strategies for reading nonfiction include the following:

- Recognizing the author's purpose
- Identifying the author's main idea
- Locating supporting details for those main ideas
- Determining the pattern of organization used by the author
- Varying reading rate to fit the reader's purpose

These strategies for reading nonfiction are modeled with "Single Room, Earth View." Each green box shows an example of how to apply each of the strategies.

Following their reading, meet with students in small groups to discuss how they used each strategy to read and understand the essay successfully. Have them tell how they might use the strategies to read other types of nonfiction.

How to Use the Reading for Success Page

- Introduce the strategies for reading nonfiction, presenting each as a problem-solving procedure. Be sure students understand what each strategy involves and under what circumstances to apply it.

- Before students read the essay, have them preview it, looking at the annotations in the green boxes that model the strategies.

- To reinforce these strategies after students have read "Single Room, Earth View," have students do the Reading for Success pages in **Selection Support,** pp. 165–166. These pages give students an opportunity to read a selection and practice strategies for reading nonfiction by writing their own annotations.

Reading for Success

Strategies for Reading Nonfiction

Nonfiction is writing about real life. A work of nonfiction may describe real people, places, events, objects, or ideas. Nonfiction includes biographies, autobiographies, and essays. Although works of nonfiction vary in topic, type, and purpose, they all share one key characteristic: They all are true. However, this does not mean that you should accept all of the writer's ideas. You need to judge the facts for yourself and form your own opinions. Use these strategies to help you get the most out of the nonfiction you read.

Recognize the author's purpose.
▶ Consider the details that the writer includes or fails to include. Think about what this tells you about the author's beliefs and purpose in writing.
▶ Based on what you discover about the author's purpose, decide whether you should accept the writer's ideas wholeheartedly—or whether you should be skeptical.

Identify the author's main points.
Ask yourself what the author wants you to learn or think as a result of reading his or her work of nonfiction. These main points are the most important ideas in the work.

Identify the evidence for the author's main points.
Each point the author makes must be supported by evidence. Evaluate the facts the author uses to back up his or her points. Ask yourself whether the writer offers enough facts to support each point thoroughly. Also look at the type of evidence the writer presents. Is it convincing?

Recognize patterns of organization.
▶ A work of nonfiction should be organized so that the main points and supporting evidence are easy for readers to follow.
▶ Transition words, such as *next, compared to,* or *most important,* will clue you into the type of organization the writer is using.

Vary your reading rate.
▶ Read quickly if you are reviewing familiar material, scanning for a particular idea, or just want the gist of a work of nonfiction.
▶ Read slowly and carefully if it is important that you fully understand the material. At times, you will even want to go back and reread key passages.

As you read the essay by Sally Ride, notice the notes along the side. The notes demonstrate how to apply these strategies to your reading.

Reading Strategies: Support and Reinforcement
Appropriate Reading Strategies Students are given a reading strategy to apply in reading each selection. For example, students will be directed to recognize the author's purpose in a selection that expresses a strong opinion. In other selections a strategy is suggested that is appropriate to the selection.

Reading Prompts To encourage application of the given reading strategy, there are occasional prompts, within green boxes, at appropriate and significant points.

In addition, there are red boxes prompting application of the Literary Focus concept and maroon boxes prompting students to connect with their lives.

Using the Boxed Annotations and Prompts
The material in the green, red, and maroon boxes along the sides of selections is intended to help students apply the literary element and the reading strategy and to make a connection with their lives.

You may use the boxed material in these ways:
- Have students pause when they come to a box and respond to its prompt before they continue reading.
- Urge students to read through the selection, ignoring the boxes. After they have read the selection completely, they may go back and review the selection, responding to the prompts.

Single Room, Earth View

Sally Ride

MODEL

Everyone I've met has a glittering, if vague, mental image of space travel. And naturally enough, people want to hear about it from an astronaut: "How did it feel . . . ?" "What did it look like . . . ?" "Were you scared?" Sometimes, the questions come from reporters, their pens poised and their tape recorders silently reeling in the words; sometimes, it's wide-eyed, ten-year-old girls who want answers. I find a way to answer all of them, but it's not easy.

> From these details, you can guess that Ride's **purpose** is to describe what space travel is like.

Imagine trying to describe an airplane ride to someone who has never flown. An <u>articulate</u> traveler could describe the sights but would find it much harder to explain the difference in perspective provided by the new view from a greater distance, along with the feelings, impressions, and insights that go with the new perspective. And the difference is enormous: Spaceflight moves the traveler another giant step farther away. Eight and one-half thunderous minutes after launch, an astronaut is orbiting high above the Earth, suddenly able to watch typhoons form, volcanoes smolder, and meteors streak through the atmosphere below.

> Here, Ride states a **main point**: Spaceflight gives the viewer a new perspective, as well as new feelings, impressions, and insights.

While flying over the Hawaiian Islands, several astronauts have marveled that the islands look just as they do on a map. When people first hear that, they wonder what should be so surprising about Hawaii looking the way it does in the atlas. Yet, to the astronauts it is an absolutely startling sensation: The islands really do look as if that part of the world has been carpeted with a big page torn out of Rand-McNally,[1] and all we can do is try to convey the <u>surreal</u> quality of that scene.

> The astronauts' surprised reaction to seeing Hawaii is **evidence** that backs up the idea that spaceflight results in new feelings.

In orbit, racing along at five miles per second, the space shuttle circles the Earth once every 90 minutes. I found that at this speed, unless I kept my nose pressed to the window, it was almost impossible to keep track of where we were at any given moment—the world below simply changes too fast. If I turned my concentration away for too long, even just to change film in a camera, I could miss an entire land mass. It's embarrassing to float up to a window, glance outside, and then have to ask a crewmate, "What continent is this?"

We could see smoke rising from fires that dotted the entire east coast of Africa, and in the same orbit only moments later, ice floes jostling for position in the Antarctic. We could see the Ganges River dumping its murky, sediment-laden water into the Indian Ocean and watch

---

1. **Rand-McNally:** Publishers of atlases.

◆ Build Vocabulary

articulate (är tik′ yə lit) *adj.*: Expressing oneself clearly and easily

surreal (sə rē′ əl) *adj.*: Strange

Single Room, Earth View ◆ 559

Develop Understanding

 **One-Minute Insight** Astronaut Sally Ride responds to the question "What is space travel like?" with a lyrical description of viewing the Earth from 200 miles above. She points out landmarks on Earth from a new perspective and shows how that perspective changes a space traveler's feelings about the Earth.

◆ Build Vocabulary

❶ **Correct Use of *Its* and *It's*** Ask students to explain why there is an apostrophe between the *t* and the *s*. Then ask students to read the sentence using "it is" in place of "it's." How does this affect the tone of the writing? *The apostrophe takes the place of the missing i in is. The contraction makes the tone more informal; substituting the full words makes the tone more formal.*

◆ Reading for Success

❷ **Identify the Evidence for the Author's Main Points** Ask students to identify the examples the author uses to show the difference between space flight and airplane flight. *She refers to seeing typhoons form, volcanoes smolder, and meteors streak through the atmosphere.*

◆ Reading for Success

❸ **Recognize the Author's Purpose** Here the author hints at one of her purposes in writing. Ask students to restate the purpose in their own words. *She wants to describe the amazing view from space.*

Comprehension Check ✓

❹ Why does the author use the word *float* here? *She is weightless in space and is floating around the cabin.*

 Block Scheduling Strategies

Consider these suggestions to take advantage of extended class time:

- As you review the information in Background for Understanding (p. 557), discuss other important "firsts" for women. Encourage students to draw upon their knowledge of sports and current events in addition to what they have learned from social studies and science classes.
- Use the Personal Response essay in **Alternative Assessment,** p. 40, to encourage students to react to a specific description in "Single Room, Earth View."
- Before students complete the Writing Mini-Lesson (p. 564), have them locate additional examples of vivid adjectives in the essay.
- Have students work on the Description From Above, Eyewitness Report, or Interview activities in the Idea Bank (p. 564). These activities do not require reference materials or resources other than those that are found in a typical classroom.
- Enrich student understanding of the essay and connect literature to science by assigning the Cross-Curricular Connection: Science page on Plate Tectonics in **Beyond Literature,** p. 40.
- Allow pairs or small groups of students to use classroom or computer lab resources to find more information about Sally Ride and NASA on the World Wide Web.

❶ Recognize Patterns of Organization Ask students what all the details in this paragraph have in common. Have them single out transitional words that signal the reader that the author is moving from one detail to the next. *All the details in this paragraph relate to how the Earth looks from space at night. Transitional words that separate one detail from another are "On one night-time pass," "When the moon is full," "One night," and "Of all the sights from orbit."*

◆ **Reading for Success**

❷ Identify the Author's Main Points The author sums up by reiterating one of her main points. Have students restate it in their own words. *The perspective of Earth from space is unfamiliar and different from anything known on Earth.*

Reinforce and Extend

Answers
◆ *Literature and Your Life*

Reader's Response Some students may want to be an astronaut because they love science and find space exploration exciting and glamorous. Others may find that the discomfort and danger of space travel make the job of an astronaut unappealing to them.

Thematic Focus They give us a "big picture" perspective on the Earth.

☑ Check Your Comprehension

1. Because space-shuttle astronauts are much closer to Earth than lunar astronauts, they cannot see the entire globe at a glance and can distinguish many manmade features. From the moon, the Earth looks like a "blue marble."
2. Ride regards nighttime lightning storms as the most spectacular sight from orbit.
3. Ride was able to see islands, mountain ranges, volcanoes, river deltas, ice floes, deserts, lakes, and oceans.
4. Ride saw fires, bridges, runways, abrupt transitions from desert to farmland caused by irrigation, cities, oil slicks, patches of pollution-damaged trees, haze due to air pollution, and contrails of airplanes.

562

---

❶ the clouds into bursting balls of light. Sometimes, when a storm extends hundreds of miles, it looks like a transcontinental brigade is tossing fireworks from cloud to cloud.

As the shuttle races the sun around the Earth, we pass from day to night and back again during a single orbit—hurtling into darkness, then bursting into daylight. The sun's appearance unleashes spectacular blue and orange bands along the horizon, a clockwork miracle that astronauts witness every 90 minutes. But, I really can't describe a sunrise in orbit. The drama set against the black backdrop of space and the magic of the materializing colors can't be captured in an astronomer's equations or an astronaut's photographs.

> The **pattern of organization** Ride uses is organizing by type. She simply groups related facts and ideas. This type of organization lends itself to an observation or a description in which all points are equally important.

I once heard someone (not an astronaut)

suggest that it's possible to imagine what space-flight is like by simply extrapolating from the sensations you experience on an airplane. All you have to do, he said, is mentally raise the airplane 200 miles, mentally eliminate the air noise and the turbulence, and you get an accurate mental picture of a trip in the space shuttle.

Not true. And while it's natural to try to liken spaceflight to familiar experiences, it can't be brought "down to Earth"—not in the final sense. The environment is different, the perspective is different. Part of the fascination with space travel is the element of the unknown—the conviction that it's different from earthbound experiences. And it is.

❷

◆ Build Vocabulary

extrapolating (ek strap′ ə lāt′ in) *v*.: Arriving at a conclusion by making inferences based on known facts

---

Guide for Responding

◆ *Literature and Your Life*

Reader's Response Would you like to be an astronaut like Sally Ride? Why or why not?

Thematic Focus How do spaceflights give us a better appreciation for the world around us?

Group Activity Brainstorm for a list of reasons why going on a spaceflight would be interesting to you. Then, as a group, come to a consensus on a "top three" list.

☑ Check Your Comprehension

1. How does the view of Earth from the space shuttle differ from the view of Earth from the moon?
2. What does Ride regard as the most spectacular sight from orbit?
3. Name three natural features that Ride saw from orbit.
4. Identify three examples that she observed of humans' effect on the environment.

562 ◆ *Nonfiction*

Beyond Literature

History Connection

The Challenger Tragedy On January 28, 1986, a six-person crew lifted off at Cape Canaveral, Florida, and thundered toward space aboard the space shuttle *Challenger*. Suddenly, disaster struck. Just 73 seconds into the flight, the *Challenger* broke up in a huge fireball, killing all on board. All future shuttle missions were canceled while a special commission determined the cause of the accident. The culprit turned out to be a faulty O ring, one of a series of circular rubber rings that seal the joints between sections of the shuttle's solid-fuel rocket boosters. After the O rings were redesigned, space shuttles once again zoomed into space. The first flight was that of the shuttle *Discovery*, on September 29, 1988. Do you think space travel is worth the risks involved? Why or why not?

Beyond the Selection

FURTHER READING

Other Works by Sally Ride
The Third Planet: Exploring Earth From Space (with Tam O'Shaughnessy)
To Space and Back (with Susan Oakie)

Other Works With the Theme of Perspectives
Matthew Henson: Explorer, Michael Gilman
The Story of Sacajawea, Guide to Lewis and Clark, Della Rowland

INTERNET

You and your students may find additional information about Sally Ride and space exploration on the Internet. We suggest the following sites. Please be aware, however, that sites may have changed from the time we published this information.

To reach NASA and the Kennedy Space Center's home page, visit **http://www.ksc.nasa.gov/ ksc.html**

To find out what Sally Ride is currently working on, see **http://sdphul.ucsd.edu/dept/pr/faculty/cssr.html**

We *strongly recommend* that you preview the sites before you send students to them.

*G*uide for Responding (continued)

◆ Critical Thinking

INTERPRET
1. According to Ride, how is riding on the space shuttle different from riding on an airplane? **[Compare and Contrast]**
2. Why did Ride find it easier to imagine geological forces from space? **[Interpret]**
3. An astronaut reported that colors did not seem as bright in 1983 as in 1973. What does this suggest? **[Infer]**
4. How does space travel help us understand conditions on Earth? **[Draw Conclusions]**

EVALUATE
5. Is the title of the essay appropriate? Explain. **[Make a Judgment]**

APPLY
6. How have Ride's descriptions of the Earth affected your thoughts about our planet? **[Relate]**

◆ Reading for Success

STRATEGIES FOR READING NONFICTION
Review the reading strategies and notes showing how to read nonfiction. Then apply those strategies to answer the following questions.
1. What is the author's purpose in writing this essay?
2. What are the author's main points?
3. How does the author support these main points?

◆ Literary Focus

OBSERVATION
In an **observation**, a writer carefully notes the facts and events that he or she witnesses firsthand, and describes them vividly so that readers feel as if they had experienced the event themselves. In "Single Room, Earth View," Sally Ride shares her observations of traveling in the space shuttle.
1. How does Ride show her talent for observation in finding civilization's "signatures"?
2. How does she prove herself to be a careful observer of Earth's oceans?
3. How does she use comparisons to everyday phenomena to help readers follow her observations?

◆ Build Vocabulary

USING THE WORD ROOT -nov-
The word root -nov- means "new." In your notebook, write a definition that incorporates the word *new* for each term.
1. novel (*adj.*) 2. innovate (*v.*) 3. renovate (*v.*)

USING THE WORD BANK
In your notebook, fill in the blanks with words in the Word Bank or forms of those words.

Normally _____?_____, the scientist felt like a tongue-tied _____?_____ speaker. The low, _____?_____ murmuring of her audience sounded frightening and _____?_____. She turned on the overhead projector, and the smell of burning dust, _____?_____ but unmistakable, _____?_____ through the air. "I know this seems _____?_____," she said, putting on the first slide. "However, what we can _____?_____ from the evidence is clear. The odd, _____?_____ patterns of _____?_____ and whirlpools on Planet X are signs of intelligent life. We are not alone."

◆ Build Grammar Skills

CORRECT USE OF *ITS* AND *IT'S*
Its is a possessive pronoun that means "belonging to it." *Its* does not have an apostrophe. *It's* is a contraction of *it is*. *It's* has an apostophe to show where a letter has been removed to create the contraction.

When in doubt about whether to use *its* or *it's*, substitute the phrase *it is* into the sentence. If the meaning of the sentence remains the same, *it's* is correct. If the sentence stops making sense or its meaning changes, *its* is correct.

Practice In your notebook, write each of these sentences. Choose *its* or *it's* to complete each one.
1. _____?_____ exciting to fly on the space shuttle.
2. Earth reveals _____?_____ features to the astonauts.
3. Sometimes _____?_____ difficult to identify what you see.
4. At times, pollution rears _____?_____ ugly head.
5. After seeing Earth from space, _____?_____ clear that people have a powerful effect on _____?_____ land and oceans.

Single Room, Earth View ◆ 563

◆ Build Vocabulary

Using the Word Root -nov-
Answers may vary, but should be similar to these:
1. Something that is novel is fresh and new.
2. When you innovate, you create a new way of doing something.
3. When you renovate, you renew the appearance of a building.

Using the Word Bank
articulate, novice, muted, ominous, subtle, diffused, surreal, extrapolate, eerie, eddies

◆ Build Grammar Skills
1. It's; 2. its; 3. it's; 4. its; 5. it's, its

🖊 Writer's Solution
For additional practice on the correct use of *its* and *it's*, use the Apostrophes With Pronouns page and Apostrophes With Contractions page in the *Writer's Solution Grammar Practice Book*, pp. 113–114.

◆ Critical Thinking
1. A ride on the space shuttle is higher, faster, and less noisy and less turbulence than a ride on an airplane. More importantly, riding on the space shuttle provides a new environment and perspective unlike anything on Earth.
2. She could better see the effects of such forces from her vantage point in space.
3. Air pollution has increased.
4. Space travel allows us to see the "big picture" of natural phenomena such as ocean dynamics, plate tectonics, and hurricane formation. It also allows us to see how human actions affect the environment.
5. Students may relate the title to a description of a hotel room that describes occupancy and view— for example, single room, ocean view. In this case, the room is the space shuttle. Some students may point out that, although Ride gives a single viewpoint, the space shuttle is actually a quintuple to septuple room.
6. Students may say that the essay has given them a new sense of the unity of our planet.

◆ Reading for Success
1. She wants to describe what it's like to travel on the space shuttle.
2. Suggested response: Space travel provides a new perspective on the Earth. Space flight is not like any earthbound experiences.
3. She provides detailed descriptions of the extraordinary sights she observed from orbit.

◆ Literary Focus
1. Suggested response: She was able to pick out the straight lines of bridges and runways and use them as a framework to see the city around them.
2. Suggested response: She describes seeing the faint traces of eddies and water currents, oil slicks, and the wakes of boats—things that are not noticed at first glance.
3. Examples of the way she compares what she observed to everyday phenomena include descriptions of "hurricanes expanding and rising like biscuits," geological features appearing "in salt-and-flour relief," and lightning looking like "fireworks."

Idea Bank

Customizing for
Performance Levels

Following are suggestions for matching the Idea Bank topics with your students' performance levels:
Less Advanced Students: 1, 5
Average Students: 2, 4, 6
More Advanced Students: 3, 7

Customizing for
Learning Modalities

Following are suggestions for matching Idea Bank topics with your students' learning modalities:
Visual/Spatial: 1, 2
Auditory: 4, 5
Logical/Mathematical: 6

Writing Mini-Lesson

Refer students to the Writing Handbook, page 962, for instruction on the writing process, and page 964 for further information on Description.

Writer's Solution

Writers at Work Videodisc

Have students view the videodisc segment (Ch. 1) featuring science-fiction writer Anne McCaffrey to see how she makes her descriptions vivid and memorable. Have students discuss how attention to detail can bring places and events to life in nonfiction as well as fiction.

Play frames 335 to 10785

Writing Lab CD-ROM

Have students complete the Tutorial on Description. Follow these steps:
1. Use the sensory word bins for gathering details.
2. Have students draft on computer.
3. Use the Vague Adjectives Checker to aid revision.

Allow approximately 50 minutes of class time to complete these steps.

Sourcebook

Have students use Chapter 1, Description (pp. 1–29), for additional support. The chapter includes indepth instruction on gathering sensory details (pp. 17–18), organizing details (pp. 19–20), and making language more precise (p. 21).

Build Your Portfolio

Idea Bank

Writing

1. **Description From Above** Write a description of a familiar place as it would appear to someone looking down from above.

2. **Eyewitness Report** In any job, you will need to describe incidents you observe—such as a meeting or someone else's job performance. Practice this skill by writing an eyewitness report about something you saw this week. **[Career Link]**

3. **Persuasive Essay** Write a persuasive essay arguing for public support for the space program. Back up your points with facts, vivid descriptions, and statistics. **[Science Link]**

Speaking and Listening

4. **Interview** With three classmates, assume the roles of three astronauts and the journalist who is interviewing them. Prepare questions and answers before conducting the interview.

5. **Description Feedback** Thoroughly describe something you observed to a partner, then have your partner restate your description in his or her own words. Discuss any differences in understanding. Then switch roles.

Projects

6. **Game** Create a board game in which the object is to travel through space to Pluto and back to Earth. Include obstacles that players must avoid to achieve success. **[Science Link]**

7. **Space Exploration Report** Prepare a report on one aspect of space exploration, such as women astronauts or the space shuttle. If possible, use NASA's World Wide Web site to obtain information and illustrations for your report. **[Science Link; Technology Link]**

564 ◆ Nonfiction

Writing Mini-Lesson

Observation From Space

Imagine that you are an astronaut in space. Perhaps you are orbiting the Earth on the space shuttle or planting a flag on the surface of Mars. Write an observation that will capture the minds and imaginations of readers on Earth.

Writing Skills Focus: Vivid Adjectives

To make your experiences come alive for your readers, use **vivid adjectives** to paint a picture in words. For example, if something is colorful, tell what colors it is. If the weather is hot, tell whether it is *scorching, steamy,* or *searing.*

Look at how Ride uses vivid adjectives to describe the Earth from space.

Model From the Essay

We could see the Ganges River dumping its *murky, sediment-laden* water into the Indian Ocean and watch *ominous* hurricane clouds expanding and rising like biscuits in the oven of the Caribbean.

Prewriting Make a sketch of what you'll describe in your observation. Annotate your drawing with details about different objects and events.

Drafting To make sure you get down all your ideas, write your first draft without stopping to change what you've written. Concentrate on getting across what you perceive through your five senses.

Revising Look for places where you can add vivid adjectives to enliven your description. For example, you might change the phrase "the surface of the moon" to "the gray, rocky, utterly desolate surface of the moon."

✓ ASSESSMENT OPTIONS

Formal Assessment, Selection Test, pp. 142–144, and Assessment Resources Software. The selection test is designed so that it can be easily customized to the performance levels of your students.
Alternative Assessment, p. 40, includes options for less advanced students, more advanced students, visual/spatial learners, and logical/mathematical learners.

PORTFOLIO ASSESSMENT
Use the following rubrics in the *Alternative Assessment* booklet to assess student writing:
Description From Above: Description Rubric, p. 90
Eyewitness Report: Description Rubric, p. 90
Persuasive Essay: Persuasion Rubric, p. 98
Writing Mini-Lesson: Description Rubric, p. 90

PART **1** *Essays and Personal Accounts*

Discussion, Milton Avery, Mount Holyoke College Art Museum, South Hadley, Massachusetts

Essays and Personal Accounts ◆ 565

One-Minute Planning Guide

This section of the "Nonfiction" unit introduces students to essays and personal accounts. "The Washwoman" is a narrative essay in which a young boy recalls a person who made a lasting impact on his life. "On Summer" is a persuasive essay about a writer's favorite season. "A Celebration of Grandfathers" is a reflective essay that reveals the author's respect for older family members. In an excerpt from *A White House Diary*, Lady Bird Johnson recounts the assassination of President Kennedy. The section ends with two biographical pieces—one on tennis-great Arthur Ashe, and the other on esteemed painter Georgia O'Keeffe.

Customize for
Varying Student Needs
When assigning the selections in this section to your students, keep in mind the following factors:

"The Washwoman"
- Setting, culture, and customs may be unfamiliar to students

"On Summer"
- Accessible essay
- Strong model for persuasion

"A Celebration of Grandfathers"
- Essay makes strong connection to family and community

from *A White House Diary*
- Moving personal account of a tragedy in American history
- History connection

"Arthur Ashe Remembered"
- Will appeal to students interested in sports

"Georgia O'Keeffe"
- Insightful, interesting portrait of a woman with whom students may not be familiar
- Fine arts link

Humanities: Art

Discussion by Milton Avery.

Avery (1885–1965) lived for his art, which has come to be widely appreciated only after his death. Born in upstate New York, he began working at a series of factory jobs at the age of sixteen. In his twenties he discovered that he loved to paint, and so he would paint landscapes by day and work an eight-hour night shift in a typewriter factory. When he was able to concentrate exclusively on his painting for the first time

in his early forties, his work began to show the influence of European painters, particularly Henri Matisse; he has come to be regarded as a link between American painting and Matisse. Avery's fresh and unpredictable use of color sets him apart from other American artists of his time.

Help students link Discussion to the focus of Part I ("Essays and Personal Accounts") by answering this question:

Do the women in this painting seem to be friends? What might they be talking about? Base your answers on any evidence you can find in the painting. *The relaxed positions of the women suggest that they are friends and that they are talking about aspects of their private lives— relationships or personal ambitions. The warm colors of the painting add to the friendly, intimate mood.*

565

Guide for Reading

More About the Authors

I. B. Singer's work has been made into numerous filmstrips, recordings, and movies: the films *Yentl* and *Enemies, a Love Story* were both based on Singer stories.

Lorraine Hansberry's *A Raisin in the Sun* was made into a film starring Sidney Poitier. Though Hansberry died at the age of thirty-five, several of her plays were published and produced after her death.

Rudolfo Anaya is widely acclaimed as the founder of modern Chicano literature. According to the *New York Times,* he is the most widely read author in Hispanic communities today.

Isaac Bashevis Singer *(1904–1991)*

I. B. Singer once said that he believed that "life itself is a story." This belief is reflected in his many short stories, novels, and nonfiction pieces that capture the lessons of everyday life. Born in Poland, Singer moved to New York City in 1935 and later became an American citizen. Writing in Yiddish, the language of some Eastern European Jews and their descendants, Singer established himself as one of the most popular and respected writers of this century, earning the Nobel Prize for Literature in 1978.

Lorraine Hansberry *(1930–1965)*

Lorraine Hansberry was born and raised in Chicago, Illinois. After high school, she studied art for two years before moving to New York City. While working at several jobs, she wrote *A Raisin in the Sun,* which, in 1959, became the first play by an African American woman to be produced on Broadway. "On Summer" is from *To Be Young, Gifted, and Black,* a collection of her writings that was published after her death.

Rudolfo Anaya *(1937–)*

Rudolfo Anaya was born in Pastura, New Mexico, and his writing reflects his Mexican American heritage. Anaya says, "For those of us who listen to the Earth, and to the old legends and the myths of the people, the whispers of the blood draw us to our past." It is the past that concerns Anaya in much of his writing. His first novel, *Bless Me, Ultima* (1972), won national acclaim for its moving depiction of the culture and history of New Mexico. Anaya has also published *The Heart of Aztlan* (1976) and *Tortuga* (1979), as well as many stories and articles. His essay "A Celebration of Grandfathers" reflects on the "old ones" he remembers from his childhood.

566 ◆ Nonfiction

◆ **Build Vocabulary**

PREFIXES: *fore-*

"The Washwoman" contains the word *forebears,* which means "ancestors"—or, more loosely, "relatives who came before us." The prefix *fore-,* meaning "before" or "occurring earlier," can help you piece together the meaning of this word and others that contain the prefix.

forebears
rancor
obstinacy
pious
aloofness
perplexes
permeate
epiphany

WORD BANK

Before you read, preview this list of words from the selections.

◆ **Build Grammar Skills**

**COMMONLY CONFUSED WORDS:
AFFECT AND *EFFECT***

When Hansberry writes that cancer was an enemy with "shape and effect and source," she uses a word that is frequently misused: *effect.* Most often, as in this sentence, *effect* is a noun meaning "the result." *Effect* can also be a verb meaning "to bring about" or "to cause." *Affect* is always a verb meaning "to influence." Look at these examples:

verb
How will reading these essays *affect* you emotionally?

noun
the *effect* that she was not certain of her own children.

And she would drop dark hints to

verb
Can an essay *effect* change?

The Washwoman ◆ On Summer ◆ A Celebration of Grandfathers ◆

◆ *Literature and Your Life*

CONNECT YOUR EXPERIENCE

These authors journey deep into their past to find people who gave them gifts that weren't in boxes or tied with bows. What are some special gifts in your life that didn't come in packages? Who gave them to you, and what did you do with them?

Journal Writing Jot down notes about the best gifts you have received and the best gifts you can ever hope to give.

THEMATIC FOCUS: APPRECIATING OTHERS

Sometimes the most special gift we can receive is a new way of viewing ourselves and the world around us. In these essays, the authors write about important people in their lives who helped them find new ways of looking at life.

◆ Background for Understanding

HISTORY

"The Washwoman" takes place in the early twentieth century prior to World War I in what is now Poland. At the time, Poland did not exist as an independent nation. Instead, it was divided into three sections ruled by Russia, Austria-Hungary, and Germany. The population consisted largely of members of the working class, who worked long hours in the fields in order to earn enough to survive. Because Poland had long been known for its religious tolerance, the population included a sizeable number of Jewish people who had settled there centuries earlier. Most of the Jews spoke Yiddish and maintained their own cultural traditions.

◆ Literary Focus

ESSAY

An **essay** is a short piece of nonfiction in which a writer expresses a personal view of a topic. There are different types of essays. "The Washwoman" is an example of a **narrative essay,** which tells a story. "On Summer" is a **persuasive essay,** which tries to convince readers to accept a position or take a course of action. In this case, Hansberry tries to convince readers to appreciate summer. "A Celebration of Grandfathers" is a **reflective essay**—a type of essay in which a writer reflects on his or her feelings about a topic of personal importance.

◆ Reading Strategy

IDENTIFY THE AUTHOR'S ATTITUDE

In any type of essay, the **author's attitude** toward his or her subject colors the presentation of information. For example, when describing a person he or she deeply respects, a writer will use descriptive words that convey this respect and include details that will help readers understand and share the respect for the subject.

As you read these essays, use a sunburst diagram like the one shown to help you identify the authors' attitudes toward their subjects. On the lines surrounding the center, jot down words and details that hint at the writer's attitude toward the subject. When you've finished, review the details you've listed and decide what they suggest about the writer's attitude. Write a statement of that attitude in the center of the diagram.

Author's Attitude:

Guide for Reading ◆ 567

Preparing for Standardized Tests

Reading and Vocabulary The Build Vocabulary lesson for this section focuses on the prefix *fore-*. Using prefixes to help determine word meaning can improve students' performance on vocabulary and reading comprehension items on standardized tests. For additional practice, use the Build Vocabulary page in *Selection Support,* p. 168.

Grammar and Language Some tests may require students to select the correct word from a pair of commonly confused words, as in the following:

> The news story had a sobering (affect, effect) on the group. *effect*

The Build Grammar Skills lesson focuses on the words *affect* and *effect*. For additional practice, use the Build Grammar Skills page in *Selection Support*, p. 169.

❶ Essay Ask students to determine what important point Singer is reflecting upon in this section. *He is reflecting on how strong and stubborn humans can be—how the will to work can exceed one's physical strength.*

❷ Clarification Explain that "fringed garments" refers to an article of clothing called the *arba kanfot*, which was once worn by most observant Jewish males. However, it is now worn only by the extremely religious. The *arba kanfot* is a sleeveless, fringed, four-cornered undergarment that is worn beneath the regular clothing and has a tassel attached to each corner. In the Bible (Numbers 15:37–40), God instructs the children of Israel to attach tassels (*tzitzit*) to the corners of their garments. These *tzitzit* are to serve as a reminder of God's commandments. The ancient Jews commonly wore a four-cornered garment, similar to modern Bedouin costume. However, styles changed over time and place. To continue obeying this religious rule, Jewish men began wearing the *arba kanfot*.

◆ Reading Strategy

❸ Identify the Author's Attitude Ask students to describe the author's attitude toward the washwoman. *He respects her pride, courage, and determination, but is also concerned about her well-being. He is worried that she might not make it home safely.*

Heart, The Book of the Covenant, and other serious philosophic works.

But to return to the washwoman. That winter was a harsh one. The streets were in the grip of a bitter cold. No matter how much we heated our stove, the windows were covered with frostwork and decorated with icicles. The newspapers reported that people were dying of the cold. Coal became dear. The winter had become so severe that parents stopped sending children to cheder,[3] and even the Polish schools were closed.

On one such day the washwoman, now nearly eighty years old, came to our house. A good deal of laundry had accumulated during the past weeks. Mother gave her a pot of tea to warm herself, as well as some bread. The old woman sat on a kitchen chair trembling and shaking, and warmed her hands against the teapot. Her fingers were gnarled from work, and perhaps from arthritis too. Her fingernails were strangely white. These hands spoke of the **❶** stubbornness of mankind, of the will to work not only as one's strength permits but beyond the limits of one's power. Mother counted and wrote down the list: men's undershirts, women's vests, long-legged drawers, bloomers, petticoats, shifts, featherbed covers, pillowcases, sheets, and the men's fringed garments. **❷** Yes, the Gentile woman washed these holy garments as well.

The bundle was big, bigger than usual. When the woman placed it on her shoulders, it covered her completely. At first she swayed, as though she were about to fall under the load. But an inner <u>obstinacy</u> seemed to call out: No, you may not fall. A donkey may permit himself **❸** to fall under his burden, but not a human being, the crown of creation.

It was fearful to watch the old woman staggering out with the enormous pack, out into the frost, where the snow was dry as salt and the air was filled with dusty white whirlwinds, like goblins dancing in the cold. Would the old woman ever reach Wola?

She disappeared, and Mother sighed and prayed for her.

---

3. **cheder** (khā′ dər) *n.*: Religious school.

570 ◆ Nonfiction

Usually the woman brought back the wash after two or, at the most, three weeks. But three weeks passed, then four and five, and nothing was heard of the old woman. We remained without linens. The cold had become even more intense. The telephone wires were now as thick as ropes. The branches of the trees looked like glass. So much snow had fallen that the streets had become uneven, and sleds were able to glide down many streets as on the slopes of a hill. Kindhearted people lit fires in the streets for vagrants[4] to warm themselves and roast potatoes in, if they had any to roast.

For us the washwoman's absence was a catastrophe. We needed the laundry. We did not even know the woman's address. It seemed certain that she had collapsed, died. Mother declared she had had a premonition, as the old woman left our house that last time, that we would never see our things again. She found some old torn shirts and washed and mended them. We mourned, both for the laundry and for the old, toil-worn woman who had grown close to us through the years she had served us so faithfully.

More than two months passed. The frost had subsided, and then a new frost had come, a new wave of cold. One evening, while Mother was sitting near the kerosene lamp mending a shirt, the door opened and a small puff of steam, followed by a gigantic bundle, entered. Under the bundle tottered the old woman, her face as white as a linen sheet. A few wisps of white hair straggled out from beneath her shawl. Mother uttered a half-choked cry. It was as though a corpse had entered the room. I ran toward the old woman and helped her unload her pack. She was even thinner now, more bent. Her face had become more gaunt, and her head shook from side to side as though she were saying no. She could not utter a clear word, but mumbled something with her sunken mouth and pale lips.

After the old woman had recovered somewhat, she told us that she had been ill, very ill.

---

4. **vagrants** (vā′ grənts) *n.*: People who wander from place to place, especially those without regular jobs.

Cultural Connection: Special Clothing

People wear special kinds of clothing or jewelry as a mark of their religious beliefs and to celebrate important occasions. For example, the Orthodox Jewish men in "The Washwoman" wear a special fringed garment beneath their regular clothes. They also undoubtedly wear a skullcap (in Hebrew, *kipah*; in Yiddish *yarmulke*) during their waking hours. These two articles of clothing represent their obedience to God.

Other religions also have special clothing, especially for religious leaders. For example, Buddhist monks and nuns may wear saffron robes, and Catholic cardinals wear scarlet robes.

Special clothing is also worn for significant occasions. For example, a Chinese bride might wear a red silk robe, a Norwegian bride might wear an elaborately embroidered white-on-white apron, and an

American bride might wear a long white gown.

Have interested students find out more about items of clothing with religious or festive significance. You may wish to have them present their findings in the form of a bulletin-board display.

Just what her illness was, I cannot remember. She had been so sick that someone had called a doctor, and the doctor had sent for a priest. Someone had informed the son, and he had contributed money for a coffin and for the funeral. But the Almighty had not yet wanted to take this pain-racked soul to Himself. She began to feel better, she became well, and as soon as she was able to stand on her feet once more, she resumed her washing. Not just ours, but the wash of several other families too.

"I could not rest easy in my bed because of the wash," the old woman explained. "The wash would not let me die."

"With the help of God you will live to be a hundred and twenty," said my mother, as a benediction.

"God forbid! What good would such a long life be? The work becomes harder and harder . . . my strength is leaving me . . . I do not want to be a burden on anyone!" The old woman muttered and crossed herself, and raised her eyes toward heaven.

◆ **Build Vocabulary**

obstinacy (ăb´ stə nə sē) *n.*: Stubbornness
pious (pī´ əs) *adj.*: Showing religious devotion

Fortunately there was some money in the house and Mother counted out what she owed. I had a strange feeling: the coins in the old woman's washed-out hands seemed to become as worn and clean and pious as she herself was. She blew on the coins and tied them in a kerchief. Then she left, promising to return in a few weeks for a new load of wash.

But she never came back. The wash she had returned was her last effort on this earth. She had been driven by an indomitable will to return the property to its rightful owners, to fulfill the task she had undertaken.

And now at last her body, which had long been no more than a shard[5] supported only by the force of honesty and duty, had fallen. Her soul passed into those spheres where all holy souls meet, regardless of the roles they played on this earth, in whatever tongue, of whatever creed. I cannot imagine paradise without this Gentile washwoman. I cannot even conceive of a world where there is no recompense for such effort.

---

5. **shard** (shärd) *n.*: Fragment or broken piece.

Guide for Responding

◆ *Literature and Your Life*

Reader's Response Whom do you know who seems to give so much and ask so little?
Thematic Focus How does looking back on people from your past make it easier to concentrate on their strengths rather than their flaws?

☑ **Check Your Comprehension**

1. Explain the relationship of the washwoman to Singer's family.
2. Retell the events of the last few months of the washwoman's life.

◆ **Critical Thinking**

INTERPRET
1. What values does the washwoman represent? **[Analyze]**
2. In what ways is the washwoman like the author's mother? **[Compare and Contrast]**
3. This washwoman is more than just a washwoman to Singer. What greater significance does she have to him? **[Make a Judgment]**

EXTEND
4. How might the washwoman's life be different if she lived in Poland in the year 2000? How might it be the same? **[Social Studies Link]**

The Washwoman ◆ 571

◆ **Critical Thinking**

1. Several answers are possible, including hard work, pride, dignity, strength, self-reliance, and persistence.
2. Like the washwoman, the author's mother is selfless in the love of her children. Despite the fact that her circumstances are better than those of the washwoman,

like the washwoman, she lives a humble life and scrapes together money. She also values and respects hard work.

3. Among other things, the washwoman represents the triumph of the human spirit and the will to endure. She represents "the force of honesty and duty": the product of her "indomitable will."

4. Today, the washwoman would have running water, electricity, a modern washing machine, and modern laundry products. She would probably travel by public transportation or car. She might still, however, be old, alone, and poor.

◆ *Literature and Your Life*

❹ Have students compare the washwoman to other older people they know. In what ways is she similar? In what ways is she different?

◆ **Critical Thinking**

❺ **Draw Conclusions** Ask students why the writer cannot imagine heaven without the washwoman. *To him, she symbolizes what is strong and admirable in humankind.*

Reinforce and Extend

Answers

Reader's Response Students' responses should be informed by their reading of the story.

Thematic Focus Students might note that time provides the distance with which to see more clearly, and it also seems to erase the small complaints of day-to-day living.

☑ **Check Your Comprehension**

1. The washwoman was the favorite washwoman that the family ever had because of the good work she did. Singer's mother also respected the washwoman and felt sympathy for her.
2. In the middle of a harsh winter, the washwoman, now eighty, had staggered away under the burden of the laundry. For more than two months, she did not return. When she did bring back the laundry, she was very weak and told about an illness that had nearly taken her life. After that visit, she did not return again.

On Summer
Lorraine Hansberry

It has taken me a good number of years to come to any measure of respect for summer. I was, being May-born, literally an "infant of the spring" and, during the later childhood years, tended, for some reason or other, to rather worship the cold aloofness of winter. The adolescence, admittedly lingering still, brought the traditional passionate commitment to melancholy autumn—and all that. For the longest kind of time I simply thought that *summer* was a mistake.

In fact, my earliest memory of anything at all is of waking up in a darkened room where I had been put to bed for a nap on a summer's afternoon, and feeling very, very hot. I acutely disliked the feeling then and retained the bias for years. It had originally been a matter of the heat but, over the years, I came actively to associate displeasure with most of the usually celebrated natural features and social by-products of the season: the too-grainy texture of sand; the too-cold coldness of the various waters we constantly try to escape into, and the icky-perspiry feeling of bathing caps.

It also seemed to me, esthetically[1] speaking, that nature had got inexcusably carried away on the summer question and let the whole thing get to be rather much. By duration alone, for instance, a summer's day seemed maddeningly excessive; an utter overstatement. Except for those few hours at either end of it, objects always appeared in too sharp a relief against backgrounds; shadows too pronounced and light too blinding. It always gave me the feeling of walking around in a motion picture which had been too artsily-craftsily exposed. Sound also had a way of coming to the ear without that muting influence, marvelously common to winter, across patios or beaches or through the woods. I suppose I found it too stark and yet too intimate a season.

My childhood Southside[2] summers were the ordinary city kind, full of the street games which the other rememberers have turned into fine ballets these days and rhymes that anticipated what some people insist on calling modern poetry:

◆ **Reading Strategy**
What is the author's attitude toward summer? **❷**

Oh, Mary Mack, Mack, Mack
With the silver buttons, buttons, buttons
All down her back, back, back
She asked her mother, mother, mother
For fifteen cents, cents, cents
To see the elephant, elephant, elephant
Jump the fence, fence, fence
Well, he jumped so high, high, high
'Til he touched the sky, sky, sky
And he didn't come back, back, back
'Til the Fourth of Ju-ly, ly, ly!

---

1. **esthetically** (es thet′ ik lē) *adv.*: Artistically.

2. **Southside:** Section of Chicago, Illinois.

572 ◆ *Nonfiction*

Cross-Curricular Connection: Music

Street Songs Point out that Hansberry has vivid memories of the street songs that children in her neighborhood sang. These songs vary from neighborhood to neighborhood and are used in games such as jump rope and ring games. Students who are interested in finding out more about street songs and poems can look in books such as *Shake It to the One That You Love Best: Play Songs and Lullabies From Black Musical Traditions* and *Anna Banana: 101 Jump-Rope Rhymes* by Joanna Cole.

▲ Critical Viewing How well does this photograph fit the essay? Explain. [Evaluate] ❹

♦ **Literary Focus**

❸ **Essay** Ask students what features of an essay are revealed in this passage. *Suggested response: The passage is nonfiction. In it, the author expresses her personal reactions to summertime activities such as camping in the park or visiting relatives.*

▶**Critical Viewing**◀

❹ **Evaluate** Students may think this photograph is extremely appropriate for the essay because it shows one of the images from the essay—city children playing street games.

Customize for
English Language Learners
Students for whom English is a second language may be confused by this mention of slavery. Explain that the writer's grandfather was a slave who ran away from his master and hid in the hills.

Evenings were spent mainly on the back porches where screen doors slammed in the darkness with those really very special summertime sounds. And, sometimes, when Chicago nights got too steamy, the whole family got into the car and went to the park and slept out in the open on blankets. Those were, of course, the best times of all because the grownups were invariably reminded of having been children in rural parts of the country and told the best stories then. And it was also cool and sweet to be on the grass and there was usually the scent of freshly cut lemons or melons in the air. And Daddy would lie on his back, as fathers must, and explain about how men thought the stars above us came to be and how far away they were. I never did learn to believe that anything could be as far away as *that*. Especially the stars.

My mother first took us south to visit her Tennessee birthplace one summer when I was seven or eight, I think. I woke up on the back seat of the car while we were still driving through some place called Kentucky and my mother was pointing out to the beautiful hills on both sides of the highway and telling my brothers and my sister about how her father had run away and hidden from his master in those very hills when he was a little boy. She said that his mother had wandered among the wooded slopes in the moonlight and left food for him in secret places. They were very beautiful hills and I looked out at them for miles and miles after that wondering who and what a master might be.

I remember being startled when I first saw my grandmother rocking away on her porch. All my life I had heard that she was a great beauty and no one had ever remarked that

♦ **Build Vocabulary**

aloofness (ə lōōf' nəs) *n.*: State of being distant, removed, or uninvolved

On Summer ♦ 573

 Speaking and Listening Mini-Lesson

Interview
This mini-lesson supports the Speaking and Listening activity in the Idea Bank on page 583.
Introduce the Concept Discuss with students the elements of a good interview. Remind them that an interviewer must prepare questions that will evoke answers that reveal the subject's personality.
Develop Background Encourage students to choose an older subject to interview. Have

them prepare their interview by writing open-ended questions for their subjects. Urge them to include questions that will reveal
• details about the subject's early life
• information about events that had a strong effect on the subject
• details that reveal the subject's feelings about various topics
Apply the Information With this background, students can interview their subjects. If they want, they can record their

interviews, or they can take notes on their subjects' answers.
Assess the Outcome Have students read their interviews or play the taped versions. Encourage the class to determine what sort of person each interview subject is. Have the class discuss how the older people in these essays might have responded to the best questions the interviewers asked. Evaluate the interviews based on the criteria listed in the Develop Background step.

▶Critical Viewing◀

❶ Connect The photograph of waves crashing against the rocky Maine coast helps the reader visualize the place that the author is describing.

◆ **Critical Thinking**

❷ Analyze Ask students to analyze what sort of woman the writer's grandmother is. *She is very old and infirm, but she can still do wonderful things that affect a child deeply.*

◆ *Literature and Your Life*

❸ Point out that Hansberry's image of what slavery was like changes as a result of hearing her grandmother's recollections of her childhood. Direct students to think about experiences that helped them to gain a more mature understanding of issues in their own lives, then record their thoughts in their journal. Ask volunteers to share their experiences with the class.

❹ Clarification Explain to the class that *Gone With the Wind* is a novel that, in many ways, romanticizes slavery. If any students have read the book or seen the movie, encourage them to describe how slavery is portrayed.

◆ **Reading Strategy**

❺ Identify the Author's Attitude Ask students how the author feels about the woman she met in Maine. *She admires her greatly for her courage and her positive attitude.*

▲ **Critical Viewing** How does this photograph of the Maine coast add to the descriptions in the essay? **[Connect]** ❶

they meant a half century before. The woman that I met was as wrinkled as a prune and could hardly hear and barely see and always seemed to be thinking of other times. But she could still rock and talk and even make wonderful cupcakes which were like cornbread, only sweet. She was captivated by automobiles and, even though it was well into the Thirties,[3] I don't think she had ever been in one before we came down and took her driving. She was a little afraid of them and could not seem to negotiate the windows, but she loved driving. She died the next summer and that is all that I remember about her, except that she was born in slavery and had memories of it and they didn't sound anything like *Gone With the Wind*.[4]

Like everyone else, I have spent whole or bits of summers in many different kinds of places since then: camps and resorts in the Middle West and New York State; on an island; in a tiny Mexican village; Cape Cod, perched atop the Truro bluffs at Longnook Beach that Millay[5] wrote about; or simply strolling the

---

3. **Thirties:** The 1930's.
4. *Gone With the Wind:* Novel set in the South during the Civil War period.

574 ◆ *Nonfiction*

streets of Provincetown[6] before the hours when the parties begin.

And, lastly, I do not think that I will forget days spent, a few summers ago, at a beautiful lodge built right into the rocky cliffs of a bay on the Maine coast. We met a woman there who had lived a purposeful and courageous life and who was then dying of cancer. She had, characteristically, just written a book and taken up painting. She had also been of radical viewpoint all her life; one of those people who energetically believe that the world *can* be changed for the better and spend their lives trying to do just that. And that was the way she thought of cancer; she absolutely refused to award it the stature of tragedy, a devastating instance of the brooding doom and inexplicability[7] of the absurdity of human destiny, etc., etc. The kind of characterization given, lately, as we all know, to far less formidable foes in life than cancer.

But for this remarkable woman it was a matter of nature in imperfection, implying, as always, work for man to do. It was an *enemy*, but a palpable one with shape and effect and

---

5. **Millay:** Edna St. Vincent Millay (1892–1950), American poet.
6. **Provincetown:** Resort town at the northern tip of Cape Cod, Massachusetts.
7. **inexplicability** (in eks´ pli kə bil´ ə tē) *n.:* Condition that cannot be explained.

 Beyond the Classroom

Community Connection

Elders in the Community Have students look into what activities, housing, and agencies are provided for elders in their community. Are there nursing homes, volunteer centers, regular reading

groups or other outings offered? Encourage them to compare how elders live in their community to how the older people in "The Washwoman" and "On Summer" live.

source; and if it existed, it could be destroyed. She saluted it accordingly, without despondency, but with a lively, beautiful and delightfully ribald anger. There was one thing, she felt, which would prove equal to its relentless ravages and that was the genius of man. Not his mysticism, but man with tubes and slides and the stubborn human notion that the stars are very much within our reach.

The last time I saw her she was sitting surrounded by her paintings with her manuscript laid out for me to read, because, she said, she wanted to know what a *young person* would think of her thinking; one must always keep up with what *young people* thought about things because, after all, they were *change*.

Every now and then her jaw set in anger as we spoke of things people should be angry about. And then, for relief, she would look out at the lovely bay at a mellow sunset settling on the water. Her face softened with love of all that beauty and, watching her, I wished with all my power what I knew that she was wishing: that she might live to see at least one more *summer*. Through her eyes I finally gained the sense of what it might mean; more than the coming autumn with its pretentious melancholy; more than an austere and silent winter which must shut dying people in for precious months; more than the frivolous spring, too full of too many false promises, would be the gift of another summer with its stark and intimate assertion of neither birth nor death but life at the apex; with the gentlest nights and, above all, the longest days.

I heard later that she did live to see another summer. And I have retained my respect for the noblest of the seasons.

◆ Reading Strategy

How does Hansberry's attitude toward summer change?

❼

Guide for Responding

◆ Literature and Your Life

Reader's Response How do Hansberry's ideas about summer compare with your own?

Thematic Focus How do Hansberry's experiences cause her to change her way of thinking about summer?

Journal Writing List associations you have with each season of the year. Include places and events that have a special significance during each season.

☑ Check Your Comprehension

1. What did Hansberry dislike about summer before she met the woman in Maine?
2. Describe some of Hansberry's memories of childhood summers.
3. Tell why meeting the woman in Maine had such a lasting effect on Hansberry.

◆ Critical Thinking

INTERPRET

1. Why does Hansberry include the section about her grandmother? **[Draw Conclusions]**
2. Why does Hansberry refer to summer as "the noblest of seasons"? **[Infer]**
3. Is this essay about summer, or is it really about something else? Explain your answer. **[Identify]**

EVALUATE

4. (a) How does Hansberry appeal to your emotions in this essay? (b) How does this emotional appeal make the essay more effective? **[Evaluate]**

EXTEND

5. For each season of the year, list three or four destinations around the globe that might persuade a person that that particular season was "the noblest of seasons." Then explain why the geography and climate of one particular season in one particular place is uplifting to the human spirit. **[Social Studies Link]**

On Summer ◆ 575

One-Minute Insight In this essay Rudolfo Anaya celebrates the respect his culture held for its elders. He focuses on the way his grandfather lived and died and appeals to readers to appreciate and respect the contributions of older people in today's society.

◆ Literary Focus

❶ Essay Have students determine what topic the author reflects on in this passage. *He reflects on the value of old people.*

◆ Reading Strategy

❷ Identify the Author's Attitude Elicit responses such as the following: *The author's childhood respect and love for the older generation make his present attitude of admiration and love easier to understand.*

◆ Build Vocabulary

❸ Using Prefixes Ask students what prefix is used in this section and what the word *inanimate* and its opposite, *animate*, mean. *The prefix is in-, which means "not." Inanimate means "not living" and its opposite, animate, means "living."*

Looking at Literature Videodisc To provide background and insight into the author of "A Celebration of Grandfathers," play Chapter 9 of the videodisc. In this interview with the writer, Anaya discusses his approach to writing. Discuss how Anaya's comments are reflected in "A Celebration of Grandfathers."

Chapter 9

A Celebration of Grandfathers

Rudolfo A. Anaya

"Buenos días le de Dios, abuelo."[1] God give you a good day, grandfather. This is how I was taught as a child to greet my grandfather, or any grown person. It was a greeting of respect, a cultural value to be passed on from generation to generation, this respect for the old ones.

The old people I remember from my childhood were strong in their beliefs, and as we lived daily with them we learned a wise path of life to follow. They had something important to **❶** share with the young, and when they spoke the young listened. These old abuelos and abuelitas[2] had worked the earth all their lives, and so they knew the value of nurturing, they knew the sensitivity of the earth. The daily struggle called for cooperation, and so every person contributed to the social fabric, and each person was respected for his contribution.

◆ Reading Strategy How do the facts **❷** about the author's past help you understand his attitude toward his subject?

The old ones had looked deep into the web **❸** that connects all animate and inanimate forms of life, and they recognized the great design of the creation.

These *ancianos*[3] from the cultures of the Rio Grande, living side by side, sharing, growing together, they knew the rhythms and cycles of time, from the preparation of the earth in the spring to the digging of the acequias[4] that brought the water to the dance of harvest in the fall. They shared good times and hard times. They helped each other through the epidemics and the personal tragedies, and they shared what little they had when the hot winds burned the land and no rain came. They learned that to survive one had to share in the process of life.

Hard workers all, they tilled the earth and farmed, ran the herds and spun wool, and carved their saints and their kachinas[5] from cottonwood late in the winter nights. All worked with a deep faith which <u>perplexes</u> the modern mind.

Their faith shone in their eyes; it was in the strength of their grip, in the creases time wove into their faces. When they spoke, they spoke plainly and with few words, and they meant what they said. When they prayed, they went straight to the source of life. When there were good times, they knew how to dance in celebration and how to prepare the foods of the fiestas.[6] All this they passed on to the young,

---

1. **Buenos días le de Dios, abuelo** (bwe´ nôs dē´ äs lā dä dē´ ōs ä bwä´ lō)
2. **abuelitas** (a bwä lē´ täs): Grandmothers.
3. **ancianos** (än cē ä´ nōs): Old people; ancestors.

4. **acequias** (ä sā´ kē əs): Irrigation ditches.
5. **kachinas** (kə chē´ nəz): Small wooden dolls, representing the spirit of an ancestor or a god.
6. **fiestas** (fē es´ təz): Celebrations; feasts.

 Beyond the Classroom

Career Connection

Farmers Point out to students that farming is one of the most important jobs a person can do. Everyone needs food, and most of the food the world eats comes from crops and livestock on farms. Farming is a business, and farmers must concentrate not only on the best way to raise crops or livestock but on accounting, marketing, and the science of farming. Interested students can find out information such as the number of farmers in the United States, reasons why that number has dropped so precipitously, the average size of farms, and the average gross income of a farm.

Encourage students to think about how today's farms differ from the farm that Anaya's grandfather worked.

Don Nemesio, 1977, Esperanza Martinez

▲ **Critical Viewing** In this essay, Rudolfo Anaya celebrates the wisdom and experience of his grandfather and of the other elders of the community in which he grew up. What lessons can you learn from your grandparents and other older members of your own community? [Generalize]

❹

so that a new generation would know what they had known, so the string of life would not be broken.

❺ Today we would say that the old abuelitos lived authentic lives.

Newcomers to New Mexico often say that time seems to move slowly here. I think they mean they have come in contact with the inner strength of the people, a strength so solid it causes time itself to pause. Think of it. Think of the high, northern New Mexico villages, or the lonely ranches on the open llano.[7] Think of the Indian pueblo[8] which lies as solid as rock in the face of time. Remember the old people whose eyes seem like windows that peer into a distant past that makes absurdity of our

7. **llano** (yä′ nō): Plain.
8. **pueblo** (pweb′ lō): Village or town.

contemporary world. That is what one feels when one encounters the old ones and their land, a pausing of time.

We have all felt time stand still. We have all been in the presence of power, the knowledge of the old ones, the majestic peace of a mountain stream or an aspen grove or red buttes rising into blue sky. We have all felt the light of dusk <u>permeate</u> the earth and cause time to pause in its flow.

❻

I felt this when first touched by the spirit of Ultima, the old *curandera*[9] who appears in my first novel, *Bless Me, Ultima*. This is how the young Antonio describes what he feels:

> When she came the beauty of the llano
> unfolded before my eyes, and the

9. **curandera** (kōō rän dä′ rä): Medicine woman.

◆ **Build Vocabulary**

perplexes (pər′ pleks′ iz) *v.*: Confuses or makes hard to understand

permeate (pur′ mē āt) *v.*: Spread or flow throughout

A Celebration of Grandfathers ◆ 577

► **Critical Viewing** ◄

❹ **Generalize** Answers should focus on what can be learned from older people with years of experience and learning behind them.

◆ **Critical Thinking**

❺ **Analyze Character** Ask students what the author means when he calls the lives of the elders "authentic." *He means that they focus on what is really important—the things that sustain life and make it good.*

◆ **Critical Thinking**

❻ **Make Inferences** What does Anaya mean when he says that time "stands still"? *He means that things of great beauty or power can cause time to seem to stop briefly.*

 Humanities: Art

Don Nemesio, 1977, by Esperanza Martinez.

An elderly man rests his head on his elbow as he either looks intently at something out of the bounds of the painting, or perhaps simply thinks quietly to himself.

Use these questions for discussion:

1. What can you tell about the man in the painting from the objects the artist chose to depict? *He is Latino, probably Mexican in* descent, because he sits beside a stack of tortillas. The bowl on the table has a design that could also be Mexican.

2. How does the man in the painting compare to your mental picture of the writer's grandfather? *Answers will vary but may mention the age of the man in the portrait and his thoughtful expression.*

◆ Literary Focus

❶ Essay Elicit responses such as the following: *Anaya uses his experiences with the strength and beauty of nature to compare with his experiences of the strength and wisdom of his elders, drawing an analogy that emphasizes his deep feelings for the old ones.*

◆ Critical Thinking

❷ Infer Ask students to determine what the grandfather's advice could mean in a larger, more universal sense. *He could mean that it is important to know where you are in relation to the world—to know where you belong and where you want to be.*

◆ Critical Thinking

❸ Compare and Contrast Ask students to analyze the difference between the boy's wish and the grandfather's prayer. *The boy is placing responsibility for rain on fate, while the grandfather believes in the strength of prayer and feels that by praying, he is doing all he can to bring the rain.*

◆ *Literature and Your Life*

❹ In this passage, Anaya's grandfather comforts him after a friend is killed in a tragic riding accident. Ask students to relate Anaya's experience to their own lives. How has a grandparent or other older person helped them to understand a significant event in their own lives?

gurgling waters of the river sang to the hum of the turning earth. The magical time of childhood stood still, and the pulse of the living earth pressed its mystery into my living blood. She took my hand, and the silent, magic powers she possessed made beauty from the raw, sun-baked llano, the green river valley, and the blue bowl which was the white sun's home. My bare feet felt the throbbing earth, and my body trembled with excitement. Time stood still . . .

At other times, in other places, when I have been privileged to be with the old ones, to learn, I have felt this inner reserve of strength upon which they draw. I have been held motionless and speechless by the power of curanderas. I have felt the same power when I hunted with Cruz, high on the Taos[10] mountain, where it was more than the incredible beauty of the mountain bathed in morning light, more than the shining of the quivering aspen, but a connection with life, as if a shining strand of light connected the particular and the cosmic. That feeling is an <u>epiphany</u> of time, a standing still of time.

> **◆ Literary Focus**
> How does Anaya use personal experience to help him reflect on his feelings about the strength and power of the old ones?

❶

But not all of our old ones are curanderos or hunters on the mountain. My grandfather was a plain man, a farmer from Puerto de Luna[11] on the Pecos River. He was probably a descendent of those people who spilled over the mountain from Taos, following the Pecos River in search of farmland. There in that river valley he settled and raised a large family.

Bearded and walrus-mustached, he stood five feet tall, but to me as a child he was a giant. I remember him most for his silence. In the summers my parents sent me to live with him on his farm, for I was to learn the ways of a farmer. My uncles also lived in that valley, the valley called Puerto de Luna, there where

---

10. **Taos** (tä´ ōs)
11. **Puerto de Luna** (pwer´ tō dā lōō´ nə): Port of the Moon, the name of a town.

578 ◆ Nonfiction

only the flow of the river and the whispering of the wind marked time. For me it was a magical place.

I remember once, while out hoeing the fields. I came upon an anthill and before I knew it I was badly bitten. After he had covered my welts with the cool mud from the irrigation ditch, my grandfather calmly said: "Know where you stand." That is the way he spoke, in short phrases, to the point.

❷

One very dry summer, the river dried to a trickle, there was no water for the fields. The young plants withered and died. In my sadness and with the impulses of youth I said, "I wish it would rain!" My grandfather touched me, looked up in the sky and whispered, "Pray for rain." In his language there was a difference. He felt connected to the cycles that brought the rain or kept it from us. His prayer was a meaningful action, because he was a participant with the forces that filled our world, he was not a bystander.

❸

A young man died at the village one summer. A very tragic death. He was dragged by his horse. When he was found I cried, for the boy was my friend. I did not understand why death had come to one so young. My grandfather took me aside and said: "Think of the death of the trees and the fields in the fall. The leaves fall, and everything rests, as if dead. But they bloom again in the spring. Death is only this small transformation in life."

❹

These are the things I remember, these fleeting images, few words.

I remember him driving his horse-drawn wagon into Santa Rosa in the fall when he brought his harvest produce to sell in the town. What a tower of strength seemed to come in that small man huddled on the seat of the giant wagon. One click of his tongue and the horses obeyed, stopped or turned as he wished. He never raised his whip. How unlike today when so much teaching is done with loud words and threatening hands.

◆ Build Vocabulary

epiphany (ē pif´ ə nē) *n.:* Moment of sudden understanding

Cross-Curricular Connection: Social Studies

The Pueblos Explain to students that the Pueblos are a group of American Indians who are centered in the Southwest. They were given the name *Pueblo* by Spanish explorers. In Spanish the word means "town"; the communities the Indians lived in looked much like Spanish towns. Most Pueblos built their homes from adobe in structures that look like apartment buildings. They can be as tall as four stories high. The Pueblos used ladders to climb to the upper stories. Often, an extended family, including grandparents, would live in connected buildings. Some of these villages, hundreds of years old, can still be visited. Discuss with students why Anaya would compare the elders in his community with the adobe buildings of the Pueblos.

El Lenador, 1934, Tom Lea, Museum of Fine Arts, Museum of New Mexico

►Critical Viewing◄

⑤ Compare and Contrast Some students may say the farmer in the painting has a sterner expression than they would have imagined the author's grandfather to have; others might think his expression only looks stern because of the lines in his face.

◆ **Literary Focus**

⑥ Essay Ask: What is Anaya saying about the lives of older people? *He is saying that watching and learning from how they move through the last years of their lives is vitally important.*

◀ Critical Viewing How does the elderly farmer in this painting compare with the image you have of the author's grandfather? [Compare and Contrast] **⑤**

I would run to greet the wagon, and the wagon would stop. "Buenos días le de Dios, abuelo," I would say. This was the prescribed greeting of esteem and respect. Only after the greeting was given could we approach these venerable old people. "Buenos días le de Dios, mi hijo,"[12] he would answer and smile, and then I could jump up on the wagon and sit at his side. Then I, too, became a king as I rode next to the old man who smelled of earth and sweat and the other deep aromas from the orchards and fields of Puerto de Luna.

⑥ We were all sons and daughters to him. But today the sons and daughters are breaking with the past, putting aside los abuelitos. The old values are threatened, and threatened most where it comes to these relationships with the old people. If we don't take the time to watch and feel the years of their final transformation, a part of our humanity will be lessened. **⑥**

I grew up speaking Spanish, and oh! how difficult it was to learn English. Sometimes I would give up and cry out that I couldn't learn. Then he would say, "Ten paciencia."[13] Have patience. *Paciencia*, a word with the strength of centuries, a word that said that someday we would overcome. *Paciencia*, how soothing a word coming from this old man who could still sling hundred-pound bags over his shoulder, chop wood for hours on end, and hitch up his own horses and ride to town and back in one day.

---

12. **mi hijo** (mē ē´ hō): My son.

13. **Ten paciencia** (ten pä sē en´ sē ä)

A Celebration of Grandfathers ◆ 579

🎼 Humanities: Art

El Lenador, 1934, by Tom Lea.

This painting shows a man guiding a heavily laden donkey. The man has a stick in his hand, which he is probably using to tap the donkey on its shoulders or side of the neck so that it knows which way to go.

Use the following questions for discussion:

1. What can you infer about the life of the farmer in this painting? *Students may say that that the farmer needs to work hard to* make a living, as the painting implies an uphill journey. The farmer appears as tough, craggy, sturdy, and patient as his donkey and the landscape around them. Judging from the load of firewood on the donkey's back, the farmer either uses wood to provide fuel for heating and cooking or sells wood to supplement his income.

2. What can you tell about the farmer's relationship with animals and nature? *Students may say that the farmer appears* to be in harmony with nature; he is even a part of nature. Despite its load of firewood, the donkey appears to be more of a co-worker than a servant. Its lack of a halter means that the farmer trusts that it will not run away or balk and that it needs no more direction than an occasional tap.

◆ Critical Thinking

❶ Draw Conclusions Ask students what Anaya is criticizing about modern life. *He thinks people pay too much attention to material gain and too little to sharing what we have so there is enough for all.*

◆ Reading Strategy

❷ Identify the Author's Attitude Have students determine how Anaya feels about his grandfather's deterioration. *He understands that it is part of the process of living.*

◆ *Literature and Your Life*

❸ Ask students to relate the ideas in this passage to their own opinions and experiences. Have them generalize to other segments of society the author's ideas about allowing the old ones to be young at heart in their own way, rather than in the image of an ever-youthful Hollywood star. What forces keep people from being true to themselves? What can be done to change this? Direct students' attention to the passage about the "return to the valley." Ask volunteers to share their experiences about getting back to their roots and becoming interested in their cultural heritage.

◆ Reading Strategy

❹ Identify the Author's Attitude Elicit responses such as the following: *The author respects and loves his elders. He feels they have valuable lessons to teach and believes that people learn important things simply by being with them, caring for them, and respecting them.*

"You have to learn the language of the Americanos,"[14] he said. "Me, I will live my last days in my valley. You will live in a new time, the time of the gringos."[15]

A new time did come, a new time is here. How will we form it so it is fruitful? We need to know where we stand. We need to speak softly and respect others, and to share what we have. **❶** We need to pray not for material gain, but for rain for the fields, for the sun to nurture growth, for nights in which we can sleep in peace, and for a harvest in which everyone can share. Simple lessons from a simple man. These lessons he learned from his past which was deep and strong as the currents of the river of life, a life which could be stronger than death.

He was a man; he died. Not in his valley, but nevertheless cared for by his sons and daughters and flocks of grandchildren. At the end, I would enter his room which carried the smell of medications and Vicks, the faint pungent odor of urine, and cigarette smoke. Gone were the aroma of the fields, the strength of his young manhood. Gone also was his patience in the face of crippling old age. Small things bothered him; he shouted or turned sour when his expectations were not met. It was because he could not care for himself, because he was returning to that state of childhood, and all those wishes and desires were now wrapped in a crumbling old body.

❷ "Ten paciencia," I once said to him, and he smiled. "I didn't know I would grow this old," he said. "Now, I can't even roll my own cigarettes." I rolled a cigarette for him, placed it in his mouth and lit it. I asked him why he smoked, the doctor had said it was bad for him. "I like to see the smoke rise," he said. He would smoke and doze, and his quilt was spotted with little burns where the cigarettes dropped. One of us had to sit and watch to make sure a fire didn't start.

I would sit and look at him and remember what was said of him when he was a young man. He could mount a wild horse and break it, and he could ride as far as any man. He

---

14. **Americanos** (ä mer′ ē kä′ nōs): Americans.
15. **gringos** (grin′ gōs): Foreigners; North Americans.

---

could dance all night at a dance, then work the acequia the following day. He helped neighbors, they helped him. He married, raised children. Small legends, the kind that make up everyman's life.

He was 94 when he died. Family, neighbors, and friends gathered; they all agreed he had led a rich life. I remembered the last years, the years he spent in bed. And as I remember now, I am reminded that it is too easy to romanticize old age. Sometimes we forget the pain of the transformation into old age, we forget the natural breaking down of the body. Not all go gentle into the last years, some go crying and cursing, forgetting the names of those they loved the most, withdrawing into an internal anguish few of us can know. May we be granted the patience and care to deal with our ancianos.

For some time we haven't looked at these changes and needs of the old ones. The American image created by the mass media is an image of youth, not of old age. It is the beautiful and the young who are praised in this society. If analyzed carefully, we see that same damaging thought has crept into the way society views the old. In response to the old, the mass media have just created old people who act like the young. It is only the healthy, pink-cheeked, outgoing, older persons we are shown in the media. And they are always selling something, as if an entire generation of old people were salesmen in their lives. Commercials show very lively old men, who must always be in excellent health according to the new myth, selling insurance policies or real estate as they are out golfing; older women selling coffee or toilet paper to those just married. That image does not illustrate the real life of the old ones.

Real life takes into account the natural cycle of growth and change. My grandfather pointed to the leaves falling from the tree. So time brings with its transformation the often painful, wearing-down process. Vision blurs, health wanes; even the act of walking carries with it the painful reminder of the autumn of life. But this process is something to be faced, not something to be hidden away by false images. Yes, the old can be young at heart, but

---

Workplace Skills Mini-Lesson

Using Tact With Others

Introduce the Concept Point out to students that those who take care of older people must use great care and tact. Tact can be useful in any kind of work situation, whether or not it involves elders. Discuss with students how using tact can help in work situations.

Develop Background Have students work in small groups to choose a workplace situation in which tact is needed. Ask them

to consider these points:

• What problem are the workers facing?

• What might happen if the situation were not treated with tact?

• How can tact help to resolve the situation?

Apply the Information Groups can write scenarios in which tact is used to bring a work situation to a successful resolution. Encourage them to present their scenarios to the class.

Assess the Outcome Have the class judge the scenarios and discuss the role tact played in the resolutions. Use criteria like the following to assess student scenarios: realistic situation; realistic characters and behaviors; clear, concise written description of the situation and how it plays out; appropriate use of tact. Students' work should reflect an understanding of the complexities of the situation and demonstrate an appreciation for tact.

in their own way, with their own dignity. They do not have to copy the always young image of the Hollywood star.

❸ My grandfather wanted to return to his valley to die. But by then the families of the valley had left in search of a better future. It is only now that there seems to be a return to the valley, a revival. The new generation seeks its roots, that value of love for the land moves us to return to the place where our ancianos formed the culture.

I returned to Puerto de Luna last summer, to join the community in a celebration of the founding of the church. I drove by my grandfather's home, my uncles' ranches, the neglected adobe[16] washing down into the earth from whence it came. And I wondered, how might the values of my grandfather's generation live in our own? What can we retain to see us through these hard times? I was to become a

16. **adobe** (ä dō´ bē): Sun-dried clay brick.

farmer, and I became a writer. As I plow and plant my words, do I nurture as my grandfather did in his fields and orchards? The answers are not simple.

"They don't make men like that anymore," is a phrase we hear when one does honor to a man. I am glad I knew my grandfather. I am glad there are still times when I can see him in my dreams, hear him in my reverie. Sometimes I think I catch a whiff of that earthy aroma that was his smell, just as in lonely times sometimes I catch the fragrance of Ultima's herbs. Then I smile. How strong these people were to leave such a lasting impression.

So, as I would greet my abuelo long ago, it would help us all to greet the old ones we know with this kind and respectful greeting: "Buenos días le de Dios."

◆ **Reading Strategy**
Sum up the author's attitude toward the "old ones." ❹

Guide for Responding

◆ *Literature and Your Life*

Reader's Response How do the "old ones" in Anaya's life compare with the "old ones" in your own life?

Thematic Focus What perspective does Anaya offer on how old people should be treated as they age and as they die?

Group Activity Make a list of recommendations for the way younger people might greet, respect, or help care for older people in their homes and neighborhoods.

✓ **Check Your Comprehension**

1. What are some of the qualities Anaya remembers about old people from his childhood?
2. What does Anaya remember about his own grandfather?
3. How does the "new time" in which Anaya lives differ from the time of his grandfather?

◆ Critical Thinking

INTERPRET

1. How does the world of the old ones compare with the modern world? [Compare and Contrast]
2. How do the author's values differ from those of his grandfather? How are his values the same? [Compare and Contrast]
3. Why do you think the essay ends with the very same words with which it begins? [Analyze]

APPLY

4. What do the grandfathers that Anaya celebrates have in common with Singer's washwoman or Singer's mother? [Synthesize]

EXTEND

5. Explain how geography and history helped shape the values of the old ones. [Social Studies Link]

A Celebration of Grandfathers ◆ 581

Beyond the Selection

FURTHER READING

Other Works by the Authors
Gimpel the Fool and Other Stories, Isaac Bashevis Singer
A Raisin in the Sun, Lorraine Hansberry
Heart of Aztlan, Rudolfo Anaya

Other Works on the Theme of Perspectives
Let Us Now Praise Famous Men, James Agee and Walker Evans
"Once More to the Lake," E. B. White

INTERNET

For more information about the authors, visit the following Web sites. Please be aware, however, that sites may have changed from the time we published this information.

Isaac Bashevis Singer: **http://www.nobel.se/laureates/literature-1978-bio.html**

Lorraine Hansberry: **http://www.csustan.edu/english/reuben/pal/chap8/hansberry bio.html**

Rudolfo Anaya: **http://www.unm.edu/~wrtgsw/anaya.html**

We *strongly recommend* that you preview the sites before you send students to them.

◆ Reading Strategy

1. Possibilities include *strong, proud, inspirational, unstoppable,* and *hard-working.*

2. Hansberry gains more experience of life, so she comes to appreciate not just summer, but life itself, more. In particular, she respects the life lived with courage, determination, and spirit—the life that yearns for more life.

3. Students may say that Anaya's reflections are convincing by themselves, or they may say that a reader does not have to have the same experience as an author to understand an author's attitude. It is also reasonable for students to say that their own grandparents embodied other values and that they are more likely to respect or try to preserve the values modeled in their own lives.

◆ Literary Focus

1. Singer is making a point about the importance of hard work, pride, dignity, strength, self-reliance, and persistence. To him, the washwoman represents the triumph of the human spirit and the will to endure.

2. Hansberry first attempts to persuade the reader of the downside of summer by citing details such as waking up in a hot room and calling summer "maddeningly excessive" and an "utter overstatement." Later, she trumpets the goodness of summer by citing the wish of a dying woman to see one more summer.

3. "A Celebration of Grandfathers" is a reflective essay because the author reflects on very personal feelings such as his love for and memories of his grandfather, as well as on such topics as how daily life has changed for his people and the place of older people in our lives.

◆ Build Vocabulary

Using Prefixes: *fore-*
1. foreground; 2. forethought;
3. foresee

Using the Word Bank
1. perplexes; 2. aloofness; 3. forebears; 4. rancor; 5. epiphany; 6. obstinacy; 7. pious; 8. palpable

---

Guide for Responding (continued)

◆ Reading Strategy

IDENTIFY THE AUTHOR'S ATTITUDE

In all three essays, the **author's attitude** toward the subject comes through clearly in the choice of words and details. For example, Rudolfo Anaya shows his admiration and respect for the older generation when he describes the older generation's strength in its beliefs and tells about how the younger people would listen carefully whenever older people spoke.

1. What three adjectives do you think Singer might select to describe his attitude toward the washwoman? Support your answers with details from the essay.

2. What is Hansberry's attitude toward summer? How can you tell?

3. Anaya's attitude comes from his heritage and his own experience. Do you think he could convince others who do not have the same background to adopt his attitude? Why or why not?

◆ Literary Focus

ESSAY

An **essay** is a short piece of nonfiction in which a writer expresses a personal view of a topic. These selections illustrate three different types of essays: narrative essays, which tell a story; persuasive essays, which try to convince readers to accept a position or take a course of action; and reflective essays—essays in which a writer reflects on his or her feelings about a topic of personal importance.

1. In addition to entertaining readers, narrative essays often make important points about life. What points does I. B. Singer make through his story about the washwoman?

2. In a persuasive essay, the writer presents facts, reasons, anecdotes, and other types of information in an attempt to sway the reader's opinion. What are some of the facts and reasons that Lorraine Hansberry presents to persuade you to accept her opinion about summer?

3. Why is "A Celebration of Grandfathers" a good example of a reflective essay? Support your answer with details from the selection.

◆ Build Vocabulary

USING THE PREFIX *fore-*

Complete the following analogies using these words: *foreground, foresee, forethought,* which all contain the prefix *fore-,* meaning "occurring earlier."
1. *Ahead* is to *behind* as ___?___ is to *background.*
2. *Reflection* is to the *past* as ___?___ is to the *future.*
3. *To anticipate* is to ___?___ as *to find* is to *discover.*

USING THE WORD BANK

On your paper, write the word from the Word Bank that best matches each clue.
1. a synonym for *confuses*
2. a three-syllable word that describes an uninvolved state
3. long-ago relatives of your relatives
4. the opposite of peace and harmony
5. the end to a state of confusion
6. a quality of donkeys
7. people with this quality may be found in a mosque, church, or temple
8. the word you might use in describing an inescapable odor

◆ Build Grammar Skills

COMMONLY CONFUSED WORDS: *AFFECT* AND *EFFECT*

These essays are about people and experiences that **affected,** or influenced, the authors deeply. One **effect,** or result, of these experiences was the essay each wrote. As these sentences illustrate, *affect* is a verb meaning "to influence," while *effect* is often a noun meaning "the result." *Effect* can also be a verb meaning "to bring about" or "to accomplish."

Practice Revise the following sentences, correcting any errors in the use of *affect* and *effect.*
1. The documentary effected Sean emotionally.
2. It was about the affects of the Great Depression.
3. There were many statements to the affect that Hoover was to blame.
4. Sean thought it was unfair to blame the affects of the Depression on President Hoover.
5. Sean did, however, know how negatively the Depression had effected his great-grandparents.

◆ Build Grammar Skills

Commonly Confused Words: *Affect* and *Effect*
1. The documentary affected Sean emotionally.
2. It was about the effects of the Great Depression.
3. There were many statements to the effect that Hoover was to blame.
4. Sean thought it was unfair to blame the effects of the Depression on President Hoover.
5. Sean did, however, know how negatively the Depression had affected his great-grandparents.

✎ Writer's Solution

For additional instruction and practice, use the lesson in the **Language Lab CD-ROM** on Using Precise Words and the Using Action Words and Using Vivid Words pages in the *Writer's Solution Grammar Practice Book,* pp. 119–120.

*B*uild *Y*our *P*ortfolio

 ## Idea Bank

Writing

1. **Summary** Write a brief essay summarizing the key points of one of these essays. Start with a paragraph in which you sum up the overall message and introduce the key points. Then write a paragraph about each of the main points.

2. **Reflective Essay** Write a reflective essay about a subject of personal importance to you. For example, you might write about why a specific person has influenced you, or you might reflect on a single experience that had a powerful impact.

3. **Essay About Themes** Each of these essays has a theme, or central message, that we can apply to our own lives. Write an essay in which you explain the lessons that you learned from the three selections. Cite details to support your points.

Speaking and Listening

4. **Interview** Interview an older person whom you know and admire. Find out key details about the person's life and important lessons that he or she has learned. Share your findings with the class. **[Community Link]**

5. **Persuasive Speech** Prepare and present a persuasive speech on the importance of respecting and learning from older generations. Use details from Anaya's and Singer's essays for support.

Projects

6. **Collage** Create a collage in which you use a collection of images to pay tribute to older generations. **[Art Link]**

7. **Medley of Songs** Find a series of songs connected to the themes of the three essays. Play them for the class, and explain how each one relates to one of the essays. **[Music Link]**

Writing Mini-Lesson

Proposal for a Celebration

Choose your favorite season of the year and think of the perfect way to celebrate it in your community. Then put together a formal proposal that you could present to the local government, outlining a series of festivities that could be held to commemorate this special season. Keep the following tip in mind as you develop your proposal:

Writing Skills Focus: Clear Explanation of Cause and Effect

To create a successful proposal, you need to outline the **causes and effects** of each activity you suggest. In fact, you should probably start by explaining what caused you to make your proposal—what it is about the season that makes it worth celebrating. Then clearly state the reasons for each activity you suggest and indicate the positive effects of that activity. For example, you might suggest a fishing contest to celebrate spring, because it would help build an appreciation of the beauty of the environment in which you live.

Prewriting Start by deciding on a season. Then brainstorm to come up with a list of activities that would capture the spirit of that season.

Drafting Propose the celebration in full detail. Tell when each event will happen, where it will take place, and who is likely to take part. As you do so, explain cause-and-effect relationships, and use cause-and-effect signal words such as *because, why, for, therefore, so, result,* and *effect.*

Revising Share your draft with a classmate. Ask him or her to decide whether each cause-and-effect relationship is clearly stated. Then discuss whether or not he or she found the proposal convincing. If not, encourage him or her to make suggestions on how you can improve it.

The Washwoman/On Summer/A Celebration of Grandfathers ◆ 583

 ### Idea Bank
Customizing for
Performance Levels
Following are suggestions for matching the Idea Bank topics with your students' performance levels:
    Less Advanced Students: 1, 6
    Average Students: 2, 4, 7
    More Advanced Students: 3, 5

Customizing for
Learning Modalities
Following are suggestions for matching the Idea Bank topics with your students' learning modalities:
    Verbal/Linguistic: 4, 5
    Interpersonal: 4
    Musical/Rhythmic: 7
    Visual/Spatial: 6

 ### Writing Mini-Lesson
Refer students to the Writing Handbook, page 962, for instruction on the writing process, and page 965 for further information on Persuasion.

 ### Writer's Solution

Writing Lab CD-ROM
Have students complete the Tutorial on Persuasion. Follow these steps:
1. Complete the Audience Profile to focus on writing for a target audience.
2. View the interactive examples of ways to organize evidence to learn more about cause-and-effect order.
3. Draft the proposal on computer.
4. Use the tips on sharing the work with others to learn more about how to send essays to people in office.
Allow approximately 90 minutes of class time to complete these steps.

Sourcebook
Have students use Chapter 4, Persuasion (pp. 97–127), for additional support. The chapter includes a workplace writing model of a persuasive essay (p. 101), instruction on using a cause-and-effect organization (p. 116), and an annotated student model of a persuasive essay (p. 123).

✓ ASSESSMENT OPTIONS

Formal Assessment, Selection Test, pp. 145–147, and Assessment Resources Software. The selection test is designed so that it can be easily customized to the performance levels of your students.
Alternative Assessment, p. 41, includes options for less advanced students, more advanced students, verbal/linguistic learners, logical/mathematical learners, visual/spatial learners, and musical/rhythmic learners.

PORTFOLIO ASSESSMENT
Use the following rubrics in the *Alternative Assessment* booklet to assess student writing:
Summary: Summary Rubric, p. 91
Reflective Essay: Expression Rubric, p. 87
Essay About Themes: Literary Analysis/ Interpretation Rubric, p. 105
Writing Mini-Lesson: Cause-Effect Rubric, p. 95

Guide for Reading

OBJECTIVES

1. To read, comprehend, and interpret three essays
2. To relate the essays to personal experience
3. To find writer's main points and support
4. To identify biographical and autobiographical writing
5. To build vocabulary in context and learn the word root -sent-/-sens-
6. To develop skill in using appositives and appositive phrases
7. To write an awards speech exhibiting coherence
8. To respond to the story through writing, speaking and listening, and projects

SKILLS INSTRUCTION

Vocabulary: Word Roots: -sent-/-sens-
Grammar: Appositives and Appositive Phrases
Reading Strategy: Find the Writer's Main Points and Support
Literary Focus: Biographical and Autobiographical Writing

Writing: Awards Speech
Speaking and Listening: News Report Speech (teacher edition);
Critical Viewing: Speculate; Deduce; Hypothesize

PORTFOLIO OPPORTUNITIES

Writing: Letter of Condolence; How-to Essay; Essay
Writing Mini-Lesson: Awards Speech
Speaking and Listening: News Report; Speech
Projects: Internet Exploration; Museum Exhibit

Lady Bird Johnson *(1912–)*

On one of the most tragic days in American history, November 22, 1963, Lady Bird Johnson became First Lady of the United States. President John F. Kennedy had just been killed by an assassin in Dallas, Texas. On board *Air Force One*, the President's airplane, Vice President Lyndon Baines Johnson took the oath of office to become the thirty-sixth President of the United States. On his left stood Kennedy's widow, Jackie, her clothing still spattered with her husband's blood. On his right stood his wife, Lady Bird Johnson.

Texas-born Claudia Alta Taylor received her nickname at age two, when a nurse said she was as pretty as a lady bird. In 1934, she married Lyndon Johnson, then a congressional secretary. Throughout Lyndon Johnson's political career, Lady Bird was a most valued advisor and campaigner.

John McPhee *(1931–)*

Nonfiction writer John McPhee has found success in writing about topics that fascinate him. One such subject is sports. After graduating from Princeton University, McPhee worked at *Time* magazine, and then at *The New Yorker*. McPhee has written many books and essays. In *Levels of the Game* (1969), an account of the 1968 U.S. Open Tennis Championships, McPhee reveals his admiration for Arthur Ashe.

Joan Didion *(1934–)*

Joan Didion is descended from a long line of pioneers. Her great-great-grandmother went west in a covered wagon in 1846. As a young woman, Didion won a writing contest sponsored by *Vogue* magazine. Eventually she became an editor there. Her reputation in the literary world, however, is based on her novels and essays. The essay "Georgia O'Keeffe" pays tribute to an artist who herself displayed a strong pioneer spirit.

584 ◆ Nonfiction

◆ Build Vocabulary

WORD ROOTS: -sent-/-sens-
In "Georgia O'Keeffe," Joan Didion refers to a sentimental appreciation of art. The word *sentimental* contains the root -sent- (sometimes spelled -sens-), which means "feeling or perceiving." The root is an important clue to the meaning of the word, which is "having excessive feelings or emotions."

WORD BANK
Before you read, preview this list of words from the selections.

tumultuous
implications
poignant
legacy
enigma
condescending
sentimental
genesis
rancor
immutable

◆ Build Grammar Skills

APPOSITIVES AND APPOSITIVE PHRASES
Look at the following passages from Lady Bird Johnson's diary. What purpose is served by words in italics?

... our Secret Service man, *Rufus Youngblood*, vaulted over the front seat ...

... Kenny O'Donnell, *the President's top aide*, ...

In both cases, the italicized words help to identify the people Johnson mentions. The first example features an **appositive**—a noun or pronoun placed near another noun or pronoun to identify, rename, or explain it. The second contains an **appositive phrase**—an appositive accompanied by other words that modify it. As you read these selections, notice how the writers use appositives.

◆ *from* A White House Diary ◆
Arthur Ashe Remembered ◆ Georgia O'Keeffe

◆ *Literature and Your Life*

CONNECT YOUR EXPERIENCE
Through the media, we have many opportunities to see and hear famous people. Seldom, however, do we find out what famous people are truly like. In the following selections, you'll have a rare chance to see the private sides of three famous Americans.

THEMATIC FOCUS: LEARNING ABOUT OURSELVES AND OTHERS
As the selections illustrate, the good times, the hard work, and—perhaps most of all—the tragedies of life can lead to discoveries about what really matters in life.

◆ Background for Understanding

HISTORY
Any American old enough to remember the day President John F. Kennedy was assassinated—November 22, 1963—will never forget it. At the moment that radio and television commentators reported the news of the fatal shooting, the United States came to a halt. A shocked nation stayed glued to television sets to get the details of the unfolding story. People wept openly in their homes and in the streets. President Kennedy had been a young, vibrant, and popular leader, who had fostered a sense of optimism about the future. With his assassination, this optimism was shattered. A stunned nation shared the feelings of newly sworn-in President Lyndon Johnson when he said, "This is a sad time for all people. We have suffered a loss that cannot be weighed. For me, it is a deep personal tragedy."

Journal Writing List a few local or world events of your lifetime that caused people either joy or sorrow.

◆ Literary Focus

BIOGRAPHICAL AND AUTOBIOGRAPHICAL WRITING
Biographical writing is a form of nonfiction in which a writer tells the story of another person's life. **Autobiographical** writing is a form of nonfiction in which a person tells about his or her own life. The entry from *A White House Diary* is an autobiographical account. As the diary reveals, autobiographical writing shows events from the author's perspective and lets you share the author's thoughts and feelings. In a piece of biographical writing, on the other hand, you are presented with a writer's view of a subject's life and do not have direct access to the subject's thoughts and feelings.

◆ Reading Strategy

FIND THE WRITER'S MAIN POINTS AND SUPPORT
A key to understanding and enjoying any literary work is the ability to **find the writer's main points** and the details—facts, events, quotations, and more—that support those points. Sometimes writers will directly state the main points in the opening paragraph. Other times, however, writers depend on the cumulative effect of their writing to communicate their message.

To find the main ideas of these selections, look closely at each paragraph to determine the main idea it conveys. A paragraph's main idea may be stated in a single sentence, or you may have to draw a conclusion about its main idea from the supporting information it presents. For example, if a paragraph in a biography describes an incident in which the subject risked her life to save someone, you might conclude that the paragraph's main point relates to the subject's bravery and selflessness. Once you've finished reading, try to piece together the key ideas of the individual paragraphs to determine the main points of the work as a whole.

Guide for Reading ◆ 585

Preparing for Standardized Tests

Reading and Vocabulary The Reading Strategy lesson for this selection focuses on finding the writer's main points and support. This strategy is important for students in addressing reading comprehension passages on standardized tests. Have students apply the strategy as they read these selections. For additional practice, use the Reading Strategy pages in *Selection Support,* pp. 174–175.

Grammar and Language The Build Grammar Skills lesson for this selection focuses on appositives and appositive phrases. Students can apply this skill to both grammar items and essays on the verbal portions of standardized tests. For additional practice, use the Build Grammar Skills page in *Selection Support,* p. 173.

Strength in times of trouble is the thread that runs through these three essays. From Lady Bird Johnson's autobiography excerpt, we learn of the strength shown by everyone aboard *Air Force One* on the flight from Dallas back to Washington, D.C., with President Kennedy's coffin on board.

◆ **Critical Thinking**

❶ **Make Inferences** Ask students: Why do you think Mrs. Johnson emphasizes the happy mood that morning? *Through contrast, the initial happiness reinforces the tragedy to follow.*

❷ **Clarification** Explain that Secret Service men guarding a President have sworn to give up their lives for him, if necessary.

▶ **Critical Viewing** ◀

❸ **Infer** The faces reveal sorrow and anxiety.

Customize for
More Advanced Students
Have these students explain how *A White House Diary* would differ if it were written as a biography from the third-person point of view. Would it have more or less impact? Why?

from *A White House Diary*

Lady Bird Johnson

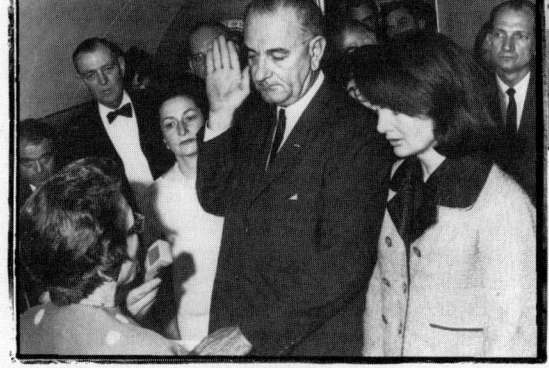

DALLAS, FRIDAY, NOVEMBER 22, 1963

It all began so beautifully. After a drizzle in the morning, the sun came out bright and clear. We were driving into Dallas. In the lead car were President and Mrs. Kennedy, John and Nellie Connally,[1] a Secret Service car full of men, and then our car with Lyndon and me and Senator Ralph Yarborough.

The streets were lined with people—lots and lots of people—the children all smiling, placards, confetti, people waving from windows. ❶ One last happy moment I had was looking up and seeing Mary Griffith leaning out of a window waving at me. (Mary for many years had been in charge of altering the clothes which I purchased at Neiman-Marcus.)

Then, almost at the edge of town, on our way to the Trade Mart for the Presidential luncheon, we were rounding a curve, going down a hill, and suddenly there was a sharp, loud report. It sounded like a shot. The sound seemed to me to come from a building on the right above my shoulder. A moment passed, and then two more shots rang out in rapid succession. There had been such a gala air about the day that I thought the noise must come from firecrackers—part of the celebration. Then the Secret Service[2] men ❷ were suddenly down in the lead car. Over the car radio system, I heard "Let's get out of here!" and our Secret Service man, Rufus Youngblood,

---

1. **John and Nellie Connally:** John Connally, then Governor of Texas, and his wife, Nellie.
2. **Secret Service:** Division of the U.S. Treasury Department, responsible for protecting the President.

586 ◆ *Nonfiction*

▲ **Critical Viewing** What do the people's facial expressions reveal about their feelings in the aftermath of President Kennedy's assassination? [Infer] ❸

vaulted over the front seat on top of Lyndon, ❷ threw him to the floor, and said, "Get down."

Senator Yarborough and I ducked our heads. The car accelerated terrifically—faster and faster. Then, suddenly, the brakes were put on so hard that I wondered if we were going to make it as we wheeled left and went around the corner. We pulled up to a building. I looked up and saw a sign, "HOSPITAL." Only then did I believe that this might be what it was. Senator Yarborough kept saying in an excited voice, "Have they shot the President? Have they shot the President?" I said something like, "No, it can't be."

As we ground to a halt—we were still the third car—Secret Service men began to pull, lead,

---

Block Scheduling Strategies

Consider these suggestions to take advantage of extended class time:

• Encourage students to research Lady Bird Johnson, Arthur Ashe, or Georgia O'Keeffe on the Internet. Students can access the Internet site listed on page 596.

• Students may listen to the selections on audiocassette. Guide students to explain how hearing the selections, especially Lady Bird Johnson's account of the assassination of President Kennedy, added to their appreciation of the author's craft.

• Have students complete the Build Vocabulary lesson and preview the words in the Word Bank. Encourage students to use a dictionary to find other words that contain the word root *-sent-*.

• Use the Daily Language Practice activities for week 22, pp. 48–49, in *Daily Language Practice*.

• Students can work in discussion groups to respond to the Critical Thinking questions (pp. 589, 591, and 596).

▲ Critical Viewing What does this photograph reveal about the mood in the moments leading up to the assassination? [Infer] **④**

guide, and hustle us out. I cast one last look over my shoulder and saw in the President's car a bundle of pink, just like a drift of blossoms, lying on the back seat. It was Mrs. Kennedy lying over the President's body.

The Secret Service men rushed us to the right, then to the left, and then onward into a quiet room in the hospital—a very small room. It was lined with white sheets, I believe.

People came and went—Kenny O'Donnell, the President's top aide, Congressman Homer Thornberry, Congressman Jack Brooks. Always there was Rufe right there and other Secret Service agents—Emory Roberts, Jerry Kivett, Lem Johns, and Woody Taylor. People spoke of how widespread this might be. There was talk about where we would go—to the plane, to our house, back to Washington.

Through it all Lyndon was remarkably calm and quiet. He suggested that the Presidential plane ought to be moved to another part of the field. He spoke of going back out to the plane in **⑤** unmarked black cars. Every face that came in,

you searched for the answer. I think the face I kept seeing the answer on was the face of Kenny O'Donnell, who loved President Kennedy so much. **⑤**

It was Lyndon who spoke of it first, although I knew I would not leave without doing it. He said, "You had better try to see Jackie and Nellie." We didn't know what had happened to John.

I asked the Secret Service if I could be taken to them. They began to lead me up one corridor and down another. Suddenly I found myself face to face with Jackie in a small hallway. I believe it was right outside the operating room. You always think of someone like her as being insulated, protected. She was quite alone. I don't think I ever saw anyone so much alone in my life. I went up to her, put my arms around her, and said something to her. I'm sure it was something like "God, help us all," because my feelings for her were too <u>tumultuous</u> to put into words.

And then I went to see Nellie. There it was different, because Nellie and I have gone through so many things together since 1938. I hugged her tight and we both cried and I said, "Nellie, John's going to be all right." And Nellie said, "Yes, John's going to be all right." Among her many other fine qualities, she is also strong.

I turned and went back to the small white room where Lyndon was. Mac Kilduff, the President's press man on this trip, and Kenny O'Donnell were coming and going. I think it was **⑥** from Kenny's face that I first knew the truth **⑦** and from Kenny's voice that I first heard the words "The President is dead." Mr. Kilduff entered and said to Lyndon, "Mr. President."

It was decided that we would go immediately to the airport. Hurried plans were made about how we should get to the cars and who was to ride in which car. Our departure from the hospital and approach to the cars was one of the swiftest walks I have ever made.

We got in. Lyndon told the agents to stop the sirens. We drove along as fast as we could. I

◆ Build Vocabulary
tumultuous (tōō mul´ chōō əs) *adj.*: Greatly disturbed

from A White House Diary ◆ 587

▶Critical Viewing◀

④ Infer The mood is cheerful and happy. President Kennedy and his wife are smiling back at the welcoming crowd.

◆ Critical Thinking

⑤ Infer Ask students: What does Mrs. Johnson mean when she says that she "searched for the answer" on everyone's face? *She is trying to find out the condition of President Kennedy.*

◆ Reading Strategy

⑥ Find the Writer's Main Points and Support Have students find the main idea of this passage. Guide them to make inferences based on the last line, ". . . Mr. President." *Mrs. Johnson has just realized the enormity of her personal loss, the nation's loss, and the sudden change in her and her husband's lives, all due to the President's death.*

◆ Build Grammar Skills

⑦ Appositives and Appositive Phrases Ask students to find the appositive phrase in this paragraph. Which word is the appositive? Which words modify that word? What information does the phrase provide? How is it punctuated? *The appositive phrase is "the President's press man on this trip." The appositive is the noun "man," modified by the other words in the phrase. The appositive phrase identifies "Mac Kilduff" and is set off by commas.*

588

❶ Clarification Explain that at this point, no one was sure if Kennedy's assassination was part of a conspiracy or an isolated act of terrorism. Johnson had to be sworn in immediately to ensure continued leadership of the United States and to prevent international panic.

◆ **Reading Strategy**

❷ Find the Writer's Main Points and Support Have students identify the main point and support in this passage. *The main point is that odd things come to mind at times of great stress, such as flashes of compassion for those at the fringes of the tragedy. This point is supported by the author's recounting that she felt terrible for a Secret Service man and then for the police chief of Dallas.*

---

looked up at a building and there, already, was a flag at half-mast. I think that was when the enormity of what had happened first struck me.

When we got to the field, we entered *Air Force One*[3] for the first time. There was a TV set on and the commentator was saying, "Lyndon B. Johnson, now President of the United States." The news commentator was saying the President had been shot with a 30-30 rifle. The police had a suspect. They were not sure he was the assassin.

❶ On the plane, all the shades were lowered. We heard that we were going to wait for Mrs. Kennedy and the coffin. There was a telephone call to Washington—I believe to the Attorney General.[4] It was decided that Lyndon should be sworn in here as quickly as possible, because of national and world implications, and because we did not know how widespread this was as to intended victims. Judge Sarah Hughes, a Federal Judge in Dallas—and I am glad it was she—was called and asked to come in a hurry to administer the oath.

Mrs. Kennedy had arrived by this time, as had the coffin. There, in the very narrow confines of the plane—with Jackie standing by Lyndon, her hair falling in her face but very composed, with me beside him, Judge Hughes in front of him, and a cluster of Secret Service people, staff, and Congressmen we had known for a long time around him—Lyndon took the oath of office.

❷ It's odd the little things that come to your mind at times of utmost stress, the flashes of deep compassion you feel for people who are really not at the center of the tragedy. I heard a Secret Service man say in the most desolate voice—and I hurt for him: "We never lost a President in the Service." Then, Police Chief Curry of Dallas came on the plane and said, "Mrs. Kennedy, believe me, we did everything we possibly could." That must have been an agonizing moment for him.

We all sat around the plane. The casket was in the corridor. I went in the small private room

---

3. **Air Force One:** Name of the airplane officially assigned to transport the president of the United States.
4. **Attorney General:** Chief law officer of the nation, head of the U.S. Department of Justice.

588 ◆ *Nonfiction*

---

to see Mrs. Kennedy, and though it was a very hard thing to do, she made it as easy as possible. She said things like, "Oh, Lady Bird, we've liked you two so much. . . . Oh, what if I had not been there. I'm so glad I was there."

I looked at her. Mrs. Kennedy's dress was stained with blood. One leg was almost entirely covered with it and her right glove was caked, it was caked with blood—her husband's blood. Somehow that was one of the most poignant sights—that immaculate woman exquisitely dressed, and caked in blood.

I asked her if I couldn't get someone in to help her change and she said, "Oh, no. Perhaps later I'll ask Mary Gallagher but not right now." And then with almost an element of fierceness—if a person that gentle, that dignified, can be said to have such a quality—she said, "I want them to see what they have done to Jack."

I tried to express how we felt. I said, "Oh, Mrs. Kennedy, you know we never even wanted to be Vice President and now, dear God, it's come to this." I would have done anything to help her, but there was nothing I could do, so rather quickly I left and went back to the main part of the airplane where everyone was seated.

❸ The flight to Washington was silent, each sitting with his own thoughts. One of mine was a recollection of what I had said about Lyndon a long time ago—he's a good man in a tight spot. I remembered one little thing he had said in that hospital room—"Tell the children to get a Secret Service man with them."

Finally we got to Washington, with a cluster of people waiting and many bright lights. The casket went off first, then Mrs. Kennedy, and then we followed. The family had come to join her. Lyndon made a very simple, very brief, and, I think, strong statement to the people there. Only about four sentences. We got in helicopters, dropped him off at the White House, and I came home in a car with Liz Carpenter.[5]

---

5. **Liz Carpenter:** Mrs. Johnson's press secretary.

◆ **Build Vocabulary**

implications (im′ pli kā′ shənz) *n.*: Suggestions or indirect indications

poignant (poin′ yənt) *adj.*: Drawing forth pity or compassion; moving

---

News Report

This mini-lesson supports the Speaking and Listening activity in the Idea Bank on page 598.

Introduce the Concept Have students discuss some radio news reports they have heard. Point out the importance of a reporter staying calm, especially when delivering tragic news such as the assassination of President Kennedy.

Develop Background Through class discussion, generate a list of "dos" and "don'ts"

for the news reports. Elicit points such as the following:

- Organize the facts logically so that the report is easy to understand.
- Make sure your facts and details are accurate.
- Summarize the most important points at the beginning and the end of the broadcast.
- Stay calm—don't let what you say or how you say it cause a panic.

Apply the Information Remind students to incorporate the elements of good oral presentation, as well as the points generated in the Develop Background step, into their news reports.

Assess the Outcome Have students evaluate the news reports on organization, accuracy, highlighting of main idea, possession of the desired impact on listeners, and delivery. You may wish to distribute the Peer Assessment: Speaker/Speech page in *Alternative Assessment,* p. 111.

▲ **Critical Viewing** This photograph shows Lyndon Johnson beginning to assume his duties as president. Based on the details in the photo, how do you think he felt at that time? Why? **[Analyze]**

❹

Beyond Literature

History Connection

Lyndon Johnson and the Vietnam War On March 31, 1968, President Johnson announced that he would not seek reelection. More than any other factor, his decision resulted from his support of the Vietnam War and the criticism that followed. During his presidency, the United States became more and more deeply involved in the war. When he took office, there were only about 16,300 American military advisors in Vietnam. By 1968, the United States had more than 500,000 troops there, and Americans were bitterly divided over the war.

Activity With a group, conduct research to learn more about the Vietnam War and the protests that resulted from it. Share your findings with the class.

◆ **Reading Strategy**

❸ **Find the Writer's Main Points and Support** Ask students to identify the main point of this paragraph. *Sometimes, especially at the time of a tragedy, it is difficult to put one's feelings into words.*

▶**Critical Viewing**◀

❹ **Analyze** Students may interpret Johnson's posture and expression to mean that he is feeling anxious about his new duties, but is determined to do a good job.

Reinforce and Extend

Answers
◆ *Literature and Your Life*

Reader's Response Answers will vary. Students may say they admire Lady Bird Johnson's compassion for Mrs. Kennedy because it shows that Lady Bird Johnson cares about the feelings of others.

Thematic Focus Suggested response: Perhaps Lady Bird Johnson discovers that life is unpredictable and fragile. She might also realize that tragedy sometimes brings out the best in people, reminding them to do what they can to help others.

☑ **Check Your Comprehension**

1. She hears the words "Let's get out of here!"
2. It is Mrs. Kennedy lying over the President's body.
3. He takes the oath of office on board *Air Force One*, the presidential airplane.
4. The sight that moves Lady Bird Johnson most is Mrs. Kennedy with her clothing caked with her husband's blood.

Guide for Responding

◆ *Literature and Your Life*

Reader's Response What do you admire most about Lady Bird Johnson? Why?

Thematic Focus What do you think Lady Bird Johnson discovers about life during the ordeal of the Kennedy assassination?

☑ **Check Your Comprehension**

1. What does Lady Bird Johnson hear over the car radio system immediately after the shots are fired?
2. What is the "bundle of pink" that Lady Bird Johnson sees lying on the back seat of the president's car?
3. Where does Lyndon Johnson take the oath of office for president of the United States?
4. When she enters the private room on the presidential airplane to speak with Mrs. Kennedy, what sight moves Lady Bird Johnson most?

◆ **Critical Thinking**

INTERPRET
1. Lady Bird Johnson says of Mrs. Kennedy at the hospital, "I don't think I ever saw anyone so much alone in my life." In what ways is Mrs. Kennedy alone? **[Deduce]**
2. Mrs. Kennedy does not change her bloodstained clothing. In what way is wearing the clothing a tribute to her husband? **[Interpret]**
3. With frightful suddenness, the assassination drastically changes the lives of Lady Bird Johnson and Lyndon Johnson. Cite examples from the diary entry that indicate they are up to the tasks before them. **[Support]**

EXTEND
4. Why is this diary an especially valuable source for people, such as historians and teachers, who are interested in the Kennedy assassination or the Lyndon Johnson presidency? **[Social Studies Link]**

from *A White House Diary* ◆ 589

◆ **Critical Thinking**

1. She is the only person in the hallway. She is alone in having just lost her husband. She is also alone in experiencing the shock and grief of losing her husband in such a sudden and brutal manner.
2. It is a stark reminder of the brutality of assassination that the President had just suffered.

3. Suggested response: Examples for Lady Bird Johnson include her lack of panic and her concern for others. Examples for Lyndon Johnson include his lack of panic and his ability to think clearly as shown by his decisions to move the presidential airplane and to drive to the airport in unmarked cars.

4. It gives a first-hand account of important events from a person, Lady Bird Johnson, who either took part in the events herself or was a witness to the events. From the vantage point of First Lady, Lady Bird Johnson can provide more information about the presidency than perhaps anyone else except the President himself.

Develop Understanding

One-Minute Insight From John McPhee, we learn how tennis great Arthur Ashe was possibly at his best in the face of defeat—even in the face of death.

◆ **Critical Thinking**

❶ **Connect** Ask students: How does this paragraph reflect on the earlier quote by Ashe that his life was "a succession of fortunate circumstances"? *Students might say that the fact that Ashe died young contradicts his earlier statement.*

❷ **Clarification** You may wish to tell students that Arthur Ashe contracted AIDS from a blood transfusion.

▶ **Critical Viewing** ◀

❸ **Speculate** Students might suggest that Ashe is feeling joy and pride.

◆ **Literary Focus**

❹ **Biographical and Autobiographical Writing** Ask: How does McPhee want you to react to Ashe's refusal to reveal his emotions on the tennis court? How can you tell? *McPhee admires Ashe for this quality and wants readers to do the same. McPhee's admiring tone throughout the essay makes this evident.*

◆ **Reading Strategy**

❺ **Find the Writer's Main Points and Support** The writer's main point is stated directly in the last sentence.

◆ **Critical Thinking**

❻ **Deduce** Ask students: How is the image of Arthur Ashe in this scene characteristic of the way he lived his entire life? *Students might suggest that it shows Ashe's dignity and "cool."*

Arthur Ashe
Remembered

John McPhee

▲ **Critical Viewing** In 1975, Arthur Ashe won the men's singles championship at Wimbledon. What do you think is going through his mind as he displays his trophy? **[Speculate]** ❸

H e once described his life as "a succession of fortunate circumstances." He was in his twenties then. More than half of his life was behind him. His memory of his mother was confined to a single image: in a blue corduroy bathrobe she stood in a doorway looking out on the courts and playing fields surrounding their house, which stood in the center of a Richmond playground. Weakened by illness, she was taken to a hospital that day, and died at the age of twenty-seven. He was six.

It was to be his tragedy, as the world knows, that he would leave his own child when she was six, that his life would be ❶ ❷ trapped in a medical irony as a result of early heart disease, and death would come to him prematurely, as it had to his mother.

His mother was tall, with long soft hair and a face that was gentle and thin. She read a lot. She read a lot to him. His father said of her, "She was just like Arthur Junior. She never argued. She was quiet, easygoing, kindhearted."

If by legacy her son never argued, he was also schooled, instructed, coached not to argue, and as he moved alone into alien country he fashioned not-arguing into an enigma and turned the enigma into a weapon. When things got tough (as I noted in these pages twenty-four years ago), he had control. Even in very tight moments, other players thought he was toying with them. They rarely knew what he was thinking. They could not tell if he was angry. It was maddening, sometimes, to play against him. Never less ❹

590 ◆ Nonfiction

 Beyond the Classroom

Career Connection

Tennis Tennis was invented in 1873 by Major Walter Clopton Wingfield, a British army officer. It took only a year for the game to come to America, where it set down deep roots. Have students research how to become a professional tennis player. They can discover the dedication, discipline, hours of daily practice, success on the amateur level, and sacrifices necessary to make it to the professional tennis circuit. They might read about such tennis stars as Steffi Graf and Pete Sampras as they conduct their research.

Community Connection

Local Sports Figures Point out that many professional athletes have short careers, due to the rigors of their sports. After they retire as athletes, they often begin second careers as coaches, teachers, and businesspersons. Encourage students to research retired sports figures in their area and to find out what they are now doing. If possible, students can interview them about their experiences. The class can create an oral history on audio- or videotape to place in the library.

than candid, he said that what he liked best about himself on a tennis court was his demeanor: "What it is is controlled cool, in a way. Always have the situation under control, even if losing. Never betray an inward sense of defeat."

And of course he never did—not in the height of his athletic power, not in the statesmanship of the years that followed, and not in the endgame of his existence. If you wished to choose a single image, you would see him standing there in his twenties, his lithe body a braid of cables, his energy without apparent limit, in a court situation indescribably bad, and all he does is put his index finger on the bridge of his glasses and push them back up the bridge of his nose. In the shadow of disaster, he hits out. Faced with a choice between a conservative, percentage return or a one-in-ten flat-out blast, he chooses the blast. In a signature manner, he extends his left arm to point upward at lobs as they fall toward him. His overheads, in fire bursts, put them away. His backhand is, if anything, stronger than his forehand, and his shots from either side for the most part are

explosions. In motions graceful and decisive, though, and with reactions as fast as the imagination, he is a master of drop shots, of cat-and-mouse, of miscellaneous dinks and chips and (riskiest of all) the crosscourt half-volley. Other tennis players might be wondering who in his right mind would attempt something like that, but that is how Ashe plays the game: at the tensest moment, he goes for the all but impossible. He is predictably unpredictable. He is unreadable. His ballistic serves move in odd patterns and come off the court in unexpected ways. Behind his impassive face—behind the enigmatic glasses, the lifted chin, the first-mate-on-the-bridge look—there seems to be, even from this distance, a smile.

◆ **Reading Strategy**
What is the writer's main point in this paragraph?
❺
❻

◆ **Literary Focus**
The writer of this remembrance has balanced the tragic and the joyful aspects of Arthur Ashe's life. What are those two aspects?
❼

◆ **Build Vocabulary**
legacy (leg′ ə sē) *n.*: Anything handed down from an ancestor
enigma (i nig′ mə) *n.*: Puzzling or baffling matter; riddle.

◆ **Literary Focus**
❼ **Biographical and Autobiographical Writing** The tragic aspects are his mother's early death and his own early death; the joyful aspects include his great tennis victories.

Reinforce and Extend

Guide for Responding

◆ *Literature and Your Life*

Reader's Response After reading this selection, what are your feelings about Arthur Ashe? Why?
Thematic Focus What does Arthur Ashe discover are the advantages of "controlled cool" during a tennis match?

 **Check Your Comprehension**

1. In what ways is Arthur Ashe like his mother?
2. How does Ashe use the traits he inherited from his mother to his advantage when playing tennis?
3. What does Arthur Ashe do in a disastrous situation in a tennis match?
4. What does Arthur Ashe never betray in tennis or in life?

◆ **Critical Thinking**

INTERPRET
1. What later proved to be tragically ironic, or surprising, about Arthur Ashe's early statement that his life is "a succession of fortunate circumstances"? **[Connect]**
2. What does Ashe's ability never to betray an inward sense of defeat say about his character? **[Draw Conclusions]**
3. Use examples to show how the writer uses the way Arthur Ashe played tennis to illustrate how Ashe lived life. **[Support]**

APPLY
4. How can one aspect of Ashe's approach to tennis—going for the difficult shot when in trouble—be applied as an approach to life? **[Apply]**

Arthur Ashe Remembered ◆ 591

Answers
◆ *Literature and Your Life*

Reader's Response Most students will like Ashe because of his even temperament and honesty.

Thematic Focus He discovers that "controlled cool" on the court keeps his opponents guessing about his tactics and state of mind.

☑ **Check Your Comprehension**
1. Like his mother, Ashe is quiet, easygoing, kindhearted. He also never argues.
2. When playing tennis, Arthur Ashe turns not arguing into a weapon. By always remaining levelheaded, he never lets his opponents feel that he fears he might lose.
3. Rather than play it safe, he goes for the difficult winning shot.
4. Arthur Ashe never betrays an inward sense of defeat.

◆ **Critical Thinking**
1. After a dazzling rise in the tennis world, Ashe's "succession of fortunate circumstances" became tragically unfortunate. Early heart disease and a tragic sequence of additional medical problems led to Ashe's untimely death.
2. Ashe's ability shows that he is a person of strong character and self-discipline.
3. Examples should demonstrate that Ashe is enigmatic, dignified, controlled, daring, and unpredictable both on the court and in real life.
4. Suggested response: As an approach to life, "going for the difficult shot when in trouble" could mean that a person should do what is necessary in difficult situations in life even if what must be

---

 Speaking and Listening Mini-Lesson

Speech
This mini-lesson supports the Speaking and Listening activity in the Idea Bank on page 598.
Introduce the Concept Have students discuss instances when calm discussions helped settle differences between people. Explore ways that Ashe's "controlled cool" behavior might have helped him deal with the tragedies of his life.
Develop Background Before students write their speeches, have them discuss ways to settle disagreements calmly, such as:

- Be willing to compromise.
- Take responsibility for your actions.
- Try to see situations from the other person's point of view.

Apply the Information Have students use this information as they write their speeches, include ample support, and deliver their speeches with conviction.

Assess the Outcome Use the Peer Assessment: Speaker/Speech page in *Alternative Assessment,* p. 110.

One-Minute Insight From Joan Didion, we learn how artist Georgia O'Keeffe fought to paint her own vision in spite of criticism from the largely male art world of her time.

◆ **Literary Focus**

❶ **Biographical and Autobiographical Writing** Ask students: Why do you suppose Didion begins this essay about Georgia O'Keeffe with a quotation? *The direct quotation by O'Keeffe gives this third-person biographical essay some of the immediacy of a first-person autobiography.*

◆ **Critical Thinking**

❷ **Interpret** Ask students: What do you think Didion means by "Style is character"? *An artist's personality and values are reflected in the style of his or her art.*

◆ **Critical Thinking**

❸ **Interpret** Have students interpret the phrase "a straight shooter." Then ask the class how this quality could make someone seem "hard." *A straight shooter tells the truth no matter what. This quality might make the person seem tactless, insensitive, or difficult to get along with.*

◆ **Critical Thinking**

❹ **Synthesize** Ask students: What do you think O'Keeffe means by "create one's own world in any of the arts"? *Students may say that an artist creates his or her own world by painting or describing it as he or she—and no one else—sees it.*

GEORGIA O'KEEFFE
Joan Didion

❶ "Where I was born and where and how I have lived is unimportant," Georgia O'Keeffe told us in the book of paintings and words published in her ninetieth year on earth. She seemed to be advising us to forget the beautiful face in the Stieglitz[1] photographs. She appeared to be dismissing the rather condescending romance that had attached to her by then, the romance of extreme good looks and advanced age and deliberate isolation. "It is what I have done with where I have been that should be of interest." I recall an August afternoon in Chicago in 1973 when I took my daughter, then seven, to see what Georgia O'Keeffe had done with where she had been. One of the vast O'Keeffe "Sky Above Clouds" canvases floated over the back stairs in the Chicago Art Institute that day, dominating what seemed to be several stories of empty light, and my daughter looked at it once, ran to the landing, and kept on looking. "Who drew it," she whispered after a while. I told her. "I need to talk to her," she said finally.

❷ My daughter was making, that day in Chicago, an entirely unconscious but quite basic assumption about people and the work they do. She was assuming that the glory she saw in the work reflected a glory in its maker, that the painting was the painter as the poem is the poet, that every choice one made alone—every word chosen or rejected, every brush stroke laid or not laid down—betrayed one's character. *Style is character.* It seemed to me that afternoon

---

1. **Stieglitz** (stēg´ lĭts): Alfred Stieglitz (1864–1946); U.S. photographer and husband of Georgia O'Keeffe.

592 ◆ *Nonfiction*

that I had rarely seen so instinctive an application of this familiar principle, and I recall being pleased not only that my daughter responded to style as character but that it was Georgia O'Keeffe's particular style to which she responded: this was a hard woman who had imposed her 192 square feet of clouds on Chicago.

"Hardness" has not been in our century a quality much admired in women, nor in the past twenty years has it even been in official favor for men. When hardness surfaces in the very old we tend to transform it into "crustiness" or eccentricity, some tonic pepperiness to be indulged at a distance. On the evidence of her work and what she has said about it, Georgia O'Keeffe is neither "crusty" nor eccentric. She is simply hard, a straight shooter, a ❸ woman clean of received wisdom and open to what she sees. This is a woman who could early on dismiss most of her contemporaries as "dreamy," and would later single out one she liked as "a very poor painter." (And then add, apparently by way of softening the judgment: "I guess he wasn't a painter at all. He ❹ had no courage and I believe that to create one's own world in any of the arts takes courage.") This is a woman who in 1939 could advise her admirers that they were missing her point, that their appreciation of her famous flowers was merely sentimental. "When I paint a red hill," she observed coolly in the catalogue for an exhibition that year, "you say it is too bad that I don't always paint flowers. A flower touches almost everyone's heart. A red hill doesn't touch everyone's heart." This is a ❺ woman who could describe the genesis of one of her most well-known paintings—the "Cow's

---

 Humanities: Art

The White Trumpet Flower, 1932, by Georgia O'Keeffe.

In this, as in many of O'Keeffe's paintings, a flower is enlarged to fill the whole canvas.

Georgia O'Keeffe was married to the famous photographer Alfred Stieglitz, who admired her personal vision of abstract design in nature.

Use these questions for discussion:
1. What do you notice about this flower that you might not notice in a real flower in nature? *Possible response: Details, such as various flower parts, are noticed in this large painted flower. These details may be too small to notice in a real flower unless one looked at it very closely.*

2. Why might it take courage to paint a picture like this one? *Possible response: It might take courage to do a painting that is so different from what is expected.*

592

The White Trumpet Flower, Georgia O'Keeffe, San Diego Museum of Art

◆ **Reading Strategy**

❺ **Find the Writer's Main Points and Support** Point out that the information about *Cow's Skull: Red, White, and Blue* supports the main point of this paragraph. Have students identify the main point and its support. *The main idea is that Georgia O'Keeffe is hard. This is supported by the artist's honest but tactless comments about other artists and her blunt comment to her admirers that they were missing the message in her work, as well as by the "derisive orneriness" behind her painting.*

▶**Critical Viewing**◀

❻ **Deduce** Students might deduce from this painting that O'Keeffe is bold, assertive, courageous, confident, and daring.

❺ Skull: Red, White and Blue" owned by the Metropolitan[2] —as an act of quite deliberate and derisive orneriness. "I thought of the city men I had been seeing in the East," she wrote. "They talked so often of writing the Great American Novel—the Great American Play—the Great American Poetry. . . . So as I was painting my cow's head on blue I thought to myself, 'I'll make it an American painting. They will not think it great with the red stripes down the sides—Red White and Blue—but they will notice it.'"

The city men. The men. They. The words crop up again and again as this astonishingly aggressive woman tells us what was on her mind when she was making her astonishingly aggressive paintings. It was those city men

---

2. **Metropolitan:** Metropolitan Museum of Art in New York City.

▲ **Critical Viewing** Georgia O'Keeffe is famous for her paintings of flowers. Notice how the white trumpet flower in this painting fills the canvas with bold lines and shapes. What can you guess about the personality of the artist from her work? [Deduce] ❻

who stood accused of sentimentalizing her flowers: "I made you take time to look at what I saw and when you took time to really notice my flower you hung all your associations with flowers on my flower and you write

◆ **Build Vocabulary**

condescending (kän′ di sen′ diŋ) *adj.*: Characterized by looking down on someone

sentimental (sen′ tə ment′ əl) *adj.*: Excessively or foolishly emotional

genesis (jen′ ə sis) *n.*: Birth; origin; beginning

Georgia O'Keeffe ◆ 593

 Cross-Curricular Connection: Social Studies

The American Southwest, O'Keeffe's home for many years and the setting of her most famous paintings, is a realm of great diversity. Woven into the fabric of the region are the threads of many cultures, which left a legacy of romance and adventure in their wake.

Ancient Native Americans built great cities that in time disappeared. Determined explorers struggled across uncharted expanses; later, soldiers clashed with Native Americans. In their turn

came trappers, prospectors, gunslingers, lawmen, cowboys—including some of the legendary figures of the Old West. Today, the Southwest blooms with settlers of a different kind, including researchers and retirees, entrepreneurs and engineers—and artists.

Have students discuss what elements of their particular region an artist might depict in his or her work.

►Critical Viewing◄

❶ Hypothesize Elicit responses such as the following: *Men may have viewed O'Keeffe's work as unfeminine because of its subject matter, as in the painting on this page, or because of the bold treatment of its subject matter, as in the painting of the white trumpet flower on page 593.*

Cultural Connection

Didion notes that "hardness has not been in our century a quality much admired in women." Ask students if they agree with this statement and why or why not. Discuss what qualities they think are admired in women in American society today; have them back up their opinions with specific examples. Stimulate discussion by asking students what people might think of a woman who is strong, clever, gentle, ambitious, shy, compassionate, tough, or aggressive.

Point out that in other cultures, the qualities most valued in a woman might be quite different from those valued in the United States. Have students select another culture and research the role of women and attitudes toward women in that culture. Try to have a broad range of societies represented. Have students report their findings to the class.

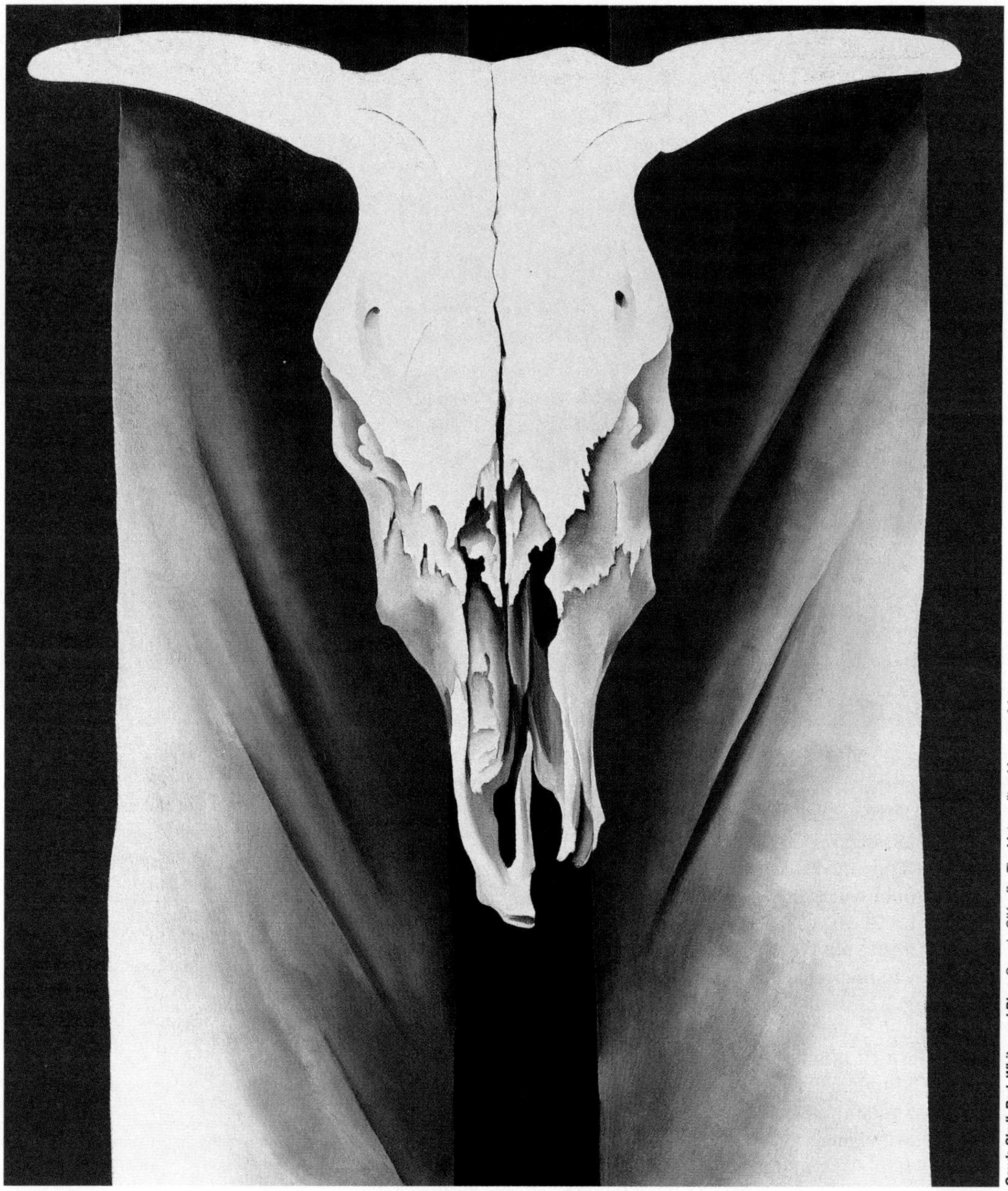

Cow's Skull: Red, White, and Blue, Georgia O'Keeffe, The Metropolitan Museum of Art

▲ **Critical Viewing** Why do you think that some critics—especially men who felt that women should adopt attitudes and behaviors traditionally thought of as feminine—found O'Keeffe's work inappropriate, disturbing, and even threatening? **[Hypothesize]**

❶

594 ◆ *Nonfiction*

 Humanities: Art

Cow's Skull: Red, White, and Blue, 1931, by Georgia O'Keeffe.

This is another of O'Keeffe's most famous paintings. For O'Keeffe, nature offered subjects that could be removed from their original context and transformed into art. Her favorite subjects were flowers and bleached bones, which she translated into larger-than-life images.

Use these questions for discussion:

1. What elements in this painting represent America? *The subject matter (a bleached cow's head found in the American Southwest); the red, white, and blue colors*

2. How is this painting both realistic and abstract? *Possible response: It has a realistic subject but the lines and colors create an abstract pattern.*

about my flower as if I think and see what you think and see—and I don't." *And I don't.* Imagine those words spoken, and the sound you hear is *don't tread on me.*[3] "The men" believed it impossible to paint New York, so Georgia O'Keeffe painted New York. "The men" didn't think much of her bright color, so she made it brighter. The men yearned toward Europe so she went to Texas, and then New Mexico. The men talked about Cézanne,[4] "long involved remarks about the 'plastic quality' of his form and color," and took one another's long involved remarks, in the view of this angelic rattlesnake in their midst, altogether too seriously. "I can paint one of those dismal-colored paintings like the men," the woman who regarded herself always as an outsider remembers thinking one day in 1922, and she did: a painting of a shed "all low-toned and dreary with the tree beside the door." She called this act of <u>rancor</u> "The Shanty" and hung it in her next show. "The men seemed to approve of it," she reported fifty-four years later, her contempt undimmed. "They seemed to think that maybe I was beginning to paint. That was my only low-toned dismal-colored painting."

◆ **Literary Focus**
❸ What does this paragraph reveal about O'Keeffe?

Some women fight and others do not. Like so many successful guerrillas in the war between the sexes, Georgia O'Keeffe seems to have been equipped early with an <u>immutable</u> sense of who she was and a fairly clear understanding that she would be required to prove it. On the surface her upbringing was conventional. She was a child on the Wisconsin prairie who played with china dolls and painted watercolors with cloudy skies because sunlight was too hard to paint and, with her brother and sisters, listened every night to her mother read stories of the Wild West, of Texas, of Kit Carson and Billy the Kid. She told adults that she wanted to be an artist and was embarrassed when they asked what kind of artist she wanted to be: she had no idea "what kind." She had no idea what artists did. She had never seen a picture that interested her, other than a pen-and-ink Maid of Athens in one of her mother's books, some Mother Goose illustrations printed on cloth, a tablet cover that showed a little girl with pink roses, and the painting of Arabs on horseback that hung in her grandmother's parlor. At thirteen, in a Dominican convent, she was mortified when the sister corrected her drawing. At Chatham Episcopal Institute in Virginia she painted lilacs and sneaked time alone to walk out to where she could see the line of the Blue Ridge Mountains on the horizon. At the Art Institute in Chicago she was shocked by the presence of live models and wanted to abandon anatomy lessons. At the Art Students League in New York one of her fellow students advised her that, since he would be a great painter and she would end up teaching painting in a girls' school, any work of hers was less important than modeling for him. Another painted over her work to show her how the Impressionists did trees. She had not before heard how the Impressionists did trees and she did not much care.

◆ **Reading Strategy**
What kind of support does Didion use in this paragraph to indicate that O'Keeffe had "an immutable sense of who she was"?

◆ **Build Vocabulary**

rancor (raŋ′ kər) *n.:* Hatred; spite

immutable (im′ myo͞ot′ ə bəl) *adj.:* Never changing

---

3. **Don't tread on me:** Motto of the first official American flag to be flown by a naval vessel, on December 3, 1775.
4. **Cézanne** (sē zän′): Paul Cézanne (1836–1906), French Impressionist and Postimpressionist painter.

Georgia O'Keeffe ◆ 595

◆ **Critical Thinking**
❷ **Draw Conclusions** Ask students: Why did O'Keeffe often do the opposite of what the art "experts" suggested she do? *She followed her own vision, rather than bend to the will of others.*

◆ **Literary Focus**
❸ **Biographical and Autobiographical Writing** Elicit responses such as the following: *This passage reveals that O'Keeffe is defiant, clever, and determined not to be influenced by others.*

◆ **Literary Focus**
❹ **Biographical and Autobiographical Writing** Elicit responses such as the following: *The support includes her determination to become an artist even though she had no idea what kind; her chagrin when the nun corrected her painting; her decision to ignore a fellow student's advice that she give up art and model for him; and her choice to ignore the Impressionists.*

Cross-Curricular Connection: Science/Art

O'Keeffe was so fascinated by the "evening star"—which is actually the planet Venus—that she created ten watercolors from her interpretation of it. Since it is the brightest planet in the sky, Venus is called the "morning star" when it appears in the East at sunrise and the "evening star" when it is visible in the West at sunset. From space probes, we have learned that Venus has a surface temperature of about 858°F and an atmosphere that is 97 percent carbon dioxide.

Invite students to track Venus in the evening and paint, draw, or sketch their own interpretation of the "evening star." Students can compare their paintings to O'Keeffe's versions of the same scene. To make it easier for students to locate Venus, point out that it is never visible more than three hours after sunset.

Idea Bank

Customizing for
Performance Levels

Following are suggestions for matching Idea Bank topics with your students' performance levels:

Less Advanced Students: 1, 7
Average Students: 2, 4, 6
More Advanced Students: 3, 5

Customizing for
Learning Modalities

Following are suggestions for matching Idea Bank topics with your students' learning modalities:

Verbal/Linguistic: 1, 3, 4, 5, 6
Logical/Mathematical: 2
Visual/Spatial: 7

Writing Mini-Lesson

Refer students to the Writing Handbook, page 962, for instruction on the writing process, and page 964 for further information on Narration.

Writer's Solution

Writing Lab CD-ROM

Have students complete the Tutorial on Narration. Follow these steps:

1. Use the Sunburst Diagram to choose a person to write about.
2. Have students draft on computer.
3. Have students use the Character Trait Word Bins to strengthen descriptions of characters.

You will need approximately 70 minutes of class time to complete these steps.

Sourcebook

Have students use Chapter 2, Narration (pp. 30–61), for additional support. The chapter includes detailed instruction on considering the purpose of a piece of writing (p. 46).

Build Your Portfolio

Idea Bank

Writing

1. **Letter of Condolence** Imagine you were alive at the time of President Kennedy's assassination. Write a letter to his widow expressing your sympathy and describing the late President's importance to the nation. **[Social Studies Link]**

2. **How-to Essay** Arthur Ashe excelled in the sport of tennis. Write a how-to essay in which you explain how to play a sport, a video game, or a board game at which you excel. Be sure to include a description of any required equipment.

3. **Essay** The subjects of these selections were all strong role models. Write a short essay in which you discuss what you can learn from the three subjects that you can apply to your own life.

Speaking and Listening

4. **News Report** Develop and present to the class a radio news report on the assassination of President Kennedy. **[Social Studies Link]**

5. **Speech** Present a speech on the advantages of practicing Arthur Ashe's "controlled cool" in daily life. Discuss how calm discussions can help settle differences. **[Social Studies Link]**

Projects

6. **Internet Exploration** Use the Internet to gather additional information about the subject of one of these selections. Present your findings to the class in an informal oral report. **[Social Studies Link; Media Link]**

7. **Museum Exhibit** Find reproductions of several of Georgia O'Keeffe's paintings. Write informational captions for each painting. Put the reproductions and the captions together to create an exhibit of O'Keeffe's work. **[Fine Art Link]**

Writing Mini-Lesson

Awards Speech

You are an official at an awards ceremony for an influential person, such as Lady Bird Johnson, Arthur Ashe, or Georgia O'Keeffe. Write a speech that introduces the award winner. To make your speech easy to follow, be sure it is coherent.

Writing Skills Focus: Coherence

A piece of writing has **coherence** when each idea flows logically out of the previous ideas. The first step in achieving coherence is to make sure that all your key points fit together and to arrange them in an order that makes sense. Then use transition words, such as *then* and *next*, to highlight the relationships among ideas. You can also repeat key words to establish clear connections among sentences or paragraphs. Notice how John McPhee links the content of one paragraph to the next by repeating an idea.

Model From the Selection

. . . She *never argued*. She was quiet, easygoing, kindhearted.

If by legacy her son *never argued*, he was also . . . .

Prewriting Select an influential person whom you admire. Then jot down the main points you'd like to make about that person.

Drafting Begin your speech with an attention-grabbing opening, such as an amusing anecdote. Then, present your main points in a logical order. You might organize them in either chronological order or order of importance.

Revising Read your speech and ask a classmate to suggest places where you can rearrange ideas or add transitions to make your speech clearer.

✓ ASSESSMENT OPTIONS

Formal Assessment, Selection Test, pp. 148–150, and Assessment Resources Software. The selection test is designed so that it can be easily customized to the performance levels of your students.
Alternative Assessment, p. 42, includes options for less advanced students, more advanced students, visual/spatial learners, intrapersonal learners, logical/mathematical learners, and musical/rhythmic learners.

PORTFOLIO ASSESSMENT

Use the following rubrics in the *Alternative Assessment* booklet to assess student writing:
Letter of Condolence: Expression Rubric, p. 87
How-to Essay: How-to/Process Explanation Rubric, p. 93
Essay: Problem-Solution Rubric, p. 94
Writing Mini-Lesson: Expression Rubric, p. 87

Writing Process Workshop

Cause-and-Effect Essay

In "Single Room, Earth View," astronaunt Sally Ride recounts viewing pollution-damaged trees from the vantage point of her orbit around Earth. In this passage, Ride is describing a cause—pollution—and its effect—damaged trees. A type of writing that explores the reasons that a particular event or situation occurred is the **cause-and-effect essay**. Write your own cause-and-effect essay on a topic of your choice. The following skills, introduced in this section's Writing Mini-Lessons, will help you write a cause-and-effect essay.

Writing Skills Focus

▶ **Use vivid adjectives** to create a clear and lively picture for readers to "see" in their minds. (See p. 564.)
▶ **Give clear explanations** of the cause and the effects. Be sure to offer reasons for the results you describe. (See p. 583.)
▶ **Create coherence** by arranging your ideas and details in a logical order. (See p. 598.)

Sally Ride uses all these skills as she explains civilization's negative effects on our environment.

MODEL FROM LITERATURE

from *Single Room, Earth View* by Sally Ride

Some of civilization's more unfortunate effects on the environment are also evident from orbit. ① Oil slicks glisten on the surface of the Persian Gulf, patches of pollution-damaged trees dot the forests of central Europe. Some cities look out of focus, and their colors muted, when viewed through a pollutant haze. ② Not surprisingly, the effects are more noticeable now than they were a decade ago. ③

① Ride begins by clearly stating the cause: civilization. She is now ready to explain the effects.

② Ride uses vivid adjectives, such as <u>pollution-damaged</u>, <u>muted</u>, and <u>pollutant</u>.

③ The essay has coherence because the ideas flow logically and the order of details makes sense.

 Cross-Curricular Connection: Social Studies

Tell students that historians and journalists often write cause-and-effect essays to describe why a certain thing is the way it is. For example, you might want to explain to them in cause-and-effect terms why sunglasses became a popular fashion item: In the 1920's, movie stars such as Rudolph Valentino and Gloria Swanson wore them to protect their eyes from the glare of the studios' arc lamps. The effect was that a fashion trend was born and people soon started wearing their sunglasses outdoors.

Develop Student Writing

Prewriting

When choosing a topic, some students may try to choose something that is too large or complex—such as the effect of fossil fuels on the ozone layer—to handle in a brief report. While such topics are worthwhile, you might want to encourage students to look closer to home for this exercise, since the idea is to learn the form of a cause-and-effect essay.

Customize for
English Language Learners

The excerpt from *Single Room, Earth View* is a good text for reviewing vivid verbs and adjectives with these students. Have students think of different words for glisten, dot, muted, pollutant, and haze. Then have students read the passage aloud using the new words.

Customize for
Less Proficient Writers

Have these students make an outline before drafting. At the top of the outline they should write the main effect they are describing. Below that they should write the main causes of that effect as well as any minor causes and effects related to the main one.

Drafting

Encourage students to write a dramatic opening paragraph to grab the reader's attention. One way to do so is to pose an intriguing question or to make a fascinating observation. After writing the opening paragraph, students should continue their essays in accord with the type of organization they have chosen. Remind students to use appropriate transition words to make their essays easy to follow.

Applying Language Skills

Coordinating and Subordinating Conjunctions
Answers

Sample responses:
1. The population grew, and the high school expanded. *or* Because the population grew, the high school expanded.
2. Our town grew, but other towns did not. *or* Although our town grew, other towns did not.

600

Applying Language Skills: Coordinating and Subordinating Conjunctions

A **coordinating conjunction** joins words or phrases:

A bridge went up, <u>and</u> more people moved to town.

A **subordinating conjunction** introduces an adverb clause:

<u>After</u> a bridge went up, more people moved to town.

Use the type of conjunction that best expresses your idea.

Practice Join each pair of sentences using a coordinating or subordinating conjunction.

1. The population grew. The high school expanded.
2. Our town grew. Other towns did not.
3. A new factory opened. More jobs were created.

Writing Application As you draft your essay, use coordinating or subordinating conjunctions to join sentences. In each case, use the type that works best for you.

Writer's Solution Connection
Writing Lab

To help you come up with a topic, use the Inspirations in the Choosing a Topic section in the tutorial on Exposition.

600 ◆ *Nonfiction*

Prewriting

Choose a Topic Choose a topic that interests you, such as changes that have occurred in your neighborhood, the impact of a new government policy, or the effects of a recent world event. Many topics may require you to do some research.

Outline Causes and Effects To help identify clearly the causes and effects you'll present in your essay, use a cluster diagram like the one shown here. Write an effect in the center circle, then write the causes in clusters around the effect.

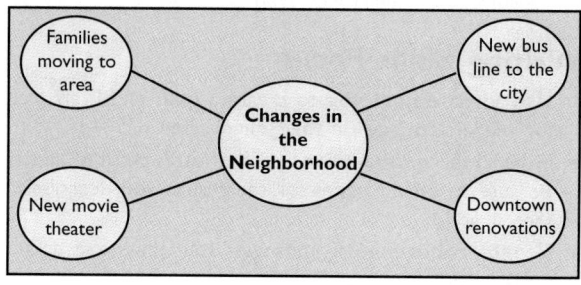

List Vivid Adjectives List adjectives you might use in your essay. Start with a general adjective, and then list vivid adjectives that will make your descriptions more precise and colorful.

General Adjective: big
Vivid Adjectives: enormous, gigantic, gargantuan

Organize Your Details Coherently Choose the best organization for your cause-and-effect essay. You might want to use chronological order, in which you arrange details according to when in time they occurred, or order of importance organization, in which you list details from most to least important (or from least to most important). Whatever organization you choose, jot down your main details on separate note cards, then arrange the cards in the proper order.

Drafting

Write a Strong Introduction Begin with an introductory paragraph that captures readers interest, highlights the importance of your topic, and touches on the main points you'll make.

Use Transitions to Show Relationships As you draft, use transition words and phrases, such as *because of* and *as a result,* to clearly indicate the causes and effects you're describing.

---

3. A new factory opened, and more jobs were created. or After a new factory opened, new jobs were created.

Writer's Solution

For additional instruction and practice, use the **Language Lab CD-ROM** lesson on Fragments and Run-On Sentences and the practice in the *Writer's Solution Grammar Practice Book* (p. 23).

Answers
1. If one business does well, another does well, too.

2. Because more drivers come here, the roads are paved. or Because more drivers came here, the roads were paved.
3. After a town expands it needs more services.
4. As elevators were installed, buildings grew.

Writer's Solution

For additional instruction and practice, use the **Language Lab CD-ROM** lesson Verb Tense and practice in the *Writer's Solution Grammar Practice Book* (p. 69)

Revising

Use a Checklist Go back to the Writing Skills Focus on the first page of the lesson, and use the items as a checklist to evaluate and revise your cause-and-effect essay.

▶ Have I used vivid adjectives rather than general ones?
Look over your draft, and identify all the adjectives. If any seem too general, replace them with more specific, lively ones.

▶ Have I clearly explained each cause and effect?
Have a peer review your essay and jot down points he or she does not understand. Then find a way to explain those ideas more clearly.

▶ Does my essay have coherence?
Reread your draft to check how smoothly the ideas flow. Is there a way to rearrange your details to improve your presentation?

REVISION MODEL

①were invented,   ②booming
After elevators, many small towns grew to big cities.
③
Before the age of elevators, the U.S. was a country made

up mainly of small towns.

① The writer explains the cause more clearly.
② The writer uses a more vivid adjective.
③ The writer rearranges details to make his ideas more coherent.

Work With a Peer Reviewer After revising your own work, have a classmate review your essay, looking for any missing details and any places where you can add transitions to make relationships clearer.

Publishing

▶ **Classroom** Share your cause-and-effect essay with your classmates.

▶ **Internet** Post your essay on an electronic bulletin board. Consult with an experienced Internet user if you're unsure about how to publish on-line.

APPLYING LANGUAGE SKILLS: Avoiding Shifts in Tense

As you write, don't shift from past tense to present tense or from present tense to past tense.

Incorrect: The bridge went up, so the town grows.

Correct: The bridge went up, so the town grew.

Practice On your paper, rewrite the sentences so that the verb tense does not shift.

1. If one business does well, another did well, too.
2. Because more drivers came here, roads are paved.
3. After a town expands, it needed more services.
4. As elevators were installed, buildings grow.

Writing Application As you revise your essay, check for shifts in the verb tense. If shifts occur, make the necessary changes.

Writer's Solution Connection Writing Lab

For more instruction on proofreading and revision, work through the Revision section of the tutorial on Exposition.

Revising

After revising their work, have students use a proofreading checklist to check for errors in spelling, grammar, punctuation, and capitalization. Make sure they pay special attention to coordinating and subordinating conjunctions to avoid run-on sentences, and the proper verb tenses.

Writer's Solution

Writing Lab CD-ROM
The Revision Checker for Language Variety identifies any words used more than once and highlights them. Students will be able to see if they have overused words and thus have the opportunity to replace them with appropriate synonyms.

Publishing

If students do not wish to share what they've written with other classmates, they should be encouraged to save their work for possible incorporation into a larger piece of writing at a later time.

Reinforce and Extend

Review the Writing Guidelines
After students have completed their papers, review the characteristics of a cause-and-effect essay. Encourage students to come up with additional criteria for an interesting cause-and-effect essay based on what they learned through completing the assignment.

Connect to Literature Unit 5 ("Visions of the Future") includes an example of a cause-and-effect essay: the excerpt from Rachel Carson's *Silent Spring* (p. 430).

✓ ASSESSMENT

PORTFOLIO ASSESSMENT		4	3	2	1
Use the rubric on Description in **Alternative Assessment** (p. 90) to assess students' writing. Add these criteria to customize the rubric to this assignment.	**Coordination and Subordination**	There are no run-on sentences. Frequent use of coordinating and subordinating conjunctions makes for varied sentence structure.	Coordination and subordination are used well but not perfectly. No egregious grammatical errors.	Coordination and subordination are used infrequently. More than a few run-on sentences.	No use of coordinating or subordinating conjunctions. Frequent run-on sentences and comma splices.
	Shifts in Verb Tense	All verbs are used correctly.	One or two shifts in verb tense.	Noticeable shifts in verb tense, though the essay has other redeeming factors.	Frequent, inexplicable shifts in tense, rendering the essay almost unreadable.

601

Students will be familiar with charts from their social studies and science textbooks, as well as from magazines and newspaper articles, even the sides of cereal boxes. Point out that reading charts is a valuable skill that they will often be called upon to use in real-world situations.

Customize for
Less Proficient Readers
Tell these students that a chart such as this one has a purpose—in this case, to show the average recommended caloric intake. Walk them through the chart step by step until they are confident enough to be able to draw conclusions from the information given.

Apply the Strategy

Have students study the chart until it is clear that they all understand its concept. Answer any lingering questions they may have, such as why the recommended caloric intake might be different for people in tropical or arctic climates.

Answers
1. The calorie allowance for a fourteen-year-old boy is 2,700 calories, for a fourteen-year-old girl, 2,200 calories.
2. The difference in calorie allowance between males and females over fifty-one years old is the 600 additional calories that males can intake.
3. The age range nineteen to fifty-one+ is the same for males, fifteen to fifty-one+ the same for females.
4. As a person grows older the recommended calorie allowance goes down.

Reading Charts | Real-World Reading Skills Workshop

Strategies for Success
There may be times when you need to get information from a chart. You might have to check the times on a bus schedule, for example, or find a chemical element on the periodic table. Charts are also included in many nonfiction articles. Get the most from charts by learning how to read them correctly.

Study the Chart When you first look at a chart, note how it is organized. The information usually appears in columns. Notice how each column is labeled. Do the columns run vertically? Horizontally? Both ways? What does each column show?

Know What You Want to Find A chart may offer more information than you need. In order to read it successfully, you must know exactly what you want to find. For example, a bus schedule might list departure and arrival times for many stations. Do you want to know when a bus will leave or when it will arrive? Which station do you need?

Read the Small Print Some charts contain special symbols that indicate footnotes at the bottom of the chart. Read the footnotes carefully. They may help clarify information on the chart.

Apply the Strategy
Use the calorie chart to answer these questions. Remember to study the chart carefully before answering.
1. What is the calorie allowance for a 14-year-old boy? For a 14-year-old girl?
2. What is the difference in calorie allowance for males and females more than 51 years old?
3. Which age ranges show the same weights for males? For females?
4. What happens to the recommended calorie allowance as a person grows older?

RECOMMENDED DAILY CALORIE ALLOWANCES*

	Age	Average Weight**	Calories
Males	11–14	99	2,700
	15–18	145	2,800
	19–22	154	2,900
	23–50	154	2,700
	51+	154	2,400
Females	11–14	101	2,200
	15–18	120	2,100
	19–22	120	2,100
	23–50	120	2,000
	51+	120	1,800

* for normally active people in temperate climates
** in pounds

✔ Here are other situations in which reading a chart is helpful:
► Finding the mileage between two cities
► Finding the populations of each of the fifty states
► Learning about former presidents
► Discovering the nutritional values of foods

PART 2

Visual Essays and Workplace Writing

Busy Office Flowchart, Celia Johnson/Stock Illustration Source, Inc.

In this section, students will encounter a visual essay, as well as different types of workplace writing. The visual essay "Understanding Comics" takes an in-depth look at a popular medium—in comic-strip format. "Earhart Redux" is the transcript of a radio interview with a modern-day Amelia Earhart. Students will also read a book review and jacket copy from a book on a high-school women's basketball team. The unit ends with an example of an Internet home page on Edgar Allan Poe.

Customize for
Varying Student Needs
When assigning the selections in this section to your students, keep in mind the following factors:

"Understanding Comics"
• Unique format will appeal to students who like reading comics
• Sophisticated concepts presented in an engaging way

"Earhart Redux"
• Inclusion of sound effects makes radio transcript engaging to students
• Can be read aloud in class

"In These Girls, Hope Is a Muscle"
• High-interest subject
• Examples of workplace writing that students are likely to encounter in daily life

"Edgar Allan Poe"
• Some students may require additional information about how the Internet works
• Technology connection will appeal to many students

Visual Essays and Workplace Writing ♦ 603

Humanities: Art

Busy Office Flowchart by Celia Johnson.
Explain that a flowchart is a diagram that shows the way work is supposed to travel in an office: who does what, who supervises or answers to whom. Most actual flowcharts are systems of lines and arrows, labeled with people's names and titles. This cartoonlike flowchart treats humans, office equipment, words, numbers, and symbols all in the same simplified, abstract style, using the same primary colors, and, above all,

offered up with a humorous, tongue-in-cheek, slightly antic, slightly frantic attitude. Call students' attention to the way the computers and phones seem as frazzled as the people, as they all struggle to make the arrow of productivity go up.

Help students link this art to the focus of Part 2 ("Visual Essays and Workplace Writing") by answering these questions:
1. A visual essay expresses ideas through images as well as through words. What

ideas about work does this artwork express, and how? *Through its jagged lines, it suggests that the workplace is a harried, frantic place where everyone scrambles.*
2. What humorous details can you point to in this work? *Examples include the man with a pointer braying out the sales graph, the noisy or sweating office equipment; the numbers that seem to pester everyone.*

OBJECTIVES

1. To read, comprehend, and interpret a visual essay
2. To relate a visual essay to students' personal experience
3. To use visuals as a key to meaning
4. To identify the characteristics of a visual essay
5. To build vocabulary in context and learn the word root -stat-
6. To develop skill in punctuating introductory words
7. To write a visual essay appropriate to the knowledge level of the audience
8. To respond to the work through writing, speaking and listening, and projects

SKILLS INSTRUCTION

Vocabulary:
Word Roots: -stat-

Grammar:
Punctuation of Introductory Words

Reading Strategy:
Use Visuals as a Key to Meaning

Literary Focus:
Visual Essay

Writing:
Knowledge Level of Audience

Speaking and Listening:
Skit (teacher edition)

PORTFOLIO OPPORTUNITIES

Writing: Letter to the Author; Definition; Essay on Humor
Writing Mini-Lesson: Visual Essay
Speaking and Listening: Skit; Panel Discussion
Projects: Comic Strip; Internet Research Report

More About the Author
Scott McCloud is a poet as well as a comic-strip artist. Like his book *Understanding Comics*, his poetry combines humor, seriousness, and autobiographical detail.

Guide for Reading

Scott McCloud (1960–   )

Like many of us, Scott McCloud had a childhood passion for comics. For McCloud, however, this passion wasn't a passing phase.

McCloud has developed his passion for comics into a successful career.

Beginnings Scott McCloud originally came from Massachusetts and now lives in California. He started drawing comics at the age of twelve and, after graduating with high honors from Syracuse University in 1982, he plunged into what quickly became a very successful career as a cartoonist. His award-winning comic book series *Zot!*, published when he was just twenty-five, uses robots and teleportation machines to tell the story of a teenager seeking the "Doorway at the Edge of the Universe." This work was followed by *Destroy!* which parodies superhero comics.

Explaining His Art Having established himself as a successful comic book writer, McCloud went on to produce a book, *Understanding Comics: The Invisible Art,* in which he combines words and pictures to explain how comics work, how they affect readers, the different forms they can take, and, above all, why he loves them and has made them his life's work. The book has won wide critical acclaim. Garry Trudeau, the creator of *Doonesbury,* said that McCloud's book "shows us how the mind processes [comics] . . . and how words combine with pictures to work their singular magic."

◆ Build Vocabulary

WORD ROOTS: -stat-

In his visual essay, Scott McCloud uses the word *static* (see p. 612) to describe each frame of a comic strip. The word *static* contains the Latin root -stat-, which means "to stand." Knowing this root, you could easily guess that *static* refers to something that stands unchanging. What other words can you think of that contain the root -stat-?

WORD BANK

As you read the comic, you will encounter the words on this list. Note the definitions so that you'll be familiar with the words when you come to them.

obsessed (əb sest´) *v.*: Greatly preoccupied with (p. 607)
aesthetic (es thet´ ik) *adj.*: Relating to the appreciation of beauty (p. 609)
arbitrary (är´ bə trer´ ē) *adj.*: Not fixed by rules but left to one's judgment (p. 612)

◆ Build Grammar Skills

PUNCTUATION OF INTRODUCTORY WORDS

Because Scott McCloud's selection takes the form of a comic strip, the reader must leapfrog from each individual frame (box containing a picture and words) to the next. To make the hops and landings smoother, McCloud uses **introductory words and phrases** at the beginning of many of the frames. Look at these examples:

Frame 5: *Soon,* I was hooked.
Frame 6: *In less than a year,* I became totally obsessed with comics!

As these examples illustrate, a comma is placed after an introductory word or phrase to set it off from the rest of a sentence. Look for other examples of introductory words and phrases as you read the selection.

604 ◆ Nonfiction

Prentice Hall Literature Program Resources

REINFORCE / RETEACH / EXTEND

Selection Support Pages
Build Vocabulary: Word Roots: -stat-, p. 176
Build Grammar Skills: Punctuation of Introductory Words, p. 177
Reading Strategy: Use Visuals as a Key to Meaning, p. 178
Literary Focus: Visual Essay, p. 179

Strategies for Diverse Student Needs, p. 43

Beyond Literature
Humanities Connection: Comic Art, p. 43

Formal Assessment Selection Test, pp. 151–153, Assessment Resources Software

Alternative Assessment, p. 43

Resource Pro CD-ROM
"Understanding Comics"—includes all resource material and customizable lesson plan

Listening to Literature Audiocassettes
"Understanding Comics"

Understanding Comics

◆ Literature and Your Life

CONNECT YOUR EXPERIENCE

What comes to mind when you think of comics? If you're like most people, you probably think of superheroes, humorous animal characters, or amusing people with exaggerated facial features. As you read this selection, however, you'll discover that comics have a much broader definition than you might expect.

Journal Writing Jot down your definition of the term *comics*. Refer to your definition again after you read McCloud's essay.

THEMATIC FOCUS: OUT OF THE ORDINARY

When people need a laugh, they often turn to the comic section of a newspaper. What is it that makes comics humorous? Is it the out-of-the-ordinary characters and situations? The words? The images? Or a combination?

◆ Background for Understanding

HUMANITIES

Comic strips began appearing in American newspapers in the late 1800's. One of the early strips, which featured a character called the Yellow Kid and was published in a New York newspaper, became so popular that the sales of the newspaper increased. As a result, other papers began to run comic strips to boost their own circulation.

Comic books were first introduced in the 1930's. One of the most popular early comic book series, *Superman,* first appeared in 1938 and has remained popular to this day. In recent years, comic books have begun addressing more sophisticated themes and the popularity of comic books has increased dramatically among adults.

◆ Literary Focus

VISUAL ESSAY

If someone read this selection aloud to you, you might get the gist of its ideas, but you would miss out on the author's unique approach, not to mention the fun of seeing the work on the page. That's because the selection is a **visual essay,** an exploration of a topic that conveys its ideas through visual elements as well as language. Like a standard essay, a visual essay presents an author's views of a single topic. Unlike other essays, however, much of the meaning in a visual essay is conveyed through illustrations or photographs.

◆ Reading Strategy

USE VISUALS AS A KEY TO MEANING

Visual essays, newspaper and magazine articles, manuals—much of the nonfiction that we read today is accompanied by illustrations or photographs. When you read these types of pieces, you can **use the visuals as a key to meaning** by looking carefully at each illustration or photograph and thinking about how it reinforces or adds to what is presented in the written text. In the following piece by Scott McCloud, you'll discover that the visuals play as important a role in conveying meaning as the words do. Some of the pictures add humor to apparently straightforward statements. Other pictures add details that it would take a great number of words to present. In still other cases, the pictures signal flashbacks in time or the presentation of a fantasy.

As you read, think about how each of the pictures reinforces or extends the words that McCloud presents.

Guide for Reading ◆ 605

Interest Grabber Ask students how they would respond to the statement that comics are "bright, colorful magazines filled with bad art, stupid stories and guys in tights." Tell students that this definition expresses author Scott McCloud's view of comics *before* he became hooked on them. Now, he is a successful creator of comics himself, and in *Understanding Comics*, he tells what he really thinks makes comic books tick. Ask students to name comics that fit the "guys in tights" description and ones that don't. Then have students suggest qualities that both kinds of comics have in common.

Customize for
Less Proficient Readers
Guide students to read each panel in three steps: first looking at the picture, then reading the words, then putting picture and words together.

Customize for
More Advanced Students
Urge students, as they read, to log or note informally the visual devices McCloud uses to add humor and clarity. After reading, discuss the idea that McCloud's visuals and words support one another perfectly, thus *showing* the value of the comics medium in a way that a prose essay could only *tell* about.

Customize for
English Language Learners
Ask students to read single panels aloud. Have them use visual clues such as boldface, italics, and exclamation marks to comprehend tone. Help English language learners with idioms such as "I was hooked," and difficult words and phrases such as "sequential art."

Customize for
Visual/Spatial Learners
Encourage students to point out pictorial details, such as the faces on the globe on page 608, that help them understand the selection.

Preparing for Standardized Tests

Reading and Vocabulary After students complete the exercise on page 614, give students additional -stat- words to define, such as *status*, *statute*, and *stature*. Using word roots to determine word meanings can help improve students' performance on the verbal sections of standardized tests. The Build Vocabulary lesson for this selection focuses on the Latin root -*stat*-. For additional practice, use the Build Vocabulary page in **Selection Support,** p. 176.

Grammar and Language For students to do well on the essay portions of standardized tests, they must use punctuation correctly. The Build Grammar Skills lesson for this selection focuses on punctuating introductory words. Do the exercise on page 614 with students. If students clearly understand the skill, you might have them correct sentences with interrupters in various locations, such as:

"I believe, *as I've said before,* that comics are enjoyable to read."

For additional practice, use the Build Grammar Skills page on Punctuating Introductory Words, p. 177, in **Selection Support.**

Develop Understanding

One-Minute Insight A comic that defines comics represents an ideal match between form and content: It uses both words and pictures to explain an art form that uses words and pictures. Students will acquire a deeper understanding of this medium by paying attention not only to what McCloud says, but to how he says it. His pictures add humor, graphically illustrate concepts, and heighten the interest of the essay by inserting unexpected, quirky, comic-style touches that illustrate what he is explaining.

Listening to Literature Audiocassettes You might have students do a first reading while listening to the audiocassette, in order to catch the "feel" of this humorous but instructive visual essay; then, have them reread at their own pace, slowing down at difficult spots for better comprehension.

❶ Clarification Begin by making sure students understand the basic conventions of comics, such as speech balloons and panel sequence. Dialogue is enclosed in speech balloons, with a balloon pointer leading to the speaker. Unspoken thoughts are enclosed in thought balloons, which are cloud-shaped. Panel sequence is usually from left to right and top to bottom, as with print, but it can vary inventively as on pages 608 and 609.

Comprehension Check ☑

❷ What was McCloud's attitude toward comics when he was a child? *He looked down on them.*

Comprehension Check ☑

❸ Who is the boy reading the comic in the last panel on this page? *The boy is McCloud as a child, having just discovered the joy of comics.*

excerpt from
UNDERSTANDING COMICS
Scott McCloud

606 ◆ Nonfiction

 Block Scheduling Strategies

Consider these suggestions to take advantage of extended class time:

• To help build prior knowledge, have students complete the journal activity in Literature and Your Life (p. 605) and relate their definitions to specific comics, such as the ones they named in the Interest Grabber activity.

• Discuss with students the reading strategy on page 605. Stress the primary importance of visuals in comics, and ask students to compare the relative importance of visuals in other print media, such as newspapers and magazines.

• Students can respond to the "Evaluate" and "Apply" Critical Thinking questions on page 614 in small groups.

• Students can work in pairs on the Comic Strip project on page 615. One student could draw the pictures while the other writes the words.

• Encourage students to show the class examples of comics they feel Scott McCloud would appreciate as fine examples of this art form.

606

Understanding Comics ◆ 607

◆ **Critical Thinking**

❹ Interpret Ask students what the phrase *hidden power* means to them. *The phrase might mean that a person or thing has potential that has not yet been fulfilled.*

◆ *Literature and Your Life*

❺ Discuss with students the influence of peer pressure on young people to conform in various ways, such as in mode of dress or, as in the case of this frame, adherence to an opinion. Ask students in what ways they can express disagreement with a peer while at the same time respecting the peer's right to his or her own way of thinking.

◆ *Literature and Your Life*

❻ Ask students to discuss briefly whether they, and people who have influenced them, look upon comics as "crude, poorly-drawn, semiliterate, cheap, disposable kiddie fare," and whether they feel that this characterization is justified in the case of *Understanding Comics*.

◆ **Literary Focus**

❼ Visual Essay Ask students how the bottom three panels show visually the same ideas they express in words. *When McCloud talks about narrowness, he is shown in a narrow, confined space; when he talks about limitless potential and about a journey, he shows himself against the background of the limitless universe.*

Customize for
English Language Learners
Ask students to guess the meaning of *comic book* as a modifier in the sentence "Don't gimme that comic book talk." *Simple-minded, crude, childish.* Point out that *gimme* is a nonstandard way of spelling and pronouncing *give me.*

Cross-Curricular Connection: Social Studies

Comics in the United States span the history of the twentieth century, and allusions to current or historical events can often be found in them. The Depression of the 1930's was often commented upon in the comic strip *Little Orphan Annie*; World War II saw numerous action heroes such as Captain America and Wonder Woman enter the fight on behalf of the Allies; the Cold War and the Vietnam War were often alluded to in *Pogo*

and other strips. A few comics, such as Gary Trudeau's *Doonesbury* newspaper strip and Art Spiegelman's *Maus* books, have been primarily about history or current events.

Ask students to find references to historical events in contemporary comics and in old comics that can be found in stores or in back issues of newspapers. Invite students to analyze the comic artists' views on the issues mentioned.

607

◆ Reading Strategy

① Use Visuals as a Key to Meaning Ask students to state the order in which they would read the four panels on this page. *Read first the large left-hand panel containing the globe, then the three right-hand panels from top to bottom.*

◆ Literary Focus

② Visual Essay Ask students how the picture of a globe helps express McCloud's point about the world of comics. *It graphically shows comics as a world; its large size makes the point that comics are a "huge" world; the individual pictures on the globe illustrate many different comic types and comic characters.*

Comprehension Check ☑

③ According to McCloud, what is the difference between the word *comic* and the words *comic strip* or *comic book*? *Comic refers to the medium of comics in general; comic strips and comic books are specific forms in which comics can be found.*

◆ Literary Focus

④ Visual Essay Invite students to find humorous visual touches that McCloud adds on this page. *Humorous visual touches include familiar faces on the globe; the fictitious comic Generic Guy in the third panel; the parody of comic-style emphasis in the lettering of the question in this last panel.*

Customize for
Visual/Spatial Learners
These students might enjoy finding on the globe as many recognizable characters from comics as they can. *Among the many characters drawn are Batman, Spiderman, Popeye, and Dick Tracy.*

608 ◆ *Nonfiction*

608

Beyond the Classroom

Career Connection
Comics—A Serious Career Scott McCloud has made a career as an independent comic artist. But creating comics is often a cooperative task: One person may invent a story idea, another might write dialogue, another might ink the drawings, and a fourth might add color. Publishers of comics employ story editors, copy editors, art directors, and people in various business positions. Invite students to look at the mastheads of their favorite comics to learn what occupations exist in this field.

Community Connection
Definitions, Definitions! Scott McCloud gives a definition of comics in *Understanding Comics.* Writers, teachers, lecturers, coaches, and tour guides are among the kinds of people who spend much of their time explaining or defining concepts to others. Invite students to brainstorm for aspects of their community that outsiders might wish to have defined or explained: for instance, ethnicity, zoning, local traditions, or politics. Invite students to create such an explanation in the form of a comic.

© and ™ 1994 Scott McCloud

Understanding Comics ◆ 609

---

❺
❻

◆ Reading Strategy

❺ Use Visuals as a Key to Meaning The sequence of panels on this page is challenging. Call attention to the arrows that lead from panel to panel as guides. Reassure students that they can move back and forth from panel to panel along several paths to enhance their understanding, just as when reading an on-line text!

◆ Build Grammar Skills

❻ Punctuating Introductory Words Point out the word *however* in the first frame. Ask students why it is followed by a comma. *It is an introductory word that makes the "hop" from the previous balloon to this one smoother.*

Customize for
Visual Learners
Invite students to describe what is unusual about the appearance of the three arrows leading from the first frame. *McCloud's face is in the arrows.* Ask them what this odd feature conveys. *It shows that he is the narrator, the one helping us follow the sequence of frames.*

Customize for
Less Proficient Readers
Have students identify the five objects that are shown in the vertical rows of pictures. *Shown are a man wearing a stovepipe hat, the sun, a pistol going off, a clock, an eye.* Then ask them to state what each object is doing in the paired sequence of pictures. *The man tips the hat, the sun sets, the gun causes a woman to scream, the clock's hands move forward, the eye blinks.*

Customize for
More Advanced Students
Ask students to explain what is meant by the difference between the form of a work of art and its content. *Form refers to the structure of a work or the category to which it belongs: It might be a novel, a movie, a comic, etc. Content refers to what the work contains or says.*

Cross-Curricular Connection: Art

Are comics art? Decades ago, the immediate answer might have been a resounding "No!" However, in the 1960's, Pop artists began to use the subjects and materials of mass culture in artworks that were collected in museums and galleries. Some of them, especially American painter Roy Lichtenstein (1923–1997), used greatly enlarged comic images as parody elements. Narrowing the popular-serious gap from the other direction, museums and galleries in recent years have sometimes exhibited cells (original drawings of single frames) from animated films, similar in appearance to, and often based upon, comics.

Invite students to search for comic-style Pop Art images in books of contemporary American art. Then invite them to discuss the similarities and differences they find between these paintings and "real" comics. Some differences are the size of the images, the presence or absence of sequencing, storytelling, and identifiable characters. The major difference may be a matter of genre label and price!

❶ **Visual Essay** Ask students how McCloud shows visually the difference between form and content. *He shows form as a container, content as the liquid inside it.*

❷ **Clarification** Explain to students that comics, perhaps more than any other print medium, utilize onomatopoeia, or the use of words that imitate sounds. Point out that all of the words in frames three, four, and five are examples of onomatopoeic words. Ask students to pronounce the words and to come up with more examples of onomatopoeic words of their own.

♦ **Critical Thinking**

❸ **Interpret** Ask students whether they are familiar with the adage "Don't mistake the message for the messenger." Ask volunteers to paraphrase it. *Possible paraphrase: We should pay attention to the contents of a message and not be prejudiced by who delivers it to us or in what form it comes to us.*

♦ **Build Grammar Skills**

❹ **Punctuating Introductory Words** Invite students to point out a place in the bottom left-hand panel where an introductory phrase should have been punctuated. *"At one time or another" should theoretically be followed by a comma.* Point out that the omission is one example of comics' being an informal medium.

♦ **Critical Thinking**

❺ **Make Judgments** Ask students whether they agree with McCloud that comics deserve critical attention. *Accept reasonable responses; the fact that McCloud has convincingly given critical attention to comic books may in itself imply a yes answer.*

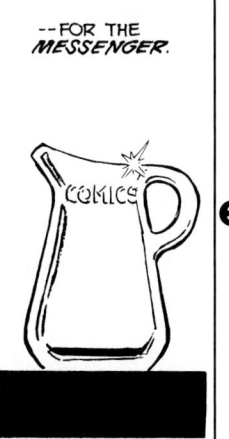

610 ♦ *Nonfiction*

◆ Speaking and Listening Mini-Lesson

Skit

This mini-lesson supports the Speaking and Listening activity in the Idea Bank on page 615.

Introduce the Concept Remind students that a skit is an informal, brief, often humorous presentation. Brainstorm for ways in which skits are similar to, and different from, comics. *Both comics and skits deal with similar subject matter, but skits contain actual people performing on stage.*

Develop Background First, ask students to name movies that have already used comic heroes. *Superman and Batman movies are examples.* Then divide students into groups and have each group decide on one comic to turn into a movie skit. As their next step, have them resolve the following issues:

• What roles need to be filled?
• Which student will play which role?
• What scene shall be acted out?

Apply the Information Have students rehearse their skits at least twice. Point out during rehearsal that skits may contain improvisation. Then have students perform their skits.

Assess the Outcome Have groups observe others' skits and give feedback on the effectiveness of the performance. Evaluate each skit on preparedness, use of action and gestures, clarity of speaking, and entertainment quality.

© and ™ 1994 Scott McCloud

Understanding Comics ◆ 611

Comprehension Check ☑

❻ What does the phrase *sequential art* mean? *Art consisting of a set of images placed one after another is called sequential art.*

❼ Clarification Ask, "Who is saying, 'There are a lot of different kinds of art'"? *A person in the audience, voicing a possible objection to something McCloud has just said.* Point out that by showing an audience, McCloud is putting his readers into his work, and is inviting them to exchange ideas.

❽ Clarification Be sure students know the meaning of the word *juxtaposed*: "Placed side by side"—as are the frames of comics.

Customize for
Less Proficient Readers
Remind students to read the placards that McCloud holds up. They show the stages in his developing definition of comics. First the placard reads, *Sequential Art*; then it reads, *Sequential Visual Art*, keeping nonvisual arts (literature, music) out of the definition. Encourage students to keep following the phrase on the placard as it changes.

Customize for
More Advanced Students
Ask students to think about the phrase "Space does for comics what time does for film." Ask a volunteer to restate the sentence as an analogy. *Space : comics :: time : film.* Then challenge students to explain McCloud's idea in their own words. *Both film and comics consist of sequences of pictures. In comics, one panel follows another on a page—in space. In film, one frame follows another, in the same space on the projection, in time. (The time intervals of motion-picture film are twenty-four frames per second.)*

  Cross-Curricular Connection: Art

Comic art has a style all its own, which has developed over more than a century. It has a set of iconic symbols all its own, as well, which help make the actions in comics clearly recognizable to readers. For example, a character running fast is shown as having many blurred feet; a character having an idea has a light bulb over his or her head. Comic artists have a specialized vocabulary to describe these symbols. For example, the blurred feet are *blurgits*; the light bulb inside a thought balloon turns it into an *idea balloon*; lines of vertical hatching are *vites* and horizontal ones are *hites*; squiggly lines that show heat are *solrads*, and wavy lines that show aromas are *waftaroms*. The symbols as a group are called *symbolia*.

Encourage students to find many different kinds of symbolia in the comics available to them, and to state what each one represents. (Source for symbolia names: David Fisher & Reginald Bragonier, Jr., *What's What: A Visual Glossary of the Physical World,* Hammond, Inc., 1981 edition, pp. 374–375.)

612 ◆ *Nonfiction*

612

③

© and ™ 1994 Scott McCloud

The complete **Understanding Comics** is 215 pages in 9 chapters and examines all aspects of comics. The above excerpt is from Chapter One.

④

Guide for Responding

◆ *Literature and Your Life*

Reader's Response Did you enjoy this selection? Why or why not?

Thematic Focus What did you find most humorous about the selection? Why?

Journal Writing Look back at the definition of comics you wrote before you read the selection. Note whether or not the selection has in any way changed your definition.

☑ Check Your Comprehension

1. When and how did McCloud become hooked on comics?
2. Why does McCloud feel that people have failed to understand comics?
3. How does McCloud ultimately define comics?

Understanding Comics ◆ 613

 Beyond the Selection

FURTHER READING

Other Works by Scott McCloud
Zot!
Destroy!

Other Sophisticated Comics
Krazy Kat, George Herriman
Maus, Art Spiegelman
Bloom County, Berkeley Breathed
For Better or for Worse, Lynn Johnston

INTERNET

You and your students may find additional information about Scott McCloud on the Internet. We suggest the following site. Please be aware, however, that the site may have changed from the time we published this information.

For poetry by McCloud, go to **http://www. dstory.com/story/McCloud/McCloud.htm**

We *strongly recommend* that you preview the site before you send students to it.

◆ **Literary Focus**

❸ **Visual Essay** Ask students to identify the humorous touches McCloud inserts as he is approaching the completion of his definition. *Someone in the audience asks about Batman and X-Men; someone else asks, "Who let him in?"* Ask what the serious point of this humorous moment is. *Comics are not just about super-heroes—and McCloud's audience should know it!*

◆ **Critical Thinking**

❹ **Identify Main Idea** Ask students how they can recognize McCloud's final definition of comics through its visual form. *It is printed as a dictionary entry and highlighted.* You might ask students to review the changes in the definition from its earliest form, "sequential art," to its final form, and to state which form they prefer or find most meaningful.

Reinforce and Extend

Answers

◆ *Literature and Your Life*

Reader's Response Some students will have enjoyed McCloud's light-hearted, clever approach; others might feel that the selection further supports the notion that comics should not be considered serious literature.

Thematic Focus Sample responses: The interaction McCloud has with his audience; the small jokes he inserts as asides, such as the "Generic Man" comic book.

☑ **Check Your Comprehension**

1. McCloud was hooked when, in eighth grade, a friend lent him his comic books to read.
2. McCloud admits that people justifiably associate comics with "crude, poorly-drawn, semiliterate, cheap, disposable, kiddie fare"— not the sort of art form that people tend to take seriously or even try to understand.
3. He defines comics as "juxtaposed pictorial and other images in deliberate sequence."

◆ Critical Thinking

1. Sample response: Most people associate comics with childhood or simple entertainment and such associations might lead to narrow definitions.
2. In this case, the message is the simple, often silly content of comics, which is the messenger. The messenger can deliver deeper, more complex messages.
3. Sample responses: Yes, in formal terms McCloud made a convincing case that the comics medium should be defined apart from its subject matter; no, the very term *comics* implies humorous or entertaining content.
4. Sample response: The "hidden power" is the ability to make a serious point in an entertaining way.
5. Sample responses: Yes, he's shown that comics is an equally valid, potentially highly complex art form; no, in failing to address the issue of content, McCloud has not supported the contention that the medium has produced great art on a par with other media.
6. Answers can include certain sports, particular hobbies, and the like.

◆ Reading Strategy

1. Sample responses: McCloud's depiction of his youthful attempts to explain his feeling about comics; the cartoon character who asks a question; the bottle/bad-tasting drink visual analogy for "Never mistake the message for the messenger."
2. Sample response: The globe showing the history and variety of comics and the presentation of the film-comics analogy make the meaning easier to understand.

◆ Literary Focus

1. The main idea is that the reader should be open to a wider definition of comics. This serious idea is effectively presented in what looks like standard comic-book form, showing the versatility of the medium.
2. If the words were deleted, we would lose the sense of many of the panels; if the pictures were deleted, the author would not have proven his point as effectively.

614

Guide for Responding (continued)

◆ Critical Thinking

INTERPRET
1. Why do you think people tend to have a narrow definition of comics? **[Infer]**
2. What does McCloud mean by the terms *message* and *messenger* when he says, "Never mistake the message for the messenger"? **[Analyze]**
3. McCloud's final definition of "comics" does not include anything about being humorous or entertaining the reader. Do you accept his definition? Why or why not? **[Make a Judgment]**
4. What do you think the "hidden power" of comics might be? **[Speculate]**

EVALUATE
5. Do you think McCloud is justified in comparing comics to art forms such as film, music, and theater? Why or why not? **[Make a Judgment]**

APPLY
6. What activities do you enjoy that you would define differently or more broadly than other people might? Explain. **[Apply]**

◆ Reading Strategy

USE VISUALS AS A KEY TO MEANING
To fully understand and appreciate McCloud's piece, it is important to **use the visuals as a key to the meaning** by considering how the illustrations reinforce and enhance the words.
1. Find three places in which the illustrations add humor to text that is straightforward and serious. Explain each example.
2. Find two illustrations that add meaning to McCloud's definition of a comic. Explain.

◆ Literary Focus

VISUAL ESSAY
McCloud's piece is a **visual essay**—a piece of nonfiction in which a writer combines words and visuals to communicate his or her ideas on a topic.
1. What is the main idea of this piece? How do both the visuals and images convey this idea?
2. Why would the selection lose its impact if either the words or the visuals were eliminated?

◆ Build Vocabulary

USING THE WORD ROOT -stat-
Each of the following words contains the root *-stat-*, which means "to stand." Write a definition of each word. Incorporate the meaning of the root in your definition.
1. statue   2. stationary (*adj.*)   3. statistics

USING THE WORD BANK
In your notebook, write the word(s) whose meaning is closest to that of the first word.
1. obsessed: (a) feverish, (b) filled the thoughts of, (c) did not interest
2. arbitrary: (a) changeable, (b) legal, (c) mediocre
3. aesthetic: (a) painless, (b) artistic, (c) romantic

◆ Build Grammar Skills

PUNCTUATION OF INTRODUCTORY WORDS
Introductory words and phrases—such as *then, as a result,* and *in contrast*—help readers to follow a piece of writing by showing how sentences and paragraphs relate to one another. Commas appear after introductory words or phrases to set them off from the rest of a sentence.

Practice Add punctuation as needed to the following sentences.
1. Of course I didn't appreciate the range of ideas that comic books could express.
2. Anyway I finally realized that I could say anything in a comic book.
3. All right so why have I bothered to define comics at such length?
4. Hey show some respect for the art of comics.
5. As comic strips became increasingly popular more newpapers began to publish them.

Writing Application Write a paragraph describing a memorable experience you've had recently. Begin each sentence with an introductory word or phrase followed by a comma.

◆ Build Vocabulary
1. a representation that stands still
2. standing still
3. facts that do not change and so are said to "stand"

Using the Word Bank
1. b   2. a   3. b

◆ Build Grammar Skills
1. Of course, I didn't appreciate the range of ideas that comic books could express.
2. Anyway, I finally realized that I could say something in a comic book.
3. All right, so why have I bothered to define comics at such length?
4. Hey, show some respect for the art of comics.
5. As comic strips became increasingly popular, more newspapers began to publish them.

✎ **Writer's Solution**

For additional instruction and practice, use the lesson in the **Language Lab CD-ROM** on Commas and the practice pages on Commas That Set Off Added Elements, pp. 101–103, in the *Writer's Solution Grammar Practice Book.*

Build Your Portfolio

 Idea Bank

Writing

1. **Letter to the Author** Write a letter to Scott McCloud responding to his ideas about comics. Tell whether you agree or disagree with his definition of comics and why.

2. **Definition** Write a brief definition of a hobby or other activity that you enjoy. Point out any ways in which your definition is different from definitions others might offer.

3. **Essay on Humor** Write a short essay about McCloud's use of humor in *Understanding Comics*. Discuss his use of visuals and other techniques, and explain how he uses humor both to entertain and to inform.

Speaking and Listening

4. **Skit** Many comic strips recently have been made into movies. With a group, plan and act out a scene from a movie based on one of your favorite comics. **[Performing Arts Link]**

5. **Panel Discussion** Hold a television-style panel discussion in which you and a group of classmates discuss whether comics can be an effective way of addressing serious issues, such as social problems and political developments.

Projects

6. **Comic Strip** Create a comic strip of your own using comics from the newspaper as models. **[Art Link]**

7. **Internet Research Report** Browse the Internet to learn more about the history of comics or about one of today's popular comic strips. Share your findings with the class. If possible, download or print visuals to use in your presentation. **[Technology Link]**

 Writing Mini-Lesson

Visual Essay

Think of an activity that especially interests you—your favorite sport, for example. Then develop an essay in which you combine words and visuals—photographs, charts, illustrations, and so on—to communicate what this activity means to you. Keep the following in mind:

Writing Skills Focus: Knowledge Level of Audience

When you write about a topic that you know well, you should recognize that your audience may not have as much knowledge of your topic as you do. For this reason, it's important to identify your **audience** and determine their **knowledge level** of your subject. If you're writing for people who share your knowledge of the subject, you can use specialized terms that a less knowledgeable audience wouldn't recognize, and you can leave out basic details. If, on the other hand, you're writing for an audience unfamiliar with your topic, you'll need to include basic details and define each term you introduce.

Prewriting Start by listing the reasons why you're interested in the activity you chose. Then gather visuals that you can use to illustrate these reasons. For example, if you appreciate the gracefulness of basketball players, you might find photographs that capture this quality. Next, decide on your audience, and determine how well they know your topic.

Drafting Assemble the visuals you've gathered into a logical order. Then write a short passage to accompany each one. As you write, keep the knowledge level of your audience in mind. Be sure to define any terms they wouldn't recognize.

Revising Review your visual essay. Does it clearly communicate what the activity means to you? What details can you add to make it clearer?

 Idea Bank
Customizing for *Performance Levels*
Following are suggestions for matching Idea Bank topics with your students' performance levels:
Less Advanced Students: 1, 4, 7
Average Students: 2, 4, 6
More Advanced Students: 3, 5

Customizing for *Learning Modalities*
Following are suggestions for matching Idea Bank topics with your students' learning modalities:
Verbal/Linguistic: 1, 3, 5, 7
Logical/Mathematical: 2
Interpersonal: 4
Auditory: 4, 5
Visual/Spatial: 6

 Writing Mini-Lesson
Refer students to the Writing Handbook, page 962, for instruction on the writing process, and page 965 for further information on Creative Writing.

 **Writer's Solution**

Writers at Work Videodisc
Have students view the videodisc segment (Ch. 6) featuring animation scriptwriter Grant Moran to see how he uses creative writing in writing and producing cartoons. Have students discuss how they can apply his techniques to their visual essays.

Play frames 12243 to 21791

Writing Lab CD-ROM
Have students complete the Tutorial on Creative Writing. Follow these steps:
1. Use the Audience Profile to determine the audience's knowledge level of the subject.
2. Draft on the computer.
3. Use the video tips on proofreading to aid revision.

Sourcebook
Have students use Chapter 6, Creative Writing (pp. 162–193), for additional support. The chapter includes a model of a script for an animated cartoon (pp. 191–193).

✓ ASSESSMENT OPTIONS

Formal Assessment, Selection Test, pp. 151–153, Assessment Resources Software. The selection test is designed so that it can be easily customized to the performance levels of your students.
Alternative Assessment, p. 43, includes options for less advanced students, more advanced students, intrapersonal learners, verbal/linguistic learners, and visual/spatial learners.

PORTFOLIO ASSESSMENT
Use the following rubrics in the *Alternative Assessment* booklet to assess student writing:
Letter to the Author: Response to Literature Rubric, p. 103
Definition: Definition/Classification Rubric, p. 92
Write About Humor: Literary Analysis/Interpretation Rubric, p. 105
Writing Mini-Lesson: Expression Rubric, p. 87, or Multimedia Report Rubric, p. 100

*G*uide for Reading

OBJECTIVES

1. To read, comprehend, and interpret a radio program transcript, a book review and a book jacket
2. To relate three pieces of workplace writing to personal experience
3. To determine the author's purpose
4. To compare types of workplace writing
5. To build vocabulary in context and learn the word root *-dyna-*
6. To develop skill in using hyphens
7. To write a radio feature story using sources
8. To respond to the work through writing, speaking and listening, and projects

SKILLS INSTRUCTION

Vocabulary: Word Roots: *-dyna-*

Grammar: Hyphens

Reading Strategy: Determine the Author's Purpose

Literary Focus: Workplace Writing

Writing: Use of Sources

Speaking and Listening: Book Chat, Dramatization (teacher edition)

Critical Viewing: Infer; Analyze

PORTFOLIO OPPORTUNITIES

Writing: Book-Jacket Blurb; Sports Article; Review

Writing Mini-Lesson: Radio Feature Story

Speaking and Listening: Book Chat; Dramatization

Projects: Research Project; Commemorative Stamp

Alex Chadwick (1947–)

As you read Alex Chadwick's interview with pilot Linda Finch, notice the references to sound effects, such as an airplane engine starting, wheels turning, and a propeller whirring. Chadwick's work as a correspondent for National Public Radio for over twenty years has been marked by his use of such sounds to anchor his stories in reality.

Before becoming a radio correspondent, Chadwick earned a degree in communications from American University in Washington, D.C., and worked in Maine as both a radio reporter and a commercial fisherman. His accomplishments in radio include his essays and features on the critically acclaimed radio programs *Morning Edition* and *All Things Considered*. He also co-hosted the Public Broadcasting Service television series *Childhood* in 1991.

Steve Gietschier (1948–)

Steve Gietschier holds the game of basketball dear to his heart: His experiences coaching his daughter's team led him to seek out the assignment of reviewing *In These Girls, Hope Is a Muscle*, author Madeleine Blais's gripping account of a high-school girls' basketball team's championship season.

Born in New York City, Gietschier earned a bachelor's degree from Georgetown University in Washington, D.C., and a doctorate from Ohio State University. Since 1986, he has been the Director of Historical Records at *The Sporting News* in St. Louis, Missouri, the newspaper that originally published his review of Madeleine Blais's book.

◆ Build Vocabulary

WORD ROOTS: *-dyna-*

aerodynamics
hydraulic
pursue
improbable
derides
legacy
riveting
ruminative
adept
compelling

When you want to find a word with power packed into it, look for one that includes the root *-dyna-*. This root comes from the Greek word *dynamikos*, which means "power" or "strength." In describing a vintage airplane, Alex Chadwick uses the word *aerodynamics*. If the prefix *aero-* means "of the air," what might *aerodynamics* mean?

WORD BANK

As you read these selections, you will encounter the words on this list. Each word is defined on the page where it first appears. Preview the list before you read.

◆ Build Grammar Skills

HYPHENS

These selections contain a variety of examples of **hyphens**—punctuation marks used to connect two or more words that function as a single word. Notice the use of hyphens in this sentence:

Alex Chadwick interviews Linda Finch, a *forty-six-year-old* grandmother who traced Amelia Earhart's *round-the-world* flight in a plane with *nine-cylinder, air-cooled* engines.

The hyphens used in this sentence form compound modifiers. Hyphens are not used in compound modifiers that include words ending in *-ly* (*badly damaged*, for example) or with compound proper adjectives (*New England* cooking, for instance). Hyphens are used, however, in many compound nouns, such as *mother-in-law*.

Prentice Hall Literature Program Resources

REINFORCE / RETEACH / EXTEND

Selection Support Pages
Build Vocabulary: Word Roots: *-dyna-*, p.180
Build Grammar Skills: Hyphens, p.181
Reading Strategy: Determine Author's Purpose, p.182
Literary Focus: Workplace Writing, p.183

Strategies for Diverse Student Needs, p. 44

Beyond Literature
Career Connection: Aviation, p. 44

Formal Assessment Selection Test, pp. 154–156, Assessment Resources Software

Alternative Assessment, p. 44

Writing and Language Transparencies
Description and Observational Writing, pp. 17–20

Resource Pro CD-ROM
"Earhart Redux," "In These Girls, Hope Is a Muscle" —includes all resource material and customizable lesson plan

Listening to Literature Audiocassettes
"Earhart Redux," "In These Girls, Hope Is a Muscle"

◆ Earhart Redux ◆
In These Girls, Hope Is a Muscle

◆ *Literature and Your Life*

CONNECT YOUR EXPERIENCE
A woman decides to fly around the Earth in an antique airplane because another woman disappeared on a similar flight in a similar plane sixty years ago. A girls' basketball team struggles to win the state championship that slipped through their fingers the previous year. Sometimes a failure can be the most powerful incentive for a new victory. If you've ever wanted something, lost it, and wanted it even more, you'll know the truth at the heart of these true stories.

THEMATIC FOCUS: WORKING TOWARD A GOAL
These selections tell about real women who are defined by the challenges they take on. What do you think it is like to live your life focused almost entirely on a single goal?

◆ Background for Understanding

HISTORY
Born in 1897, Amelia Earhart became interested in aviation in her twenties. In 1932, she became the first woman to fly solo across the Atlantic Ocean. In May 1937, she began an attempt to fly around the world, accompanied only by a navigator. After having flown three quarters of the way around the globe, they disappeared on July 1, near New Guinea. Earhart's final message reported empty fuel tanks. Although a wide-ranging search was made, her plane was never found. Sixty years later, in May 1997, Linda Finch successfully re-created Earhart's flight around the Earth in a similar aircraft.

Journal Writing Write about a time when you achieved a goal after trying and failing several times.

◆ Literary Focus

WORKPLACE WRITING
You don't have to be a novelist or a poet to write for a living. Writing is an important part of a wide range of occupations—television reporting, advertising, police work, even automechanics. Any writing that is done as part of a person's job responsibilities is called **workplace writing.** Following are three examples of workplace writing: a radio interview; a review of a book; and book-jacket copy created by a publisher. What qualities do the pieces share?

◆ Reading Strategy

DETERMINE THE AUTHOR'S PURPOSE
Workplace writing is shaped most of all by its **purpose**—the goal the writer sets out to achieve. On a basic level, the purpose of workplace writing is usually quite easy to see. For example, one of the pieces you are about to read is a radio interview, and you know without even reading it that the interview will present inside information straight from the interviewee's mouth. However, when you actually read the interview, you'll need to look a little further: What *particular* purposes is this interviewer trying to achieve? Does he want to create suspense? Is his goal to make you admire his subject? You can determine the writer's purpose from clues within the interview: what he asks about, how he describes the subject, how he begins and ends the interview.

As you read these three pieces, look for words and details that provide clues to each author's purpose.

Guide for Reading ◆ 617

 Preparing for Standardized Tests

Reading and Vocabulary Knowing how to determine the meaning of an unfamiliar word from word parts can help students answer vocabulary questions on standardized tests. The Build Vocabulary Skills lesson for this selection focuses on determining word meanings through recognition of the word root -*dyna*-. Have students complete the Build Vocabulary lesson on page 624. Then give students more -*dyna*- words, such as *dynamic* and *dynamite,* to define. For additional practice, use the Build Vocabulary page in **Selection Support,** p. 180.

Grammar and Language Grammar and usage sections of some standardized tests may ask students to revise sentences that contain errors in punctuation, such as:

We have a four-month old puppy. (*. . . . four-month-old puppy*)

The Build Grammar Skills lesson for this selection focuses on using hyphens in compound modifiers. After students complete the exercise on page 624, extend their learning with the Build Grammar Skills page in **Selection Support,** p. 181.

The primary purpose of this radio feature report is to convey information to viewers in a lively, engaging way that will hold an audience's attention. Alex Chadwick skillfully weaves clips of Amelia Earhart into an interview with aviator Linda Finch to link the past with the present, that is, to link Amelia Earhart's ill-fated attempt in 1937 to fly around the world with Linda Finch's plan to complete the same flight in an identical vintage airplane.

◆ **Literary Focus**

❶ **Workplace Writing** Ask students what they think is the purpose of this opening passage. What other kind of workplace writing starts out in a similar way? *Students should recognize in this passage the "5 Ws and an H": Who, What, Where, When, Why, and How. This passage, like the lead paragraph in a news article, conveys essential information to the audience.*

◆ **Reading Strategy**

❷ **Determine Author's Purpose** Ask students why Chadwick introduces the interview in this particular way. *Chadwick makes his subject sound very exciting by comparing the door to a big-theater movie screen and describing how it opens to reveal the plane.*

◆ **Critical Thinking**

❸ **Identify Character Traits** Ask students what kind of person they think Linda Finch is after they read this passage. *Students may answer that she is an impressive or unusual person who is good at many things. She has raised a family and is a business executive as well as a skilled mechanic.*

◆ **Critical Thinking**

❹ **Make Inferences** Ask students to suggest why Linda Finch refers to Amelia Earhart by her first name. *Students may answer that Finch may feel a closeness or kinship to Amelia Earhart that would account for her desire to attempt this risky project.*

Earhart Redux

Alex Chadwick

Date: March 17, 1997

BOB EDWARDS, HOST: This is *Morning Edition*. I'm Bob Edwards.

In Oakland, California, this morning, pilot Linda Finch takes off on an adventure that actually started 60 years ago. On this day in 1937, Amelia Earhart began her attempt to become the first person to fly around the world at the equator. She failed.

Her plane disappeared over the Pacific Ocean, but in that, she achieved a measure of immortality.

In the latest National Geographic Radio Expedition, NPR's[1] Alex Chadwick reports Linda Finch hopes to finish what Amelia Earhart began.

SOUNDS OF MACHINERY

ALEX CHADWICK, NPR REPORTER: The door to the hangar is bigger than any big theater movie screen. And it's opening slowly and improbably, folding outward on a horizontal midline and upward from the bottom. And there is Linda Finch's amazing airplane: 1930's aerodynamics, like an artifact from an old movie, or a dream.

LINDA FINCH, PILOT: The aircraft is very rare. There were only fifteen manufactured initially in the twenties and thirties, and there are only two left in the world.

CHADWICK: Ms. Finch is pretty rare herself. A 46-year-old grandmother who owns several nursing homes in Texas, and a pilot who restores and flies vintage fighters. Even so, replicating Amelia Earhart's flight is difficult. And though she doesn't like to say so, a little risky.

SOUNDS OF DOORS OPENING AND CLOSING

FINCH: We'll be flying in an aircraft that is the exact same model Amelia flew. And we'll be following the same route that she flew around the world.

---

1. **NPR's:** National Public Radio's.

618   *Nonfiction*

Block Scheduling Strategies

Consider these suggestions to take advantage of extended class time:

• Begin by discussing with students the Literature and Your Life section (p. 618). Stress how failure can be an incentive for a new victory. Ask students "Why is it important to focus on a goal?"

• A radio interview is meant to be listened to. Let students listen to the audiocassette recording of the radio interview. Discuss elements that make the radio broadcast effective.

• Have students work in discussion groups to answer the Critical Thinking questions (p. 623).

• Purpose is of paramount importance in workplace writing. Discuss author's purpose with students, stressing that a writer's purpose can be determined by clues within a piece of writing. Have students jot down clues to purpose as they read the selections.

CHADWICK: Well, I'm sure some people hearing about this flight would say, what is the point of setting off in an aircraft that's already failed in this once? I mean, it's dangerous. Maybe recklessly dangerous.

FINCH: Well, I have a lot of advantages that Amelia didn't have. We will have modern navigation, communication, and flight instruments that she just didn't have available at the time. The flight, I believe, needs to be done in the right airplane, to be historically correct, to generate the excitement in order to communicate our message.

I started learning about Amelia and really feel like I came to know her. And although I think that flying was definitely a part of her being, that she really flew to get the recognition to convince people that they could do what they wanted. Especially women in the 1930's. That people weren't limited to small lives. That they could have their dreams.

CHADWICK: Amelia Earhart was an aviation pioneer, daring and determined. The second flyer after Lindbergh[2] to solo across the Atlantic. Fourteen others had died trying to repeat his flight, and Amelia nearly did when a crucial instrument failed in bad weather.

Here's that earlier flyer after her Atlantic flight, when President Hoover presented her with a gold medal from the National Geographic Society.

AMELIA EARHART, PILOT: I came down until I could see the flight path blinking in the darkness. If it had been a smooth sea, I might have come too far. Whether I was 50 feet off the water or 150, I do not know, without my altimeter. I was too close, however.

CHADWICK: The plane that Amelia used on her round-the-world attempt, the Lockheed Electra 10-E, is 38.5 feet long, with a 55-foot wingspan. The tail angles back on a small, solid rubber rear wheel. The nose tilts upwards toward the sky. She glows like a polished aluminum athlete, broad-shouldered. Beautiful as a swan dive.

SOUND OF AIRPLANE ENGINE

She carries two nine-cylinder radial Pratt and Whitney Wasp engines. These are the first

2. **Lindbergh:** Charles Lindbergh (1902–1974) made the first solo nonstop flight across the Atlantic Ocean on May 20–21, 1927.

air-cooled engines developed. At 650 pounds, they produced more than 400 horsepower when they were introduced in 1926, and that was an extraordinary weight-power ratio for the time.

Linda Finch's plane has later, more powerful versions of that engine, as did Amelia Earhart's. Except for new navigation and communication gear, their planes are identical.

FINCH: The aircraft was in boxes and pieces and parts. And one of the things that I discovered was that prior to World War II, there were no parts manuals. You get just a big box of pieces, and it's like a jigsaw puzzle, you have to figure out how to put it together.

CHADWICK: She describes the Electra as graceful and slow in flight. Almost peaceful. Amelia did all her flying, but carried a navigator co-pilot. And so will Linda. The cockpit is a narrow, confined space, barely enough room for twin controls. And the enormous, banquet-sized steering wheels.

SOUND OF WHEELS TURNING

What do these wheels feel like? They look like they came out of 1940's British sports cars or something.

FINCH: Exactly, and the wood is so worn. We actually had some new ones we could have put in. But I like these because they're worn and they've been in the airplane, obviously, since it was new.

CHADWICK: So, this is all human-powered controls for turning things and making the airplane fly?

FINCH: Absolutely. People are very surprised that there is just a thin cable and actually you move the cable. Everyone always says, does it have hydraulic controls? Absolutely not.

CHADWICK: These things here, these switches and hand controls. Those are original on the plane. This is what Amelia Earhart flew.

FINCH: Exactly. There are many things, the controls, throttle, and the propeller and mixture controls, the fuel selector gauges, the magneto

◆ Build Vocabulary

aerodynamics (er´ ō dī nam´ iks) *n.*: Branch of mechanics dealing with the forces exerted by air or other gases in motion

hydraulic (hī drô´ lik) *adj.*: Operated by the movement and pressure of liquid

Earhart Redux ◆ 619

Speaking and Listening Mini-Lesson

Dramatization

This mini-lesson supports the Speaking and Listening activity in the Idea Bank on page 625.

Introduce the Concept Explain that a radio dramatization utilizes actors' voices and sound effects to communicate ideas.

Develop Background If possible, have the class divide into groups of six so that each student in a group can play one role (Bob Edwards, Alex Chadwick, Linda Finch, Amelia Earhart), one can do sound effects, and one can direct. (Casting need not be gender-specific.) With smaller groups, students can double up in roles. Students should rehearse in their groups.

Apply the Information The groups can take turns recording their dramatizations, which can then be played for the class.

Assess the Outcome Lead a class discussion about the effectiveness of each dramatization. Evaluate dramatizations on clarity of vocal expression, use of vocal inflections, to express emotions, and appropriate overall tone, or mood.

Blais followed their efforts throughout 1992–93, an epic campaign dedicated to overcoming a long legacy of being good, but just not good enough.

On the surface, then, this book is a simple tale of a singular basketball season, following in the footsteps of "Friday Night Lights" and "Fall River Dreams" (reviewed in TSN, January 23, 1995). Readers looking for no more than a good story can chart the season game by game and turn one page after another in anticipation of the next victory.

But there is so much more here to savor and absorb. The young women who give themselves so completely to their team's quest are extraordinary each in her own way. Burdened with the pains of adolescence, the duties that high school imposes and, in some cases, the tough circumstances of families rent asunder,[3] they learn from one another how to dig deep to find the resources they need to reach their goal.

In the process, they journey in so many ways to places Amherst women have never gone before, proving to themselves, their families, their town and all who will look with open eyes that women's sports can be an astoundingly fulfilling and moving experience.

---

3. **rent** (rent) **asunder** (ə sun′ dər): Torn apart.

♦ **Build Vocabulary**

legacy (leg′ ə sē) *n.*: Anything handed down from an ancestor

▲ **Critical Viewing** How does this picture capture the team's emotions? [**Analyze**]

622 ♦ *Nonfiction*

Book-Jacket Copy for

In These Girls,

Advance praise for *In These Girls, Hope Is a Muscle:*

This book is the product of a perfect marriage. The subject is timely and fascinating, and Madeleine Blais is a first-rate reporter and writer.   —Tracy Kidder

Blais's narrative gift has produced a touching, exciting book about a subject largely ignored until now, namely women athletes. Her story of a year in the life of a high school basketball team and its hometown goes far beyond the obvious to illuminate how people really feel, how things really work.   —Anne Bernays

Begun as an article that appeared in the *New York Times Magazine, In These Girls, Hope Is a Muscle* offers a riveting close-up of the girls on a high school basketball team whose passion for the sport is rivaled only by their loyalty to one another. Reminiscent of John McPhee's *A Sense of Where You Are* and H. G. Bissinger's *Friday Night Lights*, Pulitzer Prize-winning journalist Madeleine Blais's book takes the reader through a singular season in the history of the Lady Hurricanes of Amherst, Massachusetts.

For years they had been known as a finesse team, talented and hardworking players who in the end lacked that final hardscrabble ingredient that would take them over the top to the state championship. They seemed doomed to mirror the college town they represented: kindly, ruminative, at times ineffectual; more adept at quoting Emily Dickinson[1] and singing nature songs than going to the basket.

One season, all that changed. Madeleine Blais takes us from tryouts to practices

---

1.   **Emily Dickinson:** (1830–1886), poet who was born and lived most of her life in Amherst, Massachusetts.

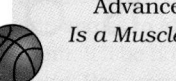

 Beyond the Classroom

Workplace Connection

Athletics Point out that students need not be star athletes to find summer jobs that are connected to physical education. Encourage interested students to learn about opportunities in their area. Public swimming pools need lifeguards and maintenance personnel. Summer sports leagues and recreation programs need coaches and assistants. Once students have learned what jobs are

available, suggest that they learn how to apply for these positions, and what qualifications are needed. Parks or Recreation departments might be a good place to start. Invite interested students to share the information they gather on summer jobs related to physical education. They might want to create a chart indicating the job openings, the job requirements, and whom to contact for further information.

Hope Is a Muscle Madeleine Blais

during the regular season, up through the final championship game against the mighty Hillies from Haverhill. The result is an astoundingly moving narrative that captures the complexities of girls' experiences in high school, in sports, and in our society. As their coach says, unlike training boys—whose arrogance and confidence often have to be eroded before a team can pull together—working with girls is all constructive. The way to build a girls' team is to build each player's self-confidence. During the course of this season we see the Amherst Lady Hurricanes in their fierce, funny, sisterhood-is-powerful quest for excellence.

As Blais reports, "This is just one team in one season. It alone cannot change the discrimination against girls and their bodies throughout history." But it is a <u>compelling</u>, funny, and touching literary exploration of one group of girls' fight for success and, perhaps

most of all, respect. *In These Girls, Hope Is a Muscle* is both a dramatization of the success of the women's movement and a testimony to all the changes that have yet to come.

Madeleine Blais worked at the *Miami Herald* for eight years. A collection of her work, *The Heart Is an Instrument: Portraits in Journalism*, was published by the University of Massachusetts Press in 1992. Now a resident of Amherst, she has been on the faculty at the University of Massachusetts for six years.

◆ Build Vocabulary

riveting (riv´ it in) *adj.*: Firmly holding attention
ruminative (rōō´ mə nə təv) *adj.*: Meditative
adept (ə dept´) *adj.*: Highly skilled; expert
compelling (kəm pel´ in) *adj.*: Forceful

♦ **Reading Strategy**
8 Determine Author's Purpose
Ask students why the book-jacket writer included this information about the author of the book. *The author's professional history and the fact that she is on the faculty of a major university may impress readers and further the purpose of the jacket blurb—to persuade people to buy the book.*

Reinforce and Extend

Answers
◆ *Literature and Your Life*

Reader's Response Many students will say yes because the blurb and review describe the book as a gripping story of courage and determination.

Thematic Focus Suggested response: To coordinate the efforts of a group of people can be more difficult, since individuals have different abilities and personalities.

☑ Check Your Comprehension

1. They're a high-school basketball team that won the state championship in 1992–1993.
2. Boys need to learn to subordinate themselves to the group; girls must learn to be aggressive.
3. They prove that women's sports give young women an opportunity to excel and provide inspiration to others.

Guide for Responding

◆ *Literature and Your Life*

Reader's Response Does reading the book-jacket blurb and the review of *In These Girls, Hope Is a Muscle* make you want to read the book itself? Explain.

Thematic Focus Most of the challenges you have read about in the stories and poems in this book involve individuals. In what ways is a challenge different when it involves a group of people, like a basketball team?

☑ Check Your Comprehension

1. Who are the Lady Hurricanes, and what did they accomplish?
2. According to the book-jacket blurb, how is working with a team of girls different from training boys to work as a team?
3. According to the book review, what do the girls prove about women's sports?

◆ Critical Thinking

INTERPRET
1. Why do you think Steve Gietschier likes the book *In These Girls, Hope Is a Muscle*? **[Infer]**
2. The commentary in the book-jacket blurb closely echoes the author's writing in the book itself. Sum up the author's main idea and her attitude toward her subject. **[Summarize]**
3. Both the book-jacket blurb and the review are positive descriptions of *In These Girls, Hope Is a Muscle*. What differences can you see between the two pieces? **[Contrast]**

EVALUATE
4. What does the title *In These Girls, Hope Is a Muscle* mean, and why might the reviewer call this title "poetic"? **[Criticize]**

In These Girls, Hope Is a Muscle ◆ 623

◆ Critical Thinking

1. Suggested response: He has coached his daughter's team, and so has a built-in interest in the subject. He also finds the story of their progress toward the championship a gripping narrative.
2. The author admires the team and feels that women's sports deserve much more attention.
3. The review emphasizes the fact that women's sports deserve admiration and attention. The book concentrates more on the story.
4. It means that the girls' spirit is almost a physical thing and that their aspiration is as important to their success as their athletic ability. It is an effective metaphor.

Beyond the Selection

FURTHER READING
Other Works About Focusing on a Goal
The Old Man and the Sea, Ernest Hemingway
"Raymond's Run," Toni Cade Bambara

INTERNET
You and your students may find additional information about the authors on the Internet. We suggest the following sites. Please be aware, however, that sites may have changed from the time we published this information.

For information about Alex Chadwick, go to **http://www.npr.org/inside/bios/achadwick.html**
For information about Steve Gietschier, go to **http://www.sportingnews.com/voices/steve_gietschier.bio/**
We *strongly recommend* that you preview the sites before you send students to them.

Answers

◆ Reading Strategy

1. He conveys the impression of a modest, determined woman, courageous enough to tackle a risky project.
2. The language and details in the blurb emphasize the appeal of the book.

◆ Build Vocabulary

1. political power in a single family
2. water-powered
3. heat-powered

Using the Word Bank

1. b 2. a 3. a 4. c 5. a
6. c 7. b 8. a 9. c 10. a

◆ Literary Focus

1. Since the audience is not distracted by visual images, as in television, the radio journalist's words receive more attention and must stand effectively on their own.
2. The interviewer needs to describe the circumstances of the interview and the appearance and manner of the interviewee, as well as to plan questions and follow-up responses.
3. Suggested response: Qualities include the interviewer's ability to listen; an engaging, interesting interviewer; quick-wittedness, and articulateness on both ends.
4. Sample responses: Yes, he creates a vivid portrait of Finch and the task ahead of her; no, we never learn the deeper motivations of Finch that make her tick.
5. Suggested response: Characteristics include a clear, accurate, appealing description of the book, and an indication of what sort of people will like the book.
6. Sample responses: Yes, it makes people want to buy the book by discussing the author's intelligent handling of a compelling topic; no, it focuses its persuasiveness toward too small an audience—for example, there may be few reasons why men who are not sports fans should read this book.
7. Suggested responses: Occupations include doctor, teacher, government employee, lawyer, and so on.

Guide for Responding (continued)

◆ Reading Strategy

DETERMINE AUTHOR'S PURPOSE

In each of these selections, the author has a general **purpose**, or reason for writing, and one or more specific purposes.

1. The general purpose of Chadwick's interview with Linda Finch is to present inside information about Finch's upcoming adventure. One of his more specific purposes is to convey a specific impression of Finch. What is that impression? Support your answer.
2. The general purpose of the book-jacket blurb for *In These Girls, Hope Is a Muscle* is to convey information about the book. Based on the words and details the writer includes, what other purpose do you think the blurb serves? Explain.

◆ Build Vocabulary

USING THE WORD ROOT -*dyna*-

These words contain the root -*dyna*-, which means "power" or "strength." Look up each word in a dictionary. Then write your own definition in which you incorporate the meaning of the root -*dyna*-.

1. dynasty 2. hydrodynamic 3. thermodynamic

USING THE WORD BANK

In your notebook, write the word whose meaning is closest to that of the first word.

1. hydraulic: (a) strong, (b) powered by liquid, (c) old-fashioned
2. pursue: (a) chase, (b) quarrel with, (c) refer to
3. aerodynamics: (a) air movement, (b) flight, (c) piloting skill
4. riveting: (a) difficult, (b) beautiful, (c) gripping
5. improbable: (a) unlikely, (b) impossible, (c) odd
6. compelling: (a) unwilling, (b) noisy, (c) fascinating
7. adept: (a) clumsy, (b) skillful, (c) modified
8. ruminative: (a) intellectual, (b) wealthy, (c) spoiled
9. legacy: (a) burden, (b) victory, (c) heritage
10. derides: (a) belittles, (b) ignores, (c) notices

◆ Literary Focus

WORKPLACE WRITING

Both of these selections are examples of **workplace writing**—writing that is performed as part of a person's job.

1. Why is it important for a radio journalist to be a good writer?
2. What is the role of writing in putting together an interview?
3. What qualities do you think make a successful interview? Support your answer.
4. Do you think that Chadwick's interview is effective? Why or why not?
5. What are the most important characteristics of a book-jacket blurb? Why?
6. Do you think that the blurb for *In These Girls, Hope Is a Muscle* is effective? Why or why not?
7. What other occupations can you think of in which writing is important?

◆ Build Grammar Skills

HYPHENS

A **hyphen** is a punctuation mark used to connect two or more words that function as a single word. Often hyphens are used to form compound modifiers, such as *quick-witted* or *slow-paced*. Hyphens *are not* used in compound modifiers that include words ending in -*ly* or with compound proper adjectives.

Practice On your paper, write the following sentences, adding hyphens where necessary.

1. Many planes once used air cooled engines.
2. The old fashioned aircraft had twin engines.
3. Finch's clear headed, calm, collected attitude impressed the interviewer.
4. Recently invented navigation technology helped Finch succeed.
5. Finch's round the world flight took several weeks.
6. Finch exhibited great self confidence in attempting her flight.

◆ Build Grammar Skills

1. air-cooled; 2. old-fashioned;
3. clear-headed; 4. no hyphens;
5. round-the-world; 6. self-confidence

⚓ Writer's Solution

For additional instruction and practice, use the practice page on hyphens (p. 111) in the *Writer's Solution Grammar Practice Book*.

Build Your Portfolio

Idea Bank

Writing

1. **Book-Jacket Blurb** Choose a book you like, and write a book-jacket blurb that makes the book appealing to readers. Decide on your target audience, and play up the features of the book that would appeal to this audience.

2. **Sports Article** Using your imagination to come up with the details, create a sports article describing the game in which the Lady Hurricanes won the state championship.

3. **Review** Choose a television or radio program that you either like or dislike very much, and write a review expressing your opinion. Support your points with examples from the program.

Speaking and Listening

4. **Book Chat** Another way in which publishers promote books is through reviews on radio programs. With classmates, stage a book chat in which you review a book that you've read recently.

5. **Dramatization** Work with classmates to perform Alex Chadwick's interview. You will need a male reader to play Chadwick, a female reader to play Finch, at least one person to create the sound effects, and a director to coordinate everyone's efforts. **[Performing Arts Link]**

Projects

6. **Research Project** Research one aspect of the role of women in aviation—for example, women who have flown in spacecraft or who piloted planes during the Persian Gulf War. Present your information as an oral report with visual displays.

7. **Commemorative Stamp** Design a commemorative stamp honoring women in sports. **[Art Link]**

Writing Mini-Lesson

Radio Feature Story

Imagine that you are a radio correspondent like Alex Chadwick. Choose a current event or issue that interests you. Then prepare and present a radio program that informs listeners about the event or issue. Use this tip to help you develop your story:

Writing Skills Focus: Use of Sources

A radio feature story is only as good as the research on which it's based. To make your feature story as thorough and convincing as possible, gather information about your topic from a variety of **sources**, such as newspapers, magazines, nonfiction books, and Internet sites. If your topic relates to a local issue or event, you may even want to conduct interviews to get a firsthand view from people who have direct involvement with your topic.

Prewriting Start by determining the best sources from which to gather information about your topic. If you're dealing with a topic that's very current, your best bet is probably newspaper and magazine articles. In addition, you'll probably have some luck using key words to browse the Internet for information. Finally, you may want to contact government agencies or other local organizations to locate people you might interview.

Drafting Use the information you've gathered to create a script for your feature. Try to begin with attention-grabbing information. Then present your information in an order that fits your topic. For example, if you're describing an event, you may want to present details in chronological order.

Revising Read your script aloud to yourself. Focus on what it says as well as how it sounds. Where necessary, add information and replace words with ones that are more lively. Finally, record your feature and share it with the class.

Earhart Redux/In These Girls, Hope Is a Muscle ◆ 625

 Idea Bank
Customizing for
Performance Levels
Following are suggestions for matching the Idea Bank topics with your students' performance levels:
Less Advanced Students: 1, 7
Average Students: 2, 4, 6
More Advanced Students: 3, 5

Customizing for
Learning Modalities
Following are suggestions for matching Idea Bank topics with your students' learning modalities:
Visual/Spatial: 6, 7
Auditory: 4, 5
Verbal/Linguistic: 1, 2, 3, 6
Interpersonal: 4, 5

 Writing Mini-Lesson
Refer students to the Writing Handbook, page 962, for instruction on the writing process, and page 964 for further information on Exposition.

Have students use the Cluster Organizer in *Writing and Language Transparencies,* p. 80, to organize their prewriting information for their radio feature stories.

 Writer's Solution

Writers at Work Videodisc
Have students view the videodisc segment (Ch. 3) featuring Gene Bryan Johnson to see how he prepares scripts for radio broadcast. Have students discuss how to use his approaches to prepare their radio feature stories.

Play frames 22539 to 32284

Writing Lab CD-ROM
Have students complete the Tutorial on Exposition. Follow these steps:
1. Have students use the interactive instruction on gathering details and on conducting library research.
2. Have students draft on computer.
3. Have them use the interactive Self-Evaluation Checklists to aid evaluation and revision.

Sourcebook
Have students use Chapter 3, Exposition (pp. 62–95), for additional support. The chapter includes an annotated model of a radio script for an informational report (pp. 93–95).

✓ ASSESSMENT OPTIONS

Formal Assessment, Selection Test, pp. 154–156, and Assessment Resources Software. The selection test is designed so that it can be easily customized to the performance levels of your students. *Alternative Assessment,* p. 44, includes options for less advanced students, more advanced students, interpersonal learners, verbal/linguistic learners, intrapersonal learners, and visual/spatial learners.

PORTFOLIO ASSESSMENT
Use the following rubrics in the *Alternative Assessment* booklet to assess student writing:
Book-Jacket Blurb: Persuasion Rubric, p. 98
Sports Article: Description Rubric, p. 90
Review: Critical Review Rubric, p. 104
Writing Mini-Lesson: Research Report/Paper Rubric, p. 99

Connections to Today's World

Office memos and movie reviews have something in common: They are both forms of workplace writing, or writing that is done on the job. By its very nature, workplace writing—such as "Earhart Redux" and the review and book-jacket blurb of *In These Girls, Hope Is a Muscle*—is based upon information gathered from one or more sources. Today, one of the best sources for finding up-to-the-minute information on virtually any topic is the Internet. These two pages illustrate some of the various kinds of information available on the Internet that could comprise the basis of a piece of workplace writing about Edgar Allan Poe.

CONNECTIONS TO TODAY'S WORLD
Internet Web Site

With the Internet explosion of the last several years, it's now possible to get information on virtually any topic with a just a few clicks of a mouse. Unlike most printed information, which doesn't change over time, the information delivered through the Internet is interactive and ever-changing. Web pages are updated regularly, and people who visit them can choose their own pathways through the information. Following are some samples from a Web site on Edgar Allan Poe. Notice that the site includes both text and images.

Edgar Allan Poe

Biographical Pages

INDEX	Short summary of Poe's life
1) Edgar's mother Eliza	2) Edgar's Childhood
3) Edgar's Teens	4) The Army and the Death of Fanny Allan
5) Al Aaraaf and West Point	6) Poems by Edgar A. Poe, Maria Clemm and Henry Poe
7) The Saturday Visitor Contest & The Death of John Allan	8) The Messenger and Marriage to Virginia Clemm
9) Break with the Messenger and the Blank Period	10) Usher and Rue Morgue
11) Virginia's Health and Tales of Ratiocination	

Edgar Allan Poe, son of actress Eliza Poe and actor David Poe, Jr., born January 19, 1809, was mostly known for his poems and short tales and his literary criticism. He has been given credit for inventing the detective story, and his psychological thrillers have been influences for many writers worldwide.

Edgar and his brother and sister were orphaned before Edgar's third birthday, and Edgar was taken in to the home of John and Fanny Allan in Richmond, Virginia. The Allans lived in England for five years (1815–1820), where Edgar also attended school. In 1826, he entered the University of Virginia. Although a good student, he was forced to gambling since John Allan did not provide well enough. Allan refused to pay Edgar's debts and Edgar had to leave the university after only one year.

In 1827, Edgar published his first book, *Tamerlane and Other Poems*, anonymously under the signature "A Bostonian." The poems were heavily influenced by Byron and showed a youthful attitude.

Later, in 1827, Edgar enlisted in the army under the name Edgar A. Perry, where his quarrels with John Allan continued. Edgar did well in the army, but in 1829 he left and decided to apply for a cadetship at West Point.

Work of Edgar Allan Poe

- Images
- Some Poe Trivia.
- Rabies?!
- Listen to the Raven
- Some of my own poems!

Credits

Images Related to Poe and these Pages

1. Based on these samples, what types of things can you learn about Poe from the Web site?
2. How is the Web site different from a book about Poe?
3. What advantages does the Internet have over books?
4. What are some of the advantages of books versus the Internet?

Answers

1. You can learn detailed information about Poe's life as well as some trivia about him. You can also view some pictures of Poe and listen to a recitation of "The Raven."
2. The Web site differs from a book in that you click on the topic you want to explore rather than look up the topic in an index. In addition, the Web site offers audio material.
3. Among the advantages are the constant updating of information, the ease of finding the topic of your choice, the ability to find audio and video materials, and a means to respond to what is presented.
4. Books are permanent and not subject to technical problems. A book lets the reader view many pages quickly, thus allowing the reader to easily flip back and forth through any number of pages.

Before Students begin, review the following key characteristics of an informational report:

- An informational report presents facts, statistics, and other types of information about a topic.

- To write a successful informational report, the writer gathers relevant information and present it in a clear and interesting way.

Refer students to the Writing Handbook, page 962, for instruction in the writing process, and page 964 for further information on Exposition.

 Writer's Solution

Writers at Work Videodisc

To spark class discussion on expository writing and show students how radio journalist Gene Bryan Johnson uses expository techniques in his writing, play the videodisc segment on Exposition (Ch. 3). Have students discuss Johnson's strategy of using a focus statement.

Play frames 22539 to 32284

Writing Lab CD-ROM

If your students have access to computers, you may want to have them work on the tutorial on Exposition to complete all or part of their informational reports. Follow these steps:
1. Have students view the interactive model of an informational report.
2. Suggest that students use the Word Bins activities to help them gather precise words for their reports.
3. Have students draft on the computer.
4. Encourage students to use the Revision Checker for transitional words.
5. Have students view the section on citing sources to help them revise.

Sourcebook

Students can find additional support, including topic ideas, models, and graphic organizers in the chapter on exposition (pp. 62–95).

Informational Report — Writing Process Workshop

Have you heard people talk about the "information super-highway"? They're referring to the vast amounts of information available to you instantly on computers. Of course, you can also find information in books, newspapers, magazines, and other printed sources, including this book. Make your own contribution to the "information age" by writing an **informational report** that provides an in-depth set of facts on a topic that interests you.

The following skills, introduced in this section's Writing Mini-Lessons, will help you write an informational report.

Writing Skills Focus

▶ **Identify your audience's knowledge level of your topic.** Consider what your readers may or may not already know about the topic you are presenting. Their level of knowledge will affect how much information you include. (See p. 615.)

▶ **Use a variety of sources** when gathering information for your report. In addition to books, newspapers, and magazines, you might use pictures, the Internet, or personal interviews, for example. (See p. 625.)

Scott McCloud uses both these skills as he shares information about comics.

① The writer considers his audience's knowledge and assumes they have all seen a comic before.

② The source of the writer's quote might be a book, a magazine article, or an interview with Will Eisner himself.

③ The writer uses pictures as an additional source for gathering information.

MODEL FROM LITERATURE

from Understanding Comics by Scott McCloud

"Comics" is the word worth defining, as it refers to the medium itself, not a specific object as "comic book" or "comic strip" do. We can all visualize a comic. ① But what is comics? Master comics artist Will Eisner uses the term sequential art when describing comics. ② Taken individually, the pictures below are merely that—pictures. However, when part of a sequence, even a sequence of only two, the art of the image is transformed into something more: the art of comics. ③

628 ◆ Nonfiction

 Beyond the Classroom

Career Connection

Tell students that writing informational reports is a task that many people have to do as part of their jobs, even though they are not paid expressly to write. For instance, an analyst at an investment bank or brokerage house will frequently write informational reports about the states of companies in which his or her company plans to invest. An assistant working at the State Department, a nonprofit group, or for a Congressman may write an informational report on human rights or economic conditions in a particular country. The ability to communicate information clearly and succinctly in writing is a skill that will help students at many jobs.

Prewriting

Choose a Topic Think about a topic that especially interests you or about which you have an in-depth knowledge. You can also choose one of the topic ideas listed here:

> ## Topic Ideas
> - Today's music or music performers
> - A widely watched spectator sport
> - An important year in history
> - A popular political leader

Consider Your Audience's Knowledge On your paper, make brief notes on the age and background of your readers. Then make a two-column list. In one column, jot down facts your audience may already know about your subject. In the other column, jot down information they may not know.

Readers' Age:	Readers' Background:
What They Know	**What They Don't Know**

Plan and Find Your Sources Make a list of facts, statistics, and quotations you will need for your report. Next to each one, note a possible source. Look for those sources in the library, or request an interview with an expert who can provide you with information.

Technology Tip The Internet is a great source of information. If you aren't sure how to use the Internet, ask a teacher, librarian, or experienced Internet user for help.

Drafting

Develop a Clear Organization Plan Using the information you've gathered, begin drafting your report. Start with a paragraph that introduces your subject and your main points. Follow with a series of paragraphs, each focusing on a single point or aspect of your subject. Make sure that each body paragraph has a topic sentence and several supporting sentences. End with a conclusion that sums up your main points.

APPLYING LANGUAGE SKILLS: Adjective Clauses

An **adjective clause** is a group of words with a subject and a verb that work together to modify a noun. You can sometimes combine information by using an adjective clause.

Without an Adjective Clause:
We drink water. The water is filtered at a plant.

With an Adjective Clause:
The water *that we drink* is filtered at a plant.

Practice On your paper, combine each pair of sentences by using an adjective clause.

1. Inspectors check the water. They go to the plant daily.
2. They carry a special instrument. It measures chlorine levels.

Writing Application As you draft your report, try to identify places where you can combine information into one sentence by using an adjective clause.

> **Writer's Solution Connection Writing Lab**
>
> For tips on interviewing an expert, work through the Prewriting section of the tutorial on Exposition.

Prewriting

Remind students that the more information they gather for their reports, the easier it will be to write them. They should therefore be persuaded to choose a topic for which there will be sufficient information.

Customize for
Less Proficient Writers
These students may find it helpful to make some preliminary charts or graphs to help guide them through the report.

Customize for
More Advanced Students
Challenge these students to pick a topic that is not immediately self-evident to them, but that flows from their initial research on a broader topic. Encourage them to convey the information in a witty, surprising way that readers will remember.

 **Writer's Solution**

Writing Lab CD-ROM
Audience and Purpose profiles are included in the Considering Audience and Purpose section of the tutorial on Exposition. Have students complete these profiles and print them out. They can later refer to them while drafting.

Drafting

Even though students should write their informational report in a single sitting—without pausing to labor over a single word or to correct a grammatical error—they should be reminded to follow a clear organizational plan as they write.

Applying Language Skills
Adjective Clauses

Answers
1. Inspectors who check the water go to the plant daily.
2. They carry a special instrument that measures chlorine levels.

 **Writer's Solution**

For additional instruction and practice, use the **Language Lab CD-ROM** lesson on Varying Sentence Structure and the practice in the *Writer's Solution Grammar Practice Book* (p. 53)

Appositives and Appositive Phrases

Answers
1. The water inspector, Mr. Jones, writes a report each month.
2. His report goes to the Health Department, an office run by the state.

 **Writer's Solution**

For additional instruction and practice, use the practice page in the *Writer's Solution Grammar Practice Book* (pp. 42–43).

Revising

Remind students that revision is a critical part of the writing process. Have them first check their own papers to see if they can add interesting and important information or make any explanations clearer. Then have them work with a peer reviewer.

Publishing

If students have access to a computer and a word processing program such as Claris Works™, or a page layout program, they can turn their informational report into a multimedia informational report by adding pictures, graphs, charts, or even video. Consult the User's Guide for the *Writing Lab/Language Lab CD-ROM* to find out how to open files from outside the *Writer's Solution*.

Reinforce and Extend

Review the Writing Guidelines
After students have completed their papers, review the characteristics of a informational report. Encourage students to come up with additional criteria for an interesting informational report based on what they learned through completing the assignment.

APPLYING LANGUAGE SKILLS: Appositives and Appositive Phrases

An **appositive** is a noun or pronoun that identifies or explains a previous noun or pronoun:

Our mayor, <u>Sara Leeds</u>, has served for six years.

An appositive phrase is an appositive plus modifiers:

The mayor, <u>our highest official</u>, will run again.

Practice On your paper, combine each pair of sentences into a single sentence by using an appositive or an appositive phrase.

1. The water inspector is Mr. Jones. He writes a report each month.
2. His report goes to the Health Department. It's an office run by the state.

Writing Application As you revise your report, see whether there are places where you can combine information by using appositives and appositive phrases.

Writer's Solution Connection Writing Lab

For help in revising, use the revision checks for transitions and language variety in the tutorial on Expositon.

Consider Your Audience's Level of Knowledge As you write, always keep your readers in mind. Don't try to impress them with information beyond their level of understanding. Use formal vocabulary, not slang, but remain "reader friendly" as you present your facts.

Science Writing Tip When writing about a science topic, provide definitions for words or terms that your audience may not know.

Revising

Have a Peer Review Your Work Ask a classmate to read your informational report and then answer the following questions:

▶ Is the main idea clear? How can it be made more specific?
▶ Does the report include facts, statistics, and quotations that support the main ideas?
▶ Is the information clear and easy to understand?
▶ Are all unfamiliar terms defined?

REVISION MODEL

Americans speak in different dialects.①, or forms of language. New Yorkers call soft
② My Arkansas aunt, on the other hand, says "soda pop."
drinks "soda." In Ohio, soft drinks are referred to as "pop."

① The writer defines a term her audience may not know.
② The writer adds information she obtained from a new source: an interview.

Publishing

▶ **Classroom** Present your report to the class as a special television or radio broadcast.
▶ **Magazine** Send a copy of your report to a magazine that publishes informational articles.
▶ **Internet** Post your report on the Internet.

☑ ASSESSMENT		4	3	2	1
PORTFOLIO ASSESSMENT Use the following rubric to assess the students' writing.	**Organization**	Organization is consistent and easy to follow. Effective transitions link ideas.	Organization is generally easy to follow. Transitions link most ideas.	Organization is at times difficult to follow.	The report is generally confusing and hard to follow.
	Grammar and Usage	There are no errors in grammar, usage, or mechanics. Word choice is precise and appropriate.	There are minor errors in grammar, usage, and mechanics. Word choice is usually appropriate.	There are some errors in grammar, usage, and mechanics.	Numerous errors in grammar, usage, and mechanics make the report difficult to understand.

Real-World Reading Skills Workshop

Adjusting Reading Rate

Strategies for Success

As you know, speed limits are not always the same. A car riding on a highway may be allowed to go 55 miles per hour. Near a hospital or school, the speed limit might be only 15 miles per hour. The speed at which you read can also vary. You need to adjust your reading rate depending on the situation.

What Are You Reading? You do many types of reading. You might look at the comics in a newspaper, or you may read a scientific report in a medical journal. Adjust your reading rate according to the type of material before you. The more serious the selection, the more slowly you should read it.

Why Are You Reading? You may read for many different reasons. You might study a chapter in your social studies textbook to prepare for a test. You may read an article in a music magazine purely for relaxation or fun. Your reading rate is determined partly by your purpose for reading. The more serious the purpose, the more slowly you should read.

When and Where Are You Reading? Your reading rate also depends on the time and place where you read. For a timed test in school, you need to read faster than for pleasure reading at home during the weekend. Know how much time you have to complete your reading, and adjust your rate accordingly.

Apply the Strategy

Consider different types of reading materials. Then answer these questions:

1. List two types of reading material you would read slowly.

2. List two types of reading material you would read quickly.

3. Describe the reading rate you would use in the following situations:
   - ▶ Reading an encyclopedia article about London, looking for information for a report on the Houses of Parliament
   - ▶ Reading an instruction manual on how to install a new computer program
   - ▶ Scanning the television listings for a program to watch

> ✔ Here are other situations in which you need to adjust your reading rate:
> - ▶ Reviewing notes the night before a test
> - ▶ Browsing through a store catalog
> - ▶ Reading a friendly letter or a business letter

Introduce the Strategy

Discuss with students how speaking in front of a group is the activity that the highest percentage of people place as their greatest fear, outranking even fear of death. Yet the ability to give an oral presentation is also one of the most useful and powerful skills a person can have. Have them think of careers and situations where good public-speaking skills would come in handy. (Possibilities include politician, teacher, businessperson, actor, and telejournalist, to name a few.)

Customize for
English Language Learners

These students may be more nervous than other students about speaking in front of the class. Remind them that this activity emphasizes such things as enunciation, intonation, volume, eye contact, and body language—things that are the same in any language. Remind other students not to judge English language learners too harshly, and ask them how they would feel if they were asked to give an oral presentation in another language.

Apply the Strategy

Have students do the following activities in pairs and then in front of the entire class.

Suggested Answers:
1. Content will vary, but students should be assessed on volume, maintaining eye contact, posture, lack of distracting hand or other movements, and general confidence.
2. See #1.
3. See #1.

Speaking and Listening Workshop

Giving an Oral Presentation

The most successful news reporters know how to present the news effectively. They speak in a way that holds viewers' interest so they don't tune out. You, too, can make successful oral presentations by following these guidelines:

Speak in a Strong, Clear Voice When you speak before a group, your words will be wasted if no one can hear them. Use a strong, confident tone of voice, and speak clearly. Don't speak too quickly, or listeners won't understand what you're saying.

Make Eye Contact As you speak, try to look at the audience as much as possible. Even if you're using notes, pause from time to time to look up. Avoid gazing at the walls or window, which will distract your listeners.

Use Your Body Effectively As you speak, practice good posture. Don't hunch over or fidget nervously with your hands or fingers. However, use body motions where it will help your presentation. For example, you might point to a visual aid or use a gesture to stress a particular idea.

Tips for Giving an Oral Presentation

✔ To give an effective oral presentation to a small or a large group, follow these strategies:
▶ Be loud and clear; don't mumble or slur your words.
▶ Maintain *good eye contact.*
▶ Stand straight; move your body naturally.

Apply the Strategies

Practice giving an oral presentation in each of the following situations. After each presentation, invite audience members to offer feedback.

1. You have applied for a job. As part of your interview, the company president and vice president ask you to make a brief presentation to them, telling why you'd like the job.

2. You have been chosen to represent your school in a statewide speaking contest. You are supposed to speak about your school and its curriculum to a group of ten judges.

3. You are a television newscaster who is broadcasting a report on an event that occurred recently in your neighborhood or town.

632 ◆ *Nonfiction*

Extended Reading Opportunities

True stories—such as histories, biographies, and articles that provide information or express the writer's opinion—can help us to understand our world. Following are just a few possibilities through which you can explore the many types of nonfiction.

Suggested Titles

Today's Nonfiction

This collection includes a variety of contemporary nonfiction by some of today's most important writers. In *Today's Nonfiction,* you will encounter biographies and personal accounts, essays, and feature articles on a wide range of interesting and relevant topics.

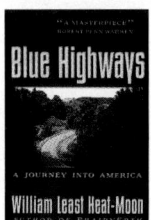

Blue Highways: A Journey Into America
William Least Heat Moon

William Least Heat Moon lives and writes in Columbia, Missouri. His best-selling book *Blue Highways: A Journey Into America* is an account of his 14,000-mile journey through the back roads of the United States in a converted van named "Ghost Dancing." Readers who go along for the ride will enjoy Least Heat Moon's sensitive descriptions of the people and places he encounters on his travels.

All Things Bright and Beautiful
James Herriott

This book is just one in a series of best-selling autobiographical works by a veterinarian living in Yorkshire, England. Through the many humorous and heartwarming anecdotes in these pages, Herriott shares his love for life, humanity, and, of course, the many animals in his care.

Other Possibilities

The Negro Leagues: The Story of Black Baseball	Jacob Margolies
Into a Strange Land: Unaccompanied Refugee Youth in America	Brent Ashbranner and Melissa Ashbranner
On Board the Titanic	Shelley Tanaka

Planning Students' Extended Reading

All of these works are good choices for students' exploration of the genre of nonfiction. Following is some information that will help you choose which to teach:

Customize for
Varying Student Needs

When assigning the selections in this part to your students, keep in mind the following factors:

• *Today's Nonfiction,* an offering in the Prentice Hall Literature Library, offers a chance for students to encounter a wide range of different types of nonfiction. The pieces vary in level of difficulty.
• *Blue Highways* is an engaging work of narrative nonfiction.
• *All Things Bright and Beautiful* is an accessible nonfiction collection that should entertain and amuse students.

Literature Study Guides A literature study guide is available for *Today's Nonfiction.* The guide includes section summaries, discussion questions, and activities.

Resources for Teaching Novels, Plays, and Literature Collections This booklet includes graphic organizers, teaching strategies, and transparencies that you can use in teaching any of these works.

Planning Instruction and Assessment

Unit Objectives

1. To read selections in different genres that develop the theme of "Drama"
2. To apply a variety of reading strategies, particularly literal comprehension strategies, appropriate for reading these selections
3. To recognize literary elements used in these selections
4. To increase vocabulary
5. To learn elements of grammar and usage
6. To write in a variety of modes and about situations based on the selections
7. To develop speaking and listening skills, by doing proposed activities

Meeting the Objectives

With each selection, you will find instructional material and portfolio opportunities through which students can meet these objectives. Further, you will find additional practice pages for reading strategies, literary elements, vocabulary, and grammar in the **Selection Support** booklet in the Teaching Resources box.

Setting Goals Work with your students at the beginning of the unit to set goals for unit outcomes. Plan what skills and concepts you wish students to acquire. You may individualize according to students' performance levels or learning modalities.

Portfolios You may have students keep portfolios of their work or of their work in progress. The activities and prompts on the Build Your Portfolio page of each selection provide opportunities for students to apply the concepts presented with the selection.

Music, 1956-57, John Koch, Butler Institute of American Art, Youngstown, Ohio

Humanities: Drama

The Stage and the Actor

Most students have some experience of theater, even if it is limited to the auditorium in their school. Point out that theater has been a part of civilization for thousands of years. Archaeologists have uncovered ruins of the outdoor theaters of the ancient Greeks. The Globe theater, which Shakespeare used, was typical of performing spaces in the sixteenth century, while later on, theaters resembled the Theater of San Carlo, as shown on page 665: grand interior spaces, with seats for more than a thousand spectators. Explain that the kinds of plays and style of performing were suited to that performance space: The plays of the eighteenth and nineteenth centuries often involved huge spectacles, impressive sets, large casts—like some Broadway musicals today. However, in the late nineteenth and early twentieth century, the pendulum began to swing toward more intimate, psychological drama. The actors who worked with the dramas of the Russian playwright Anton Chekhov developed a highly personal, intense mode of acting, which has come to be known as the "Method." Actors today—whether they perform the works of Shakespeare, Chekhov, or contemporary late-twentieth-century playwrights—are influenced by this acting style, which has as its goal the discovery of the character's inner experience and the communication of that experience to an audience.

Drama

When you read a play, you're likely to get completely swept up in the experience. This is because reading a play exercises your imagination. All the action unfolds through dialogue, so you, the reader, must infer each character's thoughts and feelings. In addition to dialogue, stage directions also help you picture the ways that characters speak and move.

Following are a teleplay by acclaimed playwright Horton Foote and a classic tragedy by William Shakespeare. As you read each one, use the dialogue, stage directions, and your own imagination to help you "see" the performance in your mind.

◆ 635

 Humanities: Art

Music, 1956–57, by John Koch.

Encourage students to find as many connections as they can between this photograph of a singer and pianist and the unit focusing on drama: for example, the fact that drama and music are both performing arts that involve interpreting a written text; both involve the human voice and body in expressing emotion; both connect performers and audiences.

Have students link this photograph with the focus of this unit ("Drama") by answering the following question:

If this picture were a still from a play or movie, what would you imagine is happening between the singer and her accompanist? *Suggested answers: This might be an emotional moment in the song being rehearsed; the singer and pianist might be involved in a relationship outside the music, and the song emphasizes their feelings; the singer may be auditioning for the pianist, trying to impress him.*

Assessing Student Progress

The following tools are available to measure the degree to which students meet the unit objectives:

Informal Assessment

The questions on the Guide for Responding sections are a first level of response to the concepts and skills presented with the selection. Students' responses are a brief informal measure of their grasp of the material. Their responses on this level can indicate where further instruction and practice are needed. You may then follow up with the practice pages in the *Selection Support* booklet.

You will find literature and reading guides in the *Alternative Assessment* booklet, which you may give students on an individual basis for informal assessment of their performance.

Formal Assessment

In the *Formal Assessment* booklet, you will find selection tests and a unit test.

Selection Tests The selection tests measure comprehension and skills acquisition for each selection or group of selections.

Unit Test The unit test applies the unit skills on a broader level. The Critical Reading section measures Unit Objectives 1, 2, and 3. The Vocabulary and Grammar section measures Objectives 4 and 5. The Essay section measures Objectives 1 and 6.

Alternative Assessment

Portfolios As you review individual pieces or the collected work in students' portfolios, you will find assessment sheets available in the portfolio section of the *Alternative Assessment* booklet.

Scoring Rubrics You will find scoring rubrics for writing modes in the *Alternative Assessment* booklet. You can apply these to Writing Mini-Lessons and to Writing Process Workshop lessons.

Speaking and Listening The *Alternative Assessment* booklet contains assessment sheets for speaking and listening activities.

Learning Modalities The *Alternative Assessment* contains activities that appeal to different learning styles. You may use these to as an alternative measurement of students' growth.

The Reading for Success page in each unit presents a set of problem-solving procedures to help readers understand authors' words and ideas on multiple levels. Good readers develop a bank of strategies from which they can draw as needed and apply to a variety of reading situations.

Unit 8 presents strategies for reading drama. Students will have encountered most of these strategies earlier. Here, however, they apply them to a very specific situation: reading plays.

How to Use the Reading for Success Page

- Introduce strategies for reading drama, presenting each as a problem-solving procedure. Be sure students understand what each strategy involves and under what circumstances to apply it.

- Before students read the plays, have them preview them, looking at the annotations in the green boxes that model the strategies.

Reading for Success

Strategies for Reading Drama

One of the earliest literary forms, drama dates back to prehistoric times when people reenacted scenes of exciting moments of a hunt or acted out their fears and hopes in religious rites. In modern drama, people continue to act out the struggles and triumphs of life.

While plays share many elements with prose, fiction, and poetry, the greatest difference is that drama is designed to be performed on a stage before an audience. The story is told mostly through dialogue and action. The stage directions indicate when and how the actors move and sometimes suggest sound and lighting effects. It is the doing or acting quality that makes drama unique in literature. Although people frequently read and enjoy a drama's text, you must always keep in mind that it was written to be performed.

When you read a drama, apply the following strategies to interact with the text:

Envision the action.
Reading a drama without envisioning the action is like watching a movie with your eyes shut. Your understanding and appreciation of the drama will be enriched if you use the stage directions and other details to help you form mental pictures of the action. How do the actors move? What tones of voice do they use?

Predict.
As you read a drama, make predictions about what you think will happen. Look for hints in the dialogue or action that seem to suggest a certain outcome. As you read on, you will see whether your predictions are correct.

Question.
Note the questions that come to mind as you read. For example, why do the characters act as they do? What causes events to happen? Why does the writer include certain information? Look for answers to your questions as you read.

Be aware of the historical context.
When does the action of the drama occur? What are the conditions of the times? If the drama takes place in a setting from the past or in a foreign city, you may have to consider that customs and accepted conduct may be different from your experiences.

Summarize.
Dramas are often broken into acts or scenes. These natural breaks give you an opportunity to review the action. What is the conflict? What is happening toward its resolution? Put the characters' actions and words together as you summarize.

You will be a more effective reader of drama if you use these strategies. You will be better able to understand the conflict and resolution of a play and apply your understanding to your own world.

636 ◆ Drama

Reading Strategies: Support and Reinforcement

Appropriate Reading Strategies Students are given a reading strategy to apply in each act of the plays. Each reading strategy is appropriate to the content of the act.

Reading Prompts To encourage application of the given reading strategy, there are occasional prompts, within green boxes, at appropriate and significant points.

In addition, there are red boxes prompting application of the Literary Focus concept and maroon boxes prompting students to connect with their lives.

Using the Boxed Annotations and Prompts
The material in the green, red, and maroon boxes along the sides of selections is intended to help students apply the literary element and the reading strategy and to make a connection with their lives.

You may use the boxed material in several ways:

- Have students pause when they come to a box and respond to its prompt before they continue reading.

- Urge students to read through the selection ignoring the boxes. After they have read the selection completely, they may go back and review the selection, responding to the prompts.

PART **1** *Today's Drama*

Balcony at the Alhambra, 1911, Spencer Gore, York City Art Gallery, England

Today's Drama ◆ 637

A teleplay by renowned playwright Horton Foote makes up this section of the "Drama" unit. In "The Dancers," a young man finds himself forced into an uncomfortable situation: He is expected to escort a girl he doesn't know to a dance he does-n't want to attend. Although the play is set in 1950's Texas, today's students will have no trouble relating to the timeless themes of teenagers struggling to fit in and trying to communicate with others.

Customize for
Varying Student Needs
When assigning the selection in this section to your students, keep in mind the following factors:

"The Dancers"
• High-interest subject matter—dating, getting along with friends and parents, learning how to behave in social situations—will appeal to most students
• Teleplay can be read aloud in class
• 1950's setting may be unfamiliar to many students

Humanities: Art

Balcony at the Alhambra, 1911, by Spencer Gore.

This painting recalls the Impressionist work of Henri Matisse, particularly in its use of the rose-violet-blue spectrum and its stylized human faces. In contrast to *Music* on the previous spread, this painting shows not the performers without their audience, but the audience without performers. Nevertheless, the performers are suggested in the intent expressions and body language of the audience members in the balcony.

Have students link the painting to the focus of Part 1 ("Today's Drama") by answering the following questions:
1. Do you think the audience is watching a thought-provoking play or an entertaining one? How can you tell? *Students should note that the people are bending toward the performance, showing great concentration.*
2. Some people would say that a work such as a play, concert, or opera is incomplete until it is performed for an audience. Do

you agree? *Accept reasonable responses.*
3. Choose one of the audience members (either in the balcony or in the seats below), and imagine what he or she is doing at the theater, what he or she thinks of the performance, and so on.
Students may wish to speculate about the figure seen in profile, who may be viewing the woman next to him as well as the performance.

Guide for Reading

OBJECTIVES

1. To read, comprehend, and interpret a play
2. To relate a play to personal experience
3. To envision the action in a play
4. To imagine the staging of a play
5. To build vocabulary in context and learn homographs
6. To develop skill in using linking verbs and predicate adjectives
7. To write a script using realistic dialogue
8. To respond to the play through writing, speaking and listening, and projects

SKILLS INSTRUCTION

Vocabulary:
Homographs
Grammar:
Linking Verbs and Predicate Adjectives
Reading Strategy:
Envision the Action
Literary Focus:
Staging

Speaking and Listening:
Role-Playing a Counseling Session (teacher edition)
Critical Viewing:
Compare and Contrast; Hypothesize; Generalize; Speculate

PORTFOLIO OPPORTUNITIES

Writing: Diary Entry; Casting Notes; News Report
Writing Mini-Lesson: Script
Speaking and Listening: Musical Accompaniment; Counseling
Projects: Dance Demonstrate ; Costume Design

More About the Author
Horton Foote won the 1995 Pulitzer Prize for Drama for his play *The Young Man from Atlanta.* He has also won Academy Awards for his screenplays for the movies *To Kill a Mockingbird* and *Tender Mercies.*

Horton Foote (1916–   )

The computer was not around when Horton Foote started writing plays over fifty years ago, so he used a pen. Today, he still uses a pen. He says, "The whole process of writing is a life force for me. I love the theater, you see. I love actors. I love directors, I love stagehands. I love the whole process."

From Actor to Writer After high school, Foote left his hometown of Wharton, Texas, to go to acting school—first in California and then in New York. While in New York, he formed friendships with fellow actors and, together, they formed an off-Broadway theater company. He began writing plays at that time, and since then, writing has been the focus of his career.

During the 1950's and early 1960's, Foote wrote scripts for live television in what is called television's "golden age." One of his first teleplays, *The Trip to Bountiful,* was later made into an award-winning film.

> *Foote is best known as a screenwriter whose characters are everyday people with everyday problems.*

A World of His Own Many of Foote's plays are set in the fictional town of Harrison, Texas. Foote bases this town on his own hometown, and his characters on people he has known. He says that his plays are often concerned "with defining what home is and where home is and how we get to home."

Some recurring themes in Foote's plays are human shortcomings, family issues, and the relationships between generations. *The Dancers,* which comes from a 1956 collection of television plays called *Harrison, Texas,* reflects these themes.

◆ Build Vocabulary

HOMOGRAPHS
In "The Dancers," a daughter tries to console her mother, who has been crying. *Console* is a homograph—a word that has two or more meanings but is always spelled the same. In this case, *console* is a verb pronounced "kun *sohl*" and meaning "to comfort." Console can also be a noun, pronounced "*kon* sohl" and meaning "a television cabinet that is made to stand on the floor." The only way to tell the proper meaning and pronunciation of a homograph is to look at the context in which it appears.

genteel
mortified
defiance
console

WORD BANK
Before you read, preview this list of words from the play.

◆ Build Grammar Skills

LINKING VERBS AND PREDICATE ADJECTIVES
A **linking verb** connects a subject to a word later in the sentence. Verbs used most often as linking verbs are forms of *be* and verbs associated with the five senses (look, sound, smell, feel, and taste), as well as a few other verbs (such as *appear, seem, become*). When the word later in the sentence describes the subject, it is a **predicate adjective**. When it renames the subject, it is a predicate noun.

Do not make the mistake of using an adverb instead of a predicate adjective after a linking verb.

Correct: Inez felt foolish.

Incorrect: Inez felt foolishly.

638 ◆ *Drama*

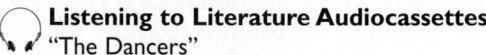
Prentice Hall Literature Program Resources

REINFORCE / RETEACH / EXTEND
Selection Support Pages
Build Vocabulary: Homographs, p. 184
Build Grammar Skills: Linking Verbs and Predicate Adjectives, p. 185
Reading Strategy: Envision the Action, p. 186
Literary Focus: Staging, p. 187
Strategies for Diverse Student Needs, p. 45
Beyond Literature
Career Connection: Performing Arts, p. 45
Formal Assessment Selection Test, pp. 161–163, Assessment Resources Software

Alternative Assessment, p. 45
Writing and Language Transparencies
Cluster Organizer, p. 80
Resource Pro CD-ROM
"The Dancers"—includes all resource material and customizable lesson plan

Listening to Literature Audiocassettes
"The Dancers"

Literature CD-ROM *How to Read and Understand Drama,* Feature 3

The Dancers

◆ Literature and Your Life

CONNECT YOUR EXPERIENCE

Like everyone, you probably experience times when your social life doesn't go smoothly. You might go to a party where you don't know anyone, or mistakenly make plans with two different people for the same evening. As you read this play, notice how the characters respond to awkward situations like these.

Journal Writing Jot down different ways of declining and accepting a social invitation.

THEMATIC FOCUS: FACING CONFLICTS

In "The Dancers," the characters face some common interpersonal problems: conflicts between mother and daughter, friends and acquaintances. As you read, think about similar problems you've faced. How do the characters' actions remind you of your own?

◆ Background for Understanding

CULTURE

In the 1950's, when "The Dancers" is set, people danced differently from the way they do now. Partners held each other, and their movements were synchronized and predetermined, depending on the type of dance. It was not uncommon for children to take dance lessons, in which they learned how to do ballroom dances such as the Waltz, the Foxtrot, and the Cha-Cha.

◆ Literary Focus

STAGING

The way a play is brought to life on the stage is called **staging.** Staging includes the sets, lighting, sound effects, costumes, and the way the actors move and deliver their lines. Staging is based on the stage directions the playwright includes in a drama. These directions, which are bracketed and italicized, describe sets, props, lighting, sound effects, and the appearance, personalities, and movements of the characters. The director, designers, actors, and other people working on the play adapt and interpret stage directions to determine how the play is staged. When you read a play, you use the dialogue, stage directions, and your imagination to stage the play in your mind's eye.

◆ Reading Strategy

ENVISION THE ACTION

Plays are meant to be performed, so it is important to **envision the action.** As you read, form a picture in your mind. Use the stage directions provided by the author to help you do so. Look at this example:

[HORACE *is smiling over the compliments, half wanting to believe what they say, but then not so sure. He is dancing with her around the room as the lights fade.*]

By carefully reading this description and drawing from your own experiences, you can picture Horace's face as he dances with his sister. The details in the description reveal that although Horace is smiling, he is feeling uncertain. Based on your experiences, you can picture how Horace might look with a tentative smile on his face.

As you read, use a graphic organizer like this one to note details of the setting and of characters' physical appearances. Recording such details will be an additional aid in picturing the action.

Details of Characters		Details of Setting
Horace		

Interest Grabber Although styles of dress and dancing have changed a lot since the 1950's, when this play is set, many of the conflicts of teenage social life remain the same. Hook students' interest in the play by having them discuss a recent dance or other boy-girl social event at your school. Ask students to list some of the concerns they had and the decisions they made in the weeks before the dance. What tensions and conflicts did students have with friends and family? Ask students to look for similar conflicts as they read the play.

Customize for
Less Proficient Readers
These students may have difficulty envisioning the action and, especially, the changes in scene, in the play. Assign roles to different students, and have them read the first few pages of the play aloud. Stop the reading frequently to explain the stage directions and to make sure students can picture the action in their minds.

Customize for
More Advanced Students
Encourage these students to imagine they are the director of a local production of the play. As they read, have them make notes on how they would stage each scene and what advice they would give to the actors.

Customize for
English Language Learners
Explain to these students that the play takes place several decades ago in a small American town. Review the photos in the text to help students imagine how American teenagers of that time looked and acted.

Preparing for Standardized Tests

Reading and Vocabulary Using context clues to understand the meaning of a homograph is a useful skill for verbal sections of standardized tests. Give students this example:

The pianist ended his recital with a <u>bow</u>.

The word *bow* means: *(C)*

(A) A ribbon with two or more loops

(B) The front end of a ship

(C) To bend the head in respect

The Build Vocabulary lesson for this selection focuses on homographs. For more practice, use

Build Vocabulary, page 184 in *Selection Support*.

Grammar and Language Some standardized tests require students to choose the correct word or words to complete a sentence. The Build Grammar Skills lesson for this selection, which focuses on placing adjectives after linking verbs and adverbs after action verbs, will improve students' performance on such items. For additional practice, use the Build Grammar Skills page on Linking Verbs and Predicate Adjectives, p. 185, in *Selection Support.*

❶ Envision the Action Students may already have suspected that Emily is reluctant to go to the dance with Horace and that her mother is forcing her to do it. As a result, she hurries out of the store to get away from her mother and Horace's sister, because she doesn't want to talk about the dance.

◆ Build Vocabulary

❷ Homographs Point out to students that there are four homographs spelled "bit," and that in this case they are all pronounced the same: the mouthpiece of a horse's bridle; a drilling tool; a small quantity of something; and the most recent meaning, a unit of computer information. Ask which meaning is used here. *The meaning is "a small quantity of something."*

◆ Literary Focus

❸ Staging Accept any reasonable responses, as students may picture this scene in a variety of ways.

◆ Critical Thinking

❹ Infer Ask students what they can infer about Horace's personality from this conversation with Inez. *Students may infer that Horace is either a bit shy or doesn't care much for small talk. Note that Horace answers most of his sister's questions with few words.*

---

❶ ◆ **Reading Strategy**
Picture in your mind how Emily looks as she starts to leave the drugstore. Is she in a hurry?

INEZ. Oh, yes. He's taking Herman's.

ELIZABETH. I just wondered. I wanted to offer ours if he didn't have one.

INEZ. That's very sweet—but we're giving him our car every night for the two weeks of his visit. Oh—I know what I'm after. Flowers. I have to order Emily's corsage for Horace. I came in here to use the telephone to call you to find out what color Emily's dress was going to be.

ELIZABETH. Blue.

INEZ. My favorite color. Walk me over to the florist.

ELIZABETH. All right.

[*They go out as the lights fade. The lights are brought up downstage left on the living room of* INEZ STANLEY. HERMAN STANLEY *and his brother-in-law,* HORACE, come in. HERMAN *is carrying* HORACE's *suitcase.* HERMAN *is in his middle thirties.* HORACE *is eighteen, thin, sensitive, but a likable boy.*]

HERMAN. Inez. Inez. We're here.

[*He puts the bag down in the living room.* INEZ *comes running in from stage right.*]

INEZ. You're early.

HERMAN. The bus was five minutes ahead of time.

INEZ. Is that so? Why, I never heard of that. [*She kisses her brother.*] Hello, honey.

HORACE. Hello, sis.

INEZ. You look fine.

HORACE. Thank you.

❷ INEZ. You haven't put on a bit of weight though.

INEZ. 'Bye, Emily.

EMILY. 'Bye.

[*She goes on out.*]

ELIZABETH. Does Horace have a car for tonight?

INEZ. Oh, yes. He's taking Herman's.

HORACE. Haven't I?

INEZ. Not a bit. I'm just going to stuff food down you and put some weight on you while you're here. How's your appetite?

HORACE. Oh, it's real good. I eat all the time.

INEZ. Then why don't you put on some weight?

HORACE. I don't know. I guess I'm just the skinny type.

INEZ. How are the folks?

HORACE. Fine.

INEZ. Mother over her cold?

HORACE. Yes, she is.

INEZ. Dad's fine?

HORACE. Just fine.

INEZ. Oh, Herman, did you ask him?

HERMAN. Ask him what?

INEZ. Ask him what? About his tux.

HERMAN. No, I didn't. . . .

INEZ. Honestly, Herman. Here we have him a date with the prettiest and most popular girl in Harrison and Herman says ask him what. You did bring it, didn't you, Bubber?

HORACE. Bring what?

INEZ. Your tux.

HORACE. Oh, sure.

INEZ. Well, guess who I've got you a date with. Aren't your curious?

HORACE. Uh. Huh.

INEZ. Well, guess . . .

[*A pause. He thinks.*]

HORACE. I don't know.

❸ ◆ **Literary Focus**
Notice that there are no directions for how Inez should play this scene. Does she feel her brother's arm, for example? Or does she just hold him at arm's length and look at him?

❹

INEZ. Well, just try guessing. . . .

HORACE. Well . . . uh . . . [*He is a little embarrassed. He stands trying to think. No names come to him.*] I don't know.

INEZ. Emily Crews. Now isn't she a pretty girl?

HORACE. Yes. She is.

INEZ. And the most popular girl in this town. You know her mother is a very close friend of mine and she called me day before yesterday and she said I hear Horace is coming to town and I said yes you were and she said that the boy Emily is going with is in summer school and couldn't get away this week-end and Emily said she wouldn't go to the dance at all but her mother said that she had insisted and wondered if you'd take her. . . .

HORACE. Her mother said. Does Emily want me to take her?

INEZ. That isn't the point, Bubber. The point is that her mother doesn't approve of the boy Emily is in love with and she likes you. . . .

HORACE. Who likes me?

INEZ. Emily's mother. And she thinks you would make a very nice couple.

HORACE. Oh. [*A pause.*] But what does Emily think?

▲ Critical Viewing During the 1950's, the neighborhood drugstore was a place to hear local gossip and get something to eat, as well as a place to obtain medicine, soap, and other necessities. Why do you think several scenes in "The Dancers" take place in the drugstore? [Hypothesize]

The Dancers ◆ 643

◆ **Critical Thinking**

❺ **Compare and Contrast** Ask students what qualities Elizabeth and Inez seem to have in common, judging from this passage. *They both seem pushy and insensitive to the feelings of others; they enjoy meddling in the affairs of younger family members.*

◆ **Critical Thinking**

❻ **Analyze** Ask students why Horace keeps asking how Emily feels about him and their upcoming date. *He senses that Emily is going out with him against her will. He is a sensitive person and considerate of Emily's feelings. He doesn't want to go out with someone who doesn't really like him.*

▶**Critical Viewing**◀

❼ **Hypothesize** Elicit responses such as the following: *The drugstore is a logical place for characters to run into each other accidentally; it is believable that characters might meet there or overhear gossip.*

After students respond to the Critical Viewing question, ask students if they have any favorite place where they like to meet with and talk to other young people. *Students may respond that they have a local fast food restaurant or shopping mall where they like to get together with other young people.*

Humanities: Art

The photos with this selection illustrate scenes from small-town teenage life in the 1950's, the setting for Horton Foote's play. Before students read the play, preview the photos with them, and help students imagine how life was different for teenagers of that time and place.

Use these questions for discussion:

1. What differences can you see between teenage life in the 1950's and teenage life today? *Students may notice differences in cloth-*

ing, dance styles, music technology, hairstyles, choice of hangouts, and attitudes—as revealed by facial expressions and body language.

2. What do you find most surprising about the images of 1950's teenage life shown in these pictures? *Responses will depend upon students' knowledge of the time period and their familiarity with contrasting images of the time, such as those portrayed in the musical Grease.*

643

▶Critical Viewing◀

① Infer You might elicit from students that young people of the 1950's dressed more formally on dates and liked going to favorite places—such as "soda fountains"—to enjoy each other's company over an ice-cream sundae or a milkshake.

◆ **Build Grammar Skills**

② Linking Verbs and Predicate Adjectives Have students identify all the linking verbs and predicate adjectives in this passage. *The linking verbs and predicate adjectives are: am, sorry; feeling, well; it's (It is), advisable.*

◆ **Critical Thinking**

③ Evaluate Ask students how Horace feels when Elizabeth tells him that Emily can't go out with him. *Some students might say that Horace feels hurt that Emily refuses to see him, but the majority of students will probably say that Horace is relieved by the news because he doesn't want someone to go out with him only because she is forced to do so.*

◆ **Build Vocabulary**

④ Homographs Point out that the word *counter* has several different meanings. Ask what the word means in this context and what other meanings students can think of for the word. *In this context, it means "a level surface over which business is conducted or food is served." Other meanings include "someone or something that counts things" or "to act in opposition to or in the opposite direction of."*

◆ **Critical Thinking**

⑤ Evaluate Character Ask students what Horace's behavior toward the waitress shows about his character. *Students may say that he is sensitive and concerned about other people's feelings. He is eager to please other people and afraid to speak up for his rights.*

① ▲ Critical Viewing What does this photograph reveal about life in the 1950's? [Infer]

downtown if you don't open that door right this very minute.

EMILY. I don't care. I won't come out.

ELIZABETH. Then I'll call him. [*She comes running in from right stage.* HORACE *quickly gets back to his chair and sits.*] Excuse me, Horace.

[*She crosses through the room and goes out upstage right.* HORACE *seems very ill at ease. He looks at the box of flowers. He is very warm. He begins to fan himself.* ELIZABETH *comes back in the room from upstage right. She is very nervous. But she tries to hide her nervousness in an overly social manner.* ELIZABETH *has decided to tell a fib.*]

②
③
Horace, I am so sorry to have to ruin your evening, but my little girl isn't feeling well. She has a headache and a slight temperature and I've just called the doctor and he says he thinks it's very advisable that she stay in this evening. She's upstairs insisting she go, but I do feel under the circumstances I had just

646 ◆ Drama

better keep her in. I hope you understand. **③**

HORACE. Oh, yes ma'am. I do understand.

ELIZABETH. How long do you plan to visit us, Horace?

HORACE. Two weeks.

ELIZABETH. That's nice. [*They start walking off-stage left.*] Please call Emily tomorrow and ask her out again. She'll just be heartbroken if you don't.

HORACE. Yes, ma'am. Good night.

ELIZABETH. Good night, Horace. [HORACE *goes out.* ELIZABETH *calls out after him.*] Can you see, Horace? [*In the distance we hear* HORACE *answer.*]

HORACE. Yes, ma'am.

ELIZABETH. Now you be sure and call us tomorrow. You hear? [*She stands waiting for a moment. Then she walks back across stage to upstage right, screaming at the top of her voice.*] Emily Carter Crews. You have mortified me. You have mortified me to death. I have, for your information, called your father and he is interrupting his work and is coming home this very minute and he says to tell you that you are not to be allowed to leave this house again for two solid weeks. Is that perfectly clear?

[*She is screaming as she goes out upstage right. The lights are brought down. They are brought up immediately downstage right on the drugstore. It is half an hour later.* HORACE *comes in. He seats himself at the counter. He still has the box of flowers. The drugstore is deserted. A* WAITRESS *is up near the front with her arms on the counter. She keeps glancing at a clock.* HORACE *is examining a menu.*] **④**

◆ **Build Vocabulary**

mortified (môr´ tə fīd) *v.*: Humiliated
defiance (di fī´ əns) *n.*: Open resistance

HORACE. Can I have a chicken salad sandwich?

WAITRESS. We're all out of that.

HORACE. Oh.

[*He goes back to reading the menu.*]

WAITRESS. If it's all the same to you. I'd rather not make a sandwich. I'm closing my doors in ten minutes.

❺ HORACE. Oh. Well, what would you like to make?

WAITRESS. Any kind of ice cream or soft drinks. [*She looks up at the ice cream menu.*] Coffee is all gone.

HORACE. How about a chocolate ice cream soda?

WAITRESS. OK. Coming up. [*She starts to mix the soda. She talks as she works.*] Going to the dance?

HORACE. No.

WAITRESS. The way you're all dressed up I thought for sure you were going.

HORACE. No. I was, but I changed my mind.

[*MARY CATHERINE DAVIS comes in the drugstore from downstage right. Somehow in her young head she has gotten the idea that she is a plain girl and in* defiance *for the pain of that fact she does everything she can to make herself look plainer.*]

◆ **Reading Strategy**
❻ What do you think Mary Catherine does to make herself look plainer?

WAITRESS. Hello, Mary Catherine. Been to the movies?

MARY CATHERINE. Yes, I have.

[*The WAITRESS puts the drink down in front of HORACE. He begins to drink.*]

WAITRESS. What'll you have, Mary Catherine?

MARY CATHERINE. Vanilla ice cream.

WAITRESS. OK. [*She gets the ice cream. She talks as she does so.*] There weren't many at

the picture show tonight, I bet. I can always tell by whether we have a crowd in here or not after the first show. I guess everybody is at the dance.

MARY CATHERINE. I could have gone, but I didn't want to. I didn't want to miss the picture show. Emily Crews didn't go. Leo couldn't get home from summer school and she said she was refusing to go. Her mother made a date for her with some boy from out of town without consulting her and she was furious about it. I talked to her this afternoon. She said she didn't know yet how she would get out of it, but she would. She said she had some rights. Her mother doesn't approve of Leo and that's a shame because they are practically engaged.

WAITRESS. I think Emily is a very cute girl, don't you?

MARY CATHERINE. Oh, yes. I think she's darling.

[*HORACE has finished his drink and is embarrassed by their talk. He is trying to get the WAITRESS's attention but doesn't quite know how. He finally calls to the WAITRESS.*]

◆ **Literary Focus:**
❽ What do you think Horace might be doing to get the waitress's attention?

HORACE. Miss. . .

WAITRESS. Yes?

HORACE. How much do I owe you?

WAITRESS. Twenty cents.

HORACE. Thank you.

[*He reaches in his pocket for the money.*]

WAITRESS. Emily has beautiful clothes, doesn't she?

MARY CATHERINE. Oh, yes. She does.

WAITRESS. Her folks are rich?

MARY CATHERINE. She has the prettiest things. But she's not a bit stuck up. . . .

[*He holds the money out to the WAITRESS.*]

◆ **Reading Strategy**
❻ **Envision the Action** Elicit responses such as the following: *Mary Catherine might wear unflattering clothes, wear no makeup, and take no care with her hair. She might walk with a slouch and not smile much.*

Comprehension Check ☑
❼ Does Mary Catherine know that Emily's date for the dance is sitting at the counter? How do you think Horace feels when he hears Mary Catherine talking about Emily's refusal to go out with him? *Mary Catherine does not know that Horace is the boy who was supposed to take Emily to the dance. Horace is embarrassed and nervous that Mary Catherine and the waitress might suddenly realize that he was supposed to be Emily's date. He might also feel a little relieved to know that Emily's reasons had to do with her feelings for another boy.*

◆ **Literary Focus**
❽ **Staging** Elicit responses such as the following: *Horace might be moving his head to try to make eye contact with the waitress, or he might be clearing his throat, standing up, or waving his hand to try to get her attention.*

◆ **Critical Thinking**
❾ **Evaluate** Ask students what Mary Catherine's comments about Emily reveal about Mary Catherine herself. *Students may say that, though Emily is rich, pretty, and popular, and Mary Catherine is not, Mary Catherine doesn't seem to feel jealous of Emily. She is kind and concerned about Emily, and it is generous of her to defend someone she has good reasons to resent or envy.*

The Dancers ◆ 647

 Workplace Skills Mini-Lesson

Negotiating, Compromising, and Being Assertive

Introduce the Concept Point out that working with others requires flexibility and an ability to stand up for one's own needs. Horace is so concerned with being nice and avoiding conflict with the waitress and his sister that he often puts aside his own needs and goes along with others.

Develop Background Tell students that being sensitive to the feelings of others is

important, but that good workers sometimes need to negotiate and compromise, rather than avoiding conflicts. Alert them to the skills they may need to do this:

- Be assertive, but not hostile, about what they need to do a job.
- In a conflict situation, try to find a compromise both parties can accept.
- Negotiate a compromise by making offers and counteroffers about ways to solve a problem.

Apply the Information Have students work in pairs to negotiate a compromise for this job situation: The worker needs Saturday off, but the employer is short of workers that weekend.

Assess the Outcome List the compromises students reached, and have the class judge those compromises. Are the compromises logical? Can they be easily implemented in the workplace?

❶ Staging Make sure students understand that Horace is not on stage at this point, so the audience cannot actually see what he is doing. Ask: How can the actors playing the waitress and Mary Catherine convey to the audience what Horace is doing and how they feel about his strange behavior? *Their words, actions, and facial expressions can convey what they see to the audience.*

◆ **Critical Thinking**

❷ Analyze Ask students what Inez's reaction to Horace's disappointment shows about her. *Inez is so insensitive that instead of feeling compassion for Horace, she actually blames him for being depressed and wanting to go home. She seems incapable of changing her pushy behavior, even when it's obviously hurting other people instead of helping them. She has no insight into her own true motivations and capacity for damaging people.*

▶Critical Viewing◀

❸ Compare and Contrast Generally, the dancers seem to be feeling relaxed, happy, and absorbed in the music and their partners, much the same as teenagers of today. However, the slow dancing shown in the photo is not done too often by today's teens. Also, some of the clothing worn by the teenagers in the photo is somewhat different from the clothing of today. Of course, the radio-phonograph being operated by the young girl is quite different from the stereo CD-player of today.

HORACE. Here you are.

WAITRESS. Thank you. [*She takes the money and rings it up in the cash register.* HORACE *goes on out.* WAITRESS *shakes her head as he goes.*] There's a goofy nut if I ever saw one. He's got flowers under his arm. He's wearing a tux and yet he's not going to the dance. Who is he?

MARY CATHERINE. I don't know. I never saw him before.

[*The* WAITRESS *walks to the edge of the area and looks out. She comes back shaking her head. She sits on the stool beside* MARY CATHERINE.]

WAITRESS. [*While laughing and shaking her head.*] I ought to call the Sheriff and have him locked up. Do you know what he's doing?

MARY CATHERINE. No. What?

WAITRESS. Standing on the corner. Dancing back and forth. He's holding his arm up like he's got a girl and everything. Wouldn't it kill you? [*Goes to the front and looks out.*] See him?

MARY CATHERINE. No. He's stopped.

WAITRESS. What's he doing?

MARY CATHERINE. Just standing there. Looking kind of lost.

[MARY CATHERINE *comes back to the counter. She starts eating her ice cream again.*]

WAITRESS. Well—it takes all kinds.

MARY CATHERINE. I guess so.

[*She goes back to eating her ice cream. The lights are brought down. The lights are brought up on the area downstage left. The living room of the* STANLEYS. INEZ *is there reading a book.* HERMAN *comes in.*]

HERMAN. Hi, hon.

INEZ. Hello. . . .

HERMAN. What's the matter with you? You look down in the dumps.

INEZ. No, I'm just disgusted.

HERMAN. What are you disgusted about?

INEZ. Horace. I had everything planned so beautifully for him and then that silly Emily has to go and hurt his feelings.

HERMAN. Well, honey, that was pretty raw, the trick she pulled.

INEZ. I know. But he's a fool to let that get him down. He should have just gone to the dance by himself and proved her wrong. . . . Why like I told him. Show her up. Rush a different girl every night. Be charming. Make yourself popular. But it's like trying to talk to

▼ Critical Viewing Look at the way these teenagers are dancing, and notice how they are dressed. How do the teens in this photo compare with teenagers today? [**Compare and Contrast**]

a stone wall. He refused to go out any more. He says he's going home tomorrow.

HERMAN. Where is he now?

INEZ. Gone to the movies.

HERMAN. Well, honey. I hate to say it, but in a way it serves you right. I've told you a thousand times if I've told you once. Leave the boy alone. He'll be all right. Only don't push him. You and your mother have pushed the boy and pushed him and pushed him.

INEZ. And I'm going to keep on pushing him. I let him off tonight because his feelings were hurt, but tomorrow I'm going to have a long talk with him.

HERMAN. Inez. Leave the boy alone.

INEZ. I won't leave him alone. He is my brother and I'm going to see that he learns to have a good time.

HERMAN. Inez. . . .

INEZ. Now you just let me handle this, Herman. He's starting to college next year and it's a most important time in his life. He had no fun in high school. . . .

HERMAN. Now. He must have had some fun. . . .

INEZ. Not like other people. And he's not going through four years of college like a hermit with his nose stuck in some old book. . . . [*She jumps up.*] I'll never forgive Elizabeth for letting Emily behave this way. And I told her so. I said Elizabeth Crews, I am very upset. . . .

[*She is angrily walking up and down as the lights fade. They are brought up downstage right on the drugstore area. The* WAITRESS *is there alone.* MARY CATHERINE *comes in from downstage right.*]

WAITRESS. Did you go to the movies again tonight?

MARY CATHERINE. Uh-huh. Lila, do you remember when I was telling you about Emily's date and how she wouldn't go out with him because he was such a bore?

WAITRESS. Uh. . . .

MARY CATHERINE. Oh, I just feel awful. That was the boy sitting in here. . . .

WAITRESS. Last night . . . ?

MARY CATHERINE. Yes. I went riding with Emily and some of the girls this afternoon and we passed by his sister's house and there sat the boy.

WAITRESS. Sh . . . sh. . . . [*She has seen* HORACE *come into the area from downstage right. He comes to the counter. He seems very silent. He picks up a menu.*] Back again tonight?

HORACE. Uh-huh.

WAITRESS. What'll you have?

The Dancers ◆ 649

◆ **Critical Thinking**

❶ Analyze Emily speaks with Horace face-to-face and tells him the truth about last night. Ask students what this shows about Emily's character. *Suggested response: Emily shows that she is mature enough to tell someone the truth, even if doing so is not a pleasant task. What Emily says also shows that she is considerate of other people's feelings.*

◆ **Critical Thinking**

❷ Make Judgments Ask students if they admire Mary Catherine for keeping her promise to Velma. *Students may say that they admire Mary Catherine because it is important to keep promises you make to a friend, or they may say they do not admire her because she seems motivated mostly by her fear of making Velma angry.*

◆ **Critical Thinking**

❸ Make Judgments Ask students to judge whether Velma is really a true friend of Mary Catherine. Would a true friend be so "sensitive"? Have students give reasons for their opinions. *Some students will say that Velma is a true friend, and being a friend includes keeping promises—even promises over inconsequential matters. Other students will disagree, saying that if Velma were a true friend, she wouldn't get upset over things that aren't very important.*

HORACE. A cup of coffee. . . .

WAITRESS. All out. We don't serve coffee after eight unless we happen to have some left over from suppertime. . . .

HORACE. Thanks. [*He gets up.*]

WAITRESS. Nothing else?

HORACE. No, thanks.

[*He goes over to the magazine rack. He picks up a magazine and starts looking through it.* EMILY CREWS *comes in from downstage right. She doesn't see* HORACE. *She goes right over to* MARY CATHERINE.]

EMILY. Leora and I were riding around the square and we saw you sitting here. . . .

[MARY CATHERINE *points to* HORACE. *She turns around and sees him.* EMILY *looks a little embarrassed. He happens to glance up and sees her.*]

HORACE. Hello, Emily.

EMILY. Hello, Horace. . . . Do you know Mary Catherine Davis?

HORACE. No. How do you do.

MARY CATHERINE. How do you do.

EMILY. I feel awfully bad about last night, Horace. My mother says you know I wasn't really sick. I just wanted to tell you that it had nothing to do with you, Horace. It was a battle between me and my mother. Mary Catherine can tell you. I promised the boy I go with not to go with any other boys. . . .

HORACE. Oh, that's all right, I understand.

EMILY. You see, we've gone steady for two years. All the other boys in town understand it and their feelings are not a bit hurt if I turn them down. Are they, Mary Catherine?

MARY CATHERINE. No.

EMILY. Mary Catherine is my best friend and she can tell you I'm not stuck up. And I would have gone, anyway, except I was so mad at my mother. . . .

MARY CATHERINE. Emily is not stuck up a bit. Emily used to date all the boys before she began going with Leo steadily. Didn't you, Emily?

EMILY. Uh-huh. How long are you going to be here, Horace?

HORACE. Well, I haven't decided, Emily.

EMILY. Well, I hope you're not still hurt with me.

HORACE. No, I'm not, Emily.

EMILY. Well, I'm glad for that. Mary Catherine, can you come with us?

MARY CATHERINE. No, I can't, Emily. Velma came in after the first show started and I promised to wait here for her and we'd walk home together.

EMILY. Come on. We can ride around and watch for her.

MARY CATHERINE. No, I don't dare. You know how sensitive Velma is. If she looked in here and saw I wasn't sitting at this counter she'd go right home and not speak to me again for two or three months.

EMILY. Velma's too sensitive. You shouldn't indulge her in it.

MARY CATHERINE. I'm willing to grant you that. But you all are going off to college next year and Velma and I are the only ones that are going to be left here and I can't afford to get her mad at me.

EMILY. OK. I'll watch out for you and if we're still riding around when Velma gets out, we'll pick you up.

MARY CATHERINE. Fine. . . .

EMILY. 'Bye. . . .

MARY CATHERINE. 'Bye. . . .

EMILY. 'Bye, Horace.

HORACE. Good-bye, Emily.

[*She goes downstage right.*]

MARY CATHERINE. She's a lovely girl. She was my closest friend until this year. Now we're still good friends, but we're not as close as we were. We had a long talk about it last week. I told her I understood. She and Eloise Dayton just naturally have a little more in common now. They're both going steady and they're going to the same college. *A pause.* They're going to Sophie Newcomb.[5] Are you going to college?

HORACE. Uh-huh.

MARY CATHERINE. You are? What college?

HORACE. The university. . . .

MARY CATHERINE. Oh. I know lots of people there. [*A pause.*] I had a long talk with Emily about my not getting to go. She said she thought it was wonderful that I wasn't showing any bitterness about it. [*A pause.*] I'm getting a job next week so I can save up enough money to go into Houston to business school. I'll probably work in Houston some day. If I don't get too lonely. Velma Morrison's oldest sister went into Houston and got herself a job but she almost died from loneliness. She's back here now working at the courthouse. Oh, well . . . I don't think I'll get lonely. I think a change of scenery would be good for me.

[VELMA MORRISON *comes in downstage right. She is about the same age as* MARY CATHERINE. *She is filled with excitement.*]

VELMA. Mary Catherine, you're going to be furious with me. But Stanley Sewell came in right after you left and he said he'd never forgive me if I didn't go riding with him. . . . I said I had to ask you first. As I had asked you to wait particularly for me and that I knew you were very sensitive.

---
5. **Sophie Newcomb:** H. Sophie Newcomb College for Women in New Orleans, Louisiana.

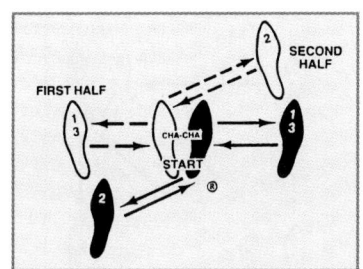

MARY CATHERINE. I'm very sensitive. You're very sensitive. . . . I have never in my life stopped speaking to you over anything.

[*A car horn is heard off stage.*]

VELMA. Will you forgive me if I go?

MARY CATHERINE. Oh, sure.

[VELMA *goes running out.*]

VELMA. Thank you.

[*She disappears out the door.*]

MARY CATHERINE. I'm not nearly as close to Velma as I am to Emily. I think Emily's beautiful, don't you?

HORACE. Yes. She's very pretty.

MARY CATHERINE. Well, Lila's going to kill us if we don't stop holding her up. Which way do you go?

HORACE. Home.

MARY CATHERINE. I go that way, too. We can walk together.

HORACE. OK. [*They go out of the area.*]

MARY CATHERINE. Good night, Lila.

WAITRESS. Good night.

[*They continue walking out downstage left as the lights fade. The lights are brought up on the living room of the* CREWS's *house.* ELIZABETH CREWS *is there, crying.* EMILY *comes in.*]

EMILY. Mother, what is it? Has something happened to Daddy?

ELIZABETH. No. He's in bed asleep.

EMILY. Then what is it?

ELIZABETH. Inez blessed me out and stopped speaking to me over last night. She says we've ruined the boy's whole vacation. You've broken his heart, given him all kinds of complexes and he's going home tomorrow. . . .

The Dancers ◆ 651

Explain that the word *nag* means "to constantly complain, scold, or urge someone to do something." To "get down on my knees to you" means "to beg." Being on one's knees is a posture of humility or supplication; thus, it is used for praying in Christian churches and it is appropriate for begging

◆ Critical Thinking

❶ Make Judgments Ask students what conclusions they can draw from the fact that Emily has to console and appease her mother over a small social embarrassment. *A possible response is: Elizabeth is childish and unfairly manipulates her daughter. In many ways, Emily has learned to behave more maturely than her own mother.*

◆ Literary Focus

❷ Staging Ask students why lighting plays such an important role in the staging of this play. *Lighting plays an important role because there are four different sets on stage at all times, the lighting must direct the audience's attention on the set where the action is currently taking place. Areas where the action is fading must be darkened, so the actors can leave the stage.*

◆ Critical Thinking

❸ Make Comparisons Ask students what social skill both Horace and Mary Catherine have struggled to learn. *They've both had to struggle to find enough confidence to learn to dance.*

EMILY. But I saw him at the drugstore tonight and I had a long talk with him and he said he understood. . . .

ELIZABETH. But Inez doesn't understand. She says she'll never forgive either of us again.

[*She starts to cry.*]

EMILY. Oh, Mother. I'm sorry. . . .

ELIZABETH. Emily. if you'll do me one favor. I promise you I'll never ask another thing of you again as long as I live. And I will never nag you about going out with Leo again as long as I live. . . .

EMILY. What is the favor, Mother?

ELIZABETH. Let that boy take you to the dance day after tomorrow. . . .

EMILY. Now, Mother. . . .

ELIZABETH. Emily. I get down on my knees to you. Do me this one favor. . . . [*A pause.*] Emily. . . . Emily. . . . [*She is crying again.*]

❶ EMILY. Now, Mother, please. Don't cry. I'll think about it. I'll call Leo and see what he says. But please don't cry like this. . . . Mother . . . Mother.

❷ [*She is trying to <u>console</u> her as the lights fade. The lights are brought up on upstage left. It is* MARY CATHERINE*'s yard and living room. Music can be heard in the distance.* HORACE *and* MARY CATHERINE *come walking in downstage left, go up the center of the stage until they reach the upstage area.*]

MARY CATHERINE. Well, this is where I live.

HORACE. In that house there?

MARY CATHERINE. Uh-huh. [*A pause.*]

HORACE. Where is that music coming from?

MARY CATHERINE. The Flats. . . .

◆ Build Vocabulary
console (kən sōl′) *v.*: Comfort

HORACE. What's the Flats?

MARY CATHERINE. I don't know what it is. That's just what they call it. It's nothing but a bunch of barbecue restaurants and beer joints down there and they call it the Flats. There used to be a creek running down there that they called Willow Creek but it's all dry now. My father says when he was a boy, every time the river flooded, Willow Creek would fill up. The river doesn't overflow any more since they took the raft[6] out of it. I like to come out here at night and listen to the music. Do you like to dance . . . ?

HORACE. Well . . . I . . . .

MARY CATHERINE. I love to dance.

HORACE. Well . . . I don't dance too well.

MARY CATHERINE. There's nothing to it but confidence.

HORACE. That's what my sister says. . . .

❸ MARY CATHERINE. I didn't learn for the longest kind of time for lack of confidence and then Emily gave me a long lecture about it and I got confidence and went ahead and learned. Would you like to come in for a while?

HORACE. Well . . . if it's all right with you. . . .

MARY CATHERINE. I'd be glad to have you.

HORACE. Thank you.

[*They go into the area.* MARY CATHERINE*'s father,* TOM DAVIS, *is seated there in his undershirt. He works in a garage.*]

MARY CATHERINE. Hello, Daddy.

TOM. Hello, baby.

MARY CATHERINE. Daddy, this is Horace.

TOM. Hello, son.

HORACE. Howdy do, sir.

---

6. **raft:** Natural dam formed by debris, leaves, and trees.

652 ◆ *Drama*

🗣 Speaking and Listening Mini-Lesson

Role-Playing a Counseling Session
This mini-lesson supports the Speaking and Listening activity in the Idea Bank on page 660.

Introduce the Concept Tell students that counselors are trained in special skills to help their clients deal with problems. In this activity, students will act as Elizabeth explaining her problem and as a counselor working out a solution to the problem.

Develop Background Give students these criteria for the role-playing:

• Explain that the counselor must first listen carefully to Elizabeth's problem and restate it so that Elizabeth feels understood. Elizabeth must describe the problem as she sees it and tell how she feels about it.

• The counselor must help Elizabeth understand Emily's feelings and point of view.

• The counselor then helps Elizabeth think

of ways to improve her relationship with Emily.

Apply the Information Have students role-play the counseling session, using the guidelines.

Assess the Outcome Use the following criteria to evaluate the counseling sessions: Were the students prepared? Did they speak clearly and use appropriate gestures? Was the problem explained well? Was the solution logical?

[*They shake hands.*]

MARY CATHERINE. Horace is Mrs. Inez Stanley's brother. He's here on a visit.

TOM. That's nice. Where's your home, son?

HORACE. Flatonia.

TOM. Oh, I see. Well, are you young people going to visit for a while?

MARY CATHERINE. Yes, sir.

TOM. Well, I'll leave you then. Good night.

MARY CATHERINE. Good night, Daddy.

HORACE. Good night, sir. [*He goes out upstage left.*] What does your father do?

MARY CATHERINE. He works in a garage. He's a mechanic. What does your father do?

HORACE. He's a judge.

MARY CATHERINE. My father worries so because he can't afford to send me to college. My mother told him that was all foolishness. That I'd rather go to business school anyway.

HORACE. Had you rather go to business school?

MARY CATHERINE. I don't know. [*A pause.*] Not really. But I'd never tell him that. When I was in the seventh grade I thought I would die if I couldn't get there, but then when I was in the ninth, Mother talked to me one day and told me Daddy wasn't sleeping at nights for fear I'd be disappointed if he couldn't send me, so I told him the next night I decided I'd rather go to business school. He seemed relieved. [*A pause.*]

HORACE. Mary Catherine. I . . . uh . . . heard you say a while ago that you didn't dance because you lacked confidence and uh . . . then I heard you say you talked it over with Emily and she told you what was wrong and you got the confidence and you went ahead . . .

MARY CATHERINE. That's right. . . .

HORACE. Well . . . It may sound silly and all to you . . . seeing I'm about to start my first year of college . . . but I'd like to ask you a question. . . .

MARY CATHERINE. What is it, Horace?

HORACE. How do you get confidence?

MARY CATHERINE. Well, you just get it. Someone points it out to you that you lack it and then you get it. . . .

HORACE. Oh, is that how it's done?

MARY CATHERINE. That's how I did it.

HORACE. You see I lack confidence. And I . . . sure would like to get it. . . .

MARY CATHERINE. In what way do you lack confidence, Horace . . . ?

HORACE. Oh, in all kinds of ways. [*A pause.*] I'm not much of a mixer.[7] . . .

MARY CATHERINE. I think you're just mixing fine tonight.

HORACE. I know. That's what's giving me a little encouragement. You're the first girl I've every really been able to talk to. I mean this way. . . .

MARY CATHERINE. Am I, Horace. . . ?

HORACE. Yes.

MARY CATHERINE. Well, I feel in some ways that's quite a compliment.

HORACE. Well, you should feel that way. [*A pause.*] Mary Catherine. . . .

MARY CATHERINE. Yes, Horace?

HORACE. I had about decided to go back home tomorrow or the next day, but I understand there's another dance at the end of the week. . . .

MARY CATHERINE. Uh-huh. Day after tomorrow.

HORACE. Well . . . I . . . don't know if you have a date or not . . . but if you don't have . . . I feel if I could take you . . . I would gain the confidence to go. . . . I mean . . .

---

7. **a mixer:** Someone who socializes easily.

The Dancers ◆ 653

Explain that "crawled on her knees"
has a similar meaning to the phrase
"get down on my knees," used on
page 652. "To eat dirt" also means to
humble oneself or humiliate oneself
in front of a person that one has
previously hurt.

◆ **Reading Strategy**

❶ **Envision the Action** Have students picture this dance in their minds. Then have them compare and contrast their image of Horace and Mary Catherine dancing with their earlier image of Horace and his sister dancing. *Even though Horace is still nervous, he wears a genuinely happy expression. As the dance continues, he may even grow more and more relaxed. He is not embarrassed and resentful, as he was with Inez. Mary Catherine, too, is genuinely happy and, unlike Inez, eager to help Horace relax and enjoy himself.*

◆ **Critical Thinking**

❷ **Predict** Ask students to predict what news Inez has for Horace. Remind them to base their predictions upon Inez's behavior up to this point. *Based upon Inez's actions thus far, students will probably predict that Inez is going to tell Horace that Emily has decided to go with Horace to the next dance.*

▶ **Critical Viewing** ◀

❸ **Speculate** Horace would probably have a better time at the dance with Mary Catherine. The primary reason is that Horace and Mary Catherine enjoy each other's company. In addition, Horace feels comfortable enough with Mary Catherine to tell her about his lack of confidence and his poor dancing skills.

MARY CATHERINE. Well, Horace. . . . You see. . .

HORACE. I know I'd gain the confidence. My sister is a swell dancer and she'll let me practice with her every living minute until it's time for the dance. Of course I don't know if I could learn to jitterbug by then or rumba or do anything fancy, you understand, but I know I could learn the fox trot and I can waltz a little now. . . .

MARY CATHERINE. I'm sure you could.

HORACE. Well, will you go with me?

MARY CATHERINE. Yes, Horace. I'd love to. . . .

HORACE. Oh, thank you, Mary Catherine. I'll just practice night and day. I can't tell you how grateful Inez is going to be to you. . . . Mary Catherine, if we played the radio softly could we dance now?

MARY CATHERINE. Why certainly, Horace.

HORACE. You understand I'll make mistakes. . .

MARY CATHERINE. I understand. . . .

[*She turns the radio on very softly.*]

HORACE. All right.

MARY CATHERINE. Yes. . . .

[*He approaches her very cautiously and takes her in his arms. He begins awkwardly to dance.* MARY CATHERINE *is very pleased and happy.*]

❶ Why, you're doing fine, Horace. Just fine.

HORACE. Thank you, Mary Catherine. Thank you.

[*They continue dancing.* HORACE *is very pleased with himself although he is still dancing quite awkwardly. The lights fade. The lights are brought up on the area downstage left. It is early next morning.* INEZ *is there reading.* HORACE *comes in*

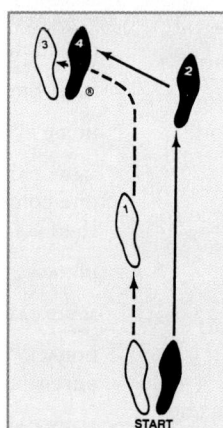

whistling. He seems brimming over with happiness.]

INEZ. What are you so happy about?

HORACE. I'm just happy.

INEZ. Wait until you hear my news and you'll be happier.

HORACE. Is that so?

INEZ. Miss Emily has seen the light.

HORACE. What? ❷

INEZ. She has succumbed.

HORACE. What do you mean?

INEZ. She has crawled on her knees.

HORACE. She's crawled on her knees? I don't get it. . . .

INEZ. She has eaten dirt.

HORACE. Sister, what's all this about?

INEZ. Last night around ten o'clock she called in the meekest kind of voice possible and said, Inez, I've called up to apologize to you. I have apologized to Horace in the drugstore. Did she?

HORACE. Uh. Huh.

INEZ. And now I want to apologize to you and to tell you how sorry I am I behaved so badly. . . .

HORACE. Well. Isn't that nice of her, Inez?

INEZ. Wait a minute. You haven't heard the whole thing. And then her highness added, tell Horace if he would like to invite me to the dance to call me and I'd be glad to accept. And furthermore, Elizabeth called this morning and said they were leaving

---

▶ **Critical Viewing** Do you think Horace would have a better time at the dance with Mary Catherine or with Emily? Why? [Speculate] ❸

Clarification Students will notice the dance steps illustrated on some pages. These steps are for the following ballroom dances that were common in the 50's:

    p. 644: Swing

    p. 651: Cha-cha

    p. 652: Rumba

    p. 654 and 656: Fox trot

You might have students who are bodily/kinesthetic learners practice the steps and demonstrate them for the class.

The Dancers ❖ 655

Cross-Curricular Connection: Social Studies

Dancing and Society The photograph on this page shows young people at a high-school prom in the 1950's. Formal dances, such as the prom pictured above, are an annual event at most high schools and they may also mark important occasions like the inauguration of a president.

The dances just described are known as social dances, as opposed to theatrical dances, because their primary function is not to entertain, as in ballet, but rather to foster recreation and companionship. Social dancing also includes less formal dancing, such as that done at parties and some restaurants or clubs.

In high school and college, social dancing serves as a means for people to get to know each other better. For the same reason, dancing is often a part of courtship.

Ask students about dances they have participated in, such as at school functions or weddings. Discuss the role of dancing in society.

Help these students understand that Inez thinks she is persuading Horace to accept her point of view by pointing out that Mary Catherine's family can't afford to buy her a dress for the dance. In fact, however, this information probably helps convince Horace to stick to his decision. Because he is so concerned about other people's feelings, the fact that Mary Catherine may have gone out and bought a dress she really can't afford is another reason he can't let her down by breaking their date.

◆ Build Vocabulary

❶ Homographs Explain that *impress* can be either a verb, with the accent on the second syllable, or a noun, with the accent on the first syllable. As a verb, it can mean either "to affect or influence someone" or "to force someone into public service, especially the military." As a noun, it means "a stamp or distinctive mark." Ask students which meaning is used here. *The meaning used here is "to affect or influence someone."*

Comprehension Check ☑

❷ What is Horace thinking after he hears that Emily wants to go to the next dance with him? *He's wondering whether to tell Inez that he already has a date, and whether he should be true to Mary Catherine, whom he really likes, or go along with his sister's plan for him, so she won't be angry with him.*

◆ Reading Strategy

❸ Envision the Action Ask students to imagine what expression Horace has on his face as his sister tells him he has to break his date with Mary Catherine. *His expression would be one of shock or anger.*

◆ Critical Thinking

❹ Make Comparisons Have students compare Inez's behavior here with the behavior Elizabeth used to convince Emily to make another date with Horace. *Both women are childish and use tears to try to manipulate a younger member of the family. They both act as if their own embarrassment is more important than the feelings of the young people involved.*

---

for Houston to buy her the most expensive evening dress in sight. **❶** Just to impress you with.

HORACE. Oh. . . . [*He sits down on a chair.*]

INEZ. Brother. What is the matter with you? **❷** Now are you gonna start worrying about this dancin' business all over again? You are the biggest fool sometimes. We've got today and tomorrow to practice.

HORACE. Inez. . . .

INEZ. Yes?

HORACE. I already have a date with someone tomorrow. . . .

INEZ. You do?

HORACE. Yes. I met a girl last night at the drugstore and I asked her.

INEZ. What girl did you ask?

HORACE. Mary Catherine Davis. . . .

INEZ. Well, you've got to get right out of it. You've got to call her up and explain what just happened.

HORACE. But, Inez. . . .

INEZ. You've got to do it, Horace. They told me they are spending all kinds of money for that dress. I practically had to threaten Elizabeth with never speaking to her again to bring this all about. Why, she will never **❸** forgive me now if I turn around and tell her you can't go. . . . Horace. Don't look that way. I can't help it. For my sake, for your sister's sake you've got to get out of this date with Mary Catherine Davis. . . . Tell her . . . tell her . . . anything. . . .

HORACE. OK. [*A pause. He starts out.*] What can I say?

INEZ. I don't know, Horace. [*A pause.*] Say . . .

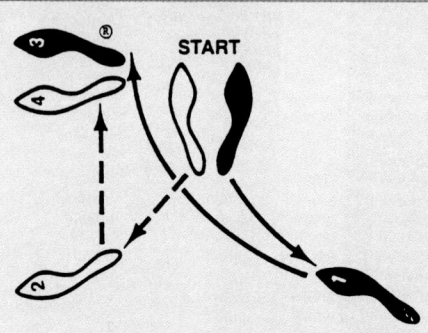

well just tell her the truth. That's the best thing. Tell her that Emily's mother is your sister's best friend and that Emily's mother has taken her into Houston to buy her a very expensive dress. . . .

HORACE. What if Mary Catherine has bought a dress . . . ?

INEZ. Well, she can't have bought an expensive dress. . . .

HORACE. Why not?

INEZ. Because her people can't afford it. Honey, you'll be the envy of every young man in Harrison, bringing Emily Crews to the dance. . . . Why, everybody will wonder just what it is you have. . . .

HORACE. I'm not going to do it.

INEZ. Horace. . . .

HORACE. I don't want to take Emily. I want to take Mary Catherine and that's just what I'm going to do.

INEZ. Horace. . . .

HORACE. My mind is made up. Once and for all. . . .

INEZ. Then what am I gonna do? [*She starts to cry.*] Who's gonna speak to Elizabeth? She'll bless me out putting her to all this trouble. Making her spend all this money and time. . . . [*She is crying loudly now.*] Horace. You just can't do this to me. You just simply can't. . . . **❹**

HORACE. I can't help it. I'm not taking Emily Crews—

INEZ. Horace. . . .

HORACE. I am not taking Emily Crews.

[*He is firm. She is crying as the lights fade. The lights are brought up on the upstage left area.* MARY CATHERINE'S FATHER *is seated there.*]

He is in his undershirt. In the distance dance music can be heard. MRS. DAVIS *comes in from stage left.*]

MRS. DAVIS. Don't you think you'd better put your shirt on, Tom? Mary Catherine's date will be here any minute.

TOM. What time is it?

MRS. DAVIS. Nine o'clock.

TOM. The dance has already started. I can hear the music from here.

MRS. DAVIS. I know. But you know young people, they'd die before they'd be the first to a dance. Put your shirt on, Tom.

TOM. OK.

MRS. DAVIS. As soon as her date arrives we'll go.

TOM. OK.

[MARY CATHERINE *comes in from stage left. She has on an evening dress and she looks very pretty.*]

❺ MRS. DAVIS. Why, Mary Catherine. You look lovely. Doesn't she look lovely, Tom?

TOM. Yes, she does.

MRS. DAVIS. Turn around, honey, and let me see you from the back. [*She does so.*] Just as pretty as you can be, Mary Catherine.

MARY CATHERINE. Thank you.

[HORACE *comes in from downstage left in his tux with a corsage box. He walks up the center of the stage to the upstage left area.*]

That's Horace. [*She goes to the corner of the area.*] Hello, Horace.

HORACE. Hello, Mary Catherine.

MARY CATHERINE. You've met my mother and father.

HORACE. Yes. I have. I met your father the other night and your mother yesterday afternoon.

MRS. DAVIS. Hello, Horace.

TOM. Hello, son.

MRS. DAVIS. Well, we were just going. You all have a good time tonight.

HORACE. Thank you.

MRS. DAVIS. Come on, Tom.

TOM. All right. Good night and have a nice time.

MARY CATHERINE. Thank you, Daddy. [*They go out stage left.* HORACE *hands her the corsage box. She takes it and opens it.*] Oh, thank you, Horace. Thank you so much. [*She takes the flowers out.*] They're just lovely. Will you pin them on for me? ❻

HORACE. I'll try. [*He takes the corsage and the pin. He begins to pin it on.*] Will about here be all right?

MARY CATHERINE. Just fine. [*He pins the corsage on.*] Emily told me about the mix-up between your sister and her mother. I appreciate your going ahead and taking me anyway. If you had wanted to get out of it I would have understood. Emily and I are very good friends . . . and. . . . ❼

HORACE. I didn't want to get out of it, Mary Catherine. I wanted to take you.

MARY CATHERINE. I'm glad you didn't want to get out of it. Emily offered to let me wear her new dress. But I had already bought one of my own.

HORACE. It's very pretty, Mary Catherine.

MARY CATHERINE. Thank you. [*A pause.*] Well, the dance has started. I can hear the music. Can't you?

HORACE. Yes.

MARY CATHERINE. Well, we'd better get going. . . .

HORACE. All right. [*They start out.*] Mary Catherine. I hope you don't think this is silly, but could we practice just once more. . . .

MARY CATHERINE. Certainly we could. . . .

[*They start to dance.* HORACE *has improved although he is no Fred Astaire. They are*

The Dancers ◆ 657

Cross-Curricular Connection: Social Studies

"The Dancers" is set in a small town in Texas, on the Gulf of Mexico, much like Horton Foote's own hometown of Wharton, Texas. Before World War I, the area was rich with cotton plantations, and the plantation owners were the local aristocracy. Later, the same land created more wealth through the oil discovered there. Thus, even in a small town like Harrison, the presence of valuable natural resources could generate large amounts of capital.

Discuss with students how government income derived from taxes on profitable local industries could benefit all citizens of Harrison—the wealthy and the not so wealthy alike. *Sample response: Government funds could be used to create better hospitals, schools, housing, and recreational facilities.*

❶ Apply Ask students to write in their journals about how they might apply Mary Catherine's words to their own lives. *Some students may write that people shouldn't let fear of embarrassment keep them from enjoying life.*

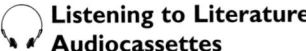

Reinforce and Extend

Customize for
Less Proficient Readers
Your less proficient readers will benefit greatly from listening to all or part of the audiocassette performance of the play after they have read it through on their own. Stop the tape at important moments to help students envision the action and to clarify important points.

🎧 **Listening to Literature Audiocassettes**

Answers

◆ *Literature and Your Life*

Reader's Response Students might say they admire his kindness and consideration for the feelings of others.

Thematic Focus Emily screams and protests vehemently, while Horace either goes along with what he is asked to do or explains why he cannot do so.

☑ Check Your Comprehension

1. Inez wants Horace to come out of his shell and have a good time once in a while.
2. Emily says that she thinks Horace is a person who rarely talks and doesn't know how to dance. She also promised the boy she's going steady with that she won't go out with anyone else.
3. Horace meets Mary Catherine by chance at the drugstore.
4. Inez wants Horace to break his date with Mary Catherine because Inez arranged a date for him with Emily. Inez also feels that Emily is the better catch because she is from a wealthy family and popular.

---

dancing around and suddenly HORACE *breaks away.*]

HORACE. Mary Catherine. I'm not good enough yet. I can't go. I'm sorry. Please let's just stay here.

MARY CATHERINE. No, Horace. We have to go.

HORACE. Please, Mary Catherine. . . .

MARY CATHERINE. I know just how you feel, Horace, but we have to go. [*A pause.*] I haven't told you the whole truth, Horace. This is my first dance, too. . . .

HORACE. It is?

MARY CATHERINE. Yes. I've been afraid to go. Afraid I wouldn't be popular. The last two dances I was asked to go and I said no.

HORACE. Then why did you accept when I asked you?

❶ **MARY CATHERINE.** I don't know. I asked myself that afterwards. I guess because you gave me a kind of confidence. [*A pause. They dance again.*] You gave me confidence and I gave you confidence. What's the sense of getting confidence, Horace, if you're not going to use it?

[*A pause. They continue dancing.*]

HORACE. That's a pretty piece.

MARY CATHERINE. Yes, it is.

[*A pause. They dance again.* HORACE *stops.*]

HORACE. I'm ready to go if you are, Mary Catherine.

MARY CATHERINE. I'm ready. [*They start out.*] Scared?

HORACE. A little.

MARY CATHERINE. So am I. But let's go.

HORACE. OK.

[*They continue out the area down the center of the stage and off downstage right as the music from the dance is heard.*]

Beyond Literature

Humanities Connection

Dance Fads Through the years, dance fads have come and gone, requiring the learning of many new dances. Among the earliest dances to sweep America in the twentieth century were the Tango, the Hesitation Waltz, the Bunny Hop, the Turkey Trot, and the Charleston. Decades later, Chubby Checker's 1960 hit record "The Twist" ushered in the new dance of the same title. Soon additional new dances swept the nation. Spurred on by hit songs, these dances included the Hucklebuck, the Pony, the Hully-Gully, the Mashed Potato, the Frug, the Watusi, the Limbo, and the Monkey.

Activity What dances do you know how to do? Form a small group of students and teach each other some popular dances.

Guide for Responding

◆ *Literature and Your Life*

Reader's Response What did you admire about Horace? Why?

Thematic Focus Compare the ways in which Emily and Horace react when asked to do something they don't want to do.

☑ Check Your Comprehension

1. Why is Inez so determined that Horace will have a social life?
2. Why does Emily refuse to go to the dance with Horace?
3. How does Horace meet Mary Catherine?
4. Why does Inez want Horace to break his date with Mary Catherine? Give two reasons.

 Beyond the Selection

FURTHER READING

Other Works by Horton Foote
Selected One-Act Plays of Horton Foote, edited by Gerald C. Wood
Horton Foote: Four New Plays, Introduction by Jerry Tallmer

Other Works With the Theme of Working It Out
"The Red Dress," Alice Munro
"The Osage Orange Tree," William Stafford

INTERNET

You and your students can find additional information about Horton Foote and other Pulitzer Prize winners on the Internet. We suggest the following site. Please be aware, however, that the site may have changed from the time we published this information.

The Pulitzer Prize site is at **http://www.pulitzer.org/winners**

We *strongly recommend* that you preview the site before you send students to it.

Guide for Responding (continued)

◆ Critical Thinking

INTERPRET

1. What types of people are Elizabeth and Inez? Use evidence from the play to support your answer. **[Support]**
2. How does Horace demonstrate that he is a sensitive and considerate person? **[Analyze]**
3. In what ways are Horace and Mary Catherine well suited to be friends? **[Infer]**

EVALUATE

4. Is Emily's behavior on the first night justified? Explain. **[Make a Judgment]**

APPLY

5. (a) Name one insight about human relationships that you gained from this play. (b) How can this insight be applied to your own life? **[Apply]**

◆ Reading Strategy

ENVISION THE ACTION

By carefully reading stage directions and drawing from your own experiences about how people and places look, you can **envision the action** of the play—viewing it in your mind just as you would on the stage.

1. Stage directions in the opening scene tell you that it is evident that Emily is unhappy. How do Emily's face, posture, and actions show this?
2. Picture the scene in which Mary Catherine tells the waitress about the date Emily Crews wanted to break. How does Horace act as he sits at the counter? What is the waitress doing as she listens?
3. Describe Mary Catherine's living room.

◆ Literary Focus

STAGING

The way a play is presented is called **staging.** Horton Foote's short, simple stage directions give theater groups or readers a great deal of freedom in staging "The Dancers."

1. Select two examples of stage directions in "The Dancers" that leave most of the specifics up to the imagination.
2. Explain in detail how you would stage the place, action, or event described in your examples.

◆ Build Vocabulary

USING HOMOGRAPHS

Choose the correct homograph for each italicized word. In your notebook, write its letter.

a. converse (kən vʉrsʹ): to talk
b. converse (känʹ vʉrs): the opposite
c. buffet (bə fāʹ): a counter for refreshments
d. buffet (bufʹ it): to strike repeatedly
e. contract (kən traktʹ): to get, as a disease
f. contract (känʹ trakt): a binding agreement

1. First go from right to left; then do the *converse*.
2. They usually *converse* for an hour after dinner.
3. Did Paul *contract* pneumonia?
4. The partners signed a *contract*.
5. The winds continued to *buffet* the little ship.
6. We arranged the food on the *buffet*.

USING THE WORD BANK

In your notebook, write the letter of the word that means the opposite of the first word.

1. genteel: (a) gentle, (b) refined, (c) impolite
2. mortified: (a) honored, (b) humiliated, (c) loved
3. defiance: (a) resistance, (b) anger, (c) cooperation
4. console: (a) cause grief, (b) ease grief, (c) table

◆ Build Grammar Skills

LINKING VERBS AND PREDICATE ADJECTIVES

A **linking verb** connects a subject with a word later in the sentence. When the later word describes the subject, it is called a **predicate adjective.** Avoid mistakenly using an adverb where a predicate adjective is needed.

Practice Copy each sentence in your notebook. Circle each linking verb and predicate adjective. Correct any sentence in which an adverb is mistakenly used by replacing the adverb with a predicate adjective.

1. At the end of the evening, John was angry.
2. When George asked her out, Donna was happily.
3. Juana looked beautifully in her gown.
4. Rick is uncertain whether he'll go to the dance.
5. Wanda felt sadly about how things turned out.

◆ Literary Focus

1. (a) p. 645: "The pounding offstage is getting louder and louder." (b) p. 647: "... she does everything she can to make herself look plainer."
2. (a) Instead of being offstage, this scene would be shown. The viewer would see the hallway outside Emily's room. Family pictures on the walls. A dog might participate in the excitement. (b) Mary Catherine is wearing plain clothes in dull colors. She doesn't stand up straight. Her hair just hangs, with no style.

◆ Build Vocabulary

1. b   2. a   3. e   4. f
5. d   6. c

Using the Word Bank
1. c   2. a   3. c   4. a

◆ Build Grammar Skills

1. LV: was; PA: angry
2. LV: was; correct PA: happy
3. LV: looked; correct PA: beautiful
4. LV: is; PA: uncertain
5. LV: felt; correct PA: sad

1. Elizabeth and Inez are people who meddle in other people's lives without caring about other people's feelings. For example, Elizabeth tries to force Emily to go to a dance with Horace, while Inez tries to force Horace to go to the same dance with Emily.
2. Horace goes to the dance with Mary Catherine, the person he asked to accompany him, even though Inez tries to convince him to break the date and go with Emily.
3. They are both sensitive to other's feelings and not as popular and confident as the other young people in the play.
4. Some students may say Emily's behavior is justified because she shouldn't have to go on a date her mother arranged. Others may say it is not justified because going on one date with a kind and polite young man isn't such a bad thing to have to do.
5. Suggested response: (a) People should not meddle in other people's relationships, and people should have the right, in most cases, to decide for themselves whom they want as friends. (b) People should not, in most cases, try to dictate the friendships.

◆ Reading Strategy

1. She might be frowning, slouching, making faces, and rolling her eyes.
2. Horace might have been sipping his soda and looking embarrassed. The waitress might have been scooping out Mary Catherine's ice cream, serving it, and making eye contact with her.
3. Mary Catherine's living room has fairly inexpensive furniture, a radio, and no TV, since TVs were not as prevalent in the early 1950's as they are now.

✎ Writer's Solution

For additional instruction and practice, use the lesson in the **Language Lab CD-ROM** on the Eight Parts of Speech and the practice pages on Linking Verbs (pp. 12–13) in the *Writer's Solution Grammar Practice Book.*

Idea Bank

Customizing for
Performance Levels

Following are suggestions for matching the Idea Bank topics with your students' performance levels:

Less Advanced Students: 1, 4
Average Students: 2, 5, 6, 7
More Advanced Students: 3

Customizing for
Learning Modalities

Following are suggestions for matching Idea Bank topics with your students' learning modalities:

Verbal/Linguistic: 1, 3
Musical/Rhythmic: 4, 6
Interpersonal: 4, 5, 6
Visual/Spatial: 7

Writing Mini-Lesson

Refer students to the Writing Handbook, page 962, for instruction on the writing process, and page 965 for information on creative writing.

Have students use the Cluster Organizer in *Writing and Language Transparencies*, p. 80, to organize their prewriting notes on characters.

Writers at Work Videodisc

Have students view the videodisc segment (Ch. 6) featuring Grant Moran to see how he writes a first draft. Have students discuss the most effective ways of developing characters.

Play frames 12243 to 21791

Writing Lab CD-ROM

Have students complete the Tutorial on Creative Writing. Use these steps:

1. Have students use the interactive models on how dialogue develops character.
2. Have students draft on computer.
3. Have students use the Interactive Self-Evaluation Checklist for Drama to aid revision.

Sourcebook

Have students use Chapter 6, Creative Writing (pp. 162–193), for additional support. The chapter includes tips for developing character traits through dialogue (p. 181).

660

*B*uild *Y*our *P*ortfolio

Idea Bank

Writing

1. **Diary Entry** Write a diary entry that Horace might have written about the first day of his visit. Have Horace explain how he felt about what happened.

2. **Casting Notes** Which actors do you think would be best for the movie roles of Horace, Emily, and Mary Catherine? Write a short paper in which you make suggestions and give a reason for each choice.

3. **News Report** Suppose you were at the dance that Horace and Mary Catherine attended. Envision what that dance might have been like. Write an article for the school paper describing the dance. **[Media Link]**

Speaking and Listening

4. **Musical Accompaniment** Put together a musical soundtrack for a movie version of "The Dancers." Play your choices for the class. **[Music Link]**

5. **Counseling** With a partner, role-play the following situation. One of you is a family counselor, and the other is Elizabeth. Elizabeth describes the problems she has with Emily. The counselor explains Elizabeth's choices. **[Career Link]**

Projects

6. **Dance Demonstration** With a partner, learn one type of ballroom dance and demonstrate it for the class. **[Performing Arts Link]**

7. **Costume Designs** Imagine that you are the costume designer for a film version of the play. Draw costumes for Horace and Mary Catherine for the dance they attend. **[Art Link]**

Writing Mini-Lesson

Script

Horton Foote is known for his ability to create characters who speak and act like people in real life. Try your hand at writing a realistic scene in which one character invites another character to go out.

Writing Skills Focus: Realistic Dialogue

Use **realistic dialogue** to make your characters believable. Keep in mind that people often don't speak in complete sentences. In addition, they sometimes pause in between thoughts. People are also likely to use contractions and may even commit grammatical errors. Look at this example from the play. Notice that Horace pauses between thoughts.

Model From the Play

HORACE. Well . . . I . . . don't know if you have a date or not . . . but if you don't have . . . I feel if I could take you . . . I would gain the confidence to go . . . I mean . . .

Prewriting Think of a situation in which one character extends an invitation to another character. Then decide on the personalities of the characters. Are they confident? Are they nervous? Do they use slang? Jot down notes about each character and the ways in which they speak.

Drafting Put yourself in the place of each character as you write the dialogue. Use words that show what the character is thinking and feeling.

Revising Read your script aloud. Does it sound realistic? Can you tell the difference between the characters by the way they speak? If not, change the dialogue until it sounds true to life.

✓ ASSESSMENT OPTIONS

Formal Assessment, Selection Test, pp. 161–163, and Assesment Resources Software. The selection test is designed so that it can be easily customized to students' performance levels.
Alternative Assessment, p. 45, includes options for less advanced students, more advanced students, musical/rhythmic learners, interpersonal learners, visual/spatial learners, verbal/linguistic learners, and logical/mathematical learners.

PORTFOLIO ASSESSMENT
Use the following rubrics in the *Alternative Assessment* booklet to assess student writing:
Diary Entry: Expression Rubric, p. 87
Casting Notes: Technical Description/Explanation Rubric, p. 108
News Reports: Summary Rubric, p. 91
Writing Mini-Lesson: Drama Rubric, p. 102

Writing Process Workshop

Dramatic Scene

William Shakespeare once wrote, "All the world's a stage." What he meant was that everyone's life—including yours—is filled with some type of drama. In literature, a drama is a story told through dialogue that is meant to be performed by actors. In most dramas, there is a central conflict, or problem, that the characters must try to solve.

Write your own **dramatic scene** in which a character faces or works out some type of problem. The following skills will help you.

Writing Skills Focus

▶ **Use realistic dialogue.** Even though the characters are imaginary, have them speak the same way that people in real life would speak. Readers will then identify with the characters and care more about them. (See p. 660.)

▶ **Use stage directions** to help readers envision the action. Stage directions convey your ideas about sets, props, and sound effects. They also tell how characters act, move, and speak.

Playwright Horton Foote uses realistic dialogue in this dramatic scene between a mother and her daughter who refuses to come out of her room to meet her date for a dance.

MODEL FROM LITERATURE

from *The Dancers* by Horton Foote

ELIZABETH. Emily. I can hear you in there. Now open that door.

EMILY. [*Screaming back.*] I won't. I told you I won't. ①

ELIZABETH. Emily Carter Crews. You open that door immediately. ②

EMILY. I won't.

ELIZABETH. I'm calling your father from downtown if you don't open that door this very minute. ③

EMILY. I don't care. I won't come out.

ELIZABETH. Then I'll call him.

① Emily angrily repeats her words, just as people often do in real life.

② Elizabeth addresses her child by her full name, as a parent might do to show anger.

③ Elizabeth resorts to a threat that is sometimes heard in real-life families.

Writing Process Workshop ◆ 661

Cross-Curricular Connection: Social Studies

Students who are interested in the past might want to put a historical spin on their dramatic scenes by re-creating a famous scene from history. Examples of such scenes might be Abraham Lincoln and his advisors having a debate about issuing the Emancipation Proclamation, or the trial of Socrates or Joan of Arc. They may also wish to be even more imaginative, perhaps staging a scene in which William Shakespeare reads the first reviews of *Hamlet*.

Develop Student Writing

Prewriting

You may want to have students work in small groups to brainstorm for topic ideas. Suggest that sounds often trigger memories, so they may want to think of sounds such as a thunderclap, a dripping faucet, or a baby crying to see if any of these stirs up a memory that could serve as the basis for a dramatic scene. They may also want to discuss current events to see if any current topic would serve well as the basis for a dramatic scene.

Customize for
English Language Learners

Take a comic strip and white out the dialogue. Then make copies of the strip and distribute it to English language learners. Have them compose dialogue for each balloon. Have them compare their dialogues to see which one is the most realistic.

Customize for
Less Proficient Writers

These student may benefit from taping a conversation and then transcribing it to see how the words appear on paper. They can then refer to the transcription as they draft.

Customize for
More Advanced Students

Challenge these students to develop their characters entirely through dialogue, using little or no stage directions. Encourage students to use indirect characterization, in which a character's personality is revealed by what he or she says and by how other characters react to him or her, rather than by the author directly stating the character's personality traits.

Drafting

Prompt students to draft realistic dialogue for their dramatic scenes, keeping each character's personality in mind as they write. Remind them, however, to draft in a single sitting, without pausing to labor over a single word—or to correct a grammatical error—until after their draft is completed. Then students can go back into their work and make extensive revisions.

662

APPLYING LANGUAGE SKILLS:
Sentence Fragments

A **fragment** is an incomplete sentence punctuated as a sentence. In formal writing, fragments are not acceptable. They can, however, be used in dialogue to capture the way people actually speak. Notice the variety of end marks that can be used.

TED. Do you mind if . . .
KIM. Whatever. But if you—
TED. If I what?
KIM. Oh, please!

Practice On your paper, add punctuation to this dialogue:

AL. It's just that
SUE. Cat got your tongue
AL. Why do you always
SUE. Interrupt

Writing Application As you draft your dramatic scene, use punctuation for fragments in the dialogue. Choose the punctuation that would best show actors how to deliver the dialogue.

Writer's Solution Connection
Writing Lab

For help on choosing an audience for your dramatic scene, use the Audience Profile in the Prewriting section of the tutorial on Creative Writing.

662 ◆ *Drama*

Prewriting

Choose an Idea Find an idea for your dramatic scene by recalling a challenging problem you once faced or witnessed. You can also make up a problem. If you like, choose one of the topic ideas listed here.

> ### Topic Ideas
> - Two students argue in the school cafeteria
> - A teenager meets a favorite celebrity
> - One family member plays a practical joke on another
> - A sales clerk has difficulty with a customer

Develop Your Characters Before you can write dialogue for a character, you must know who that character is. For each character in your scene, answer these questions:
- ▶ What is the person's name?
- ▶ How old is the person?
- ▶ What does the person look like?
- ▶ Where is the person from? Where does the person live now?
- ▶ What kind of education does the person have?
- ▶ What job does the person have?

Think About the Dialogue Once you have defined your characters, consider how they think and behave. Answer these questions:
- ▶ How does the character feel about himself or herself? About other people?
- ▶ Is the person shy? Polite? Loud? Rude? Caring? Callous?
- ▶ What other character traits does the person possess?

Based on your answers, imagine how each character might speak to someone else in a dramatic situation.

Drafting

Write Realistic Dialogue As you write, always keep in mind who your characters are. Make their words sound believable. Try to hear the conversation in your mind as you write. Write their lines so that readers will exclaim, "Yes, I know someone who would say the same thing!"

Style Tip Formal prose requires you to write in complete sentences, but playwriting allows you more freedom. Characters may speak in incomplete sentences, with pauses, or in slang if it makes the dialogue sound realistic.

Applying Language Skills
Sentence Fragments
Answers

Al. It's just that . . .
Sue. Cat got your tongue?
Al. Why do you always—
Sue. Interrupt?

 Writer's Solution

For additional instruction and practice, use the **Language Lab CD-ROM** lesson on Fragments and Run-on Sentences and the practice pages in the *Writer's Solution Grammar Practice Book* (pp. 62–63).

Brackets and Parentheses
Answers

Bob. (Whirling around.) You scared me!
Meg. I'm sorry. (She laughs.) You looked so funny.
or
Bob. [Whirling around.] You scared me!
Meg. I'm sorry. [She laughs.] You looked so funny.

 **Writer's Solution**

For additional instruction and practice, use the practice in the *Writer's Solution Grammar Practice Book* (p. 109).

Use Stage Directions As you draft your dramatic scene, include stage directions that will communicate your specific ideas about sets, props, and sound effects. Through stage directions, you can also describe the appearance, speaking style, and movements of any of the characters. Refer to the plays in this section to see how playwrights use stage directions.

Revising

Use a Checklist Go back to the Writing Skills Focus on the first page of this lesson to evaluate and revise your dramatic scene.

▶ Have I used realistic dialogue?

Reread your dialogue aloud with a classmate. Listen to the way it sounds. If any part of a character's conversation sounds unnatural, consider how you may rewrite it to make it sound more realistic.

▶ Does the dialogue remain consistent?

Listen again to the way your characters speak throughout the scene. Decide whether each character's personality remains the same from beginning to end. If any dialogue doesn't reflect the speaker's basic character traits, change it to make the manner of speech consistent.

REVISION MODEL

ERIC. Excuse me,① Hey, Sharon! Wait up. We gotta talk.

SHARON. [*Sarcastically.*] Yeah, right.②Like I really want to!

① The writer uses a word more consistent with the rest of the character's speech.

② The writer adds an expression often heard in real-life conversations.

Publishing

Stage Your Scene Mount a production of your scene for the class. Working with other students, gather costumes, props, and musical accompaniment or sound effects. Perform the scene live, or videotape the scene to share with other students.

APPLYING LANGUAGE SKILLS: Brackets and Parentheses

In a dramatic scene, stage directions appear either in **brackets** or in **parentheses.**

MEG. [*Whispering.*] Are you asleep?

MEG. (*Whispering.*) Are you asleep?

Be consistent when writing stage directions. Use brackets only or parentheses only. Do not alternate between the two.

Practice Use either brackets or parentheses to set off the stage directions.

BOB. Whirling around. You scared me!

MEG. I'm sorry. She laughs. You looked so funny.

Writing Application Review your dramatic scene to find where you used stage directions. If they aren't in brackets or parentheses, or if your usage isn't consistent, make revisions.

Writer's Solution Connection Writing Lab

To help you revise your scene, use the instruction and activities in the Revision section of the tutorial on Creative Writing.

Revising

You may want to have students use the following peer revision checklist for a dramatic scene:

1. What is the subject of the scene? How can the focus be made clearer?
2. What is the central conflict, and how is it resolved? Would you prefer a different ending?
3. Are the characters believable? How might they be made more convincing?
4. Is the characters' language consistent in the dialogue? How does the dialogue contribute to the conflict and plot in general?
5. What kinds of information do the stage directions provide? How might they be improved?

Publishing

In addition to performing their dramatic scenes, some students may want to videotape theirs. Have these students experiment with camera angles and types of shots (long, medium, close-up). Have them find a realistic or otherwise interesting place to shoot the scene. Afterward, have them assess what difficulties they encountered while filming their scene and how those might be rectified in the future.

Reinforce and Extend

Review the Writing Guidelines After students have completed their papers, review the characteristics of a dramatic scene. Encourage students to come up with additional criteria for an interesting dramatic scene based on what they learned through completing the assignment.

✓ ASSESSMENT		4	3	2	1
PORTFOLIO ASSESSMENT Use the rubric on Drama in *Alternative Assessment* (p. 102) to assess students' writing. Add these criteria to customize the rubric to this assignment.	**Sentence Fragments**	The dialogue is realistic, and sentence fragments are punctuated correctly. The writer consistently uses vivid verbs.	The dialogue sounds good and for the most part sentence fragments are punctuated correctly.	The dialogue makes sense but could clearly be improved. Numerous errors in punctuation.	There is no rhyme or reason to the sentence fragments. Punctuation is nonexistent.
	Parentheses and Brackets	All stage directions are in either parentheses or brackets.	Most stage directions are in parentheses or brackets.	Most stage directions are in parentheses or brackets, but use is inconsistent.	Stage directions are neither in parentheses nor brackets and are extremely difficult to follow.

Introduce the Strategy

Make sure that students realize that an editorial is a form of persuasive writing in which the writer wants to convince readers to agree with his or her position. Students should read an editorial with the same wariness with which they would read an advertisement for a new kitchen cleanser.

Customize for
Less Proficient Readers

These students might be easily convinced by the editorial writer's argument because of its overall authoritative tone rather than because of its logic. Suggest that as students read an editorial, they make a list of its facts and a list of its opinions. Then, using the list as a guide, students can make an informed judgment as to the credibility of the editorial opinion.

Apply the Strategy

Remind students that a fact can be checked by other sources and that an opinion cannot. Be sure that students can distinguish between the facts and opinions in this editorial. Point out some of the typical kinds of information that are factual, such as statistical data and examples.

Answers

1. The writer thinks American children watch too much television. The opinion is stated in the very first sentence.
2. The writer states that children between the ages of six and seventeen view four and a half hours of television per day. He or she claims that television is ruining the minds of young people by being used as a baby sitter that turns viewers into zombies.
3. The statistics cited are probably reliable because they can be checked for accuracy. The rest of the writer's claims are mainly opinions.
4. The writer says nothing about the positive side of television. The writer avoids the argument that some television programs—such as news programs and historical documentaries and biographies—are educational.
5. Students should support their opinions with citations from the editorial.

Strategies for Success

Sometimes in a newspaper or magazine, you'll find an editorial, which expresses the writer's personal opinion on an issue. Analyze the writer's position before deciding whether or not you agree with it.

Identify the Opinion Before you can accept or reject an opinion, you need to know what the opinion is. Usually in an editorial, the writer states his or her opinion near the beginning. Words such as *think, believe, personally, should, best,* and *worst* can signal that an opinion is being expressed.

Identify Supporting Details Once you have determined the writer's opinion, analyze how the writer supports the opinion. Types of support may include facts, examples, and details. If the writer offers facts, judge them for their reliability. This may require checking the facts yourself. Reject an opinion that is supported only by other opinions.

The World's Worst Baby Sitter

The average American child today watches entirely too much television. Recent studies show that on average, a child between the ages of six and seventeen views four and a half hours of television per day. That's more than thirty hours per week! In other words, every week children spend more than one full day watching television!

Television is ruining the minds of our youth. Before television, families actually carried on a conversation together. Today, parents use television as a convenient baby sitter, but there is a large price to pay for that in the long run. Children don't receive the mental stimulation they need. They become zombies who learn only to look, not think.

664 ◆ *Drama*

Look at Both Sides Remember that there are always two sides to an issue. Responsible writers will address both sides, explaining why they feel their point of view is the more acceptable one. Beware of writers who purposely omit facts that might hurt their case or who fail to answer their critics' concerns.

Apply the Strategy

Read the editorial "The World's Worst Baby Sitter." Then analyze the writer's position by answering these questions.

1. What is the writer's opinion about television? Where in the article is it stated?
2. What facts, examples, and details does the writer give to support that opinion?
3. How reliable do you feel the writer's facts are? Where might you check them for accuracy?
4. How much does the writer say about the positive side of watching television? What arguments do you feel he or she avoids that opponents might raise?
5. Do you ultimately agree or disagree with the writer? Why?

✔ Here are other situations in which analyzing a position is helpful:
▶ Reading a political candidate's speech
▶ Reading a letter to the editor
▶ Reading a fund-raising advertisement
▶ Reading a petition you are asked to sign

PART 2 *History and Traditions*

Interior of the Theater of San Carlo in Naples, (detail), 19th C. Musee Conde, Chantilly, France, Giraudon/Art Resource, NY

One-Minute Planning Guide

This section of the "Drama" unit features *The Tragedy of Romeo and Juliet,* perhaps the best-known love story of all time. Also in this section are song lyrics from the movie *West Side Story,* a twentieth-century version of Shakespeare's tragic tale of star-crossed lovers.

Customize for
Varying Student Needs
When assigning the selection in this section to your students, keep in mind the following factors:

The Tragedy of Romeo and Juliet
- Language and vocabulary will challenge all but the most advanced students
- Setting, time period, and many social customs described in the play may be unfamiliar to most students
- Students unfamiliar with using glosses may need additional direction
- Reading parts of the play aloud will help students read in sentences for better comprehension
- Timeless themes of romantic love, longstanding resentment, and youthful rebellion will appeal to most students.

 Humanities: Art

Interior of the Theater of San Carlo in Naples (detail).

Help students to contrast this traditional, grand theater with theaters they might visit today. Point out the way the audience is separated from the very deep stage by the elaborate proscenium arch. The balconies that ring the audience space are usually seen only in opera houses today. The staging looks more old-fashioned than what we would see today in a theater; the gestures and postures of the performers seem grander and less subtle and naturalistic; the fact that these postures and gestures had to "read" at some distance from the stage precluded intimacy and subtlety.

Help students link this artwork with the focus of Part 2 ("History and Traditions") by answering the following questions:
1. What kind of play seems to be being performed on the stage? *The performance may be an opera, with singers and troupes of dancers leading the storyline.*

2. How is this play different from a play like *The Dancers? The theater is designed for a formal theatrical presentation, whereas* The Dancers *could be staged much more informally and intimately.*

the Shakespearean theater

Romeo and Juliet

Of all the love stories ever written, that of Romeo and Juliet is the most famous. To many people, Shakespeare's tragic lovers represent the essence of romantic love. When Shakespeare wrote *The Tragedy of Romeo and Juliet*, he was a young man, and the play is a young man's play about young love.

THE THEATER IN SHAKESPEARE'S DAY

Romeo and Juliet, like most of Shakespeare's plays, was produced in a public theater. Public theaters were built around roofless courtyards without artificial light. Performances, therefore, were given only during daylight hours. Surrounding the courtyard were three levels of galleries with benches where wealthier playgoers sat. Less wealthy spectators, called groundlings, stood and watched a play from the courtyard, which was called the pit.

Most of Shakespeare's plays were performed in the Globe theater. No one is certain exactly what the Globe looked like, though Shakespeare tells us it was round or octagonal. We know that it was open to the sky and held between 2,500 and 3,000 people. Scholars disagree about its actual dimensions and size. The discovery of its foundation in 1990 was exciting because the eventual excavation will reveal clues about the plays, actors, and the audience. The tiny part of the foundation initially uncovered yielded a great number of hazelnut shells. Hazelnuts were Elizabethan popcorn; people munched on them all during the performance.

The stage was a platform that extended into the pit. Actors entered and left the stage from doors located behind the platform. The portion of the galleries behind and above the stage was used primarily as dressing and storage rooms. The second-level gallery right above the stage, however, was used as an upper stage. It would have been here that the famous balcony scene in *Romeo and Juliet* was enacted.

There was no scenery in the theaters of Shakespeare's day. Settings were indicated by references in the dialogue. As a result, one scene could follow another in rapid succession. The actors wore elaborate clothing. It was, in fact, typical Elizabethan clothing, not costuming. Thus, the plays produced in Shakespeare's day were fast-paced, colorful productions. Usually a play lasted two hours.

One other difference between Shakespeare's theater and today's is that acting companies in the sixteenth century were made up only of men and boys. Women did not perform on the stage. This was not considered proper for a woman. Boys of eleven, twelve, or thirteen—before their voices changed—performed the female roles, and no one in the audience thought it the least bit odd, because they were accustomed to it.

THE GLOBE TODAY

Building a replica of Shakespeare's Globe was the dream of American actor Sam Wanamaker. After long years of fund-raising and construction, the theater opened to its first full season on June 8, 1997, with a production of *Henry V.* Like the earlier Globe, this one is made of wood, with a thatched roof and lime plaster covering the walls. The stage and the galleries are covered, but the "bear pit," where the modern-day groundlings stand, is open to the skies, exposing the spectators to the weather.

The Shakespearean Theater ◆ 667

INTERNET

For additional information, see *Shakespeare and the Globe: Then and Now* on the Internet at this address: **http://shakespeare.eb.com/shakespeare/index2.html**

This beautifully illustrated site includes biographies, videos, articles, and images relating to the works of Shakespeare and the reconstructed Globe theater.

More About the Authors

West Side Story was composed by Leonard Bernstein with lyrics by Stephen Sondheim

Composer **Leonard Bernstein** (1918–1990) wrote musicals, classical music, operas, ballets, and film scores. He was also a pianist, a conductor, and a lecturer whose TV appearances inspired millions of people with a love of music.

Besides *West Side Story,* he is famous for *On the Town* (1944), was based on a jazz ballet, and *Fancy Free* (1944), which Bernstein created with the choreographer Jerome Robbins. Bernstein also won fame as musical director of the New York Philharmonic (1958–1969).

Lyricist **Stephen Sondheim,** born in 1930, is known as one of the most innovative lyricists and composers of our time. The inspirations for his musicals include an Ingmar Bergman film (*A Little Night Music*), fairy tales (*Into the Woods*), French Impressionism (*Sunday in the Park With George*), nineteenth-century Japan (*Pacific Overtures*), and infamous murderers (*Sweeny Todd, Assassins*).

Thematic Focus

Ask students to compare the verse that Tony sings with the words that Romeo speaks. *Students should notice that both Tony and Romeo are passionately in love. Also, both Tony and Romeo use the image of a star.*

Thematic Focus

Ask students what images appear in both the balcony scene from *Romeo and Juliet* and "Tonight." *Students should note the images of light, suns, moons, and stars in both plays.*

Answers

1. Being in love may cause a person to perceive the world as a happier, more exciting place.
2. Circumstances might include different sides of a conflict, such as a war; or a rivalry between political factions. To create happy endings, conflicts need to be resolved in a manner that is fair to all sides.

CONNECTIONS TO TODAY'S WORLD

The story of Romeo and Juliet is retold in *West Side Story,* a musical set in New York City. Tony, a founding member of an Anglo gang, and Maria, sister of the leader of a rival Puerto Rican gang, meet at a dance. Maria's brother, angry to see his sister dancing with an Anglo, sends her home. Tony finds where Maria lives and joins her on the fire escape outside her window. In a scene that mirrors the balcony scene in Romeo and Juliet, they sing of their love for each other.

from West Side Story

MARIA

. . . Tonight, tonight,
It all began tonight,
I saw you and the world went away.
Tonight, tonight,
There's only you tonight,
What you are, what you do, what you
    say.

TONY

Today, all day I had a feeling
A miracle would happen—
I know now I was right.
For here you are
And what was just a world is a star
Tonight!

BOTH

Tonight, tonight
The world is full of light,
With suns and moons all over the
    place,
Tonight, tonight,
The world is wild and bright,
Going mad, shooting sparks into
    space.
Today the world was just an address,
A place for me to live in,
No better than all right,
But here you are
And what was just a world is a star
    Tonight!

668 ◆ Drama

1. How can love change a person's perception of the world?

2. In *Romeo and Juliet,* the lovers come from feuding families; in *West Side Story,* rival gangs. What other types of circumstances create a setting for a tragic love story? What might be done to work out these situations to create happy endings?

Beyond the Selection

FURTHER LISTENING

Other Works by Leonard Bernstein
On the Town
Candide

Other Works by Stephen Sondheim
A Funny Thing Happened on the Way to the Forum
"Send in the Clowns"
Into the Woods

INTERNET

The Internet provides excellent opportunities for students to learn about Bernstein and Sondheim. We suggest the following sites. Please be aware, however, that sites may have changed from the time we published this information.

For more about Bernstein, go to **http://www.nyphilharmon. org/archive/archive2.htm** or **http://www.classicalinsites.com /live/hallfame/gallery/**

For information about Sondheim, go to **http://www.geocities. com/Broadway/9432**

Please preview the sites before you send students to them.

Guide for Reading

William Shakespeare
(1564–1616)

William Shakespeare is widely regarded as the greatest writer in English Literature.

Almost 400 years after Shakespeare's death, his 37 plays continue to be read widely and produced frequently throughout the world. They have as powerful an impact on audiences today as when they were first staged.

Stage Celebrity Not much is known about Shakespeare's early life. We do know, however, that by 1594 Shakespeare had developed a reputation as an actor, had written several plays, and had become the principal playwright of the Lord Chamberlain's Men, a successful London theater company. In 1599, the company built the famous Globe theater, where most of Shakes-peare's plays were performed. When James I became king in 1603, following Queen Elizabeth I's death, he took control of the Lord Chamberlain's Men and renamed the company The King's Men. He continued in that role until 1610, when he retired to Stratford-on-Avon.

When Were They Written? Because Shakespeare wrote his plays to be performed, not published, no one knows exactly when each play was written. However, scholars have charted periods in Shakespeare's development as a playwright. During his early years, he wrote a number of comedies, several histories, and two tragedies. *Romeo and Juliet*—inspiration for the musical *West Side Story*, ballets, songs, stories, and movies—was written around 1595. Just before, and at the turn of the seventeenth century, Shakespeare wrote several of his finest romantic comedies (*As You Like It, Twelfth Night,* and *Much Ado About Nothing*). During the first decade of the seventeenth century, Shakespeare created his greatest tragedies (*Hamlet, Othello, King Lear,* *Macbeth, Antony and Cleopatra,* and *Coriolanus*). Finally, toward the end of his life, Shakespeare wrote several plays referred to as romances or tragicomedies.

Shakespeare's Impact on English No other individual has played a more significant role in shaping the English language than Shakespeare. In addition to introducing many new words into the language, Shakespeare penned hundreds of memorable lines that are familiar to millions of people throughout the world—even people who have never read one of Shakespeare's plays. Following are just a few of his most famous lines. See how many you recognize.

From *Hamlet*:
To be, or not to be: that is the question:
Whether 'tis nobler in the mind to suffer
The slings and arrows of outrageous fortune,
Or take arms against a sea of troubles, . . .

From *Romeo and Juliet*:
What's in a name? That which we call a rose
By any other name would smell as sweet.

. . . parting is such sweet sorrow, . . .

From *Macbeth*:
Fair is foul, and foul is fair.

From *Julius Caesar*:
Friends, Romans, countrymen, lend me your ears;
I come to bury Caesar, not to praise him.

From *As You Like It*:
All the world's a stage,
And all the men and women merely players . . .

From *Richard the Third*:
A horse, a horse! My kingdom for a horse!

From *Twelfth Night*:
If music be the food of love, play on . . .

Romeo and Juliet ◆ 669

Literature CD-ROMs To acquaint students with William Shakespeare's life, use *The Time, Life, and Works of Shakespeare* CD-ROM. In Feature 2, students can learn about Shakespeare's early life. Shakespeare's career as an actor is described in Feature 3. Feature 4 documents Shakespeareís rise as a playwright. Feature 5 focuses on the historical context that shaped Shakespeare's later work, and includes information about the Essex rebellion, the ascent to the throne of James I, other major dramatists of Shakespeare's day, and the publication of the first folio of Shakespeare's plays.

To build background on drama, use the CD-ROM *How to Read and Understand Drama,* Feature 3. This video focuses on the way in which stage directions suggest dramatic elements, how scenery and lighting indicate transitions in time and place, and how stage devices and conventions help to reveal a character's inner thoughts.

Objectives and Program Resources for Act I are listed on page 670. Objectives and Program Resources for each act are listed on the Guide for Reading page for that act.

◆ Literature and Your Life

CONNECT YOUR EXPERIENCE

The world is filled with rivalries—among countries, families, schools, groups of friends. Sometimes rivalries can become so fierce that the members of one group will refuse to associate with their rivals. In the most extreme instances, rivalries can even erupt into violence. This is the case in Shakespeare's play, which captures a long-standing feud between two families in Renaissance Italy.

THEMATIC FOCUS: FACING CONFLICTS

As you read about the conflict between the rival families in this play, you'll probably find yourself wondering what might have caused the conflict and what could have been done to resolve it.

Journal Writing Describe a rivalry with which you are familiar, then jot down your thoughts about what might be done to put an end to the rivalry.

◆ Background for Understanding

LITERATURE

The story of star-crossed lovers from feuding families was told and retold many times before Shakespeare first produced this play. Shakespeare's play is based on *The Tragicall Historye of Romeus and Juliet* by Arthur Brooke, which was published in 1562. Brooke's 3,000-line poem has a highly moral tone: disobedience, as well as fate, leads to the deaths of the two lovers. Brooke's poem, in turn, was based on a French version of the story, written in 1559. The earliest version of the story that sets the action in Verona was written around 1530.

LANGUAGE

As you read, most of the unfamiliar words you will encounter are explained in footnotes. The following, however, appear so frequently that learning them now will make your reading of the play easier.

against: for; in preparation for	**happy:** fortunate
alack: alas (an exclamation of sorrow)	**hence:** away; from here
an, and: if	**hie:** hurry
anon: soon	**hither:** here
aye: yes	**marry:** indeed
but: only; except	**whence:** where
e'en: even	**wilt:** will
e'er: ever	**withal:** in addition; notwithstanding
haply: perhaps	**would:** wish

◆ Reading Strategy

USE TEXT AIDS

While watching reruns of old sitcoms from the 1970's, you may be amazed and amused by the clothes people wear and the language they use. The way people speak in casual conversation has changed noticeably in thirty years, and it has changed even more since Shakespeare's time, over 400 years ago. As a result, much of the language in Shakespeare's play, and in other early works of literature, will probably be unfamiliar to you. To make sure that you understand the dialogue, it is crucial that you **use the text aids**— the numbered explanations of Shakespeare's language that appear beside the text. Each time you come across a footnoted term, read the corresponding explanation to ensure that you grasp the meaning of the passage.

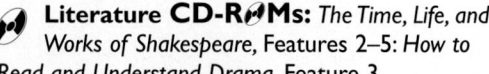

The Tragedy of Romeo and Juliet

◆ Literary Focus

CHARACTER

Characters are the people or animals who take part in a literary work. **Round characters** have many personality traits, like real people. **Flat characters**, on the other hand, are one-dimensional, embodying only a single trait. Shakespeare's plays often include flat characters who provide comic relief.

In a play, the personalities of characters are revealed largely through their interactions with other characters, who often possess contrasting traits. Such characters, who highlight or bring out the personality traits of another character in a play, are called **dramatic foils.** For example, In Act I of *Romeo and Juliet,* Benvolio, who tries to quiet a group of brawling servants, is a dramatic foil to Tybalt, a character with a fiery, hot temper. As you read, use a graphic organizer like this one to note each character's personality traits. Look for characters who have contrasting traits. This will help you identify dramatic foils.

Character	Personality Traits

◆ Build Vocabulary

PREFIXES: TRANS-

In the first act of *The Tragedy of Romeo and Juliet,* Romeo, on discovering that his own sadness is making his sympathetic friend Benvolio unhappy, speaks of "love's transgression." The word *transgression* includes the prefix *trans-,* which means "through" or "across." Notice how the prefix contributes to the overall meaning of the word *transgression:* "the act of going across a boundary of right behavior." What other words can you think of that contain the prefix *trans-* and what do they mean?

WORD BANK

Before you read, preview this list of words from the selection.

> pernicious
> augmenting
> grievance
> transgression
> heretics

◆ Build Grammar Skills

PUNCTUATING WORDS OF DIRECT ADDRESS

In a play, most of what the audience learns about the characters—even the characters' names—is revealed through dialogue. As a result, you'll find that the characters often use words of direct address, interrupters that clearly indicate to whom a character is speaking. Commas are used to set off the words of direct address from the other words in a sentence. Look at these examples:

> You, *Capulet,* shall go
> along with me; . . .

> My *noble uncle,* do you
> know the cause?

Customize for
Less Proficient Readers

Point out the complete cast of characters that appears on page 673. Have less proficient readers keep their own annotated list of the play's major characters. Suggest that students use the lists to note character traits as well as major actions by the characters.

Customize for
More Advanced Students

Explain to these students that Shakespeare often used "comic relief"—comic scenes that give the audience a moment's relief from the tragic plot. Encourage students to notice and discuss the purpose of the comic-relief scenes as they read the first act of *Romeo and Juliet.*

Customize for
English Language Learners

Arrange for language learners to work closely with native speakers. Pairs or small groups of students can work together to read aloud and paraphrase difficult passages and summarize the action of each scene within the act.

Customize for
Visual/Spatial Learners

Encourage visual/spatial learners to use the still photos from the film *Romeo and Juliet* to preview as well as review the events that take place in this act.

Preparing for Standardized Tests

Reading and Vocabulary The Build Vocabulary lesson for this selection focuses on determining word meaning through the use of the prefix *trans-.* Using prefixes to determine the meanings of unfamiliar words will help students improve their performance on vocabulary items of standardized tests. For additional practice, use the Build Vocabulary page in *Selection Support,* p. 188.

Grammar and Language Portions of some standardized tests require students to demonstrate their mastery of grammar, usage, and punctuation. Students may be asked to select between correctly and incorrectly punctuated items, as in the following:

> Thank you ladies and gentlemen. *incorrect*
> Thank you, ladies and gentlemen. *correct*

The Build Grammar Skills lesson for this selection focuses on punctuation—specifically, on punctuating words of direct address. For additional practice, use the Build Grammar Skills page on Punctuating Words of Direct Address, p. 189, in *Selection Support.*

One-Minute Insight "A pair of star-crossed lovers. . . / Doth with their death bury their parents' strife. . . ." The Prologue that opens this act tells briefly of the terrible events that mark a tender but tragic love, while the five scenes that follow set these events in motion. We first meet Romeo just after a bitter and long-standing feud between members of his family, the Montagues, and their foes, the Capulets, has erupted into a street brawl. Romeo's kinsman, Benvolio, suggests that they secretly attend a feast being given that night by the Capulets. There, Romeo and Juliet meet for the first time. Only after they have exchanged kisses and words of love do they learn each other's names and discover their misfortune at being the son and daughter of bitter enemies.

Looking at Literature Videodisc To capture the interest of students, play Chapter 10 of the videodisc. This segment features a scene from *The Tragedy of Romeo and Juliet.* Ask students to discuss the similarities and differences between reading a play and seeing it performed.

Chapter 10

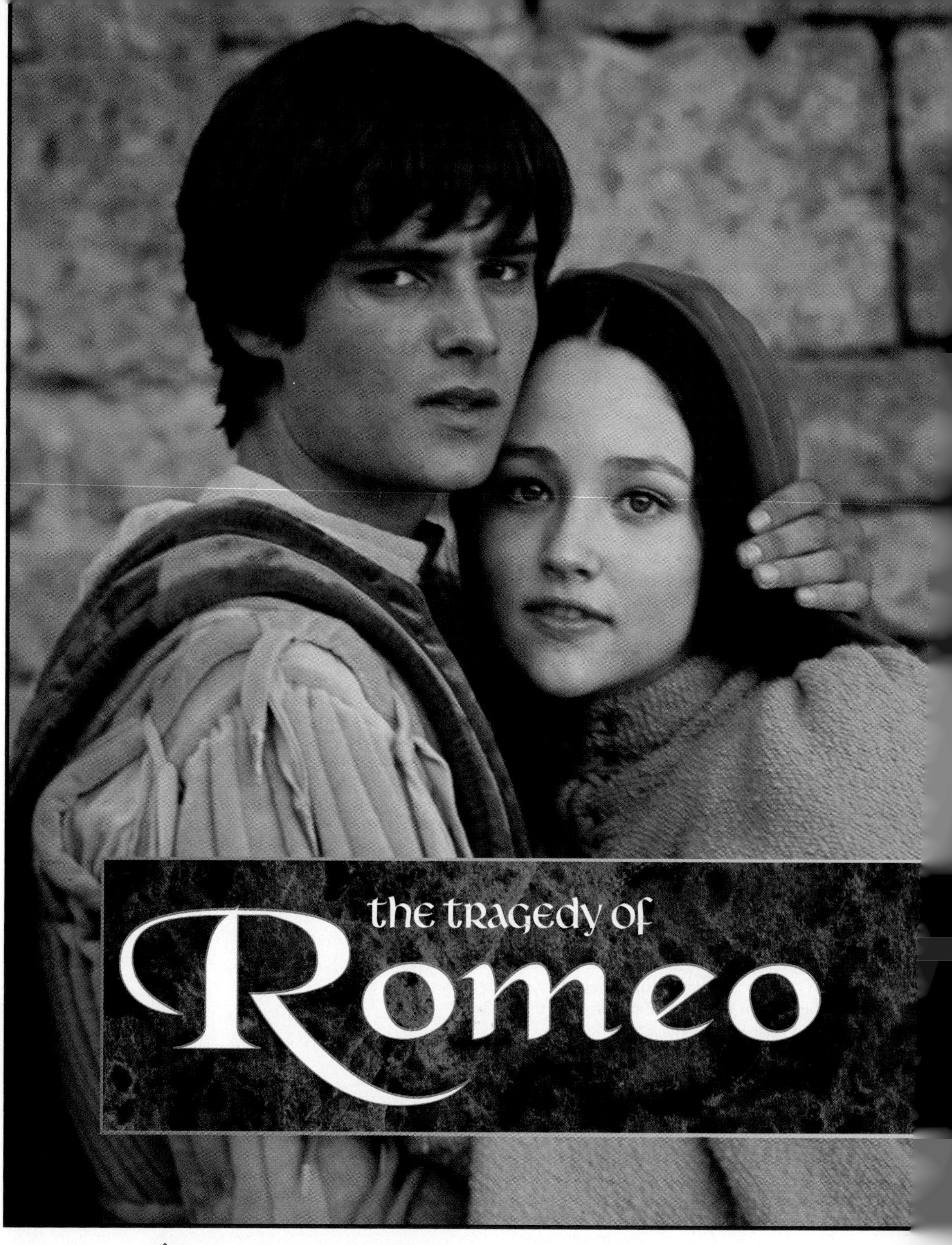

the tragedy of Romeo

Block Scheduling Strategies

Consider these suggestions to take advantage of extended class time:

- Direct students to complete the journal activity in Literature and Your Life (p. 670). Then have them meet in small groups to discuss their entries.
- Students can learn more about Shakespeare's historical context by working on the Cross-Curricular Connection: Social Studies page on Elizabethan England in **Beyond Literature,** p. 46

- Have small groups of students select portions of Act I that they would like to hear on audiocassette. Then have students discuss how hearing the play read increased their understanding and enjoyment of it. Encourage them to cite specific passages during their discussion.
- Use the Literary Focus information on pages 671 and 696 as the basis of a class discussion on character. Then have students work in pairs or small groups to

answer the Literary Focus questions on page 696.

- Have students work on the Advice Column and Character Analysis writing activities on page 696.
- Instruct students to complete the Stage Directions activity in **Alternative Assessment,** p. 46

PROLOGUE

Scene: Verona; Mantua

❶ [*Enter* CHORUS]

CHORUS. Two households, both alike in dignity.[1]
    In fair Verona, where we lay our scene,
    From ancient grudge break to new mutiny,[2]
      Where civil blood makes civil hands
      unclean.[3]
5   From forth the fatal loins of these two foes
    A pair of star-crossed[4] lovers take their
    life;
    Whose misadventured piteous overthrows[5]
❷   Doth with their death bury their parents'
      strife.
    The fearful passage of their death-marked
    love,
10   And the continuance of their parents' rage,
    Which, but[6] their children's end, naught
      could remove,
      Is now the two hours' traffic[7] of our stage;
    The which if you with patient ears attend,
    What here shall miss, our toil shall strive to
    mend.[8]   [*Exit.*]

---

1. dignity: High social rank.
2. mutiny: Violence.
3. Where . . . unclean: In which the blood of citizens stains citizens' hands.
4. star-crossed: Ill-fated by the unfavorable positions of the stars.
5. Whose . . . overthrows: Whose unfortunate, sorrowful destruction.
6. but: Except.
7. two hours' traffic: Two hours' business.
8. What . . . mend: What is not clear in this prologue we actors shall try to clarify in the course of the play.

CHARACTERS

CHORUS
ESCALUS, Prince of Verona
PARIS, a young count, kinsman to the Prince
MONTAGUE
CAPULET
AN OLD MAN, of the Capulet family
ROMEO, son to Montague
MERCUTIO, kinsman to the Prince and friend to Romeo
BENVOLIO, nephew to Montague and friend to Romeo
TYBALT, nephew to Lady Capulet
FRIAR LAURENCE, Franciscan
FRIAR JOHN, Franciscan
BALTHASAR, servant to Romeo
SAMPSON, servant to Capulet
GREGORY, servant to Capulet
PETER, servant to Juliet's nurse
ABRAM, servant to Montague
AN APOTHECARY
THREE MUSICIANS
AN OFFICER
LADY MONTAGUE, wife to Montague
LADY CAPULET, wife to Capulet
JULIET, daughter to Capulet
NURSE TO JULIET
CITIZENS OF VERONA, Gentlemen and Gentlewomen of both houses, Maskers, Torchbearers, Pages, Guards, Watchmen, Servants, and Attendants

Romeo and Juliet, Prologue ◆ 673

Humanities: Film

The photos that illustrate this play are stills from Franco Zeffirelli's film *Romeo and Juliet*, which was released in 1968.

Born in Florence, Italy, in 1923, Zeffirelli is an internationally acclaimed director of films, plays, and operas. Several years before *Romeo and Juliet*, he directed Elizabeth Taylor and Richard Burton in a rollicking film version of Shakespeare's *The Taming of the Shrew*. More recently, he directed a film ver-

sion of *Hamlet*, with Mel Gibson in the title role.

Use the following as springboards for discussion:

1. Tell students that Zeffirelli's *Romeo and Juliet* is known for its opulent re-creation of the period in which it is set. Have students identify elements in the photos that support this description. *Elements include the costumes and the authentic-look-*

ing outdoor locations.

2. Also tell students that the film has been acclaimed for the freshness and naturalness that Zeffirelli's young actors—playing Romeo and Juliet as believable teenaged heroes—brought to their roles. Invite students to discuss whether the actors in the photos resemble the pictures they formed of the characters as they read. Why or why not?

Act 1

◆ Critical Thinking

❶ Analyze Have students use the notes at the side to look up the meanings of the footnoted terms. Point out the words *collier, choler,* and *collar.* How would students describe the effect of this rapid sequence of similar-sounding words?

Students may describe the examples as puns or plays on words; the effect is playful and humorous.

◆ Reading Strategy

❷ Use Text Aids SAMPSON: Gregory, upon my words, we'll not endure insults. GREGORY: No, for them we would be sellers of coal. SAMPSON: I mean, if we are angered, we'll draw our swords. GREGORY: Ay, while you live, keep your neck out of the hangman's noose.

◆ Literary Focus

❸ Character What can students tell about Samson and Gregory's traits as the two continue to banter about what they would do if they met someone from the house of Montague? Do students think that they are flat or round characters?

Students should point out that they seem to be flat characters—the only traits they exhibit are boastfulness and flippancy.

◆ Literary Focus

❹ Character It reveals that there is great hostility between the two houses.

Scene i. *Verona. A public place.*

[*Enter* SAMPSON *and* GREGORY, *with swords and bucklers,*[1] *of the house of Capulet.*]

❶ **SAMPSON.** Gregory, on my word, we'll not carry coals.[2]

GREGORY. No, for then we should be colliers.[3]

SAMPSON. I mean, and we be in choler, we'll draw.[4]

GREGORY. Ay, while you live, draw your neck out of collar.[5]

5 **SAMPSON.** I strike quickly, being moved.

GREGORY. But thou art not quickly moved to strike.

SAMPSON. A dog of the house of Montague moves me.

GREGORY. To move is to stir, and to be valiant is to stand. Therefore, if thou art moved, thou run'st away.

10 **SAMPSON.** A dog of that house shall move me to stand. I will take the wall[6] of any man or maid of Montague's.

GREGORY. That shows thee a weak slave; for the weakest goes to the wall.

SAMPSON. 'Tis true; and therefore women, being the weaker
15 vessels, are ever thrust to the wall. Therefore I will push Montague's men from the wall and thrust his maids to the wall.

❸ **GREGORY.** The quarrel is between our masters and us their men.

SAMPSON. 'Tis all one. I will show myself a tyrant. When I have fought with the men, I will be civil with the maids—I will cut
20 off their heads.

GREGORY. The heads of the maids?

SAMPSON. Ay, the heads of the maids or their maidenheads. Take it in what sense thou wilt.

GREGORY. They must take it in sense that feel it.

25 **SAMPSON.** Me they shall feel while I am able to stand; and 'tis known I am a pretty piece of flesh.

GREGORY. 'Tis well thou art not fish; if thou hadst, thou hadst been Poor John. Draw thy tool![7] Here comes two of the house of Montagues.

[*Enter two other Servingmen,* ABRAM *and* BALTHASAR.]

674 ◆ Drama

1. bucklers: Small shields.

2. carry coals: Endure insults.
3. colliers: Sellers of coal.

4. and . . . draw: If we are angered, we'll draw our swords.
5. collar: The hangman's noose.

◆ **Reading Strategy**
Restate each line, substituting the words in the footnotes. ❷

6. take the wall: Assert superiority by walking nearest the houses and therefore farthest from the gutter.

◆ **Literary Focus**
What does this conversation reveal about the Capulets and the Montagues? ❹

7. tool: Weapon.

Reading Shakespeare

Many students may find Shakespeare's language a challenge. He uses words and structures not familiar to the modern ear. This would probably not be a problem in a theater, when actors communicate word meanings through their interpretation, but it does pose a problem for readers. Students will need to develop skill in recognizing Elizabethan language and unusual sentence structures.

The reading strategies provided for each act of the play support students in reading *Romeo and Juliet.* In addition, you may share with them the following tips that will give them an overview and an approach to Shakespeare's language.

Shakespeare's Vocabulary Some of Shakespeare's words are no longer in use and some of the words that are still in use have different meanings. Make these points to students:

- A list of common Elizabethan words and phrases appears on page 670. Refer students to this list.

- Glosses and notes are provided alongside the text lines. Remind students to make use of these notes, which explain many usages that are not recognizable to a modern reader.

Shakespeare's Sentences Shakespeare frequently plays with the normal English word order of subject-verb-complement. A reader—and especially a novice reader of Shakespeare—may have to go

30 **SAMPSON.** My naked weapon is out. Quarrel! I will back thee.

GREGORY. How? Turn thy back and run?

SAMPSON. Fear me not.

GREGORY. No, marry. I fear thee!

SAMPSON. Let us take the law of our sides;[8] let them begin.

35 **GREGORY.** I will frown as I pass by, and let them take it as they list.[9]

SAMPSON. Nay, as they dare. I will bite my thumb[10] at them, which is
disgrace to them if they bear it.

ABRAM. Do you bite your thumb at us, sir?

SAMPSON. I do bite my thumb, sir.

40 **ABRAM.** Do you bite your thumb at us, sir?

SAMPSON. [*Aside to* GREGORY] Is the law of our side if I say ay?

GREGORY. [*Aside to* SAMPSON] No.

SAMPSON. No, sir, I do not bite my thumb at you, sir; but I bite my
thumb, sir.

45 **GREGORY.** Do you quarrel, sir?

ABRAM. Quarrel, sir? No, sir.

SAMPSON. But if you do, sir, I am for you. I serve as good a man as you.

ABRAM. No better.

SAMPSON. Well, sir.

[*Enter* BENVOLIO.]

50 **GREGORY.** Say "better." Here comes one of my master's kinsmen.

SAMPSON. Yes, better, sir.

ABRAM. You lie.

SAMPSON. Draw, if you be men. Gregory, remember thy swashing[11]
blow.   [*They fight.*]

55 **BENVOLIO.** Part, fools!
Put up your swords. You know not what you do.

[*Enter* TYBALT.]

TYBALT. What art thou drawn among these heartless hinds?[12]
Turn thee, Benvolio; look upon thy death.

BENVOLIO. I do but keep the peace. Put up thy sword,

8. take . . . sides: Make
sure the law is on our side.
9. list: Please.

10. bite . . . thumb: Make
an insulting gesture.

11. swashing: Hard
downward swordstroke.

12. heartless hinds:
Cowardly servants. Hind
also meant "a female deer."

Romeo and Juliet, Act I, Scene i ◆ 675

◆ **Build Grammar Skills**

❺ **Punctuating Words of Direct
Address** Ask students what word of
direct address is used repeatedly in
this exchange. *The word* sir *is used
repeatedly.* How is the word punctuated when it appears in the middle of
a sentence? *It is preceded and followed
by a comma.* How is it punctuated
when it appears at the end? *It is preceded by a comma.*

Enrichment

Tybalt's name comes from a word
that means "bold." Benvolio is from
Latin words that mean "I wish and
"well." Ask students to comment on
the appropriateness of their names,
based on what students know about
them so far.

over the lines slowly and carefully, using the notes
provided, and puzzling out the meaning of the lines.
Share these tips with students:

- Look for the placement of the subject and the
  verb. Shakespeare often places the verb before
  the subject. For example, when Montague says
  "Away from light steals home my heavy son," (I, i,
  128) he is inverting the subject and verb. The normal order would be "My son steals home. . . ."
  Often he places the complement before the verb,
  as in Montague's line "Black and portentous must
  this humor prove" (I, i, 132) where the normal
  order would be "This humor must prove black
  and portentous."

- Shakespeare often separates words that belong
  together in meaning. A subject may have a number
  of other constructions following it that separate it
  from the verb. For example, the Prince, speaking
  to the citizens of Verona (I, i, 80–82), separates
  the subject from the verb: "*Three civil brawls* bred
  of any airy word/By thee, Old Capulet, and
  Montague,/*Have* thrice *disturbed* the quiet . . ."

- Shakespeare's lines are not necessarily sentences.
  A sentence may extend over a number of lines.
  Students should not stop at the end of a line
  unless the punctuation dictates a stop. The reading strategy with Act II reinforces this point.

675

1 Punctuating Words of Direct Address Have students identify the words of direct address in these lines. Where in the sentence does each term appear? How is it punctuated? *In line 134, the words of direct address are* my noble uncle, *which occur at the beginning of the sentence and are followed by a comma. In line 150, the word* madam *appears in the middle of the sentence and is preceded and followed by a comma. In line 151, the word* cousin *appears at the end of the sentence and is preceded by a comma.*

◆ *Literature and Your Life*

2 Students may say that Romeo's moody behavior is very much like that they have observed in teens who are having problems with their romantic relationships.

---

135   **MONTAGUE.** I neither know it nor can learn of him.

     BENVOLIO. Have you importuned[31] him by any means?

     MONTAGUE. Both by myself and many other friends;
      But he, his own affections' counselor,
      Is to himself—I will not say how true—
140   But to himself so secret and so close,
      So far from sounding[32] and discovery,
      As is the bud bit with an envious worm
      Ere he can spread his sweet leaves to the air
      Or dedicate his beauty to the sun.
145   Could we but learn from whence his sorrows grow,
      We would as willingly give cure as know.

[*Enter* ROMEO.]

     BENVOLIO. See, where he comes. So please you step aside;
      I'll know his <u>grievance</u>, or be much denied.

     MONTAGUE. I would thou wert so happy by thy stay
150   To hear true shrift.[33] Come, madam, let's away.

                                    [*Exit* MONTAGUE *and* WIFE.]

     BENVOLIO. Good morrow, cousin.

     ROMEO.   Is the day so young?

     BENVOLIO. But new struck nine.

     ROMEO.   Ay me! Sad hours seem long.
      Was that my father that went hence so fast?

     BENVOLIO. It was. What sadness lengthens Romeo's hours?

155   **ROMEO.** Not having that which having makes them short.

     BENVOLIO. In love?

     ROMEO. Out—

     BENVOLIO. Of love?

     ROMEO. Out of her favor where I am in love.

160   **BENVOLIO.** Alas that love, so gentle in his view,[34]
      Should be so tyrannous and rough in proof![35]

     ROMEO. Alas that love, whose view is muffled still,[36]
      Should without eyes see pathways to his will!
      Where shall we dine? O me! What fray was here?
165   Yet tell me not, for I have heard it all.
      Here's much to do with hate, but more with love.[37]
      Why then, O brawling love, O loving hate,

678 ◆ Drama

---

31. importuned: Questioned deeply.

32. sounding: Understanding.

33. I . . . shrift: I hope you are lucky enough to hear him confess the truth.

◆ *Literature and Your Life*
How does Romeo's moody behavior compare with that of teens you know who are having problems with their girlfriend or boyfriend?

34. view: Appearance.
35. in proof: When experienced.
36. whose . . . still: Cupid is traditionally represented as blindfolded.
37. but . . . love: Loyalty to family and love of fighting. In the following lines, Romeo speaks of love as a series of contradictions—a union of opposites.

◆ **Build Vocabulary**

grievance (grē′ vəns) *n.*: Injustice; complaint

transgression (trans gresh′ ən) *n.*: Wrongdoing; sin

▲ **Critical Viewing** In this scene, Benvolio coaxes Romeo into explaining why he's been so moody lately. How does what Benvolio says and does compare with the way you would find out what's troubling a friend? [Compare and Contrast]

❸ 170

O anything, of nothing first created!
O heavy lightness, serious vanity,
Misshapen chaos of well-seeming forms,
Feather of lead, bright smoke, cold fire, sick health,
Still-waking sleep, that is not what it is!
This love feel I, that feel no love in this.
Dost thou not laugh?

BENVOLIO.   No, coz,[38] I rather weep.

ROMEO. Good heart, at what?

175 **BENVOLIO.**   At thy good heart's oppression.

ROMEO. Why, such is love's <u>transgression</u>.
Griefs of mine own lie heavy in my breast,
Which thou wilt propagate, to have it prest
With more of thine.[39] This love that thou hast shown
180 Doth add more grief to too much of mine own.
Love is a smoke made with the fume of sighs;
Being purged, a fire sparkling in lovers' eyes;
Being vexed, a sea nourished with loving tears.
What is it else? A madness most discreet,[40]
185 A choking gall,[41] and a preserving sweet.
Farewell, my coz.

BENVOLIO.   Soft![42] I will go along.
And if you leave me so, you do me wrong.

ROMEO. Tut! I have lost myself; I am not here;

38. **coz:** Cousin.

39. **Which . . . thine:** Which griefs you will increase by adding your own sorrow to them.

40. **discreet:** Intelligently sensitive.
41. **gall:** A bitter liquid.

42. **Soft!:** Hold on a minute.

Romeo and Juliet, Act I, Scene i ◆ 679

Comprehension Check ☑

1 Have students carefully reread lines 193–195 and then explain why Romeo does not reveal the name of the woman he loves. *Her name is a painful reminder of the fact that she does not love him back, just as the mention of a will is painful to someone who is seriously ill.*

◆**Reading Strategy**

2 Use Text Aids Have students review the numbered notes that correspond to this passage. Then have them explain in their own words why the woman Romeo loves does not return his love. *Students should note that she has apparently committed herself to a life of chastity.*

Customize for
English Language Learners
Some of these students might not be familiar with the mythological beings Romeo alludes to in his speech beginning on line 199. Besides telling students that Cupid is the Roman god of love and that Diana is the Roman goddess of chastity, explain to them that according to ancient mythology, whoever is struck by one of Cupid's arrows falls in love.

This is not Romeo, he's some other where.

190 **BENVOLIO.** Tell me in sadness,[43] who is that you love?

ROMEO. What, shall I groan and tell thee?

BENVOLIO.   Groan? Why, no;
But sadly tell me who.

1
ROMEO. Bid a sick man in sadness make his will.
Ah, word ill urged to one that is so ill!
195 In sadness, cousin, I do love a woman.

BENVOLIO. I aimed so near when I supposed you loved.

ROMEO. A right good markman. And she's fair I love.

BENVOLIO. A right fair mark, fair coz, is soonest hit.

ROMEO. Well, in that hit you miss. She'll not be hit
200 With Cupid's arrow. She hath Dian's wit,[44]
And, in strong proof[45] of chastity well armed,
From Love's weak childish bow she lives uncharmed.
She will not stay[46] the siege of loving terms,
Nor bide th' encounter of assailing eyes,
205 Nor ope her lap to saint-seducing gold.
O, she is rich in beauty; only poor
That, when she dies, with beauty dies her store.[47]

2
BENVOLIO. Then she hath sworn that she will still live chaste?

ROMEO. She hath, and in that sparing make huge waste;
210 For beauty, starved with her severity,
Cuts beauty off from all posterity.[48]
She is too fair, too wise, wisely too fair
To merit bliss by making me despair.[49]
She hath forsworn to[50] love, and in that vow
215 Do I live dead that live to tell it now.

BENVOLIO. Be ruled by me; forget to think of her.

ROMEO. O, teach me how I should forget to think!

BENVOLIO. By giving liberty unto thine eyes.
Examine other beauties.

3
ROMEO.   'Tis the way
220 To call hers, exquisite, in question more.[51]
These happy masks that kiss fair ladies' brows,
Being black puts us in mind they hide the fair.
He that is strucken blind cannot forget
The precious treasure of his eyesight lost.

680 ◆ Drama

43. **in sadness:** Seriously.

44. **Dian's wit:** The mind of Diana, goddess of chastity.
45. **proof:** Armor.

46. **stay:** Endure; put up with.

47. **That . . . store:** In that her beauty will die with her if she does not marry and have children.

48. **in . . . posterity:** By denying herself love and marriage, she wastes her beauty, which will not live on in future generations.
49. **She . . . despair:** She is being too good—she'll earn happiness in heaven by dooming me to live without her love.
50. **forsworn to:** Sworn not to.

51. **'Tis . . . more:** That way will only make her beauty more strongly present in my mind.

225 Show me a mistress that is passing fair:
What doth her beauty serve but as a note
Where I may read who passed that passing fair?[52]
Farewell. Thou canst not teach me to forget.

BENVOLIO. I'll pay that doctrine, or else die in debt.[53] [*Exit.*]

Scene ii. *A street.*

[*Enter* CAPULET, COUNTY PARIS, *and the* CLOWN, *his servant.*]

CAPULET. But Montague is bound as well as I,
In penalty alike; and 'tis not hard, I think,
For men so old as we to keep the peace.

PARIS. Of honorable reckoning[1] are you both,
5   And pity 'tis you lived at odds so long.
But now, my lord, what say you to my suit?

CAPULET. But saying o'er what I have said before:
My child is yet a stranger in the world,
She hath not seen the change of fourteen years;
10   Let two more summers wither in their pride
Ere we may think her ripe to be a bride.

PARIS. Younger than she are happy mothers made.

CAPULET. And too soon marred are those so early made.
Earth hath swallowed all my hopes[2] but she;
15   She is the hopeful lady of my earth.[3]
But woo her, gentle Paris, get her heart;
My will to her consent is but a part.
And she agreed, within her scope of choice
Lies my consent and fair according voice,[4]
20   This night I hold an old accustomed feast,
Whereto I have invited many a guest,
Such as I love; and you among the store,
One more, most welcome, makes my number more.
At my poor house look to behold this night
25   Earth-treading stars[5] that make dark heaven light.
Such comfort as do lusty young men feel
When well-appareled April on the heel
Of limping Winter treads, even such delight
Among fresh fennel buds shall you this night
30   Inherit at my house. Hear all, all see,
And like her most whose merit most shall be;
Which, on more view of many, mine, being one,

---

52. who . . . fair: Who surpassed in beauty that very beautiful woman.
53. I'll . . . debt: I'll teach you to forget, or else die trying.

1. reckoning: Reputation.

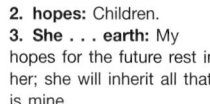
◆ **Literary Focus**
What can you tell about Lord Capulet's character traits based on his talk with Paris?

2. hopes: Children.
3. She . . . earth: My hopes for the future rest in her; she will inherit all that is mine.

4. and . . . voice: If she agrees, I will consent to and agree with her choice.

5. Earth-treading stars: Young ladies.

Romeo and Juliet, Act I, Scene ii ◆ *681*

❶ | May stand in number, though in reck'ning none.[6]
❷ Come, go with me. [*To* SERVANT, *giving him a paper*]
    Go, sirrah, trudge about
35 Through fair Verona; find those persons out
Whose names are written there, and to them say
My house and welcome on their pleasure stay.[7]   [*Exit with* PARIS.]

❸ SERVANT. Find them out whose names are written here? It is written
40 that the shoemaker should meddle with his yard and the tailor with
his last, the fisher with his pencil and the painter with his nets;[8] but
I am sent to find those persons whose names are here writ, and can
never find what names the writing person hath here writ. I must to
the learned. In good time![9]

[*Enter* BENVOLIO *and* ROMEO.]

BENVOLIO. Tut, man, one fire burns out another's burning;
45   One pain is less'ned by another's anguish;
Turn giddy, and be holp by backward turning;[10]
    One desperate grief cures with another's languish.
Take thou some new infection to thy eye,
And the rank poison of the old will die.

50 ROMEO. Your plantain leaf[11] is excellent for that.

BENVOLIO. For what, I pray thee?

ROMEO.   For your broken shin.

BENVOLIO. Why, Romeo, art thou mad?

ROMEO. Not mad, but bound more than a madman is;
    Shut up in prison, kept without my food,
55 Whipped and tormented and—God-den,[12] good fellow.

SERVANT. God gi' go-den. I pray, sir, can you read?

❹ ROMEO. Ay, mine own fortune in my misery.

SERVANT. Perhaps you have learned it without book. But, I pray, can you read anything you see?

60 ROMEO. Ay, if I know the letters and the language.

SERVANT. Ye say honestly. Rest you merry.[13]

ROMEO. Stay, fellow; I can read. [*He reads the letter.*]
"Signior Martino and his wife and daughters;
County Anselm and his beauteous sisters;
65 The lady widow of Vitruvio;
Signior Placentio and his lovely nieces;
Mercutio and his brother Valentine;

682 ◆ *Drama*

Cross-Curricular Connection: Social Studies

Like all of Shakespeare's dramas, *Romeo and Juliet* features characters from all social classes and all walks of life. The diversity of characters on the stage reflects the diversity found within the audiences who watched the plays when they were first performed.

Shakespeare's London was a bustling, rapidly growing city. The age of overseas exploration and colonization had recently begun; people poured into the city; scores of new businesses were springing up.

Against this backdrop, London's first large theaters were built. Known as *public theaters,* they offered a range of accommodations and ticket prices to attract both wealthy patrons and those of more modest means. The performances themselves were noisy and bustling—refreshments were sold, and audience members cheered, jeered, and talked among themselves.

• Have students identify characters of various social classes who appear in Act I. *The Capulets, the Montagues, and the Prince all belong to the wealthy or ruling class; the Nurse and other servants belong to the lower classes.*

• Have students research and report on the size, seating arrangements, and stage design of Shakespeare's Globe theater.

Mine uncle Capulet, his wife and daughters;
My fair niece Rosaline; Livia;
70 Signior Valentio and his cousin Tybalt;
Lucio and the lively Helena."
A fair assembly. Whither should they come?

SERVANT. Up.

ROMEO. Whither? To supper?

75 **SERVANT.** To our house.

ROMEO. Whose house?

SERVANT. My master's.

ROMEO. Indeed I should have asked you that before.

SERVANT. Now I'll tell you without asking. My master is the great
80 rich Capulet; and if you be not of the house of Montagues, I pray
come and crush a cup of wine. Rest you merry. [*Exit.*]

BENVOLIO. At this same ancient[14] feast of Capulet's
Sups the fair Rosaline whom thou so loves;
With all the admirèd beauties of Verona.
85 Go thither, and with unattainted[15] eye
Compare her face with some that I shall show,
And I will make thee think thy swan a crow.

ROMEO. When the devout religion of mine eye
Maintains such falsehood, then turn tears to fires:
90 And these, who, often drowned, could never die,
Transparent <u>heretics</u>, be burnt for liars![16]
One fairer than my love? The all-seeing sun
Ne'er saw her match since first the world begun.

BENVOLIO. Tut! you saw her fair, none else being by,
95 Herself poised with herself in either eye;[17]
But in that crystal scales[18] let there be weighed
Your lady's love against some other maid
That I will show you shining at this feast,
And she shall scant show well that now seems best.

100 **ROMEO.** I'll go along, no such sight to be shown,
But to rejoice in splendor of mine own.[19]
[*Exit.*]

14. **ancient:** Long-established; traditional.

15. **unattainted:** Unprejudiced.

◆ **Reading Strategy**
How does the text aid help you understand Romeo's assertion in lines 90–95?

16. **When . . . liars!:** When I see Rosaline as just a plain-looking girl, may my tears turn to fire and burn my eyes out!

17. **Herself . . . eye:** Rosaline compared with no one else.
18. **crystal scales:** Your eyes.

19. **mine own:** My own love, Rosaline.

◆ **Build Vocabulary**
heretics (her′ ə tiks) *n.*: Those who hold to a belief opposed to the established teachings of a church

Romeo and Juliet, Act I, Scene ii ◆ 683

◆ *Literature and Your Life*
❺ Have two volunteers read these lines aloud, bringing out the comic nature of the exchange. Does this dialogue remind students of any comic routines they have seen in movies or television shows? *Students probably can describe—and even reproduce—a number of similar pieces of comic dialogue.*

◆ **Critical Thinking**
❻ **Speculate** Invite students to describe what may happen if Romeo follows Benvolio's suggestion and goes to Capulet's feast. *Some students may say that his presence will lead to another feud-related brawl. Others may say that he will meet and fall in love with Juliet.*

◆ **Reading Strategy**
❼ **Use Text Aids** In their explanations, students may cite such difficult phrases as: "devout religion of mine eye," "maintains such falsehood," and so on. They should note that the lines in which these phrases appear are explained in note 16.

◆ **Build Vocabulary**
❽ **Prefixes: *trans-*** Point out the word *transparent* contains the prefix *trans-,* which means "through" or "across." Have students use this information to explain the meaning of the word. *Something that is transparent can be seen through.*

◆ Literary Focus

❶ Character Ask students what trait or tendency the Nurse shows when the subject of Juliet's age comes up. *Students should note her tendency to digress, or be long-winded.* Tell students to pay attention to whether the Nurse shows only one trait or several different traits as the scene progresses—in other words, whether she proves to be a flat or a round character.

Scene iii. *A room in* CAPULET's *house.*

[*Enter* CAPULET'S WIFE, *and* NURSE.]

LADY CAPULET. Nurse, where's my daughter? Call her forth to me.

NURSE. Now, by my maidenhead at twelve year old,
I bade her come. What, lamb! What, ladybird!
God forbid, where's this girl? What, Juliet!

[*Enter* JULIET.]

JULIET. How now? Who calls?

NURSE.   Your mother.

5 **JULIET.** Madam, I am here
What is your will?

LADY CAPULET. This is the matter—Nurse, give leave[1] awhile;
We must talk in secret. Nurse, come back again.
I have rememb'red me; thou's hear our counsel.[2]
10 Thou knowest my daughter's of a pretty age.

NURSE. Faith, I can tell her age unto an hour.

LADY CAPULET. She's not fourteen.

NURSE.   I'll lay fourteen of my teeth—
And yet, to my teen[3] be it spoken, I have but four—
She's not fourteen. How long is it now
To Lammastide?[4]

15 **LADY CAPULET.**   A fortnight and odd days.[5]

NURSE. Even or odd, of all days in the year,
Come Lammas Eve at night shall she be fourteen.
Susan and she (God rest all Christian souls!)
Were of an age.[6] Well, Susan is with God;
20 She was too good for me. But, as I said,
On Lammas Eve at night shall she be fourteen;
That shall she, marry; I remember it well.
'Tis since the earthquake now eleven years.
And she was weaned (I never shall forget it),
25 Of all the days of the year, upon that day;
For I had then laid wormwood to my dug,
Sitting in the sun under the dove house wall.
My lord and you were then at Mantua.
Nay, I do bear a brain. But, as I said,
30 When it did taste the wormwood on the nipple
Of my dug and felt it bitter, pretty fool,

1. **give leave:** Leave us alone.
2. **thou's . . . counsel:** You shall hear our conference.

3. **teen:** Sorrow.

4. **Lammastide:** August 1, a holiday celebrating the summer harvest.
5. **A fortnight and odd days:** Two weeks plus a few days.

6. **Susan . . . age:** Susan, the Nurse's child, and Juliet were the same age.

684 ◆ *Drama*

♫ Cross-Curricular Connection: Social Studies

The date of Juliet's birthday, Lammas Eve, marked a time of celebration for Elizabethans. Lammas (loaf mass) Day, an annual August celebration of the summer harvest, usually began by thanking God for a good harvest and blessing the grains and breads and was followed by a glorious feast.

The Lammas feast featured breads and pastries of all types that were paraded through the feast hall. The highlight of the day was the bread making. Bakers baked bread in all shapes and sizes, including geometric, animal, and celestial shapes. They also sculpted bread into castles and multi-decked warships. The meal was served on bread, or the courses themselves consisted of breads, such as currant buns, shortbread, gingerbread, and cucumber bread.

After the meal the feasters participated in a playlet called "Bringing Home the Bacon" that reminded them that true love is hard work.

The last event of the day was a candlelight procession around the feast hall. Everyone carried a loaf of bread in which a candle was placed. Afterward, they would set aside three quarters of the bread to be eaten the following day. They preserved the remaining quarter for the next year's celebration, at which time the bread would be made into crumbs and fed to the birds to indicate the beginning of the new festival.

▲ **Critical Viewing** What do this picture and the conversation among Juliet, her nurse, and her mother tell you about their relationship and personalities? [Infer]

❷

To see it tetchy and fall out with the dug!
Shake, quoth the dovehouse! 'Twas no need, I trow,
To bid me trudge.
35   And since that time it is eleven years,
For then she could stand high-lone; nay, by th' rood,
She could have run and waddled all about;
For even the day before, she broke her brow;
And then my husband (God be with his soul!
40   'A was a merry man) took up the child.
"Yea," quoth he, "dost thou fall upon thy face?
Thou wilt fall backward when thou hast more wit;
Wilt thou not, Jule?" and, by my holidam,
The pretty wretch left crying and said, "Ay."
45   To see now how a jest shall come about!
I warrant, and I should live a thousand years,
I never should forget it. "Wilt thou not, Jule?" quoth he,
And, pretty fool, it stinted and said, "Ay."

❸

LADY CAPULET. Enough of this. I pray thee hold thy peace.

50 **NURSE.** Yes, madam. Yet I cannot choose but laugh
  To think it should leave crying and say, "Ay."

Romeo and Juliet, Act I, Scene iii ◆ *685*

▶Critical Viewing◀

❷ **Infer** Students may infer that the women share a close relationship, Lady Capulet is kind but firm, the nurse is a humorous character; and Juliet is an obedient daughter.

◆ **Literary Focus**

❸ **Character** Encourage students to identify the traits that the Nurse shows in these lines. *Students should note that she shows sentimentality and genuine affection as she recalls Juliet as a young child.*

Customize for
Less Proficient Readers

Less proficient readers who enjoy art and visual/spatial learners will get more out of this play if they interact with and respond to it through art. The Costume Design activity in *Alternative Assessment,* p. 46, provides such an opportunity. This activity will also encourage students to develop their research skills. You may want to point out to students that they will have to do research; they cannot simply adapt the costumes shown in the movie stills. These costumes show the styles of Renaissance Italy, and not Elizabethan England.

❶ **Character** The Nurse is earthy and somewhat coarse. She is also very long-winded and tends to repeat herself, as indicated by the way she keeps on repeating the story about Juliet falling down when she was a toddler. The reactions of Lady Capulet and Juliet suggest that others tend to lose patience with the Nurse, either because the Nurse chatters on and on, or because she is saying something off-color and embarrassing.

◆ *Literature and Your Life*

❷ Encourage students to express their opinions on the following question: Are Lady Capulet and the Nurse acting in Juliet's best interest by encouraging her to marry Paris? *Responses may include: No—Juliet is too young to get married, especially to someone she hardly knows; yes—the two women truly believe that Paris will make an excellent husband; in the context of the time in which she lives, Juliet is not too young for marriage.*

◆ **Reading Strategy**

❸ **Use Text Aids** Students may say that it is necessary because the meaning of the line is not obvious.

◆ **Reading Strategy**

❹ **Use Text Aids** Have students read note 9, which explains that, throughout her speech, Lady Capulet compares Paris to a book. Have students identify some specific phrases or images that she uses to make this comparison. *Possibilities include: "the volume of young Paris' face," "delight writ there," "beauty's pen," and so on.*

And yet, I warrant, it had upon it brow
A bump as big as a young cock'rel's stone;
A perilous knock; and it cried bitterly.
55 "Yea," quoth my husband, "fall'st upon thy face?
Thou wilt fall backward when thou comest to age,
Wilt thou not, Jule?" It stinted and said, "Ay."

JULIET. And stint thou too, I pray thee, nurse, say I.

NURSE. Peace, I have done. God mark thee to His grace!
60 Thou wast the prettiest babe that e'er I nursed.
And I might live to see thee married once,
I have my wish.

LADY CAPULET. Marry, that "marry" is the very theme
I came to talk of. Tell me, daughter Juliet,
65 How stands your dispositions to be married?

JULIET. It is an honor that I dream not of.

NURSE. An honor? Were not I thine only nurse,
I would say thou hadst sucked wisdom from thy teat.

LADY CAPULET. Well, think of marriage now. Younger than you,
70 Here in Verona, ladies of esteem,
Are made already mothers. By my count,
I was your mother much upon these years
That you are now a maid.[7] Thus then in brief;
The valiant Paris seeks you for his love.

75 **NURSE.** A man, young lady! Lady, such a man
As all the world—why, he's a man of wax.[8]

LADY CAPULET. Verona's summer hath not such a flower.

NURSE. Nay, he's a flower, in faith—a very flower.

LADY CAPULET. What say you? Can you love the gentleman?
80 This night you shall behold him at our feast.
Read o'er the volume of young Paris' face,
And find delight writ there with beauty's pen;
Examine every married lineament,
And see how one another lends content;[9]
85 And what obscured in this fair volume lies
Find written in the margent[10] of his eyes.
This precious book of love, this unbound lover,
To beautify him only lacks a cover.[11]
The fish lives in the sea, and 'tis much pride
90 For fair without the fair within to hide.
That book in many's eyes doth share the glory,

7. **I . . . maid:** I was your mother when I was as old as you are now.

8. **he's . . . wax:** He's a model of a man.

9. **Examine . . . content:** Examine every harmonious feature of his face, and see how each one enhances every other. Throughout this speech, Lady Capulet compares Paris to a book.
10. **margent:** margin. Paris's eyes are compared to the margin of a book, where whatever is not clear in the text (the rest of his face) can be explained by notes.
11. **cover:** Metaphor for wife.

(4) That in gold clasps locks in the golden story;
So shall you share all that he doth possess,
(5) By having him making yourself no less.

95 **NURSE.** No less? Nay, bigger! Women grow by men.

LADY CAPULET. Speak briefly, can you like of Paris' love?

JULIET. I'll look to like, if looking liking move;[12]
But no more deep will I endart mine eye
Than your consent gives strength to make it fly.[13]

[*Enter* SERVINGMAN.]

100 **SERVINGMAN.** Madam, the guests are come, supper served up, you
called, my young lady asked for, the nurse cursed in the pantry,
and everything in extremity. I must hence to wait. I beseech you
follow straight. [*Exit.*]

LADY CAPULET. We follow thee. Juliet, the County stays.[14]

105 **NURSE.** Go, girl, seek happy nights to happy days. [*Exit.*]

Scene iv. *A street*

[*Enter* ROMEO, MERCUTIO, BENVOLIO, *with five or six other* MASKERS;
TORCHBEARERS.]

(7) **ROMEO.** What, shall this speech[1] be spoke for our excuse?
Or shall we on without apology?

BENVOLIO. The date is out of such prolixity.[2]
We'll have no Cupid hoodwinked with a scarf,
5 Bearing a Tartar's painted bow of lath,
Scaring the ladies like a crowkeeper,
Nor no without-book prologue, faintly spoke
After the prompter, for our entrance;
But, let them measure us by what they will,
10 We'll measure them a measure and be gone.

ROMEO. Give me a torch. I am not for this ambling.
Being but heavy,[3] I will bear the light.

MERCUTIO. Nay, gentle Romeo, we must have you dance.

ROMEO. Not I, believe me. You have dancing shoes
15 With nimble soles; I have a soul of lead
So stakes me to the ground I cannot move.

MERCUTIO. You are a lover. Borrow Cupid's wings
And soar with them above a common bound.

---

12. I'll . . . move: If
looking favorably at
someone leads to liking
him, I'll look at Paris in a
way that will lead to liking
him.

13. But . . . fly: But I
won't look harder than you
want me to.

♦ *Literature
and Your Life*

Relate Juliet's reac-
tion to times when
you've been asked
to perform a chore
you don't want to
do.
(6)

14. the County stays: The
Count, Paris, is waiting.

1. this speech: Romeo
asks whether he and his
companions, being
uninvited guests, should
follow custom by
announcing their arrival
in a speech.
2. The . . . prolixity: Such
wordiness is outdated. In
the following lines,
Benvolio says, in sum:
"Let's forget about
announcing our entrance
with a show. The other
guests can look over as
they see fit. We'll dance a
while, then leave."
3. heavy: Weighed down
with sadness.

Romeo and Juliet, Act I, Scene iv ♦ 687

Comprehension Check ☑

5 Have students express the main
points of Lady Capulet's speech. *Main
points are that when Juliet observes
Paris at the banquet, she will be pleased
with what she sees; Paris is a fine
man—both in appearance and within;
Juliet would be fortunate to have him as
a husband.*

♦ *Literature and Your Life*

6 Students may note that in her
response, Juliet stresses her mother's
wishes and expectations. They might
relate this to grudging agreements in
which they have used such expressions as "if you say so" or "if it's really important to you."

♦ **Reading Strategy**

7 Use Text Aids Have students use
the notes at the side to summarize
the meaning of this scene's opening
lines. *Summaries should include the following: Romeo asks whether he and his
companions should announce their
arrival; Benvolio says that they should
not; other guests can watch them dance
and then they'll leave.*

Customize for
More Advanced Students

You might suggest that more
advanced students compare and contrast Lady Capulet's speech with
Lord Capulet's speech to Paris in
Scene ii, lines 13–33. Among the similarities they may note: Both Lord and
Lady Capulet urge the young people
to observe their prospective spouses
at the banquet. Among the differences: Lady Capulet makes more of
an effort to persuade Juliet of Paris's
outstanding qualities; Lord Capulet
gives the impression of being more
objective.

◈ **Beyond the Classroom**

Career Connection
Costume Design Any professional production
of a play like *Romeo and Juliet* involves artistic
decisions of the many specialists, such as those of
the production's costume designer.

Costume designers help to communicate the
mood, period, and meaning of a play. If the play is
set in a specific region, country, or historical period they must do research to learn about authentic designs and materials. They then put artistic
skills to use by sketching preliminary designs.

Costume designers who work on large and
expensive theatrical productions must also develop management skills in order to oversee budgets and supervise other professionals.

Have interested students gather further information about this career. Some students might list
industries and organizations—for example, the
movie industry, the television industry, theater
and dance companies—that employ costume
designers. Others might request information on
courses from colleges and universities.

❶ **Character** Remind students that a dramatic foil is a character whose traits contrast with and bring out those of another character. Then ask students how Mercutio acts as a dramatic foil for Romeo in this conversation. *The cheerful Mercutio tells Romeo he has to dance at the feast; this prompts a contrasting response from Romeo about love's torments. The loftiness of Romeo's thoughts about love are highlighted by Mercutio's irreverent comment in line 28, which has an extremely crude double meaning.*

◆ **Literary Focus**

❷ **Character** Ask students what Mercutio's remarks about his face and his mask reveal about his personality. *Elicit the following: He does not mind making fun of himself; he has a lively sense of humor.*

◆ *Literature and Your Life*

❸ Point out that Romeo continues to express his pain and sorrow while Mercutio remains determined to draw him out of his state of dejection. Encourage students to discuss which character they identify with more and why. *Some students may say that Romeo is being too dramatic and gloomy about his situation, thereby identifying with Mercutio. Others may identify with Romeo, saying that Mercutio should be more sensitive and sympathetic to his friend.*

Comprehension Check ☑

❹ Explain that audiences in Shakespeare's time were especially fond of puns, and Shakespeare's dialogue is full of such wordplay. Then challenge students to explain the pun in these lines. *Shakespeare plays on the double meaning of lie—which can be used in the sense of "to lie in bed asleep" as well as mean "to tell untruths."*

◆ **Literary Focus**

❺ **Character** Students may say that Mercutio has a good-natured, outgoing personality; he is a foil for the moody, too-serious Romeo in that he is able to enjoy life and poke fun at himself and others.

ROMEO. I am too sore enpiercèd with his shaft
20   To soar with his light feathers; and so bound
I cannot bound a pitch above dull woe.
Under love's heavy burden do I sink.

MERCUTIO. And, to sink in it, should you burden love—
Too great oppression for a tender thing.

25   **ROMEO.** Is love a tender thing? It is too rough,
Too rude, too boist'rous, and it pricks like thorn.

MERCUTIO. If love be rough with you, be rough with love.
Prick love for pricking, and you beat love down.
Give me a case to put my visage[4] in.
30   A visor for a visor![5] What care I
What curious eye doth quote deformities?[6]
Here are the beetle brows shall blush for me.

BENVOLIO. Come, knock and enter; and no sooner in
But every man betake him to his legs.[7]

35   **ROMEO.** A torch for me! Let wantons light of heart
Tickle the senseless rushes[8] with their heels;
For I am proverbed with a grandsire phrase,[9]
I'll be a candleholder and look on;
The game was ne'er so fair, and I am done.[10]

40   **MERCUTIO.** Tut! Dun's the mouse, the constable's own word![11]
If thou art Dun,[12] we'll draw thee from the mire
Of this sir-reverence love, wherein thou stickest
Up to the ears. Come, we burn daylight, ho!

ROMEO. Nay, that's not so.

MERCUTIO.   I mean, sir, in delay
45   We waste our lights in vain, like lights by day.
Take our good meaning, for our judgment sits
Five times in that ere once in our five wits.[13]

ROMEO. And we mean well in going to this masque,
But 'tis no wit to go.

MERCUTIO.   Why, may one ask?

ROMEO. I dreamt a dream tonight.

50   **MERCUTIO.**   And so did I.

ROMEO. Well, what was yours?

MERCUTIO.   That dreamers often lie.

ROMEO. In bed asleep, while they do dream things true.

---

4. **visage:** Mask.

5. **A visor . . . visor!:** A mask for a mask—which is what my real face is like!

6. **quote deformities:** Notice my ugly features.

7. **betake . . . legs:** Start dancing.

8. **Let . . . rushes:** Let fun-loving people dance on the floor coverings.

9. **proverbed . . . phrase:** Directed by an old saying.

10. **The game . . . done:** No matter how much enjoyment may be had, I won't have any.

11. **Dun's . . . word!:** Lie low like a mouse—that's what a constable waiting to make an arrest might say.

12. **Dun:** Proverbial name for a horse.

13. **Take . . . wits:** Understand my intended meaning. That shows more intelligence than merely following what your senses perceive.

◆ **Literary Focus**
What can you tell about Mercutio's personality from his jokes and fanciful stories? In what way is he a foil for the sulky Romeo? ❺

▶Critical Viewing◀
6 Infer Students should infer the
following: *Romeo and his friends need
to disguise their identities—specifically,
by wearing masks—in order to attend
the Capulets' feast.*

Comprehension Check ☑
7 According to Mercutio, how does
Queen Mab affect people? *She brings
them dreams.*

Customize for
Visual/Spatial Learners
Visual/spatial learners might create
illustrations based on the imagery in
the speech, particularly the imagery
that occurs between the lines beginning "She is the fairies' midwife" and
"Made by the joiner squirrel."

6 ▲ **Critical Viewing** Their way lit by torchbearers, Romeo and his
friends prepare to invite themselves to the Capulet's feast. What
do these uninvited guests need to do to attend the feast? [Infer]

MERCUTIO. O, then I see Queen Mab[14] hath been with you.
    She is the fairies' midwife, and she comes
55 In shape no bigger than an agate stone
    On the forefinger of an alderman,
    Drawn with a team of little atomies[15]
    Over men's noses as they lie asleep;
    Her wagon spokes made of long spinners'[16] legs,
60 The cover, of the wings of grasshoppers;
    Her traces, of the smallest spider web;
    Her collars, of the moonshine's wat'ry beams;
    Her whip, of cricket's bone; the lash, of film;[17]
    Her wagoner, a small gray-coated gnat,
65 Not half so big as a round little worm
    Pricked from the lazy finger of a maid;
    Her chariot is an empty hazelnut,
    Made by the joiner squirrel or old grub,[18]
    Time out o' mind the fairies' coachmakers.
70 And in this state she gallops night by night
    Through lovers' brains, and then they dream of love;
7 On courtiers' knees, that dream on curtsies straight;
    O'er lawyers' fingers, who straight dream on fees;
    O'er ladies' lips, who straight on kisses dream,
75 Which oft the angry Mab with blisters plagues,

14. Queen Mab: The
queen of fairyland.

15. atomies: Creatures.

16. spinners: Spiders.

17. film: Spider's thread.

18. old grub: An insect
that bores holes in nuts.

Romeo and Juliet, Act I, Scene iv ◆ *689*

Customize for
Musical/Rhythmic Learners

Mercutio's Queen Mab speech is one of the finest and most famous passages of poetry in Shakespeare's early works. Have musical/rhythmic learners practice the speech and perform it for the class. Encourage students to bring out the musical rhythms as well as the vivid imagery of Shakespeare's lines.

◆ **Critical Thinking**

❶ Connect Have students refer to note 28, which paraphrases Romeo's speech. Then have them identify the phrases or images in this speech that echo back to the Prologue.
Possibilities include: "some consequences yet hanging in the stars" and "star-crossed lovers" (Prologue, line 6); "fearful date" and "fearful passage" (Prologue, line 9); and "untimely death" and "death-marked love" (Prologue, line 9).

Because their breath with sweetmeats[19] tainted are.
Sometimes she gallops o'er a courtier's nose,
And then dreams he of smelling out a suit;[20]
And sometime comes she with a tithe pig's[21] tail
80 Tickling a parson's nose as 'a lies asleep,
Then he dreams of another benefice.[22]
Sometime she driveth o'er a soldier's neck,
And then dream he of cutting foreign throats,
Of breaches, ambuscadoes,[23] Spanish blades,
85 Of healths[24] five fathom deep; and then anon
Drums in his ear, at which he starts and wakes,
And being thus frighted, swears a prayer or two
And sleeps again. This is that very Mab
That plats[25] the manes of horses in the night
90 And bakes the elflocks[26] in foul sluttish hairs,
Which once untangled much misfortune bodes.
This is the hag, when maids lie on their backs,
That presses them and learns them first to bear,
Making them women of good carriage.[27]
This is she—

95 **ROMEO.**   Peace, peace, Mercutio, peace!
Thou talk'st of nothing.

MERCUTIO.   True, I talk of dreams;
Which are the children of an idle brain,
Begot of nothing but vain fantasy;
Which is as thin of substance as the air,
100 And more inconstant than the wind, who woos
Even now the frozen bosom of the North
And, being angered, puffs away from thence,
Turning his side to the dew-dropping South.

BENVOLIO. This wind you talk of blows us from ourselves.
105 Supper is done, and we shall come too late.

ROMEO. I fear, too early; for my mind misgives
Some consequence yet hanging in the stars
Shall bitterly begin his fearful date
With this night's revels and expire the term
110 Of a despisèd life, closed in my breast,
By some vile forfeit of untimely death.[28]
But he that hath the steerage of my course
Direct my sail! On, lusty gentlemen!

BENVOLIO. Strike, drum.
[*They march about the stage, and retire to one side.*]

19. sweetmeats: Candy.

20. smelling . . . suit: Finding someone who has a petition (suit) for the king and who will pay the courtier to gain the king's favor for the petition.
21. tithe pig: A pig donated to a parson.
22. benefice: A church appointment that included a guaranteed income.
23. ambuscadoes: Ambushes.
24. healths: Toasts ("To your health!").
25. plats: Tangles.
26. elflocks: Tangled hair.

27. carriage: Posture.

28. my mind . . . death: My mind is fearful that some future event, fated by the stars, shall start to run its course tonight and cut my life short.

Cross-Curricular Connection: Social Studies

At the end of Scene iv, Romeo says that he is fearful that his life will be cut short as determined by the stars. Point out to students that belief in the star's influence was common in the sixteenth century.

Many Elizabethans believed that the positions of the moon, sun, and planets were responsible for their general dispositions. For example, they believed that the Zodiac sign under which a person was born and the position of the planets at that time

determined his or her general character.

Elizabethans also believed that planetary influences that determine a person's character were separate from the control the stars had on people. They believed the stars determined a person's fate. For example, it was the stars that determined if a person would live a long and happy life or a short life filled with unhappiness. It is this belief that causes Romeo to be fearful that his life will be cut short as the stars have fated.

Ask students why Romeo and Juliet might have been referred to as "star-crossed lovers" and their love said to be "death-marked" in the play's Prologue. *Students may respond that Romeo and Juliet were fated by the stars to fall in love in spite of all the obstacles to their love and that their love was doomed. Because of the stars, they had no control over the situation.*

Scene v. *A hall in* CAPULET'*s house.*

[SERVINGMEN *come forth with napkins.*]

FIRST SERVINGMAN. Where's Potpan, that he helps not to take away? He shift a trencher![1] He scrape a trencher!

SECOND SERVINGMAN. When good manners shall lie all in one or two men's hands, and they unwashed too, 'tis a foul thing.

5 **FIRST SERVINGMAN.** Away with the join-stools, remove the court cupboard, look to the plate. Good thou, save me a piece of marchpane,[2] and, as thou loves me, let the porter let in Susan Grindstone and Nell. Anthony, and Potpan!

SECOND SERVINGMAN. Ay, boy, ready.

10 **FIRST SERVINGMAN.** You are looked for and called for, asked for and sought for, in the great chamber.

THIRD SERVINGMAN. We cannot be here and there too. Cheerly, boys! Be brisk awhile, and the longer liver take all. [*Exit.*]

[*Enter* CAPULET, *his* WIFE, JULIET, TYBALT, NURSE, *and all the* GUESTS *and* GENTLEWOMEN *to the* MASKERS.]

15 **CAPULET.** Welcome, gentlemen! Ladies that have their toes
Unplagued with corns will walk a bout[3] with you.
Ah, my mistresses, which of you all
Will now deny to dance? She that makes dainty,[4]
She I'll swear hath corns. Am I come near ye now?
20 Welcome, gentlemen! I have seen the day
That I have worn a visor and could tell
A whispering tale in a fair lady's ear,
Such as would please. 'Tis gone, 'tis gone, 'tis gone.
You are welcome, gentlemen! Come, musicians, play.
[*Music plays, and they dance.*]
25 A hall,[5] a hall! Give room! And foot it, girls.
More light, you knaves, and turn the tables up,
And quench the fire; the room is grown too hot.
Ah, sirrah, this unlooked-for sport comes well.
Nay, sit; nay, sit, good cousin Capulet;
30 For you and I are past our dancing days.
How long is't now since last yourself and I
Were in a mask?

SECOND CAPULET. By'r Lady, thirty years.

CAPULET. What, man? 'Tis not so much, 'tis not so much;

1. **trencher:** Wooden platter.

2. **marchpane:** Marzipan, a confection made of sugar and almonds.
3. **walk a bout:** Dance a turn.
4. **makes dainty:** Hesitates, acts shy.
5. **A hall:** Clear the floor, make room for dancing.

▲ **Critical Viewing** What can you tell about Romeo's personality from his words and behavior regarding Rosaline? [**Draw Conclusions**]

Romeo and Juliet, Act I, Scene v ◆ 691

◆ **Build Grammar Skills**

❷ **Punctuating Words of Direct Address** Have students identify the words of direct address that Lord Capulet uses as he greets his guests and shouts at his servants in lines 15–28. Then have students explain the way in which each term is punctuated and why. *The words of direct address are as follows: Gentlemen (lines 15, 20, 24) and girls (line 25) are preceded by commas because they occur at the end of a sentence. My mistresses (line 17), musicians (line 24), you knaves (line 26), and sirrah (line 28) are used in the middle of sentences and so are preceded and followed by a comma.*

▶**Critical Viewing**◀

❸ **Draw Conclusions** Based on his reactions to Rosaline and Juliet, some students may describe Romeo as idealistic, poetic, and romantic; others may say that he is impulsive and easily infatuated.

Humanities: Performing Arts

Music and Dance During the Renaissance

The Renaissance saw a flowering of music and dance. Shakespeare's plays often contained both songs and dances.

In Italy, a new form of composition, the *madrigal*, appeared. Composers wrote lyrics in their own language rather than in Latin, or set poetry of the time to music. Madrigals, written by composers such as John Dowland and William Byrd, were popular in England in Shakespeare's time.

During the Renaissance, especially in Italy, it was the custom for the nobility of one city to compete with the nobles of another in staging elaborate musical entertainments. Professional dancing masters were hired to create original *balli* or *balletti.* Leading composers wrote the music and talented artists, including Leonardo da Vinci, designed costumes.

If possible, play a recording of English Renaissance music for the class.

Use the following questions for discussion:
1. Which scene in *Romeo and Juliet* includes music and dance? *The Capulets' ball might include music and dance.*
2. What do music and dance add to a stage or film production of a play? *Students may say they make the play more interesting and more appealing to the senses of sight and hearing.*

❶ Have students use these lines to identify a theme that runs through Capulet's speeches so far in this scene. *The theme is age and the passage of time.* Then invite students to consider possible reasons why Shakespeare would bring up this theme in relation to Capulet. *Students may suggest that Capulet's concern with the passage of time makes him more of a round character, or that conflict between the older generation—represented by Capulet—and the younger generation—represented by Romeo and Juliet—will develop as the play unfolds.*

◆ Critical Thinking

❷ Interpret Ask students whose beauty Romeo speaks of in these lines. How do they know? *He speaks about Juliet's. Line 41, in which he asks a servingman who the lady is and lines 51–52, "Did my heart love till now? Forswear it, sight!" reveal that he is not speaking about Rosaline.*

◆ Reading Strategy

❸ Use Text Aids Ask students: Why is Tybalt outraged at Romeo's presence at the feast? *Tybalt interprets Romeo's presence and his mask as signs of scorn; he believes that Romeo has come to the banquet to mock the Capulets.*

◆ Literary Focus

❹ Character Have students contrast Tybalt's reaction to Romeo's presence with Capulet's. Then ask: In what way is each character's behavior consistent with his earlier behavior? *Tybalt reacts with anger, while Capulet urges patience and tolerance. Students should note that Tybalt behaved in a similar way when he met Benvolio on the street; Capulet urged Paris to show patience by not rushing Juliet into marriage.*

---

35 'Tis since the nuptial of Lucentio,
Come Pentecost as quickly as it will,
Some five-and-twenty years, and then we masked.

SECOND CAPULET. 'Tis more, 'tis more. His son is elder, sir;
His son is thirty.

CAPULET. Will you tell me that?
40 His son was but a ward[6] two years ago.

6. **ward:** Minor.

ROMEO. [*To a* SERVINGMAN] What lady's that which doth enrich the hand
Of yonder knight?

SERVINGMAN. I know not, sir.

ROMEO. O, she doth teach the torches to burn bright!
It seems she hangs upon the cheek of night
45 As a rich jewel in an Ethiop's ear—
Beauty too rich for use, for earth too dear!
So shows a snowy dove trooping with crows
As yonder lady o'er her fellows shows.
The measure done, I'll watch her place of stand
50 And, touching hers, make blessèd my rude hand.
Did my heart love till now? Forswear[7] it, sight!
For I ne'er saw true beauty till this night.

7. **Forswear:** Deny.

TYBALT. This, by his voice, should be a Montague.
Fetch me my rapier, boy. What! Dares the slave
55 Come hither, covered with an antic face,[8]
To fleer[9] and scorn at our solemnity?
Now, by the stock and honor of my kin,
To strike him dead I hold it not a sin.

8. **antic face:** Strange, fantastic mask.
9. **fleer:** Mock.

CAPULET. Why, how now, kinsman? Wherefore storm you so?

60 **TYBALT.** Uncle, this is a Montague, our foe,
A villain, that is hither come in spite
To scorn at our solemnity this night.

CAPULET. Young Romeo is it?

TYBALT. 'Tis he, that villain Romeo.

CAPULET. Content thee, gentle coz,[10] let him alone.
65 'A bears him like a portly gentleman,[11]
And, to say truth, Verona brags of him
To be a virtuous and well-governed youth.
I would not for the wealth of all this town
Here in my house do him disparagement.[12]
70 Therefore be patient; take no note of him.
It is my will, the which if thou respect,

10. **coz:** Here coz is used as a term of address for a relative.
11. **'A . . . gentleman:** He behaves like a dignified gentleman.
12. **disparagement:** Insult.

692 ◆ Drama

Enrichment: Shakespeare's Imagery

Imagery is the use of words and phrases that appeal to the senses—of sight, sound, smell, touch, and taste—throughout a work to give an overall picture, tone, or impression.

In *Romeo and Juliet,* a dominant image is light. Have students find lines in Act I, Scene v, that contain images of light, for example, "O, she doth teach the torches to burn bright!"

Read the quotation that follows by Caroline Spurgeon, from *Shakespeare's Imagery and What It Tells Us,* in which she comments on the light imagery in *Romeo and Juliet:*

To Juliet, Romeo is "day in night"; to Romeo Juliet is the sun rising from the east, and when they soar to love's ecstasy, each alike pictures the other as stars in heaven, shedding such brightness as puts to shame the heavenly bodies themselves.

In contrast to the light imagery, Shakespeare also uses images of darkness, which generate a different tone or impression. Have students compare the images of darkness in the following passages with the light imagery in the preceding quotation.

More light and more light; more dark and dark our woes! (Act III, Scene v, l. 36)

Show a fair presence and put off these frowns,
An ill-beseeming semblance[13] for a feast.

❹ **TYBALT.** It fits when such a villain is a guest.
I'll not endure him.

75 **CAPULET.**   He shall be endured.
What, goodman[14] boy! I say he shall. Go to![15]
Am I the master here, or you? Go to!
You'll not endure him, God shall mend my soul![16]
You'll make a mutiny among my guests!

80 You will set cock-a-hoop.[17] You'll be the man!

TYBALT. Why, uncle, 'tis a shame.

CAPULET.   Go to, go to!
You are a saucy boy. Is't so, indeed?
This trick may chance to scathe you.[18] I know what.
You must contrary me! Marry, 'tis time–

85 Well said, my hearts!—You are a princox[19]—go!
Be quiet, or—more light, more light!—For shame!
I'll make you quiet. What!—Cheerly, my hearts!

TYBALT. Patience perforce with willful choler meeting[20]
Makes my flesh tremble in their different greeting.

❺ 90 I will withdraw; but this intrusion shall,
Now seeming sweet, convert to bitt'rest gall.   [*Exit.*]

ROMEO. If I profane with my unworthiest hand
This holy shrine,[21] the gentle sin is this:
My lips, two blushing pilgrims, ready stand

95 To smooth that rough touch with a tender kiss.

JULIET. Good pilgrim, you do wrong your hand too much,
Which mannerly devotion shows in this;
For saints have hands that pilgrims' hands do touch
And palm to palm is holy palmers'[22] kiss.

❼ 100 **ROMEO.** Have not saints lips, and holy palmers too?

JULIET. Ay, pilgrim, lips that they must use in prayer.

ROMEO. O, then, dear saint, let lips do what hands do!
They pray; grant thou, lest faith turn to despair.

JULIET. Saints do not move,[23] though grant for prayers' sake.

105 **ROMEO.** Then move not while my prayer's effect I take.
Thus from my lips, by thine my sin is purged.   [*Kisses her.*]

JULIET. Then have my lips the sin that they have took.

13. **ill-beseeming semblance:** Inappropriate appearance.
14. **goodman:** Term of address for someone below the rank of gentleman.
15. **Go to!:** Expression of angry impatience.
16. **God . . . soul!:** Expression of impatience, equivalent to, "God save me!"
17. **You will set cock-a-hoop:** You want to swagger like a barnyard rooster.
18. **This . . . you:** This trait of yours may turn to hurt you.
19. **princox:** Rude youngster; wise guy.
20. **Patience . . . meeting:** Enforced self-control mixing with strong anger.
21. **shrine:** Juliet's hand.
22. **palmers:** Pilgrims who at one time carried palm branches from the Holy Land.

◆ **Literary Focus**
What character traits do Romeo and Juliet reveal in the words they say to each other?   ❻

23. **move:** Initiate involvement in earthly affairs.

Romeo and Juliet, Act I, Scene v ◆ 693

1 Use Text Aids Have students use the note at the side of the page to look up the meaning of these lines. Then ask what the Nurse's words reveal about her. *She can be boastful, crass, and money-conscious.*

◆ **Reading Strategy**

2 Use Text Aids Using the text aid for help, have students explain the purpose behind Capulet's remarks to Romeo and Benvolio. *Students should note that Capulet knows who they really are and is teasing them.*

▶**Critical Viewing**◀

3 Infer Romeo and Juliet talk about love, using imagery of religion and worship. Students may infer that, within the story's time and culture, ideas were often expressed poetically and symbolically; that worship was a popular metaphor for love; and that courtship was conducted in a courtly and formal manner.

Customize for
Less Proficient Readers
These students may have difficulty keeping track of the events in the play. To help them with this, assign the Summary activity in **Alternative Assessment,** p. 46.

ROMEO. Sin from my lips? O trespass sweetly urged!²⁴
Give me my sin again.

[*Kisses her.*]

JULIET.   You kiss by th' book.²⁵

110 **NURSE.** Madam, your mother craves a word with you.

ROMEO. What is her mother?

NURSE.   Marry, bachelor,
Her mother is the lady of the house,
And a good lady, and a wise and virtuous.
I nursed her daughter that you talked withal.
1 115 I tell you, he that can lay hold of her
Shall have the chinks.²⁶

ROMEO.   Is she a Capulet?
O dear account! My life is my foe's debt.²⁷

BENVOLIO. Away, be gone; the sport is at the best.

ROMEO. Ay, so I fear; the more is my unrest.

2 120 **CAPULET.** Nay, gentlemen, prepare not to be gone;
We have a trifling foolish banquet towards.²⁸
Is it e'en so?²⁹ Why then, I thank you all.
I thank you, honest gentlemen. Good night.
More torches here! Come on then; let's to bed.
125 Ah, sirrah, by my fay,³⁰ it waxes late;
I'll to my rest.
[*Exit all but* JULIET *and* NURSE.]

24. **O . . . urged!:** Romeo is saying, in substance, that he is happy. Juliet calls his kiss a sin, for now he can take it back—by another kiss.

25. **by th' book:** As if you were following a manual of courtly love.

26. **chinks:** Cash.
27. **My life . . . debt:** since Juliet is a Capulet, Romeo's life is at the mercy of the enemies of his family.

28. **towards:** Being prepared.
29. **Is . . . so?:** Is it the case that you really must leave?
30. **fay:** Faith.

▼ **Critical Viewing** What does Romeo and Juliet's formal, stylized conversation reveal about the time and culture in which the story takes place? [**Infer**] **3**

694 ◆ *Drama*

◆ **Speaking and Listening Mini-Lesson**

Reading

This mini-lesson supports the Speaking and Listening activity on page 696.

Introduce the Concept Point out that Act I contains comic scenes, action-packed scenes, and scenes that build toward tragedy. Students will now have a chance to choose and perform their own scenes.

Develop Background Help students identify approaches that will help them better understand their roles and their lines:

• Using text aids: The numbered notes will explain some of the words and lines that the characters speak.

• Discussion with other cast members: Sharing insights into what the characters are thinking and feeling will help cast members interact in believable ways as they perform.

Apply the Information Have students prepare, practice, and perform their scenes.

Assess the Outcome After each scene, discuss: Did the actors capture the right mood? Did they deliver their lines smoothly and with feeling? What did the actors and the audience learn about Shakespeare's language and characters as a result of the performance? You might have students use the Peer Assessment form for Oral Interpretation, p. 112 in **Alternative Assessment.**

JULIET. Come hither, nurse. What is yond gentleman?

NURSE. The son and heir of old Tiberio.

JULIET. What's he that now is going out of door?

130 **NURSE.** Marry, that, I think, be young Petruchio.

JULIET. What's he that follows here, that would not dance?

NURSE. I know not.

JULIET. Go ask his name—If he is married,
My grave is like to be my wedding bed.

135 **NURSE.** His name is Romeo, and a Montague,
The only son of your great enemy.

JULIET. My only love, sprung from my only hate!
Too early seen unknown, and known too late!
Prodigious³¹ birth of love it is to me

31. **Prodigious:** Monstrous; foretelling misfortune.

140 That I must love a loathèd enemy.

NURSE. What's this? What's this?

JULIET.   A rhyme I learnt even now.
Of one I danced withal. [*One calls within, "Juliet."*]

NURSE.   Anon, anon!
Come, let's away; the strangers all are gone.   [*Exit.*]

Guide for Responding

◆ Literature and Your Life

Reader's Response If you were Romeo and Juliet, would you pursue a relationship? Explain.

Thematic Focus What are some signs that the Capulet-Montague feud might be worked out peacefully? What are some obstacles to achieving this goal?

☑ **Check Your Comprehension**

1. How does Romeo's attitude change during the course of this act?
2. What possible threats to Romeo's and Juliet's love already exist in Act I?

◆ Critical Thinking

INTERPRET

1. Compare and contrast the personalities of Romeo and Juliet in Act I. **[Compare and Contrast]**
2. How does Juliet's comment when she sends her nurse to find out Romeo's name echo back to the Prologue? **[Connect]**
3. How does Shakespeare generate suspense in the first act? **[Support]**

EXTEND

4. Based on the Prologue and other hints provided in the first act, what do you think will happen as the plot unfolds? Why? **[Predict]**

Romeo and Juliet, Act I, Scene v ◆ 695

695

Answers

◆ Reading Strategy

1. Students should substitute the definitions from the text aids into Capulet's speech.
2. Student responses may be similar to the following: Leave him alone. I said, *leave him alone.* Who's in charge here, me or you? If you don't leave him alone, my guests will riot. But you want to act macho. Real adult behavior.

◆ Literary Focus

1. They embody antagonism. As well as providing some off-color comic relief, they show the enmity between the two houses.
2. Student lists may be similar to the following. Romeo: moody, romantic, impulsive, pessimistic. Benvolio: cautious, loyal, diplomatic, practical, talkative. Mercutio: carefree, outgoing, joking, playful, talkative.
3. Students may say that Benvolio's practicality contrasts with Romeo's moody romanticism, and that Mercutio's carefree antics serve to underscore Romeo's basically bleak outlook.

◆ Build Vocabulary

Using the Prefix *trans-*

1. transcontinental: extending across a continent
2. transport: to carry something from one place across to another
3. translate: to move from one place or condition across to another
4. transplant: to remove from one place across to another
5. transform: to change from one form across to another

Using the Word Bank

1. a   2. b   3. c   4. a   5. c

◆ Build Grammar Skills

1. Nurse, where's my daughter?
2. Good morrow, cousin.
3. Turn thee, Benvolio . . .
4. My noble uncle, do you . . .
5. I thank you, honest gentlemen.

 Writer's Solution

For additional instruction and practice, use the lesson in the **Language Lab CD-ROM** on commas, and the Commas That Set Off Added Elements page in the *Writer's Solution Grammar Practice Book,* p. 101.

696

Guide for Responding (continued)

◆ Reading Strategy

USE TEXT AIDS

Using **text aids**—the explanations of words and passages appearing in the margins—makes it easier to understand the English of Shakespeare's day.

1. Rewrite Capulet's scolding of Tybalt in Scene iv, lines 77–89, substituting the words in the text aids for the annotated words in the play.
2. Using your answer to question 1, express Capulet's meaning in your own words.

◆ Build Grammar Skills

PUNCTUATING WORDS OF DIRECT ADDRESS

When **words of direct address** appear in the middle of a sentence, they are preceded and followed by commas; when used at the beginning of a sentence, they are followed by a comma; and when used at the end, they are preceded by a comma.

Practice On a sheet of paper, correct the following sentences of dialogue from *The Tragedy of Romeo and Juliet.*

1. Nurse where's my daughter?
2. Good morrow cousin.
3. Turn thee Benvolio; look upon thy death.
4. My noble uncle do you know the cause?
5. I thank you honest gentlemen.

◆ Literary Focus

CHARACTER

Shakespeare's play includes a variety of memorable **characters**—people who take part in the action of a literary work.

1. Gregory and Sampson are both **flat characters**—characters with one dimension—who appear only in the first scene. What personality trait do they embody and what purpose do they serve in the play?
2. Romeo, Mercutio, and Benvolio are all **round characters**—characters with many personality traits. List the character traits of each one.
3. A **dramatic foil** is a character whose personality traits contrast with and highlight those of another character. In what ways are Benvolio and Mercutio dramatic foils for Romeo?

696 ◆ Drama

◆ Build Vocabulary

USING THE PREFIX *trans-*

The prefix *trans-* means "through" or "across." Define each of these words. Incorporate the definition of *trans-* into each answer.

1. transcontinental   3. translate   5. transform
2. transport   4. transplant

USING THE WORD BANK

Write the letter of the word that is the best synonym of the first word.

1. pernicious: (a) harmful, (b) courageous, (c) helpful
2. augmenting: (a) propelling, (b) increasing, (c) decreasing
3. grievance: (a) confusion, (b) praise, (c) complaint
4. transgression: (a) crime, (b) deed, (c) travel
5. heretics: (a) believers, (b) learners, (c) dissenters

Idea Bank

Writing

1. **Advice Column** Write a letter from Romeo or Juliet to an advice columnist in which he or she asks what to do about falling in love with the wrong person. Then write the advice columnist's response. **[Career Link]**

2. **Character Analysis** Choose one of the main characters introduced in the first act. Then write a short essay in which you analyze this character's personality traits.

Speaking and Listening

3. **Reading** Select a scene from Act I to perform with the appropriate number of classmates. Practice reading your lines aloud so that you can deliver them meaningfully. Pay attention to other people's lines so that you can respond to what they say with feeling. After you have practiced several times, perform your reading for the class. **[Performing Arts Link]**

 Idea Bank

Customizing for
Performance Levels

Following are suggestions for matching the Idea Bank topics with your students' performance levels:

Less Advanced Students: 3
Average Students: 1
More Advanced Students: 2

Customizing for
Learning Modalities

Following are suggestions for matching Idea Bank topics with your students' learning modalities:

Interpersonal: 1
Verbal/Linguistic: 2, 3

☑ ASSESSMENT OPTIONS

Formal Assessment, pp. 164-166.
Alternative Assessment, p. 46.
PORTFOLIO ASSESSMENT
Use the following rubrics in the *Alternative Assessment* booklet:
Advice Column: Problem-Solution Rubric, p. 94
Character Analysis: Literary Analysis/Interpretation Rubric, p. 105

Guide for Reading, Act II

◆ Review and Anticipate

In Act I, you learned of a bitter, long-standing feud between two families, the Montagues and the Capulets. You were also introduced to the play's title characters, who meet at a feast at the Capulets' house. Having immediately fallen in love, Romeo and Juliet discover that they come from opposing sides of the Capulet-Montague feud.

Based on what you've learned about the personalities of Romeo and Juliet, how do you expect them to respond to their love for each other? Will they pursue their love? Will they reveal their love to their families? How do you think their families would react?

◆ Literary Focus

BLANK VERSE

Blank verse is unrhymed verse written in iambic pentameter, or ten-syllable lines in which every second syllable is stressed. For example, when Romeo sees Juliet appear at her window, he exclaims,

> But soft! What light through yonder window breaks?
> It is the east, and Juliet is the sun!

Much of *Romeo and Juliet* is written in blank verse. This formal meter is well suited to serious subjects and has been used in many of the greatest poems and verse dramas in English. In Shakespeare's plays, important or aristocratic characters typically speak in blank verse. Minor or comic characters most often do not speak in verse.

Lines in iambic pentameter can also be rhymed. This gives extra emphasis to the words a character speaks. In addition, a sense of completeness or finality is created when two successive lines rhyme, forming a rhymed couplet. Because of this, the exits of major characters and the ends of scenes are often marked by a rhymed couplet.

◆ Build Grammar Skills

LOGICAL COMPARISONS

Shakespeare frequently uses memorable, striking comparisons in his plays. Look at the following example, which compares the name *rose* to all other flower names.

> That which we call a rose / By any other name would smell as sweet.

Whenever one member of a group is compared to other members—as in this example—the word *other* or *else* must be included to create a **logical comparion.** You'll notice that if the word *other* were omitted from the previous passage, the name *rose* would be illogically compared with itself as well as with all other names.

◆ Reading Strategy

READING BLANK VERSE

Blank verse can be a little distracting if you are not used to it. Like a really good song, blank verse can get you so absorbed in admiring the skill needed to produce it that you miss the meaning. To get the most meaning out of blank verse, keep in mind that thoughts or phrases do not necessarily end with the end of the line. Whether you read the words aloud or to yourself, read blank verse in sentences, pausing where the punctuation indicates and not necessarily at the end of every line.

◆ Build Vocabulary

PREFIXES: *inter-*

In Act II, you'll encounter the word *intercession,* which includes the prefix *inter-,* meaning "between" or "among." The word *intercession* refers to the act of going between two people or groups involved in a dispute in an effort to resolve the dispute. What other words can you think of that contain the prefix *inter-?*

WORD BANK

Before you read, preview this list of words.

cunning
procure
vile
predominant
intercession
sallow
waverer
lamentable
unwieldy

Guide for Reading ◆ 697

Prepare and Engage

OBJECTIVES

1. To read, comprehend, and interpret a play
2. To relate a play to personal experience
3. To read blank verse effectively
4. To identify blank verse
5. To build vocabulary in context and learn the prefix *inter-*
6. To make logical comparisons
7. To respond to a play through writing, speaking and listening, and projects

SKILLS INSTRUCTION

Vocabulary:
Prefixes: *inter-*

Grammar: Logical Comparisons

Reading Strategy: Read Blank Verse

Literary Focus:
Blank Verse

Critical Viewing:
Draw Conclusions; Generalize; Interpret

PORTFOLIO OPPORTUNITIES

Writing: Poem in Iambic Pentameter; Adaptation
Speaking and Listening: Persuasion
Projects: Set Design, Shakespeare Display

 To inspire students' interest in Act II of *Romeo and Juliet,* invite them to share their thoughts about teenage love and marriage. You might prompt discussion with questions like these:

- Are teenagers capable of real love, or only infatuation?
- How do you distinguish between love and infatuation?
- Are Romeo and Juliet in love or infatuated with each other?
- What do you think of the custom of parents choosing a husband or wife for their daughter or son?

 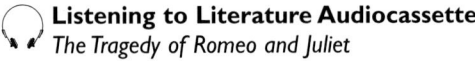
Prentice Hall Literature Program Resources

REINFORCE / RETEACH / EXTEND

Selection Support Pages
Build Vocabulary: Prefixes: *inter-,* p. 192
Build Grammar Skills: Logical Comparisons, p. 193
Reading Strategy: Read Blank Verse, p. 194
Literary Focus: Blank Verse, p. 195

Strategies for Diverse Student Needs, p. 47

Beyond Literature
Media Connection: Film Adaptations, p. 47

Formal Assessment Selection Test, pp. 167–169, Assessment Resources Software

Alternative Assessment, p. 46

Resource Pro CD-RM
The Tragedy of Romeo and Juliet—includes all resource material and customizable lesson plan

🎧 **Listening to Literature Audiocassettes**
The Tragedy of Romeo and Juliet

💿 **Looking at Literature Videodisc**
The Tragedy of Romeo and Juliet

Romeo and Juliet

One-Minute Insight

The main action of *Romeo and Juliet,* Act II, is the young couple's betrothal, which occurs the night they meet, and their marriage, which occurs the day after. The act invites the audience to speculate about Romeo and Juliet's love for each other. On the one hand, Romeo and Juliet are the archetypal teenage lovers—reckless, impulsive, passionate, head over heels in love. On the other hand, they are growing toward an adult version of love— marriage, devotion, and a willingness to make sacrifices and take risks. As the play progresses, their love will continue to be tested.

Customize for
Less Proficient Readers

Before they read each scene, review the plot with these readers. After they finish each scene, have them summarize the story in their own words.

Customize for
More Advanced Students

Some critics say that Juliet is more mature than Romeo and teaches him the meaning of true love. Invite more advanced students to discuss whether they agree with this idea and to explain why or why not.

◆ Literary Focus

❶ Blank Verse Invite students to read these two lines aloud, focusing on the iambic pentameter. How must the words *bewitched* and *supposed* be pronounced to fit the meter?
Bewitched must be pronounced with three syllables and supposed with two.

◆ Reading Strategy

❷ Read Blank Verse Invite students to read this passage aloud. Then ask how the passage would differ in feel if it were in blank verse.
The rhymes make the passage more formal. Blank verse would make the lines seem more like ordinary speech.

◆ Critical Thinking

❸ Interpret Invite students to tell why Romeo calls himself "dull earth," i.e., a "lifeless body." *Romeo is saying that without Juliet, he is nothing more than a corpse; that Juliet is his soul—his "center"—and without her, he is as good as dead.*

698

Act II

Prologue

[*Enter* CHORUS.]

    CHORUS. Now old desire[1] doth in his deathbed lie,
        And young affection gapes to be his heir;[2]
        That fair[3] for which love groaned for and would die,
          With tender Juliet matched, is now not fair.
5   Now Romeo is beloved and loves again,
          Alike bewitchèd[4] by the charm of looks;
        But to his foe supposed he must complain,[5]
          And she steal love's sweet bait from fearful hooks.
        Being held a foe, he may not have access
10   To breathe such vows as lovers use to swear,
        And she as much in love, her means much less
          To meet her new belovèd anywhere;
        But passion lends them power, time means to meet,
          Temp'ring extremities with extreme sweet.[6]
                              [*Exit.*]

Scene i. *Near* CAPULET'S *orchard.*

[*Enter* ROMEO *alone.*]

    ROMEO. Can I go forward when my heart is here?
        Turn back, dull earth,[1] and find thy center[2] out.

[*Enter* BENVOLIO *with* MERCUTIO. ROMEO *retires.*]

    BENVOLIO. Romeo! My cousin Romeo! Romeo!

    MERCUTIO.   He is wise.
        And, on my life, hath stol'n him home to bed.

5   BENVOLIO. He ran this way and leapt this orchard wall.
        Call, good Mercutio.

    MERCUTIO.   Nay, I'll conjure[3] too.
        Romeo! Humors! Madman! Passion! Lover!
        Appear thou in the likeness of a sigh;
        Speak but one rhyme, and I am satisfied!
10   Cry but "Ay me!" pronounce but "love" and "dove";
        Speak to my gossip[4] Venus one fair word,
        One nickname for her purblind son and heir,
        Young Abraham Cupid, he that shot so true

698 ◆ *Drama*

1. old desire: Romeo's love for Rosaline.
2. young . . . heir: Romeo's new love for Juliet is eager to replace his love for Rosaline.
3. fair: Beautiful woman (Rosaline).
4. Alike bewitched: Both Romeo and Juliet are enchanted.
5. complain: Address his words of love.

6. Temp'ring . . . sweet: Easing their difficulties with great delights.

1. dull earth: Lifeless body.
2. center: Heart, or possibly soul (Juliet).

3. conjure: Recite a spell to make Romeo appear.

4. gossip: Merry old lady.

 Preparing for Standardized Tests

Reading and Vocabulary Vocabulary development will enable students to improve performance on the verbal portions of standardized tests—both reading comprehension and vocabulary items. The Build Vocabulary lesson focuses on learning word meaning through the use of the prefix *inter-*. Students can apply this skill to infer the meanings of unfamiliar words that contain this prefix. For additional practice, use the Build Vocabulary page in *Selection Support,* p. 192.

Grammar and Language Portions of some standardized tests standardized require students

to understand logical comparisons and to be able to determine if a comparison is not logical. Students may be asked to correct sentences like the following:

    Romeo thought that Juliet was more beautiful than any woman he had ever seen. *Romeo thought that Juliet was more beautiful than any other woman he had ever seen.*

The Build Grammar Skills lesson for this selection focuses on this topic. For additional practice, use the Build Grammar Skills page on Logical Comparisons, p. 193, in *Selection Support.*

When King Cophetua loved the beggar maid!
15 He heareth not, he stirreth not, he moveth not;
The ape is dead,[5] and I must conjure him.
I conjure thee by Rosaline's bright eyes,
By her high forehead and her scarlet lip,
By her fine foot, straight leg, and quivering thigh,
20 And the demesnes that there adjacent lie,
That in thy likeness thou appear to us!

BENVOLIO. And if he hear thee, thou wilt anger him.

MERCUTIO. This cannot anger him. 'Twould anger him
To raise a spirit in his mistress' circle
25 Of some strange nature, letting it there stand
Till she had laid it and conjured it down.
That were some spite; my invocation
Is fair and honest; in his mistress' name,
I conjure only but to raise up him.

30 **BENVOLIO.** Come, he hath hid himself among these trees
To be consorted[6] with the humorous[7] night.
Blind is his love and best befits the dark.

MERCUTIO. If love be blind, love cannot hit the mark.
Now will he sit under a medlar tree
35 And wish his mistress were that kind of fruit
As maids call medlars[8] when they laugh alone.
O, Romeo, that she were, O that she were
An open *et cetera*, thou a pop'rin pear!
Romeo, good night. I'll to my truckle bed;[9]
40 This field bed is too cold for me to sleep.
Come, shall we go?

BENVOLIO.   Go then, for 'tis in vain
To seek him here that means not to be found.

[*Exit with others.*]

Scene ii. CAPULET'S *orchard.*

ROMEO. [*Coming forward*] He jests at scars that never felt a wound.

[*Enters* JULIET *at a window.*]

But soft! What light through yonder window breaks?
It is the East, and Juliet is the sun!
Arise, fair sun, and kill the envious moon,
5 Who is already sick and pale with grief
That thou her maid art far more fair than she.
Be not her maid, since she is envious.

5. The ape is dead:
Romeo, like a trained monkey, seems to be playing.

6. consorted: Associated.
7. humorous: Humid; moody, like a lover.

8. medlars: Applelike fruits.

9. truckle bed: Trundlebed, placed under a larger bed when not in use.

◆ **Literary Focus**
What effect does Shakespeare achieve by breaking up a rhymed couplet into two separate scenes?

Romeo and Juliet, Act II, Scene ii ◆ 699

---

❹ **Clarification** Help students understand that Mercutio is teasing Romeo about his love for Rosaline, whom he thinks Romeo still loves. Point out that kids today, too, sometimes tease each other about having a boyfriend or girlfriend. They just use different language.

◆ **Critical Thinking**

❺ **Interpret** Invite students to explain Benvolio's remark about why Romeo wants to be in the dark.
Benvolio sees Romeo as lovesick and "blindly" in love. Benvolio is making a joke: that since Romeo loves blindly, he prefers to be in the darkness, where he can't see anyway.

◆ **Literary Focus**

❻ **Blank Verse** By breaking up the rhymed couplet, one scene flows smoothly and quickly to the next.

❼ **Clarification** Point out to students that this is the beginning of the famous "balcony scene" in *Romeo and Juliet*—one of the most famous scenes in all of Shakespeare's plays. Help them understand that Romeo is making an extended comparison here that reveals his strong feelings for Juliet. First he says that Juliet's beauty is so great that she lights up the world, as the sun does when it rises. Then he says that even the moon is envious of her, the way the moon might be envious of the brighter, "more fair" sun. You may want to point out that the moon symbolizes Romeo's love for Rosaline, who is likened to Diana, goddess of the moon, in Act I.

◆ **Block Scheduling Strategies**

Consider these suggestions to take advantage of extended class time:
- Have students work in groups to review the events in *Romeo and Juliet,* Act I. Encourage them to predict what might happen in Act II.
- Play the audiocassette recording of portions of the play while students read along. Point out places where one line of blank verse flows into the next without a pause.

Remind students to read blank verse as if it were normal speech.
- Have students listen to a recording of "Tonight" from *West Side Story.* Then ask small groups to answer the questions on page 668.
- Obtain videotapes of *Romeo and Juliet* and *West Side Story.* Have students view related scenes in the two films and compare and contrast them.

- Have students work on the Poem in Iambic Pentameter activity on page 719.
- Have students complete the Media Connection: Film Adaptations activity in *Beyond Literature,* p. 47.
- Have students perform the Persuasion role-play on page 719. This activity is supported by a Speaking and Listening Mini-Lesson on page 717 in the teacher edition.

❶ Draw Conclusions Students might conclude that Juliet is passionate (she is clearly attracted to Romeo), shy (she wishes he had not overheard her), cautious (she tells him she does not trust his vows), assertive (she asks him to marry her), religious (she does not want to see him again if he *won't* marry her), and brave (she is willing to defy her entire family and follow Romeo to the ends of the earth). Encourage students to support their opinions about character traits by citing evidence from the scene.

◆ Critical Thinking

❷ Infer Invite students to explain what this passage reveals about Juliet's feelings. Ask them how the darkness may make it easier for her to handle those feelings. *Juliet is embarrassed that Romeo heard her express her love for him. She would prefer to take back her words and act more conventionally—but she is also glad to throw convention aside and admit her true feelings. The darkness may make it easier for her to behave more freely, since she thinks Romeo cannot see her face clearly and since she probably cannot see him clearly, either.*

◆ *Literature and Your Life*

❸ Point out that in Shakespeare's time, it was proper to maintain a mask of courtly formality. However, Juliet decides to break the rules of conduct and speak plainly to Romeo. Ask students how her behavior relates to situations they have observed in which people must choose between politeness and bluntness. *Students may describe times they have seen others tell a "white lie," or discuss situations in which they wish they had been more open or more diplomatic. Students may say that Juliet's behavior is like that of other women who decide not to be coy, but rather to tell the truth about their feelings. They may also compare her behavior to people who choose to be honest with their families, their employers, their teachers, or their friends.*

◀ **Critical Viewing**
When Romeo enters the Capulets' orchard, he overhears Juliet talking to herself. What do Juliet's musings to herself and her later conversation with Romeo reveal about her character? [Draw Conclusions] ❶

85   **JULIET.** Thou knowest the mask of night is on my face;
     Else would a maiden blush bepaint my cheek
     For that which thou hast heard me speak tonight.
     Fain would I dwell on form[13]—fain, fain deny
     What I have spoke; but farewell compliment![14]
90   Dost thou love me? I know thou wilt say "Ay";
     And I will take thy word. Yet, if thou swear'st,
     Thou mayst prove false. At lovers' perjuries,
     They say Jove laughs. O gentle Romeo,
     If thou dost love, pronounce it faithfully.
95   Or if thou thinkest I am too quickly won,
     I'll frown and be perverse[15] and say thee nay,
     So thou wilt woo; but else, not for the world.
     In truth, fair Montague, I am too fond,[16]
     And therefore thou mayst think my havior light;[17]
100   But trust me, gentleman, I'll prove more true
     Than those that have more <u>cunning</u> to be strange.[18]
     I should have been more strange, I must confess,
     But that thou overheard'st, ere I was ware,
     My truelove passion. Therefore pardon me,
105   And not impute this yielding to light love,
     Which the dark night hath so discoverèd.[19]

❹ **ROMEO.** Lady, by yonder blessèd moon I vow,

702 ◆ Drama

13. Fain . . . form: Eagerly would I follow convention (by acting reserved).
14. compliment: Conventional behavior.

15. be perverse: Act contrary to my true feelings.
16. fond: Affectionate.
17. my havior light: My behavior immodest or unserious.
18. strange: Distant and cold.
19. discoverèd: Revealed.

◆ **Build Vocabulary**
cunning (kun´ iŋ) *adj.*: Cleverness; slyness

 Humanities: Film

This still from the movie *Romeo and Juliet* shows the young actress Olivia de Hussey as Juliet.
Use questions like these for discussion:
1. Based on this image, how do you think the director envisioned Juliet? What kind of character did he want to present to the audience? *The director seemed to see Juliet as young, naive, passionate, and intense.*

2. In this particular still, the actress playing Juliet stares out of the screen directly into the eyes of the audience. What is the effect of that stare? *Having Juliet make direct eye contact with the audience draws the audience in, makes them sympathize with her, makes them believe or take seriously what she has said, gets them on her side.*

That tips with silver all these fruit-tree tops—

JULIET. O, swear not by the moon, th' inconstant moon,
110 That monthly changes in her circle orb,
    Lest that thy love prove likewise variable.

ROMEO. What shall I swear by?

JULIET.   Do not swear at all;
    Or if thou wilt, swear by thy gracious self,
115 Which is the god of my idolatry,
    And I'll believe thee.

ROMEO.   If my heart's dear love—

JULIET. Well, do not swear. Although I joy in thee,
    I have no joy of this contract[20] tonight.
    It is too rash, too unadvised, too sudden;
    Too like the lightning, which doth cease to be
120 Ere one can say it lightens. Sweet, good night!
    This bud of love, by summer's ripening breath,
    May prove a beauteous flow'r when next we meet.
    Good night, good night! As sweet repose and rest
    Come to thy heart as that within my breast!

125 **ROMEO.** O, wilt thou leave me so unsatisfied?

JULIET. What satisfaction canst thou have tonight?

ROMEO. Th' exchange of thy love's faithful vow for mine.

JULIET. I gave thee mine before thou didst request it;
    And yet I would it were to give again.

130 **ROMEO.** Wouldst thou withdraw it? For what purpose, love?

JULIET. But to be frank[21] and give it thee again.
    And yet I wish but for the thing I have.
    My bounty[22] is as boundless as the sea,
    My love as deep; the more I give to thee,
135 The more I have, for both are infinite,
    I hear some noise within. Dear love, adieu!

[NURSE *calls within.*]

    Anon, good nurse! Sweet Montague, be true.
    Stay but a little, I will come again.   [*Exit.*]

ROMEO. O blessèd, blessèd night! I am afeard,
140 Being in night, all this is but a dream,
    Too flattering-sweet to be substantial.[23]

[*Enter* JULIET *again.*]

Romeo and Juliet, Act II, Scene ii ◆ *703*

◆ **Reading Strategy**
How would you rephrase in standard English what Romeo and Juliet are saying to each other? ❺

20. **contract:** Betrothal.

21. **frank:** Generous.

22. **bounty:** What I have to give.

23. **substantial:** Real.

◆ **Critical Thinking**

❹ **Compare and Contrast** Ask students to compare and contrast the two characters' approaches to love. *Romeo is trying to make extravagant vows, while Juliet is concerned that Romeo's vows are not trustworthy. Both characters are strongly attracted to one another, but Romeo seems willing to abandon himself to his feelings, whereas Juliet seems more concerned with finding out whether she can trust such a "sudden," "rash," and "unadvised" connection.*

◆ **Reading Strategy**

❺ **Read Blank Verse** Students may rephrase lines 90–131 in a manner similar to the following.

JULIET: If you tell me you love me, I will believe you, so be honest. If you think I fall in love too easily, I'll hide my true feelings and act aloof. However, you know how I really feel, so it's pointless to play games. ROMEO: I promise. . . . JULIET: Don't make promises; I believe you. I'm happy with you, but I'm not happy with how fast we're rushing into things. Goodnight. ROMEO: Wait. Aren't you going to promise you love me, too? JULIET: I promised to love you even before you asked me to, but I want to take back my promise. ROMEO: Why? JULIET: So I could make it again.

◆ **Reading Strategy**

❻ **Read Blank Verse** Invite students to read this passage in two ways. First, have them stress every other syllable. What do they notice about the word *blessed*? *To fit the meter, blessed must be pronounced with two syllables— bles-sed.* Then ask students to read the passage aloud more naturally, though still pronouncing *blessed* with two syllables. Instruct them to use the punctuation, pausing slightly at each exclamation point or comma. Finally, ask students how the blank verse helps to convey Romeo's feelings. *The blank verse, while sounding natural, also helps the actor playing Romeo draw out his words, conveying the intensity of his love for Juliet.*

❶ Ask: What is Juliet asking for in this passage? What is she offering? *Juliet is asking Romeo to commit to marrying her. She is offering to follow him "throughout the world" if he does marry her.*

❷ Clarification Help students to see how Juliet's sentence would have read if the Nurse had not interrupted her: "But if thou meanest not well, I do beseech thee to cease thy strife and leave me to my grief." Make sure that students understand her meaning: "If your intentions are not honorable (if you do not intend to marry me), I beg you to stop your efforts (to win me) and leave me alone with my sad feelings (since I love you and my heart will be broken)."

Comprehension Check ☑

❸ Ask students to explain Juliet's words. *Juliet is comparing the action she would like to take (shouting "My Romeo!" loud enough for her voice to echo) with the action she is forced to take (whispering).* **Point out that the word** *else* **indicates the comparison. Ask students for a definition of the word** *else* **in this context.** *Else means "otherwise."*

◆ Reading Strategy

❹ Read Blank Verse You can count the number of syllables (ten) and see that every other syllable is stressed. In addition, the characters' lines are offset so that if they were compressed vertically, they would form a single line. Point out that Romeo and Juliet's sharing of a line emphasizes their bond.

---

❶
JULIET. Three words, dear Romeo, and good night indeed.
  If that thy bent[24] of love be honorable,
  Thy purpose marriage, send me word tomorrow,
145 By one that I'll <u>procure</u> to come to thee,
  Where and what time thou wilt perform the rite;
  And all my fortunes at thy foot I'll lay
  And follow thee my lord throughout the world.

NURSE. [*Within*] Madam!

JULIET. I come anon.—But if thou meanest not well,
150 I do beseech thee—

❷ NURSE.   [*Within*] Madam!

JULIET.   By and by[25] I come.—
  To cease thy strife[26] and leave me to my grief.
  Tomorrow will I send.

ROMEO.   So thrive my soul—

JULIET. A thousand times good night!   [*Exit.*]

155 **ROMEO.** A thousand times the worse, to want thy light!
  Love goes toward love as schoolboys from their books;
  But love from love, toward school with heavy looks.

[*Enter* JULIET *again.*]

JULIET. Hist! Romeo, hist! O for a falc'ner's voice
  To lure this tassel gentle[27] back again!
❸ 160 Bondage is hoarse[28] and may not speak aloud,
  Else would I tear the cave where Echo[29] lies
  And make her airy tongue more hoarse than mine
  With repetition of "My Romeo!"

ROMEO. It is my soul that calls upon my name.
165 How silver-sweet sound lovers' tongues by night,
  Like softest music to attending ears!

JULIET. Romeo!

ROMEO.   My sweet?

JULIET.   What o'clock tomorrow
  Shall I send to thee?

ROMEO.   By the hour of nine.

JULIET. I will not fail. 'Tis twenty year till then.
170 I have forgot why I did call thee back.

ROMEO. Let me stand here till thou remember it.

---

24. **bent:** Purpose; intention.

25. **By and by:** At once.
26. **strife:** Efforts.

27. **tassel gentle:** Male falcon.
28. **Bondage is hoarse:** Being bound in by my family restricts my speech.
29. **Echo:** In classical mythology, the nymph Echo, unable to win the love of Narcissus, wasted away in a cave until nothing was left of her but her voice.

◆ Reading Strategy
Notice that Juliet's question (ll.167–168), although broken into two lines, is actually a single sentence.

❹

◆ Build Vocabulary
procure (prō kyōōr') *v.*: Get; obtain

704 ◆ *Drama*

JULIET. I shall forget, to have thee still stand there,
Rememb'ring how I love thy company.

ROMEO. And I'll stay, to have thee still forget,
175   Forgetting any other home but this.

JULIET. 'Tis almost morning. I would have thee gone—
And yet no farther than a wanton's[30] bird,
That lets it hop a little from his hand,
Like a poor prisoner in his twisted gyves,[31]
180   And with a silken thread plucks it back again,
So loving-jealous of his liberty.

ROMEO. I would I were thy bird.

JULIET.   Sweet, so would I.
Yet I should kill thee with much cherishing.
Good night, good night! Parting is such sweet sorrow
❺ 185   That I shall say good night till it be morrow. [*Exit.*]

❻ **ROMEO.** Sleep dwell upon thine eyes, peace in thy breast!
Would I were sleep and peace, so sweet to rest!
Hence will I to my ghostly friar's[32] close cell,[33]
His help to crave and my dear hap[34] to tell.   [*Exit.*]

Scene iii. FRIAR LAURENCE'S *cell.*

[*Enter* FRIAR LAURENCE *alone, with a basket.*]

FRIAR. The gray-eyed morn smiles on the frowning night,
Check'ring the eastern clouds with streaks of light;
And fleckèd[1] darkness like a drunkard reels
From forth day's path and Titan's burning wheels.[2]
5   Now, ere the sun advance his burning eye
The day to cheer and night's dank dew to dry,
I must upfill this osier cage[3] of ours
With baleful[4] weeds and precious-juicèd flowers.
The earth that's nature's mother is her tomb.
❼ 10   What is her burying grave, that is her womb;
❽   And from her womb children of divers kind[5]
We sucking on her natural bosom find,
Many for many virtues excellent,
None but for some, and yet all different.
15   O, mickle[6] is the powerful grace[7] that lies
In plants, herbs, stones, and their true qualities;
For naught so vile that on the earth doth live
But to the earth some special good doth give;
Nor aught so good but, strained[8] from that fair use,

---

30. **wanton's:** Spoiled, playful child's.

31. **gyves** (jivz): Chains.

---

32. **ghostly friar's:** Spiritual father's.
33. **close cell:** Small room.
34. **dear hap:** Good fortune.

---

1. **fleckèd:** Spotted.

2. **Titan's burning wheels:** Wheels of the sun god's chariot.

3. **osier cage:** Willow basket.
4. **baleful:** Poisonous.

5. **divers kind:** Different kinds.
6. **mickle:** Great.
7. **grace:** Divine power.
8. **strained:** Turned away.

◆ **Build Vocabulary**

vile (vīl) *adj.*: Worthless; cheap; low

◆ **Critical Thinking**

❺ Speculate The sentence, "Parting is such sweet sorrow . . . ," is well known. Ask students to speculate about why this is so. *Students may propose that the sentence is memorable because of its rhythm and rhyme, its intriguing contradiction in terms (sweet/sorrow), or its position at the end of the famous "balcony scene." Other answers are possible.*

◆ **Literary Focus**

❻ Blank Verse Ask students how these four lines differ from the lines that went before. *The lines rhyme.* Why did Shakespeare construct the lines in this manner? *By convention, rhymed couplets mark the end of a scene. Rhyming gives a sense of completion or closure.*

❼ Clarification Make sure students understand Friar Lawrence's point: The earth gives birth to creatures and is also where creatures are buried when they die.

◆ **Critical Thinking**

❽ Make Inferences Ask students why Shakespeare has chosen to have Friar Lawrence make this connection between birth and death. *Students may think that Shakespeare wants to characterize the Friar as a philosophical character; they may see this speech about death as foreshadowing the ultimate deaths of Romeo and Juliet.*

Romeo and Juliet, Act II, Scene iii ◆ 705

Cross-Curricular Connection: Social Studies

Friar, which comes from the Latin word for *brother,* is a general term for members of religious orders of men who originally lived only as *mendicants,* or beggars. They had no worldly possessions or fixed place to live so that they could devote themselves exclusively to preaching, missionary work, or other charitable undertakings. Friars wore robes or *habits* that were either gray, black, or white.

Students should understand the difference between a friar, like Friar Lawrence, and a monk.

A monk is a man who has taken religious vows of poverty, chastity, and obedience and has retired from worldly life to live with other monks, studying the Scriptures, praying, and meditating. A friar lives among ordinary people and helps them, as Friar Lawrence tried, unsuccessfully, to help the two star-crossed lovers.

Students might discuss where Friar Lawrence lives and imagine what his dwelling place looks like.

20   Revolts from true birth,[9] stumbling on abuse.
     Virtue itself turns vice, being misapplied,
     And vice sometime by action dignified.

[*Enter* ROMEO.]

     Within the infant rind[10] of this weak flower
     Poison hath residence and medicine power;[11]
25   For this, being smelt, with that part cheers each part;[12]
     Being tasted, stays all senses with the heart.[13]
     Two such opposèd kings encamp them still[14]
     In man as well as herbs—grace and rude will;
     And where the worser is <u>predominant</u>,
30   Full soon the canker[15] death eats up that plant.

ROMEO. Good morrow, father.

FRIAR.   *Benedicite!*[16]
     What early tongue so sweet saluteth me?
     Young son, it argues a distemperèd head[17]
     So soon to bid good morrow to thy bed.
35   Care keeps his watch in every old man's eye,
     And where care lodges, sleep will never lie;
     But where unbruisèd youth with unstuffed[18] brain
     Doth couch his limbs, there golden sleep doth reign,
     Therefore thy earliness doth me assure
40   Thou art uproused with some distemp'rature;[19]
     Or if not so, then here I hit it right—
     Our Romeo hath not been in bed tonight.

ROMEO. That last is true. The sweeter rest was mine.

FRIAR. God pardon sin! Wast thou with Rosaline?

45 **ROMEO.** With Rosaline, my ghostly father? No.
     I have forgot that name and that name's woe.

FRIAR. That's my good son! But where hast thou been then?

ROMEO. I'll tell thee ere thou ask it me again.
     I have been feasting with mine enemy,
50   Where on a sudden one hath wounded me
     That's by me wounded. Both our remedies
     Within thy help and holy physic[20] lies.
     I bear no hatred, blessèd man, for, lo,
     My <u>intercession</u> likewise steads my foe.[21]

55 **FRIAR.** Be plain, good son, and homely in thy drift.[22]
     Riddling confession finds but riddling shrift.[23]

ROMEO. Then plainly know my heart's dear love is set

706 ◆ *Drama*

9. Revolts . . . birth: Conflicts with its real purpose.

10. infant rind: Tender skin.
11. and medicine power: And medicinal quality has power.
12. with . . . part: With that quality—odor—revives each part of the body.
13. stays . . . heart: Kills (stops the working of the five senses along with the heart).
14. still: Always.
15. canker: A destructive caterpillar.
16. *Benedicite!*: God bless you!
17. distemperèd head: Troubled mind.

18. unstuffed: Not filled with cares.
19. distemp'rature: Illness.
20. physic (fiz´ ik): Medicine.
21. My . . . foe: My plea also helps my enemy (Juliet, a Capulet).
22. and . . . drift: And simple in your speech.
23. Riddling . . . shrift: A confusing confession will get you uncertain forgiveness. The Friar means that unless Romeo speaks clearly, he will not get clear and direct advice.

◆ **Build Vocabulary**

predominant (prē däm´ ə nənt) *adj.*: Having dominating influence over others

intercession (in´ tər sesh´ ən) *n.*: The act of pleading on behalf of another

On the fair daughter of rich Capulet;
As mine on hers, so hers is set on mine,
60 And all combined, save[24] what thou must combine
By holy marriage. When and where and how
We met, we wooed, and made exchange of vow,
I'll tell thee as we pass; but this I pray,
That thou consent to marry us today.

65 **FRIAR.** Holy Saint Francis! What a change is here!
Is Rosaline, that thou didst love so dear,
So soon forsaken? Young men's love then lies
Not truly in their hearts, but in their eyes.
Jesu Maria! What a deal of brine[25]
70 Hath washed thy <u>sallow</u> cheeks for Rosaline!
How much salt water thrown away in waste
To season love, that of it doth not taste!
The sun not yet thy sighs from heaven clears,
Thy old groans ring yet in mine ancient ears.
75 Lo, here upon thy cheek the stain doth sit
Of an old tear that is not washed off yet.
If e'er thou wast thyself, and these woes thine,
Thou and these woes were all for Rosaline.
And art thou changed? Pronounce this sentence then:
80 Women may fall[26] when there's no strength[27] in men.

ROMEO. Thou chidst me oft for loving Rosaline.

FRIAR. For doting,[28] not for loving, pupil mine.

ROMEO. And badst[29] me bury love.

FRIAR.   Not in a grave
To lay one in, another out to have.

85 **ROMEO.** I pray thee chide me not. Her I love now
Doth grace[30] for grace and love for love allow.[31]
The other did not so.

FRIAR.   O, she knew well
Thy love did read by rote, that could not spell.[32]
But come, young <u>waverer</u>, come go with me.
90 In one respect I'll thy assistant be;
For this alliance may so happy prove
To turn your households' rancor[33] to pure love.

ROMEO. O, let us hence! I stand on[34] sudden haste.

FRIAR. Wisely and slow. They stumble that run fast.

[*Exit.*]

24. And . . . save: And we are united in every way, except for (save).

25. brine: Salt water (tears).

◆ **Literary Focus**
Which syllables are stressed and which are unstressed in Friar Laurence's speech ?

26. fall: Be weak or inconstant.
27. strength: Constancy; stability.
28. doting: Being infatuated.
29. badst: Urged.
30. grace: Favor.
31. allow: Give.
32. Thy . . . spell: Your love was someone who recites words from memory with no understanding of them.
33. rancor: Hatred.
34. stand on: Insist on.

◆ **Build Vocabulary**

sallow (sal´ ō) *adj.:* Of a sickly, pale-yellowish complexion

waverer (wā´ vər ər) *n.:* One who changes or is unsteady

Romeo and Juliet, Act II, Scene iii ◆ 707

❺

❻

◆ *Literature and Your Life*

❺ Ask students if they think this is a realistic portrayal of an adult talking to a teenager in love. Invite them to identify the elements that they think are or are not realistic. *Students may find it realistic that the Friar scolds Romeo for being so fickle—loving Rosaline one moment and Juliet the next. They might also find realistic Friar Lawrence's refusal to take Romeo's love for Juliet seriously.*

◆ **Literary Focus**

❻ **Blank Verse** Friar Lawrence's speech is almost completely straight iambic pentameter. (There are, however, trochaic substitutions in the first foot of line 65 and the first foot of line 69.) Students should realize that in blank verse, the first syllable is unstressed, the second syllable is stressed, and so on. Encourage students to read each line with exaggerated meter, then more naturally.

Nurse's. Similarly, in the Nurse's circle, students should list her traits that are different from Mercutio's. In the intersecting section of both circles, students should list the traits that the two characters share. Use the following example as a guide:

Student Activity
Using the same procedure, select two other characters from the play to compare and contrast. You might want to compare and contrast Montague and Capulet, for example.

❶ Ask students to repeat the Nurse's point in their own words.

Students might say: "I am so upset, I'm shaking all over. You villain! Please, sir, my mistress has asked me to ask you this. I won't tell you what she told me to say, but I will tell you that if you deceive her, you will be behaving very badly, because she is very young, and so if you cheat her, that is a very bad way to treat a good woman, and not the way a gentleman would behave."

◆ Literary Focus

❷ **Blank Verse** Help students see that the Nurse is an unromantic, comic character from a lower class than Romeo and Juliet. In Shakespeare's plays, the servants and lower-class characters typically speak in prose, as do the comic characters. The romantic characters speak in blank verse, to show that they are more thoughtful, poetic, and passionate than those who speak prose.

---

that is something stale and hoar ere it be spent.

[*He walks by them and sings.*]

125
An old hare hoar,
And an old hare hoar,
Is very good meat in Lent;
But a hare that is hoar
Is too much for a score
130
When it hoars ere it be spent.

Romeo, will you come to your father's? We'll to dinner thither.

ROMEO. I will follow you.

MERCUTIO. Farewell, ancient lady. Farewell, [*singing*]
"Lady, lady, lady."³³   [*Exit* MERCUTIO, BENVOLIO.]

135 **NURSE.** I pray you, sir, what saucy merchant was this that was so full of his ropery?³⁴

ROMEO. A gentleman, nurse, that loves to hear himself talk and will speak more in a minute than he will stand to in a month.

140 **NURSE.** And 'a³⁵ speak anything against me, I'll take him down, and 'a were lustier than he is, and twenty such Jacks; and if I cannot, I'll find those that shall. Scurvy knave! I am none of his flirt-gills;³⁶ I am none of his skainsmates.³⁷ And thou must stand by too, and suffer
145 every knave to use me at his pleasure!

PETER. I saw no man use you at his pleasure. If I had, my weapon should quickly have been out, I warrant you. I dare draw as soon as another man, if I see occasion in a good quarrel, and the law on my side.

150 **NURSE.** Now, afore God, I am so vexed that every part about me quivers. Scurvy knave! Pray you, sir, a word; and, as I told you, my young lady bid me inquire you out. What she bid me say, I will keep to myself; but first let me tell ye, if ye should lead her in a fool's paradise, as
155 they say, it were a very gross kind of behavior, as they say; for the gentlewoman is young; and therefore, if you should deal double with her, truly it were an ill thing to be off'red to any gentlewoman, and very weak³⁸ dealing.

160 **ROMEO.** Nurse, commend³⁹ me to thy lady and mistress. I protest unto thee—

712 ◆ *Drama*

---

33. **"Lady . . . lady":** Line from an old ballad, "Chaste Susanna."

34. **ropery:** The Nurse means roguery, the talk and conduct of a rascal.

35. **'a:** He.

36. **flirt-gills:** Common girls.
37. **skainsmates:** Criminals; cutthroats.

◆ **Literary Focus**
Why didn't Shakespeare have the Nurse speak in blank verse?   **❷**

38. **weak:** Unmanly.
39. **commend:** Convey my respect and best wishes.

NURSE. Good heart, and i' faith I will tell her as much.
Lord, Lord, she will be a joyful woman.

ROMEO. What wilt thou tell her, nurse? Thou dost not
165 mark me.

NURSE. I will tell her, sir, that you do protest, which, as I
take it, is a gentlemanlike offer.

ROMEO. Bid her devise
Some means to come to shrift[40] this afternoon;
170 And there she shall at Friar Laurence' cell
Be shrived and married. Here is for thy pains.

40. **shrift:** Confession.

NURSE. No, truly, sir; not a penny.

ROMEO. Go to! I say you shall.

NURSE. This afternoon, sir? Well, she shall be there.

175 **ROMEO.** And stay, good nurse, behind the abbey wall.
Within this hour my man shall be with thee
And bring thee cords made like a tackled stair.[41]
Which to the high topgallant[42] of my joy
Must be my convoy[43] in the secret night.
180 Farewell. Be trusty, and I'll quit[44] thy pains.
Farewell. Commend me to thy mistress.

41. **tackled stair:** Rope
ladder.
42. **topgallant:** Summit.
43. **convoy:** Conveyance.
44. **quit:** Reward; pay you
back for.

NURSE. Now God in heaven bless thee! Hark you, sir.

ROMEO. What say'st thou, my dear nurse?

NURSE. Is your man secret? Did you ne'er hear say,
185 Two may keep counsel, putting one away?[45]

45. **Two . . . away:** Two
can keep a secret if one is
ignorant, or out of the way.

ROMEO. Warrant thee my man's as true as steel.

NURSE. Well, sir, my mistress is the sweetest lady. Lord,
Lord! When 'twas a little prating[46] thing—O, there is a
nobleman in town, one Paris, that would fain lay knife
190 aboard;[47] but she, good soul, had as lieve[48] see a toad,
a very toad, as see him. I anger her sometimes, and tell
her that Paris is the properer man; but I'll warrant
you, when I say so, she looks as pale as any clout[49]
in the versal world.[50] Doth not rosemary and Romeo be-
195 gin both with a letter?

46. **prating:** Babbling.

47. **fain . . . aboard:**
Eagerly seize Juliet for
himself.
48. **had as lieve:** Would as
willingly.
49. **clout:** Cloth.
50. **versal world:** Universe.

ROMEO. Ay, nurse; what of that? Both with an *R*.

NURSE. Ah, mocker! That's the dog's name.[51] *R* is for the—
No; I know it begins with some other letter; and she
hath the prettiest sententious[52] of it, of you and rosemary,

51. **dog's name:** *R* sounds
like a growl.
52. **sententious:** The Nurse
means *sentences*—clever,
wise sayings.

Romeo and Juliet, Act II, Scene iv ◆ 713

❸ **Blank Verse** Ask students why
Romeo suddenly breaks into blank
verse after an entire scene in prose.
*Students should see that the blank verse
conveys the intensity of Romeo's feelings
as well as showing his romantic ideas
about this plan.*

❹ **Clarification** Rosemary symbolizes fidelity and remembrance.

Cross-Curricular Connection: Social Studies

In Shakespeare's day, it would not be unusual for parents to choose husbands or wives for their children. Nor would it be unusual for a girl as young as thirteen or fourteen to be married, as Juliet is. Women were seen as the property of the family, and they might easily be forced to marry—or prevented from marrying. Indeed, later in the play, Juliet's father offers her a choice between marrying the man of his choice and becoming a nun.

Women who married were expected to bring their husbands a *dowry*—a certain amount of goods, property, or money to compensate the husband and his family for the expense of caring for the wife for the rest of her life. Women without property were naturally at a disadvantage in the marriage market.

Invite students to discuss how the conditions surrounding marriage help to shape the plot of *Romeo and Juliet.*

◆ **Literature and Your Life**

❶ Students might cite personal examples of waiting impatiently for such occasions as a date, telephone call, visit, party, or holiday.

◆ **Critical Thinking**

❷ **Analyze** Ask students what this passage tells them about Juliet's state of mind. *Students might say that she is impatient for news of Romeo, which makes her critical of old people, since she is waiting for her aged nurse. Because the Nurse seems slow to the impatient Juliet, she says angrily that young people are fast but old people are slow.*

200   that it would do you good to hear it.

ROMEO. Commend me to thy lady.

NURSE. Ay, a thousand times. [*Exit* ROMEO.] Peter!

PETER. Anon.

NURSE. Before, and apace.[53]   [*Exit, after* PETER.]

53. **Before, and apace:** Go ahead of me, and quickly.

Scene v. CAPULET'S *orchard.*

[*Enter* JULIET.]

JULIET. The clock struck nine when I did send the nurse;
     In half an hour she promised to return.
     Perchance she cannot meet him. That's not so.
     O, she is lame! Love's heralds should be thoughts,
5   Which ten times faster glides than the sun's beams
     Driving back shadows over low'ring[1] hills.
     Therefore do nimble-pinioned doves draw Love,[2]
     And therefore hath the wind-swift Cupid wings.
     Now is the sun upon the highmost hill
10   Of this day's journey, and from nine till twelve
     Is three long hours; yet she is not come.
     Had she affections and warm youthful blood,
     She would be as swift in motion as a ball;
     My words would bandy her[3] to my sweet love,
15   And his to me.
     But old folks, many feign[4] as they were dead—
     Unwieldy, slow, heavy and pale as lead.

◆ **Literature and Your Life**
How does this passage capture how time drags when you're waiting for something to happen? ❶

1. **low'ring:** Darkening.

2. **Therefore . . . Love:** Therefore, doves with quick wings pull the chariot of Venus, goddess of love.

3. **bandy her:** Send her rapidly.

4. **feign:** Act.

[*Enter* NURSE *and* PETER.]

     O God, she comes! O honey nurse, what news?
     Hast thou met with him? Send thy man away.

20 **NURSE.** Peter, stay at the gate.   [*Exit* PETER.]

JULIET. Now, good sweet nurse—O Lord, why lookest thou
     sad?
     Though news be sad, yet tell them merrily;
     If good, thou shamest the music of sweet news
     By playing it to me with so sour a face.

25 **NURSE.** I am aweary, give me leave[5] awhile.
     Fie, how my bones ache! What a jaunce[6] have I!

JULIET. I would thou hadst my bones, and I thy news.
     Nay, come, I pray thee speak. Good, good nurse, speak.

5. **give me leave:** Excuse me; give me a moment's rest.

6. **jaunce:** Rough trip.

◆ **Build Vocabulary**

unwieldy (un wēl′ dē) *adj.*: Awkward; clumsy

NURSE. Jesu, what haste? Can you not stay a while?
30 Do you not see that I am out of breath?

JULIET. How art thou out of breath when thou hast breath
To say to me that thou art out of breath?
The excuse that thou dost make in this delay
Is longer than the tale thou dost excuse.
Is thy news good or bad? Answer to that.
35 Say either, and I'll stay the circumstance.[7]
Let me be satisfied, is't good or bad?

NURSE. Well, you have made a simple[8] choice; you know
not how to choose a man. Romeo? No, not he. Though
his face be better than any man's, yet his leg excels all
40 men's; and for a hand and a foot, and a body, though
they be not to be talked on, yet they are past compare.
He is not the flower of courtesy, but, I'll warrant him,
as gentle as a lamb. Go thy ways, wench; serve God.
What, have you dined at home?

45 **JULIET.** No, no. But all this I did know before.
What says he of our marriage? What of that?

NURSE. Lord, how my head aches! What a head have I!
It beats as it would fall in twenty pieces.
My back a[9] t'other side—ah, my back, my back!
50 Beshrew[10] your heart for sending me about
To catch my death with jauncing up and down!

JULIET. I' faith, I am sorry that thou art not well.
Sweet, sweet, sweet nurse, tell me, what says my love?

NURSE. Your love says, like an honest gentleman, and a
55 courteous, and a kind, and a handsome, and, I warrant,
a virtuous—Where is your mother?

JULIET. Where is my mother? why, she is within.
Where should she be? How oddly thou repliest!
"Your love says, like an honest gentleman,
'Where is your mother?'"

60 **NURSE.**   O God's Lady dear!
Are you so hot?[11] Marry come up, I trow.[12]
Is this the poultice[13] for my aching bones?
Henceforward do your messages yourself.

JULIET. Here's such a coil![14] Come, what says Romeo?

7. stay the circumstance: Wait for the details.

8. simple: Foolish; simpleminded.

9. a: On.
10. Beshrew: Shame on.

11. hot: Impatient; hot-tempered.
12. Marry . . . trow: Indeed, cool down, I say.
13. poultice: Remedy.
14. coil: Disturbance.

Romeo and Juliet, Act II, Scene v ◆ 715

715

◆ Literary Focus

❶ Blank Verse The two lines form a rhymed couplet, signaling the end of the scene.

◆ Critical Thinking

❷ Make Inferences Invite students to explain why Shakespeare has his characters discuss sorrow and death just before a joyful event like a wedding. *Students may speculate that the Friar is preoccupied with death and that Romeo is just being dramatic; that both Romeo and the Friar are well aware of the dangers involved in the marriage of children from two feuding families; or that Shakespeare is foreshadowing the end of the tragedy.*

❸ Clarification Explain that *ghost* was another word for *spirit* in Shakespeare's day (much as the phrase "Holy Ghost" is still used to mean "Holy Spirit"). Thus by calling Friar Lawrence "ghostly," Juliet is calling him "spiritual."

---

65   **NURSE.** Have you got leave to go to shrift today?

     JULIET. I have.

     NURSE. Then hie you hence to Friar Laurence' cell;
       There stays a husband to make you a wife.
       Now comes the wanton[15] blood up in your cheeks:
70   They'll be in scarlet straight at any news.
       Hie you to church: I must another way,
       To fetch a ladder, by the which your love
       Must climb a bird's nest soon when it is dark.
       I am the drudge, and toil in your delight:
75   But you shall bear the burden soon at night.
       Go; I'll to dinner; hie you to the cell.

     JULIET. Hie to high fortune! Honest nurse, farewell.   [*Exit.*]

15. wanton: Excited.

◆ Literary Focus
Why does Juliet's last line rhyme with the Nurse's last line? ❶

Scene vi. FRIAR LAURENCE'S *cell.*

[*Enter* FRIAR LAURENCE *and* ROMEO.]

     FRIAR. So smile the heavens upon this holy act
       That afterhours with sorrow chide us not![1]

     ROMEO. Amen, amen! But come what sorrow can,
       It cannot countervail[2] the exchange of joy
5   That one short minute gives me in her sight.
       Do thou but close our hands with holy words,
       Then love-devouring death do what he dare—
       It is enough I may but call her mine.

     FRIAR. These violent delights have violent ends
10   And in their triumph die, like fire and powder,[3]
       Which, as they kiss, consume. The sweetest honey
       Is loathsome in his own deliciousness
       And in the taste confounds[4] the appetite.
       Therefore love moderately: long love doth so;
15   Too swift arrives as tardy as too slow.

[*Enter* JULIET.]

     Here comes the lady. O, so light a foot
       Will ne'er wear out the everlasting flint.[5]
       A lover may bestride the gossamers[6]
       That idles in the wanton summer air,
20   And yet not fall; so light is vanity.[7]

❸| **JULIET.** Good even to my ghostly confessor.

❹| **FRIAR.** Romeo shall thank thee, daughter, for us both.

1. That . . . not!: That the future does not punish us with sorrow.

2. countervail: Equal.

3. powder: Gunpowder.

4. confounds: Destroys.

5. flint: Stone.
6. gossamers: Spider webs.

7. vanity: Foolish things that cannot last.

716 ◆ Drama

Cross-Curricular Connection: Social Studies

Elizabethan Weddings

Tell students that unlike Romeo and Juliet's secret marriage, most Elizabethan weddings were all-day extravaganzas in which almost the whole village or town participated.

A wedding celebration began in the morning when the bridesmaids awakened and dressed the bride. Shortly thereafter, the groom, his groomsmen, friends, relatives, and musicians would arrive at the bride's house to claim her. The entire wedding party then paraded through the town to the church. The bride in her white gown and loose-flowing hair was the center of attraction.

After the ceremony, the wedding party went to the groom's house for a great feast and celebration. The party lasted the rest of the day with plenty of food, dances, and games. Sometime during the evening, the bride and groom left the party with their attendants, who would prepare the couple for the night. In the morning of the following day, musicians awakened the couple with a song at their bedroom window. The newlyweds did not have a honeymoon.

Have students compare and contrast Elizabethan weddings with contemporary weddings. Ask students of various cultural backgrounds to describe wedding customs unique to their cultures.

4 | JULIET. As much to him,[8] else is his thanks too much.

　　ROMEO.　Ah, Juliet, if the measure of thy joy
25　Be heaped like mine, and that thy skill be more
　　To blazon it,[9] then sweeten with thy breath

8. **As . . . him:** The same greeting to him.

9. **and . . . it:** And if you are better able to proclaim it.

◆ **Reading Strategy**
Although Romeo's words are in blank verse, the ideas he expresses do not end at the line breaks. How can you read these lines to grasp most effectively their meaning as well as their poetry?　**5**

◀ Critical Viewing
What do Romeo and Juliet's words and actions reveal about their feelings for each other? [Interpret]　**6**

Romeo and Juliet, Act II, Scene vi　◆　717

◆ **Critical Thinking**
4 Make Judgments Ask students what they think of Romeo's decision to marry Juliet? *Some students may think that Romeo's desire to marry Juliet shows that their love is strong; others may think that Romeo and Juliet are not using good judgment.*

◆ **Reading Strategy**
5 Read Blank Verse Suggested response: *You should pause at the commas rather than at the ends of the lines and read with feeling.*

▶ **Critical Viewing** ◀
6 Interpret Students may say that Romeo and Juliet have developed a deep love and devotion, which means that they are now willing to make sacrifices and take risks for one another.

Listening to Literature Audiocassettes Now that students have read and discussed Act 2 of *Romeo and Juliet,* invite them to listen to the recorded version on the audiocassette. Remind them that they can now bring to their listening experience what they have learned about blank verse.

Speaking and Listening Mini-Lesson

Persuasion
This mini-lesson supports the Speaking and Listening activity on page 719.

Introduce the Concept Point out that persuasion plays an important role in everyday life. Ask volunteers to describe examples of times they have tried to convince others to embrace an idea or to take a desired action. Let students know that they will now have a chance to practice their powers of persuasion through a role-play.

Develop Background Help students understand that some basic principles are involved in any type of persuasion. Lead them to consider the following:

- Whom are you trying to persuade? What are his or her needs and opinions?
- What do you need to convince him or her? What counterarguments might he or she pose? How will you respond?

Apply the Information Have students select the situation they want to role-play.

You may want to point out that students should avoid role-playing any potentially sensitive situations. Remind students to stay in their roles during the exercise.

Assess the Outcome At the end of each role-play, the partners should constructively criticize the persuader's performance. What did the persuader do well? Did he or she tailor his or her arguments to suit the target audience? Was he or she prepared to deal with counterarguments?

717

Answers

◆ *Literature and Your Life*

Reader's Response Students may say that Friar Lawrence is right because Romeo and Juliet seem sincere in their love for each other and because their marriage would unify the warring families.

Thematic Focus Students may suggest that Romeo and Juliet use their marriage as an opportunity to persuade their families to stop fighting.

☑ Check Your Comprehension

1. She wonders why Romeo has to be a Montague.
2. She fears for his life at the hands of her relatives. She fears that his love is shallow. She questions whether he can truly be in love when they barely know each other.
3. He says that Romeo is fickle. Romeo argues that the situation with Rosaline was a different matter because Rosaline did not return his love and Juliet does.
4. Friar Lawrence thinks that the marriage may end the feuding. The Nurse dotes on Juliet, and will do anything to make her happy.

◆ Critical Thinking

1. Darkness conceals Romeo from Juliet's relatives. It also provides an illusion of privacy so that Juliet feels she can speak her thoughts aloud. Her words of love for Romeo prompt him to come out of hiding and declare his love.
2. She is impatient as she waits for the Nurse to return. She is even more impatient and exasperated as she tries to prod the Nurse into giving her the message.
3. He hopes to end the feud between the two families.
4. Students may point out Scene ii, lines 78–79 and 117–120; Scene iii, lines 23–26; Scene iv, lines 6–8; and Scene vi, lines 1–2 and 9–11.
5. Most students will say that Romeo and Juliet's concern for each other indicates that they are in love, and not merely infatuated.
6. Students may say that the romantic words and images, the vivid descriptions, and the expressions of devotion are extremely effective.

This neighbor air, and let rich music's tongue
Unfold the imagined happiness that both
Receive in either by this dear encounter.

30 **JULIET.** Conceit, more rich in matter than in words,
Brags of his substance, not of ornament.[10]
They are but beggars that can count their worth;
But my true love is grown to such excess
I cannot sum up sum of half my wealth.

35 **FRIAR.** Come, come with me, and we will make short work;
For, by your leaves, you shall not stay alone
Till Holy Church incorporate two in one.   [*Exit.*]

10. Conceit . . . ornament: Understanding does not need to be dressed up in words.

Guide for Responding

◆ *Literature and Your Life*

Reader's Response Do you think Friar Lawrence is right in agreeing to marry Romeo and Juliet? Explain.

Thematic Focus What can Romeo and Juliet do to overcome the obstacles that stand in the way of their happiness?

Journal Entry In Scene ii, Juliet says "'Tis twenty year till then," meaning that it will seem like a very long time until the following morning, when she can send a messenger to Romeo. Describe an incident, real or imaginary, in which time seemed to drag too slowly or fly too quickly.

☑ Check Your Comprehension

1. Why does Juliet cry out in Scene ii, "O Romeo, Romeo, Romeo! Wherefore (Why) art thou Romeo?"
2. What doubts and fears does Juliet express even as she realizes that Romeo loves her?
3. What weakness in Romeo's character does Friar Lawrence point out before agreeing to assist the lovers in their plan to wed? How does Romeo defend himself?
4. Why does Friar Lawrence finally agree to marry Romeo and Juliet? Why does the Nurse help them carry out their plan?

718 ◆ *Drama*

◆ Critical Thinking

INTERPRET

1. Explain the role that darkness plays in helping Romeo and Juliet learn of their love for each other. **[Support]**
2. Describe Juliet's feelings in Scene v as she waits for the Nurse and then as she waits for the Nurse to reveal Romeo's message. **[Interpret]**
3. Aside from wanting Romeo and Juliet to be happy, what other motives does Friar Lawrence have for marrying the couple? **[Compare and Contrast]**
4. Although the events of Act II are joyful ones, Shakespeare foreshadows, or hints at, more sinister events that will occur later. Find at least two examples of foreshadowing and explain each example. **[Support]**
5. Are the feelings that Romeo and Juliet have for each other true love or infatuation? Explain. **[Draw Conclusions]**

EVALUATE

6. Why do you think the love scene in Capulet's garden is the most famous in all of literature? **[Assess]**

APPLY

7. Juliet is thirteen years old and Romeo not much older. In what way is their love typical of adolescence, and in what way is it not? **[Relate]**

---

7. Students may suggest that, like typical adolescents, Romeo and Juliet make up their minds and rush into love very quickly. On the other hand, the depth of their attachment and concern for each other is not typical of the usual adolescent crush. Students may also point out that modern adolescents of Romeo and Juliet's age are not yet interested in marriage.

◆ Literary Focus

Juliet's speech is straight iambic pentameter. Some students may consider the name Romeo to consist of three syllables, in which case the last two syllables of the name (*-meo*) and the following accented syllable represents an anapest (˘ ˘ ´) substituting for an iamb (˘ ´).

Guide for Responding (continued)

◆ Literary Focus

BLANK VERSE

Blank verse is unrhymed iambic pentameter—ten-syllable lines in which every second syllable is stressed. Poets and playwrights like Shakespeare often depart from the normal pattern to avoid monotony, to imitate the rhythms of real speech, or to vary the "music" of the verse.

On a separate piece of paper, indicate the pattern of unaccented and accented syllables in Scene ii, lines 43–51. Use the ˘ mark for an unaccented syllable and the ´ mark for an accented one. This is how the first line should look:

Whăt's ĭn ă náme? Thăt whĭch wĕ cáll ă róse

◆ Reading Strategy

READING BLANK VERSE

When you **read blank verse**, there's no need to be intimidated by the way the verse appears on the page. Simply read the words as if they were normal speech, without worrying about line breaks or the singsong rhythm of iambic pentameter.

To help you practice focusing on the meaning of the lines in a Shakespeare play, do the following.
1. Copy lines 1 through 8 of Juliet's speech at the beginning of Scene v as a single double-spaced paragraph. Read your paragraph aloud. Then mark your paragraph to indicate where it is natural to take a breath or pause.
2. Rewrite the paragraph in your own words.

◆ Build Grammar Skills

LOGICAL COMPARISONS

Include the word *other* or *else* when comparing one member of a group with the other members.

Writing Application Rewrite each sentence or passage, correcting any illogical comparisons.
1. Romeo is more open-minded than the Montagues.
2. Juliet appears as does the sun, brighter than any object in the heavens.
3. Juliet's eyes are twinkling stars, fairer than any stars in the universe.
4. "...Though his face be better than any man's."

◆ Build Vocabulary

USING THE PREFIX *inter-*

Match each word on the left with its meaning on the right.
1. international   a. between or among states
2. interpersonal   b. between planets
3. interstate   c. between or among nations
4. interplanetary   d. between persons

USING THE WORD BANK

Match each expression on the left with its meaning on the right. (Some expressions contain two vocabulary words.)
1. lamentable intercession   a. low slyness
2. to procure quickly   b. dominating hue
3. vile cunning   c. sickly skin tone
4. predominant color   d. awkward tool
5. sallow complexion   e. sad pleading
6. unwieldy implement   f. cowardly fluctuator
7. spineless waverer   g. to obtain fast

Idea Bank

Writing

1. **Poem in Iambic Pentameter** Create a poem that consists of at least eight lines in iambic pentameter. Your poem may be in blank verse, consist of rhymed couplets, or follow some other rhyme scheme.

2. **Modern Adaptation** Create a modern adaptation of Shakespeare's famous balcony scene. You can either use Romeo and Juliet as your two characters or invent new characters. Update the language and the setting to fit today's world, but retain the underlying meaning of the dialogue.

Project

3. **Set Design** Imagine that you're a set designer for a production of this play. Create a detailed sketch of a set for one of the scenes in Act II. Include labels and instructions to make it easy to build a set based on your sketch. **[Career Link]**

◆ Build Grammar Skills

1. Romeo is more open-minded than the other Montagues.
2. Juliet appears as does the sun, brighter than any other object in the heavens.
3. Juliet's eyes are like twinkling stars, fairer than any other stars in the universe.
4. "...Though his face be better than any other man's."

◆ Build Vocabulary

Using the Prefix *inter-*
1. c   2. d   3. a   4. b

Using the Word Bank
1. e   2. g   3. a   4. b   5. c   6. d   7. f

 Writer's Solution

For additional instruction and practice, use the lesson in the **Language Lab CD-ROM** on Double and Illogical Comparisons and the Clear Comparisons page in the *Writer's Solution Grammar Practice Book,* p. 91.

 Idea Bank

Customizing for
Performance Levels
Following are suggestions for matching the Idea Bank topics with your students' performance levels:
    Less Advanced Students: 3
    Average Students: 2
    More Advanced Students: 1

Customizing for
Learning Modalities
Following are suggestions for matching Idea Bank topics with your students' learning modalities:
    Interpersonal: 3
    Verbal/Linguistic: 1, 2, 3

◆ Reading Strategy

1. Suggested response: "The clock struck nine when I did send the nurse; in half an hour she promised to return. [pause] Perchance she cannot meet him. [pause] That's not so. [pause] O, she is lame! [pause] Love's heralds should be thoughts, which ten times faster glides than the sun's beams driving back shadows over low'ring hills. [pause] Therefore do nimble-pinioned doves draw Love, and therefore hath the wind-swift Cupid wings."

2. Suggested response: "It was nine o'clock when I sent the nurse, and she promised to return in half an hour. Maybe she can't meet him. No, that can't be so. Oh, she is so slow! Love's messengers should be like thoughts, which move ten times faster than sunbeams chase back shadows. Speed is the reason Love is drawn by fast-moving doves and Cupid has wings."

Guide for Reading, Act III

OBJECTIVES

1. To read, comprehend, and interpret a play
2. To relate a play to personal experience
3. To paraphrase
4. To identify soliloquies, asides, and monologues
5. To build vocabulary in context and learn words derived from myths
6. To develop skill in using *who* and *whom*
7. To respond to the play through writing and speaking and listening

SKILLS INSTRUCTION

Vocabulary:
Words From Myths

Grammar:
Who and *Whom*

Reading Strategy:
Paraphrase

Literary Focus:
Soliloquy, Aside, and Monologue

Speaking and Listening:
Debate (teacher edition)

Critical Viewing:
Make a Judgment; Analyze

PORTFOLIO OPPORTUNITIES

Writing: Editorial; Soliloquy
Speaking and Listening: Debate

Interest Grabber In Scene ii of this act, the Nurse throws Juliet into a state of suspense by excitedly telling her that someone is dead while forgetting to tell her who. You might borrow Shakespeare's dramatic device to hook students' interest in Act III. Dramatically shout to the class these words:

"He's dead! He's dead! He's dead!"

Have students use this dramatic but incomplete information to make predictions about the action in Act III. Then have them read to find out who dies.

◆ Review and Anticipate

You'll recall that in Act II, Romeo and Juliet express their love for each other and enlist the aid of Juliet's nurse and Friar Laurence to arrange a secret marriage ceremony. As the act closes, the young couple are about to be married. Before performing the ceremony, however, Friar Lawrence warns Romeo: "These violent delights have violent ends. . . ." What does he mean? How might this statement hint at events that will occur in Act III and the others that follow?

◆ Literary Focus

SOLILOQUY, ASIDE, AND MONOLOGUE

A **soliloquy** is a speech in which a character, alone on stage, expresses his or her thoughts to the audience. An **aside** is a remark made to the audience, unheard by the other characters. There are two differences between these devices. First, a soliloquy is usually lengthy; an aside is brief. Second, a soliloquy is usually spoken when no other characters are present; an aside is delivered with other characters present but unable to hear. Both devices, however, let the audience know what a character is really thinking or feeling.

Similar to a soliloquy is a **monologue**, which is a lengthy speech. Unlike a soliloquy, however, a monologue is addressed to other characters, not to the audience.

◆ Build Grammar Skills

COMMONLY CONFUSED WORDS: WHO AND WHOM

You'll find that Act III is filled with examples of the pronouns *who* and *whom*. Notice that the pronoun *who* is used when the pronoun is the subject of the verb or is a predicate nominative (a noun or pronoun that renames or explains the subject of a sentence). The pronoun *whom* is used when the pronoun receives the action of the verb or when it is the object of a preposition (as in "With *whom* are you speaking?"). Look at these examples:

> subject
> . . .*who* began this bloody fray?
>
> direct object
> Tybalt, . . . , *whom* Romeo's hand did slay.

Sometimes it's helpful to reword a sentence to determine whether *who* or *whom* is correct. For example, rewording the second example—". . . Romeo's hand did slay *whom*"—makes it clear that the pronoun receives the action of the verb.

◆ Reading Strategy

PARAPHRASE

Because Shakespeare writes in long passages of blank verse and uses unfamiliar language, his plays can be difficult to understand. One way to make sure you don't miss the meaning of key passages is to **paraphrase**—to identify key ideas and words and express them in your own words. Example:

Shakespeare's version

This gentleman, the Prince's near ally / My very friend, hath got his mortal hurt / In my behalf . . .

Paraphrased

My good friend, a close relative of the prince, has been fatally wounded defending me . . .

◆ Build Vocabulary

WORDS FROM MYTHS

In this act, the word *martial,* meaning "military" or "warlike," is used to describe a sword fight. The word *martial* is one of many English words that come from mythology, ancient stories that seek to explain natural phenomena. The word is derived from the Roman god of war, Mars.

WORD BANK

Before you read, preview this list of words.

gallant
fray
martial
exile
eloquence
fickle

Prentice Hall Literature Program Resources

REINFORCE / RETEACH / EXTEND

Selection Support Pages
Build Vocabulary: Words From Myths, p. 196
Build Grammar Skills: Commonly Confused Words: *Who* and *Whom*, p. 197
Reading Strategy: Paraphrase, p. 198
Literary Focus: Soliloquy, Aside, and Monologue, p. 199

Strategies for Diverse Student Needs, p. 48

Beyond Literature

Humanities Connection: The Globe Theater, p. 48

Formal Assessment Selection Test, p. 170–172, Assessment Resources Software

Alternative Assessment, p. 47

Resource Pro CD-ROM
The Tragedy of Romeo and Juliet—includes all resource material and customizable lesson plan

Listening to Literature Audiocassettes
The Tragedy of Romeo and Juliet

Romeo and Juliet

Act III

Scene i. *A public place.*

[*Enter* MERCUTIO, BENVOLIO, *and* MEN.]

BENVOLIO. I pray thee, good Mercutio, let's retire.
The day is hot, the Capels are abroad,
And, if we meet, we shall not 'scape a brawl,
For now, these hot days, is the mad blood stirring.

5 **MERCUTIO.** Thou art like one of these fellows that, when he enters
the confines of a tavern, claps me his sword upon the table and
says, "God send me no need of thee!" and by the operation of
the second cup draws him on the drawer,[1] when indeed there is
no need.

10 **BENVOLIO.** Am I like such a fellow?

MERCUTIO. Come, come, thou art as hot a Jack in thy mood as any in
Italy; and as soon moved to be moody, and as soon moody to be
moved.[2]

BENVOLIO. And what to?

15 **MERCUTIO.** Nay, and there were two such, we should have none
shortly, for one would kill the other. Thou! Why, thou wilt quarrel
with a man that hath a hair more or a hair less in his beard than
thou hast. Thou wilt quarrel with a man for cracking nuts, having
no other reason but because thou hast hazel eyes. What eye but
20 such an eye would spy out such a quarrel? Thy head is as full of
quarrels as an egg is full of meat; and yet thy head hath been
beaten as addle[3] as an egg for quarreling. Thou hast quarreled
with a man for coughing in the street, because he hath wakened
thy dog that hath lain asleep in the sun. Didst thou not fall out
25 with a tailor for wearing his new doublet[4] before Easter? With an
other for tying his new shoes with old riband?[5] And yet thou wilt
tutor me from quarreling![6]

BENVOLIO. And I were so apt to quarrel as thou art, any man should
buy the fee simple[7] of my life for an hour and a quarter.[8]

30 **MERCUTIO.** The fee simple? O simple![9]

[*Enter* TYBALT, PETRUCHIO, *and* OTHERS.]

◆ **Reading Strategy**
How would you restate Benvolio's comments in your own words? ❶

1. **and . . . drawer:** And by the effect of the second drink, draws his sword against the waiter.

2. **and . . . moved:** And as quickly stirred to anger as you are eager to be so stirred.

3. **addle:** Scrambled; crazy.

4. **doublet:** Jacket.
5. **riband:** Ribbon.
6. **tutor . . . quarreling:** Instruct me not to quarrel.
7. **fee simple:** Complete possession.
8. **an hour and a quarter:** Length of time that a man with Mercutio's fondness for quarreling may be expected to live.
9. **O simple!:** O stupid!

Romeo and Juliet, Act III, Scene i ◆ 721

Preparing for Standardized Tests

Reading and Vocabulary Most standardized tests require students to read a passage and answer critical reading questions about it. The Reading Strategy for Act III focuses on paraphrasing, a key skill that students can use to help them understand reading passages. After students complete the Reading Strategy activities on page 745, expand their learning by having them paraphrase another excerpt from *Romeo and Juliet.* For additional practice, use the Reading Strategy page in *Selection Support,* p. 198.

Grammar and Language Portions of some standardized tests require students to distinguish between subjective case and objective case pronouns, including the pronouns *who* and *whom.* Students may be asked to select the correct word to complete a sentence, as in the following:

   (Who, Whom) has Romeo invited to the dance? *Whom*

The Build Grammar Skills lesson focuses on this topic. For additional practice, use the preceding example and the Build Grammar Skills page on *Who* and *Whom,* p. 197, in *Selection Support.*

Develop Understanding

One-Minute Insight Circumstances and Romeo's impulsive, passionate nature conspire to wreck Romeo and Juliet's happiness in the wake of their secret wedding. Events move toward the tragic outcome that follows from Romeo's killing of Tybalt and banishment from Verona, and the Capulets' plan to marry Juliet to Paris.

Customize for
English Language Learners
Paraphrasing will be more difficult for English language learners than for native speakers. To help these students with paraphrasing, provide as many opportunities as possible for them to work closely with a partner or with small groups of classmates. Encourage students to identify difficult passages and help each other express Shakespeare's lines in simple, contemporary English.

◆ **Reading Strategy**

❶ **Paraphrase** Suggested paraphrase: *"Let's go home, Mercutio. It's a hot day, and the Capulets are out. If we meet, there's bound to be a fight, because tempers are running high."*

Comprehension Check ☑

❷ Have students express the main idea behind this exchange. *Mercutio is telling Benvolio how quarrelsome he is, while Benvolio disagrees, telling Mercutio that he is the more quarrelsome of the two.* Follow up by having students explain the irony or humor of the situation. *Benvolio is right—Mercutio is wildly exaggerating; Mercutio is being much more argumentative than Benvolio.*

◆ **Literary Focus**

❸ **Soliloquy, Aside, and Monologue** Is Mercutio's long speech—beginning with the word *Nay*—a soliloquy or a monologue? How can students tell? *Students should identify the speech as a monologue, citing the fact that Mercutio addresses his words to Benvolio.*

Have students recall the event that caused Tybalt to bear a grudge against Romeo. If necessary, have them review Tybalt's words and actions in Act I, Scene v. *Students should recall that, upon spotting Romeo at Lord Capulet's banquet, Tybalt assumed that Romeo had come to mock the Capulets. He declared that he would not forget Romeo's intrusion and that it would bring on trouble.*

◆ **Reading Strategy**

❶ **Paraphrase** Sample paraphrase:

TYBALT: Hello gentlemen. I'd like a word with one of you.

MERCUTIO: Just a word? You can do better. Make it a word and a punch.

TYBALT: I might just do that if you give me a reason.

MERCUTIO: Can't you find a reason of your own?

TYBALT: Mercutio, you consort with Romeo.

MERCUTIO: Consort? What do you think we are—a bunch of musicians? If you're going to call us musicians, you'll be hearing some sour notes. Here's my sword—this will make you dance. Consort, my foot!

◆ **Reading Strategy**

❷ **Paraphrase** To help students understand Romeo's state of mind as he enters this scene, have them paraphrase these lines. *Sample paraphrase: "Tybalt, the reason that I have to love you is stronger than the anger I should feel because of your insult. So, good-bye. I see that you are wrong about me."*

BENVOLIO. By my head, here comes the Capulets.

MERCUTIO. By my heel I care not.

TYBALT. Follow me close, for I will speak to them.
35   Gentlemen, good-den. A word with one of you.

MERCUTIO. And but one word with one of us? Couple it with something; make it a word and a blow.

TYBALT. You shall find me apt enough to that, sir, and you will give me occasion.[10]

40 **MERCUTIO.** Could you not take some occasion without giving?

TYBALT. Mercutio, thou consortest[11] with Romeo.

MERCUTIO. Consort?[12] What, dost thou make us
45   minstrels? And thou make minstrels of us, look to hear nothing but discords.[13] Here's my fiddlestick; here's that shall make you dance. Zounds,[14] consort!

BENVOLIO. We talk here in the public haunt of men.
    Either withdraw unto some private place,
    Or reason coldly of your grievances,
50   Or else depart. Here all eyes gaze on us.

MERCUTIO. Men's eyes were made to look, and let them gaze.
    I will not budge for no man's pleasure, I.

[*Enter* ROMEO.]

TYBALT. Well, peace be with you, sir. Here comes my man.[15]

MERCUTIO. But I'll be hanged, sir, if he wear your livery.[16]
55   Marry, go before to field,[17] he'll be your follower!
    Your worship in that sense may call him man.

TYBALT. Romeo, the love I bear thee can afford
    No better term than this: thou art a villain.[18]

60 **ROMEO.** Tybalt, the reason that I have to love thee
    Doth much excuse the appertaining[19] rage
    To such a greeting. Villain am I none.
    Therefore farewell. I see thou knowest me not.

TYBALT. Boy, this shall not excuse the injuries
    That thou hast done me; therefore turn and draw.

65 **ROMEO.** I do protest I never injured thee,
    But love thee better than thou canst devise[20]
    Till thou shalt know the reason of my love;

722 ◆ *Drama*

◆ **Reading Strategy**
How would you paraphrase the words Tybalt and Mercutio exchange to make their tone and meaning readily apparent to a contemporary reader? ❶

10. occasion: Cause; reason.

11. consortest: Associate with.
12. Consort: Associate with; consort also meant a group of musicians.
13. discords: Harsh sounds.
14. Zounds: Exclamation of surprise or anger ("By God's wounds").

15. man: The man I'm looking for; "man" also meant "manservant."
16. livery: Servant's uniform.
17. field: Dueling place.

18. villain: Low, vulgar person.

19. appertaining: Appropriate.

20. devise: Understand; imagine.

🚩 **Block Scheduling Strategies**

Consider these suggestions to take advantage of extended class time:

- Use Daily Language Practice for Week 17. You may dictate the passages to students, or you may use the transparency and have students correct the passages in groups.
- Students may work in pairs or small groups to choose, practice, and perform short scenes from Act III. Let students listen to the same scenes on the Listening to Literature audiocassette. Encourage

them to use the reading of the actors on the recording to guide their own reading.

- Have groups of students choose a short scene and work together to paraphrase all of the lines within it. Invite the students to perform their paraphrased scenes for the class.
- Use the information and examples in Build Grammar Skills (p. 720) as the basis of a class discussion on the difference between *who* and *whom*. Then have stu-

dents work with partners to complete the Practice items on page 745.

- Have students choose and complete one of the writing assignments in the Idea Bank (p. 745).
- Students may form teams to prepare the Speaking and Listening activity on page 745.

And so, good Capulet, which name I tender²¹
As dearly as mine own, be satisfied.

❸ 70 **MERCUTIO.** O calm, dishonorable, vile submission!
*Alla stoccata*²² carries it away. [*Draws.*]
Tybalt, you ratcatcher, will you walk?

TYBALT. What wouldst thou have with me?

MERCUTIO. Good King of Cats, nothing but one of your nine lives.
75 That I mean to make bold withal,²³ and, as you shall use me hereafter, dry-beat²⁴ the rest of the eight. Will you pluck your sword
out of his pilcher²⁵ by the ears? Make haste, lest mine be about
your ears ere it be out.

TYBALT. I am for you. [*Draws.*]

80 **ROMEO.** Gentle Mercutio, put thy rapier up.

MERCUTIO. Come, sir, your *passado*! [*They fight.*]

❹ **ROMEO.** Draw, Benvolio; beat down their weapons.
Gentlemen, for shame! Forbear this outrage!
Tybalt, Mercutio, the Prince expressly hath
85 Forbid this bandying in Verona streets.
Hold, Tybalt! Good Mercutio!

[TYBALT *under* ROMEO's *arms thrusts* MERCUTIO *in, and flies.*]

MERCUTIO.   I am hurt.
A plague a²⁶ both houses! I am sped.²⁷
Is he gone and hath nothing?

BENVOLIO.   What, art thou hurt?

MERCUTIO. Ay, ay, a scratch, a scratch. Marry, 'tis enough.
90 Where is my page? Go, villain, fetch a surgeon. [*Exit* PAGE.]

ROMEO. Courage, man. The hurt cannot be much.

MERCUTIO. No, 'tis not so deep as a well, nor so wide as a church
door; but 'tis enough, 'twill serve. Ask for me tomorrow, and you
shall find me a grave man. I am peppered,²⁸ I warrant, for this
95 world. A plague a both your houses! Zounds, a dog, a rat, a mouse,
a cat, to scratch a man to death! A braggart, a rogue, a villain,
that fights by the book of arithmetic!²⁹ Why the devil came you
between us? I was hurt under your arm.

ROMEO. I thought all for the best.

100 **MERCUTIO.** Help me into some house, Benvolio,

21. **tender:** Value.

22. *Alla stoccata:* At the thrust—an Italian fencing term that Mercutio uses as a nickname for Tybalt.

23. **make bold withal:** Make bold with; take.
24. **dry-beat:** Thrash.
25. **pilcher:** Scabbard.

26. **a:** On.
27. **sped:** Wounded; done for.

28. **peppered:** Finished off.

29. **by . . . arithmetic:** By formal rules.

Romeo and Juliet, Act III, Scene i ◆ 723

❶ Like many lines and phrases from Shakespeare's works, Mercutio's exclamation, "A plague [on] both your houses," has become extremely famous, even among people who have never read Shakespeare. Ask students whether they have ever heard this expression before. What was the context? Did they recognize the words as Shakespeare's?

◆ Critical Thinking

❷ Identify Cause and Effect
Have students express the observation that Romeo makes about himself in terms of a cause-effect relationship. *Elicit the following: According to Romeo, his love for Juliet—cause—has made him too forgiving and too weak—effect.*

◆ Reading Strategy

❸ Paraphrase Encourage students to restate these key lines in their own words. *Sample paraphrase: "This terrible day will be followed by more terrible days; this is just the beginning of the troubles that other days—and other actions—must end."*

Comprehension Check ☑

❹ Have students identify the resolutions that Romeo makes in this passage. *He resolves to be merciless; he also resolves that either he or Tybalt must die—that is, that he must now fight Tybalt.*

---

❶ I Or I shall faint. A plague a both your houses!
They have made worms' meat of me. I have it,[30]
And soundly too. Your houses!

30. **I have it:** I've got my deathblow

[*Exit* MERCUTIO *and* BENVOLIO.]

ROMEO. This gentleman, the Prince's near ally,[31]
105   My very friend, hath got his mortal hurt
In my behalf—my reputation stained
With Tybalt's slander—Tybalt, that an hour
Hath been my cousin. O sweet Juliet,
❷ Thy beauty hath made me effeminate
110   And in my temper soft'ned valor's steel!

31. **ally:** Relative.

[*Enter* BENVOLIO.]

BENVOLIO. O Romeo, Romeo, brave Mercutio is dead!
That gallant spirit hath aspired[32] the clouds,
Which too untimely here did scorn the earth.

32. **aspired:** Climbed to.

❸ ROMEO. This day's black fate on moe[33] days doth depend;[34]
115   This but begins the woe others must end.

33. **moe:** More.
34. **depend:** Hang over.

[*Enter* TYBALT.]

BENVOLIO. Here comes the furious Tybalt back again.

ROMEO. Alive in triumph, and Mercutio slain?
Away to heaven respective lenity,[35]
And fire-eyed fury be my conduct[36] now!
120   Now, Tybalt, take the "villain" back again
❹ That late thou gavest me; for Mercutio's soul
Is but a little way above our heads,
Staying for thine to keep him company.
Either thou or I, or both, must go with him.

35. **respective lenity:** Thoughtful mercy.
36. **conduct:** Guide.

125   TYBALT. Thou, wretched boy, that didst consort him here,
Shalt with him hence.

ROMEO.   This shall determine that.

[*They fight.* TYBALT *falls.*]

BENVOLIO. Romeo, away, be gone!
The citizens are up, and Tybalt slain.
Stand not amazed. The Prince will doom thee death
130   If thou art taken. Hence, be gone, away!

37. **fool:** Plaything.

ROMEO. I am fortune's fool![37]

◆ Build Vocabulary

gallant (gal´ ənt) *adj.*: Brave and noble

BENVOLIO.   Why dost thou stay?

[*Exit* ROMEO.]

724 ◆ *Drama*

Cross-Curricular Connection: Physical Education

Fencing When Tybalt, Mercutio, and Romeo fence, they fight to kill. Fencing became a sport in the late 1700's, and today it is played at the Olympic Games.

The object in fencing is to touch the opponent with a sword and to avoid being touched. Three different weapons may be used: The *foil,* the *epee,* and the *saber.* They differ in size, weight, and appearance, and each has its own set of strict rules.

Fencers wear a strong wire-mesh mask and protective clothing to avoid injury. They must develop precision, speed, timing, and tactical judgment. Many professional actors study and practice fencing for use on the stage.

Have students discuss what a dueling scene adds to a performance. Have them compare and contrast the dueling scenes in *Romeo and Juliet* with action scenes in contemporary movies, such as fist fights, car chases, and shoot-outs.

◀ Critical Viewing Because
Romeo refuses to fight with
Tybalt, Mercutio decides it is
up to him to defend
Romeo's honor. Mercutio's
death goads Romeo into
dueling with Tybalt. What do
you think of Romeo's
actions? Are they justifiable?
Are they right? [Make a
Judgment]

❺

[*Enter* CITIZENS.]

    CITIZEN. Which way ran he that killed Mercutio?
       Tybalt, that murderer, which way ran he?

    BENVOLIO. There lies that Tybalt.

    CITIZEN.   Up, sir, go with me.
135 I charge thee in the Prince's name obey.

[*Enter* PRINCE, OLD MONTAGUE, CAPULET, *their* WIVES, *and all.*]

    PRINCE. Where are the vile beginners of this <u>fray</u>?

❻

    BENVOLIO. O noble Prince, I can discover[38] all
       The unlucky manage[39] of this fatal brawl.
       There lies the man, slain by young Romeo,
140   That slew thy kinsman, brave Mercutio.

    LADY CAPULET. Tybalt, my cousin! O my brother's child!
       O Prince! O cousin! Husband! Oh, the blood is spilled
       Of my dear kinsman! Prince, as thou art true,
       For blood of ours shed blood of Montague.
145   O cousin, cousin!

    PRINCE. Benvolio, who began this bloody fray?

    BENVOLIO. Tybalt, here slain, whom Romeo's hand
       did slay.
       Romeo, that spoke him fair, bid him bethink
150   How nice[40] the quarrel was, and urged withal
       Your high displeasure. All this—uttered
       With gentle breath, calm look, knees humbly bowed—

38. discover: Reveal.

39. manage: Course.

◆ **Literary Focus**
Is Benvolio's speech
a soliloquy, aside, or
monologue? Explain.

❼

40. nice: Trivial.

◆ **Build Vocabulary**
fray (frā) *n.:* Noisy fight

Romeo and Juliet, Act III, Scene i ◆ 725

▶ Critical Viewing ◀
❺ **Make a Judgment** Elicit
responses such as the following:
*(a) Romeo's actions are neither justifi-
able nor right—his anger and new-
found thirst for revenge only lead to
more violence. (b) Romeo's actions are
justifiable, or at least understandable—
he cannot help being overwhelmed by
feelings of anger and betrayal over
Mercutio's death.*

◆ **Reading Strategy**
❻ **Paraphrase** Encourage students
to paraphrase the Prince's question
and Benvolio's reply.
Sample paraphrase:

   *PRINCE: Where are the ones who
began this fight?*
   *BENVOLIO: I can explain everything
that happened. There lies Tybalt—
he was killed by Romeo—after he,
Tybalt, had killed your kinsman,
Mercutio.*

◆ **Literary Focus**
❼ **Soliloquy, Aside, and
Monologue** Students should identify the speech as a monologue; it is a
long speech addressed to another
character—in this case, the Prince—
and not to the audience.

 Humanities: Film

Romeo and Juliet, 1968, directed by Franco
Zeffirelli.

   The photos from Zeffirelli's *Romeo and Juliet*
bring to life three pivotal encounters within this
act.

   Use the following questions for discussion:
1. Have students identify the main characters in
each photo. *Scene I: Romeo, Benvolio—standing,
Mercutio—slain; Scene iii: Romeo and Friar
Lawrence; Scene v: Juliet and Lady Capulet.*
2. Have students describe the specific event that
they think each photo illustrates as well as

speculate on the exact lines that the characters might be speaking. Encourage students to
defend their choices by citing visual evidence
such as facial expressions, body language, and
gestures. For example, based on the fact that
Juliet is kneeling before Lady Capulet, students
might say that she is begging for understanding
and mercy with the lines "O, sweet my mother, cast me not away;/Delay this marriage for a
month, a week. . . ."

❶ Have students determine if Benvolio's account of what happened is accurate by comparing it to the incidents themselves. If so, why does Lady Capulet insist that it took twenty men to kill Tybalt? *Students should confirm that Benvolio's account is accurate. They may point out that the explanation that Lady Capulet gives for his supposed distortion of the facts— "affection makes him false"—is in fact truer of her than of Benvolio.*

◆ **Critical Thinking**

❷ **Interpret** Have students explain Lord Montague's argument about why Romeo should not be punished for Mercutio's death. *Romeo killed Tybalt, who, by law, was supposed to die for killing Mercutio.* Then have students explain what effect this line of reasoning seems to have on the Prince. *Students may say that the Prince is swayed by it, as he exiles Romeo instead of sentencing him to death—the penalty he had set in Act I.*

Could not take truce with the unruly spleen[41]
Of Tybalt deaf to peace, but that he tilts[42]
155 With piercing steel at bold Mercutio's breast;
Who, all as hot, turns deadly point to point,
And, with a <u>martial</u> scorn, with one hand beats
Cold death aside and with the other sends
It back to Tybalt, whose dexterity
160 Retorts it. Romeo he cries aloud,
"Hold, friends! Friends, part!" and swifter than his tongue,
His agile arm beats down their fatal points,
And 'twixt them rushes; underneath whose arm
An envious[43] thrust from Tybalt hit the life
165 Of stout Mercutio, and then Tybalt fled;
But by and by comes back to Romeo,
Who had but newly entertained[44] revenge,
And to't they go like lightning; for, ere I
Could draw to part them, was stout Tybalt slain;
170 And, as he fell, did Romeo turn and fly.
This is the truth, or let Benvolio die.

❶   **LADY CAPULET.** He is a kinsman to the Montague;
Affection makes him false, he speaks not true.
Some twenty of them fought in this black strife,
175 And all those twenty could but kill one life.
I beg for justice, which thou, Prince, must give.
Romeo slew Tybalt; Romeo must not live.

PRINCE. Romeo slew him; he slew Mercutio.
Who now the price of his dear blood doth owe?

❷   180 **MONTAGUE.** Not Romeo, Prince; he was Mercutio's friend;
His fault concludes but what the law should end,
The life of Tybalt.[45]

PRINCE.   And for that offense
Immediately we do <u>exile</u> him hence.
I have an interest in your hate's proceeding.
185 My blood[46] for your rude brawls doth lie a-bleeding;
But I'll amerce[47] you with so strong a fine
That you shall all repent the loss of mine.
I will be deaf to pleading and excuses;
Nor tears nor prayers shall purchase out abuses.
190 Therefore use none. Let Romeo hence in haste,
Else, when he is found, that hour is his last.
Bear hence this body and attend our will.[48]
Mercy but murders, pardoning those that kill.

                                                     [*Exit with others.*]

41. **spleen:** Angry nature.
42. **tilts:** Thrusts.

43. **envious:** Full of hatred.

44. **entertained:** Considered.

45. **His fault . . . Tybalt:** By killing Tybalt, he did what the law would have done.
46. **My blood:** Mercutio was related to the Prince.
47. **amerce:** Punish.
48. **attend our will:** Await my decision.

◆ **Build Vocabulary**

martial (mär´ shəl) *adj.*: Military

exile (eg´ zīl) *v.*: Banish

Enrichment: Stage Directions

Historians and scholars generally believe that stage directions in Elizabethan plays were the author's notations and not the director's or prompter's. We can assume, therefore, that the stage directions, which were found in the original first and second quartos of *Romeo and Juliet*, were written by Shakespeare himself. The first quarto for *Romeo and Juliet* was printed in London in 1597, approximately two years after Shakespeare wrote the play.

Read the following passages from the introduction of *Shakespeare, The Complete Works*, edited by G. B. Harrison, to your students. The stage directions from the first quarto are shown in italics and single quotation marks; those from the second quarto are shown in italics and double quotation marks. The other directions are purely conjectural; Harrison is showing how the rest of the scene might have been staged. "RIGHT" means as the actor faces the audience—the viewer's left.

Act III, Scene I:
"Enter Mercutio, Benvolio and men," by the LEFT door. By the RIGHT door, enter Tybalt and others. Romeo enters through the RECESS curtains. Tybalt draws attention to his entry with "Here comes my man."

◆ Literary Focus

❸ **Soliloquy, Aside, and Monologue** Students should identify the speech as a soliloquy, as Juliet is alone on stage, and she expresses her thoughts for the audience. Students may also point out that, unlike an aside, which is also addressed to the audience, a soliloquy is usually a lengthy speech.

Scene ii. CAPULET'S *orchard.*

[*Enter* JULIET *alone.*]

JULIET. Gallop apace, you fiery-footed steeds,[1]
   Towards Phoebus' lodging![2] Such a wagoner
   As Phaëton[3] would whip you to the west
   And bring in cloudy night immediately.
5   Spread thy close curtain, love-performing night,
   That runaways' eyes may wink,[4] and Romeo
   Leap to these arms untalked of and unseen.
   Lovers can see to do their amorous rites,
   And by their own beauties; or, if love be blind,
10 It best agrees with night. Come, civil night,
   Thou sober-suited matron all in black,
   And learn me how to lose a winning match,
   Played for a pair of stainless maidenhoods.
   Hood my unmanned blood, bating in my cheeks,[5]
15 With thy black mantle till strange[6] love grow bold,
   Think true love acted simple modesty,
   Come, night; come, Romeo; come, thou day in night;
   For thou wilt lie upon the wings of night
   Whiter than new snow upon a raven's back.
20 Come, gentle night; come, loving, black-browed night;
   Give me my Romeo; and when I shall die,
   Take him and cut him out in little stars,
   And he will make the face of heaven so fine
   That all the world will be in love with night
25 And pay no worship to the garish sun
   O, I have bought the mansion of a love,
   But not possessed it; and though I am sold,
   Not yet enjoyed. So tedious is this day
   As is the night before some festival
30 To an impatient child that hath new robes
   And may not wear them. O, here comes my nurse,

[*Enter* NURSE, *with cords.*]

   And she brings news; and every tongue that speaks
   But Romeo's name speaks heavenly eloquence.
   Now, nurse, what news? What hast thou there, the cords
   That Romeo did thee fetch?

35 NURSE.   Ay, ay, the cords.

JULIET. Ay me! What news? Why dost thou wring thy hands?

NURSE. Ah, weraday![7] He's dead, he's dead, he's dead!

1. **fiery-footed steeds:** Horses of the sun god, Phoebus.
2. **Phoebus' lodging:** Below the horizon.
3. **Phaëton:** Phoebus' son, who tried to drive his father's horses but was unable to control them.
4. **That runaways' eyes may wink:** So that the eyes of busybodies may not see.

5. **Hood . . . cheeks:** Hide the untamed blood that makes me blush.
6. **strange:** Unfamiliar.

◆ **Literary Focus**
Should Juliet's speech be classified as a soliloquy, aside, or monologue? Why? ❸

7. **Ah, weraday!:** Alas!

◆ **Build Vocabulary**
eloquence (el´ ə kwəns) *n.:* Speech that is vivid, forceful, graceful, and persuasive

◆ **Reading Strategy**

❹ **Paraphrase** Have students paraphrase the comparison that Juliet makes here. Then encourage them to explain the thoughts and situation that Juliet speaks of in her soliloquy. *Sample paraphrase: "This day is as long and tedious as the night before a party is to a child eager to wear a new party dress." Students should note that Juliet is eager for night to fall, so that Romeo can come to her unseen.*

❺ **Clarification** The *cords* referred to here are the ropes that Romeo asked the Nurse to bring to Juliet in Act II, Scene iv; he planned to use them to climb up to Juliet's room in secret.

Romeo and Juliet, Act III, Scene ii ◆ 727

Tybalt and Mercutio fight; *'Tybalt under Romeo's arm thrusts Mercutio in, and flies'* through the RIGHT door. The Page goes out by the LEFT door. Mercutio, supported by Benvolio, goes out through the LEFT door, whence Benvolio emerges to say that Mercutio is dead. Tybalt reenters by the RIGHT door. Romeo and Tybalt fight and Tybalt is slain. Romeo runs out by the LEFT door. The citizens enter through the curtains of the RECESS, followed by the Prince. Capulet and his wife enter by the RIGHT door. Montague and his wife enter by the LEFT. At the end of the scene, all go out by the ways in which they have entered, the body of Tybalt being carried out through the RIGHT door.

Student Activity:
Choose a scene from the play and write the stage directions for it, keeping in mind the structure and layout of the Elizabethan theater.

Comprehension Check ✓

❶ Ask students to identify the source of confusion and misunderstanding in this exchange. *The Nurse delivers the news of Tybalt's death and Romeo's banishment in a very unclear and roundabout way. As a result, Juliet is tormented by the thought that Romeo may be dead.*

◆ **Build Grammar Skills**

❷ ***Who* and *Whom*** Point out the pronoun *who* in Juliet's question. Ask students whether this pronoun is used as a subject or an object. *subject*

Comprehension Check ✓

❸ In this passage, Juliet describes Romeo in contrary terms. Why does she do this? What does she mean when she calls him "just opposite to what thou justly seem'st"? *On one hand, she is thinking of the Romeo that she fell in love with; on the other, she is thinking of the Romeo that killed Tybalt.*

We are undone, lady, we are undone!
Alack the day! He's gone, he's killed, he's dead!

JULIET. Can heaven be so envious?

40 **NURSE.**   Romeo can,
Though heaven cannot. O Romeo, Romeo!
Who ever would have thought it? Romeo!

JULIET. What devil art thou that dost torment me thus?
This torture should be roared in dismal hell.
45 Hath Romeo slain himself? Say thou but "Ay,"
And that bare vowel "I" shall poison more
Than the death-darting eye of cockatrice.[8]
I am not I, if there be such an "Ay,"[9]
Or those eyes' shot[10] that makes thee answer "Ay."
50 If he be slain, say "Ay"; or if not, "No."
Brief sounds determine of my weal or woe.

NURSE. I saw the wound, I saw it with mine eyes,
(God save the mark![11]) here on his manly breast.
A piteous corse,[12] a bloody piteous corse;
55 Pale, pale as ashes, all bedaubed in blood,
All in gore-blood. I sounded[13] at the sight.

JULIET. O, break, my heart! Poor bankrout,[14] break at once!
To prison, eyes; ne'er look on liberty!
Vile earth, to earth resign;[15] end motion here,
60 And thou and Romeo press one heavy bier![16]

NURSE. O Tybalt, Tybalt, the best friend I had!
O courteous Tybalt! Honest gentleman!
That ever I should live to see thee dead!

JULIET. What storm is this that blows so contrary?[17]
65 Is Romeo slaught'red, and is Tybalt dead?
My dearest cousin, and my dearer lord?
Then, dreadful trumpet, sound the general doom![18]
For who is living, if those two are gone?

NURSE. Tybalt is gone, and Romeo banishèd;
70 Romeo that killed him, he is banishèd.

JULIET. O God! Did Romeo's hand shed Tybalt's blood?

NURSE. It did, it did! Alas the day, it did!

JULIET. O serpent heart, hid with a flow'ring face!
Did ever dragon keep so fair a cave?
75 Beautiful tyrant! Fiend angelical!

8. **cockatrice:** Serpent that, in fables, could kill with its glance.
9. **"Ay":** Yes.
10. **eyes' shot:** The Nurse's glance.

11. **God save the mark!:** May God save us from evil!
12. **corse:** Corpse.

13. **sounded:** Swooned; fainted.
14. **bankrout:** Bankrupt.

15. **Vile . . . resign:** Let my body return to the earth.
16. **bier:** Platform on which a corpse is displayed before burial.

17. **contrary:** In opposite directions.

18. **dreadful . . . doom:** Let the trumpet that announces doomsday be sounded.

728 ◆ Drama

Cross-Curricular Connection: Social Studies

The Renaissance in England

The Renaissance was an age of culture and learning that began in Italy around 1300. Whereas earlier, in the Middle Ages, art and philosphy centered on the Church, Renaissance thinkers, taking the ancient Greeks and Romans as models, made the individual their focus. Great artists and thinkers associated with the Italian Renaissance are Petrarch, Michelangelo, Leonardo da Vinci, and Raphael.

During the early Renaissance in Italy, England was involved in the Hundred Years' War with France, and then the Wars of the Roses—a struggle for the throne between two royal families. When the wars ended in 1485, the Renaissance spread to England. Under the reign of Queen Elizabeth I (1558–1603), English literature flowered with the works of such great writers as Francis Bacon, Ben Jonson, Christopher Marlowe, Edmund Spenser, and, above all, William Shakespeare.

Have students discuss how *Romeo and Juliet* reflects the importance the Renaissance placed on the individual.

3 Dove-feathered raven! Wolvish-ravening lamb!
Despisèd substance of divinest show!
Just opposite to what thou justly seem'st—
A damnèd saint, an honorable villain!

80 O nature, what hadst thou to do in hell
When thou didst bower the spirit of a fiend
In mortal paradise of such sweet flesh?
Was ever book containing such vile matter
So fairly bound? O, that deceit should dwell
In such a gorgeous palace!

85 **NURSE.**   There's no trust,
No faith, no honesty in men; all perjured,
All forsworn,[19] all naught, all dissemblers.[20]
Ah, where's my man? Give me some *aqua vitae*.[21]
These griefs, these woes, these sorrows make me old.
Shame come to Romeo!

90 **JULIET.**   Blistered be thy tongue
For such a wish! He was not born to shame.
Upon his brow shame is ashamed to sit;
4 For 'tis a throne where honor may be crowned
Sole monarch of the universal earth.
95 O, what a beast was I to chide at him!

NURSE. Will you speak well of him that killed your cousin?

JULIET. Shall I speak ill of him that is my husband?
Ah, poor my lord, what tongue shall smooth thy name
When I, thy three-hours wife, have mangled it?
100 But wherefore, villain, didst thou kill my cousin?
That villain cousin would have killed my husband.
Back, foolish tears, back to your native spring!
Your tributary[22] drops belong to woe,
Which you, mistaking, offer up to joy.
6 105 My husband lives, that Tybalt would have slain;
And Tybalt's dead, that would have slain my husband.
All this is comfort; wherefore weep I then?
Some word there was, worser than Tybalt's death,
That murd'red me. I would forget it fain;
110 But O, it presses to my memory
Like damnèd guilty deeds to sinners' minds!
"Tybalt is dead, and Romeo—banishèd."
That "banishèd," that one word "banishèd,"
Hath slain ten thousand Tybalts. Tybalt's death
115 Was woe enough, if it had ended there;

19. **forsworn:** Are liars.
20. **dissemblers:**
Hypocrites.
21. *aqua vitae:* Brandy.

◆ Reading Strategy
5 How would Juliet express these thoughts in contemporary language?

---

22. **tributary:** In tribute.

Romeo and Juliet, Act III, Scene ii ◆ 729

◆ **Reading Strategy**

5 **Paraphrase** *Sample paraphrase: "How can I say such terrible things about my husband? Ah, Romeo, who will stand by you, when I, your brand new wife, have accused you?"*

◆ **Build Grammar Skills**

6 ***Who* and *Whom*** You might point out that instead of *who* or *whom,* Shakespeare sometimes uses *that.* Follow up by challenging students to replace each *that* in these lines with either *who* or *whom. "My husband lives,* whom *Tybalt would have slain;/And Tybalt's dead,* who *would have slain my husband."*

◆ Reading Strategy

1 Paraphrase How would students paraphrase these lines from Juliet's speech? *Sample paraphrase: "Romeo is banished—there is no limit to the pain that this news brings; words cannot describe my sorrow."*

◆ Critical Thinking

2 Connect Point out that earlier in this scene, the Nurse denounces Romeo. Why does she now offer to bring Romeo out of hiding to comfort Juliet? *Students may say that she acts as she does because she is moved by Juliet's grief; students may also discuss the tendency she has shown so far in the play to be somewhat fickle and impulsive.*

Customize for
Less Proficient Readers

Encourage less proficient readers to recall and describe Romeo's situation as this scene opens. *Romeo fled after killing Tybalt; he does not know that the Prince sentenced him to exile rather than death.*

      Or, if sour woe delights in fellowship
      And needy will be ranked with[23] other griefs,
      Why followed not, when she said "Tybalt's dead,"
      Thy father, or thy mother, nay, or both,
120   Which modern[24] lamentation might have moved?
      But with a rearward[25] following Tybalt's death,
      "Romeo is banishèd"—to speak that word
      Is father, mother, Tybalt, Romeo, Juliet,
      All slain, all dead. "Romeo is banishèd"—
125   There is no end, no limit, measure bound,
      In that word's death; no words can that woe sound.
      Where is my father and my mother, nurse?

NURSE. Weeping and wailing over Tybalt's corse.
      Will you go to them? I will bring you thither.

130 **JULIET.** Wash they his wounds with tears? Mine shall be spent,
      When theirs are dry, for Romeo's banishment.
      Take up those cords. Poor ropes, you are beguiled,
      Both you and I, for Romeo is exiled.
      He made you for a highway to my bed;
135   But I, a maid, die maiden-widowèd.
      Come, cords; come, nurse. I'll to my wedding bed;
      And death, not Romeo, take my maidenhead!

NURSE. Hie to your chamber. I'll find Romeo
      To comfort you. I wot[26] well where he is.
140   Hark ye, your Romeo will be here at night.
      I'll to him; he is hid at Lawrence' cell.

JULIET. O, find him! Give this ring to my true knight
      And bid him come to take his last farewell.

                              [*Exit with* NURSE.]

Scene iii. FRIAR LAWRENCE'S *cell.*

[*Enter* FRIAR LAWRENCE.]

FRIAR. Romeo, come forth, thou fearful man.
      Affliction is enamored of thy parts.[1]
      And thou art wedded to calamity.

[*Enter Romeo.*]

ROMEO. Father, what news? What is the Prince's doom?[2]
5   What sorrow craves acquaintance at my hand
      That I yet know not?

FRIAR.   Too familiar

730 ◆ *Drama*

---

23. needly . . . with: Must be accompanied by.

24. modern: Ordinary.

25. rearward: Follow up: literally, a rear guard.

26. wot: know.

1. Affliction . . . parts: Misery is in love with your attractive qualities.

2. doom: Final decision.

 Cross-Curricular Connection: Social Studies

Tell students about the following points of geographical interest related to Shakespeare and *Romeo and Juliet*:

• Stratford-on-Avon: This small English town is famous as Shakespeare's birthplace. Shakespeare's father was elected its bailiff, or mayor, in 1568.

• London: In Shakespeare's time, this English capital was thriving with commerce and entertainment. It was here that

Shakespeare found work as an actor and success as a playwright and, with his company, the Lord Chamberlain's men, built the Globe theater.

• Verona (Italy): The play's main setting, this small city was a Roman colony in ancient times and a center of Italian art and culture in medieval times. Today, the house where Juliet is said to have lived is visited by tourists from around the world.

• Mantua (Italy): Like Verona, the city where Romeo seeks refuge during his banishment is rich in ancient and medieval history and culture.

Have students do research to learn more about each of these places. Students may work together to present their findings in the form of travel brochures for a "Romeo and Juliet Tour," complete with maps, illustrations, itineraries, and descriptions.

Is my dear son with such sour company.
I bring thee tidings of the Prince's doom.

    ROMEO. What less than doomsday[3] is the Prince's doom?

10 FRIAR. A gentler judgment vanished[4] from his lips—
    Not body's death, but body's banishment.

    ROMEO. Ha, banishment? Be merciful, say "death";
    For exile hath more terror in his look,
    Much more than death. Do not say "banishment."

15 FRIAR. Here from Verona art thou banishèd.
    Be patient, for the world is broad and wide.

    ROMEO. There is no world without[5] Verona walls,
    But purgatory, torture, hell itself.
    Hence banishèd is banished from the world,
20   And world's exile is death. Then "banishèd"
    Is death mistermed. Calling death "banishèd,"
    Thou cut'st my head off with a golden ax
    And smilest upon the stroke that murders me.

    FRIAR. O deadly sin! O rude unthankfulness!
25   Thy fault our law calls death;[6] but the kind Prince,
    Taking thy part, hath rushed[7] aside the law,
    And turned that black word "death" to "banishment."
    This is dear mercy, and thou seest it not.

    ROMEO. 'Tis torture, and not mercy. Heaven is here,
30   Where Juliet lives; and every cat and dog
    And little mouse, every unworthy thing,
    Live here in heaven and may look on her;
    But Romeo may not. More validity,[8]
    More honorable state, more courtship lives
35   In carrion flies than Romeo. They may seize
    On the white wonder of dear Juliet's hand
    And steal immortal blessing from her lips,
    Who, even in pure and vestal modesty,
    Still blush, as thinking their own kisses sin;
40   But Romeo may not, he is banishèd.
    Flies may do this but I from this must fly;
    They are freemen, but I am banishèd.
    And sayest thou yet that exile is not death?
    Hadst thou no poison mixed, no sharp-ground knife,
45   No sudden mean[9] of death, though ne'er so mean,[10]
    But "banishèd" to kill me—"banishèd"?
    O friar, the damned use that word in hell;

3. doomsday: My death.

4. vanished: Escaped; came forth.

5. without: Outside.

6. Thy fault . . . death: For what you did our law demands the death penalty.
7. rushed: Pushed.

8. validity: Value.

◆ Literary Focus
What characteristics of a monologue are present in Romeo's lament?
④

9. mean: Method.
10. mean: Humiliating.

Romeo and Juliet, Act III, Scene iii ◆ 731

◆ **Critical Thinking**

❸ **Contrast** Encourage students to contrast the traits that Friar Lawrence and Romeo show in this exchange. In what ways is Romeo's behavior reminiscent of his behavior earlier in the scene? *Students may note that Friar Lawrence stresses patience and reason, while Romeo is emotional and excitable. They may also note that Romeo acted out of emotion and impulsiveness when he fought and killed Tybalt.*

◆ **Literary Focus**

❹ **Soliloquy, Aside, and Monologue** Elicit the following response: *Romeo's speech is lengthy, and it is addressed to another character—Friar Lawrence.*

◆ **Reading Strategy**

❺ **Paraphrase** Invite students to paraphrase these lines. Then have them briefly describe the key thoughts and ideas in Romeo's monologue. *Sample paraphrase: "You say that exile isn't death? Don't you have any poison, a sharp knife, or anything else that would kill me? Whatever it is, it could not be as devastating as the word banished." In his monologue Romeo compares himself to all kinds of small, humble creatures and finds that they are better off because they can be near Juliet. He also describes in dramatic terms the pain that the word banished causes him.*

① Analyze Elicit the following: *Romeo is in a highly emotional and excitable state of mind; he feels that being separated from Juliet is a fate worse than death.*

◆ *Literature and Your Life*

② Friar Lawrence suggests that Romeo is mad and irrational, while Romeo insists that the Friar does not understand what it means to be young and in love. Invite students to express their opinions about whether one or both characters are right and why. *Sample response: The Friar is right—Romeo is acting with the rashness of youth; Romeo is right—the Friar does not understand his feelings; both are right to some degree.*

▲ **Critical Viewing** Friar Lawrence explains that the Prince has decided to be merciful: Instead of being put to death for killing Tybalt, Romeo is to be banished. Why does Romeo react so badly to this news? [Analyze]

Howling attends it! How hast thou the heart,
Being a divine, a ghostly confessor,
50   A sin-absolver, and my friend professed,
To mangle me with that word "banishèd"?

FRIAR. Thou fond mad man, hear me a little speak.

ROMEO. O, thou wilt speak again of banishment.

FRIAR. I'll give thee armor to keep off that word;
55   Adversity's sweet milk, philosophy,
To comfort thee, though thou art banishèd.

ROMEO. Yet "banished"? Hang up philosophy!
Unless philosophy can make a Juliet,
Displant a town, reverse a prince's doom,
60   It helps not, it prevails not. Talk no more.

FRIAR. O, then I see that madmen have no ears.

ROMEO. How should they, when that wise men have no eyes?

FRIAR. Let me dispute[11] with thee of thy estate.[12]

 ROMEO. Thou canst not speak of that thou dost not feel.
65   Wert thou as young as I, Juliet thy love,
An hour but married, Tybalt murderèd,
Doting like me, and like me banishèd,
Then mightst thou speak, then mightst thou tear thy hair,
And fall upon the ground, as I do now,

11. **dispute:** Discuss.
12. **estate:** Condition; situation.

732 ◆ Drama

🏰 **Beyond the Classroom**

Career Connection

Film Editing Surprisingly, certain stage conventions in Shakespeare's time produced effects much like those we see in movies. Elizabethan stages had no scenery; therefore a play's scenes and changes of setting could flow swiftly and smoothly, just as they do in a modern motion picture.

In movies, television shows, and all other kinds of films, the pace and rhythm of the action is achieved through film editing. Editors may work with hundreds of hours of shots to put together a film that is one or two hours long. One brief scene of Zeffirelli's *Romeo and Juliet,* for example, would have been shot by several different cameras from several different angles and several different points of view, including close-ups, mid-range shots, and long shots. Conferring with the director, the film's edi-tor would have chosen and assembled the shots that produce the dramatic and visual effects that work best for the scene.

Have interested students gather more information about film editing and share their findings with the class. Students might also explore other technical aspects of film-making, such as cinematography and sound recording.

❷ | 70   Taking the measure of an unmade grave.

[*Enter* NURSE *and knock.*]

   FRIAR. Arise, one knocks. Good Romeo, hide thyself.

   ROMEO. Not I; unless the breath of heartsick groans
      Mistlike infold me from the search of eyes. [*Knock.*]

   FRIAR. Hark, how they knock! Who's there? Romeo, arise;
75   Thou wilt be taken.—Stay awhile!—Stand up; [*Knock.*]
      Run to my study.—By and by!¹³—God's will,
      What simpleness¹⁴ is this.—I come, I come! [*Knock.*]
   ❹ | Who knocks so hard? Whence come you? What's your will?

[*Enter* NURSE.]

   NURSE. Let me come in, and you shall know my errand.
      I come from Lady Juliet.

80 **FRIAR.**   Welcome then.

   NURSE. O holy friar, O, tell me, holy friar,
      Where is my lady's lord, where's Romeo?

   FRIAR. There on the ground, with his own tears made drunk.

   NURSE. O, he is even in my mistress' case,
85   Just in her case! O woeful sympathy!
      Piteous predicament! Even so lies she,
      Blubb'ring and weeping, weeping and blubb'ring.
      Stand up, stand up! Stand, and you be a man.
      For Juliet's sake, for her sake, rise and stand!
90   Why should you fall into so deep an O?¹⁵

   ROMEO. [*Rises.*] Nurse—

   NURSE. Ah sir, ah sir! Death's the end of all.

   ROMEO. Spakest thou of Juliet? How is it with her?
      Doth not she think me an old murderer,
❺ | 95   Now I have stained the childhood of our joy
      With blood removed but little from her own?
      Where is she? And how doth she? And what says
      My concealed lady¹⁶ to our canceled love?

   NURSE. O, she says nothing, sir, but weeps and weeps;
100   And now falls on her bed, and then starts up,
      And Tybalt calls; and then on Romeo cries,
      And then down falls again.

   ROMEO.   As if that name,

Romeo and Juliet, Act III, Scene iii ◆ 733

◆ **Reading Strategy**

How would you paraphrase Friar Lawrence's words if the scene were set in modern times? **❸**

13. By and by!: In a minute! (said to the person knocking).
14. simpleness: Silly behavior (Romeo does not move).

15. O: Cry of grief.

16. concealed lady: Secret bride.

◆ **Reading Strategy**

❸ Paraphrase Sample paraphrase: *"Someone's knocking! Who's there? Get up, Romeo, or they'll find you—Hold on!—Stand up. [Knock.] Run to my study—Just a minute!—I can't believe you're acting like this.—Coming! [Knock.] Who's there? What do you want?"*

◆ **Build Grammar Skills**

❹ Who and Whom Point out the pronoun *who* in the first question. Ask whether it is used as a subject or an object. *It is used as a subject.*

◆ **Reading Strategy**

❺ Paraphrase How would students paraphrase Romeo's questions to the Nurse? *Sample paraphrase: "Are you talking about Juliet? How is she? Does she think of me as a murderer now that I have ruined our happiness by killing Tybalt? Where is she? How is she? What does my secret bride say about our broken-off love?"*

◆ **Critical Thinking**

❶ **Connect** Ask: In what way is Romeo's attempt to stab himself consistent with the rest of his behavior in this act? In what way is it reminiscent of Friar Lawrence's warning from Act II, "These violent delights have violent ends . . . ."? *Suggested response: Romeo continues to act rashly and impulsively; he continues to give in to his emotions and go to extremes.*

◆ **Literary Focus**

❷ **Soliloquy, Aside, and Monologue** Invite a volunteer to read aloud the first few lines of Friar Lawrence's speech. Then have students tell whether it is a soliloquy, an aside, or a monologue. How do they know? *It is a monologue. Friar Lawrence addresses Romeo; the speech is lengthy, as monologues usually are.*

◆ **Reading Strategy**

❸ **Paraphrase** Have students identify and paraphrase the key idea in this portion of Friar Lawrence's speech. *Possible paraphrase: "You should count your blessings; happiness has come your way."* Then have students identify the "blessings" that the Friar points out to Romeo. *Juliet is alive; Romeo killed Tybalt before Tybalt could kill him; Romeo has been exiled instead of being sentenced to death.*

Shot from the deadly level[17] of a gun,
Did murder her; as that name's cursèd hand
105 Murdered her kinsman. O, tell me, friar, tell me,
In what vile part of this anatomy
Doth my name lodge? Tell me, that I may sack[18]
The hateful mansion.

❶ [*He offers to stab himself, and* NURSE *snatches the dagger away.*]

FRIAR.   Hold thy desperate hand.
Art thou a man? Thy form cries out thou art;
❷ 110 Thy tears are womanish, thy wild acts denote
The unreasonable fury of a beast.
Unseemly[19] woman in a seeming man!
And ill-beseeming beast in seeming both![20]
Thou hast amazed me. By my holy order,
115 I thought thy disposition better tempered.
Hast thou slain Tybalt? Wilt thou slay thyself?
And slay thy lady that in thy life lives,
By doing damnéd hate upon thyself?
Why railest thou on thy birth, the heaven, and earth?
120 Since birth and heaven and earth, all three do meet
In thee at once; which thou at once wouldst lose.
Fie, fie, thou shamest thy shape, thy love, thy wit,[21]
Which, like a usurer,[22] abound'st in all,
And usest none in that true use indeed
125 Which should bedeck[23] thy shape, thy love, thy wit.
Thy noble shape is but a form of wax,
Digressing from the valor of a man;
Thy dear love sworn but hollow prejury,
Killing that love which thou hast vowed to cherish;
130 Thy wit, that ornament to shape and love,
Misshapen in the conduct[24] of them both,
Like powder in a skilless soldier's flask,[25]
Is set afire by thine own ignorance,
And thou dismemb'red with thine own defense.[26]
❸ 135 What, rouse thee, man! Thy Juliet is alive,
For whose dear sake thou wast but lately dead.[27]
There art thou happy.[28] Tybalt would kill thee,
But thou slewest Tybalt. There art thou happy.
The law, that threat'ned death, becomes thy friend
140 And turns it into exile. There art thou happy.
A pack of blessings light upon thy back;
Happiness courts thee in her best array;
But, like a misbehaved and sullen wench,[29]

17. **level:** Aim.

18. **sack:** Plunder.

19. **Unseemly:** Inappropriate (because unnatural).
20. **And . . . both!:** That is, Romeo inappropriately has lost his human nature because he seems like a man and woman combined.

21. **wit:** Mind; intellect.
22. **Which, like a usurer:** Who, like a rich money-lender.
23. **bedeck:** Do honor to.

24. **conduct:** Management.
25. **flask:** Powder flask.

26. **And thou . . . defense:** The friar is saying that Romeo's mind, which is now irrational, is destroying rather than aiding him.
27. **but lately dead:** Only recently declaring yourself dead.
28. **happy:** Fortunate.

29. **wench:** Low, common girl.

Comprehension Check ☑

4 What practical instructions and advice does the Friar give Romeo in this passage? *He instructs Romeo to go to Juliet but to leave before he can be discovered. Romeo should then wait in the town of Mantua until the time is right to announce his marriage and ask the Prince for a pardon.*

◆ **Reading Strategy**

5 Paraphrase Ask students to paraphrase the instructions that Friar Lawrence gives to Romeo in this passage. *Sample paraphrase: Now go from here; good night. This is your situation: Either go away before the watch is set, or leave by daybreak in a disguise. Remain in Mantua. I'll find your man, and he will let you know from time to time everything that happens here that can make you happy. Shake hands. It's late. Farewell; good night.*

Thou puts up[30] thy fortune and thy love.
145   Take heed, take heed, for such die miserable.
Go get thee to thy love, as was decreed,
Ascend her chamber, hence and comfort her.
But look thou stay not till the watch be set,[31]
For then thou canst not pass to Mantua,
4 150   Where thou shalt live till we can find a time
To blaze[32] your marriage, reconcile your friends,
Beg pardon of the Prince, and call thee back
With twenty hundred thousand times more joy
Than thou went'st forth in lamentation.
155   Go before, nurse. Commend me to thy lady,
And bid her hasten all the house to bed,
Which heavy sorrow makes them apt unto.[33]
Romeo is coming.

NURSE. O Lord, I could have stayed here all the night
160   To hear good counsel. O, what learning is!
My lord, I'll tell my lady you will come.

ROMEO. Do so, and bid my sweet prepare to chide.[34]
              [NURSE *offers to go in and turns again.*]

NURSE. Here, sir, a ring she bid me give you, sir.
Hie you, make haste, for it grows very late.   [*Exit.*]

165 **ROMEO.** How well my comfort is revived by this!

FRIAR. Go hence; good night; and here stands all your state:[35]
Either be gone before the watch be set,
Or by the break of day disguised from hence.
Sojourn[36] in Mantua. I'll find out your man,
5 170   And he shall signify[37] from time to time
Every good hap to you that chances here.
Give me thy hand. 'Tis late. Farewell; good night.

ROMEO. But that a joy past joy calls out on me,
It were a grief so brief to part with thee.
175   Farewell.   [*Exit.*]

Scene iv. *A room in* CAPULET'S *house.*

[*Enter old* CAPULET, *his* WIFE, *and* PARIS.]

CAPULET. Things have fall'n out, sir, so unluckily
That we have had no time to move[1] our daughter.
Look you, she loved her kinsman Tybalt dearly,
And so did I. Well, we were born to die.

30. puts up: Pouts over.

31. watch be set: Watchmen go on duty.

32. blaze: Announce publicly.

33. apt unto: Likely to do.

34. chide: Rebuke me (for slaying Tybalt).

35. here . . . state: This is your situation.

36. Sojourn: Remain.
37. signify: Let you know.

1. move: Discuss your proposal with.

Romeo and Juliet, Act III, Scene iv ◆ 735

❶ Paraphrase Ask students what brought on Lord Capulet's more hurried approach to his daughter's marriage. *Tybalt's death brought on the approach.* Then have them paraphrase these lines. *Sample paraphrase: "It may seem as if we don't care about Tybalt if we throw a big party. Therefore we'll invite a few friends, and that will be it. What do you say to Thursday?"*

Customize for
Less Proficient Readers
Point out that this scene focuses around a single event. Encourage less proficient readers to identify that event. *Juliet's parents arrange her marriage to Paris.*

Customize for
More Advanced Students
Encourage more advanced students to consider this scene together with the end of the previous scene. Have them identify the irony that emerges here. *By the end of Scene iii, Friar Lawrence had convinced Romeo that everything could still work out happily; in Scene iv, an event that will be disastrous for Romeo and Juliet begins to take shape.*

5   'Tis very late; she'll not come down tonight.
     I promise you, but for your company,
     I would have been abed an hour ago.

     PARIS. These times of woe afford no times to woo.
     Madam, good night. Commend me to your daughter.

10 LADY. I will, and know her mind early tomorrow;
     Tonight she's mewed up to her heaviness.[2]

     CAPULET. Sir, Paris, I will make a desperate tender[3]
     Of my child's love. I think she will be ruled
     In all respects by me; nay more, I doubt it not.
15 Wife, go you to her ere you go to bed;
     Acquaint her here of my son[4] Paris' love
     And bid her (mark you me?) on Wednesday next—
     But soft! What day is this?

     PARIS.   Monday, my lord.

     CAPULET. Monday! Ha, ha! Well, Wednesday is too soon.
20 A[5] Thursday let it be—a Thursday, tell her,
     She shall be married to this noble earl.
     Will you be ready? Do you like this haste?
     We'll keep no great ado[6]—a friend or two;
     For hark you, Tybalt being slain so late,
25 It may be thought we held him carelessly,[7]
     Being our kinsman, if we revel much.
     Therefore we'll have some half a dozen friends,
     And there an end. But what say you to Thursday?

     PARIS. My lord, I would that Thursday were tomorrow.

30 CAPULET. Well, get you gone. A Thursday be it then.
     Go you to Juliet ere you go to bed;
     Prepare her, wife, against[8] this wedding day.
     Farewell, my lord.—Light to my chamber, ho!
     Afore me,[9] it is so very late
35 That we may call it early by and by.
     Good night.   [*Exit.*]

Scene v. CAPULET'S *orchard.*

[*Enter* ROMEO *and* JULIET *aloft.*]

     JULIET. Wilt thou be gone? It is not yet near day.
     It was the nightingale, and not the lark,[1]
     That pierced the fearful hollow of thine ear.
     Nightly she sings on yond pomegranate tree.

2. **mewed . . . heaviness:** Locked up with her sorrow.
3. **desperate tender:** Risky offer.

4. **son:** Son-in-law.

5. **A:** On.

6. **We'll . . . ado:** We won't make a great fuss.

7. **held him carelessly:** Did not respect him enough.

8. **against:** For.

9. **Afore me:** Indeed (a mild oath).

1. **nightingale . . . lark:** The nightingale was associated with the night, the lark with dawn.

736 ◆ Drama

Beyond the Classroom

Community Connection
Community Theater Every year across the United States, more theater productions are put on by noncommercial—that is, not-for-profit—theater groups than by commercial theater producers. The main driving forces behind noncommercial theater are high-school, college, and community theater groups.

Community theater is made possible by local talent—community members who perform the many functions involved in putting on a play, including acting, costume and stage design, and technical and administrative support. People involved in community theater generally are not paid for their work; they take part for the sheer love of theater and a desire to bring live theater experiences to local audiences.

Encourage students to gather information about community theater in your area. Students might interview company members involved in the creative, technical, and administrative areas of a production to learn about the responsibilities and rewards that come with their roles.

5   Believe me, love, it was the nightingale.

   ROMEO. It was the lark, the herald of the morn;
         No nightingale. Look, love, what envious streaks
         Do lace the severing² clouds in yonder East.
         Night's candles³ are burnt out, and jocund day
10   Stands tiptoe on the misty mountaintops.
         I must be gone and live, or stay and die.

   JULIET. Yond light is not daylight; I know it, I.
         It is some meteor that the sun exhales⁴
         To be to thee this night a torchbearer
15   And light thee on thy way to Mantua.
         Therefore stay yet; thou need'st not to be gone.

   ROMEO. Let me be ta'en, let me be put to death.
         I am content, so thou wilt have it so.
         I'll say yon gray is not the morning's eye,
20   'Tis but the pale reflex of Cynthia's brow;⁵
         Nor that is not the lark whose notes do beat
         The vaulty heaven so high above our heads.
         I have more care to stay than will to go.
         Come, death, and welcome! Juliet wills it so.
25   How is't, my soul? Let's talk; it is not day.

   ❷ **JULIET.** It is, it is! Hie hence, be gone, away!
         It is the lark that sings so out of tune,
         Straining harsh discords and unpleasing sharps.⁶
         Some say the lark makes sweet division;⁷
30   This doth not so, for she divideth us.
         Some say the lark and loathèd toad change eyes;⁸
         O, now I would they had changed voices too,
         Since arm from arm that voice doth us affray,⁹
         Hunting thee hence with hunt's-up¹⁰ to the day.
35   O, now be gone! More light and light it grows.

   ROMEO. More light and light—more dark and dark our woes.

[*Enter* NURSE.]

   NURSE. Madam!

   JULIET. Nurse?

   NURSE. Your lady mother is coming to your chamber.
40   The day is broke; be wary, look about.   [*Exit.*]

   JULIET. Then, window, let day in, and let life out.

   ROMEO. Farewell, farewell! One kiss, and I'll descend. [*He goeth down.*]

Romeo and Juliet, Act III, Scene v ◆ 737

---

2. **severing:** Parting.
3. **Night's candles:** Stars.

4. **exhales:** Sends out.

5. **reflex . . . brow:**
Reflection of the moon
(Cynthia was a name for
the moon goddess).

6. **sharps:** Shrill high
notes.
7. **division:** Melody.

8. **change eyes:**
Exchange eyes (because
the lark has a beautiful
body with ugly eyes and
the toad has an ugly body
with beautiful eyes).
9. **affray:** Frighten.
10. **hunt's-up:** Morning
song for hunters.

◆ **Reading Strategy**
How might you trans-
late Romeo and
Juliet's conversation
into plain contempo-
rary English?   ❸

Comprehension Check ☑

❷ Why are Romeo and Juliet so concerned with signs of night and day?
Encourage students to cite specific
lines to support their answers. *Romeo
must leave before he is discovered; the
Prince had declared that he would be
executed if he did not leave Verona.
Students may cite the following: "Let me
be ta'en, let me be put to death;"
"Come, death, and welcome! Juliet wills
it so;" "Since arm from arm that voice
(the lark's) doth us affray,/Hunting thee
hence with hunt's-up to the day."*

◆ **Reading Strategy**

❸ **Paraphrase** Sample paraphrase:
*JULIET: Then, window, let daylight in and
my life out. ROMEO: Goodbye, goodbye!
Just one kiss and I'll go down. JULIET:
When you're gone, I must hear from you
every hour of every day. For minutes
seem like days, and it will seem like
years before I again see Romeo. ROMEO:
Goodbye! I'll send my good wishes and
love to you whenever I can. JULIET: Do
you think we'll ever meet again? ROMEO:
I have no doubt that these sorrows will
become conversation topics in good
times to come. JULIET: I fear the worst. I
keep thinking that some disaster will
happen and that you'll be found dead in
a tomb. ROMEO: Trust me, my love.
Goodbye, goodbye! JULIET: Oh, fortune,
fortune! All men call you fickle. If you
are fickle, what will you do? I hope that
you won't keep him long, but will send
him back.*

737

JULIET. Art thou gone so, love-lord, ay husband-friend?
I must hear from thee every day in the hour,
45 For in a minute there are many days.
O, by this count I shall be much in years[11]
Ere I again behold my Romeo!

ROMEO. Farewell!
I will omit no opportunity
50 That may convey my greetings, love, to thee.

JULIET. O, think'st thou we shall ever meet again?

ROMEO. I doubt it not; and all these woes shall serve
For sweet discourses[12] in our times to come.

JULIET. O God, I have an ill-divining[13] soul!
55 Methinks I see thee, now thou art so low,
As one dead in the bottom of a tomb.
Either my eyesight fails, or thou lookest pale.

ROMEO. And trust me, love, in my eye so do you.
Dry sorrow drinks our blood.[14] Adieu, adieu! [*Exit.*]

60 **JULIET.** O Fortune, Fortune! All men call thee <u>fickle</u>.
If thou art fickle, what dost thou[15] with him
That is renowned for faith? Be fickle, Fortune,
For then I hope thou wilt not keep him long
But send him back.

[*Enter* MOTHER.]

65 **LADY CAPULET.** Ho, daughter! Are you up?

JULIET. Who is't that calls? It is my lady mother.
Is she not down so late,[16] or up so early?
What unaccustomed cause procures her hither?[17]

LADY CAPULET. Why, how now, Juliet?

JULIET.   Madam, I am not well.

70 **LADY CAPULET.** Evermore weeping for your cousin's death?
What, wilt thou wash him from his grave with tears?
And if thou couldst, thou couldst not make him live.
Therefore have done. Some grief shows much of love;
But much of grief shows still some want of wit.

75 **JULIET.** Yet let me weep for such a feeling[18] loss.

LADY CAPULET. So shall you feel the loss, but not the friend
Which you weep for.

11. **much in years:** Much older.

12. **discourses:** Conversations.
13. **ill-divining:** Predicting evil.

14. **Dry sorrow . . . blood:** It was once believed that sorrow drained away the blood.
15. **dost thou:** Do you have to do.

16. **Is she . . . late:** Has she stayed up so late?
17. **What . . . hither?:** What unusual reason brings her here?

18. **feeling:** Deeply felt.

◆ **Build Vocabulary**
fickle (fik´əl) *adj.*: Changeable

738 ◆ *Drama*

JULIET.   Feeling so the loss,
I cannot choose but ever weep the friend.

LADY CAPULET. Well, girl, thou weep'st not so much for his death
80   As that the villain lives which slaughtered him.

JULIET. What villain, madam?

LADY CAPULET.   That same villain Romeo.

JULIET. [*Aside*] Villain and he be many miles asunder.[19]—
God pardon him! I do, with all my heart;
And yet no man like he doth grieve my heart.

85 **LADY CAPULET.** That is because the traitor murderer lives.

❷ **JULIET.** Ay, madam, from the reach of these my
        hands.
Would none but I might venge my cousin's death!

LADY CAPULET. We will have vengeance for it, fear thou not.
Then weep no more. I'll send to one in Mantua,
90   Where that same banished runagate[20] doth live,
Shall give him such an unaccustomed dram[21]
That he shall soon keep Tybalt company;
And then I hope thou wilt be satisfied.

JULIET. Indeed I never shall be satisfied
95   With Romeo till I behold him—dead[22]—
Is my poor heart so for a kinsman vexed.
Madam, if you could find out but a man
To bear a poison, I would temper[23] it;
That Romeo should, upon receipt thereof,
100 Soon sleep in quiet. O, how my heart abhors
To hear him named and cannot come to him,
To wreak[24] the love I bore my cousin
Upon his body that hath slaughtered him!

LADY CAPULET. Find thou the means, and I'll find such a man.
105 But now I'll tell thee joyful tidings, girl.

JULIET. And joy comes well in such a needy time.
What are they, beseech your ladyship?

LADY CAPULET. Well, well, thou hast a careful[25] father, child;
One who, to put thee from thy heaviness,
❸ 110 Hath sorted out[26] a sudden day of joy
That thou expects not nor I looked not for.

JULIET. Madam, in happy time![27] What day is that?

◆ **Literary Focus**
What characteristics of an aside do you see in Juliet's words in lines 82–84?   ❶

19. **asunder:** Apart.

20. **runagate:** Renegade; runaway.
21. **unaccustomed dram:** Unexpected dose of poison.

22. **dead:** Juliet is deliberately ambiguous here. Her mother thinks *dead* refers to Romeo. But Juliet is using the word with the following line, in reference to her heart.
23. **temper:** Mix; weaken.

24. **wreak** (reek): Avenge; express.

25. **careful:** Considerate.

26. **sorted out:** Selected.

27. **in happy time:** Just in time.

◆ **Literary Focus**

❶ **Soliloquy, Aside, and Monologue** Juliet's aside is brief; it is made to the audience while other characters are on stage but unable to hear it.

Comprehension Check ☑

❷ Encourage students to explain how this remark contrasts with Juliet's aside. *Now that Juliet speaks directly to her mother, she speaks in double meanings. Lady Capulet can interpret these words to mean that, like the rest of her family, Juliet would like to take revenge on Romeo. What Juliet really means, however, is that she wishes that she could be near Romeo and save him from everyone else.*

◆ **Build Grammar Skills**

❸ *Who* and *Whom* Point out Lady Capulet's use of the pronoun *who.* Help students reword the sentence in a way that shows why *who*—which acts as or refers to a subject—is correct in this case. *Suggested rewording: "Thou hast a careful father, child; he is someone who put thee from thy heaviness. . . ."*

Romeo and Juliet, Act III, Scene v ◆ 739

❶ Soliloquy, Aside, and Monologue Have students identify Juliet's speech as a soliloquy, aside, or monologue; have them explain their answers. *It is a soliloquy. Alone on stage, Juliet expresses her thoughts to the audience.* Follow up by asking why this is a particularly appropriate way for Juliet to make her exit from this act. Elicit the following: *Juliet has been let down and betrayed by the adults in her life—her father, her mother, and the Nurse. Her soliloquy reinforces the fact that from now on she must act alone.*

🎧 **Listening to Literature Audiocassettes** Now that students have read Act III, you might have them listen to some or all of the scenes within it on the Listening to Literature audiocassette.

Reinforce and Extend

Answers
◆ *Literature and Your Life*

Reader's Response Some students may say that Romeo and Juliet should confess that they are married.

Thematic Focus Students may observe that sometimes intervention with the best of intentions serves only to get the antagonists angry at the person who intervenes.

☑ **Check Your Comprehension**

1. Romeo controls his anger and tries to make light of the challenge to a duel. Mercutio becomes angry and begins to fight with Tybalt. As Romeo tries to separate them, Tybalt kills Mercutio and runs away. When Tybalt returns, Romeo avenges his friend's death by killing Tybalt. Romeo runs away. The Prince banishes Romeo.

2. At first Juliet believes Romeo is evil and begins to speak against him, although she can only half-curse him. But when the Nurse also attacks Romeo, Juliet defends him, feeling guilty that she had even thought he was villainous. She is upset that Tybalt is dead and Romeo is banished.

3. Friar Lawrence thinks Romeo should feel fortunate because Juliet is alive, he is alive, and he has only been banished—not sentenced to death.

744

---

❶
240

Is it more sin to wish me thus forsworn,
Or to dispraise my lord with that same tongue
Which she hath praised him with above compare
So many thousand times? Go, counselor!
Thou and my bosom henceforth shall be twain.⁶¹
I'll to the friar to know his remedy.
If all else fail, myself have power to die.   [*Exit.*]

61. Thou . . . twain: You will from now on be separated from my trust.

Guide for Responding

◆ *Literature and Your Life*

Reader's Response What would you do if you were in Romeo's or Juliet's situation?
Thematic Focus Why is it that when people make an effort to work out a conflict it sometimes makes matters worse?

☑ **Check Your Comprehension**

1. Trace the sequence of events that begins with Tybalt's insult to Romeo and ends with Tybalt's death and Romeo's banishment.
2. Describe the clashing emotions Juliet feels when the Nurse reports Tybalt's death and Romeo's banishment.
3. In his long speech to Romeo, Friar Lawrence mentions three things for which Romeo should consider himself fortunate. What are they?
4. What decision concerning Paris and Juliet does Lord Capulet make in Scene iv? Describe Juliet's reaction to this plan.
5. What advice does the Nurse give Juliet at the end of Act III? Describe Juliet's reaction to this advice.

744 ◆ *Drama*

◆ **Critical Thinking**

INTERPRET
1. What does Romeo mean when he says, after killing Tybalt, "I am fortune's fool!"? **[Interpret]**
2. Why didn't Escalus sentence Romeo to death, in keeping with his speech in Act I? **[Draw Conclusions]**
3. As Romeo and Juliet are about to part, how do they differ in their views of the future? **[Compare and Contrast]**
4. Explain why you think Romeo and Juliet's troubles do or do not result primarily from fate. Support your answer with details from the play. **[Support]**

EVALUATE
5. How should Romeo have acted in Scene I? Support your answer. **[Criticize]**

EXTEND
6. Up to this point, the Nurse has acted as a counselor for Juliet. What qualities should a counselor have? **[Career Link]**

---

4. Capulet has decided that Paris and Juliet will marry in three days. Juliet's reaction is explosive and definite. She will not marry Paris.
5. The Nurse advises Juliet to forget Romeo and marry Paris. Juliet reacts by secretly rejecting the Nurse as a confidante.

◆ **Critical Thinking**

1. Romeo feels he is a victim of fate.

2. The Prince was lenient because Romeo killed a person who had himself killed the Prince's relative.
3. Juliet is pessimistic, Romeo more positive. She wonders if they will ever see each other again. Romeo assures her that they will.
4. Many students will conclude that most of the troubles arise from the feud between their families; as a result, their love is dangerous and

bound to lead to trouble. Tybalt's anger at Romeo and the need to keep the marriage a secret are the result of the feud.
5. Some students might say that Romeo should have taken part in the duel so that Mercutio would not have been killed.
6. A good counselor should be consistent, intelligent, and not afraid to speak his or her mind.

Guide for Responding (continued)

◆ Literary Focus

SOLILOQUY, ASIDE, AND MONOLOGUE

A **soliloquy** is a speech in which a character, alone on stage, speaks directly to the audience. An **aside** is a brief remark to the audience, uttered while other characters are nearby but unable to hear. A **monologue** is a lengthy speech addressed to other characters, rather than to the audience.

1. What thoughts and feelings does Juliet reveal in her soliloquy that opens Scene ii?
2. When Lady Capulet, in Scene v, refers to Romeo as a villain, Juliet utters the aside "Villain and he be many miles asunder." In your own words, what is Juliet saying? Why is it important that the audience, but not Lady Capulet, hear this remark?
3. Reread Friar Lawrence's monologue in Scene iii beginning "Hold thy desperate hand." What criticisms is he addressing to Romeo?

◆ Build Vocabulary

USING WORDS FROM MYTHOLOGY

Use the clues that follow to help you complete these sentences with the words provided.

a. nemesis   **b.** mercurial   **c.** odyssey

1. The mood of a ___?___ person can change quickly.
2. An ___?___ is a very long journey.
3. A ___?___ is a person who punishes.

MYTHOLOGICAL CLUES

Nemesis: Greek goddess of vengeance
Mercury: Swift Roman messenger to the gods
Odyssey: Ancient Greek epic about the wanderings of Odysseus

USING THE WORD BANK

Write the letter of the word that is the best synonym of the first word.

1. gallant: (a) enchanting, (b) courageous, (c) cowardly
2. fray: (a) brawl, (b) condition, (c) truce
3. martial: (a) financial, (b) deputy, (c) warlike
4. exile: (a) expel, (b) travel, (c) arrive
5. eloquence: (a) beauty, (b) expressiveness, (c) value
6. fickle: (a) fruitful, (b) erratic, (c) constant

◆ Reading Strategy

PARAPHRASE

Paraphrasing involves identifying key ideas and restating them in your own words.

1. Paraphrase lines 29 through 51 of scene iii.
2. Extend your paraphrasing skills by choosing a paragraph that you've written and restating it in language that Shakespeare might have used.

◆ Build Grammar Skills

COMMONLY CONFUSED WORDS: *WHO* AND *WHOM*

The pronoun *who* is used when the pronoun is the subject of the verb or is a predicate nominative. The pronoun *whom* is used when the pronoun receives the action of the verb or when it is the object of a preposition.

Practice On a sheet of paper, complete the following sentences by adding *who* or *whom*.

1. ___?___ began the argument that resulted in two deaths and Romeo's banishment?
2. Romeo, ___?___ has good intentions, tries to separate the combatants.
3. Romeo is a person to ___?___ banishment seems worse than death.
4. Juliet states that Romeo is the man ___?___ she will marry.

Idea Bank

Writing

1. **Editorial** Imagine that you're the editor of the Verona newspaper. Write an editorial on whether the Prince's response to Tybalt's death was appropriate. Support your argument with details from Acts I through III.
2. **Soliloquy** Write a brief soliloquy, either in prose or in blank verse, that Juliet might deliver just before meeting with the Friar.

Speaking and Listening

3. **Debate** Form two teams to debate the following issue: Is Romeo a victim of fate or of his own character?

◆ Literary Focus

1. Juliet is impatient for the night to arrive, so that she can be with her new husband.
2. Juliet says there is a big difference between Romeo and a villain. It is important that Lady Capulet not hear how she feels but also important that the audi-ence knows that she does not think that Romeo is a villain.
3. Friar Lawrence thinks that Romeo is acting irrationally and self-destructively.

✓ ASSESSMENT OPTIONS

Formal Assessment, pp. 170–172.
Alternative Assessment, p. 47.
PORTFOLIO ASSESSMENT
Use the following rubrics in the *Alternative Assessment* booklet:
Editorial: Persuasion Rubric, p. 98
Soliloquy: Drama Rubric, p. 102

Answers

◆ Build Vocabulary

1. mercurial;   2. odyssey;   3. nemesis

Using the Word Bank

1. b   2. a   3. c   4. a   5. b   6. b

◆ Reading Strategy

1. Sample paraphrase: Banishment is torture, not mercy, for heaven is here where Juliet lives. While every little creature may look upon Juliet, I cannot. Even flies have it better than me, for they can hear Juliet speak. But I cannot hear Juliet's voice because I am banished. You say that exile is not death, but it is. The damned howl the word *banished* in hell. How can you torture me with the word *banished*?
2. Students' paragraphs should reflect Shakespeare's language.

◆ Build Grammar Skills

1. Who;   2. who;   3. whom;   4. whom

 **Writer's Solution**

For additional practice, use the lesson in the **Language Lab CD-ROM** on Using Pronouns Correctly and the practice pages on Pronoun Usage (pp. 78–81) in the *Writer's Solution Grammar Practice Book.*

 Idea Bank

Customizing for
Performance Levels
Following are suggestions for matching the Idea Bank topics with your students' performance levels:
     Less Advanced Students: 1
     Average Students: 2
     More Advanced Students: 3

Customizing for
Learning Modalities
Following are suggestions for matching Idea Bank topics with your students' learning modalities:
     Verbal/Linguistic: 1, 2
     Logical/Mathematical: 3

Guide for Reading, Act IV

1. To read, comprehend, and interpret a play
2. To relate a play to personal experience
3. To make predictions
4. To identify dramatic irony
5. To build vocabulary in context and learn the suffix *-ward*
6. To recognize and use parallel structure
7. To respond to the play through writing and speaking and listening

SKILLS INSTRUCTION

Vocabulary:
Suffixes: *-ward*

Grammar:
Parallel Structure

Reading Strategy:
Predict

Literary Focus:
Dramatic Irony

Speaking and Listening:
Renaissance Music Presentation (teacher edition)

Critical Viewing:
Evaluate

PORTFOLIO OPPORTUNITIES

Writing: Love Letter; Your Own Ending
Speaking and Listening: Renaissance Music Presentation

Interest Grabber

Both prime time and daytime serials tell many tales about teenagers in love. Although the characters, settings, and plot details vary, one thing is always certain. The course of love never runs smoothly. Encourage students to consider what they know about "soap operas." Ask: If *Romeo and Juliet* were a soap opera, what would likely happen now that Juliet is secretly married to Romeo, a young man whom her parents have forbidden her to see?

◆ Review and Anticipate

Romeo and Juliet are married for only a few hours when disaster strikes. Mercutio is killed by Tybalt in a duel meant for Romeo; enraged by Mercutio's death, Romeo fights with Tybalt and kills him. As a result, Romeo is banished forever from Verona. To make matters worse, Juliet's parents are determined to marry her to Paris. What do you think is going to happen to Romeo and Juliet? What, if anything, can they do to preserve their relationship?

◆ Reading Strategy

PREDICT

Dramatic irony, which occurs when the audience knows more about a situation than a character does, keeps the audience guessing about what will happen next. Will a character find out what the audience knows, and, if so, how will this happen and how will he or she react? What will happen if the character doesn't get the necessary information? As you continue reading, **predict**—make educated guesses—about what will happen next. Base your predictions on what you know about the characters' personalities and the information available to each of them. Also look for places where the author foreshadows, or hints at, future events. Jot down your predictions in a chart like this one.

Prediction	Actual Outcome

◆ Build Grammar Skills

PARALLEL STRUCTURE

To emphasize how a character thinks or feels, Shakespeare often uses **parallel structure**, or the expression of similar ideas in similar grammatical forms. For example, in Act IV, Juliet expresses to Friar Lawrence the magnitude of her contempt at the thought of marrying Paris by voicing a string of commands, each beginning with the words *bid me,* followed by a verb.

> O, bid me leap . . . /From off the battlements of any tower . . .
> . . . or bid me lurk / Where serpents are . . .
> Or bid me go into a new-made grave . . .

◆ Literary Focus

DRAMATIC IRONY

Dramatic irony is a contradiction between what a character thinks or says and what the audience or reader knows to be true. For example, in Act III, Scene iv, Lord Capulet decides that the way to ensure Juliet's future happiness is to have her wed Paris. He does not know what you know—that Juliet is already married. Such dramatic irony adds suspense and involves us emotionally in the action. It can even make us want to step into the world of the play and give the characters a correct understanding of the situation they are in.

◆ Build Vocabulary

SUFFIXES: *-ward*

In Act IV, Lord Capulet says that he is happy because his once *wayward* daughter is again obedient. The word *wayward* contains the suffix *-ward,* meaning "in a direction." Based on your knowledge of this suffix, you might guess that the definition of the word is "in the direction of a specific route." This is close to the actual definition: "insistent upon having one's own way."

WORD BANK

Before you read, preview these words.

pensive
vial
enjoined
wayward
dismal
loathsome
pilgrimage

Prentice Hall Literature Program Resources

REINFORCE / RETEACH / EXTEND

Selection Support Pages
Build Vocabulary: Suffixes: *-ward,* p. 200
Build Grammar Skills: Parallel Structure, p. 201
Reading Strategy: Predict, p. 202
Literary Focus: Dramatic Irony, p. 203

Strategies for Diverse Student Needs, p. 49

Beyond Literature
Career Connection: Medicine, p. 49

Formal Assessment Selection Test, pp. 173–175, Assessment Resources Software

Alternative Assessment, p. 47

Resource Pro CD-ROM
The Tragedy of Romeo and Juliet—includes all resource material and customizable lesson plan

Listening to Literature Audiocassettes
The Tragedy of Romeo and Juliet

Romeo and Juliet

Act IV

Scene i. FRIAR LAURENCE'S *cell.*

[*Enter* FRIAR LAURENCE *and* COUNTY PARIS.]

    FRIAR. On Thursday, sir? The time is very short.

    PARIS. My father[1] Capulet will have it so,
    And I am nothing slow to slack his haste.[2]

    FRIAR. You say you do not know the lady's mind.
5   Uneven is the course;[3] I like it not.

    PARIS. Immoderately she weeps for Tybalt's death,
    And therefore have I little talked of love;
    For Venus smiles not in a house of tears.
    Now, sir, her father counts it dangerous
10   That she do give her sorrow so much sway,
    And in his wisdom hastes our marriage
    To stop the inundation[4] of her tears,
    Which, too much minded[5] by herself alone,
    May be put from her by society.
15   Now do you know the reason of this haste.

    FRIAR. [*Aside*] I would I knew not why it should be slowed.—
    Look, sir, here comes the lady toward my cell.

[*Enters* JULIET.]

    PARIS. Happily met, my lady and my wife!

    JULIET. That may be, sir, when I may be a wife.

20   **PARIS.** That "may be" must be, love, on Thursday next.

    JULIET. What must be shall be.

    FRIAR.   That's a certain text.[6]

    PARIS. Come you to make confession to this father?

    JULIET. To answer that, I should confess to you.

    PARIS. Do not deny to him that you love me.

25   **JULIET.** I will confess to you that I love him.

    PARIS. So will ye, I am sure, that you love me.

1. father: Future father-in-law.
2. I . . . haste: I won't slow him down by being slow myself.
3. Uneven . . . course: Irregular is the plan.

4. inundation: Flood.
5. minded: Thought about.

6. That's . . . text: That's a certain truth.

Romeo and Juliet, Act IV, Scene i ◆ 747

One-Minute Insight Act IV belongs to Juliet as she interacts with the Friar, Paris, her parents, and the Nurse. Using witty wordplay and misleading statements, Juliet avoids suspicion about her true intent. Her unwillingness to confront her parents along with her putting her trust in the Friar leads her further along the road to tragedy. Thus, Act IV illustrates a dichotomy at work within Juliet. Because Juliet is deeply in love with Romeo, she is brave enough to take the Friar's potion, but she is at the same time afraid to tell her parents the truth.

Customize for
Less Proficient Readers
At the end of each scene, have these students write a three- to five-sentence summary of the action. Encourage them to share and discuss their summaries with one another.

◆ Critical Thinking

❶ **Make Judgments** Have students consider what Paris tells the Friar about his impending marriage to Juliet. Then ask: Do you believe that Paris truly loves Juliet? Why or why not? *Suggested responses: Paris truly loves Juliet because he is anxious to marry her; Paris does not truly love Juliet because he hardly knows her and has not talked to her about love.*

◆ Build Vocabulary

❷ **Suffixes: -ward** Point out the word *toward.* Have students identify the base word *to* and the suffix *-ward.* Have them explain how analyzing the word by separating the base word from the suffix gives them more insight into the word's meaning and history. *The suffix -ward means "in a direction," so toward means "in a direction to a person or place."*

❸ **Clarification** Juliet is cleverly playing with words in order to avoid lying. She says that if she confesses to the Friar that she loves Paris, it will be more valuable than if she told Paris himself. If she told Paris she loved him, she might be lying, but she would not lie in a confession to a priest.

Preparing for Standardized Tests

Reading and Vocabulary Standardized tests include items, such as analogies, that assess a student's knowledge of vocabulary. Recognizing a familiar suffix as part of an unfamiliar word can help students determine the meaning of the word. The Build Vocabulary lesson for this selection focuses on the suffix *-ward.* For additional practice, use the Build Vocabulary page in *Selection Support,* p. 200.

Grammar and Language Standardized tests often require students to improve a sentence by choosing the best option, as in this example

focusing on parallel structure:

I enjoy playing tennis, to exercise, and swimming. *(B)*

    (A) ...tennis, to exercise often, and ...

    (B) ...tennis, exercising, and ...

    (C) ...tennis, some exercise, and ...

The Build Grammar Skills lesson focuses on parallel structure. After students complete the activities on page 759, have them correct the previous example. For more practice, use the Build Grammar Skills page on parallel structure in *Selection Support,* p. 201.

These students may be confused by
the inverted word order often used
by Shakespeare. Call their attention
to sentences such as "And therefore
have I little talked of love" and have
students reword them in more
customary word order ("Therefore
I have talked little of love.")

◆ **Literary Focus**

❶ **Dramatic Irony** Ask: Why is
this exchange between Paris and
Juliet an example of irony? *Paris says
that Juliet's face belongs to him. Juliet
seems to agree with him because she
says, "it is not mine own." However, the
audience knows that Juliet means that it
belongs to Romeo.*

◆ **Reading Strategy**

❷ **Predict** Sample responses: Juliet
will run away; Juliet will find the
courage to tell her parents that she
is married to Romeo; Juliet will do
something desperate.

◆ **Build Grammar Skills**

❸ **Parallel Structure** Point out
the use of parallel structure in the
phrases "past hope, past care, past
help." Ask: How does this use of
parallel structure affect your understanding of the situation? *It emphasizes Juliet's hopelessness.*

◆ **Reading Strategy**

❹ **Predict** Ask: Why might Juliet
have a knife? *Elicit that the knife is an
example of foreshadowing, a hint to the
audience of what might occur.*

JULIET. If I do so, it will be of more price,[7]
   Being spoke behind your back, than to your face.

PARIS. Poor soul, thy face is much abused with tears.

30 **JULIET.** The tears have got small victory by that,
   For it was bad enough before their spite.[8]

PARIS. Thou wrong'st it more than tears with that report.

JULIET. That is no slander, sir, which is a truth;
   And what I spake, I spake it to my face.

❶ 35 **PARIS.** Thy face is mine, and thou hast sland'red it.

JULIET. It may be so, for it is not mine own.
   Are you at leisure, holy father, now,
   Or shall I come to you at evening mass?

FRIAR. My leisure serves me, <u>pensive</u> daughter, now.
40 My lord, we must entreat the time alone.[9]

PARIS. God shield[10] I should disturb devotion!
   Juliet, on Thursday early will I rouse ye.
   Till then, adieu, and keep this holy kiss.   [*Exit.*]

❸ 45 **JULIET.** O, shut the door, and when thou hast done so,
   Come weep with me—past hope, past care, past help!

FRIAR. O Juliet, I already know thy grief;
   It strains me past the compass of my wits.[11]
   I hear thou must, and nothing may prorogue[12] it,
   On Thursday next be married to this County.

❹ 50 **JULIET.** Tell me not, friar, that thou hearest of this,
   Unless thou tell me how I may prevent it.
   If in thy wisdom thou canst give no help,
   Do thou but call my resolution wise
   And with this knife I'll help it presently.[13]
55 God joined my heart and Romeo's, thou our hands;
   And ere this hand, by thee to Romeo's sealed,
   Shall be the label to another deed,[14]
   Or my true heart with treacherous revolt
   Turn to another, this shall slay them both.
60 Therefore, out of thy long-experienced time,
   Give me some present counsel; or, behold,
   'Twixt my extremes and me[15] this bloody knife
   Shall play the umpire, arbitrating[16] that
   Which the commission of thy years and art
65 Could to no issue of true honor bring.[17]

748 ◆ *Drama*

---

7. **price:** Value.

8. **before their spite:**
Before the harm that the
tears did.

◆ **Reading Strategy**
What do you pre-
dict Juliet will do if
there is no way to
prevent her
marriage to Paris? ❷

9. **entreat . . . alone:**
ask to have this time to
ourselves.
10. **shield:** Forbid.

11. **past . . . wits:** Beyond
the ability of my mind to
find a remedy.
12. **prorogue:** Delay.

13. **presently:** At once.
14. **Shall . . . deed:** Shall
give the seal of approval to
another marriage contract.
15. **'Twixt . . . me:**
Between my misfortunes
and me.
16. **arbitrating:** Deciding.
17. **Which . . . bring:**
Which the authority that
derives from your age and
ability could not solve
honorably.

◆ **Build Vocabulary**
pensive (pen´ siv) *adj.*
Thinking deeply or seriously

◆ **Block Scheduling Strategies**

Consider these suggestions to take advantage of extended class time:
• Suggest that students use a prediction
  chart (p. 746) as they read Act IV.
• Have students listen to the audiocassette
  recording of Act IV before they read the
  text so that they can better understand
  the emotions of the characters.
• Dramatic irony is central to Act IV. Have
  students discuss the use of irony using the

Literary Focus questions (p. 759) as a
guide.
• Students can work in small groups to
  answer the Critical Thinking questions (p.
  758). Suggest that each group appoint a
  facilitator to keep the answers on track, a
  questioner to draw out more complete
  responses, a recorder to keep track of the
  group's answers, and a speaker to present
  the responses to the other groups.

• Discuss parallel structure and have students complete the Writing Application
  on page 759. After they have finished, have
  them share and compare their questions
  with partners.
• Students interested in doing the Speaking
  and Listening activity on Renaissance
  music (p. 759) might search the Internet
  for background information before they
  consult other sources.

Be not so long to speak. I long to die
If what thou speak'st speak not of remedy.

FRIAR. Hold, daughter. I do spy a kind of hope,
Which craves[18] as desperate an execution
70 As that is desperate which we would prevent
If, rather than to marry County Paris,
Thou hast the strength of will to slay thyself,
Then is it likely thou wilt undertake
A thing like death to chide away this shame,
75 That cop'st with death himself to scape from it;[19]
And, if thou darest, I'll give thee remedy.

JULIET. O, bid me leap, rather than marry Paris.
From off the battlements of any tower,
Or walk in thievish ways,[20] or bid me lurk
80 Where serpents are; chain me with roaring bears,
Or hide me nightly in a charnel house,[21]
O'ercovered quite with dead men's rattling bones,
With reeky[22] shanks and yellow chapless[23] skulls;
Or bid me go into a new-made grave
85 And hide me with a dead man in his shroud—
Things that, to hear them told, have made me tremble—
And I will do it without fear or doubt,
To live an unstained wife to my sweet love.

FRIAR. Hold, then. Go home, be merry, give consent
90 To marry Paris. Wednesday is tomorrow.
Tomorrow night look that thou lie alone;
Let not the nurse lie with thee in thy chamber.
Take thou this <u>vial</u>, being then in bed,
And this distilling liquor drink thou off;
95 When presently through all thy veins shall run
A cold and drowsy humor;[24] for no pulse
Shall keep his native[25] progress, but surcease;[26]
No warmth, no breath, shall testify thou livest;
The roses in thy lips and cheeks shall fade
100 To wanny ashes,[27] thy eyes' windows[28] fall
Like death when he shuts up the day of life;
Each part, deprived of supple government,[29]
Shall, stiff and stark and cold, appear like death;
And in this borrowed likeness of shrunk death
105 Thou shalt continue two-and-forty hours,
And then awake as from a pleasant sleep.
Now, when the bridegroom in the morning comes
To rouse thee from thy bed, there art thou dead.

18. craves: Requires.

19. That cop'st . . . it: That bargains with death itself to escape from it.

20. thievish ways: Roads where criminals lurk.

21. charnel house: Vault for bones removed from graves to be reused.
22. reeky: Foul-smelling.
23. chapless: Jawless.

24. humor: Fluid; liquid.
25. native: Natural.
26. surcease: Stop.
27. wanny ashes: To the color of pale ashes.
28. eyes' windows: Eyelids.
29. supple government: Ability for maintaining motion.

◆ **Build Vocabulary**

vial (vī′ əl) *n.*: Small bottle containing medicine or other liquids

Romeo and Juliet, Act IV, Scene i ◆ 749

Comprehension Check ☑

❺ Summarize the things that Juliet would rather do than marry Paris.
She would rather leap from a tower, walk in the worst part of town, step on snakes, be chained to bears, be put in a vault with human bones, or be lowered in a grave with a dead person.

❻ **Clarification** Be sure students recognize that in the phrase "when he shuts up the day of life," the word *he* refers to death. This is an example of personification.

Beyond the Classroom

Community Connection
Where to Get Help Juliet went to the Friar when she felt that she had nowhere else to turn, but where do people in your community go when all seems hopeless? Have students make a list of both individual sources of help (members of the clergy, teachers, counselors) and organizations that offer support to people in trouble. Encourage students to make a list of such organizations with phone numbers that people can use if they feel they need help coping with their problems.

❶ **Predict** The Friar's plan is complicated, which means there are many ways for it to go wrong. Ask: What might happen to the Friar's letter? *Sample responses: The letter can get lost. It might be intercepted or stolen. It might not be delivered on time.*

❷ **Clarification** Be sure that students understand that the Capulet family is beginning preparations for the wedding. Capulet has given a servant a list of guests to invite.

Then, as the manner of our country is,
110 In thy best robes uncovered on the bier[30]
Thou shalt be borne to that same ancient vault
Where all the kindred of the Capulets lie.
In the meantime, against[31] thou shalt awake,
Shall Romeo by my letters know our drift;[32]
115 And hither shall he come; and he and I
Will watch thy waking, and that very night
Shall Romeo bear thee hence to Mantua.
And this shall free thee from this present shame,
If no inconstant toy[33] nor womanish fear
120 Abate thy valor[34] in the acting it.

JULIET. Give me, give me! O, tell not me of fear!

❶ FRIAR. Hold! Get you gone, be strong and prosperous
In this resolve. I'll send a friar with speed
To Mantua, with my letters to thy lord.

125 JULIET. Love give me strength, and strength shall help afford.
Farewell, dear father. [*Exit with* FRIAR.]

Scene ii. *Hall in* CAPULET's *house.*

[*Enter* FATHER CAPULET, MOTHER, NURSE *and* SERVINGMEN *two or three.*]

❷ CAPULET. So many guests invite as here are writ. [*Exit a* SERVINGMAN.]
Sirrah, go hire me twenty cunning[1] cooks.

SERVINGMAN. You shall have none ill, sir; for I'll try[2] if they can lick
their fingers.

5 CAPULET. How canst thou try them so?

SERVINGMAN. Marry, sir, 'tis an ill cook that cannot lick his own fingers[3]
Therefore he that cannot lick his fingers goes not with me.

CAPULET. Go, begone. [*Exit* SERVINGMAN.]
We shall be much unfurnished[4] for this time.
10 What, is my daughter gone to Friar Laurence?

NURSE. Ay, forsooth.[5]

CAPULET. Well, he may chance to do some good on her.
A peevish self-willed harlotry it is.[6]

[*Enter* JULIET.]

NURSE. See where she comes from shrift with merry look.

15 CAPULET. How now, my headstrong? Where have you been gadding?

30. uncovered on the bier: Displayed on the funeral platform.

31. against: Before.
32. drift: Purpose; plan.

33. inconstant toy: Passing whim.
34. Abate thy valor: Lessen your courage.

1. cunning: Skillful.

2. try: Test.

3. 'tis . . . fingers: It's a bad cook that won't taste his own cooking.
4. unfurnished: Unprepared.
5. forsooth: In truth.
6. A peevish . . . it is: It is the ill-tempered, selfish behavior of a woman without good breeding.

◆ **Build Vocabulary**

enjoined (en joind´) *v.:* Ordered

wayward (wā´ wərd) *adj.:* Insistent upon having one's own way; headstrong

JULIET. Where I have learnt me to repent the sin
Of disobedient opposition
To you and your behests,[7] and am <u>enjoined</u>
By holy Laurence to fall prostrate[8] here
20 To beg your pardon. Pardon, I beseech you!
Henceforward I am ever ruled by you.

CAPULET. Send for the County. Go tell him of this.
I'll have this knot knit up tomorrow morning.

JULIET. I met the youthful lord at Laurence' cell
25 And gave him what becomèd[9] love I might,
Not stepping o'er the bounds of modesty.

CAPULET. Why, I am glad on't. This is well. Stand up.
This is as't should be. Let me see the County.
Ay, marry, go, I say, and fetch him hither.
❸ 30 Now, afore God, this reverend holy friar,
All our whole city is much bound[10] to him.

JULIET. Nurse, will you go with me into my closet[11]
To help me sort such needful ornaments[12]
As you think fit to furnish me tomorrow?

❹ 35 **LADY CAPULET.** No, not till Thursday. There is time enough.

CAPULET. Go, nurse, go with her. We'll to church tomorrow.
[*Exit* JULIET *and* NURSE.]

LADY CAPULET. We shall be short in our provision.[13]
'Tis now near night.

CAPULET.   Tush, I will stir about,
And all things shall be well, I warrant thee, wife.
40 Go thou to Juliet, help to deck up her.[14]
I'll not to bed tonight; let me alone.
I'll play the housewife for this once. What, ho![15]
They are all forth; well, I will walk myself
❺ To County Paris, to prepare up him
45 Against tomorrow. My heart is wondrous light,
Since this same <u>wayward</u> girl is so reclaimed.
[*Exit with* MOTHER.]

Scene iii. JULIET'S *chamber.*

[*Enter* JULIET *and* NURSE.]

❼ **JULIET.** Ay, those attires are best; but, gentle nurse,
I pray thee leave me to myself tonight;
For I have need of many orisons[1]

---

7. **behests:** Requests.
8. **fall prostrate:** Lie face down in humble submission.

9. **becomèd:** Suitable; proper.

10. **bound:** Indebted.

11. **closet:** Private room.
12. **ornaments:** Clothes.

13. **short . . . provision:** Lacking time for preparation.

14. **deck up her:** Dress her; get her ready.

15. **What, ho!:** Capulet is calling for his servants.

◆ **Literary Focus**
What is ironic about Lord Capulet's relief and joy? **❻**

1. **orisons:** Prayers.

Romeo and Juliet, Act IV, Scene iii ◆ 751

◆ **Literary Focus**

❸ Dramatic Irony Point out that Capulet states that the whole city is indebted to the Friar. Ask: How is this an example of dramatic irony? *Capulet thinks that the Friar has convinced Juliet to marry Paris, but the audience knows that the Friar is helping Juliet avoid the marriage to Paris.*

◆ **Reading Strategy**

❹ Predict Ask: How might the change in the wedding date affect the outcome of the Friar's plan? *Elicit from students that the change in date gives the Friar less time to notify Romeo, and so Romeo might not be at the tomb when Juliet awakes.*

Comprehension Check ☑

❺ Why does Capulet say that he will go tell Paris? *All the servants are gone, either inviting guests to the wedding or making other preparations.*

◆ **Literary Focus**

❻ Dramatic Irony Capulet is joyous because he believes his daughter is going to marry Paris the following day according to his wishes when, in fact, the change of the date and haste of the marriage is going to bring tragedy to his family.

Comprehension Check ☑

❼ Why does Juliet tell the Nurse to leave her to herself? *Juliet does not want the Nurse to stop her from drinking the potion.*

Cross-Curricular Connection: Social Studies

Renaissance Weddings Act IV involves preparations for Juliet's wedding. Since the Capulets were an upper-class family, the Renaissance wedding would have been quite elaborate. Have interested students research Renaissance wedding celebrations. Some questions they might like to consider include:

• Where would the actual ceremony take place?

• Who would perform the ceremony?

• What kind of clothing would the bridal party and guests wear?

• What kind of food would be served and what kind of entertainment would occur?

• How long would the celebration last?

After students have done their research, have them share their findings with the class. In addition, encourage students of various cultural backgrounds to share and compare their wedding customs with the class.

To move the heavens to smile upon my state,[2]
5   Which, well thou knowest, is cross[3] and full of sin.

[*Enter* MOTHER.]

LADY CAPULET. What are you busy, ho? Need you my help?

JULIET. No, madam; we have culled[4] such necessaries
As are behoveful[5] for our state tomorrow.
So please you, let me now be left alone,
10   And let the nurse this night sit up with you:
For I am sure you have your hands full all
In this so sudden business.

❶ **LADY CAPULET.**   Good night.
Get thee to bed, and rest: for thou hast need.

[*Exit* MOTHER *and* NURSE.]

JULIET. Farewell! God knows when we shall meet again.
15   I have a faint cold fear thrills through my veins
That almost freezes up the heat of life.
I'll call them back again to comfort me.
Nurse!—What should she do here?
My <u>dismal</u> scene I needs must act alone.
20   Come, vial.
What if this mixture do not work at all?
Shall I be married then tomorrow morning?
No, no! This shall forbid it. Lie thou there.

[*Lays down a dagger.*]

❸   What if it be a poison which the friar
25   Subtly hath minist'red[6] to have me dead,
Lest in this marriage he should be dishonored
Because he married me before to Romeo?
I fear it is; and yet methinks it should not,
For he hath still been tried[7] a holy man.
30   How if, when I am laid into the tomb,
I wake before the time that Romeo
Come to redeem me? There's a fearful point!
Shall I not then be stifled in the vault,
To whose foul mouth no healthsome air breathes in,
35   And there die strangled ere my Romeo comes?
Or, if I live, is it not very like
The horrible conceit[8] of death and night,
Together with the terror of the place—
As in a vault, an ancient receptacle
40   Where for this many hundred years the bones
Of all my buried ancestors are packed;

752 ◆ *Drama*

2. state: Condition.
3. cross: Selfish; disobedient.

4. culled: Chosen.
5. behoveful: Desirable; appropriate.

◆ **Reading Strategy**
What do you predict will happen to Juliet? Do you think that everything will turn out as she and the Friar planned? ❷

6. minist'red: Given me.

7. tried: Proved.

8. conceit: Idea; thought.

◆ **Build Vocabulary**
dismal (diz´ məl) *adj.*: Causing gloom or misery

Beyond the Classroom

Career Connection
Pharmacology Central to Act IV is the potion given to Juliet by the Friar. In Act IV, Romeo visits an apothecary to get a remedy. Nowadays, "potions" would be dispensed by a pharmacist, the modern equivalant of an apothecary. Today, the demand for pharmacists is high as pharmacies are now found in grocery stores and discount department stores, as well as in drugstore chains and hospitals. Have interested students investigate the field of pharmacy, focusing on qualifications, job description, responsibilities, and salary.

 ◀ **Critical Viewing** Juliet decides to take Friar Laurence's potion despite her fears and misgivings. Do you think her decision is courageous. Why or why not? [Evaluate]

4 Evaluate Sample responses: *Yes, her decision is courageous because she is not sure that the plan will work but she believes that this is her only chance for happiness with Romeo. No, her decision is foolish because she is not certain that the Friar is trustworthy and there are too many ways the plan can go awry.*

5 Clarification Students might be confused by Juliet's apparently telling the ghost of Tybalt to stay. Tell them that in this context, *stay* means "stop."

Where bloody Tybalt, yet but green in earth,[9]
Lies fest'ring in his shroud; where, as they say,
At some hours in the night spirits resort—
45 Alack, alack, is it not like[10] that I,
So early waking—what with loathsome smells,
And shrieks like mandrakes[11] torn out of the earth,
That living mortals, hearing them, run mad—
O, if I wake, shall I not be distraught,[12]
50 Environèd[13] with all these hideous fears,
And madly play with my forefathers' joints,
And pluck the mangled Tybalt from his shroud,
And, in this rage, with some great kinsman's bone
As with a club dash out my desp'rate brains?
55 O, look! Methinks I see my cousin's ghost
Seeking out Romeo, that did spit his body
Upon a rapier's point. Stay, Tybalt, stay!
Romeo, Romeo, Romeo, I drink to thee.
[*She falls upon her bed within the curtains.*]

9. **green in earth:** Newly entombed.

10. **like:** Likely.

11. **mandrakes:** Plants with forked roots that resemble human legs. The mandrake was believed to shriek when uprooted and cause the hearer to go mad.
12. **distraught:** Insane.
13. **Environèd:** Surrounded.

Scene iv. *Hall in* CAPULET'S *house.*

[*Enter* LADY OF THE HOUSE *and* NURSE.]

LADY CAPULET. Hold, take these keys and fetch more spices, nurse.

NURSE. They call for dates and quinces[1] in the pastry.[2]

[*Enter old* CAPULET.]

CAPULET. Come, stir, stir, stir! The second cock hath crowed,
5 The curfew bell hath rung, 'tis three o'clock.
Look to the baked meats, good Angelica;[3]
Spare not for cost.

NURSE. Go, you cotquean,[4] go,
Get you to bed! Faith, you'll be sick tomorrow
For this night's watching.[5]

1. **quinces:** Golden apple-shaped fruit.
2. **pastry:** Baking room.
3. **Angelica:** This is probably the Nurse's name.
4. **cotquean** (kät′ kwēn): Man who does housework.
5. **watching:** Staying awake.

◆ **Build Vocabulary**
loathsome (lōth′ səm) *adj.*: Disgusting

Romeo and Juliet, Act IV, Scene iv ◆ 753

 Humanities: Film

Juliet Praying, scene from the film by Franco Zeffirelli.

Juliet kneels as she prays in this scene from the Zeffirelli film. The image of the young girl praying moves the hearts of the audience to feel pity and grief for her impending tragic fate.

Use the following questions for discussion:
1. Look at Juliet's expression. What emotion or emotions is she experiencing? *Students may*

say that Juliet's expression reflects her fear of death, her love for Romeo, and her intense desire to find a way out of her desperate situation.

2. What elements of the setting help to reinforce these emotions? *Students may say the dimly lit atmosphere emphasizes the impending tragedy; Juliet's white robes emphasize her youth and purity.*

CAPULET. No, not a whit. What, I have watched ere now
10   All night for lesser cause, and ne'er been sick.

LADY CAPULET. Ay, you have been a mouse hunt[6] in your time;
But I will watch you from such watching now.

[*Exit* LADY *and* NURSE.]

6. **mouse hunt:** Woman chaser.

CAPULET. A jealous hood,[7] a jealous hood!

7. **jealous hood:** Jealousy.

[*Enter three or four* FELLOWS *with spits and logs and baskets.*]
Now, fellow,
What is there?

15   FIRST FELLOW. Things for the cook, sir; but I know not what.

CAPULET. Make haste, make haste.   [*Exit* FIRST FELLOW.]
Sirrah, fetch drier logs.
Call Peter; he will show thee where they are.

SECOND FELLOW. I have a head, sir, that will find out logs
20   And never trouble Peter for the matter.

CAPULET. Mass,[8] and well said; a merry whoreson, ha!
Thou shalt be loggerhead.[9]   [*Exit* SECOND FELLOW, *with the others.*]
Good faith, 'tis day.
The County will be here with music straight,
For so he said he would.   [*Play music.*] |❸
25   I hear him near.
Nurse! Wife! What, ho! What, nurse, I say!

[*Enter* NURSE.]
Go waken Juliet; go and trim her up.
I'll go and chat with Paris. Hie, make haste,
Make haste! The bridegroom he is come already:
30   Make haste, I say.   [*Exit.*]

8. **Mass:** By the Mass (an oath).
9. **loggerhead:** Blockhead.

◆ **Literary Focus**
How is the bustle and excitement in the Capulet household an example of dramatic irony? |❶

Scene v. JULIET'S *chamber.*

NURSE. Mistress! What, mistress! Juliet! Fast,[1] I warrant her, she.
Why, lamb! Why, lady! Fie, you slugabed.[2]
Why, love, I say! Madam; Sweetheart! Why, bride!
What, not a word? You take your pennyworths now;
5   Sleep for a week; for the next night, I warrant,
The County Paris hath set up his rest
That you shall rest but little. God forgive me!
Marry, and amen. How sound is she asleep!
I needs must wake her. Madam, madam, madam!
10   Ay, let the County take you in your bed;
He'll fright you up, i' faith. Will it not be?

1. **Fast:** Fast asleep.
2. **slugabed:** Sleepy head.

754 ◆ *Drama*

I needs must wake her. Madam, madam, madam!

[*Draws aside the curtains.*]

What, dressed, and in your clothes, and down again?[3]

I must needs wake you. Lady! Lady! Lady!

15 Alas, alas! Help, help! My lady's dead!

O weraday that ever I was born!

Some *aqua vitae*, ho! My lord! My lady!

[*Enter* MOTHER.]

LADY CAPULET. What noise is here?

NURSE.   O lamentable day!

LADY CAPULET. What is the matter?

NURSE.   Look, look! O heavy day!

20 **LADY CAPULET.** O me, O me! My child, my only life!

Revive, look up, or I will die with thee!

Help, help! Call help.

[*Enter* FATHER.]

CAPULET. For shame, bring Juliet forth; her lord is come.

NURSE. She's dead, deceased; she's dead, alack the day!

LADY CAPULET. Alack the day, she's dead, she's dead, she's dead!

25 **CAPULET.** Ha! Let me see her. Out alas! She's cold,

Her blood is settled, and her joints are stiff;

Life and these lips have long been separated.

Death lies on her like an untimely frost

30 Upon the sweetest flower of all the field.

NURSE. O lamentable day!

LADY CAPULET.   O woeful time!

CAPULET. Death, that hath ta'en her hence to make me wail,

Ties up my tongue and will not let me speak.

[*Enter* FRIAR LAURENCE *and the* COUNTY PARIS, *with* MUSICIANS.]

FRIAR. Come, is the bride ready to go to church?

35 **CAPULET.** Ready to go, but never to return.

O son, the night before thy wedding day

Hath Death lain with thy wife. There she lies,

Flower as she was, deflowerèd by him.

Death is my son-in-law, Death is my heir;

40 My daughter he hath wedded. I will die

And leave him all. Life, living, all is Death's.

3. **down again:** Back in bed.

Romeo and Juliet, Act IV, Scene v ◆ 755

Comprehension Check ☑

5 What are Lady Capulet and the Nurse trying to do? *They are trying to revive Juliet.*

◆ **Critical Thinking**

6 Analyze Ask students the meaning of Capulet's simile, "Death lies on her like an untimely frost." *Capulet is saying that Juliet has died before she has lived a complete life, like a flower that is not yet in full bloom being killed by an early frost.*

PARIS. Have I thought, love, to see this morning's face,
And doth it give me such a sight as this?

LADY CAPULET. Accursed, unhappy, wretched, hateful day!
45 Most miserable hour that e'er time saw
In lasting labor of his pilgrimage!
But one, poor one, one poor and loving child,
But one thing to rejoice and solace⁴ in,
And cruel Death hath catched it from my sight.

50 **NURSE.** O woe! O woeful, woeful, woeful day!
Most lamentable day, most woeful day
That ever ever I did yet behold!
O day, O day, O day! O hateful day!
Never was seen so black a day as this.
55 O woeful day! O woeful day!

❶ **PARIS.** Beguiled,⁵ divorcèd, wrongèd, spited, slain!
Most detestable Death, by thee beguiled,
By cruel, cruel thee quite overthrown.
O love! O life!—not life, but love in death!

60 **CAPULET.** Despised, distressèd, hated, martyred, killed!
Uncomfortable⁶ time, why cam'st thou now
To murder, murder our solemnity?⁷
O child, O child! My soul, and not my child!
Dead art thou—alack, my child is dead,
❷ 65 And with my child my joys are burièd!

FRIAR. Peace, ho, for shame! Confusion's cure lives not
In these confusions.⁸ Heaven and yourself
Had part in this fair maid—now heaven hath all,
And all the better is it for the maid.
70 Your part in her you could not keep from death,
But heaven keeps his part in eternal life.
The most you sought was her promotion,
For 'twas your heaven she should be advanced;
And weep ye now, seeing she is advanced
75 Above the clouds, as high as heaven itself?
O, in this love, you love your child so ill
That you run mad, seeing that she is well.⁹
❸ She's not well married that lives married long,
But she's best married that dies married young.
80 Dry up your tears and stick your rosemary¹⁰
On this fair corse, and, as the custom is,
And in her best array bear her to church:
For though fond nature¹¹ bids us all lament,

4. **solace:** Find comfort.

5. **Beguiled:** Cheated.

6. **Uncomfortable:** Painful, upsetting.
7. **solemnity:** Solemn rites.

8. **Confusion's . . . confusions:** The remedy for this calamity is not to be found in these outcries.

9. **well:** Blessed in heaven.
10. **rosemary:** An evergreen signifying love and remembrance.
11. **fond nature:** Mistake-prone human nature.

◆ **Build Vocabulary**
pilgrimage (pil′ grəm ij) *n.*: Long journey

756 ◆ *Drama*

Humanities: Theater Design

The Globe Theater

Many of Shakespeare's plays, were originally staged at London's Globe theater—a large, roofless, wooden building with a raised stage at one end of a central courtyard. Wealthy viewers sat in galleries along the sides, while poor people, or "groundlings," crowded around the stage, yelling and throwing things at actors they did not like.

At the rear of the *main stage* was an open room called the *inner below,* for intimate indoor scenes. A balcony, the *above,* was set above this room. Painted backdrops and simple props—like a throne or a table—were used instead of elaborate sets. Refer students to the feature on the Globe on pages 666–667.

Use the following questions for discussion:
1. In what performance areas would scenes from *Romeo and Juliet,* such as the duel scene, the balcony scene, or the tomb scene have taken place? *Duel scene—main stage; balcony scene—the above; tomb scene—inner below.*

scene—*inner below.*
2. Compare and contrast the Globe with modern theaters. *Comparisons: A modern theater has a raised stage, with higher-priced ticket holders having a better view. Some modern productions have sparse sets. Contrasts: A modern theater has only one playing area. All audience members remain seated and quiet. Some modern productions have elaborate sets.*

Yet nature's tears are reason's merriment.[12]

85 **CAPULET.** All things that we ordainèd festival[13]
Turn from their office to black funeral—
❹ Our instruments to melancholy bells,
Our wedding cheer to a sad burial feast;
Our solemn hymns to sullen dirges[14] change;
90 Our bridal flowers serve for a buried corse;
And all things change them to the contrary.

FRIAR. Sir, go you in; and, madam, go with him;
And go, Sir Paris. Everyone prepare
To follow this fair corse unto her grave.
95 The heavens do low'r[15] upon you for some ill;
Move them no more by crossing their high will.

[*Exit, casting rosemary on her and shutting the curtains.
The* NURSE *and* MUSICIANS *remain.*]

FIRST MUSICIAN. Faith, we may put up our pipes and be gone.

NURSE. Honest good fellows, ah, put up, put up!
For well you know this is a pitiful case.[16]   [*Exit*]

100 **FIRST MUSICIAN.** Ay, by my troth, the case may be amended.

[*Enter* PETER.]

PETER. Musicians, O, musicians, "Heart's ease," "Heart's ease"! O, and
you will have me live, play "Heart's ease."

FIRST MUSICIAN. Why "Heart's ease"?

PETER. O, musicians, because my heart itself plays "My heart is full."
105 O, play me some merry dump[17] to comfort me.

FIRST MUSICIAN. Not a dump we! 'Tis no time to play now.

PETER. You will not then?

FIRST MUSICIAN. No.

PETER. I will then give it you soundly.

110 **FIRST MUSICIAN.** What will you give us?

PETER. No money, on my faith, but the gleek.[18] I will give you[19] the
minstrel.[20]

FIRST MUSICIAN. Then will I give you the serving-creature.

PETER. Then will I lay the serving-creature's dagger on your pate.
115 I will carry no crotchets.[21] I'll *re* you, I'll *fa* you. Do you note me?

FIRST MUSICIAN. And you *re* us and *fa* us, you note us.

SECOND MUSICIAN. Pray you put up your dagger, and put out your wit.

Romeo and Juliet, Act IV, Scene v ◆ 757

12. Yet . . . merriment:
While human nature causes
us to weep for Juliet,
reason should cause us to
be happy (since she is in
heaven).
13. ordainèd festival:
Planned to be part of a
celebration.
14. dirges: Funeral hymns.

◆ **Literary Focus**
What is ironic about
Friar Laurence saying
in line 84 that
"nature's tears are
reason's merriment"?   ❺

15. low'r: Frown.

16. case: Situation;
instrument case.

17. dump: Sad tune.

18. gleek: Scornful speech.
19. give you: Call you.
20. minstrel: A
contemptuous term (as
opposed to *musician*).

21. crotchets: Whim;
quarter notes.

◆ **Build Grammar Skills**
❹ **Parallel Structure** Have students identify the parallel structure in Capulet's speech and explain its effect. *"Our instruments to . . . , Our wedding cheer to . . . , Our solemn hymns to . . ."; the parallel structure emphasizes how each symbol of happiness has changed to a symbol of sadness.*

◆ **Literary Focus**
❺ **Dramatic Irony** The Friar is telling them that they should not be weeping because Juliet's in heaven, even though he knows that Juliet is not dead. The irony is that the Friar doesn't realize that soon Juliet will really be dead, and he will be responsible.

Speaking and Listening Mini-Lesson

Renaissance Music Presentation

This mini-lesson supports the Speaking and Listening activity in the Idea Bank on page 759.

Introduce the Concept Tell students that a music presentation requires that they choose and organize information to present to a group. Remind students that every generation has its own style of music, and the Renaissance was no exception. Have students discuss possible sources for Renaissance music material.

Develop Background Have students discuss the elements of a successful oral presentation. Elicit the following:

• Consider the purpose: What kind of information about Renaissance music should be included?

• Consider the audience: How many recordings will be needed to provide insight into Renaissance music?

• Organize the material so that samples of music flow naturally from the facts that the speaker imparts.

• Entertain questions from the audience to clarify points or to satisfy curiosity.

Apply the Information After students have done their research, they should develop and deliver their presentation.

Assess the Outcome Listeners can evaluate the presentation, considering purpose, audience, organization, and ability to handle questions.

758

❶ Clarification Explain that the scene with the musicians, culminating with their decision to have dinner, is a reminder that life goes on for the many, even when a few have suffered a great tragedy.

👂 Listening to Literature Audiocassettes Now that students have read and discussed Act IV of *Romeo and Juliet*, invite them to listen to the audiocassette recording. Remind them that they can bring to their listening experience all that they have learned about dramatic irony.

Reinforce and Extend

Answers
◆ *Literature and Your Life*

Reader's Response Encourage students to consider the possibilities as well as the probabilities. Ask students what could unexpectedly happen to ruin Friar Lawrence's plan.

Thematic Focus Encourage students to discuss various types of situations, such as those involving parents and other relatives, teachers, and friends.

☑ **Check Your Comprehension**

1. Friar Lawrence will give Juliet a potion to make her fall into a coma for forty-two hours. She will be placed in the tomb. Friar Lawrence will call Romeo and the Friar and Romeo will be in the tomb when Juliet wakes. Romeo will then take her back to Mantua.
2. The potion may not work; it may kill her; she may wake up before Romeo comes.

◆ **Critical Thinking**

1. The soliloquy reveals that Juliet is somewhat fearful and inclined to weigh probabilities before making a decision. It also reveals that she has the courage to do what is most frightening.
2. Suggested response: Juliet has developed a more mature and serious outlook. She is no longer a little girl, but a woman in love and determined not to be married to someone other than Romeo.
3. Suggested response: Paris is not worthy of Juliet because he is selfishly concerned only with his own

---

Then have at you with my wit!

120 **PETER.** I will dry-beat you with an iron wit, and put up my iron dagger. Answer me like men.

"When griping grief the heart doth wound,
    And doleful dumps the mind oppress,
        Then music with her silver sound"—

125 Why "silver sound"? Why "music with her silver sound"? What say you, Simon Catling?

FIRST MUSICIAN. Marry, sir, because silver hath a sweet sound.

PETER. Pretty! What say you, Hugh Rebeck?

130 **SECOND MUSICIAN.** I say "silver sound" because musicians sound for silver.

PETER. Pretty too! What say you, James Soundpost?

135 **THIRD MUSICIAN.** Faith, I know not what to say.

PETER. O, I cry you mercy,[22] you are the singer. I will say for you. It is "music with her silver sound" because musicians have no gold for sounding.

"Then music with her silver sound
    With speedy help doth lend redress." [*Exit.*]

FIRST MUSICIAN. What a pestilent knave is this same!

❶ 140 **SECOND MUSICIAN.** Hang him, Jack! Come, we'll in here, tarry for the mourners, and stay dinner.

[*Exit with others.*]

22. cry you mercy: Beg your pardon.

Guide for Responding

◆ *Literature and Your Life*

Reader's Response Should Romeo and Juliet have followed Friar Lawrence's advice? Why or why not?

Thematic Focus When is it better to work things out through a direct confrontation? When is it better to use indirect means?

☑ **Check Your Comprehension**

1. Describe Friar Lawrence's plan for Juliet.
2. What three fears rise up in Juliet just before she drinks the potion?

◆ **Critical Thinking**

INTERPRET
1. What does Juliet's soliloquy in Scene iii reveal about her personality? **[Interpret]**
2. How has Juliet's character developed since the start of the play? Support your answer. **[Draw Conclusions]**
3. Do you think Paris is worthy of Juliet? Explain. **[Analyze]**

EVALUATE
4. Evaluate Friar Lawrence's plan. What do you anticipate might go wrong with it? **[Assess]**

758 ◆ *Drama*

---

happiness and not that of Juliet.
4. Suggested response: The plan is complicated and risky. The potion may not work; Romeo may receive the message too late; the potion may kill Juliet; Romeo may not arrive at the tomb in time.

Guide for Responding (continued)

◆ Literary Focus

DRAMATIC IRONY

Dramatic irony is a contradiction between what a character thinks, says, or does and what the audience or reader knows to be true. Because the audience has knowledge that the characters do not, it can foresee events to come even as the characters rush blindly toward their fate.

1. How is Juliet's meeting with Paris in Friar Lawrence's cell an example of dramatic irony?
2. Review Scene iv, in which Capulet is preparing for Juliet's wedding to Paris. What makes this scene an example of dramatic irony?
3. Find at least one other example of dramatic irony in the first four acts. Explain the example.

◆ Build Grammar Skills

PARALLEL STRUCTURE

Shakespeare often uses **parallel structures**—such as strings of similarly constructed sentences or phrases—to emphasize similar ideas.

Writing Application Rewrite the following to include a series of questions with parallel structures.

> Just before she drinks the Friar's potion, Juliet is tormented by questions. She asks herself what will happen if the mixture does not work. Voicing her worst fears, Juliet wonders whether the potion is poison. In agony, she finds herself contemplating what might happen if she wakes before Romeo arrives.

◆ Reading Strategy

PREDICT

You can **predict**—or make educated guesses about—the direction of future events in a literary work by considering what you know about the characters and thinking about how they'd be most likely to respond to their situations. You can also use **foreshadowing**—clues about events yet to occur—to help you in making predictions.

1. Find at least three examples of foreshadowing in the first four acts and explain how each example can help you predict future events.
2. What do you predict will happen in the final act?

◆ Build Vocabulary

USING THE SUFFIX -ward

Knowing that the suffix -ward means "in a direction," match each word on the left with its meaning.

1. forward   **a.** in the direction of the sky
2. skyward   **b.** toward or on the outside
3. outward   **c.** in the direction of the front; ahead

USING THE WORD BANK

Complete each analogy with a word from the Word Bank.

1. ____?____ is to *gloomy* as *bright* is to *glistening*
2. ____?____ is to *commanded* as *requested* is to *asked*
3. *exhausted* is to *rested* as *beautiful* is to ____?____
4. *long* is to ____?____ as *destructive* is to *tornado*
5. *sedan* is to *car* as ____?____ is to *container*
6. *day* is to *night* as *obedient* is to ____?____
7. ____?____ is to *thoughtful* as *leaping* is to *jumping*

Idea Bank

Writing

1. **Love Letter** Create a love letter that Juliet might have written for Romeo to read if she were never to awaken. For a challenge, try using language similar to that spoken by Juliet in the play.

2. **Your Own Ending** If you were to write your own ending for the play, what would it be? Write a narrative of events that would occur in your version of Act V. Make sure that your version develops naturally out of the events in Acts I through IV.

Speaking and Listening

3. **Renaissance Music Presentation** Collect examples of the kind of music that would have been played by the musicians in Scene v. Using the recordings you collect, along with facts you obtain through library research, prepare and deliver an informal oral presentation on Renaissance music. **[Social Studies Link; Music Link]**

Romeo and Juliet, Act IV ◆ 759

◆ Literary Focus

1. When Juliet goes to Friar Lawrence for help in avoiding a marriage with Paris, she finds him there arranging for the ceremony.
2. The entire household is busy and in good humor, getting ready for a large and happy wedding. They do not know, as the audience does, that Juliet has taken the potion and that the wedding will turn into a funeral.
3. Sample response: In the scene at the beginning of Act II, Romeo goes to the orchard to be near Juliet, and Mercutio teases him by talking about Rosaline.

✓ ASSESSMENT OPTIONS

Formal Assessment, pp. 173–175.
Alternative Assessment, p. 47.
PORTFOLIO ASSESSMENT
Use the following rubrics in the *Alternative Assessment* booklet:
Love Letter: Expression Rubric, p. 87
Your Own Ending: Narration: Fictional Narrative Rubric, p. 88

Answers

◆ Build Grammar Skills

Writing Application: Students should begin sentences two through four with the same grammatical form, such as "She asks herself . . .".

 *Writer's Solution*

For additional instruction and practice, use the lesson in the **Language Lab CD-ROM** on Varying Sentence Structure and Combining Sentences.

◆ Reading Strategy

1. Sample responses: In Act I, Tybalt's promise that he will challenge Romeo helps predict a future confrontation. In Act I, the fears that Romeo and Juliet express when they learn each other's identities help predict future problems. In Act IV, Juliet's fears concerning Friar Lawrence's plan help predict real difficulties.
2. Some students may predict tragedy because of the gloomy foreshadowing thus far.

◆ Build Vocabulary

Using the Suffix -ward
1. c   2. a   3. b

Using the Word Bank
1. dismal;   2. enjoined;   3. loathsome;   4. pilgrimage;   5. vial;   6. wayward;   7. pensive

🔲 Idea Bank

Customizing for
Performance Levels
Following are suggestions for matching the Idea Bank topics with your students' performance levels:
Less Advanced Students: 1
Average Students: 2
More Advanced Students: 3

Customizing for
Learning Modalities
Following are suggestions for matching Idea Bank topics with your students' learning modalities:
Verbal/Linguistic: 1, 2, 3
Musical/Rhythmic: 3

*G*uide for Reading, Act V

On the board, write: "Whatever can go wrong— will." Ask students what this means. *Students may say that it means that when you make plans, assume that something will go wrong, and figure out how to deal with it in advance.* Ask students to describe examples of times when things have gone wrong.

With the class, review Friar Lawrence's scheme for rejoining the two lovers. Then ask students to list everything they can think of that could go wrong. Did Friar Lawrence prepare to deal with any of these potential slip-ups when he devised his scheme?

◆ Review and Anticipate

You'll recall that in Act IV, Juliet escapes her unwanted marriage to Paris by taking a potion that puts her into a deathlike sleep for forty-two hours. Believing that she is dead, her family plans a funeral in place of her wedding. Having instructed Juliet to take the potion as part of a scheme to save her marriage to Romeo, Friar Lawrence sends a fellow friar to Mantua to tell Romeo about the plan of the ruse and to bring him back to rescue Juliet from her family tomb. What do you think might go wrong with Friar Lawrence's scheme?

◆ Literary Focus

TRAGEDY

A **tragedy** is a drama in which the central character meets with disaster or great misfortune. In the great tragedies of the past, including Shakespeare's, the central character's downfall is usually the result of fate, a serious character flaw, or a combination of the two. Other causes, however, may also be involved. Though flawed, the tragic hero or heroine is usually of noble stature and basically good. The downfall, therefore, always seems worse than what the character deserves. Yet a great tragedy is not depressing. It uplifts the audience by showing the greatness of spirit of which people are capable.

◆ Build Grammar Skills

SUBJECT AND VERB AGREEMENT IN INVERTED SENTENCES

Shakespeare's characters often use sentences with an **inverted word order**—sentences in which the verb comes before the subject. For example, Friar Lawrence uses a sentence with inverted word order in Act V when he asks, "What says Romeo?" When using inverted sentences such as this one, it is easy to make errors in **subject and verb agreement**. However, you can easily check to make sure that the subject agrees with its verb in number by changing the word order of the sentence so that the subject comes before the verb. Notice that if you change the order of the previous example to "Romeo says what?" you can clearly see that both the subject and the verb are singular.

◆ Reading Strategy

IDENTIFY CAUSES AND EFFECTS

A **cause** is an action, event, or situation that produces a result. An **effect** is the result produced by a cause. One way to understand a play or other kind of story is to analyze the chain of causes and effects that advances the plot. To do this, you need to notice how one event causes another event—its effect—and how that event in turn has its own effect.

Juliet takes the Friar's potion → Juliet falls into a deathlike sleep → Everyone thinks Juliet is dead →____ →____ →____

◆ Build Vocabulary

PREFIXES: *ambi-*

Toward the end of the fifth act of *The Tragedy of Romeo and Juliet*, the Prince speaks of clearing up ambiguities. The word *ambiguities* contains the prefix *ambi-*, which means "both." Notice how the meaning of the prefix contributes to the overall meaning of the word: "statements or events that have two or more possible meanings."

WORD BANK

Before you read, preview this list of words.

remnants
penury
haughty
sepulcher
ambiguities
scourge

Romeo and Juliet

Act V

Scene i. *Mantua. A street.*

[*Enter* ROMEO.]

ROMEO. If I may trust the flattering truth of sleep,[1]
My dreams presage[2] some joyful news at hand.
My bosom's lord[3] sits lightly in his throne,
And all this day an unaccustomed spirit
5 Lifts me above the ground with cheerful thoughts.
I dreamt my lady came and found me dead
(Strange dream that gives a dead man leave to think!)
And breathed such life with kisses in my lips
That I revived and was an emperor.
10 Ah me! How sweet is love itself possessed,
When but love's shadows[4] are so rich in joy!

❶

[*Enter* ROMEO'S MAN, BALTHASAR, *booted.*]

News from Verona! How now, Balthasar?
Dost thou not bring me letters from the friar?
How doth my lady? Is my father well?
15 How fares my Juliet? That I ask again,
For nothing can be ill if she be well.

MAN. Then she is well, and nothing can be ill.
Her body sleeps in Capels' monument,[5]
And her immortal part with angels lives.
❷ 20 I saw her laid low in her kindred's vault
And presently took post[6] to tell it you.
O, pardon me for bringing these ill news,
Since you did leave it for my office,[7] sir.

ROMEO. Is it e'en so? Then I defy you, stars!
25 Thou knowest my lodging. Get me ink and paper
And hire post horses. I will hence tonight.

MAN. I do beseech you, sir, have patience.
Your looks are pale and wild and do import
Some misadventure.[8]

ROMEO. Tush, thou art deceived.
30 Leave me and do the thing I bid thee do.
Hast thou no letters to me from the friar?

1. **flattering . . . sleep:** Pleasing illusions of dreams.
2. **presage:** Foretell.
3. **bosom's lord:** Heart.

4. **shadows:** Dreams; unreal images.

5. **Capels' monument:** The Capulets' burial vault.

6. **presently took post:** Immediately set out on horseback.
7. **office:** Duty.

8. **import/Some misadventure:** Suggest some misfortune.

Romeo and Juliet, Act V, Scene i ◆ 761

Customize for
More Advanced Students

Tell these students that according to the ancient Greek philosopher Aristotle's definition of tragedy, the tragic hero (or heroine) must be of noble stature, and the action must take place within a twenty-four hour period. In addition, the audience should feel such pity and fear at the end of the play that they experience a "catharsis" or cleansing of their emotions. In modern terms, we might say they feel "wrung out" by the intense emotions they experienced during the play. Have students meet in groups to discuss in which ways *Romeo and Juliet* meets or does not meet Aristotle's criteria for tragedy. They might also evolve their own definition for tragedy and compare and contrast it with Aristotle's.

◆ Build Grammar Skills

❶ Subject-Verb Agreement
Have students identify the subject of the verb *is*. Remind students to rearrange the word order to check for accuracy. *The subject is love. The sentence may be restated as: Love itself is [very] sweet when its [mere] shadows are so rich in joy!*

◆ Reading Strategy

❷ Identify Causes and Effects
Ask students what effects they predict will be set in motion by Balthasar's message. *Students might predict that Romeo will find out who is responsible for Juliet's death and kill that person; they might predict that he will kill himself. Accept all reasonable answers.*

Preparing for Standardized Tests

Reading and Vocabulary Identifying causes and effects will help students improve their performance on the reading comprehension portions of standardized tests. For more practice, use the Reading Strategy page in *Selection Support,* p. 206.

The Build Vocabulary lesson focuses on using the prefix *ambi-* to help students determine meanings of words such as *ambivalent* and *ambidextrous.* Students can apply this skill to vocabulary items on standardized tests. For additional practice, use the Build Vocabulary page in *Selection Support,* p. 204.

Grammar and Language Portions of some standardized tests require students to identify subject-verb agreement in inverted sentences.

Choose the correct sentence in each pair: *(A)*
    (A) Have Romeo and Juliet met yet?
    (B) Has Romeo and Juliet met yet?

The Build Grammar Skills lesson for this selection focuses on this topic. For additional practice, use the Build Grammar Skills page on Subject and Verb Agreement in Inverted Sentences, p. 205, in *Selection Support.*

◆ Literary Focus

❶ Tragedy Unfortunately for Friar Lawrence's plan, Balthasar saw Juliet's funeral and intercepted Romeo before the Friar's explanation could reach him. Romeo's remark "Then I defy you, stars!" suggests he believes that fate has played a role in events, and that he plans to do something that will spare him from the fate of a life without Juliet. A series of events that render a tragic outcome inevitable has been set in motion.

◆ Build Grammar Skills

❷ Subject-Verb Agreement Have students identify the subject and verb in "Meager were his looks." Ask them to change the word order so that the subject and verb are easier to identify. *The subject is* looks, *and the verb is* were. *The sentence could also read, "His looks were meager."*

Comprehension Check ☑

❸ Ask students what Romeo has asked the apothecary to supply. *Romeo wants a quick-acting poison that will bring about a speedy death.*

Customize for
Visual/Spatial Learners

Have visual/spatial learners use the descriptive details in Romeo's speech to draw a sketch of the apothecary's shop.

MAN. No, my good lord.

ROMEO. No matter. Get thee gone.
And hire those horses. I'll be with thee straight.

Well, Juliet, I will lie with thee tonight.   [*Exit* BALTHASAR.]
35 Let's see for means. O mischief, thou art swift
To enter in the thoughts of desperate men!
I do remember an apothecary,[9]
And hereabouts 'a dwells, which late I noted
In tatt'red weeds, with overwhelming brows,
40 Culling of simples.[10] Meager were his looks, ❷
Sharp misery had worn him to the bones;
And in his needy shop a tortoise hung,
An alligator stuffed, and other skins
Of ill-shaped fishes; and about his shelves
45 A beggarly account[11] of empty boxes,
Green earthen pots, bladders, and musty seeds,
Remnants of packthread, and old cakes of roses[12]
Were thinly scattered, to make up a show.
Noting this penury, to myself I said,
50 "And if a man did need a poison now
Whose sale is present death in Mantua,
Here lives a caitiff[13] wretch would sell it him."
O, this same thought did but forerun my need,
And this same needy man must sell it me.
55 As I remember, this should be the house.
Being holiday, the beggar's shop is shut.
What, ho! Apothecary!

[*Enter* APOTHECARY.]

❸ **APOTHECARY.** Who calls so loud?

ROMEO. Come hither, man. I see that thou art poor.
Hold, there is forty ducats.[14] Let me have
60 A dram of poison, such soon-speeding gear[15]
As will disperse itself through all the veins
That the life-weary taker may fall dead,
And that the trunk[16] may be discharged of breath
As violently as hasty powder fired
65 Doth hurry from the fatal cannon's womb.

APOTHECARY. Such mortal drugs I have; but Mantua's law
Is death to any he that utters[17] them.

ROMEO. Art thou so bare and full of wretchedness
And fearest to die? Famine is in thy cheeks,

762 ◆ Drama

◆ Literary Focus

How does the exchange between Romeo and the man suggest the role of fate in bringing about the tragedy? ❶

9. **apothecary:** One who prepares and sells drugs and medicines.

10. **In tatt'red . . . simples:** In torn clothing, with overhanging eyebrows, sorting out herbs.

11. **beggarly account:** Small number.

12. **cakes of roses:** Pressed rose petals (used for perfume).

13. **caitiff:** Miserable.

14. **ducats:** Gold coins.
15. **soon-speeding gear:** Fast-working stuff.

16. **trunk:** Body.
17. **utters:** Sells.

◆ Build Vocabulary

remnants (rem´ nənts) *n.:* Remaining persons or things
penury (pen´ yə rē) *n.:* Extreme poverty

Block Scheduling Strategies

Consider these suggestions to take advantage of extended class time:

- Students may listen to the audiocassette recording of *Romeo and Juliet*, focusing on the series of events that cause the tragedy.
- Have students complete the Writing Mini-Lesson (p. 777). They can share their persuasive letters in a group, evaluating them and discussing how they could be more persuasive.

- Have students complete the Letter from Juliet activity in *Alternative Assessment,* p. 48.
- Suggest that students who choose the Alternate Ending from the writing activities in the Idea Bank (p. 777) put together a cast to act out their endings.
- Have the students who choose the Set Design from the projects in the Idea Bank (p. 777) make a model based on their description.

- Encourage interested students who choose the Response to Literary Criticism from the writing activities in the Idea Bank (p. 777) to do further reading of works by literary critics about Shakespeare.
- Have students work in small groups on the Guide to Preventing Civil Strife, as described in *Alternative Assessment,* p. 48.

70   Need and oppression starveth in thy eyes.
      Contempt and beggary hangs upon thy back:
      The world is not thy friend, nor the world's law;
      The world affords no law to make thee rich;
      Then be not poor, but break it and take this.

75 **APOTHECARY.** My poverty but not my will consents.

    ROMEO. I pay thy poverty and not thy will.

    APOTHECARY. Put this in any liquid thing you will
      And drink it off, and if you had the strength
      Of twenty men, it would dispatch you straight.

80 **ROMEO.** There is thy gold—worse poison to men's souls,
      Doing more murder in this loathsome world,
      Than these poor compounds[18] that thou mayst not sell.

      18. compounds: Mixtures.

      I sell thee poison; thou hast sold me none.
      Farewell. Buy food and get thyself in flesh.
85   Come, cordial[19] and not poison, go with me
      To Juliet's grave; for there must I use thee.

      [*Exit.*]

      19. cordial: Health-giving drink.

Scene ii. FRIAR LAURENCE'S *cell.*

[*Enter* FRIAR JOHN *to* FRIAR LAURENCE.]

    JOHN. Holy Franciscan friar, brother, ho!

[*Enter* FRIAR LAURENCE.]

    LAURENCE. This same should be the voice of Friar John.
      Welcome from Mantua. What says Romeo?
      Or, if his mind be writ, give me his letter.

5   **JOHN.** Going to find a barefoot brother out,
      One of our order, to associate[1] me

      1. associate: Accompany.

      Here in this city visiting the sick,
      And finding him, the searchers[2] of the town,
      Suspecting that we both were in a house

      2. searchers: Health officers who search for victims of the plague.

10   Where the infectious pestilence did reign,
      Sealed up the doors, and would not let us forth,
      So that my speed to Mantua there was stayed.

    LAURENCE. Who bare my letter, then, to Romeo?

    JOHN. I could not send it—here it is again—
15   Nor get a messenger to bring it thee,
      So fearful were they of infection.

    LAURENCE. Unhappy fortune! By my brotherhood,

> ◆ **Reading Strategy**
> What do you think will be the effects of the failure of Friar John to deliver the letter to Romeo?

Romeo and Juliet, Act V, Scene ii ◆ 763

Cross-Curricular Connection: Science

For thousands of years, herbs and spices have been used to enhance the flavor of foods and to cure ailments. The healing properties of herbs were well known in ancient Greece, and indeed, some herbal remedies are still used today. Gentian roots, for example, are used as a stomach medicine, and balm tea is used to reduce fever. The Chinese use ginseng root to treat many illnesses. Tansy, on the other hand, is rarely used as medicine today—it is far too poisonous.

However, it is still used as a substitute for mothballs or flea powder.

In Shakespeare's time, apothecaries dispensed myriad herbal remedies. Fresh or dried herb sprigs steeped in alcohol, vinegar, or oil were taken as an elixir; strained liquids were ingested as tea.

Have interested students do research to find out which herbs and natural ingredients are used today in the treatment of various illnesses.

Sidebar (teacher notes):

◆ **Critical Thinking**

❷ **Assess** Have students assess Paris's behavior and express their opinions over whether his sorrow seems genuine. *Some students will say that Paris seems genuinely grieved over the loss of Juliet. Other students will say that Paris is in love with the idea of being in love, and is simply being melodramatic. They might liken Paris's behavior to Romeo's mooning over Rosaline at the beginning of the play.*

❶
20
The letter was not nice,[3] but full of charge,
Of dear import;[4] and the neglecting it
May do much danger. Friar John, go hence,
Get me an iron crow and bring it straight
Unto my cell.

JOHN.   Brother, I'll go and bring it thee.   [*Exit.*]

LAURENCE. Now must I to the monument alone.
Within this three hours will fair Juliet wake.
25
She will beshrew[5] me much that Romeo
Hath had no notice of these accidents;[6]
But I will write again to Mantua,
And keep her at my cell till Romeo come—
Poor living corse, closed in a dead man's tomb!   [*Exit.*]

3. **nice:** Trivial.

4. **full of charge, Of dear import:** Urgent and important.

5. **beshrew:** Blame.

6. **accidents:** Happenings.

Scene iii. *A churchyard; in it a monument belonging to the* CAPULETS

[*Enter* PARIS *and his* PAGE *with flowers and sweet water.*]

PARIS. Give me thy torch, boy. Hence, and stand aloof.[1]
Yet put it out, for I would not be seen.
Under yond yew trees lay thee all along,[2]
Holding thy ear close to the hollow ground.
5
So shall no foot upon the churchyard tread
(Being loose, unfirm, with digging up of graves)
But thou shalt hear it. Whistle then to me,
As signal that thou hearest something approach.
Give me those flowers. Do as I bid thee, go.

10 **PAGE.** [*Aside*] I am almost afraid to stand alone
Here in the churchyard; yet I will adventure.[3]   [*Retires.*]

1. **aloof:** Apart.

2. **lay . . . along:** Lie down flat.

3. **adventure:** Chance it.

❷
15
PARIS. Sweet flower, with flowers thy bridal bed I strew
(O woe! thy canopy is dust and stones)
Which with sweet[4] water nightly I will dew;
Or, wanting that, with tears distilled by moans.
The obsequies[5] that I for thee will keep
Nightly shall be to strew thy grave and weep.

4. **sweet:** Perfumed.

5. **obsequies:** Memorial ceremonies.

[*Whistle* BOY.]

The boy gives warning something doth approach.
What cursèd foot wanders this way tonight
20
To cross[6] my obsequies and true love's rite?
What, with a torch? Muffle me, night, awhile.   [*Retires.*]

6. **cross:** Interrupt.

[*Enter* ROMEO, *and* BALTHASAR *with a torch, a mattock, and a crow of iron.*]

ROMEO. Give me that mattock and the wrenching iron.

Hold, take this letter. Early in the morning
See thou deliver it to my lord and father.
25 Give me the light. Upon thy life I charge thee,
Whate'er thou hearest or seest, stand all aloof
And do not interrupt me in my course.
Why I descend into this bed of death
Is partly to behold my lady's face,
30 But chiefly to take thence from her dead finger
A precious ring—a ring that I must use
In dear employment.[7] Therefore hence, be gone.
But if thou, jealous,[8] dost return to pry
In what I farther shall intend to do,
35 By heaven, I will tear thee joint by joint
And strew this hungry churchyard with thy limbs.
The time and my intents are savage-wild,
More fierce and more inexorable[9] far
Than empty[10] tigers or the roaring sea.

40 **BALTHASAR.** I will be gone, sir, and not trouble ye.

ROMEO. So shalt thou show me friendship. Take thou that.
Live, and be prosperous; and farewell, good fellow.

7. dear employment:
Important business.
8. jealous: Curious.

9. inexorable:
Uncontrollable.
10. empty: Hungry.

 ▲ **Critical Viewing** What is Romeo thinking and feeling as he enters the Capulets' tomb? [Interpret]

Romeo and Juliet, Act V, Scene iii ◆ 765

Customize for
Less Proficient Readers

❸ Check that students understand Romeo's instructions to Balthasar by asking questions like the following: **What does Romeo want Balthasar to deliver?** *Romeo gives Balthasar a letter, and tells him to deliver it to his father.* **What do you think is the subject of the letter?** *Students may correctly guess that Romeo writes about his secret marriage to Juliet and explains why he plans to kill himself.* **What reason does Romeo give for breaking into the tomb?** *He needs to take a ring from Juliet's body because he requires the ring in important business.* **What does Romeo threaten to do if he catches Balthasar spying on him?** *He threatens to tear him limb from limb.* **Do you think that Balthasar believes Romeo's excuse and threat?** *Students may say that Balthasar is not convinced that Romeo merely intends to steal a ring, but is concerned that Romeo might beat him up if he catches him spying.* **Ask students to predict what Balthasar will do.** *Some students will predict that Balthasar will follow Romeo's orders. Other may say that Balthasar will hide somewhere and spy upon Romeo.*

▶Critical Viewing◀

❹ **Interpret** Students may say that Romeo is determined to die, and so he is fearless. He is furious at Juliet's death, and defiant of the fates he believes have conspired against him.

Humanities: Film

The movie still shows Romeo entering the recesses of the Capulet crypt. He has just arrived, breathless and distraught, from Mantua, and his worst fears are about to be realized as he interrupts Paris, mourning over Juliet.

Have students discuss the following questions:
1. What mixture of emotions are captured in the portrayal of Romeo here? *Have students share their ideas. Recall that Romeo has just said good-bye to his trusted friend and is facing Juliet's*

death as well as his own. Some may say that he is reaching for the pillar to steady himself as he enters the tomb.

2. How does Zeffirelli's vision of the tomb differ from what students imagine? *Students may have had a "creepier" tomb in mind. Have them share their own descriptions and discuss how the features of the tomb could be used to enhance the downward spiral of the tragedy.*

① Tragedy Students may say that Romeo's intention is especially tragic because his death will be so unnecessary. Some may add that his dead body will be discovered by Juliet when she wakes up.

◆ **Build Grammar Skills**

② Subject-Verb Agreement Have students identify the subject and verb in the sentence. Suggest that they paraphrase the sentence. *The subject is I, and the verb came. The sentence can be rearranged to read: "I must indeed, and that is why I came here."*

◆ **Critical Thinking**

③ Connect Point out that Romeo is rash and impulsive, but he is not murderous. Ask students to identify another point in the play where Romeo tried to avoid a fight. *In Act III, Scene i, Romeo tried to avoid dueling with Tybalt.* How are the two scenes similar? *In both scenes, Romeo says that he "loves" the other man, and has no wish to fight. However, Romeo and the other man end up fighting, and Romeo kills the other man.*

Customize for
Less Proficient Readers
Play the audiocassette recording so that less proficient readers can use the tone and escalation of the exchange between Romeo and Paris as clues to meaning.

🎧 **Listening to Literature Audiocassettes**

BALTHASAR. [*Aside*] For all this same, I'll hide me hereabout.
His looks I fear, and his intents I doubt. [*Retires.*]

45 **ROMEO.** Thou detestable maw,[11] thou womb of death,
Gorged with the dearest morsel of the earth,
Thus I enforce thy rotten jaws to open,
And in despite[12] I'll cram thee with more food.
[ROMEO *opens the tomb.*]

PARIS. This is that banished haughty Montague
50 That murd'red my love's cousin—with which grief
It is supposed the fair creature died—
And here is come to do some villainous shame
To the dead bodies. I will apprehend[13] him.
Stop thy unhallowèd toil, vile Montague!
55 Can vengeance be pursued further than death?
Condemnèd villain, I do apprehend thee.
Obey, and go with me; for thou must die.

② ROMEO. I must indeed; and therefore came I hither.
Good gentle youth, tempt not a desp'rate man.
60 Fly hence and leave me. Think upon these gone;
Let them affright thee. I beseech thee, youth,
Put not another sin upon my head
By urging me to fury. O, be gone!
By heaven, I love thee better than myself,
65 For I come hither armed against myself.
Stay not, be gone. Live, and hereafter say
A madman's mercy bid thee run away.

③ PARIS. I do defy thy conjurations.[14]
And apprehend thee for a felon[15] here.

70 **ROMEO.** Wilt thou provoke me? Then have at thee, boy!
[*They fight.*]

PAGE. O Lord, they fight! I will go call the watch.
[*Exit.* PARIS *falls.*]

PARIS. O, I am slain! If thou be merciful,
Open the tomb, lay me with Juliet. [*Dies.*]

ROMEO. In faith, I will. Let me peruse[16] this face.
75 Mercutio's kinsman, noble County Paris!
What said my man when my betossèd[17] soul
Did not attend[18] him as we rode? I think
He told me Paris should have married Juliet.
Said he not so, or did I dream it so?

11. **maw:** Stomach.

12. **despite:** Scorn.

◆ **Literary Focus**
Why is Romeo's intention to feed himself to the tomb especially tragic? **①**

13. **apprehend:** Seize; arrest.

14. **conjurations:** Solemn appeals.
15. **felon:** Criminal.

16. **peruse:** Look over.
17. **betossèd:** Upset.
18. **attend:** Give attention to.

◆ **Build Vocabulary**
haughty (hôt´ ē) *adj.:* Arrogant

766 ◆ *Drama*

►Critical Viewing◄

4 Support Juliet does not look as if she has been dead for two days. According to lines 94–95, her lips and cheeks are rosy, rather than pallid.

4 ▲ **Critical Viewing** In the tomb, Romeo pulls back the shroud to reveal what he thinks is Juliet's dead body. What clues about her appearance should have led him to realize she was still alive? **[Support]**

80 Or am I mad, hearing him talk of Juliet,
     To think it was so? O, give me thy hand,
     One writ with me in sour misfortune's book!
     I'll bury thee in a triumphant grave.
     A grave? O, no, a lanthorn,[19] slaught'red youth,
85   For here lies Juliet, and her beauty makes
     This vault a feasting presence[20] full of light.
     Death, lie thou there, by a dead man interred.

                                    [*Lays him in the tomb.*]

     How oft when men are at the point of death
     Have they been merry! Which their keepers[21] call
90   A lightning before death. O, how may I
     Call this a lightning? O my love, my wife!
     Death, that hath sucked the honey of thy breath,
     Hath had no power yet upon thy beauty.
     Thou art not conquered. Beauty's ensign[22] yet
95   Is crimson in thy lips and in thy cheeks,
     And death's pale flag is not advanced there.

19. lanthorn: Windowed structure on top of a room to admit light; also, a lantern.
20. feasting presence: Chamber fit for a celebration.

21. keepers: Jailers.

22. ensign: Banner.

Romeo and Juliet, Act V, Scene iii ◆ 767

 Humanities: Film

In this scene from Zeffirelli's *Romeo and Juliet* Romeo bids farewell to Juliet, promising to stay with her forever. Have students discuss the following questions:

1. How would you describe Romeo's demeanor in this scene? *Romeo's tender expression has a calming effect on the scene; he has up until now displayed rash behavior, exhibited wild mood* *swings, taken bold risks, jumped to conclusions. All of these actions have brought him to this moment of quiet tenderness.*

2. How does this scene reflect "the calm before the storm"? *Romeo's composure and control in this scene give way to the tragic, horrifying events that follow.*

❶ Tragedy "Death's pale flag is not advanced" in Juliet's face because she is not dead. In fact, her coloring suggests that the potion she took to feign the appearance of death is wearing off.

◆ **Critical Thinking**

❷ Draw Conclusions Ask students what might have happened if the argument and fight with Paris had lasted longer. *Students may suggest that Friar Lawrence would have had time to arrive; Juliet might have awakened.*

Customize for
Musical/Rhythmic Learners

❸ Pique the interest of these students by pointing out that Romeo's last words have been used as lyrics to a song. If possible, play the appropriate portion of "Let the Sun Shine In" from the musical *Hair* for students. Explain that in the musical, hippies are protesting the Vietnam War. Ask: Why did the lyricist quote Shakespeare in an anti-war protest? *Romeo's famous words are applicable because they allude to a tragedy and premature death. The song also includes Hamlet's last words: "The rest is silence."* Students who enjoy music might enrich their experience of the play and of Shakespeare's work by assembling an anthology album of songs that use quotations from Shakespeare or refer to Shakespeare's plays.

◆ **Reading Strategy**

❹ Causes and Effects Students should answer: *If Friar Lawrence had been faster, he would have gotten to the tomb earlier and could have prevented Romeo's death.*

Tybalt, liest thou there in thy bloody sheet?
O, what more favor can I do to thee
Than with that hand that cut thy youth in twain
100   To sunder[23] his that was thine enemy?
Forgive me, cousin!, Ah, dear Juliet,
Why art thou yet so fair? Shall I believe
That unsubstantial Death is amorous,[24]
And that the lean abhorrèd monster keeps
105   Thee here in dark to be his paramour?
For fear of that I still will stay with thee
And never from this pallet[25] of dim night
Depart again. Here, here will I remain
With worms that are thy chambermaids. O, here
110   Will I set up my everlasting rest
And shake the yoke of inauspicious[26] stars
From this world-wearied flesh. Eyes, look your last!
Arms, take your last embrace! And, lips, O you
The doors of breath, seal with a righteous kiss
115   A dateless[27] bargain to engrossing[28] death!
Come, bitter conduct;[29] come, unsavory guide!
Thou desperate pilot,[30] now at once run on
The dashing rocks thy seasick weary bark!
Here's to my love! [*Drinks.*] O true apothecary!
120   Thy drugs are quick. Thus with a kiss I die.   [*Falls.*]

[*Enter* FRIAR LAURENCE, *with lanthorn, crow, and spade.*]

FRIAR. Saint Francis be my speed![31] How oft tonight
Have my old feet stumbled[32] at graves! Who's there?

BALTHASAR. Here's one, a friend, and one that knows you well.

FRIAR. Bliss be upon you! Tell me, good my friend,
125   What torch is yond that vainly lends his light
To grubs[33] and eyeless skulls? As I discern,
It burneth in the Capels' monument.

BALTHASAR. It doth so, holy sir; and there's my master,
One that you love.

FRIAR.   Who is it?

130 **BALTHASAR.**   Romeo.

FRIAR. How long hath he been there?

BALTHASAR.   Full half an hour.

FRIAR. Go with me to the vault.

---

23. **sunder:** Cut off.
24. **amorous:** Full of love.

25. **pallet:** Bed.

26. **inauspicious:** Promising misfortune.

27. **dateless:** Eternal.
28. **engrossing:** All-encompassing.
29. **conduct:** Guide (poison).
30. **pilot:** Captain (Romeo himself).

31. **speed:** Help.
32. **stumbled:** Stumbling was thought to be a bad omen.

33. **grubs:** Worms.

◆ **Reading Strategy**
How is Friar Laurence's late arrival another example of chance contributing to this tragedy? ❹

 Cross-Curricular Connection: Performing Arts

Actor, director, and writer David Garrick (1717–1779) is credited with reviving the popularity of Shakespeare's plays. In so doing, he also set the precedent for directors to cut material and rewrite scenes. Following is Garrick's rewrite:

ROMEO: . . . Arms take your last embrace; and lips do you / the doors of breath seal with a righteous kiss. / Soft! soft! She breaths and stirs! (*Juliet wakes.*)
JULIET: Where am I? Defend me, powers!

ROMEO: She speaks, she lives! And we shall still be blessed!/ My kind propitious stars o'erpay me now/For all my sorrows past. Rise, rise, my Juliet,/ And from this cave of death, this house of horror,/ Quick let me snatch thee to Romeo's arms. There breathe a vital spirit in thy lips,/ And call thee back to life and love! (*Takes her hand.*)

Critics praised Garrick's changes. In her biography *David Garrick*, author Margaret

Barton records the enthusiastic response:

[Francis Gentleman wrote] ". . . Bringing Juliet to life before Romeo dies is undoubtedly a change of infinite merit. The whole dying scene does Mr. Garrick great credit."

And generation after generations of playgoers agreed with him. It was not until 1845 that Garrick's additions to the play were scrapped.

BALTHASAR.   I dare not, sir.
My master knows not but I am gone hence,
⑤ And fearfully did menace me with death
If I did stay to look on his intents.

135 **FRIAR.** Stay then; I'll go alone. Fear comes upon me.
⑥ O, much I fear some ill unthrifty³⁴ thing.

34. **unthrifty:** Unlucky.

BALTHASAR. As I did sleep under this yew tree here,
I dreamt my master and another fought,
And that my master slew him.

FRIAR.   Romeo!
140 Alack, alack, what blood is this which stains
The stony entrance of this sepulcher?
What mean these masterless³⁵ and gory swords
To lie discolored by this place of peace?

35. **masterless:** Discarded (without masters).

[Enters the tomb.]

Romeo! O, pale! Who else? What, Paris too?
145 And steeped in blood? Ah, what an unkind³⁶ hour
Is guilty of this lamentable chance!
The lady stirs.

36. **unkind:** Unnatural.

[JULIET rises.]

JULIET. O comfortable³⁷ friar! Where is my lord?
I do remember well where I should be,
150 And there I am. Where is my Romeo?

37. **comfortable:** Comforting.

FRIAR. I hear some noise. Lady, come from that nest
Of death, contagion, and unnatural sleep.
⑦ A greater power than we can contradict
Hath thwarted our intents. Come, come away.
155 Thy husband in thy bosom there lies dead;
And Paris too. Come, I'll dispose of thee
⑧ Among a sisterhood of holy nuns.
Stay not to question, for the watch is coming.
⑨ Come, go, good Juliet. I dare no longer stay.

[Exit FRIAR.]

160 **JULIET.** Go, get thee hence, for I will not away.
What's here? A cup, closed in my truelove's hand?
Poison, I see, hath been his timeless³⁸ end.
O churl!³⁹ Drunk all, and left no friendly drop
To help me after? I will kiss thy lips.
165 Haply some poison yet doth hang on them
To make me die with a restorative.⁴⁰
Thy lips are warm!

38. **timeless:** Untimely; too soon.
39. **churl:** Rude fellow.

[Kisses him.] 40. **restorative:** Medicine.

CHIEF WATCHMAN. *[Within]* Lead, boy. Which way?

◆ **Build Vocabulary**
sepulcher (sep′ əl kər) *n.:* Tomb

Romeo and Juliet, Act V, Scene iii ◆ 769

❶ Tragedy The tragedy is now complete. Ask students whether they think the tragedy uplifts the audience or celebrates the greatness of the human spirit. *Students may say that the two lovers, although they may have acted foolishly at times, show complete loyalty to each other over and above what is expected of people in real life.*

❷ Clarification Point out that the watch is acting as police would in a modern police drama or real-life crime scene: They are securing the scene of the crime and rounding up suspects.

◆ **Reading Strategy**

❸ Identify Causes and Effects Students may point out that if the Friar had arrived first, he could have explained the circumstances to Romeo, or that if Paris had arrived after Romeo, there might not have been a duel—or Paris might have convinced the widowed Juliet to marry him.

Customize for
Bodily/Kinesthetic Learners
These students can act out the events in the tomb, beginning with Romeo's confrontation with Paris and ending with Juliet's death.

---

❶
JULIET. Yea, noise? Then I'll be brief. O happy[41] dagger!
[*Snatches* ROMEO'S *dagger.*]
This is thy sheath; there rust, and let me die.
[*She stabs herself and falls.*]

41. happy: Convenient; opportune.

[*Enter* PARIS' *boy and watch.*]

170 **BOY.** This is the place. There, where the torch doth burn.

CHIEF WATCHMAN. The ground is bloody. Search about the churchyard.
Go, some of you; whoe'er you find attach.[42]
[*Exit some of the* WATCH.]

42. attach: Arrest.

Pitiful sight! Here lies the County slain;
And Juliet bleeding, warm, and newly dead,
175 Who here hath lain this two days burièd.
Go, tell the Prince; run to the Capulets;
Raise up the Montagues; some others search.
[*Exit others of the* WATCH.]
We see the ground whereon these woes do lie,
But the true ground[43] of all these piteous woes
❷ 180 We cannot without circumstance descry.[44]

43. ground: Cause.
44. without circumstance descry: See clearly without details.

[*Enter some of the* WATCH, *with* ROMEO'S *MAN,* BALTHASAR.]

SECOND WATCHMAN. Here's Romeo's man. We found him in the churchyard.

CHIEF WATCHMAN. Hold him in safety till the Prince come hither.

[*Enter* FRIAR LAURENCE *and another* WATCHMAN.]

THIRD WATCHMAN. Here is a friar that trembles, sighs and weeps.
We took this mattock and this spade from him
185 As he was coming from this churchyard's side.

CHIEF WATCHMAN. A great suspicion! Stay the friar too.

[*Enter the* PRINCE *and* ATTENDANTS.]

PRINCE. What misadventure is so early up,
That calls our person from our morning rest?

◆ **Reading Strategy**
How might the outcome have been different if the characters had come to the churchyard in a different order? **❸**

[*Enter* CAPULET *and his* WIFE *with others.*]

CAPULET. What should it be, that is so shrieked abroad?

190 **LADY CAPULET.** O, the people in the street cry "Romeo,"
Some "Juliet," and some "Paris"; and all run
With open outcry toward our monument.

PRINCE. What fear is this which startles in your ears?

CHIEF WATCHMAN. Sovereign, here lies the County Paris slain;

770 ◆ *Drama*

Speaking and Listening Mini-Lesson

Modern Scene
This mini-lesson supports the Speaking and Listening activity in the Idea Bank (p. 777).

Introduce the Concept To make literature more accessible to modern audiences, stories and plays may be reset in a time and place that is familiar to the audience.

Develop Background Urge writers to consider a contemporary situation that would make the same basic point as Shakespeare does.

Apply the Information Students will need to do the following:

- Decide how to change the characters, actions, and dialogue in their chosen scene to fit a contemporary setting.
- Read through the draft, revising it to fit the setting and flow smoothly.
- Rehearse the scene, paying careful attention to delivery.

Assess the Outcome Have students critique the performances. Were the characters and dialogue appropriate for the modern setting? Did the modern scene convey the essence of Shakespeare's original? Were the performers familiar with the script? Did they gesture deliberately and meaningfully and deliver their lines with feeling? You might also wish to use the Scoring Rubric for Drama, p. 102 in *Alternative Assessment.*

195 And Romeo dead; and Juliet, dead before,
     Warm and new killed.

     PRINCE. Search, seek, and know how this foul murder comes.

     CHIEF WATCHMAN. Here is a friar, and slaughtered Romeo's man,
     With instruments upon them fit to open
200 These dead men's tombs.

     CAPULET. O heavens! O wife, look how our daughter bleeds!
     This dagger hath mista'en, for, lo, his house⁴⁵   **45. house:** Sheath.
     Is empty on the back of Montague,
     And it missheathèd in my daughter's bosom!

205 **LADY CAPULET.** O me, this sight of death is as a bell
     That warns my old age to a sepulcher.

     [*Enter* MONTAGUE *and others.*]

     PRINCE. Come, Montague; for thou art early up
     To see thy son and heir more early down.

     MONTAGUE. Alas, my liege,⁴⁶ my wife is dead tonight!   **46. liege** (lēj)**:** Lord.
210 Grief of my son's exile hath stopped her breath.
     What further woe conspires against mine age?

     PRINCE. Look, and thou shalt see.

     MONTAGUE. O thou untaught! What manners is in this,
     To press before thy father to a grave?

215 **PRINCE.** Seal up the mouth of outrage⁴⁷ for a while,   **47. mouth of outrage:**
     Till we can clear these ambiguities   Violent cries.
     And know their spring, their head, their true descent;
     And then will I be general of your woes⁴⁸   **48. general . . . woes:**
     And lead you even to death. Meantime forbear,   Leader in your sorrow.
220 And let mischance be slave to patience.⁴⁹   **49. let . . . patience:** Be
     Bring forth the parties of suspicion.   patient in the face of
                                                                    misfortune.

     FRIAR. I am the greatest, able to do least,
     Yet most suspected, as the time and place
     Doth make against me, of this direful⁵⁰ murder;   **50. direful:** Terrible.
225 And here I stand, both to impeach and purge⁵¹   **51. impeach and purge:**
     Myself condemnèd and myself excused.   Accuse and declare
                                                             blameless.
     PRINCE. Then say at once what thou dost know in this.   **52. date of breath:** Term of
                                                                   life.
     FRIAR. I will be brief, for my short date of breath⁵²
230 Is not so long as is a tedious tale.
     Romeo, there dead, was husband to that Juliet;
     And she, there dead, that's Romeo's faithful wife.

◆ **Build Vocabulary**

ambiguities (am´ bə gyoo͞ ´ ə
tēz) *n.:* Statements or events
whose meanings are unclear

Romeo and Juliet, Act V, Scene iii ◆ *771*

Comprehension Check ☑

❹ Ask students what the Prince is asking all present to do. *The Prince is asking everyone to be quiet so that he can determine what has happened and why.*

Customize for
More Advanced Students
Explain that, in the action on these pages, everyone is being brought on stage for the *denouement,* the outcome or solution of a complex sequence of events. In the denouement, all the pieces come together and, for the first time, everyone knows the whole story. Have students relate the action in *Romeo and Juliet* to the conclusions of film and television mysteries, in which the detective calls together the various characters and explains the solution to the mystery.

285   PRINCE.   This letter doth make good the friar's words,
       Their course of love, the tidings of her death;
       And here he writes that he did buy a poison
       Of a poor pothecary and therewithal
       Came to this vault to die and lie with Juliet.
290   Where be these enemies? Capulet, Montague.
       See what a scourge is laid upon your hate,
       That heaven finds means to kill your joys with love.
       And I, for winking at[58] your discords too,
       Have lost a brace[59] of kinsmen. All are punished.

295   CAPULET.   O brother Montague, give me thy hand.
       This is my daughter's jointure,[60] for no more
       Can I demand.

     MONTAGUE.   But I can give thee more;
       For I will raise her statue in pure gold,
       That whiles Verona by that name is known,
300   There shall no figure at such rate[61] be set
       As that of true and faithful Juliet.

     CAPULET.   As rich shall Romeo's by his lady's lie—
       Poor sacrifices of our enmity![62]

     PRINCE.   A glooming[63] peace this morning with it brings.
305   The sun for sorrow will not show his head.

Beyond Literature

Media Connection

Shakespeare Comes to Hollywood If William Shakespeare were alive today, he would be making a fortune collecting residuals for *The Tragedy of Romeo and Juliet*. Residuals are fees collected by performers and writers for each rerun of filmed or taped material. Since the dawning of the motion-picture industry, many of Shakespeare's plays have been made into movies. Hollywood producers and directors realize that Shakespeare's plays combine dramatic situations with universal themes, a combination that translates into success at the box office. The movies based upon Shakespearean plays include *Romeo and Juliet*, *Macbeth*, *Othello*, *Hamlet*, *Henry V*, *Richard III*, *Kiss Me Kate* (based upon *The*

Taming of the Shrew), *Julius Caesar*, *King Lear*, and *Antony and Cleopatra*. In the case of some of the plays, such as *Hamlet* and *King Lear*, several film versions have been made. In addition, the stars of Shakespearean movies comprise some of the world's finest actors. A partial list includes Laurence Olivier, Charlton Heston, Kathryn Grayson, John Gielgud, Deborah Kerr, James Mason, Marlon Brando, Diana Rigg, Orson Welles, Richard Chamberlain, Paul Scofield, and Lynn Redgrave. What specific elements and qualities of *The Tragedy of Romeo and Juliet* have made it a candidate for a great motion picture?

Beyond the Selection

FURTHER READING

Other Works by William Shakespeare
A Midsummer Night's Dream
The Taming of the Shrew
Antony and Cleopatra

Other Works About Rivalries and Feuds
The Iliad, Homer
Animal Farm, George Orwell
Ivanhoe, Sir Walter Scott

INTERNET

You and you students may find additional information about Shakespeare and *Romeo and Juliet* on the Internet. We suggest the following sites. Please be aware, however, that sites may have changed from the time we published this information.
     For "The Bard" Web site, direct student to the following Internet address: **http://www.gh.cs.usyd.edu.au/~matty/Shakespeare**
     The "William Shakespeare" Web site links students to the complete works of Shakespeare and an "interactive hypermedia environment." The address is: **http://library. luhsd.k12.ca.us/library/shakes.html**
     For information on programs available at the Folger Shakespeare Library in Washington, D.C., send an e-mail to **educate@folger.edu**

3 Go hence, to have more talk of these sad things;
 Some shall be pardoned, and some punishèd;
For never was a story of more woe
Than this of Juliet and her Romeo.

[Exit all.]

Guide for Responding

◆ *Literature and Your Life*

Reader's Response Were you in any way surprised by the way in which this play ends? Why or why not?

Thematic Focus Why do you think that a tragedy or a disaster often has to occur before rival groups make the effort to work out their conflicts?

Group Activity Suppose that you could have stepped into the action of the play for exactly one minute. In a small group, discuss when you would have stepped in and what you would have said or done.

☑ Check Your Comprehension

1. At the start of Scene i, why is Romeo happy and expecting joyful news?
2. Why does the Friar go to Juliet's tomb?
3. What causes Paris and Romeo to fight?
4. How do Romeo and Juliet die?
5. How does the relationship of the feuding families change at the end of the play?

◆ Critical Thinking

INTERPRET

1. Why isn't it surprising that Friar Laurence's scheme fails? Base your answer both on your own experience and on events from the play. **[Analyze]**
2. (a) Hearing Balthasar's report of Juliet's death (Scene i), Romeo exclaims, "Then I defy you, stars!" What might he mean by this? (b) How are his words consistent with what you know of his character? **[Connect]**
3. (a) In what ways is chance to blame for the deaths of Romeo and Juliet? (b) In what ways are Romeo and Juliet to blame for their deaths? (c) In what ways are their families to blame? **[Analyze]**
4. What lessons can be learned from Shakespeare's play about the destructive effects of hatred? Support your answer. **[Draw Conclusions]**

EVALUATE

5. Was it necessary for Romeo and Juliet to die for the feud between the Montagues and Capulets to end? Explain. **[Assess]**

APPLY

6. Explain how the lesson that the play teaches could be applied to a specific situation in today's world. **[Apply]**

Romeo and Juliet, Act V, Scene iii ◆ 775

775

◆ Literary Focus

1. Suggested response: The lovers are impulsive and insistent on having their way.
2. Students may cite Romeo and Juliet's falling in love, Romeo overhearing Juliet as she stands on her balcony, Romeo encountering Tybalt immediately after his marriage, the Friar's message not reaching Romeo, Paris being at Juliet's tomb when Romeo gets there, and Juliet reviving a few minutes too late to prevent Romeo from taking the poison.
3. One key circumstance is the feud between the two families. Other answers are possible.
4. Some students may say that a combination of character flaws and unlucky circumstances results in the destruction of the hero and heroine. Other students may say that unreasoning hatred results in the destruction of things that are beautiful and good, like young lovers.

◆ Reading Strategy

1. Romeo hears of Juliet's death, which causes him to buy poison and rush to Verona. Paris goes to Juliet's tomb to strew perfume and flowers, which causes him to be there when Romeo arrives. Because Romeo is too distraught to explain himself, he ends up fighting with and killing Paris. Romeo does not realize that Juliet is still alive and takes the poison that results in his death. Juliet, finding Romeo dead, takes his dagger and stabs herself, causing her death.
2. Romeo marries Juliet → Romeo kills Tybalt → Romeo is banished → Juliet grieves → Juliet's parents betroth her to Paris → Juliet demands a way to avoid the second marriage → Friar gives Juliet a potion → potion causes Juliet to seem dead → Friar writes to Romeo → Friar's letter does not reach Romeo → Friar goes to tomb and finds Paris and Romeo dead → Juliet wakes and the Friar flees → Juliet kills herself.

Guide for Responding (continued)

◆ Literary Focus

TRAGEDY

A **tragedy** is a drama in which the central character or characters suffer disaster or great misfortune. In many tragedies, the downfall results from fate, a serious character flaw, or a combination of the two. Other contributing causes may be present as well. The theme of a tragedy is the central idea or insight about life that explains why the downfall occurred.

1. What character traits of the lovers may have led to their destruction?
2. What events reveal the tragic influence of fate or chance?
3. What other causes or conditions are important to the way events turn out?
4. Using your answers to the preceding questions, write a one-sentence statement of the theme, or central message, of *Romeo and Juliet*. You might put your sentence in a form like the following: "The theme of the play is that ____?____ leads to the destruction of ____?____."

◆ Build Grammar Skills

SUBJECT AND VERB AGREEMENT IN INVERTED SENTENCES

To determine whether the verb of an **inverted sentence**—one in which the verb precedes the subject—should be singular or plural, rearrange the sentence so that the subject comes before the verb.

Practice Write the form of the verb in parentheses that correctly completes each sentence.
1. Through the churchyard (walks, walk) the watchman.
2. Where (is, are) Romeo and Juliet?
3. Upon ghastly sights (stumbles, stumble) the watchman.
4. Silent and still (is, are) the couple.
5. Into deepest sorrow (plunges, plunge) the Montagues and the Capulets.

Writing Application Write a brief dialogue between two of the characters in the play. Include five sentences with inverted word order.

◆ Reading Strategy

IDENTIFY CAUSES AND EFFECTS

A **cause** is an event that produces a result, or **effect**. This effect may then cause effects of its own. The plot of a play or other story consists of a chain of events linked by cause-and-effect relationships.
1. Describe the chain of events in Act V that lead up to the deaths of Paris, Romeo, and Juliet.
2. Summarize Friar Lawrence's monologue in Scene iii, lines 230–263 in a form similar to the one used on page 758.

◆ Build Vocabulary

USING THE PREFIX *ambi-*

The prefix *ambi-* means "both." Using the clues for help, complete each of the following sentences with one of the words below. Write your answers on a separate sheet of paper.

a. ambidextrous   **b.** ambilateral

1. An ____?____ person can use both hands with equal skill.
2. A condition affecting both sides of the body is ____?____.

CLUES

dexter: skillful   *later-:* side

USING THE WORD BANK

On a separate sheet of paper, write the letter of the word that is the best synonym of the first word.
1. remnants: (a) cloths, (b) remains, (c) factors
2. penury: (a) poverty, (b) currency, (c) disease
3. haughty: (a) timid, (b) friendly, (c) egotistical
4. sepulcher: (a) monument, (b) tomb, (c) cemetery
5. ambiguities: (a) courtesies, (b) details, (c) uncertainties
6. scourge: (a) sorrow, (b) whip, (c) hatred

◆ Build Vocabulary

Using the Prefix *ambi-*
1. ambidextrous; 2. ambilateral

Using the Word Bank
1. b 2. a 3. c 4. b 5. c
6. b

◆ Build Grammar Skills

1. walks; 2. are;
3. stumbles; 4. is; 5. plunge

✎ Writer's Solution

For additional instruction and practice, use the lesson in the **Language Lab CD-ROM** on Special Problems in Agreement I. For additional practice on Subject and Verb Agreement, use the practice page in the *Writer's Solution Grammar Practice Book*, p. 82.

Build Your Portfolio

Idea Bank

1. **Executive Summary** Imagine that Prince Escalus has asked you to brief him on the events leading up to the deaths of Romeo and Juliet. Write a short, factual account of events, paying careful attention to causes and effects.

2. **Alternate Ending** Write a new version of Act V that develops naturally out of Acts I–IV. Your new ending can be happy or tragic, and it can involve the deaths of some or none of the characters.

3. **Response to Literary Criticism** W. H. Auden, a well-known poet and critic, has said that *Romeo and Juliet* "is not simply a tragedy of two individuals, but the tragedy of a city. Everybody in the city is in one way or another involved in and responsible for what happens." Write a brief essay in which you explain why you agree or disagree with this statement.

Speaking and Listening

4. **Modern Scene** With a group, rewrite a scene from *Romeo and Juliet* to fit a contemporary setting of your choice. Rehearse your scene, then perform it for the class. **[Performing Arts Link]**

5. **Rap Song** Compose and perform a rap song about *Romeo and Juliet* that both summarizes the story and includes your reactions to it. **[Music Link; Performing Arts Link]**

Projects

6. **Set Design** Imagine that you and a group of classmates have been hired as set designers for a modern-day version of the play. Decide on an appropriate setting for the adaptation. Then create a description, with diagrams, of the set. **[Art Link]**

7. **Shakespeare Display** As a class, create a Shakespeare display. Include a variety of materials, such as biographies, versions of the plays, student compositions, and artwork.

Writing Mini-Lesson

Persuasive Letter

If Friar Lawrence had tried to persuade both the Montagues and the Capulets to end their feud, Romeo and Juliet might have been saved. As Friar Lawrence, develop a letter to both families, written immediately after the wedding, to persuade them to end the feud.

Writing Skills Focus: Precise Details

To be persuasive, your letter must **appeal both to reason and to the emotions**. Emotional appeals attempt to touch the hearts of readers. You might touch the heart by asking both families if they want their children to be miserable. Appeals to reason present facts that support an argument. For example, you might cite the senseless bloodshed the feud has engendered. Note the appeal to reason the Nurse employs to try to persuade Juliet to marry Paris.

Model From the Selection

Romeo is banishèd; and all the world to nothing / That he dares ne'er come back to challenge you; / Or if he do, it needs must be by stealth. / Then, since the case so stands as now it doth, / I think it best you married with the County.

Prewriting Jot down all of the factual evidence and the emotional pleas you will present to persuade the families to end their feud.

Drafting Begin your letter by announcing the marriage ceremony you have just performed. Then arrange your persuasive points in a logical order. One method is to lead your readers up to your strongest argument.

Revising Read your draft as if you were a Montague or a Capulet. Does the letter present, in a logical order, arguments that appeal to reason and to the emotions? Might anything in the letter seem offensive to members of either family?

Romeo and Juliet, Act V ◆ 777

Prepare and Engage

Establish Writing Guidelines

Before students begin, review the following key characteristics of an editorial:

- An editorial concerns an issue the writer believes is important to the community.

- It states a viewpoint and tries to get readers to agree with it.

You may want to distribute the scoring rubric for Persuasion (p. 98 in *Alternative Assessment*) to make students aware before they begin of the criteria on which they will be evaluated. See the suggestions on page 780 for how you can customize the rubric for this workshop.

Refer students to the Writing Handbook, page 962, for instruction in the writing process, and page 965 for further information on Persuasive Writing.

 Writer's Solution

Writers at Work Videodisc

To introduce students to the key elements of persuasion and show them how National Basketball Association writer Larry Weitzman uses persuasive techniques in his writing, play the videodisc segment on Persuasion (Ch. 4). Have students discuss what Weitzman says are the goals of persuasive writing.

Play frames 33836 to 42938

Writing Lab CD-ROM

If your students have access to computers, you may want to have them work on the tutorial on Persuasion to complete all or part of their editorials. Follow these steps:

1. Have the students review the Inspirations for Persuasion to help find a topic.
2. Suggest that students complete audience and purpose profiles.
3. Have students draft on computer.
4. Have students complete the screen Avoiding Faulty Logic.
5. Encourage students to complete the screen, checking for Errors in Comparisons.

Sourcebook

Students can find additional support in the chapter on Persuasion. (pp. 96–127).

Editorial | # Writing Process Workshop

In an **editorial**, a writer offers his or her personal views on an issue and provides facts and examples that support those views. Many newspapers and magazines carry editorials on a wide range of topics.

Write an editorial based on an idea in one of the plays in this section—for example, on dating or on resolving a long-standing feud—or on one of the plays itself. The following skills will help you write an editorial on any topic.

Writing Skills Focus

▶ **Make persuasive appeals to readers' emotions and to their reason.** In an emotional appeal, you attempt to touch the reader's heart and arouse a feeling such as pity or anger. In an appeal to reason, you present facts, details, and examples that support your argument. (See p. 777.)

▶ **Support your opinions with facts.** Facts are statements that can be proved true; opinions cannot be proved true or false. In your editorial, provide facts to support each of your opinions

In the following passage from an editorial, the writer uses these skills in trying to persuade readers to accept her point of view.

MODEL FROM LITERATURE

① The writer states her opinion early in the editorial.

② The writer appeals to reason by offering facts and examples to support her opinion.

③ The writer appeals to emotion by stirring readers' pride and anger.

Some publishers now print simplified versions of Shakespeare's plays. I feel that is very wrong. ① By not having the original text, readers are deprived of the beauty of the language. "Wherefore art thou Romeo?" becomes simply, "Why do you have to be Romeo?" Studies show that readers of such texts often don't go on to more challenging material. ② Soon publishers will be revising our Declaration of Independence! Is that what we want? I say stick to the original! ③

778 ◆ Drama

 Beyond the Classroom

Career Connection

Tell students that persuasive writing is one of the most common and useful modes in the workplace. Nonprofit organizations and foundations use persuasive writing to solicit donations from corporations and wealthy individuals. Advertisers use persuasive writing to entice people to buy products or use services. Politicians use persuasive writing in their speeches. Editors use persuasive writing in editorials. Most people who have applied for a job haved used persuasive writing in the cover letters that accompany their résumés.

Prewriting

Choose a Topic Base your topic on an idea presented in either *The Dancers* or *Romeo and Juliet*, or write about one of the plays or playwrights. Choose an idea listed here or come up with your own idea.

> ## Topic Ideas
>
> - Should a parent tell a child whom to date?
> - What is the best way to turn down a date?
> - Should a long-standing feud be allowed to continue?
> - Are Shakespeare's plays still relevant today?

Plan an Appeal to Reason Jot down your point of view on your topic, then list facts, examples, and details to support your point of view. First list the facts you already know. Then go to the library to find more information. Ask yourself:

▶ What supporting facts and examples can I find in books, encyclopedias, and almanacs?

▶ What information might I use from newspapers and magazines?

▶ What other sources might have useful information?

To help you distinguish facts from opinions, look at this chart:

> ## Distinguishing Fact From Opinion
>
> | Opinions | Facts |
> |---|---|
> | ■ This is a responsible newspaper. | ■ This newspaper won a Pulitzer Prize for Meritorious Public Service. |
> | ■ Mr. Tsao isn't boring. | ■ Mr. Tsao alternates between lectures and hands-on demonstrations. |
> | ■ We need more pet shelters. | ■ Last year, more than 600 stray animals were destroyed because shelters had no room for them. |
> | ■ Americans eat too much fat. | ■ The average American diet is 40 percent fat. |

Plan an Appeal to Emotion On another piece of paper, identify the emotions you wish to stir in your readers. Do you want them to feel anger, fear, or sorrow? Take notes on emotional arguments you might use to achieve your goal. Also, consider how you might use pictures to arouse readers' feelings.

Applying Language Skills: Compound-Complex Sentences

A **compound-complex sentence** has two or more independent clauses and one or more subordinate clauses:

The plays that Shakespeare wrote are great, but simplified texts ruin them.

The plays are great and *simplified texts ruin them* are independent clauses; *that Shakespeare wrote* is a subordinate clause.

Practice Rewrite each pair of sentences as a compound-complex sentence.

1. If you're treated like a child, you'll act like one. You'll never grow up.
2. The text is hard at first. If you read it long enough, it gets easier.

Writing Application As you draft your editorial, look for places where you can combine information into a compound-complex sentence.

> ## Writer's Solution Connection Writing Lab
>
> To help you gather evidence for your editorial, use the Pros and Cons organizer in the Prewriting section of the Persuasion tutorial.

Prewriting

To help students choose a topic, you might want to have them poll other students or residents of the community to find out what issues the other students and residents consider most important. Students can tabulate their results and use them to come up with a topic for an editorial.

Customize for
English Language Learners

Have these students conduct three sets of surveys to improve their speaking and listening skills and build up confidence. First, have them survey one another as you observe. Resolve any communication problems that might result. Next, have them survey other class members. Finally, have them survey members of the community.

Customize for
Less Proficient Writers

These students may benefit from a review of the types of faulty logic: circular reasoning, bandwagon appeals, overgeneralization, either/or arguments, loaded language, and questionable cause-and-effect arguments.

Customize for
More Advanced Students

Challenge these students to write from a point of view that is the opposite of their own. For example, a student in favor of stricter environmental regulations might write from the point of view of an oil company executive.

 Writer's Solution

Writing Lab CD-ROM
The Gathering Evidence section of the tutorial on Persuasion includes the following options to help students write their editorials: video tips on gathering evidence, interactive instruction on gathering evidence using library resources, interactive instruction on detecting bias in sources, interactive hints on gathering evidence, and a pro-and-con chart.

Applying Language Skills
Compound-Complex Sentences
Answers

1. If you're treated like a child, you'll act like one and you'll never grow up.
2. Although the text is hard at first, if you read it long enough, it gets easier.

 **Writer's Solution**

For additional instruction and practice, use the **Language Lab CD-ROM** lesson on Varying Sentence Structure and the practice pages in the *Writer's Solution Grammar Practice Book* (pp. 57–58).

Infinitives
Answers

1. Try to understand the text fully.
2. Don't be afraid to ask questions occasionally.
3. It feels good to face a challenge bravely.

 **Writer's Solution**

For additional instruction and practice, use the **Language Lab CD-ROM** lesson on Principal Parts of Verbs and the practice pages in the *Writer's Solution Grammar Practice Book* (pp. 46–47).

779

Drafting

Discuss with students the importance of a strong introduction and a logical organization in writing any persuasive piece of writing. Remind students to draft their editorial in a single sitting, without pausing to labor over a single word or a grammatical error. After an initial draft is completed is the best time to revise a piece of writing.

Revising

Make sure students proofread their drafts thoroughly. Have them look for run-on sentences and fragments, problems with subject-verb agreement, spelling errors, double negatives, and capitalization and punctuation errors. Tell peer reviewers to look for these as well.

Publishing

Often the purpose of an editorial is to get people to act on an issue. Encourage students to read their editorials in front of the class to spark a discussion on the issue. Another alternative is to have students read the editorials of their classmates, who, to prevent embarrassment, can remain anonymous during the readings.

Reinforce and Extend

Review the Writing Guidelines
After students have completed their papers, review the characteristics of an editorial. Encourage students to come up with additional criteria for a persuasive editorial based on what they learned through completing the assignment.

APPLYING LANGUAGE SKILLS: Infinitives

An **infinitive** is a verb form preceded by the word *to*. Avoid splitting an infinitive by inserting a word between *to* and the verb.

Correct: It is hard to read Shakespeare quickly.

Incorrect: It is hard to quickly read Shakespeare.

Practice Rewrite each sentence to avoid a split infinitive.

1. Try to fully understand the text.
2. Don't be afraid to occasionally ask questions.
3. It feels good to bravely face a challenge.

Writing Application Review your editorial and check to see whether it contains any split infinitives. If it does, revise the sentences so the word *to* is not separated from its verb.

Writer's Solution Connection Writing Lab

For your additional help in revising your editorial, use the instruction and activities in the tutorial on Persuasion in the Writing Lab. You'll find an interactive student model and instruction on identifying faulty reasoning.

Drafting

Use a Solid Organization As you draft, be sure to use a solid organization to present the reasons that support your point of view. You might choose to go from the most important reasons to the least important, or do the reverse. You might also use a cause-and-effect organization, which will explain the reasons why something happened or will happen.

Write a Strong Introduction, Body, and Conclusion Begin your editorial with a strong statement that will capture readers' interest. In the body of your editorial, support your position with facts and examples. In the conclusion, restate your position and summarize your most important points.

Revising

Use a Peer Reviewer Ask a classmate to read your editorial, then answer the following questions:
- ▶ What is the writer's position?
- ▶ What details support the writer's position?
- ▶ What details do not support the writer's position?
- ▶ Has the writer appealed to reason? How?
- ▶ Has the writer appealed to emotion? How?

Use your peer reviewer's comments to guide your revision. However, use your judgment—you don't have to do everything your peer reviewer suggests.

Publishing

- ▶ **Classroom** Deliver your editorial in the form of a "live broadcast" to your class.
- ▶ **Newspaper** Send your editorial to your school newspaper or a local newspaper.
- ▶ **Magazine** Submit your editorial to a magazine that publishes editorials related to your topic.

✓ ASSESSMENT		4	3	2	1
PORTFOLIO ASSESSMENT Use the rubric on Persuasion in *Alternative Assessment* (p. 98) to assess students' writing. Add these criteria to customize the rubric to this assignment.	**Sentence Style**	Sentence style is varied, interesting, and powerful. No split infinitives or style mistakes.	Sentences are for the most part interesting. Style mistakes are minor.	Sentences are slightly varied but could be more so. Noticeable split infinitives or other style mistakes.	Sentence structure is monotonous. Numerous style errors including split infinitives.
	Persuasive Elements	The argument convincingly appeals to the reader's emotions and reason and is supported with facts.	The argument is effective but not watertight. It is predominantly supported with facts.	The argument tends to manipulate the reader's emotions rather than try to sway him or her by reason.	The argument relies entirely on emotional appeals. Facts are nonexistent or confused with opinions.

780

Real-World Reading Skills Workshop

Break Down Difficult Texts

Strategies for Success

At times, you may be faced with reading a difficult selection, such as a play by William Shakespeare. Just looking at the material might discourage you, but don't lose hope! There are strategies for breaking down the text to make it easier to understand.

Get an Overview Whether the text is a long book, short story, poem, or play, first look at the overall selection. Note its title—it may signal the content of the selection. Next, note whether the text is divided into chapters, stanzas, or paragraphs. If there are subtitles, read them for clues to the content.

Tackle One Section at a Time Begin with the first section you plan to read. Look at captions or highlighted words that may appear in the section. Also, look for footnotes or glosses (notes in the side columns) that will illuminate the meaning. Next, go through the text line by line. If a sentence is long, break it into parts where a comma appears. Read the text once for general meaning. Then go back and reread those parts you didn't understand fully.

Do a Vocabulary Search As you read a difficult text, jot down any words that are unfamiliar. Try to get a sense of a word's meaning by its context—how it is used in the passage. If that doesn't work, look up the word in a dictionary before rereading the passage.

Apply the Strategy

Here is your chance to succeed with a challenging text. Read "The True Tragedy of Romeo and Juliet" article. Then answer these questions.

1. How is the text divided? What do you learn about the article from its title and subtitle?
2. What specific topic does the author discuss in each paragraph?
3. Which longer sentences did you break into parts? Where did you break them?
4. Which vocabulary words were you able to figure out from the context? What clues in the passage hinted at the meaning?

The True Tragedy of Romeo and Juliet

Shakespeare's tragedy *Romeo and Juliet* may be centuries old, yet its message is as timely as any contemporary tome. The two star-crossed lovers ultimately meet with tragedy because of a senseless feud between their clans.

A Message for Today

One only has to peruse today's newspaper headlines to conclude that baseless hatred remains rampant in modern society. Countries, armies, and families wage war with one another. If humans don't learn how to coexist in harmony, tragedy will continue to manifest itself with international, national, and personal repercussions.

✔ Here are other situations in which breaking down difficult text will help your understanding:
- ▶ Reading a scientific report
- ▶ Reading a contract
- ▶ Reading the results of a government study
- ▶ Reading a scholarly work

Introduce the Strategy

Students will be familiar with difficult texts from most, if not all, of their classes. Remind them that one of the benefits of reading and breaking down difficult texts is that it improves one's overall reading ability.

Customize for
Less Proficient Readers

These students may benefit from being walked through the instructional text as well as being reminded that speed is not the primary goal here; comprehension is.

Apply the Strategy

Before reading the passage, have students look at the title and subhead to get an idea of the passage's message. Have them follow the instructions while reading; for example, look up any unknown words, break up longer sentences, and tackle the piece one section at a time.

Answers

1. The text is divided into two sections, an introductory paragraph and one paragraph from the body. From the title and subtitle, we learn that Shakespeare's tragedy has relevance today.
2. In the first paragraph, the author discusses the play itself and mentions that its message is timeless. In the second paragraph, he gives contemporary examples of feuding parties.
3. Ask students to explain exactly what breaking up of the sentences helped them to understand.
4. Words that might give students difficulty include *tome, ultimately, clans, peruse, baseless, rampant, coexist, manifest, repercussions.*

Introduce the Strategy

Remind students that persuasive speeches are a common part of everyday life. Politicians trying to get elected aren't the only ones who speak persuasively. For example, a student trying to convince his or her parent to let him or her go see a movie is also making a persuasive speech.

Customize for
English Language Learners

Emphasize the importance of body language and the tone of one's voice to these students. Let them know that they can still be persuasive and convincing even if their English-speaking ability is limited.

Apply the Strategy

Remind students that in speaking, body language and the tone of one's voice are extremely important, sometimes almost as important as the words themselves. Before they give their speeches, have students practice adjusting their tone of voice and using appropriate gestures.

Answers

1. A good speech will give reasons why the speaker is the best candidate, rather than *ad hominem* attacks on other candidates.
2. A good speech will be one that convinces listeners that their lives will be enriched in some abstract or concrete way if they buy the product.
3. Good speeches will offer specific examples and facts to back up opinions.

Speaking and Listening Workshop

Giving a Persuasive Speech

Imagine giving a speech in which you try to persuade the Capulets and the Montagues to give up their terrible feud. When you give a persuasive speech, your aim is to persuade listeners to accept your opinion about a subject. Knowing how to present yourself can help you to convince your listeners.

Appear Confident To persuade an audience, you must make them feel that you really believe what you're telling them. Speak in a tone of voice that is strong and confident. Also, be enthusiastic about your reasons. If you aren't excited about your views, chances are your listeners won't be, either.

Use Strong, Persuasive Language Choose words that will have an emotional impact on your listeners. Note the difference in these speeches. Which is more effective? Why?

> This feud is harmful to everyone involved. I think you should give it up.

> Your ridiculous feud has sent your precious children to their graves. I urge you to make peace with each other—before more innocent lives are lost.

Be Animated When you speak, don't stand stiffly. Also, don't look bored or tired. Move your arms or hands to emphasize a point you are making.

Tips for Giving a Persuasive Speech

✔ *If you want to convince your audience to agree with your opinions, follow these strategies:*
- ▶ Speak loudly and clearly.
- ▶ Use an enthusiastic tone of voice.
- ▶ Maintain good eye contact.
- ▶ Move your body effectively.

Apply the Strategies

Role-play these situations in front of your classmates. Then invite classmates to share feedback on how effective you were.

1. You plan to run for class office. Give a persuasive speech telling why students should vote for you.
2. Select an item of clothing you are wearing, such as your shoes. Try to convince your audience to buy the same product for themselves.
3. Think of a controversial school issue that many students are discussing. Give your personal opinion about the issue. Offer as many strong reasons as you can to support your view. Then, do a flip! Pretend you have the opposite opinion, and offer reasons to support *that* view.

782 ◆ *Drama*

 Workplace Skills Mini-Lesson

Careers in Sales

Persuasive speaking is important in many workplace situations. One of the most common is in sales, whether it's selling vacuum cleaners door to door, clothing in a department store, or stock options to a giant corporation.

As an extension activity, have pairs of students test out their persuasive skills in mock selling situation.

Extended Reading Opportunities

As you read a play, try to envision the action, which is meant to be performed on stage. Following are just a few possibilities for extending your exploration of drama.

Suggested Titles

A Midsummer Night's Dream
William Shakespeare

In this comedy by William Shakespeare, the road to love is winding and rocky. Hermia loves Lysander, although she has been promised by her father to Demetrius—who is in turn adored by Helena. In the forest, where all the lovers flee, the merry fairy Puck further confuses matters by doling out a magic love potion that causes a person to fall asleep, then fall in love with the first object he or she sees upon awakening.

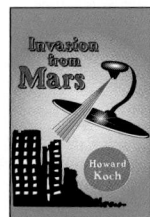

Invasion From Mars
Howard Koch

This radio play, based on *The War of the Worlds* by H. G. Wells, caused a huge sensation in 1938 when it first aired on Orson Welles's radio show, the *Mercury Theater*. At the time, many listeners thought it was an actual news report of a Martian landing! The play pretends to be an authentic evening of radio, including weather reports, musical interludes, and special news bulletins—which are accounts of an invasion by hostile beings from Mars.

Twelve Angry Men
Reginald Rose

In this courtroom drama, the life of a young boy hangs in the balance as a jury deliberates whether or not to convict him for killing his father. Locked in the jury room, the jurors— twelve men of varying ages and temperaments—argue with increasing violence as they struggle to come to a unanimous decision. This teleplay, which won an Emmy Award and was later adapted into a movie, was inspired by Reginald Rose's own experience on a jury.

Other Possibilities

All the World's a Stage: Speeches, Poems and Songs from William Shakespeare   Dorothy Boux

Two Gentlemen of Verona   William Shakespeare
Calisto 5   Alan Ayckbourn

Planning Students' Extended Reading

All of these works are good choices for students' exploration of the genre of drama. Following is some information that will help you choose which to teach.

Customize for
Varying Student Needs

When assigning the selections in this part to your students, keep in mind the following factors:

- *A Midsummer Night's Dream* is an engaging Shakespearian comedy that offers an excellent alternative to *Romeo and Juliet*. The play is especially well suited for your less advanced students.

- *Invasion from Mars* will appeal to students with an interest in science-fiction.

- *Twelve Angry Men* deals with realistic subject matter that students will be able to relate to because of their frequent exposure to courtroom scenes on television.

Literature Study Guides A literature study guide is available for *A Midsummer Night's Dream*. The guide includes section summaries, discussion questions, and activities.

Resources for Teaching Novels, Plays, and Literature Collections This booklet includes graphic organizers, teaching strategies, and transparencies that you can use in teaching any of these works.

Customize for
Special Needs

To meet the needs of your special needs students, you may want to consider using the version of *A Midsummer Night's Dream* in Globe Fearon's Pacemaker Classics series.

Planning Instruction and Assessment

Unit Objectives

1. To develop skills in reading poetry.
2. To apply a variety of reading strategies, particularly literal comprehension strategies, appropriate for reading these selections
3. To recognize literary elements used in these selections
4. To increase vocabulary
5. To learn elements of grammar and usage
6. To write in a variety of modes and about situations based on the selections
7. To develop speaking and listening skills, by doing proposed activities

Meeting the Objectives

With each selection, you will find instructional material and portfolio opportunities through which students can meet these objectives. Further, you will find additional practice pages for reading strategies, literary elements, vocabulary, and grammar in the *Selection Support* booklet in the Teaching Resources box.

Setting Goals Work with your students at the beginning of the unit to set goals for unit outcomes. Plan what skills and concepts you wish students to acquire. You may individualize according to students' performance levels or learning modalities.

Portfolios You may have students keep portfolios of their work or of their work in progress. The activities and prompts on the Build Your Portfolio page of each selection provide opportunities for students to apply the concepts presented with the selection.

The Library, Jacob Lawrence, National Museum of American Art, Washington, D.C.

Humanities: Art

The Library by Jacob Lawrence.

Born in 1917 in Atlantic City, New Jersey, Jacob Lawrence is best known for painting scenes of African American life. His subjects have included street scenes and people working or relaxing; he has also painted several series of artworks focusing on such historical figures as Toussaint L'Ouverture (begun in 1937) and Frederick Douglass (painted in 1938–1939). His style of painting often incorporates bright colors and shapes with heavy outlines, to create geometric patterns.

Help students link the painting with the focus of Unit 9 ("Poetry") by answering the following questions:

1. What attitude toward reading does the art communicate, and how? *The art expresses a reverence for and love of reading, through the intense concentration of the readers in the library.*

2. A poem is a highly structured piece of writing. Each line is carefully shaped, sometimes lines are grouped into stanzas, and words in different lines are often

linked together through sound. The poem's structure also gives certain words special emphasis. Find some resemblances between this work of art and a poem as described here. *The artwork is structured into geometric patterns, the way a poem is structured into lines and verses; with a few colors, the different parts of the painting are tied together, the way sound ties a poem together.*

Poetry

In poetry, each word rings with meaning. In some poems, repetition and rhyme create musical rhythms. In other poems, figurative language can help you see the world in a whole new way. In this section, you'll encounter narrative poetry, which tells a story; lyric poetry, which expresses an emotional response toward a subject; haiku, which celebrates the wonders of nature; and several other types of poetry. Try reading some of the poems aloud to help you experience the full impact of what the poet is communicating.

◆ 785

Assessing Student Progress

The following tools are available to measure the degree to which students meet the unit objectives:

Informal Assessment

The questions on the Guide for Responding sections are a first level of response to the concepts and skills presented with the selection. Students' responses are a brief informal measure of their grasp of the material. Their responses on this level can indicate where further instruction and practice are needed. You may then follow up with the practice pages in the *Selection Support* booklet.

You will find literature and reading guides in the *Alternative Assessment* booklet, which you may give students on an individual basis for informal assessment of their performance.

Formal Assessment

In the *Formal Assessment* booklet, you will find selection tests and a unit test.

Selection Tests The selection tests measure comprehension and skills acquisition for each selection or group of selections.

Unit Test The unit test applies the unit skills on a broader level. The Critical Reading section measures Unit Objectives 1, 2, and 3. The Vocabulary and Grammar section measures Objectives 4 and 5. The Essay section measures Objectives 1 and 6.

Alternative Assessment

Portfolios As you review individual pieces or the collected work in students' portfolios, you will find assessment sheets available in the portfolio section of the *Alternative Assessment* booklet.

Scoring Rubrics You will find scoring rubrics for writing modes in the *Alternative Assessment* booklet. You can apply these to Writing Mini-Lessons and to Writing Process Workshop lessons.

Speaking and Listening The *Alternative Assessment* booklet contains assessment sheets for speaking and listening activities.

Learning Modalities The *Alternative Assessment* contains activities that appeal to different learning styles. You may use these as an alternative measurement of students' growth.

*G*uide for Reading

OBJECTIVES

1. To read, comprehend, and interpret a poem
2. To relate a poem to personal experience
3. To use interactive reading strategies to read for success
4. To identify rhyme scheme
5. To build vocabulary in context and become familiar with poetic contractions
6. To recognize inverted word order
7. To write a word picture of a natural scene, avoiding unnecessary details
8. To respond to the poem through writing, speaking and listening, and projects

SKILLS INSTRUCTION

Vocabulary:
Specialized
Vocabulary: Poetic
Contractions
Grammar:
Inverted Word
Order
**Reading for
Success:**
Interactive Reading
Strategies

Literary Focus:
Rhyme Scheme
Writing:
Avoiding
Unnecessary
Details

PORTFOLIO OPPORTUNITIES

Writing: Personal Response; Poem With Similes; Support for a Definition
Writing Mini-Lesson: Word Picture of a Natural Scene
Speaking and Listening: Speech; Memorized Presentation
Projects: Anthology; Illustration

William Wordsworth
(1770–1850)

Wordsworth began his career as a revolutionary firebrand and ended it as an honored, conservative member of England's establishment.

During all the stages of his long literary career, however, he made major contributions to British literature. In fact, Wordsworth is regarded as the father of the British Romantic Movement—a major literary movement of the early 1800's that emphasized the importance of the emotions, the imagination, and an appreciation of nature.

A Passion for Change Wordsworth was born on the northern edge of the rural Lake District in England. As a young man, he spent a period of time in France and became a supporter of the French Revolution's ideals of freedom, equality, and brotherhood. Although Wordsworth abandoned his desire for political change as the French Revolution grew increasingly bloody, he was able to bring about revolutionary changes in British literature.

Lyrical Ballads The revolution that Wordsworth prompted in British literature began in 1798 when he and fellow poet Samuel Taylor Coleridge published a book of poetry entitled *Lyrical Ballads*. Unlike the formal, highly intellectual poems that were popular at the time, the poems in the book used simple language to memorialize the remarkable moments of everyday life. In the preface, Wordsworth presented a definition of poetry that would influence the next generation of British poets.

Nature and Intuition Wordsworth's most memorable poetry, including much of the verse in *Lyrical Ballads*, rejoices in the powers of intuition and the kinship between people and nature. Written in 1804, his poem "I Wandered Lonely as a Cloud" was prompted by observations his sister Dorothy had made in her journal after she and William had suddenly come upon the sight of a field crowded with daffodils. Wordsworth took his sister's fragmented comments and turned them into this poem.

◆ Build Vocabulary

**SPECIALIZED VOCABULARY:
POETIC CONTRACTIONS**

To maintain rhythm and rhyme, poets sometimes use **poetic contractions**—words in which a letter is replaced by an apostrophe. For example, you'll find the contraction *o'er* (over) in this poem. Notice the rhythm of this line: "That *floats* on *high* o'er *vales* and *hills*." The word *over* would have disrupted the iambic rhythm (soft/*stressed*), but the word *o'er* fits right in.

WORD BANK
host
glee
pensive
bliss

Before you read, preview this list of words from the poem.

◆ Build Grammar Skills

INVERTED WORD ORDER

"Ten thousand saw I at a glance...." What makes this sentence sound unusual is the **inverted word order**. Normal word order follows a subject-verb-complement pattern. In the sentence from Wordsworth's poem, the complement (*Ten thousand*) comes at the beginning, followed by the verb (*saw*) and then the subject (*I*). Wordsworth intentionally uses inverted word order to draw your attention to what he is seeing: ten thousand daffodils waving in a field. When you see other instances of inverted word order, imagine the sentence in normal order and think about what the writer hoped to do by inverting it.

More About the Author
In the preface to the second edition of *Lyrical Ballads,* William Wordsworth outlined ideas about poetry that have been identified with the movement in art and literature known as *romanticism.* He argued that a serious poem could describe "situations from common life" and be written in ordinary language. He further insisted that poetry is the imaginative expression of emotions based on experiences and memories of the sights and sounds of nature. Although his poems are often praised for their descriptions of nature, Wordsworth claimed that his primary interest was the "mind of man."

Prentice Hall Literature Program Resources

I Wandered Lonely as a Cloud

◆ *Literature and Your Life*

CONNECT YOUR EXPERIENCE

You see the ocean for the first time. Your baby brother says your name and smiles. There are moments in your life that you replay in your memory, images that photographs and home videos can't do justice to because they can't capture your feelings. In this poem, Wordsworth captures both the images and the feelings connected to a special moment in his life when he and his sister came across a beautiful field of daffodils.

Journal Writing Make a list of natural scenes you've seen that stand out in your memory. What feelings do the scenes stir up in you?

THEMATIC FOCUS: OBSERVATIONS

Like many of the poems of Wordsworth and the other Romantic poets, this poem captures the poet's observations of the tranquil beauty of the natural world.

◆ Background for Understanding

LITERATURE

In his sister, Dorothy, William Wordsworth found not only a companion, but also a kindred spirit who shared his vision of life and his love of nature. Dorothy kept a daily journal of their activities, and, after their walks together through the hills and valleys of the Lake District, Dorothy would often record what they had seen. Sometimes her observations fed one of William's poems. "I Wandered Lonely as a Cloud" is probably the most famous example of this partnership of imagination. Here are Dorothy's observations on April 15, 1802:

> I never saw daffodils so beautiful they grew among the mossy stones about and about them, some rested their heads upon these stones as on a pillow for weariness and the rest tossed and reeled and danced and seemed as if they verily laughed when the wind that blew upon them over the lake, they looked so gay ever glancing, ever changing.

Compare Dorothy's observations with those presented in the poem you're about to read.

◆ Literary Focus

RHYME SCHEME

A **rhyme scheme** is a regular pattern of the rhyming words at the end of each line in a poem. You indicate the pattern of a poem's rhymes by using letters of the alphabet, assigning a new letter to each new rhyme. For example, the first stanza of "I Wandered Lonely as a Cloud" uses an *ababcc* rhyme scheme, which tells you that line 1 rhymes with line 3, line 2 with line 4, and line 5 with line 6.

As you read "I Wandered Lonely as a Cloud," see if Wordsworth keeps to this rhyme scheme in the other stanzas or if he tries something different. You might use a graphic organizer like this one to help you. Notice that the first stanza has been done for you.

Stanza	Rhyme Scheme
Stanza 1	ababcc
Stanza 2	
Stanza 3	
Stanza 4	

Interest Grabber Pique students' interest in the poem by showing them a Peanuts cartoon of Linus clutching his security blanket, a video of the song "My Favorite Things" from the musical *The Sound of Music,* or another image conveying the idea of a comforting object or memory. Ask volunteers to share their ideas about things that people think about to cheer themselves up. Tell them to close their eyes for a moment and think of something that makes them happy. Point out that special memories like these are often a person's secret treasures. Then explain that in this poem, a poet reveals one of his special, treasured memories.

Customize for
Less Proficient Readers
Have students skim the poem before reading to find the periods that mark the ends of thoughts. That way they will be less inclined to look for closure at the end of a line. If they wish, they might copy the poem out in sentence form before rereading it in stanza form.

Customize for
More Advanced Students
Wordsworth believed that poetry should be an expression of emotions based on personal experience. Have students keep this purpose in mind as they read. Discuss how the poem fits that purpose.

Customize for
English Language Learners
These students might benefit from hearing the poem read aloud before tackling it themselves.

 Listening to Literature Audiocassettes

Customize for
Verbal/Linguistic Learners
Ask students to look for vivid adjectives and lively verbs as they read. How do these words help them envision the scene the poet saw? Why is it important for the reader to be able to "see" the scene?

 Preparing for Standardized Tests

Reading and Vocabulary The ability to read and understand poetry will help students improve their performance on standardized achievement tests that measure students' ability to interpret literature. The Build Vocabulary lesson familiarizes students with poetic contractions. Such contractions may appear in reading selections on standardized tests. For more practice, use the Build Vocabulary page in *Selection Support,* p. 208.

Grammar and Language The more-advanced reading-comprehension items on standardized tests

may include a variety of sentence structures, so it is an important skill for students to be able to handle sentences with inverted word order. Students should be comfortable with recasting a sentence to figure out its meaning, as in the following:

> Into the valley of death rode the six hundred.
> *The six hundred rode into the valley of death.*

The Build Grammar Skills lesson for this selection focuses on this topic. For additional practice, use the Build Grammar Skills page on Inverted Word Order, p. 209, in *Selection Support.*

Notice that stanzas 3 and 4 can be read as a single sentence.

20 For oft, when on my couch I lie
In vacant or in <u>pensive</u> mood,
They flash upon that inward eye
Which is the <u>bliss</u> of solitude;
And then my heart with pleasure fills,
And dances with the daffodils.

❶
❷

◆ **Build Vocabulary**
pensive (pen´ siv) *adj.*: Thinking deeply
bliss (blis) *n.*: Great joy or happiness

Guide for Responding

◆ *Literature and Your Life*

Reader's Response Why do you think this experience created such a strong impression in Wordsworth's memory?

Thematic Focus Have you ever made an observation that caused you to feel the type of connection to nature that the poet describes? Explain.

Discussion With other students, create a "top ten" list of favorite (most beautiful, most powerful, strangest) scenes from nature.

☑ **Check Your Comprehension**

1. What terms does the speaker use to describe himself in the beginning of the poem?
2. Where are the daffodils, and what are they doing?
3. What does the speaker say happens when he is alone in a "pensive" mood?

790 ◆ Poetry

Beyond the Selection

FURTHER READING

Other Works by William Wordsworth
"She Dwelt Among the Untrodden Ways"
"My Heart Leaps Up"
"The Solitary Reaper"

Other Works With the Theme of the World Around Us
"The Tide Rises, the Tide Falls," Henry Wadsworth Longfellow
"I Saw in Louisiana a Live-Oak Growing," Walt Whitman

INTERNET

You and your students may find additional information about William Wordsworth and the Romantic movement on the Internet. We suggest the following sites. Please be aware, however, that sites may have changed from the time we published this information.

For biographical information on Wordsworth, visit **http://www.penguin.co.uk/Penguin/Authors/662.html** and **http://iu.newi.ac.uk/rdover/words/**

We *strongly recommend* that you preview the site before you send students there.

Guide for Responding (continued)

◆ Critical Thinking

INTERPRET

1. (a) What does the speaker suggest by comparing himself to a cloud? (b) To what are the daffodils compared in Stanza 2, and what does the comparison suggest about the daffodils? **[Analyze]**
2. What effect does the scene have on the speaker while he is present? **[Synthesize]**
3. What "wealth" is he later aware of, according to the fourth stanza? **[Connect]**

APPLY

4. Of what value to people are natural scenes such as the one the poem presents? **[Apply]**

EXTEND

5. Wordsworth's poem paints a vivid portrait of the daffodils. What does his poem add that would not be conveyed by a photograph, videotape, or painting of the same scene? **[Art Link]**

◆ Reading for Success

STRATEGIES FOR READING POETRY

Review the reading strategies and the notes showing how to read poetry. Then apply these strategies to answer the following questions.

1. How does the speaker change from the beginning to the end of the poem?
2. Which sense(s) do you use most in reading this poem? Support your answer.
3. Review the structure of the poem. What idea does each stanza develop?

◆ Literary Focus

RHYME SCHEME

A **rhyme scheme** is a regular pattern of rhyming words at the end of each line in a poem. A sequence of letters is used to indicate rhyme scheme. For example, if every other line in each stanza rhymes, the rhyme scheme is *abab*.

1. What is the rhyme scheme of this poem?
2. How does the rhyme scheme help to set off the final two lines of each stanza?
3. How does setting off the final two lines of each stanza reinforce the meaning?

◆ Build Vocabulary

POETIC CONTRACTIONS

Poets sometimes use **poetic contractions**—words in which one or more letters are left out—to sustain a rhythm or rhyme scheme. For example, Wordsworth uses the contraction *o'er*—short for *over*—to maintain the rhythm of line 2.

Identify what these contractions actually mean. Then make up a line or two using each contraction.

1. 'twill
2. twasn't
3. fore'er
4. ne'er

USING THE WORD BANK

Choose the word whose meaning is most opposite to that of the first word.

1. glee: (a) intelligence, (b) happiness, (c) sorrow
2. pensive: (a) careless, (b) cheerful, (c) thoughtful
3. host: (a) guest, (b) small number, (c) parasite
4. bliss: (a) depression, (b) joy, (c) horror

◆ Build Grammar Skills

INVERTED WORD ORDER

Poets sometimes use **inverted word order** to emphasize words or to make their writing fit a rhythm. In the line, "Ten thousand saw I at a glance," Wordsworth uses inverted word order, following the pattern of complement-verb-subject. By inverting the words, he gives emphasis to the words *Ten thousand*.

> **Inverted word order** changes the subject-verb-complement pattern of normal word order in English.

Practice Find three other examples of inverted word order from Wordsworth's poem. Identify the pattern of each. Then, in each case, explain the effect Wordsworth created by using inverted word order.

Writing Application Rewrite these sentences, changing them from inverted to normal order or normal to inverted order, whichever applies.

1. Bright they were, and golden too.
2. I wandered lonely as a cloud.
3. A host of daffodils saw I.
4. They stretched in never-ending line along the margin of a bay.

I Wandered Lonely as a Cloud ◆ 791

◆ Build Grammar Skills

Examples of inverted word order include the following:

"What wealth the show to me had brought"; complement-subject-verb; this word order emphasizes the word *wealth*.

"For oft when on my couch I lie"; complement-subject-verb; this word order emphasizes the frequency with which the speaker remembers the scene.

"And then my heart with plea-sure fills"; subject-complement-verb; this word order highlights the cause-and-effect relationship between remembrance and mood.

1. They were bright and gold-en too.
2. Lonely as a cloud wandered I.
3. I saw a host of daffodils.
4. In never-ending line stretched they along the margin of the bay. In never-ending line along the margin of the bay stretched they.

Writer's Solution

For additional instruction and practice, use the lesson in the **Language Lab CD-ROM** on Varying Sentence Structure and the Hard-to-Find Subjects page in the *Writer's Solution Grammar Practice Book*, p. 31.

791

Idea Bank

Customizing for
Performance Levels

Following are suggestions for matching the Idea Bank topics with your students' performance levels:

Less Advanced Students: 1, 5, 7
Average Students: 2, 4
More Advanced Students: 3, 6

Customizing for
Learning Modalities

Following are suggestions for matching Idea Bank topics with your students' learning modalities:

Visual/Spatial: 7
Verbal/Linguistic: 4, 5
Intrapersonal: 1, 2, 7

Writing Mini-Lesson

Refer students to the Writing Handbook, page 962, for instruction on the writing process, and page 964 for further information on Description. To guide students through the process of writing a description, use Writing Process Model 3: Descriptive and Observational Writing, in *Writing and Language Transparencies,* pp. 17–20.

Writer's Solution

Writers at Work Videodisc

Have students view the videodisc segment (Ch. 1) featuring science-fiction writer Anne McCaffrey to see how she generates and selects details for her descriptions. Have students discuss how attention to sensory details plays a part in creating a vivid description.

Play frames 335 to 10785

Writing Lab CD-ROM

Have students complete the Tutorial on Description. Follow these steps:
1. Use a cluster diagram to narrow the topic.
2. Have students draft on computer.
3. Obtain feedback from a peer reviewer to aid revision.
Allow approximately 50 minutes of class time to complete these steps.

Sourcebook

Have students use Chapter 1, Description (pp. 1–29), for additional support. The chapter includes in-depth instruction on considering audience and purpose (p. 17).

*B*uild *Y*our *P*ortfolio

Idea Bank

Writing

1. **Personal Response** Describe your reactions to this poem. Did you like it? Why or why not? What emotions did it evoke? What personal experiences did it call to mind?

2. **Poem With Similes** Wordworth's poem contains several similes—comparisons between strikingly different items, signaled by the words *like* or *as*. Using the poem as a model, write a poem in which you use similes to capture your feelings about a personal experience involving nature.

3. **Support for a Definition** Wordsworth defined poetry as "emotion recollected in tranquillity." How well does this poem illustrate his definition? Write an essay in which you apply Wordsworth's definition to the poem. Support your points.

Speaking and Listening

4. **Speech** Wordsworth freely shared his ideas about poetry with his audience. Share your ideas about poetry with your classmates by giving a brief speech in which you explain the qualities you think contribute to a good poem. Cite examples to support your opinion. **[Career Link]**

5. **Memorized Presentation** Memorize this poem and recite it to the class. Use the poem's rhymes to help you remember it. **[Performing Arts Link]**

Projects

6. **Anthology** Wordsworth is one of the most famous British Romantic poets. Find out about other Romantic poets. Collect examples of their poetry and put them together in an anthology. Include an explanation of each choice.

7. **Illustration** Create an illustration to accompany this poem. Show your illustration and explain how it connects to the poem. **[Art Link]**

792 ◆ *Poetry*

Writing Mini-Lesson

Word Picture of a Natural Scene

In "I Wandered Lonely as a Cloud," Wordsworth uses words to create a vivid portrait of a natural scene. Create your own word picture—either in the form of a few paragraphs or in the form of a brief poem—of a beautiful natural scene that you've seen either in person or in photographs. Use the following tip to help you.

Writing Skills Focus: Avoiding Unnecessary Details

Too many details, especially details that don't fit together, can create a confusing picture. It's important to be selective when deciding which details to include in a description. Decide on your purpose in writing the word picture. Is it to create a particular mood or overall impression? To persuade the reader to visit the spot? **Avoid unnecessary details**—those that do not serve your purpose. For example, if you wanted to create a vivid impression of flowers bobbing in the wind, you wouldn't want to mention an earthworm you noticed or the taste of the crisp apple in your picnic lunch.

Prewriting Jot down as many details as you can think of that are related to the scene you've chosen. Next, decide on the purpose of your word picture. Then go through your details and eliminate those that don't fit your purpose.

Drafting Decide whether your word picture will take the form of a few paragraphs or a short poem. Then use the details you've gathered to write your first draft.

Revising Use these questions to help you revise: How well have you achieved your purpose? Have you left out important or memorable details? What details can you eliminate? Which words can you replace with ones that are more precise?

✓ ASSESSMENT OPTIONS

Formal Assessment, Selection Test, pp. 183–185, and Assessment Resources Software. The selection test is designed so that it can be easily customized to the performance levels of your students.

Alternative Assessment, p. 49, includes options for less advanced students, more advanced students, verbal/linguistic learners, and musical/rhythmic learners.

PORTFOLIO ASSESSMENT

Use the following rubrics in the *Alternative Assessment* booklet to assess student writing:
Personal Response: Response to Literature Rubric, p. 103
Poem With Similes: Poetry Rubric, p. 101
Support for a Definition: Definition/Classification Rubric, p. 92
Writing Mini-Lesson: Description Rubric, p. 90

PART **1** *Meaning and Sound*

Fantastic Horse Cart, 1949, Marc Chagall, Blanden Memorial Art Museum

Meaning and Sound ◆ 793

One-Minute Planning Guide

This section introduces students to meaning and sound in poetry. The grouping that includes "The Eagle," "'Hope' is the thing with feathers—," "Dream Deferred," and "Dreams," reveals the impact that figurative language can have on a poem. In the grouping of "Blackberry Eating," "Memory," "Woman's Work," "Meciendo," and "Eulogy for Hermit Crab," students will see imaginative and powerful examples of word choice and imagery. Finally, reading "Uphill," "Summer," "Ecclesiastes 3: 1–8," "The Bells," and the song lyrics for "The Long and Winding Road," will show students the close connection between poetry and music.

Customize for
Varying Student Needs
When assigning the selections in this section to your students, keep in mind the following factors:

"The Eagle," "'Hope' is the thing with feathers—," "Dream Deferred," "Dreams"
• Some examples of simile, metaphor, and personification may present a challenge to English Language Learners

"Blackberry Eating," "Memory," "Woman's Work," "Meciendo," "Eulogy for Hermit Crab"
• Literal language and strong imagery make poems accessible to less proficient readers and English language learners

"Uphill," "Summer," "Ecclesiastes 3:1–8," "The Bells," "The Long and Winding Road"
• Reading these poems aloud will help students hear the musicality of the language
• Vocabulary in "The Bells" will challenge some students

Humanities: Art

Fantastic Horse Cart, 1949, by Marc Chagall.

Born in Russia, the great, exuberant painter Marc Chagall (1887–1985) incorporated elements of several different schools of art—including Cubism and Surrealism—into a highly personal style that celebrated both physical and spiritual life. He left the village of his birth to study art in Paris in 1910, but his art fondly recalled his devout upbringing and the Russian-Jewish village of his childhood, often in a dreamlike style with vibrant, glowing colors. During Chagall's long career (he lived almost a century), he produced many great works of art in different media: He designed for the ballet, was a lithographer as well as a painter, and created monumental stained-glass art, including murals for the Metropolitan Opera in New York City and the Hadassh-Hebrew Medical Center in Jerusalem.

Help students to link the art with the focus of Part 1 ("Meaning and Sound") by answering the following question:
How might a poem transform the things of ordinary life the way the fiddler seems to affect the horse cart? *Poetry can take ordinary things, like a horse cart, and bring out their fantastic or dreamlike side or it can make us see ordinary everyday things in an extraordinary way.*

Guide for Reading

More About the Authors

As a young man, **Langston Hughes** lived with his father in Mexico for more than a year, served on the crew of a merchant ship bound for Africa, studied for a year at Columbia University, and lived in Paris, Venice, and Genoa.

Alfred, Lord Tennyson, was the son of a minister in the marsh country of Lincolnshire; he entered Cambridge University but never got a degree.

Emily Dickinson rarely left her family's house, and always dressed in white. She published only seven poems during her lifetime.

Alfred, Lord Tennyson (1809–1892)

The most popular of British poets during his lifetime, Tennyson rose from humble beginnings to the glory of being named poet laureate of England. Although he was enthralled by the technological advances of the Victorian era, Tennyson remained a poet of nature who brought both imagination and feeling to the landscape and its inhabitants.

Emily Dickinson (1830–1886)

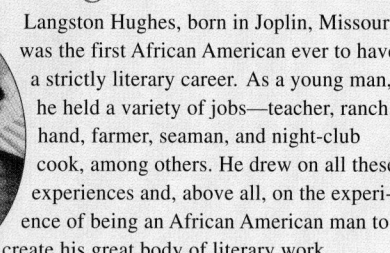

Shy, solitary, and brilliant, Dickinson led a life of nearly piercing loneliness in Amherst, Massachusetts. Yet, despite her quiet exterior, an inner life raged, enabling her to produce at least 1,775 poems. A fly and a bird coming down a walk are among her deceptively simple subjects from nature. She also wrote about death, love, and some of her religious beliefs. No matter what her subject, however, Dickinson's treatment was imaginative, complex, and thought-provoking. (For more on Emily Dickinson, see p. 244.)

Langston Hughes (1902–1967)

Langston Hughes, born in Joplin, Missouri, was the first African American ever to have a strictly literary career. As a young man, he held a variety of jobs—teacher, ranch hand, farmer, seaman, and night-club cook, among others. He drew on all these experiences and, above all, on the experience of being an African American man to create his great body of literary work.

"Dream Deferred" and "Dreams" illustrate his ability to express the spirit of black America.

◆ Build Vocabulary

COLOR WORDS

Alfred, Lord Tennyson, uses the word *azure,* instead of its near-synonym, *blue,* to describe the sky that surrounds the eagle. Why doesn't Tennyson use *blue*? Azure says more, because it refers to the exact color of a clear blue sky, rather than to just any blue. Other specific color words, such as *vermilion,* which is a flaming red, help poets convey meaning with more exactness and feeling.

WORD BANK

Before you read, preview this list of words from the poems.

| azure |
| sore |
| abash |
| deferred |
| fester |
| barren |

◆ Build Grammar Skills

COORDINATING CONJUNCTIONS

Coordinating conjunctions join words, phrases, and clauses of equal rank. For example, when Hughes dramatically ends "Dream Deferred" with the question "Or does it explode?" he begins the question with the coordinating conjunction *or,* which presents an alternative. Tennyson ends "The Eagle" with a similar last line: "And like a thunderbolt he falls." This line begins with *and,* which signals an addition or, in a narrative sequence like this one, tells what happens next. Other coordinating conjunctions are *but* and *yet,* which show contrast or exception; *or* and *nor,* which signal an alternative; and *for,* which shows cause.

The Eagle ◆ "Hope" is the thing with feathers—
Dream Deferred ◆ Dreams

◆ Literature and Your Life

CONNECT YOUR EXPERIENCE

In your dreams, you can accomplish anything. You can hit a game-winning home run, perform in a rock band in front of thousands of fans, or be the first person to set foot on Mars. Your hopes and dreams can provide you with the motivation you need to keep working toward a goal. These poems explore the significance of our hopes and dreams and look at what happens when dreams are shattered.

THEMATIC FOCUS: LOOKING INWARD

How do our hopes and dreams help define who we are?
Journal Writing Briefly describe one of your personal dreams.

◆ Background for Understanding

HISTORY

"Dream Deferred" begins with a reference to *Harlem*. Harlem has been a center for the African American population in New York City since about 1900. In the 1920's, a literary and cultural movement called the Harlem Renaissance flowered there. At the time this poem was written in 1951, however, a large percentage of the people in Harlem were living in extreme poverty and much of the neighborhood was in a state of decay. Furthermore, the advances of the civil rights era, though just around the corner, had not yet begun. As a result, many of those who lived in Harlem at the time felt a sense of hopelessness.

◆ Literary Focus

FIGURATIVE LANGUAGE

Figurative language is language that uses figures of speech. A figure of speech is a way of saying one thing and meaning another. Simile, metaphor, and personification are three common figures of speech. A **simile** compares one thing to another using the word *like* or *as*. Hughes uses a simile when he asks whether a dream deferred "stinks like rotten meat." A **metaphor** compares one thing to another without using *like* or *as*. Hughes uses a metaphor when he writes, "Life is a barren field." **Personification** gives human characteristics to an animal, object, or idea. Tennyson personifies an eagle by giving it "hands."

◆ Reading Strategy

PARAPHRASE

When you **paraphrase,** you use your own words to express what someone else has written. All of the following are examples of paraphrasing. Notice how each example uses simpler language to express ideas originally written in more complex language.

From "Dreams"

Hold fast to dreams

Paraphrased

Don't let go of dreams.

From "The Eagle"

Close to the sun in
lonely lands,

Paraphrased

very high in the sky; alone

From "'Hope' is the thing with feathers—"

And sore must be the
storm—/That could abash
the little Bird

Paraphrased

A storm would have to be
really bad to stop the bird.

Guide for Reading ◆ 795

One-Minute Insight These four poems are linked by imagery and theme. In "The Eagle," Tennyson expresses awe and admiration for the bird's strength and majesty.

◆ Critical Thinking

❶ Analyze Ask students what the word *lonely* contributes to their impression of the eagle. *The eagle's solitude makes it more majestic and awe-inspiring.*

◆ Reading Strategy

❷ Paraphrase Ask students to paraphrase "ring'd with the azure world, he stands." *He stands surrounded by blue sky.*

◆ Literary Focus

❸ Figurative Language Ask students how "wrinkled sea" is a metaphor. *Water cannot be "wrinkled." Therefore, Tennyson is comparing the sea to a wrinkled fabric.*

◆ Literary Focus

❹ Figurative Language Ask students in which ways the eagle descending from the mountain crag can be compared to a thunderbolt. *A thunderbolt, like the eagle, is swift, powerful, and deadly.*

►Critical Viewing◄

Analyze How is the eagle in the photograph similar to Tennyson's eagle? *Both are awesome creatures and fierce predators.*

The Eagle

Alfred, Lord Tennyson

He clasps the crag[1] with crooked hands;
❶ Close to the sun in lonely lands,
❷ Ring'd with the <u>azure</u> world, he stands.

❸ The wrinkled sea beneath him crawls;
5   He watches from his mountain walls,
❹ And like a thunderbolt he falls.

1. **crag** (krag) *n.:* Steep, rugged rock that juts out from a rock mass.

796 ◆ *Poetry*

Block Scheduling Strategies

Consider these suggestions to take advantage of extended class time:

- Use Daily Language Practice for Week 31. You may dictate the passages to students, or you may use the transparency and have students correct the passages in groups.
- Students can research Tennyson, Dickinson, and Hughes on the Internet either before reading the poems or while doing the

Biographical Report project in the Idea Bank on page 801.

- Have students answer the Critical Thinking questions (pp. 797 and 799) in groups of three or four students, with each member leading the discussion for one poet or poem.
- Students might create ads or guidebook descriptions in pairs, with one partner

producing copy (text) and the other producing an illustration. (See writing activities in the Idea Bank, p. 801.)

- Help students begin the Writing Mini-Lesson (p. 801) by having the class brainstorm for possible subjects.

"Hope" is the thing with feathers— Emily Dickinson

"Hope" is the thing with feathers— **⑤**
That perches in the soul— **⑥**
And sings the tune without the words—
And never stops—at all—

5   And sweetest—in the Gale[1]—is heard—
And <u>sore</u> must be the storm—
That could <u>abash</u> the little Bird
That kept so many warm—

I've heard it in the chillest land—
10 And on the strangest Sea—
Yet, never, in Extremity,
It asked a crumb—of Me. **⑦**

1.   **Gale** (gāl) *n*.: Strong wind.

◆ **Build Vocabulary**

azure (azh´ ər) *adj*.: Blue
sore (sôr) *adj*.: Fierce; cruel
abash (ə bash´) *v*.: Embarrass

Guide for Responding

◆ *Literature and Your Life*

Reader's Response How do your views about hope compare with those expressed in Dickinson's poem?

Thematic Focus What is unique about Dickinson's definition of hope?

☑ Check Your Comprehension

1. What actions of the eagle are described in Tennyson's poem?
2. According to the speaker of Dickinson's poem, what does hope do?
3. Where has the speaker heard hope?

◆ Critical Thinking

INTERPRET
1. Why do you think Tennyson begins "The Eagle" by placing the eagle so high up? **[Analyze]**
2. Is *falls* the right word for the action of the eagle? Why or why not? **[Make a Judgment]**
3. Why do you think Dickinson compares hope to a bird? **[Speculate]**
4. According to the speaker, is it easy or difficult to lose hope? Support your answer. **[Interpret]**

EVALUATE
5. Why do you think Tennyson breaks up such a short poem into two stanzas? **[Evaluate]**
6. How does Dickinson define hope in a fresh and unexpected way? **[Synthesize; Evaluate]**

The Eagle/"Hope" is the thing with feathers— ◆ 797

Develop Understanding

One-Minute Insight

What are the characteristics of hope? In "'Hope' is the thing with feathers—," Dickinson compares hope to a bird—small and delicate, yet constant and indomitable.

◆ Critical Thinking

⑤ Analyze Ask students why they think Dickinson uses the words "the thing with feathers," instead of the words "a bird." *Students might say that "the thing with feathers" leaves more to the reader's imagination.*

◆ Literary Focus

⑥ Figurative Language Point out that "perches in the soul" contains an implied metaphor for "soul." Ask students: If something perches in the soul, with what is the poet indirectly comparing the soul? *Students might answer that the soul is being compared to a tree, or a bird cage.*

◆ Reading Strategy

⑦ Paraphrase Ask students to paraphrase the last stanza. What is Dickinson saying about her own experience of hope? *She has felt hope during hard times, and felt it as a free gift that asked nothing in return.*

Reinforce and Extend

Answers
◆ *Literature and Your Life*

Reader's Response When making comparisons, students should cite lines from the poem.

Thematic Focus Dickinson's portrayal of hope as a little bird perched on the soul is unique.

☑ Check Your Comprehension
1. The eagle is swooping to the ground with the speed of a thunderbolt.
2. Hope perches on the soul and continuously sings a wordless tune.
3. The speaker has heard hope in the chilliest land and on the strangest sea.

◆ Critical Thinking
1. One reason may be that the eagle is very majestic on its high perch.
2. If students say *falls* is the wrong word, they may mention that the eagle's action is deliberate and aimed. If students say the word is appropriate, they might say the eagle's fall is a metaphor: At the end of the poem, the eagle metaphorically falls from its great height. In short, *falls* brings the eagle "down to earth."
3. Perhaps Dickinson wants to create an image of hope as a song bird that can give joy to anyone.
4. It is difficult to lose hope because hope survives even the worst moments of our lives.
5. The two stanzas provide two different visions of the eagle. In the first stanza the eagle is high above the earth. In the second, the eagle moves, first by watching and then by suddenly swooping downward.
6. Defining hope as a bird that perches upon the soul and sings sweetest during the most turbulent times is fresh and unexpected.

797

One-Minute Insight

What happens when dreams are dashed by frustration? "Dream Deferred" by Langston Hughes uses powerful images to depict the despair of shattered dreams.

◆ **Reading Strategy**

❶ **Paraphrase** Ask students to explain in their own words the meaning of the phrase "a dream deferred." *"A dream deferred" is a dream or hope that has been put off until later.*

◆ **Literary Focus**

❷ **Figurative Language** This poem consists of a series of similes (lines 3–4, 5, 7, 8–9 and 10–11). Ask students to compare and contrast the effectiveness of these similes. Which similes are the most effective? Why? *Students' responses should contain interpretations and comparisons of the following similes: like a raisin in the sun, fester like a sore, stink like rotten meat, crust over like a syrupy sweet, sag like a heavy load.*

◆ **Critical Thinking**

❸ **Make Inferences** Ask students to state what overall question the poem asks. *Sample responses: "What happens to people when their dreams and hopes are dashed?" or "What should people do who are denied freedom and equality?"*

▶ **Critical Viewing** ◀

❹ **Support** Students' opinions should be supported by examples from the poems.

Humanities: Art

Bernard's Daddy by Raymond Lark.
   This graphite drawing shows a young African American. The person's body position could be interpreted as looking discouraged or depressed.
   Use these questions for discussion:
1. In what ways does the picture show the effects of a dream deferred? *The figure looks sad and hopeless.*
2. Which simile from Hughes's poem best fits this picture, and why? *Students' responses should be supported with reasons.*

798

Dream Deferred

Langston Hughes

Harlem

❶ What happens to a dream <u>deferred</u>?

Does it dry up
like a raisin in the sun?
5 Or <u>fester</u> like a sore—
And then run?
Does it stink like rotten meat?
Or crust and sugar over—
like a syrupy sweet?

10 Maybe it just sags
like a heavy load.

❸ *Or does it explode?*

◆ **Build Vocabulary**
deferred (di furd´) *v*.: Put off until a future time
fester (fes´ tər) *v*.: Form pus

▲ **Critical Viewing** Explain why you do or do not think this piece of art is an effective illustration for the two poems. **[Support]** ❹

798 ◆ Poetry

Speaking and Listening Mini-Lesson

Inspirational Speech
This mini-lesson supports the Speaking and Listening activity in the Idea Bank on page 801.
Introduce the Concept Have students cite examples of inspirational speeches they have heard or read, such as Martin Luther King, Jr.'s, "I Have a Dream" speech, political speeches, or speeches at school pep rallies.
Develop Background Have students prepare as follows:
• Reread the Dickinson and Hughes poems.

• Jot down specific inspiring passages.
• Work the passages into an inspiring message.
• Rehearse alone or in front of a trusted listener.

Apply the Information Have students give their speeches. Remind them that, while the most inspiring speech is not necessarily the loudest, they should use expression in their voices.

Assess the Outcome To evaluate the speeches, have students use the Peer-Assessment: Speaker/ Speech page in *Alternative Assessment,* p. 111.

Bernard's Daddy, Raymond Lark, Edward Smith and Company

Dreams

Langston Hughes

Hold fast to dreams
For if dreams die
Life is a broken-winged bird ❺
That cannot fly.

5   Hold fast to dreams
For when dreams go
Life is a <u>barren</u> field ❻
Frozen with snow.

◆ **Build Vocabulary**

barren (bar´ən) *adj*.: Empty

Develop Understanding

One-Minute Insight

Is life worth living without hopes and dreams? In "Dreams," Langston Hughes uses two vivid metaphors to communicate the fundamental importance of a dream to the life of the individual.

◆ **Literary Focus**

❺ **Figurative Language** Ask students what they think Hughes means by calling life without dreams a "broken-winged bird." *As a bird cannot fly with a broken wing, people without dreams are unable to rise above the challenges of everyday life.*

◆ **Literary Focus**

❻ **Figurative Language** Ask students what they think Hughes means by calling life without dreams "a barren field/Frozen with snow." *Life without dreams is cold and empty.*

◆ **Build Grammar Skills**

Coordinating Conjunctions Ask students what coordinating conjunction is used in lines 2 and 6. Ask what subordinating conjunction has the same meaning. *The conjunction used is for. The conjunction because has the same meaning.*

Reinforce and Extend

Answers

◆ **Literature and Your Life**

Reader's Response Life might be frustrating or without hope.

Thematic Focus Sample response: A person must have perseverance, tenacity, persistence, determination, and resiliency.

Guide for Responding

◆ Literature and Your Life

Reader's Response Describe what your life would be like if you were prevented from pursuing your dreams or goals.

Thematic Focus What types of qualities does it take for a person to hold onto dreams in the face of adversity?

Journal Entry Write about what you think people can do to hold onto their dreams when it seems that their dreams might never become a reality.

☑ Check Your Comprehension

1. List the verbs that Hughes uses to tell what can happen to a "dream deferred."
2. To what two things does the speaker in "Dreams" compare life?
3. Tell how the two poems are alike.

◆ Critical Thinking

INTERPRET

1. "Dream Deferred" is full of questions. Why do you think Hughes uses six questions and only one statement? **[Speculate]**
2. Interpret the last line of "Dream Deferred." **[Draw Conclusions]**
3. What is the message of "Dream Deferred"? **[Draw Conclusions]**
4. Restate in your own words the advice that "Dreams" offers. **[Interpret]**

APPLY

5. How might you apply the advice Hughes gives in "Dreams" to your own life? **[Apply]**

EXTEND

6. How might civil rights leaders have used these poems in support of their cause? **[Social Studies Link]**

Dream Deferred/Dreams ◆ 799

☑ Check Your Comprehension

1. The verbs are *dry up, fester, run, stink, crust and sugar over, sags,* and *explode.*
2. The speaker compares life to a broken-winged bird that cannot fly and to a barren, snowy field.
3. Both poems are about dreams. Both poems suggest that life will go seriously wrong if dreams are not part of it.

◆ Critical Thinking

1. By asking questions, Hughes invites the reader to explore with him the idea of dreams deferred. The repetition of questions underscores the many possible tragedies of not being allowed to follow one's dreams. The single statement near the end of the poem breaks the rhythm of the questioning pattern, giving the final question even greater impact.
2. The word *explode* may suggest violence; it certainly suggests grave repercussions—perhaps for both the dreamer and others—for not following dreams.
3. If dreams are deferred, the results can be deleterious or catastrophic.
4. "Dreams" tells the reader to hold on to dreams because, without them, life is crippled and empty.
5. Students might apply the advice to their dreams for future careers.
6. Civil rights leaders might have cited the enormous human cost of deferring dreams. They might have warned of the possibility of explosions, in the form of violence, if dreams continued to be deferred.

Guide for Reading

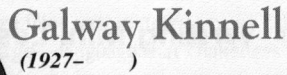

OBJECTIVES

1. To read, comprehend, and interpret poems
2. To relate the poems to personal experience
3. To envision the imagery in a poem
4. To appreciate imagery
5. To build vocabulary in context and learn the word root *-primo-*
6. To develop skill in using parallel structure
7. To write a "remember-when . . ." letter focusing on a main impression
8. To respond to the poems through writing, speaking and listening, and projects

SKILLS INSTRUCTION

Vocabulary:
Word Roots:
-primo-
Grammar: Parallel
Structure
Reading Strategy:
Envision the
Imagery
Literary Focus:
Imagery

Writing:
Main Impression
**Speaking and
Listening:**
Monologue
(teacher edition)
Critical Viewing:
Explain; Connect;
Infer

PORTFOLIO OPPORTUNITIES

Writing: Menu; Diary Entry; Evaluation
Writing Mini-Lesson: "Remember-When . . ." Letter
Speaking and Listening: Dramatic Reading Monologue
Projects: Concrete Image; Research Project

More About the Authors

Galway Kinnell won both the Pulitzer Prize for Poetry and the American Book Award for *Selected Poems* in 1982.

Margaret Walker earned her Ph.D. in 1966, when she was more than fifty years old.

Julia Alvarez has served as Kentucky's poet in the schools. She is now a professor of English and creative writing at Middlebury College in Vermont.

Gabriela Mistral was only fifteen years old when she went to teach in a remote town in the Andean mountains.

Pattiann Rogers taught high-school English in Missouri and elementary school in Texas before focusing on her career as a poet.

Galway Kinnell
(1927–)

Galway Kinnell is an American poet concerned with the themes of the inevitability of death, selfhood, and the power of nature. He has taught at various universities and has been active in the civil rights movement.

Margaret Walker
(1915–)

A poet and a novelist, Walker is considered one of the legends of African American literature. As an artist, she focuses on the experiences and hardships of black people in America.

Julia Alvarez
(1950–)

Julia Alvarez moved from the Dominican Republic to New York City with her family when she was ten. She says that the complexity of the many cultures in America is "part of what makes us rich and makes us strong."

Gabriela Mistral
(1889–1957)

Born in Chile and named Lucila Godoy y Alcayaga, this writer formed her pen name from the names of two of her favorite writers, Gabriele D'Annunzio and Frederic Mistral. The 1945 recipient of the Nobel Prize for Literature, Mistral wrote many poems about children and motherhood.

Pattiann Rogers
(1940–)

Known for the scientifically exact language of her poems, Pattiann Rogers says that the natural world has always provided a way for her to consider the important questions of why we are here.

◆ Build Vocabulary

WORD ROOTS: *-primo-*
In her poem "Woman's Work," Julia Alvarez uses the phrase, "I was primed. . . ." The word *prime* comes from the word root *-primo-*, which means "first in time or in importance." In this case, *primed* means "coached beforehand."

WORD BANK
Before you read, preview this list of words from the poems.

| unbidden |
| sinister |
| primed |
| divine |
| meticulously |

◆ Build Grammar Skills

PARALLEL STRUCTURE
In these poems, the poets use **parallel structure** to create rhythm and emphasize meaning. Parallel structure is the expression of similar ideas in similar grammatical form. Look at this example from Walker's poem:

> **Memory**
> I can remember wind-swept streets . . .
> I can remember seeing them alone . . .
> I can remember hearing all they said . . .

By repeating the phrase "I can remember," Walker draws attention to the content of the speaker's memories and creates a pleasing rhythm.

802 ◆ Poetry

Prentice Hall Literature Program Resources

REINFORCE / RETEACH / EXTEND

Selection Support Pages
Build Vocabulary: Word Roots: *-primo-*, p. 217
Build Grammar Skills: Parallel Structure, p. 219
Reading Strategy: Envision the Imagery, p. 220
Literary Focus: Imagery, p. 221

Strategies for Diverse Student Needs, p. 51

Beyond Literature
Cross-Curricular Connection: Science, p. 53

Formal Assessment Selection Test, pp. 189–191,
Assessment Resources Software

Alternate Assessment, p. 51

Writing and Language Transparencies
Personal Narrative, pp. 21–27

Resource Pro CD-ROM
"Blackberry Eating," "Memory," "Woman's Work," "Meciendo," "Eulogy for a Hermit Crab"—includes all resource material and customizable lesson plan

Listening to Literature Audiocassettes
"Blackberry Eating," "Memory," "Woman's Work," "Meciendo," "Eulogy for a Hermit Crab"

Blackberry Eating ◆ Memory
Woman's Work ◆ Meciendo
◆ Eulogy for a Hermit Crab ◆

◆ *Literature and Your Life*

CONNECT YOUR EXPERIENCE

It's often possible to find deeper meaning in routine events and observations. For example, looking out at the ocean might make you think of the immensity and timelessness of nature. As these poems illustrate, one of the great qualities of poetry is that it can help lead you toward such insights.

Journal Writing Describe a time when you had an important insight that was inspired by a routine event or observation.

THEMATIC FOCUS: LOOKING INWARD

What role do the poets' experiences and attitudes play in shaping the insights that they gather from everyday occurrences and observations?

◆ Background for Understanding

SCIENCE

One of the poems is about a hermit crab, an animal that carries around an abandoned shell to cover its own unprotected abdomen. The hermit crab uses the tip of its tail to grip the inside of the shell. The claws of the crab are formed in such a way that when the crab withdraws into the shell, the claws close the opening. As the hermit crab grows, it becomes too big for the shell and must find a new one. There is a lot of competition among hermit crabs for suitable shells.

◆ Literary Focus

IMAGERY refers to language that paints pictures in readers' minds. An image may appeal to any one of the five senses. For example, when Margaret Walker speaks of "wind-swept streets of cities/on cold and blustery nights," she is using imagery that appeals to the senses of touch and sight. As you read, use a chart like this one to note memorable images and the senses to which each appeals. Note that one image is already included.

Image	Sight	Sound	Taste	Smell	Touch
fat, overripe, icy, black blackberries	X		X		X

◆ Reading Strategy

ENVISION THE IMAGERY

To appreciate the images that the poets use, form a mental picture of each image. Use your memory and imagination to *see, feel, hear, smell,* and *taste* what the poets describe. For example, when Kinnell refers to "fat, overripe, icy, black blackberries," try to imagine what the blackberries would look, feel, and taste like. Use the descriptive words to help you. For example, Kinnell's use of the word *black* in describing the blackberries clues you in to the fact that they're especially dark; his use of the word *icy* reveals that they're cold to the touch; and his use of the word *fat* and *overripe* suggest that the blackberries are large and swollen with flavor.

Guide for Reading ◆ 803

On the chalkboard, write the words *woman's work*. Ask students what kinds of work they would list under this heading and record their responses. The lively discussion that this exercise will spark can be harnessed in a brief, informal debate. Have the students on one side of the classroom take the affirmative position and the other side the negative position on the following statement: "There is no kind of work that should be considered exclusively 'man's work' or 'woman's work.'" Give the members of each side a chance to make several points and to respond to their opponents' points. Then tell the class that one of the group of poems they will read is about the subject of their debate.

Customize for
Less Proficient Readers
To help these readers find the imagery in the poems, have them complete a chart for each poem that lists its sensory images and names the sense to which each image appeals. To help students construct their charts, distribute copies of the Grid Organizer in **Writing and Language Transparencies,** p. 76.

Customize for
More Advanced Students
Challenge these students to identify the personification, similes, and metaphors in these poems. Have students analyze the effects of these figures of speech on imagery.

Customize for
English Language Learners
Walk students through the complex sentences in the poems and help them extract the subject and verb. Then help them identify the functions of other elements in the sentence. Ask questions to verify that they understand the poems at a literal level.

Customize for
Visual/Spatial Learners
Have these students preview the poems and draw the images that they find most striking, such as a fat, ripe blackberry; an urban street scene; a girl sweeping; a mother cradling a child; a hermit crab; or a seascape.

Preparing for Standardized Tests

Reading and Vocabulary Students can improve their performance on verbal analogies, sentence completion, and synonym items on standardized tests by learning how to use word roots to determine meanings of unfamiliar words. The Build Vocabulary lesson focuses on the word root *-primo-*. For additional practice, use the Build Vocabulary page in *Selection Support,* p. 217.

Grammar and Language Grammar items in the verbal portions of standardized tests may ask students to correct sentences such as the following.

My favorite activities are guitar, running marathons, and to write poetry. *My favorite activities are playing the guitar, running marathons, and writing poetry.*

The Build Grammar Skills lesson for this selection focuses on parallel structure. For additional practice, use the Build Grammar Skills page in *Selection Support,* p. 219.

One-Minute Insight "Blackberry Eating" describes not just the sensuous experience of eating ripe fruit but also the process of writing poetry. In this poem, words are likened to blackberries—they, too, must be savored as they are taken in.

◆ **Critical Thinking**

❶ Deduce Ask students: How can a stalk on a blackberry bush know "the black art of blackberry-making"? *Because the stalk is a blackberry stalk, it is genetically programmed by nature to make blackberries. This can be thought of as a kind of "knowing."*

◆ **Critical Thinking**

❷ Compare Have students compare what the speaker does with the blackberries to what the speaker does with words. *The speaker eats the blackberries, getting every possible bit of the delicious taste; because the speaker is a poet, he or she squeezes every possible sound and meaning out of words.*

◆ **Build Grammar Skills**

❸ Parallel Structure Ask students to find a line elsewhere in the poem that is parallel in structure to this line. Have them explain why the two lines are parallel. *Line 2 is parallel to line 13. Each line begins with a preposition and an article followed by four adjectives, the last two of which are* icy *and* black, *then ends with a noun.*

Customize for
More Advanced Students
Ask: How does the parallel structure of lines 2 and 13 support the meaning of the poem? *In lines 7, 8, and 9, Kinnell joins* blackberries *and* words *in a simile: ". . . the ripest berries/fall almost unbidden to my tongue,/as words sometimes do. . . ." Using the words* blackberries *and* language *as the final words in two parallel sentences supports their joined meanings.*

BLACKBERRY EATING

Galway Kinnell

I love to go out in late September
among the fat, overripe, icy, black blackberries
to eat blackberries for breakfast,
the stalks very prickly, a penalty
5 they earn for knowing the black art
of blackberry-making; and as I stand among them
lifting the stalks to my mouth, the ripest berries
fall almost <u>unbidden</u> to my tongue,
as words sometimes do, certain peculiar words
10 like *strengths* or *squinched*,
many-lettered, one-syllabled lumps,
which I squeeze, squinch open, and splurge well
in the silent, startled, icy, black language
of blackberry-eating in late September.

◆ **Build Vocabulary**

unbidden (un bid´ ən) *adj.*: Without being asked; uninvited

sinister (sin´ is tər) *adj.*: Threatening harm; ominous

804 ◆ *Poetry*

Block Scheduling Strategies

Consider these suggestions to take advantage of extended class time:

• Have students set up a sensory image chart, like the one on page 803, and fill it out while reading these poems.
• Instruct students to preview the words in the Word Bank and complete the Build Vocabulary lesson on page 810. Encourage students to look through a dictionary to find other words that

contain the word root *-primo-*. For additional practice, assign the Build Vocabulary page in *Selection Support,* p. 217.
• Direct students to work in pairs to answer the Literature and Your Life and Critical Thinking questions on pages 805, 807, and 809.
• Students may work in small groups to create a children's book about a hermit crab, as described in *Alternative Assessment,* p. 51.

804

Memory
Margaret Walker

I can remember wind-swept streets of cities
on cold and blustery nights, on rainy days;
heads under shabby felts[1] and parasols
and shoulders hunched against a sharp concern;
5 seeing hurt bewilderment on poor faces,
smelling a deep and <u>sinister</u> unrest
these brooding people cautiously caress;
hearing ghostly marching on pavement stones
and closing fast around their squares of hate.
10 I can remember seeing them alone,
at work, and in their tenements at home.
I can remember hearing all they said:
their muttering protests their whispered oaths,
and all that spells their living in distress.

---

1. **felts:** Felt hats.

▶ **Critical Viewing** Why would the poem's first line make a good caption for this photograph? **[Explain]**

Guide for Responding

◆ Literature and Your Life

Reader's Response Which lines helped you to envision the blackberries in "Blackberry Eating"?

Thematic Focus What thoughts and feelings did "Memory" evoke in you? Explain.

☑ Check Your Comprehension

1. What words does Galway Kinnell use to describe the blackberries?
2. How does the speaker get the berries into his mouth?
3. In "Memory," what clues does the poet give that the people are poor?
4. How do you know that the people are unhappy?

◆ Critical Thinking

INTERPRET

1. What do "certain peculiar words" have in common with the blackberries? **[Interpret]**
2. What special meaning does eating blackberries have to the speaker of "Blackberry Eating"? **[Analyze]**
3. What kinds of lives do the people in "Memory" lead? **[Interpret]**
4. Explain how "Memory" can be seen as a poem that criticizes an injustice in society. **[Support]**

EVALUATE

5. W. H. Auden once said that to be a good poet, one had to "like to hang around words and overhear them talking to one another." How do these poems show that Kinnell and Walker fit this description? **[Evaluate]**

Blackberry Eating/Memory ◆ 805

Develop Understanding

⏱ One-Minute Insight

"Woman's Work" recalls how as a young girl the speaker resented having to help her mother with the housework. As an adult, the speaker realizes that she is still very similar to her mother. At a deeper level, the poem examines how people obsess over tasks to hide or suppress their emotional needs.

▶Critical Viewing◀

❶ Connect Students may point out the broom, dustpan, and sunbeams.

◆ Literary Focus

❷ Imagery Ask students: To what senses does this image appeal? *Sight, touch, smell, hearing are all reasonable answers.*

◆ Build Grammar Skills

❸ Parallel Structure Ask students to identify which parts of this line are parallel. What impression does the parallel structure create of the speaker's mother? *"The tines of forks" and "the wheels of carts" are parallel. It makes the mother seem so obsessed with cleaning that she would clean just about anything—even a cart wheel.*

◆ Critical Thinking

❹ Infer The speaker says she wanted to be different from her mother. Ask: In which way did the speaker turn out to be different from her mother? In which one important way is she like her mother? *She is different from her mother because she writes poetry and is not obsessed with housekeeping. They are similar in that they both put their hearts into their work.*

Customize for
More Advanced Students

You might want to point out that this poem is a modern variation of a traditional form called a villanelle. Encourage interested students to compare the structure of "Woman's Work" to a traditional villanelle, such as Dylan Thomas's "Do Not Go Gentle Into That Good Night." *A traditional villanelle is also nineteen lines long and has the same rhyme scheme and meter. However, a traditional villanelle repeats entire lines, whereas "Woman's Work" repeats only the key words art and heart.*

806

The Broom, Joseph Solman, The Phillips Collection, Washington, D.C.

❶ ▲ Critical Viewing Which details in this painting connect it to Alvarez's poem? [Connect]

806 ◆ Poetry

Woman's Work
Julia Alvarez

Who says a woman's work isn't high art?
She'd challenge as she scrubbed the bathroom tiles. **❷**
Keep house as if the address were your heart.

5 We'd clean the whole upstairs before we'd start
downstairs. I'd sigh, hearing my friends outside.
Doing her woman's work was a hard art

to practice when the summer sun would bar
the floor I swept till she was satisfied.
She kept me prisoner in her housebound heart.

10 She'd shine the tines of forks, the wheels of carts, **❸**
cut lacy lattices[1] for all her pies.
Her woman's work was nothing less than art.

And, I, her masterpiece since I was smart,
was <u>primed</u>, praised, polished, scolded and advised
15 to keep a house much better than my heart.

I did not want to be her counterpart!
I struck out . . . but became my mother's child: **❹**
a woman working at home on her art,
housekeeping paper as if it were her heart.

---

1. **lattices** (lat´ is əz): Narrow strips of pastry laid on the pie in a crisscross pattern.

◆ Build Vocabulary
primed (prīmd) *v*.: Made ready; prepared

 **Humanities: Art**

The Broom by Joseph Solman.

This piece of art illustrates a room with a broom and dustpan standing against the wall. Joseph Solman, an American artist, was born in 1909. He has been called an "urban scholar," perhaps because his work reflects close observation of the urban working class.

Use these questions for discussion:

1. Compare how the speaker of the poem "Woman's Work" and her mother would react to this piece of art. *The speaker would probably find this piece of art depressing. It might* remind her of her childhood, when she couldn't go outside because she had to sweep the floor. The speaker's mother, however, might have considered it inspiring or motivating.

2. Do you think that sweeping and other household chores should be considered "woman's work," or do you think these jobs should be shared equally by women and men? *The women's movement notwithstanding, opinions may differ on this question. Accept all answers that are supported. This question may lead to a debate.*

Meciendo ("Rocking")

Gabriela Mistral
Translated by Doris Dana

Develop Understanding

One-Minute Insight "Meciendo" ("Rocking") uses images of the sea, the wind, and the stars to express a mother's love. The alternation of long and short lines captures the rhythmic back-and-forth motion of waves or a rocking chair.

El mar sus millares de olas
mece, divino.
Oyendo a los mares amantes,
mezo a mi niño.

5 El viento errabundo en la noche
mece a los trigos.
Oyendo a los vientos amantes,
mezo a mi niño.

10 Dios Padre sus miles de mundos
mece sin ruido.
Sintiendo su mano en la sombra,
mezo a mi niño.

❺

The sea rocks her thousands of waves.
The sea is <u>divine</u>.
Hearing the loving sea
I rock my son.

5 The wind wandering by night
rocks the wheat.
Hearing the loving wind
I rock my son.

10 God, the Father, soundlessly rocks
His thousands of worlds.
Feeling His hand in the shadow
I rock my son.

❻

◆ **Build Vocabulary**
divine (də vīn´) *adj.*: Holy; sacred

◆ Critical Thinking

❺ Compare and Contrast
Students can learn something about a poem just by looking at it in its original language—even if they don't know that language! Ask them to compare the uses of rhyme and repetition in the two versions. *The Spanish version rhymes, while the translation does not. The Spanish version has slightly more repetition, since the second line in each stanza begins with the word mece.*

◆ Reading Strategy

❻ Envision the Imagery To which of the senses do these images appeal? *They appeal to hearing, touch, and sight.*

Customize for
English Language Learners
If there are any Spanish-speaking students in your class, ask a volunteer to read the poem to the class in Spanish so that they can hear the sound of the original. Then play the audiocassette recording for the class.
Listening to Literature Audiocassettes

Guide for Responding

◆ Literature and Your Life

Reader's Response Do the images created in these poems appeal to you? Why or why not?
Thematic Focus What do these poems reveal about the poets' feelings toward motherhood?

☑ Check Your Comprehension

1. What ambition does the mother in "Woman's Work" have for her daughter?
2. How does the daughter react to her mother's wishes?
3. Whom is the speaker rocking in "Meciendo"?
4. In the third stanza, what does the speaker feel?

◆ Critical Thinking

INTERPRET
1. How can you tell that the daughter in "Woman's Work" both admires and resents her mother? **[Infer]**
2. Compare the mother's attitude toward housekeeping and her attitude toward the education of her daughter. **[Compare and Contrast]**
3. In "Meciendo," what is the connection between the image the speaker describes in each stanza and her rocking of her son? **[Connect]**
EVALUATE
4. What universal truths about motherhood do you think Mistral is addressing in "Meciendo"? **[Apply]**

Woman's Work/Meciendo ◆ 807

Answers
◆ **Literature and Your Life**
Reader's Response
Students may find the images in "Woman's Work" unpleasant because they remind students of disliked chores. Students may find the images in "Rocking" comforting.
Thematic Focus Students may say that both poems reveal that the poets appreciate how mothers influence the lives of their children.

☑ **Check Your Comprehension**
1. She wants her to become as good at keeping a house as she is.
2. She rebels.
3. She is rocking her son.
4. She feels akin to God nurturing His creation.

◆ **Critical Thinking**
1. Her admiration for her mother is conveyed in lines 12 and 17; her resentment is revealed in lines 8, 9, 15, and 16.
2. Her attitude toward both is similar; she fusses over her house and her daughter to make them come out perfect.
3. Each image is eternal, as is the rocking of a baby.

4. Students may say that motherhood is empowering, loving, and a powerful natural force.

One-Minute Insight "Eulogy for a Hermit Crab" describes and praises a hermit crab. The awe and appreciation the speaker expresses for this humble animal is indirect praise for nature, and for universal virtues such as persistence, constancy, and being true to oneself.

◆ **Critical Thinking**

❶ **Infer** Ask students what the image in this sentence suggests about the life of a hermit crab. *It suggests the crab always faces great danger and hardship.*

◆ **Critical Thinking**

❷ **Interpret** Ask students: Why does the crab stay in the face of this danger? *Students may say that the crab is brave and determined to survive.*

▶ **Critical Viewing** ◀

❸ **Infer** Students may say that hermit crabs live in snail shells, have a spiny body covering, walk on two pairs of legs, and sense their environment with their antennae and beady eyes. Students may also infer that hermit crabs use their large front claws in manipulating food, examining new shells, pinching enemies, and blocking the opening of their shell.

Eulogy for a Hermit Crab
Pattiann Rogers

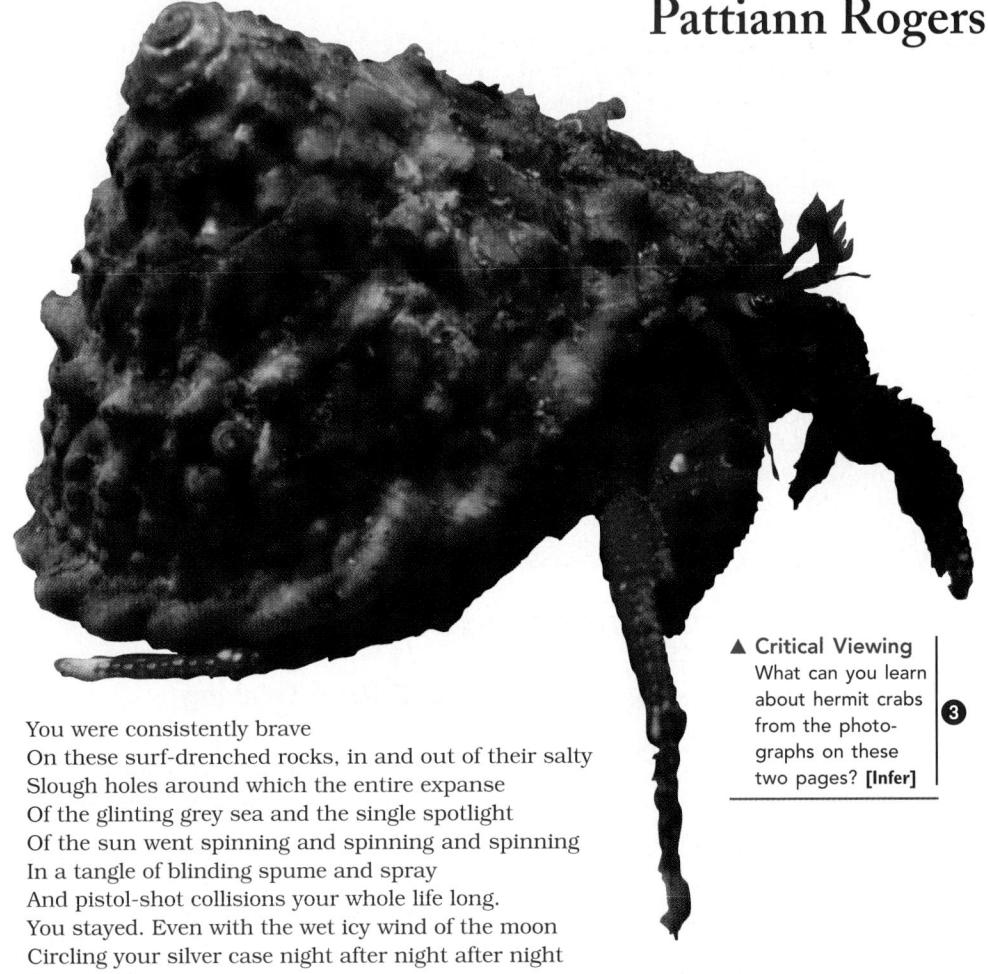

▲ **Critical Viewing**
What can you learn about hermit crabs from the photographs on these two pages? [Infer] ❸

❶ 5

You were consistently brave
On these surf-drenched rocks, in and out of their salty
Slough holes around which the entire expanse
Of the glinting grey sea and the single spotlight
Of the sun went spinning and spinning and spinning
In a tangle of blinding spume and spray
And pistol-shot collisions your whole life long.
You stayed. Even with the wet icy wind of the moon
Circling your silver case night after night after night

❷ 10

You were here.

And by the gritty orange curve of your claws,
By the soft, wormlike grip
Of your hinter body, by the unrelieved wonder

808 ◆ Poetry

Monologue
This mini-lesson supports the Speaking and Listening activity on page 811.
Introduce the Concept Tell students that a monologue is a speech by one character. In this activity, they will assume the role of a politician and give a speech on behalf of their constituents.
Develop Background To check that students understand the concept, ask questions like these:

• What are some techniques for grabbing the audience's attention in a speech?
• How can you organize the body of your speech to make your points clear?
• What are some techniques for concluding a speech?
• What are some tips for improving oral presentations?

Help students generate guidelines for the monologue based on their responses.
Apply the Information Before they start

drafting their monologue, instruct students to provide answers to questions character, audience, and purpose, such as Who is your audience? Is it friendly or unfriendly? What will it take to get your point across?
Assess the Outcome Use the guidelines generated in the Develop the Concept step as an evaluation checklist. Other criteria might include appropriateness of the speech to the student's selected character, audience and purpose, clarity; and persuasiveness.

15 Of your black-pea eyes, by the mystified swing
And swing and swing of your touching antennae,
You maintained your name <u>meticulously</u>, you kept
❹ Your name intact exactly, day after day after day.
No one could say you were less than perfect
In the hermitage of your crabness.

20 Now, beside the racing, incomprehensible racket
Of the sea stretching its great girth forever
Back and forth between this direction and another,
Please let the words of this proper praise I speak
Become the identical and proper sound
25 Of my mourning.

◆ **Build Vocabulary**
meticulously (mə tik′ yoō ləs lē) *adj.*: Very carefully;
scrupulously

◆ **Build Grammar Skills**

❹ Parallel Structure Have students identify other phrases in the poem that are parallel to "day after day after day." *Parallel phrases are found in lines 5, 9, and 14–15.*

Reinforce and Extend

Answers
◆ *Literature and Your Life*

Reader's Response There are many images in this poem from which students may choose. Some students may like the image of frantic, swirling motion conveyed in lines 5–6. Others may enjoy the image of the curious crab in lines 13–15.

Thematic Focus Students may say that the crab's life consists of never-ending change.

☑ **Check Your Comprehension**
1. She has been observing it in rocky tide pools at the edge of the sea.
2. The crab's world is limited to the "surf-drenched rocks" where it lives.

◆ **Critical Thinking**
1. She describes the adverse conditions in which it lives, which include pounding surf and cold nights.
2. There were waves that confused and battered it, and the nights were cold.
3. She praises it for its bravery, constancy, and ability to be true to itself.
4. Students may say that people can learn about courage, persistence, and being true to oneself.

Guide for Responding

◆ *Literature and Your Life*

Reader's Response What image in the poem do you like best? Explain.

Thematic Focus From the crab's point of view, what is its life like?

Journal Entry Write a paragraph or two about a day in the life of a hermit crab as the crab sees it.

☑ **Check Your Comprehension**
1. Where has the poet been observing the crab she describes?
2. What are the limits of the crab's world?

◆ **Critical Thinking**

INTERPRET
1. What evidence does the speaker use to prove the crab was "consistently brave"? **[Interpret]**
2. How was the crab's environment a constant challenge to it? **[Infer]**
3. As in any eulogy, the speaker praises the dead. For what qualities does the poet praise the dead hermit crab? **[Classify]**

APPLY
4. Based on the depiction of the crab in this poem, what lesson can people learn from hermit crabs? Support your answer. **[Relate]**

Eulogy for a Hermit Crab ◆ 809

Beyond the Selection

FURTHER READING

Other Works by the Poets
Imperfect Thirst, Galway Kinnell
For My People, Margaret Walker
Lagar, Gabriela Mistral
The Family Is All There Is, Pattiann Rogers

Other Works About Looking Inward
"When I Was One-and-Twenty," A. E. Housman
"Desert Places," Robert Frost

INTERNET

You and your students may find additional information about the authors of these selections on the Internet. We suggest the following sites. Please be aware, however, that sites may have changed from the time we published this information.

For information about Margaret Walker's life and career, go to **http://www.virginia.edu/~history/ courses/hius323/walker.html**

For information about Gabriela Mistral's life and career, go to **http://www.tdo.com/ features/stories/whold/whold4.htm**

To read an interview with Pattiann Rogers and see some of her poems, go to **http://morpo.com/morpo/v3i3/**

We *strongly recommend* that you preview the sites before you send students to them.

◆ Literary Focus

Sample responses:
1. Two words that appeal to the sense of touch are *prickly* and *squeeze*.
2. Three examples of images that appeal to the sense of hearing are "ghostly marching," "muttering protests," and "whispered oaths."
3. An image that appeals to the sense of sight is ". . . when the summer sun would bar/the floor. . . ."
4. An image that appeals to the sense of touch is "feeling His hand in the shadow."
5. A particularly appealing image is "a tangle of blinding spume and spray," which appeals to the sense of sight.

◆ Reading Strategy

1. In their responses, students should clearly describe the image, identify the poem from which it comes, and provide well thought out reasons for why they like that particular image.
2. Student paragraphs should include details that appeal to all five senses, and relate the image to personal experience.

◆ Build Vocabulary

Using the Word Root -primo-
1. prime minister;   2. prime witness;
3. prime coat

Using the Word Bank
1. a   2. b   3. b   4. a   5. a

◆ Build Grammar Skills

Sample responses:
1. The prickly stalks knew the art of blackberry-making. The man liked blackberry eating.
2. I can remember all they said. I can also recall their faces.
3. First she scrubbed the bathroom tiles. Then she washed the kitchen floor.

Julia Alvarez not only writes poetry, but she also writes novels. Her first novel, *How the Garcia Girls Lost Their Accents,* is based on her own experience as an immigrant in America. *In the Time of the Butterflies,* her second novel, is based on a true story about four sisters who remained in the Dominican Republic.

Guide for Responding (continued)

◆ Literary Focus

IMAGERY

These poems are filled with vivid **images**—groups of words that create pictures in our minds by appealing to one or more of our senses.
1. In "Blackberry Eating," find two words that appeal to your sense of touch.
2. Find three examples in "Memory" of images that appeal to your sense of hearing.
3. Find an image in "Woman's Work" that is especially appealing to your sense of sight.
4. Find an image in "Meciendo" that appeals to your sense of touch.
5. Find a particularly appealing image in "Eulogy for a Hermit Crab." To which of your senses does it appeal?

◆ Build Grammar Skills

PARALLEL STRUCTURE

Parallel structure is the expression of similar ideas in similar grammatical form. When you use parallel structure, be careful to use the same grammatical form for repeated elements.

Practice In your notebook, change one of each pair of italicized parts to match the other in grammatical form.
1. The prickly stalks knew the art of *blackberry making.* The man liked *to eat blackberries.*
2. *I can remember* all they said. *I also recall* their faces.
3. First she scrubbed *the bathroom tiles.* Then she washed *the floor of the kitchen.*

Writing Application In your notebook, rewrite this paragraph, replacing the underlined sections to achieve parallel structure.

Julia Alvarez not only writes poetry, but she also <u>is a novelist.</u> Her first novel, *How the Garcia Girls Lost Their Accents,* is based on her own experience as an immigrant in America. *In the Time of the Butterflies* <u>is the title of her second novel. It is based on a true story about four sisters who remained in the Dominican Republic.</u>

◆ Reading Strategy

ENVISION THE IMAGERY

To appreciate the images in these poems, you have to create a mental picture of what each image describes.
1. Which image in these poems were you able to picture most clearly? Why?
2. Write a paragraph in which you expand on one of the images. Use the associations the image calls to mind to expand on what the writer describes.

◆ Build Vocabulary

USING THE WORD ROOT -primo-

In your notebook, write each sentence, completing it with one of these phrases.
a. prime witness **b.** prime minister **c.** prime coat
1. The ___?___ has a great deal of political power.
2. The ___?___ in the trial was nervous.
3. The painter had to wait for the ___?___ to dry.

USING THE WORD BANK

In your notebook, write the letter of the word that means about the same as the first word.
1. unbidden: (a) uninvited, (b) unusual, (c) ordered
2. sinister: (a) innocent, (b) evil, (c) sisterly
3. primed: (a) allowed, (b) coached, (c) followed
4. meticulously: (a) carefully, (b) sloppily, (c) quickly
5. divine: (a) godlike, (b) deep, (c) divided

Beyond Literature

Community Connection

Keeping the Past Alive Memories are worth saving. Personal memories (like those in Margaret Walker's poem) are often saved in photographs and journals. Historical memories are preserved in books, historical sites, and monuments. In many locations throughout America, historic buildings are preserved and monuments are erected to commemorate important people and events. What are some historic places in your area? Why is it important for a community to preserve its past?

Writer's Solution

For additional instruction and practice, use the lesson in the **Language Lab CD-ROM** on Unity and Coherence in Paragraphs and the Understanding Unity and Coherence page in the *Writer's Solution Grammar Practice Book,* p. 129.

Build Your Portfolio

 Idea Bank

Writing

1. **Menu** Imagine that you own a restaurant which serves crabs, blackberries, and other dishes of your choice. Write a menu in which you use vivid descriptive words to make the dishes sound appealing. **[Career Link]**

2. **Diary Entry** Write an entry that the mother in "Woman's Work" might have written in her diary. Have her comment on her daughter's behavior and attitude. **[Social Studies Link]**

3. **Evaluation** Write a critical evaluation of one of the poems. In your evaluation, discuss the effectiveness of the poet's word choice and use of imagery. Tell why you would or would not recommend the poem to readers. Cite lines from the poem to support your opinions.

Speaking and Listening

4. **Dramatic Reading** Deliver a dramatic reading of one of these poems. Use the tone and volume of your voice to emphasize key ideas and details. **[Performing Arts Link]**

5. **Monologue** Imagine that you're a politician representing the people described in "Memory." Deliver a speech in which you argue for better social services for the people who voted you into office. **[Career Link]**

Projects

6. **Concrete Image** Choose an image from one of the poems that appeals to the sense of sight. Draw a picture that shows what you see in your mind's eye. **[Art Link]**

7. **Research Project** Conduct research to learn how women's roles have changed over the past several decades. Share your findings with the class.

 Writing Mini-Lesson

Remember When . . .

The imagery used by Margaret Walker in "Memory" creates a main impression of despair, hopelessness, and poverty as the speaker reflects on her past. Choose a memorable moment or event from your own life and write a letter about it, using imagery to create a main impression.

Writing Skills Focus: Main Impression

Is your **main impression** of the event one of joy, fear, pride, or awe? Whatever it is, use imagery that contributes to that main impression. For example, if you want to convey a main impression of misery, use sensory details that support this main impression, and avoid details that contradict it.

Model From the Poem

I can remember wind-swept streets of cities
on cold and blustery nights, on rainy days;

Prewriting Once you've chosen an event to describe, list sensory details that contribute to your main impression of that event. What did you see, hear, taste, feel, and smell?

Drafting Using your prewriting notes, write a letter about the event you remember. Organize your details in order of time, space, or importance so your reader can follow your description. Refer to a grammar or etiquette book if you aren't sure about proper letter form.

Revising Put yourself in the place of your reader. Reread your letter, asking yourself whether the sensory details create your intended main impression. Revise as necessary. Check your work for proper letter form.

 Idea Bank

Customizing for
Performance Levels

Following are suggestions for matching Idea Bank topics with your students' performance levels:
Less Advanced Students: 1, 6
Average Students: 2, 4, 7
More Advanced Students: 3, 5

Customizing for
Learning Modalities

Following are suggestions for matching Idea Bank topics with your students' learning modalities:
Visual/Spatial: 6
Verbal/Linguistic: 1, 2, 3 4, 5

 Writing Mini-Lesson

Refer students to the Writing Handbook, page 962, for instruction on the writing process, and page 964 for further information on Description.

To review and reinforce the steps of drafting, peer reviewing, and revision, use the Writing Process Models for a Personal Narrative, pages 21–27 in *Writing and Language Transparencies*

✎ Writer's Solution

Writers at Work Videodisc

Have students view the videodisc segment (Ch. 1) featuring science-fiction writer Anne McCaffrey to see how she develops vivid descriptions. Have students discuss how the careful selection of details helps to convey the main impression of an event.

Play frames 335 to 10785

Writing Lab CD-ROM

Have students complete the Tutorial on Description. Follow these steps:
1. Use the Sensory Word Bins for gathering details.
2. Have students draft on computer.
3. Use the Revision Checklist to aid revision.

Allow approximately 60 minutes of class time for completing these steps.

Sourcebook

Have students use Chapter 1, Description (pp. 1–29), for additional support. The chapter includes in-depth instruction on gathering sensory details (pp. 17–18).

✓ ASSESSMENT OPTIONS

Formal Assessment, Selection Test, pp. 189–191, and Assessment Resources Software. The selection test is designed so that it can be easily customized to the performance levels of your students.
Alternative Assessment, p. 51, includes options for less advanced students, more advanced students, visual/spatial learners, interpersonal learners, intrapersonal learners, and verbal/linguistic learners.

PORTFOLIO ASSESSMENT

Use the following rubrics in the *Alternative Assessment* booklet to assess student writing:
Menu: Description Rubric, p. 90
Diary Entry: Expression Rubric, p. 87
Evaluation: Critical Review Rubric, p. 104
Writing Mini-Lesson: Description Rubric, p. 90

OBJECTIVES

1. To read, comprehend, and interpret poems
2. To relate the poems to personal experience
3. To listen to poems to increase appreciation for sound and structure
4. To identify lyric poetry and sound devices
5. To build vocabulary in context and learn the prefix *mono-*
6. To interpret and use end punctuation
7. To write a rap song using repetition effectively
8. To respond to the poems through writing, speaking and listening, and projects

SKILLS INSTRUCTION

Vocabulary:
Prefixes: *mono-*

Grammar: End Punctuation

Reading Strategy: Listen

Literary Focus: Lyric Poetry and Sound Devices

Writing: Repetition

Speaking and Listening: Dramatic Reading (teacher edition)

Critical Viewing: Compare and Contrast; Connect; Interpret

PORTFOLIO OPPORTUNITIES

Writing: Written Recommendation; Lyric Poem; Comparison-and-Contrast Essay

Writing Mini-Lesson: Rap Song

Speaking and Listening: Dramatic Reading; Listening Activity

Projects: Illustration; Multimedia Presentation

More About the Authors
London-born **Christina Rossetti** published her first book of poems at age seventeen. She lived a quiet religious life and never married.

Walter Dean Myers worked as an editor before becoming a full-time writer at age forty. He has said, "As a Black writer I had not only the personal desire to find myself, but the obligation to use my abilities to fill a void."

Edgar Allan Poe is considered the father of the short story and a pioneer of the detective, horror, and science-fiction genres.

The **King James Bible** was based partly on sixteenth-century translations by Englishmen William Tyndale and Miles Coverdale.

Guide for Reading

Christina Rossetti *(1830–1894)*

Christina Rossetti is considered by some critics to be the best female poet in English literature. Her father had come from Italy to live in England. The famous poet and painter Dante Gabriel Rossetti was her brother. Christina Rossetti's best-known work is the long poem "Goblin Market," a kind of supernatural fairy tale. Many of her other poems, however, reflect concern for religion. A number of them, like "Uphill," deal with the theme of death.

Walter Dean Myers *(1937–　)*

As a child, acclaimed author Walter Dean Myers never imagined himself becoming a writer. He was born into poverty in West Virginia, and even though he was writing award-winning poems and stories by his early teens, he believed his dream of becoming a professional writer would never be fulfilled. His dream became a reality, however, when he won a writing contest sponsored by the Council on Interracial Books for Children.

The King James Bible

The King James, or Authorized, Version of the Bible was published in 1611. It was the work of a committee of English churchmen led by Lancelot Andrews. The language of the King James Version is so beautiful that the Bible is ranked in English literature with the works of Shakespeare. According to tradition, Ecclesiastes, the section from which this selection is taken, was written by Solomon, the wise Hebrew king, who died around 932 B.C.

Edgar Allan Poe *(1809–1849)*

Edgar Allan Poe is best known for chilling tales like "The Cask of Amontillado." He was also a talented poet, however. As poems like "The Bells" illustrate, Poe was a master at using rhythm and sound effects to emphasize meaning and create a musical effect.

Many scholars believe that the idea for "The Bells" was suggested to Poe by Marie Louise Shew, a woman with medical training who treated Poe when his health began to fail during his final years. (For more on Edgar Allan Poe, see pp. 2 and 830.)

◆ Build Vocabulary

PREFIXES: *mono-*

In "The Bells," Poe describes the tolling of iron bells as a "muffled *monotone.*" The word *monotone* contains the prefix *mono-*, which means "one." Knowing the meaning of the prefix, you might guess that the meaning of the word *monotone* is "one tone," which is close to the actual meaning, "uninterrupted repetition of the same tone."

wayfarers
voluminously
palpitating
monotone
paean

WORD BANK
Before you read, preview this list of words from the poems.

◆ Build Grammar Skills

END PUNCTUATION

End punctuation—the period, question mark, or exclamation mark at the end of a sentence—does more than merely signal the end of a sentence. These marks often indicate meaning or feeling. This is especially true in poetry, in which words and punctuation are used with precision. Notice how the exclamation mark adds terror and the question mark adds anxiety in these examples.

How they scream out their affright!

Shall I find comfort, travel-sore and weak?

812 ◆ Poetry

Prentice Hall Literature Program Resources

REINFORCE / RETEACH / EXTEND

Selection Support Pages
Build Vocabulary: Prefixes: *mono-*, p. 221
Build Grammar Skills: End Punctuation, p. 222
Reading Strategy: Listen, p. 223
Literary Focus: Lyric Poetry and Sound Devices, p. 224

Strategies for Diverse Student Needs, p. 54

Beyond Literature
Humanities Connection: Seasons in Literature, p. 54

Formal Assessment Selection Test, pp. 192–194,

Assessment Resources Software

Alternative Assessment, p. 52

Writing and Language Transparencies
Cluster Organizer, p. 80

Resource Pro CD-ROM
"Uphill," "Summer," "Ecclesiastes 3: 1–8," "The Bells"—includes all resource materials and customizable lesson plan

Listening to Literature Audiocassettes
"Uphill," "Summer," "Ecclesiastes 3: 1–8," "The Bells"

Uphill ◆ Summer
Ecclesiastes 3:1–8 ◆ The Bells

◆ *Literature and Your Life*

CONNECT YOUR EXPERIENCE

You feel the heat of a steamy August day and you think about how the broiling heat of summer will change to the chill of autumn. You see parents and children enjoying the outdoors and realize that toddlers grow up to be adults. Nature and life have predictable cycles and stages. In the following poems, you will explore these cycles.

THEMATIC FOCUS: SEASONS AND CYCLES

As these poems illustrate, the world around us is filled with patterns and stages. What can you learn from the patterns of nature that you can apply to your life?

◆ Background for Understanding

SCIENCE AND LITERATURE

Poets through the ages have explored the variety, stages, and patterns found in life. For example, "The Bells" speaks of how different sounds made by bells signal the variety of life, while the poem "Uphill" concentrates on one particular stage of life. Cycles and seasons, stages and patterns: These are what comprise life. While each life is unique, each life can also be similar. People are born, then many grow to adulthood, grow old, and die. Advances in medicine have extended life expectancy far beyond what people centuries ago could have imagined. However, medicine has been unable to alter the basic cycles of life.

Journal Writing Jot down patterns or rhythms that you experience in your own life and that you see in the world around you.

◆ Literary Focus

LYRIC POETRY AND SOUND DEVICES

These poems are all examples of **lyric poetry**—highly musical verse that expresses the observations and feelings of a single speaker. In ancient times, lyric poems were sung to the accompaniment of the lyre, a type of stringed instrument. Modern lyric poems are not usually sung. However, they still have a musical quality that is achieved through various **sound devices** such as rhythm (the pattern of beats or stresses in language), alliteration (the repetition of initial consonant sounds), rhyme (the repetition of sounds at the ends of words), and onomatopoeia (the use of words that imitate the sounds).

◆ Reading Strategy

LISTEN

While the sound of words is important in all kinds of poetry, sound is especially significant in lyric poetry. To appreciate the musical quality of lyric poems, read them aloud and **listen** to your speech as you do so. For example, only by listening to the following lines from "The Bells" can you truly hear how onomatopoeia, rhyme, and rhythm combine to re-create the delightful sound and cheerful mood of sleigh bells.

> How they tinkle, tinkle, tinkle,
> In the icy air of night!
> While the stars, that oversprinkle
> All the heavens, seem to twinkle
> With a crystalline delight;

Read each of the following poems aloud to yourself or to a partner. Listen carefully for the musical effect created by the use of sound devices. Think about how the use of sound reinforces each poem's meaning.

Guide for Reading ◆ 813

Interest Grabber To introduce "Uphill," put on a brief skit for students by acting out the role of someone who is weary of life's struggle. Gripe that life sometimes seems all uphill. In a comic tone, moan about real and exaggerated difficulties: Students don't pay attention, you spend all evening grading papers, the coffee in the teacher's lounge tastes like turpentine, and so on. Ask students if they ever feel that way about life. Encourage them to mention specific difficulties from their points of view. Inform them that in "Uphill," they will read a poem that expresses the same feeling.

Customize for
Less Proficient Readers
Have students read "Uphill" aloud in pairs, alternating lines, to help them understand that the poem is a dialogue between two speakers.

Customize for
More Advanced Students
Encourage students to discuss real-life examples of the different "times" listed in "Ecclesiastes 3: 1–8." Then have students create personal responses in forms they choose.

Customize for
English Language Learners
Have students read "Summer" along with the audiocassette, stopping to review the gist of the meaning.
🎧 **Listening to Literature Audiocassettes**

Customize for
Musical/Rhythmic Learners
Have students prepare dramatic readings of "Uphill," "Summer," and "Ecclesiastes 3: 1–8" to supplement the Speaking and Listening activity for "The Bells" in the Idea Bank, p. 824.

 Preparing for Standardized Tests

Reading and Vocabulary To do well on the verbal portions of standardized tests, students should apply knowledge of word parts. The Build Vocabulary lesson for these selections focuses on using the meaning of the prefix *mono-* to help define words containing it. After students have completed the activities on page 823, give them additional *mono-* words to define, such as *monogram* and *monologue*. For additional practice, use the Build Vocabulary page in *Selection Support,* p. 221.

Grammar and Language Some standardized tests require students to demonstrate how end punctuation affects the meaning of a sentence, as in the following reading comprehension example:

> "'Watch out'?" Jim echoed, bewildered.

Which of the following terms best describes how Jim feels? (A) alarmed; (B) frightened; (C) puzzled; (D) bored *(C)*

The Build Grammar Skills lesson focuses on using end punctuation to indicate meaning. When students complete the activities on page 823, have them answer the preceding example. For additional practice, use the Build Grammar Skills page on End Punctuation, p. 222, in *Selection Support.*

One-Minute Insight

"Uphill," seemingly a conversation between a traveler seeking directions and a helpful expert, has serious overtones. The uphill road is life's journey, and the beds at journey's end are graves. The traveler is thus asking about the difficulty of life and whether there is hope for peace in the end.

◆ Critical Thinking

❶ Analyze Ask students what the words *road, uphill,* and *end* symbolize in the poem. *The word* road *symbolizes a person's life,* uphill *symbolizes struggles along life's way, and* end *symbolizes death.*

◆ Literary Focus

❷ Lyric Poetry and Sound Devices Lead students to notice the simple rhyme scheme *abab* in each stanza. Point out that in each stanza, the questioner's lines and the responder's lines rhyme.

Answers

◆ Literature and Your Life

Reader's Response Some students may find the journey depressing because it is long and uphill. Others may find it hopeful because there is comfort at the end.

Thematic Focus The poem describes life's journey.

☑ **Check Your Comprehension**

The journey is uphill and takes all day, but there is a welcoming inn with beds at the end of the road.

◆ Critical Thinking

1. Students may say that the absolute certainty of the person giving directions indicates that this is not just an ordinary trip.
2. It symbolizes a person's life.
3. It might represent life's difficulties.
4. The final destination is an inn, or a final resting place.

Uphill
Christina Rossetti

❶ Does the road wind uphill all the way?
    Yes, to the very end.
Will the day's journey take the whole long day?
    From morn to night, my friend.

5 But is there for the night a restingplace?
    A roof for when the slow dark hours begin.
May not the darkness hide it from my face?
    You cannot miss that inn.

❷ Shall I meet other wayfarers at night?
10   Those who have gone before.
Then must I knock, or call when just in sight?
    They will not keep you standing at that door.

Shall I find comfort, travel-sore and weak?
    Of labor you shall find the sum.
15 Will there be beds for me and all who seek?
    Yea,[1] beds for all who come.

---

1. **yea** (yā): Indeed; truly.

◆ Build Vocabulary

wayfarers (wā´ fer ərz) *n.*: Travelers

Guide for Responding

◆ Literature and Your Life

Reader's Response How do you feel about the journey described in this poem? Why?
Thematic Focus The questions and answers in many ways reflect a typical journey in the world. What kind of journey does the poem describe?

☑ **Check Your Comprehension**

Cite four details of the journey.

◆ Critical Thinking

INTERPRET
1. What evidence is there that this journey is not just an ordinary trip? **[Analyze]**
2. What does the journey along a road symbolize, or represent? **[Interpret]**
3. What might the uphill winding represent? **[Interpret]**
4. What is the final destination of the journey? **[Infer]**

 Block Scheduling Strategies

Consider these suggestions to take advantage of extended class time:

- To introduce the musical qualities of these poems to students, have students do a "first listening" rather than a "first reading." Have them look at the printed texts of the poems only after they have heard them spoken on the Listening to Literature audiocassette.
- Discuss with students the cycles found in life and in nature and the relationship of those cycles to these poems. Then have students complete the Humanities Connection: Seasons in Literature, found in **Beyond Literature,** p. 54.

- Let students answer the Critical Thinking questions (pp. 814, 815, 817, 822) in pairs or small groups.
- When students begin work on the Writing Mini-Lesson, you might suggest that they use one of the poems in the section as the basis for a rap song, revising as much as necessary to fit the new form.

Summer

Walter Dean Myers

3 I like hot days, hot days
Sweat is what you got days
Bugs buzzin from cousin to cousin
Juices dripping
5 Running and ripping
Catch the one you love days

Birds peeping
Old men sleeping
Lazy days, daisies lay
4 10 Beaming and dreaming
Of hot days, hot days,
Sweat is what you got days

▶ **Critical Viewing** What feeling do these images of summer evoke in you? How are they similar to or different from the images evoked by the poem? **[Compare and Contrast]**

Guide for Responding

◆ *Literature and Your Life*

Reader's Response Do you like hot summer days? Why or why not?

Thematic Focus Each season fills the world around us with an infinite number of images. What are some of your favorite images of summer?

☑ Check Your Comprehension

1. What happens to bugs and juices in the summer?
2. What do birds and old men do in summer?
3. What pair of lines sums up the way the speaker feels about summer?

◆ Critical Thinking

INTERPRET
1. What kinds of juices might be dripping? **[Interpret]**
2. What might the words "daisies lay beaming and dreaming" mean? **[Speculate]**
3. From what is said in the poem, how do people and living things from the world of nature act on hot days? **[Infer]**

EVALUATE
4. How does the poet use repetition to help communicate meaning? **[Evaluate]**

Uphill/Summer ◆ 815

 Beyond the Classroom

Workplace Skills Connection
Summer-Job Search While for some students summer represents a time of leisure, for others it represents a time to find a summer job. The process of finding a job can be less anxiety ridden if a student draws up a search plan beforehand.

Major sources of job information include personal contacts, classified ads, employment agencies, school guidance offices, state employment offices, and the personnel departments of companies. For young entrepreneurs, the library is a

good place to start gathering information about how to set up one's own business.

Invite students to list two or three possible summer jobs they would like to have. For each job possibility, ask students to state, orally or in their journals, the specific search procedures that would be most likely to land that particular job—for example, "send résumé to personnel office." Discuss students' job search plans with them and provide informal suggestions where appropriate.

815

One-Minute Insight Ecclesiastes 3: 1–8 says that every event, good or bad, has its place and purpose in the grand scheme of things, and implies that people should accept life's ups and downs as part of nature's cycles or as divine will. The stately rhythms and repeated phrases reinforce the passage's message.

▶Critical Viewing◀

❶ Connect This series of illustrations effectively illustrates the poem because the series represents the four seasons, or the repeating cycles of nature. Similarly, the poem represents the repeating cycles of life.

◆ Critical Thinking

❷ Analyze Ask students what is meant by the words *season* and *time* mean in the passage. *Suggested response: The words* season *and* time *may mean a particular phase or moment in the cycle of a person's life. The words might also mean a particular phase or moment in the grand scope of time itself.*

◆ Critical Thinking

❸ Evaluate Point out that some of the pairs of opposites are extreme: killing and healing, love and hate, war and peace. Ask students how one can be comfortable accepting both sides of each pair. *Students may say that each side is a part of life.*

◆ Literary Focus

Lyric Poetry and Sound Devices Invite students to describe the rhythm of this passage and to discuss how that rhythm might help create its mood. *Students may say that the rhythm is stately, majestic, and calm. These qualities help establish a mood of calm, all-accepting wisdom.*

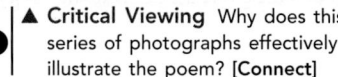

▲ Critical Viewing Why does this series of photographs effectively illustrate the poem? [Connect]

816 ◆ Poetry

Cross-Curricular Connection: Science

Seasonal Weather Many people in the United States think of the four seasons as having weather clearly distinct from one another. However, manifestations of the seasons vary in different regions of the world; even large parts of the United States, such as the Sun Belt, Alaska, and Hawaii, do not fit the classic pattern. In India and sub-Saharan Africa, wet and dry seasons alternate. In some fortunate spots, such as Costa Rica or Tahiti, warm, springlike conditions prevail year-round. In some places, fierce, hot winds affect life at specific times of the year; these winds include the mistral of France, the Santa Ana of southern California, the sirocco of Italy, the meltemi of Greece, the harmattan of West Africa, and the khamsin of Egypt.

Ask students to choose two or three different spots on the globe and find out what the seasons there are like. Suggest that students select one place they'd wish to visit, one place they'd not wish to visit, and one place on the opposite side of the world from them.

Ecclesiastes 3:1-8
(King James Version)

❷ To every thing there is a season, and a time to
every purpose under the heaven:
A time to be born, and a time to die; a time to
plant, and a time to pluck up that which is planted;
A time to kill, and a time to heal; a time to break
down, and a time to build up;
A time to weep, and a time to laugh; a time to
mourn, and a time to dance;
5 A time to cast away stones, and a time to gather
❸ stones together; a time to embrace, and a time to
refrain from embracing;
A time to get, and a time to lose; a time to keep,
and a time to cast away;
A time to rend,[1] and a time to sew; a time to keep
silence, and a time to speak;
A time to love, and a time to hate; a time of war,
and a time of peace.

---

1. **rend** (rend) *v.*: Tear.

Guide for Responding

◆ Literature and Your Life

Reader's Response Do you find this passage comforting? Why or why not?

Thematic Focus How does this poem connect the cycles of nature with the cycles of human life?

☑ Check Your Comprehension

1. Name four pairs of actions mentioned in the passage.
2. What verse contains the main idea?
3. How would you describe the way this passage is organized?

◆ Critical Thinking

INTERPRET

1. What does "To every thing there is a season" mean? **[Infer]**
2. What is the purpose of the repetition of the phrase "a time"? **[Speculate]**
3. What activity is suggested by the words "A time to cast away stones, and a time to gather stones together ..."? **[Infer]**

EVALUATE

4. This passage is balanced by pairs of phrases that are opposites. How does the pairing of opposite ideas help to communicate the message of the passage? **[Evaluate]**

Ecclesiastes 3:1–8 ◆ *817*

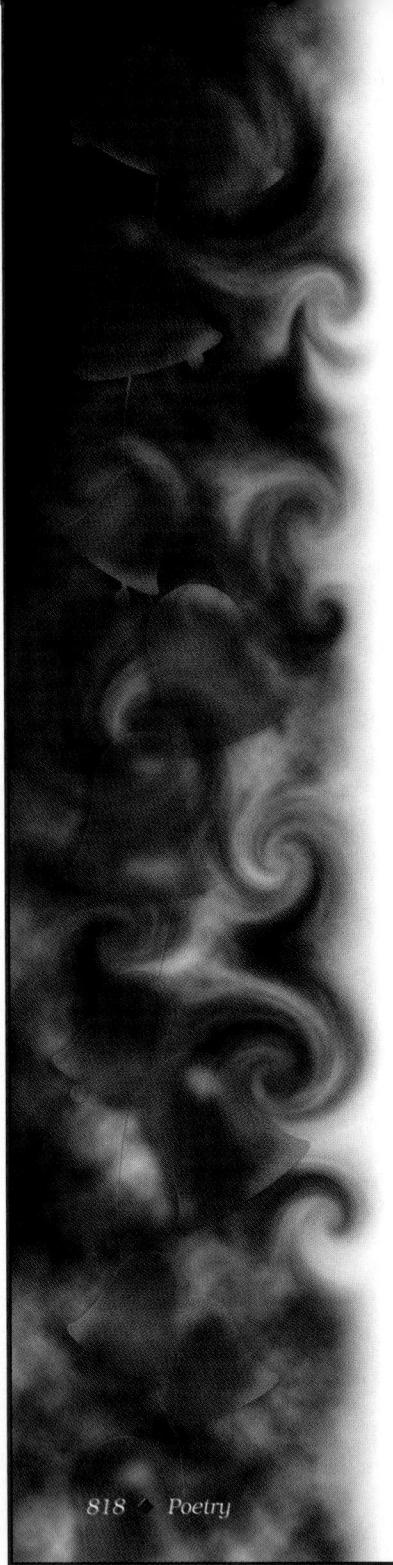

One-Minute Insight "The Bells" uses repetition and onomatopoeia to capture the sound and symbolism of four sets of bells. The silver bells are playful and merry, the golden bells are exultant, the brazen bells are terrified and terrify, and the iron bells are menacing.

◆ **Critical Thinking**

❶ **Support** Ask students what season is depicted here. What words or phrases indicate the season? *It is winter, as indicated by terms like* sledges *and* icy air.

◆ **Literary Focus**

❷ **Sound Devices** Ask students to identify the example of onomatopoeia in these lines and have them explain their answers. *Tintinnabulation is an example of onomatopoeia because the word itself suggests the sound of bells ringing.*

◆ **Critical Thinking**

❸ **Analyze** Ask students to cite words that establish the mood of Part II. *Words that establish mood include:* mellow, wedding, golden, happiness, harmony, balmy, delight, turtledove, gush, *and* euphony.

◆ **Build Grammar Skills**

❹ **End Punctuation** Discuss how exclamation points affect the mood in Part II. *Most students will say they enhance the sense of happy excitement.*

The Bells
Edgar Allan Poe

I

Hear the sledges[1] with the bells—
　　　　Silver bells!
What a world of merriment their melody foretells!
　　How they tinkle, tinkle, tinkle,
5　　　　In the icy air of night!
While the stars, that oversprinkle
All the heavens, seem to twinkle
　　　With a crystalline delight;
　　Keeping time, time, time,
10　　In a sort of Runic[2] rhyme,
To the tintinnabulation[3] that so musically wells ❷
　　From the bells, bells, bells, bells,
　　　　Bells, bells, bells—
From the jingling and the tinkling of the bells.

❶

II

15　　Hear the mellow wedding bells,
　　　　Golden bells!
What a world of happiness their harmony foretells!
　　Through the balmy air of night
　　How they ring out their delight!
20　　　From the molten golden-notes,
　　　　And all in tune,
　　What a liquid ditty[4] floats
To the turtle-dove[5] that listens, while she gloats
　　　　On the moon!
25　　Oh, from out the sounding cells,
What a gush of euphony[6] voluminously wells!
　　　How it swells!
　　　How it dwells
　　On the future! how it tells
30　　Of the rapture that impels
To the swinging and the ringing

❸

❹

---

1. **sledges** (slej´ əz) *n.*: Sleighs.
2. **Runic** (rōō´ nik) *adj.*: Songlike; poetical.
3. **tintinnabulation** (tin ti nab yōō la´ shən) *n.*: Ringing of bells.
4. **ditty** (dit´ ē) *n.*: Song.
5. **turtle-dove:** The turtle-dove is traditionally associated with love.
6. **euphony** (yōō´ fə nē) *n.*: Pleasing sound.

◆ **Speaking and Listening Mini-Lesson**

Dramatic Reading

This mini-lesson supports the Speaking and Listening activity in the Idea Bank on p. 824.

Introduce the Concept Explain that a dramatic reading involves more than simply reciting words. Readers need to bring a poem to life. Delivery includes phrasing the lines as if they were music—deciding where to take a breath, where to pause dramatically, where to get louder, and where to get quieter. It also involves the use of vocal effects—such as

whispering, bellowing, or using different voices or accents.

Develop Background Have students discuss the following questions before rehearsing their dramatic reading:

• What mood or moods should the reader strive for in each part?

• How can different vocal effects help create mood?

• How can a reading of "The Bells" be made seriously dramatic without crossing the

line into corny humor?

Apply the Information Ask students to rehearse their readings and then to perform them for the class.

Assess the Outcome Have students evaluate each dramatic reading by using the following criteria: appropriate moods, musicality, vocal effects, overall delivery, and expression.

You might have students use the Peer Assessment form for Oral Interpretation, p. 112 in *Alternative Assessment*.

Of the bells, bells, bells,
Of the bells, bells, bells, bells
Bells, bells, bells—
35　To the rhyming and the chiming of the bells!

III

Hear the loud alarum[7] bells!
Brazen[8] bells!
What a tale of terror now their turbulency tells!
In the startled ear of night
40　　　How they scream out their affright!
Too much horrified to speak,
They can only shriek, shriek,
Out of tune,
In a clamorous appealing to the mercy of the fire,
45　In a mad expostulation[9] with the deaf and frantic fire
Leaping higher, higher, higher,
With a desperate desire,
And a resolute endeavor
Now—now to sit or never,
50　By the side of the pale-faced moon.
Oh, the bells, bells, bells!
What a tale their terror tells
Of Despair!
How they clang, and clash, and roar!
55　What a horror they outpour
On the bosom of the <u>palpitating</u> air!
Yet the ear it fully knows,
By the twanging
And the clanging,
60　How the danger ebbs and flows;
Yet the ear distinctly tells,
In the jangling,
And the wrangling,
How the danger sinks and swells,
65　By the sinking or the swelling in the anger of the bells—
Of the bells—
Of the bells, bells, bells, bells,
Bells, bells, bells—
In the clamor and the clangor of the bells!

IV

70　Hear the tolling of the bells—
Iron bells!
What a world of solemn thought their monody[10] compels!
In the silence of the night,

---

7. **alarum** (ə ler´ əm) *n.*: Sudden call to arms; alarm.
8. **brazen** (brā´ zən) *adj.*: Made of brass; having the sound of brass.
9. **expostulation** (ik späs chə lā´ shən) *n.*: Objection; complaint.
10. **monody** (män´ ə dē) *n.*: Poem of mourning; a steady sound; music in which one instrument or voice is dominant.

◆ **Build Vocabulary**
voluminously (və lōō´ mə nəs lē) *adv.*: Fully; in great volume
palpitating (pal´ pə tāt´ iŋ) *v.*: Beating rapidly; throbbing

The Bells　819

◆ **Literary Focus**

❺ Sound Devices Ask students why Poe repeated the word *bells* so many times. Before they answer, suggest they repeat any single-syllable word over and over. What seems to happen? *Students may say that the continuously repeated word begins to lose its meaning and become nothing but sound. This may have been Poe's reason for repeating the word bells over and over again.*

◆ **Critical Thinking**

❻ Analyze Ask students which words set the scene in Part III. *The words* alarum *and* fire *set the scene.*

◆ **Critical Thinking**

❼ Analyze Ask students to cite words that establish a mood in Part III. *Students may cite the following words:* terror, turbulency, startled, scream, affright, horrified, shriek, mad, frantic, desperate, despair, horror, fury, *and* danger.

◆ **Literary Focus**

❽ Sound Devices Ask students what consonant sound is repeated for alliteration in lines 64–65. *The sound of the letter* s. Why might this sound have been chosen? *Students may say that the hissing sound suggests the roar of a fire or the sound of water putting out a fire.*

◆ **Build Vocabulary**

❾ Prefixes: mono- Tell students that the suffix *-ody* means "song," as in the word *melody*. Challenge students to analyze the parts of the word *monody*. *Mono- means "one"; -ody means "song." A monody is a song in which one voice or instrument is dominant.*

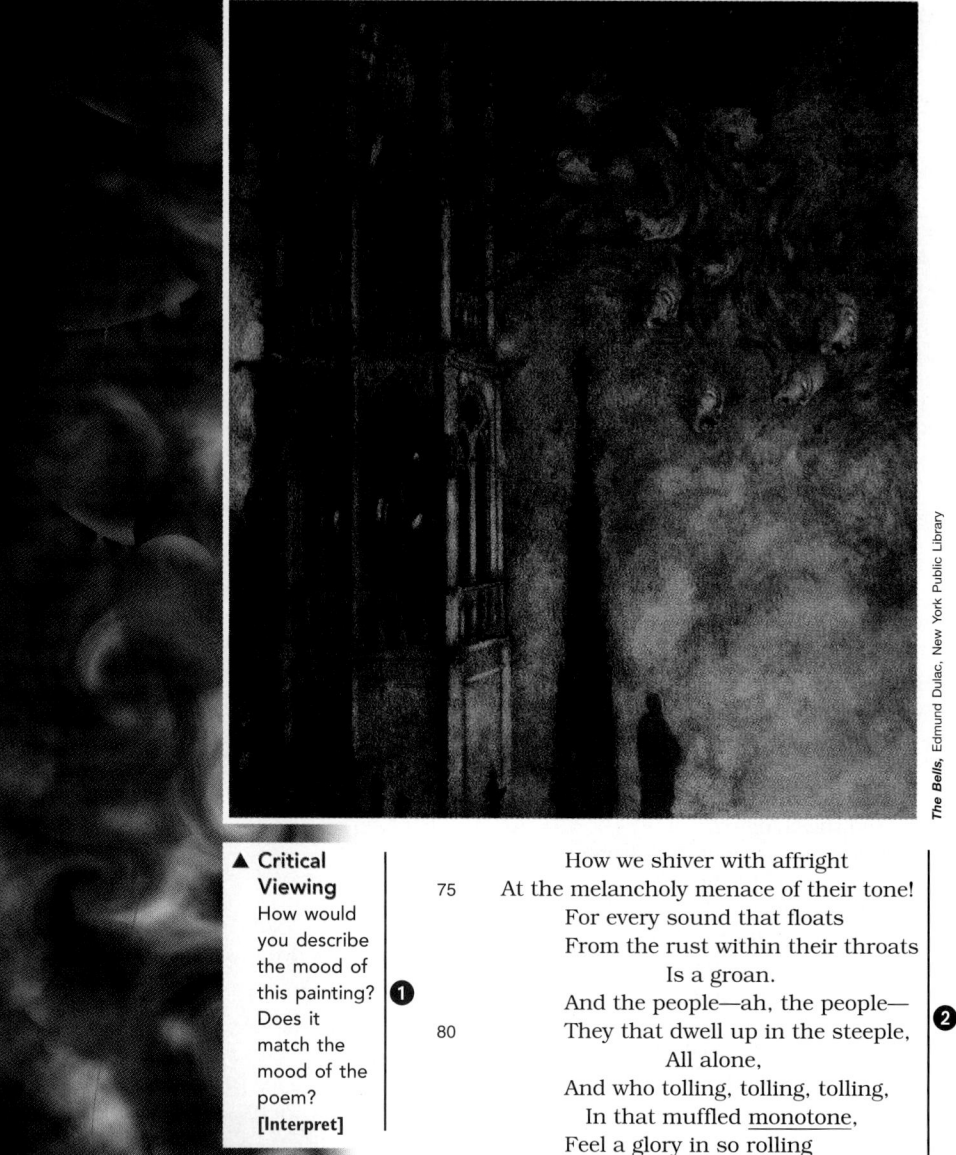

The Bells, Edmund Dulac, New York Public Library

►Critical Viewing◄

❶ Interpret Some students might describe the mood of the painting as somber because of the predominantly dark scene with only an eerie source of light. Others might say the mood is bizarre because of the oddly rendered faces to the right of the steeple. The painting matches the mood of only the part of the poem that speaks of the iron bells (Part IV) and their melancholy tone.

◆ Literary Focus

❷ Sound Devices Have a volunteer read this passage aloud, drawing out long vowel sounds. Ask students to identify the rhyming words that suggest the tolling of bells. *These words are* tone, groan, alone, monotone, *and* stone.

◆ Critical Thinking

❸ Interpret Ask students to identify the mood of the ghoul king. *He is merry, somewhat eccentric or playful, and perhaps gloating.*

Customize for
English Language Learners

Many unusual words, such as *euphony* and *monody*, are scattered throughout this poem. You may want to make sure that those words do not present an obstacle to basic comprehension of the poem. Discuss the meanings of any words in the poem that English language learners do not understand.

▲ **Critical Viewing**
How would you describe the mood of this painting? **❶** Does it match the mood of the poem?
[Interpret]

How we shiver with affright
75 At the melancholy menace of their tone!
    For every sound that floats
    From the rust within their throats
        Is a groan.
    And the people—ah, the people— **❷**
80 They that dwell up in the steeple,
        All alone,
    And who tolling, tolling, tolling,
        In that muffled <u>monotone</u>,
    Feel a glory in so rolling
85   On the human heart a stone—
    They are neither man nor woman—
    They are neither brute nor human—
        They are Ghouls:[11]
    And their king it is who tolls; **❸**
90 And he rolls, rolls, rolls,
        Rolls

---

11. **Ghouls** (go͞olz) *n.*: Evil spirits that rob graves.

820 Poetry

◆ **Build Vocabulary**

monotone
(män´ ə tōn´)
Uninterrupted repetition of the same tone

  Humanities: Art

The Bells by Edmund Dulac.
Edmund Dulac (1882–1953) was a French illustrator known for the color and imagination of his work. This painting, with its somber overall mood, illustrates Part IV of "The Bells."
Use these questions for discussion:
1. Using this painting as an example, what are some of the advantages of illustrating a literary work with paintings as opposed to photographs? *Sample response: One advantage is an artist's prerogative to stray from reality in order to create a certain impression or mood. Another is the ability to use light and composition in any way desired for emphasis or effect.*
2. How else could this poem be illustrated? *Students might suggest that paintings or photographs of sleighs, weddings, or fires might be used to illustrate the other parts of the poem.*

820

CONNECTIONS TO TODAY'S WORLD

Although you may not have thought of it, song lyrics are a form of poetry. Like poetry, good song lyrics use sound devices, imagery, and figurative language. Among the most highly regarded modern songwriters are Paul McCartney and John Lennon, who were both members of the Beatles, a rock group that disbanded in 1970 but remain popular to this day. "The Long and Winding Road" is just one of their many hits.

The Long and Winding Road

The Beatles

John Lennon and Paul McCartney

The long and winding road that leads to your door,
Will never disappear,
I've seen that road before
It always leads me here,
Leads me to your door.

The wild and windy night the rain washed away,
Has left a pool of tears crying for the day.
Why leave me standing here, let me know the way.
Many times I've been alone and many times I've cried.
Anyway you'll never know the many ways I've tried, but
Still they lead me back to the long and winding road.
You left me standing here a long, long time ago.
Don't leave me waiting here, lead me to your door.

---

1. What might the "long and winding road" symbolize?
2. Find two especially effective images, and explain what each represents.
3. Compare and contrast this song with one of the poems you've just read.

The Long and Winding Road ◆ 821

Cross-Curricular Connection: Music

Rock-and-Roll Rock-and-roll music appeared in the American mainstream in the 1950's, when artists such as Chuck Berry, Elvis Presley, Little Richard, Jerry Lee Lewis, Carl Perkins, and Buddy Holly attained fame. British groups such as the Beatles and the Rolling Stones added new energy in the mid-1960's. Around 1965, rock merged with the folk music of Bob Dylan and his followers; it was also influenced by the counterculture movement of the late 1960's. After a period of stagnation in the 1970's, it received new impetus from the British punk movement of the late 1970's, and from the popularity of music videos in the 1980's and 1990's.

In its beginnings, rock was a hybrid of several American musical forms: blues, rhythm and blues, country and western, gospel, and mainstream pop. In turn, rock has influenced other forms of music, including jazz and classical. Ask students to research the history of rock from its origins in the blues and other forms, and to present an illustrated report.

More About the Authors
The four Beatles were John Lennon (1940–1980; rhythm guitar), Paul McCartney (1942–   ; bass guitar), George Harrison (1943–   ; lead guitar), and Ringo Starr (1940–   ; drums). All four Beatles sang, and all four sometimes played other instruments such as piano, harmonica, or sitar. In addition to Lennon and McCartney, Harrison wrote several classic Beatles hits.

Beginning by playing in clubs in Liverpool, England, and in Hamburg, Germany, in the 1960's, the Beatles became idols in England in 1963, and attained American superstardom the following year. They influenced countless musicians and young people through their music, hair styles, and appealingly irreverent personalities.

The music and lyrics for "The Long and Winding Road" were written by Paul McCartney in late 1968 or early 1969. Because of an agreement McCartney and Lennon made with each other, all of the songs they wrote for the Beatles, whether written individually or in collaboration, are credited to both of them.

Answers
1. The long and winding road might symbolize the road of life's struggles or the path to love.
2. Sample response: One image is "the long and winding road." Another image is "the pool of tears crying for a day," probably representing the pain of life or of unrequited love.
3. "The Long and Winding Road" and "Uphill" are especially appropriate to compare and contrast.

Thematic Connection
Invite students to compare and contrast the mood of acceptance of life's troubles in "The Long and Winding Road" with that in Ecclesiastes.
Accept reasonable responses. Students may say that the speaker in "The Long and Winding Road" does not accept the current situation, but the speaker in the passage from Ecclesiastes does.

Develop Understanding

◆ Build Grammar Skills

❶ End Punctuation Ask how the final period affects the poem's mood, in contrast to the frequent use of exclamation points. *It suggests a quiet, sober ending; it conveys a sense of finality.*

Reinforce and Extend

Answers
◆ *Literature and Your Life*

Reader's Response Students may say that the first two sections made them happy and the last two sections were disturbing.

Thematic Focus Students may say that door bells and telephone rings arouse a sense of anticipation or the bell at the end of the class period fills them with relief.

☑ Check Your Comprehension

1. The four sections of the poem describe silver sleigh bells, golden wedding bells, brazen alarum bells, and iron funeral bells, respectively.
2. The first, third, and fourth sections describe bells in the night.
3. Students may note that the first line in each part begins with an exhortation to hear the bells. The second line consists of two words, an adjective and the word *bells,* followed by an exclamation mark. All stanzas contain the word *bells* repeated many times.

◆ Critical Thinking

1. The parts each suggest, respectively, a sleigh ride, a wedding, a fire, and a celebration of ghouls.
2. Students may say that the different line lengths add interest.
3. The mood varies greatly from one part to another. The mood of the first two parts is happy; the mood of the last two parts is spooky.
4. Poe is successful. The delicate sound of the sleigh bells, for example, is captured in ono-matopoetic words like *tinkle, twinkle, tintinnabulation,* and *jingling.*
5. Students may agree, noting that the interesting sounds of the words make a person interested in their meaning.

A pæan from the bells!
And his merry bosom swells
   With the pæan of the bells!
95   And he dances and he yells;
Keeping time, time, time,
In a sort of Runic rhyme,
   To the pæan of the bells—
     Of the bells:
100   Keeping time, time, time,
In a sort of Runic rhyme,
   To the throbbing of the bells—
Of the bells, bells, bells—
     To the sobbing of the bells;
105   Keeping time, time, time,
As he knells, knells, knells,
In a happy Runic rhyme,
   To the rolling of the bells—
     Of the bells, bells, bells—
110   To the tolling of the bells,
Of the bells, bells, bells, bells,
   Bells, bells, bells—
To the moaning and the groaning of the bells. ❶

◆ Build Vocabulary
pæan (pē´ ən) *n.:* Song of joy or triumph

Guide for Responding

◆ *Literature and Your Life*

Reader's Response What feelings did each section of "The Bells" evoke in you?

Thematic Focus In "The Bells," the sounds of different kinds of bells evoke different scenes. What scenes or events from your world do the sounds of different kinds of bells evoke in you?

☑ Check Your Comprehension

1. What kinds of bells are described in each of the four sections of "The Bells"?
2. How many of the four sections of the poem speak of bells ringing in the night?
3. What similarities among the four sections do you see? Describe at least three.

◆ Critical Thinking

INTERPRET
1. What scene or situation is suggested in each of the sections? **[Infer]**
2. Why do you think Poe varies the length of the lines in "The Bells"? **[Draw Conclusions]**
3. Does the mood or spirit of the poem vary from one section to another or is it basically the same throughout? Explain. **[Compare and Contrast]**

EVALUATE
4. How successful is Poe in capturing the sounds of bells in words? Cite excerpts from one section of the poem to explain your answer. **[Criticize]**

APPLY
5. The poet T. S. Eliot once said that poetry can be enjoyed before it is understood. Could "The Bells" be used as evidence in support of this idea? Give reasons for your opinion. **[Synthesize]**

822 ◆ Poetry

Beyond the Selection

FURTHER READING

Other Works by the Poets
Sing-Song, Christina Rossetti
The Young Landlords, Walter Dean Myers
"The Raven," Edgar Allan Poe

INTERNET
For additional information on the poets represented in this section, we suggest the following sites. Please be aware, however, that sites may have changed from the time we published this information.

For more on Christina Rossetti, go to **ht.//www.Lexmark.com/data/poem/roset02.html**

For more on Walter Dean Myers, go to **http:// www.bdd.com/teacher/myer.html**

For more on the Bible, go to **http://www.bythesea.org/Bible/**

For more on Edgar Allan Poe, go to **http://www.iptweb.com/www/lib/authors/poe.html**

We *strongly recommend* that you preview the sites before you send students to them.

Guide for Responding (continued)

◆ Literary Focus

LYRIC POETRY AND SOUND DEVICES

These poems are all examples of **lyric poetry**—highly musical verses that express the thoughts and feelings of a single speaker. The musical effect of the poems is created through the use of **sound devices** such as rhythm (the pattern of beats or stresses in language), alliteration (the repetition of initial consonant sounds), rhyme (the repetition of sounds at the ends of words), and onomatopoeia (the use of words that imitate sounds).

1. How does the speaker of "Uphill" feel about life's journey and its ultimate destination? Support your answer.
2. If you were to give "Summer" a different title, what would it be? Why?
3. The musical quality of "The Bells" is achieved in part through rhymes at the ends of lines and within lines. Point out three examples of rhymes within lines of "The Bells."
4. List at least four words in "The Bells" that are examples of onomatopoeia.
5. Much of the musical quality of Ecclesiastes 3:1–8 is achieved through the repetition of similarly constructed pairs of phrases opposite in meaning. List four such pairs of phrases.
6. Do all of the lines of Ecclesiastes 3:1–8 have the same rhythm or does the rhythm vary somewhat? Explain your answer.

◆ Reading Strategy

LISTEN

Because sound is so important in lyric poetry, reading a lyric poem aloud and **listening** as you do so is a good way to appreciate the poem fully. In a group, take turns reading sections from one or more of the four poems. Then answer these questions.

1. How does reading the poems aloud help you appreciate the use of rhyme in the poems?
2. How does reading the poems help draw your attention to the use of other sound devices such as alliteration and onomatopoeia?
3. How does reading aloud help you grasp each poem's meaning?

◆ Build Vocabulary

USING THE PREFIX *mono-*

Match each word containing the prefix *mono-*, meaning "one," with its definition on the right.

1. monorail   a. single large block of stone
2. monopoly   b. railway with a single rail as a track
3. monolith   c. exclusive control of the selling of something

USING THE WORD BANK

Write the paragraph in your notebook. Then complete it with words from the Word Bank.

Commuters, ____?____ heading home from work, ____?____ packed the railroad platform. With their hearts ____?____, they listened to an announcement delivered in a ____?____. When the voice proclaimed that their train was about to arrive, they sang a ____?____ as one!

◆ Build Grammar Skills

END PUNCTUATION

Beside signaling the end of a sentence, **end punctuation**—periods, question marks, and exclamation marks—often indicates meaning or feeling, especially in poetry. Notice how the end punctuation affects the meaning of these sentences:

> The road winds uphill.
> The road winds uphill?
> The road winds uphill!

Practice Change the meaning or feeling of each sentence to that given in parentheses by changing only the end punctuation.

1. I will meet other wayfarers at night. (anxiety)
2. You like hot days. (disbelief)
3. Please, listen to the bells. (anger)
4. It's time to destroy what we've built. (resignation)

Writing Application Write a brief dialogue that might take place between you and your friends. Use each type of end mark within your dialogue to convey the emotions of the participants.

Uphill/Summer/Ecclesiastes 3:1–8/The Bells ◆ 823

Answers
◆ Literary Focus

1. The traveler in "Uphill" is concerned about the journey, as indicated by the many questions he or she asks.
2. Students may suggest the title "Hot Days" to emphasize the central image of the poem.
3. Internal rhymes (or near-rhymes) are found in lines 31, 35, 65, 69, and 113.
4. Onomatopoetic words include *tinkle, tintinnabulation, jingling, shriek, clang, crash, roar, twanging, groan,* and *tolls.*
5. There are fourteen pairs of phrases from which students can choose.
6. The rhythm varies somewhat, as can be seen in the different lengths of lines 4 and 5.

◆ Reading Strategy

1. It reveals words that rhyme even though their spelling is not similar—*before/door* and *sum/come* in "Uphill," for example.
2. Reading silently tends to make you focus on the meaning of the words; reading aloud makes you listen to the sounds of the words, making alliteration and onomatopoeia more obvious and easier to appreciate.
3. It diminishes the impact of line breaks and helps you distinguish phrases and sentences. This facilitates comprehension.

◆ Build Vocabulary

Using the Prefix *mono-*
1. b   2. c   3. a

Using the Word Bank
Commuters, <u>wayfarers</u> heading home from work, <u>voluminously</u> packed the railroad platform. With their hearts <u>palpitating</u>, they listened to an announcement delivered in a <u>monotone</u>. When the voice proclaimed that their train was about to arrive, they sang a <u>paean</u> as one!

◆ Build Grammar Skills

1. question mark;   2. question mark;   3. exclamation mark; 4. period

✏ Writer's Solution

For additional instruction and practice, use the lesson in the **Language Lab CD-ROM** on Fragments and Run-On Sentences. For additional practice on end marks, use the practice page in the *Writer's Solution Grammar Practice Book,* p. 99.

823

Idea Bank

Customizing for
Performance Levels

Following are suggestions for matching the Idea Bank topics with your students' performance levels:

Less Advanced Students: 1, 5, 6
Average Students: 2, 4, 7
More Advanced Students: 3

Customizing for
Learning Modalities

Following are suggestions for matching Idea Bank topics with your students' learning modalities:

Verbal/Linguistic: 1, 2, 3, 4, 5, 7
Visual/Spatial: 6
Interpersonal: 1, 5

Writing Mini-Lesson

Refer students to the Writing Handbook, page 962, for instruction on the writing process, and page 965 for further information on creative writing.

Have students use the Cluster Organizer in *Writing and Language Transparencies,* p. 80, to organize their prewriting key ideas and words to repeat.

Writer's Solution

Writers at Work Videodisc

Have students view the videodisc segment (Ch. 6) featuring animation scriptwriter Grant Moran to see how he uses his imagination to devise clever dialogue for cartoons. Have students discuss how concepts are transformed into creative works.

Play frames 12243 to 21791

Writing Lab CD-ROM

Have students complete the Tutorial on Creative Writing. Use these steps:

1. Students may use the Poetry Topic Wheel to find images to spark ideas for their rap poem.
2. Have students draft on computer.
3. Use the Interactive Self-Evaluation Checklist for Poetry to aid revision.

Sourcebook

Have students use Chapter 6, Creative Writing (pp. 163–193), for additional support. The chapter includes in-depth instruction on using sound devices in a poem or song lyric (p. 183).

*B*uild *Y*our *P*ortfolio

Idea Bank

Writing

1. **Written Recommendation** If you had to recommend one of these poems to people interested in learning about lyric poetry, which poem would you choose? Write a short paper presenting and supporting your recommendation.

2. **Lyric Poem** Write a lyric poem about your favorite season of the year. Include vivid images that you associate with the season. In addition, be sure to express your feelings about the season clearly. As a challenge, try using musical devices, such as rhyming or alliteration.

3. **Comparison-and-Contrast Essay** Write an essay comparing and contrasting Sections III and IV of "The Bells." Explore similarities and differences in mood, word choice, rhythm, rhyme, and repetition. Use details from both for support.

Speaking and Listening

4. **Dramatic Reading** "The Bells" was meant to be read aloud. Practice and present a dramatic reading of the poem. Try to capture the poem's musical quality. **[Performing Arts Link]**

5. **Listening Activity** The rock group The Birds recorded a musical adaptation of Ecclesiastes 3:1–8 entitled "Turn, Turn, Turn." Find a recording of the song, share it with the class, and discuss whether the music adds to the poem. **[Music Link]**

Projects

6. **Illustration** Draw or paint a picture to illustrate the poem "Summer." Include as many of the images mentioned in the poem as possible. Also, try to capture the mood of the poem. **[Art Link]**

7. **Multimedia Presentation** Create a multimedia presentation on bells. The presentation should include both pictures and sounds.

824 ◆ Poetry

Writing Mini-Lesson

Rap Song

Like lyric poems, rap songs are musical expressions of a speaker's thoughts and feelings. Write a rap song that conveys your feelings about a season, a stage of life, or some other topic that interests you. Use repetition to emphasize your message.

Writing Skills Focus: Repetition

When you think about your favorite songs, certain repeated words or lines probably stand out in your mind. The **repetition** of key words, groups of words, or lines is one of the most effective ways of getting a message across to readers or listeners. In addition, repetition helps to create a musical effect. As you plan and write your rap song, use the repetition of sounds, words, and lines to leave a strong impression in the minds of your audience. Be careful not to overuse repetition, however. If you repeat too many different words or lines, none of them will stand out.

Prewriting Start by deciding on your topic and jotting down your thoughts about that topic. Decide which key ideas or messages you want to leave in the minds of your audience. Then think about which words or lines you could repeat to help drive home your points.

Drafting As you draft your rap song, focus on establishing a strong rhythm. Use rhymes at the ends of lines to help create a musical effect. In addition, establish a refrain—a line or group of lines that is repeated throughout the song.

Revising Read your rap song aloud to make sure that it has a strong rhythm and that your use of repetition highlights your main ideas. Make revisions to improve the sound and the meaning. Then perform your song for the class.

✓ ASSESSMENT OPTIONS

Formal Assessment, Selection Test, pp. 192–194, and Assessment Resources Software. The selection test is designed so that it can be easily customized to the performance levels of your students. *Alternative Assessment,* p. 52, includes options for less advanced students, more advanced students, musical/rhythmic learners, bodily/kinesthetic learners, logical/mathematical learners, intrapersonal learners, and interpersonal learners.

PORTFOLIO ASSESSMENT

Use the following rubrics in the *Alternative Assessment* booklet to assess student writing:
Written Recommendation: Critical Review Rubric, p. 104
Lyric Poem: Poetry Rubric, p. 101
Comparison-and-Contrast Essay: Comparison/Contrast Rubric, p. 96
Writing Mini-Lesson: Poetry Rubric, p. 101

Writing Process Workshop

Song Lyrics

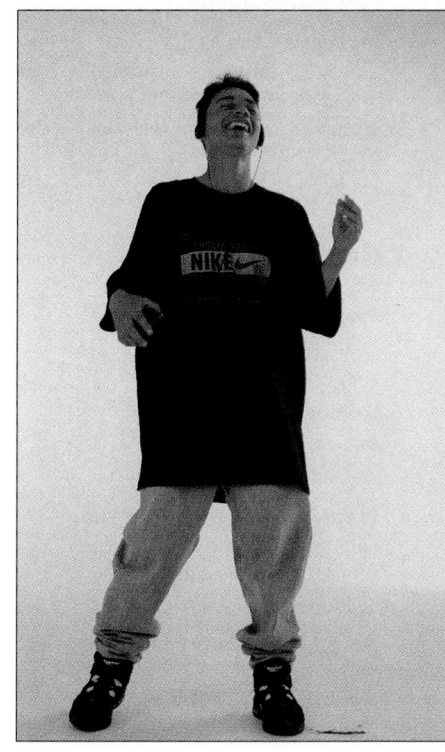

Songs may be described as "poetry set to music." Like poems, **song lyrics** often contain poetic elements such as rhythm, rhyme, repetition, and imagery. In addition, song lyrics also spark emotional reactions in listeners and often convey important messages about life.

Using your favorite songs as both models and sources of inspiration, write a set of song lyrics that convey emotions as well as interesting ideas. The following skills, introduced in this section's Writing Mini-Lessons, will help you to write song lyrics.

Writing Skills Focus

▶ **Create a main impression** of your subject that will remain in listeners' minds. (See p. 811.)

▶ **Avoid unnecessary details in your writing.** Songs are brief, so every word counts. Use only those details that convey the ideas you wish to present. (See p. 792.)

▶ **Use figurative language,** such as similes and metaphors, to create interesting images and spark new ideas in listeners' minds. A simile compares one thing to another using the word *like* or *as.* A metaphor compares one thing to another without using *like* or *as.* (See p. 801.)

▶ **Use repetition of key words** to get your ideas across and to give the song a catchy sound. (See p. 824.)

The writer of the folk song "Clementine" uses these skills as he mourns the loss of his daughter.

MODEL

from "Clementine"

Oh, my darling, oh, my darling,
Oh, my darling Clementine, ①
You are lost and gone forever,
Dreadful sorry, Clementine. ②
Light she was and like a fairy, ③
And her shoes were number nine;
Herring boxes without topses,
Sandals were for Clementine. ④

① The phrase "Oh, my darling" is repeated several times, emphasizing the speaker's feelings.

② The writer focuses the song on his sorrow over the loss of Clementine.

③ Here, the writer uses a simile.

④ Notice the writer's use of rhyme.

Writing Process Workshop ◆ 825

825

Prepare and Engage

Establish Writing Guidelines

Before students begin, review the following key characteristics of song lyrics:

- Song lyrics can express a wide range of emotions and moods.
- When effective, song lyrics remain with listeners, both because of the power of their words and because of how those words work with the music.
- Song lyrics can often contain elements of poetry, such as rhyme, rhythm, repetition, and imagery.

You may want to distribute the scoring rubric for Poetry (p. 101 in *Alternative Assessment*) to make students aware before they begin of the criteria on which they will be evaluated. See the suggestions on page 827 as to how you can customize the rubric to this workshop.

 Writer's Solution

Writing Lab CD-ROM

If your students have access to computers, you may want to have them work on the tutorial on Creative Writing to complete all or part of their song lyrics. Have students follow these steps:

1. Review the Audio-annotated model of song lyrics.
2. Use Word Bins to gather details for their song lyrics, including sensory details, rhyming words, and colors.
3. Draft their song lyrics on computer.
4. Use the Language Variety Revision Checker.
5. Respond to the Self-Evaluation Checklist to help them judge the effectiveness of their song lyrics.

Sourcebook

Students can find additional support in the chapter on Creative Writing (pp. 162–193).

 Cross-Curricular Connection: Performing Arts

Have students—especially those with a background in the performing arts, as musicians, singers, or actors in a musical play—share with the class their opinions about what makes a song memorable. Student opinions might include a catchy melody or lyrics and music that are particularly well suited to each other. Follow this question by asking what devices lyricists use in these songs to facilitate the performance of the song in front of an audience. *Student replies might include the lyricist's repetition of images or individual words and phrases that come to provide important emotional touchstones for both singer and audience. Remind students that when writing song lyrics they are actually always writing for two audiences—the listeners and the performers themselves.*

Develop Student Writing

Prewriting

When deciding on an audience, students may find it helpful to keep in mind various musical genres and styles. Point out that blues or rock-and-roll songs will have quite different purposes and forms from ballads or humorous songs. Students may be motivated by a specific musical idiom to write a particular type of song, or the reverse may take place. Students may decide on a subject and theme for their songs and then choose the proper format. Tell students that either process is acceptable when prewriting, but remind them that in all cases they should have familiarity with the conventions of the genre in which they choose to work.

Customize for
More Advanced Students

To help these students create a context for their song lyrics that will motivate their writing, have them situate their songs in a musical or opera whose plot outline they will create. Ask them who is singing the song, to what other character(s), and for what purpose. Students can write brief synopses of longer musical works that do not actually exist, but that inform the songs they are to create. By providing this kind of dramatic backdrop for their song lyrics, these students can integrate their work here with their skills at other forms of creative writing.

APPLYING LANGUAGE SKILLS: Figurative Language

Figurative language can include similes, metaphors, or personification, which gives human characteristics to an animal, object, or idea.

Simile: *Books are like a magic carpet ride.*

Metaphor: *Books are a magic carpet ride.*

Personification: *Books smile and take your hand.*

Notice how figurative language creates colorful images and new ways of looking at familiar things.

Practice On your paper, state each idea more colorfully by using figurative language.
1. Flowers are pretty.
2. Flowers smell good.
3. Flowers blow in the wind.
4. Flowers grow in a garden.

Writing Application As you draft your song lyrics, use figurative language such as simile, metaphor, and personification to create vivid images.

Writer's Solution Connection Writing Lab

To help you gather details for your songs, use the Word Bins activities in the Prewriting section of the tutorial on Creative Writing.

Prewriting

Choose a Topic Find a topic for your song lyrics by thinking of an idea or message about which you have strong feelings. You can also choose one of the topic ideas listed here.

Topic Ideas
- Something or someone you love
- A beautiful gift you have given or received
- A happy or special occasion
- An event that surprised you

Identify the Main Impression You'll Create Does your topic make you feel happy or sad? Fulfilled or empty? List words and phrases that describe the main impression of your topic. You may also wish to draw pictures that express your impression. Later, you can use the pictures as inspiration for your song lyrics.

Use of Figurative Language Next, make a list of similes or metaphors that convey the images you picture in your mind.

Similes	Metaphors
as red as a rose	the moon is a balloon
as fresh as morning dew	sun rays of happiness
blossomed like a flower	an explosion of love
as deep as the ocean	a chain around my heart

Choose the figurative language that you sense is most effective. Plan to use those phrases in your song.

Drafting

Choose a Tune To help you "hear" your lyrics in your head, set them to music. If you don't write music yourself, choose an existing song that you like, and use that tune.

Repeat Key Words and Phrases Popular lyrics often have a hook—a catchy phrase that is repeated throughout the song. As you write, find one or more phrases to repeat. The phrases should express the essence of your ideas and help convey the main impression you wish to share with readers.

Applying Language Skills
Figurative Language
Answers
Suggested responses:
1. Flowers bring the colors of the rainbow down to the Earth.
2. Flowers on a hillside wash the slopes with their spilled perfume.
3. Flowers sway in the wind as if dancing with invisible partners.
4. Flowers grow in the garden like hopes and dreams, renewing themselves despite winter's frost.

 Writer's Solution

For additional practice, use the Figurative Language lesson in the **Language Lab CD-ROM**. This multimedia lesson contains interactive instruction and writing applications on metaphor, simile, and personification.

Punctuating Song Lyrics
Answers
Suggested response:
Whether it's raining,

Whether it's snowing,
My love for you
Is always growing.

 Writer's Solution

For additional instruction and practice on punctuation, use the **Language Lab CD-ROM** lesson on Commas and the practice pages on commas and end marks in the *Writer's Solution Grammar Practice Book* (pp. 99–101).

Music Writing Tip Since song lyrics are set to music with a steady rhythmic beat, it is important that repeated words or phrases be easy to pronounce. Many phrases sound catchy because they contain a repeated consonant sound, as in "feeling foolish falling fast."

Avoid Unnecessary Details Be economical when using words to express your ideas. If your song is about love, stick to that idea. Don't introduce details that stray from your topic. If other subjects occur to you as you write, save them for another song.

Revising

Use a Checklist Go back to the Writing Skills Focus on the first page of this lesson to evaluate and revise your song lyrics.

▶ How well have I conveyed my main impression?
Invite a peer to read your song lyrics and describe his or her main impression. If the intended impression is not conveyed, revise the lyrics.

▶ How effective is my figurative language?
Find where you have used similes, metaphors, or personification. Does each phrase create a vivid image? If not, use different language.

▶ Have I repeated words and phrases?
Find the words that are repeated in your song. If they don't sound catchy or convey your main idea, revise them.

▶ Have I avoided unnecessary details?
Look for details that direct the focus away from your main idea, and remove them.

Publishing

▶ **Songbook** Collect lyrics from other students and create a class song book.
▶ **Performance** Recite or sing your lyrics for an audience. If you play a musical instrument, you may choose to accompany yourself. If your school has its own radio station, perform your song on the air.

APPLYING LANGUAGE SKILLS: Punctuating Song Lyrics

In a song, use a comma at the end of a line if there is a pause. Omit punctuation if there is no pause. Use a period at the end of a verse or stanza.

When sorrow or pain
Come close to me,
I try to flee.

Practice On your paper, add punctuation to these song lyrics:

Whether it's raining
Whether it's snowing
My love for you
Is always growing

Writing Application As you revise your song lyrics, note how you punctuated the lines. If you find a place where you used the wrong punctuation, make the necessary corrections.

Writer's Solution Connection Writing Lab

To help you revise, use the Language Variety Checker in the Revision section of the tutorial on Creative Writing.

Drafting

Students may discover while drafting that an innovative or appealing rhyme or rhythmic element suddenly occurs to them. Encourage them to incorporate such ideas into their songs if a way for doing so readily suggests itself—If not, they can jot down—or tape-record—new elements and decide how to use them after completing their first draft.

Revising

You may want to have students work with peer reviewers to revise their song lyrics. Remind peer reviewers to use the Revision Checklist to guide their review, regardless of whether, according to their own personal tastes, they might freely choose to listen to songs with such subject matter or written in a particular style. Emphasize the need for evaluating the formal aspects of the song lyrics, as summarized in the checklist.

Publishing

Another presentation option, in addition to the Student Edition suggestions on performance, is for song writers to recruit other students with a musical background to perform their lyrics. Point out that while there are many successful singer-songwriters, the work of many more lyricists reaches audiences only when talented performers decide to make it part of their repertoire.

Reinforce and Extend

Review the Writing Guidelines After students have completed their writing, review the characteristics of song lyrics. Encourage students to come up with additional criteria based on what they learned through completing the assignment.

ASSESSMENT		4	3	2	1
PORTFOLIO ASSESSMENT Use the rubric on Poetry in *Alternative Assessment* (p. 101) to assess students' writing. Add these criteria to customize the rubric to this assignment.	**Creates a Main Impression**	The writer creates a main impression of the subject of the song lyrics that will remain in listeners' minds.	The writer does create a main impression, but not one that will necessarily be memorable for listeners.	The writer creates several different impressions of the song's subject.	The song lyrics do not create a main impression of a subject.
	Repeats Key Words	The writer consistently repeats key words to get ideas across and lend a catchy sound to the song.	Key words are consistently repeated, sometimes effectively, sometimes not.	The writer for the most part fails to repeat key words.	The writer avoids repeating any key words.

Real-World Reading Skills Workshop

Introduce the Strategy

Tell students that though they may intuitively understand certain song lyrics, often the best songs can bear close examination and interpretation in much the same way that poetry does. While song lyrics are often considered part of "popular" culture, point out that they deserve the same sort of serious appreciation that other forms of creative writing merit—an approach that need not diminish the basic enjoyment of the song. Explain that applying reading strategies in this context might at first seem unusual in that song lyrics are not usually presented in text form, as they are here, but are per-formed. Point out, however, that these days it is a common practice for music CDs to include the com-plete lyrics of every song on an album. Ask students whether they have ever read these lyrics carefully. Have new meanings become appar-ent as a result? Use students' famil-iarity with their own favorite lyrics as a springboard for applying this work-shop's strategies.

Apply the Strategy

Start by asking students how the lyrics immediately establish both the tone and the basic intention of the speaker by using precise words and phrases. Elicit that the first word, *alas*, signals right away that this song is somewhat melancholy; while the second line is a dependent clause that sustains the mood with the vivid verb phrase *cast me off* and the pre-cise adverb *discourteously*. Once stu-dents have established the mood of the lyrics and the speaker's motiva-tion, they can speculate as to whether the lyrics would still be effective if the gender roles were reversed. Whereas some students will believe that the fundamental human emotions of love and the fear of being unloved are equally natural to men and women, others may argue that though the emotions expressed in the song may be univer-sal, women would express them-selves differently. Ask these students to give specific examples to support this assertion. When exploring the purpose of the lyrics, point out that several different things could be going on at the same time and that, indeed, the speaker's mixture of emotions—which range from sad-

Strategies for Success

Songwriters, like poets, wish to convey to their audience a special feeling or idea. Consider the following points to help you interpret song lyrics.

What Is the Mood of the Music? Even before hearing a song's lyrics, the music can be a clue to their message. Is the melody lively and happy? Is it slow and sad? Remember that music is usually composed to match the feeling of the lyrics. The mood of the melody can signal the narrator's feelings.

Who Are the Speaker and the Audience? As you read song lyrics, consider who is narrating them. Is it one person, a pair, or a group? Also consider the intended audience. Is the song directed specifically to a male? To a female? To anyone at all? How easily could references to "he" in the lyrics be switched to "she," or vice versa?

What Is the Purpose? Consider the speaker's purpose in expressing his or her words. Is the person celebrating? Mourning? Giving a warning? Also consider the language that the speaker's uses to express his or her message. What images do they create in your mind? The images you "see" are a clue to the narrator's purpose.

Apply the Strategy

Read carefully the lyrics to "Greensleeves." Then, if possible, listen to a recording of the song. Interpret the song lyrics by answering these questions.

1. Who is the speaker in the song? Whom is the speaker addressing?
2. What is the speaker's purpose in addressing Greensleeves? What is the speaker's message to her?
3. Why do you think the speaker is afraid of losing Greensleeves?
4. How relevant do you think this song is to modern-day audiences? To which lyrics can you relate the most? The least?

Greensleeves
Old English Folk Song (1620)

Alas, my love, you will do me wrong
If you cast me off so discourteously;
And I have loved you so very long
Delighted in your winning company.

Greensleeves, you were all my joy,
And you know, Greensleeves, you were my
  delight;
Greensleeves, you're my heart of gold,
No one else but my dear Lady Greensleeves.

✔ Here are other situations in which interpreting song lyrics can be helpful:
- ▶ Hearing a popular new song on the radio
- ▶ Interpreting the lyrics of a love song
- ▶ Appreciating a historical folk song
- ▶ Understanding the lyrics to a rap song

828 ◆ *Poetry*

---

ness to affection—contributes to the song's effectiveness. This combination of different feel-ings simultaneously washing over the speaker is very true to life.

Answers

1. An anonymous man addresses his lost love, the Lady Greensleeves.
2. The speaker's purpose is to keep Greensleeves from leaving him.
3. The lyrics themselves are inconclusive. However, the fact that the speaker takes great pains to express his appreciation for Greensleeves possi-bly reflects a concern that to date he has taken her for granted.
4. Some students will find the sentiments and lan-guage somewhat archaic and conclude that the lyrics are irrelevant to a modern-day audience. Others will take the opposite position, contend-ing that the lyrics clearly express a timeless theme, and that the simple effectiveness of the language has helped the song survive for nearly four centuries.

PART 2 *Structure*

Transection #1, 1966, Clarence H. Carter, The Newark Museum

In this section, students will encounter some of the many different forms of poetry. "The Raven" is a narrative poem that tells a frightening story. "The Seven Ages of Man" is an example of dramatic poetry. "On the Grasshopper and the Cricket" and Sonnet 30 are examples of a Petrarchan Sonnet and a Shakespearean sonnet respectively. The unit ends with several examples of Haiku—some by traditional Japanese poets and others by a twentieth-century American writer.

Customize for
Varying Student Needs
When assigning the selections in this section to your students, keep in mind the following factors:

"The Raven"
• Very long poem
• Vocabulary will challenge some students
• Eeriness of the poem will appeal to some students

"The Seven Ages of Man"
• Poem may challenge less proficient readers and English language learners

"On the Grasshopper and Cricket," Sonnet 30
• Students may need to be reminded to read according to punctuation, and not according to line breaks in order for these poems to make sense

Three Haiku, Hokku Poems
• Short lines and simple language make these poems very accessible

 Humanities: Art

Transection #1, 1966, by Clarence H. Carter.

Born in Ohio in 1904, Clarence Carter studied at the Cleveland School of Architecture and taught art at a number of colleges and art schools. He works primarily in watercolors and has been honored by the states of Ohio, his birth state, and New Jersey, where he has spent much of his adult life.

Explain that a transection, literally, is something that has been cut across or has been divided by being cut. Elicit that this is an abstract work of art, being composed of geometric shapes, rather than recognizable objects.

Help students link the art with the focus of Part 2 ("Structure") by answering the following questions:

1. Describe the structure you see in this artwork: What three shapes do you see, and how are they arranged? *The three shapes are a transparent white oval, a black rectangle, and a grayish-white cross-shaped grid, repeated over and over with the rectangles lying between the lines of the grid and the ovals seeming to hover at different heights above each rectangle.*

2. What ideas, images, or situations does this abstract picture suggest to you? *Sample answers: The picture could suggest workers in cubicles, ghosts coming out of graves, or an idea like conformity.*

*G*uide for Reading

More About the Authors

The death of **Edgar Allan Poe** is shrouded in mystery. He was found dead in the street, wearing someone else's clothing. His supposed friend, Rufus Griswold, issued a scurrilous biography in which he claimed that Poe had died of alcoholism; thus the legend of Poe's dissipation was born. Modern scholars, in contrast, think Poe was more likely diabetic. They theorize that from near starvation Poe may have lapsed into a diabetic coma that night.

William Shakespeare was not only a great poet, but he is considered to be the greatest playwright in the English-speaking world.

Edgar Allan Poe *(1809–1849)*

Although he is remembered mostly for his suspenseful, often horrifying, short stories, Edgar Allan Poe was also a gifted poet. "The Raven," his best-known poem, is haunting and mournful, reflecting the impact of the many misfortunes that Poe experienced during his brief, tragic life.

Early Life After losing both of his parents as a young boy, Poe was taken in by a wealthy Virginia merchant, John Allan. Poe had a stormy relationship with his stepfather, which completely disintegrated when Poe was a young man.

Literary Career Poe published numerous short stories, several collections of poetry, and a novel, but never achieved financial success as a writer. Despite his financial struggles, Poe experienced a period of happiness following his marriage to Virginia Clemm in 1835. This happiness was shattered, however, by his wife's death in 1847. (For more on Edgar Allan Poe, see pp. 2 and 812.)

William Shakespeare *(1564–1616)*

Theatergoers of Shakespeare's time expected to see action, humor, and passion played out on the stage. At a time when the English language was rapidly developing into a rich and powerful means of expression, they were also eager to hear impressive, fully developed speeches modeled on those in classical drama. Shakespeare was able to forge a perfect blend of high drama and exalted language that met his audience's twin expectations.

Memorable Speeches Altogether, Shakespeare wrote more than three dozen plays, most of which continue to be read and performed today. Because of the beauty of his language and the timelessness of the themes he addressed, speeches and scenes in his plays are quoted more often than the works of any other writer. "The Seven Ages of Man," from the play *As You Like It,* is considered one of his best speeches. (For more on William Shakespeare, see pp. 669 and 840.)

◆ Build Vocabulary

WORD ROOTS: *-sol-*
In "The Raven," the word *desolate* is used to help capture the speaker's state of mind as he struggles to come to terms with the death of the woman he loves. The word contains the root *-sol-*, which means "alone." How does the meaning of the root relate to the overall meaning of the word, which is "deserted" or "abandoned"?

WORD BANK
Here is a list of words from the selection. With a group of classmates, try to come up with a sentence using each of the words. If necessary, check meanings in the dictionary.

quaint
beguiling
respite
desolate
pallid
woeful
treble

◆ Build Grammar Skills

PARTICIPIAL PHRASES
Both poets use participial phrases (participles with modifiers and complements) to create detailed images. Participial phrases may be restrictive or nonrestrictive. A **restrictive participial phrase** is necessary to complete the meaning of the noun or pronoun it modifies. It is not set off by commas. A **nonrestrictive participial phrase** is not necessary but adds meaning. It is set off with commas.

Restrictive: . . . filled me with fantastic terrors *never felt before.*

Nonrestrictive: And then the whining schoolboy, with his satchel,
And shining morning face, *creeping like a snail
Unwillingly to school.*

 Prentice Hall Literature Program Resources

REINFORCE / RETEACH / EXTEND
Selection Support Pages
Build Vocabulary: Word Roots: *-sol-*, p. 225
Build Grammar Skills: Participial Phrases, p. 226
Reading Strategy: Make Inferences About the Speaker, p. 227
Literary Focus: Narrative and Dramatic Poetry, p. 228
Strategies for Diverse Student Needs, p. 55
Beyond Literature
Cross-Curricular Connection: Music, p. 55
Formal Assessment Selection Test, pp.

195–197, Assessment Resources Software
Alternative Assessment, p. 53
Writing and Language Transparencies
Descriptive and Observational Writing, pp. 17–20
Resource Pro CD-ROM
"The Raven," "The Seven Ages of Man"—includes all resource material and customizable lesson plan

Listening to Literature Audiocassettes
"The Raven," "The Seven Ages of Man"

Looking at Literature Videodisc
"The Seven Ages of Man"

The Raven ◆ The Seven Ages of Man

◆ *Literature and Your Life*

CONNECT YOUR EXPERIENCE

Why do people act the way they do? Adults often explain the behavior of young people by saying, "It's just a phase he or she is going through." In "The Seven Ages of Man," the speaker argues that each person goes through seven phases in a lifetime. "The Raven" presents a different perspective. It seems to suggest that the individual events of a person's life shape that person's behavior.

Journal Writing What do you think the "seven ages of man" might be? Jot down your ideas in your journal.

THEMATIC FOCUS: LOOKING INWARD

These two poems present different perspectives on human life. As you read, think about how the authors' perspectives compare with your own perspective.

◆ Background for Understanding

LITERATURE

"The Seven Ages of Man" is a speech from Shakespeare's comedy *As You Like It*. A comedy, in the Shakespearean sense, is a play in which humorous things are said and done, and in which a multitude of problems arise and are easily solved by the end of the play. Usually, Shakespeare's comedies end with one or more weddings.

As You Like It is about a duke who has been deprived of his rights and exiled to the forest by his own brother. "The Seven Ages of Man" is a speech addressed to the duke by his attendant, Jacques. The speech reveals the character and outlook on life of Jacques, who is a bitter realist.

◆ Literary Focus

NARRATIVE AND DRAMATIC POETRY

"The Raven" is a poem that has characters, a setting, and a plot. This makes it **narrative poetry**—poetry that tells a story. "The Seven Ages of Man," on the other hand, is an example of **dramatic poetry**—poetry in which the lines are spoken by one or more characters. When a dramatic poem has a single speaker who is a fictional character expressing his or her thoughts or feelings within a developing situation, it is called a **dramatic monologue**. "The Seven Ages of Man," which is a speech delivered by a character in a full-length play, is a dramatic monologue.

◆ Reading Strategy

MAKE INFERENCES ABOUT THE SPEAKER

Readers sometimes mistakenly assume that a poem's **speaker**—the voice of a poem—is always the poet. Though in some cases the speaker is in fact the poet, often the speaker is an imaginary voice assumed by the poet. To understand a poem, it is important to identify who the speaker is and then to **make inferences,** or draw conclusions, about his or her situation, attitudes, and personality traits by looking closely at the words and details. For example, from the first line of "The Raven"—"Once upon a midnight dreary, while I pondered, weak and weary"—you can infer that the speaker is in a gloomy, depressed state of mind. What does this knowledge of the speaker's situation lead you to expect in the rest of the poem?

Use a chart like this one to record words and details that reveal important information about each speaker. Jot down the inference you can make based on each detail.

Key Details	Inferences
——— ➤ ———
——— ➤ ———
——— ➤ ———
——— ➤ ———

Guide for Reading ◆ 831

One-Minute Insight

In "The Raven," the speaker and main character is a man whose life has been shattered by a single experience—the death of the woman he loved. Therefore, "The Raven" presents a picture of a hopeless and gloomy life.

◆ **Build Grammar Skills**

❶ **Restrictive and Nonrestrictive Participial Phrases** Have students identify the participial phrase and discuss the image it creates. Ask: Why is there no comma before the word *gently*? *The participial phrase is "gently rapping, rapping at my chamber door." It appeals to the sense of hearing. No comma is necessary because the phrase is restrictive—it is necessary to complete the meaning of the pronoun, someone, which it modifies.*

◆ **Reading Strategy**

❷ **Make Inferences About the Speaker** Ask students who Lenore might have been, and why the speaker is so sad. *Lenore is the woman the speaker loved. He grieves for her loss.*

◆ **Reading Strategy**

❸ **Make Inferences About the Speaker** Ask students: What is scaring the speaker? Why does he repeat to himself that it is just some visitor, "and nothing more"? *The tapping at the door and the rustling of the curtains are frightening the speaker. He imagines that something horrible is going to happen, so he tries to calm his nerves by telling himself that it is just a visitor at the door.*

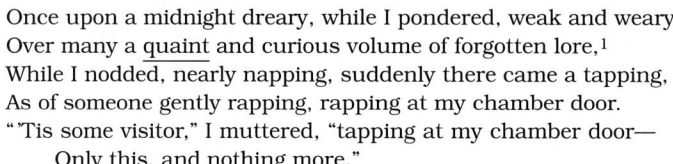

The Raven

Edgar Allan Poe

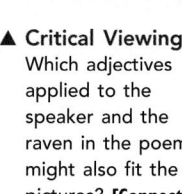

Illustration to E.A. Poe's "The Raven," Edouard Manet, Museum of Fine Arts, Boston

Once upon a midnight dreary, while I pondered, weak and weary,
Over many a <u>quaint</u> and curious volume of forgotten lore,[1]
❶ While I nodded, nearly napping, suddenly there came a tapping,
As of someone gently rapping, rapping at my chamber door.
5 " 'Tis some visitor," I muttered, "tapping at my chamber door—
    Only this, and nothing more."

Ah, distinctly I remember it was in the bleak December,
And each separate dying ember wrought its ghost upon the floor.
Eagerly I wished the morrow—vainly I had tried to borrow
❷ 10 From my books surcease[2] of sorrow—sorrow for the lost Lenore—
For the rare and radiant maiden whom the angels name Lenore—
    Nameless here for evermore.

And the silken, sad, uncertain rustling of each purple curtain
Thrilled me—filled me with fantastic terrors never felt before;
❸ 15 So that now, to still the beating of my heart, I stood repeating
" 'Tis some visitor entreating entrance at my chamber door—
Some late visitor entreating entrance at my chamber door—
    This it is and nothing more."

Presently my soul grew stronger; hesitating then no longer,
20 "Sir," said I, "or Madam, truly your forgiveness I implore;
But the fact is I was napping, and so gently you came rapping,
And so faintly you came tapping, tapping at my chamber door,
That I scarce was sure I heard you"—here I opened wide the door—
    Darkness there, and nothing more.

---

1. **quaint . . . lore:** Strange book of ancient learning.
2. **surcease** (sʉr sēs´) *n.:* End.

▲ **Critical Viewing** Which adjectives applied to the speaker and the raven in the poem might also fit the pictures? **[Connect]**

◆ **Build Vocabulary**
quaint (kwānt) *adj.:* Strange; unusual

 Block Scheduling Strategies

Consider these suggestions to take advantage of extended class time:
- Use Daily Language Practice for Week 2. You may dictate the passages to students, or you may use the transparency and have students correct the passages in groups.
- Before students begin reading the poems, discuss the ideas presented in Literature and Your Life (p. 831). Ask students if they think people behave as they do because of

phases, or because of the impact of certain events.
- Either before or after reading the poems, students can research Edgar Allan Poe and William Shakespeare on the Internet. Have students access the Internet sites listed on page 837.
- Students can work in discussion groups to respond to the Critical Thinking questions

for "The Raven" (p. 835) and "The Seven Ages of Man" (p. 837).
- Have students complete the Writing Mini-Lesson (p. 839). Students can make charts with the heads *sight, sound, touch, smell,* and *taste* to help them generate images that appeal to all five senses.

25   Deep into that darkness peering, long I stood there wondering, fearing,
     Doubting, dreaming dreams no mortal ever dared to dream before;
     But the silence was unbroken, and the darkness gave no token,[3]
     And the only word there spoken was the whispered word, "Lenore!"
     This *I* whispered, and an echo murmured back the word, "Lenore!"
30   Merely this, and nothing more.

     Then into the chamber turning, all my soul within me burning,
     Soon I heard again a tapping somewhat louder than before.
     "Surely," said I, "surely that is something at my window lattice;[4]
     Let me see, then, what thereat[5] is, and this mystery explore— ❹
35   Let my heart be still a moment and this mystery explore—
         'Tis the wind, and nothing more!"

     Open here I flung the shutter, when, with many a flirt[6] and flutter,
     In there stepped a stately raven of the saintly days of yore;
     Not the least obeisance[7] made he; not an instant stopped or stayed he; ❺
40   But, with mien[8] of lord or lady, perched above my chamber door—
     Perched upon a bust of Pallas[9] just above my chamber door—
         Perched, and sat, and nothing more.

     Then this ebony bird beguiling my sad fancy[10] into smiling,
     By the grave and stern decorum of the countenance[11] it wore,
45   "Though thy crest be shorn and shaven, thou," I said, "art sure no craven,[12]
     Ghastly grim and ancient raven wandering from the Nightly shore—
     Tell me what thy lordly name is on the Night's Plutonian[13] shore!" ❻
         Quoth[14] the raven, "Nevermore."

     Much I marveled this ungainly fowl to hear discourse so plainly,
50   Though its answer little meaning—little relevancy bore;
     For we cannot help agreeing that no sublunary[15] being
     Ever yet was blessed with seeing bird above his chamber door—
     Bird or beast upon the sculptured bust above his chamber door,
         With such name as "Nevermore."

55   But the raven, sitting lonely on the placid bust, spoke only
     That one word, as if his soul in that one word he did outpour. ❼

---

3. **token** (tō´ kən) *n.*: Sign.
4. **lattice** (lat´ is) *n.*: Framework of wood or metal.
5. **thereat** (ther at´) *adv.*: There.
6. **flirt** (flʉrt) *n.*: Quick, uneven movement.
7. **obeisance** (ō bā´ səns) *n.*: Bow or another sign of respect.
8. **mien** (mēn) *n.*: Manner.
9. **bust of Pallas** (pal´ əs): Sculpture of the head and shoulders of Pallas Athena (ə thē´ nə), the ancient Greek goddess of wisdom.
10. **fancy** (fan´ sē) *n.*: Imagination.
11. **countenance** (koun´ tə nəns) *n.*: Facial appearance.
12. **craven** (krā´ vən) *n.*: Coward (usually an adjective).
13. **Plutonian** (plōō tō´ nē ən) *adj.*: Like the underworld, ruled over by the ancient Roman god Pluto.
14. **quoth** (kwōth) *v.*: Said.
15. **sublunary** (sub lōōn´ ər ē) *adj.*: Earthly.

Illustration to E.A. Poe's "The Raven,"
Edouard Manet, Museum of Fine Arts, Boston

The Raven ◆ 833

Customize for
English Language Learners
The elevated diction in this poem may pose difficulty for English language learners. Help these students through the poem by letting them follow along in their text as they listen to the audiocassette recording of the selection.

🎧 **Listening to Literature Audiocassettes**

💿 **Literature CD-ROM** To build background, use the CD-ROM *The History of American Literature:* Part I, Disk 2, Feature 6, "The Raven."

◆ **Literary Focus**

❹ **Narrative and Dramatic Poetry** Remind students that narrative poems contain all the elements of a plot: exposition, rising action, climax, falling action, and resolution. Ask students: What part of the plot occurs here? How do you know? *This is the rising action, during which Poe builds the conflict—here, the speaker against the unknown—and develops the speaker's character.*

◆ **Critical Thinking**

❺ **Clarification** Point out that a raven is a large, all-black bird of the crow family found in Europe, Asia, North America, and North Africa. A raven's voice sounds like deep croaking.

◆ **Literary Focus**

❻ **Narrative and Dramatic Poetry** Ask students: How does Poe use the raven to build an eerie, suspenseful mood? *The "ghastly grim" raven wandering from the underworld's "nightly shore" is spooky and unnerving.*

Comprehension Check ☑

❼ What does Poe accomplish by having the raven speak only one word? *The repeated word* nevermore *builds tension; it becomes more frightening each time it is spoken.*

🎵 **Humanities: Art**

Illustration to E. A. Poe's "The Raven,"
1875, by Edouard Manet.
   In this painting, a man sees a raven flying into his house through a window with open shutters. The mood of the painting matches that of Poe's poem.
   The French painter Edouard Manet (1832–1883) was one of the earliest and most famous members of the Impressionist school of painting.
   Use these questions for discussion:
1. What event in the first half of the poem does this scene illustrate? *The picture illustrates the moment when the raven comes into the house.*
2. How does Manet capture the eerie, suspenseful mood of Poe's poem? *Manet uses bold brush strokes and deep shadows to capture the poem's mysterious mood.*
3. What words applied to the speaker and the raven in the poem might also fit the picture? *Some of the words that apply to the picture are* fearing, doubting, grave decorum, ghastly grim, lonely, ominous.

◆ **Critical Thinking**

❶ **Interpret** Ask students: How does the speaker explain the raven's odd behavior? Why is the speaker so concerned with finding a rational explanation for the bird's actions? *The speaker infers that the raven repeats the only word it learned from its former master, who must have been unhappy or depressed. The speaker seeks rational explanations for irrational events because the rational is safe, while the irrational is frightening.*

◆ **Critical Thinking**

❷ **Infer** Ask students: Why does the speaker think the raven has been sent by angels? If so, why does he call the raven "Wretch"? *The speaker thinks that God has taken pity on him for his grieving, and the angels have sent the raven to offer the speaker a drug to cause forgetfulness of sorrow. He calls the raven "Wretch" because he thinks the raven is keeping the drug of forgetfulness from him.*

◆ **Critical Thinking**

❸ **Connect** Ask students: Why is the speaker becoming so upset? How are his feelings now different from his earlier emotions? *The speaker is becoming more and more agitated; he seems to be going mad. First he thought the bird was amusing, but now he thinks the bird is a "thing of evil."*

Comprehension Check ☑

❹ To ensure literal comprehension, ask students what the speaker is asking the raven to do for him. How does the raven respond? How does the speaker interpret that response? *The speaker wants the raven to tell him that, when he dies, he will be reunited with Lenore. The raven repeats "nevermore" again, but now the speaker imagines it to be a cruel negative answer to his desperate question.*

◆ **Literary Focus**

❺ **Narrative and Dramatic Poetry** Ask students: What does the speaker want the raven to do now? How does the raven respond? Is this the rising action, climax, or falling action of the plot? *The speaker shrieks at the raven to leave, but the raven says, "nevermore." This is the climax of the plot. The speaker has now gone completely mad, and believes the raven will torture him forever.*

Nothing farther then he uttered—not a feather then he fluttered—
Till I scarcely more than muttered, "Other friends have flown before—
On the morrow *he* will leave me, as my hopes have flown before."
60   Quoth the raven, "Nevermore."

Wondering at the stillness broken by reply so aptly spoken,
"Doubtless," said I, "what it utters is its only stock and store,
Caught from some unhappy master whom unmerciful Disaster
❶ Followed fast and followed faster—so, when Hope he would adjure,[16]
65 Stern Despair returned, instead of the sweet Hope he dared adjure—
      That sad answer, "Nevermore."

But the raven still <u>beguiling</u> all my sad soul into smiling,
Straight I wheeled a cushioned seat in front of bird, and bust, and door;
Then upon the velvet sinking, I betook myself to linking
70 Fancy unto fancy, thinking what this ominous bird of yore—
What this grim, ungainly, ghastly, gaunt, and ominous bird of yore
      Meant in croaking "Nevermore."

This I sat engaged in guessing, but no syllable expressing
To the fowl whose fiery eyes now burned into my bosom's core;
75 This and more I sat divining,[17] with my head at ease reclining
On the cushion's velvet lining that the lamplight gloated o'er,
But whose velvet violet lining with the lamplight gloating o'er,
      She shall press, ah, nevermore!

Then, methought, the air grew denser, perfumed from an unseen censer[18]
80 Swung by angels whose faint footfalls tinkled on the tufted floor.
"Wretch," I cried, "thy God hath lent thee—by these angels he hath sent thee
Respite—respite and Nepenthe[19] from thy memories of Lenore!
❷ Let me quaff[20] this kind Nepenthe and forget this lost Lenore!"
      Quoth the raven, "Nevermore."

85 "Prophet!" said I, "thing of evil!—prophet still, if bird or devil!—
Whether Tempter[21] sent, or whether tempest tossed thee here ashore,
❸ <u>Desolate</u>, yet all undaunted, on this desert land enchanted—
On this home by Horror haunted—tell me truly, I implore—
Is there—*is* there balm in Gilead?[22]—tell me—tell me, I implore!"
90   Quoth the raven, "Nevermore."

---

16. **adjure** (ə joor′) *v*.: Appeal to.
17. **divining** (də vīn′ in) *v*.: Guessing.
18. **censer** (sen′ sər) *n*.: Container for burning incense.
19. **Nepenthe** (ni pen′ thē) *n*.: Drug used in ancient times to cause forgetfulness of sorrow.
20. **quaff** (kwäf) *v*.: Drink.
21. **Tempter**: Devil.
22. **balm** (bäm) **in Gilead** (gil′ ē əd): Cure for suffering; the Bible refers to a medicinal ointment, or balm, made in a region called Gilead.

◆ **Build Vocabulary**

beguiling (bi gīl′ in) *v*.: Tricking; charming
respite (res′ pit) *n*.: Rest; relief
desolate (des′ ə lit) *adj*.: Deserted; abandoned
pallid (pal′ id) *adj*.: Pale

834 ◆ *Poetry*

Speaking and Listening Mini-Lesson

Choral Reading

This mini-lesson supports the first Speaking and Listening activity in the Idea Bank on page 839.

Introduce the Concept Have students discuss performances of choral music they have heard. Have them list ways in which the choral reading of a poem is similar to and different from a choral musical performance. Guide students to see how "The Raven" is ideal for a choral reading because of its building drama.

Develop Background Have students follow these guidelines:

- Survey the poem to find the high points in the plot—the moments of tension and key action.
- Use your voice to create the mood. Don't shout! Rather, project your voice so everyone can hear you.

Apply the Information Have students use these suggestions as they prepare and perform their choral readings.

Assess the Outcome To evaluate the oral interpretations, have students use the Peer Assessment: Oral Interpretation page in *Alternative Assessment*, p. 112.

"Prophet!" said I, "thing of evil!—prophet still, if bird or devil!
By that Heaven that bends above us—by that God we both adore—
Tell this soul with sorrow laden if, within the distant Aidenn,[23]
It shall clasp a sainted maiden whom the angels name Lenore—
95 Clasp a rare and radiant maiden whom the angels name Lenore."
        Quoth the raven, "Nevermore."

❹

"Be that word our sign of parting, bird or fiend!" I shrieked, upstarting—
"Get thee back into the tempest and the Night's Plutonian shore!
Leave no black plume as a token of that lie thy soul hath spoken!
100 Leave my loneliness unbroken!—quit the bust above my door!
Take thy beak from out my heart, and take thy form from off my door!"
        Quoth the raven, "Nevermore."

❺

And the raven, never flitting, still is sitting, still is sitting
On the pallid bust of Pallas just above my chamber door;
105 And his eyes have all the seeming of a demon that is dreaming,
And the lamplight o'er him streaming throws his shadow on the floor;
And my soul from out that shadow that lies floating on the floor
        Shall be lifted—nevermore!

❻

---

23. **Aidenn:** Name meant to suggest Eden or paradise.

Guide for Responding

◆ Literature and Your Life

Reader's Response How do you feel about the speaker of the poem? Explain.

Thematic Focus How does the speaker's perspective on the raven change throughout the poem?

☑ Check Your Comprehension

1. What is the setting (time and place) of the poem?
2. Who is Lenore?
3. What one word does the raven speak?
4. What question does the speaker ask the raven near the end of the poem?

◆ Critical Thinking

INTERPRET
1. What can you infer, or conclude, about Lenore and the speaker's relationship with her? **[Infer]**
2. (a) Describe how your impression of the raven changes as the poem progresses. (b) What causes your impression to change? **[Connect]**
3. (a) How does the speaker's state of mind change as the poem progresses? (b) What causes these changes? **[Connect]**
4. What does the raven come to represent to the speaker? **[Draw Conclusions]**

EVALUATE
5. When Poe set out to write this poem, he thought of having a parrot repeat the word "Nevermore." Would the poem have been as effective if Poe had used a parrot instead of a raven? Explain. **[Evaluate]**

The Raven ◆ 835

Cross-Curricular Connection: Science

Ravens The raven, a member of the crow family (*Corvidae*), is commonly found in Europe, Asia, North America, and North Africa. The largest of all songbirds, an adult raven can grow to more than two feet in length and have a wing span of three feet. The raven is a beautiful bird. Its feathers are so black they have a metallic, bluish shine; its bill is long and powerful.

Since the raven is friendly, bright, and docile, it is sometimes trained as a house pet. With patience, one can teach a raven to repeat a few simple words, a fact Poe likely knew when he chose the raven as the creature to use in his poem. In addition, the raven has become the subject of many folk songs, folk tales, and legends.

The Seven Ages of Man

William Shakespeare

The Seven Ages of Man, Folger Shakespeare Library, Washington, D.C.

❶ All the world's a stage,
And all the men and women merely players:[1]
They have their exits and their entrances;
And one man in his time plays many parts,
5 His acts being seven ages.[2] At first the infant,
Mewling[3] and puking in the nurse's arms.
And then the whining schoolboy, with his satchel,
And shining morning face, creeping like snail
Unwillingly to school. And then the lover,
❷ 10 Sighing like furnace, with a <u>woeful</u> ballad
Made to his mistress' eyebrow. Then a soldier,
Full of strange oaths, and bearded like the pard,[4]
Jealous in honor,[5] sudden and quick in quarrel,
Seeking the bubble reputation
❸ 15 Even in the cannon's mouth. And then the justice,[6]
In fair round belly with good capon[7] lined,
With eyes severe and beard of formal cut,
Full of wise saws and modern instances;[8]

---

1. **players:** Actors.
2. **ages:** Periods of life.
3. **mewling** (myōōl′ iŋ) *v.*: Whimpering; crying like a baby.
4. **pard** (pärd) *n.*: Leopard or panther.
5. **Jealous in honor:** Very concerned about his honor.
6. **justice:** Judge.
7. **capon** (kā′ pän) *n.*: Roasted chicken.
8. **wise saws and modern instances:** Wise sayings and modern examples that show the truth of the sayings.

◆ Build Vocabulary

woeful (wō′ fəl) *adj.*: Full of sorrow

treble (treb′ əl) *adj.*: High-pitched voice

 Humanities: Art

The Seven Ages of Man, stained-glass window, Folger Shakespeare Library, Washington, D.C.

Stained glass is a term used for windows or other display pieces composed of small pieces of dyed and painted glass joined with pieces of lead and mounted in a metal framework. The art achieved its greatest expression in the Gothic cathedrals of the twelfth through the fourteenth centuries. Twentieth-century masters of the art included Louis Comfort Tiffany, Henri Matisse, and Marc Chagall.

Use these questions for discussion:

1. This window represents the seven ages of man described by Shakespeare. Why do you think the panels were arranged as they are? *They were meant to rise to the fourth age, which was considered the age when man is "in his prime," and then fall to the seventh age when man is back on the same level with the first.*

2. Do you agree that the fourth age (the soldier) is man's prime? If not, which would you place in that position? *Accept all responses that are supported with logical reasons.*

And so he plays his part. The sixth age shifts
20 Into the lean and slippered pantaloon,[9]
With spectacles on nose and pouch on side,
His youthful hose[10] well saved, a world too wide
For his shrunk shank;[11] and his big manly voice,
Turning again toward childish <u>treble</u>, pipes
25 And whistles in his sound. Last scene of all,
That ends this strange eventful history,
Is second childishness, and mere oblivion,
Sans[12] teeth, sans eyes, sans taste, sans everything.

4

5

---

9. **pantaloon** (pan´ təl ōon´) *n*.: Thin, foolish old man—originally a character in old comedies.
10. **hose** (hōz) *n*.: Stockings.
11. **shank** (shank) *n*.: Leg.
12. **sans** (sanz) *prep*.: Without; lacking.

◀ **Critical Viewing** How do the images in this stained glass window add to your understanding of the poem? [Relate] **6**

Critical Thinking

5 **Interpret** Ask students: Why do you think Shakespeare ends with a reference to man's "second childhood"? *Having man ending up back where he began shows the pointlessness of life.*

▶**Critical Viewing**◀

6 **Relate** The images represent the seven stages described in the poem. Their relative heights in the window might represent the rising and falling of physical and mental powers throughout life.

Reinforce and Extend

Answers

◆ *Literature and Your Life*

Reader's Response Students may suggest other divisions or other occupations more appropriate for today.

Thematic Focus Students may agree that people are like actors playing parts in a play that will end.

☑ **Check Your Comprehension**

1. The speaker compares the world to a stage.
2. He is unwilling to go to school.
3. The soldier's main concern is his reputation.
4. The last stage of man is a second childhood.

◆ **Critical Thinking**

1. He doesn't take human beings very seriously.
2. Suggested response: They represent infancy, school age, youth, adulthood, advanced middle age, old age, and senility.
3. The soldier is a bearded man, very proud and quarrelsome, who acts bravely to gain fame. The judge is a fat man with a trim beard who likes to display his wisdom.
4. During this last stage, human beings resemble children again.
5. Suggested response: The speaker seems to be expressing a detached, somewhat cynical, and ironical view of life.
6. Most students will say that people do pass through phases similar to the ones that Shakespeare describes.

Guide for Responding

◆ *Literature and Your Life*

Reader's Response Do you agree with the speaker's view of the seven ages of life? Explain.

Thematic Focus Does this poem in any way change your perspective about the stages of life? Why or why not?

Group Activity In a group, discuss how you would modernize this poem for today. What would the seven ages be?

☑ **Check Your Comprehension**

1. To what does the speaker compare the world?
2. What is the schoolboy's attitude toward school?
3. What is the soldier's main concern?
4. What is the last age of man?

◆ **Critical Thinking**

INTERPRET

1. What attitude does the speaker reveal by using the word *merely* in the second line? [Analyze]
2. What period of life does each person referred to in the poem represent? [Interpret]
3. What characterizes the periods of life represented by the soldier and the judge? [Interpret]
4. How does the last age bring us back full circle to the start? [Interpret]
5. What attitude toward life does the speaker seem to be expressing? [Draw Conclusions]

APPLY

6. Explain whether you think that most people who live long lives pass through seven periods similar to those described in the poem. [Apply]

The Seven Ages of Man ◆ 837

Beyond the Selection

FURTHER READING

Other Works by Edgar Allan Poe
"Annabel Lee"
"The Black Cat"

Other Works by William Shakespeare
The Tragedy of Macbeth
The Tragedy of Julius Caesar

Other Works With the Theme of Perspectives
My Antonia, Willa Cather
To Kill a Mockingbird, Harper Lee

INTERNET

Students can learn more about Poe and Shakespeare at the following Internet sites. Please be aware, however, that sites may have changed from the time we published this information.

For essays about Poe and his life, go to **hhttp://www. yasuda-u.ac. jp/staff/ptervin/HAL/hamlit07.html**

For information about William Shakespeare, go to **http://the-tech.mit.edu/Shakespeare/**

We *strongly recommend* that you preview the sites before you send students to them.

◆ **Reading Strategy**

1. The speaker is well educated and financially comfortable to support the kind of home he describes.
2. The speaker is a reader, has gentlemanly manners, and is highly suggestible, unhappy, and imaginative.
3. He thinks that lovers are foolish and soldiers are foolhardy.
4. Students may say that the speaker is cynical.

◆ **Build Vocabulary**

1. Only;   2. Quiet aloneness;
3. Alone and apart from other things

Using the Word Bank

1. respite;   2. quaint;   3. desolate;
4. pallid;   5. woeful;   6. beguiling;
7. treble

◆ **Literary Focus**

1. They tie the story together very tightly and keep it flowing.
2. Sample response: The poem is clear and complete by itself because, as it stands, its meaning is obvious.

◆ **Build Grammar Skills**

At ten o'clock, I opened my literature book. "The Raven," <u>assigned by my English teacher three nights earlier</u>, stared up at me from the page. With eyes <u>tingling from sleep deprivation</u>, I began to read.

 Writer's Solution

For additional instruction and practice, use the lesson in the **Language Lab CD-ROM** on Misplaced Modifiers and the practice pages on Participles and Participial Phrases (pp. 44–45) in the *Writer's Solution Grammar Practice Book*.

Guide for Responding (continued)

◆ **Reading Strategy**

MAKE INFERENCES ABOUT THE SPEAKER
  Making inferences about the **speaker** of a poem means seeing what is suggested about him or her through the choice of words and details. When, for example, the speaker of "The Raven" says, "Eagerly I wished the morrow—vainly I had tried to borrow/From my books surcease of sorrow . . . ," you can infer that he is sorrowful and that the night worsens the way he feels.

1. In "The Raven," what can you infer about the speaker's level of education and social class from the way he speaks throughout the poem?
2. What else can you infer about the speaker of "The Raven" from other details in the poem?
3. Look at lines 9 through 15 of "The Seven Ages of Man." What do the speaker's words reveal about his attitude toward lovers and soldiers?
4. Based on his ideas about the stages of life, what are your overall impressions of the speaker of "The Seven Ages of Man"? Support your answer.

◆ **Build Vocabulary**

USING THE WORD ROOT *-sol-*
  Knowing that the root *-sol-* means "alone," write a definition of each italicized word.
1. Al was the *sole* owner of Al's Tackle Shop.
2. Maria enjoyed the *solitude* of a morning walk.
3. The *isolated* cottage at the end of the country road has been uninhabited for years.

USING THE WORD BANK
  In your notebook, write the word from the Word Bank that belongs in each blank.
  Entering the town, we thought to seek (1)___?___ from a long day of travel. A (2)___?___ inn tucked into a (3)___?___ corner far from the center of town caught our eye. The innkeeper, whose (4)___?___ complexion contrasted sharply with her black dress, launched into a (5)___?___ tale about a tragic event that had occurred in one of the rooms. When we looked dismayed, she broke into a (6)___?___ smile and admitted, in her high (7)___?___ voice, that the story wasn't really true.

◆ **Literary Focus**

NARRATIVE AND DRAMATIC POETRY
  "The Raven" is a **narrative poem**—a poem that tells a story. "The Seven Ages of Man" is a **dramatic monologue**—a poem in which a fictional character directly expresses his or her thoughts in the midst of a developing situation.
1. How do the rhythm and rhyme scheme of "The Raven" enhance the telling of the story?
2. "The Seven Ages of Man" is from Shakespeare's play *As You Like It*. Tell why you think the poem is or is not clear and complete by itself.

◆ **Build Grammar Skills**

PARTICIPIAL PHRASES
  Restrictive participial phrases are not set off by commas because they are necessary to the meaning of the word they modify. **Nonrestrictive participial phrases,** which are not necessary but add to the meaning, are set off by commas.

  Writing Application Rewrite this paragraph:
  At ten o'clock, I opened my literature book. "The Raven" assigned by my English teacher three nights earlier stared up at me from the page. With eyes tingling from sleep deprivation I began to read.

Beyond Literature

Cultural Connection

The Raven as a Symbol Through the ages, the raven has often been seen as a symbol of evil or negativity. For example, in Greek mythology, the raven is portrayed as indiscreetly revealing secrets, prompting the god Apollo to blacken the raven's white feathers as punishment. In many fairy tales, people who have had spells cast upon them have been depicted as ravens. In contrast, however, some Native American myths depict the raven more positively—as a creator of the natural world. What other birds might have made an effective symbol in Poe's poem?

 Speaking and Listening Mini-Lesson

Debate
This mini-lesson supports the second Speaking and Listening activity in the Idea Bank on page 839.

Introduce the Concept Point out that a debate is an organized discussion of two sides of an issue. Have students discuss debates, such as political debates, that they have witnessed.

Develop Background Before students hold their debate, have them plan the following:
• First clarify the proposition to be debated,

number and role of participants on each team, and time limit.
• Select a moderator or chairperson.
• Prepare specific examples and details to support the sides of the issue.

Apply the Information Have students use these guidelines as they debate.

Assess the Outcome Evaluate the debate by using the following criteria: logic of arguments, adherence to debating format, speech clarity.

Build Your Portfolio

 Idea Bank

Writing

1. **Poem Summary** Write a summary of one of these poems. Capture the key details of the poem in the order in which they are presented.

2. **Story** Write a story about the relationship between Lenore and the speaker of "The Raven." End with the details of Lenore's death.

3. **Essay About the Stages of Life** Write an essay entitled "The Stages of Life." Like Shakespeare, choose a type of person to represent each stage. Begin with an introduction revealing the types of people you've chosen. Then write a paragraph explaining each choice.

Speaking and Listening

4. **Choral Reading** With a group of classmates, prepare a choral reading of "The Raven." Decide on the best arrangement of group and individual voices. For example, you might have a different person read the first five lines of each stanza and all read the last line. **[Performing Arts Link]**

5. **Debate** Stage a debate between a group of students supporting the views of the speaker of "The Seven Ages of Man" and a group with a more optimistic view. Each group should support its view with examples from real life.

Projects

6. **Photo Exhibit** Prepare a photo exhibit on the theme "Ages of Humankind." Decide what ages you will represent. Gather photos for each age. Then write a label for each photo. **[Art Link]**

7. **Fact Sheet** Gather information about ravens— what they look like, where they're found, and so on. Present your findings in an illustrated fact sheet. **[Science Link]**

 Writing Mini-Lesson

Scene for a Movie

Imagine that you've been hired by a film studio to create a movie based on "The Raven." Come up with an idea for the movie's opening scene. Then write a detailed description of the scene that a scriptwriter could use as the basis for developing a script for the scene. In your description, provide detailed instructions about the setting, characters, and events in the scene. Pay special attention to the mood, or atmosphere, that should be established.

Writing Skills Focus: Setting a Mood

Edgar Allan Poe was a master at establishing specific **moods** through his careful choice of descriptive details. Follow his example by using precise details to describe the mood that you would like the scriptwriter to capture in your scene. Look at this example. Notice how Edgar Allan Poe uses the italicized words to establish a gloomy mood in the first line of "The Raven."

Model From the Selection
Once upon a midnight *dreary*, while I pondered, *weak* and *weary* . . .

Prewriting Start by thinking about how the poem could be expanded into a movie. Jot down the events that might take place in the opening scene. Then brainstorm for details related to the characters, setting, and mood. Keep in mind that the ideas you come up with must fit in with Poe's poem.

Drafting Using the ideas you've gathered, draft your description. Start with a paragraph describing the mood you want to establish. Then follow with paragraphs about the plot, characters, and setting.

Revising Have one of your classmates assume the role of the scriptwriter and read your description. Make sure that after reading your description, your classmate's impression of what the script should be like matches what you intended.

The Raven/The Seven Ages of Man ◆ 839

 Idea Bank

Customizing for
Performance Levels

Following are suggestions for matching the Idea Bank topics with your students' performance levels:

Less Advanced Students: 1, 6
Average Students: 2, 4, 7
More Advanced Students: 3, 5

Customizing for
Learning Modalities

Following are suggestions for matching Idea Bank topics with your students' learning modalities:

Logical/Mathematical: 1, 5, 7
Verbal/Linguistic: 2, 3, 4, 5
Interpersonal: 4, 5
Visual/Spatial: 6, 7

 Writing Mini-Lesson

Refer students to the Writing Handbook, page 962, for instruction on the writing process, and page 964 for further information on description.

Use the Writing Process Model 3: Descriptive and Observational Writing in **Writing and Language Transparencies,** pp. 17–20, to guide students through the writing process.

 **Writer's Solution**

Writers at Work Videodisc
Have students view the videodisc segment (Ch. 1) featuring science-fiction writer Anne McCaffrey to see how she includes details to improve her descriptions. Have students discuss how description of characters can be worked into a story line.

Play frames 335 to 10785

Writing Lab CD-ROM
Have students complete the Tutorial on Description. Follow these steps:
1. Use the Video Tips on gathering details.
2. Have students draft on computer.
3. Use the Interactive Self-Evaluation Checklist to aid revision.

Sourcebook
Have students use Chapter 1, Description (pp. 1–29), for additional support. The chapter includes in-depth instruction on creating a main impression (p. 19).

OBJECTIVES

1. To read, comprehend, and interpret poems
2. To relate poems to personal experience
3. To read in sentences to understand the literal meaning of a poem
4. To identify features of sonnets and haiku
5. To build vocabulary in context and learn the suffix -ness
6. To differentiate between concrete and abstract nouns and develop skill in using concrete nouns
7. To write a haiku series, keeping to a format
8. To respond to the poems through writing, speaking and listening, and projects

SKILLS INSTRUCTION

Vocabulary:
Suffixes: -ness
Grammar:
Concrete and Abstract Nouns
Reading Strategy:
Read in Sentences
Literary Focus:
Sonnets and Haiku

Writing: Keeping to a Format
Speaking and Listening:
Dialogue (teacher edition)
Critical Viewing:
Infer

PORTFOLIO OPPORTUNITIES

Writing: Journal Entry; Introduction; Literary Analysis
Writing Mini-Lesson: Haiku Series
Speaking and Listening: Poetry Reading; Dialogue
Projects: Illustrated Book; Internet Research

More About the Authors
Just as works by **Shakespeare** and **Keats** are considered part of the canon of Western classics and an important part of students' education in English-language literature, **Bashō** is an important contributor to the Eastern canon. Poets **Chiyojo** and **Richard Wright** are more modern and less well known, but both poets' works are well on their way to joining the list of "classics."

Guide for Reading

John Keats (1795–1821)

John Keats's poems are among the most admired in the English language. Remarkably, Keats accomplished this distinction in spite of his early death at the age of twenty-five.
Keats is considered one of the main poets of the Romantic Movement, a group of writers who stressed the importance of individual experience and the spiritual connection between people and nature.

William Shakespeare (1564–1616)

William Shakespeare was as much a poet as a playwright. Not only are his 37 plays written in verse, he also composed 154 sonnets. Taken together, the sonnets seem to tell a story. The "plot" is not always clear, but it seems obvious that the main characters are a young nobleman, a lady, a poet (probably Shakespeare himself), and a rival poet. Some of the best sonnets, like "Sonnet 30," are addressed to the nobleman. (For more on William Shakespeare, see pp. 669 and 830.)

Bashō (1644–1694)

Bashō (bash´ō) is regarded as one of the greatest Japanese poets. In his youth, he knew luxury as the companion to the son of a lord. Later, however, he lived apart and devoted himself to writing haiku. Many of his best poems were inspired by travels in which he observed nature.

Chiyojo (1887–1959)

Chiyojo (chē yō´ jō) was the wife of a samurai's servant. When her husband died, she became a nun and she began studying poetry with a well-known teacher of haiku. Scholars value the lightness of spirit in her poems.

Richard Wright (1908–1960)

Richard Wright is best known for his acclaimed novel *Native Son* (1940), which chronicles the life of a boy raised in poverty in Chicago. However, Wright also produced a wide range of other types of works, including essays and poems. As a poet, Wright experimented with different forms, including the traditional Japanese haiku.

◆ Build Vocabulary

SUFFIXES: -ness
In his sonnet "On the Grasshopper and the Cricket," Keats describes a person half lost in drowsiness. *Drowsiness* ends in the suffix -ness, meaning "in the state or condition of." When added to the adjective *drowsy*, the suffix -ness forms the noun *drowsiness*, meaning "in the state of being drowsy or sleepy."

ceasing
wrought
drowsiness
woes

WORD BANK
Before you read, preview this list of words from the poems.

◆ Build Grammar Skills

CONCRETE AND ABSTRACT NOUNS
In his sonnet, Keats uses many concrete nouns to create images of grasshoppers and crickets in your mind. A **concrete noun** names something that can be perceived by the senses. The noun *birds,* for example, is a concrete noun. In "Sonnet 30," Shakespeare uses several abstract nouns to express ideas. An **abstract noun** names an idea, a belief, or a quality. The word *remembrance,* for example, is an abstract noun.

840 ◆ *Poetry*

Prentice Hall Literature Program Resources

REINFORCE / RETEACH / EXTEND

Selection Support Pages
Build Vocabulary: Suffixes: -ness, p. 229
Build Grammar Skills: Concrete and Abstract Nouns, p. 230
Reading Strategy: Read in Sentences, p. 231
Literary Focus: Sonnets and Haiku, p. 232

Strategies for Diverse Student Needs, p. 56

Beyond Literature
Humanities Connection: Poetry Reading, p. 56

Formal Assessment Selection Test, pp. 198–200,

Assessment Resources Software

Alternative Assessment, p. 54

Writing and Language Transparencies
Sunburst Organizer, p. 64

Resource Pro CD-ROM
—includes all resource material and customizable lesson plan

🎧 **Listening to Literature Audiocassettes**
"On the Grasshopper and the Cricket," "Sonnet 30," Three Haiku, "Hokku Poems"

◆ On the Grasshopper and the Cricket ◆
Sonnet 30 ◆ Three Haiku ◆ Hokku Poems

◆ *Literature and Your Life*

CONNECT YOUR EXPERIENCE

Almost everyone has regrets—memories of losses, disappointments, and mistakes—that can ruin the enjoyment of the present. What can be done when regrets crowd out the present? In "Sonnet 30," Shakespeare offers a way to put aside regrets about the past. The other poems in this section present a way to keep focused on the present—through the careful observation of nature.

Journal Writing Nature includes animals, plants, weather, and more. List some aspects of nature you enjoy.

THEMATIC FOCUS: OBSERVATIONS

Each person experiences the world in a different way. As you read, think about how the poets' observations about the natural world compare with your own.

◆ Background for Understanding

SCIENCE

It is not surprising that Keats chose the cricket and the grasshopper when he wanted to write about the poetry of nature. These two members of the order Orthoptera are among the most musical of insects. The males of both groups produce sounds by rubbing one part of the body against another. Male crickets rub the rough surfaces of their wing covers together. Male grasshoppers usually rub a leg against a wing with a sawing motion.

◆ Literary Focus

SONNETS AND HAIKU

The poems in this section represent two poetic forms with strict rules. The poems by Shakespeare and Keats are sonnets. A **sonnet** is a lyric poem of fourteen lines, usually written in rhymed iambic pentameter (ten-syllable lines in which every second syllable is accented). This meter can be seen in the first line from Keats's poem.

The seven other poems in this section are haiku, a form of poetry developed in Japan. A **haiku** consists of three lines of verse. The first and third lines have five syllables each. The second line has seven syllables. In a very few words, the poet creates a dominant impression in the reader's mind with one or two striking images.

◆ Reading Strategy

READ IN SENTENCES

Like prose, many poems are written in sentences. They are also written in lines. However, poets don't always complete a sentence at the end of a line. A sentence may extend for several lines and then end in the middle of a line so that the poet can keep to the chosen rhythm and rhyme scheme.

To understand the literal meaning of a poem, **read in sentences**. Notice the punctuation. Don't make a full stop at the end of a line unless there is a period, comma, colon, semicolon, or dash. Notice where the stops are in the following lines from Keats' sonnet:

> That is the Grasshopper's—
>   he takes the lead
> In summer luxury,—he has
>   never done
> With his delights; for when
>   tired out with fun
> He rests at ease beneath
>   some pleasant weed.

Guide for Reading ◆ 841

Preparing for Standardized Tests

Reading and Vocabulary The Reading Strategy lesson for this selection focuses on reading poetry in sentences. Practicing this skill will help students interpret poetic language and thus improve their performance on reading comprehension items on standardized tests. For additional practice, use the Reading Strategy page in **Selection Support,** p. 231.

Grammar and Language The Build Grammar Skills lesson for this selection focuses on concrete and abstract nouns. Students' familiarity with types of nouns can help them make distinctions that will enable them to score well on standardized tests. For additional practice, use the Build Grammar Skills page on Concrete and Abstract Nouns in **Selection Support,** p. 230.

 **Interest Grabber** Provide students with the following template, which represents the syllables of a haiku:

___ ___ ___ ___ ___

___ ___ ___ ___ ___ ___ ___

___ ___ ___ ___ ___

Give students time to fill the blanks with syllables of words about a subject of their choice. The only rule is that the completed set of words make sense. Invite students to share what they've written. Tell them that the *haiku*—a form of Japanese poetry—follows this same form. If anyone in the class has written something she or he would consider a poem, ask the student to explain why she or he thinks it qualifies as poetry. Does it create a striking image? Does the last line add some special meaning?

Customize for
Less Proficient Readers

Sonnet 30 may cause readers some difficulty because of the Elizabethan language and use of inverted word order. Invite students to listen to the sonnet before reading it. When they read it for the first time, they should pay attention to the footnotes.

 Listening to Literature Audiocassettes

Customize for
More Advanced Students

Bashō's haiku and Shakespeare's sonnet could not be much more different. Ask these students what qualities these works share that qualifies them both for membership in the same genre—poetry.

Customize for
English Language Learners

You may wish to begin with the haiku to help these students achieve some success with poetry before moving on to the more complex and concept-heavy sonnets.

Customize for
Bodily/Kinesthetic Learners

Students who are interested in movement and dance might like to choose two haiku and choreograph interpretive dances to be performed as the haiku are read aloud. The dances should reflect the differences between the chosen poems.

"On the Grasshopper and the Cricket" is an expression of delight in the world of nature. Keats writes of how the cricket's song from the hearth in winter brings to mind the song of the grasshopper, and with it, summer.

◆ Literary Focus

❶ Sonnet A Petrarchan sonnet, of which this is an example, contains an octave, eight lines that develop a problem, followed by a sestet, six lines that resolve the problem. Ask: At what point in the poem does the speaker change the subject? *The speaker changes the subject at line 9.*

◆ Critical Thinking

❷ Interpret What is the meaning of the last two lines of the sonnet? *The cricket's song in winter reminds the speaker of the grasshopper's song and summer.*

Reinforce and Extend

Answers
◆ Literature and Your Life

Reader's Response Accept all answers supported by logical reasons.

Thematic Focus He suggests that the world around us is filled with natural poetry.

☑ Check Your Comprehension

1. The birds hide in cooling trees.
2. The grasshopper takes the lead.
3. The cricket resides in the stove.

◆ Critical Thinking

1. They both make music, but the grasshopper's song is noticed in summer, while the cricket's song is noticed in winter.
2. They both produce the poetry, or music, of nature.
3. Nature is always alive with the music of its creatures and the poetry of its landscape.
4. Students should suggest elements of nature and their respective poetic attributes.
5. Sample response: A musical collage featuring sounds from nature would illustrate the theme.

842

On the Grasshopper and the Cricket John Keats

◆ Build Vocabulary

ceasing (sēs´ in) *v.*: Stopping

wrought (rôt) *v.*: Formed; fashioned

drowsiness (drou´ zē nes) *n.*: Sleepiness

The poetry of earth is never dead:
When all the birds are faint with the hot sun,
And hide in cooling trees, a voice will run
From hedge to hedge about the new-mown mead;[1]
5   That is the Grasshopper's—he takes the lead
In summer luxury,—he has never done
With his delights; for when tired out with fun
He rests at ease beneath some pleasant weed. ❶
The poetry of earth is ceasing never:
10 On a lone winter evening, when the frost
Has wrought a silence, from the stove there shrills
The Cricket's song, in warmth increasing ever, ❷
And seems to one in drowsiness half lost,
The Grasshopper's among some grassy hills.

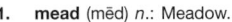

1. **mead** (mēd) *n.*: Meadow.

Guide for Responding

◆ Literature and Your Life

Reader's Response Which scene painted by the poet appeals more to you? Why?
Thematic Focus What does the poet suggest about the world around us?

☑ Check Your Comprehension

1. What do birds do when summer gets too hot?
2. Who "takes the lead in summer luxury"?
3. Where does the cricket reside in winter?

◆ Critical Thinking

INTERPRET
1. How are the grasshopper and the cricket alike and different? **[Compare and Contrast]**
2. How are the two insects connected in the speaker's mind? **[Associate]**
3. What does the speaker mean when he says that the "poetry of earth is never dead"? **[Explain]**
APPLY
4. In your environment, what "poetry of nature" do you experience at different times of the year? **[Specify]**
EXTEND
5. How could you illustrate the theme of this poem in music? **[Music Link]**

Block Scheduling Strategies

Consider these suggestions to take advantage of extended class time:

- Students might enjoy participating in a grammar game following their work on Build Grammar Skills (p. 846). Challenge them to think of one concrete noun and one abstract noun that can fit into the form, "The (abstract noun) of the (concrete noun)." (Examples: "The beauty of the sunset," "The smell of the flowers")
- Students who complete the journal activity in

Literature and Your Life (p. 841) might share their entries in small groups.

- As you review the information in Background for Understanding (p. 846), ask students to share any facts they know about crickets and grasshoppers from their science classes or their own observations.
- To reinforce the Reading Strategy instruction (p. 846), present copies of several additional poems to students and have students read the poems aloud in sentences.

Sonnet 30

William Shakespeare

When to the sessions of sweet silent thought
I summon up remembrance of things past,
I sigh the lack of many a thing I sought,
And with old <u>woes'</u> new wail my dear times waste:[1]
5 Then can I drown an eye, unused to flow,
For precious friends hid in death's dateless[2] night,
❸ And weep afresh love's long since cancelled woe,
❹ And moan the expense[3] of many a vanished sight:
Then can I grieve at grievances foregone,[4]
10 And heavily from woe to woe tell o'er[5]
The sad account of fore-bemoanèd moan,[6]
Which I new pay as if not paid before.
But if the while I think on thee, dear friend,
All losses are restored and sorrows end.

---

1. **And . . . waste:** And by grieving anew for past sorrows, ruin the precious present.
2. **dateless:** Endless.
3. **expense:** Loss.
4. **foregone:** Past and done with.
5. **tell o'er:** Count up.
6. **fore-bemoanèd moan:** Sorrows suffered in the past.

◆ **Build Vocabulary**

woes (wōz) *n.*: Great sorrows

Guide for Responding

◆ Literature and Your Life

Reader's Response Would you want the speaker of the poem as a friend? Explain.

Thematic Focus What two different "worlds" around him does the speaker describe?

☑ Check Your Comprehension

1. In general, what are the speaker's feelings when he recalls the past?
2. How does the speaker feel when he thinks of his friend?

◆ Critical Thinking

INTERPRET

1. What does "drown an eye" mean? **[Infer]**
2. In lines 10–12, the words "tell o'er" (count up) "account," "pay," and "paid" suggest someone going over bills. What action is the speaker describing through this metaphor, or implied comparison? **[Clarify]**
3. How is the metaphor extended in line 14? **[Identify]**
4. How does the poet's use of metaphor add interest to the sonnet? **[Explain]**

APPLY

5. What does the sonnet imply about the value of friendship? **[Generalize]**

On the Grasshopper and the Cricket/Sonnet 30 ◆ 843

✦ Speaking and Listening Mini-Lesson

Dialogue

This mini-lesson supports the second Speaking and Listening activity in the Idea Bank on page 847.

Introduce the Concept Explain that a dialogue is a conversation between characters. An interesting dialogue uses convincing, real-life language and has a specific purpose.

Develop Background Have partners brainstorm for opinions the cricket and grasshopper might have about the seasons.

Apply the Information Have students use these questions to organize their work.

- What main point does each insect wish to make? How might it support its points?
- How would one insect counter the other's arguments?

Instruct students to rehearse their dialogue until they can perform it from memory.

Assess the Outcome Use criteria such as the following: Main points are presented in a logical order and supported with details; lines are delivered with feeling; counterarguments match original arguments.

Although the haiku by Bashō, Chiyojo, and Richard Wright differ in subject matter, they share one quality—each one creates a dominant impression in the reader's mind with one or two striking images from nature.

◆ Literary Focus

❶ Haiku Ask students to identify the two striking images in this haiku. Then ask them to describe the dominant impression the haiku suggests. *The two images are the sound of the bells dying out and the fragrance of the blossoms. The dominant image is a peaceful evening.*

◆ Reading Strategy

❷ Read in Sentences Ask students to describe how a reader should read this poem to show that it is a single sentence. *The reader should pause after the word* catcher *and use his or her voice to express the question in the poem.*

►Critical Viewing◄

❸ Infer One can infer that the Japanese appreciate the delicate beauty of nature and that they take pride in highlighting that beauty with such items as a lantern to illuminate blossoms.

◆ *Literature and Your Life*

❹ Have students relate this poem to their own experiences of giving and receiving directions. How does the poem differ from ordinary directions? *It is in haiku form and contains an unexpected and striking image from nature.*

Clarification The word *hokku* is not precisely equivalent to *haiku*. The first refers to the "opening stanza" in a series of related verse; while the second translates as "amusing sentence." They are, nevertheless, often used interchangeably. Ask students to examine Wright's poems to see whether they are genuine haiku. *They are, although the first one has a third line of only four syllables.*

Three Haiku

Girl With Lantern on a Balcony at Night, c. 1768 (detail), Suzuki Harunobu, The Metropolitan Museum of Art

Temple bells die out.
The fragrant blossoms remain.　❶
A perfect evening!
　　　　　　　　—BASHŌ

Dragonfly catcher,
How far have you gone today　❷
In your wandering?
　　　　　　　　—CHIYOJO

Bearing no flowers,
I am free to toss madly
Like the willow tree.
　　　　　　　　—CHIYOJO

▲ Critical Viewing What inferences, or conclusions, can you make about Japanese culture based on this painting? [Infer]

844 ◆ Poetry

♪ Humanities: Art

Girl with Lantern on a Balcony at Night, 1768, by Suzuki Harunobu.

Like Japanese haiku, Japanese prints capture a moment or a mood. Suzuki Harunobu (1725–1770) is considered the first of—and one of the greatest of—Japan's early full-color printmakers. It usually took three craftspersons to create a full-color print: the artist who designed it, the carver of the wood blocks, and the printer who dipped the blocks in ink and pressed them onto a background. Only the artist received credit for the work. The technique for making a full-color print, which used many carved wood blocks and a variety of colors, was developed in 1765, only three years before this print was made.

Use these questions for discussion:
1. How does this print illustrate the first haiku on the page? *The girl may be contemplating a perfect evening, as in the Bashō poem.*
2. Bashō lived nearly 100 years before Harunobu made this print. Is it still a reasonable illustration for his work? Why or why not? *Students will probably say yes, because the mood and theme of his haiku are timeless.*

Hokku Poems

Richard Wright

Make up your mind snail!
You are half inside your house
And halfway out!

In the falling snow
A laughing boy holds out his palms
Until they are white

4 Keep straight down this block
Then turn right where you will find
A peach tree blooming

Whose town did you leave
O wild and drowning spring rain
And where do you go?

Guide for Responding

◆ Literature and Your Life

Reader's Response Which of the seven haiku do you like best? Why?

Thematic Focus Choose one of the haiku and explain how it heightens your awareness of the world around you.

Group Activity In a group, brainstorm to come up with a list of topics for a contemporary haiku.

✓ Check Your Comprehension

1. To which senses does Bashō's haiku appeal?
2. How does Chiyojo compare herself to the willow tree?
3. What two weather events does Richard Wright refer to in his haiku?

◆ Critical Thinking

INTERPRET

1. Describe the kind of evening that you imagine based on Bashō's haiku. **[Support]**
2. In Chiyojo's second haiku, what might the speaker be suggesting about herself? **[Analyze]**
3. What is the "house" in Wright's first haiku? **[Analyze]**
4. What feelings are stirred in you by the scene Wright depicts in his second haiku?
5. Compare the language of the three Japanese haiku with the language of Richard Wright's haiku. **[Compare and Contrast]**

EVALUATE

6. Which do you think are more effective—Wright's haiku or the Japanese haiku? Support your answer with details from the poems. **[Evaluate]**

Three Haiku/Hokku Poems ◆ 845

Beyond the Selection

FURTHER READING

Other Works by the Poets
Sonnet 18: "Shall I Compare Thee," William Shakespeare
"To Autumn," John Keats
"When I Have Fears," John Keats
Narrow Road to the Interior, Bashō

Other Works With the Theme of the World Around Us
"Cobwebs," Christina Rossetti
The Tosa Diary, Ki Tsurayuki

INTERNET

The Internet provides opportunities for students to learn more about poets and their poetry. We suggest the following sites. Please be aware, however, that sites may have changed from the time we published this information.

For haiku by Bashō, go to **http://www.dmu.ac.uk/~pka/haiku.html**

For information about Richard Wright, go to **http://www.itvs.org/programs/RW/more_info.html**

We *strongly recommend* that you preview the sites before you send students to them.

Reinforce and Extend

Answers

◆ **Literature and Your Life**

Reader's Response Encourage students to share the experiences, places, and emotions that their favorite haiku brings to mind.

Thematic Focus Student responses should reflect the images and the dominant impression of the chosen poem.

☑ **Check Your Comprehension**

1. Bashō's haiku appeals to the senses of hearing (bells) and smell (fragrant blossoms).
2. She is as flexible and free in motion as the willow tree.
3. He refers to "falling snow" and "drowning spring rain."

◆ **Critical Thinking**

1. Students might say that they imagine a warm spring evening.
2. Suggested response: She is expressing freedom to follow her impulses.
3. The house is the shell of the snail.
4. Students might say the scene gives them a happy, joyous feeling.
5. Sample response: The language of both groups is similar in its level of formality. However, the language of the three haiku poems might seem a bit less spontaneous than that of the hokku poems due to its translation from Japanese.
6. Suggested response: The Japanese haiku are probably a little less effective because, when you translate a poem, you cannot translate the meaning and the images that a poet had in mind. Because Wright's haiku were already in English, the meaning is not affected.

845

◆ Reading Strategy

1. Lines 1 and 10 do not end in punctuation marks because the complete ideas expressed by those lines continue into lines 2 and 11 respectively.

2. Lines 1 and 9 end in colons because an example of what each line states—line 1 states that "the poetry of earth is never dead," and line 9 states that "the poetry of earth is ceasing never"—follows each of the lines.

3. Sample response: The punctuation marks at the ends of lines of "Sonnet 30" give the sonnet a more formal tone. The lack of punctuation at the ends of some lines of "On the Grasshopper and the Cricket" make the poem read more like an informal narrative.

◆ Build Grammar Skills

1. poetry, abstract; earth, concrete; birds, concrete; sun, concrete; trees, concrete; voice, concrete; hedge, concrete; mead, concrete; lead, abstract; luxury, abstract; delights, abstract; fun, abstract

2. Suggested response: Because Shakespeare's sonnet deals with abstract human emotions, it contains more abstract nouns than the other poems.

Writing Application
Sample responses follow:
1. Though surrounded by expensive *toys,* the child was not happy.
2. His *cries* were many.
3. The family lacked the most basic *clothes.*
4. There was no want of glowing *eyes* in her face.

 **Writer's Solution**

For additional instruction and practice, use the lesson in the **Language Lab CD-ROM** on Types of Nouns.

◆ Literary Focus

1. Suggested response: Yes. Each quatrain reflects a sad feeling or expresses a loss. The feeling in the last two lines changes to reflect a sense of hope and promise.

2. Suggested response: The content of the octave is about summer, while the content of the sestet is about winter.

Guide for Responding (continued)

◆ Reading Strategy

READ IN SENTENCES
You were better able to understand and appreciate these poems if you **read in sentences**—that is, if you paused or stopped only at punctuation marks rather than automatically at the ends of lines. The punctuation of the two sonnets may seem unusual by today's standards. In these poems, colons are used in place of periods to show a close connection between one sentence and the next.

1. In "Sonnet 30," why do lines 1 and 10 not end in punctuation marks?
2. In "On the Grasshopper and the Cricket," why do lines 1 and 9 end in colons rather than in periods?
3. Most of the lines in Shakespeare's sonnet end in punctuation marks. Several of the lines in Keats's poem do not end in punctuation marks. Explain the effect of the punctuation of each poem.

◆ Build Grammar Skills

CONCRETE AND ABSTRACT NOUNS
When Chiyojo writes about a dragonfly catcher, she creates a specific image in the reader's mind by using a **concrete noun**—one that names something that can be perceived by the senses. When Shakespeare writes about remembrance, he conveys an idea by using an **abstract noun**—one that names a concept, idea, belief, or quality.

Practice
1. List the nouns in the first eight lines of "On the Grasshopper and the Cricket." Label each one as concrete or abstract.
2. Why might Shakespeare's sonnet have more abstract nouns than the other poems?

Writing Application Rewrite these sentences, adding concrete nouns to paint a more vivid picture.
1. Though surrounded by luxury, the child was not happy.
2. His woes were many.
3. The family lacked the most basic necessities.
4. There was no want of beauty in her face.

◆ Literary Focus

SONNETS AND HAIKU
A **sonnet** is a lyric poem of fourteen lines, usually written in rhymed iambic pentameter. A **haiku** has three lines. The first and third lines have five syllables, and the second line has seven syllables.

A haiku generally consists of two concise, contrasting images that spark associations in the reader's mind. In a sonnet, the rhyme scheme reflects the content of the poem. A Shakespearean sonnet usually presents an idea or question in the first quatrain (four lines), explores the idea for the next two quatrains, and reaches a conclusion in the couplet (two lines) at the end. The rhyme scheme is *abab cdcd efef gg.* A Petrarchan sonnet, named for the Italian poet Petrarch, consists of an octave (eight lines) and a sestet (six lines). The octave always uses two rhymes in the pattern *abbaabba.* The rhyme scheme of the sestet can vary.

1. Can the thought content of "Sonnet 30" be divided into units that correspond to the divisions of three quatrains and a couplet? Explain.
2. In Keats's sonnet, how is the content of the octave related to that of the sestet?
3. What are the two main images in Wright's second haiku?

◆ Build Vocabulary

USING THE SUFFIX -ness
Rewrite each sentence by adding the suffix -*ness,* meaning "state of," to change the italicized adjective into a noun.

1. Elwood insisted that all he wanted was for me to be *happy.*
2. To become *drowsy* behind the wheel of a car can lead to a serious accident.
3. She was known throughout the town for being *friendly.*

USING THE WORD BANK
Identify the correct antonym for each first word.
1. wrought: (a) create, (b) seen, (c) destroyed
2. ceasing: (a) escaping, (b) rewarding, (c) beginning
3. drowsiness: (a) frankness, (b) alertness, (c) quietness
4. woe: (a) terror, (b) ease, (c) joy

3. The two main images are the falling snow and a laughing boy holding out his hands to catch snow.

◆ Build Vocabulary

1. Elwood insisted that all he wanted was my *happiness.*
2. *Drowsiness* behind the wheel of a car can lead to a serious accident.

3. She was known throughout the town for her *friendliness.*

Using the Word Bank
1. c 2. c 3. b 4. c

Build Your Portfolio

Idea Bank

Writing

1. **Journal Entry** Write a journal entry describing something interesting in nature that you recently observed. **[Science Link]**

2. **Introduction** Write a brief passage that could serve as the introduction to one of these poems in a poetry collection. Offer your interpretation of the poem and explain why it is worth reading.

3. **Literary Analysis** Write an essay analyzing the relationship between the form and content of Shakespeare's sonnet. Explain how the thought content of the sonnet can be divided into sections that correspond to the sections of the sonnet. Cite details from the poem for support.

Speaking and Listening

4. **Poetry Reading** Prepare and deliver a reading of one of the sonnets that will help your audience understand its meaning.

5. **Dialogue** With a partner, write a dialogue between the grasshopper and the cricket in which they discuss the merits of summer and winter. Rehearse the dialogue and present it to the class.

Projects

6. **Illustrated Book** Put together an illustrated book of haiku. Choose three of the haiku you just read. Create an illustration or find a photograph to accompany each one. **[Art Link]**

7. **Internet Research** Conduct research on the Internet to learn more about haiku and their connection to Japanese culture. Gather examples of haiku, along with illustrations and background information. Present your findings to the class. **[Technology Link]**

Writing Mini-Lesson

Haiku Series

Shakespeare wrote 154 sonnets with the same cast of characters. Yet each of the poems expresses a fresh new idea. Write three related haiku—either about the same subject or on the same theme. Remember that a haiku captures a feeling with one or two concrete images and follows a strict format: three lines of five, seven, and five syllables.

Writing Skills Focus: Keeping to a Format

When you write a poem that fits into a specific form, it is essential to **keep to the format** of that form. For example, when you write a haiku, you must compose three lines with the correct number of syllables in each line. This requires you to use one- or two-syllable words that spark strong associations. Notice how Bashō uses brief, evocative words in this haiku.

Model From the Selection

Temple bells die out.
The fragrant blossoms remain.
A perfect evening!

Prewriting Think of the topics for the three haiku and decide what will be the connection among them. Jot down a few images you will include.

Drafting In each haiku, capture one or two images and create one impression. Don't worry about getting exactly the right number of syllables as you draft.

Revising Count the syllables in each line. If you don't have the correct number, see what words you can change, leave out, or add to achieve the desired number of syllables. In addition, work with a classmate to make sure that your haiku convey the impression you intended.

On the Grasshopper and the Cricket/Sonnet 30/Three Haiku/Hokku Poems ◆ 847

Idea Bank

Customizing for *Performance Levels*

Following are suggestions for matching Idea Bank topics with your students' performance levels:
  Less Advanced Students: 1, 4
  Average Students: 2, 5, 6
  More Advanced Students: 3, 7

Customizing for *Learning Modalities*

Following are suggestions for matching Idea Bank topics with your students' learning modalities:
  Verbal/Linguistic: 1, 2, 3, 4, 5
  Logical/Mathematical: 3, 7
  Musical/Rhythmic: 4
  Interpersonal: 5
  Visual/Spatial: 6

Writing Mini-Lesson

Have students use the Sunburst Organizer in *Writing and Language Transparencies,* p. 64, to organize the topics and images of their three haiku.

Writer's Solution

Writers at Work Videodisc

Have students view the videodisc segment (Ch. 6) featuring animation scriptwriter Grant Moran to see how he chooses a topic. Have students discuss how to choose a topic that is best for them to write about.

Play frames 12243 to 21791

Writing Lab CD-ROM

Have students complete the Tutorial on Creative Writing. Use these steps:
1. Use the Poetry Topic Wheel to spark ideas for a poem.
2. Use the Audio-annotated Literary Models of poetic forms to see an example of a haiku.
3. Have students draft on computer.
4. Use the Interactive Self-Evaluation Checklist for Poetry to aid revision.
Allow approximately 60 minutes of class time to complete these steps.

Sourcebook

Have students use Chapter 6, Creative Writing (pp. 162–193), for additional support. The chapter includes tips for gathering sensory images (p. 179).

✓ ASSESSMENT OPTIONS

Formal Assessment, Selection Test, pp. 198–200, and Assessment Resources Software. The selection test is designed so that it can be easily customized to the performance levels of your students. **Alternative Assessment,** p. 54, includes options for less advanced students, more advanced students, visual/spatial learners, logical/mathematical learners, intrapersonal learners, and verbal/linguistic learners.

PORTFOLIO ASSESSMENT
Use the following rubrics in the **Alternative Assessment** booklet to assess student writing:
Journal Entry: Description Rubric, p. 90
Introduction: Literary Analysis/Interpretation Rubric, p. 105
Literary Analysis: Literary Analysis/Interpretation Rubric, p. 105
Writing Mini-Lesson: Poetry Rubric, p. 101

Establish Writing Guidelines

Before students begin, review the following key characteristics of a poem:

- A poem usually expresses a writer's deepest thoughts and feelings about a subject.

- When effective, a poem makes use of such sound devices as rhyme, rhythm, and alliteration.

- A lyric poem is an intense, highly musical form of poetry; whereas a narrative poem features elements such as plot, character, and theme in much the same way that a short story does.

You may want to distribute the scoring rubric for Poetry (p. 101 in **Alternative Assessment**) to make students aware of the criteria on which they will be evaluated before they begin. See the suggestions on page 850 for how you can customize the rubric to this workshop.

 Writer's Solution

Writing Lab CD-ROM

If your students have access to computers, you may want to have them work on the tutorial on Creative Writing to complete all or part of their song lyrics. Have students follow these steps:

1. Have students review the Audio-annotated Model from Literature of a poem, then spin a Poetry Topic Wheel to see words and images that might spark ideas for their own poems.

2. To gather details for their poems, have students explore the annotated examples of poetic details, including sensory details, rhyming words, and colors.

3. Have students draft their poems on computer.

4. To make the imagery in their poems more striking, have students incorporate words or phrases from the Sensory or Colors Word Bins.

Sourcebook

Students can find additional support in the chapter on Creative Writing (pp. 162–193).

Poem | Writing Process Workshop

Edgar Allan Poe once described poetry as "the rhythmical creation of beauty." When you write a **poem**, you express an image or idea in a special way that focuses on form, feeling, and sound. A poem requires far fewer words than a short story or a novel, yet its impact on readers can be just as great. Write your own poem, using the following skills introduced in this section's Writing Mini-Lessons.

Writing Skills Focus

▶ **Keep to the format of the type of poem you are writing.** You might choose to write a limerick, haiku, sonnet, or free verse, for example. Regardless of your choice, follow the form that the poem requires. (See p. 847.)

▶ **Set the mood in your poem through your choice of descriptive details.** Make your audience experience a specific feeling as they read—whether it's joy, sadness, fear, or surprise. (See p. 839.)

▶ **Use sound devices** such as rhythm, rhyme, and repetition to give your poem a musical quality and to emphasize your main ideas.

Japanese poets Bashō and Chiyojo use the above skills in haiku poetry, which celebrates the joys and wonders of life.

---

① Basho creates a mood of joy and satisfaction in his description of the evening.

② Chiyojo sticks to the format of haiku: three lines of verse with five, seven, and five syllables, respectively.

MODEL FROM LITERATURE

from "Three Haiku" by Bashō and Chiyojo

Temple bells die out.
The fragrant blossoms remain.
A perfect evening! ①

—BASHŌ

Dragonfly catcher,
How far have you gone today
In your wanderings? ②

—CHIYOJO

848 ◆ Poetry

 Cross-Curricular Connection: Science

The haiku presented on this page are an effective introduction to poetry writing because they succinctly illustrate both the formal and aesthetic/emotional characteristics of poems. Point out to students that traditional Japanese haiku always connect closely observed natural phenomena—such as wildlife, weather, or a particular landscape—to an inner state of being. This connection is what lends haiku its power, as inner and outer worlds serve to illuminate each other in unexpected ways. Ask students to share specific observable events in the natural world that evoke special feelings in them. Then encourage students to use such moments as the basis for a poem, or as an effective line or stanza for a poem that deals with a different theme. Discuss how this "unscientific" approach to nature might actually foster a greater appreciation for it and inspire scientific enquiry. Guide students to understand that the close observation of nature is something scientists and poets through the ages have had in common.

Prewriting

Analyze Formats Decide on a topic, then choose the type of poem you will compose. First, study a variety of poems to note how each is set up. Ask yourself these questions:
- ▶ How many lines are in the poem?
- ▶ How many syllables are in each line?
- ▶ How many stanzas are there?
- ▶ Does the poem rhyme? If so, in what order do the rhyming words appear?

After analyzing different formats, choose the one that you feel works best with your topic.

Choose Sensory Images Brainstorm for a list of sensory images that will describe how the subject of your poem looks, sounds, smells, tastes, and feels. The examples in the chart can help spark your own ideas.

Sensory Images

Sights	Sounds	Smells	Tastes	Physical Sensations
green fields	gurgling	roses	honey	hot sand
flashing neon	sobbing	garbage	salt water	velvet
towering tree	whispering	ocean air	bitterness	soft fur

Plan Your Mood The topic of your poem can help you determine the feeling, or mood, you wish to create, but topic alone is not enough. After all, a poem about love might be serious, sad, or funny. Ask yourself this question: If you read your poem aloud, what kind of music would you play in the background? Jot down details that will help create that mood.

Drafting

Develop Your Mood As you draft your poem, include the details you planned for creating the mood. Use colorful and powerful language to help readers form a precise picture of your subject in their minds. Pay particular attention to nouns, verbs, adjectives, and adverbs that you use.

Writing Tip If your poem rhymes, you may find it helpful to consult a rhyming dictionary. Make your rhymes conform to your ideas, however, not the other way around.

APPLYING LANGUAGE SKILLS: Concrete Nouns

A **concrete noun** is a word that names a person, place, or thing in a specific way, rather than in a general way.

General Noun:
I like <u>music</u>.

Concrete Noun:
I like <u>rock-and-roll</u>.

Notice how a concrete noun creates a clearer picture.

Practice On your paper, replace each general noun with a concrete noun.
1. I met a man.
2. I enjoyed the book.
3. The food is good.
4. The machine broke.
5. Your shoes look nice.

Writing Application As you draft your poem, use concrete nouns to name people, places, and things. Use nouns that readers can imagine clearly.

Writer's Solution Connection Writing Lab

For more on sensory images, use the Sensory Word Bin in the Prewriting section of the tutorial on Creative Writing.

Prewriting

If students feel daunted or put off by choosing a format for their poems, feeling perhaps that it constrains their free expression, explain that a well-chosen format should have the opposite effect on their creativity. A particular format and organization will dictate a rhythm that will enable readers to appreciate more fully the sensory images, sound devices, and mood of the poem. Because readers will find specific formats somewhat predictable and reliable, they can concentrate more on the poem's subtleties than on basic comprehension.

Customize for
Visual/Spatial Learners

To help these students choose sensory images for their poems and plan mood, suggest that they close their eyes and visualize the setting and specific items in it. Visual/spatial learners can then describe these "mind's eye" images to another student who transcribes the descriptive words. In this way these students are freed to concentrate on what they want to describe before focusing on revising the word choices made to support their descriptions.

Drafting

Encourage students to draft their poems in one sitting, putting themselves in a state of mind that helps them focus on sustaining a particular mood.

Applying Language Skills
Concrete Nouns

Answers
Suggested responses:
1. I met an undercover police officer.
2. I enjoyed the anthology of Latin American poetry.
3. The appetizer of smoked oysters is good.
4. The laptop computer broke.
5. Your high-top basketball sneakers look nice.

Writer's Solution

For additional instruction and practice on concrete nouns, complete the **Language Lab CD-ROM** lesson on Types of Nouns and the practice pages on nouns (p. 5) and choosing precise words (p. 119) in the *Writer's Solution Grammar Practice Book*.

Parallel Structure

Answers
Suggested responses:
1. The girl ran quickly, carefully, and gracefully.

2. Running isn't the same as jogging.
3. She has confidence, pride, and intelligence.

Writer's Solution

For additional instruction and practice on parallel structure, have students complete the **Language Lab CD-ROM** lesson on Varying Sentence Structure.

Revising

You may want to have students work with peer reviewers to revise their poems. Reviewers should use the Revision Checklist to guide their review, but may want to begin by reading the piece aloud so that the poet can listen for overused words, dull or contrived imagery, and other areas that need improvement. Students can then reverse roles and serve as the readers of their reviewers' work.

 Writer's Solution

Writing Lab CD-ROM

The Revision Checker for Language Variety in the tutorial on Creative Writing can help students make sure that their poems do not overuse specific descriptive words.

Publishing

Students may wish to illustrate their poetry anthologies or magazines with contributions from the visual artists of the class. Another option is to have the poetry printed in a special calligraphic hand or computer font. With either of these possibilities, the poet should act as a consultant on how best to present the poem. When a writer works with a graphic artist in this manner, the result is usually a close review of the writer's vision and perhaps a greater understanding of it by both parties.

Reinforce and Extend

Review the Writing Guidelines
After students have completed their writing, review the characteristics of a poem. Encourage students to come up with additional criteria based on what they learned through completing the assignment.

Writing Process Workshop

APPLYING LANGUAGE SKILLS: Parallel Structure

In a sentence with **parallel structure**, details that are parallel in meaning are expressed in the same form.

Incorrect:
I love to swim, to run, and dancing.

Correct:
I love to swim, to run, and to dance.

or

I love swimming, running, and dancing.

Practice On your paper, rewrite each sentence so it has parallel structure.

1. The girl ran quickly, carefully, and with grace.
2. Running isn't the same as to jog.
3. She has confidence, pride, and is intelligent.

Writing Application Review your poem to see whether it contains any structure that is not parallel. If it does, rephrase the words so they become parallel.

Writer's Solution Connection Writing Lab

For help revising your poem, use the instruction and activities in the Revision section of the tutorial on Creative Writing.

850 ◆ Poetry

Stick to Your Format As you write, follow the rules for the style of poetry you have chosen. For example, if you've chosen haiku, do not deviate from its format. Remember that the way you express yourself is as important as what you say.

Revising

Use a Checklist Return to the Writing Skills Focus on the first page of this lesson, and use the items as a checklist to evaluate and revise your poem.

▶ Have I set a distinct mood in my poem?
Ask a classmate to read your poem and describe the mood he or she felt was expressed. If it isn't the mood you intended, consider details you can add, remove, or change to create the mood you want.

▶ Have I kept to the poem's format?
Check your poem for the number of lines, lines per stanza, syllables per line, and rhyme scheme. Compare it with a published poem of the same type. If you discover that you have not followed the format, make the necessary adjustments in your work.

REVISION MODEL

① Crackling! Booming!   ② attack the
See the many streaks of light! Thunderstorms

are attacking hard at night!

① The poet adds a line to help establish a mood of excitement and terror.
② The poet adjusts the words because the line can have only seven syllables.

Publishing

▶ **Classroom** Set up a Poetry Cafe in your classroom and read your poem to the audience.
▶ **Library** Collect your classmates' poems to make a poetry book that you donate to the school library.
▶ **Magazine** Submit your poem to a magazine that publishes poetry.

✓ ASSESSMENT		4	3	2	I
PORTFOLIO ASSESSMENT Use the rubric on Poetry in *Alternative Assessment* (p. 101) to assess students' writing. Add these criteria to customize the rubric to this assignment.	**Developing Mood**	The writer thoughtfully develops and sustains a mood through the choice of descriptive details and precise words.	The writer occasionally develops a mood in the poem by choosing particular words.	The writer hints at a mood in the poem, but does not sustain or develop it.	The writer avoids establishing a mood, or appears to attempt to create one or more moods, but does so in an unclear manner.
	Range of Sensory Details	In the course of the poem the writer engages three or more of the reader's five senses.	The writer includes details that appeal to at least two senses, at times evocatively.	The writer uses details that relate to only one of the five senses.	The writer avoids using sensory details altogether.

850

Real-World Reading Skills Workshop

Using Headlines and Text Structure

Strategies for Success

You may read a newspaper for your own enjoyment or for a school assignment. The newspaper offers a vast amount of interesting information on a variety of topics. To help you find the information, use these strategies:

Look at the Headlines Most articles in a newspaper are preceded by a large headline in bold type. The headline gives a very brief summary of the information to follow. If you are in search of a particular story or news report, scan the various headlines until you find the reference you need.

Look at the Subheads Most newspaper articles are several paragraphs long. Often, a new paragraph or section is introduced with a subhead. The subhead, which appears in smaller type than the main headline, signals the specific information to come in that part of the article.

Look at the Section Headings Newspapers are usually divided into several sections. The first section often contains the international and national news stories. There may be other sections for features such as sports, entertainment, and comics. Often, an index tells you where each section is located within the newspaper.

Apply the Strategy

Use the newspaper to answer these questions:

1. What information can you learn about the new tax bill from the article's headline and subhead?
2. What do the plant workers seek?
3. How much money did the lottery winner get?
4. Where would you find the television listings?
5. Where would you learn about a death?

THE DAILY GAZETTE

President Signs New Tax Bill; House Approves

Benefits Both Rich and Poor

The President signed a bill today that will cut taxes across the board. The new bill, which was approved by the House by a vote of 246–188, is part of a long-term plan that calls for $70 billion in tax cuts over the next five years. Supporters have announced that Americans of all income levels will benefit from the new tax bill.

Resident Wins $3 Million Lottery

Inez Torres of Pine Hollow learned last night that she had won Monday's lottery jackpot of $3.2 million. "I've never won anything in my whole life!" an ecstatic Torres exclaimed to reporters. Torres said she plans to attend next month's High Rollers Ball, a yearly dinner dance for lottery winners and their families.

Workers Strike at Local Plant

Demand More Pay, Fewer Hours

Workers at the Orangewood Motors Plant announced their decision to strike last night. The decision followed the refusal of plant management to meet workers' demands for higher wages and shorter work shifts. A spokesperson for the workers told reporters that the strike will continue for as long as necessary. "We won't back down or settle for less than we deserve," said foreman Milton Lanier.

Section Index

International. . . . A
National. . . . . . . A
City . . . . B
Entertainment . . B
Sports C
Obituaries. . . . . . D

> ✔ Here are other situations in which using headlines and text structure can be helpful:
> ▶ Reading a magazine
> ▶ Reading an encyclopedia article
> ▶ Using an almanac or yearbook

Real-World Reading Skills ◆ 851

Answers

1. We learn that the new tax bill had the backing of both the President and the House of Representatives and that a wide spectrum of society should benefit from it.
2. The plant workers seek a reduction in the duration of their shifts as well as higher wages.
3. The lottery winner won $3.2 million.
4. The television listings can be found in section B (Entertainment) of the newspaper.
5. The details about recent deaths are provided in the Obituaries, section D.

Unit Objectives

1. To develop skill in reading epics
2. To apply a variety of reading strategies, particularly literal comprehension strategies, appropriate for reading these selections
3. To recognize literary elements used in these selections
4. To increase vocabulary
5. To learn elements of grammar and usage
6. To write in a variety of modes and about situations based on the selections
7. To develop speaking and listening skills, by doing proposed activities.

Meeting the Objectives

With each selection, you will find instructional material and portfolio opportunities through which students can meet these objectives. Further, you will find additional practice pages for reading strategies, literary elements, vocabulary, and grammar in the **Selection Support** booklet in the Teaching Resources box.

Setting Goals Work with your students at the beginning of the unit to set goals for unit outcomes. Plan what skills and concepts you wish students to acquire. You may individualize according to students' performance levels or learning modalities.

Portfolios You may have students keep portfolios of their work or of their work in progress. The activities and prompts on the Build Your Portfolio pages of each selection provide opportunities for students to apply the concepts presented with the selection.

Ulysses Deriding Polyphemus, 1819,
J. M. W. Turner, The National Gallery, London

 Humanities: Art

Ulysses Deriding Polyphemus, 1819, by J. M. W. Turner.

Born in London, Turner (1775–1851) had a traditional training at the Royal Academy of Arts. Turner began as a watercolor painter, influenced by the baroque landscape paintings of the seventeenth century. As he matured, Turner's work began to show his intoxication with the effects of light and atmosphere. Like those of the much later Impressionists, Turner's paintings do not treat scenes as made up of solid entities, but as images

carved by light. Not surprisingly, many of Turner's paintings explore the images created by fire and water, smoke and mist. As a result, although Turner's paintings always had real subjects, they seem almost abstract explosions of light and color.

Help students link this painting to the focus of Unit 10 ("The Epic") by answering the following questions:

1. This painting portrays one of the adventures of Odysseus, the hero of Homer's epic the Odyssey. what clue does this

painting supply about Odysseus' adventure with Polyphemus, a one- eyed giant? *The painting hints that Odysseus defeats Polyphemus in some way, and that he and his men barely escape from the giant.*

2. In this painting, the characters are difficult to see in the swirling mist and half-light. What mood does the play of light and dark in the painting lend to the story? *It lends a mood of otherworldliness, mystery, and danger.*

854

UNIT 10

The Epic

Turn the page to enter a world of heroes, gods, and sweeping adventures. In the *Odyssey,* Odysseus, a hero of the Trojan War, embarks on a journey home that takes him ten years to complete and brings him many thrilling and death-defying experiences. As you read the *Odyssey,* keep in mind that this epic poem began in the oral tradition and was passed down through word of mouth by wandering Greek minstrels. Can you think of a modern-day hero who could inspire stories that would span many generations?

◆ 855

Assessing Student Progress

The following tools are available to measure the degree to which students meet the unit objectives:

Informal Assessment

The questions on the Guide for Responding sections are a first level of response to the concepts and skills presented with the selection. Students' responses are a brief informal measure of their grasp of the material. Their responses on this level can indicate where further instruction and practice are needed. You may then follow up with the practice pages in the **Selection Support** booklet.

You will find literature and reading guides in the **Alternative Assessment** booklet, which you may give students on an individual basis for informal assessment of their performance.

Formal Assessment

In the **Formal Assessment** booklet, you will find selection tests and a unit test.

Selection Tests The selection tests measure comprehension and skills acquisition for each selection or group of selections.

Unit Test The unit test applies the unit skills on a broader level. The Critical Reading section measures Unit Objectives 1, 2, and 3. The Vocabulary and Grammar section measures Objectives 4 and 5. The Essay section measures Objectives 1 and 6.

Alternative Assessment

Portfolios As you review individual pieces or the collected work in students' portfolios, you will find assessment sheets available in the portfolio section of the **Alternative Assessment** booklet.

Scoring Rubrics You will find scoring rubrics for writing modes in the **Alternative Assessment** booklet. You can apply these to Writing Mini-Lessons and to Writing Process Workshop lessons.

Speaking and Listening The **Alternative Assessment** booklet contains assessment sheets for speaking and listening activities.

Learning Modalities The **Alternative Assessment** contains activities that appeal to different learning styles. You may use these as an alternative measurement of students' growth.

855

The Reading for Success page in each unit presents a set of problem-solving procedures to help readers understand authors' words and ideas on multiple levels. Good readers develop a bank of strategies from which they can draw as needed and apply in a variety of reading situations.

Unit 10 presents strategies for reading an epic, particularly the *Odyssey*. Students will have encountered these strategies earlier. Here, however, they apply them to a particular reading situation: the *Odyssey*.

How to Use the Reading for Success Page

- Introduce the strategies for reading an epic, presenting each as a problem-solving procedure. Be sure students understand what each strategy involves and under what circumstances to apply it.

- Before students read the *Odyssey*, have them preview it, looking at the annotations in the green boxes that encourage them to apply the strategies.

Reading for Success

Strategies for Reading an Epic

In ancient societies, stories were passed from one person to another by word of mouth. Storytellers who arrived in a village, court, or camp would entertain eager listeners with tales of the gods or great heroes. The longer stories, now called epics, might be told over several days. To help the storytellers remember these lengthy pieces, the tales were composed in poetic lines and were often recited to the accompaniment of stringed instruments. Although these stories were filled with fantastic deeds and exploits, many were based on historical events and were accepted as fact by the listeners. Two epics, the *Iliad* and the *Odyssey*, had their roots in the events of the Trojan War, which occurred about 1200 B.C. While legend credits the abduction of Helen, the wife of a Greek king, as the reason for the war, most probably economic conflict over control of trade in the Aegean Sea was the cause.

As you read the *Odyssey*, you may find a few areas that cause some difficulty. Apply the following strategies to help you get the most from your reading.

Reread or read ahead.

If you don't understand a certain passage, reread it, looking for connections among the words or sentences. It might also help you to read ahead, because a word or idea may be clarified further on.

In the *Odyssey*, some of the long, involved, and ornate comparisons—called epic similes—may give you trouble. You might choose to skim through these on your first reading so that you don't lose the plot line. Later, reread the epic similes to appreciate their imagery.

Read in sentences, according to punctuation.

Although epics are written in poetic form, you should read the sentences according to the punctuation, instead of line by line. It might also help you to read parts aloud with your classmates.

Paraphrase.

As you read, pause periodically to restate in your own words what you have read. By doing this in your mind, you can check your own understanding of the key concepts and events in the epic.

Be aware of the historical context.

The *Odyssey* took place long ago and far away. Customs and attitudes in this epic are very different from those of today, and places may be unfamiliar. Being aware of the historical context of the epic will aid your understanding. Before you begin the *Odyssey*, familiarize yourself with the names of the characters. It will also help you to look at the map on p. 891.

By using these strategies as you read the *Odyssey*, you will be better able to follow the plot and apply your understanding to your own world.

Reading Strategies: Support and Reinforcement

Appropriate Reading Strategies Students are given a reading strategy to apply with each part of the *Odyssey* and with the poems. The strategies are appropriate to each reading selection.

Reading Prompts To encourage application of the given reading strategy, there are occasional prompts, within green boxes, at appropriate and significant points.

In addition, there are red boxes prompting application of the Literary Focus concept and maroon boxes prompting students to connect with their lives.

Using the Boxed Annotations and Prompts

The material in the green, red, and maroon boxes along the sides of selections is intended to help students apply the literary element and the reading strategy and to make a connection with their lives.

You may use the boxed material in several ways:

- Have students pause when they come to a box and respond to its prompt before they continue reading.

- Urge students to read through the selection ignoring the boxes. After they have read the selection completely, they may go back and review the selection, responding to the prompts.

PART **1** *Heroic Adventure*

The Cyclops (Odysseus Series), 1977, Romare Bearden, collage, 14 x 11″
© 1997 Romare Bearden Foundation/Licensed by VAGA, New York, NY

One-Minute
Planning Guide

This section introduces students to Homer's *Odyssey*, one of the greatest epics of all time. Part I recounts the adventures of Odysseus as he sails home to Ithaca following the Trojan War. On his journey Odysseus narrowly escapes from the one-eyed Cyclops, the hypnotic Sirens, and other perilous foes. In Part II, having at last reached his homeland, Odysseus must reestablish himself in his household and do away with his wife's would-be suitors.

Customize for
Varying Student Needs
When assigning the *Odyssey* to your students, keep in mind the following factors:

• Students may need to be reminded to read according to punctuation, and not according to line breaks in order for the epic to make sense.

• Language and vocabulary will challenge some students.

• Setting, time period, and many social customs described in the epic may be unfamiliar to most students.

• Themes of daring adventure and death-defying acts will appeal to students.

Humanities: Art

The Cyclops, from The Odysseus Suite, 1977, by Romare Bearden.

    Born in North Carolina, African American artist Romare Bearden (1914–1988) grew up in New York and New Jersey and graduated from New York University. He later studied art at the Art Students League of New York, advanced mathematics at Columbia University, and philosophy and art history at the Sorbonne in Paris. Bearden traveled widely but maintained his home base in New York City, where he was Art Director

for the Harlem Cultural Council and designed sets and costumes for the Alvin Ailey Ballet Company. His work is most remarkable for his highly sophisticated use of the artistic idiom of Cubism to portray the everyday realities of African American urban life. Many of his most famous compositions are collages incorporating fragments of photocopies and paper cutouts.

    Help students to link the art to the focus of Part 1 ("Heroic Adventure") by answering this question:

What image does Bearden's collage create of the Cyclops? Is it serious or comic? If you didn't know what the epic was about, would you think this collage illustrates a heroic adventure? Why or why not? *Sample answer: Bearden's collage creates a slightly ludicrous but possibly sympathetic view of the Cyclops, trapped helplessly in his cave. The style of the collage might make it equally appropriate for a modern novel or children's story.*

Guide for Reading

OBJECTIVES

1. To read, comprehend, interpret, and respond to an epic
2. To relate an epic to personal experience
3. To read in sentences to facilitate comprehension
4. To identify the epic hero
5. To build vocabulary in context and become familiar with words from myths
6. To develop skill in using restrictive and nonrestrictive appositives
7. To respond to the epic through writing, speaking and listening, and projects

SKILLS INSTRUCTION

Vocabulary:
Word Origins: Words From Myths

Grammar:
Restrictive and Nonrestrictive Appositives

Reading Strategy:
Reading Sentences

Literary Focus:
The Epic Hero

Writing:
Sequence of Events

Speaking and Listening:
Play-by-Play Broadcast (teacher edition)

Critical Viewing:
Compare and Contrast; Analyze; Infer; Deduce

PORTFOLIO OPPORTUNITIES

Writing: Letter; Comparison-and-Contrast Essay
Writing Mini-Lesson: Letter Home
Speaking and Listening: Play-by-Play Broadcast
Projects: *Odyssey* Map; Board Game

More About the Author

Some twenty cities in Greece claim to be Homer's birthplace. Some scholars believe that Homer lived during the period of the Trojan War—that is, during the eleventh or twelfth century B.C. If this is correct, Homer would have been telling about current events and people in his own time. However, the more accepted belief, based on the ancient Greek historian Herodotus, is that Homer lived in the eighth century B.C.—more than 300 years after the Trojan War. Linguistic and archaeological evidence also suggests that the *Iliad* and the *Odyssey* date from this later period. This would mean that Homer was writing about legendary people and events of long before his time.

Homer (circa 800 B.C.)

This legendary poet-historian is credited with writing two of the most famous and enduring epics of all time: the *Iliad* and the *Odyssey*. The length of these impressive works has resulted in an adjective being coined from the author's name.

From Homer's name comes the adjective homeric, meaning large-scale, massive, and enormous.

Indeed, the *Iliad* and the *Odyssey*, which consist of thousands of lines of verse, are both homeric efforts.

Man of Mystery The facts about Homer's life have been lost in the mists of antiquity. In fact, scholars disagree about whether the *Iliad* and the *Odyssey* were written by the same person and even whether Homer existed at all! Homer is thought to have been born in western Asia Minor, the setting for many of the events in the *Iliad* and the *Odyssey*. According to tradition, he was blind. He did not write his two great epics as a modern novelist writes a novel. Rather, he composed them orally by assembling a number of earlier and shorter narrative songs. He probably traveled around the Greek-speaking world reciting them on many occasions. In later centuries, the two epics were the basis of Greek and Roman education.

◆ Build Vocabulary

WORD ORIGINS: WORDS FROM MYTHS

Many words and expressions in English come from Greek myths. For example, in line 496, a one-eyed giant is described as "titanic for the cast," as he prepares to hurl a boulder at Odysseus' fleeing ship. The word *titanic* comes from the mythical giants called Titans, who once ruled the world but were conquered by Zeus and the other Olympian deities. Like a mythical giant, anything enormous and powerful is described as titanic. From movies and musicals you might be familiar with the name *Titanic*—an enormous luxury ship that was sunk by an iceberg on its first voyage.

As you read, look for the myth behind other words, such as *siren* and *music* (muse).

WORD BANK

Before you read, preview this list of words from the *Odyssey*.

plundered
squall
dispatched
mammoth
titanic
assuage
bereft
ardor
insidious

◆ Build Grammar Skills

RESTRICTIVE AND NONRESTRICTIVE APPOSITIVES

An **appositive** is a noun or pronoun placed near another noun or pronoun to provide more information about it. An **appositive phrase** is a group of words that provides more information about a noun or pronoun. A **restrictive appositive** or appositive phrase is essential to the meaning of the sentence and is not set off by commas. A **nonrestrictive appositive** or appositive phrase provides additional information but is not necessary to the meaning of the sentence, and it is set off by commas.

nonrestrictive
The *Odyssey, an epic consisting of thousands of verses,*

restrictive
is attributed to the Greek poet *Homer*.

The nonrestrictive appositive phrase gives additional but unnecesary information about the *Odyssey*. The restrictive appositive is necessary to identify which Greek poet.

Prentice Hall Literature Program Resources

REINFORCE / RETEACH / EXTEND

Selection Support Pages
Build Vocabulary: Words From Myths, p. 233
Build Grammar Skills: Appositives, p. 234
Reading Strategy: Reading Sentences, p. 235
Literary Focus: The Epic Hero, p. 236

Strategies for Diverse Student Needs, p. 57

Beyond Literature
Cross-Curricular Connection: Geography. p. 57

Formal Assessment Selection Test, pp. 205–207, Assessment Resources Software

Alternative Assessment, p. 55

Writing and Language Transparencies
Responding to Literature, pp. 45–51

Resource Pro CD-ROM

Literature CD-ROMs Myths and Legends of Ancient Greece

 Listening to Literature Audiocassettes
The *Odyssey*, Part 1

Looking at Literature Videodisc
The *Odyssey*

The Odyssey

◆ *Literature and Your Life*

CONNECT YOUR EXPERIENCE

Whether you're journeying across town or to another country, it sometimes seems to take forever to get to your destination. Getting there may not be half the fun—but it can be quite an adventure. In the *Odyssey*, you'll learn about a journey that took far longer than expected and experience the strange and exciting adventures that took place along the way.

Journal Writing Describe your own adventures—real, imaginary, or exaggerated—on a particularly long trip.

THEMATIC FOCUS: WORKING TOWARD A GOAL

Odysseus faces many challenges and adventures as he struggles to reach his goal—returning home to Ithaca. Why is returning home to one's loved ones after a long absence a goal worth fighting for?

◆ Background for Understanding

LITERATURE

The *Odyssey* describes what happened to one of the Greek heroes in the aftermath of the Trojan War. According to legend, the Trojan War was sparked when Paris, son of the king of Troy, ran off with Helen, the most beautiful woman in the world and daughter of the god Zeus. Unfortunately, Helen was already married to Menelaus of Sparta. To recapture the lovely Helen, Agamemnon, Menelaus' brother, led a Greek force to Troy. The seige of Troy dragged on for ten years and ended when the Greeks pretended to depart, leaving a giant wooden horse behind. Thinking themselves victorious, the Trojans dragged the horse within their city walls. That night, Greek warriors hiding within the horse crept out and opened the city gates to their waiting comrades, who then conquered the city.

◆ Reading Strategy

READ IN SENTENCES

To get the most out of a story told in verse, ignore the line breaks and **read in sentences**. Often, sentences flow from one line to the next or end in the middle of a line. Although the line breaks reveal the structure of the verse, they generally have little to do with the meaning of the author's words. Thus, you can read the *Odyssey* the same way you might read a magazine article or a novel. Ignore the line breaks, and let the words flow to you in complete sentences.

◆ Literary Focus

THE EPIC HERO

An epic is a long poem that tells the story about the adventures of gods or heroes. The central character of an epic, called the **epic hero,** is a figure of great, sometimes larger-than-life, stature. The hero may be a character from history or from legend and generally possesses the character traits that are most valued by the society in which the epic originates. Complete a cluster diagram similar to the one shown by filling in words and phrases you associate with the word *hero.*

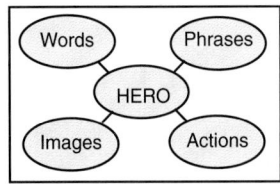

Guide for Reading ◆ 859

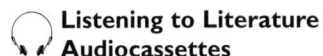

One-Minute Insight

The *Odyssey* is a classic adventure story. It combines realistic elements of historical events with wildly imagined scenes of fantastic places and creatures. The epic also includes skillful characterizations. Odysseus, for example, represents the model epic hero: A leader of courage, daring, and wit, he pursues his goal—to return home after many years at war—in the face of many setbacks. However, he has human traits and failings that make him seem like a real person: He enjoys life, is too curious for his own good, is foolishly cocky at times, and is clever to the point of being tricky. Some critics have interpreted the *Odyssey* as representing an individual's journey through life and the search for self-knowledge.

◆ Build Vocabulary

❶ Word Origins: Words From Myths Ask students to suggest words in English that sound as if they come from the word *muse*. *Students may suggest* music, museum, *and* muse—*the verb that means "to mull over."* Then ask students what the connections might be between the words they have identified and the Muses as goddesses of the arts. *Students might suggest that music is one of the arts presided over by the Muses, and that a museum is a kind of temple of the arts.* Explain that the Muses were believed to inspire artists by whispering in their ears.

◆ Literary Focus

❷ The Epic Hero Ask students what qualities of Odysseus mark him as a hero. *Odysseus is determined (he "weathered many bitter days and nights. . . at sea"), has a "deep heart," and fought only for the noble purposes of saving his own life and bringing "his shipmates home."*

The Odyssey

Homer
Translated by Robert Fitzgerald

Part 1
The Adventures of Odysseus

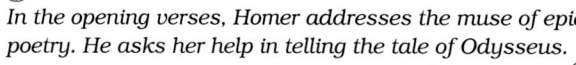

In the opening verses, Homer addresses the muse of epic poetry. He asks her help in telling the tale of Odysseus.

❶ Sing in me, Muse,[1] and through me tell the story
of that man skilled in all ways of contending,
the wanderer, harried for years on end,
after he <u>plundered</u> the stronghold
5 on the proud height of Troy.[2]
                                    He saw the townlands and
learned the minds of many distant men,
❷ and weathered many bitter nights and days
in his deep heart at sea, while he fought only
to save his life, to bring his shipmates home.

860 ◆ *The Epic*

1. Muse (myo͞oz): Any one of the nine goddesses of the arts, literature, and the sciences.

2. Troy (troi): City in northwest Asia Minor, site of the Trojan War.

◆ Build Vocabulary

plundered (plun´ dərd) *v.*: Took goods by force from; looted

Block Scheduling Strategies

Consider these suggestions to take advantage of extended class time:

- Invite students to share what they know about Greek mythology. Use this discussion to start building a word bank of terms that originated in myths. Encourage students to watch for these words as they read the *Odyssey*.
- Use the Cross-Curricular Connection: Geography page in **Beyond Literature** (p. 57) to familiarize students with the epic's setting.

- Have students work in pairs to answer the Check Your Comprehension and Critical Thinking questions (pp. 865, 881, 892).
- Students may work in groups to create the Play-by-Play Broadcast described in the Idea Bank (p. 893). This activity is supported by a Mini-Lesson in the teacher edition (p. 890).
- Students can relate Odysseus' traits to their own by working on the Cause-and-Effect Chart described in **Alternative Assessment** (p. 55).

La Nef de Telemachus, The New York Public Library Picture Collection

▲ Critical Viewing In the *Odyssey,* Telemachus searches for his father in a ship like this one. From what you observe in the painting, how does this ship compare with modern ships? [Compare and Contrast]

❸

❸ **Compare and Contrast**
Students should note that ships today are powered by engines rather than by the wind and are steered by complicated mechanical devices. They may also point out that today's ships make use of highly advanced technology both to navigate and to communicate with other ships.

Looking at Literature Videodisc To help capture students' interest and to provide background for the *Odyssey,* play Chapter 12 of the videodisc. This segment traces the route of Odysseus and his crew as they wandered the Mediterranean. Ask students to discuss what impact the landscapes and waterways shown in the segment might have on the events in the *Odyssey.*

Chapter 12

Cultural Connection

Remind students that the hero of an epic often portrays the goals and values of a society; thus, an epic can reveal much about the culture from which it comes. Ask students to imagine that they are going to write an epic about a larger-than-life character from the past century. Discuss what heroes or heroines they might want to write about, what factual material they would include, and what legends they would use, whether actual legends or ones they made up.

As an extension of the class discussion, assign students to write a descriptive summary of their own modern-day epic, including plot, characters, and setting. Have students read their "epics" to the class. Discuss how students' epic heroes and heroines and their actions differ, and how they reflect cultural values.

Humanities: Art

La Nef De Telemachus (The Ship of Telemachus).

This picture is an illustration for the *Odyssey* of Homer. The modern style of this rendering in no way interferes with its ancient flavor. This illustration was inspired by statues, pottery, and frescoes from ancient Greece. The rich blue of the ocean, echoed in the duller blue of the cloudy sky, forms a striking frame for the massive black ship. Powered by sail and oar, this craft is the kind on which Odysseus and his men would have sailed to and from Troy.

Use the following questions for discussion:
1. How do you think this ship compares in size with Columbus's vessels or with a modern ocean liner? *This ship is smaller than a fifteenth-century wooden ship, and is much smaller than a hotel-sized ocean liner.*

2. How do you think this ship would fare in a storm? *As a relatively small ship, this craft would be buffeted by a storm and might be damaged or even sunk.*

CHARACTERS

Alcinous (al sin´ ō əs)—king of the Phaeacians, to whom Odysseus tells his story

Odysseus (ō dis´ ē əs)—king of Ithaca

Calypso (kə lip´ sō)—sea goddess who loved Odysseus

Circe (sʉr´ se)—enchantress who helped Odysseus

Zeus (zōōs)—king of the gods

Apollo (ə pal´ ō)—god of music, poetry, and medicine

Agamemnon (ag´ ə mem´ nän)—king and leader of Greek forces

Poseidon (pō sī´ dən)—god of sea and earthquakes

Athena (ə thē´ nə)—goddess of wisdom, skills, and warfare

Polyphemus (päl´ ə fē´ məs)—the Cyclops who imprisoned Odysseus

Laertes (lā ʉr´ tēz)—Odysseus' father

Cronus (krō´ nəs)—Titan ruler of the universe; father of Zeus

Perimedes (per´ ə mē´ dēz)—member of Odysseus' crew

Eurylochus (yōō ril´ ə kes)—another member of the crew

Tiresias (tī rē´ sē əs)—blind prophet who advised Odysseus

Persephone (pər sef´ ə nē)—wife of Hades

Telemachus (tə lem´ ə kəs)—Odysseus and Penelope's son

Sirens (sī´ rənz)—creatures whose songs lure sailors to their deaths

Scylla (sil´ ə)—sea monster of gray rock

Charybdis (kə rib´ dis)—enormous and dangerous whirlpool

Lampetia (lam pē´ shə)—nymph

Hermes (hʉr´ mēz)—herald and messenger of the gods

Eumaeus (yōō me´ əs)—old swineherd and friend of Odysseus

Antinous (an tin´ ō əs)—leader among the suitors

Eurynome (yōō rin´ ə mē)—housekeeper for Penelope

Penelope (pə nel´ ə pē)—Odysseus' wife

Eurymachus (yōō ri´ mə kəs)—suitor

Amphinomus (am fin´ ə məs)—suitor

10 But not by will nor valor could he save them,
for their own recklessness destroyed them all—
❶ children and fools, they killed and feasted on
❷ the cattle of Lord Helios,³ the Sun,
and he who moves all day through heaven
15 took from their eyes the dawn of their return.

❸ Of these adventures, Muse, daughter of Zeus,⁴
tell us in our time, lift the great song again.

3. Helios (hē´ lē äs´): Sun god.

4. Zeus (zōōs): King of the gods.

Sailing from Troy

*Ten years after the Trojan War, Odysseus departs
from the goddess Calypso's island. He arrives in
Phaeacia, ruled by Alcinous. Alcinous offers a ship to
Odysseus and asks him to tell of his adventures.*

"I am Laertes'[5] son, Odysseus.
                                    Men hold me
    formidable for guile[6] in peace and war:
20 this fame has gone abroad to the sky's rim.

    My home is on the peaked sea-mark of Ithaca[7]
    under Mount Neion's wind-blown robe of leaves,
    in sight of other islands—Dulichium,
    Same, wooded Zacynthus—Ithaca
25 being most lofty in that coastal sea
    and northwest, while the rest lie east and south.
    A rocky isle, but good for a boy's training;
    I shall not see on earth a place more dear,
    though I have been detained long by Calypso,[8]
30 loveliest among goddesses, who held me
    in her smooth caves, to be her heart's delight,
    as Circe of Aeaea,[9] the enchantress,
    desired me, and detained me in her hall.
    But in my heart I never gave consent.
35 Where shall a man find sweetness to surpass
    his own home and his parents? In far lands
    he shall not, though he find a house of gold.

    What of my sailing, then, from Troy?
                                    What of those years
    of rough adventure, weathered under Zeus?
40 The wind that carried west from Ilium[10]
    brought me to Ismarus, on the far shore,
    a strongpoint on the coast of Cicones.[11]
    I stormed that place and killed the men who fought.
    Plunder we took, and we enslaved the women,
45 to make division, equal shares to all—
    but on the spot I told them: 'Back, and quickly!

◆ **Reading Strategy**
Why do the opening
lines of Odysseus
sound more natural
when you ignore
the line breaks?

5. **Laertes** (lā ʉr´ tēz)
6. **guile** (gīl) *n.*:
Craftiness; cunning.
7. **Ithaca** (ith´ ə kə):
Island off the west coast of
Greece.
8. **Calypso** (kə lip´ sō)

9. **Circe** (sʉr´ sē) of
Aeaea (ē´ ē ə)

10. **Ilium** (il ē əm): Troy.

11. **Cicones** (si kō´ nēz)

Note: In his translation of the *Odyssey*, Fitzgerald spelled Greek names in a way that suggests the sound and flavor of the original Greek. In the excerpts included here, more
familiar spellings have been used. Where, for example, Fitzgerald wrote "Kirkê," "Kyklops,"
and "Seirênês," you will here find "Circe," "Cyclops," and "Sirens."

The Odyssey, Part 1, Sailing from Troy ◆ 863

◆ **Literary Focus**
❹ The Epic Hero Ask students
which qualities cited in this passage
suggest that Odysseus is a hero.
*Students should notice that Odysseus is
famous for his guile, which makes him
effective in both peace and war.* You
may want to tell students that the
idea for the Trojan horse is traditionally attributed to Odysseus.

◆ **Reading Strategy**
❺ Read in Sentences Suggested
response: *"Men hold me formidable for
guile in peace and war. This fame has
gone abroad to the sky's rim."*

❻ Clarification Tell students that
in other parts of the epic, Odysseus
falls under the spell of two
enchantresses—Calypso and Circe.
Calypso is a sea nymph who holds
Odysseus in her spell for seven years.
Circe turns Odysseus' men into pigs.

◆ **Critical Thinking**
❼ Interpret Ask students how
Odysseus feels about his home on
Ithaca. Why did he stay with Calypso
and Circe, if he was so eager to
return to Ithaca? *Odysseus is eager to
return to his home. He says that he
"never gave consent" to stay with
Calypso or Circe, indicating that he was
under a spell and not in control of his
own actions.*

◆ **Reading Strategy**

❷ **Read in Sentences** Invite students to read this passage aloud, pausing where necessary to convey the sense of the sentence. Students may find it helpful to paraphrase the passage first and then to read the original words aloud. When at least one student has read the passage effectively, ask students what they gained from the strategy of reading in sentences. *Students should see that reading in sentences helps them grasp the author's meaning.*

◆ **Critical Thinking**

❸ **Evaluate** Ask students whether Maron was a good host. Then ask them to cite evidence from the passage to support their opinions. *Students should see that Maron was an excellent host who gave Odysseus many valuable gifts, including a highly prized kind of brandy.*

The Cyclops

110　In the next land we found were Cyclopes,[15]
　　giants, louts, without a law to bless them.
　　In ignorance leaving the fruitage of the earth in
　　　mystery
　　to the immortal gods, they neither plow
　　nor sow by hand, nor till the ground, though
　　　grain—
115　wild wheat and barley—grows untended, and
　　wine grapes, in clusters, ripen in heaven's rains.
　　Cyclopes have no muster and no meeting,
　　no consultation or old tribal ways,
　　but each one dwells in his own mountain cave
　　dealing out rough justice to wife and child,
120　indifferent to what the others do. . . .

　　As we rowed on, and nearer to the mainland,
　　at one end of the bay, we saw a cavern
　　yawning above the water, screened with laurel,
　　and many rams and goats about the place
125　inside a sheepfold—made from slabs of stone
　　earthfast between tall trunks of pine and rugged
　　towering oak trees.
　　　　　　　　　　　　A prodigious[16] man
　　slept in this cave alone, and took his flocks
　　to graze afield—remote from all companions,
130　knowing none but savage ways, a brute
　　so huge, he seemed no man at all of those
　　who eat good wheaten bread; but he seemed rather
　　a shaggy mountain reared in solitude.
　　We beached there, and I told the crew
135　to stand by and keep watch over the ship:
　　as for myself I took my twelve best fighters
　　and went ahead. I had a goatskin full
　　of that sweet liquor that Euanthes' son,
　　Maron, had given me. He kept Apollo's[17]
140　holy grove at Ismarus; for kindness
　　we showed him there, and showed his wife and child,
　　he gave me seven shining golden talents[18]
　　perfectly formed, a solid silver winebowl,
　　and then this liquor—twelve two-handled jars
145　of brandy, pure and fiery. Not a slave
　　in Maron's household knew this drink; only
　　he, his wife and the storeroom mistress knew;
　　and they would put one cupful—ruby-colored
　　honey—smooth—in twenty more of water,

866 ◆ *The Epic*

15. Cyclopes (sī klō′ pēz) *n.*: Plural form of Cyclops (sī′ kläps), a race of giants with one eye in the middle of the forehead.

◆ *Literature and Your Life*

The description of the Cyclopes reveals what the ancient Greeks regarded as the benefits of civilization. What in your opinion are the benefits of civilization?

16. prodigious (prə dij′ əs) *adj.*: Enormous.

17. Apollo (ə päl′ ō): God of music, poetry, prophecy, and medicine.

18. talents: Units of money in ancient Greece.

3
150 but still the sweet scent hovered like a fume
over the winebowl. No man turned away
when cups of this came round.

                                        A wineskin full
4
I brought along, and victuals[19] in a bag,
155 for in my bones I knew some towering brute
would be upon us soon—all outward power,
a wild man, ignorant of civility.

We climbed, then, briskly to the cave. But Cyclops
had gone afield, to pasture his fat sheep,
so we looked round at everything inside:
160 a drying rack that sagged with cheeses, pens
crowded with lambs and kids,[20] each in its class:
firstlings apart from middlings, and the 'dewdrops,'
or newborn lambkins, penned apart from both.
And vessels full of whey[21] were brimming there—
165 bowls of earthenware and pails for milking.
My men came pressing round me, pleading:

                                        'Why not
take these cheeses, get them stowed, come back,
throw open all the pens, and make a run for it?
We'll drive the kids and lambs aboard. We say
5
170 put out again on good salt water!'
6

                                        Ah,
how sound that was! Yet I refused. I wished
to see the cave man, what he had to offer—
no pretty sight, it turned out, for my friends.
We lit a fire, burnt an offering,
175 and took some cheese to eat: then sat in silence
around the embers, waiting. When he came
he had a load of dry boughs[22] on his shoulder
to stoke his fire at suppertime. He dumped it
with a great crash into that hollow cave,
180 and we all scattered fast to the far wall.
Then over the broad cavern floor he ushered
the ewes he meant to milk. He left his rams
and he-goats in the yard outside, and swung
high overhead a slab of solid rock
7
185 to close the cave. Two dozen four-wheeled wagons,
with heaving wagon teams, could not have stirred
the tonnage of that rock from where he wedged it
over the doorsill. Next he took his seat
and milked his bleating ewes. A practiced job
190 he made of it, giving each ewe her suckling;

19. **victuals** (vit´ əls) *n.*: Food or other provisions.

20. **kids** (kids) *n.*: Young goats.

21. **whey** (hwā) *n.*: Thin, watery part of milk separated from the thicker curds.

22. **boughs** (bouz) *n.*: Tree branches.

The Odyssey, Part 1, The Cyclops ◆ 867

◆ **Build Grammar Skills**

4 Restrictive and Nonrestrictive Appositives Ask students to identify the appositives in this sentence and to tell whether they are restrictive or nonrestrictive. Encourage them to explain their answers. Why are they set off by commas? *Students should identify "all outward power" and "a wild man" as nonrestrictive appositives. None of the appositives restricts the meaning of "towering brute." Instead, they flesh out the meaning of the phrase and therefore are set off by commas and a dash.*

◆ **Literary Focus**

5 The Epic Hero In this passage, Odysseus shows one of the qualities that gets him into trouble. Ask students to identify that flaw. Ask them, also, if Odysseus is aware of this character trait himself. *Students should see that Odysseus' curiosity leads him to disregard a "sound" idea, to the cost of his friends. He knows it would be wise to stock up on food and then leave, but he is too curious to see "the cave man." Odysseus seems to be aware of his overactive curiosity because he takes care to explain that he knew his men's idea was sound.*

6 Clarification The Greek laws of hospitality mandated an exchange of gifts. A host was expected to welcome his guests *and* give them gifts.

Comprehension Check ☑

7 What does the Cyclops do that puts Odysseus and his men in grave danger? *He seals the opening of the cave with a huge rock that "two dozen four-wheeled wagons" could not have moved.*

① Clarification Explain that the Cyclops is asking whether Odysseus and his men are traders or pirates.

◆ *Literature and Your Life*

② Invite students to suggest how they think someone should handle a situation like this: being caught trespassing by a powerful, dangerous opponent. Encourage them to compare real-life strategies for handling this situation with the approaches taken by heroes in action movies. *Students might say that in real life it would pay to be cautious, whereas in an action movie, the hero is usually confident of being able to use force to overcome his opponent.*

◆ **Build Grammar Skills**

③ Restrictive and Nonrestrictive Appositives Ask students to identify the appositive in this sentence, to tell whether it is restrictive or nonrestrictive, and to explain the way it is punctuated in the text. *"Son of Atreus" is a nonrestrictive appositive for "Agamemnon," and, as such, is set off by a comma.*

◆ **Critical Thinking**

④ Analyze Ask students to explain why Odysseus makes a point of referring first to Agamemnon, the king who led the Greeks in the Trojan War, and then to Zeus, king of the gods. *First, Odysseus is trying to impress the Cyclops by letting him know he was part of a powerful army; then he is reminding him that Zeus punishes those who are not polite to guests. He is using words and reasoning to talk the Cyclops into letting him and his men go.*

◆ **Literary Focus**

⑤ The Epic Hero Students may say that he or she might have learned that it is important to be polite, to honor the laws of hospitality, and to respect the gods.

Customize for
More Advanced Students
⑥ Point out that the Cyclops' words are an example of *hubris,* the excessive arrogance or insolence that results from too much pride, ambition, or passion. In Greek myths and in tragedies, hubris leads to the ruin of its possessor. Ask students to relate the concept of hubris to other works of literature.

thickened his milk, then, into curds and whey,
sieved out the curds to drip in withy[23] baskets,
and poured the whey to stand in bowls
cooling until he drank it for his supper.
195   When all these chores were done, he poked the fire,
heaping on brushwood. In the glare he saw us.

① 'Strangers,' he said, 'who are you? And where from?
What brings you here by seaways—a fair traffic?
Or are you wandering rogues, who cast your lives
200   like dice, and ravage other folk by sea?'

② We felt a pressure on our hearts, in dread
of that deep rumble and that mighty man.
But all the same I spoke up in reply:

'We are from Troy, Achaeans, blown off course
205   by shifting gales on the Great South Sea;
homeward bound, but taking routes and ways
uncommon; so the will of Zeus would have it.
③ We served under Agamemnon,[24] son of Atreus—
the whole world knows what city
210   he laid waste, what armies he destroyed.
It was our luck to come here; here we stand,
beholden for your help, or any gifts
④ you give—as custom is to honor strangers.
We would entreat you, great Sir, have a care
215   for the gods' courtesy; Zeus will avenge
the unoffending guest.'

                    He answered this
         from his brute chest, unmoved:

                         'You are a ninny,
or else you come from the other end of nowhere,
telling me, mind the gods! We Cyclopes
⑥ 220   care not a whistle for your thundering Zeus
or all the gods in bliss; we have more force by far.
⑦ I would not let you go for fear of Zeus—
you or your friends—unless I had a whim[25] to.
Tell me, where was it, now, you left your ship—
225   around the point, or down the shore, I wonder?'

He thought he'd find out, but I saw through this,
and answered with a ready lie:

868   ◆   *The Epic*

23. **withy** (with´ ē) *adj.*: Tough, flexible twigs.

24. **Agamemnon** (ag´ ə mem´ nän): King who led the Greek army during the Trojan War.

◆ **Literary Focus**
An epic hero like Odysseus served as a role model for ancient Greeks. What can be learned about conduct and respect for the gods from Odysseus' speech?   **⑤**

25. **whim** (hwim) *n.*: Sudden thought or wish to do something.

◆ **Build Vocabulary**
dispatched (dis pacht´) *v.*: Finished quickly

 Cross-Curricular Connection: Social Studies

The *Odyssey* takes place during the years immediately following the Trojan War. According to tradition, the Helladic people of southern Greece, whom Homer called the Achaeans and whom historians consider to be the earliest Greeks, fought against Troy in Asia Minor. Mycenae was the Achaeans' largest city, and Agamemnon, the legendary king of Mycenae, was the richest and most powerful ruler on the mainland of Greece. It was he who is said to have led the Achaeans against the Trojans.

Homer is believed to have lived on the main-land of Greece in the eighth century B.C., at a time following a period of invasions from Asia Minor and from the north. By 750 B.C., Greece had become overpopulated and many people emigrated to form Greek colonies in the Black Sea, Sicily and southern Italy, France, and Spain. The Greek colonies traded with their home cities, sending great wealth to Greece. However, it was the aristocrats who became rich while the poor became discontented. It may have been this development that first led to the idea of democratic government, which took form much later in Greek history.

'My ship?
Poseidon[26] Lord, who sets the earth a-tremble,
broke it up on the rocks at your land's end.
230 A wind from seaward served him, drove us there.
We are survivors, these good men and I.'

Neither reply nor pity came from him,
but in one stride he clutched at my companions
and caught two in his hands like squirming puppies
235 to beat their brains out, spattering the floor.
Then he dismembered them and made his meal,
gaping and crunching like a mountain lion—
everything: innards, flesh, and marrow bones.
We cried aloud, lifting our hands to Zeus,
240 powerless, looking on at this, appalled;
but Cyclops went on filling up his belly
with manflesh and great gulps of whey,
then lay down like a mast among his sheep.
My heart beat high now at the chance of action,
245 and drawing the sharp sword from my hip I went
along his flank to stab him where the midriff
holds the liver. I had touched the spot
when sudden fear stayed me: if I killed him
we perished there as well, for we could never
250 move his ponderous doorway slab aside.
So we were left to groan and wait for morning.

When the young Dawn with fingertips of rose
lit up the world, the Cyclops built a fire
and milked his handsome ewes, all in due order,
255 putting the sucklings to the mothers. Then,
his chores being all dispatched, he caught
another brace[27] of men to make his breakfast,
and whisked away his great door slab
to let his sheep go through—but he, behind,
260 reset the stone as one would cap a quiver.[28]
There was a din[29] of whistling as the Cyclops
rounded his flock to higher ground, then stillness.
And now I pondered how to hurt him worst,
if but Athena[30] granted what I prayed for.
265 Here are the means I thought would serve my turn:

a club, or staff, lay there along the fold—
an olive tree, felled green and left to season[31]
for Cyclops' hand. And it was like a mast
a lugger[32] of twenty oars, broad in the beam—

The Odyssey, Part 1, The Cyclops ◆ 869

---

26. Poseidon (pō sī′ dən):
God of the sea and of earthquakes.

◆ **Reading Strategy**
Read lines 244–250
in complete
sentences, ignoring
the line breaks. How
does doing so help
your understanding
of the passage?

27. brace (brās) *n.*: Pair.

28. cap (kap) **a quiver**
(kwiv′ ər): Close a case
holding arrows.
29. din (din) *n.*: Loud,
continuous noise; uproar.
30. Athena (ə thē′ nə):
Goddess of wisdom, skills,
and warfare.

**31. felled green and left to
season:** Chopped down and
exposed to the weather to
age the wood.
32. lugger (lug′ ər) *n.*: Small
sailing vessel.

◆ **Literary Focus**

2 The Epic Hero Students may say that Odysseus is resourceful, creative, and brave. He also joins his men in the most dangerous tasks, and is apparently a good judge of his men's abilities and characters.

◆ **Build Grammar Skills**

3 Restrictive and Nonrestrictive Appositives Ask students to identify the appositive in the first sentence, to tell whether it is restrictive or nonrestrictive, to explain why, and to identify the correct punctuation.
"His woolly flock" is a nonrestrictive appositive for "his flock." It is nonrestrictive because it gives additional information about the flock, and is therefore set off by a comma.

◆ **Background for Understanding**

4 Help students understand that the Greeks took hospitality very seriously. Someone who violated the laws of hospitality was considered a criminal. Remind students that in ancient Greece, there were no cars, hotels, or roadside food stands. Hospitality might literally make the difference between a traveler's life and death. Therefore, a bad host might indeed be a kind of murderer.

◆ *Literature and Your Life*

5 Cyclops drinks three bowls of wine and becomes drunk. Invite students to relate this scene to their own understanding of the dangers of drinking, particularly to excess.
Students may point out that drinking, especially to the point of drunkenness, impairs judgment and puts a person in danger.

270
   a deep-sea-going craft—might carry:
   so long, so big around, it seemed. Now I
   chopped out a six foot section of this pole
   and set it down before my men, who scraped it;
   and when they had it smooth, I hewed again
275
   to make a stake with pointed end. I held this
   in the fire's heart and turned it, toughening it,
   then hid it, well back in the cavern, under
   one of the dung piles in profusion there.
   Now came the time to toss for it: who ventured
280
   along with me? whose hand could bear to thrust
   and grind that spike in Cyclops' eye, when mild
   sleep had mastered him? As luck would have it,
   the men I would have chosen won the toss—
   four strong men, and I made five as captain.

285
   At evening came the shepherd with his flock,
   his woolly flock. The rams as well this time,
   entered the cave: by some sheepherding whim—
   or a god's bidding—none were left outside.
   He hefted his great boulder into place
290
   and sat him down to milk the bleating ewes
   in proper order, put the lambs to suck,
   and swiftly ran through all his evening chores.
   Then he caught two more men and feasted on them.
   My moment was at hand, and I went forward
295
   holding an ivy bowl of my dark drink,
   looking up, saying:

                   'Cyclops, try some wine.
   Here's liquor to wash down your scraps of men.
   Taste it, and see the kind of drink we carried
   under our planks. I meant it for an offering
300
   if you would help us home. But you are mad,
   unbearable, a bloody monster! After this,
   will any other traveler come to see you?'

   He seized and drained the bowl, and it went down
   so fiery and smooth he called for more:
305
   'Give me another, thank you kindly. Tell me,
   how are you called? I'll make a gift will please you.
   Even Cyclopes know the wine grapes grow
   out of grassland and loam in heaven's rain,
   but here's a bit of nectar and ambrosia!'[33]
310
   Three bowls I brought him, and he poured them
     down.
   I saw the fuddle and flush come over him,

870 ◆ The Epic

33. nectar (nek´ tər) **and ambrosia** (am brō´ zhə): Drink and food of the gods.

then I sang out in cordial tones:

                              'Cyclops,
    you ask my honorable name? Remember
    the gift you promised me, and I shall tell you.
315 My name is Nohbdy: mother, father, and friends,
    everyone calls me Nohbdy.'

                              And he said:
    "Nohbdy's my meat, then, after I eat his friends.
    Others come first. There's a noble gift, now.'

    Even as he spoke, he reeled and tumbled backward,
320 his great head lolling to one side; and sleep
    took him like any creature. Drunk, hiccuping,
    he dribbled streams of liquor and bits of men.

    Now, by the gods, I drove my big hand spike
    deep in the embers, charring it again,
325 and cheered my men along with battle talk
    to keep their courage up; no quitting now.
    The pike of olive, green though it had been,
    reddened and glowed as if about to catch.
    I drew it from the coals and my four fellows
7 330 gave me a hand, lugging it near the Cyclops
    as more than natural force nerved them; straight
    forward they sprinted, lefted it, and rammed it
    deep in his crater eye, and leaned on it
    turning it as a shipwright turns a drill
335 in planking, having men below to swing
    the two-handled strap that spins it in the groove.
    So with our brand we bored[34] that great eye socket
    while blood ran out around the red-hot bar.
    Eyelid and lash were seared; the pierced ball
340 hissed broiling, and the roots popped.

                      8 In a smithy
    one sees a white-hot axhead or an adze
    plunged and wrung in a cold tub, screeching steam—
    the way they make soft iron hale and hard—:
    just so that eyeball hissed around the spike.
345 The Cyclops bellowed and the rock roared round him,
    and we fell back in fear. Clawing his face
    he tugged the bloody spike out of his eye,
    threw it away, and his wild hands went groping;
    then he set up a howl for Cyclopes
350 who lived in caves on windy peaks nearby.

The Odyssey, Part 1, The Cyclops ◆ 871

34. bored (bôrd) *v.*: Made a hole in.

◆ **Reading Strategy**
How would you write Odysseus' sly lie in regular prose? **6**

◆ **Reading Strategy**

6 Read in Sentences Students might paraphrase Odysseus' lie as follows: *"Do you want to know my name, Cyclops? If you remember that you promised to give me a gift, I'll tell you my name. It is 'Nohbdy' [Nobody.] My mother, father, friends, and everyone else call me 'Nobody.'"*

◆ **Critical Thinking**

7 Connect Have students connect this passage with Odysseus' prayer to Athena (line 264). *Students may say that the "more than natural force" that gives the men strength and courage shows that the goddess is helping them.*

8 Clarification A *smithy* is a blacksmith's forge.

  Cultural Connection

Ask students to describe what makes the Cyclops such a dreadful monster. Discuss the feelings evoked by his gigantic size and his single eye. Ask whether these traits would be considered monstrous by people of any time and culture or whether they were horrible only to the ancient Greeks. Have students give reasons for their opinions.

Assign students to do research to find out more about the portrayal of monsters in different cultures. Ask them to do a multicultural literature search for examples of giants, one-eyed monsters, and other kinds of monsters. Discuss their findings, comparing their examples with the original Cyclops of Homer's *Odyssey.*

 Beyond the Classroom

Community Connection
Shipbuilding and Boatbuilding Odysseus and his men rely absolutely on their ship. Without a sturdy vessel, they would not be able to escape their enemies and return home.

Shipbuilding and boatbuilding have been highly prized skills for centuries. Today, large, oceangoing vessels are built in shipyards, whereas smaller craft are still built by hand in many places. Many boats are constructed out of prefabricated pieces of fiberglass, which requires a different technology than is needed for boats made of wood.

Students might enjoy finding out about shipbuilding and boatbuilding in your area. Perhaps there is a shipyard or naval yard that you might visit as a class, or from which you might invite an expert to address the class. You might also visit a smaller boatbuilding business or invite someone from such a business to speak to your class. Finally, you might visit a naval museum or a whaling museum, if one is available.

Comprehension Check ☑

❶ Ask: What does Polyphemus mean? What do the other Cyclopes understand? *Polyphemus means that the man he knows as Nohbdy— Odysseus—has hurt him. The other Cyclopes understand that "Nobody" hurt Polyphemus, which means that his trouble must be natural and there is no one on whom to take revenge.*

◆ Literary Focus

❷ The Epic Hero Ask students which personality traits Odysseus exhibits in this passage. Do they think these are heroic qualities? *Odysseus is pleased with his cleverness that tricked Polyphemus and the other Cyclopes. Some students will think a hero should be more modest and should not gloat. Others will think that under the circumstances Odysseus has every right to be self-congratulatory.*

◆ Reading Strategy

❸ Read in Sentences Invite students to read this passage aloud for sense, pausing at the punctuation rather than the ends of lines. Encourage them to read the passage aloud more than once, until they can make it sound natural and meaningful. Ask them what this process tells them about how to read this type of verse. *Students should see that their first focus in reading an epic poem should be to understand the literal meaning of the poet's words.*

◆ Literary Focus

❹ The Epic Hero Ask students to explain Odysseus' plan. *He will smuggle his men out of the cave by tying the sheep together, three abreast, and tying one man under the belly of each middle sheep. This way, Polyphemus will not be able to feel the men under the sheep.* Which important heroic qualities does Odysseus exhibit by devising this plan? *This plan shows cleverness and resourcefulness.*

Some heard him; and they came by divers[35] ways
to clump around outside and call:

'What ails you,
Polyphemus?[36] Why do you cry so sore
355 in the starry night? You will not let us sleep.
Sure no man's driving off your flock? No man
has tricked you, ruined you?'

Out of the cave
the mammoth Polyphemus roared in answer:
'Nohbdy, Nohbdy's tricked me, Nohbdy's ruined me!'
To this rough shout they made a sage[37] reply:
❶ 360 'Ah well, if nobody has played you foul
there in your lonely bed, we are no use in pain
given by great Zeus. Let it be your father,
Poseidon Lord, to whom you pray.'
So saying
❷ 365 they trailed away. And I was filled with laughter
to see how like a charm the name deceived them.
Now Cyclops, wheezing as the pain came on him,
fumbled to wrench away the great doorstone
and squatted in the breach with arms thrown wide
370 for any silly beast or man who bolted—
hoping somehow I might be such a fool.
But I kept thinking how to win the game:
death sat there huge; how could we slip away?
❸ I drew on all my wits, and ran through tactics,
reasoning as a man will for dear life,
375 until a trick came—and it pleased me well.
The Cyclops' rams were handsome, fat, with heavy
fleeces, a dark violet.

Three abreast
I tied them silently together, twining
cords of willow from the ogre's bed
380 then slung a man under each middle one
to ride there safely, shielded left and right.
❹ So three sheep could convey each man. I took
the woolliest ram, the choicest of the flock,
and hung myself under his kinky belly,
385 pulled up tight, with fingers twisted deep
in sheepskin ringlets for an iron grip.
So, breathing hard, we waited until morning.

When Dawn spread out her fingertips of rose
the rams began to stir, moving for pasture,

872 ◆ The Epic

35. divers (dī′ vərz) *adj.*: Several; various.

36. Polyphemus (päl′ ə fē′ məs)

37. sage (sāj) *adj.*: Wise.

◆ Build Vocabulary
mammoth (mam′ əth) *adj.*: Enormous

872

◆ **Reading Strategy**

❺ **Read in Sentences** Invite students to read this passage aloud with the vocal expression that they imagine the giant might use. Ask students: Where will you pause? How will you treat the endings of lines? *Students should plan to pause at question marks, commas, and periods, but not at line-endings unless the sense of the sentence requires it.*

◆ **Literary Focus**

❻ **The Epic Hero** Students may say that Odysseus is allowing his anger and relief to get the best of him; it would be much wiser to be quiet. He is acting in a boastful and vindictive manner.

390 and peals of bleating echoed round the pens
where dams with udders full called for a milking.
Blinded, and sick with pain from his head wound,
the master stroked each ram, then let it pass,
but my men riding on the pectoral[38] fleece

395 the giant's blind hands blundering never found.
Last of them all my ram, the leader, came,
weighted by wool and me with my meditations.
The Cyclops patted him, and then he said:

'Sweet cousin ram, why lag behind the rest
400 in the night cave? You never linger so,
but graze before them all, and go afar
to crop sweet grass, and take your stately way
leading along the streams, until at evening
you run to be the first one in the fold.
405 Why, now, so far behind? Can you be grieving
over your Master's eye? That carrion rogue[39]
and his accurst companions burnt it out
when he had conquered all my wits with wine.
Nohbdy will not get out alive, I swear.
410 Oh, had you brain and voice to tell
where he may be now, dodging all my fury!
Bashed by this hand and bashed on this rock wall
his brains would strew the floor, and I should have
rest from the outrage Nohbdy worked upon me.'

415 He sent us into the open, then. Close by,
I dropped and rolled clear of the ram's belly,
going this way and that to untie the men.
With many glances back, we rounded up
his fat, stiff-legged sheep to take aboard,
420 and drove them down to where the good ship lay.
We saw, as we came near, our fellows' faces
shining; then we saw them turn to grief
tallying those who had not fled from death.
I hushed them, jerking head and eyebrows up,
425 and in a low voice told them: 'Load this herd;
move fast, and put the ship's head toward the
   breakers.'
They all pitched in at loading, then embarked
and struck their oars into the sea. Far out,
as far offshore as shouted words would carry,
430 I sent a few back to the adversary:
'O Cyclops! Would you feast on my companions?
Puny, am I, in a cave man's hands?
How do you like the beating that we gave you,

38. pectoral (pek´ tər əl) *adj.*: Located on the chest.

39. carrion (kar´ ē ən) **rogue** (rōg): Repulsive scoundrel.

◆ **Literary Focus**
An epic hero is larger than life but usually also has some human failings. What human weakness does Odysseus' behavior reveal? ❻

The Odyssey, Part 1, The Cyclops ◆ 873

◆ Reading Strategy

❶ Read in Sentences Ask: If this epic is meant to be read exactly like prose, why did Fitzgerald bother to retain the verse form? Why didn't he just write in prose? Before students answer, have them read this passage aloud, paying attention to the rhythm of the verse as well as the sense of the sentences. For example, they might emphasize the repeated word *row,* read the last line in the passage more slowly than the others, and pause *very slightly* at the ends of lines. Let students know it is tricky to achieve the right balance between sense and verse. Actors who perform in Shakespearean plays, which are also in verse, must practice this skill very carefully. *After practicing reading for both sense and rhythm, students should see that the poetic form adds to the epic because, as in any poetry, the sounds and rhythms of the verse add to the meaning and emotional appeal of the story. Also, the poetic form gives the epic a grander, more important stature than if it were written in prose.*

◆ *Literature and Your Life*

❷ Students may see that, like people with "big mouths," Odysseus keeps talking even when it's likely to get him into trouble. His need to boast and to express his anger to the giant who killed his men makes him irrational and incautious.

---

you damned cannibal? Eater of guests
435   under your roof! Zeus and the gods have paid you!'

The blind thing in his doubled fury broke
a hilltop in his hands and heaved it after us.
Ahead of our black prow it struck and sank
whelmed in a spuming geyser, a giant wave
440   that washed the ship stern foremost back to shore.
I got the longest boathook out and stood
fending us off, with furious nods to all
❶   to put their backs into a racing stroke—
row, row, or perish. So the long oars bent
445   kicking the foam sternward, making head
until we drew away, and twice as far.
Now when I cupped my hands I heard the crew
in low voices protesting:

                              'Godsake, Captain!
Why bait the beast again? Let him alone!'

450   'That tidal wave he made on the first throw
all but beached us.'

                              'All but stove us in!'
'Give him our bearing with your trumpeting,
he'll get the range and lob a boulder.'

                              'Aye
He'll smash our timbers and our heads together!'
455   I would not heed them in my glorying spirit,
but let my anger flare and yelled:

                              'Cyclops,
if ever mortal man inquire
how you were put to shame and blinded, tell him
Odysseus, raider of cities, took your eye:
460   Laertes' son, whose home's on Ithaca!'

At this he gave a mighty sob and rumbled:

'Now comes the weird[40] upon me, spoken of old.
A wizard, grand and wondrous, lived here—Telemus,[41]
a son of Eurymus;[42] great length of days
❸   465   he had in wizardry among the Cyclopes,
and these things he foretold for time to come:
my great eye lost, and at Odysseus' hands.
Always I had in mind some giant, armed

874 ◆ *The Epic*

◆ *Literature and Your Life*

When they are angry or boasting, people sometimes say things that they later regret. How do Odysseus' words relate to your own observations of a person "having a big mouth"? ❷

40. **weird** (wird) *n.*: Fate or destiny.
41. **Telemus** (tel e´ məs)
42. **Eurymus** (yo͞o rim´ əs)

◀ **Critical Viewing**
Odysseus and his surviving men escape in their ship as the blinded Cyclops hurls boulders and curses. What events provoke this scene? [Analyze]

❸ Invite students to identify how Polyphemus feels. *He is amazed that he was defeated by a "small, pitiful and twiggy" man.* Then ask students to relate this response to other ways that people are surprised by defeat. *Students may compare Polyphemus to a politician who does not expect to be defeated by a less well-known opponent; to an athlete who is beaten by an unknown contender; or to a famous actor whose movie is outsold by a "sleeper" with no big-name stars.*

▶**Critical Viewing**◀

❹ **Analyze** Odysseus and his men sneaked into the Cyclops' cave and then could not get out because the Cyclops had blocked the entrance with a heavy stone. Later the Cyclops ate some of the men and made it clear that he would eventually eat the rest. Odysseus directed his men to sharpen the trunk of a tree, temper its point in the fire, and be ready to put out the giant's eye. He then told the Cyclops his name was Nohbdy. After Odysseus and his men blinded the Cyclops, the other Cyclopes did not come to help him, since they thought he said nobody had harmed him. Odysseus and his men then they sneaked out of the cave by hiding under the bellies of the Cyclops' sheep.

in giant force, would come against me here.
470 But this, but you—small, pitiful and twiggy—
you put me down with wine, you blinded me.
Come back, Odysseus, and I'll treat you well,
praying the god of earthquake[43] to befriend you—
his son I am, for he by his avowal
475 fathered me, and, if he will, he may
heal me of this black wound—he and no other
of all the happy gods or mortal men.'

Few words I shouted in reply to him:

'If I could take your life I would and take
480 your time away, and hurl you down to hell!

43. god of earthquake:
Poseidon.

The Odyssey, Part 1, The Cyclops ◆ 875

Humanities: Art

Polyphemus, the Cyclops (detail), 1929, by N. C. Wyeth.

This piece of art illustrates the moment at which Polyphemus tries to smash Odysseus' ship.

N. C. (Newell Convers) Wyeth (1882–1945) was an American artist whose enchanting illustrations of children's classics made him popular and successful. Works he illustrated include several novels by Robert Louis Stevenson and James Fenimore Cooper.

The illustration *Polyphemus, the Cyclops* was commissioned for a luxury edition of the *Odyssey* published in 1929. The illustration demonstrates the skill with which Wyeth was able to depict fantastic creatures.

Use the following questions for discussion:
1. Which lines in the *Odyssey* match the moment portrayed by Wyeth in this painting? Why do you think the artist chose this particular moment to illustrate? *The picture illustrates the lines "The*

blind thing in his doubled fury broke/a hilltop in his hands and heaved it after us." Students should note that the artist actually chose the moment just before Polyphemus hurled the "hilltop" into the sea. Perhaps he thought that portraying the moment at which something is about to happen would be more suspenseful than the moment after.

2. How does the mood of the illustration reflect that of the story? *The gloomy, stormy skies and seas suggest the danger and tension surrounding the event.*

◆ Critical Thinking

❶ Make Predictions In this passage Polyphemus calls on his father to curse Odysseus. Ask students to predict what will happen to Odysseus in the end. *It will take a long time for Odysseus to get home, he will lose all his companions and his ships along the way, and he will find troubled times at his home when he gets there.*

◆ Literary Focus

❷ The Epic Hero Odysseus shows a sense of fairness by dividing the sheep equally among his men— "share and share alike."

◆ Background for Understanding

❸ Explain that sacrifices to the gods were common in ancient Greek society. The gods were frequently pictured as petty, jealous, and overly concerned with how humans treated them. Thus, Odysseus wants to be sure to observe the proper ceremonies with regard to Zeus, in order not to offend him, and perhaps to counteract Poseidon's ill will, which he has now incurred.

◆ Critical Thinking

❹ Relate This passage hints at events yet to come. Ask students to cite other examples of foreshadowing that they have encountered so far. *Students may cite the opening verses, lines 1–15; Sailing from Troy, lines 28–33; and The Cyclops, lines 488–494.*

The god of earthquake could not heal you there!'

At this he stretched his hands out in the darkness
toward the sky of stars, and prayed Poseidon:

485 'O hear me, lord, blue girdler of the islands,
if I am thine indeed, and thou art father:
grant that Odysseus, raider of cities, never
see his home: Laertes' son, I mean,
who kept his hall on Ithaca. Should destiny
490 intend that he shall see his roof again
among his family in his father land,
far be that day, and dark the years between.
Let him lose all companions, and return
under strange sail to bitter days at home.'

In these words he prayed, and the god heard him.
495 Now he laid hands upon a bigger stone
and wheeled around, <u>titanic</u> for the cast,
to let it fly in the black-prowed vessel's track.
But it fell short, just aft the steering oar,
and whelming seas rose giant above the stone
500 to bear us onward toward the island.

There
as we ran in we saw the squadron waiting,
the trim ships drawn up side by side, and all
our troubled friends who waited, looking seaward.
We beached her, grinding keel in the soft sand,
505 and waded in, ourselves, on the sandy beach.
Then we unloaded all of Cyclops' flock
to make division, share and share alike.
Only my fighters voted that my ram,
the prize of all, should go to me. I slew him
510 by the seaside and burnt his long thighbones
to Zeus beyond the stormcloud, Cronus'[44] son,
who rules the world. But Zeus disdained my
  offering:
destruction for my ships he had in store
and death for those who sailed them, my
  companions.
515 Now all day long until the sun went down
we made our feast on mutton and sweet wine,
till after sunset in the gathering dark
we went to sleep above the wash of ripples.

When the young Dawn with fingertips of rose

876 ◆ *The Epic*

> ## ◆ Literary Focus
> What admirable qualities does Odysseus show in what he does with the stolen sheep?
>
> ❷

44. Cronus (krō′ nəs): Titan who was ruler of the universe until he was overthrown by his son Zeus.

◆ Build Vocabulary
titanic (tī tan′ ik) *adj.*: Of great size or strength

520 touched the world, I roused the men, gave orders
to man the ships, cast off the mooring lines:
and filing in to sit beside the rowlocks
oarsmen in line dipped oars in the gray sea.
So we moved out, sad in the vast offing,[45]
525 having our precious lives, but not our friends.

45. **offing** (ôf′ əiŋ) *n.*: Distant part of the sea visible from the shore.

The Land of the Dead

Odysseus and his men sail to Aeolia,[46] where Aeolus, king of the winds, sends Odysseus on his way with a gift: a sack containing all the winds except the favorable west wind. When they are near home, Odysseus' men open the sack, letting loose a storm that drives them back to Aeolia. Aeolus casts them out, having decided that they are detested by the gods. They sail seven days and arrive in the land of the Laestrygonians,[47] a race of cannibals. These creatures destroy all of Odysseus' ships except the one he is sailing in. Odysseus and his reduced crew escape and reach Aeaea, the island ruled by the sorceress-goddess Circe. She transforms half of the men into swine. Protected by a magic herb, Odysseus demands that Circe change his men back into human form. Before Odysseus departs from the island a year later, Circe informs him that in order to reach home he must journey to the land of the dead, Hades, and consult the blind prophet Tiresias.

46. **Aeolia** (ē ō′ li ə)

47. **Laestrygonians** (les tri gō′ ni anz)

We bore down on the ship at the sea's edge
and launched her on the salt immortal sea,
stepping our mast and spar in the black ship;
embarked the ram and ewe and went aboard
530 in tears, with bitter and sore dread upon us.
But now a breeze came up for us astern—
a canvas-bellying land breeze, hale shipmate
sent by the singing nymph with sunbright hair;[48]
⑤ so we made fast the braces, took our thwarts,
535 and let the wind and steersman work the ship
with full sail spread all day above our coursing,
till the sun dipped, and all the ways grew dark
upon the fathomless unresting sea.

48. **singing nymph . . . hair:** Circe.

                    By night
⑥
⑦ 540 our ship ran onward toward the Ocean's bourn,
the realm and region of the Men of Winter,
hidden in mist and cloud. Never the flaming
eye of Helios lights on those men
at morning, when he climbs the sky of stars,

The Odyssey, Part 1, The Land of the Dead ◆ 877

Customize for
English Language Learners
⑥ These students may be confused by homophones—words that sound the same, but have a different meaning and spelling—such as *bourn, born,* and *borne.* In this context, bourn means "boundary." *Bourn* can also mean "stream," "goal," or "domain." Point out that the word *bourn* does not show up very often, but its homophones born and borne do. Born means "brought into life or being," and borne means "carried."

◆ Build Grammar Skills
⑦ Restrictive and Nonrestrictive Appositives Have students identify the appositive in this passage, tell whether it is restrictive or nonrestrictive, and tell what punctuation it needs and why. *"The realm and region of the Men of Winter" is an appositive for "the Ocean's bourn." As a nonrestrictive appositive, which provides additional information, it takes a comma.*

Writing Mini-Lesson

Letter

This mini-lesson supports the writing activity in the Idea Bank on page 893.

Introduce the Concept Invite students to tell about letters they have written or received. Explain that they will be writing a letter from the point of view of one of the sailors traveling with Odysseus.

Develop Background As a class, list the elements of a good letter home. Spark discussion with questions like these:

• What do people at home want to know about the adventures of someone traveling abroad?

• How can information be presented so that readers can understand what's going on?

• What can writers do to tailor their letters for the intended recipient?

• What emotions might people at home be feeling? How can writers respond to those emotions?

Apply the Information Have students draft their letters. Have writing partners role-play the recipients and give feedback to writers.

Assess the Outcome Have students evaluate their own letters and those of their writing partner by using criteria such as these: clarity, organization, vivid detail, use of precise words, knowledge of the text, creativity in filling in details not provided in the text, and appropriateness of details to the intended audience.

877

►Critical Viewing◄

❶ Infer From the illustration, we can infer that the Greeks believed that a person's spirit continued to exist after death. The spirit had to make a long journey to the under-world, and could not complete its journey unless the proper rites were observed. The spirits that had not yet reached the underworld were frightening, restless, and hungry.

◆ Background for Understanding

❷ Explain to students that the Greeks believed that after a person died, his or her spirit went to the underworld, a land below the earth. The ruler of the underworld was the god Hades, brother of Zeus (ruler of the sky) and of Poseidon (ruler of the sea). In this passage, Odysseus is placating the spirits of the dead with milk, honey, wine, water, barley, and animal sacrifices.

Odysseus in the Land of the Dead, N. C. Wyeth, Delaware Art Museum

◀ **Critical Viewing** What can you infer about ancient Greek beliefs about death and the afterlife from the text and this illustration? [Infer] **❶**

nor in descending earthward out of heaven;
545 ruinous night being rove over those wretches.
We made the land, put ram and ewe ashore,
and took our way along the Ocean stream
to find the place foretold for us by Circe.
There Perimedes and Eulylochus,[49]
550 pinioned[50] the sacred beasts. With my drawn blade
I spaded up the votive[51] pit, and poured
libations[52] round it to the unnumbered dead:
sweet milk and honey, then sweet wine, and last
clear water; and I scattered barley down.
555 Then I addressed the blurred and breathless dead,
❷ vowing to slaughter my best heifer for them
before she calved, at home in Ithaca,
and burn the choice bits on the altar fire;
as for Tiresias, I swore to sacrifice
560 a black lamb, handsomest of all our flock.
Thus to <u>assuage</u> the nations of the dead
I pledged these rites, then slashed the lamb and
      ewe,
letting their black blood stream into the wellpit.

878 ◆ The Epic

49. Perimedes (per′ ə mē′ dēz) **and Eurylochus** (yōō ril′ ə kas)
50. pinioned (pin′ yənd) *v.*: Confined or shackled.
51. votive (vōt′ iv) *adj.*: Done in fulfillment of a vow or pledge.
52. libations (lī bā′ shənz) *n.*: Wine or other liquids poured upon the ground as a sacrifice.

◆ **Build Vocabulary**

assuage (ə swāj′) *v.*: Calm; pacify

🎵 **Humanities: Art**

Odysseus in the Land of the Dead, 1929, by N. C. Wyeth.

This piece of art illustrates the scene in the *Odyssey* in which Odysseus visits the underworld. The painting was commissioned for a 1929 limited edition of the *Odyssey.* The 500 copies of this edition included sixteen full-color illustrations by N. C. Wyeth and were signed by the artist.

Besides being a noted illustrator, Wyeth was also a successful muralist. His public art includes panels in the Missouri state capitol;

the Federal Reserve Bank in Boston; the Metropolitan Life Insurance Building in New York City; and the Hubbard Memorial Building and the National Cathedral, both in Washington, D.C.

Use the following questions for discussion:
1. Which lines in Homer's *Odyssey* are illustrated by this picture? *The picture illustrates lines 564–578.* Do you think the artist portrayed Odysseus as Homer pictured him at this moment? *Most students will say that the artist has successfully cap-*

tured Homer's image of Odysseus crouching by the "bloody pit" with his drawn sword, sick with fear but determined to achieve his goal of consulting Tiresias.

2. Do you agree with the way Wyeth portrayed the dead? *Some students will agree with Wyeth's portrayal, noting that Homer says that the dead appear in "their bloody gear," or as they were when they died. Others might disagree, pointing out that the dead look skeletal and long dead, rather than recently deceased.*

565 Now the souls gathered, stirring out of Erebus,[53]
brides and young men, and men grown old in pain,
and tender girls whose hearts were new to grief;

❸ many were there, too, torn by brazen lanceheads,
battle-slain, bearing still their bloody gear.
From every side they came and sought the pit
570 with rustling cries; and I grew sick with fear.
But presently I gave command to my officers
to flay those sheep the bronze cut down, and make
burnt offerings of flesh to the gods below—
to sovereign Death, to pale Persephone.[54]
575 Meanwhile I crouched with my drawn sword to keep
the surging phantoms from the bloody pit
till I should know the presence of Tiresias.[55]

❺ One shade came first—Elpenor, of our company,
who lay unburied still on the wide earth
580 as we had left him—dead in Circe's hall,
untouched, unmourned, when other cares compelled us.
Now when I saw him there I wept for pity
and called out to him:

'How is this, Elpenor,
❻ how could you journey to the western gloom
585 swifter afoot than I in the black lugger?'
He sighed, and answered:

'Son of great Laertes,
Odysseus, master mariner and soldier,
bad luck shadowed me, and no kindly power;
ignoble death I drank with so much wine.
590 I slept on Circe's roof, then could not see
the long steep backward ladder, coming down,
and fell that height. My neckbone, buckled under,
snapped, and my spirit found this well of dark.
Now hear the grace I pray for, in the name
595 of those back in the world, not here—your wife
and father, he who gave you bread in childhood,
and your own child, your only son, Telemachus,[56]
long ago left at home.

When you make sail
and put these lodgings of dim Death behind,
600 you will moor ship, I know, upon Aeaea Island;
there, O my lord, remember me, I pray,
do not abandon me unwept, unburied,
to tempt the gods' wrath, while you sail for home;
❼ but fire my corpse, and all the gear I had,
605 and build a cairn[57] for me above the breakers—
an unknown sailor's mark for men to come.

53. Erebus (er´ ə bəs):
Dark region under the earth
through which the dead
pass before entering the
realm of Hades.

◆ **Literary Focus**
How is Odysseus'
courage revealed
even as he admits
to being "sick with
fear"?

---

54. Persephone (pər sef´
ə nē): Wife of Hades.
55. Tiresias (tī rē´ si as)

56. Telemachus
(tə lem´ ə kəs)

57. cairn (kern) n.: Conical
heap of stones built as a
monument.

The Odyssey, Part 1, The Land of the Dead ◆ 879

 Cultural Connection

Begin a discussion about the many different customs and rituals surrounding death by asking students what kind of ritual they would want when they die. Would they want to have a funeral, to be buried in a cemetery, to be cremated, to have their ashes strewn in a special place? Discuss the similarities among students' ideas. Point out that the rites surrounding death are important in every culture and always have been, but that they vary widely. Cite, for example, the funeral pyre of the Hindus, the Jewish custom of sitting shiva, and the Mandan Indian tradition of leaving the dead body outside on an elevated platform to decay naturally.

Ask students to choose a religion or culture other than their own and research the customs surrounding death in that culture. Have them share their findings with the class.

880

◆ Critical Thinking

❶ Assess Ask: How does Odysseus demonstrate his heroic qualities in this passage? *Although Odysseus grieves for his mother, who he did not realize until this moment was dead, and would probably like to talk to her, he remains steadfast in his duty.*

◆ Reading Strategy

❷ Read in Sentences Students might rephrase lines 626–629 as follows: *"Get out of the way, put your sword away. If you just let me taste the blood, I will tell you the truth." When I heard this, I stepped aside and let my sword slide all the way back into its scabbard.*

Comprehension Check ☑

❸ Whom is Tiresias referring to when he speaks of the "son whose eye you blinded"? *Tiresias is referring to Polyphemus.* Who is that son's father, and what is he up to? *Polyphemus' father is Poseidon, who is preparing trouble ahead for Odysseus.*

Customize for
Less Proficient Readers

❹ Have students prepare a two-column chart. Instruct them to write down the events Tiresias foretells in one column. As they read on, have them fill in the adventures to which the prophesies refer. *Students will discover that line 637 refers to "Scylla and Charybdis"; line 638 refers to "The Sirens"; lines 639–646 refer to "The Cattle of the Sun God"; lines 649–650 refer to "'. . . Twenty years gone, and I am home again'" (Part 2); and line 651 refers to "Odysseus' Revenge" (Part 2).*

Heap up the mound there, and implant upon it
the oar I pulled in life with my companions.'

He ceased, and I replied:
                                'Unhappy spirit,
610   I promise you the barrow and the burial.'

So we conversed, and grimly, at a distance,
with my long sword between, guarding the blood,
while the faint image of the lad spoke on.
Now came the soul of Anticlea, dead,
615   my mother, daughter of Autolycus,[58]
dead now, though living still when I took ship
for holy Troy. Seeing this ghost I grieved,
but held her off, through pang on pang of tears,
till I should know the presence of Tiresias.
620   Soon from the dark that prince of Thebes[59] came
       forward
bearing a golden staff; and he addressed me:

'Son of Laertes and the gods of old,
Odysseus, master of landways and seaways,
why leave the blazing sun, O man of woe,
625   to see the cold dead and the joyless region?
Stand clear, put up your sword;
let me but taste the blood, I shall speak true.'

At this I stepped aside, and in the scabbard
let my long sword ring home to the pommel silver,
630   as he bent down to the somber blood. Then spoke
the prince of those with gift of speech:

                                'Great captain,
a fair wind and the honey lights of home
are all you seek. But anguish lies ahead;
the god who thunders on the land prepares it,
635   not to be shaken from your track, implacable,
in rancor for the son whose eye you blinded.
One narrow strait may take you through his blows:
denial of yourself, restraint of shipmates.
When you make landfall on Thrinacia first
640   and quit the violet sea, dark on the land
you'll find the grazing herds of Helios
by whom all things are seen, all speech is known.
Avoid these kine,[60] hold fast to your intent,
and hard seafaring brings you all to Ithaca.
645   But if you raid the beeves, I see destruction

880 ◆ The Epic

58. Autolycus (ô täl′ i kus)

59. Thebes (thēbz)

◆ **Reading Strategy**
Rephrase in ordinary language the verses about Odysseus putting his sword away. How can rephrasing Homer's verses help you read the *Odyssey* in sentences?   ❷

60. kine (kīn) *n.:* Cattle.

for ship and crew. Though you survive alone,
<u>bereft</u> of all companions, lost for years,
under strange sail shall you come home, to find
your own house filled with trouble: insolent men
650 eating your livestock as they court your lady.
Aye, you shall make those men atone in blood!
But after you have dealt out death—in open
combat or by stealth—to all the suitors,
go overland on foot, and take an oar,
655 until one day you come where men have lived
with meat unsalted, never known the sea,
nor seen seagoing ships, with crimson bows
and oars that fledge light hulls for dipping flight.
The spot will soon be plain to you, and I
660 can tell you how: some passerby will say,
'What winnowing fan is that upon your shoulder?'
Halt, and implant your smooth oar in the turf
and make fair sacrifice to Lord Poseidon:
a ram, a bull, a great buck boar: turn back,
665 and carry out pure hecatombs[61] at home
to all wide heaven's lords, the undying gods,
to each in order. Then a seaborne death
soft as this hand of mist will come upon you
when you are wearied out with rich old age,
670 your country folk in blessed peace around you.
And all this shall be just as I foretell.'

61. **hecatombs** (hek´ ə tōmz´) *n.:* Large-scale sacrifices: often the slaughter of 100 cattle at one time.

◆ **Build Vocabulary**

bereft (bi reft´) *v.:* Deprived

Guide for Responding

◆ *Literature and Your Life*

Reader's Response What do you think of Odysseus' plan for escaping from Polyphemus?

Thematic Focus What are some constructive ways of working out conflicts with powerful or unreasonable opponents?

☑ Check Your Comprehension

1. What does Odysseus do to blind Polyphemus?
2. How do Odysseus and his companions ultimately escape from the Cyclops?
3. What does Tiresias foretell?

◆ Critical Thinking
INTERPRET

1. What does the encounter with Maron tell you about ancient Greek attitudes toward hospitality? [Interpret]
2. What "laws" of behavior and attitude does Polyphemus violate? Explain. [Infer]

EVALUATE

3. (a) What survival qualities does Odysseus exhibit in his conflict with Polyphemus? (b) What character trait does Odysseus display in "The Land of the Dead" that he did not reveal in his adventure with the Cyclops? [Assess]

The Odyssey, Part 1, The Land of the Dead ◆ 881

◆ Critical Thinking

1. Hospitality is highly valued; a host is judged by his courteousness and the richness of the gifts he presents to his guests.

2. He violates the laws of hospitality, of honoring the gods, and of not being a cannibal.
3. (a) Students may say that Odysseus shows guile, courage, and foresight.
(b) Students may say that

Odysseus shows compassion for his mother and for Elpenor, or reveals determination to achieve his goal even when he is afraid.

Comprehension Check ☑

❺ Ask students why the passerby would ask the question in line 661.
The passerby, having never seen or heard of an oar, would assume that the oar is a tool for fanning away chaff from grain. Because an oar has a longer handle and a narrower blade than a fan, the passerby would wonder at its shape.

◆ **Critical Thinking**

❻ **Interpret** Ask students why Odysseus must make these sacrifices.
He needs to put himself in the good graces of the gods, particularly Poseidon. What desired consequence will come from following Tiresias' advice?
Odysseus' country will be peaceful. Odysseus will live happily to a ripe old age, and die a painless death.

Answers

◆ *Literature and Your Life*

Reader's Response Students may say that Odysseus' plan was well thought out; he did not act on his first impulse, which was to kill the Cyclops immediately.

Thematic Focus Students may suggest looking for a solution that has advantages for both sides or having a neutral party help to work things out.

☑ **Check Your Comprehension**

1. He stabs him in the eye with a red-hot spike.
2. They attach themselves to the underside of the Cyclops' sheep. Thus camouflaged from the Cyclops' groping hands, they escape when Polyphemus lets his flocks out to graze.
3. Tiresias foretells the many ordeals that Poseidon has arranged for Odysseus and what Odysseus will do when he returns home. He advises Odysseus in cryptic terms on how to get past the Sirens, why the cattle should be left alone, and how to make peace with the gods.

881

◆ **Build Grammar Skills**

❶ Restrictive and Nonrestrictive Appositives Ask students to identify the appositives in this passage. Ask them to tell whether they are restrictive or nonrestrictive. *"A canvas-bellying breeze" and "a lusty shipmate…" are both nonrestrictive appositives for "an offshore breeze."*

◆ **Literary Focus**

❷ The Epic Hero Suggested response: *Odysseus is a caring leader. He also understands that by sharing information with his men, he wins their trust and is more able to get them to do what he wants.*

◆ *Literature and Your Life*

❸ Odysseus asks his men to help him resist the Sirens' song. Ask students to suggest other situations in which people ask their friends to help them resist temptation. *Students might suggest that people with addictions turn to friends for support; dieters may ask friends to help them avoid fattening foods; and people who are trying to study or get work done may ask friends not to tempt them with invitations to go out and have fun.*

The Sirens

Odysseus returns to Circe's island. The goddess reveals his course to him and gives advice on how to avoid the dangers he will face: the Sirens, who lure sailors to their destruction; the Wandering Rocks, sea rocks that destroy even birds in flight; the perils of the sea monster Scylla and, nearby, the whirlpool Charybdis;[62] and the cattle of the sun god, which Tiresias has warned Odysseus not to harm.

62. Charybdis (ka rib′ dis)

As Circe spoke, Dawn mounted her golden throne,
and on the first rays Circe left me, taking
her way like a great goddess up the island.
675 I made straight for the ship, roused up the men
to get aboard and cast off at the stern.
They scrambled to their places by the rowlocks
and all in line dipped oars in the gray sea.
But soon an offshore breeze blew to our liking—
❶ 680 a canvas-bellying breeze, a lusty shipmate
sent by the singing nymph with sunbright hair.
So we made fast the braces, and we rested,
letting the wind and steersman work the ship.
The crew being now silent before me, I
685 addressed them, sore at heart:

                                'Dear friends,
more than one man, or two, should know those
   things
Circe foresaw for us and shared with me,
so let me tell her forecast: then we die
with our eyes open, if we are going to die,
690 or know what death we baffle if we can. Sirens
weaving a haunting song over the sea
we are to shun, she said, and their green shore
all sweet with clover; yet she urged that I
alone should listen to their song. Therefore
❸ 695 you are to tie me up, tight as a splint,
erect along the mast, lashed to the mast,
and if I shout and beg to be untied,
take more turns of the rope to muffle me.'

I rather dwelt on this part of the forecast,
700 while our good ship made time, bound outward
   down
the wind for the strange island of Sirens.
Then all at once the wind fell, and a calm

◆ Literary Focus
What does Odysseus reveal about his character by sharing information with his men?

❷

882 ◆ *The Epic*

④ Deduce Students may say that Circe looks seductive, confident of her power, mysterious, and a bit mischievous.

◆ Literary Focus

❺ The Epic Hero Ask students: Why does Odysseus put wax in his men's ears but not his own? *He wants to make sure the men don't hear the Sirens' song, so that they won't sail to their own destruction. However, his curiosity, coupled with Circe's advice, makes him want to hear the song himself. Tied to the mast, he will be safe.*

Circe Meanwhile Had Gone Her Ways . . ., 1924, William Russell Flint Collection of the New York Public Library; Astor, Lenox, and Tilden Foundations

▲ **Critical Viewing** The beautiful sorceress Circe both helps and hinders Odysseus on his long journey home. What can you tell about Circe's character from this illustration? **[Deduce]**

❹

came over all the sea, as though some power
lulled the swell.

                The crew were on their feet
705   briskly, to furl the sail, and stow it; then
each in place, they poised the smooth oar blades
and sent the white foam scudding by. I carved
a massive cake of beeswax into bits
and rolled them in my hands until they softened—
710   no long task, for a burning heat came down
from Helios, lord of high noon. Going forward
I carried wax along the line, and laid it
thick on their ears. They tied me up, then, plumb

❺

The Odyssey, Part 1, The Sirens ◆ 883

Humanities: Art

Circe Meanwhile Had Gone Her Ways . . . , 1924, by William Russell Flint.

The Scottish painter and illustrator William Russell Flint (1880–1969) was the son of landscape painter F. Wrighton Flint. In 1900, the young artist became interested in the medium of watercolor. For many years, this was his favorite medium, and his works were exhibited in England and Europe to much acclaim. He added another dimension to his work when he began to create illustrations for various literary works.

The watercolor *Circe Meanwhile Had Gone Her Ways . . .* was executed in 1924 for an edition of the *Odyssey.* Flint created a beautiful Circe, who looks as if she has stepped from a Grecian urn. In keeping with this stylized effect, the perspective of the painting is basically flat.

Use the following questions for discussion:

1. What special abilities does Circe seem to have? *She seems to command the attention and obedience of animals, such*
as the two sheep.

2. What elements in the painting give a sense of the setting of the *Odyssey? The time and place are suggested in Circe's clothes and pose; the carved marble pedestal; the sensuous, stylized spirals of the ram's horns and wool and of the blue-and-purple decorations on the ship; and the form of the ship in the background.*

◆ Critical Thinking

❶ Analyze Ask students to explain the dilemma that Odysseus and his men are in. How is it that whatever they do, they are facing trouble? *If the ship sails left—"to port"—they will be near Scylla, a sea monster. However, if the ship sails right—"starboard"— they will be sucked into Charybdis, a whirlpool.*

◆ Critical Thinking

❷ Infer Ask students what would happen to a ship that sailed too near to Charybdis. *The ship would probably be sucked into the whirlpool, so that everyone on it would die.*

Customize for
Visual/Spatial Learners

❸ Encourage visual/spatial learners to illustrate the episode with Scylla and Charybdis based on the details in the text and the following additional information:

* According to legend, Charybdis swallowed and threw up the sea three times a day.

* Representations of Scylla often show her with twelve feet, six heads, and jaws containing three rows of fangs.

Remind students that the only limit on an illustrator is not to contradict the words being illustrated. He or she can deviate from traditional images as desired.

to roll for cover under the decking. Circe's
bidding against arms had slipped my mind,
so I tied on my cuirass[66] and took up
790   two heavy spears, then made my way along
to the foredeck—thinking to see her first from there,
the monster of the gray rock, harboring
torment for my friends. I strained my eyes
upon the cliffside veiled in cloud, but nowhere
could I catch sight of her.

And all this time,
795   in travail,[67] sobbing, gaining on the current,
we rowed into the strait—Scylla to port
❶ and on our starboard beam Charybdis,[68] dire
gorge[69] of the salt-sea tide. By heaven! when she
vomited, all the sea was like a cauldron
800   seething over intense fire, when the mixture
suddenly heaves and rises.

The shot spume
soared to the landside heights, and fell like rain.

But when she swallowed the sea water down
we saw the funnel of the maelstrom,[70] heard
805   the rock bellowing all around, and dark
❷ sand raged on the bottom far below.
My men all blanched against the gloom, our eyes
were fixed upon that yawning mouth in fear
of being devoured.

Then Scylla made her strike,
❸ 810   whisking six of my best men from the ship.
I happened to glance aft at ship and oarsmen
and caught sight of their arms and legs, dangling
high overhead. Voices came down to me
in anguish, calling my name for the last time.

815   A man surfcasting on a point of rock
for bass or mackerel, whipping his long rod
to drop the sinker and the bait far out,
will hook a fish and rip it from the surface
to dangle wriggling through the air:

so these
820   were borne aloft in spasms toward the cliff.
❹ She ate them as they shrieked there, in her den,
in the dire grapple, reaching still for me—

886 ◆ *The Epic*

66. cuirass (kwi ras´) *n.*: Armor for the upper body.

67. travail (trav āl´) *n.*: Very hard work.

68. Charybdis (ka rib´ dis)

69. gorge (gôrj) *n.*: Hungry, consuming mouth.

70. maelstrom (māl´ strəm) *n.*: Large, violent whirlpool.

Cross-Curricular Connection: Geography

The monster Scylla is thought to have been located at what is today known as the Strait of Messina, the passage between Sicily and the toe of the boot of Italy. With the abundance of islands and narrow straits in the Mediterranean and Aegean Seas, it is not surprising that a legend arose about a ship passing between two deadly dangers.

Have students examine a map of the Mediterranean and locate the Strait of Messina. Then have them examine a map of the world to locate other "dire straits" such as the Strait of Gibraltar, the Strait of Magellan, or the Bering Strait. Encourage students to do library or Internet research to learn more about dangerous sea passages.

4 and deathly pity ran me through
at that sight—far the worst I ever suffered,
825 questing the passes of the strange sea.

We rowed on.
The Rocks were now behind; Charybdis, too,
and Scylla dropped astern. . . .

The Cattle of the Sun God

In the small hours of the third watch, when stars
that shone out in the first dusk of evening
830 had gone down to their setting, a giant wind
blew from heaven, and clouds driven by Zeus
shrouded land and sea in a night of storm;
so, just as Dawn with fingertips of rose
touched the windy world, we dragged our ship
5 835 to cover in a grotto, a sea cave
where nymphs had chairs of rock and sanded floors.
I mustered all the crew and said:

'Old shipmates,
Our stores are in the ship's hold, food and drink;
the cattle here are not for our provision,
6 840 or we pay dearly for it.

Fierce the god is
who cherishes these heifers and these sheep:
Helios; and no man avoids his eye.'

To this my fighters nodded. Yes. But now
we had a month of onshore gales, blowing
845 day in, day out—south winds, or south by east.
As long as bread and good red wine remained
to keep the men up, and appease their craving,
they would not touch the cattle. But in the end,
when all the barley in the ship was gone,
850 hunger drove them to scour the wild shore
with angling hooks, for fishes and seafowl,
whatever fell into their hands; and lean days
wore their bellies thin.

The storms continued.
So one day I withdrew to the interior
855 to pray the gods in solitude, for hope
that one might show me some way of salvation.
Slipping away, I struck across the island

◆ **Literary Focus**
The characteristics of
an epic hero reflect
the values of his or
her culture. What
does this passage tell
you about ancient
Greek values? **7**

The Odyssey, Part 1, Cattle of the Sun God ◆ *887*

888

to a sheltered spot, out of the driving gale.
I washed my hands there, and made supplication
860 to the gods who own Olympus,[71] all the gods—
but they, for answer, only closed my eyes
under slow drops of sleep.

             Now on the shore Eurylochus
made his <u>insidious</u> plea:

             'Comrades,' he said,
You've gone through everything; listen to what I say.
865 All deaths are hateful to us, mortal wretches,
but famine is the most pitiful, the worst
end that a man can come to.

             Will you fight it?
Come, we'll cut out the noblest of these cattle
for sacrifice to the gods who own the sky;
870 and once at home, in the old country of Ithaca,
if ever that day comes—
we'll build a costly temple and adorn it
with every beauty for the Lord of Noon.[72]
But if he flares up over his heifers lost,
875 wishing our ship destroyed, and if the gods
make cause with him, why, then I say: Better
open your lungs to a big sea once for all
than waste to skin and bones on a lonely island!'

         Thus Eurylochus: and they murmered 'Aye!'
880 trooping away at once to round up heifers.
Now, that day tranquil cattle with broad brows
were gazing near, and soon the men drew up
around their chosen beasts in ceremony.
They plucked the leaves that shone on a tall oak—
885 having no barley meal—to strew the victims,
performed the prayers and ritual, knifed the kine
and flayed each carcass, cutting thighbones free
to wrap in double folds of fat. These offerings,
with strips of meat, were laid upon the fire.
890 Then, as they had no wine, they made libation
with clear spring water, broiling the entrails first;
and when the bones were burnt and tripes shared,
they spitted the carved meat.
             Just then my slumber
left me in a rush, my eyes opened,
895 and I went down the seaward path. No sooner
had I caught sight of our black hull, than savory

888 ◆ The Epic

71. Olympus (ō lim´ pəs): Mount Olympus, home of the gods.

72. Lord of Noon: Helios.

◆ Build Vocabulary

insidious (in sid´ ē əs) *adj.:* Characterized by craftiness and betrayal

---

Cross-Curricular Connection: Art and Architecture

Greek art and architecture are generally associated with ruins of stately temples, ideally proportioned marble statues, and elegantly painted vases—relics of the Golden Age of Athens, which started in 461 B.C., when Pericles came to power, and ended in 431 B.C., when Athens was defeated by Sparta in the Peloponesian War.

The Trojan War, however, predates this period by 700 years or more. The people living in Greece at that time built fortress-like citadels fortified by massive walls. Their palaces had a rectangular main room called the *megaron,* built around a central hearth, with four columns supporting the roof. The walls were decorated with colorful frescoes. Odysseus' palace was built on this plan. (See Part 2 of the *Odyssey,* lines 1204–1205: "Eumaeus crossed the court and went straight forward into the *megaron* among the suitors.")

Typical art objects from Homer's time, the eighth century B.C., are clay vases decorated with intricate patterns and geometric figures of animals and humans. They look primitive and rugged compared to art of the classical period.

If possible, obtain an art history book with illustrations of art and architecture from both the Mycenaean period and the eighth century B.C. They will give students an idea of what the civilization of each of these periods was like.

odors of burnt fat eddied around me;
grief took hold of me, and I cried aloud:

900 'O Father Zeus and gods in bliss forever,
you made me sleep away this day of mischief!
O cruel drowsing, in the evil hour!
Here they sat, and a great work they contrived.'[73]

Lampetia[74] in her long gown meanwhile
had borne swift word to the Overlord of Noon:

905 'They have killed your kine.'

                    And the Lord Helios
burst into angry speech amid the immortals:

'O Father Zeus and gods in bliss forever,
punish Odysseus' men! So overweening,
now they have killed my peaceful kine, my joy
910 at morning when I climbed the sky of stars,
and evening, when I bore westward from heaven.
Restitution or penalty they shall pay—
and pay in full—or I go down forever
to light the dead men in the underworld.'
915 Then Zeus who drives the stormcloud made reply:

'Peace, Helios: shine on among the gods,
shine over mortals in the fields of grain.
Let me throw down one white-hot bolt, and make
splinters of their ship in the winedark sea.'
920 —Calypso later told me of this exchange,
as she declared that Hermes[75] had told her.
Well, when I reached the sea cave and the ship,
I faced each man, and had it out; but where
could any remedy be found? There was none.
925 The silken beeves[76] of Helios were dead.
The gods, moreover, made queer signs appear:
cowhides began to crawl, and beef, both raw
and roasted, lowed like kine upon the spits.
Now six full days my gallant crew could feast
930 upon the prime beef they had marked for slaughter
from Helios' herd; and Zeus, the son of Cronus,
added one fine morning.

                    All the gales
had ceased, blown out, and with an offshore breeze
we launched again, stepping the mast and sail,
935 to make for the open sea. Astern of us

The Odyssey, Part 1, Cattle of the Sun God ◆ *889*

---

73. contrived (kən trīvd′)
v.: Thought up; devised.

74. Lampetia (lam pē′
she): A nymph.

75. Hermes (hʉr′ mēz):
The herald and messenger
of the gods.

76. beeves (bēvz) *n.*:
Plural of beef.

◆ **Literary Focus**

❷ **The Epic Hero** Have students
discuss why a hero would blame his
mistakes on the gods. *The ancient
Greeks believed that the gods had a
hand in whatever happened. Some students may refer back to the passage in
which Odysseus says that the gods, "for
answer, only closed my eyes under slow
drops of sleep."*

Comprehension Check ☑

❸ Ask students what Helios is
threatening to do. *He is threatening to
leave and stay in the underworld.* **What
would happen if he carried out his
threat?** *Without the sun, the world
would be cold and dark. Plants could not
grow, and people would not survive.*

◆ **Build Vocabulary**

❹ **Word Origins: Words From
Myths** Ask students if they know
another meaning of the word *calypso*.
*Students might know that calypso is
also the name of a type of music popular in the Caribbean.*

◆ *Literature and Your Life*

❺ Have students compare the eerie
behavior of the hides and meat with
other ominous events they've seen in
television shows and movies. Then
ask students to explain how such
strange scenes create a sense of
anticipation in the audience. *Students
should realize that strange events create
a sense of anticipation as readers/view-
ers try to figure out what might be causing these unusual occurrences.*

① Compare Invite students to compare this description of a storm to storms they have seen in movies or television shows. How do they imagine the men on ship are reacting? *Students might have seen movies set at sea or seen news footage of hurricanes and winter storms. They will probably imagine that some men on board are terrified, while others are bravely going about their business.*

◆ *Literature and Your Life*

② Students may say that the description of the impending storm makes them wonder what is going to happen to Odysseus and his ships.

◆ Literary Focus

③ The Epic Hero Ask students what heroic qualities Odysseus shows in this passage. *Odysseus is brave, resourceful, and skillful at seafaring. He is also determined; even though it would seem that he is destined for certain death, he refuses to give up.*

◆ Reading Strategy

④ Read in Sentences Invite students to read this passage aloud, trying to make sense of sentences. Encourage them to read the words the way they imagine Odysseus would say them as he is telling the story. Then ask, "If you had a friend who had never read the *Odyssey*, what advice would you give him or her about how to read it? Why?"

Students should be able to explain that reading in sentences is the best way to understand the author's meaning and follow the story. They might want to add that, after understanding the story, awareness of the verse adds to or enriches the reading experience.

---

the island coastline faded, and no land
showed anywhere, but only sea and heaven,
when Zeus Cronion piled a thunderhead
above the ship, while gloom spread on the ocean.

① 940 We held our course, but briefly. Then the squall
struck whining from the west, with gale force, breaking
both forestays, and the mast came toppling aft
along the ship's length, so the running rigging
showered into the bilge.

                On the afterdeck
945 the mast had hit the steersman a slant blow
bashing the skull in, knocking him overside,
as the brave soul fled the body, like a diver.
With crack on crack of thunder, Zeus let fly
a bolt against the ship, a direct hit,
950 so that she bucked, in reeking fumes of sulphur,
and all the men were flung into the sea.
They came up 'round the wreck, bobbing awhile
like petrels[77] on the waves.

               No more seafaring
homeward for these, no sweet day of return;
955 the god had turned his face from them.

               I clambered
fore and aft my hulk until a comber
split her, keel from ribs, and the big timber
floated free; the mast, too, broke away.
③ A backstay floated dangling from it, stout
960 rawhide rope, and I used this for lashing
mast and keel together. These I straddled,
riding the frightful storm.

               Nor had I yet
seen the worst of it: for now the west wind
dropped, and a southeast gale came on—one more
965 twist of the knife—taking me north again,
straight for Charybdis. All that night I drifted,
and in the sunrise, sure enough, I lay
off Scylla[78] mountain and Charybdis deep.
④ There, as the whirlpool drank the tide, a billow
970 tossed me, and I sprang for the great fig tree,
catching on like a bat under a bough.
Nowhere had I to stand, no way of climbing,
the root and bole[79] being far below, and far
above my head the branches and their leaves,
975 massed, overshadowing Charybdis pool.

890 ◆ The Epic

77. petrels (pet′ rəlz): Small, dark sea birds.

78. Scylla (sil′ ə)

79. bole (bōl) *n.*: Tree trunk.

Speaking and Listening Mini-Lesson

Play-by-Play Broadcast

This mini-lesson supports the Speaking and Listening activity in the Idea Bank (p. 893).

Introduce the Concept Ask students who have watched sports events to define the concept of a play-by-play broadcast for the class. Point out that the announcer describes everything that is happening as it happens, so that people who cannot see for themselves what is going on can visualize the action. Tell students that in this activity,

they will create a play-by-play broadcast of a scene from the *Odyssey*.

Develop Background As a class, list the elements of a good play-by-play broadcast. Use questions like these to create your list:
• Why do audiences need a play-by-play?
• What elements of a play-by-play help audiences follow the action?
• What mistakes should a play-by-play broadcast avoid?

Apply the Information With this back-

ground, students might work in pairs or small groups to create a play-by-play broadcast of an incident, which they can take turns performing in class.

Assess the Outcome Have students use the list of the elements of a good play-by-play broadcast (generated during the Develop Background phase) to assess their own play-by-play broadcasts and constructively criticize other students' broadcasts.

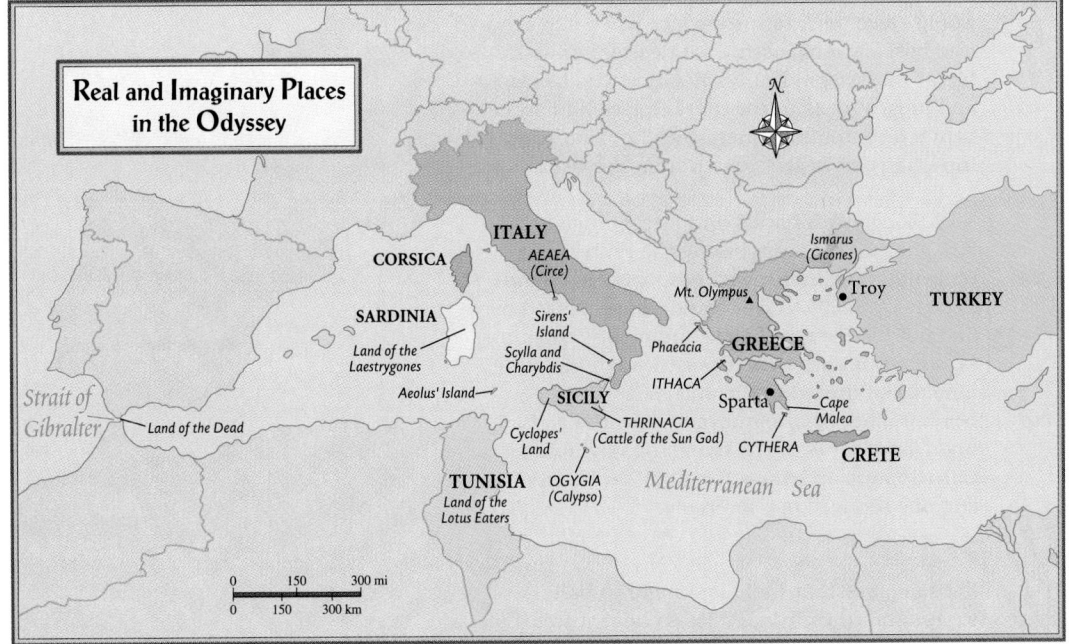

Real and Imaginary Places in the Odyssey

ITALY
CORSICA
AEAEA (Circe)
Ismarus (Cicones)
Troy
TURKEY
SARDINIA
Sirens' Island
Mt. Olympus
Land of the Laestrygones
Scylla and Charybdis
Phaeacia
GREECE
Aeolus' Island
SICILY
ITHACA
Sparta
Cape Malea
Strait of Gibralter
Land of the Dead
Cyclopes' Land
THRINACIA (Cattle of the Sun God)
CYTHERA
CRETE
TUNISIA
OGYGIA (Calypso)
Mediterranean Sea
Land of the Lotus Eaters

0   150   300 mi
0   150   300 km

▲ Critical Viewing The entrance to the Land of the Dead is believed
to be the Strait of Gibraltar. Why might the ancient Greeks have
considered this location frightening? [Analyze]

❺

Beyond Literature

Geography Connection

Tracing Odysseus' Route Odysseus' journey carries him to real places, such as Troy and Sparta, as well as to fictitious places, such as Aeolia and Aeaea. In modern times, historians and explorers have tried to retrace the epic journey of Odysseus to determine the actual locations of the places with fictional names and thus to determine Odysseus' exact route. What follows is just one of many theories of the actual route of Odysseus: From Troy in present-day Turkey, Odysseus proceeded briefly northward and then southwestward on the Aegean Sea, passing between the Greek

lands of Peloponnesus and Crete. Then, sailing westward on the Mediterranean Sea, Odysseus traveled near Sicily, where he found the Cyclops and where nearby islands were homes to the Lotus Eaters, the Sirens, and Aeolus, among others. After circling Sicily clockwise, Odysseus sailed northeastward and finally reached the Ionian Islands of Greece and his home, Ithaca.

Activity Choose either another piece of literature or a movie in which one or more characters take a journey. Draw a map of that journey.

The Odyssey, Part 1, Cattle of the Sun God ◆ 891

◆ Literary Focus

❶ The Epic Hero Ask students what heroic qualities Odysseus reveals in this passage. *Odysseus is protected by Zeus, who saves him from Scylla. He thus reveals two heroic qualities: enjoying the gods' special protection and being appropriately grateful for that protection.*

Comprehension Check ☑

❷ Ask students to whom Odysseus is addressing these remarks. *Students should recall that Odysseus is telling his story to Alcinoüs, ruler of Phaeacia.*

▶▶ Reinforce and Extend

Answers

◆ *Literature and Your Life*

Reader's Response Some students might admire Odysseus' skill and bravery when faced with the lose-lose choice between Scylla and Charybdis.

Thematic Focus Odysseus seems to be able to put powerful emotions on hold, whether they are fear or desire, in order to reach his goals. He tackles problems with whatever skill the situation calls for—verbal or physical.

☑ Check Your Comprehension

1. (a) Tiresias foretells the many ordeals that Poseidon has arranged for Odysseus and what Odysseus will do when he returns home. (b) He advises Odysseus in cryptic terms on how to get past the Sirens, why the cattle should be left alone, and how to make peace with the gods.
2. He seals their ears with wax, so they cannot hear the songs.
3. Eurylochus claims that there is no worse fate than starving to death; in addition, he claims that Helios can be appeased later on.
4. Zeus placates Helios by striking Odysseus' ship with a lightning bolt.

◆ Critical Thinking

1. Both episodes involve the perils of giving in to temptation. The Sirens lure sailors to their destruction by singing a seductive song. The Lotus-Eaters cause men to forget their homes and the

---

But I clung grimly, thinking my mast and keel
would come back to the surface when she spouted.
And ah! how long, with what desire, I waited!
980 till, at the twilight hour, when one who hears
and judges pleas in the marketplace all day
between contentious men, goes home to supper,
the long poles at last reared from the sea.

Now I let go with hands and feet, plunging
985 straight into the foam beside the timbers,
pulled astride, and rowed hard with my hands
❶ to pass by Scylla. Never could I have passed her
had not the Father of gods and men,[80] this time,
kept me from her eyes. Once through the strait,
nine days I drifted in the open sea
990 before I made shore, buoyed up by the gods,
upon Ogygia[81] Isle. The dangerous nymph
Calypso lives and sings there, in her beauty,
and she received me, loved me.

But why tell
the same tale that I told last night in hall
❷ 995 to you and to your lady? Those adventures
made a long evening, and I do not hold
with tiresome repetition of a story."

80. **Father . . . men:** Zeus.

81. **Ogygia** (o jij´ ī a).

Guide for Responding

◆ *Literature and Your Life*

Reader's Response In your opinion, when does Odysseus act most heroically? Explain.

Thematic Focus What personal qualities are useful when it comes to working out problems and reaching goals?

☑ Check Your Comprehension

1. (a) What does Tiresias foretell? (b) What directions and warnings does he give?
2. What does Odysseus do to protect his men from the Sirens?
3. How does Eurylochus persuade Odysseus' men to slaughter and eat Helios' cattle?
4. What is Zeus' response to Helios' demand for revenge?

892 ◆ The Epic

◆ Critical Thinking

INTERPRET
1. Compare and contrast the peril of the Sirens and the peril of the Lotus-Eaters. **[Compare and Contrast]**
2. Why do you think Odysseus chooses to sail toward Scylla rather than Charybdis? **[Analyze]**
3. In these adventures, how does Odysseus show himself to be an effective leader? **[Draw Conclusions]**

EVALUATE
4. Is Odysseus right to keep his decision to sail toward Scylla a secret from his men? Give reasons for your opinion. **[Make a Judgment]**

APPLY
5. What is the meaning of the saying "caught between Scylla and Charybdis"? **[Apply]**

---

purpose for journeying by feeding them the lotus. The Sirens seem to be aware that they are doing something wrong, whereas the Lotus-Eaters do not.
2. Odysseus might reason that Charybdis endangers the entire ship while Scylla can cause only partial losses.
3. Bravery, piety, cleverness, coolheadedness, and concern for his men allow

Odysseus to lead effectively and serve as a role model.
4. Some students might reply that Odysseus is wise to keep the information from his men in order to minimize their panic. Others might think that the men have a right to know which danger lies in store for them in order to prepare for it better.

5. The phrase is used to describe situations in which there is no easy choice to be made—because both options are potentially disastrous. The same meaning is captured by the phrase "between a rock and a hard place."

Guide for Responding *(continued)*

◆ Reading Strategy

READ IN SENTENCES

Read the words of an epic **in complete sentences**, without worrying about line breaks.

1. Copy Odysseus' description of preparing to meet the Sirens on pp. 883–884 from the second part of line 704 through the first part of line 713 as a single paragraph. Read your paragraph aloud.
2. Rewrite the paragraph in your own words.

◆ Literary Focus

THE EPIC HERO

The **epic hero**—the central character of an epic—possesses qualities superior to those of most people yet remains recognizably human.

1. (a) How is Odysseus different from ordinary men? (b) How is he similar to ordinary men?
2. Do you admire Odysseus? Explain.

◆ Build Vocabulary

USING WORDS FROM MYTHS

The words that follow come from mythology. Use one word to complete each sentence.

a. museum **b.** odyssey **c.** *Titanic* **d.** siren

1. Because the enormous ocean liner was thought to be unsinkable, it was named the ___?___.
2. The treasures from ancient Troy were housed in a ___?___.
3. The archaeologist's study of ancient ruins took her on an ___?___ across Turkey and Greece.
4. Unlike its mythical namesake, a modern ___?___ makes an unpleasant warning sound.

USING THE WORD BANK

Match each word with its opposite.

1. dispatch   a. restore to its owner
2. bereft   b. finish slowly
3. plunder   c. joyfully acquiring
4. squall   d. tiny
5. mammoth   e. small and weak
6. assuage   f. calm, sunny weather
7. insidious   g. honest
8. titanic   h. aggravate
9. ardor   i. lack of interest

◆ Build Grammar Skills

RESTRICTIVE AND NONRESTRICTIVE APPOSITIVES

Appositives add information about the nouns and pronouns in a sentence. A **restrictive appositive** is essential to the meaning of the sentence and is not set off by commas. A **nonrestrictive appositive** or appositive phrase provides nonessential information and is set off with commas.

Practice In your notebook, identify the appositives in these phrases from the *Odyssey* and tell whether each is restrictive or nonrestrictive.

1. Of these adventures, Muse, daughter of Zeus, tell us in our time, lift the great song again.
2. Sweet cousin ram, why lag behind the rest in the night cave?
3. We Cyclopes care not a whistle for your thundering Zeus . . .
4. . . . grant that Odysseus, raider of cities, never see his home: Laertes' son, I mean, who kept his hall on Ithaca.
5. . . . a burning heat came down from Helios, lord of high noon.

Idea Bank

Writing

1. **Letter** Imagine that you are a sailor aboard Odysseus' ship. Write a letter home, telling your family about your adventures.

2. **Comparison-and-Contrast Essay** Write an essay in which you explore the concept of the hero. In your essay, compare and contrast Odysseus with other heroes, real or imaginary.

Speaking and Listening

3. **Play-by-Play Broadcast** Select an exciting, action-filled incident from Part 1 of the *Odyssey*. Using the text and your imagination, describe the action as it unfolds. When you have worked out all the details, perform your broadcast for an audience. **[Performing Arts Link; Career Link]**

Answers

◆ Reading Strategy

1. Students' paragraphs should follow the conventions of paragraph writing, including indentation and correct punctuation.
2. Students' rewritten paragraphs should retain the key elements of this passage: that Odysseus seals his men's ears so they cannot hear the Sirens, then has himself tied to the mast.

◆ Literary Focus

1. (a) He is both protected and punished by the gods; he is able to remain true to himself and his goals under impossible circumstances; he is exceptionally clever and daring. (b) He is more like ordinary men when he is homesick or curious, when he cannot resist boasting after besting the Cyclops, and when he is afraid during his encounter with the dead.
2. Some students will admire Odysseus' tenacity and courage. Others might find him too single-minded or compassionless to identify with.

◆ Build Vocabulary

Using Word Origins: Words From Myths
1. Titanic; 2. museum; 3. odyssey; 4. siren

Using the Word Bank
1. b   2. c   3. a   4. f   5. d   6. h
7. g   8. e   9. i

◆ Build Grammar Skills

1. daughter of Zeus—nonrestrictive
2. ram—restrictive
3. Cyclopes—restrictive
4. raider of cities—nonrestrictive
5. lord of high noon—nonrestrictive

 Writer's Solution

For additional instruction and practice, use the lesson on Commas in the **Language Lab CD-ROM** and the page on Commas That Set Off Added Elements in the *Writer's Solution Grammar Practice Book*, p. 101.

Idea Bank

Customizing for Performance Levels

Following are suggestions for matching the Idea Bank topics with your students' performance levels:

    Less Advanced Students: 1
    Average Students: 2
    More Advanced Students: 3

Customizing for *Learning Modalities*

Following are suggestions for matching Idea Bank topics with your students' learning modalities:
    Verbal/Linguistic: 1, 2, 3

✓ ASSESSMENT OPTIONS

Formal Assessment, pp. 205–207.
Alternative Assessment, p. 55.
PORTFOLIO ASSESSMENT
Use the following rubrics in the **Alternative Assessment** booklet:
Letter: Fictional Narrative Rubric, p. 88
Comparison-and-Contrast Essay: Comparison/Contrast Rubric, p. 96

OBJECTIVES

1. To read, comprehend, and interpret an epic
2. To relate an epic to personal experience
3. To summarize
4. To identify epic simile
5. To build vocabulary in context and learn the word root *-equi-*
6. To develop skill in using participial phrases
7. To write a letter home using sequence of events
8. To respond to the epic through writing, speaking and listening, and projects

SKILLS INSTRUCTION

Vocabulary:
Word Roots: *-equi-*

Grammar:
Participial Phrases

Reading Strategy:
Summarize

Literary Focus:
Epic Simile

Writing:
Sequence of Events

Speaking and Listening:
Debate (teacher edition)

PORTFOLIO OPPORTUNITIES

Writing: Epic Simile; Modern Heroic Poem; Literary Essay

Speaking and Listening: Debate; Oral Report

Projects: Odyssey Map; Board Game

Interest Grabber

Have students form teams to come up with various scenarios that might take place when Odysseus finally reaches his home. In developing their scenarios, groups should consider what might have happened in Ithaca during Odysseus' absence. Have groups present their scenarios to the class. Then have them read the second part of the *Odyssey* to see which group's scenario is closest to what actually happens in the epic.

Guide for Reading

◆ Review and Anticipate

In Part I of the *Odyssey*, Odysseus and his companions face many perils on their voyage from Troy to Ithaca, including the hypnotic Lotus, a man-eating Cyclops, the Sirens, and the monsters Scylla and Charybdis. Odysseus journeys to the Land of the Dead to consult the prophet Tiresias and learns of still more challenges to come. Although warned by the prophet to leave the cattle of the sun god Helios alone, Odysseus' men fail to heed this advice and are killed when a lightning bolt hurled by the god Zeus destroys their ship.

The events you will read about in Part 2 of the *Odyssey* take place in Ithaca, Odysseus' homeland and the goal of all his travels. Predict what you think will happen when Odysseus arrives home.

◆ Literary Focus

EPIC SIMILE

An **epic simile,** sometimes called a Homeric simile, is an elaborate comparison that may extend for a number of lines. Epic similes may use the words, *like* or *as, just as,* or *so* to make the comparison. In lines 268–271, Odysseus uses an epic simile to describe the fallen tree from which he will create the weapon to blind the Cyclops.

> And it was like a mast
> a lugger of twenty oars, broad in the beam—
> a deep-sea-going craft—might carry:
> so long, so big around, it seemed.

◆ Build Vocabulary

WORD ROOTS: *-equi-*

A disguised Odysseus, speaking to his wife Penelope, tells her that her good name is like the honor of a just king "who rules in equity." The word *equity* means "fairness" or "justice" and contains the word root *-equi-*, which means "same" or "equal." Thus, a king who rules in equity treats all his subjects the same.

dissemble
lithe
incredulity
bemusing
glowering
equity
maudlin
contempt

WORD BANK

Preview these words from the selection.

◆ Reading Strategy

SUMMARIZE

You can better understand what is going on in an epic like the *Odyssey*—or in any other work of literature with a complicated plot—if you first **summarize** the events. When you summarize, you retell the plot briefly in your own words. Ideally, your summary should tell not only what happened but why it happened. To assist you in summarizing Part 2 of the *Odyssey*, you may find it helpful to jot down some notes about important events and their causes as you read.

◆ Build Grammar Skills

PARTICIPIAL PHRASES

A participle is a verb form that is used as an adjective to modify a noun or pronoun. A **participial phrase** is a phrase that consists of a participle and the words that work with it. The entire participial phrase then serves as an adjective to modify a noun or pronoun. Here are some examples of participial phrases from the *Odyssey*.

> past participle
> This was an army *trained to fight on horseback* ...

> present participle
> So, *breathing hard*, we waited until morning.

894 ◆ *The Epic*

Prentice Hall Literature Program Resources

REINFORCE / RETEACH / EXTEND

Selection Support Pages
Build Vocabulary: Word Roots: *-equi-*, p. 237
Build Grammar Skills: Participial Phrases, p. 238
Reading Strategy: Summarize, p. 239
Literary Focus: Epic Simile, p. 240

Strategies for Diverse Student Needs, p. 58

Beyond Literature
Humanities Connection: Greek Gods, p. 58

Formal Assessment Selection Test, pp. 208–210, Assessment Resources Software

Alternative Assessment, p. 56

Writing and Language Transparencies
Personal Narrative, pp. 21–27

Resource Pro CD-ROM
The *Odyssey*—includes all resource material and customizable lesson plan

🎧 **Listening to Literature Audiocassettes**
The *Odyssey*

The Odyssey

Homer

Translated by Robert Fitzgerald

Part 2
The Return of Odysseus

"Twenty years gone, and I am back again"

Odysseus has finished telling his story to the Phaeacians. The next day, young Phaeacian noblemen conduct him home by ship. He arrives in Ithaca after an absence of twenty years. The goddess Athena appears and informs him of the situation at home. Numerous suitors, believing Odysseus to be dead, have been continually seeking the hand of his wife, Penelope, in marriage, while overrunning Odysseus' palace and enjoying themselves at Penelope's expense. Moreover, they are plotting to murder Odysseus' son, Telemachus, before he can inherit his father's lands. Telemachus, who, like Penelope, still hopes for his father's return, has journeyed to Pylos and Sparta to learn what he can about his father's fate. Athena disguises Odysseus as a beggar and directs him to the hut of Eumaeus,[1] his old and faithful swineherd. While Odysseus and Eumaeus are eating breakfast, Telemachus arrives. Athena then appears to Odysseus.

1. **Eumaeus** (yōō mē´ əs)

    . . . . From the air
she walked, taking the form of a tall woman,
handsome and clever at her craft, and stood
1000 beyond the gate in plain sight of Odysseus,
unseen, though, by Telemachus, unguessed,
for not to everyone will gods appear.

The Odyssey, Part 2, The Return of Odysseus ◆ 895

Develop Understanding

One-Minute Insight

With its heroes, monsters, magic, and suspense, the *Odyssey* has always appealed strongly to readers' imaginations. Another reason for its enduring popularity is its "time machine" quality; reading it is like looking through a window at a world that is very different from ours. Despite this, the *Odyssey* is timeless. As a quest narrative, it conveys a universal lesson about determination and overcoming obstacles. In addition, readers will find important similarities to themselves and their time. Odysseus, Penelope, Telemachus—even the dog, Argus—have concerns and feelings that today's readers can understand and share.

Customize for
More Advanced Students

Remind these students that Homer's *Odyssey* was written in verse, as is Fitzgerald's translation. Whereas the translation is quite irregular in rhythm, the original was written in *dactylic hexameter*—lines of six feet or "beats," usually of three syllables each, with the stress on the first syllable. Challenge students to rewrite one or two lines in this rhythm to get an idea of how Homer's version sounded when read aloud. Example: "She set up/weaving and wove ev'ry /day but at/night she would/unweave it." Students might also look for examples of rhyme; for example, "For Zeus who views the wide world takes away/half the manhood of a man, that day/he goes into captivity and slavery," or "These men have bread to throw away on you/because it is not theirs. Who cares? Who spares/. . ."

Customize for
Less Proficient Readers

Have these students work with partners to paraphrase the difficult opening passage. *The goddess Athena, looking like a beautiful, intelligent woman, appeared to Odysseus, though she remained invisible to Telemachus, for gods appear only to certain special people. The dogs saw her, and were frightened. She nodded to Odysseus, and he crossed the yard and passed through the gate to face the goddess.*

Preparing for Standardized Tests

Reading The ability to summarize is one of the key skills tested in critical reading sections of standardized tests. Once students have completed the Reading Strategy section that follows this selection (p. 917), have them apply this skill to a standardized test format by completing the following class activity. Have students bring in newspaper articles. Have them work in groups to create brief (two- or three-sentence) summaries of

each article. In addition to creating an accurate summary for each article, students should create three additional summaries for each article that are incomplete or only partially accurate. Have the groups turn in the articles, along with the summaries they developed. Use these materials to create a multiple-choice practice test focusing on the skill of summarizing.

◆ Critical Thinking

❶ Analyze Ask students how they would describe Odysseus' reaction to seeing his son after all these years. What do they think is the reason for this reaction? *Odysseus is very calm and unemotional at this point. Students may say he acts that way because he knows how important it is for Telemachus to believe in him. He will need his son's loyal support in the battle to come.*

◆ Critical Thinking

❷ Make Inferences Ask students why Athena uses this charm on Odysseus. Does she wish to glorify him or "bring him low"? You might connect this part of the *Odyssey* to Part I by asking students to recall which god would like to bring him low. *Athena is on Odysseus' side. She wishes to glorify him. Poseidon, god of the sea, is not on Odysseus' side, because Odysseus blinded his son, Polyphemus the Cyclops.*

◆ Literary Focus

❸ Epic Simile Elicit the following response: *The crying of the reunited father and son is compared to the cries of a hawk whose babies have been taken from its nest.*

◆ Build Grammar Skills

❹ Participial Phrases Ask students to identify the participial phrase that modifies *I* in this passage. Have them identify the past participle. *The participial phrase is "directed by Athena." The past participle is directed.*

---

❶
1050

"This is not princely, to be swept
away by wonder at your father's presence.
No other Odysseus will ever come,
for he and I are one, the same; his bitter
fortune and his wanderings are mine.
Twenty years gone, and I am back again
on my own island.

                          As for my change of skin,

❷ 1055

that is a charm Athena, Hope of Soldiers,
uses as she will; she has the knack
to make me seem a beggar man sometimes
and sometimes young, with finer clothes about me.
It is no hard thing for the gods of heaven
to glorify a man or bring him low."

When he had spoken, down he sat.

                                   Then, throwing

1060

his arms around this marvel of a father
Telemachus began to weep. Salt tears
rose from the wells of longing in both men,
and cries burst from both as keen and fluttering

1065

as those of the great taloned hawk,
whose nestlings farmers take before they fly.
So helplessly they cried, pouring out tears,
and might have gone on weeping so till sundown,
had not Telemachus said:

                                   "Dear father! Tell me

what kind of vessel put you here ashore

1070

on Ithaca? Your sailors, who were they?
I doubt you made it, walking on the sea!"

Then said Odysseus, who had borne the barren sea:

"Only plain truth shall I tell you, child.
Great seafarers, the Phaeacians, gave me passage

1075

as they give other wanderers. By night
over the open ocean, while I slept,
they brought me in their cutter,³ set me down
on Ithaca, with gifts of bronze and gold
and stores of woven things. By the gods' will

1080

these lie all hidden in a cave. I came

❹

to this wild place, directed by Athena,
so that we might lay plans to kill our enemies.
Count up the suitors for me, let me know
what men at arms are there, how many men.

◆ Literary Focus
What is being compared in the epic simile in lines 1063–1065? **❸**

3. cutter (kut′ər) *n.*: Small, swift ship or boat.

898 ◆ The Epic

◆ **Critical Thinking**

❺ **Compare and Contrast** Ask
students what this passage shows
about Odysseus' confidence in the
gods, compared with that of
Telemachus. *Odysseus feels that, with
Athena and Zeus as allies, he can overcome any odds. Telemachus, to whom no
gods have appeared, is not as sure of
the gods' loyalty to any mortal.*

1085   I must put all my mind to it, to see
     if we two by ourselves can take them on
     or if we should look round for help."

Telemachus

replied:

"O Father, all my life your fame

     as a fighting man has echoed in my ears—
1090   your skill with weapons and the tricks of war—
     but what you speak of is a staggering thing,
     beyond imagining, for me. How can two men
     do battle with a houseful in their prime?[4]
     For I must tell you this is no affair
1095   of ten or even twice ten men, but scores,
     throngs of them. You shall see, here and now.
     The number from Dulichium alone
     is fifty-two, picked men, with armorers,
     a half dozen: twenty-four came from Same,
1100   twenty from Zacynthus; our own island
     accounts for twelve, high-ranked, and their retainers,
     Medon the crier, and the Master Harper,
     besides a pair of handymen at feasts.
     If we go in against all these
1105   I fear we pay in salt blood for your vengeance.
     You must think hard if you would conjure up
     the fighting strength to take us through."

Odysseus

who had endured the long war and the sea answered:

"I'll tell you now.

1110   Suppose Athena's arm is over us, and Zeus
     her father's, must I rack my brains for more?"

❺   Clearheaded Telemachus looked hard and said:

     "Those two are great defenders, no one doubts it,
     but throned in the serene clouds overhead;
1115   other affairs of men and gods they have
     to rule over."

And the hero answered:

     "Before long they will stand to right and left of us
     in combat, in the shouting, when the test comes—
     our nerve against the suitors' in my hall.
1120   Here is your part: at break of day tomorrow

4. in their prime: In the
best or most vigorous stage
of their lives.

The Odyssey, Part 2, The Return of Odysseus ◆ 899

 Speaking and Listening Mini-Lesson

Oral Report

This mini-lesson supports the second
Speaking and Listening activity in the Idea
Bank on page 918.

Introduce the Concept Tell students that
they will be preparing an oral report on the
Trojan War. Review with the class how to do
research on the Internet and library computer catalog.

Develop Background Remind students
that another of Homer's epics, the *Iliad*, tells

the story of the Trojan War. They can read
that epic or find summaries of it in a good
encyclopedia. Other sources and the
Internet will shed more light on what are
believed to be the historical facts about the
war.

Apply Information Have students prepare and present their oral reports. After
each student gives his or her report, allow
time for questions.

Assess the Outcome Students can evaluate their classmates' oral reports based
upon the following criteria:
1. Organization: Was the content presented
   in a logical order, such as chronological
   order or order of importance?
2. Content: Were there sufficient facts for
   an understanding of the war?
3. Presentation: Did the presenter speak
   clearly and at an appropriate pace?

◆ Critical Thinking

❶ Speculate Ask students to speculate about how Odysseus knows what Athena will do. *Students may speculate that Athena has instructed Odysseus what to do, or has told him her plans.*

◆ Reading Strategy

❷ Summarize Elicit summaries that cover the following events: *Telemachus does not recognize his father, who is disguised as an old beggar. Athena appears to Odysseus, tells him to reveal his identity to his son, and transforms him into a nobleman in the prime of life. Telemachus is frightened and suspicious, but is finally persuaded, and the father and son have an emotional reunion. Odysseus explains that, with the help of Telemachus and the gods Zeus and Athena, he plans to kill all the suitors in his palace.*

◆ Critical Thinking

❸ Make Inferences Ask students what Odysseus' attitude is toward his wife at this point. How do they react to the words "you and I alone must learn how far/the women are corrupted"? *Students may say that Odysseus is not sure he can trust Penelope, or that he fears she and her servants may have been won over by one or more of the suitors. Some students may think that Odysseus has an unfair mistrust of women.*

home with you, go mingle with our princes.
The swineherd later on will take me down
the port-side trail—a beggar, by my looks,
hangdog and old. If they make fun of me
1125 in my own courtyard, let your ribs cage up
your springing heart, no matter what I suffer,
no matter if they pull me by the heels
or practice shots at me, to drive me out.
Look on, hold down your anger. You may even
1130 plead with them, by heaven! in gentle terms
to quit their horseplay—not that they will heed you,
rash as they are, facing their day of wrath.
Now fix the next step in your mind.

                    Athena,

❶ counseling me, will give me word, and I
1135 shall signal to you, nodding: at that point
round up all armor, lances, gear of war
left in our hall, and stow the lot away
back in the vaulted storeroom. When the suitors
miss those arms and question you, be soft
1140 in what you say: answer:

                         'I thought I'd move them
out of the smoke. They seemed no longer those
bright arms Odysseus left us years ago
when he went off to Troy. Here where the fire's
hot breath came, they had grown black and drear.
1145 One better reason, too, I had from Zeus:
suppose a brawl starts up when you are drunk,
you might be crazed and bloody one another,
and that would stain your feast, your courtship.
  Tempered
iron can magnetize a man.'

                         Say that
1150 But put aside two broadswords and two spears
for our own use, two oxhide shields nearby
when we go into action. Pallas Athena
and Zeus All-Provident will see you through,
<u>bemusing</u> our young friends.

                     Now one thing more.
1155 If son of mine you are and blood of mine,
let no one hear Odysseus is about.
Neither Laertes, nor the swineherd here,
nor any slave, nor even Penelope.
❸ But you and I alone must learn how far
1160 the women are corrupted; we should know

900 ◆ *The Epic*

◆ **Reading Strategy**
Summarize the events of Odysseus' reunion with Telemachus.

Workplace Skills Mini-Lesson

Seeing a Project Through to the End

Introduce the Concept Point out that Odysseus takes ten years to reach home after the war and faces many hardships, but never loses sight of his goal—to reach Ithaca. While Odysseus may be a fictional character, his persistence is a real and valuable quality.

Develop Background Ask students to cite instances in which persistence, or the ability to see a project through to the end, would be a useful quality in an after-school or summer job. Students might mention that just getting the job may require persistence.

Apply Information Divide the class into groups and have them exchange ideas on how to develop the ability to overcome obstacles in reaching goals. Possible ideas include keeping a real or fictional role model in mind, or visualizing a successful outcome to their struggle.

Assess the Outcome Suggest that students keep notes on whether they have been able to employ the ideas suggested by the groups to help them see things through more effectively. Students can evaluate their persistence by listing projects (getting a summer job, homework, and other pursuits) that because of their persistence they have either completed or are in the process of completing.

3 how to locate good men among our hands,
the loyal and respectful, and the shirkers[5]
who take you lightly, as alone and young."

Argus

*Odysseus heads for town with Eumaeus. Outside the
palace, Odysseus' old dog, Argus, is lying at rest as his
long-absent master approaches.*

                                        While he spoke
      an old hound, lying near, pricked up his ears
1165 and lifted up his muzzle. This was Argus,
      trained as a puppy by Odysseus,
      but never taken on a hunt before
      his master sailed for Troy. The young men, afterward,
      hunted wild goats with him, and hare, and deer,
1170 but he had grown old in his master's absence.
      Treated as rubbish now, he lay at last
      upon a mass of dung before the gates—
      manure of mules and cows, piled there until
      fieldhands could spread it on the king's estate.
1175 Abandoned there, and half destroyed with flies,
4 old Argus lay.

                        But when he knew he heard
      Odysseus' voice nearby, he did his best
5 to wag his tail, nose down, with flattened ears,
      having no strength to move nearer his master.
1180 And the man looked away,
      wiping a salt tear from his cheek; but he
      hid this from Eumaeus. Then he said:

      "I marvel that they leave this hound to lie
      here on the dung pile;
1185 he would have been a fine dog, from the look of him,
      though I can't say as to his power and speed
      when he was young. You find the same good build
      in house dogs, table dogs landowners keep
      all for style."

                        And you replied, Eumaeus:
1190 "A hunter owned him—but the man is dead
      in some far place. If this old hound could show
      the form he had when Lord Odysseus left him,
      going to Troy, you'd see him swift and strong.

---

5. shirkers (shurk´ ərz)
n.: People who get out of
doing or leave undone
something that needs to be
done.

♦ **Build Vocabulary**

bemusing (bi myo͞o´ ziŋ)
v.: Stupefying or muddling

The Odyssey, Part 2, Argus ♦ 901

---

4 Clarification Tell students that
in Greek mythology Argus was a
creature who had one hundred eyes.
Why is "Argus" a good name for a
watchdog? *A dog with one hundred
eyes would make an excellent watchdog.*

◆ *Literature and Your Life*

5 Ask students who have dogs
whether they think this scene is realistic. Would their pets behave like
Argus under similar circumstances?
*Most students will agree that most dogs
are loyal to their owners, and in this
respect, the scene is realistic.*

 Cultural Connection

Begin an examination of cultural
attitudes toward dogs by asking students what other famous dogs they
can think of. Responses might
include Lassie, Rin Tin Tin, Benji, and
White Fang. Ask students why they
think dogs are often called "man's
best friend" and discuss their ideas.
Point out that the bond between
dogs and people may go back as far
as 25,000 years, as evidenced by
Paleolithic cave drawings of dogs.
     Have students find out more
about how dogs are viewed in different cultures. Since the dog has
been portrayed in art from the
Stone Age through all phases of
Eastern and Western art, assign
some students to find and bring in a
variety of pictures of dogs in art and
photography books. Assign other
students to research the roles dogs
have played in diverse societies, such
as the hunting dog, farm dog, lap
dog, sled dog, and even, in ancient
Egypt, Dog God. Assign other students to do a multicultural literature
search to find written portrayals of
dogs. Have students share their findings with the class.

◆ *Literature and Your Life*

1 Students may say that a person might not recognize a loved one after so many years of separation. Telemachus, for example, was not as sure of Odysseus' identity as was Argus.

◆ **Critical Thinking**

2 **Analyze** Ask students how Antinous' words must have made Odysseus feel. What would Odysseus want to do at this moment? Why are his actions described as being guileful? *Odysseus would want to hit or kill Antinous, but he has too much guile. Instead, he restrains his emotions until the time is right to reveal his identity.*

He never shrank from any savage thing
1195 he'd brought to bay in the deep woods; on the scent
no other dog kept up with him. Now misery
has him in leash. His owner died abroad,
and here the women slaves will take no care of him.
You know how servants are: without a master
1200 they have no will to labor, or excel.
For Zeus who views the wide world takes away
half the manhood of a man, that day
he goes into captivity and slavery."

Eumaeus crossed the court and went straight forward
1205 into the megaron[6] among the suitors:
but death and darkness in that instant closed
the eyes of Argus, who had seen his master,
Odysseus, after twenty years.

The Suitors

*Still disguised as a beggar, Odysseus enters his home.
He is confronted by the haughty[7] suitor Antinous.[8]*

But here Antinous broke in, shouting:

> "God!

1210 What evil wind blew in this pest?
> Get over,
> stand in the passage! Nudge my table, will you?
> Egyptian whips are sweet
> to what you'll come to here, you nosing rat,
> making your pitch to everyone!
1215 These men have bread to throw away on you
> because it is not theirs. Who cares? Who spares
> another's food, when he has more than plenty?"

With guile Odysseus drew away, then said:
"A pity that you have more looks than heart.
1220 You'd grudge a pinch of salt from your own larder
to your own handyman. You sit here, fat
on others' meats and cannot bring yourself
to rummage out a crust of bread for me!"

Then anger made Antinous' heart beat hard,
1225 and, glowering under his brows, he answered:

◆ *Literature and Your Life*

1 Pet owners will sometimes contend that animals are more perceptive than people. How does the story of Argus support this contention?

6. megaron (meg ə´ rön) *n.*: Great, central hall of the house, usually containing a center hearth.

7. haughty (hôt´ ē) *adj.*: Arrogant.
8. Antinous (an tin´ ō əs)

◆ **Build Vocabulary**

glowering (glou´ ər iŋ) *v.*: Staring with sullen anger; scowling

"Now!
You think you'll shuffle off and get away
after that impudence?[9] Oh, no you don't!"

1230 The stool he let fly hit the man's right shoulder
on the packed muscle under the shoulder blade—
like solid rock, for all the effect one saw.
❸ Odysseus only shook his head, containing
thoughts of bloody work, as he walked on,
then sat, and dropped his loaded bag again
upon the door sill. Facing the whole crowd
1235 he said, and eyed them all:

"One word only,
my lords, and suitors of the famous queen.
One thing I have to say.
There is no pain, no burden for the heart
when blows come to a man, and he defending
❹ 1240 his own cattle—his own cows and lambs.
Here it was otherwise. Antinous
hit me for being driven on by hunger—
how many bitter seas men cross for hunger!
If beggars interest the gods, if there are Furies[10]
1245 pent in the dark to avenge a poor man's wrong, then may
Antinous meet his death before his wedding day!"

Then said Eupeithes' son, Antinous:

"Enough.
Eat and be quiet where you are, or shamble elsewhere,
unless you want these lads to stop your mouth
1250 pulling you by the heels, or hands and feet,
over the whole floor, till your back is peeled!"

But now the rest were mortified, and someone
spoke from the crowd of young bucks to rebuke him:
"A poor show, that—hitting this famished tramp—
❺ 1255 bad business, if he happened to be a god.
You know they go in foreign guise, the gods do,
looking like strangers, turning up
in towns and settlements to keep an eye
on manners, good or bad."

But at this notion
1260 Antinous only shrugged.

9. impudence (im´ pyōō dəns) *n.*: Quality of being shamelessly bold; disrespectful.

10. Furies (fyōōr´ ēz): Three terrible spirits who punish those whose crimes have not been avenged.

The Odyssey, Part 2, The Suitors ◆ 903

 Cross-Curricular Connection: Social Studies

At the time of the Trojan War—the twelfth or thirteenth century B.C.—written language had not yet been introduced in Greece. Stories about the war were told from one generation to the next, handed down through an *oral tradition.* Over the years, bards, or poets who composed and sang their work, composed poems about the events of the Trojan War. The story, naturally, was told somewhat differently by each bard.

During Homer's life, the Greeks did have an alphabet and a written language. Homer, however, is thought to have been an illiterate bard, though one of exceptional talent. According to this theory, Homer sang the stories of the *Iliad* and the *Odyssey* on many occasions. At the end of his life, he dictated the poems to someone who knew how to write.

After Homer's time, the Greek people came to know Homer's poems by hearing

them recited or by reading handwritten copies of them. The *Iliad* and the *Odyssey* were recited as part of great religious festivals. Copies of the poems became the textbooks that Greek children used to learn to read.

❶ Compare and Contrast Ask students to compare and contrast Penelope's feelings about the suitors to Eurynome's. Which one judges them more harshly? *Eurynome says she would like to see all the suitors killed. Penelope, her "gentle mistress," agrees that they are all bad, but judges the others less harshly than she judges Antinous.*

Telemachus,
after the blow his father bore, sat still
without a tear, though his heart felt the blow.
Slowly he shook his head from side to side,
containing murderous thoughts.

Penelope
1265   on the higher level of her room had heard
the blow, and knew who gave it. Now she murmured:

"Would god you could be hit yourself, Antinous—
hit by Apollo's bowshot!"

And Eurynome,[11]
her housekeeper, put in:

11. **Eurynome:** (yoo rin′ əm ē)

"He and no other?
1270   If all we pray for came to pass, not one
would live till dawn!"

❶

Her gentle mistress said:

"Oh, Nan, they are a bad lot; they intend
ruin for all of us; but Antinous
appears a blacker-hearted hound than any.
1275   Here is a poor man come, a wanderer,
driven by want to beg his bread, and everyone
in hall gave bits, to cram his bag—only
Antinous threw a stool, and banged his shoulder!"

So she described it, sitting in her chamber
1280   among her maids—while her true lord was eating.
Then she called in the forester and said:

"Go to that man on my behalf, Eumaeus,
and send him here, so I can greet and question him.
Abroad in the great world, he may have heard
1285   rumors about Odysseus—may have known him!"

Penelope

In the evening. Penelope questions the old beggar about himself.

"Friend, let me ask you first of all:
who are you, where do you come from, of what nation

and parents were you born?"

And he replied:
"My lady, never a man in the wide world

2 1290   should have a fault to find with you. Your name
has gone out under heaven like the sweet
honor of some god-fearing king, who rules
in equity over the strong: his black lands bear
both wheat and barley, fruit trees laden bright,
1295   new lambs at lambing time—and the deep sea
gives great hauls of fish by his good strategy,
so that his folk fare well.

O my dear lady,
this being so, let it suffice to ask me
of other matters—not my blood, my homeland.
1300   Do not enforce me to recall my pain.
4   My heart is sore; but I must not be found
sitting in tears here, in another's house:
it is not well forever to be grieving.
One of the maids might say—or you might think—
1305   I had got maudlin over cups of wine."

And Penelope replied:

"Stranger, my looks,
my face, my carriage,[12] were soon lost or faded
when the Achaeans crossed the sea to Troy,
Odysseus my lord among the rest.
1310   If he returned, if he were here to care for me,
I might be happily renowned!
But grief instead heaven sent me—years of pain.
Sons of the noblest families on the islands,
Dulichium, Same, wooded Zacynthus,[13]
1315   with native Ithacans, are here to court me,
against my wish; and they consume this house.
Can I give proper heed to guest or suppliant
or herald on the realm's affairs?

How could I?
wasted with longing for Odysseus, while here
1320   they press for marriage.

Ruses[14] served my turn
to draw the time out—first a close-grained web
I had the happy thought to set up weaving
on my big loom in hall. I said, that day:
'Young men—my suitors, now my lord is dead,

◆ **Literary Focus**
Identify the epic simile in Odysseus' response to Penelope's question.   **3**

---

12. carriage (kar´ ij) *n.*: Posture.

13. Zacynthus (za sin´ thus)

14. Ruses (rō̄o̅z´ əz) *n.*: Tricks.

◆ **Build Vocabulary**
equity (ek´ wit ē) *n.*: Fairness; impartiality; justice
maudlin (môd´ lin) *adj.*: Tearfully or foolishly sentimental

The Odyssey, Part 2, Penelope ◆ 905

---

2 **Clarification** In complimenting Penelope, his hostess, Odysseus not only speaks from his heart but also abides by the Greek laws of hospitality.

◆ **Literary Focus**
3 **Epic Simile** The epic simile is found in lines 1290–1297. Ask students to paraphrase the simile, then identify the two ideas being compared. *Paraphrase: "Your name is as honored as that of a good, just, and wise king who sees to it that his lands prosper so that his subjects will be well-off." The two ideas being compared are Penelope's name or reputation and the name or reputation of a good and wise king.*

Comprehension Check ☑
4 Ask students what excuse Odysseus gives for not revealing his background. *Odysseus claims that thinking of his home and family makes him sad enough to cry. He does not want to show his grief and thus be thought of as being excessively sentimental or suspected of being drunk.*

 Cultural Connection

Point out that the idea underlying Penelope's web—a work that is always in progress but never finished—occurs, with variations, in the stories, fables, and folk tales of many cultures. Ask students if they know of any, and discuss their ideas. Responses might include the Greek myth of Sisyphus, a greedy king who is doomed forever to roll uphill a huge boulder that always rolls back down; or one of Grimm's fairy tales, "Rumpelstiltskin," in which the king's bride, who

has to spin flax endlessly, makes a bargain with Rumpelstiltskin. Discuss how the tasks in the stories differ from culture to culture.

Ask students to search the literature and folk tales of other cultures to find more stories with this theme. Suggest that students choose from among Native American, African American, Asian, Scandinavian, Latin American, European, Arab, and Jewish folk tales. Have them share the stories they find with the class.

◆ **Reading Strategy**

❶ **Summarize** Summaries should include the following: *Penelope's fame has not given her pleasure, but grief. It has drawn an army of unwanted suitors, who live off her wealth and demand that she choose one for a husband. She had held them off by saying that she first had to weave a burial shroud for her father-in-law, but then, at night, undoing all the work she had completed each day. Now, however, they have found out her trick and she cannot see how to hold them off any longer. In addition, her parents are urging her to remarry, and Telemachus is angry at having to host the suitors and wants to fight them.*

1325   let me finish my weaving before I marry,
       or else my thread will have been spun in vain.
       It is a shroud I weave for Lord Laertes
       when cold Death comes to lay him on his bier.
       The country wives would hold me in dishonor

1330   if he, with all his fortune, lay unshrouded.'
       I reached their hearts that way, and they agreed.
       So every day I wove on the great loom,
       but every night by torchlight I unwove it;
       and so for three years I deceived the Achaeans.

1335   But when the seasons brought a fourth year on,
       as long months waned, and the long days were spent,
       through impudent folly in the slinking maids
       they caught me—clamored up to me at night;
       I had no choice then but to finish it.

1340   And now, as matters stand at last,
       I have no strength left to evade a marriage,
       cannot find any further way; my parents
       urge it upon me, and my son
       will not stand by while they eat up his property.

1345   He comprehends it, being a man full-grown,
       able to oversee the kind of house
       Zeus would endow with honor.

                                 But you too

       confide in me, tell me your ancestry.
       You were not born of mythic oak or stone."

Penelope again asks the beggar to tell about himself. He makes up a tale in which Odysseus is mentioned and declares that Penelope's husband will soon be home.

1350   "You see, then, he is alive and well, and headed
       homeward now, no more to be abroad
       far from his island, his dear wife and son.
       Here is my sworn word for it. Witness this,
       god of the zenith, noblest of the gods,[15]

1355   and Lord Odysseus' hearthfire, now before me:
       I swear these things shall turn out as I say.
       Between this present dark and one day's ebb,
       after the wane, before the crescent moon,
       Odysseus will come."

◆ **Reading Strategy**
Summarize what Penelope tells the disguised Odysseus. How has she demonstrated her loyalty to her husband?

15. **god of the zenith, noblest of the gods:** Zeus.

The Challenge

Pressed by the suitors to choose a husband from among them, Penelope says she will marry whoever can string Odysseus' bow and shoot an arrow through twelve axhandle sockets. The suitors try and fail. Still in disguise, Odysseus asks for a turn and gets it.

1360	. . . And Odysseus took his time,
	turning the bow, tapping it, every inch,
	for borings that termites might have made
	while the master of the weapon was abroad.
	The suitors were now watching him, and some
	jested among themselves:

"A bow lover!"

1365 "Dealer in old bows!"

"Maybe he has one like it
at home!"

"Or has an itch to make one for himself."

❷ "See how he handles it, the sly old buzzard!"

And one disdainful suitor added this:

"May his fortune grow an inch for every inch he
  bends it!"

1370	But the man skilled in all ways of contending,
	satisfied by the great bow's look and heft,
	like a musician, like a harper, when
	with quiet hand upon his instrument
	he draws between his thumb and forefinger
1375	a sweet new string upon a peg: so effortlessly
	Odysseus in one motion strung the bow.
	Then slid his right hand down the cord and plucked it,
	so the taut gut vibrating hummed and sang
	a swallow's note.

In the hushed hall it smote the suitors
1380 and all their faces changed. Then Zeus thundered
❸ overhead, one loud crack for a sign.
❹ And Odysseus laughed within him that the son
of crooked-minded Cronus had flung that omen down.

The Odyssey, Part 2, The Challenge ◆ 907

◆ **Critical Thinking**

❷ **Compare and Contrast** Have students describe how Odysseus' behavior differs from that of the suitors. *The suitors' crude, noisy, scornful remarks serve to highlight Odysseus' quiet dignity, skill, patience, and strength.*

◆ **Critical Thinking**

❸ **Infer** Ask students why they think Zeus sends the thunderbolt. *Students might say that Zeus is letting Odysseus know that he is watching and ready to help, and that the time for action is here. They might also think that Zeus wants to cast fear into the hearts of the suitors.*

◆ **Background for Understanding**

❹ Explain that in Greek mythology Zeus' father is the Titan Cronus. Cronus swallowed his first five children to keep them from attacking him. But Cronus' wife, Rhea, hid their sixth child, Zeus, until he grew up. Zeus made his father spit up the other children, and they overthrew Cronus. Zeus then became king of the gods.

❶ Interpret Students may suggest that the tension of the moment is captured in the stretched bowstring, bent bow, and the way all the people are focusing on the targets set up in the courtyard. Additional suspense comes from the point in time the picture shows; the arrow has not been released, and the viewer, like the people in the painting, is wondering and worrying about what happens next.

The Trial of the Bow, N. C. Wyeth, Delaware Art Museum

❶ ▲ **Critical Viewing** The winner of the archery contest will win Penelope's hand in marriage. How does the artist capture the tension in this scene? [Interpret]

908 ◆ *The Epic*

Humanities: Art

The Trial of the Bow, 1929, by N. C. Wyeth.

Penelope promises that she will marry the man who can string Odysseus' bow and shoot an arrow through twelve ax handle sockets. In this painting, Odysseus, disguised as a beggar, has succeeded in the first part of this challenge, and is about to complete the second part.

N. C. Wyeth (1882–1945) was one of the most prolific artists of the century. As well as painting many murals and canvases, he also illustrated over 200 books. Wyeth is also regarded as the first in a dynasty of American painters. His son Andrew (1917–   ), creator of the famous painting *Christina's World,* became one of America's most successful painters. Andrew's son Jamie became the third generation of Wyeths to win acclaim as a painter.

Use these questions for discussion:
1. Why do you think Wyeth chose this particular moment in the story to illustrate? *This is an especially dramatic moment because Odysseus is about to win the contest, reveal his true identity to the suitors, and then take his revenge.*

2. Why didn't the artist illustrate the scene a few moments later, when the arrow goes through the ax handles? *At that point, Odysseus would no longer be focusing on the target, but would be giving instructions to Telemachus. This moment shows Odysseus at his best—muscles flexed and all his attention fixed on his target.*

He picked one ready arrow from his table
1385 where it lay bare: the rest were waiting still
in the quiver for the young men's turn to come.
He nocked[16] it, let it rest across the handgrip,
and drew the string and grooved butt of the arrow,
aiming from where he sat upon the stool.
                              Now flashed
1390 arrow from twanging bow clean as a whistle
through every socket ring, and grazed not one,
to thud with heavy brazen head beyond.
                              Then quietly
Odysseus said:

                    "Telemachus, the stranger
you welcomed in your hall has not disgraced you.
1395 I did not miss, neither did I take all day
stringing the bow. My hand and eye are sound,
not so contemptible as the young men say.
The hour has come to cook their lordships' mutton—
supper by daylight. Other amusements later,
1400 with song and harping that adorn a feast."

He dropped his eyes and nodded, and the prince
Telemachus, true son of King Odysseus,
belted his sword on, clapped hand to his spear,
and with a clink and glitter of keen bronze
1405 stood by his chair, in the forefront near his father.

16. nocked: Set an arrow
against the bowstring.

Guide for Responding

◆ Literature and Your Life

Reader's Response How would you react if
you were in Telemachus' or Penelope's place?
Thematic Focus How should Odysseus work to
solve the problems caused by his long absence?

☑ Check Your Comprehension

1. How do Odysseus and Telemachus plan to handle Penelope's unwanted suitors?
2. What is Argus? What was he like in his youth?
3. Describe Antinous' treatment of Odysseus.
4. Describe the trick Penelope used to delay
choosing a husband from among the suitors.

◆ Critical Thinking

INTERPRET
1. Compare Odysseus' emotions with Telemachus'
when they are reunited. **[Compare and Contrast]**
2. Is Argus' death just when Odysseus returns a coincidence? Explain. **[Analyze]**
3. What impression of Penelope do you get from
her conversation with the disguised Odysseus?
[Interpret]
APPLY
4. Why do you think Odysseus chooses not to reveal his identity to his wife? **[Speculate]**

The Odyssey, Part 2, The Challenge ◆ 909

◆ Critical Thinking

② **Predict** Ask students how much
longer it will be before Odysseus
reveals his true identity, now that he
has won the contest. What do they
think will happen next? *Odysseus has
probably already revealed his identity by
winning the contest. It will soon be time
to begin the battle against the suitors.*

Answers
◆ Literature and Your Life

Reader's Response Students may
respond that if they were Telemachus
they would be more suspicious and
that if they were Penelope they might
think immediately that the stranger
was Odysseus.

Thematic Focus Students may
respond that Odysseus should be
less guileful in solving his problems.

☑ Check Your Comprehension

1. They plan to keep Odysseus' identity a secret for the time being,
hide the arms and armor that usually decorated the great hall, and
put aside weapons for themselves.
In time, they will battle the suitors.
2. Argus is Odysseus' faithful hunting
dog. In his youth he was swift,
strong, and afraid of nothing.
3. Antinous treats Odysseus, disguised as a beggar, with cruelty
and scorn.
4. Saying that before she married
again she had to weave a shroud
for Lord Laertes, she would undo
at night the weaving she did by
day.

◆ Critical Thinking

1. Telemachus and Odysseus
are equally moved when
they are reunited.
2. It is not a coincidence.
Some students may say that
the dog is so loyal that he
had to keep watch and not
permit himself to die until
his master came home.
Others may say that Argus'
condition symbolizes the

ruin that has come to
Odysseus' home, and the
dog's death is a symbol of
the end of bad times.
3. Students may say that
Penelope is clever and very
much in love with her husband.
4. Odysseus might not be
sure of his wife's feelings at
this point.

909

Background for Understanding

1 Among his other attributes, Apollo is also the god of archery.

Reading Strategy

2 **Summarize** Student responses should indicate the following: *First, Antinous speaks rudely to Odysseus, then hits him with a stool. Other suitors rebuke Antinous, but do not help the supposed beggar. During "The Challenge," the suitors mock Odysseus. When Odysseus shoots Antinous, the other suitors are appalled and frightened. They look for weapons, but find none, since Telemachus has removed them from the hall.*

Critical Thinking

3 **Interpret** Ask students how Odysseus sees the suitors—as individuals or as an undifferentiated group. *Odysseus sees the suitors as a unit. He calls them "You yellow dogs ...," and he has not questioned any of them about their motives; nor did he ask Penelope if any of them stood out as being better behaved than the rest.*

Odysseus' Revenge

Now shrugging off his rags the wiliest[17] fighter of the islands
leapt and stood on the broad doorsill, his own bow in his hand.
He poured out at his feet a rain of arrows from the quiver
and spoke to the crowd:
     "So much for that. Your clean-cut game is over.
1410 Now watch me hit a target that no man has hit before,
if I can make this shot. Help me, Apollo."
He drew to his fist the cruel head of an arrow for Antinous
just as the young man leaned to lift his beautiful drinking cup,
embossed, two-handled, golden: the cup was in his fingers:
1415 the wine was even at his lips: and did he dream of death?
How could he? In that revelry[18] amid his throng of friends
who would imagine a single foe—though a strong foe indeed—
could dare to bring death's pain on him and darkness on his eyes?
Odysseus' arrow hit him under the chin
1420 and punched up to the feathers through his throat.
Backward and down he went, letting the winecup fall
from his shocked hand. Like pipes his nostrils jetted
crimson runnels, a river of mortal red,
and one last kick upset his table
1425 knocking the bread and meat to soak in dusty blood.
Now as they craned to see their champion where he lay
the suitors jostled in uproar down the hall,
everyone on his feet. Wildly they turned and scanned
the walls in the long room for arms; but not a shield,
1430 not a good ashen spear was there for a man to take and throw.
All they could do was yell in outrage at Odysseus:
"Foul! to shoot at a man! That was your last shot!"
"Your own throat will be slit for this!"
     "Our finest lad is down!
You killed the best on Ithaca."
     "Buzzards will tear your eyes out!"
1435 For they imagined as they wished—that it was a wild shot,
an unintended killing—fools, not to comprehend
they were already in the grip of death.
But glaring under his brows Odysseus answered:

"You yellow dogs, you thought I'd never make it
1440 home from the land of Troy. You took my house to plunder.
. . . You dared
bid for my wife while I was still alive.
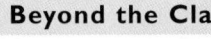
Contempt was all you had for the gods who rule wide heaven,
contempt for what men say of you hereafter.
Your last hour has come. You die in blood."

17. **wiliest** (wī´ ə əst) *adj.*: Most tricky.

18. **revelry** (rev´ əl rē) *n.*: Boisterous festivity.

◆ **Reading Strategy**
Summarize Odysseus' interactions with the suitors to this point. Why does he catch them by surprise? What do you think will happen next?

◆ **Build Vocabulary**
contempt (kən tempt´) *n.*: Actions or attitude of a person toward someone or something he or she considers low or worthless

Beyond the Classroom

Career Connection

Archaeology Because there are no written records of the Trojan War, which dates back about 3,200 years, there are many unanswered questions about it. However, archaeologists have found and examined pieces of buildings, objects, and works of art that Odysseus might have entered, used, or admired. Tell students that archaeology is the study of past cultures. These cultures may be thousands of years old, such as ancient Greece, or fairly recent, such as colonial America.

Archaeologists often camp at the sites of past human habitations to dig for buried evidence. As well as having extensive knowledge on many subjects, an archaeologist must make careful observations and keep accurate records. Other traits helpful in archaeology include the strength to use a pick and shovel, the patience to uncover an artifact with a needle probe and small paintbrush, and the ability to cope with primitive and uncomfortable field conditions.

Encourage interested students to find out what preparation they would need to pursue a career in archaeology. Suggest that they visit local colleges to find out more about what archaeologists do. If possible, they should visit museums that exhibit artifacts from ancient cultures.

1445 As they all took this in, sickly green fear
pulled at their entrails, and their eyes flickered
looking for some hatch or hideaway from death.
Eurymachus[19] alone could speak. He said:

19. **Eurymachus** (yoo ri´
mə kəs)

"If you are Odysseus of Ithaca come back,
1450 all that you say these men have done is true.
Rash actions, many here, more in the countryside.
But here he lies, the man who caused them all.
Antinous was the ringleader, he whipped us on
to do these things. He cared less for a marriage
1455 than for the power Cronion has denied him
❹ as king of Ithaca. For that
he tried to trap your son and would have killed him.
He is dead now and has his portion. Spare
your own people. As for ourselves, we'll make
1460 restitution of wine and meat consumed,
and add, each one, a tithe of twenty oxen
with gifts of bronze and gold to warm your heart.
Meanwhile we cannot blame you for your anger."

Odysseus glowered under his black brows
1465 and said:

"Not for the whole treasure of your fathers,
❺ all you enjoy, lands, flocks, or any gold
put up by others, would I hold my hand.
There will be killing till the score is paid.
You forced yourselves upon this house. Fight your way out,
1470 or run for it, if you think you'll escape death.
I doubt one man of you skins by."
They felt their knees fail, and their hearts—but heard
Eurymachus for the last time rallying them.

❻ "Friends," he said, "the man is implacable.
1475 Now that he's got his hands on bow and quiver
he'll shoot from the big doorstone there
until he kills us to the last man.
                              Fight, I say,
let's remember the joy of it. Swords out!
Hold up your tables to deflect his arrows.
1480 After me, everyone: rush him where he stands.
If we can budge him from the door, if we can pass
into the town, we'll call out men to chase him.
This fellow with his bow will shoot no more."

He drew his own sword as he spoke, a broadsword of fine
  bronze,

◆ *Literature*
and Your Life
What other "last
stands" from
movies and televi-
sion shows are
brought to mind
by Eurymachus'
brave but hollow
words?

❼

The Odyssey, Part 2, Odysseus' Revenge ◆ 911

911

◆ **Reading Strategy**

❶ Summarize Have students summarize this scene in which Telemachus and Odysseus kill the remaining suitors. Have them tell what happened and why it happened.

Telemachus runs to get spears and armor for Odysseus, Eumaeus, and the cowherd. They arm themselves in order to help Odysseus kill the suitors. Odysseus uses up his arrows, killing a suitor with every shot, then puts on a helmet and shield, and picks up his spears to finish the job.

1485   honed like a razor on either edge. Then crying hoarse and loud
      he hurled himself at Odysseus. But the kingly man let fly
      an arrow at that instant, and the quivering feathered butt
      sprang to the nipple of his breast as the barb stuck in his liver.
      The bright broadsword clanged down. He lurched and fell aside,
1490   pitching across his table. His cup, his bread and meat,
      were spilt and scattered far and wide, and his head slammed
        on the ground.
      Revulsion, anguish in his heart, with both feet kicking out,
      he downed his chair, while the shrouding wave of mist closed on
        his eyes.

      Amphinomus now came running at Odysseus,
1495   broadsword naked in his hand. He thought to make
      the great soldier give way at the door.
      But with a spear throw from behind Telemachus hit him
      between the shoulders, and the lancehead drove
      clear through his chest. He left his feet and fell
1500   forward, thudding, forehead against the ground.
      Telemachus swerved around him, leaving the long dark spear
      planted in Amphinomus. If he paused to yank it out
      someone might jump him from behind or cut him down with a
        sword
      at the moment he bent over. So he ran—ran from the tables
1505   to his father's side and halted, panting, saying:

      "Father let me bring you a shield and spear,
      a pair of spears, a helmet.
      I can arm on the run myself; I'll give
      outfits to Eumaeus and this cowherd.
1510   Better to have equipment."

                         Said Odysseus:

      "Run then, while I hold them off with arrows
      as long as the arrows last. When all are gone
      if I'm alone they can dislodge me."

                           Quick
      upon his father's word Telemachus
1515   ran to the room where spears and armor lay.
      He caught up four light shields, four pairs of spears,
      four helms of war high-plumed with flowing manes,
❶   and ran back, loaded down, to his father's side.
      He was the first to pull a helmet on
1520   and slide his bare arm in a buckler strap.
      The servants armed themselves, and all three took their stand
      beside the master of battle.

912 ◆ The Epic

The Slaughter of the Suitors, N. C. Wyeth, Delaware Art Museum

◀ Critical Viewing Do you think the fight against the suitors was a "fair fight"? Why or why not? [Make a Judgment; Support] ❷

While he had arrows
he aimed and shot, and every shot brought down
one of his huddling enemies.

1525 But when all barbs had flown from the bowman's fist,
❶ he leaned his bow in the bright entryway
beside the door, and armed: a four-ply shield
hard on his shoulder, and a crested helm,
horsetailed, nodding stormy upon his head,

1530 then took his tough and bronze-shod spears. . . .

*Aided by Athena, Odysseus, Telemachus, Eumaeus,
and another faithful herdsman kill all the suitors.*

And Odysseus looked around him, narrow eyed,
❸ for any others who had lain hidden
while death's black fury passed.

In blood and dust
he saw that crowd all fallen, many and many slain.

The Odyssey, Part 2, Odysseus' Revenge ◆ 913

▶Critical Viewing◀

❷ **Make a Judgment; Support**
Some students will say that this was a "fair fight" because Odysseus and the defenders are far outnumbered by the suitors, but have arms and armor to even the odds. Others may say that the fight was not fair, because the defenders had all the weapons and the protection and aid of the gods.

◆ **Critical Thinking**

❸ **Assess** Ask students: What other options did Odysseus have than to kill all the suitors? *Students may say he could have had the suitors tried in a court of law or could have taken more trouble to find out, at least, if any of them were less guilty than the others. Perhaps he would have found out that some of them stayed in the palace in order to protect Penelope, for example. On the other hand, some will say that if Odysseus left any of the suitors alive, he would have been considered weak; the suitors left living might have plotted to overthrow him.*

Humanities: Art

The Slaughter of the Suitors, 1929, by N. C. Wyeth.

In this painting of Odysseus and his three companions killing Penelope's suitors, Wyeth adds drama and animation to an already exciting story.

N. C. Wyeth was born in Needham, Massachusetts, and educated in Boston. He later attend art schools there and studied with the noted illustrator Howard Pyle in Wilmington, Delaware. During much of his life, he made his home in Chadds Ford, Pennsylvania.

Use the following questions for discussion:
1. Which lines from the Odyssey does this painting illustrate? *It illustrates lines 1521–1530, plus the lines that are covered by the synopsis on page 913.*
2. Who are the four figures on the right-hand side of the painting? How do you know? *They are Odysseus, Telemachus,* *Eumaeus, and the cowherd. They are wearing armor, have weapons, and are obviously winning the battle.*

3. What details make the painting exciting? *Students may cite the flung spear, the spears about to be thrown, the position of the men's bodies, or the dust of battle. The giant columns in the background create a heroic mood for the scene.*

◆ Literary Focus
How does the epic simile in lines 1535–1539 help you to picture the scene in your imagination?

1

Literary Focus

1 Epic Simile Although shore fishing is no longer a familiar sight in the United States, the simile suggests a similar image, familiar from nature documentaries and ads for frozen fish, of modern fishing boats hauling up nets with a winch and then dumping the catch onto the deck. Students may say that they can apply this familiar image to see the aftermath of the battle, with the dead and dying suitors covering the floor.

◆ Critical Thinking

2 Speculate If Penelope is not certain that Odysseus is himself, even though she recognizes him by his appearance, who might she think he could be? *Students might think Penelope is afraid that Odysseus might be another man, disguised by a god, as Odysseus was disguised by Athena as a beggar earlier in the epic. Alternatively, she might hope so much that this man is, indeed, Odysseus, that she is afraid to "believe her own eyes" or trust her own judgment.*

1535   Think of a catch that fishermen haul in to a half-moon bay
in a fine-meshed net from the whitecaps of the sea:
how all are poured out on the sand, in throes for the salt sea,
twitching their cold lives away in Helios' fiery air:
so lay the suitors heaped on one another.

Penelope's Test

Penelope tests Odysseus to prove that he really is her husband.

1540   Greathearted Odysseus, home at last,
was being bathed now by Eurynome
and rubbed with golden oil, and clothed again
in a fresh tunic and a cloak. Athena
lent him beauty, head to foot. She made him
1545   taller, and massive, too, with crisping hair
in curls like petals of wild hyacinth
but all red-golden. Think of gold infused
on silver by a craftsman, whose fine art
Hephaestus[20] taught him, or Athena: one
1550   whose work moves to delight: just so she lavished
beauty over Odysseus' head and shoulders.
He sat then in the same chair by the pillar,
facing his silent wife, and said:

        "Strange woman,
the immortals of Olympus made you hard,
1555   harder than any. Who else in the world
would keep aloof as you do from her husband
if he returned to her from years of trouble,
cast on his own land in the twentieth year?

Nurse, make up a bed for me to sleep on.
1560   Her heart is iron in her breast."

        Penelope
spoke to Odysseus now. She said:

        "Strange man,
if man you are . . . This is no pride on my part
nor scorn for you—not even wonder, merely.
I know so well how you—how he—appeared
1565   boarding the ship for Troy. But all the same . . .

Make up his bed for him, Eurycleia.
Place it outside the bedchamber my lord

20. Hephaestus (hi fes´təs): God of fire and the forge and of metalworking.

914 ◆ *The Epic*

Speaking and Listening Mini-Lesson

Debate

This mini-lesson supports the first Speaking and Listening activity on page 918.

Introduce the Concept Tell students that they will be staging a debate, explaining that a formal debate begins with a statement, such as, "Odysseus should be prosecuted for murder." One team is the "pro" team, and the other is the "con" team. The pros and the cons alternate giving opinions on the statement, backing up their opinions

with facts. Then, each team gets to speak again, rebutting, or showing why an argument by the other team is invalid.

Develop Background Team members should exchange ideas and make notes on these questions:

• What arguments support their position?

• What arguments might the other team make, and how can they be rebutted, or answered?

Apply Information The debates should

be held in front of the class. Speakers should be limited to three minutes, with one minute each for rebuttals.

Assess the Outcome Students can vote on which side was more convincing, using the following criteria: *Strength of Argument:* Was the argument logical and effectively supported? *Rebuttals:* Did rebuttals include good counter arguments? *Presentation:* Did team members speak clearly and follow the rules of debating?

built with his own hands. Pile the big bed
with fleeces, rugs, and sheets of purest linen."

1570 With this she tried him to the breaking point,
and he turned on her in a flash raging:
"Woman, by heaven you've stung me now!
Who dared to move my bed?
No builder had the skill for that—unless
1575 a god came down to turn the trick. No mortal
in his best days could budge it with a crowbar.
There is our pact and pledge, our secret sign,
built into that bed—my handiwork
and no one else's!

                    An old trunk of olive
1580 grew like a pillar on the building plot,
and I laid out our bedroom round that tree,
lined up the stone walls, built the walls and roof,
❸ gave it a doorway and smooth-fitting doors.
Then I lopped off the silvery leaves and branches,
1585 hewed and shaped that stump from the roots up
into a bedpost, drilled it, let it serve
as model for the rest. I planed them all,
inlaid them all with silver, gold and ivory,
and stretched a bed between—a pliant web
1590 of oxhide thongs dyed crimson.

                    There's our sign!
I know no more. Could someone else's hand
have sawn that trunk and dragged the frame away?"

Their secret! as she heard it told, her knees
grew tremulous and weak, her heart failed her.
1595 With eyes brimming tears she ran to him,
throwing her arms around his neck, and kissed him,
murmuring:

                    "Do not rage at me, Odysseus!
No one ever matched your caution! Think
what difficulty the gods gave: they denied us
1600 life together in our prime and flowering years,
kept us from crossing into age together.
❹ Forgive me, don't be angry. I could not
welcome you with love on sight! I armed myself
long ago against the frauds of men,
1605 impostors who might come—and all those many
whose underhanded ways bring evil on! . . .
But here and now, what sign could be so clear

The Odyssey, Part 2, Penelope's Test ◆ 915

Beyond Literature

Media Connection

Modern-Day Epics In film, the term *epic* applies to a movie of great scope and spectacle that features a heroic character who takes part in thrilling adventures. Lavish sets, enormous casts, and spectacular action—such as the parting of the Red Sea in the 1956 film *The Ten Commandments*—are hallmarks

Luke Skywalker, Princess Leia, and Han Solo in the epic film *Star Wars*.

of epic films. The advent of the wide screen in the 1950's ushered in a number of epics whose panoramic action was ideal for the new giant screens. Among those epics were *Ben Hur* (1959), *El Cid* (1961), *Cleopatra* (1963), and *Zulu* (1964). More recent epic films include *Roots* (1977), a chronicle of eighteenth- and nineteenth-century black life from enslavement to Reconstruction after the Civil War; *Star Wars* (1977), a depiction of adventures in a distant galaxy; and *Raiders of the Lost Ark* (1981), a film featuring the hair-raising adventures of Indiana Jones. What epic movies have you seen? What qualifies them to be called epic films?

◆ **Reading Strategy**

❸ Summarize Ask students to summarize Odysseus' account of how he built the bed. *Odysseus had the bedroom built around a large, old olive tree. Once the room was finished, he cut off the tree's branches, and shaped the trunk into a bedpost. He then carved the other bedposts to match, inlaid them with precious metals and ivory, and built the bed among the posts. Because of the rooted post, the bed could not be moved.*

◆ **Critical Thinking**

❹ Analyze Ask students to examine Penelope's explanation of her test. What techniques does she use to persuade Odysseus not to be angry? *Penelope reminds Odysseus that he, too, is a cautious person, implying that he shouldn't fault her for a trait he also possesses. She then justifies her test by explaining that, over the years, experience has taught her not to be too trusting.*

♦ **Reading Strategy**
Summarize Pene-
lope's test and
Odysseus' reaction to
what she says.
❶

❶ **Summarize** Penelope tests
Odysseus by seeing if he knows the
secret of their bed. Odysseus is
angered by what she says.

♦ **Reading Strategy**
❷ **Epic Simile** Ask students to
identify the epic simile in this passage
and explain the two items being
compared. *The simile begins with the
words "longed for as the sunwarmed
earth is longed for" and ends with "gale
winds, and tons of sea." The simile compares the way an exhausted swimmer
longs for land to the way Odysseus has
longed for Penelope.*

♦ **Critical Thinking**
❸ **Interpret** Ask students to interpret this passage that describes
Odysseus' and Penelope's rejoicing.
*Odysseus and Penelope rejoiced as
would a man who had almost drowned
in the sea but then crawled up on the
beach, happy, yet unable to forget the
horror of his ordeal. In other words, they
were happy to be reunited, but would
always remember the unhappiness of
the years during which they were
separated.*

Reinforce and Extend

Answers
♦ *Literature and Your Life*

Reader's Response Students may
believe that some sort of revenge
was justified, but that Odysseus perhaps overreacted to the situation.

Thematic Focus Students may say
that Odysseus should have simply
forced them to leave, rather than
wage war on them.

☑ **Check Your Comprehension**

1. They react with humor and scorn
   at a beggar daring to pick up the
   bow.
2. They react with anger and
   threats, thinking that it was unjus-
   tifiable murder.
3. He kills all the suitors.
4. She probes to see if he knows the
   secret of their bed. He describes
   how he constructed the bed.

916

---

as this of our own bed?
No other man has ever laid eyes on it—
1610 only my own slave, Actoris, that my father
sent with me as a gift—she kept our door.
You make my stiff heart know that I am yours."

Now from his breast into his eyes the ache
of longing mounted, and he wept at last,
1615 his dear wife, clear and faithful, in his arms,
longed for as the sunwarmed earth is longed for by a swimmer
❷ spent in rough water where his ship went down
under Poseidon's blows, gale winds and tons of sea.
Few men can keep alive through a big surf
1620 to crawl, clotted with brine, on kindly beaches
❸ in joy, in joy, knowing the abyss[21] behind:
and so she too rejoiced, her gaze upon her husband,
her white arms round him pressed as though forever.

The Ending

*Odysseus is reunited with his father. Athena commands that
peace prevail between Odysseus and the relatives of the slain
suitors. Odysseus has regained his family and his kingdom.*

21. **abyss** (ə bis´) *n.*:
Ocean depths.

Guide for Responding

♦ *Literature and Your Life*

Reader's Response Do you think Odysseus' revenge is justified? Why or why not?
Thematic Focus How do you think the problem
of the suitors should have been handled?
Activity With a partner, role-play the exchange between Eurymachus and Odysseus.

☑ **Check Your Comprehension**

1. What is the suitors' reaction when Odysseus,
   still in disguise, takes up the bow?
2. Describe the immediate reaction of the suitors
   to the killing of Antinous.
3. How does Odysseus get revenge on the suitors?
4. What is Penelope's test, and how does Odysseus
   pass it?

Beyond the Selection

FURTHER READING
Other Works by Homer
The *Iliad*
**Other Works With the Theme of Striving
for a Goal**
"Ulysses," Alfred, Lord Tennyson
O Pioneers! Willa Cather
Kon-Tiki, Thor Heyerdahl

INTERNET
Students can find out more about Homer, the
Odyssey, and Greek mythology at the following
Internet Web site. Please be aware, however, that
the site may have changed from the time we pub-
lished this information.
   Go to **http://www.intergate.net/uhtml/
.jhunt/greek_myth/greek_myth.html**
   We *strongly recommend* that you preview the
site before you send students to it.

Guide for Responding (continued)

◆ Critical Thinking

INTERPRET

1. What does Odysseus mean in "The Challenge" when he says, "The hour has come to cook their lordships' mutton—/supper by daylight"? [Interpret]
2. What are Odysseus' reasons for slaying all the suitors? [Analyze]
3. Since Odysseus has abandoned his disguise, why does Penelope still need to test him? [Infer]
4. Describe the mood of the scene at the end of "Penelope's Test." Is it altogether happy or does it include some sadness? Explain. [Support]

EVALUATE

5. Does Odysseus' success in the contest show that he is a skilled archer or merely that he has a god on his side? Support your answer. [Assess]

APPLY

6. Compare justice at the hands of Odysseus with justice in a modern society. [Distinguish]

◆ Reading Strategy

SUMMARIZE

Summarizing what you have read is a good way to check your understanding. It is also a useful skill when you need to demonstrate your knowledge on a test or when you want to share what you have learned with a friend.

1. List the main events in Part 2 in order.
2. For each event you listed, tell what caused it and what was the result of it.
3. Retell Part 2 of the *Odyssey* in a summary that explains why events occurred as they did.

◆ Literary Focus

EPIC SIMILE

An **epic simile** is a long, elaborate comparison between two dissimilar actions or objects. Many epic similes compare familiar objects and events with imaginative occurrences.

Identify three epic similes from Part 2 of the *Odyssey* and tell what two dissimilar objects or actions each one compares.

◆ Build Vocabulary

USING THE WORD ROOT -equi-

Keeping in mind that the word root -equi- means "equal," complete each sentence with one of these words.

    a. equinox   **b.** equivalent

1. Two nickels are ___?___ to a dime.
2. At the ___?___, the day and the night are of the same duration.

USING THE WORD BANK

Write the letter of the word or phrase that is the best synonym of the first word.

1. dissemble: (a) lie, (b) take apart, (c) disguise
2. lithe: (a) limber, (b) thin, (c) agile
3. incredulity: (a) disbelief, (b) naiveté, (c) anger
4. bemusing: (a) muddling, (b) entertaining, (c) allowing
5. glowering: (a) shining, (b) scowling, (c) laughing
6. equity: (a) fairness, (b) horses, (c) calmness
7. maudlin: (a) boring, (b) tired, (c) sentimental
8. contempt: (a) scorn, (b) pity, (c) pavillion

◆ Build Grammar Skills

PARTICIPIAL PHRASES

A **participial phrase** is a phrase that contains a participle and serves as an adjective to modify a noun or pronoun.

Practice Copy each excerpt below from Part 2 of the *Odyssey* in your notebook. Underline the participial phrase, identify the participle as *past* or *present*, and draw an arrow from the participial phrase to the noun or pronoun it modifies.

1. Crossing the yard, he passed out through the gate in the stockade to face the goddess.
2. Held back too long, the tears ran down his cheeks as he embraced his son.
3. Athena, counseling me, will give me word, and I shall signal to you, nodding . . .
4. Then anger made Antinous' heart beat hard, and, glowering under his brows, he answered . . .

The Odyssey, Part 2 ◆ 917

✒ Writer's Solution

For additional instruction and practice, use the lesson on Misplaced Modifiers in the **Language Lab CD-ROM** and the page on Participles and Participial Phrases in the *Writer's Solution Grammar Practice Book*, p. 44.

Idea Bank

Customizing for
Performance Levels

Following are suggestions for matching Idea Bank topics with your students' performance levels:

Less Advanced Students: 1, 7
Average Students: 2, 4, 6
More Advanced Students: 3, 5

Customizing for
Learning Modalities

Following are suggestions for matching Idea Bank topics with your students' learning modalities:

Verbal/Linguistic: 1, 2, 3, 4, 5
Visual/Spatial: 6, 7

Writing Mini-Lesson

Refer students to the Writing Handbook, page 962, for instruction on the writing process, and page 964 for further information on narration. For additional instruction, use the Writing Process Model 4: Personal Narrative in *Writing and Language Transparencies,* pp. 21–27.

Writer's Solution

Writers at Work Videodisc

Have students view the videodisc segment (Ch. 2) featuring fiction writer Isabel Allende to see how she uses imagination to create fiction. Have students discuss how an understanding of real events can add life to an imaginary narrative.

[barcode]

Play frames 10786 to 22536

Writing Lab CD-ROM

Have students complete the Tutorial on Narration. Follow these steps:

1. Use the Chain of Events for plot to organize plot details.
2. Use the audio-annotated literary model to see an example of chronological order.
3. Revise with the interactive instructions on avoiding anachronisms.

Sourcebook

Have students use Chapter 2, Narration (pp. 30–61), for additional support. The chapter includes in-depth instruction on organizing your narrative (p. 50).

Build Your Portfolio

Idea Bank

Writing

1. **Epic Simile** Describe an action by a hero—such as Odysseus or your favorite comic book superhero—using an epic simile to make the hero's action easy for your audience to imagine.

2. **Modern Heroic Poem** Write a narrative poem about a real-life modern-day hero.

3. **Literary Essay** Poet and critic W. H. Auden said: "Though it would be unfair to describe the Homeric hero as a mere puppet of the gods, his area of free choice and responsibility is pretty circumscribed. In the first place he is born, not made . . . so that though he does brave deeds, he cannot be called brave in our sense of the word because he never feels fear." Write an essay responding to this criticism.

Speaking and Listening

4. **Debate** Form two teams of two to four people each to debate the following issue: Should Odysseus be prosecuted for murder in the killing of Penelope's suitors?

5. **Oral Report** Odysseus is returning home from the Trojan War. Find out more about this conflict and, in an oral report, share your findings with the class. **[Social Studies Link]**

Projects

6. **Odyssey Map** Create a map that shows Odysseus' voyage. Calculate the actual straight-line distance from Troy to Ithaca. Based on your map, approximate how far Odysseus traveled. **[Social Studies Link; Math Link]**

7. **Board Game** Create a board game based on the *Odyssey,* decorating your board with scenes from the epic. **[Art Link]**

Writing Mini-Lesson

Letter Home

Imagine that Odysseus could have sent a letter home to Penelope and Telemachus. As Odysseus, write a letter home that vividly describes at least two of your adventures.

Writing Skills Focus: Sequence of Events

Your letters will be easier for your readers to understand if you pay attention to the **sequence of events**. Most of the time, you will want to recount events in chronological order—start off describing what happened first, then describe what happened next, and continue your narrative until you reach the final event.

Model

Dear Penelope and Telemachus,

I hope this letter reaches you. Hermes promised he would deliver it. Anyway, it's been a busy week. First, I had to get past the Sirens. . . .

Prewriting Decide which adventures you will describe in your letter, then jot down the most important events on separate note cards, along with details about each event. Arrange the note cards in the proper order.

Drafting Using your prewriting notes as a guide, draft your letter in one sitting, without taking a break. Relate details about each adventure in chronological order. Don't worry that your draft isn't perfect. You can fix your letter in the revision stage.

Revising Read your letter aloud, noting where you need more details or where the order of events seems jumbled. Then revise your letter as needed. Make sure that participial phrases are close to the nouns and pronouns they modify so they do not seem to be modifying the wrong words.

✓ ASSESSMENT OPTIONS

Formal Assessment, Selection Test, pp. 208–210, and Assessment Resources Software. The selection test is designed so that it can be easily customized to the performance levels of your students.
Alternative Assessment, p. 56, includes options for less advanced students, more advanced students, verbal/linguistic learners, interpersonal learners, bodily/kinesthetic learners, logical/mathematical learners, and visual/spatial learners.

PORTFOLIO ASSESSMENT
Use the following rubrics in the *Alternative Assessment* booklet to assess student writing:
Epic Simile: Description Rubric, p. 90
Modern Heroic Poem: Poetry Rubric, p. 101
Literary Essay: Literary Analysis/Interpretation Rubric, p. 105
Writing Mini-Lesson: Fictional Narrative Rubric, p. 88

Writing Process Workshop

Biographical Report

There are probably many people, living or deceased, who interest you greatly. They may fascinate you because of their unusual personalities or outstanding achievements. Perhaps you even feel they have influenced you as a person. Research and write a **biographical report** about an individual who interests you. In your report, describe the person's life, work, and the time in which he or she lived.

The following skill, introduced in this section's Writing Mini-Lesson, will help you write a biographical report about any individual.

Writing Skills Focus

▶ **Follow a sequence of events** in presenting your facts and details. Begin by describing the earliest significant events in the person's life. Then move on to describe the later significant events, all in the order in which they occurred in time. (See p. 918.)

In the following example, the writer practices the above skill by offering factual information about Homer's life in chronological order.

MODEL

Homer is thought to have been born somewhere between 1000 B.C. and 700 B.C., possibly in western Asia Minor. ① According to tradition, he was blind. He did not write his two great epics, the *Iliad* and the *Odyssey*, as a modern novelist writes a novel. Rather, he composed them orally by assembling a number of earlier and shorter narrative songs. ② He probably traveled around Greece reciting them on many occasions. ③ In later centuries, the two epics were the basis of Greek and Roman education. ④

① The writer begins with the earliest event: Homer's birth.

② The report continues by describing Homer's special method of writing.

③ The report tells what Homer did after composing his works.

④ The writer ends by telling what happened centuries later.

Writing Process Workshop ◆ 919

Cross-Curricular Connection: History

Discuss with the class the purpose of research, bringing out that research skills are important in virtually every school subject. History is a good example because papers assigned for that subject are often biographical reports about important historical figures. Before students begin drafting an introduction, body, and conclusion, they need to know how to choose a good topic, use a variety of research sources to gather information, and record and organize their notes. Lead a brief discussion about how writing a biographical report for a language arts class might differ from writing a report on the same subject for history. *Students may note that a biographical report written for a history class will focus on the influence the subject had on historical events, ideas, or culture, while a report written for a language arts class might be more concerned with the subject and with presenting a comprehensive portrait of him or her.*

Prepare and Engage

Establish Writing Guidelines

Before students begin, review the following key characteristics of a biographical report:

- A biographical report examines the life and achievements of someone who interests the writer and his or her audience.

- It includes the main events in the person's life as well as specific dates and other related details.

- It may include the writer's inferences about the reasons behind actions and events.

- In addition to researching the subject's life and achievements, the writer may have to research the times in which the subject lived.

- You may want to distribute the scoring rubric for Research Report/Paper (p. 99 in **Alternative Assessment**) to make students aware of the criteria on which they will be evaluated before they begin. See the suggestions on page 921 for how you can customize the rubric to this workshop.

Writer's Solution

Writers at Work Videodisc

To introduce students to the key elements and to show them how biographer and nonfiction writer Ellen Harkins Wheat uses them in her writing, play the videodisc segment on Research Writing (Ch. 5). Have students discuss what Wheat has to say about arranging her ideas and starting to write.

Play frames 3 to 10167

Writing Lab CD-ROM

If your students have access to computers, you may want to have them work in the tutorial on Research Writing to complete all or part of their papers. Follow these steps:

1. Encourage students to use the Inspirations to come up with possible topics.
2. Have students draft on computer.
3. Encourage students to use Revision Checkers to check for coherence and unity within and between paragraphs.
4. Direct students to the Interactive Self-Evaluation Checklist to help them evaluate their writing.

Develop Student Writing

Prewriting

You might suggest that students form small groups to brainstorm for additional topic ideas, for example, a well-known sports figure, a popular entertainer, a famous inventor.

Customize for
More Advanced Students

More advanced students may have gone into greater depth in their research than others. With these, students, you might introduce additional levels for their formal outlines; for example:

I. Homer's life as a storyteller
  A. Creating the epics
    1. Composing songs
    2. Composing the music
      a) Music without words
      b) Music with lyrics

Tell students that a formal outline should not have only one letter or number of any particular level; for example, if there is an *(a)*, there must be at least a *(b)*; if there is a *(1)*. there must be at least a *(2)*.

Customize for
English Language Learners

These students may not yet have developed a reading vocabulary broad enough to use higher-level resources such as specialized encyclopedias and biographical dictionaries. Help English language learners locate books in the library that are appropriate for their fluency in English. The more adult-looking books from a children's library may be helpful.

Drafting

Advise students to draft directly from their outlines, but remind them that outlines have to be filled out with additional information and transitional words and phrases. Point out that their outlines are not written in stone. Research writers, as they draft, are likely to change the wording and order of some of the items in their outlines.

APPLYING LANGUAGE SKILLS:
Using *Who* and *Whom*

When writing a biographical report, you'll find yourself frequently using pronouns. Make sure you use them correctly. Use *who* as the subject of a clause:

Homer is the person <u>who</u> wrote the *Odyssey*.

Use *whom* as the object in a clause:

Homer is a writer <u>whom</u> many critics praise.

Practice On your paper, complete each sentence using the correct word form.

1. Homer was a blind man (who, whom) told stories.
2. Do you know (who, whom) recorded his stories?
3. He was someone to (who, whom) scribes listened.
4. Odysseus is the hero of (who, whom) Homer speaks.

Writing Application As you draft your report, use *who* and *whom* correctly. Be sure to use *who* as a subject and *whom* as an object.

Writer's Solution Connection
Writing Lab

For additional support in gathering information for your report, use the instruction and activities in the Prewriting section of the tutorial on Research Writing.

Prewriting

Choose a Topic Think of a person from the past or present whom you admire or find interesting. You can also choose one of these topic ideas:

> ### Topic Ideas
> - Your favorite author
> - A famous political leader
> - A well-known artist
> - A famous scientist

Conduct Library Research List the information you need before going to the library. Take notes on what you learn.

Source	How to Find It
Nonfiction Books	Check library catalog, in card files or in electronic form
Newspapers and Magazines	Use indexes like *Readers' Guide to Periodical Literature*
Reference Works	Check library catalog for encyclopedias, atlases, and almanacs; some may be on CD-ROM

Organize Your Information Use an outline to help organize your ideas. Next to each Roman numeral, list your main points. Next to the capital letters, enter the topics you'll cover under each main point. Finally, list details about each topic next to the numbers.

    I. Homer's Life as a Storyteller
      A. Creating the epics
          1. Composing songs
      B. Traveling throughout Greece

Drafting

Present Facts in Sequence As you draft your report, give information about the person's life in chronological order. Your first few sentences may be general statements about the person and why he or she is special. Afterward, begin presenting facts about the subject's early years.

Applying Language Skills
Using *Who* and *Whom*
Answers
1. who;   2. who;   3. whom;   4. whom

Writer's Solution

For additional instruction and practice, use the practice page on special problems with pronouns in the *Writer's Solution Grammar Practice Book* (p. 81).

Special Problems in Agreement
Answers
1. fare;   2. is;   3. speak

Writer's Solution

For additional instruction and practice, use the **Language Lab CD-ROM** lesson on special problems in agreement and the compound subjects page in the *Writer's Solution Grammar Practice Book* (p. 83).

End With a Summary At the end of your report, offer a brief summary of the person's accomplishments and his or her effects on you or on society in general. Although your report should be factual, your summary may offer your own theories or opinions about the person, based on facts you have already presented.

Revising

Use a Checklist The following checklist will help you revise:

▶ Have I followed the proper sequence for presenting my information?
   Read over your report. Make a timeline that lists the events you include. Does your timeline move in chronological order? If not, rearrange details as necessary.

▶ Have I included all of the key details of my subject's life?
   Your paper should present a complete picture of the person's life. Read over your work to see if there are any gaps. Then fill in these gaps by adding information. You may need to do some additional research to learn more about your subject.

▶ Will my paper capture the interest of my readers?
   Have a classmate read your paper and suggest ways that you can make it more interesting.

▶ Is all of the information in my report accurate?
   Ideally, you should be able to find each piece of information in your report in at least two sources. As you revise, take the time to verify any details that are found only in one source.

Publishing

▶ **Classroom** Share your biographical report with classmates by reading it aloud.

▶ **Library Book** Collect all class reports into a "Book of Biographies" to present to your school library.

▶ **Internet** Post your biographical report on the Internet.

APPLYING LANGUAGE SKILLS: Special Problems in Agreement

When a singular subject and a plural subject are joined by *or* or *nor*, the verb agrees with the closer subject.

Neither Homer nor his <u>critics</u> <u>have</u> left much information about him.

Neither Homer's critics nor <u>Homer</u> <u>has</u> left much information about him.

Practice On your paper, complete each sentence with the correct verb form.

1. Odysseus or his men (fare, fares) poorly.
2. Neither the poems nor the prose (is, are) accurate.
3. Homer's life or times (speak, speaks) for him.

Writing Application Review your draft and check your use of *or* or *nor* to join subjects. If the subject and verb do not agree, change the form of the verb.

Writer's Solution Connection Writing Lab

For help revising your paper, use the Interactive Models provided in the Revising section of the tutorial on Research Writing.

Revising

Students might add to their checklists items that remind them to check for clear organization. For example, they might add the following: Does my report have a thesis statement? Does each of my paragraphs have a topic sentence that states the main idea and supports the thesis statement? Does every detail in each of my paragraphs support the main idea expressed in the topic sentence?

 Writer's Solution

Writing Lab CD-ROM
The Revision Checkers for Coherence and Transitions in the Revision section of the tutorial on Research Writing help students check for coherence and unity within and between paragraphs and highlight transitional words.

Publishing

Students might both enjoy and benefit from sharing their biographical reports with friends and relatives outside of school.

Reinforce and Extend

Review the Writing Guidelines
After students have completed their papers, review the characteristics of a biographical report. Encourage students to come up with additional criteria for an effective report based on what they learned from completing the assignment.

Connect to Literature Unit 7 ("Nonfiction") includes an example of a biographical essay: Joan Didion's "Georgia O'Keeffe"(p. 592)

✓ ASSESSMENT		4	3	2	1
PORTFOLIO ASSESSMENT Use the rubric on Research Report/Paper in *Alternative Assessment* (p. 99) to assess students' writing. Add these criteria to customize the rubric to this assignment.	**Sequence of Events**	The writer presents facts and details in accurate chronological order.	Facts and details are in accurate order, but the writer leaves unexplained gaps between events.	Most facts and details are in accurate chronological order, but some are out of order.	The writer skips back and forth in time so the reader has little sense of the sequence of events.
	Summary	The paper ends with a brief summary of the subject's accomplishments.	The writer summarizes some but not all of the subject's accomplishments.	The writer's summary is lacking in detail.	The writer neglects to include a summary.

Strategies for Success

When you prepare a report, research is very important. You may find many books, magazines, and other materials that contain information on your topic. How do you know which resources contain the most useful information? Follow these guidelines for evaluating your sources.

Consider the Author The first thing to ask about a source is, Who wrote it? Is the author an expert on the subject? If you've never heard of the author, look for biographical information in the book.

Also note the company that published the book. Is it a reputable publisher? An older, larger publishing house may be more reliable than a newer, smaller company you don't know.

Consider the Date Look to see when a book was published. As a rule, books published more recently are more reliable than older books. A newer book may contain information that wasn't available previously. If it's a science book, it might correct misinformation that appeared in earlier books.

Compare Information Sometimes you find conflicting information in two different books—even in different encyclopedias. Check other sources to see what they say about the topic. In the end, let the majority opinion rule.

Apply the Strategy

Imagine you are doing research for a paper on nuclear fallout. Look at the sources available to you. Answer these questions:

1. Which would you prefer to use—the encyclopedia or the book of facts? Why?
2. Which of the two newspapers would you prefer to use? Why?
3. Which of the two books would you prefer to use? Why?
4. Of all the resources, which one do you consider most reliable? Why?

The World Book Encyclopedia, Volume N, © 1998

Dave's Book of Amazing Facts, by Dave Smith, © 1983

"New Studies on Nuclear Fallout," *The New York Times*, March 6, 1998

"Fallout," *Neighbor's Gazette*, May 9, 1999

Nuclear Fallout, by Dr. E. Baird, © 1998 by Prentice-Hall

✔ *Here are other situations in which it is helpful to evaluate sources of information:*
▶ *Reading a political pamphlet*
▶ *Reading a newspaper editorial*
▶ *Investigating a rumor*
▶ *Reading a medical report*

PART 2 *Responding to the Past*

The Fall of Troy from *The Odysseus Suite,* 1979, Romare Bearden, serigraph 18 x 24,
© Romare Bearden Foundation/Licensed by VAGA, New York, NY.

Responding to the Past ◆ 923

 Humanities: Art

The Fall of Troy, from The Odysseus Suite, 1979, by Romare Bearden.
(See the biographical information about Bearden on page 857.)

Explain that this is another collage from the series done by Bearden on the adventures of Odysseus. Elicit that *The Fall of Troy* is a vivid portrayal of a city in flames; they should recognize that the large white horse to the right is the Trojan Horse, and the boats in the harbor are waiting to carry Odysseus and his men far from Troy to numerous adventures.

Help students link the art to the focus of Part 2 ("Responding to the Past") by answering the following questions:

1. The artwork represents a twentieth-century response to the heroic events of the *Odyssey,* just as the selections in Part 2 are contemporary approaches to Homer's epic. Which aspects of Bearden's collage recall what you have read from the *Odyssey*? Which aspects of the collage reflect a modern mind at work? *Students should note among recognizable references to the epic the Trojan Horse, the burning towers, the sea and ships; the modern aspects of the work include the use of the collage medium; the flat, childlike style of the cutouts; and the whimsical inclusion of the dolphins and other sea creatures.*

2. If you were going to create a picture about an event from the *Odyssey,* which one would you choose? Why? *Students should mention a specific event from the epic.*

Guide for Reading

More About the Authors

Edna St. Vincent Millay won a scholarship to Vassar College on the strength of her first published poem, "Renascence."

Margaret Atwood is a celebrated novelist and essayist, as well as a poet.

In **Derek Walcott**, West Indian culture has found its great poet. Walcott now lives in Trinidad and also teaches English at Boston University.

Before **Constantine Cavafy** began writing poetry, he worked as a clerk in a government office in Egypt.

Edna St. Vincent Millay
(1892–1950)

Like many other American writers of her time, Millay is remembered for her artistic experimentation and her rebelliousness. She published several successful poetry collections, including *The Harp-Weaver, and Other Poems* (1923), which earned her a Pulitzer Prize.

Margaret Atwood
(1939–)

For almost forty years, this Canadian author has been writing about what it means to be a woman in a period of social change. Another of her central themes is the role of mythology in people's lives. These two concerns come together in "Siren Song," a startling new look at Homer's Sirens.

Derek Walcott *(1930–)*

Born on the Caribbean island of St. Lucia, this author writes poems that reflect the influence of his background. His work has won worldwide acclaim, and in 1992 he won the Nobel Prize for Literature. In addition to being a poet, Walcott is a successful playwright and director. "Prologue" and "Epilogue" are from his stage version of the *Odyssey*.

Constantine Cavafy
(1863–1933)

Considered the most important Greek poet of the first half of the twentieth century, Cavafy was born to Greek parents in Alexandria, Egypt. In "Ithaca," you can see his basic creative method—to use the world of Greek mythology to write poems that speak to today's reader.

◆ Build Vocabulary

SUFFIXES: *-esque*

In "Siren Song," one of the Sirens complains of having to look picturesque. You can easily determine the meaning of this word if you recognize that it is formed by adding the suffix *-esque,* meaning "like" or "having the quality of," to a familiar word—*picture.*

WORD BANK

As you read, you will encounter the words on this list. Each word is defined on the page where it first appears. Preview the list before you read.

beached
picturesque
tempests
amber
ebony
defrauded

◆ Build Grammar Skills

ADVERB CLAUSES

These poets sometimes show the relationships among ideas by using **adverb clauses,** which modify verbs, adjectives, and adverbs and show when, why, or under what conditions something happened. Adverb clauses may appear in the beginning, middle, or end of a sentence. Thus, they can be useful to poets who are trying to find just the right rhyme or rhythm for a line. Notice the placement of the adverb clause in this line from "An Ancient Gesture":

I thought, *as I wiped my eyes on the corner of my apron:*
Penelope did this too.

An Ancient Gesture ◆ Siren Song
The Odyssey ◆ Ithaca

◆ *Literature and Your Life*

CONNECT YOUR EXPERIENCE

If you've ever listened to two people describe the same argument or the same traffic accident, you know that people can have very different perspectives of the same event. In these selections, four writers bring their own perspectives to the events in Homer's *Odyssey*.

Journal Writing Jot down each writer's reactions to the events and characters in the *Odyssey*.

THEMATIC FOCUS: LOOKING INWARD

As you read these selections, think about how the authors' own ideas and feelings shape each of their interpretations of Homer's *Odyssey*.

◆ Background for Understanding

HISTORY

"An Ancient Gesture" and "Siren Song" are both written by twentieth-century women whose perspectives on the role of women in society are very different from Homer's. For much of history in most cultures, women have had fewer legal rights and fewer educational and job opportunities than men. In fact, women in the United States didn't even have the right to vote until the passage of a constitutional amendment in 1920. Even after winning the right to vote, women didn't begin to gain better career and educational opportunities until the last few decades.

◆ Literary Focus

CONTEMPORARY INTERPRETATIONS

The characters and events of the *Odyssey* are timeless and universal in their interest and significance. They are so rich in meaning that every generation sees in them ideas and values relevant to the present. Hence, countless writers have mined the *Odyssey* for material to create original poems, plays, novels, and essays. Though these **contemporary interpretations** differ widely in purpose, theme, and artistic method, they usually have two features in common. They present persons, places, and events whose origins are in Homer's writings, but they use Homer's material in original ways to express contemporary thoughts, values, beliefs, and feelings.

◆ Reading Strategy

COMPARE AND CONTRAST

To fully understand a piece of writing based on an earlier work, it's important to **compare and contrast** the details, characters, and events in the updated work with those in the original. For example, when you read Margaret Atwood's poem "Siren Song," think about the way in which Atwood's portrayal of a Siren is similar to and different from Homer's portrayal. Once you've identified the similarities and differences, try to determine the reasons behind these similarities and differences. If, for instance, a writer has portrayed a character very differently from the way the character was portrayed originally, consider what the writer is trying to accomplish through the contrasting portrayal.

As you read, use a Venn diagram like this one to identify similarities and differences. Note differences in the outer sections of the two circles. Jot down similarities where the circles overlap.

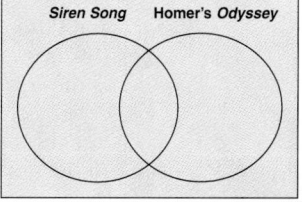

Siren Song   Homer's *Odyssey*

 Draw a cluster diagram on the chalkboard and in the center write the following name: "Penelope." Ask students what they associate with her character. Then ask: What would today's woman have done in her place? Elicit from students that today's woman would probably not want to be expected to wait faithfully at home for twenty years for a husband who is presumed dead to return from wars or other adventures. Tell students that the poems they are going to read look at characters and events from the *Odyssey* in a fresh, new light—the perspective of today's world.

Customize for
Less Proficient Readers
To help readers understand these poems, have them read the text as they listen to the audiocassette recording of the poems.

Listening to Literature Audiocassettes

Customize for
More Advanced Students
Explain to these students the concept of literary allusion—a reference in a work of literature to a character, place, or event in another literary work. Suggest that students focus on the literary allusions in these poems, researching any that are unfamiliar.

Customize for
English Language Learners
To help these students understand the relationship of these poems to the *Odyssey*, have them use the page on recognizing allusions in **Strategies for Diverse Student Needs,** p. 59.

Customize for
Musical/Rhythmic Learners
Have these students prepare oral readings of their favorite poems from this selection to perform for a group.

 Preparing for Standardized Tests

Vocabulary Students can use the suffix *-esque* to piece together the meaning of unfamiliar words on vocabulary portions of standardized tests. Often, the suffix may be attached to a word with which they are familiar. By removing the suffix and adding the words *like* or *having the quality of* to the root word, students are likely to discover that they are able to determine the meaning of the word.

Reading Critical Reading portions of standardized tests often call on students to make comparisons. Encourage students to use a Venn diagram graphic organizer like the one on this page to note similarities and differences in critical reading passages. Students can then use the details in the organizer to help them come up with the correct responses to multiple-choice items.

One-Minute Insight In "An Ancient Gesture," Penelope's actions are viewed from a modern perspective. Millay compares the emotions Penelope felt with the emotions that modern women feel today.

►Critical Viewing◄

❶ Infer; Support Penelope wants the suitors to go away and leave her alone, so she is pointedly ignoring them. Even though she is undoubtably aware of the proffered gifts and lyre-playing, she refuses to look at them and focuses on her weaving.

Comprehension Check ☑

❷ Ask students why the speaker in "An Ancient Gesture" wipes her eyes on the corner of her apron. *She is crying.*

❸ Clarification With Odysseus presumed dead, Penelope was besieged by unwanted suitors. She told them she would remarry when she finished her weaving. To stall them, every night she unraveled what she had woven during the day.

◆ **Critical Thinking**

❹ Infer Ask students: Why does the speaker call wiping her eyes on her apron an "ancient gesture"? *The gesture connects the speaker with women from earlier times who, too, have dried their eyes after weeping.*

❺ Clarification *Ulysses* is the Roman name for *Odysseus.*

◆ **Literary Focus**

❻ Contemporary Interpretations Ask students: How does Millay use the characters of Penelope and Odysseus to express contemporary thoughts? *Millay compares Penelope and Odysseus from a feminist point of view, accusing men of using the appearance of feelings for ulterior motives.*

Penelope and The Suitors, 1912, J. M. Waterhouse, Aberdeen Art Gallery and Museum, Scotland

❶ ▲ Critical Viewing What is Penelope's attitude toward the suitors? How can you tell? [Infer; Support]

An Ancient Gesture

Edna St. Vincent Millay

❷ I thought, as I wiped my eyes on the corner of my apron:
 Penelope did this too.
❸ And more than once: you can't keep weaving all day
 And undoing it all through the night;
5 Your arms get tired, and the back of your neck gets tight;
 And along towards morning, when you think it will never be light,
 And your husband has been gone, and you don't know where, for years,
 Suddenly you burst into tears;
 There is simply nothing else to do.

10 And I thought, as I wiped my eyes on the corner of my apron:
❹ This is an ancient gesture, authentic, antique,
 In the very best tradition, classic, Greek;
❺ Ulysses did this too.
 But only as a gesture,—a gesture which implied
15 **❻** To the assembled throng that he was much too moved to speak.
 He learned it from Penelope . . .
 Penelope, who really cried.

926 ◆ *The Epic*

Humanities: Art

Penelope and the Suitors, 1912, by J. W. Waterhouse.

This painting illustrates Penelope working at her loom in an attempt to stave off her suitors.

Born in Rome in 1849, John William Waterhouse was deeply influenced by Italy's classical heritage. This sparked his interest in ancient myths such as the *Odyssey.*

Use the following questions for discussion:
1. Waterhouse was a master storyteller in art, celebrated for his ability to capture the most dramatic point in a story. How is this skill apparent in "Penelope and the Suitors"? *He captures Penelope at the height of her struggle against the suitors. She is shown intent upon her weaving, but the viewer knows she must be aware of the suitors close behind her with their offers of gifts and music.*
2. What details in the painting can you find in the *Odyssey*? Which ones do you think came from the artist's imagination? *The characters in the painting can be found in the Odyssey. The lyre, the flowers and other gifts, and the clothing and furniture are from the artist's imagination.*

Siren Song

Margaret Atwood

This is the one song everyone
would like to learn: the song
that is irresistible:

the song that forces men
5 to leap overboard in squadrons
even though they see the <u>beached</u> skulls

the song nobody knows
because anyone who has heard it
is dead, and the others can't remember.

10 Shall I tell you the secret
and if I do, will you get me
out of this bird suit?[1]

I don't enjoy it here
squatting on this island
15 looking <u>picturesque</u> and mythical

with these two feathery maniacs,
I don't enjoy singing
this trio, fatal and valuable.

I will tell the secret to you,
20 to you, only to you.
Come closer. This song

is a cry for help: Help me!
Only you, only you can,
you are unique

25 at last. Alas
it is a boring song
but it works every time.

---

1. **bird suit:** Sirens are usually represented as half bird and half woman.

◆ **Build Vocabulary**

beached (bēcht) *adj.*: Washed up and lying on a beach

picturesque (pik´ chər esk´) *adj.*: Like or suggesting a picture

---

Guide for Responding

◆ *Literature and Your Life*

Reader's Response Do these poems make you feel more or less sympathetic to Penelope and the Sirens than the *Odyssey* did? Explain.

Thematic Focus How are these poets' perspectives different from Homer's?

Journal Writing Imagine that you are the speaker of "Siren Song." Write a journal entry about the encounter described in the poem.

☑ **Check Your Comprehension**

1. What similarity does the speaker of "An Ancient Gesture" see between herself and Penelope?
2. How does the speaker of "Siren Song" feel about being a Siren?

◆ **Critical Thinking**

INTERPRET

1. What is the "ancient gesture"? **[Infer]**
2. What difference between Penelope and Odysseus does the speaker point out? **[Compare and Contrast]**
3. To whom might the Siren in "Siren Song" be speaking? **[Infer]**
4. What is the speaker saying about some relationships between women and men? **[Draw Conclusions]**

EVALUATE

5. Do you agree with Millay's and Atwood's views of male/female relationships? **[Support]**

An Ancient Gesture/Siren Song ◆ 927

One-Minute Insight In "Siren Song," one of the Sirens says that she is unhappy in her role of singing a song that is irresistible to men. She says that her song is actually a cry for help. However, the last stanza holds the ironic key to this poem; it is precisely the woman's cry for help that is the Siren song men find irresistible.

◆ **Reading Strategy**

❼ **Compare and Contrast** Have students compare this Siren's song to the one in the *Odyssey* (p. 882).
Students may observe that both songs flatter the listener and tell him what he wants to hear. Homer's sirens promise an end to lonliness, whereas Atwood's siren offers to share a secret and begs for rescue.

Reinforce and Extend

Answers

◆ *Literature and Your Life*

Reader's Response Students may say that the poems made them feel more sympathetic because the poems describe personal feelings.

Thematic Focus They describe events from a point of view other than Odysseus'.

☑ **Check Your Comprehension**

1. The speaker cries and wipes away the tears as she believes Penelope must have done.
2. The speaker of "Siren Song" claims she does not like being a Siren.

◆ **Critical Thinking**

1. It is wiping away tears with the corner of an apron.
2. The speaker points out that Penelope "really cried," whereas Odysseus feigned tears to manipulate the crowd.
3. She might be speaking to a man she is trying to entice.
4. Some relationships between men and women are based upon a pretense of need.
5. Student responses on relationships should illustrate a logical interpretation of the poems.

 Block Scheduling Strategies

Consider these suggestions to take advantage of extended class time:

- Have students read and discuss the Background for Understanding (p. 925) to place these poems in their historical context.
- Students may complete the journal activity in Literature and Your Life (p. 925) and work in pairs to compare and contrast their entries.
- Suggest that students use the Internet to research the four poets included here.

Students can access the Internet sites listed on page 931.

- Have students complete the Build Grammar Skills practice and writing application on page 932. Students can work in small groups to check their answers.
- Work with students to complete the Writing Mini-Lesson (p. 933). Guide students to double-check their notes to make sure they have copied material accurately.

One-Minute Insight

"Prologue and Epilogue *from* The Odyssey" presents a modern vision of the epic's beginning and ending. This piece shows the relevance of the *Odyssey* in the modern world.

Customize for
Less Proficient Readers

Help these students through the poem by pointing out references to characters or events in the *Odyssey*.

◆ **Build Grammar Skills**

❶ **Adverb Clauses** Have students identify the adverb clause in this passage. Ask them to tell which word the clause modifies and which part of speech that word is. Then have them explain what kind of information the clause adds to the sentence. *The adverb clause is "because his stories please us." It modifies the word sing, a verb. It tells why the speaker is going to sing about Odysseus.*

❷ **Clarification** Explain that the first line in this stanza shows the pronunciation of a line from Homer's *Odyssey* as it would sound in the original Greek.

❸ **Clarification** Explain that Achilles and Hector are characters not from the *Odyssey*, but from the *Iliad*, Homer's earlier epic about the Trojan War. Achilles was the greatest of the Greek warriors (with Odysseus second), and Hector, son of the king of Troy, was the greatest of the Trojan warriors. Hector is slain by Achilles, and Achilles is killed shortly thereafter.

◆ **Reading Strategy**

❹ **Compare and Contrast** Let students know that Achilles was known for being swift. How does Walcott change the characterization of Achilles in this passage? Ask students to conjecture about why the poet made this change. *Achilles is called "slow-striding." Perhaps this describes the way a contemporary "tough guy" would walk better than "swift-of-foot."*

Prologue and Epilogue *from* The Odyssey

Derek Walcott

PROLOGUE

Sound of surf.

BILLY BLUE *(Sings)*

❶ Gone sing 'bout that man because his stories please us,
Who saw trials and <u>tempests</u> for ten years after Troy.

I'm Blind Billy Blue, my main man's sea-smart Odysseus,
Who the God of the Sea drove crazy and tried to destroy.

5 ❷ Andra moi ennepe mousa polutropon hos mala polla . . .
The shuttle of the sea moves back and forth on this line,

All night, like the surf, she shuttles and doesn't fall
Asleep, then her rosy fingers at dawn unstitch the design.

When you hear this chord
(Chord)
10   Look for a swallow's wings,
A swallow arrowing seaward like a messenger

Passing smoke-blue islands, happy that the kings
Of Troy are going home and its ten years' siege is over.

So my blues drifts like smoke from the fire of that war,
15 ❸ Cause once Achilles was ashes, things sure fell apart.

❹ Slow-striding Achilles, who put the hex on Hector
A swallow twitters in Troy. That's where we start.
(Exit.)

◆ **Build Vocabulary**

tempests (tem´ pists) *n.*: Violent storm with strong winds

◆ Critical Thinking

❺ **Make Inferences** Ask: Why does Walcott write that the sea "still rages" against Odysseus? *Odysseus is an immortal character because people will always read his story. Therefore, his adventures go on eternally.*

EPILOGUE

BILLY BLUE *(Sings)*

❺ I sang of that man against whom the sea still rages,
  Who escaped its terrors, that despair could not destroy,

20 Since that first blind singer, others will sing down the ages
  Of the heart in its harbour, then long years after Troy, after Troy.

  And a house, happy for good, from a swallow's omen,
  Let the trees clap their hands, and the surf whisper amen.

  For a rock, a rock, a rock, a rock-steady woman
25 ❻ Let the waves clap their hands and the surf whisper amen.

  For that peace which, in their mercy, the gods allow men.
(Fade. Sound of surf.)

◆ Critical Thinking

❻ **Interpret** Ask students: Who is the "rock-steady" woman? Why does Walcott use this description for her? *The woman is Penelope. She was faithful to Odysseus for twenty years, never giving up hope that he would return.*

Reinforce and Extend

Answers

◆ *Literature and Your Life*

Reader's Response Students may say they would like to know the narrator because he speaks in the idiom of popular culture.

Thematic Focus The language is contemporary, as is the name "Billy Blue," which takes the place of "Homer."

Check Your Comprehension

1. The narrator is Billy Blue.
2. The God of the Sea is the main enemy.
3. Homer is the first blind singer.

◆ Critical Thinking

1. He mentions Achilles and Hector in the "Prologue" because they were chief foes in the Trojan War from which Odysseus is journeying home.
2. The speaker likes Penelope for remaining true, or "rock-steady," to Odysseus during all the time he was away.
3. Although the language is contemporary and some new elements—such as the "blues"—are added, the interpretation is fairly consistent with Homer.
4. Sample response: The story is relevant to today's readers because it deals with courage, honor, and other timeless values.

Guide for Responding

◆ *Literature and Your Life*

Reader's Response Is the narrator someone you would like to know? Explain.

Thematic Focus In what ways is this a contemporary perspective on the *Odyssey*?

☑ **Check Your Comprehension**

1. Who is the narrator?
2. According to the narrator, who is the main enemy of Odysseus?
3. Who is the "first blind singer" mentioned in the Epilogue?

◆ **Critical Thinking**

INTERPRET
1. Why does Billy Blue mention Achilles and Hector in the "Prologue"? **[Explain]**
2. What is the speaker's attitude toward Penelope? **[Infer]**
3. How faithful is this interpretation of the *Odyssey* to Homer? **[Associate]**

APPLY
4. Derek Walcott presents the Odysseus story in contemporary language. From your perspective, how is the story relevant to today's readers? **[Generalize]**

Prologue and Epilogue from *The Odyssey* ◆ 929

Constantine Cavafy

One-Minute Insight To Cavafy, the journey to Ithaca means more than the voyage of one epic hero, Odysseus, to his home. The trip is symbolic of life's journey for anyone.

◆ **Build Grammar Skills**

❶ **Adverb Clauses** Ask students to identify the adverb clause in this sentence. Have students explain what question the clause answers. *The adverb clause is "When you start on your long journey to Ithaca." It answers the question "when."*

◆ **Critical Thinking**

❷ **Interpret** Ask students: Why will you never encounter the dangers the poet mentions "if your thoughts remain lofty"? *Sample response: People who succumb to jealousy, greed, anger, or other such thoughts endanger themselves.*

◆ **Literary Focus**

❸ **Contemporary Interpretations** Ask students: Which characters from Homer are mentioned in this passage? How does the poet use them in an original way? *The characters from Homer are the Lestrygonians, the Cyclopes, and the angry Poseidon. In Homer, they are actual characters; in the poem, they are thoughts or ideas. Cavafy uses them to express his own thoughts and values.*

◆ **Critical Thinking**

❹ **Make Inferences** Ask students: Why does the speaker advise readers to let the voyage "last for long years"? *Suggested response: The longer life's journey is, the more that can be experienced and learned.*

▶ **Critical Viewing** ◀

❺ **Connect** Students might say that "Phoenician markets" correspond to opportunities for new experiences, and that allusions to fearful creatures, such as the Lestrygonians, might represent difficult challenges or obstacles in life.

When you start on your journey to Ithaca,
❶ then pray that the road is long,
full of adventure, full of knowledge.
Do not fear the Lestrygonians[1]
5 and the Cyclopes and the angry Poseidon.
You will never meet such as these on your path,
❷ if your thoughts remain lofty, if a fine
emotion touches your body and your spirit.
❸ You will never meet the Lestrygonians,
10 the Cyclopes and the fierce Poseidon,
if you do not carry them within your soul,
if your soul does not raise them up before you.

Then pray that the road is long.
That the summer mornings are many,
15 that you will enter ports seen for the first time
with such pleasure, with such joy!
Stop at Phoenician markets,
and purchase fine merchandise,
mother-of-pearl and corals, amber and ebony,
20 and pleasurable perfumes of all kinds,
buy as many pleasurable perfumes as you can;
visit hosts of Egyptian cities,
to learn and learn from those who have knowledge.

Always keep Ithaca fixed in your mind.
25 To arrive there is your ultimate goal.
But do not hurry the voyage at all.
It is better to let it last for long years;
and even to anchor at the isle when you are old,
❹ rich with all that you have gained on the way,
30 not expecting that Ithaca will offer you riches.

---

1. **Lestrygonians** (les tri gō′ nē ənz): Cannibals who destroy all of Odysseus' ships except his own and kill the crews.

Amphora with Grapes, Loran Speck, Loran Speck Art Gallery, Carmel, CA

▲ **Critical Viewing** The poet uses classical images from the *Odyssey*, like those pictured here, to make a connection to modern life. What experiences in *your* life could correspond to some of the classical images mentioned in the poem? **[Connect]** ❺

930 ◆ *The Epic*

Speaking and Listening Mini-Lesson

Choral Reading

This mini-lesson supports the Speaking and Listening activity in the Idea Bank (p. 933).

Introduce the Concept Tell students that in a choral reading, a group reads together, the way a chorus sings together.

Develop Background Lead students to follow these steps:

• Skim the "Prologue and Epilogue" to find the most dramatic and important moments.

• Focus on punctuation for clues to pacing. For example, pause briefly at commas and longer at periods, colons, and semicolons.

• Be sure to enunciate every word clearly so the audience can understand what you are saying.

Apply the Information Have students use these suggestions as they prepare and perform their choral readings.

Assess the Outcome Students should evaluate the performances for clarity of diction and expressivity of voice.

Ithaca has given you the beautiful voyage.
Without her you would never have taken the road.
But she has nothing more to give you.

And if you find her poor, Ithaca has not <u>defrauded</u> you.
35 With the great wisdom you have gained, with so much experience,
You must surely have understood by then what Ithaca means.

◆ **Build Vocabulary**

amber (am´ bər) *n.*: Yellowish resin used in jewelry

ebony (eb´ ə nē) *n.*: Hard, dark wood used for furniture

defrauded (di frôd´ əd) *v.*: Cheated

Guide for Responding

◆ *Literature and Your Life*

Reader's Response Does the journey to Ithaca as described in this poem appeal to you? Explain.

Thematic Focus Choose three or four words from the poem that symbolize the speaker's perspective on the journey to Ithaca.

☑ **Check Your Comprehension**

1. According to the speaker, how can you avoid meeting the Lestrygonians, the Cyclopes, and Poseidon on the road to Ithaca?
2. What two things should you pray for on the journey to Ithaca?
3. Why is Ithaca important?

◆ **Critical Thinking**

INTERPRET

1. What might the journey to Ithaca symbolize? **[Infer]**
2. What might Ithaca symbolize? **[Infer]**
3. In what way could a person carry the Lestrygonians, the Cyclopes, and the angry Poseidon in his or her own soul? **[Infer]**

APPLY

4. What do you think the speaker of this poem might have said to Odysseus if he could have advised him during his journey? **[Speculate]**

Ithaca ◆ 931

Reinforce and Extend

Answers
◆ *Literature and Your Life*

Reader's Response Most students will find that a long journey of discovery appeals to them.

Thematic Focus Student lists of words that capture the speaker's perspective may include: *long, adventure, knowledge, pleasurable, learn, beautiful, wisdom,* and *experience*

Check Your Comprehension ☑

1. You can avoid them by maintaining lofty thoughts and fine emotions, and by not carrying the Lestrygonians and the Cyclopes within your soul.
2. You should pray that the road is long, that the summer mornings are many, and that you will enter ports seen for the first time.
3. Suggested response: Ithaca is important because it marks the end of the journey. Because the journey does eventually end, it is important to get as much out of it as possible.

◆ Critical Thinking

1. Suggested response: The journey probably represents the journey through life.
2. Suggested response: Ithaca might be a metaphor for old age or death.
3. Suggested response: People create their own opportunities or difficulties, depending on how they respond to life.
4. Sample response: The speaker might have advised Odysseus to travel slowly and, if possible, to learn all he could from each encounter—both friendly and dangerous—he had along the way.

Beyond the Selection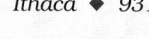

FURTHER READING

Other Works by the Poets

A Few Figs from Thistles, Edna St. Vincent Millay
The Animals in That Country, Margaret Atwood
Collected Poems 1948–1984, Derek Walcott
Walls, Constantine Cavafy

Other Works With the Theme of Perspectives

The King Must Die, Mary Renault
The Once and Future King, T. H. White
In Search of the Trojan War, Michael Wood

INTERNET

The Internet provides excellent opportunities for students to learn more about these poets. We suggest the following sites. Please be aware, however, that sites may have changed from the time we published this information.

For more Edna St. Vincent Millay poems, visit **http://wiretap.spies.com/ftp.items/ Library/Classic/renasc.evm**

For more on Margaret Atwood, visit

http://alvin. lbl.gov/bios/Atwood.html

For more on Derek Walcott, visit
http://www. nobel.se/laureates/ literature-1992-press. html

For more on Constantine Cavafy, go to
http://users.hol.gr/~barbanis/cavafy

We *strongly recommend* that you preview the sites before you send students to them.

Answers

◆ Reading Strategy

1. Students may say that some contemporary women might not enjoy acting in a particular way—rather than being themselves—to attract men.
2. She implies that she is unhappy.
3. Suggested response: Homer's journey is one filled with danger, while Cavafy's journey is one filled with opportunities for new experiences and to acquire wisdom.

◆ Literary Focus

1. Sample response: She sees the theme of separation from a loved one.
2. Sample response: Atwood's Siren is irresistible to men, as is Homer's Siren. Unlike Homer's Siren, Atwood's Siren does not enjoy her role as a singer. Atwood might be saying that modern women don't want the attracting of men to be their chief role in life.
3. Suggested response: Walcott uses contemporary language, with expressions such as "my main man's sea-smart Odysseus," to bring the Odyssey into the late twentieth century.
4. Suggested response: On his journey, Odysseus encountered a wide range of experiences—physical, emotional, and psychological. This journey therefore reflects the variety of experiences one encounters during a lifetime.
5. Students should cite literary works with timeless themes.

◆ Build Vocabulary

1. picturesque;   2. arabesque;
3. statuesque

Using the Word Bank

picturesque, amber, ebony, tempests, beached

◆ Build Grammar Skills

Practice

1. Clause: "When I read the Odyssey"; modifies "dream"
2. Clause: "because I would like to visit Hawaii"; modifies "would sail"
3. Clause: "If time permitted"; modifies "would spend"
4. Clause: "because I get seasick on all kinds of boats"; modifies "is"

Writing Application

Sample adverb clauses:

1. When the time was right
2. If he weren't blinded
3. Because many men believed Odysseus was dead

Guide for Responding (continued)

◆ Reading Strategy

COMPARE AND CONTRAST

As you read these poems, you were reminded of characters, events, or situations in Homer's *Odyssey*. **Comparing and contrasting**—seeing the likenesses and differences between—each poem and the *Odyssey* can not only add to your comprehension of the modern adaptations, but can also enhance your understanding of Homer's work.

1. What similarities do you see between Atwood's Siren and some contemporary women?
2. What does the speaker in Millay's poem imply about her life by comparing herself to Penelope?
3. Cavafy uses the journey to Ithaca as a metaphor—a comparison between two essentially unlike things. How is the journey he describes essentially different from the one Homer describes?

◆ Literary Focus

CONTEMPORARY INTERPRETATIONS

When modern writers **interpret** the *Odyssey* or some part of it creatively, they frequently use it to organize and express their own feelings, beliefs, and experiences. Atwood, for example, uses the Sirens to say something about women. Cavafy uses a basic plot thread of the *Odyssey*—the journey home of Odysseus—to say something about life and living. In the hands of these writers, Homer's subject matter takes on new meanings according to the special purpose of each artist.

1. What timeless theme does Edna St. Vincent Millay see in the *Odyssey*?
2. How does Margaret Atwood use similarities and differences between her Siren and Homer's to make a point about modern women?
3. How does Derek Walcott use language to bring Homer into the late twentieth century?
4. Why is Odysseus' journey home such excellent material for a literary work concerned with the course of human life?
5. What other literary works can you think of that are especially well suited for modern interpretations? Explain your answer.

◆ Build Vocabulary

USING THE SUFFIX *-esque*

Complete each sentence with one of the words containing the suffix *-esque*, meaning "like."

a. statuesque   **b.** arabesque   **c.** picturesque

1. The ___?___ mountain view lingered in my mind.
2. The carpet was covered in ___?___ designs resembling Moorish calligraphy.
3. The ___?___ actress commanded the attention of the audience by her regal bearing.

USING THE WORD BANK

On your paper, rewrite the paragraph, filling in the blanks with words from the Word Bank.

A ___?___ view could be seen from the rocky cliff that overlooked the entrance to the harbor. At dusk, tourists climbed the steep hills to watch an ___?___ sunset eventually fade to a deep ___?___ canopy dotted with twinkling stars. When ___?___ brewed, the sky turned a leaden gray. Afterwards, the townspeople would sometimes find a small boat ___?___ on the shore.

◆ Build Grammar Skills

ADVERB CLAUSES

An **adverb clause** is a subordinate clause that functions as an adverb, modifying a verb, adjective, or adverb in the main clause. These poets use adverb clauses to add important details to their poems.

Practice Identify the adverb clause in each sentence and tell what word it modifies.

1. When I read the *Odyssey*, I always dream of going on a long sea voyage.
2. I would sail first across the Pacific, because I would like to visit Hawaii.
3. If time permitted, I would spend time in Polynesia.
4. Unfortunately, this is probably not a realistic dream because I get seasick on all kinds of boats.

Writing Application Add details to each sentence by adding an adverb clause.

1. Odysseus left Troy with all his men.
2. The Cyclops might have destroyed their ship.
3. Penelope was besieged by suitors.

✎ Writer's Solution

For additional instruction and practice, use the lesson in the **Language Lab CD-ROM** on Varying Sentence Structure and the practice page on Adverb Clauses (p. 55) in the *Writer's Solution Grammar Practice Book*.

Build Your Portfolio

 Idea Bank

Writing

1. **Metaphor** Constantine Cavafy used Odysseus' journey to Ithaca as a metaphor for life. Come up with your own metaphor for life, and write a paragraph describing it.

2. **Comparison–and–Contrast Essay** Write an essay in which you compare and contrast one of the selections with the appropriate portion of Homer's original work. Support your points with passages from both selections.

3. **Adaptation** Follow the lead of these writers by creating your own adaptation of a section from the *Odyssey* in the form of a poem, a story, or a dramatic scene. You can either keep the original setting or use a more contemporary setting.

Speaking and Listening

4. **Monologue** Choose a character from the *Odyssey* and prepare a monologue modeled after "Siren Song." Show the character's innermost thoughts and feelings. Read your monologue aloud to the class. **[Performing Arts Link]**

5. **Choral Reading** Greek drama usually had a chorus that provided a commentary on events. With a group, prepare a choral reading of "Prologue" and "Epilogue." Rehearse several times so that you can read in unison. Then do your choral reading for the class. **[Performing Arts Link]**

Projects

6. **Illustration** Create a painting, collage, or drawing to illustrate one of these selections. Display your artwork for the class. **[Art Link]**

7. **Collection** Create a collection of literature inspired by the *Odyssey* or another famous work. Include an introduction to each piece.

 Writing Mini-Lesson

Now-and-Then Report

These poems remind readers that times have changed since the writing of the *Odyssey*—and so has Greece. Write a research report comparing ancient Greece and modern Greece. Of course, you won't be able to cover every aspect of life in Greece. Focus on just two or three—for example, government, the arts, or sports. Your report doesn't have to be all-encompassing, but the facts you do include should be accurate.

Writing Skills Focus: Accuracy

When you write a research report, it's essential that you make sure that your details are **accurate**—a true reflection of reality. To ensure accuracy, use as many sources as possible. Check each detail you find in another source. If a detail appears in two sources, you can generally be assured of its accuracy. Also, make sure that you are careful when recording the details you find. Do not change the meaning when you put the facts into your own words.

Prewriting Once you have chosen two or three areas to explore and have taken notes on note cards, make a comparison chart like this one and fill it in point by point.

Ancient Greece	Modern Greece
1.	
2.	

Drafting As you draft, use words that show points of comparison—*like, unlike, in contrast,* and so on.

Revising When you revise, make sure that your paper is clearly organized by points of comparison and contrast. Also, double-check your facts.

An Ancient Gesture/Siren Song/Prologue and Epilogue from The Odyssey/Ithaca ◆ 933

Connections to Today's World

Like the epic journey of Odysseus long ago, the nearly catastrophic journey of the Apollo 13 spacecraft was fraught with excitement and danger. Have students conjecture why this conversation was grouped with the *Odyssey* and the related poems. What connections do they see among the different literary works? *Students might say that the astronauts are like Odysseus because their journey was full of dangers and they arrived home safely; the oxygen leak can be compared with monsters and other dangers Odysseus encountered on his voyage.*

About the Author The first astronaut to make four spaceflights, Jim Lovell commanded Gemini 7, Gemini 12, Apollo 8, and Apollo 13. Born in 1928 in Cleveland, Ohio, Lovell graduated from the United States Naval Academy at Annapolis. During his space training, Lovell logged over 5,000 hours of flying time! After his dramatic flight on Apollo 13, Lovell took a post with the Johnson Space Center. In 1973, he left NASA to enter the business world.

Customize for
Less Proficient Readers
To help less proficient readers, explain that Lovell uses *jargon,* or language unique to a particular field. Point out examples of NASA jargon, such as "Copy that" (for "Did you hear that?") and "Rog" (for "understand"). As they read, have students list examples of NASA jargon and figure out their meanings through context.

Customize for
English Language Learners
Explain to nonnative speakers that English has taken many words from mythological names. A word derived from Odysseus' name, *odyssey,* now refers to any difficult voyage of discovery. Invite students to share some words from their native language that come from names in mythology.

Customize for
Interpersonal Learners
Have these students suggest ways that people can work together to stay calm in life-threatening situations such as the one described here.

CONNECTIONS TO TODAY'S WORLD

In April 1970, the three-man crew of the *Apollo 13* spacecraft embarked on a modern-day odyssey to the moon. Like Odysseus, they set out with a spirit of anticipation and adventure. Their mission almost ended tragically, however, when an oxygen tank ruptured on board, but after several nerve-wracking days, the crew finally managed to return safely to Earth.

Jim Lovell, one of the astronauts on that flight, co-authored a book about this frightening adventure. The book, in turn, inspired a feature film. In this excerpt from the book, Lovell has just reported a gas leak to controllers on the ground.

From APOLLO 13

JIM LOVELL
AND
JEFFREY KLUGER

"It looks to me," Lovell told the ground uninflectedly, "that we are venting something." Then, for impact, and perhaps to persuade himself, he repeated "We are venting something into space."

"Roger," Lousma responded, in the mandatory matter-of-factness of the Capcom, "we copy your venting."

"It's a gas of some sort," Lovell said.

"Can you tell us anything about it? Where is it coming from?"

"It's coming out of window one right now, Jack," Lovell answered, offering only as much detail as his vantage point provided.

The understated report from the spacecraft tore through the control room like a bullet.

"Crew thinks they're venting something," Lousma said to the loop at large.

934 ◆ *The Epic*

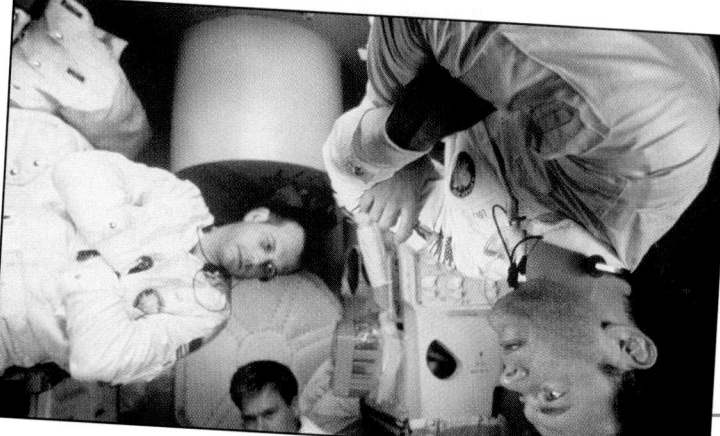

"I heard that," Kranz said.

"Copy that, Flight?" Lousma asked, just to be sure.

"Rog," Kranz assured him. "O.K. everybody, let's think of the kinds of things we'd be venting. GNC, you got anything that looks abnormal on your system?"

"Negative, Flight."

"How about you, EECOM? You see anything with the instrumentation you've got that could be venting?"

"That's affirmed, Flight," Liebergot said, thinking, of course, of oxygen tank two. If a tank of gas is suddenly reading empty and a cloud of gas is surrounding the spacecraft, it's a good bet the two are connected, especially if the whole mess had been preceded by a suspicious ship-shaking bang. "Let me look at the system as far as venting is concerned," Liebergot said to Flight.

"O.K., let's start scanning," Kranz agreed. "I assume you've called in your backup EECOM to see if we can get some brain power on this thing."

"We got one here."

"Rog."

The change on the loop and in the room was palpable. No one said anything out loud, no one declared anything officially, but the controllers began to recognize that the *Apollo 13*, which had been launched in triumph just over two days earlier, might have just metamorphosed from a brilliant mission of exploration to one of simple survival.

---

1. In what ways is the flight of *Apollo 13* similar to the journey of Odysseus? In what ways is it different?
2. When the oxygen leak is detected, both the astronauts and the controllers try to think clearly and act calmly. How can keeping your head under pressure help you to achieve your goals?

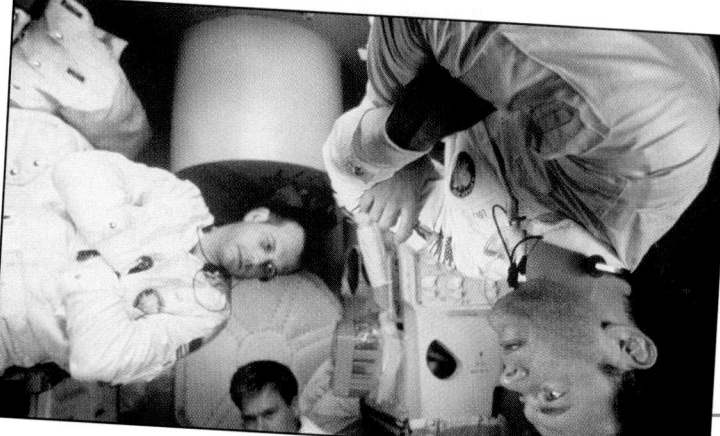

Genre Connection

This nonfiction excerpt and the four poems represent two different genres. Have students explain how the difference in genre affects the way the theme is expressed. *Suggested response: The nonfiction excerpt states the theme more directly; the poems, in contrast, are allusive by their very nature.*

Answers

1. Suggested response: The flight of Apollo 13 is similar to the journey of Odysseus in that both the spaceflight and the sea voyage were marked by adventure and danger. The journeys differed in destinations and in the levels of technology represented by a sailing ship of ancient times and a spacecraft of the twentieth century.
2. Students might say that keeping your head can help guard against making rash decisions that can adversely affect progress toward achieving a goal.

Establish Writing Guidelines
Review the following key characteristics of a research paper:

- A research paper uses information gathered from a variety of sources to explore a topic.

- It usually includes an introduction that states the main point, a body that supports the main point, and a conclusion that summarizes the main points.

- The sources used by the writer should be credited in footnotes or other types of citation.

- A bibliography is provided at the end of a research paper.

Distribute the scoring rubric for Research Report/Paper (p. 99 in **Alternative Assessment**) to make students aware of the criteria on which they will be evaluated before they begin. See the suggestions on page 938 for how you can customize the rubric to this workshop.

 Writer's Solution

Writers at Work Videodisc
Play the videodisc segment on Research Writing (Ch. 5). Have students discuss what Wheat has to say about creating a research plan.

Play frames 3 to 10167

Writing Lab CD-ROM
If your students have access to computers, you may want to have them work in the tutorial on Research Writing to complete all or part of their research papers. Follow these steps:

1. Suggest students use the Transition Word Bin to find transition words or phrases that help readers see connections among ideas.
2. Have students draft on computer.
3. Encourage students to use the Video Tip From a Writer to hear Ellen Harkins Wheat's thoughts on revising a draft.
4. Suggest students use the Peer Evaluation Checklist, which provides guiding questions to help them edit another student's work.

Sourcebook
Students can find additional support, in the chapter on Research Writing (pp. 128–161).

936

Research Paper

Writing Process Workshop

When you present factual information on a topic you've researched—such as the Trojan War or modern interpretations of the *Odyssey*—you're writing a **research paper**. A research paper usually includes an introduction that states the main idea of your topic; a body that offers information on all the subtopics in your report; and a conclusion that summarizes your main points. On each page, you cite the sources of your information in footnotes. You also include a bibliography at the end of the paper that lists all the sources you used.

Write a research paper on a topic that interests you. The following skill, introduced in this section's Writing Mini-Lesson, will help.

Writing Skills Focus

▶ **Be accurate** when researching and writing your paper. Make sure that you get your facts from reliable sources. Also be sure that you don't change the meaning of any information you rephrase in your own words. (See p. 933.)

In the following brief excerpt from a research paper, the writer uses the above skill when discussing modern interpretations of the *Odyssey*.

MODEL

① The writer clearly states her main idea.

② The writer offers details to support her main idea.

③ The names of the authors and their work are accurately recorded.

The characters and events in the *Odyssey* are timeless and universal in their interest and significance. ① They are so rich in meaning that every generation sees in them ideas and values relevant to the present. ② As a result, countless writers have mined the *Odyssey* for material to create original poems, plays, novels, and essays. Two such writers are Margaret Atwood, author of the poem "Siren Song," and Constantine Cavafy, author of the poem "Ithaca." ③ Though their interpretations differ widely in purpose and theme, they both use Homer's material in original ways to express contemporary thoughts, values, beliefs, and feelings.

936 ◆ The Epic

 Beyond the Classroom

Workplace Connection
Nonfiction Writer Tell students that the term *nonfiction writer* includes all professional writers whose writing is other than stories, novels, poetry, and plays. In other words, the term includes journalists, biographers, historical writers, science writers, and so on. Let students know that all these nonfiction writers do a great deal of research for their work. Their research can include anything from finding out about a per-son's background, to investigating the story behind a new scientific discovery, to exploring the historical causes of a current event. Discuss with the class how a professional nonfiction writer's work would differ from a high-school student's. *Professional writers might not write actual research papers, but rather use their notes, taken during research, to include information that would help readers better understand their topics and that would make their writing more interesting.*

Prewriting

Choose a Topic Pick a topic for your research paper by thinking of a subject that interests you. Your topic should also be one for which there is a good amount of information available. If you can't think of a topic on your own, consider one of the topic ideas listed here.

> ### Topic Ideas
> - An important historical event
> - A historic landmark
> - A famous scientific experiment
> - A highly regarded theory or philosophy

Find Accurate Sources In the library, locate the resources that will help you the most. These may include history books, newspapers, and magazines. Use the most up-to-date resources, because they may contain information not included in older materials. To further ensure accuracy, try to find the same facts or details in at least two different sources.

Use the Internet Use key words relating to your topic to search the Internet for additional information.

Take Accurate Notes Use note cards and source cards to record your information. Here are some tips:

Note Cards	Source Cards
• Enter only one piece of information on each card.	• Create one source card for each source you use.
• Include the page number from which you obtained the information.	• List all the information you will need for crediting the source: author, title, publisher, date, and so on.
• Write a subhead at the top of each card telling on which aspect of your topic the note focuses.	

Drafting

Copy Your Notes Accurately Use your note cards to help you draft your research paper. Copy information accurately from each note card, double-checking to make sure you've rephrased all the information in your own words.

APPLYING LANGUAGE SKILLS: Citing Sources

When you quote a passage directly, **cite the source** in a footnote. Include the title of the work, the larger work it comes from, the city in which the publisher is located, the year of publication, and the page number of the quote.

Footnote:
1. Margaret Atwood, "Siren Song," You Are Happy (New York, 1974), p. 129.

Practice Identify the information that is missing in each footnote.
1. "Ithaca," (New York, 1976)
2. The World Book, Volume 4, p. 174.

Writing Application As you draft your paper, use a footnote at the bottom of the page to cite any passage on that page that you have quoted directly.

**Writer's Solution Connection
Writing Lab**

For additional help in gathering informtion for your paper, use the instruction and activities in the Prewriting section of the tutorial on Research Writing.

Prewriting

Emphasize to students the importance of writing only one piece of information on each card. Elicit the concept that this is important because if more than one piece of information is written on a card, the individual pieces of information cannot be moved around and organized. If students limit themselves to one piece of information per card, they can place the cards in the order in which they plan to use the information when they draft their papers.

Customize for
Less Proficient Writers
Remind these students to choose a topic that is practical—one for which they will easily be able to find information in sources that are on their level. Invite them to go over their topics with you before they begin their research. In conference with students, you can suggest a direction in which to go in order to choose an appropriate topic.

Customize for
English Language Learners
These students may be less readily able than native English speakers to choose the best key words relating to their topics to search the Internet for information. Suggest they try reducing the number of words used to describe their topic as much as possible and try the remaining words as key words. By a process of trial and error, they are likely to come up with the words that will access the information they need.

 **Writer's Solution**

Writing Lab CD-ROM
The Narrowing Your Topic section of the tutorial on Research Writing includes a Topic Web to help students divide and subdivide their topics.

Drafting

Advise students that, no matter how well they have organized their note cards, just copying the information from their note cards without adding transitional words and phrases will result in choppy writing that sounds unfinished and unpolished.

Applying Language Skills
Citing Sources
Answers
1. The author and title of the larger work are missing.
2. The name of the article and the place and year of publication are missing.

 **Writer's Solution**

For additional instruction and practice, use the practice page on understanding research papers page in the *Writer's Solution Grammar Practice Book* (p. 136).

Quotation Marks and Underlining
Answers
1. "The Hero Odysseus," *Scholar's Magazine*
2. "Colleges Drop Homer," *The New York Times*

 **Writer's Solution**

For additional instruction and practice, use the practice page on underlining and other uses of quotation marks page in the *Writer's Solution Grammar Practice Book* (p. 108).

937

Revising

Students might add to their checklists an item that will remind them to be sure their theses are well supported. Each paragraph following the thesis statement should back up the thesis, or main idea. Paragraphs that do not relate to the thesis should be revised or deleted.

 **Writer's Solution**

Writing Lab CD-ROM

The Tips on Improving Content in the Revision section of the tutorial on Research Writing provide strategies students can use to check their work for accuracy, clarity, and consistency. Audio annotations allow students to hear about ways to check their writing for logical fallacies.

Publishing

Suggest students contribute copies of their research papers for inclusion in a class book that can be donated to the school library.

Reinforce and Extend

Review the Writing Guidelines
After students have completed their papers, review the characteristics of a research paper. Invite discussion on how the strategies they learned helped them to write better-organized and more interesting papers.

Connect to Literature Unit 5 ("Visions of the Future") includes an excerpt from Bill Gates's *The Road Ahead*. Although this work is mostly autobiographical, Gates is careful to cite sources and provide accurate information. Have students obtain a copy of the book from the library to see how Gates's book is an example of research writing.

APPLYING LANGUAGE SKILLS: Quotation Marks and Underlining

In a footnote, use **quotation marks** around the title of a poem, magazine article, or newspaper article. **Underline** or italicize the title of a book, magazine, or newspaper.

1. *Constantine Cavafy, "Ithaca," The Complete Poems of Cavafy (New York, 1976), p. 59.*

Practice On your paper, add quotation marks or underline where necessary.

1. E. Gray, The Hero Odysseus, Scholar's Magazine (Chicago, 1991), p. 32.
2. Colleges Drop Homer, The New York Times, May 3, 1988, p. B 7.

Writing Application As you review your research paper, check that you have written all footnotes correctly. Correct any errors you find.

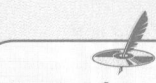

Writer's Solution Connection Writing Lab

For additional help with revising, work through the Revision section of the tutorial on Research Writing. You'll find revision checkers for coherence and transitions that will help you improve your organizaiton.

938 ◆ The Epic

Organize Your Ideas Begin with an introduction stating your thesis, the main point that you want to make about your topic. Follow with a series of body paragraphs, each focusing on a single subpoint and providing supporting details. End with a conclusion that drives home your main idea.

Quote Your Sources Accurately At some points in your paper, you will wish to quote a source directly. Be sure that you record those passages word for word. For each quotation, write a footnote that cites the author and source of the quote. List your source again in your bibliography.

Revising

Use a Checklist The following checklist will help you revise.

▶ Does my paper center around a thesis—a main point that I make about my topic?
Make sure that you've actually made a point about your topic, rather than just restating information you've gathered. For example, if you're writing a paper about Abraham Lincoln, you wouldn't simply state the facts of his life, you'd want to draw some conclusions about why he was a great leader.

▶ Have I accurately recorded my information?
Invite a peer to read your draft. If the reader questions the accuracy of any information, go back to your notes and check them. If you have copied something incorrectly, correct it.

▶ Have I accurately cited my sources of information?
Make sure that every passage that you haven't rephrased is marked with a footnote. If you have omitted a footnote, use your note cards to help you write one.

▶ Does my paper have a clear organization?
Read through your paper from start to finish, looking for any places where it seems to jump around or where one idea doesn't seem to flow logically from the previous one. Rearrange your ideas to make the organization clearer.

Publishing

▶ **Classroom** Share your research paper by presenting it to classmates as a special news report.
▶ **Audio Corner** Make an audiotape recording of your report. Create a classroom corner where classmates can listen to it.

✓ ASSESSMENT		4	3	2	1
PORTFOLIO ASSESSMENT Use the rubric on Research Report/Paper in *Alternative Assessment* (p. 99) to assess students' writing. Add these criteria to customize the rubric to this assignment.	**Organization**	There is a clear introduction, body, and conclusion. Each paragraph has one focus.	There's a clear introduction, body, and conclusion. Some paragraphs lack focus.	Many paragraphs lack focus.	The paper lacks a clear organization.
	Citation of Sources	All sources are thoroughly documented.	Most sources are thoroughly documented.	The writer often fails to cite sources.	The writer has completely failed to cite sources.

938

Real-World Reading Skills Workshop

Sorting Information on the Internet

Strategies for Success

When you have access to the Internet, it's like having an entire library at your fingertips. The problem is that sometimes you can find so much information, it's hard to decide which is the most useful. How can you evaluate the information you find? Use these tips.

Don't Judge a Web Site by Its Appearance A Web site that looks slick and professional doesn't necessarily contain the most accurate information. Look past the flashy graphics to evaluate the information critically.

Try to Determine Why the Information Was Posted Sometimes companies and professional organizations post information that will promote their products, services, or philosophies. For example, a sneaker company will most likely promote their shoes as the best, without necessarily providing the facts about other brands. Look for objectivity in the information you uncover.

Verify the Information Elsewhere When evaluating any kind of information, try to verify facts in at least one, and preferably two, other sources.

Apply the Strategy

You can get more information about the reliability of a Web site by consulting a review guide that evaluates Web sites. Here are two you might want to try:

Argus Clearinghouse
http://www.clearinghouse.net/chhome.html

Mining Company
http://miningco.com

✔ Here are other situations in which sorting information on the Internet can be helpful:
▶ Learning about today's news
▶ Planning a vacation
▶ Finding want ads
▶ Locating a particular book

939

Speaking and Listening Workshop

Critically Viewing News Reports

Every day you encounter news reports on television, radio, and in the newspaper. Many of these reports offer an objective account of events, but it's not safe to assume that *every* news report is fair and accurate. Critically viewing news reports will help you to evaluate the information you learn through news media.

Know Your News There are different types of news reports. Straightforward "hard" news reports are meant to be objective. These reports address all sides of an issue. Feature stories offer a more personal, and therefore less objective look at a topic. A news feature may present only one side of an issue. Understanding which type of news you're viewing or listening to will help you be a more critical observer.

Listen to the Language Pay close attention to the language used in a news report. Listen for words that might sway the audience—that is, persuade viewers to think in a certain way.

• *A roving pack of teenagers terrorized the mall today.*

• *A group of teenagers overwhelmed the mall today.*

Which report sounds fairer to you?

Tips for Viewing News Reports Critically

✔ *If you want to be a good judge of a news report, consider these points as you listen:*
  ▶ Who is reporting the news?
  ▶ Does the report address all sides of the issue?
  ▶ Is the language fair?

Apply the Strategies

With a partner, perform each of these activities. Apply the strategies you have learned for critically viewing a news report.

1. Have your partner read you a news report from the newspaper. Listen carefully to analyze it for fairness. Stop your partner along the way to identify content that you question.

2. Tape a news broadcast from radio or television. Have your partner play the tape for you in class. When you hear content that you question, ask your partner to stop the tape, and then describe your concerns.

3. Have your partner write a news report on any topic, real or imaginary. As your partner reads the report to you, identify points at which you question the content.

After you and your partner have finished, switch roles and repeat each activity.

 Preparing for Standardized Tests

Verbal portions of some standardized tests may require students to distinguish between words that have similar meanings but different connotations. For example:

Which sentence contains a word with a negative connotation? *(B)*

  (A) My sister kept reminding me to return the books to the library.
  (B) My sister kept nagging me to return the books to the library.
  (C) My sister kept telling me to return the books to the library

Experience with viewing news reports critically will provide practice in recognizing words with connotations that persuade readers to think in a certain way.

Extended Reading Opportunities

The world of the epic is the world of great heroes, classic struggles, and extraordinary deeds. Following are just a few possibilities for extending your exploration of the genre.

Suggested Titles

The Iliad
Homer

The *Iliad* is an epic poem that tells the story of the Trojan War. The fighting began after Paris, son of the king of Troy, ran off with the beautiful Helen, daughter of the god Zeus and wife of Menelaus of Sparta. The war between Troy and Greece dragged on for ten years and ended when the Greeks pretended to depart, leaving a giant wooden horse behind. The story of what lay waiting inside that horse, as well as many other thrilling events, has been engaging readers for centuries.

Mythology:
Timeless Tales
of Gods and Heroes
Edith Hamilton

This collection includes tales of the Greek and Roman gods and heroes, as well as the mythology of the Norse people. In it, Hamilton introduces Zeus and the other gods of Olympus and tells famous love stories, like that of Cupid and Psyche. In *Mythology*, readers also encounter thrilling tales of adventure, including Jason's perilous quest for the Golden Fleece, the epic story of the Trojan War, and the Norse legends of Signy and Sigurd.

Other Possibilities

The *Odyssey*   Homer
The Shining Company   Rosemary Sutcliff

Planning Students' Extended Reading

All of these works are good choices for extending students' exploration of epics and mythology. Following is some information that will help you choose which to teach.

Customize for
Varying Student Needs

When assigning the selections in this part to your students, keep in mind the following factors:

• The *Iliad* offers an alternative to the *Odyssey*. Be aware that the epic may pose difficulty for less proficient readers. However, your more advanced students may want to read it after completing the *Odyssey*.

• Mythology offers an excellent opportunity for extending students exploration of the Ancient Greek folk traditions.

Resources for Teaching Novels, Plays, and Literature Collections

This booklet includes graphic organizers, teaching strategies, and transparencies that you can use in teaching any of these works

Sensitive Issues

By nature, mythology touches on sensitive issues. The religious beliefs of the ancient Greeks, for example, may be considered offensive by those who are monotheistic or have different views of the afterlife.

The *Iliad* includes violent battle scenes, implied adultery (Helen runs off with Paris), suicide (Ajax kills himself when Achilles' armor is awarded to Odysseus), and human sacrifice (Polyxena is sacrificed on Achilles' tomb).

ACCESS GUIDE TO WORD BANKS

```
┌──────────────────────────────────────────────────────────────────┐
│                  KEY TO PRONUNCIATION SYMBOLS USED                 │
```

Symbol	Key Words	Symbol	Key Words
a	asp, fat, parrot	b	bed, fable, dub
ā	ape, date, play	d	dip, beadle, had
ä	ah, car, father	f	fall, after, off
e	elf, ten, berry	g	get, haggle, dog
ē	even, meet, money	h	he, head, hotel
i	is, hit, mirror	j	joy, agile, badge
ī	ice, bite, high	k	kill, tackle, bake
		l	let, yellow, ball
ō	open, tone, go	m	met, camel, trim
ô	all, horn, law	n	not, flannel, ton
o͞o	ooze, tool, crew	p	put, apple, tap
oo	look, pull, moor	r	red, port, dear
yo͞o	use, cute, few	s	sell, castle, pass
yoo	united, cure, globule	t	top, cattle, hat
oi	oil, point, toy	v	vat, hovel, have
ou	out, crowd, plow	w	will, always, swear
u	up, cut, color	y	yet, onion, yard
ʉr	urn, fur, deter	z	zebra, dazzle, haze
ə	a in ago	ch	chin, catcher, arch
	e in agent	sh	she, cushion, dash
	i in sanity	th	thin, nothing, truth
	o in comply	th	then, father, lathe
	u in focus	zh	azure, leisure
ər	perhaps, murder	ŋ	ring, anger, drink

abash, 795

acclaimed, 154

accosted, 6

acutely, 215

adept, 623

aerodynamics, 619

aesthetic, 604

afflicted, 6

aloofness, 573

amber, 931

ambiguities, 771

amicably, 168

anonymous, 310

arbitrary, 604

archaeologist, 113

archaic, 416

ardent, 478

ardor, 884

articulate, 239, 559

assuage, 878

astutely, 545

astuteness, 93

augmenting, 677

avail, 88

awry, 178

azure, 795

bafflement, 347

barren, 797

beached, 927

beguiling, 832

beleaguered, 437

bemusing, 901

benevolently, 229

bereft, 881

bizarre, 21

blandly, 25

blight, 432

bliss, 788

brazen, 239

buffet, 313

buffeted, 369

cannonading, 302

capacious, 387

cascade, 460

ceasing, 840

censure, 131

charged, 215

chasms, 445

chaste, 460

chattel, 129

chortled, 353

cipher, 131

circumvent, 398

cloister, 524

compelling, 623

complied, 144

concessions, 230

condescending, 593

condolence, 264

confer, 443

confounds, 415

console, 652

contempt, 910

conundrums, 93

covenant, 415, 445

creed, 141

cunning, 702

cur, 302

dallying, 171

déclassé, 537

decoy, 321

deferred, 796

defiance, 646

defrauded, 931

deity, 193

deleterious, 526

demure, 241

depravity, 347

depreciate, 460

derides, 621

derisive, 304

desolate, 832

despair, 189

despotic, 129

desultory, 528

determination, 145

detritus, 217

diffused, 560

disconsolately, 508

discreet, 463

disheveled, 540

dishevelment, 239

dismal, 752

dispatched, 868

disperse, 250

dissemble, 896

distraught, 301

diverged, 167

divine, 805

dogmas, 113

droll, 134

drowsiness, 840

ebony, 931

eddies, 560

eerie, 560

effervesce, 217

effigies, 250

eloquence, 727

elucidate, 216

encroaching, 471

endangered, 478

endeavoring, 365

endurance, 145

enigma, 591

enjoined, 750

entrails, 491

epiphany, 578

epithets, 250

equity, 905

erratic, 395

evanesced, 493

exalted, 141

exile, 726

explicit, 6

extrapolating, 562

extrapolation, 216

feint, 199

feline, 347

fester, 796

fetid, 506

fickle, 738

ford, 359

forebears, 569

formality, 501

formidable, 93

fray, 725

fretful, 67

furtive, 475

furtively, 60

futile, 27

gallant, 724

garish, 50

gaunt, 133

genesis, 593

genteel, 645

glee, 787

glowering, 902

gossamer, 478

grievance, 678

grisly, 395

grotesque, 25

haggard, 301

hamlet, 142

harness, 171

harried, 239

harrowed, 543

haughty, 766

heretics, 683

hieroglyphics, 442

hoax, 89

host, 787

hurtling, 299

hydraulic, 619

ideology, 445

imbued, 252

imminent, 489

immortalized, 336

immutable, 595

impassive, 506

imperative, 60, 180

imperialist, 113

impertinent, 371

imperturbable, 395

implications, 588

impose, 6, 277

improbable, 621

improbably, 478

inalienable, 445

incognito, 310

incredulity, 896

indolently, 18

indulged, 241

ineffable, 217

infallibility, 489

infrared, 387

ingeniously, 277

insatiable, 369

inscrutable, 304

insidious, 217, 888

insinuatingly, 302

insolent, 301

instigates, 459

intent, 282

intercession, 706

interpretation, 323

interval, 9

introspective, 92

intuition, 236

iridescent, 489

irradiated, 364

jibed, 199

judicious, 528

keener, 246

kindred, 186

laden, 272

lamentable, 708

languid, 284

languor, 264

larder, 347

lassoed, 499

lateral, 319

legacy, 591, 622

legendary, 106

levitation, 347

lingered, 240

literally, 180

lithe, 896

loathsome, 753

loitered, 365

longevity, 180

malevolence, 334

malodorous, 229

mammoth, 872

manhandled, 144

marauders, 262

martial, 726

maudlin, 905

medley, 264

menacing, 475

metaphors, 332

metaphysical, 199

meticulously, 168, 807

microcosms, 332

monotone, 818

moribund, 433

mortified, 189, 646

muted, 560

myriad, 217

naive, 24

novice, 560

oasis, 141

obsessed, 604

obstinacy, 571

omen, 371

ominous, 170, 528, 560

ominously, 366

oppression, 141

oracle, 395

paean, 820

pagans, 524

pallid, 504, 832

pallor, 37

palpable, 17

palpitating, 817

pandemonium, 154

parched, 113

parlance, 388

pensive, 748, 788

penury, 762

perennial, 428

perish, 412

permeate, 577

pernicious, 445, 677

perpetuated, 252

perplexed, 104

perplexes, 577

perverse, 239, 524

picturesque, 927

pilgrimage, 756

pinions, 442

pious, 571

placid, 47

placidly, 528

plaiting, 282

plundered, 860

poignant, 334, 588

portents, 153

postulated, 437

precariously, 491

precipitous, 262

precluded, 5

precursors, 387

predominant, 706

preposterous, 478

primed, 804

procure, 704

prodigious, 142, 526

prodigy, 229

profoundly, 540

projectiles, 351

pungent, 225

purged, 426

pursue, 621

pyre, 428

quaint, 830

rakishly, 299

rancor, 569, 595

ravages, 463

ravenous, 153

reciprocate, 476

recoiling, 9

reconcile, 115

reconciled, 193

reconnaissance, 63

recounted, 55

refrain, 359

remnants, 762

respite, 832

resplendent, 539

retort, 229

retribution, 5

revelry, 191

reverie, 238

riveting, 623

rueful, 537

ruminative, 623

sallow, 707

schism, 437

scourge, 774

scowling, 359

scruples, 24

sentimental, 593

sepulcher, 769

shard, 239

simultaneously, 385

singular, 84

sinister, 803

skeptical, 325

slouching, 131

sobriety, 177

sore, 795

specters, 170

spurn, 154

squall, 864

steeds, 416

stout, 283

strafing, 107

suavity, 349

subjugation, 115

submerged, 171

subsided, 9

subsidiary, 396

subtle, 560

succession, 9

succor, 267

suffice, 412

sullen, 56

surcease, 396

surge, 200

surpassed, 9

surreal, 559

tantalizing, 472

tempests, 928

termination, 9

thronging, 104

titanic, 876

transgression, 678

treble, 834

tremulous, 414

trundle, 310

tumult, 38

tumultuous, 587

unbidden, 802

unpalatable, 170

unrequited, 510

unwieldy, 714

valet, 312

vanquished, 504

venture, 180

vex, 93

vial, 749

vigorously, 9

vile, 153, 705

voluminously, 817

vortex, 489

warp, 249

waverer, 707

wavering, 191

wayfarers, 812

wayward, 750

woeful, 834

woes, 841

wreathed, 37

writhing, 37

wrought, 840

yearned, 321

LITERARY TERMS HANDBOOK

ACT See Drama.

ALLITERATION *Alliteration* is the repetition of initial consonant sounds. Writers use alliteration to give emphasis to words, to imitate sounds, and to create musical effects. Notice, in the following lines from Walter de la Mare's "The Listeners," how the s sound imitates a whisper:

Ay, they heard his foot upon the stirrup,

And the sound of iron on stone,

And how the silence surged softly backward,

When the plunging hoofs were gone.

Prose writers use alliteration too, but not as frequently as poets do. Jane Austen used the technique for the titles of her novels *Pride and Prejudice* and *Sense and Sensibility*. Notice, too, that alliteration is the basis of tongue twisters: She sells seashells by the seashore.

See Repetition.

ALLUSION An *allusion* is a reference to a well-known person, place, event, literary work, or work of art. In "The Gift of the Magi," on p. 459, O. Henry writes about a young couple and the Christmas gifts they give to each other. At the end of the story, the narrator explains the biblical allusion in the title: "The Magi, as you know, were wise men—wonderfully wise men—who brought gifts to the Babe in the manger. They invented the art of giving Christmas presents. Being wise, their gifts were no doubt wise ones. . . ."

ANECDOTE An *anecdote* is a brief story about an interesting, amusing, or strange event. Anecdotes are told to entertain or to make a point. In "A Lincoln Preface," on p. 129, Carl Sandburg tells anecdotes about Abraham Lincoln.

See Narrative.

ANTICLIMAX Like a climax, an *anticlimax* is the turning point in a story. However, an anticlimax is always a letdown. It's the point at which you learn that the story will not turn out the way you'd expected. In Thayer's "Casey at the Bat," the anticlimax occurs when Casey strikes out instead of hitting a game-winning run as everyone had expected.

ASIDE An *aside* is a short speech delivered by an actor in a play, expressing the character's thoughts. Traditionally, the aside is directed to the audience and is presumed to be inaudible to the other actors.

ASSONANCE *Assonance* is the repetition of vowel sounds followed by different consonants in two or more stressed syllables. Assonance is found in the phrase "weak and weary" in Edgar Allan Poe's "The Raven," on p. 832.

ATMOSPHERE See Mood.

AUTOBIOGRAPHY An *autobiography* is a form of nonfiction in which a person tells his or her own life story. An autobiography may tell about the person's whole life or only a part of it.

See Biography and Nonfiction.

BIOGRAPHY A *biography* is a form of nonfiction in which a writer tells the life story of another person. Biographies have been written about many famous people, historical and contemporary, but they can also be written about "ordinary" people.

A *biographical essay* is shorter than a biography. In "Georgia O'Keeffe," on p. 592, Joan Didion writes about the independent spirit of the famous painter.

See Autobiography and Nonfiction.

BLANK VERSE *Blank verse* is poetry written in unrhymed iambic pentameter lines. This verse form was widely used by Elizabethan dramatists like William Shakespeare.

See Meter.

CHARACTER A *character* is a person or an animal who takes part in the action of a literary work. The main character, or protagonist, is the most important character in a story. This character often changes in some important way as a result of the story's events. In Richard Connell's "The Most Dangerous Game," on p. 16, Rainsford is the main character and General Zaroff is the antagonist, or character who opposes the main character.

Characters are sometimes classified as round or flat, dynamic or static. A *round character* shows many different traits—faults as well as virtues. Walter Mitty, in James Thurber's "The Secret Life of Walter Mitty," on p. 299, is a round character. We know him not only as a

▲ Two of the most famous characters in literature are William Shakespeare's Romeo and Juliet.

mousy husband but also a man who has a means of escape: his fantasies. His wife is a *flat character*. We see her only as a shrew. A *dynamic character* develops and grows during the course of the story, as does Doodle's brother in "The Scarlet Ibis," on p. 484. A *static character* does not change. Walter Mitty, for example, is just as mousy and just as inclined to fantasize at the end of the story as he was at the beginning.

See Characterization and Motivation.

CHARACTERIZATION *Characterization* is the act of creating and developing a character. In *direct characterization*, the author directly states a character's traits. In "Uncle Marcos," for example, a character states that "Uncle Marcos's manners were those of a cannibal."

In *indirect characterization*, an author tells what a character looks like, does, and says, and how other characters react to him or her. It is up to the reader to draw conclusions about the character based on this indirect information. Toni Cade Bambara describes Granny Cain indirectly in the following

passages from her story, "Blues Ain't No Mockin Bird," on p. 498:

> "I don't know about the thing, the it, and the stuff," said Granny, still talkin with her eyebrows.

> Me and Cathy were waitin, too, cause Granny always got something to say. She teaches steady with no letup.

The most effective indirect characterizations usually result from showing characters acting or speaking. In Saki's "The Interlopers," on p. 262, two enemies lie trapped under a fallen tree. When one of them, Ulrich, suddenly offers a drink of wine to the other, the reader knows that Ulrich is beginning to change his mind about the old feud.

See Character.

CLIMAX The *climax* of a story, novel, or play is the high point of interest or suspense. The events that make up the rising action lead up to the climax. The events that make up the falling action follow the climax.

See Conflict, Plot, and Anticlimax.

CONFLICT A *conflict* is a struggle between opposing forces. Characters in conflict form the basis of stories, novels, and plays.

There are two kinds of conflict: external and internal. In an external conflict, the main character struggles against an outside force. This force may be another character, as in Richard Connell's "The Most Dangerous Game," on p. 16, in which Rainsford struggles with General Zaroff. The outside force could also be the standards or expectations of a group, such as the family prejudices that Romeo and Juliet struggle against. Their story, on p. 672, shows them in conflict with society. The outside force may be nature itself, a person-against-nature conflict. The two men trapped by a fallen tree in Saki's "The Interlopers," on p. 262, face such a conflict.

An *internal conflict* involves a character in conflict with himself or herself. An example is "Checkouts," on p. 236, in which two young people who meet by chance in a supermarket agonize over whether they should speak to each other.

A story may have more than one conflict. In addition to the person-against-nature conflict of "The Interlopers," there are also a person-against-nature conflict between the two men and an internal conflict for the main character, who must decide whether he should forgive his enemy.

See Plot.

Think of a catch that fishermen haul in to a
   half-moon bay

in a fine-meshed net from the whitecaps of the sea:

how all are poured out on the sand, in throes
   for the salt sea,

twitching their cold lives away in Helios' fiery air:

so lay the suitors heaped on one another.

See Figurative Language and Simile.

ESSAY An *essay* is a short nonfiction work about a
particular subject. While classification is difficult, four
types of essays are sometimes identified. A descriptive
essay seeks to convey an impression about a person,
place, or object. In "A Celebration of Grandfathers," on
p. 576, Rudolfo Anaya describes the cultural values that
his grandfather and other "old ones" from his childhood
passed down.

A *narrative essay* tells a true story. In "The Washwoman," I. B. Singer tells of his childhood in Poland, and
the hardworking woman who washed the family
clothes.

An *expository essay* gives information, discusses ideas,
or explains a process. In "Single Room, Earth View," on
p. 559, Sally Ride describes what it's like to be in outer
space.

A *persuasive essay* tries to convince readers to do

▲ In her essay "Single Room, Earth View," astronaut Sally Ride describes her observations of
Earth from the space shuttle.

something or to accept the writer's point of view. In
the essay, "To the Residents of 2029," on p. 434, Bryan
Woolley advises future generations on how to avoid
calamities.

A *visual essay* is an exploration of a topic that conveys its ideas through visual elements as well as language. Like a standard essay, a visual essay presents an
author's views of a single topic. Unlike other essays,
however, much of the meaning in a visual essay is conveyed through illustrations or photographs.

This classification of essays is loose at best. Most
essays contain passages that could be classified differently from the essay as a whole. For example, a
descriptive passage may be found in a narrative essay,
or a factual, expository section may be used to support
a persuasive argument.

See Description, Exposition, Genre, Narration, Nonfiction, and Persuasion.

EXPOSITION *Exposition* is writing or speech that
explains a process or presents information. In the plot
of a story or drama, the exposition is the part of the
work that introduces the characters, the setting, and
the basic situation.

EXTENDED METAPHOR In an *extended metaphor*, as in regular metaphor, a subject is spoken or written of as though it were something else. However, extended metaphor differs from regular metaphor in that several comparisons are made. All extended metaphor sustains the comparison for several lines or for an entire poem. The "caged bird" of Paul Laurence Dunbar's "Sympathy," on p. 246, is an extended metaphor for a person who is not free.

See Figurative Language and Metaphor.

FALLING ACTION See Plot.

FANTASY A *fantasy* is highly imaginative writing that contains elements not found in real life. Examples of fantasy include stories that involve supernatural elements, stories that resemble fairy tales, and stories that deal with imaginary places and creatures, such as Ray Bradbury's "The Golden Kite, the Silver Wind," on p. 152.

Some writers consider science fiction a type of fantasy. Other writers make a distinction between the two kinds of writing.

See Science Fiction.

FICTION *Fiction* is prose writing that tells about imaginary characters and events. The term is usually used for novels and short stories, but it also applies to dramas and narrative poetry. Some writers rely on their imaginations alone to create their works of fiction. Others base their fiction on actual events and people, to which they add invented characters, dialogue, and plot situations.

See Genre, Narrative, and Nonfiction.

FIGURATIVE LANGUAGE *Figurative language* is writing or speech not meant to be interpreted literally.

Figurative language is often used to create vivid impressions by setting up comparisons between dissimilar things.

Though figures of speech are especially important in poetry, they are used in prose as well. Look, for example, at this description from James Hurst's "The Scarlet Ibis," on p. 484:

> . . . the oriole nest in the elm was untenanted and rocked back and forth like an empty cradle. The last graveyard flowers were blooming, and their smell drifted across the cotton field and through every room of our house, speaking softly the names of our dead.

Some frequently used figures of speech are *metaphors*, *similes*, and *personifications*.

See Literal Language.

FOOT See Meter.

FORESHADOWING *Foreshadowing* is the use in a literary work of clues that suggest events that have yet to occur. Use of this technique helps to create suspense, keeping readers wondering and speculating about what will happen next.

See Suspense.

FREE VERSE *Free verse* is poetry not written in a regular rhythmical pattern, or meter. Free verse seeks to capture the rhythms of speech. It is the dominant form of contemporary poetry.

See Meter.

GENRE A *genre* is a category or type of literature. Literature is commonly divided into three major genres: poetry, prose, and drama. Each major genre is in turn divided into smaller genres, as follows:

1. Poetry: Lyric Poetry, Concrete Poetry, Dramatic Poetry, Narrative Poetry, and Epic Poetry

2. Prose: Fiction (Novels and Short Stories) and Nonfiction (Biography, Autobiography, Letters, Essays, and Reports)

3. Drama: Serious Drama and Tragedy, Comic Drama, Melodrama, and Farce

See Drama, Poetry, and Prose.

HAIKU The *haiku* is a three-line verse form. The first and third lines of a haiku each have five syllables. The second line has seven syllables. A haiku seeks to convey a single vivid emotion by means of images from nature. The poems on p. 844 are haiku.

Translators of Japanese haiku try to maintain the syllabic requirements. Western writers, however, sometimes use the form more loosely.

HOMERIC SIMILE See Epic Simile.

IAMB See Meter.

IMAGE An *image* is a word or phrase that appeals to one or more of the five senses—sight, hearing, touch, taste, or smell. Writers use images to re-create

▲ In his lyric poem "The Eagle," Alfred, Lord Tennyson pays tribute to one of nature's creatures.

sensory experiences in words.
See Description.

IMAGERY *Imagery* is the descriptive or figurative language used in literature to create word pictures for the reader. These pictures, or images, are created by details of sight, sound, taste, touch, smell, or movement.

INDIRECT CHARACTERIZATION *See* Characterization.

INTERNAL RHYME *See* Rhyme.

IRONY *Irony* is the general term for literary techniques that portray differences between appearance and reality, expectation and result, or meaning and intention. In *verbal irony* words are used to suggest the opposite of what is meant. In *dramatic irony* there is a contradiction between what a character thinks and what the reader or audience knows to be true. In *irony of situation*, an event occurs that directly contradicts the expectations of the characters, the reader, or the audience. The humor in Ernest Laurence Thayer's "Casey at the Bat," on p. 36, derives in part from irony of situation. The speaker creates the expectation that Casey will save the day. However, at the end of the poem "there is no joy in Mudville" because "Mighty Casey has struck out."

LITERAL LANGUAGE *Literal language* uses words in their ordinary senses. It is the opposite of *figurative language*. If you tell someone standing on a diving board to jump in, you are speaking literally. If you tell someone standing on the street corner to jump in the lake, you are speaking figuratively.

See Figurative Language.

LYRIC POEM A *lyric poem* is a highly musical verse that expresses the observations and feelings of a single speaker. In ancient times lyric poems were sung to the accompaniment of the lyre, a type of stringed instrument. Modern lyric poems are not usually sung. However, they still have a musical quality that is achieved through rhythm and other devices such as alliteration and rhyme. Alfred, Lord Tennyson's "The Eagle," on p. 796, is a lyric poem expressing the speaker's feeling of wonder as he watches an eagle dive from a cliff.

MAIN CHARACTER *See* Character.

METAPHOR A *metaphor* is a figure of speech in which one thing is spoken of as though it were something else. Unlike a simile, which compares two things using *like* or *as*, a metaphor implies a comparison between them. In "Dreams," on p. 799, Langston Hughes uses a metaphor to show what happens to a life without dreams:

Hold fast to dreams

For if dreams die

Life is a broken-winged bird

That cannot fly.

See Extended Metaphor and Figurative Language.

METER The *meter* of a poem is its rhythmical pattern. This pattern is determined by the number and types of stresses, or beats, in each line. To describe the meter of a poem, you must *scan* its lines. *Scanning* involves marking the stressed and unstressed syllables, as shown with the following two lines from "I Wandered Lonely as a Cloud" by William Wordsworth, on p. 789.

Ĭ wán|dĕred lóne|lў ás| ă clóud

Thăt floáts | ŏn hígh | ŏ'er váles | ănd hĭlls.

As you can see, each strong stress is marked with a slanted line (´) and each unstressed syllable with a horseshoe symbol (˘). The stressed and unstressed syllables are then divided by vertical lines (|) into groups called feet. The following types of feet are common in English poetry:

1. *Iamb:* a foot with one unstressed syllable followed by a stressed syllable, as in the word "again"

2. *Trochee:* a foot with a stressed syllable followed by an unstressed syllable, as in the word "wonder"

3. *Anapest:* a foot with two unstressed syllables followed by one strong stress, as in the phrase "on the beach"

4. *Dactyl:* a foot with one strong stress followed by two unstressed syllables, as in the word "wonderful"

5. *Spondee:* a foot with two strong stresses, as in the word "spacewalk"

Depending on the type of foot that is most common in them, lines of poetry are described as *iambic, trochaic, anapestic,* and so forth.

Lines are also described in terms of the number of feet that occur in them, as follows:

1. *Monometer:* verse written in one-foot lines

   All things

   Must pass

   Away.

2. *Dimeter:* verse written in two-foot lines

   Thomas | Jefferson

   What do | you say

   Under the | gravestone

   Hidden | away?

   — Rosemary and Stephen Vincent Benet,

   "Thomas Jefferson 1743–1826"

3. *Trimeter:* verse written in three-foot lines

   I know | not whom | I meet

   I know | not where | I go.

4. *Tetrameter:* verse written in four-foot lines

5. *Pentameter:* verse written in five-foot lines

6. *Hexameter:* verse written in six-foot lines

7. *Heptameter:* verse written in seven-foot lines

Blank verse is poetry written in unrhymed iambic pentameter. Poetry that does not have a regular meter is called *free verse.*

MONOLOGUE A *monologue* is a speech by one character in a play, story, or poem. An example from Shakespeare's *Romeo and Juliet*, on p. 672, is the speech in which the Prince of Verona commands the Capulets and Montagues to cease feuding (Act 1, Scene I, lines 62–84).

See Dramatic Poetry and Soliloquy.

MONOMETER *See* Meter.

MOOD *Mood,* or *atmosphere,* is the feeling created in the reader by a literary work or passage. The mood is often suggested by descriptive details. Often the mood can be described in a single word such as lighthearted, frightening, or despairing. Notice how this passage from Edgar Allen Poe's "The Cask of Amontillado," on p. 5, contributes to an eerie, fearful mood:

"The niter!" I said; "see, it increases. It hangs like moss upon the vaults. We are below the river's

bed. The drops of moisture trickle among the bones. Come, we will go back ere it is too late."

See Tone.

MORAL A *moral* is a lesson taught by a literary work. A fable usually ends with a moral that is directly stated.

MOTIVATION *Motivation* is a reason that explains or partially explains why a character thinks, feels, acts, or behaves in a certain way. Motivation results from a combination of the character's personality and the situation he or she must deal with. Nat Hocken, in "The Birds," on p. 46, is motivated by his fear of dying by bird attacks to board up windows and stay inside.

When the motives of a main character are not clear and logical, neither that character nor the story seems believable. Adventure stories often do not concern themselves much with the character's motivations. In contrast, serious fiction usually explores motivations in depth.

See Character and Characterization.

▼ Fear is the motivation for many of Nat Hocken's actions in "The Birds."

MYTH A *myth* is a fictional tale that explains the actions of gods or the causes of natural phenomena. Unlike legends, myths have little historical truth and involve supernatural elements. Every culture has its collections of myths. Among the most familiar are the myths of the ancient Greeks and Romans. The *Odyssey*, on p. 860, is a mythical story, attributed to the ancient poet Homer.

See Oral Tradition.

NARRATION *Narration* is writing that tells a story. The act of telling a story in speech is also called narration. Novels and short stories are fictional narratives. Nonfiction works such as news stories, biographies, and autobiographies are also narratives. A narrative poem tells a story in verse.

See Anecdote, Essay, Narrative Poem, Nonfiction, Novel, and Short Story.

NARRATIVE A *narrative* is a story told in fiction, nonfiction, poetry, or drama.

See Narration.

NARRATIVE POEM A *narrative poem* is one that tells a story. "Casey at the Bat," on p. 36, is a humorous narrative poem about the last inning of a baseball game. Edgar Allan Poe's "The Raven," on p. 832, is a serious narrative poem about a man's grief over the loss of a loved one.

See Dramatic Poetry, Epic, and Narration.

NARRATOR A *narrator* is a speaker or character who tells a story. The narrator may be either a character in the story or an outside observer. The writer's choice of narrator determines the story's *point of view*, which in turn determines the type and amount of information the writer can reveal.

When a character in the story tells the story, that character is a *first-person narrator*. This narrator may be a major character, a minor character, or just a witness. Readers see only what this character sees, hear only what he or she hears, and so on. The first-person narrator may or may not be reliable. We have reason, for example, to be suspicious of the first-person narrator of Edgar Allan Poe's "The Cask of Amontillado," on p. 5.

When a voice outside the story narrates, the story has a *third-person narrator*. An omniscient, or all-knowing, third-person narrator can tell readers what any character thinks and feels. For example, in Guy de Maupassant's "The Necklace," on p. 536, we know the feelings of both Monsieur and Madame Loisel. A *limited* third-person narrator, on the other hand, sees the world through one character's eyes and reveals only that character's thoughts. For example, in James Thurber's "The Secret Life of Walter Mitty," on p. 299, we share only Mitty's experiences and feelings.

See Speaker.

NONFICTION *Nonfiction* is prose writing that presents and explains ideas or that tells about real people, places, objects, or events. Nonfiction narratives are about actual people, places, and events, unlike fictional narratives, which present imaginary characters and events. To be classified as nonfiction, a work must be true. Arthur C. Clarke's "If I Forget Thee, Oh Earth . . . ," on p. 426, presents a fictional account of the Earth as viewed from space. "Single Room, Earth View," on p. 559, presents a nonfictional account of the same subject.

Among nonfiction forms are essays, newspaper and magazine articles, journals, travelogues, biographies, and autobiographies. Historical, scientific, technical, political, and philosophical writings are also nonfiction.

See Autobiography, Biography, and Essay.

NOVEL A *novel* is a long work of fiction. Like a short story, a novel has a plot that explores characters in conflict. However, a novel is much longer than a short story and may have one or more subplots, or minor stories, and several themes.

OCTAVE See Stanza.

ONOMATOPOEIA *Onomatopoeia* is the use of words that imitate sounds. *Whirr, thud, sizzle,* and *hiss* are typical examples. Writers can deliberately choose words that contribute to a desired sound effect. In the following lines, from Edgar Allen Poe's "The Bells," on p. 818, *clang, crash, roar,* and *twang* are onomatopoeic:

Oh, the bells, bells, bells!

What a tale their terror tells

Of Despair!

How they clang, and clash, and roar!

What a horror they outpour

On the bosom of the palpitating air!

Yet the ear it fully knows,

In some stories, setting serves merely as a backdrop for action, a context in which the characters move and speak. In others, however, setting is a crucial element. Both the desert and Native American culture are important in Leslie Marmon Silko's "The Man to Send Rain Clouds," on p. 222, and the lunar landscape and the future are important in Arthur C. Clarke's "If I Forget Thee, Oh Earth . . . ," on p. 426.

Description of the setting often helps establish the mood of a story. For example, in Edgar Allan Poe's "The Cask of Amontillado," on p. 5, the setting contributes to the growing horror.

See Mood.

SHORT STORY A *short story* is a brief work of fiction. A *novel,* by contrast, is a long work of fiction. In most short stories, one main character faces a conflict that is resolved in the plot of the story. Great craftsmanship must go into the writing of a good story, for it has to accomplish its purpose in relatively few words.

The short story as a distinct literary form emerged in the nineteenth century. The American writers Edgar

▲ Arthur C. Clarke uses the moon as the setting for his science-fiction story "If I Forget Thee, Oh Earth . . . "

Allan Poe and Nathaniel Hawthorne were especially important in the development of the short story.

See Fiction and Genre.

SIMILE A *simile* is a figure of speech in which *like* or *as* is used to make a comparison between two basically unlike ideas. "Claire is as flighty as Roger" is a comparison, not a simile. "Claire is as flighty as a sparrow" is a simile.

Poets often use similes. The following example from William Wordsworth's "I Wandered Lonely as a Cloud," on p. 789, compares a mass of daffodils to a flood of stars:

Continuous as the stars that shine

And twinkle on the milky way,

They stretched in never-ending line

Along the margin of a bay.

▲ In his poem "I Wandered Lonely as a Cloud," William Wordsworth uses a simile to compare a field of daffodils to stars in the Milky Way.

Prose writers also use similes. Here is one from James Hurst's "The Scarlet Ibis," on p. 484:

> We were down in Old Woman Swamp and it was spring and the sick-sweet smell of bay flowers hung everywhere like a mournful song.

See Figurative Language.

SOLILOQUY A *soliloquy* is a long speech expressing the thoughts of a character alone on stage. In William Shakespeare's *Romeo and Juliet* (p. 672), Romeo gives a soliloquy after the servant has fled and Paris has died (Act V, Scene iii, lines 74–120).

See Monologue.

SONNET A *sonnet* is a fourteen-line lyric poem, usually written in rhymed iambic pentameter. The *English*, or *Shakespearean, sonnet* consists of three quatrains (four-line stanzas) and a couplet (two lines), usually rhyming *abab cdcd efef gg*. The couplet usually comments on the ideas contained in the preceding twelve lines. The sonnet is usually not printed with the stanzas divided, but a reader can see distinct ideas in each. See the English sonnet by William Shakespeare on p. 843.

The *Italian*, or *Petrarchan, sonnet* consists of an octave (eight-line stanza) and a sestet (six-line stanza). Often the octave rhymes *abbaabba* and the sestet rhymes *cdecde*. The octave states a theme or asks a question. The sestet comments on or answers the question.

The Petrarchan sonnet took its name from Petrarch, a fourteenth-century Italian poet. Once the form was

introduced in England, it underwent change. The Shakespearean sonnet is, of course, named after William Shakespeare.

See Lyric Poem, Meter, and Stanza.

SPEAKER The *speaker* is the imaginary voice assumed by the writer of a poem. In many poems the speaker is not identified by name. When reading a poem, remember that the speaker within the poem may be a person, an animal, a thing, or an abstraction. The speaker in the following stanza by Emily Dickinson is a person who has died:

> Because I could not stop for Death—
>
> He kindly stopped for me—
>
> The Carriage held but just Ourselves—
>
> And Immortality.

STAGE DIRECTIONS *Stage directions* are notes included in a drama to describe how the work is to be performed or staged. These instructions are printed in italics and are not spoken aloud. They are used to describe sets, lighting, sound effects, and the appearance, personalities, and movements of characters.

See Drama.

STANZA A *stanza* is a formal division of lines in a poem, considered as a unit. Often the stanzas in a poem are separated by spaces.

Stanzas are sometimes named according to the number of lines found in them. A couplet, for example, is a two-line stanza. A tercet is a stanza with three lines. Other types of stanzas include the following:

1. Quatrain: a four-line stanza

2. Cinquain: a five-line stanza

3. Sestet: a six-line stanza

4. Heptastich: a seven-line stanza

5. Octave: an eight-line stanza

Sonnets, limericks, and haiku all have distinct stanza forms. A *sonnet* is a fourteen-line poem that is made up either of three quatrains and a couplet or of an octave followed by a sestet. A *limerick* consists of a single five-line stanza with a particular pattern of rhymes. A *haiku* is made up of a single three-line stanza.

See Haiku and Sonnet.

Literary Terms Handbook ◆ *959*

◄ A rare bird is the central symbol in James Hurst's story, "The Scarlet Ibis."

STATIC CHARACTER See *Character.*

SURPRISE ENDING A *surprise ending* is a conclusion that violates the expectations of the reader but in a way that is both logical and believable. O. Henry's "The Gift of the Magi," on p. 459, and Guy de Maupassant's "The Necklace," on p. 536, have surprise endings. Both authors were masters of this form.

SUSPENSE *Suspense* is a feeling of curiosity or uncertainty about the outcome of events in a literary work. Writers create suspense by raising questions in the minds of their readers.

SYMBOL A *symbol* is anything that stands for or represents something else. An object that serves as a symbol has its own meaning, but it also represents abstract ideas. Marks on paper can symbolize spoken words. A flag symbolizes a country. A flashy car may symbolize wealth. Writers sometimes use such conventional symbols in their work, but sometimes they also create symbols of their own through emphasis or repetition.

In James Hurst's "The Scarlet Ibis," on p. 484, the ibis symbolizes the character named Doodle. Doodle and the ibis have many traits in common. Both are beautiful and otherworldly. Both struggle against great odds. Both

meet an unfortunate fate. Since a story says something about life or people in general, the ibis, in a larger sense, becomes a symbol for those who struggle.

TETRAMETER See *Meter.*

THEME A *theme* is a central message or insight into life revealed through the literary work. The theme is not a condensed summary of the plot. Instead, it is a generalization about people or about life that is communicated through the literary work.

The theme of a literary work may be stated directly or implied. In James Hurst's "The Scarlet Ibis," on p. 484, the narrator directly states one theme of the story: ". . . pride is a wonderful, terrible thing, a seed that bears two vines, life and death."

When the theme of a work is implied, readers think about what the work seems to say about the nature of people or about life. The story or poem can be viewed as a specific example of the generalization the writer is trying to communicate.

Note that there is usually no single correct statement of a work's theme, though there can be incorrect ones. Also, a long work, like a novel or a full-length play, may have several themes. Finally, not all literary works have themes. A work meant only to entertain may have no theme at all.

TONE The *tone* of a literary work is the writer's attitude toward his or her audience and subject. The tone can often be described by a single adjective, such as *formal* or *informal, serious* or *playful, bitter,* or *ironic.* When O. Henry discusses the young married couple in "The Gift of the Magi," on p. 459, he uses a sympathetic tone. By contrast, Margaret Walker uses a grieving tone in her poem "Memory," on p. 805.

See *Mood.*

TRAGEDY A *tragedy* is a work of literature, especially a play, that results in a catastrophe for the main character. In ancient Greek drama, the main character was always a significant person, a king or a hero, and the cause of the tragedy was a tragic flaw, or weakness, in his or her character. In modern drama the main character can be an ordinary person, and the cause of the tragedy can be some evil in society itself. The purpose of tragedy is not only to arouse fear and pity in the

960 ◆ *Literary Terms Handbook*

audience, but also, in some cases, to convey a sense of the grandeur and nobility of the human spirit.

Shakespeare's *Romeo and Juliet*, on p. 672, is a tragedy. Romeo and Juliet both suffer from the tragic flaw of impulsiveness. This flaw ultimately leads to their deaths.

See Drama.

TRIMETER *See Meter.*

VERBAL IRONY *See Irony.*

VISUAL ESSAY A *visual essay* is an exploration of a topic that conveys its ideas through visual elements as well as language. Like a standard essay, a visual essay presents an author's views of a single topic. Unlike other essays, however, much of the meaning in a visual essay is conveyed through illustrations or photographs.

In her poem "Memory," Margaret Walker uses words and images that create a grieving tone.

WRITING HANDBOOK

THE WRITING PROCESS

A polished piece of writing can seem to have been effortlessly created, but most good writing is the result of a process of writing, rethinking, and rewriting. The process can be roughly divided into a series of stages: prewriting, drafting, revising, editing, proofreading, and publishing.

It's important to remember that the writing process is one that moves backward as well as forward. Even while you are moving forward in the creation of your composition, you may still return to a previous stage—to rethink or rewrite.

Following are stages of the writing process, with key points to address during each stage.

Prewriting

In this stage you plan out the work to be done. You prepare to write by exploring ideas, gathering information, and working out an organization. Following are the key steps to take at this stage.

Step 1: Analyze the writing situation. Start by clarifying your assignment, so that you know exactly what you are supposed to do.

- *Focus your topic.* If you need to, narrow the topic—the subject you are writing about—so that you can write about it fully in the space you have.
- *Know your purpose.* What is your goal for this paper? What do you want to accomplish? Your purpose will determine what you include in it.
- *Know your audience.* Who will read your paper influences what you say and how you say it.

Step 2: Gather ideas and information. You can do this in a number of ways:

- *Brainstorm.* When you brainstorm, either alone or with others, you come up with possible ideas to use in your paper. Not all of your brainstormed ideas will be useful or suitable. You'll need to evaluate them later.
- *Consult other people about your subject.* Speaking informally with others may suggest an idea or approach you did not see at first.
- *Make a list of questions about your topic.* Then find the answers to your questions.

- *Do research.* Your topic may require information that you don't have, so you will need to go to other sources to find information. There are numerous ways to find information on a topic. See the Research Handbook on p. 979 for suggestions.

The ideas and information you gather will become the content of your paper. Not all of the information you gather will be needed. As you develop and revise your paper, you will make further decisions about what to include and what to leave out.

Step 3: Organize. First, make a rough plan for how you want to present your information. Sort your ideas and notes; decide what goes with what, and which points are the most important. You can make an outline to show the order of ideas, or you can use some other organizing plan that works for you.

There are many ways in which you can organize and develop your material. Use a method that works for your topic. Following are common methods of organizing information in the development of a paper.

- *Chronological Order* In this method, events are presented in the order in which they occurred. This organization works best for presenting narrative material or explaining in a "how to."
- *Spatial Order* In spatial order, details are presented as seen in space, for example, from left to right or from foreground to background. This order is good for descriptive writing.
- *Order of Importance* This order helps readers see the relative importance of ideas. You present ideas from most to least important or from least to most important.
- *Main Idea and Details* This logical organization works well to support an idea or opinion.

Drafting

When you draft, you put down your ideas on paper in rough form. Working from your prewriting notes and your outline or plan, you develop and present your ideas in sentences and paragraphs.

Don't worry about getting everything perfect at the drafting stage. Concentrate on getting your ideas down.

Draft in a way that works for you. Some writers work best by writing a quick draft—putting down all their ideas without stopping to evaluate them. Other writers prefer to develop each paragraph carefully and thoughtfully, making sure each main idea is supported by details.

As you are developing a draft, keep in mind your purpose and your audience. These determine what you say and how you say it.

Don't be afraid to change your original plans during drafting. Some of the best ideas are those that were not planned at the beginning. Write as many drafts as you like. You can draft over and over until you've got it the way you like.

Most papers, regardless of the topic, are developed with an introduction, a body, and a conclusion. Here are tips for developing these parts.

Introduction In the introduction to a paper, you want to engage your readers' attention and let them know the purpose of your paper. You may use the following strategies in your introduction:

- State your main idea.
- Take a stand.
- Use an anecdote.
- Quote someone.
- Startle your readers.

Body of the paper In the body of your paper, you present your information and make your points. Your **organization** is an important factor in leading readers through your ideas. Your elaboration on your main ideas is also important. **Elaboration** is the development of ideas to make your written work precise and complete. You can use the following kinds of details to elaborate your main ideas:

- Facts and statistics
- Anecdotes
- Sensory details
- Examples
- Explanation and definition
- Quotations

Conclusion The ending of your paper is the final impression you leave with your readers. Your conclusion should give readers the sense that you have pulled everything together. Following are some effective ways to end your paper:

- Summarize and restate.
- Ask a question.
- State an opinion.
- Tell an anecdote.
- Call for action.

Revising

Once you have a draft, you can look at it critically or have others review it. This is the time to make changes—on many levels. Revising is the process of reworking what you have written to make it as good as it can be. You may change some details so that your ideas flow smoothly and are clearly supported. You may discover that some details don't work and you'll need to discard them. Two strategies may help you start the revising process:

1. Read your work aloud. This is an excellent way to catch any ideas or details that have been left out and to notice errors in logic.
2. Ask someone else to read your work. Choose someone who can point out its strengths as well as suggest how to improve it.

How do you know what to look for and what to change? Here is a checklist of major writing issues. If the answer to any of these questions is no, then that is an area that needs revision.

1. Does the writing achieve your purpose?
2. Does the paper have unity? That is, does it have a single focus, with all details and information contributing to that focus?
3. Is the arrangement of information clear and logical?
4. Have you elaborated enough to give your audience adequate enough information?

Editing

When you edit, you look more closely at the language you have used, so that the way you express your ideas is most effective.

- Replace dull language with vivid, precise words.
- Cut or change redundant expressions (unnecessary repetition).
- Cut empty words and phrases, those that do not add anything to the writing.
- Check passive voice. Usually active voice is more effective.
- Replace wordy expressions with shorter, more precise ones.

Proofreading

After you finish your final draft, the last step is to proofread the draft to make it ready for a reader. You may do this on your own or with the help of a partner.

It's useful to have handy both a dictionary and a usage handbook to help you check for correctness. Here are the tasks in proofreading:

- Correct errors in grammar and usage.
- Correct errors in punctuation and capitalization.
- Correct errors in spelling.

that convey your ideas about sets, props, sound effects, and the speaking style and movements of the characters.

Response to Literature

In a **response to literature,** you express your thoughts and feelings about a work and often, in so doing, gain a better understanding of what the work is all about. Your response to literature can take many forms—oral or written, formal or informal. During the course of your reading, you may be asked to respond to a work of literature in one of these forms:

Literary Analysis In a literary analysis, you take a critical look at various important elements in the work. You then attempt to explain how the author has used those elements and how they work together to convey the author's message.

Retelling of a Fairy Tale Most fairy tales—stories about good and evil characters, giants, and magic deeds—have been handed down from generation to generation, and often the original authors are unknown. When you retell a fairy tale in your own way, you can add to the original or change it. For example, you might set it in another place or time period or write it as a poem or a drama.

Reader's Response Journal Entry Your reader's response journal is a record of your thoughts and feelings about works you have read. Use it to remind you of writers and works that you particularly liked or disliked, or to provide a source of writing ideas.

Letter to an Author People sometimes respond to a work of literature by writing a letter to the author. You can praise the work, ask questions, or offer constructive criticism.

Critical Review In a critical review of a literary work, you discuss various elements in the work and offer opinions about them. You may also give a summary of the work and a recommendation to readers.

Practical and Technical Writing

Practical writing is fact-based writing that people do in the workplace or in their day-to-day lives. Business letters, memos, school forms, and job applications are examples of practical writing. **Technical writing,** which is also based on facts, explains procedures, provides instructions, or presents specialized information. You encounter technical writing every time you read a manual or a set of instructions.

In the following descriptions, you'll find tips for tackling several types of practical and technical writing.

Letter Requesting Information In a letter requesting information, you state the information you're searching for and ask any specific questions you have. In your letter, include your name and address so that you can receive a response. Include the date, which can help you or the recipient keep track of correspondence. It is also customary to include the address of the party to whom you are writing. Use a formal greeting followed by a colon. Keep the body of the letter as brief and clear as possible. Use a polite closing, and remember to sign as well as type or print your name.

News Release News releases announce factual information about upcoming events. Also called press releases, they are usually sent to local newspapers, local radio stations, and other media. When you write a news release, use this format: Position your name and phone number in the upper right corner. Then capture your main point in a centered headline, which will allow the recipient to see at a glance what the news release is about. In the body, present factual information in a concise way. You may begin with an opening location tag that tells in which town or city the news release originated. The numeral 30 or number signs (###) customarily indicate the end of the news release.

Guidelines When you write guidelines, you give information about how people should act or you provide tips on how to do something. List guidelines one by one, using somewhat formal language. Your guidelines may or may not be numbered. In addition to factual information, which should be complete and accurate, guidelines may contain your opinions.

Process Explanation In a process explanation, you offer a step-by-step explanation of how to do something. Your explanation should be specific, using headings, labels, or numbers to make the process clear. You may also include diagrams or other illustrations to further clarify the process.

GRAMMAR AND MECHANICS HANDBOOK

Nouns A **noun** is the name of a person, place, or thing. A **common noun** names any one of a class of people, places, or things. A **proper noun** names a specific person, place, or thing.

Common Noun	Proper Noun
city	Washington, D.C.

Pronouns A **pronoun** is a word that stands for a noun or for a word that takes the place of a noun.

A **personal pronoun** refers to (1) the person speaking, (2) the person spoken to, or (3) the person, place, or thing spoken about.

	Singular	Plural
First Person	I, me, my, mine	we, us, our, ours
Second Person	you, your, yours	you, your, yours
Third Person	he, him, his, she, her, hers it, its	they, them, their, theirs

A **reflexive pronoun** ends in -self or -selves and adds information to a sentence by pointing back to a noun or a pronoun earlier in the sentence.

> As I said these words I busied *myself* among the pile of bones of which I have before spoken.
> —"The Cask of Amontillado," Edgar Allan Poe, p. 9

An **intensive pronoun** ends in -self or -selves and simply adds emphasis to a noun or a pronoun in the same sentence.

> And Spring *herself,* when she woke at dawn, Would scarcely know that we were gone.
> —"There Will Come Soft Rains," Sara Teasdale, p. 414

A **demonstrative pronoun** directs attention to a specific person, place, or thing.

> this   these   that   those

> *These* are the juiciest pears I've ever tasted.

A **relative pronoun** begins a subordinate (relative) clause and connects it to another idea in the sentence.

> The poet *who* wrote "Fire and Ice" is Robert Frost.
> The president *whom* Sandburg admired was Lincoln.

An **indefinite pronoun** refers to a person, place, or thing, often without specifying which one.

> *Some* of the flowers were in bloom.
> *Everybody* chose something.

Verbs A **verb** is a word that expresses time while showing an action, a condition, or the fact that something exists.

An **action verb** indicates the action of someone or something.

An action verb is **transitive** if it directs action toward someone or something named in the same sentence.

> Henderson *shook* his head.
> — "The Machine That Won the War," Isaac Asimov, p. 396

An action verb is **intransitive** if it does not direct action toward something or someone named in the same sentence.

> Earth *had won* so all *had been* for the best.
> — "The Machine That Won the War," Isaac Asimov, p. 396

A **linking verb** is a verb that connects the subject of a sentence with a noun or pronoun that renames or describes the subject. All linking verbs are intransitive.

> Life *is* a broken-winged bird . . .
> — "Dreams," Langston Hughes, p. 799

A **helping verb** is a verb that can be added to another verb to make a verb phrase.

> Nor *did* I suspect that these experiences could be part of a novel's meaning.

Adjectives An **adjective** describes a noun or a pronoun or gives a noun or a pronoun a more specific meaning. Adjectives answer these questions:

What kind?	*blue* lamp, *large* tree
Which one?	*this* table, *those* books
How many?	*five* stars, *several* buses
How much?	*less* money, *enough* votes

The articles *the, a,* and *an* are adjectives. *An* is used before a word beginning with a vowel sound.

A noun may sometimes be used as an adjective.

> *diamond* necklace   *summer* vacation

Grammar and Mechanics Handbook ◆ 967

Adverbs An **adverb** modifies a verb, an adjective, or another adverb. Adverbs answer the questions where? when? in what way? to what extent?

He could stand *there*. (modifies verb *stand*)
He was *blissfully* happy. (modifies adjective *happy*)
It ended *too* soon. (modifies adverb *soon*)

Prepositions A **preposition** relates a noun or a pronoun that appears with it to another word in the sentence.

before the end   *near* me   *inside* our fence

Conjunctions A **conjunction** connects other words or groups of words.

A **coordinating conjunction** connects similar kinds or groups of words.

mother *and* father   simple *yet* stylish

Correlative conjunctions are used in pairs to connect similar words or groups of words.

both Sue *and* Meg   *neither* he *nor* I

A **subordinating conjunction** connects two complete ideas by placing one idea below the other in rank or importance.

You would know him *if* you saw him.

Interjections An **interjection** expresses feeling or emotion and functions independently of a sentence.

"*Oh*, my poor, poor, Mathilde!"
— "The Necklace,"
Guy de Maupassant, p. 541

Sentences A **sentence** is a group of words with a subject and a predicate. Together, these parts express a complete thought.

I closed my eyes and pondered my next move.
— "Rules of the Game,"
Amy Tan, p. 231

A **fragment** is a group of words that does not express a complete thought.

The Swan Theater in London

Subject and Verb Agreement To make a subject and verb agree, make sure that both are singular or both are plural.

Many *storms are* the cause of beach erosion.
Either the *cats* or the *dog is* hungry.
Neither *Angie* nor her *sisters were* present.
The *conductor*, as well as the soloists, *was applauded*.

Phrase A **phrase** is a group of words, without a subject and a verb, that functions in a sentence as one part of speech.

A **prepositional phrase** is a group of words that includes a preposition and a noun or a pronoun that is the object of the preposition.

outside my window   below the counter

An **adjective phrase** is a prepositional phrase that modifies a noun or a pronoun by telling *what kind* or *which one*.

The wooden gates *of that lane* stood open.

An **adverb phrase** is a prepositional phrase that modifies a verb, an adjective, or an adverb by pointing out *where, when, in what way*, or *to what extent*.

On December the third, the wind changed overnight, and it was winter.
— "The Birds,"
Daphne du Maurier, p. 46

An **appositive phrase** is a noun or pronoun with modifiers, placed next to a noun or a pronoun to add information and details.

"It is a very great pleasure and honor to welcome Mr. Sanger Rainsford, *the celebrated hunter*, to my home."
— "The Most Dangerous Game,"
Richard Connell, p. 21

A **participial phrase** is a participle with its modifiers or complements. The entire phrase acts as an adjective.

"Try the settee," said Holmes, *relapsing into his armchair . . .*
— "The Red-headed League,"
Sir Arthur Conan Doyle, p. 82

A **gerund phrase** is a gerund with modifiers or a complement, all acting together as a noun.

The baying of the hounds drew nearer, . . .
— "The Most Dangerous Game,"
Richard Connell, p. 30

An **infinitive phrase** is an infinitive with modifiers, complements, or a subject, all acting together as a single part of speech.

I continued, as was my wont, *to smile in his face, . . .*
— "The Cask of Amontillado,"
Edgar Allan Poe, p. 5

Clauses A **clause** is a group of words with a subject and a verb.

An **independent clause** has a subject and a verb and can stand by itself as a complete sentence.

A **subordinate clause** has a subject and a verb but cannot stand by itself as a complete sentence; it can only be part of a sentence.

An **adjective clause** is a subordinate clause that modifies a noun or a pronoun by telling what kind or which one.

> Walter Mitty stopped the car in front of the building *where his wife went to have her hair done.*
>> — "The Secret Life of Walter Mitty," James Thurber, p. 299

An **adverb clause** modifies a verb, an adjective, an adverb, or a verbal by telling *where, when, in what way, to what extent, under what condition,* or *why.*

> The hunter shook his head several times, *as if he was puzzled.*
>> — "The Most Dangerous Game," Richard Connell, p. 28

A **noun clause** is a subordinate clause that acts as a noun.

> . . . I discovered *that the intoxication had worn off . . .*
>> — "The Cask of Amontillado," Edgar Allan Poe, p. 9

Summary of Capitalization and Punctuation

Capitalization Capitalize the first word of a sentence and also the first word in a quotation if the quotation is a complete sentence.

> I said to him, "My dear Fortunato, you are luckily met."
>> — "The Cask of Amontillado," Edgar Allan Poe, p. 6

Capitalize all proper nouns and adjectives.

> O. Henry   Ganges River   Great Wall of China

Capitalize a person's title when it is followed by the person's name or when it is used in direct address.

> Madame   Dr. Mitty   General Zaroff

Capitalize titles showing family relationships when they refer to a specific person, unless they are preceded by a possessive noun or pronoun.

> Uncle Marcos   Granddaddy Cain

Capitalize the first word and all other key words in the titles of books, periodicals, poems, stories, plays, paintings, and other works of art.

> *Rosa Parks: My Story*
> "I Wander'd Lonely as a Cloud"

Punctuation

End Marks Use a **period** to end a declarative sentence, an imperative sentence, an indirect question, and most abbreviations.

> Mr. Jabez Wilson laughed heavily.
>> — "The Red-headed League," Sir Arthur Conan Doyle, p. 85

Use a **question mark** to end a direct question, an incomplete question, or a statement that is intended as a question.

> Shall I meet other wayfarers at night?
>> — "Uphill," Christina Rossetti, p. 814

Use an **exclamation mark** after a statement showing strong emotion, an urgent imperative sentence, or an interjection expressing strong emotion.

> Free at last! Free at last!
> Thank God almighty, we are Free at last!
>> — "I Have a Dream," Martin Luther King, Jr., p. 142

Commas Use a **comma** before the coordinating conjunction to separate two independent clauses in a compound sentence.

> All at once . . . she came upon a superb diamond necklace, and her heart started beating with overwhelming desire.
>> — "The Necklace," Guy de Maupassant, p. 538

Use commas to separate three or more words, phrases, or clauses in a series.

> My brothers and I would peer into the medicinal herb shop, watching old Li dole out onto a stiff sheet of white paper the right amount of insect shells, saffron-colored seeds, and pungent leaves for his ailing customers.
>> — "Rules of the Game," Amy Tan, p. 224

Use commas to separate adjectives of equal rank. Do not use commas to separate adjectives that must stay in a specific order.

Grammar and Mechanics Handbook ◆ *969*

The big cottonwood tree stood apart from a small group of winterbare cottonwoods which grew in the wide, sandy arroyo.

— "The Man to Send Rain Clouds,"
Leslie Marmon Silko, p. 522

In autumn those that had not migrated overseas . . . were caught up in the same driving urge . . .

— "The Birds,"
Daphne du Maurier, p. 46

Use a comma after an introductory word, phrase, |or clause.

When Marvin was ten years old, his father took him through the long, echoing corridors . . .

— "If I Forget Thee, Oh Earth . . . ,"
Arthur C. Clarke, p. 426

Use commas to set off parenthetical and nonessential expressions.

An evil place can, so to speak, broadcast vibrations of evil.

— "The Most Dangerous Game,"
Richard Connell, p. 18

Use commas with places, dates, and titles.

Poe was raised in Richmond, Virginia.
On September 1, 1939, World War II began.
Dr. Martin Luther King, Jr., was born in 1929.

Use a comma to indicate words left out of an elliptical sentence, to set off a direct quotation, and to prevent a sentence from being misunderstood.

In the *Odyssey*, the Cyclops may symbolize brutishness; the Sirens, knowledge.

Semicolons Use a **semicolon** to join independent clauses that are not already joined by a conjunction.

The lights of cities sparkle; on nights when there was no moon, it was difficult for me to tell the Earth from the sky. . . .

— "Single Room, Earth View,"
Sally Ride, p. 563

Use a semicolon to join independent clauses separated by either a conjunctive adverb or a transitional expression.

Edward Way Teale wrote nearly thirty books; moreover, he was also an artist and a naturalist.

Use semicolons to avoid confusion when independent clauses or items in a series already contain commas.

Unable to afford jewelry, she dressed simply; but she was as wretched as a *déclassé,* for women have neither caste nor breeding— in them beauty, grace, and charm replace pride of birth.

— "The Necklace,"
Guy de Maupassant, p. 536

Colons Use a **colon** in order to introduce a list of items following an independent clause.

The authors we are reading include a number of poets: Robert Frost, Lewis Carroll, and Emily Dickinson.

Use a colon to introduce a formal quotation.

I have a dream that one day this nation will rise up and live out the true meaning of its creed: "We hold these truths to be self-evident; . . ."

— "I Have a Dream,"
Martin Luther King, Jr., p. 141

Quotation Marks A **direct quotation** represents a person's exact speech or thoughts and is enclosed in quotation marks.

"Where I was born and where and how I have lived is unimportant," Georgia O'Keeffe told us in the book of paintings and words published in her ninetieth year on earth.

— "Georgia O'Keeffe,"
Joan Didion, p. 592

An **indirect quotation** reports only the general meaning of what a person said or thought and does not require quotation marks.

The driver of the bus saw me still sitting there, and he asked was I going to stand up . . .

— from *Rosa Parks: My Story,*
Rosa Parks, p. 144

Always place a comma or a period inside the final quotation mark.

"I don't know," he said slowly. "It says here the birds are hungry."

— "The Birds,"
Daphne du Maurier, p. 54

Place a question mark or an exclamation mark inside the final quotation mark if the end mark is part of the quotation; if it is not part of the quotation, place it outside the final quotation mark.

> "That pig will devour us, greedily!"
> —"The Golden Kite, the Silver Wind,"
> Ray Bradbury, p. 153

Have you ever read the poem "Dreams"?

Use single quotation marks for a quotation within a quotation.

> " 'But,' said I, 'there would be millions of red-headed men who would apply.' "
> — "The Red-headed League,"
> Sir Arthur Conan Doyle, p. 87

Use quotation marks around the titles of short written works, episodes in a series, songs, and titles of works mentioned as parts of a collection.

> "I Hear America Singing"   "Both Sides Now"

Dashes Use **dashes** to indicate an abrupt change of thought, a dramatic interrupting idea, or a summary statement.

> The streets were lined with people—lots and lots of people—the children all smiling, placards, confetti, people waving from windows.
> —from *A White House Diary*,
> Lady Bird Johnson, p. 586

Parentheses Use **parentheses** to set off asides and explanations only when the material is not essential or when it consists of one or more sentences.

> One last happy moment I had was looking up and seeing Mary Griffith . . . (Mary for many years had been in charge of altering the clothes which I purchased) . . .
> —from *A White House Diary*,
> Lady Bird Johnson, p. 586

Hyphens Use a **hyphen** with certain numbers, after certain prefixes, with two or more words used as one word, and with a compound modifier coming before a noun.

> seventy-six   Post-Modernist

Apostrophes Add an **apostrophe** and *-s* to show the possessive case of most singular nouns.

> Thurmond's wife   the playwright's craft

Add an apostrophe to show the possessive case of plural nouns ending in *-s* and *-es*.

> the sailors' ships   the Wattses' daughter

Add an apostrophe and *-s* to show the possessive case of plural nouns that do not end in *-s* or *-es*.

> the children's games   the people's friend

Use an apostrophe in a contraction to indicate the position of the missing letter or letters.

> You'll be lonely at first, they admitted, but you're so nice you'll make friends fast.
> — "Checkouts," Cynthia Rylant, p. 236

GLOSSARY OF COMMON USAGE

among, between
Among is usually used with three or more items. *Between* is generally used with only two items.

> *Among* the poems we read this year, Margaret Walker's "Memory" was my favorite.

> Mark Twain's "The Invalid's Story" includes a humorous encounter *between* the narrator and a character named Thompson.

amount, number
Amount refers to a mass or a unit, whereas *number* refers to individual items that can be counted. Therefore, *amount* generally appears with a singular noun, and *number* appears with a plural noun.

> Annie Sullivan's work with Helen Keller must have required a huge *amount* of patience.

> In her poem, "Uphill," Christina Rossetti uses a *number* of intriguing symbols.

any, all
Any should not be used in place of *any other* or *all.*

> Rajika liked Amy Tan's "Rules of the Game" better than *any other* short story.

> Of *all* O. Henry's short stories, "The Gift of the Magi" is one of the most famous.

around
In formal writing, *around* should not be used to mean *approximately* or *about.* These usages are allowable, however, in informal writing or in colloquial dialogue.

> Shakespeare's *Romeo and Juliet* had its first performance in *approximately* 1595.

Shakespeare was *about* thirty when he wrote this play.

as, because, like, as to

The word *as* has several meanings and can function as several parts of speech. To avoid confusion, use *because* rather than *as* when you want to indicate cause and effect.

> *Because* Cyril was interested in the history of African American poetry, he decided to write his report on Paul Laurence Dunbar.

Do not use the preposition *like* to introduce a clause that requires the conjunction *as.*

> Dorothy Parker conversed *as* she wrote—wittily.

The use of *as to* for *about* is awkward and should be avoided.

> Rosa has an interesting theory *about* E. E. Cummings's unusual typography in his poems.

bad, badly

Use the predicate adjective *bad* after linking verbs such as *feel, look,* and *seem.* Use *badly* whenever an adverb is required.

> Sara Teasdale's poem "There Will Come Soft Rains" shows clearly that the author felt *bad* about the destruction of war.

> In O'Henry's "The Gift of the Magi," Della *badly* wants to buy a wonderful Christmas present for her husband, Jim.

because of, due to

Use *due to* if it can logically replace the phrase *caused by.* In introductory phrases, however, *because of* is better usage than *due to.*

> The popularity of Frank Stockton's "The Lady or the Tiger?" is largely *due to* the story's open ending.

> *Because* of her feeling that Bennie's mother had enough to worry about already, Bennie's grandmother keeps the doctor's conclusions to herself.

being as, being that

Avoid these expressions. Use *because* or *since* instead.

> *Because* the protagonist of James Hurst's "The Scarlet Ibis" is a dynamic character, he changes significantly in the course of the story.

> *Since* Romeo and Juliet were from feuding families, their relationship involved secrecy and risk.

beside, besides

Beside is a preposition meaning "at the side of" or "close to." Do not confuse beside with besides, which means "in addition to." Besides can be a preposition or an adverb.

> When our group discussed William Least Heat Moon's "Nameless, Tennessee," Luis sat *beside* Eileen.

> *Besides* "The Bells," can you think of any other poems by Edgar Allan Poe?

> John Updike is a celebrated novelist; he is a gifted poet and essayist, *besides.*

can, may

The verb *can* generally refers to the ability to do something. The verb *may* generally refers to permission to do something.

> The mysterious listeners in Walter de la Mare's poem *can* hear the words of the lonely traveler.

> *May* I tell you why I admire Edgar Lee Masters's "George Gray"?

compare, contrast

The verb *compare* can involve both similarities and differences. The verb *contrast* always involves differences. Use *to* or *with* after compare. Use *with* after contrast.

> Theo's paper *compared* James Weldon Johnson's style in "The Creation" with the style of African American sermons of the same period.

> In the opening lines of the famous speech in Shakespeare's *As You Like It,* the world is *compared* to a stage and men and women to actors or players.

> The speaker's tone of hysteria in the closing stanzas of Poe's "The Raven" *contrasts* with the quiet opening of the poem.

different from, different than

The preferred usage is *different from*.

> The structure of "The Meadow Mouse" is quite *different from* that of "I Wandered Lonely as a Cloud."

farther, further

Use *farther* when you refer to distance. Use *further* when you mean "to a greater degree" or "additional."

> The *farther* Rainsford traveled in the jungle in "The Most Dangerous Game," the nearer the baying of the hounds sounded.

> Despite his men's advice, Odysseus *further* insults the Cyclops and provokes the monster's curse.

fewer, less

Use *fewer* for things that can be counted. Use *less* for amounts or quantities that cannot be counted.

> Poetry often uses *fewer* words than prose to convey ideas and images.

> T. S. Eliot's humorous poems have received *less* critical attention than his serious verse has.

good, well

Use the adjective *good* after linking verbs such as *feel, look, smell, taste,* and *seem.* Use *well* whenever you need an adverb.

> In Walt Whitman's "I Hear America Singing," the "varied carols" sound *good* to the speaker.

> Dickens wrote especially *well* when he described eccentric characters.

hopefully

You should not loosely attach this adverb to a sentence, as in "*Hopefully,* the rain will stop by noon." Rewrite the sentence so that *hopefully* modifies a specific verb. Other possible ways of revising such sentences include using the adjective *hopeful* or a phrase such as, "everyone *hopes* that."

> Dr. Martin Luther King, Jr., wrote and spoke *hopefully* about his dream of racial harmony.

> Akko was *hopeful* that he could find some of the unusual words from Lewis Carroll's "Jabberwocky" in an unabridged dictionary.

> Everyone *hopes* that the class production of *Romeo and Juliet* will be a big success.

its, it's

Do not confuse the possessive pronoun *its* with the contraction *it's,* used in place of "it is" or "it has."

> Ancient Greek society must have recognized many of *its* ideal values in the *Odyssey.*

> In Walter de la Mare's "The Listeners," the traveler thinks *it's* strange that no one replies to his call.

just, only

When you use *just* as an adverb meaning "no more than," be sure you place it directly before the word it logically modifies. Likewise, be sure you place *only* before the word it logically modifies.

> Shakespeare's "Sonnet 30" offers *just* one remedy for the speaker's grief and depression: the thought of a dear friend.

> A stereotyped character exhibits *only* those traits or behavior patterns that are assumed to be typical.

kind of, sort of

In formal writing, you should not use these colloquial expressions. Instead, use a word such as *rather* or *somewhat.*

> Alfred is *rather* irresponsible in Morley Callaghan's story "All the Years of Her Life."

> In "The Secret Life of Walter Mitty," James Thurber characterizes Mitty as *somewhat* absent-minded.

lay, lie

Do not confuse these verbs. *Lay* is a transitive verb meaning "to set or put something down." Its principal parts are *lay, laying, laid, laid. Lie* is an intransitive verb meaning "to recline." Its principal parts are *lie, lying, lay, lain.*

> In Heyerdahl's *Kon-Tiki* the narrator says that after the ship hit the reef, Herman *lay* pressed flat across the ridge of the cabin roof.

> Homer describes the slaughtered suitors *lying* dead in a heap on the floor of Odysseus' hall.

Grammar and Mechanics Handbook ◆ *973*

leave, let

Be careful not to confuse these verbs. *Leave* means "to go away" or "to allow to remain." *Let* means "to permit."

> In Tennyson's "The Eagle," the bird *leaves* the crag and plunges like a thunderbolt toward the sea.

> The love-sick Romeo asks his friends to *leave* him alone while they go to Capulets' party.

> "*Let* wantons light of heart / Tickle the senseless rushes with their heels," he says.

literally, figuratively

Literally means "word for word" or "in fact." The opposite of *literally* is *figuratively*, meaning "metaphorically." Be careful not to use *literally* as a synonym for *nearly,* as in informal expressions like this: "He was *literally* beside himself with rage."

> Certain specific details in "I Hear an Army" show that James Joyce does not intend us to interpret the army *literally*; instead, the army and the speaker's nightmare are meant *figuratively* to suggest his despair at his abandonment by his love.

of, have

Do not use *of* in place of *have* after auxiliary verbs like *would, could, should, may,* or *might.*

> Sir Arthur Conan Doyle might *have* continued to practice medicine, but soon after the publication *of* his first Sherlock Holmes stories, he decided to write full time.

raise, rise

Raise is a transitive verb that usually takes a direct object. *Rise* is an intransitive verb and never takes a direct object.

> In "Casey at the Bat," Ernest Lawrence Thayer suspensefully *raises* the reader's expectations throughout the poem, only to end the narrative with a mighty anticlimax.

> Jorge *rose* to the challenge of interpreting Gabriel García Márquez's story "A Very Old Man With Enormous Wings."

set, sit

Do not confuse these verbs. *Set* is a transitive verb meaning "to put (something) in a certain place." Its principal parts are *set, setting, set, set. Sit* is an intransitive verb meaning "to be seated." Its principal parts are *sit, sitting, sat, sat.*

> The opening sentence of Saki's "The Interlopers" *sets* a tone of tension and conflict for the story.

> While Walter Mitty *sat* in a big leather chair in the hotel lobby, he picked up a copy of a magazine.

so, so that

Be careful not to use the coordinating conjunction *so* when your context requires *so that. So* means "accordingly" or "therefore" and expresses a cause-and-effect relationship. *So that* expresses purpose.

> He wanted to check the clues, *so* he read "The Red-headed League" again.

> The priest wanted to locate Teofilo's body *so that* he could give him the Last Rites.

than, then

The conjunction *than* is used to connect the two parts of a comparison. Do not confuse *than* with the adverb *then*, which usually refers to time.

> I enjoyed reading "Jacob Lawrence: American Painter" more *than* "Autumn Gardening."

> Sally Ride earned a doctorate in physics and *then* became the first American woman in space.

that, which, who

Use the relative pronoun *that* to refer to things or people. Use *which* only for things and *who* only for people.

> The phrase *that* James Thurber dislikes is "you know."

> Donald Justice wrote "Incident in a Rose Garden," *which* is a dramatic poem.

> The sea goddess *who* loved Odysseus was Calypso.

unique

Because *unique* means "one of a kind," you should not use it carelessly to mean "interesting" or "unusual." Avoid such illogical expressions as "most unique," "very unique," and "extremely unique."

> Homer occupies a *unique* position in the history of Western literature.

when, where

Do not directly follow a linking verb with *when* or *where*. Also, be careful not to use *where* when your context requires *that*.

> *Faulty:* Foreshadowing is *when* an author uses clues to suggest future events.
>
> *Revised:* In foreshadowing, an author uses clues to suggest future events.
>
> *Faulty:* Ithaca was *where* Penelope awaited Odysseus.
>
> *Revised:* Penelope awaited Odysseus on Ithaca.

who, whom

In formal writing, remember to use *who* only as a subject in clauses and sentences and *whom* only as an object.

> Richard Wright, *who* is widely admired for his novel *Native Son*, also wrote haiku verse.
>
> Leslie Marmon Silko, *whom* Mark quoted in his oral report, was raised on the Laguna Pueblo reservation in New Mexico.

Speaking and Listening Handbook

Language is both spoken and written. The literature in this book is written, which is one form of communication, but most of your communication is probably oral. Oral communication involves both speaking and listening. Having strong speaking and listening skills benefits you both in your school life and your life outside of school.

Many of the assignments accompanying the literature in this textbook involve speaking and listening. This handbook identifies some of the terminology related to speaking and listening, both the oral communication you experience every day and the assignments you may do in conjunction with the literature in this book.

Oral Communication

You use many different kinds of oral communication each day. When you communicate with your friends, when you communicate with your teachers or your parents, when you interact with a cashier in a store, you are communicating orally. In addition to ordinary, every-day conversation, oral communication includes class discussions, speeches, interviews, presentations, debates. When you communicate face to face, you usually use more than your voice to get your message across. If you communicate by telephone, however, you must rely solely on your verbal skills.

The following terms will give you a better understanding of the many elements that are part of oral communication.

ARTICULATION is the process of forming sounds into words; it is the way in which the tongue, teeth, lower jaw, and soft palate are used to produce speech sounds.

BODY LANGUAGE refers to the use of facial expressions, eye contact, gestures, posture, and movement to communicate a feeling or idea.

CONNOTATION is the set of associations a word calls to mind. The connotations of the words you choose influence the message you send. For example, most people respond more favorably to being described as "slim" rather than as "skinny." The connotation of *slim* is more appealing than that of *skinny*.

EYE CONTACT is direct visual contact with another person's eyes.

FEEDBACK is the set of verbal and nonverbal reactions that indicate to a speaker that a message has been received and understood.

GESTURES are the movements made with arms, hands, face, and fingers to communicate.

INFLECTION refers to the rise and fall in the pitch of the voice in speaking; it is also called **intonation.**

LISTENING is understanding and interpreting sound in a meaningful way. You listen differently for different purposes.

Listening for key information: For example, when a teacher gives an assignment, or when someone gives you directions to a place, you listen for key information.

Listening for main points: In a classroom exchange of ideas or information, or while watching a television documentary, you listen for main points.

Listening critically: When you evaluate a performance, song, or a persuasive or political speech, you listen critically, questioning and judging the speaker's message.

NONVERBAL COMMUNICATION is communication without the use of words. People communicate nonverbally through gestures, facial expressions, posture, and body movements. Sign language is an entire language based on nonverbal communication.

PROJECTION is speaking in such a way that the voice carries clearly to an audience. It's important to project your voice when speaking in a large space like a classroom or auditorium.

VOCAL DELIVERY is the way in which you present a message. Your vocal delivery involves all of the following elements:

Volume: the loudness or quietness of your voice
Pitch: the high or low quality of your voice
Rate: the speed at which you speak; also called pace
Stress: the amount of emphasis placed on different syllables in a word or on different words in a sentence

All of these elements individually, and the way in which they are combined, contribute to the meaning of a spoken message.

Speaking and Listening Situations

The following are some of the many types of situations in which you apply your speaking and listening skills.

AUDIENCE Your audience in any situation refers to the person or people to whom you direct your message. An audience can be a group of people sitting in a classroom or auditorium observing a performance or just one person to whom you address a question or a comment. When preparing for any speaking situation, it's useful to analyze your audience, learning what you can about their background, interests, and attitudes so that you can tailor your message to them.

DEBATE A debate is a formal public-speaking situation in which participants prepare and present arguments on opposing sides of a question, stated as a **proposition.** The proposition must be controversial: It must concern an issue that may be solved in two different, valid ways.

The two sides in a debate are the *affirmative* (pro) and the *negative* (con). The affirmative side argues in favor of the proposition, while the negative side argues against it. The affirmative side begins the debate, since it is seeking a change in belief or policy. The opposing sides take turns presenting their arguments, and each side has an opportunity for *rebuttal,* in which they may challenge or question the other side's argument.

GROUP DISCUSSION results when three or more people meet to solve a common problem, arrive at a decision, or answer a question of mutual interest. Group discussion is one of the most widely used forms of interpersonal communication in modern society. **Meetings** are a kind of organized group discussion for a specific purpose.

INTERVIEW An interview is a form of interaction in which one person, the interviewer, asks questions of another person, the interviewee. Interviews may take place for many purposes: to obtain information, to discover a person's suitability for a job or a college, or to inform the public of a notable person's opinions.

ORAL INTERPRETATION is the reading or speaking of a piece of literature aloud for an audience. Oral interpretation involves giving expression to the ideas, meaning, or even the structure of a piece of literature. The speaker interprets the piece through his or her vocal delivery. **Storytelling,** in which a speaker reads or tells a story expressively, is a form of oral interpretation.

PANEL DISCUSSION is a group discussion on a topic of interest common to all members of a panel and to a listening audience. A panel is usually composed of four to six experts on a particular topic who are brought together to share information and opinions.

PANTOMINE is a form of nonverbal communication in which an idea or a story is communicated completely through the use of gesture, body language, and facial expressions, without any words at all.

PARLIAMENTARY PROCEDURE refers to the set of rules used to conduct a meeting in an orderly manner. Parliamentary procedure makes discussions at meetings more efficient and productive, and protects the rights of individuals attending the meeting.

All of the business conducted according to parliamentary procedure is handled through motions. Motions are proposals for action made by members of the meeting. For example, beside main motions that set forth the items of business that will be considered, a motion can be made to adjourn—or end the meeting—or to amend, or alter the wording of a motion.

The following are the main principles of parliamentary procedure:

1. Only one item of business may be considered at a time.
2. Everyone has a right to express an opinion, and each opinion is treated as valuable.
3. Every member of the group has the right to vote, and each vote is counted as equal.
4. The group always follows the decision of the majority.

Speaking and Listening Handbook ◆ 977

READERS' THEATER is a dramatic reading of a piece of literature in which participants take parts from a story or play and read aloud in expressive voices. Unlike a play, however, sets and costumes are not part of the performance, and the participants remain seated as they deliver their lines.

ROLE PLAY To role-play is to take the role of a person or character and, as that character, act out a given situation, speaking, acting, and responding in the manner of the character.

SPEECH A speech is a talk or address given to an audience. A speech may be **impromptu**—delivered on the spur of the moment with no preparation—or formally prepared and delivered for a specific purpose or occasion.

informative, as appropriate. The following are common occasions for speeches.

Introduction: Introducing a speaker or presenter at a meeting or assembly

Presentation: Giving an award or acknowledging the contributions of someone

Acceptance: Accepting an award or tribute

Keynote: Giving an inspirational address at a large meeting or convention

Commencement: Honoring the graduates of a school or university

- ***Purposes:*** The most common purposes of speeches are to persuade (for example, political speeches), to entertain, to explain, and to inform.
- ***Occasions:*** Different occasions call for different types of speeches. Speeches given on these occasions could be persuasive, entertaining, or

978 ◆ *Speaking and Listening Handbook*

RESEARCH HANDBOOK

Many of the assignments and activities in this literature book require you to find out more about your topic. Whenever you need ideas, details, or information, you must conduct research. You can find information by using library resources and computer resources, as well as by interviewing experts in a field.

Before you begin, create a research plan that lists the questions you want answered about your topic. Then decide which sources will best provide answers to those questions. When gathering information, it is important to use a variety of sources and not to rely on one main source of information. It is also important to document where you find different pieces of information you use so that you can cite those sources in your work.

The suggestions that follow can help you locate your sources.

Library Resources

Libraries contain many sources of information in both print and electronic form. You'll save time if you plan your research before actually going to the library. Make a list of the information you think you will need, and for each item list possible sources for the information. Here are some sources to consider:

NONFICTION BOOKS An excellent starting point for researching your topic, nonfiction books can provide either broad coverage or specific details, depending on the book. To find appropriate nonfiction books, use the library catalog, which may be in card files or in electronic form on computers. In either case, you can search by author, title, or subject; in a computer catalog, you can also search by key word. When you find the listing for a book you want, print it out or copy down the title, author, and call number. The call number, which also appears on the book's spine, will help you locate the book in the library.

NEWSPAPERS AND MAGAZINES Books are often not the best places for finding up-to-the-minute information. Instead, you might try newspapers and magazines. To find information about an event that occurred on a specific date, go directly to newspapers and magazines for that date. To find articles on a particular topic, use indexes like the *Readers' Guide to Periodical Literature*, which lists magazine articles under subject headings. For each article that you want, jot down the title, author (if given), page number or numbers, and the name and date of the magazine in which the article appears. If your library does not have the magazine you need, either as a separate issue or on microfilm, you may still be able to obtain photocopies of the article through an interlibrary loan.

REFERENCE WORKS The following important reference materials can also help you with your research.

- *General encyclopedias* have articles on thousands of topics and are a good starting point for your research, although they shouldn't be used as primary sources.
- *Specialized encyclopedias* contain articles in particular subject areas, such as science, music, or art.
- *Biographical dictionaries and indexes* contain brief articles on people and often suggest where to find more information.
- *Almanacs* provide statistics and data on current events and act as a calendar for the upcoming year.
- *Atlases*, or books of maps, usually include geographical facts and may also include information like population and weather statistics.
- *Indexes and bibliographies*, such as the *Readers' Guide to Periodical Literature*, tell you in what publications you can find specific information, articles, or shorter works (such as poems or essays).
- *Vertical files* (drawers in file cabinets) hold pamphlets, booklets, and government publications that often provide current information.

Computer Research

The Internet Use the Internet to get up-to-the-minute information on virtually any topic. The Internet provides access to a multitude of resource-rich sources such as news media, museums, colleges and universities, and government institutions. There are a number of indexes and directories organized by subject to help you locate information on the Internet, including Yahoo!, the World Wide Web Virtual Library, the Kids Web, and the Webcrawler. These indexes and directories will help you find direct links to information related to your topic.

Internet Sources and Addresses

- *Yahoo! Directory* allows you to do word searches or link directly to your topic by clicking on such subjects as the arts, computers, entertainment, or government.
http://www.yahoo.com
- *World Wide Web Virtual Library* is a comprehensive and easy-to-use subject catalog that provides direct links to academic subjects in alphabetical order.
http://celtic.stanford.edu/vlib/Overview.html
- *Kids Web* supplies links to reference materials, such as dictionaries, *Bartlett's Familiar Quotations*, a thesaurus, and a world fact book.
http://www.npac.syr.edu/textbook/kidsweb/
- *Webcrawler* helps you to find links to information about your topic that are available on the Internet when you type in a concise term or key word.
http://www.webcrawler.com

CD-ROM References

Other sources that you can access using a computer are available on CD-ROM. The Wilson Disk, Newsquest, the *Readers' Guide to Periodical Literature*, and many other useful indexes are available on CD-ROM, as are encyclopedias, almanacs, atlases, and other reference works. Check your library to see which are available.

Interviews as Research Sources

People who are experts in their field or who have experience or knowledge relevant to your topic are excellent sources for your research. If such people are available to you, the way to obtain information from them is through an interview. Follow these guidelines to make your interview successful and productive:

- Make an appointment at a time convenient to the person you want to interview, and arrange to meet in a place where he or she will feel comfortable talking freely.
- If necessary, do research in advance to help you prepare the questions you will ask.
- Before the interview, list the questions you will ask, wording them so that they encourage specific answers. Avoid questions that can be answered simply with *yes* or *no*.

- Make an audiotape or videotape of the interview if possible. If not, write down the answers as accurately as you can.
- Include the date of the interview at the top of your notes or on the tape.
- Follow up with a thank-you note or phone call to the person you interviewed.

Sources for a Multimedia Presentation

When preparing a multimedia presentation, keep in mind that you'll need to use some of your research findings to illustrate or support your main ideas when you actually give the presentation. Do research to find media support, such as visuals, CD's, and so on—in addition to those media you might create yourself. Here are some media that may be useful as both sources and illustrations:

- Musical recordings on audio cassette or compact disk (CD) (often available at libraries)
- Videos- that you prepare yourself
- Fine art reproductions (often available at libraries and museums)
- Photographs that you or others have taken
- Computer presentations using slide shows, graphics, and so on
- Video or audio cassette recordings of interviews that you conduct.

INDEX OF AUTHORS AND TITLES

INDEX OF SKILLS

Index of Skills ◆ 985

Defend, 171
Describe, 63, 68, 133, 282, 303
Discuss, 435
Distinguish, 105, 135, 249, 353, 475, 917
Draw conclusions, 38, 73, 114, 141,
157, 167, 171, 187, 190, 194, 219, 241,
252, 278, 283, 305, 323, 327, 337, 360,
372, 389, 400, 406, 433, 445, 465, 480,
503, 525, 563, 575, 591, 596, 691, 702,
718, 744, 758, 775, 799, 822, 835, 837,
892, 909, 927
Evaluate, 11, 73, 100, 116, 146, 167, 240,
386, 480, 543, 575, 620, 753, 797, 805,
815, 817, 835, 845
Explain, 5, 104, 201, 842, 843, 929
Extend, 397
Generalize, 241, 249, 278, 337, 372,
445, 465, 480, 577, 709, 843, 929
Hypothesize, 32, 167, 360, 432, 594,
643
Identify, 575, 843
Infer, 11, 32, 43, 59, 100, 105, 107, 116,
130, 142, 155, 157, 167, 171, 182, 194,
200, 201, 219, 240, 241, 268, 278, 285,
305, 314, 323, 327, 337, 346, 353, 360,
368, 372, 389, 400, 405, 413, 429, 465,
480, 487, 494, 499, 503, 512, 525, 539,
541, 544, 545, 563, 568, 575, 586, 587,
596, 614, 623, 646, 659, 685, 689, 694,
758, 807, 808, 809, 814, 815, 817, 822,
835, 843, 844, 865, 878, 881, 897, 917,
926, 927, 929, 931
Interpret, 107, 135, 145, 146, 182, 201,
219, 268, 285, 337, 413, 416, 443, 465,
512, 541, 545, 563, 589, 596, 717, 718,
744, 758, 765, 797, 799, 805, 809, 814,
815, 820, 837, 865, 881, 908, 909, 917
Make a judgment, 11, 135, 146, 157,
194, 314, 323, 327, 337, 433, 465, 494,
503, 563, 571, 614, 659, 725, 797, 892,
913
Modify, 360
Predict, 19, 46, 73, 194, 389, 408, 477,
529, 695
Relate, 252, 413, 431, 490, 523, 563,
718, 809
Specify, 842
Speculate, 24, 30, 38, 73, 100, 107, 152,
159, 177, 189, 268, 311, 326, 348, 349,
367, 413, 416, 437, 444, 471, 480, 504,
509, 531, 560, 590, 614, 620, 654, 797,
799, 815, 817, 909, 931
Summarize, 623
Support, 135, 142, 167, 179, 192, 227,
241, 247, 337, 349, 353, 409, 437, 445,
465, 494, 512, 527, 589, 591, 659, 695,
718, 744, 767, 798, 805, 845, 913, 917,
926
Synthesize, 105, 146, 581, 596, 791, 797,
822, 865

WRITING

Writing Opportunities
Adaptation, 933
Advertisement, 801
   classified, 243, 373
   job, 315
   public service, 74, 158
   real estate, 183
Advice, 158

Advice column, 315, 696
Alternate ending, 777
American dream, 149
Anecdote, 136
Animal organizer, 338
Argument for the defense, 149
Awards speech, 598
Biographical report, 919
Bird's-eye view, 74
Book vs. movie, 74
Book jacket, 117, 361, 625
Bug story, 338
Bumper sticker slogan, 439
Business proposal, 390
Casting notes, 660
Cause-and-effect essay, 101, 599
Celebration, proposal for, 583
Character analysis, 696
Character profile, 136, 306
Character sketch, 495, 514, 547
Classified advertisement, 243, 373
Comic strip, 109
Comparison-and-contrast essay, 255,
824, 893, 933
Comparison poem, 801
Consistency, 75
Continuation, 481
Critical evaluation, 374
Daydream, 306
Definition, 615, 792
Description, 203
   from above, 564
   of the future, 390
   of a future invention, 409
Details, precise, 75
Detective story, 101
Dialogue, 173, 220, 254, 287, 315
Diary entry, 306, 373, 401, 418, 660,
811
Directions for simple machine, 401
Dramatic scene, 101, 109, 279, 329,
661
Editorial, 254, 745, 778
Endings, 759, 777
   happy, 269
   surprise, 466
Environmental report, 439
Epic similes, 918
Essay, 533, 598
   about stages of life, 839
   about a symbol, 495
   about themes, 583
   about use of irony, 547
   cause-and-effect, 101, 599
   comparison-and-contrast, 255, 824,
    893, 933
   futuristic, 447
   how-to, 598
   on humor, 615
   literary, 918
   persuasive, 204, 220, 514, 564
   problem-and-solution, 288
   reflective, 583
   for a test, 448
   visual, 615
Eulogy, 533
Evaluation, 481, 811
Executive summary, 777
Extension, 233
Eyewitness report, 564

Fable, 158
Fantastic poem, 355
Feature article, 195
Field guide, 220
Figurative language, 173
Final outcome, 74
Folk tale, 361
Future, 390, 409
Futuristic essay, 447
Game rule proposal, 233
Gettysburg Address, 136
Guidebook description, 801
Haiku series, 847
Happy ending, 269
Heroic poem, 918
How-to essay, 598
Humorous essay, 615
Humorous folk tale, 361
Humorous narrative, 329
Information report, 628
Interview questions, 390
Introduction, 847
Job advertisement, 315
Job description, 173, 373
Job evaluation, 243
Journal entry, 287, 495, 847
Letter, 233, 254, 514, 893
   of appreciation, 466
   to an author, 339, 615
   of complaint, 279
   of condolence, 598
   to the czar, 315
   to Edgar Allan Poe, 12
   to an expert, 338
   last letter, 269
   letter home, 918
   love letter, 759
   to Nelson Mandela, 447
   persuasive, 158, 777
   suggestion, 533
   thank-you, 466
   for a time capsule, 390
Literary analysis, 847
Literary criticism response, 777
Literary essay, 918
Love letter, 759
Love poem, 243
Lyric poem, 824
Magazine article, 233, 514
Memo, 439, 481
Memorable event, 811
Menu, 811
Metaphors, 933
Modern adaptation, 719
Modern heroic poem, 918
Modern-day myth, 195
Monologue, 12
Movie scene, 839
Movie script, 33
Movie set, 12
Movie summary, 109
Movie vs. book, 74
Myth, modern-day, 195
Natural scene, 792
News report, 136, 355, 361, 481, 660
News story, 117, 269, 401
Notes for a magazine article, 233
Now-and-then report, 933
Obituary, 183
Observation, 75

Index of Skills ◆ *987*

INDEX OF FINE ART

ACKNOWLEDGMENTS (continued)

Arte Público Press
"The Harvest" from *La Cosecha* by Tomás Rivera, translated by Julián Olivares. Copyright © 1989 by Tomás Rivera Archives/Concepción Rivera. Reprinted by permission of Arte Público Press.

Atlantic Monthly Press
Book-jacket copy for *In These Girls, Hope Is a Muscle*, book written by Madeleine Blais, copyright © 1995 by Madeleine Blais. Reprinted by permission of Atlantic Monthly Press.

Margaret Atwood and Oxford University Press Canada
"Siren Song" from *You Are Happy* by Margaret Atwood. Copyright © 1974 by Margaret Atwood. Reprinted by permission of Margaret Atwood.

Bantam Books, a division of Bantam, Doubleday, Dell Publishing Group, Inc.
"One Ordinary Day, With Peanuts," excerpts from *Just an Ordinary Day: The Uncollected Stories* by Shirley Jackson. Copyright © 1997 by The Estate of Shirley Jackson. Used by permission of Bantam Books, a division of Bantam, Doubleday, Dell Publishing Group, Inc.

Elizabeth Barnett, literary executor
"An Ancient Gesture" by Edna St. Vincent Millay. From *Collected Poems*, HarperCollins. Copyright © 1954, 1982 by Norma Millay Ellis. All rights reserved. Reprinted by permission of Elizabeth Barnett, literary executor.

Brandt & Brandt Literary Agents, Inc.
"The Most Dangerous Game" by Richard Connell. Copyright, 1924 by Richard Connell. Copyright renewed © 1952 by Louise Fox Connell. "Sonata for Harp and Bicycle" from *The Green Flash* by Joan Aiken. Copyright © 1957, 1958, 1959, 1960, 1965, 1968, 1969, 1971 by Joan Aiken. Reprinted by permission of Brandt & Brandt Literary Agents, Inc.

Helen Brann Agency, Inc., agent for the author
"All Watched Over by Machines of Loving Grace," by Richard Brautigan, from *Trout Fishing in America, The Pill versus the Springhill Mine Disaster, and In Watermelon Sugar.* Copyright © 1967, 1968. Reprinted by permission of The Helen Brann Agency, Inc., agent for the author.

Abigail de Oliveria Carvalho
"Echo" by Henriqueta Lisboa, from *Poems Escolbidos: Chosen Poems*, translated by Helcio Veiga Costa, copyright © 1981 by Ed. Editora e Distribuidora, Ltda. Reprinted by permission of Abigail de Oliveira Carvalho, Henriqueta Lisboa's niece.

Arthur C. Clarke and Scott Meredith Literary Agency, Inc.
"If I Forget Thee, Oh Earth . . ." from *Expedition to Earth* by Arthur C. Clarke. Copyright © 1953, 1970 by Arthur C. Clarke; copyright 1951 by Columbia Publications, Inc. Reprinted by permission of the author and the author's agent, Scott Meredith Literary Agency, Inc., 845 Third Avenue, New York, NY 10022.

Coffee House Press
"Problems With Hurricanes" originally appeared in *Red Beans* by Victor Hernández Cruz, Coffee House Press, 1991. Copyright © 1991 by Victor Hernandez Cruz. Reprinted by permission of the publisher.

Don Congdon Associates
"The Golden Kite, the Silver Wind" by Ray Bradbury. Copyright © 1953 by Epoch Associates, renewed 1981 by Ray Bradbury. Reprinted by permission of Don Congdon Associates, Inc.

Richard Curtis Associates, Inc.
"Fly Away," from *The Beauty of the Beasts: Tales of Hollywood's Wild Animal Stars* by Ralph Helfer. Copyright © 1990 by Ralph Helfer. Reprinted by permission of Richard Curtis Associates, Inc.

Dial Books for Young Readers, a division of Penguin Books USA Inc.
From *Rosa Parks: My Story* by Rosa Parks with Jim Haskins. Copyright © 1992 by Rosa Parks. Used by permission of Dial Books for Young Readers, a division of Penguin Books USA Inc.

Doubleday, a division of Bantam, Doubleday, Dell Publishing Group, Inc.
"The Machine That Won the War," copyright © 1961 by Mercury Press, Inc. from *Nightfall and Other Stories* by Isaac Asimov. "The Gift of the Magi" by O. Henry from *The Complete Works of O. Henry.* Copyright © 1905 by Press Publications Company. "The Invalid's Story" by Mark Twain from *The Comic Mark Twain Reader,* edited by Charles Neider. Copyright © 1977 by Charles Neider. Used by permission of Doubleday, a division of Bantam, Doubleday, Dell Publishing Group, Inc.

Doubleday, a division of Bantam, Doubleday, Dell Publishing Group, Inc., and Curtis Brown Ltd.
"The Birds," copyright 1952 by Daphne du Maurier, from *Kiss Me Again Stranger* by Daphne du Maurier. Reprinted by permission of Doubleday, a division of Bantam, Doubleday, Dell Publishing Group, Inc., and Curtis Brown Ltd.

Farrar, Straus & Giroux, Inc.
"Georgia O'Keeffe" from *The White Album* by Joan Didion. Copyright © 1979 by Joan Didion. Prologue from *In My Place* by Charlayne Hunter-Gault. Copyright © 1992 by Charlayne Hunter-Gault. "The Washwoman" from *A Day of Pleasure* by Isaac Bashevis Singer. Copyright © 1963, 1965, 1966, 1969 by Isaac Bashevis Singer. The Prologue and The Epilogue from *The Odyssey: A Stage Version* by Derek Walcott. Copyright © 1993 by Derek Walcott. All rights reserved. Reprinted by permission of Farrar, Straus & Giroux, Inc.

Harcourt Brace & Company
"A Lincoln Preface," copyright 1953 by Carl Sandburg and renewed 1981 by Margaret Sandburg, Janet Sandburg, and Helga Sandburg Crile. "Ithaca" from *The Complete Poems of Cavafy,* copyright © 1961 and renewed 1989 by Rae Dalven. "Women" from *Revolutionary Petunias & Other Poems,* copyright